AF342057

Pattern Recognition Techniques, Technology and Applications

Pattern Recognition Techniques, Technology and Applications

Edited by
Peng-Yeng Yin

Pattern Recognition Techniques, Technology and Applications

Edited by Peng-Yeng Yin

CBS, Edition **2017**

Published by InTech

Janeza Trdine 9, 51000 Rijeka, Croatia

Notice

Statements and opinions expressed in the chapters are these of the individual contributors and not necessarily those of the editors or publisher. No responsibility is accepted for the accuracy of information contained in the published chapters. The publisher assumes no responsibility for any damage or injury to persons or property arising out of the use of any materials, instructions, methods or ideas contained in the book.

Publishing Process Manager Iva Simcic

Technical Editor InTech DTP team

Cover Designer InTech Design Team

Additional hard copies can be obtained from orders@intechopen.com

Pattern Recognition Techniques, Technology and Applications, Edited by Peng-Yeng Yin
p. cm.
ISBN 978-953-7619-24-4

Preface

A wealth of advanced pattern recognition algorithms are emerging from the inter-discipline between technologies of effective visual features and the human-brain cognition process. Effective visual features are made possible through the rapid developments in appropriate sensor equipments, novel filter designs, and viable information processing architectures. While the understanding of human-brain cognition process broadens the way in which the computer can perform pattern recognition tasks. The present book is intended to collect representative researches around the globe focusing on low-level vision, filter design, features and image descriptors, data mining and analysis, and biologically inspired algorithms. The 27 chapters coved in this book disclose recent advances and new ideas in promoting the techniques, technology and applications of pattern recognition.

Editor

Peng-Yeng Yin
National Chi Nan University,
Taiwan

Contents

Contents

Contents

1

Local Energy Variability as a Generic Measure of Bottom-Up Salience

Antón Garcia-Diaz, Xosé R. Fdez-Vidal, Xosé M. Pardo and Raquel Dosil
Universidade de Santiago de Compostela
Spain

1. Introduction

In image analysis, complexity reduction by selection of regions of interest is considered a biologically inspired strategy. In fact, Human Visual System (HVS) is constantly moving away less relevant information in favour of the most salient objects or features, by means of highly selective mechanisms forming an overall operation referred to as visual attention. This is the evolutionary solution to the well known complexity reduction problem (Tsotsos, 2005), when dealing with the processing and interpretation of natural images; a problem that is a major challenge for technical systems devoted to the processing of images or video sequences in real time. Hence, attention seems to be an adequate bio-inspired solution which can be applied in a variety of computing problems. Along with available technical advances, this fact is key to explain why the description and computational modelling of the attentional function of the HVS has experienced an enormous increase in the last two decades. In fact, applications of computing visual conspicuity are already found in many different fields: image segmentation and object learning and recognition (Rutishauser et al., 2004); vision system for robots (Witkowski & Randell, 2004) and humanoid robots (Orabona et al., 2005); visual behaviour generation in virtual human animation (Peters & O'Sullivan, 2003); processing data from 3D laser scanner (Frintrop et al., 2003); content-based image retrieval (Marques et al., 2003), etc.

In models of attention it is common to differentiate between two types of attention, the bottom-up from an image-based saliency, which accounts for features that stand out from the context, and the top-down attention as task-dependent and knowledge-based. These two kinds of attention are widely assumed to interact each other, delivering a global measure of saliency that drives visual selection. In fact, neurophysiological results suggest that these two mechanisms of attention take place in separate brain areas which interact in a visual task (Corbetta & Shulman, 2002) (Buschman & Miller 2007).

Regarding bottom-up attention, there are both psychophysical and neurophysiological experiments supporting the existence of some kind of an image-based saliency map in the brain, and it can be also argued that understanding of bottom-up saliency should definitely help to elucidate the mechanisms of attention (Zhaoping, 2005).

Moreover, from a technical point of view, mainly concerned with a generic approach to active vision tasks, the modelling of bottom-up component of attention can play a crucial role in the reduction of the amount of information to process, regardless of the knowledge managed by a given system, providing salient locations (regions of interest) or salient features. But it can also be suitable to learn salient objects, to measure the low level salience of a given object in a scene, etc. Hence, improvements on generic approaches to the modelling of bottom-up, image-based saliency are of great importance for computer vision.

The feature integration theory by Treisman & Gelade (1980) marked the starting point for the development of computational models of visual attention. Its main contribution lies on the proposal of parallel extraction of feature maps representing the scene in different feature dimensions and the integration of these maps in a central one, which would be responsible for driving attention. As a remarkable result from this parallel processing of few features proposed and maintained by Treisman in several works, arises the explanation of pop-out effects observed in visual search experiments with humans. It is well known that a stimulus that is clearly different from a homogeneous surrounding in a single feature rapidly attract our glance without the need to search the scene, regardless of the number of nearby objects acting as distractors. In contrast, when distractors are clearly heterogeneous, or when the target differs from all of them in a combination of features rather than in only one, subjects need to examine the scene object by object to check for a match with the target, so the time wasted in search linearly grows with the number of distractors. Treisman held that this can be understood if parallel processing of features exhibiting pop-out effects is assumed, and thus the feature map corresponding to the unique different feature in the first case will strongly respond in the location of the target attracting attention to it. On the other hand, in the heterogeneous and in the conjunctive cases none or several maps in different locations will fire, without provide for a clear salient location, so explaining the need for a serial search.

These ideas were gathered by Koch & Ullman (1985), to conceive a saliency-based computational architecture, in which they also introduced a Winner Takes All (WTA) network to determine the next most salient region, combined with a mechanism of Inhibition Of Return (IOR) to allow for a dynamic selection of different regions of a scene in the course of time. This architecture is essentially bottom-up, although they pointed the possibility of introducing top-down knowledge through bias of the feature maps.

An important subsequent psychophysical model of attention trying to explain more results on visual search experiments is the Guided Search Model, hold by Wolfe, in which feature dimensions (colour and orientation) rather than features (vertical, green, horizontal, etc.) are assumed to be processed in parallel and so to have an independent map of salience (Wolfe, 1994). In this model also top-down influences are considered by means of top-down maps for each feature dimension. More recent psychophysical models of attention are focusing more on top-down than in bottom-up aspects of attention, introducing the reasoning on the gist of a scene and its layout as driving attention (Rensink, 2005) (Oliva, 2005).

We have already mentioned the Guided Search Model by Wolfe, but we can cite a number of examples of computational models of bottom-up visual attention, many incorporating also a top-down component. Some of them are conceived more to explain psychophysical and neurophysiological results than to reach a performance in machine vision or other technical applications dealing with natural images. This is the case of the FeatureGate model by Cave (1999), the adaptive resonance theory to model attention proposed by Grossberg (2005), the neurodynamical approach hold by Deco et al. (2005), the model of bottom-up saliency coded in V1 cells by Zhaoping (2005), etc. Other models are motivated by the study of attention from an information theoretical point of view, trying to catch and describe the strategy of information processing of the HVS with statistical and computational tools. This is the case of Tsotsos et al. (1995) who have hold the Selective Tuning Model exploiting the complexity analysis of the problem of viewing, and achieving by this way several predictions on the real behaviour of the HVS. It is also the case of Rajashekhar et al. (2006), who have studied the statistical structure of the points that attract the eye fixations of human observers in natural images, in surveillance and search task. From this study they have derived models for a set have modelled a set of low level gaze attractors, in the form of filter kernels.

Focusing in the computational models that are the most relevant for our work, we find two particular previous implementations of the Koch and Ullman architecture being of special interest. The first was made by Milanese and was initially only bottom-up (Milanese, 1993), employing colour (or intensity), orientation and edge magnitude, in a centre-surround approach, as low level conspicuity maps; and proposing a relaxation rule for the integration process in a final saliency map. In a later work (Milanese et al., 1993), a top-down component was added in the form of an object recognition system that, applied to a few small regions of interest provided by the bottom-up component, delivered a top-down map favouring regions of the recognized objects. This map was combined with the conspicuity maps to give a final saliency in which known objects were highlighted against unknown ones.

The second implementation of the Koch and Ullman architecture was hold by Itti et al. (1998) who similarly made use of contrast, colour and orientation as features, in a centre-surround approach, but introducing a simpler integration process of weighting and addition of maps at first and of iterative spatial competition and addition in a subsequent work (Itti & Koch 2000). These two approaches to integration were significantly faster than the relaxation rule proposed by Milanese. This model can be seen as the most developed and powerful among all models of bottom-up visual attention, considering the fact that its performance has been compared with human performance (Itti & Koch, 2000)(Itti, 2006)(Ouerhani et al., 2006)(Parkhurst & Niebur, 2005), and tested in a variety of applications (Walther, 2006)(Ouerhani & Hugli, 2006). Recently, Navalpakkam & Itti (2005) introduced a top-down module in the model, based on the learning of target features from training images. This produces a feature vector which is subsequently used to bias the feature maps of the bottom-up component, hence speeding up the detection of a known object, in relation to the plain bottom-up model.

Now turning back to the problem of modelling bottom-up attention, we still have to ask, as a first question to delimit, which guidelines or requirements are currently imposed to the modelling of early low level features?. An interesting and worthy approach to attentional relevant features can be found in a recent exhaustive review on psychophysical works dealing with pop-out generation in visual attention, where Wolfe & Horowitz (2004) have provided a list classifying a variety of features, from lowest level, like contrast, colour or orientation, to highest level, like words or faces, making the classification dependent on the evidence and probability of each feature being causing pop-out or not. Hence, there would be features with enough observed evidences of causing pop-out (as intensity contrast, orientation, colour, size), others with high probability, others with low probability and finally others without probability at all. Then, a model of visual attention should be able to account for at least those features which give rise to clear pop-out effects as deduced from all of these cumulated results.

A starting issue underlying the selection of low level features lies in the assumption of a basis of "receptive fields", suitable to efficiently extract all the information needed from an image. Therefore, an obliged reference should be the cumulated knowledge about visual receptive fields in five decades, from the seminal work of Hubel and Wiesel in the 60's. In this sense, there is a general agreement in viewing the region V1 region of the visual cortex as a sort of Gabor-like filter bank. However, we also should to have in mind the shadows threatening this sight, as have been pointed out in a recent review by Olshausen and Field (2005) on the emerging challenges to the standard model of V1, to the point of assessing that we only understand up to a 15% of the V1 function.

On the other hand, information theory has also provided a number of requirements for the construction and processing of early low level features. Hence many studies have oriented their work to discover the statistical structure of what we see and link it to the known neurological processing strategies of the HVS. The intrinsic sparseness of natural images has been pointed out by Olshausen & Field (1996) , who have demonstrated that an efficient coding maximizing sparseness is sufficient to account for neural receptive fields, because of the statistical structure of natural images. Likewise, Bell & Sejnowski (1997) found that the independent components of natural images were localised edge detectors, similar to neural receptive fields. Following this idea, Hoyer & Hyvärinen (2000) have applied the Independent Component Analysis (ICA) to the feature extraction on colour and stereo images, obtaining features resembling simple cell receptive fields, and thereby reinforcing this prediction.

This idea has been strongly supported by parallel neurophysiological works, showing increased population sparseness as well as decorrelated responses during experiments of observation of natural scenes, or when non classical receptive fields receive natural-like stimuli as input (Weliky et al. 2003) (Vinje & Gallant 2000).

Hence, what we can expect in a plausible, adapted to natural images, computing model of visual attention is that any representation of information to be processed, should be coded in a sparse way, and it should also lead to a decorrelation of the information captured by the vision system, in accordance with the structure of information in natural images and the results from neurophysiological experiments, as well as efficiency requirements.

Other important reference more directly related to attention is the work of Zetzsche, who, with basis on the analysis of the statistical properties of fixated regions in natural images, hold that i2D signals are preferred by saccadic selection in comparison to i1D and i0D signals, that is, regions containing different orientations (corners, curves, etc) do attract attention much more than regions with little structural content (simple edges, constant luminance, etc) (Zetzsche, 2005). We find this approach to low level conspicuity very enlightening, and pointing in the direction of a more formal approach to the definition of what is a low level feature.

1.1 Our approach

Intensity contrast, orientation, symmetry, edges, corners, circles,... all designate different but overlapping concepts. Then, a question arises: is there a formal and more general low-level measure capable of retaining and managing with all of the information related to them? We consider that local energy meets this condition, and we hold that its relative variability in a given region can produce a pop-out effect. Moreover, we expect early unguided attention to be driven by any pop-out stimulus present in the scene, and this is the basis for our working hypothesis: variability on local energy (as well as on colour) can be considered as driving attention by means of pop-out phenomena.

Local energy has proved to be a powerful tool for the extraction and segmentation of a variety of perceived features related to phase -from edges and corners to Mach bands or motion- and, in general, regions exhibiting phase congruency and phase symmetry, be in space or in spacetime (Kovesi 1993; 1996), (Morrone & Owens 1987), (Dosil et al. 2008).

In this chapter, exploiting the basic Koch and Ullman architecture, we present a saliency measure for the computational modelling of bottom-up attention, based on the detection of regions with maximum local energy variability, as a measure of local feature contrast and relative amount of structural content, which we have outlined in a previous brief paper (Garcia-Diaz et al. 2007).

We hold that this way, regions with maximum feature contrast and maximum structural content are extracted from a given image, providing a suitable map of salience to drive bottom-up attention.

We focus on local energy conspicuity computation in static scenes, while other relevant feature dimensions, like colour and motion, remain beyond the scope of this chapter. Likewise, we limit our study to the bottom-up component, without task or target constraints.

Qualitative and quantitative observations on a variety of results on natural images, suggest that our model ensures reproduction of both sparseness population increase, decorrelated responses and pop-out phenomena deployment of orientation, size, shape, and contrast singletons, widely observed in the human visual system (Vinje & Gallant 2000),(Weliky et al. 2003), (Zhaoping 2005), (Wolfe & Horowitz 2004).

To provide for results comparable with those found in literature, we carry out here the reproduction of several experiments already published by Itti & Koch (2000), improving the performance achieved by them in the deployment of orientation pop-out, and equalizing their results in the detection of military vehicles within cluttered natural scenes, in our case without the use of colour information.

Beyond the success in these tests of technical performance, other relevant contribution of this work lies on the new elements provided for the computational interpretation of different observed psychophysical pop-out phenomena (intensity contrast, edge, shape, etc.), as probably different faces or appearances of a pop-out effect bound to a unique low level feature dimension (local energy). Unlike the extended use of intuitive features conceived from natural language, we think that the results achieved by our model help to highlight the importance of tackling the modelling of feature dimensions in a more formal way, thereby, avoiding misleading conclusions when we assess the results from psychophysical experimental observations, with the aim of translating them in computational constraints or requirements.

This paper is organized as follows, in the section 2 we describe the model proposed; in section 3 we show the experimental results obtained and make a brief discussion of them; section 4 deals with conclusions; and finally an appendix offers a brief formal explanation of T^2 Hotelling statistic.

2. Extraction of salience and fixations

The model of bottom-up attention presented here involves the extraction of local energy variability as a measure of salience and the subsequent selection of fixations.

Thus, we extract initial local energy maps obtaining by this way a multi-scale and multi-oriented representation of the image. For each orientation we decorrelate the multi-scale information by means of a PCA. Next we fuse each of the new sets of *principal* scaled maps in corresponding oriented conspicuity measures, extracting variability with the computation of the statistical distance of each pixel from the centre of the distribution. Afterwards we locally excite and gather regions exhibiting maximum variability by a non-linear and centre-surround spatial competition. Therefore we reach a unique and final saliency map, on which we perform fixations. The following subsections detail the process.

2.1 Local energy from log Gabor receptive fields

As we have previously pointed out, one first question to tackle is related to the starting basis of receptive fields. A variety of elections have been made on the subject in previous models of bottom-up attention: Gabor functions (Itti et al., 1998) (Torralba, 2005), Difference of oriented gaussians (Milanese et al. 1995), Oriented derivative of Gaussians (Rao & Ballard, 1995), non linear i2D selective operators (Schill et al., 2001), etc...

We use, instead, a bank of log Gabor filters (Field 1987), which besides a number of advantages against Gabor filters, have complex valued responses. Hence, they provide in each scale and orientation a pair of filters in phase quadrature (Kovesi 1996), an even symmetric -real part- filter and its Hilbert transform, an odd, antisymmetric -imaginary part- filter, allowing us to extract local energy as the modulus (Morrone & Burr 1988) of this filter vector.

$$(r, g, b) = (R, G, B) / 255;$$
$$I = (r + g + b) / 3; \tag{1}$$

$$\mathrm{Resp}_{so}(x, y) = (I * \log \mathrm{Gabor}_{so})(x, y) = f_{so}(x, y) + h_{so}(x, y)i \tag{2}$$

$$e_{so}(x, y) = \sqrt{f_{so}^2(x, y) + h_{so}^2(x, y)} \tag{3}$$

All Gabor filters present a non-zero DC component, as well non-zero values for negative frequencies, which gives rise to artefacts. Field (1987) proposed to construct Gabors in a logarithmic frequency scale, the so called log Gabor filters, overcoming these pointed drawbacks. Besides this advantages the symmetric profile in a logarithmic frequency scale, characteristic of log Gabor filters, confers them one additional advantage: a long tail towards the high frequencies. Since natural images present scale invariance, this is, they present amplitude profiles that decay with the inverse of the frequency (Field, 1993), then a filter that presents a similar behaviour, should be able to properly encode those images (Kovesi, 1996). Moreover, they gain in biological plausibility respecto to Gabor, since they reproduce better the response of simple cells from cortex, logarithmic in the frequency domain.

The fact that log Gabors have no analytic representation in the spatial domain, forces us to construct the bank of filters in the frequency domain, performing the inner product between their transfer functions and the Fourier transform of the intensity of the image. This should not be seen as a problem, as the use of Fast Fourier Transform and Inverse Fast Fourier Transform algorithms, speed up a filtering process respect to a convolution operation. Anyway the log Gabor are given by the expression:

$$\log \mathrm{Gabor}(f,\alpha; f_i,\alpha_i) = e^{-\frac{(\log(f/f_i))^2}{2(\log(\sigma_{fi}/f_i))^2}}\, e^{-\frac{(\alpha-\alpha_i)^2}{2(\sigma_\alpha)^2}} \tag{4}$$

We have used 6 scales and the central frequencies of the filters were spaced by one octave; other parameters were the minimum wavelength (λ_{min} = 2), the angular standard deviation (σ_α = 37.5°) or the frequency bandwidth (two octaves). This election of scales simply stretches the possible number of scales of the smallest images within the sets used in this work, and for simplicity it has not been modified for the rest of them since it has been observed to not significantly alter the results. In relation to the number of orientations the election accounts for the facts that pop-out effects are observed preferentially for deviations from four "canonical" orientations (Treisman 1993) -horizontal, vertical and right and left diagonal-, and is also needed a minimum difference of orientation angle of nearly 10° between distractors and target to generate a pop-out.

Once the initial receptive field responses have been extracted, the next step is necessarily related to the *feature* to extract from them. Again, a number of combined possibilities have been explored on the matter in previous models: intensity contrast, orientations, edges, predefined shapes, etc. But we put in question here the suitability of dividing the non-colour information in a number of feature dimensions in an early - low level- approach to attention. We hold instead the extraction of a low level, structurally meaningful, and multifaceted feature as local energy has proven to be. We obtain it as the modulus of the log Gabor responses.

2.2 Decorrelation and variability extraction

The next step to take is related to the integration of the initial feature maps in a final measure of saliency, and here we find again a variety of approaches in previous models. Focusing in the mentioned implementations of the Koch and Ullman architecture, Milanese et al. (1995) implemented a relaxation process by means of a non-linear updating rule which updates all the feature maps to satisfy a convergence criterion, and defining a heuristic energy function to minimize; in the other hand Itti & Koch (2000) have proposed an integration process based on the summation after the filtering of maps with iterative DoG filters, providing local within-feature and inter-feature competition.

Instead of convergence or summation for intra-feature integration we hold a *relative variability hypothesis*, by which one region is conspicuous as far as it contributes to the variability of responses in the ensemble of scales, leading to a measure of structural difference from the surround. So that, regarding local energy as a feature dimension split in oriented sub-dimensions, each characterized by a multi-scaled sub-feature vector, we propose a bottom-up attentional integration process based on the decorrelation of information and the subsequent extraction of the statistical distance from the average sub-feature vector.

A relevant point (or region) is expected to have a scale composition vector (structure) far from the mean. Given the huge number of samples (pixels) as well as the high dimensionality (number of scales) to manage, we propose to perform an information decorrelation process and the further gathering of the T^2 value of each point, providing a measure of statistical distance in a space of decorrelated scales, as a measure of multi-scale relevance.

Going more into detail, we start from six local energy scale maps for each of the four orientations computed. From them we define at each point four sub-feature vectors, one for each orientation, with six components corresponding to the local energy values at each of the scales. We have as many sample vectors for each orientation as pixels are in the single local energy maps, that is

$$\mathbf{x_i} = (x_{i1}, x_{i2}, \cdots, x_{is})' ; (i=1,2,\ldots,n)$$
(5)

Arranging these original vectors as columns -samples- in a matrix of data X for each orientation, we treat the rows -scales- as original -partially correlated- coordinates, and we perform a PCA on it. From the new -decorrelated- coordinates, we can extract the T² statistical distance of each sample -pixel- from the centre of the distribution.

$$\mathbf{X_o} = \begin{pmatrix} x_{11} & \cdots & x_{1n} \\ \vdots & \vdots & \vdots \\ x_{s1} & \cdots & x_{sn} \end{pmatrix} \rightarrow (PCA) \rightarrow T_o^2 = (T_{o1}^2, T_{o2}^2, \cdots, T_{on}^2)$$
(6)

where T² is defined as:

$$T_i^2 = (\mathbf{x_i} - \overline{\mathbf{x_i}})'\mathbf{S^1}(\mathbf{x_i} - \overline{\mathbf{x_i}})$$
(7)

being **S** the covariance matrix of the samples -pixels-, and $\mathbf{x_i}$ a sample vector with the scale values as components.

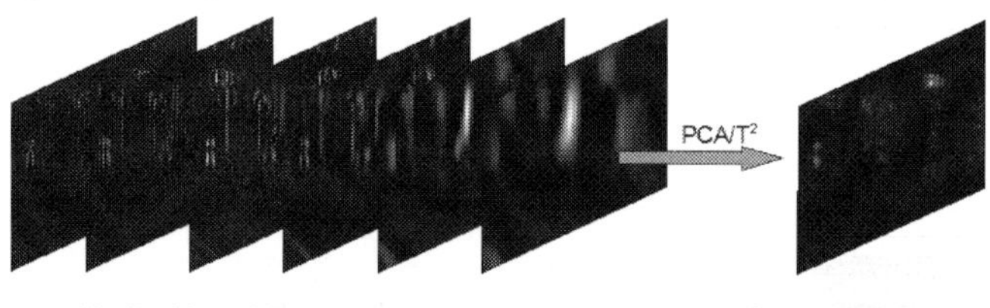

Vertical Local Energy Maps   T² Conspicuity

Fig. 1. T² conspicuity from PCA on local energy.

We take the resulting map of statistical distances as a relevance map for the analysed sub-feature. In figure 1 we can observe the high selectivity of this process, leading to an enhancement in population sparseness, synonym for code efficiency.

2.3 Local maxima excitation

We combine the previous procedure with a local maxima excitation to provide for a more robust and locally reinforced conspicuity. Next, to further compose a final saliency from oriented conspicuities, we gather the maximum values from the previous maps.

Local maxima excitation is addressed by means of a non-linear and centre-surround spatial competition. With preciseness, we apply iterative non-linear filtering of Difference of Gaussians (DoG), in a close but modified version of that implemented by Itti & Koch (2000). As well as minor differences in the inhibitory mechanisms, we reduce the number of iterations by modifying the last one. Thus, we take the excitatory signal (the response to the higher and narrower Gaussian) instead of the response to the difference (excitatory less inhibitory), avoiding the influence of the inhibitory signal, that is to say, achieving a strengthening of the regions with a high contribution to structure variability.

Hence, the excitatory and the inhibitory gaussian filters hold the following expressions:

$$Exc = \frac{c_{ex}^2}{2\pi\sigma_{ex}^2} e^{-(x^2+y^2)/2\sigma_{ex}^2} \tag{8}$$

$$Inh = \frac{c_{inh}^2}{2\pi\sigma_{inh}^2} e^{-(x^2+y^2)/2\sigma_{inh}^2} \tag{9}$$

Where we have used the values σ_{ex} = 2% and c_{ex} = 0.5 for the excitatory signal and σ_{in} = 25% and c_{in} = 1.5 for the inhibitory signal.

$$DoG = Exc - Inh = \frac{c_{ex}^2}{2\pi\sigma_{ex}^2} e^{-(x^2+y^2)/2\sigma_{ex}^2} - \frac{c_{inh}^2}{2\pi\sigma_{inh}^2} e^{-(x^2+y^2)/2\sigma_{inh}^2} \tag{10}$$

We perform a number of iterations (two in all of the experiments described here) for the following non-linear transformation:

$$\left| M_i + M_i * DoG - C_{inh} \right|_{>0} \rightarrow M_{i+1} \tag{11}$$

where the non-linear inhibitory term C_{inh} is established to the 2% of the maximum of the map. So far we have essentially followed the proposal made by Itti & Koch (2000) but in addition to these intermediate steps we finally impose the convolution of the map with the excitation signal, without any kind of inhibition:

$$M_{i+1} = M_i * Exc \tag{12}$$

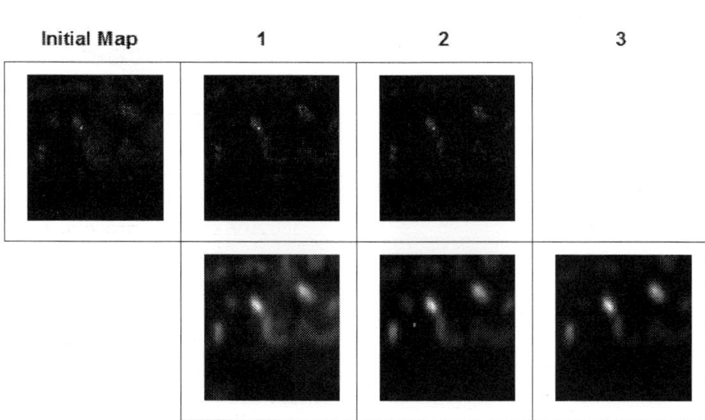

Fig. 2. Example of spatial Competition Process. First row: evolution of the map; second row: excitatory signal in each iteration and final conspicuity map

The overall effect of this spatial competition operation can be summarized in two main assessments, namely it favours small regions with many strong peaks, removing single isolated pixels and wide and constant regions, and it also reinforces the maxima, grading them in a conspicuity map. One example illustrates all of this in figure 2.

An example summarizing the whole integration process up to here can be seen in the figure 3, where we can check how the resulting relevance maps are actually a representation of regions with maximum contribution to structural variability, which have proven perceptually relevant and are supposed to strongly attract gaze. Furthermore, the highly competitive character of this procedure removes most noise and irrelevant regions, and reaches an important gain in population sparseness, retaining one or very few relevant regions, depending on the variability and thus low level significance of the feature considered. Hence, it seems to perform an efficient within feature competition, and also set the basis for a good inter feature competition.

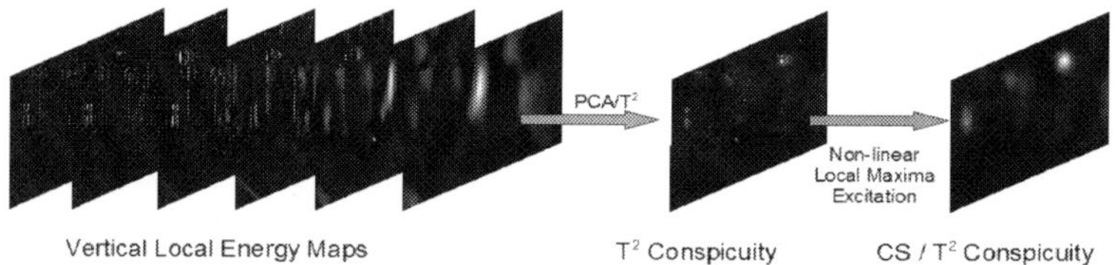

Fig. 3. Effect of non-linear local maxima excitation

After local maxima reinforcement, the next integration step is the obtaining of a final measure of saliency. This is done by taking the maximum values at each point from the previous conspicuity maps, giving rise to a horizontal competition between orientations, indeed reinforcing our strategy which aims to maximize the variability distance in structural content.

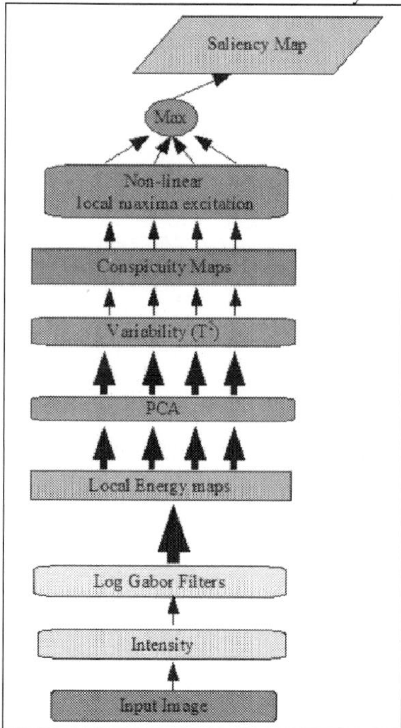

Figure 4. Extraction of Saliency from Local Energy

In the figure 4 is shown a complete scheme of our approach to the extraction of a bottom-up saliency map.

2.4 Fixations selection

Finally, making use of the extracted saliency map, the model should deploy a series of ordered fixations on the image. To do this, we have implemented a simplified version of the WTA neural network used by Itti & Koch (2000) in their experiments, but maintaining the basic assumptions for the focus of attention (FOA) size and considering the target detected when the FOA intersects its mask. This WTA is modelled by a two dimensional layer of integrate-and-fire neurons, with a mechanism of inhibition of return to prevent from attending always the same location. Therefore, neuron firing shifts the FOA to the correspondent location, and immediately afterwards a transient inhibitory feedback is applied to the surrounding region in the saliency map to allow for the subsequent selection of other salient locations.

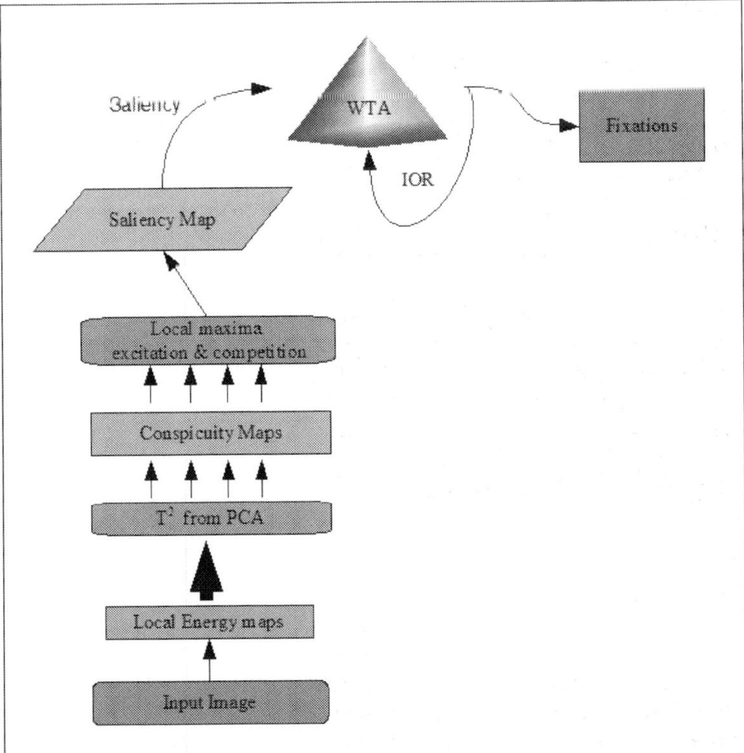

Fig. 5. Complete model of bottom-up attention based on local energy saliency

In the figure 5 is shown a scheme summarizing our local energy-based model of bottom-up attention.

3. Results

In this section we present the results obtained with the described model of bottom-up attention. We start, in the following subsection, with a qualitative analysis of its performance in psychophysically relevant situations. Other two subsections deal with the reproduction of quantitative experiments with public sets of images to evaluate both the capability to capture pop-out, as well as the search performance in a general purpose images dataset containing military vehicles in a landscape.

3.1 Reproduction of psychophysical phenomena and qualitative performance on natural scenes.

In this section we tackle the qualitative description of the behaviour of the model, showing the accordance with a variety of psychophysical results.

It is commonplace to relate the low-level saliency of a given target to the efficiency -in terms of wasted time- to find it. Thereby, a line for the qualitative analysis of a bottom-up attention model consists in checking the suitable reproduction of some relevant phenomena described in experiments of visual search.

The main and most characteristic of these phenomena is the pop-out, produced by an element differing in one unique feature from all of the others, that is to say, when a singleton is present in the image. Thus, one important aspect in a visual attention system consists in explaining saliency for singletons showing a pattern or feature unique in the image, be by the orientation, the size, the frequency content, etc. This kind of phenomena are the basis of the Treisman's FIT, which explains them by a privileged parallel processing of certain features.

Therefore, the pop-out of a target in a given image is strongly dependent on the context in which the target is present, and in the other hand it implies a behaviour highly non-linear: there is pop-out and the target is immediately found, or there is no pop-out and a serial search takes place, in which each of several elements with similar relevance are checked until the target is found. In this paper we show a wide range of pop-out phenomena successfully reproduced by our model, from local maxima in the variability of a structure descriptor as local energy is. In figure 6 we can see two first examples in which an element with a differing size fires a pop-out effect and rapidly attracts attention. It is not the size of the element itself, but the relative size respect to the others what causes a predominant salience.

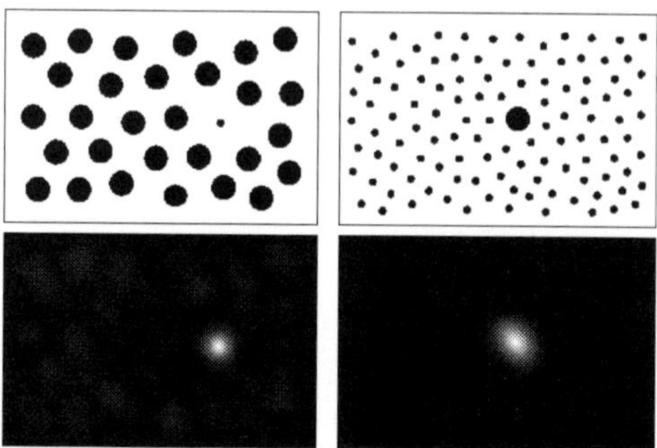

Fig. 6. Two examples of size pop-out

As we have seen, a singleton between many similar distractors shows a very high saliency, but what happens if distractors present differences themselves? As can be expected, differentiation of distractors leads to appearance of new singletons competing with the target, reducing its relative saliency. This effect of the distractor heterogeneity on target saliency, is well understood in our model as a reduction of the relative contribution to structure variability. In figure 7 we can see a meaningful example which illustrates well this question.

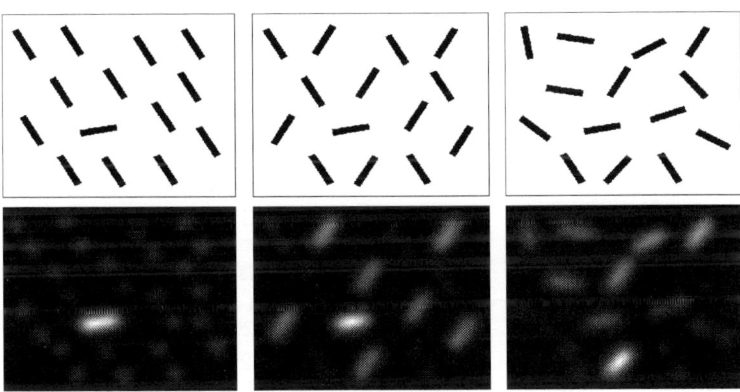

Fig. 7. Distractor heterogeneity reduces saliency of the target up to prevent for pop-out. In the three images the unique feature of the target is the same, but in the left image the distractor heterogeneity makes less relevant the orientation than other structural features.

Another factor reducing saliency is related to resemblance between the searched element and the surrounding ones, usually referred as the target-distractor similarity. Here it is this similarity with surrounds what threatens the status of singleton of the target. In the frame of our model, this can be explained again as a reduction in the local contribution to structure variability in the image. In figure 8 is shown how our model reproduces well this behaviour observed in psychophysical experiments. As can be seen there is no a linear relation between difference in size and relative saliency, since the model collects local variability maxima in a non-linear approach, aiming decorrelated and sparse responses.

There is another important set of phenomena observed in visual searches, commonly denoted as "search asymmetries". The related to visual search experiments designed on a given feature space, where target and distractors exchange its characterization, giving rise to different behaviours and therefore "asymmetric" attentional performance in such feature spaces. Disregarding the common discussion on the feature definitions involved, and on the suitability in talking of such asymmetries, we show the behaviour of our model in two typical situations and how it coincides basically with that described in psychophysical observations, providing with an simple explanation for them. The first of these cases has to see with the so called presence/absence asymmetry, in which target and distractors are the same element except by the presence or absence of an additional simple feature. What typically happens in these experiments is that the presence of the additional feature generates a pop-out while its absence remains unnoticed and does not fire any pop-out.

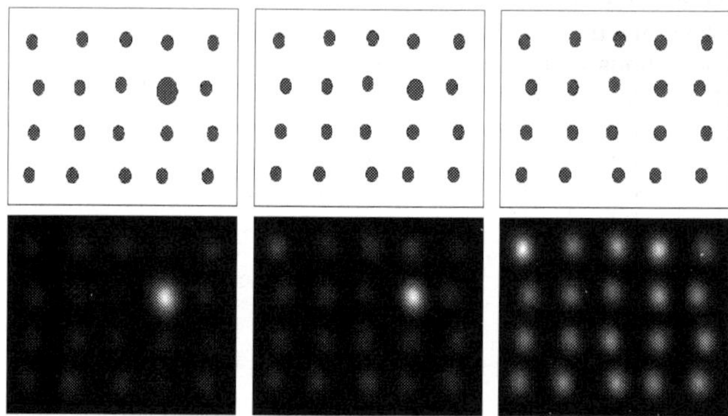

Fig. 8. Target-Distractor similarity reduces saliency of the target abruptly

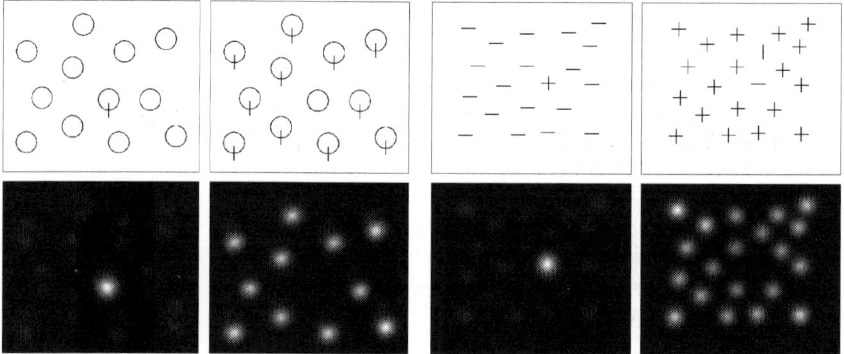

Fig. 9. Reproduction of the so called presence/absence asymmetry

In figure 9 we can see two examples of this asymmetry, in the left all the elements are circles which can have or not a vertical bar, in the rigth elements are horizontal bars and the aditional feature is again a vertical bar. As can be seen in both cases the model reproduces well psychophysical observations. In other hand the explanation is simple: the structure of the element(s) labelled by the "absence" is present in all the elements, so this contribution to structure variability in the image is equalled by all the other stimuli, while the element(s) with the additional feature present an additional contribution to structure variability, increasing its relative salience. Thus, such asymmetry is not an asymmetry in our model and the observed behaviour is perfectly understandable.

Another classical example of search assymetry is found in experiments in which target and distractor differing only in orientation exchange the value of this feature. It has been observed in such cases that the threshold in orientation difference needed to fire pop-out varies in a significant amount between the two possibilities. Treisman & Gormican (1988) have explained this phenomenon with basis in a privileged treatment of certain "canonical" orientations which would break the expected symmetry. As figure 10 shows this is well reproduced by our model. This should not result surprising, as the model computes four different orientations, which in spite of gathering all the possible orientations existing in the image, they make it in a unequal way. So, our low level descriptor makes use in fact of a set of canonical orientations and thus, is not symmetric respect to any orientation. But this seems to be in accordance with the performance observed for the HVS.

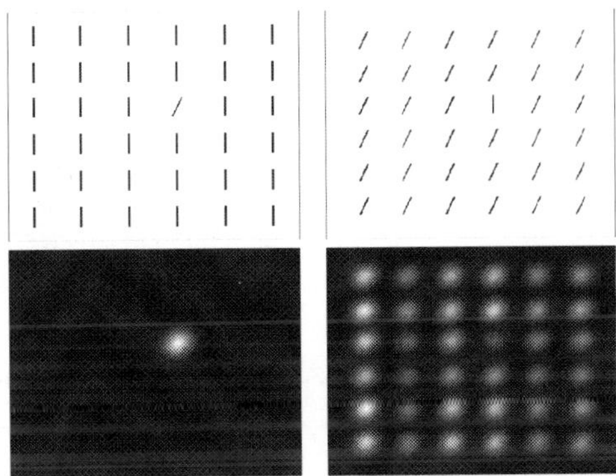

Fig. 10. Asymmetry in orientation pop-out threshold

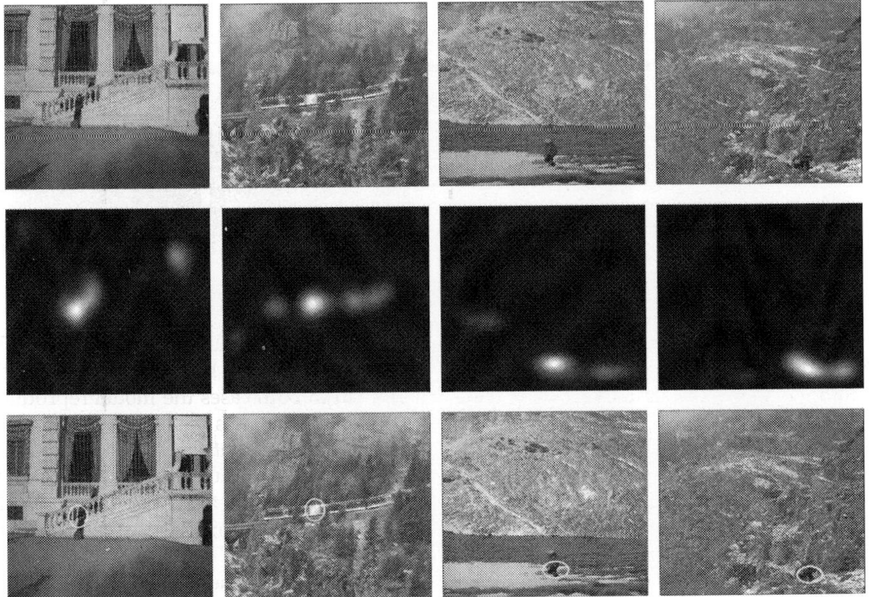

Fig. 11. Performance on natural scenes. Top: original image; centre: saliency map; bottom: first fixation.

Finally, to complete this qualitative description of the performance of the model figure 11 shows the saliency map and the first fixation for five cluttered natural scenes with different relevant objects, different visibilities, and different contexts. We should remember at this point that colour information was discarded in this work. As we can appreciate saliency maps are sparse, present few concentrated salient regions, corresponding in all cases to elements of obvious relevance. Therefore, the capability of the model to reproduce pop-out phenomena is not limited to artificial stimuli in synthetic images but it is also confirmed with different targets in natural scenes.

3.2 Performance on orientation pop-out

In this section we dealt with the reproduction of the orientation pop-out effects observed in the human visual system, parallel to that already carried out by Itti & Koch (2000). All the images, and their respective binary versions with the masks for target detection, are public and can be found in (http://ilab.usc.edu).

In the figure 12 we can see twenty examples of the obtained results, with the saliency map obtained and the correspondent fixations performed, they can give an idea of the robustness of the model in capturing orientation pop-out.

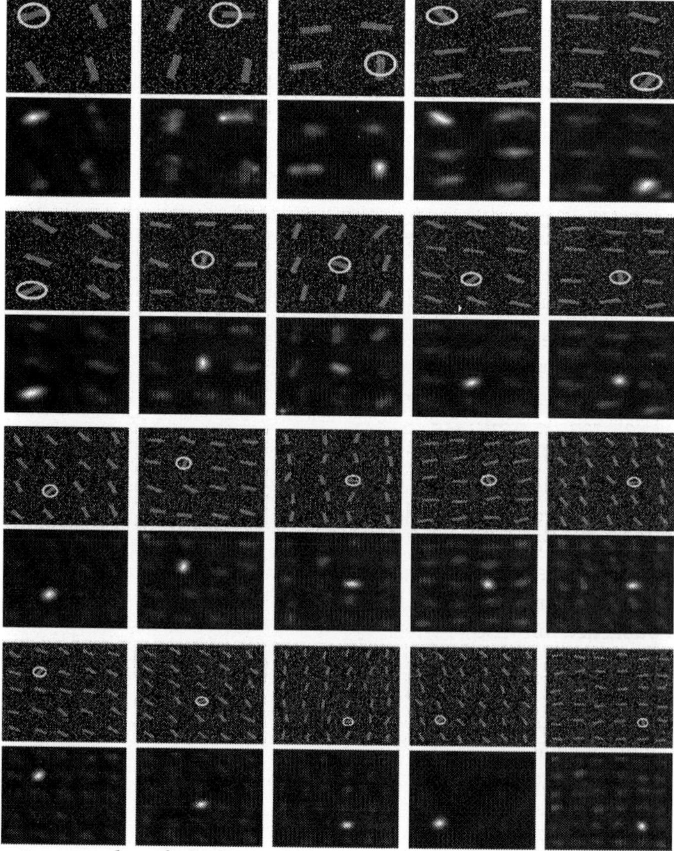

Fig. 12. Twenty examples of results in the pop-out orientation experiment.. For each case, fixations (top) and saliency (bottom) are shown.

In figure 11, the overall results are shown as the mean number of false fixations before target detection faced to the number of distractors present in the image. The dashed line represents the chance value corresponding to a pure serial search without any orientation pop-out effect (supposed half of distractors visited before the detection), and the blue points connected by a solid line, the average performance of our model, with the error bars being one standard deviation.

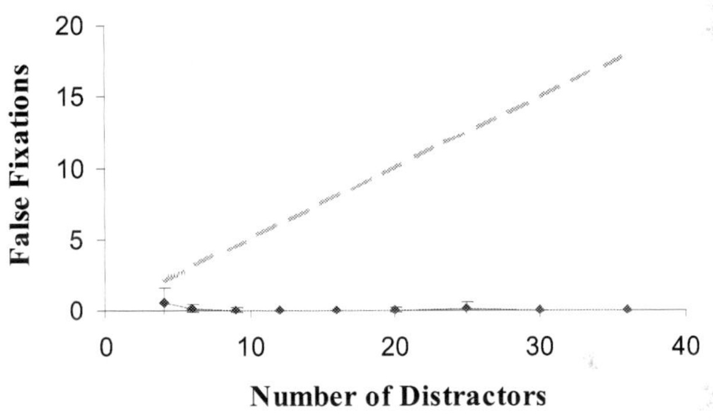

Fig. 13. Number of fixations against number of distractors. The dashed green line represents what could be expected in a serial search (half of distractors attended before target detection). Blue points connected by a blue solid line, and black bars, show the correspondent average and standard deviation values obtained.

We can assess that the model assures for a robust capture of orientation pop-out, independently of the number of distractors, since we obtained a flat slope in the number of false fixations. The performance became slightly poorer when the number of distractors was very small, which can be explained in terms of a reduction of the pop-out effect by the expectable reduction in the relative contribution of the target to structure variability in the image.

Our results clearly improve those obtained by Itti & Koch (2000), regarding the visible reduction of the mean value and even more important, the remarkable reduction of the standard deviation values; giving account for the fact that with our procedure there are not cases with a large number of false detections, thereby achieving a more robust performance. They haven't published numerical results so we can't carry out a numerical comparison.

3.3 Search performance on natural scenes

In this section we handle with target detection within natural scenes in a set of images containing a military vehicle in a landscape, again parallel to that already carried out by Itti & Koch (2000). The images from this set were sub sampled versions of images belonging to the search_2 database described by Toet et al. (2001). They correspond to 44 natural scenes containing a military vehicle of variable relative dimensions, identical to those used by Itti & Koch, except for the resolution of the images: ours had the fourth part size (1536x1024 pixels). Some of these images can be seen in figure 14.

We also assumed the same relative size for the FOA, which would imply a mean result of 61.5 fixations for random target detection.

One interesting feature of this database is the availability of the search time distribution curves obtained for human observers for each of the 44 images, allowing for a comparison with human performance in a search task in natural scenes. Simulated search times have been calibrated so that a mean of 330 ms elapse between two fixations, and an additional time of 1.5 s has then added to account for human motor response time.

Fig. 14. Examples of natural images from the military vehicles set. As can be seen many of them present a very low visibility of the target.

The main results take the very close overall values than Itti & Koch (2000), and so the model found the target with the first fixation in seven of the 44 images, and with fewer than twenty fixations in 23 images. The model has failed in two cases. Figure 13 shows the saliency map and the correspondent fixations performed for five images of high visibility of the target.

As Itti's model did, our model reached a poor correlation with human, and can also be considered faster than them finding the target, under the exposed search time calibration assumptions. In any case, this is a very inaccurate approach, because of the fact that search time distributions for humans are not well represented by the mean value.

But in other hand, qualitative analysis allows to see an agreement on the classification of an image, when it is considered as one with a high visibility of the target. This classification in humans has been done by comparison of the curves of search time distribution, and in the model selecting those images with less of 6s of search time. This comparison yields the result of eleven images classified like showing high visibility both by humans and the model, and only two images classified with medium visibility by the model while showing high visibility for humans.

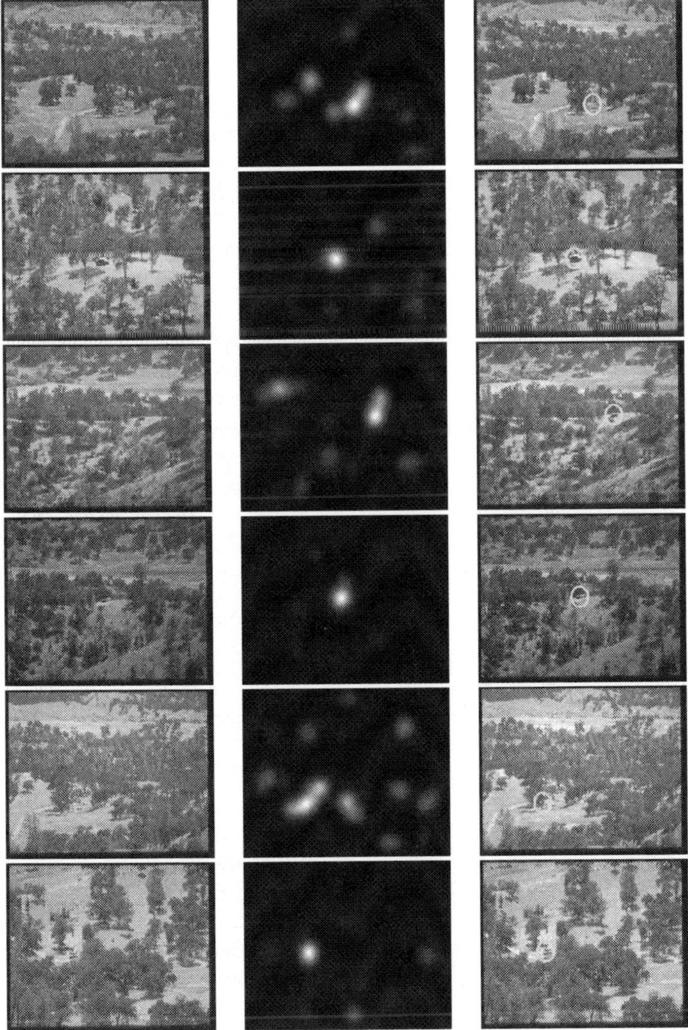

Fig. 15. Six examples of high visibility of the target, where a bottom-up approach makes sense. Left: original image; centre: saliency map; right: fixations performed.

In images with poor visibility for humans the agreement didn't exist, but these images, without a conspicuous target are expected to be processed by humans in a top-down manner, not bottom-up, the only one that is being modelled here.

Another comment to be made is related to the sparse maps obtained, particularly when a pop-out effect is clear. In the other hand, when the visibility of the target is lower, more elements from the landscape gain relative salience.

4. Conclusions

In this chapter we have exposed a particular approach to model bottom-up saliency, based in the hypothesis that variability of local energy is capable of capture the pop-out produced by the local contrast in a variety of non-colour features.

Hence, we have employed local energy as a suitable general descriptor of non-colour structure in the image, combined with information decorrelation, statistical distance computation and non-linear maxima excitation to detect local maxima of structure variability. The biological plausibility of the model arises from the combination of known features from V1 behaviour with a highly non-linear and collective performance, as well as assumptions based on psychophysical considerations (e.g. election of orientations).

The model is implemented in a meaningful and understandable fashion, thereby providing for a complete and robust computational frame to reproduce and formally explain the main observed features of static and non-colour bottom-up attention in humans.

Tested in synthetic as well as natural images, this approach gives rise to a simple model of bottom-up attention with a high performance, which accounts for pop-out effects and other psychophysical phenomena, and also solves conspicuity-driven search tasks more efficiently and robustly than a powerful state of art approach to bottom-up attention as it is that hold by Itti and colleagues. All of this is achieved with a simple scheme: while other models need for the separate use of intensity contrast and orientation (Itti et al. 2000), edges and orientation (Milanese 1993), and other combinations, we only make use of local energy as low-level descriptor to characterize non-colour structure.

It is important to remark that the model makes a generic approach to bottom-up saliency, without the use of any kind of knowledge or feature constraints, related to the target nor the task, and it is expected to reproduce human performance in corresponding situations, as unguided surveillance or conspicuity-driven visual search, on non-colour scenes or when relevance does not lie in colour.

Although local energy is not an intuitive feature from common language, it can account for many of these perceived intuitive features in a more reliable way for computational modelling purposes. In fact, it is underlying them. Moreover, conceived as a descriptor of structure is a powerful tool to understand a variety of features and the phenomena related to them without loss of meaning.

Furthermore, this approach takes into account and incorporates important features of HVS as expected and observed increased population sparseness and response decorrelation in comparison to previous Gabor-like and feature extraction models of saliency computation.

In progress and future work will deal with other feature dimensions, like colour and motion, in order to allow the model to work with real dynamic scenes; and also with a more depth study on the comparison with human performance.

5. Acknowledgements

This work has been financially supported by the Ministry of Education and Science of the Spanish Government through the research project AVISTA (TIN2006-08447), and by the Ministry of Industry and Innovation of the Galician Government through the project (PGIDIT07PXIB206028PR).

6. References

Bell, A. J. & Sejnowski, T. J. (1997). The 'independent components' of natural scenes are edge filters. Vision Research, 37,23, 3327-3338

Buschman, T. J. & Miller, E. K. (2007). Top-Down Versus Bottom-Up Control of Attention in the Prefrontal and Posterior Parietal Cortices Science Vol. 315. no. 5820, pp. 1860 - 1862

Cave K.R. The FeatureGate Model of Visual Selection Psychological Research 1999 62 182-194

Corbetta M. & Shulman G. L. (2002). Control of goal-directed and stimulus-driven attention in the brain. Nature Reviews, 3(3); 201–215.

R. Dosil; X. R. Fdez-Vidal, X. M. Pardo & A. Garcia (2008) Motion Representation Using Composite Energy Features Pattern Recognition, 41(3):1110-1123, 2008

Deco G.; Rolls E.T. & Zihl J. A (2005). Neurodynamical Model of Visual Attetion In L. Itti, G. Rees, J.K. Tsotsos (eds) Neurobiology of Attention (Elsevier Academia Press, 2005, 593-599).

Field D. J. (1987) Relations Between the Statistics of Natural Images and the Response Properties of Cortical Cells. Journal of the Optical Society of America A, 4(12), 1987, 2379–2394.

Field D. J.(1993). Scale-invariance and self-similar 'wavelet' transforms: an analysis of natural scenes and mammalian visual systems. In M. Farge, J. Hunt & J. Vassilicos(eds.), Wavelets, Fractals and Fourier Transforms (Oxford, Clarendon Press, 1993, 151–193).

Frintrop S.; Rome E.; Nüchter A. & Surmann H. (2005) A Bimodal Laser-Based Attention System Journal of Computer Vision and Image Understanding (CVIU), 100(1-2), 2005,

Garcia-Diaz, A.; Fdez-Vidal, X.R.; Dosil, R.; Pardo, X.M. (2007) Local energy saliency for bottom-up visual attention. Proceedings of the IASTED International Conference on Visualization, Imaging and Image Processing.

Grossberg S. (2005). Linking attention to learning, expectation, competition and consciousness. n L. Itti, G. Rees, J.K. Tsotsos (eds) Neurobiology of Attention (Elsevier Academia Press, 2005, 652-662).

Hoyer P. O. & HyvärinenA. (2000). Independent component analysis applied to feature extraction from colour and stereo images. Network: Computation in Neural Systems, 11, 2000 191-210.

Itti L.; Koch C. & Niebur E. (1998) A model of saliency-based visual attention for rapid scene analysis. IEEE Transactions on Pattern Analysis and Machine Intelligence, 20 (11), 1998,1254-59.

Itti L. & C. Koch (2000), A saliency-based search mechanism for overt and covert shifts of visual attention. Vision Research, 40, 2000, 1489-1506.

Itti L. (2006). Quantitative modelling of perceptual salience at human eye position. Visual Cognition, 14(4/5/6/7/8), 2006, 959-984.

Jackson J.E. (1991). A User's Guide to Principal Components., Wiley-Interscience, John Wiley & Sons, New York,.USA. 1991.

Koch C. & Ullman (1985) S. Shifts in selective visual attention: towards the underlying neural circuitry. Human neurobiology, 4(4), 1985, 219-227.

Kovesi P. (1996). Invariant Measures of Image Features from Phase Information. Ph.D. (The University or Western Australia, 1996).

Kovesi P (1999).Image Features from Phase Congruency. Videre: Journal of Computer Vision Research The MIT Press, 1(3), 1999, 1-26

Marques O. ; Mayron L. M., Borba G. B. & Gamba H. R. (2006). Using visual attention to extract regions of interest in the context of image retrieval Proceedings of the ACM SE'06, Melbourne, FL, 2006, 638-643.

Milanese R. (1993). Detecting Salient Regions in an Image: from Biological Evidence to Computer Implementation. Ph.D. thesis, Univ. of Geneva,1993.

Milanese R. , Gil S. & Pun T. (1995). Attentive mechanisms for dynamic and static scene analysis. Optical engineering, 34(8), 1995 2428-34.

Morrone, M.C. & Owens, R.A. (1987) Feature detection from local energy. Pattern Recognition Letters 6, 303-313, 1987.

Morrone M.C. & Burr D.C.(1988). Feature Detection in Human Vision: A Phase-Dependent Energy Model. Proceedings of the Royal Society of London B, 235, 1988, 221–245.

Navalpakkam V. & Itti L. (2005) Modeling the influence of task on attention, Vision Research, 45(2), 2005, 205-231.

Nothdurft H.C. (2005) Salience of Feature Contrast In L. Itti, G. Rees, J.K. Tsotsos (eds) Neurobiology of Attention (Elsevier Academia Press, 2005, 233-239)

Oliva A. (2005). Gist of the scene. In L. Itti, G. Rees, J.K. Tsotsos (eds) Neurobiology of Attention (Elsevier Academia Press, 2005, 251-256).

Olshausen B. A. & Field D.J. (1996). Emergence of Simple-Cell Receptive Field Properties by Learning a Sparse Code for Natural Images. Nature, 381, 1996, 607-609.

Olshausen B. A. & Field D.J. (2005) How close are we to understanding V1? Neural Computation 17, 2005, 1665-1699

Orabona F.; Metta G. & Sandini G. (2005). Object-based Visual Attention: a Model for a Behaving Robot Proceedings of the 2005 IEEE Computer Society Conference on Computer Vision and Pattern Recognition (CVPR'05) - Workshops – 03, 2005, 89.

Ouerhani N. & Hugli H. (2003) Maps: Multiscale attention-based presegmentation of color images, Lecture Notes in Computer Science, 2695, 2003, 537-549.

Ouerhani N. , R.Wartburg, , H.,Hugli R. Mueri (2004) Empirical validation of the saliency-based model of visual attention, Electronic letters on computer vision and image analysis, 3(1), 2004, 13-24.

Parkhurst D.J. & Niebur E. (2005) Stimulus-Driven Guidance of Visual attention in Nattural Scenes In L. Itti, G. Rees, J.K. Tsotsos (eds) Neurobiology of Attention (Elsevier Academia Press, 2005, 240-245).

Peters C. & O'Sullivan C. (2003). Bottom-Up Visual Attention for Virtual Human Animation CASA, 2003, 111-117.

Rajashekhar U.; Bovik A.C., & Cormack L.K. (2006). Visual search in noise. Journal of Vision, 6, 2006, 379-386

Rao R. P. N. & Ballard D. (1995) An Active Vision Architecture Based on Iconic Representations Artificial Intelligence 78, 1995, 461-505

Rensink R. A. (2000). The dynamic representation of scenes. Visual Cognition, 7; 2000; 17–42.

Rutishauser U.; Walther D.; Koch C. & Perona P. (2004). Is bottom-up attention useful for object recognition? IEEE Conference on Computer Vision and Pattern Recognition, 2, 2004, 37-44.

Schill K.; Umkehrer E.; Beinlich S.; Krieger G. & Zetzsche C. Scene analysis with saccadic eye movements: Top-Down and Bottom-Up Modelling. J. Electron. Imaging 10, 2001, 152-160.

Toet A. , Bijl P. & Valeton J.M. (2001), Image dataset for testing search and detection models. Optical Engineering 40(9), 2001, 1760-1767

Torralba A. (2005). Contextual Influences on Saliency In L. Itti, G. Rees, J.K. Tsotsos (eds) Neurobiology of Attention (Elsevier Academia Press, 2005, 586-592).

Treisman A. & Gelade G. A (1980), Feature-Integration Theory of Attention. Cognitive Psychology, 12, 1980, 97–136.

Treisman A. & Gormican, S. (1988) Feature analysis in early vision: Evidence from search asymmetries. Psychological Review, 95(1), 15-48

Treisman A. (1993). The perception of features and objects In Baddeley, A. and Weiskrantz, L. (eds) Attention: Selection, awareness, and control, Clarendon Press, Oxford, 1993 5–35..

Tsotsos J. K.; Culhane S.; Wai. W.; Lai Y.; Davis N.& F. Nuflo, Modeling visual attention via selective tuning, Artificial Intelligence, 8(1-2), 1995, 507 – 547.

Tsotsos J. K. (2005) Computacional foundations for attentive Processes. In L. Itti, G. Rees, J.K. Tsotsos (eds) Neurobiology of Attention (Elsevier Academia Press, 2005, 3-7).

Walther D. , (2006) Interactions of visual attention and object recognition: computational modelling, algorithms, and psychophysics. PhD. (California Institute of Technology, 2006).

Weliky M. , J. Fiser, R. H. Hunt & D. N. Wagner, Coding of natural scenes in primary visual cortex. Neuron 37, 2003, 703-718.

Witkowski M. & Randell D. (2006) Modes of Attention and Inattention for a Model of Robot Perception. Proc. Towards Autonomous Robotic Systems, 2006, 246-253.

Wolfe J. M. (1994). Guided Search 2.0 A Revised model of visual search. Psychonomic Bulletin, 1(2), 1994, 202-238.

Wolfe J. M. & Horowitz T. S. (2004). What attributes guide the deployment of visual attention and how do they do it?. Nature Reviews. Neuroscience, 5(6), 2004, 495-501.

Zetzsche C. (2005). Natural Scene Statistics and Salient Visual Features In L. Itti, G. Rees, J.K. Tsotsos (eds) Neurobiology of Attention (Elsevier Academia Press, 2005, 226-232).

Zhaoping L. (2005). The primary visual cortex creates a bottom-up saliency map In L. Itti, G. Rees, J.K. Tsotsos (eds) Neurobiology of Attention (Elsevier Academia Press, 2005, 570-575)

2

Real-Time Detection of Infrared Profile Patterns and Features Extraction

Rubén Usamentiaga, Daniel F. García and Julio Molleda
University of Oviedo
Spain

1. Introduction

The pressing demand to improve quality of manufactured products requires the use of the latest technologies in order to enhance the control systems that adjust manufacturing parameters. Computer vision inspection and control are already standard technologies which are frequently used to improve the quality of manufactured products. Recently, due to the availability of fast and affordable infrared acquisition devices, computer vision beyond the spectrum is also becoming an essential technology for quality control and improvement. For example, during steel strips manufacturing, uneven temperature across the width of the strips during rolling generates defects, due to differences in the contraction of the longitudinal fibers that make up a strip. Detecting the infrared profile pattern of the strip which is being manufactured makes it possible to use this information to modify the manufacturing parameters to compensate for the temperature differences in the strip (Gonzalez et al., 2002).

This work proposes a robust method to detect infrared profile patterns in real-time. The proposed method is based on the acquisition and processing of infrared profiles using an infrared line scanner. The detection of infrared patterns, and the change of pattern which occur during manufacturing, need to be carried out online with the production process in order to use this information to enhance the control systems during manufacturing. The method proposed to detect these patterns in real-time is based on the segmentation of the stream of infrared profiles acquired from the infrared line scanner. The segmentation aims to find regions of homogeneous temperature, that is, regions formed by a set of adjacent profiles which have a similar temperature pattern. The proposed method to segment infrared images into regions of common temperature patterns is by means of boundary detection, which, in this case, is accomplished through edge detection. The first step of the segmentation is the calculation of the gradient, which is obtained as the result of the convolution of the image with a gradient operator. Two different gradient operators, Gaussian and difference, are evaluated to test which one is best suited to solve the current problem. The next step is the projection of the gradient, which simplifies the thresholding that must be carried out to eliminate noise from the gradient. Once the projection of the gradient is available, it is thresholded. The objective of the thresholding is to differentiate noise from real edges. An edge is found when there is data in the projection over the threshold. All these processes are designed to require low computational power, which makes a real-time implementation possible. The information about the current infrared profile pattern and about the changes in the infrared pattern obtained in real-time can be used to improve the quality of the product during manufacturing.

In addition to real-time detection of infrared profile patterns, methods to extract distinguishing features from infrared patterns are explored in this work. These features aim to characterize infrared patterns to be recognized by measurements whose values are very similar for patterns in the same category, and very different from patterns in different categories. Polynomial fit using orthogonal polynomials is studied as a method capable of providing a compact and meaningful description of infrared profile patterns.

2. Infrared images

Temperature in infrared images is computed from the measured radiation, according to Planck's law. The conversion is affected by the emissivity of the object radiating energy, which is a parameter of the device used to acquire infrared images. Among infrared acquisition devices, infrared line scanners are the most commonly used to measure the temperature of very long moving objects, such as steel strips. Image acquisition using these devices is carried out by capturing infrared profiles from objects which move forward along a track. The repetitive line-scanning ($\approx$100Hz) and the movement of the object make the acquisition of a rectangular image possible. Fig. 1 shows a diagram of the operation of an infrared line scanner.

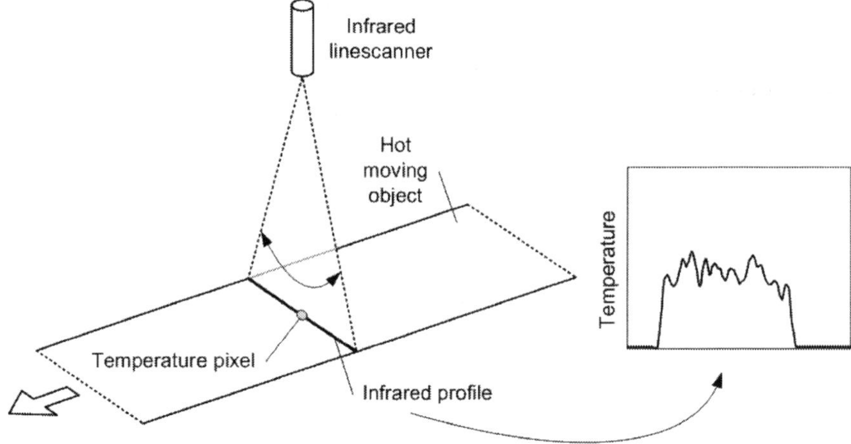

Fig. 1. Operation of an infrared line scanner

The resulting infrared image consists of a sequence of infrared profiles, each of which is made up of a set of pixels which represent temperature. Fig. 2 shows an example of infrared image acquired from a hot steel strip. Infrared images acquired from steel strips using infrared line scanners have an approximated resolution of 130 rows and 10,000 columns, where each pixel of the image represents a temperature value in the range [100, 200ºC].

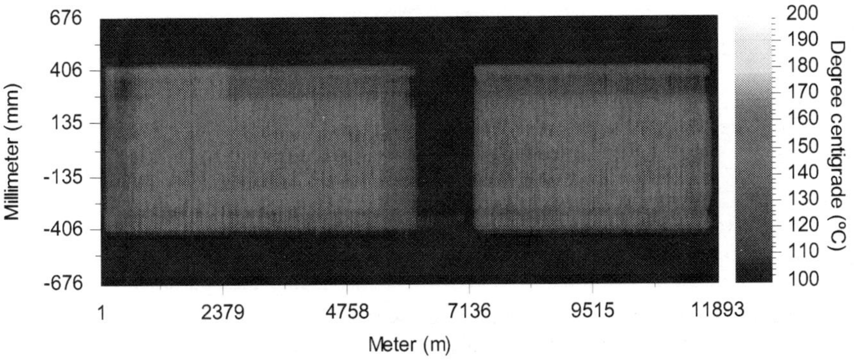

Fig. 2. Example of infrared image acquired from a steel strip

2.1 Infrared profile patterns

One of the objectives of this work is the detection of infrared profile patterns. This means detection regions of homogeneous temperature, that is, regions formed by a set of adjacent profiles which have a similar temperature pattern.

Different regions in the infrared image appear as a consequence of the changes of the manufacturing conditions over time. The following is an example of how different regions can appear in an image acquired from a steel strip. For an instant during a strip manufacturing (Fig. 3, moment A) the speed is reduced, which produces a decrement in the temperature of the strip. Before the speed reduction, the profiles acquired show a high infrared profile pattern (Fig. 3, pattern 1), and after the speed reduction they show a lower one (Fig. 3, pattern 2). Later (Fig. 3, moment B), the speed strip is recovered and the pattern is again high (Fig. 3, pattern 3). After this, a typical change in the manufacturing conditions is produced (Fig. 3, moment C), which consists of the application of excessive pressure on one part of the strip. The excess of pressure generates heat and the infrared pattern rises where high pressure is applied to the strip (Fig. 3, pattern 4). When the excess of pressure disappears (Fig. 3, moment D) a flat infrared pattern appears again (Fig. 3, pattern 5). Finally, a new decrement of the speed (Fig. 3, moment E) produces a new infrared pattern (Fig. 3, pattern 6).

In the case of steel strips, information about the current temperature pattern can be used during the manufacturing process to activate the cooling nozzles where the temperature is higher. However, to do this, infrared profile patterns must be detected in real-time with the manufacturing process, making the real-time adjustment of the cooling feedback possible.

3. Detection of infrared profile patterns

The method proposed to detect these infrared profile patterns in real-time is based on the segmentation of the stream of infrared profiles acquired from the infrared line scanner. The proposed method to segment infrared images into regions of common temperature patterns is by means of boundary detection, which, in this case, is accomplished through edge detection.

Segmentation techniques based on edge detection rely on edges found in an image by edge detection operators. These edges mark image discontinuities regarding some image attribute. Usually, the attribute is the luminance level; in this case, the temperature level will be used.

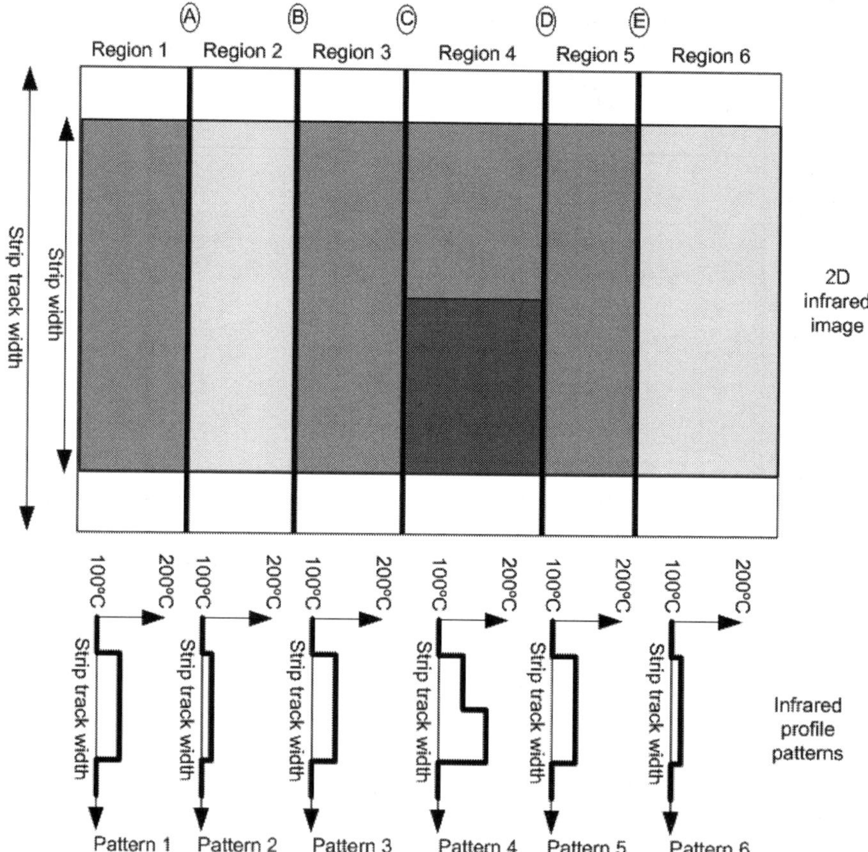

Fig. 3. Infrared profile patterns

The general edge-based segmentation process consists of several steps. It starts by applying a convolution kernel (or gradient operator) over an image (Pratt, 2001). The result obtained from the convolution is the gradient of the image, which is obviously dependent on the gradient operator used. The next step involves the analysis of the gradient in order to eliminate the noise while keeping the real edges. Usually, this process is carried out by using thresholding techniques or morphological operators. The last step consists of linking the edges in order to determine the boundary of the regions, and in this way, to accomplish the segmentation of the image into regions.

The steps for the proposed edge-based segmentation method for the infrared images considered in this work are described below.

3.1 Calculation of the gradient

The gradient of an image is obtained as the result of the convolution of the image with a gradient operator, also called convolution kernel (Canny, 1986).

When choosing a gradient operator, three important issues must be carefully selected: the direction, the size, and the shape. The fact that the edges will only be searched in the direction of the object movement makes the selection of direction and size easier. The direction of the operator will be the same as the object movement, that is, longitudinal. Furthermore, the size, normally defined as A rows x B columns, can be simplified as 1xB, since only the modification of the number of columns of the operator (B) will make significant changes to the resulting gradient. To simplify the next operations, N, defined as (B-1)/2, will be used when referring to the operator length.

In order to decide which operator shape best fits the images considered, two operators were analyzed: the difference operator and the FDoG (first derivative of Gaussian). The difference operator consists of a convolution kernel where the first N coefficients are -1, the next is 0, and the last N are 1. Summarizing, this operator calculates the difference between the next and the previous window (both of size N) of the current pixel. On the other hand, the FDoG operator consists of the derivative of a Gaussian function. The representation of both operators can be seen in Fig. 4.

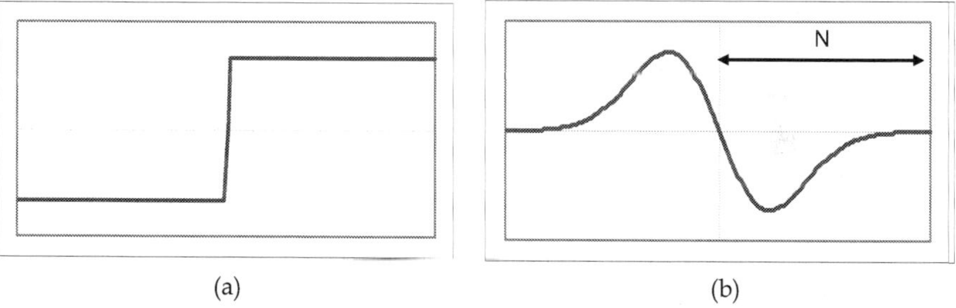

(a)   (b)

Fig. 4. Gradient operators. (a) difference, (b) FDoG

To apply the FDoG operator, a convolution operation must be carried out. This operation can be calculated using (1), where LS[i, j] is the pixel j of the infrared profile i, and FDoG[i] is the ith coefficient of the FDoG operator.

$$FDoG\_Grad[i,j] = \sum_{k=i-N}^{k=i+N} LS[k,j] \, FDoG\big[k-(i-N)\big] \tag{1}$$

To apply the difference operator (Dif), the same convolution operation with different coefficients can be used. However, since the application of the difference operator in one pixel corresponds to the calculation of the difference between two averages, it can also be applied in Eq. (2).

Eq. (2) can also be seen as (3), the difference between the next and previous window (size N), where ALS[f, t, j] is the average pixel j from the profile f to t.

$$Dif\_Grad[i,j] = \frac{\displaystyle\sum_{k=i+1}^{k=i+N} LS[k,j]}{N} - \frac{\displaystyle\sum_{k=i-N}^{k=i-1} LS[k,j]}{N} \tag{2}$$

$$Dif\_Grad[i,j] = ALS[i+1, i+N, j] - ALS[i-N, i-1, j] \tag{3}$$

The average of a signal from point a to point b can be calculated using Eq. (4), which can be transformed into a recursive equation as seen in Eq. (5).

$$\overline{x_{a,b}} = \frac{\sum_{i=a}^{b} x_i}{b-a+1} \tag{4}$$

$$\overline{x_{a,b}} = \frac{\sum_{i=a-1}^{b-1} x_i + x_b - x_{a-1}}{b-a+1} = \overline{x_{a-1,b-1}} + \frac{x_b - x_{a-1}}{b-a+1} \tag{5}$$

Using the recursive definition of the average given in Eq. (5), Eq. (6) can be proposed for the calculation of ALS, which makes it possible to calculate the operator recursively, therefore requiring a lower number of operations.

$$ALS[a,b,j] = ALS[a-1,b-1,j] + \frac{LS[b,j] - LS[a-1,j]}{b-a+1} \tag{6}$$

The segmentation method must be applied in real-time. This means that the time necessary to calculate the gradient in a profile will be a part of the total time necessary to process a new acquired profile (maximum of 10ms using an infrared line-scanner of 100Hz). Applying a convolution operation with an operator of window size N, and a profile of length L requires the operations included in Table 1. The recursive version is seen to need far fewer mathematical operations than the convolution. For example, the calculations of the gradient using an operator of window size 100 over a profile of 100 points, would need 40,000 mathematical operations using the convolution, but only 700 using the recursive approach. This difference makes the recursive approach 57 times faster than the convolution, which, depending on the computation speed, could represent the difference between being able to calculate the gradient before the deadline or not.

	Convolution	Recursive
Multiplications:	2*N*L	0
Additions:	2*N*L	2*L
Subtraction:	0	3*L
Divisions:	0	2*L
Total:	4*N*L	7*L

Table 1. Number of operations required to calculate the gradient

Fig. 5 shows the gradient produced by the difference and FDoG operators (both using N=100) when applied to the infrared image shown in Fig. 2.

Taking the previous considerations into account, the most suitable operator in this case is the difference, for three reasons:

- The multiple response effect in the produced gradient is not avoided by any of the operators (Canny, 1986).
- The gradient produced by the difference operator maximizes the SNR (signal to noise ratio) (Canny, 1986).

- Since the difference operator can be applied recursively, its implementation is much faster than the convolution operation. This constitutes a significant advantage when designing a segmentation method to work in real time.

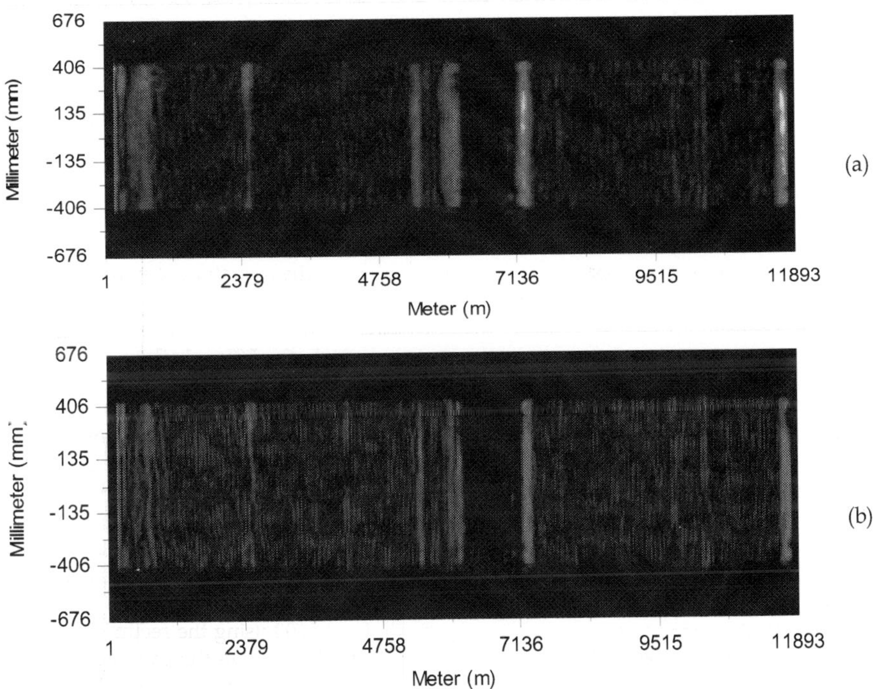

Fig. 5. Gradient produced by the difference (a) and FDoG (b) operators

3.2 Projection of the gradient

The next step is the projection of the gradient, which simplifies the thresholding that must be carried out to eliminate noise from the gradient. This projection is carried out using Eq. (7), where LSL is the profile length (number of pixels in the profile), and P is a parameter of the projection.

$$GradProj[i] = \frac{1}{LSL} \sum_{j=1}^{LSL} \left(Grad[i,j] \right)^{P} \tag{7}$$

Fig. 6 shows the projection (using P=2) of the gradients obtained using the difference and FDoG gradient operators, which can be seen in Fig. 5. This figure shows that the difference operator identifies the edges of the image more clearly and with more responses per edge, which corroborates the conclusions drawn in Canny's work (Canny, 1986) on the proper gradient operator under his constraints of SNR (signal to noise ratio) and simple response.

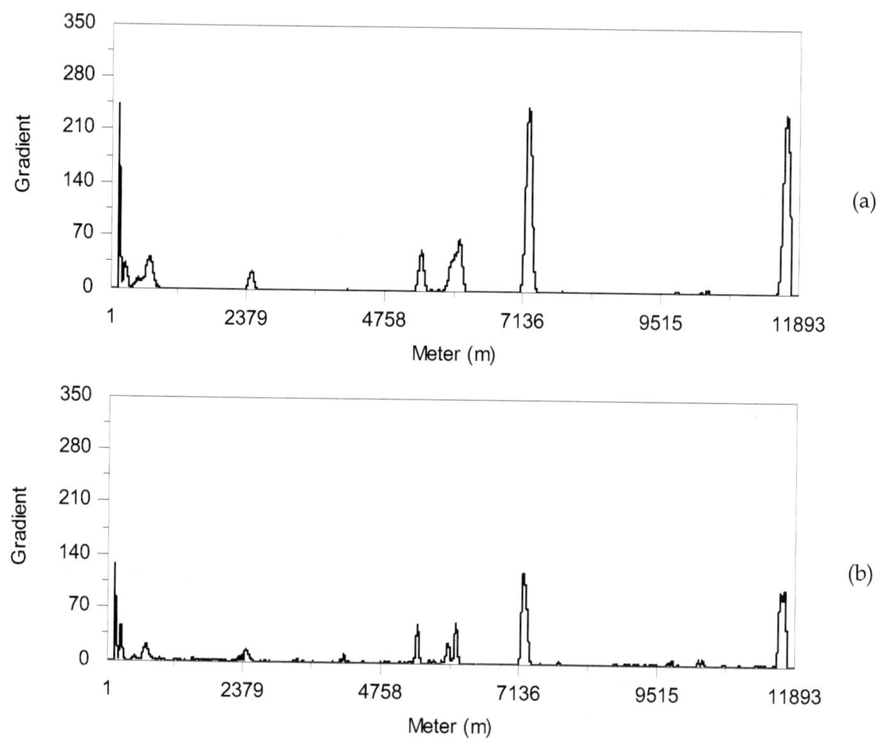

Fig. 6. Projection of the gradient. (a) using difference operator, (b) using FDoG operator

3.3 Thresholding of the projection

Once the projection of the gradient is available, it is thresholded. The objective of the thresholding is to differentiate noise from real edges. An edge is found when there is data in the projection over the threshold value T. When adjacent edges are found (adjacent values of the projection over the threshold), only the edge with the higher value in the projection of all of the adjacent positions will be considered. This can be interpreted as a morphological operator.

Fig. 7a shows an example of the thresholding (T=25) carried out over the projection (P=2) of the gradient produced by the difference operator (N=100, shown in Fig. 6a) over the image in Fig. 2. As can be seen, the noise is below the threshold value and edges are obtained from the peaks above it (Fig. 7b). Only the highest value of each peak will be considered to establish the longitudinal position of its corresponding edge. The segmented image consists of the set of regions bounded by the found edges (Fig. 7c).

3.4 Summary of the segmentation method

The proposed segmentation method for infrared images is based on edge detection. Edges are detected by means of the thresholding of the projection of the gradient calculated with

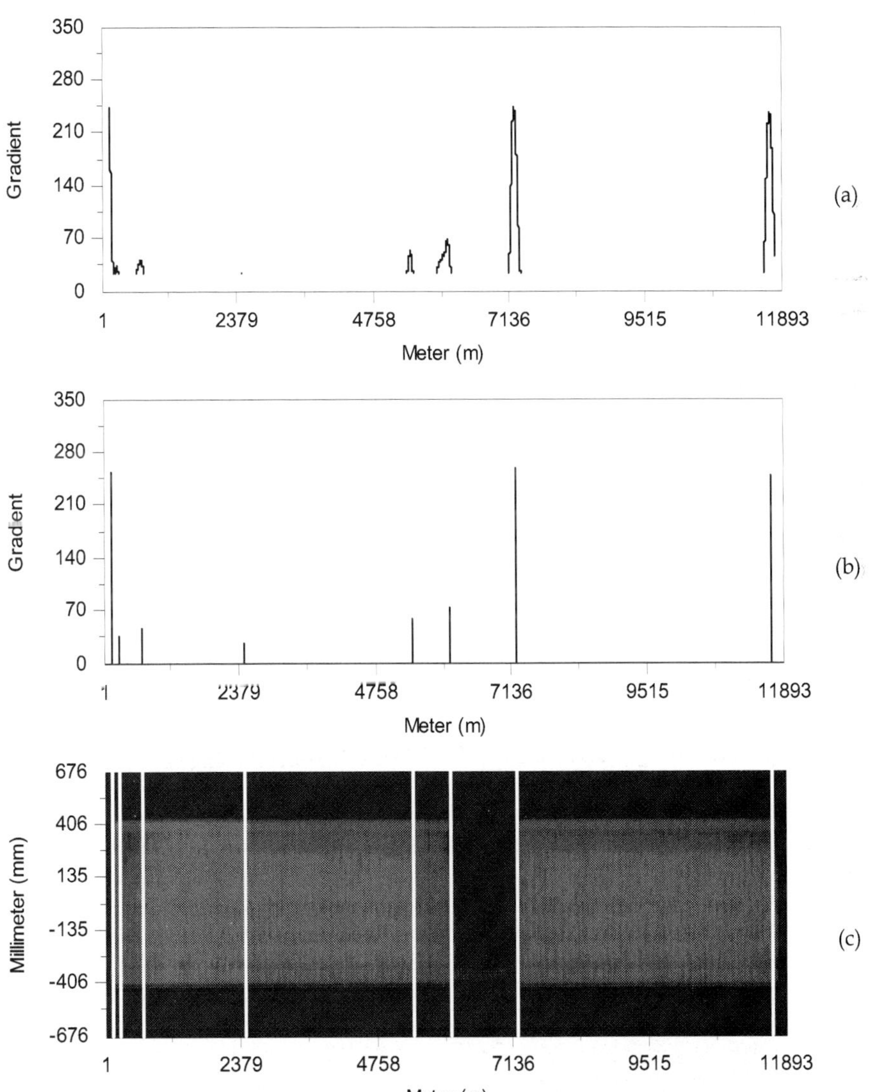

Fig. 7. Final steps of the detection process. (a) thresholding of the projection, (b) resulting position of the edges as the maximums of every peak, (c) segmented image

the difference operator. This process is carried out in real time with the infrared profile acquisition, detecting changes in the temperature pattern shortly after they appear.
The implementation of the segmentation method was successfully tested to fit the real time requirements imposed by a line acquisition rate of 100 Hz (10 ms period).

The configuration parameters of the algorithm are the following:
- Operator length (N).
- Projection power (P).
- Threshold level (T).

The results of the segmentation depend on the use of the proper values for these configuration parameters.

4. Tuning of the pattern detector

In order to tune the pattern detection process the best configuration for the parameters N, P, and T must be found.

The approach proposed to carry out automatic tuning of the pattern detection process is by means of evolutionary computation. This kind of computation method encompasses a variety of population-based problem solving techniques that mimic the biological process of Darwinian evolution, based on the principle of natural selection. Evolutionary algorithms provide versatile problem-solving mechanisms for search, adaptation, learning, and optimization in a variety of application domains (Bhandarkar & Zhang, 1999). The automatic segmentation tuning proposed in this work uses a genetic algorithm (Holland, 1992; Goldberg, 1989), an important member of the wider class of evolutionary algorithms which has been successfully used in the image processing field (Chun & Yang, 1996; Bhanu at al., 1995; Andrey, 1999; Pignalberi et al., 2003).

A genetic algorithm (GA) is an adaptive procedure that searches for viable solutions using a collection of search points, known as population, in order to maximize desirable criterion (Chun & Yang, 1996). Each search point, or member of the population, is known as an individual, and is represented as a chromosome encoded as a string of genes which are used to codify parameters. During iterations, each individual is evaluated and combined with others on the basis of its overall quality.

In this case, each chromosome contains the information about a configuration for the parameters of the segmentation algorithm. The quality of the chromosome is defined as the result provided by the combined objective function.

The first issue which must be defined in order to apply the genetic algorithm is the way the chromosomes are codified. Chromosomes contain information about parameters of the problem whose optimal values must be found. In this case, these values are the parameters of the segmentation process: N, P, and T. Each parameter is codified as a floating point number, thus, the chromosome is a vector of three numbers, as is represented in (8) for a generic chromosome i.

$$C_i = \left[N_i, P_i, T_i \right] \tag{8}$$

It is interesting to note that chromosomes are usually codified using binary methods; however, the use of floating point numbers has proved to provide similar or even better results than the binary codification for classical problems (Haupt & Haupt, 2003).

In this case, the population is defined as an array of 100 individuals, each represented by a chromosome which is initially filled with random numbers. Individuals are the search points of the genetic algorithm, and their quality is evaluated through Eq. (9), where C is a chromosome, which codifies the information about N, P and T, and OF is the objective function which indicates the success level of the segmentation using that parameter set.

$$Quality(C) = OF\left(N_i, P_i, T_i\right) \qquad (9)$$

The genetic algorithm used is an iterative process which repeats the following four steps: natural selection, pairing, crossing, and mutation. These steps are described below.

4.1 Natural selection

The natural selection process decides which chromosomes in the population are fit enough to survive and possibly produce offspring in the next generation. To carry out this task, the quality of every chromosome in the population is calculated. Then, the array of chromosomes is sorted. Only the best half of the chromosomes survives (elitism), the rest are discarded to make room for the new offspring.

4.2 Pairing

The surviving chromosomes form the mating pool. The pairing process randomly creates pairs of fathers and mothers from this pool. Each pair produces two offspring which inherit traits from each parent. Enough pairs are created to fill the room left by the discarded chromosomes. In addition, the parents survive to form part of the next generation.

4.3 Crossing

Crossing is the process which produces offspring as a combination of the parents. Many different approaches for crossing have been tested (Michalewicz, 1994). In this case, a combination of blending (Radcliff, 1991) and extrapolation (Wright, 1991) is applied. The pseudocode of the crossing method can be seen in Algorithm 1.

```
function crossover(chromosome f, chromosome m)
  : chromosome o1, o2
begin
  beta = random[0, 1];

  switch (random_int[0, 1, 2])
  begin
    case 0: // N
      No1 = Nf - beta*(Nf - Nm);
      Po1 = Pf * random[0.5, 1.5];
      To1 = Tf * random[0.5, 1.5];

      No2 = Nm + beta*(Nf - Nm);
      Po2 = Pm * random[0.5, 1.5];
      To2 = Tm * random[0.5, 1.5];
    case 1: // P
      // Similar for P
      ...

    case 2: // T
      // Similar for T
      ...

  end_switch
end_function
```

Algorithm 1. Crossover strategy

4.4 Mutation

A common problem in any optimization technique setting out to find the global optimum is how to deal with local maximums. To avoid this problem, genetic algorithms force the exploration of other areas of the solution space by randomly introducing changes or mutations, in some of the chromosomes. The mutation method applied in this case mutates 5% of the population per iteration. The mutated chromosomes are selected randomly from the new generation resulting from the crossing process. The mutation process of a chromosome consists of the modification of one of its genes.

4.5 Objective function

Different evaluation methods for image segmentation which could be used as an objective function for the segmentation method have been proposed. (Zhang, 1996) proposes a classification of existing methods as "analytical", "empirical goodness", and "empirical discrepancy". The empirical discrepancy methods provide a value which indicates the similarity between the segmentation results and the ground truth. It is esteemed to be the most suitable method to be used as the objective function.

Jaccard (Sneath & Sokal, 1973) proposed a metric (JC) for classification purposes which has also been used as an empirical discrepancy method (Rosin & Ioannidis, 2003). This metric is defined in Eq. (10), where N_{TP} is the number of true positive detections, that is, the number of pixels correctly defined as edge pixels, N_{FP} is the number of false positive detections, that is, the number of pixels erroneously defined as edge pixels, and N_{FN} is the number of false negative detections, that is, the number of pixels erroneously defined as non-edge pixels.

$$JC = \frac{N_{TP}}{N_{TP} + N_{FP} + N_{FN}} \tag{10}$$

JC is a suitable method to be used as the objective function; therefore it will be used in this work.

The ground truth, necessary to determine the effectiveness of a detection method, is created by manually segmenting the images in a test set. This ground truth will be used to calculate the objective function (JC) during the tuning of the parameters of the pattern detector.

4.6 Results

After 250 iterations the best chromosome codifies the following parameter set:

- N: 118.
- P: 13.810.
- T: 5.869e12.

Fig. 8 and Fig. 9 show the infrared profile patterns detected in two images using the configuration obtained in the tuning procedure.

5. Feature extraction

Features extracted from an object aim to characterize the object to be recognized by measurements whose values are very similar for objects in the same category, and very different from objects in different categories (Duda et al., 2001). This leads to the idea of seeking distinguishing features.

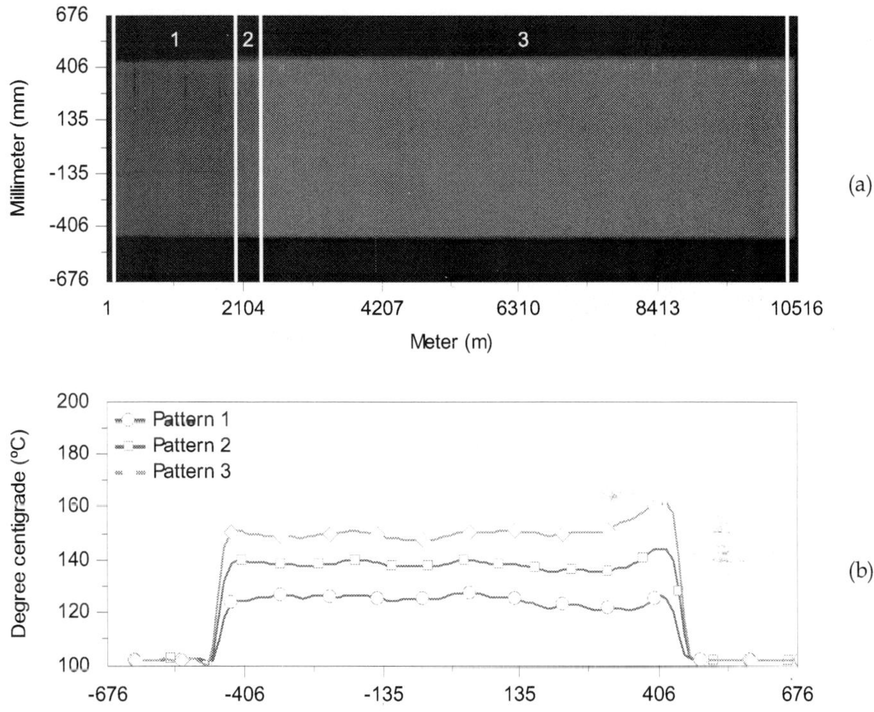

Fig. 8. Infrared profile patterns detected in image 1. (a) Segmented image, (b) infrared profile patterns for each segmented region

The proposed approach in this work is to extract features is by means of a polynomial fit. In particular, the shape of the infrared profile will be approximated by orthogonal polynomials (Abramowitz & Stegun, 1972). This approach has several advantages, including the elimination of the low frequency components of the signal (noise), and a reduction of the amount o information about the profile (Mukundan, 2004). However, the most important advantage of this approach is that the coefficients of the polynomials can be used to effectively describe the shape of the profile pattern.

To carry out the polynomial fit, several alternatives are available, including Chebyshev or Hermite orthogonal polynomials. However, in this case, Gram polynomials (sometimes called discrete Legendre orthogonal polynomials), are used due to their simplicity and accuracy.

Gram polynomials can be calculated using Eq. (11).

$$P_m(i) = c_{mN} \sum_{j=0}^{m} \frac{(-1)^j (m+j)^{2j}}{(j!)^2} \frac{i^j}{(N-1)^j} \tag{11}$$

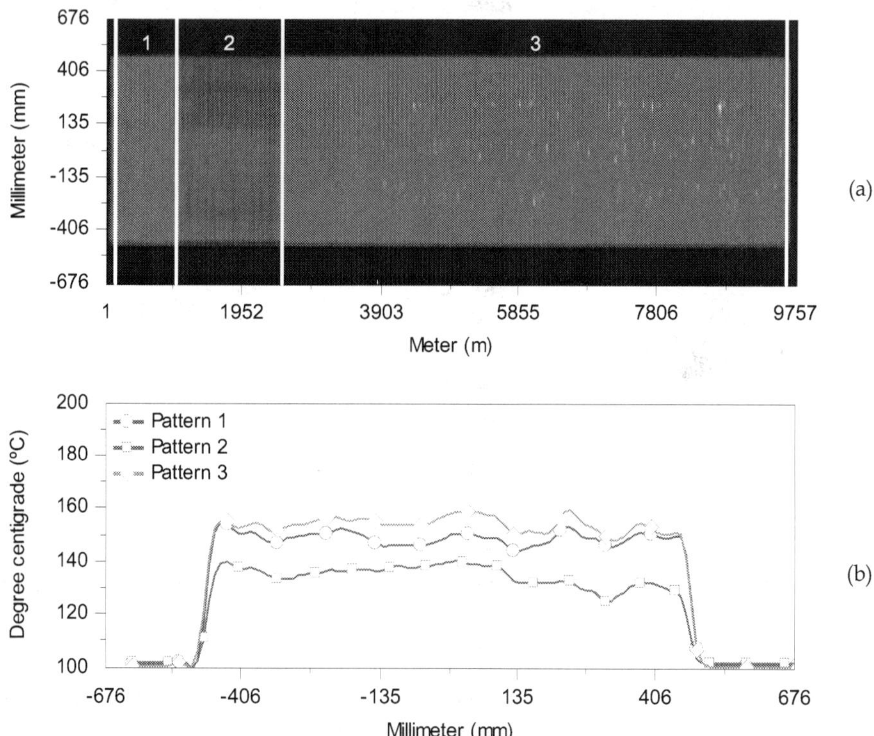

Fig. 9. Infrared profile patterns detected in image 2. (a) Segmented image, (b) infrared profile patterns for each segmented region

Gram polynomials, with $c_{mN}=1$, are constructed, for N equally spaced points in the interval [-1, 1] by the recurrence relationship shown in Eq. (12).

The matrix, X, consisting of the first p orthogonal polynomials evaluated at N points can be seen in (13). The profile or shape, Ω, can be expressed as (14), where ε consists of terms of order p+1 and higher (as a polynomial of order N–1 will match the measurements at the N data points), and c is the vector of coefficients of the orthogonal polynomials.

$$P_{-1}(i) = 0$$
$$P_0(i) = 1$$
$$P_j(i) = \alpha(i,j)P_{j-1}(i) - \beta(j)P_{j-2}(i) \qquad j \geq 1 \tag{12}$$
$$\alpha(i,j) = \frac{(N-1)(2j-1)}{j(N-j)}\left(1 - \frac{2i}{N-1}\right) \qquad i = 1,\ldots,N$$
$$\beta(j) = \frac{(j-1)(N-1+j)}{j(N-j)}.$$

The least-squares estimate of the parameter vector c can be seen in (15).

$$\hat{c} = \left(\mathbf{XX}^{\mathrm{T}}\right)^{-1}\mathbf{X\Omega} \equiv \mathbf{Q\Omega}$$ (15)

Thus, the Gram polynomial approximation of the profile shape can be given by (16), where X^{T} is a diagonal matrix.

$$\hat{\mathbf{\Omega}} = \mathbf{X}^{\mathrm{T}}\mathbf{Q\Omega}$$ (16)

The main advantage of the representation using orthogonal polynomials is that the polynomial coefficients, Cj, can be calculated independently of each other. If more coefficients are needed, the next (p+1) coefficient can be determined from Eq. (17), hence more coefficients can be added without affecting those already calculated.

$$\hat{c}(p+1) = \frac{1}{\mathbf{P}_{p+1}^{\mathrm{T}}\mathbf{P}_{p+1}}\mathbf{P}_{p+1}^{\mathrm{T}}\mathbf{\Omega}$$ (17)

From the Gram Polynomial, coefficients Ci can be used as features to describe effectively the shape of the profile. C0 is the constant coefficient and describes the average of the profile. C1 is the coefficient of the first order polynomial and describes the leveling of the profile, and thus, the symmetry when it is null. C1 will be positive when the temperature on the left border is higher than the one on the right border and negative otherwise. C2 is the coefficient of the second order polynomial and describes the curvature of the profile, which will be positive when the temperature of the borders is higher than the temperature in the middle or negative otherwise. Depending on the applications, more coefficients could be used, but these three coefficients are enough to describe common features of infrared profiles patterns.

Before extracting features from infrared profiles patterns, background and foreground need to be separated to avoid an incorrect fit. This process can be carried out using any thresholding technique (Sezgin & Sankur, 2004). In this work, the limits of the foreground were calculated using the zero crossing positions of the second derivative of the profile.

Fig. 10 shows the representation of the Gram polynomial fit for the infrared profile patterns detected in Fig 8 and Fig. 9. Table 2 shows the features extracted from these patterns.

Features shown in Table 2 contain very interesting information. For example, the right border in pattern 3 of image 1 has higher temperature than the left border. Pattern 2 of image 2 has the left border with higher temperature than the right border, and also, the temperature in the middle is higher than in the borders. Many other conclusions could be easily drawn form the extracted features.

These features make it possible to develop a pattern classifier. They can also be used directly by the manufacturing control systems to correct anomalous situations in real-time.

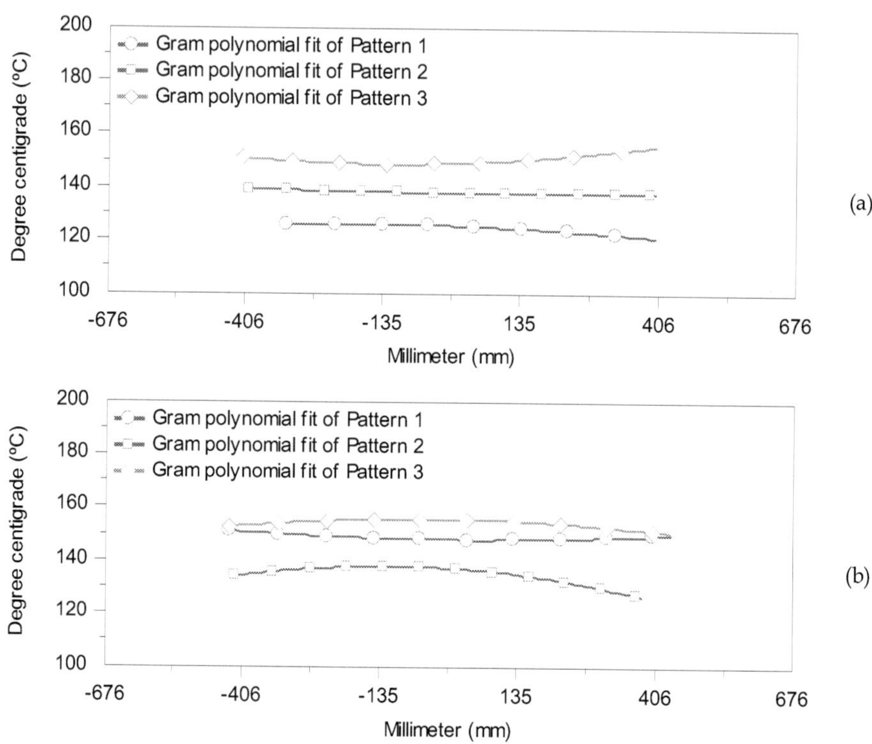

Fig. 10. Gram polynomial fit. (a) patterns in image 1, (b) patterns in image 2

Image	Pattern	Average (C0)	Leveling (C1)	Curvature (C2)
1	1	124.851	2.438	-1.150
1	2	138.424	0.632	0.481
1	3	150.616	-2.355	2.818
2	1	149.077	0.621	1.566
2	2	135.296	3.633	-4.637
2	3	154.526	1.023	-2.636

Table 2. Features extracted from the detected patterns

6. Conclusions

In this work, a method to detect infrared profiles patterns in real-time is proposed. The method is based on real-time segmentation of infrared images acquired using an infrared line-scanner. The segmentation is based on the detection of edges which indicate the change of the current infrared profile pattern. The segmentation consists of the calculation of the gradient, its projection, and its thresholding. These three steps are designed to be applied in real-time. Therefore, the information about the current infrared profile pattern can be used during manufacturing. A procedure to tune the pattern detector based on evolutionary computation is also proposed. The procedure produced the best configuration parameters of the proposed detector. The results of the pattern detector meet the functional and the real-time requirements.

Methods to extract distinguishing features from infrared patterns are also explored in this work. The results obtained indicate that polynomial fit using Gram orthogonal polynomials provide a compact and meaningful description of infrared profile patterns. The coefficients of the polynomials can describe interesting features, such as average, levelling, or curvature. These features could be easily used in many types of applications which aim to classify the patterns in different groups. These features are also an excellent method to describe images with only a few numbers, which can make the analysis or the storage of the information much more effective.

The proposed methods are very likely to find potential applications in a number of different areas, such as robotics, manufacturing control, or any other applications based on the processing of a stream of infrared profiles in real-time. Furthermore, even if the proposed method has been described for infrared images, its use with images taken from the visible spectrum is straightforward.

7. References

Abramowitz, M. & Stegun, I. A. (1972). Handbook of Mathematical Functions with Formulas, Graphs, and Mathematical Tables, Dover Publications, ISBN: 0486612724.

Andrey, P. (1999). Selectionist relaxation: genetic algorithms applied to image segmentation. Image and Vision Computing, Vol. 17, No. 3-4, 175-187.

Canny, J. (1986). A computational approach to edge detection. IEEE Transactions on Pattern Analysis and Machine Intelligence, Vol. 8, No. 6, 679-698.

Bhanu, B.; Lee, S. & Ming J. (1995). Adaptive image segmentation using a genetic algorithm. IEEE Transactions on Systems, Man and Cybernetics, Vol. 25, No. 2, 1543-1567.

Bhandarkar, S. M. & Zhang, H. (1999). Image Segmentation Using Evolutionary Computation. IEEE Transactions on Evolutionary Computation, Vol. 3, No. 1, 1-21.

Chun, D. N. & Yang H. S. (1996). Robust Image Segmentation Using Genetic Algorithm with a Fuzzy Measure. Pattern Recognition, Vol. 29, No. 7, 1195-1211.

Duda, R. O.; Hart, P. E. & Stork, D. G. (2001). Pattern Classification, Wiley-Interscience, ISBN: 0471056693, New York.

Goldberg, D. E. (1989). Genetic Algorithms in Search, Optimization, and Machine Learning, Addison-Wesley, ISBN 0201157675, Reading, MA.

Gonzalez, J. A.; Obeso, F.; García, D. F.; Usamentiaga, R. & Falessi, R. (2002). Application of thermographic analysis for the detection of longitudinal defects in cold mills. Revue de Metallurgie. Cahiers D'Informations Techniques, Vol. 99, No. 6, 537-543.

Haupt, R. L. & Haupt, S. E. (2004). Practical genetic algorithms, Wiley-Interscience, ISBN: 0471188735, New York.

Holland, J. H. (1992). Adaptation in Natural and Artificial Systems, MIT Press, ISBN 0-262-58111-6, Cambridge, MA

Michalewicz, Z. (1994). Genetic Algorithms + Data Structures = Evolution Programs, Springer-Verlag, ISBN: 3540606769, Berlin.

Mukundan, R. (2004). Some Computational Aspects of Discrete Moments. IEEE Transactions on Image Processing, Vol. 13, No. 8, 1055-1059.

Pignalberi, G.; Cucchiara, R.; Cinque, L. & Levialdi S. (2003). Tuning range image segmentation by genetic algorithm. Eurasip Journal on Applied Signal Processing, Vol. 2003, No. 8, 780-790.

Pratt, W. K. (2001). Digital Image Processing, Wiley-Interscience, ISBN: 0471374075, New York.

Radcliff, N. J. (1991). Forma analysis and random respectful recombination, Proc. 4th Int. Conf. on Genetic Algorithms, pp. 222-229, San Marco CA, 1991, Morgan Kauffman.

Rosin, P. L. & Ioannidis E. (2003). Evaluation of global image thresholding for change detection. Pattern Recognition Letters, Vol. 24, No. 14, 2345-2356.

Sezgin, M. & Sankur, B. (2004). Survey over image thresholding techniques and quantitative performance evaluation. Journal of Electronic Imaging, Vol. 13, No. 1, 146-168.

Sneath, P. & Sokal R. (1973). Numerical Taxonomy, The principle and practice of numerical classification, W H Freeman & Co, ISBN: 0716706970, San Francisco.

Wright, A. H. (1991). Genetic algorithms for real parameter optimization. Foundations of Genetic Algorithms, Vol. 1, 205-218.

Zhang, Y. J. (1996). A Survey on Evaluation Methods for Image Segmentation. Pattern Recognition Elsevier Science, Vol. 29, No. 8, 1335-1346.

3

A Survey of Shape Feature Extraction Techniques

Yang Mingqiang[1,2], Kpalma Kidiyo[1] and Ronsin Joseph[1]
[1]IETR-INSA, UMR-CNRS 6164, 35043 Rennes,
[2]Shandong University, 250100, Jinan,
[1]France
[2]China

1. Introduction

"A picture is worth one thousand words". This proverb comes from Confucius - a Chinese philosopher about 2500 years ago. Now, the essence of these words is universally understood. A picture can be magical in its ability to quickly communicate a complex story or a set of ideas that can be recalled by the viewer later in time.

Visual information plays an important role in our society, it will play an increasingly pervasive role in our lives, and there will be a growing need to have these sources processed further. The pictures or images are used in many application areas like architectural and engineering design, fashion, journalism, advertising, entertainment, etc. Thus it provides the necessary opportunity for us to use the abundance of images. However, the knowledge will be useless if one can't find it. Face to the substantive and increasing apace images, how to search and to retrieve the images that we are interested in facility is a fatal problem: it brings a necessity for image retrieval systems. As we know, visual features of the images provide a description of their content. Content-based image retrieval (CBIR), emerged as a promising mean for retrieving images and browsing large images databases. CBIR has been a topic of intensive research in recent years. It is the process of retrieving images from a collection based on automatically extracted features from those images.

This paper focuses on presenting a survey of the existing approaches of shape-based feature extraction. Efficient shape features must present some essential properties such as:

- identifiability: shapes which are found perceptually similar by human have the same features that are different from the others.
- translation, rotation and scale invariance: the location, the rotation and the scaling changing of the shape must not affect the extracted features.
- affine invariance: the affine transform performs a linear mapping from coordinates system to other coordinates system that preserves the "straightness" and "parallelism" of lines. Affine transform can be constructed using sequences of translations, scales, flips, rotations and shears. The extracted features must be as invariant as possible with affine transforms.
- noise resistance: features must be as robust as possible against noise, i.e., they must be the same whichever be the strength of the noise in a give range that affects the pattern.

- occultation invariance: when some parts of a shape are occulted by other objects, the feature of the remaining part must not change compared to the original shape.
- statistically independent: two features must be statistically independent. This represents compactness of the representation.
- reliability: as long as one deals with the same pattern, the extracted features must remain the same.

In general, shape descriptor is a set of numbers that are produced to represent a given shape feature. A descriptor attempts to quantify the shape in ways that agree with human intuition (or task-specific requirements). Good retrieval accuracy requires a shape descriptor to be able to effectively find perceptually similar shapes from a database. Usually, the descriptors are in the form of a vector. Shape descriptors should meet the following requirements:

- the descriptors should be as complete as possible to represent the content of the information items.
- the descriptors should be represented and stored compactly. The size of a descriptor vector must not be too large.
- the computation of the similarity or the distance between descriptors should be simple; otherwise the execution time would be too long.

Shape feature extraction and representation plays an important role in the following categories of applications:

- shape retrieval: searching for all shapes in a typically large database of shapes that are similar to a query shape. Usually all shapes within a given distance from the query are determined or the first few shapes that have the smallest distance.
- shape recognition and classification: determining whether a given shape matches a model sufficiently, or which of representative class is the most similar.
- shape alignment and registration: transforming or translating one shape so that it best matches another shape, in whole or in part.
- shape approximation and simplification: constructing a shape with fewer elements (points, segments, triangles, etc.), so that it is still similar to the original.

Many shape description and similarity measurement techniques have been developed in the past. A number of new techniques have been proposed in recent years. There are 3 main classification methods as follows:

- contour-based methods and region-based methods [1]. This is the most common and general classification and it is proposed by MPEG-7. It is based on the use of shape boundary points as opposed to shape interior points. Under each class, different methods are further divided into structural approaches and global approaches. This sub-class is based on whether the shape is represented as a whole or represented by segments/sections (primitives).
- space domain and transform domain [2]. Methods in space domain match shapes on point (or point feature) basis, while feature domain techniques match shapes on feature (vector) basis.
- information preserving (IP) and non-information preserving (NIP). IP methods allow an accurate reconstruction of a shape from its descriptor, while NIP methods are only capable of partial ambiguous reconstruction. For object recognition purpose, IP is not a requirement.

Unlike the traditional classification, the approaches of shape-based feature extraction and representation are classified according to their processing approaches: One-dimensional function for shape representation, Polygonal approximation, Spatial interrelation feature, Moments, Scale space approaches, Shape transform domains. The figure 1 shows the hierarchy of the classification of shape feature extraction approaches.

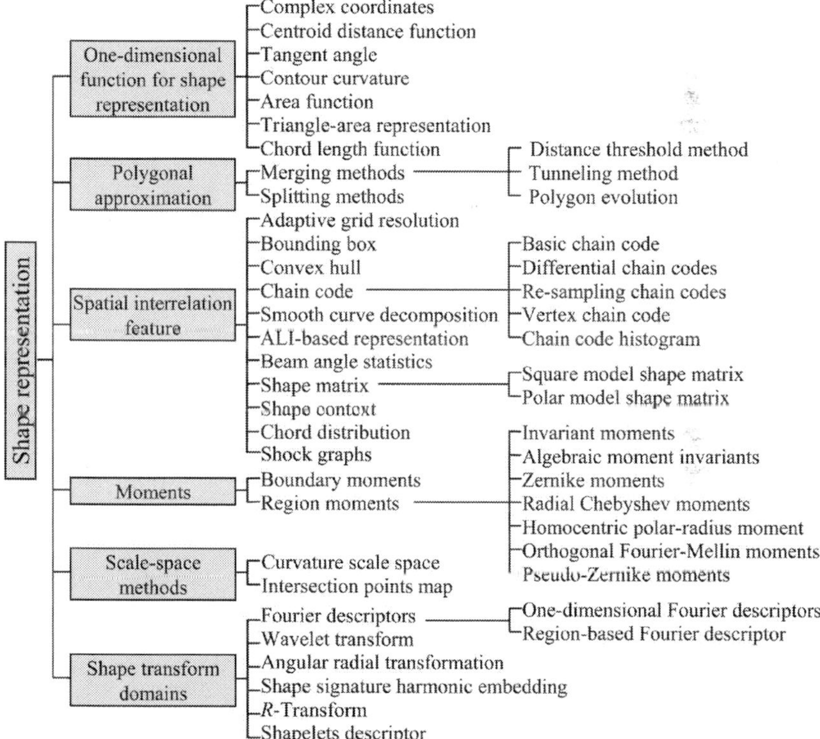

Fig. 1. An overview of shape description techniques

Without being complete, in the following sections, we will describe and group a number of these methods together.

2. Shape parameters

Basically, shape-based image retrieval consists of measuring the similarity between shapes represented by their features. Some simple geometric features can be used to describe shapes. Usually, the simple geometric features can only discriminate shapes with large differences; therefore, they are usually used as filters to eliminate false hits or combined with other shape descriptors to discriminate shapes. They are not suitable to be stand alone shape descriptors. A shape can be described by different aspects. These shape parameters are Center of gravity, Axis of least inertia, Digital bending energy, Eccentricity, Circularity ratio, Elliptic variance, Rectangularity, Convexity, Solidity, Euler number, Profiles, Hole area ratio. They will be introduced in this section.

2.1 Center of gravity

The center of gravity is also called centroid. Its position should be fixed in relation to the shape. In shape recognition field, it is of particular interest to consider the case where the general function $f(x, y)$ is

$$f(x,y) = \begin{cases} 1 & if \ (x,y) \in D \\ 0 & otherwise \end{cases} \tag{1}$$

where D is the domain of the binary shape. Its centroid (g_x, g_y) is:

$$\begin{cases} g_x = \frac{1}{N} \sum_{i=1}^{N} x_i \\ g_y = \frac{1}{N} \sum_{i=1}^{N} y_i \end{cases} \tag{2}$$

where N is the number of point in the shape, $(x_i, y_i) \in \{(x_i, y_i) \mid f(x_i, y_i) = 1\}$.
A contour is a closed curve, the discrete parametric equation in Cartesian coordinate system is

$$\Gamma(n) = (x(n), y(n)) \tag{3}$$

where $n \in [0, N - 1]$; a contour may be parametrized with any number N of vertices and $\Gamma(N) = \Gamma(0)$. The position of its centroid is given below:

$$\begin{cases} g_x = \frac{1}{6A} \sum_{i=0}^{N-1} (x_i + x_{i+1})(x_i y_{i+1} - x_{i+1} y_i) \\ g_y = \frac{1}{6A} \sum_{i=0}^{N-1} (y_i + y_{i+1})(x_i y_{i+1} - x_{i+1} y_i) \end{cases} \tag{4}$$

where A is the contour's area given by

$$A = \frac{1}{2} \left| \sum_{i=0}^{N-1} (x_i y_{i+1} - x_{i+1} y_i) \right| \tag{5}$$

The position of shape centroid is fixed with different points distribution on a contour. One can notice that the position of the centroid in Figure 2 is fixed no matter how the points distribution is.

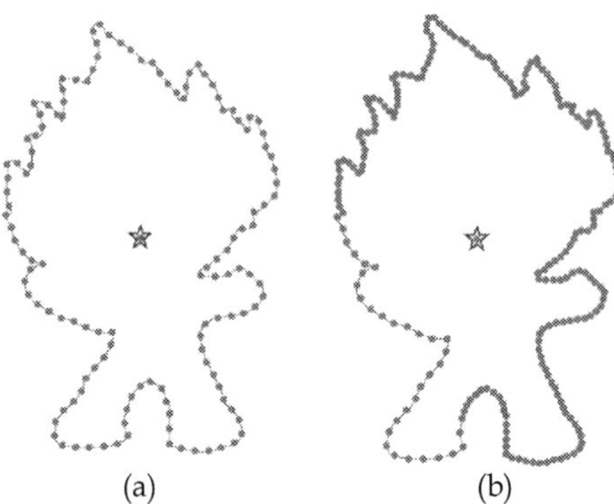

(a)   (b)

Fig. 2. Centroid of contour. The dots are points distributed on the contour uniformly (a) and non-uniformly (b). The star is the centroid of original contour and the inner dot is the centroid of sampled contour.

So using Eq. 4, we can obtain the genuine centroid of a contour under whatever the contour is normalized.

2.2 Axis of least inertia

The axis of least inertia is unique to the shape. It serves as a unique reference line to preserve the orientation of the shape. The axis of least inertia (ALI) of a shape is defined as the line for which the integral of the square of the distances to points on the shape boundary is a minimum.

Since the axis of inertia pass through the centroid of a contour, to find the ALI, transfer the shape and let the centroid of the shape be the origin of Cartesian coordinates system. Let $x\sin\theta - y\cos\theta = 0$ be the parametric equation of ALI. The slope angle θ is estimated as follows: Let α be the angle between the axis of least inertia and the x-axis. The inertia is given by [3, 4]:

$$I = \frac{1}{2}(a + c) - \frac{1}{2}(a - c)\cos(2\alpha) - \frac{1}{2}b\sin(2\alpha)$$

where $a = \sum_{i=0}^{N-1} x_i^2$, $b = 2\sum_{i=0}^{N-1} x_i y_i$, $c = \sum_{i=0}^{N-1} y_i^2$.

Hence,

$$\frac{dI}{d\alpha} = (a - c)\sin(2\alpha) - b\cos(2\alpha)$$

$$\frac{d^2 I}{d\alpha^2} = 2(a - c)\cos(2\alpha) + 2b\sin(2\alpha)$$

Let $dI/d\alpha = 0$, we obtain

$$\alpha = \frac{1}{2}\arctan\left(\frac{b}{a - c}\right), \quad -\frac{\pi}{2} < \alpha < \frac{\pi}{2}$$

The slope angle θ is given by

$$\theta = \begin{cases} \alpha + \frac{\pi}{2} & if\ \frac{d^2 I}{d\alpha^2} < 0 \\ \alpha & otherwise \end{cases}$$

2.3 Average bending energy

Average bending energy BE is defined by

$$BE = \frac{1}{N}\sum_{s=0}^{N-1} K(s)^2$$

where $K(s)$ is the curvature function, s is the arc length parameter, and N is the number of points on a contour [5]. In order to compute the average bending energy more efficiently, Young et. al. [6] did the Fourier transform of the boundary and used Fourier coefficients and Parseval's relation.

One can prove that the circle is the shape having the minimum average bending energy.

2.4 Eccentricity

Eccentricity is the measure of aspect ratio. It is the ratio of the length of major axis to the length of minor axis. It can be calculated by principal axes method or minimum bounding rectangle method.

2.4.1 Principal axes method

Principal axes of a given shape can be uniquely defined as the two segments of lines that cross each other orthogonally in the centroid of the shape and represent the directions with zero cross-correlation [7]. This way, a contour is seen as an instance from a statistical distribution. Let us consider the covariance matrix C of a contour:

$$C = \frac{1}{N} \sum_{i=0}^{N-1} \begin{pmatrix} x_i - g_x \\ y_i - g_y \end{pmatrix} \begin{pmatrix} x_i - g_x \\ y_i - g_y \end{pmatrix}^T = \begin{pmatrix} c_{xx} & c_{xy} \\ c_{yx} & c_{yy} \end{pmatrix} \tag{6}$$

where

$c_{xx} = \frac{1}{N} \sum_{i=0}^{N-1} (x_i - g_x)^2$

$c_{xy} = \frac{1}{N} \sum_{i=0}^{N-1} (x_i - g_x)(y_i - g_y)$

$c_{yx} = \frac{1}{N} \sum_{i=0}^{N-1} (y_i - g_y)(x_i - g_x)$

$c_{yy} = \frac{1}{N} \sum_{i=0}^{N-1} (y_i - g_y)^2$

$G(g_x, g_y)$ is the centroid of the shape. Clearly, here $c_{xy} = c_{yx}$.

The lengths of the two principal axes equal the eigenvalues λ_1 and λ_2 of the covariance matrix C of a contour, respectively.

So the eigenvalues λ_1 and λ_2 can be calculated by

$$det(C - \lambda_{1,2} I) = det \begin{pmatrix} c_{xx} - \lambda_{1,2} & c_{xy} \\ c_{yx} & c_{yy} - \lambda_{1,2} \end{pmatrix} = (c_{xx} - \lambda_{1,2})(c_{yy} - \lambda_{1,2}) - c_{xy}^2 = 0$$

So

$$\begin{cases} \lambda_1 = \frac{1}{2} \left[c_{xx} + c_{yy} + \sqrt{(c_{xx} + c_{yy})^2 - 4(c_{xx}c_{yy} - c_{xy}^2)} \right] \\ \lambda_2 = \frac{1}{2} \left[c_{xx} + c_{yy} - \sqrt{(c_{xx} + c_{yy})^2 - 4(c_{xx}c_{yy} - c_{xy}^2)} \right] \end{cases}$$

Then, eccentricity can be calculated:

$$E = \lambda_2 / \lambda_1 \tag{7}$$

2.4.2 Minimum bounding rectangle

Minimum bounding rectangle is also called minimum bounding box. It is the smallest rectangle that contains every point in the shape. For an arbitrary shape, eccentricity is the ratio of the length L and width W of minimal bounding rectangle of the shape at some set of orientations. Elongation, Elo, is an other concept based on eccentricity (cf. Figure 3):

$$Elo = 1 - W/L \tag{8}$$

Elongation is a measure that takes values in the range [0,1]. A symmetrical shape in all axes such as a circle or square will have an elongation value of 0 whereas shapes with large aspect ratio will have an elongation closer to 1.

2.5 Circularity ratio

Circularity ratio represents how a shape is similar to a circle [2]. There are 3 definitions:

- Circularity ratio is the ratio of the area of a shape to the area of a circle having the same perimeter:

$$C_1 = \frac{A_s}{A_c} \tag{9}$$

where A_s is the area of the shape and A_c is the area of the circle having the same perimeter as the shape. Assume the perimeter is $\mathcal{O}$, so $A_c = \mathcal{O}^2/4\pi$. Then $C_1 = 4\pi \cdot A_s = \mathcal{O}^2$. As 4π is a constant, we have the second circularity ratio definition.

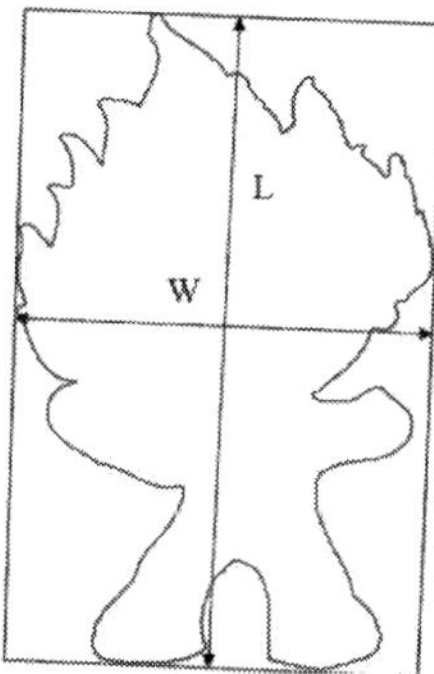

Fig. 3. Minimum bounding rectangle and corresponding parameters for elongation

- Circularity ratio is the ratio of the area of a shape to the shape's perimeter square:

$$C_2 = \frac{A_s}{\mathcal{O}^2} \tag{10}$$

- Circularity ratio is also called circle variance, and defined as:

$$C_{va} = \frac{\sigma_R}{\mu_R} \tag{11}$$

where μ_R and σ_R are the mean and standard deviation of the radial distance from the centroid (g_x, g_y) of the shape to the boundary points (x_i, y_i), $i \in [0, N\text{-}1]$. They are the following formulae respectively:

$$\mu_R = \frac{1}{N} \sum_{i=1}^{N-1} d_i \quad and \quad \sigma_R = \sqrt{\frac{1}{N} \sum_{i=1}^{N-1} (d_i - \mu_R)^2}$$

where $d_i = \sqrt{(x_i - g_x)^2 + (y_i - g_y)^2}$.

The most compact shape is a circle. See Figure 4.

2.6 Ellipse variance

Ellipse variance E_{va} is a mapping error of a shape to fit an ellipse that has an equal covariance matrix as the shape: $C_{ellipse} = C$ (cf. Eq.6). It is practically effective to apply the inverse approach yielding.

We assume

$$V_i = \begin{pmatrix} x_i - g_x \\ y_i - g_y \end{pmatrix}$$

Fig. 4. Circle variance

$$d'_i = \sqrt{V_i^T \cdot C_{ellipse}^{-1} \cdot V_i}$$

$$\mu'_R = \frac{1}{N} \sum_{i=1}^{N-1} d'_i \quad and \quad \sigma'_R = \sqrt{\frac{1}{N} \sum_{i=1}^{N-1} (d'_i - \mu'_R)^2}$$

Then

$$E_{va} = \frac{\sigma'_R}{\mu'_R} \tag{12}$$

Comparing with Eq. 11, intuitively, E_{va} represents a shape more accurately than C_{va}, cf. Figure 5.

Fig. 5. Ellipse variance

2.7 Rectangularity

Rectangularity represents how rectangular a shape is, i.e. how much it fills its minimum bounding rectangle:

$$Rectangularity = A_S/A_R$$

where A_S is the area of a shape; A_R is the area of the minimum bounding rectangle.

2.8 Convexity

Convexity is defined as the ratio of perimeters of the convex hull $\mathcal{O}_{Convexhull}$ over that of the original contour $\mathcal{O}$ [7]:

$$Convexity = \frac{\mathcal{O}_{Convexhull}}{\mathcal{O}} \tag{13}$$

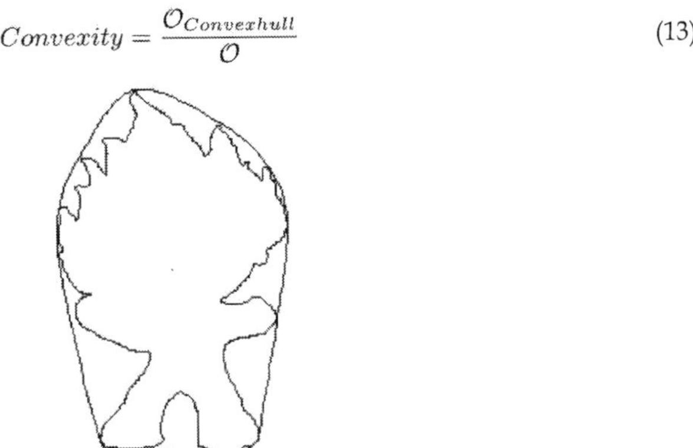

Fig. 6. Illustration of convex hull

The region R^2 is a convex if and only if for any two points $P_1, P_2 \in R^2$, the entire line segment P_1P_2 is inside the region. The convex hull of a region is the smallest convex region including it. In Figure 6, the outline is the convex hull of the region.

In [7], the authors presented the algorithm for constructing a convex hull by traversing the contour and minimizing turn angle in each step.

2.9 Solidity

Solidity describes the extent to which the shape is convex or concave [8] and it is defined by

$$Solidity = A_s/H$$

where, A_s is the area of the shape region and H is the convex hull area of the shape. The solidity of a convex shape is always 1.

2.10 Euler number

Euler number describes the relation between the number of contiguous parts and the number of holes on a shape. Let S be the number of contiguous parts and N be the number of holes on a shape. Then the Euler number is:

$$Eul = S - N$$

For example

3 B 9

Euler Number equal to *1, -1* and *0*, respectively.

2.11 Profiles

The profiles are the projection of the shape to x-axis and y-axis on Cartesian coordinates system. We obtain two one-dimension functions:

$$Pro_x(i) = \sum_{j=j_{min}}^{j_{max}} f(i,j) \quad and \quad Pro_y(j) = \sum_{i=i_{min}}^{i_{max}} f(i,j)$$

where $f(i, j)$ represents the region of shape Eq. 1. See Figure 7.

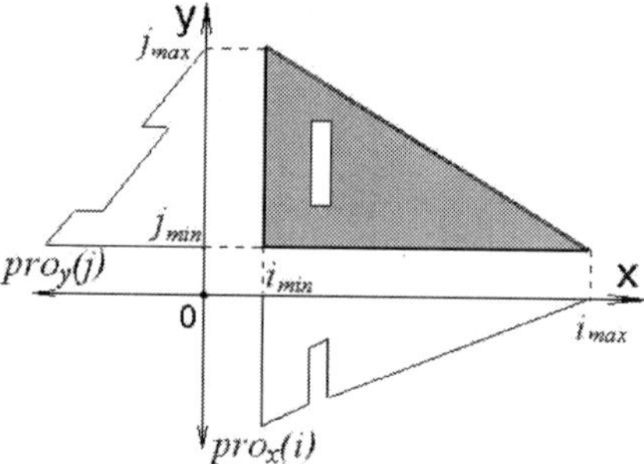

Fig. 7. Profiles

2.12 Hole area ratio

Hole area ratio HAR is defined as

$$HAR = \frac{A_h}{A_s}$$

where A_s is the area of a shape and A_h is the total area of all holes in the shape. Hole area ratio is most effective in discriminating between symbols that have big holes and symbols with small holes [9].

3. One-dimensional function for shape representation

The one-dimensional function which is derived from shape boundary coordinates is also often called shape signature [10, 11]. The shape signature usually captures the perceptual feature of the shape [12]. Complex coordinates, Centroid distance function, Tangent angle (Turning angles), Curvature function, Area function, Triangle-area representation and Chord length function are the commonly used shape signatures.

Shape signature can describe a shape all alone; it is also often used as a preprocessing to other feature extraction algorithms, for example, Fourier descriptors, wavelet description. In this section, the shape signatures are introduced.

3.1 Complex coordinates

A complex coordinates function is simply the complex number generated from the coordinates of boundary points, $P_n(x(n), y(n))$, $n \in [1,N]$:

$$z(n) = [x(n) - g_x] + i[y(n) - g_y]$$

where (g_x, g_y) is the centroid of the shape, given by Eq. 4.

3.2 Centroid distance function

The centroid distance function is expressed by the distance of the boundary points from the centroid (g_x, g_y) (Eq. 4) of a shape

$$r(n) = [(x(n) - g_x)^2 + (y(n) - g_y)^2]^{1/2}$$

Due to the subtraction of centroid, which represents the position of the shape, from boundary coordinates, both complex coordinates and centroid distance representation are invariant to translation.

3.3 Tangent angle

The tangent angle function at a point $P_n(x(n), y(n))$ is defined by a tangential direction of a contour at that point [13]:

$$\theta(n) = \theta_n = \arctan \frac{y(n) - y(n - w)}{x(n) - x(n - w)}$$

since every contour is a digital curve; w is a small window to calculate $\theta(n)$ more accurately. Tangent angle function has two problems. One is noise sensitivity. To decrease the effect of noise, a contour is filtered by a low-pass filter with appropriate bandwidth before calculating the tangent angle function. The other is discontinuity, due to the fact that the tangent angle function assumes values in a range of length 2π, usually in the interval of $[-\pi, \pi]$ or $[0, 2\pi]$. Therefore θ_n in general contains discontinuities of size 2π. To overcome the discontinuity problem, with an arbitrary starting point, the cumulative angular function φ_n is defined as the angle differences between the tangent at any point P_n along the curve and the tangent at the starting point P_0 [14, 15]:

$$\varphi(n) = [\theta(n) - \theta(0)]$$

In order to be in accordance with human intuition that a circle is "shapeless", assume $t = 2\pi n/N$, then $\varphi(n) = \varphi(tN/2\pi)$. A periodic function is termed as the cumulative angular deviant function (t) and is defined as

$$\psi(t) = \varphi(\frac{N}{2\pi}t) - t \quad t \in [0, 2\pi]$$

where N is the total number of contour points.

In [16], the authors proposed a method based on tangent angle. It is called tangent space representation. A digital curve C simplified by polygon evolution is represented in the tangent space by the graph of a step function, where the x-axis represents the arc length coordinates of points in C and the y-axis represents the direction of the line segments in the decomposition of C. Figure 8 shows an example of a digital curve and its step function representation in the tangent space.

3.4 Contour curvature

Curvature is a very important boundary feature for human to judge similarity between shapes. It also has salien perceptual characteristics and has proven to be very useful for shape recognition [17]. In order to use curvature for shape representation, we quote the function of curvature, $K(n)$, from [18, 19] as:

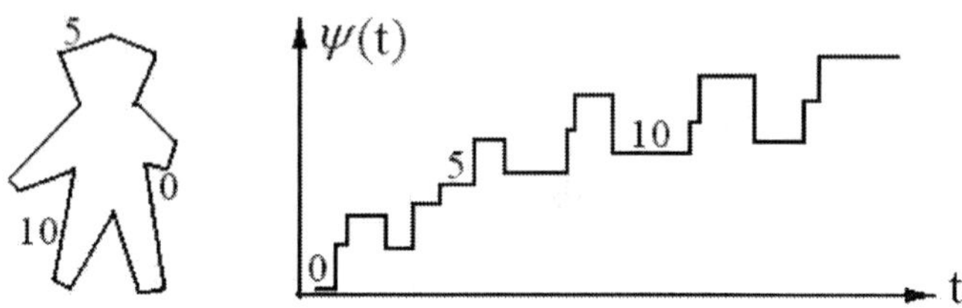

Fig. 8. Digital curve and its step function representation in the tangent space

$$K(n) = \frac{\dot{x}(n)\ddot{y}(n) - \dot{y}(n)\ddot{x}(n)}{(\dot{x}(n)^2 + \dot{y}(n)^2)^{3/2}} \tag{14}$$

Therefore, it is possible to compute the curvature of a planar curve from its parametric representation. If n is the normalized arc length parameter s, then Eq. 14 can be written as:

$$K(s) = \dot{x}(s)\ddot{y}(s) - \dot{y}(s)\ddot{x}(s) \tag{15}$$

As given in Eq. 15, the curvature function is computed only from parametric derivatives, and, therefore, it is invariant under rotations and translations. However, the curvature measure is scale dependent, i.e., inversely proportional to the scale. A possible way to achieve scale independence is to normalize this measure by the mean absolute curvature, i.e.,

$$K'(s) = \frac{K(s)}{\frac{1}{N} \sum_{s=1}^{N} |K(s)|}$$

where N is the number of points on the normalized contour.

When the size of the curve is an important discriminative feature, the curvature should be used without the normalization; otherwise, for the purpose of scale-invariant shape analysis, the normalization should be performed.

An approximate arc length parametrization based on the centripetal method is given by the following [19]:

Let $P = \sum_{n=1}^{N} d_n$ be the perimeter of the curve and $L = \sum_{n=1}^{N} \sqrt{d_n}$, where d_n is the length of the chord between points P_n and P_{n+1}, n=1, 2, . . . , N-1. The approximate arc length parametrization relations are following:

$$s_1 = 0;$$
$$s_k = s_{k-1} + \frac{P\sqrt{d_{k-1}}}{L}, k = 2, 3, \ldots, N.$$

Starting from an arbitrary point and following the contour clockwise, we compute the curvature at each interpolated point using Eq. 15. Convex and concave vertices will imply negative and positive values, respectively (the opposite is verified for counterclockwise sense). Figure 9 is an example of curvature function. Clearly, as a descriptor, the curvature function can distinguish different shapes.

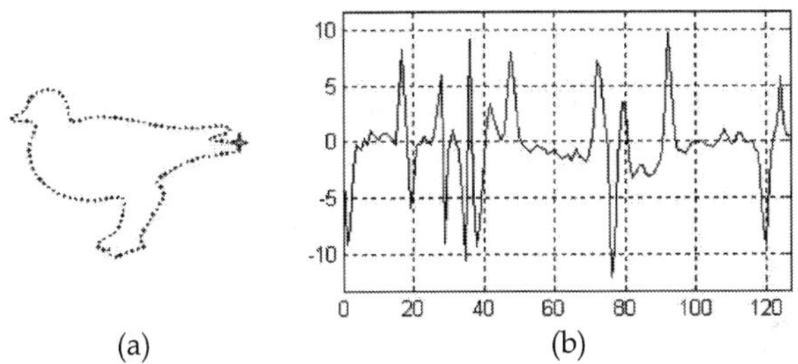

(a)   (b)

Fig. 9. Curvature function (a) Contour normalized to 128 points; the dot marked with a star is the starting point on the contour; (b) curvature function; the curvature is computed clockwise.

3.5 Area function

When the boundary points change along the shape boundary, the area of the triangle formed by two successive boundary points and the center of gravity also changes. This forms an area function which can be exploited as shape representation. Figure 10 shows an example. Let $S(n)$ be the area between the successive boundary points P_n, P_{n+1} and the center of gravity G.

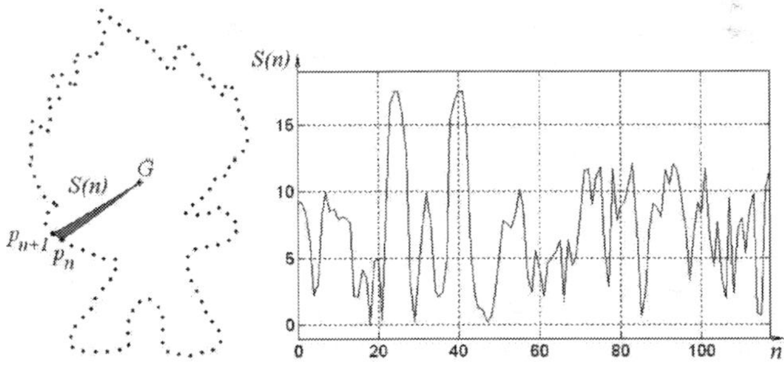

Fig. 10. Area function (a) Original contour; (b) the area function of (a).

The area function is linear under affine transform. However, this linearity only works for shape sampled at its same vertices.

3.6 Triangle-area representation

The triangle-area representation (TAR) signature is computed from the area of the triangles formed by the points on the shape boundary [20, 21]. The curvature at the contour point (x_n, y_n) is measured using the TAR as follows.

For each three points $P_{n-t_s}(x_{n-t_s}, y_{n-t_s})$, $P_n(x_n, y_n)$, and $P_{n+t_s}(x_{n+t_s}, y_{n+t_s})$, where $n \in [1, N]$ and $t_s \in [1, N/2 - 1]$, N is assumed to be even. The signed area of the triangle formed by these points is given by:

$$TAR(n, t_s) = \frac{1}{2} \begin{vmatrix} x_{n-t_s} & y_{n-t_s} & 1 \\ x_n & y_n & 1 \\ x_{n+t_s} & y_{n+t_s} & 1 \end{vmatrix} \tag{16}$$

When the contour is traversed in counter clockwise direction, positive, negative and zero values of TAR mean convex, concave and straight-line points, respectively. Figure 11 demonstrates these three types of the triangle areas and the complete TAR signature for the hammer shape.

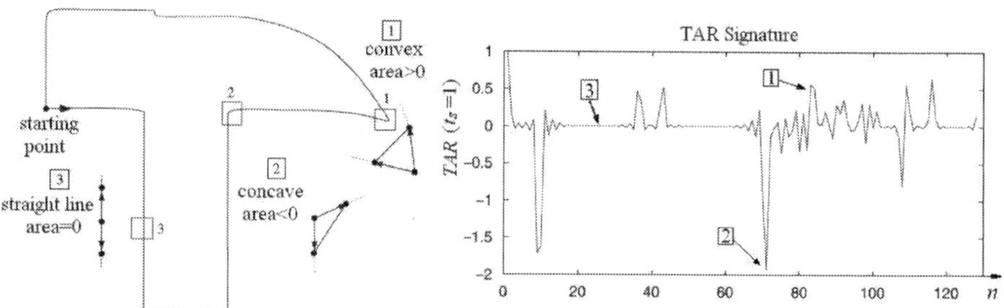

Fig. 11. Three different types of the triangle-area values and the TAR signature for the hammer shape

By increasing the length of the triangle sides, i.e., considering farther points, the function of Eq. 16 will represent longer variations along the contour. The TARs with different triangle sides can be regarded as different scale space functions. The total TARs, $t_s \in [1, N/2 - 1]$, compose a multi-scale space TAR.

In [21], authors show that the multi-scale space TAR is relatively invariant to the affine transform and robust to non-rigid transform.

3.7 Chord length function

The chord length function is derived from shape boundary without using any reference point. For each boundary point P, its chord length function is the shortest distance between P and another boundary point P' such that line PP' is perpendicular to the tangent vector at P [10].

The chord length function is invariant to translation and it overcomes the biased reference point (which means the centroid is often biased by boundary noise or defections) problems. However, it is very sensitive to noise, so that there may be drastic burst in the signature of even smoothed shape boundary.

3.8 Discussions

A shape signature represents a shape by a 1-D function derived from shape contour. To obtain the translation invariant property, they are usually defined by relative values. To obtain the scale invariant property, normalization is necessary. In order to compensate for orientation changes, shift matching is needed to find the best matching between two shapes. Having regard to occultation, Tangent angle, Contour curvature and Triangle-area representation have invariance property. In addition, shape signatures are computationally simple.

Shape signatures are sensitive to noise, and slight changes in the boundary can cause large errors in matching procedure. Therefore, it is undesirable to directly describe shape using a shape signature. Further processing is necessary to increase its robustness and reduce the matching load. For example, a shape signature can be simplified by quantizing the signature into a signature histogram, which is rotationally invariant.

4. Polygonal approximation

Polygonal approximation can be set to ignore the minor variations along the edge, and instead capture the overall shape information. This is useful because it reduces the effects of discrete pixelization of the contour. In general, there are two ways to realize it: one is merging methods and the other is splitting ones [22].

4.1 Merging methods
Merging methods add successive pixels to a line segment if each new pixel that is added doesn't cause the segment to deviate too much from a straight line.

4.1.1 Distance threshold method
Choose a point of the contour as a starting point. For each new point that we add, let a line go from the starting point to this new point. Then, compute the squared error for every point along the segment/line. If the error exceeds some threshold, we keep the line from the starting point to the previous point and start a new line at the current point.
In practice, the most of practical error measures in use are based on distance between vertices of the input curve and the approximation linear segments. The distance $d_k(i, j)$ from curve vertex $P_k = (x_k, y_k)$ to the corresponding approximation linear segments (P_i, P_j) is defined as follows (cf. Figure 12):

$$d_k(i,j) = \frac{|(x_j - x_i)(y_i - y_k) - (x_i - x_k)(y_j - y_i)|}{\sqrt{(x_j - x_i)^2 + (y_j - y_i)^2}}$$

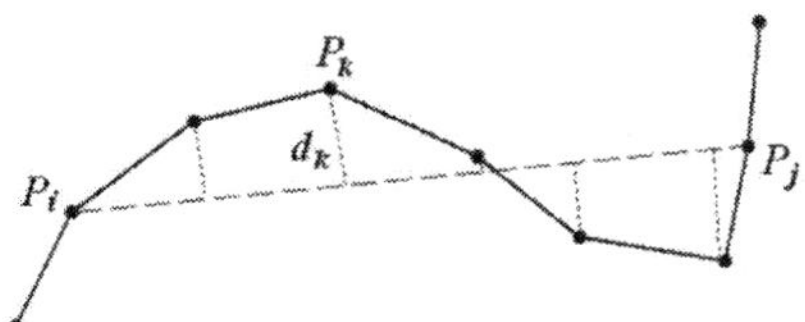

Fig. 12. Illustration of the distance from a point on the boundary to a linear segment

4.1.2 Tunneling method
If we have thick boundaries rather than single-pixel thick ones, we can still use a similar approach called tunneling. Imagine that we're trying to lay straight rods along a curved tunnel, and that we want to use as few as possible. We can start at any point and lay as long a straight rod as possible. Eventually, the curvature of the "tunnel" won't let us go any further, so we lay another rod and another until we reach the end.
Both the distance threshold and tunneling methods can do polygonal approximation efficiently. However, the great disadvantage is that the position of the starting point will affect greatly the approximate polygon.

4.1.3 Polygon evolution
The basic idea of polygons evolution in [23] is very simple: in every evolution step, a pair of consecutive line segments (the line segment is the line between two consecutive vertices) s_1, s_2 is substituted with a single line segment joining their farther endpoints of s_1 and s_2.

The key property of this evolution is the order of the substitution. The substitution is done according to a relevance measure K given by

$$K(s_1, s_2) = \frac{\beta(s_1, s_2)l(s_1)l(s_2)}{l(s_1) + l(s_2)},$$

where $\beta(s_1, s_2)$ is the turn angle at the common vertex of segments s_1, s_2 and $l(\alpha)$ is the length of α, $\alpha = s_1$ or s_2, normalized with respect to the total length of a polygonal curve. The evolution algorithm is assuming that vertices which are surrounded by segments with a high value of $K(s_1, s_2)$ are important while those with a low value are not. Figure 13 is an example.

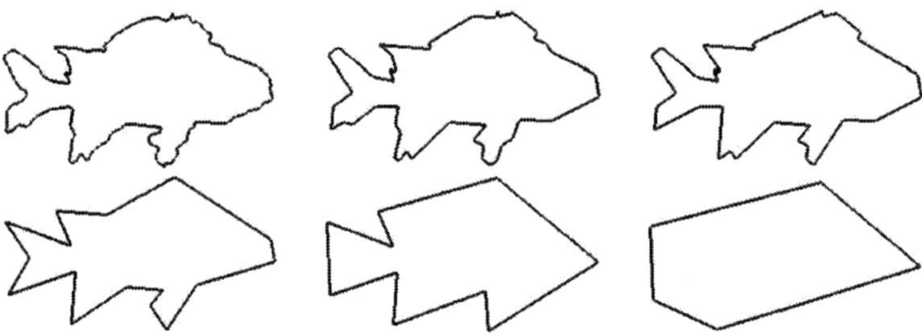

Fig. 13. Few stages of polygon evolution according to a relevant measure

The curve evolution method achieves the task of shape simplification, i.e., the process of evolution compares th significance of vertices of the contour based on a relevance measure. Since any digital curve can be regarded as a polygon without loss of information (with possibly a large number of vertices), it is sufficient to study evolutions of polygonal shapes for shape feature extraction.

4.2 Splitting methods

Splitting methods work by first drawing a line from one point on the boundary to another. Then, compute the perpendicular distance from each point along the boundary segment to the line. If this exceeds some threshold, break the line at the point of greatest distance. Repeat the process recursively for each of the two new lines until no longer need to break any more. See Figure 14 for an example.

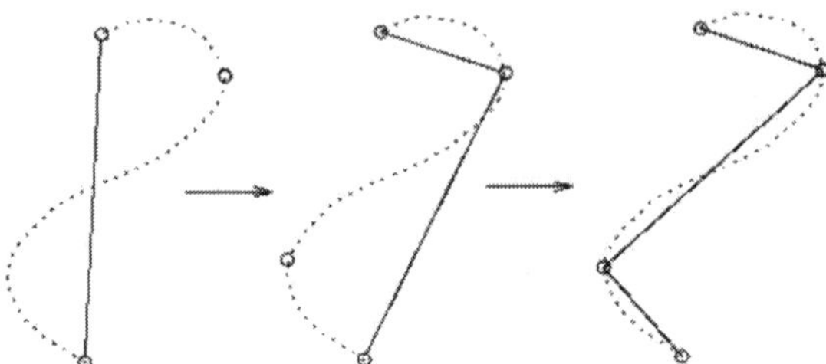

Fig. 14. Splitting method for polygonal approximation

This is sometimes known as the 'fit and split" algorithm. For a closed contour, we can find the two points that lie farthest apart and fit two lines between them, one for one side and one for the other. Then, we can apply the recursive splitting procedure to each side.

4.3 Discussions

Polygonal approximation technique can be used as a simple method for contour representation and description. The polygon approximation have some interesting properties:

- it leads to simplification of shape complexity with no blurring effects.
- it leads to noise elimination.
- although irrelevant features vanish after polygonal approximation, there is no dislocation of relevant features.
- the remaining vertices on a contour do not change their positions after polygonal approximation.

Polygonal approximation technique can also be used as preprocessing method for further extracting features from a shape.

5. Spatial interrelation feature

Spatial interrelation feature describes the region or the contour of a shape by the relation of their pixels or curves. In general, the representation is done by using their geometric features: length, curvature, relative orientation and location, area, distance and so on.

5.1 Adaptive grid resolution

The adaptive grid resolution (AGR) was proposed by [24]. In the AGR, a square grid that is just big enough to cover the entire shape is overlaid on a shape. A resolution of the grid cells varies from one portion to another according to the content of the portion of the shape. On the borders or the detail portion on the shape, the higher resolution, i.e. the smaller grid cells, are applied; on the other hand, in the coarse regions of the shape, lower resolution, i.e. the bigger grid cells, are applied.

To guarantee rotation invariance, it is necessary to convert an arbitrarily oriented shape into a unique common orientation. First, find the major axis of the shape. The major axis is the straight line segment joining the two points P_1 and P_2 on the boundary farthest away from each other. Then we rotate the shape so that its major axis is parallel to the x-axis. This orientation is still not unique as there are two possibilities: P_1 can be on the left or on the right. This problem is solved by computing the centroid of the polygon and making sure that the centroid is below the major axis, thus guaranteeing a unique orientation.

Let us now consider scale and translation invariance. We define the bounding rectangle (BR) of a shape as the rectangle with sides parallel to the x and y axes just large enough to cover the entire shape (after rotation). Note that the width of the BR is equal to the length of the major axis. To achieve scale invariance, we proportionally scale all shapes so that their BRs have the same fixed width (pixels).

The method of computation of the AGR representation of a shape applies quad-tree decomposition on the bitmap representation of the shape. The decomposition is based on successive subdivision of the bitmap into four equal-size quadrants. If a bitmap-quadrant does not consist entirely of part of shape, it is recursively subdivided into smaller and smaller quadrants until we reach bitmap-quadrants, i.e., termination condition of the recursion is that the predefined resolution is reached. Figure 15(a) is an example of AGR.

To represent the AGR image, in [24], quad-tree method is applied. Each node in the quad-tree covers a square region of the bitmap. The level of the node in the quad-tree determines the size of the square. The internal nodes (shown by gray circles) represent "partially covered" regions; the leaf nodes shown by white boxes represent regions with all 0s while the leaf nodes shown by black boxes represent regions with all 1s. The "all 1s" regions are used to represent the shape, Figure 15(b). Each rectangle can be described by 3 numbers: its center $C = (C_x, C_y)$ and its size (i.e. side length) S. So each shape can be mapped to a point in $3n$-dimensional space (n is the number of the rectangles occupied by the shape region).

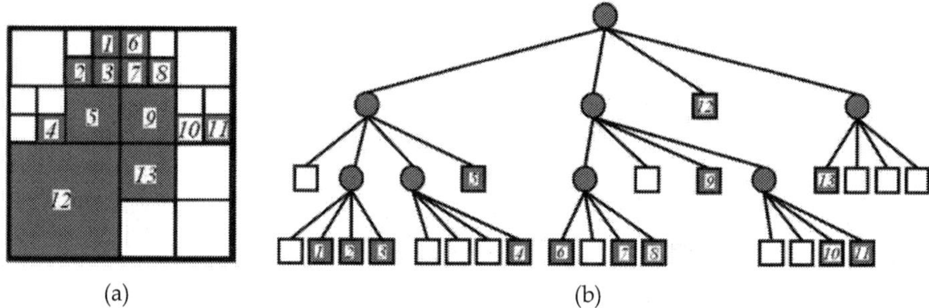

(a)   (b)

Fig. 15. Adaptive resolution representations (a) Adaptive Grid Resolution (AGR) image; (b) quad-tree decomposition of AGR.

Due to the fact that the normalization before computing AGR, AGR representation is invariant under rotation, scaling and translation. It is also computationally simple.

5.2 Bounding box

Bounding box computes homeomorphisms between 2D lattices and its shapes. Unlike many other methods, this mapping is not restricted to simply connected shapes but applies to arbitrary topologies [25].

To make bounding box representation invariant to rotation, a shape should be normalized by the same method as for AGR (Subsection 5.1) before further computation. After the normalization, a shape S is a set of L pixels, $S = \{p_k \in R^2 \mid k = 1, 2, \dots, L\}$ and also write $|S| = L$. The minimum bounding rectangle or bounding box of S is denoted by $B(S)$; its width and height, are called w and h, respectively.

Figure 16 shows the algorithm flowchart based on bounding box that divides a shape S into $m(row) \times n\ (column)$ parts. The output $\mathbf{B}$ is a set of bounding boxes.

An illustration of this procedure and its result is shown in Figure 17.

To represent each bounding box, one method is that partial points of the set of bounding boxes are sampled. Figure 18 shows an example.

If $\mathbf{v} = (v_x, v_y)^T$ denotes the location of the bottom left corner of the initial bounding box of S, and $\mathbf{u}_{ij} = (u_x^{ij}, u_y^{ij})$ denotes the center of sample box $\mathbf{B}_{ij}$, then the coordinates

$$\begin{pmatrix} \mu_x^{ij} \\ \mu_y^{ij} \end{pmatrix} = \begin{pmatrix} \left(u_x^{ij} - v_x\right)/w \\ \left(u_y^{ij} - v_y\right)/h \end{pmatrix}$$

provide a scale invariant representation of S. Sampling k points of an $m{\times}n$ lattice therefore allows to represent S as a vector

$$r = \left[\mu_x^{i(1)j(1)}, \mu_y^{i(1)j(1)}, \cdots , \mu_x^{i(k)j(k)}, \mu_y^{i(k)j(k)} \right]$$

where $i(\alpha) < i(\beta)$ if $\alpha < \beta$ and likewise for the index j.

Bounding box representation is a simple computational geometry approach to compute homeomorphisms between shapes and lattices. It is storage and time efficient. It is invariant to rotation, scaling and translation and also robust against noisy shape boundaries.

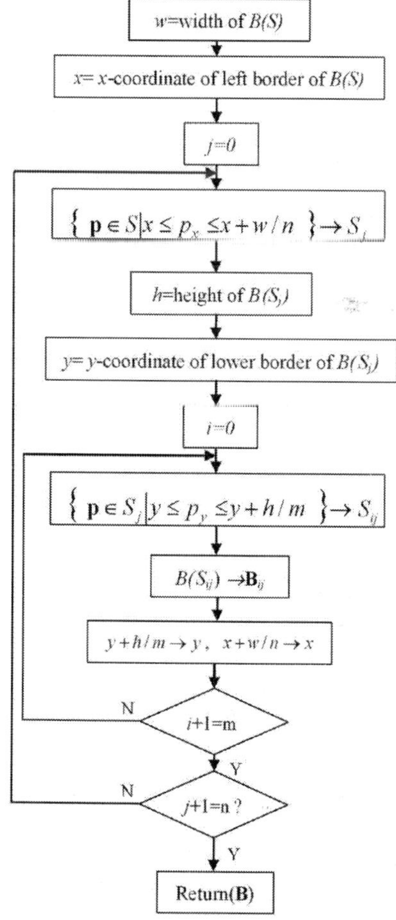

Fig. 16. Flowchart of shape divided by bounding box

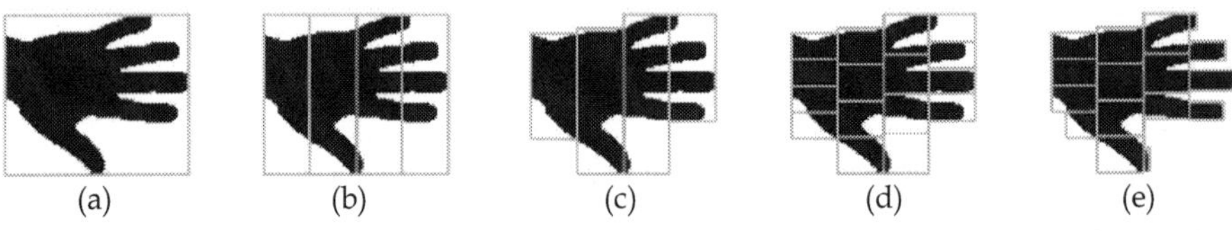

(a)   (b)   (c)   (d)   (e)

Fig. 17. Five steps of bounding box splitting (a) Compute the bounding box $B(S)$ of a pixel set S; (b) subdivide S into n vertical slices; (c) compute the bounding box $B(S_j)$ of each resulting pixel set S_j, where $j = 1, 2,..., n$, (d) subdivide each $B(S_j)$ into m horizontal slices; (e) compute the bounding box $B(S_{ij})$ of each resulting pixel set S_{ij}, where $i = 1, 2, ...,m$.

Fig. 18. A sample points on lattice and examples of how it is mapped onto different shapes

5.3 Convex hull

The approach is that the shape is represented by a serie of convex hulls. The convex region has be defined in Sebsection 2.8. The convex hull H of a region is its smallest convex region including it. In other words, for a region S, the convex hull $conv(S)$ is defined as the smallest convex set in R^2 containing S. In order to decrease the effect of noise, common practice is to first smooth a boundary prior to partitioning.

The representation of the shape may be obtained by a recursive process which results in a concavity tree. See Figure 19. Each concavity can be described by its area, chord (the line connecting the cut of the concavity) length, maximum curvature, distance from maximum curvature point to the chord. The matching between shapes becomes a string or a graph matching.

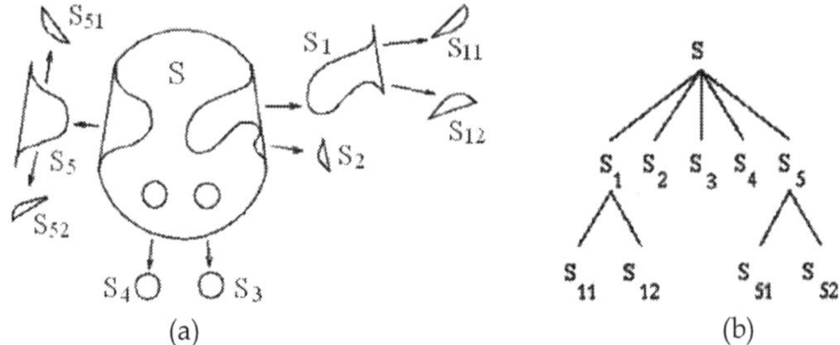

(a)   (b)

Fig. 19. Illustrates recursive process of convex hull (a) Convex hull and its concavities; (b) concavity tree representation of convex hull.

Convex hull representation has a high storage efficiency. It is invariant to rotation, scaling and translation and also robust against noisy shape boundaries (after filtering). However, extracting the robust convex hulls from the shape is where the shoe pinches. [26, 27] and [28] gave the boundary tracing method and morphological methods to achieve convex hulls respectively.

5.4 Chain code

Chain code is a common approach for representing different rasterized shapes as line-drawings, planar curves, or contours. Chain code describes an object by a sequence of unit-size line segments with a given orientation [2]. Chain code can be viewed as a connected sequence of straight-line segments with specified lengths and directions [29].

5.4.1 Basic chain code

Freeman [30] first introduced a chain code that describes the movement along a digital curve or a sequence of border pixels by using so-called 8-connectivity or 4-connectivity. The direction of each movement is encoded by the numbering scheme $\{i \mid i = 0, 1, 2, \ldots, 7\}$ or $\{i \mid i = 0, 1, 2, 3\}$ denoting a counter-clockwise angle of $45° \times i$ or $90° \times i$ regarding the positive x-axis, as shown in Figure 20.

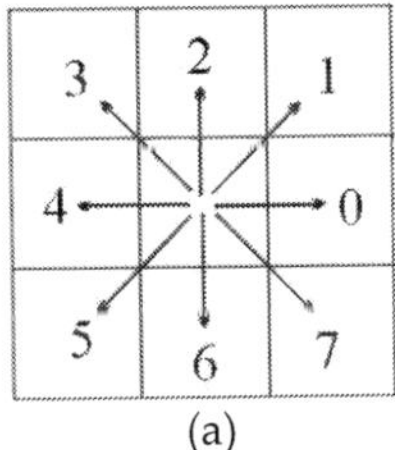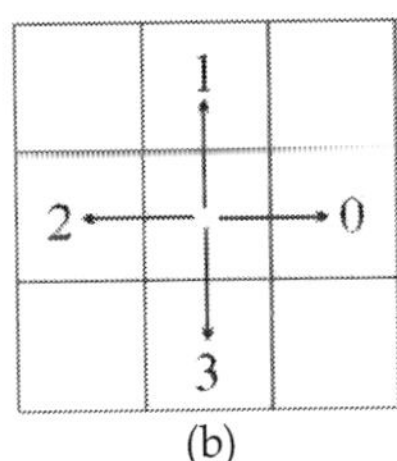

(a)   (b)

Fig. 20. Basic chain code direction (a) Chain code in eight directions (8-connectivity); (b) chain code in four directions (4-connectivity).

By encoding relative, rather than absolute position of the contour, the basic chain code is translation invariant. We can match boundaries by comparing their chain codes, but with the two main problems: 1) it is very sensitive to noise; 2) it is not rotationally invariant. To solve these problems, differential chain codes (DCC) and resampling chain codes (RCC) were proposed.

Differential chain codes (DCC) is encoding differences in the successive directions. This can be computed by subtracting each element of the chain code from the previous one and taking the result modulo n, where n is the connectivity. This differencing allows us to rotate the object in 90-degree increments and still compare the objects, but it doesn't get around the inherent sensitivity of chain codes to rotation on the discrete pixel grid.

Re-sampling chain codes (RCC) consists in re-sampling the boundary onto a coarser grid and then computing the chain codes of this coarser representation. This smoothes out small variations and noise but can help compensate for differences in chain-code length due to the pixel grid.

5.4.2 Vertex chain code (VCC)

To improve chain code efficiency, in [29] the authors proposed a chain code for shape representation according to vertex chain code (VCC). An element of the VCC indicates the number of cell vertices, which are in touch with the bounding contour of the shape in that element's position. Only three elements "1", "2" and "3" can be used to represent the bounding contour of a shape composed of pixels in the rectangular grid. Figure 21 shows the elements of the VCC to represent a shape.

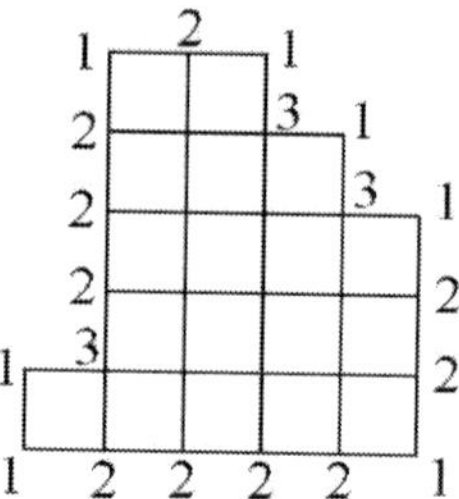

Fig. 21. Vertex chain code

5.4.3 Chain code histogram (CCH)

Iivarinen and Visa derive a chain code histogram (CCH) for object recognition [31]. The CCH is computed as h_i = #$\{i \in M$, M is the range of chain code$\}$, #$\{\alpha\}$ denotes getting the number of the value α.

The CCH reflects the probabilities of different directions present in a contour.

If the chain code is used for matching it must be independent of the choice of the starting pixel in the sequence. The chain code usually has high dimensions and is sensitive to noise and any distortion. So, except the CCH, the other chain code approaches are often used as contour representations, but is not as contour attributes.

5.5 Smooth curve decomposition

In [32], the authors proposed smooth curve decomposition as shape descriptor. The segment between the curvature zero-crossing points from a Gaussian smoothed boundary are used to obtain primitives, called tokens. The feature for each token is its maximum curvature and its orientation. In Figure 22(b), the first number in the parentheses is its maximum curvature and the second is its orientation.

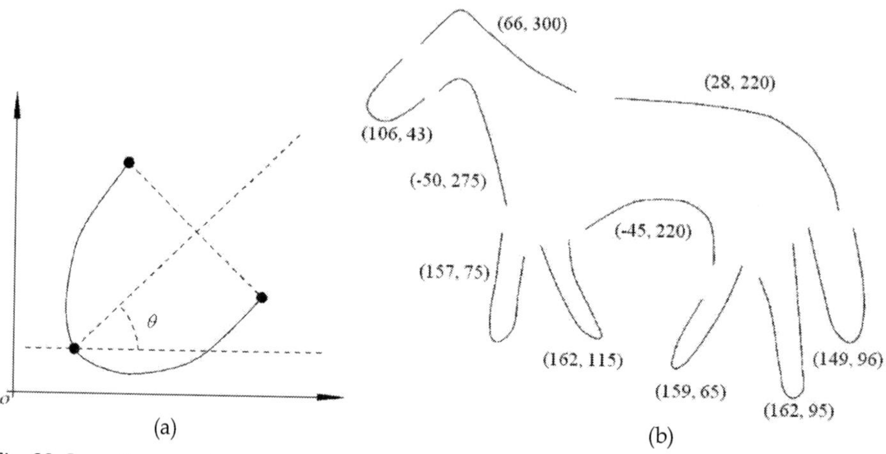

Fig. 22. Smooth curve decomposition (a) θis the orientation of this token; (b) an example of smooth curve decomposition.

The similarity between two tokens is measured by the weighted Euclidean distance. The shape similarity is measured according to a non-metric distance. Shape retrieval based on token representation has shown to be robust in the presence of partially occulted objects, translation, scaling and rotation.

5.6 Symbolic representation based on the axis of least inertia

In [33], a method of representing a shape in terms of multi-interval valued type data is proposed. The proposed shape representation scheme extracts symbolic features with reference to the axis of least inertia, which is unique to the shape. The axis of least inertia (ALI) of a shape is defined as the line for which the integral of the square of the distances to points on the shape boundary is a minimum (cf. Subsection 2.2).

Once the ALI is calculated, each point on the shape curve is projected on to ALI. The two farthest projected points say E_1 and E_2 on ALI are chosen as the extreme points as shown in Figure 23. The Euclidean distance between these two extreme points defines the length of ALI. The length of ALI is divided uniformly by a fixed number n; the equidistant points are called feature points. At every feature point chosen, an imaginary line perpendicular to the ALI is drawn. It is interesting to note that these perpendicular lines may intersect the shape curve at several points. The length of each imaginary line in shape region is computed and the collection of these lengths in an ascending order defines the value of the feature at the respective feature point.

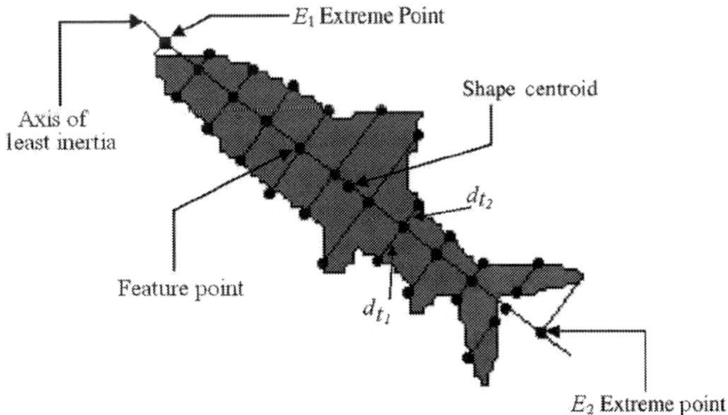

Fig. 23. Symbolic features based axis of least inertia

Let S be a shape to be represented and n the number of feature points chosen on its ALI. Then the feature vector F representing the shape S, is in general of the form $F = [f_1, f_2, \ldots, f_t, \ldots, f_n]$, where $f_t = \{d_{t_1}, d_{t_2}, \ldots d_{t_k}\}$ for some $t_k \geq 1$.

The feature vector F representing the shape S is invariant to image transformations viz., uniform scaling, rotation, translation and flipping (reflection).

5.7 Beam angle statistics

Beam angle statistics (BAS) shape descriptor is based on the beams originating from a boundary point, which are defined as lines connecting that point with the rest of the points on the boundary [34].

Let B be the shape boundary. $B = \{P_1, P_2,.. , P_N\}$ is represented by a connected sequence of points, $P_i = (x_i, y_i)$, $i = 1, 2,\ldots ,N$, where N is the number of boundary points. For each point P_i, the beam angle between the forward beam vector $V_{i+k} = \overrightarrow{P_i P_{i+k}}$ and backward beam vector $V_{i-k} = \overrightarrow{P_i P_{i-k}}$ in the kth order neighborhood system, is then computed as (see Figure 24, k=5 for example)

$$C_k(i) = (\theta_{V_{i+k}} - \theta_{V_{i-k}})$$

where $\theta_{V_{i+k}} = \arctan \dfrac{y_{i+k} - y_i}{x_{i+k} - x_i}$, $\theta_{V_{i-k}} = \arctan \dfrac{y_{i-k} - y_i}{x_{i-k} - x_i}$

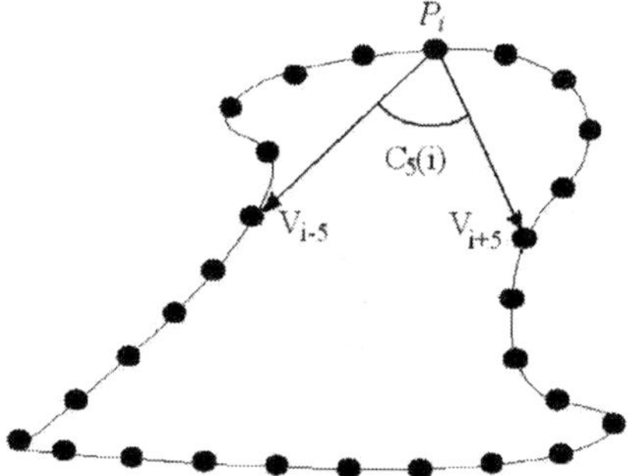

Fig. 24. Beam angle in the 5th neighborhood system for a boundary point

For each boundary point P_i of the contour, the beam angle $C_k(i)$ can be taken as a random variable with the probability density function $P(C_k(i))$. Therefore, beam angle statistics (BAS), may provide a compact representation for a shape descriptor. For this purpose, m^{th} moment of the random variable $C_k(i)$ is defined as follows:

$$E[C^m(i)] = \sum_{k=1}^{(N/2)-1} C_k^m(i) \cdot P_k(C_k(i)) \quad m = 1, 2, \cdots$$

In the above formula E indicates the expected value. See Figure 25 as an example.

Beam angle statistics shape descriptor captures the perceptual information using the statistical information based on the beams of individual points. It gives globally discriminative features to each boundary point by using all other boundary points. BAS descriptor is also quite stable under distortions and is invariant to translation, rotation and scaling.

5.8 Shape matrix

Shape matrix descriptor is an $M \times N$ matrix to represent a shape region. There are two basic modes of shape matrix: Square model [35] and Polar model [36].

5.8.1 Square model shape matrix

Square model of shape matrix, also called grid descriptor [37, 35], is constructed by the following: for the shape S, construct a square centered on the center of gravity G of S; the size of each side is equal to $2L$, L is the maximum Euclidean distance from G to a point M on the boundary of the shape. Point M lies in the center of one side and GM is perpendicular to this side.

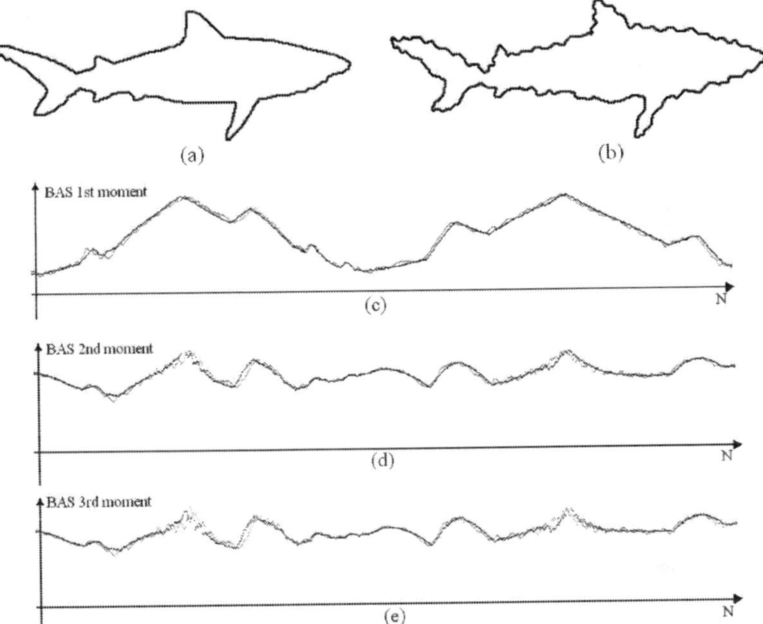

Fig. 25. The BAS descriptor for original and noisy contour (a) Original contour; (b) noisy contour; (c), (d) and (e) are the BAS plot 1st, 2nd and 3rd moment, respectively.

Divide the square into $N \times N$ subsquares and denote S_{kj}, $k, j = 1, \dots, N$, the subsquares of the constructed grid. Define the shape matrix $SM = [B_{kj}]$,

$$B_{kj} = \begin{cases} 1 \Leftrightarrow & \mu(S_{kj} \cap S) \geq \mu(S_{kj})/2 \\ 0 & otherwise \end{cases}$$

where $\mu(F)$ is the area of the planar region F. Figure 26 shows an example of square model of shape matrix.

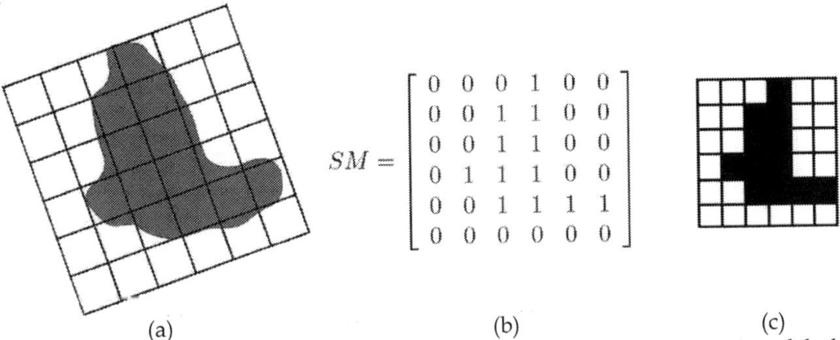

Fig. 26. Square model shape matrix (a) Original shape region; (b) square model shape matrix; (c) reconstruction of the shape region.

For a shape with more than one maximum radius, it can be described by several shape matrices and the similarity distance is the minimum distance between these matrices. In [35], authors gave a method to choose the appropriate shape matrix dimension.

5.8.2 Polar model shape matrix

Polar model of shape matrix is constructed by the following steps. Let G be the center of gravity of the shape, and GA is the maximum radius of the shape. Using G as center, draw n circles with radii equally spaced. Starting from GA, and counterclockwise, draw radii that divide each circle into m equal arcs. The values of the matrix are same as in square model shape matrix. Figure 27 shows an example, where n = 5 and m =12. Its polar model of shape matrix is

$$PSM = \begin{bmatrix} 1 & 1 & 1 & 1 & 1 & 1 & 1 & 1 & 1 & 1 & 1 & 1 \\ 1 & 1 & 1 & 1 & 1 & 1 & 1 & 1 & 1 & 1 & 1 & 1 \\ 1 & 1 & 1 & 1 & 1 & 1 & 1 & 1 & 0 & 1 & 1 & 1 \\ 1 & 0 & 0 & 0 & 0 & 1 & 1 & 0 & 0 & 0 & 0 & 1 \\ 1 & 0 & 0 & 0 & 0 & 1 & 1 & 0 & 0 & 0 & 0 & 0 \end{bmatrix}$$

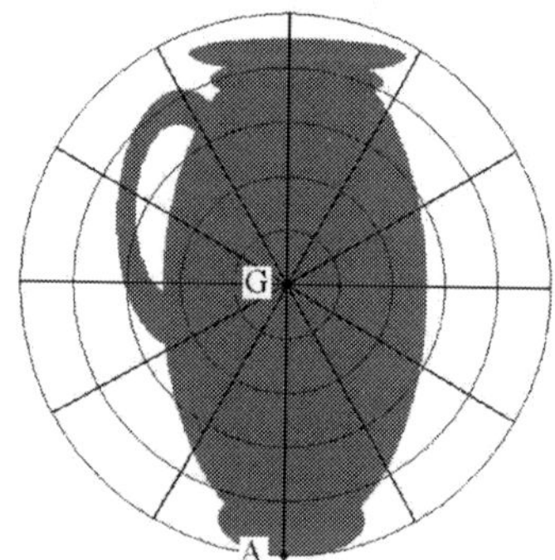

Fig. 27. Polar model shape

Polar model of shape matrix is simpler than square model because it only uses one matrix no matter how many maximum radii are on the shape. However, since the sampling density is not constant with the polar sampling raster, a weighed shape matrix is necessary. For the detail, refer to [36].

The shape matrix exists for every compact shape. There is no limit to the scope of the shapes that the shape matrix can represent. It can describe even shapes with holes. Shape matrix is also invariant under translation, rotation and scaling of the object. The shape of the object can be reconstructed from the shape matrix; the accuracy is given by the size of the grid cells.

5.9 Shape context

In [38], the shape context has been shown to be a powerful tool for object recognition tasks. It is used to find corresponding features between model and image.

Shape contexts analysis begins by taking N samples from the edge elements on the shape. These points can be on internal or external contours. Consider the vectors originating from a point to all other sample points on the shape. These vectors express the appearance of the entire shape relative to the reference point. The shape context descriptor is the histogram of the relative polar coordinates of all other points:

$$h_i(k) = \sharp\{Q \neq P_i \ : \ (Q - P_i) \in bin(k)\}$$

An example is shown in Figure 28. (c) is the diagram of log-polar histogram that has 5 bins for the polar direction and 12 bins for the angular direction. The histogram of a point P_i is formed by the following: putting the center of the histogram bins diagram on the point P_i, each bin of this histogram contains a count of all other sample points on the shape falling into that bin. Note on this figure, the shape contexts (histograms) for the points marked by $\circ$ (in (a)), $\Diamond$ (in (b)) and $\lhd$ (in (a)) are shown in (d), (e) and (f), respectively. It is clear that the shape contexts for the points marked by $\circ$ and $\Diamond$, which are computed for relatively similar points on the two shapes, have visual similarity. By contrast, the shape context for $\lhd$ is quite different from the others. Obviously, this descriptor is a rich description, since as N gets large, the representation of the shape becomes exact.

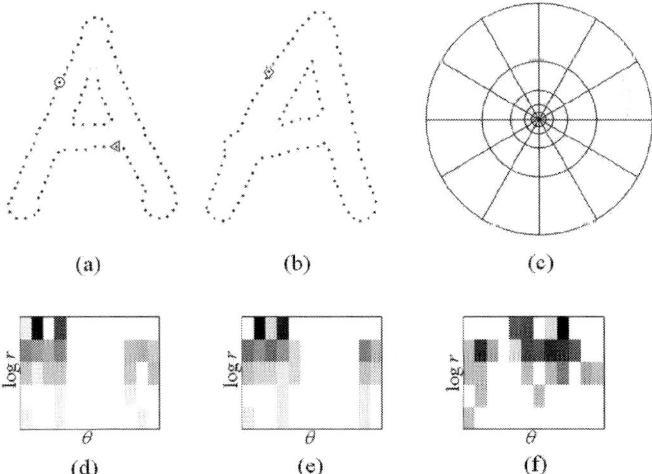

Fig. 28. Shape context computation and graph matching (a) and (b) Sampled edge points of two shapes; (c) diagram of log-polar histogram bins used in computing the shape contexts; (d), (e) and (f) shape contexts for reference sample points marked by $\circ$, $\Diamond$ and $\lhd$ in (a) and (b), respectively. (Dark=large value).

Shape context matching is often used to find the corresponding points on two shapes. It has been applied to a variety of object recognition problems [38, 39, 40, 41]. The shape context descriptor has the following invariance properties:

- translation: the shape context descriptor is inherently translation invariant as it is based on relative point locations.
- scaling: for clutter-free images the descriptor can be made scale invariant by normalizing the radial distances by the mean (or median) distance between all point pairs.

- rotation: it can be made rotation invariant by rotating the coordinate system at each point so that the positive x-axis is aligned with the tangent vector.
- shape variation: the shape context is robust against slight shape variations.
- few outliers: points with a final matching cost larger than a threshold value are classified as outliers. Additional 'dummy' points are introduced to decrease the effects of outliers.

5.10 Chord distribution

The basic idea of chord distribution is to calculate the lengths of all chords in the shape (all pair-wise distances betwee boundary points) and to build a histogram of their lengths and orientations [42]. The "lengths" histogram is invariant to rotation and scales linearly with the size of the object. The "angles" histogram is invariant to object size and shifts relative to object rotation. Figure 29 gives an example of chord distribution.

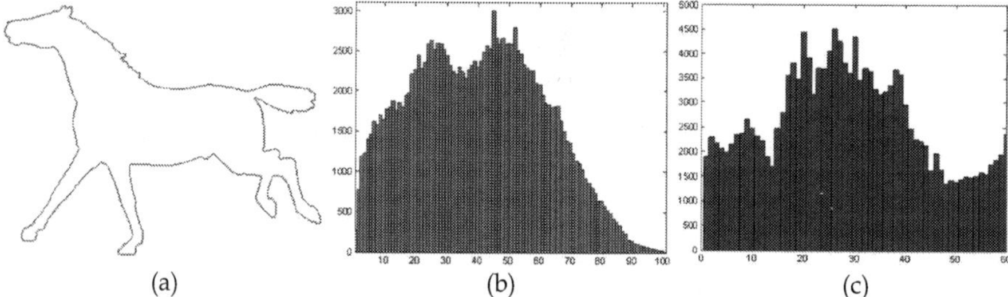

(a)   (b)   (c)

Fig. 29. Chord distribution (a) Original contour; (b) chord lengths histogram; (c) chord angles histogram (each stem covers 3 degrees).

5.11 Shock graphs

Shock graphs is a descriptor based on the medial axis. The medial axis is the most popular method that has been proposed as a useful shape abstraction tool for the representation and modeling of animate shapes. Skeleton and medial axes have been extensively used for characterizing objects satisfactorily using structures that are composed of line or arc patterns. Medial axis is an image processing operation which reduces input shapes to axial stick-like representations. It is as the loci of centers of bi-tangent circles that fit entirely within the foreground region being considered. Figure 30 illustrates the medial axis for a rectangular shape.

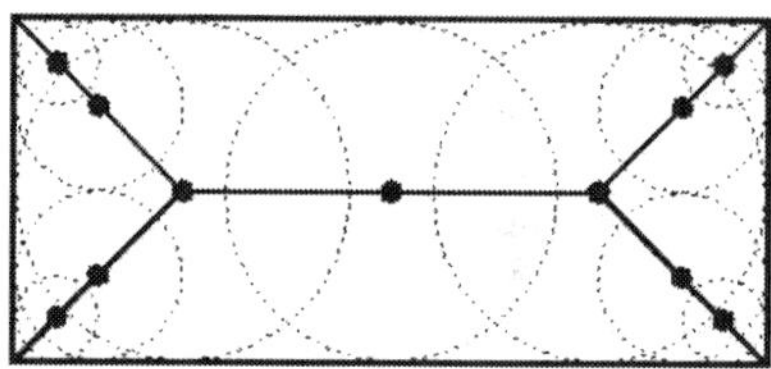

Fig. 30. Medial axis of a rectangle defined in terms of bi-tangent circles

We notice that the radius of each circle is variable. This variable is a function of the loci of points on the medial axis. This function is called radius function.

A shock graph is a shape abstraction that decomposes a shape into a set of hierarchically organized primitive parts. Siddiqi and Kimia define the concept of a shock graph [43] as an abstraction of the medial axis of a shape onto a directed acyclic graph (DAG). Shock segments are curve segments of the medial axis with monotonic flow, and give a more refined partition of the medial axis segments. Figure 31 is for example.

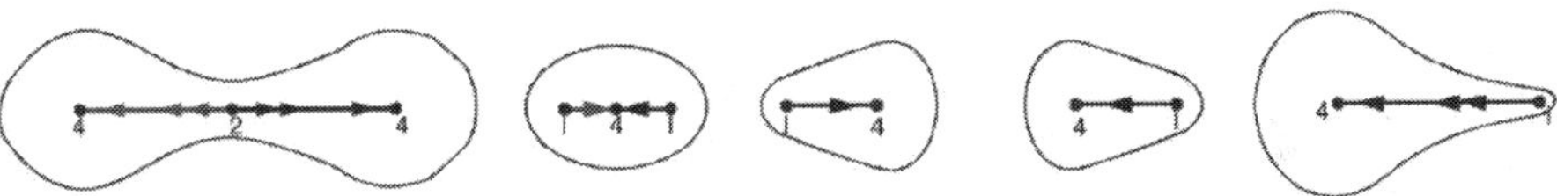

Fig. 31. Shock segments

The skeleton points are first labeled according to the local variation of the radius function at each point. Shock graph can distinguish the shapes but the medial axis cannot. Figure 32 shows two examples of shapes and their shock graphs.

Fig. 32. Examples of shapes and their shock graphs

To calculate the distance between two shock graphs, in [44], the authors employ a polynomial-time edit-distance algorithm. This algorithm is shown to have the good performances for boundary perturbations, articulation and deformation of parts, segmentation errors, scale variations, viewpoint variations and partial occultation. However the authors also indicate that the computation complexity is very high. The matching shape typically takes about 3-5 minutes on an SGI Indigo II (195 MHz), which limits the number of shapes that can be practically matched.

5.12 Discussions
Spacial feature descriptor is a direct method to describe a shape. These descriptors can apply the theory of tree-based (Adaptive grid resolution and Convex hull), statistic (Chain code histogram, Beam angle statistics, Shape context and Chord distribution) or syntactic analysis (Smooth curve decomposition) to extract or represent the feature of a shape. This description scheme not only compresses the data of a shape, but also provides a compact and meaningful form to facilitate further recognition operations.

6. Moments

The concept of moment in mathematics evolved from the concept of moment in physics. It is an integrated theory system. For both contour and region of a shape, one can use moment's theory to analyze the object.

6.1 Boundary moments

Boundary moments, analysis of a contour, can be used to reduce the dimension of boundary representation [28]. Assume shape boundary has been represented as a 1-D shape representation $z(i)$ as introduced in Section 3, the rth moment m_r and central moment μ_r can be estimated as

$$m_r = \frac{1}{N} \sum_{i=1}^{N} [z(i)]^r \quad and \quad \mu_r = \frac{1}{N} \sum_{i=1}^{N} [z(i) - m_1]^r$$

where N is the number of boundary points.

The normalized moments $\bar{m}_r = m_r/(\mu_2)^{r/2}$ and $\bar{\mu}_r = \mu_r/(\mu_2)^{r/2}$ are invariant to shape translation, rotation and scaling. Less noise-sensitive shape descriptors can be obtained from

$$F_1 = \frac{(\mu_2)^{1/2}}{m_1}, \quad F_2 = \frac{\mu_3}{(\mu_2)^{3/2}} \quad and \quad F_3 = \frac{\mu_4}{(\mu_2)^2},$$

The other approaches of boundary moments treats the 1-D shape feature function $z(i)$ as a random variable $\mathbf{v}$ and creates a K bins histogram $p(v_i)$ from $z(i)$. Then, the rth central moment is obtained by

$$\mu_r = \sum_{i=1}^{K} (v_i - m)^r p(v_i) \quad and \quad m = \sum_{i=1}^{K} v_i p(v_i)$$

The advantage of boundary moment descriptors is that it is easy to implement. However, it is dificult to associate higher order moments with physical interpretation.

6.2 Region moments

Among the region-based descriptors, moments are very popular. These include invariant moments, Zernike moments Radial Chebyshev moments, etc.

The general form of a moment function m_{pq} of order $(p + q)$ of a shape region can be given as:

$$m_{pq} = \sum_x \sum_y \Psi_{pq}(x, y) f(x, y) \quad p, q = 0, 1, 2 \cdots$$

where Ψ_{pq} is known as the *moment weighting kernel* or the *basis set*; $f(x, y)$ is the shape region Eq. 1.

6.2.1 Invariant moments (IM)

Invariant moments (IM) are also called geometric moment invariants. Geometric moments, are the simplest of the moment functions with basis $\Psi_{pq} = x_p y_q$, while complete, it is not orthogonal [30]. Geometric moment function m_{pq} of order $(p + q)$ is given as:

$$m_{pq} = \sum_x \sum_y x^p y^q f(x, y) \quad p, q = 0, 1, 2 \cdots$$

The geometric central moments, which are invariant to translation, are defined as:

$$\mu_{pq} = \sum_x \sum_y (x - \bar{x})^p (y - \bar{y})^q f(x, y) \quad p, q = 0, 1, 2 \cdots$$

where $\bar{x} = m_{10}/m_{00}$ and $\bar{y} = m_{01}/m_{00}$

A set of 7 invariant moments (IM) are given by [30]:

$$\phi_1 = \eta_{20} + \eta_{02}$$
$$\phi_2 = (\eta_{20} - \eta_{02})^2 + 4\eta_{11}^2$$
$$\phi_3 = (\eta_{30} - 3\eta_{12})^2 + (3\eta_{21} - \eta_{03})^2$$
$$\phi_4 = (\eta_{30} + \eta_{12})^2 + (\eta_{21} + \eta_{03})^2$$
$$\phi_5 = (\eta_{30} - 3\eta_{12})(\eta_{30} + \eta_{12})\left[(\eta_{30} + \eta_{12})^2 - 3(\eta_{21} + \eta_{03})^2\right] + (3\eta_{21} - \eta_{03})(\eta_{21} + \eta_{03})$$
$$\cdot \left[3(\eta_{30} + \eta_{12})^2 - (\eta_{21} + \eta_{03})^2\right]$$
$$\phi_6 = (\eta_{20} - \eta_{02})\left[(\eta_{30} + \eta_{12})^2 - (\eta_{21} + \eta_{03})^2\right] + 4\eta_{11}^2(\eta_{30} + \eta_{12})(\eta_{21} + \eta_{03})$$
$$\phi_7 = (3\eta_{21} - \eta_{03})(\eta_{30} + \eta_{12})\left[(\eta_{30} + \eta_{12})^2 - 3(\eta_{21} + \eta_{03})^2\right] + (3\eta_{12} - \eta_{03})(\eta_{21} + \eta_{03})$$
$$\cdot \left[3(\eta_{30} + \eta_{12})^2 - (\eta_{21} + \eta_{03})^2\right]$$

where $\eta_{pq} = \mu_{pq}/\mu_{00}^{\gamma}$ and $\gamma = 1 + (p + q)/2$ for $p + q = 2, 3, \cdots$

IM are computationally simple. Moreover, they are invariant to rotation, scaling and translation. However, they have several drawbacks [45]:

- information redundancy: since the basis is not orthogonal, these moments suffer from a high degree of information redundancy.
- noise sensitivity: higher-order moments are very sensitive to noise.
- large variation in the dynamic range of values: since the basis involves powers of p and q, the moments computed have large variation in the dynamic range of values for different orders. This may cause numerical instability when the image size is large.

6.2.2 Algebraic moment invariants

The algebraic moment invariants are computed from the first m central moments and are given as the eigenvalues of predefined matrices, $M_{[j,k]}$, whose elements are scaled factors of the central moments [46]. The algebraic moment invariants can be constructed up to arbitrary order and are invariant to affine transformations. However, algebraic moment invariants performed either very well or very poorly on the objects with different configuration of outlines.

6.2.3 Zernike moments (ZM)

Zernike Moments (ZM) are orthogonal moments [45]. The complex Zernike moments are derived from orthogonal Zernike polynomials:

$$V_{nm}(x, y) = V_{nm}(r \cos\theta, \sin\theta) = R_{nm}(r) \exp(jm\theta)$$

where $R_{nm}(r)$ is the orthogonal radial polynomial:

$$R_{nm}(r) = \sum_{s=0}^{(n-|m|)/2} (-1)^s \frac{(n - s)!}{s! \times \left(\frac{n-2s+|m|}{2}\right)! \left(\frac{n-2s-|m|}{2}\right)!} r^{n-2s}$$

$n = 0, 1, 2, \ldots, 0 \leq |m| \leq n$; and $n - |m|$ is even.

Zernike polynomials are a complete set of complex valued functions orthogonal over the unit disk, i.e., $x^2 + y^2 \leq 1$. The Zernike moment of order n with repetition m of shape region $f(x, y)$ (Eq. 1) is given by:

$$Z_{nm} = \frac{n + 1}{\pi} \sum_r \sum_\theta f(r \cos\theta, r \sin\theta) \cdot R_{nm}(r) \cdot exp(jm\theta) \quad r \leq 1$$

Zernike moments (ZM) have the following advantages [47]:

- rotation invariance: the magnitudes of Zernike moments are invariant to rotation.
- robustness: they are robust to noise and minor variations in shape.
- expressiveness: since the basis is orthogonal, they have minimum information redundancy.

However, the computation of ZM (in general, continuous orthogonal moments) pose several problems:

- coordinate space normalization: the image coordinate space must be transformed to the domain where the orthogonal polynomial is defined (unit circle for the Zernike polynomial).
- numerical approximation of continuous integrals: the continuous integrals must be approximated by discrete summations. This approximation not only leads to numerical errors in the computed moments, but also severely affects the analytical properties such as rotational invariance and orthogonality.
- computational complexity: computational complexity of the radial Zernike polynomial increases as the order becomes large.

6.2.4 Radial Chebyshev moments (RCM)

The radial Chebyshev moment of order p and repetition q is defined as [48]:

$$S_{pq} = \frac{1}{2\pi\rho(p,m)} \sum_{r=0}^{m-1} \sum_{\theta=0}^{2\pi} t_p(r) \cdot exp(-jq\theta) \cdot f(r,\theta)$$

where $t_p(r)$ is the scaled orthogonal Chebyshev polynomials for an image of size $N \times N$:

$$t_0(x) = 1$$
$$t_1(x) = (2x - N + 1)/N$$
$$t_p(x) = \frac{(2p-1)t_1(x)t_{p-1}(x) - (p-1)\left\{1 - \frac{(p-1)^2}{N^2}\right\} t_{p-2}(x)}{p}, \quad p > 1$$

$\rho(p,N)$ is the squared-norm:

$$\rho(p,N) = \frac{N\left(1 - \frac{1}{N^2}\right)\left(1 - \frac{2^2}{N^2}\right) \cdots \left(1 - \frac{p^2}{N^2}\right)}{2p+1} \quad p = 0, 1, \cdots, N-1$$

and $m = (N/2) + 1$.

The mapping between (r, θ) and image coordinates (x, y) is given by:

$$x = \frac{rN}{2(m-1)} \cos(\theta) + \frac{N}{2}$$

$$y = \frac{rN}{2(m-1)} \sin(\theta) + \frac{N}{2}$$

Compared to Chebyshev moments, radial Chebyshev moments possess rotational invariance property.

6.3 Discussions

Besides the previous moments, there are other moments for shape representation, for example, homocentric polar-radius moment [49], orthogonal Fourier-Mellin moments (OFMMs) [50], pseudo-Zernike Moments [51], etc. The study shows that the moment-based shape descriptors are usually concise, robust and easy to compute. It is also invariant to scaling, rotation and translation of the object. However, because of their global nature, the disadvantage of moment-based methods is that it is dificult to correlate high order moments with a shape's salient features.

7. Scale space approaches

In scale space theory a curve is embedded into a continuous family $\{\Gamma_\sigma: \sigma \geq 0\}$ of gradually simplified versions. The main idea of scale spaces is that the original curve $\Gamma = \Gamma_0$ should get more and more simplified, and so small structures should vanish as parameter σ increases. Thus due to different scales (values of σ), it is possible to separate small details from relevant shape properties. The ordered sequence $\{\Gamma_\sigma: \sigma \geq 0\}$ is referred to as evolution of Γ. Scale-spaces find wide application in computer vision, in particular, due to smoothing and elimination of small details.

A lot of shape features can be analyzed in scale-space theory to get more information about shapes. Here we introduced 2 scale-space approaches: curvature scale-space (CSS) and intersection points map (IPM).

7.1 Curvature scale-space

The curvature scale-space (CSS) method, proposed by F. Mokhtarian in 1988, was selected as a contour shape descriptor for MPEG-7. This approach is based on multi-scale representation and curvature to represent planar curves. The nature parametrization equation is shown as following:

$$\Gamma(\mu) = (x(\mu), y(\mu)) \tag{17}$$

An evolved version of that curve is defined by

$$\Gamma_\sigma(\mu) = (X(\mu, \sigma), Y(\mu, \sigma))$$

where $X(\mu, \sigma) = x(\mu) * g(\mu, \sigma)$ and $Y(\mu, \sigma) = y(\mu) * g(\mu, \sigma)$, $*$ is the convolution operator, and $g(\mu, \sigma)$ denotes a Gaussian filter with standard deviation σ defined by

$$g(\mu, \sigma) = \frac{1}{\sigma\sqrt{2\pi}} exp(\frac{-\mu^2}{2\sigma^2})$$

Functions $X(\mu, \sigma)$ and $Y(\mu, \sigma)$ are given explicitly by

$$X(\mu, \sigma) = \int_{-\infty}^{\infty} x(v) \frac{1}{\sigma\sqrt{2\pi}} exp(\frac{-(\mu - v)^2}{2\sigma^2}) dv$$

$$Y(\mu, \sigma) = \int_{-\infty}^{\infty} y(v) \frac{1}{\sigma\sqrt{2\pi}} exp(\frac{-(\mu - v)^2}{2\sigma^2}) dv$$

The curvature of is given by

$$k(\mu,\sigma) = \frac{X_\mu(\mu,\sigma)Y_{\mu\mu}(\mu,\sigma) - X_{\mu\mu}(\mu,\sigma)Y_\mu(\mu,\sigma)}{(X_\mu(\mu,\sigma)^2 - Y_\mu(\mu,\sigma)^2)^{3/2}}$$

where

$$X_\mu(\mu,\sigma) = \frac{\partial}{\partial\mu}(x(\mu) * g(\mu,\sigma)) = x(\mu) * g_\mu(\mu,\sigma)$$

$$X_{\mu\mu}(\mu,\sigma) = \frac{\partial^2}{\partial\mu^2}(x(\mu) * g(\mu,\sigma)) = x(\mu) * g_{\mu\mu}(\mu,\sigma)$$

$$Y_\mu(\mu,\sigma) = \frac{\partial}{\partial\mu}(y(\mu) * g(\mu,\sigma)) = y(\mu) * g_\mu(\mu,\sigma)$$

$$Y_{\mu\mu}(\mu,\sigma) = \frac{\partial^2}{\partial\mu^2}(y(\mu) * g(\mu,\sigma)) = y(\mu) * g_{\mu\mu}(\mu,\sigma)$$

Note that σ is also referred to as a scale parameter. The process of generating evolved versions of Γ_σ as σ increases from 0 to ∞ is referred to as the evolution of Γ_σ. This technique is suitable for removing noise and smoothing a planar curve as well as gradual simplification of a shape.

The function defined by $k(\mu, \sigma) = 0$ is the CSS image of Γ. Figure 33 is a CSS image examples.

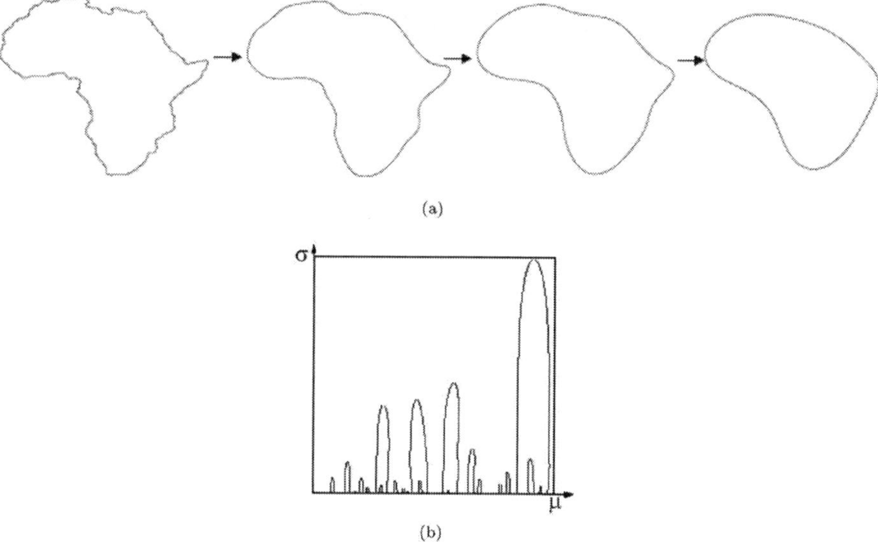

Fig. 33. Curvature scale-space image (a) Evolution of Africa: from left to right $\sigma = 0$(original), $\sigma = 4$, $\sigma = 8$ and $\sigma = 16$, respectively; (b) CSS image of Africa.

The representation of CSS is the maxima of CSS contour of an image. Many methods for representing the maxima of CSS exist in the literatures [52, 53, 19] and the CSS technique has been shown to be robust contour-based shape representation technique. The basic properties of the CSS representation are as follows:

- it captures the main features of a shape, enabling similarity-based retrieval;
- it is robust to noise, changes in scale and orientation of objects;

- it is compact, reliable and fast;
- it retains the local information of a shape. Every concavity or convexity on the shape has its own corresponding contour on the CSS image.

Although CSS has a lot of advantages, it does not always give results in accordance with human vision system. The main drawbacks of this description are due to the problem of shallow concavities/convexities on a shape. It can be shown that the shallow and deep concavities/convexities may create the same large contours on the CSS image. In [54, 55], the authors gave some methods to alleviate these effects.

7.2 Intersection points map

Similarly to the CSS, many methods also use a Gaussian kernel to progressively smooth the curve relatively to the varying bandwidth. In [56], the authors proposed a new algorithm, intersection points map (IPM), based on this principle, instead of characterizing the curve with its curvature involving 2nd order derivatives, it uses the intersection points between the smoothed curve and the original. As the standard deviation of the Gaussian kernel increases, the number of the intersection points decreases. By analyzing these remaining points, features for a pattern can be defined. Since this method deals only with curve smoothing, it needs only the convolution operation in the smoothing process. So this method is faster than the CSS one with equivalent performances. Figure 34 is an example of IPM.

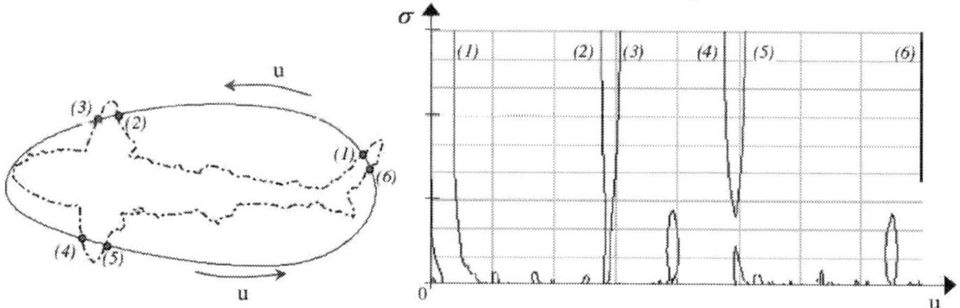

Fig. 34. Example of the IPM (a) An original contour; (b) an IPM image in the (u, σ) plane. The IPM points indicated by (1)-(6) refer to the corresponding intersection points in (a).

The IPM pattern can be identified regardless of its orientation, translation and scale change. It is also resistant to noise for a range of noise energy. The main weakness of this approach is that it fails to handle occulted contours and those having undergone a non-rigid deformation.

7.3 Discussions

As multi-resolution analysis in signal processing, scale-space theory can obtain abundant information about a contour with different scales. In scale-space, global pattern information can be interpreted from higher scales, while detailed pattern information can be interpreted from lower scales. Scale-space algorithm benefit from the boundary information redundancy in the new image, making it less sensitive to errors in the alignment or contour extraction algorithms. The great advantages are the high robustness to noise and the great coherence with human perception.

8. Shape transform domains

The transform domain class includes methods which are formed by the transform of the detected object or the transform of the whole image. Transforms can therefore be used to characterize the appearance of images. The shape feature is represented by the all or partial coefficients of a transform.

8.1 Fourier descriptors

Although, Fourier descriptor (FD) is a 40-year-old technique, it is still considered as a valid description tool. The shape description and classification using FD either in contours or regions are simple to compute, robust to noise and compact. It has many applications in different areas.

8.1.1 One-dimensional Fourier descriptors

In general, Fourier descriptor (FD) is obtained by applying Fourier transform on a shape signature that is a one-dimensional function which is derived from shape boundary coordinates (cf. Section 3). The normalized Fourier transformed coefficients are called the Fourier descriptor of the shape. FD derived from different signatures has significant different performance on shape retrieval. As shown in [10, 53], FD derived from centroid distance function $r(t)$ outperforms FD derived from other shape signatures in terms of overall performance. The discrete Fourier transform of $r(t)$ is then given by

$$a_n = \frac{1}{N} \sum_{t=0}^{N-1} r(t) exp\left(\frac{-j2\pi nt}{N}\right), \quad n = 0, 1, \cdots, N - 1$$

Since the centroid distance function $r(t)$ is only invariant to rotation and translation, the acquired Fourier coefficients have to be further normalized so that they are scaling and start point independent shape descriptors. From Fourier transform theory, the general form of the Fourier coefficients of a contour centroid distance function $r(t)$ transformed through scaling and change of start point from the original function $r(t)^{(o)}$ is given by

$$a_n = exp(jn\tau) \cdot s \cdot a_n^{(o)}$$

where a_n and $a_n^{(o)}$ are the Fourier coefficients of the transformed shape and the original shape, respectively, τ is the angles incurred by the change of start point; s is the scale factor. Now considering the following expression:

$$b_n = \frac{a_n}{a_1} = \frac{exp(jn\tau) \cdot s \cdot a_n^{(o)}}{exp(j\tau) \cdot s \cdot a_1^{(o)}} = \frac{a_n^{(o)}}{a_1^{(o)}} exp[j(n-1)\tau] = b_n^{(o)} exp[j(n-1)\tau]$$

where b_n and $b_n^{(o)}$ are the normalized Fourier coefficients of the transformed shape and the original shape, respectively. If we ignore the phase information and only use magnitude of the coefficients, then $|b_n|$ and $|b_n^{(o)}|$ are the same. In other words, $|b_n|$ is invariant to translation, rotation, scaling and change of start point.

The set of magnitudes of the normalized Fourier coefficients of the shape $\{|b_n|, 0 < n < N\}$ are used as shape descriptors, denoted as

$$\{FD_n, 0 < n < N\}.$$

One-dimensional FD has several nice characteristics such as simple derivation, simple normalization and simple to do matching. As indicated by [53], for efficient retrieval, 10 FDs are sufficient for shape description.

8.1.2 Region-based Fourier descriptor

The region-based FD is referred to as generic FD (GFD), which can be used for general applications. Basically, GFD is derived by applying a modified polar Fourier transform (MPFT) on shape image [57, 12]. In order to apply MPFT, the polar shape image is treated as a normal rectangular image. The steps are

1. the approximated normalized image is rotated counter clockwise by an angular step sufficiently small.
2. the pixel values along positive x-direction starting from the image center are copied and pasted into a new matrix as row elements.
3. the steps 1 and 2 are repeated until the image is rotated by 360°.

The result of these steps is that an image in polar space plots into Cartesian space. Figure 35 shows the polar shape image turning into normal rectangular image.

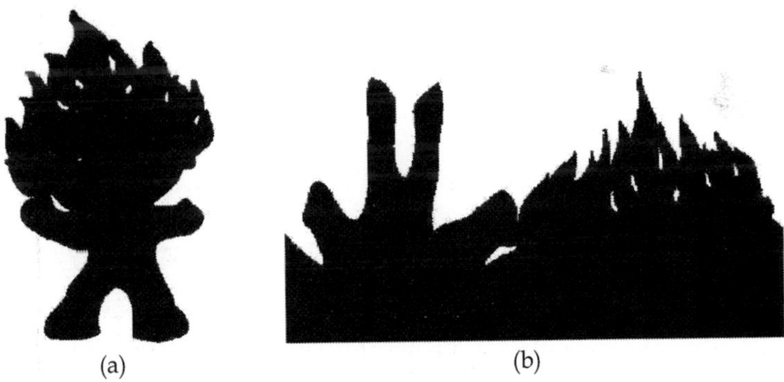

(a)   (b)

Fig. 35. The polar shape image turns into normal rectangular image. (a) Original shape image in polar space; (b) polar image of (a) plotted into Cartesian space.

The Fourier transform is acquired by applying a discrete 2D Fourier transform on this shape image.

$$pf(\rho, \phi) = \sum_r \sum_i f(r, \theta_i) exp[j2\pi(\frac{r}{R}\rho + \frac{2\pi i}{T}\phi)]$$

where $0 \leq r = \sqrt{[(x - g_x)^2 + (y - g_y)^2]} < R$, and $\theta_i = i(2\pi/T)$; $0 \leq \rho < R, 0 \leq \phi < T$. (g_x, g_y) is the center of mass of the shape; R and T are the radial and angular resolutions. The acquired Fourier coefficients are translation invariant. Rotation and scaling invariance are achieved by the following:

$$GFD = \left\{ \frac{|pf(0,0)|}{area}, \frac{|pf(0,1)|}{|pf(0,0)|}, \cdots, \frac{|pf(0,n)|}{|pf(0,0)|}, \cdots, \frac{|pf(m,0)|}{|pf(0,0)|}, \cdots, \frac{|pf(m,n)|}{|pf(0,0)|} \right\}$$

where $area$ is the area of the bounding circle in which the polar image resides. m is the maximum number of the radial frequencies selected and n is the maximum number of angular frequencies selected. m and n can be adjusted to achieve hierarchical coarse to fine representation requirement.

For efficient shape description, in the implementation of [57], 36 GFD features reflecting $m = 4$ and $n = 9$ are selected to index the shape. The experimental results have shown GFD as invariant to translation, rotation, and scaling. For obtaining the affine and general minor distortions invariance, in [57], the authors proposed Enhanced Generic Fourier Descriptor (EGFD) to improve the GFD properties.

8.2 Wavelet transform

A hierarchical planar curve descriptor is developed by using the wavelet transform [58]. This descriptor decomposes a curve into components of different scales so that the coarsest scale components carry the global approximation information while the finer scale components contain the local detailed information. The wavelet descriptor has many desirable properties such as multi-resolution representation, invariance, uniqueness, stability, and spatial localization. In [59], the authors use dyadic wavelet transform deriving an affine invariant function. In [60], a descriptor is obtained by applying the Fourier transform along the axis of polar angle and the wavelet transform along the axis of radius. This feature is also invariant to translation, rotation, and scaling. At same time, the matching process of wavelet descriptor can be accomplished cheaply.

8.3 Angular radial transformation

The angular radial transformation (ART) is based in a polar coordinate system where the sinusoidal basis functions are defined on a unit disc. Given an image function in polar coordinates, $f(\rho, \theta)$, an ART coefficient F_{nm} (radial order n, angular order m) can be defined as [61]:

$$F_{nm} = \int_0^{2\pi} \int_0^1 V_{nm}(\rho, \theta) f(\rho, \theta) \rho \, d\rho \, d\theta$$

$V_{nm}(\rho, \theta)$ is the ART basis function and is separable in the angular and radial directions so that:

$$V_{nm}(\rho, \theta) = A_m(\theta) R_n(\rho)$$

The angular basis function, A_m, is an exponential function used to obtain orientation invariance. This function is defined as:

$$A_m(\theta) = \frac{1}{2\pi} e^{jm\theta}$$

R_n, the radial basis function, is defined as:

$$R_n(\rho) = \begin{cases} 1 & if \ n = 0 \\ 2\cos(\pi n \rho) & if \ n \neq 0 \end{cases}$$

In MPEG-7, twelve angular and three radial functions are used ($n < 3$, $m < 12$). Real parts of the 2-D basis functions are shown in Figure 36.

For scale normalization, the ART coefficients are divided by the magnitude of ART coefficient of order $n = 0$, $m = 0$.

MPEG-7 standardization process showed the efficiency of 2-D angular radial transformation. This descriptor is robust to translations, scaling, multi-representation (remeshing, weak distortions) and noises.

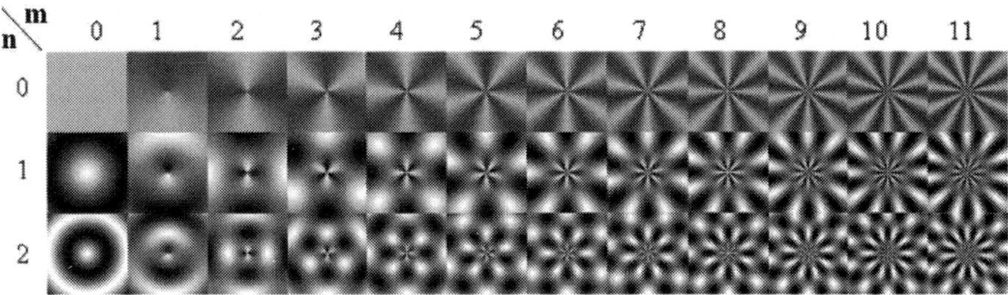

Fig. 36. Real parts of the ART basis functions

8.4 Shape signature harmonic embedding

A harmonic function is obtained by a convolution between the Poisson kernel $P_R(r, \theta)$ and a given boundary function $u(Re^{j\phi})$. Poisson kernel is defined by

$$P_R(r, \theta) = \frac{R^2 - r^2}{R^2 - 2Rr\cos(\theta) + r^2}$$

The boundary function could be any real- or complex-valued function, but here we choose shape signature functions for the purpose of shape representation. For any shape signature $s[n]$, $n = 0, 1, \ldots, N - 1$, the boundary values for a unit disk can be set as

$$u(Re^{j\phi}) = u(Re^{j\omega_0 n}) = s[n]$$

where $\omega_0 = 2\pi/N$, $\phi = \omega_0 n$.

So the harmonic function u can be written as

$$u(re^{j\theta}) = \frac{1}{2\pi} \int_0^{2\pi} u(Re^{j\phi})P_R(r, \phi - \theta)d\phi \tag{18}$$

The Poisson kernel $P_R(r, \theta)$ has a low-pass filter characteristic, where the radius r is inversely related to the bandwidth of the filter. The radius r is considered as scale parameter of a multi-scale representation [62]. Another important property is $P_R(0, \theta) = 1$, indicating $u(0)$ is the mean value of boundary function $u(Re^{j\phi})$.

In [62], the authors proposed a formulation of a discrete closed-form solution for the Poisson's integral formula Eq. 18, so that one can avoid the need for approximation or numerical calculation of the Poisson summation form.

As in Subsection 8.1.2, the harmonic function inside the disk can be mapped to a rectilinear space for a better illustration. Figure 37 shows an example for a star shape. Here, we used curvature as the signature to provide boundary values.

The zero-crossing image of the harmonic functions is extracted as shape feature. This shape descriptor is invariant to translation, rotation and scaling. It is also robust to noise. Figure 38 is for example. The original curve is corrupted with different noise levels, and the harmonic embeddings show robustness to the noise.

At same time, it is more efficient than CSS descriptor. However, it is not suitable for similarity retrieval, because it is unconsistent to non-rigid transform.

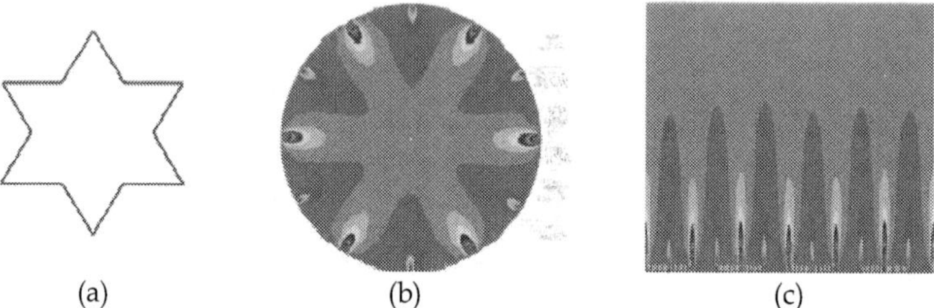

(a)   (b)   (c)

Fig. 37. Harmonic embedding of curvature signature (a) Example shape; (b) harmonic function within the unit disk; (c) rectilinear mapping of the function.

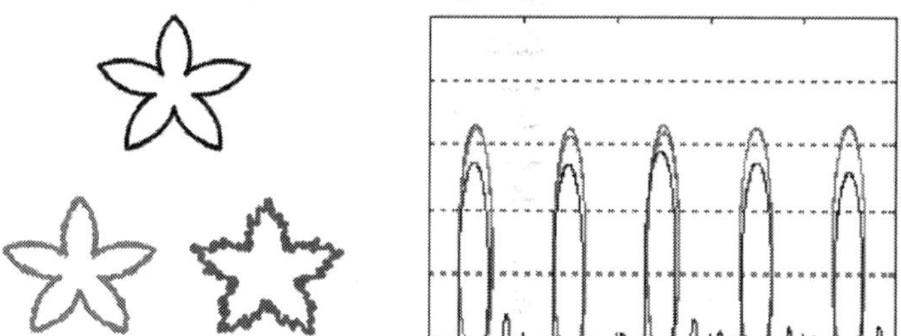

Fig. 38. centroid distance signature harmonic embedding that is robust to noisy boundaries (a) Original and noisy shapes; (b) harmonic embedding images for centroid distance signature.

8.5 $\Re$-Transform

The $\Re$-Transform to represent a shape is based on the Radon transform. The approach is presented as follow. We assume that the function f is the domain of a shape, cf. Eq. 1. Its Radon transform is defined by:

$$T_R(\rho, \theta) = \int_{-\infty}^{\infty} \int_{-\infty}^{\infty} f(x, y)\delta(x\cos\theta + y\sin\theta - \rho)dxdy$$

where $\delta(.)$ is the Dirac delta-function:

$$\delta(x) = \begin{cases} 1 & if\ x = 0 \\ 0 & otherwise \end{cases}$$

$\theta \in [0, \pi]$ and $\rho \in (-\infty, \infty)$. In other words, Radon transform $T_R(\rho, \theta)$ is the integral of f over the line $L_{(\rho, \theta)}$ defined by $\rho = x\cos\theta + y\sin\theta$.

Figure 39 is an example of a shape and its Radon transform.

The following transform is defined as $\Re$-transform:

$$\Re_f(\theta) = \int_{-\infty}^{\infty} T_R^2(\rho, \theta)d\rho$$

where $T_R(\rho, \theta)$ is the Radon transform of the domain function f. In [63], the authors show the following properties of $\Re_f(\theta)$:

- periodicity: $\Re_f(\theta \pm \pi) = \Re_f(\theta)$
- rotation: a rotation of the image by an angle θ_0 implies a translation of the $\Re$-transform of θ_0: $\Re_f(\theta + \theta_0)$.
- translation: the $\Re$-transform is invariant under a translation of the shape f by a vector $\vec{u} = (x_0, y_0)$.
- scaling: a change of the scaling of the shape f induces a scaling in the amplitude only of the $\Re$-transform.

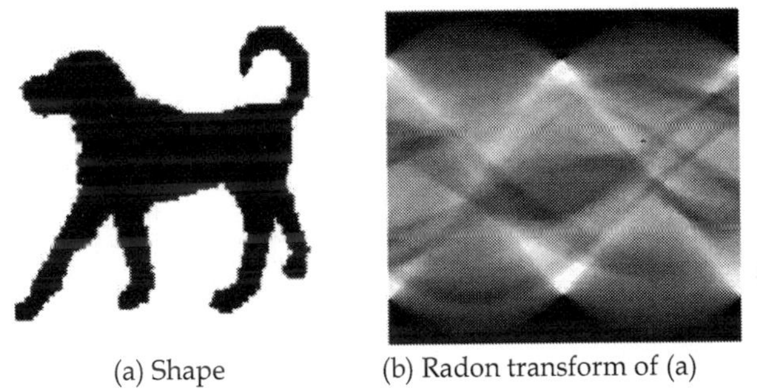

(a) Shape   (b) Radon transform of (a)

Fig. 39. A shape and its Radon transform

Given a large collection of shapes, one $\Re$-transform per shape is not efficient to distinguish from the others because the $\Re$-transform provides a highly compact shape representation. In this perspective, to improve the description, each shape is projected in the Radon space for different segmentation levels of the Chamfer distance transform. Chamfer distance transform is introduced in [64, 65].

Given the distance transform of a shape, the distance image is segmented into N equidistant levels to keep the segmentation isotropic. For each distance level, pixels having a distance value superior to that level are selected and at each level of segmentation, an $\Re$-transform is computed. In this manner, both the internal structure and the boundaries of the shape are captured.

Since a rotation of the shape implies a corresponding shift of the $\Re$-transform. Therefore, a one-dimensional Fourier transform is applied on this function to obtain the rotation invariance. After the discrete one-dimensional Fourier transform F, $\Re$-transform descriptor vector is defined as follows:

$$RTD = \left(\frac{F\Re^1(\frac{\pi}{M})}{F\Re^1(0)}, \cdots, \frac{F\Re^1(\frac{i\pi}{M})}{F\Re^1(0)}, \cdots, \frac{F\Re^1(\pi)}{F\Re^1(0)}, \cdots, \frac{F\Re^N(\frac{\pi}{M})}{F\Re^N(0)}, \cdots, \frac{F\Re^N(\frac{i\pi}{M})}{F\Re^N(0)}, \cdots, \frac{F\Re^N(\pi)}{F\Re^N(0)} \right)$$

where $i \in [1, M]$, M is the angular resolution. $F\Re^\alpha$ is the magnitude of Fourier transform to $\Re$-transform. $\alpha \in [1, N]$, is the segmentation level of Chamfer distance transform.

8.6 Shapelets descriptor

Shapelets descriptor was proposed to present a model for animate shapes and extracting meaningful parts of objects. The model assumes that animate shapes (2D simple closed curves) are formed by a linear superposition of a number of shape bases. A basis function $(s; \mu, \sigma)$ is defined in [66]: $\mu \in [0, 1]$ indicates the location of the basis function relative to the domain of the observed curve, and σ is the scale of the function ψ. Figure 40 shows the shape of the basis function ψ at different σ values. It displays variety with different parameter and transforms.

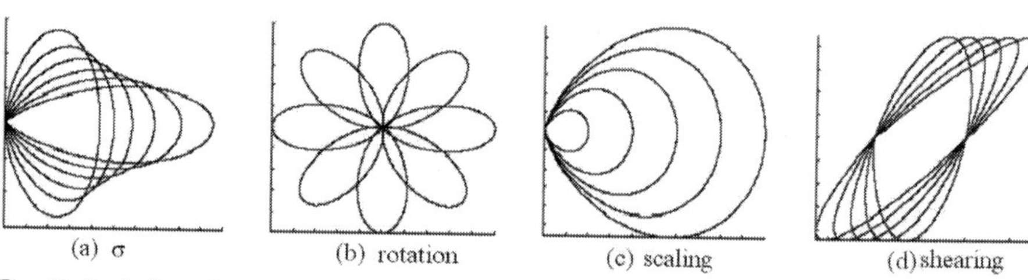

Fig. 40. Each shape base is a lobe-shaped curve

The basis functions are subject to affine transformations by a 2 × 2 matrix of basis coefficients:

$$A_k = \begin{bmatrix} a_k & b_k \\ c_k & d_k \end{bmatrix}$$

The variables for describing a base are denoted by $b_k = (A_k, \mu_k, \sigma_k)$ and are termed basis elements. The shapelet is defined by

$$\gamma(s; \mathbf{b}_k) = A_k \psi(s; \mu_k, \sigma_k)$$

Figure 40 (b,c,d) demonstrates shapelets obtained from the basis functions ψ by the affine transformations of rotation, scaling, and shearing respectively, as indicated by the basis coefficient A_k. By collecting all the shapelets at various μ, σ, A and discretizing them at multiple levels, an over-complete dictionary is obtained

$$\Delta = \{\gamma(s; \mathbf{b}_k) : \forall \mathbf{b}; \, a\gamma_0, \, a > 0\}.$$

A special shapelet γ_0 is defined as an ellipse.

Shapelets are the building blocks for shape contours, and they form closed curves by linear addition:

$$\Gamma(s) = \begin{bmatrix} x_0 \\ y_0 \end{bmatrix} + \sum_{k=1}^{K} \begin{bmatrix} a_k & b_k \\ c_k & d_k \end{bmatrix} \psi(s; \mu_k, \sigma_k) + \mathbf{n}(s)$$

Here (x_0, y_0) is the centroid of the contour and n is residue.

A discrete representation $\mathbf{B} = (K, \mathbf{b}_1, \mathbf{b}_2, ..., \mathbf{b}_K)$, shown by the dots in second row of Figure 41, represents a shape. $\mathbf{B}$ is called the "shape script" by analogy to music scripts, where each shapelet is represented by a dot in the (μ, σ) domain. The horizontal axis is $\mu \in [0, 1]$ and the vertical axis is the σ. Large dots correspond to big coefficient matrix

$$A_k^2 = a_k^2 + b_k^2 + c_k^2 + d_k^2$$

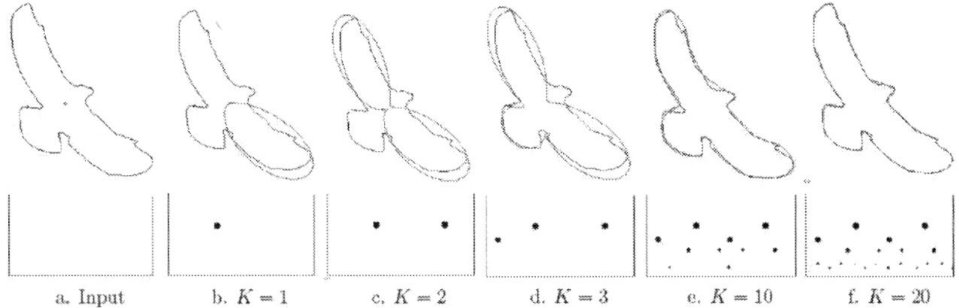

Fig. 41. Pursuit of shape bases for an eagle contour

Clearly, computing the shape script **B** is a non-trivial task, since Δ is over-complete and there will be multiple sets of bases that reconstruct the curve with equal precision. [66] gave some pursuit algorithms to use shapelets representing a shape.

8.7 Discussions

As a kind of global shape description technique, shape analysis in transform domains takes the whole shape as th shape representation. The description scheme is designed for this representation. Unlike the spacial interrelation feature analysis, shape transform projects a shape contour or region into an other domain to obtain some of its intrinsic features. For shape description, there is always a trade-off between accuracy and efficiency. On one hand, shape should be described as accurate as possible; on the other hand, shape description should be as compact as possible to simplify indexing and retrieval. For a shape transform analysis algorithm, it is very flexible to accomplish a shape description with different accuracy and efficiency by choosing the number of transform coefficients.

9. Summary table

For convenience to compare these shape feature extraction approaches in this chapter, we summarize their properties in Table 1.

Frankly speaking, it is not equitable to affirm a property of an approach by rudely speaking "good" or "bad". Because certain approaches have great different performances under different conditions. For example, the method area function is invariant with affine transform under the condition of the contours sampled at its same vertices; whereas it is not robust to affine transform if the condition can't be contented. In addition, some approaches have good properties for certain type shapes; however it is not for the others. For example, the method shapelets representation is especially suitable for blobby objects, and it has shortcomings in representing elongated objects. So the simple evaluations in this table are only as a reference. These evaluations are drawn by assuming that all the necessary conditions have been contented for each approach.

10. Conclusion

In this chapter we made a study and a comparison the methods of shape-based feature extraction and representation. About 40 techniques for extraction of shape features have been shortly described and compared. Unlike the traditional classification, the approaches of shape-based feature extraction and representation were classified by their processing

Shape representation			Reconstructure	Invariance				Resistance			Computational complexity
				Translation	Rotation	Scale	Affine transform	Noise	Occultation	Non-rigid deformation	
Shape signatures	Complex coordinates		Yes	Bad	Bad	Bad	Bad	Average	Good	Bad	Low
	Central distance		No	Good	Good	Good	Bad	Average	Good	Bad	Low
	Tangent angle		No	Good	Good	Good	Bad	Bad	Good	Average	Low
	Curvature function		No	Good	Good	Good	Bad	Bad	Good	Average	Low
	Area function		No	Good	Good	Good	Good	Good	Good	Bad	Low
	Triangle-area representation		No	Good	Good	Good	Good	Good	Average	Average	Low
	Chord length function		No	Good	Good	Good	Bad	Bad	Bad	Bad	Low
Polygonal approximation	Merging	Distance threshold	No	Good	Good	Good	Bad	Good	Bad	Bad	Average
		Tunneling	No	Good	Good	Good	Bad	Good	Bad	Bad	Average
		Polygon evolution	No	Good	Good	Good	Bad	Good	Bad	Bad	Average
	Splitting		No	Good	Good	Good	Bad	Good	Bad	Bad	Average
Space interrelation Feature	Adaptive grid resolution		Yes	Good	Good	Good	Bad	Good	Good	Bad	Low
	Bounding box		Yes	Good	Good	Good	Average	Good	Good	Average	Average
	Convex hull		No	Good	Good	Good	Good	Average	Bad	Bad	High
	Chain code	Basic chain code	Yes	Good	Bad	Bad	Bad	Bad	Good	Bad	Low
		Vertex chain code	Yes	Good	Bad	Bad	Bad	Bad	Good	Bad	Low
		Statistic chain code	No	Good	Bad	Bad	Bad	Bad	Bad	Bad	Low
	Smooth curve decomposition		No	Good	Good	Good	Bad	Good	Good	Average	Average
	ALI-based representation		No	Good	Good	Good	Average	Good	Average	Bad	Average
	Beam angle statistics		No	Good	Good	Good	Bad	Good	Bad	Bad	Low
	Shape matrix	Square model	Yes	Good	Good	Good	Bad	Bad	Good	Bad	Average
		Polar model	Yes	Good	Good	Good	Bad	Bad	Good	Bad	Low
	Shape context		No	Good	Good	Good	Bad	Bad	Average	Average	Average
	Chord distribution		No	Good	Good	Good	Bad	Good	Bad	Bad	Low
	Shock graphs		Yes	Good	Good	Good	Good	Good	Good	Good	High
Moments	Boundary moments		No	Good	Good	Good	Bad	Average	Bad	Bad	Low
	Region moments	Invariant moments	No	Good	Good	Good	Bad	Bad	Bad	Bad	Average
		Algebraic Moment	No	Good	Good	Good	Good	Average	Bad	Bad	Average
		Zernike Moments	No	Good	Good	Good	Bad	Good	Average	Average	High
		Radial Chebyshev Moments	No	Good	Good	Good	Bad	Good	Average	Average	High
Scale-space methods	Curvature scale space		No	Good	Good	Good	Average	Good	Good	Average	Average
	Intersection points map		No	Good	Good	Good	Average	Good	Good	Bad	Average
Shape transform domains	Fourier descriptors	1-D Fourier descriptor	No	Good	Good	Good	Bad	Bad	Bad	Bad	Average
		Region-based Fourier descriptor	No	Good	Good	Good	Good	Good	Average	Average	High
	Wavelet transform		No	Good	Good	Good	Good	Average	Average	Bad	Average
	Angular radial transformation		No	Good	Good	Good	Bad	Good	Bad	Bad	High
	Signature harmonic embedding		No	Good	Good	Good	Average	Good	Average	Bad	High
	$\Re$ -Transform		No	Good	Good	Good	Bad	Good	Average	Average	High
	Shapelets descriptor		No	Good	Good	Good	Bad	Good	Bad	Bad	High

Table 1. Properties of shape feature extraction approaches

approaches. These processing approaches included shape signatures, polygonal approximation methods, spatial inter-relation feature, moments approaches, scale-space methods and shape transform domains: in such way, one can easily select the appropriate processing approach. A synthetic table has been established for a fast and global comparison of the performances of these approaches.

Extracting a shape feature in accordance with human perception is not an easy task. Due to the fact that huma vision and perception are an extraordinary complicated system, it is a utopia to hope that the machine vision has super excellent performance with small complexity. In addition, choosing appropriate features for a shape recognition system must consider what kinds of features are suitable for the task. There exists no general feature which would work best for every kind of images.

11. References

"MPEG-7 overview (version 10)," ISO/IEC JTC1/SC29/WG11, Tech. Rep., 2004.

D. Zhang and G. Lu, "Review of shape representation and description techniques," *Pattern Recognition*, vol. 37, pp. 1-19, 2004.

B. Horn, *Robot Vision*. MIT Press, Cambridge, 1986.

D.-M. Tsai and M. fong Chen, "Object recognition by a linear weight classifier." *Pattern Recognition Letters*, vol. 16, pp. 591-600, 1995.

S. Loncaric, "A survey of shape analysis techniques," *Pattern Recognition*, vol. 31(8), pp. 983-1001, 1998.

I. Young, J. Walker, and J. Bowie, "An analysis technique for biological shape," *Comput. Graphics Image Processing*, vol. 25, pp. 357-370, 1974.

M. Peura and J. Iivarinen, "Efficiency of simple shape descriptors," in *Proc. 3rd International Workshop on Visual Form (IWVF3)*, May 1997.

C. Cheng, W. Liu, and H. Zhang, "Image retrieval based on region shape similarity," in Proc. 13th SPIE symposium on Electronic Imaging, Storage and Retrieval for Image and Video Databases, 2001.

A. SOFFER, "Negative shape features for image databases consisting of geographic symbols," in *Proc. 3rd International Workshop on Visual Form*, May 1997.

D. Zhang and G. Lu, "A comparative study of fourier descriptors for shape representation and retrieval," in *Proc. 5th Asian Conference on Computer Vision*, 2002.

H. Kauppinen, T. Seppanen, and M. Pietikainen, "An experimental comparison of auto-regressive and fourier-based descriptors in 2-D shape classification," *IEEE Trans. Pattern Analysis and Machine Intelligence*, vol. 17(2), pp. 201-207, 1995.

R. B. Yadava, N. K. Nishchala, A. K. Gupta, and V. K. Rastogi, "Retrieval and classification of shape-based objects using fourier, generic fourier, and wavelet-fourier descriptors technique: A comparative study," *Optics and Lasers in Engineering*, vol. 45(6), pp. 695-708, 2007.

D. S. Zhang and G. Lu, "A comparative study on shape retrieval using fourier descriptors with different shape signatures," in *Proc. International Conference on Intelligent Multimedia and Distance Education (ICIMADE01)*, 2001.

C. T. Zahn and R. Z. Roskies., "Fourier descriptors for plane closed curves," *IEEE Trans. Computer*, vol. c-21(3), pp. 269-281, 1972.

K.-J. Lu and S. Kota, "Compliant mechanism synthesis for shape-change applications: Preliminary results," in *Proceedings of SPIE Modeling, Signal Processing, and Control Conference*, vol. 4693, March 2002, pp. 161-172.

L. J. Latecki and R. Lakamper, "Shape similarity measure based on correspondence of visual parts," *IEEE Trans. Pattern Analysis and Machine Intelligence*, vol. 22(10), pp. 1185-1190, 2000.

Y. P. Wang, K. T. Lee, and K.Toraichi, "Multiscale curvature-based shape representation using B-spline wavelets," *IEEE Trans. Image Process*, vol. 8(10), pp. 1586-1592, 1999.

F. Mokhtarian and A. K. Mackworth, "A theory of multiscale, curvature-based shape representation for planar curves," *IEEE Trans. Pattern Analysis and Machine Intelligence*, vol. 14(8), pp. 789-805, 1992.

A. C. Jalba, M. H. F. Wilkinson, and J. B. T. M. Roerdink, "Shape representation and recognition through morphological curvature scale spaces," *IEEE Trans. Image Processing*, vol. 15(2), pp. 331-341, 2006.

N. Alajlan, M. S. Kamel, and G. Freeman, "Multi-object image retrieval based on shape and topology," *Signal Processing: Image Communication*, vol. 21, pp. 904-918, 2006.

N. Alajlan, I. E. Rube, M. S. Kamel, and G. Freeman, "Shape retrieval using triangle-area representation and dynamic space warping," *Pattern Recognition*, vol. 40(7), pp. 1911-1920, 2007.

S. Han and S. Yang, "An invariant feature representation for shape retrieval," in Proc. Sixth International Conference on Parallel and Distributed Computing, Applications and Technologies, 2005.

L. J. Latecki and R. Lakamper, "Convexity rule for shape decomposition based on discrete contour evolution," *Computer Vision and Image Understanding*, vol. 73(3), pp. 441-454, 1999.

K. Chakrabarti, M. Binderberger, K. Porkaew, and S. Mehrotra, "Similar shape retrieval in mars," in Proc. IEEE International Conference on Multimedia and Expo, 2000.

C. Bauckhage and J. K. Tsotsos, "Bounding box splitting for robust shape classification," in *Proc. IEEE International Conference on Image Processing*, 2005, pp. 478-481.

E. Davies, Machine Vision: Theory, Algorithms, Practicalities. Academic Press, New York, 1997.

R. Gonzalez and R. Woods, *Digital image processing, Second Edition*. PEARSON EDUCATION NORTH ASIA LIMITED and Publishing House of Electronics Industry, 2002.

M. Sonka, V. Hlavac, and R. Boyle, *Image Processing, Analysis and Machine Vision*. Chapman and Hall, London, UK, 1993.

Y. K. Liu, W. Wei, P. J. Wang, and B. Zalik, "Compressed vertex chain codes," *Pattern Recognition*, vol. 40(11), pp. 2908-2913, 2007.

M.-K. Hu, "Visual pattern recognition by moment invariants," *IRE Trans. Information Theory*, vol. IT-8, pp. 179- 187, 1962.

J. Iivarinen and A. Visa, "Shape recognition of irregular objects," in Proc. SPIE, Intelligent Robots and Computer Vision XV: Algorithms, Techniques, Active Vision, and Materials Handling, vol. 2904, 1996, pp. 25-32.

S. Berretti, A. D. Bimbo, and P. Pala, "Retrieval by shape similarity with perceptual distance and effective indexing," *IEEE Trans. on Multimedia*, vol. 2(4), pp. 225-239, 2000.

D. Guru and H. Nagendraswam, "Symbolic representation of two-dimensional shapes," *Pattern Recognition Letters*, vol. 28, pp. 144-155, 2007.

N. Arica and F. Vural, "BAS: a perceptual shape descriptor based on the beam angle statistics," *Pattern Recognition Letters*, vol. 24(9-10), 2003.

J. Flusser, "Invariant shape description and measure of object similarity," in *Proc. 4th International Conference on Image Processing and its Applications*, 1992, pp. 139-142.

A. Taza and C. Suen, "Discrimination of planar shapes using shape matrices," *IEEE Trans. System, Man, and Cybernetics*, vol. 19(5), pp. 1281-1289, 1989.

G. Lu and A. Sajjanhar, "Region-based shape representation and similarity measure suitable for content based image retrieval," *ACM Multimedia System Journal*, vol. 7(2), pp. 165-174, 1999.

S. Belongie, J. Malik, and J. Puzicha, "Shape matching and object recognition using shape context," *IEEE Trans. Pattern Analysis and Machine Intelligence*, vol. 24(4), pp. 509-522, 2002.

G. Mori and J. Malik, "Estimating human body configurations using shape context matching," in *Proc. 7th European Conference on Computer Vision*, vol. III, 2002, pp. 666-680.

H. Zhang and J. Malik, "Learning a discriminative classifier using shape context distances," in *Proc. IEEE Computer Society Conference on Computer Vision and Pattern Recognition*, 2003.

A. Thayananthan, B. Stenger, P. H. S. Torr, and R. Cipolla, "Shape context and chamfer matching in cluttered scenes," in *Proc. IEEE Computer Society Conference on Computer Vision and Pattern Recognition*, 2003.

S. P. Smith and A. K. Jain, "Chord distribution for shape matching," *Computer Graphics and Image Processing*, vol. 20, pp. 259-271, 1982.

K. Siddiqi and B. Kimia, "A shock grammar for recognition," in *Proceedings of the IEEE Conference Computer Vision and Pattern Recognition*, June 1996, pp. 507-513.

T. Sebastian, P. Klein, and B. Kimia, "Recognition of shapes by editing their shock graphs," *IEEE Trans. Pattern Analysis and Machine Intelligence*, vol. 26(5), pp. 550-571, 2004.

M. E. Celebi and Y. A. Aslandogan, "A comparative study of three moment-based shape descriptors," in *Proc. of the International Conference of Information Technology: Coding and Computing*, 2005, pp. 788-793.

G. Taubin and D. Cooper, "Recognition and positioning of rigid objects using algebraic moment invariants," in *SPIE Conference on Geometric Methods in Computer Vision*, vol. 1570, 1991, pp. 175-186.

R. Mukundan, S. Ong, and P. Lee, "Image analysis by tchebichef moments," *IEEE Trans. Image Processing*, vol. 10(9), pp. 1357-1364, 2001.

R. Mukundan, "A new class of rotational invariants using discrete orthogonal moments," in *Sixth IASTED International Conference on Signal and Image Processing*, 2004, pp. 80-84.

K. Jin, M. Cao, S. Kong, and Y. Lu, "Homocentric polar-radius moment for shape classification," in *Proc. Signal Processing, The 8th International Conference on*, 2006.

C. Kan and M. D. Srinath, "Invariant character recognition with Zernike and orthogonal Fourier-Mellin moments," *Pattern Recognition*, vol. 35, pp. 143-154, 2002.

B. M. Mehtre, M. S. Kankanhalli, and W. F. Lee, "Shape measures for content based image retrieval: A comparison," *Pattern Recognition*, vol. 33(3), pp. 319-337, 1997.

J. Peng, W. Yang, and Z. Cao, "A symbolic representation for shape retrieval in curvature scale space," in Proc. International Conference on Computational Inteligence for

Modelling Control and Automation and International Conference on Intelligent Agents Web Technologies and International Commerce, 2006.

D. Zhang and G. Lu, "A comparative study of curvature scale space and fourier descriptors for shape-based image retrieval," *Visual Communication and Image Representation*, vol. 14(1), 2003.

S. Abbasi, F. Mokhtarian, and J. Kittler, "Enhancing css-based shape retrieval for objects with shallow concavities," *Image and Vision Computing*, vol. 18(3), pp. 199-211, 2000.

M. Yang, K. Kpalma, and J. Ronsin, "Scale-controlled area difference shape descriptor," in *Proc. SPIE, Electronic Imaging science and Technology*, vol. 6500, 2007.

K. Kpalma and J. Ronsin, "Multiscale contour description for pattern recognition," *Pattern Recognition Letters*, vol. 27, pp. 1545-1559, 2006.

D. S. Zhang and G. Lu, "Enhanced generic fourier descriptors for object-based image retrieval," in *Proc. IEEE International Conference on Acoustics, Speech, and Signal Processing (ICASSP2002)*, pp. 3668-3671.

G. C.-H. Chuang and C.-C. J. Kuo, "Wavelet descriptor of planar curves: Theory and applications," *IEEE Trans. Image Processing*, vol. 5(1), pp. 56-70, 1996.

M. Khalil and M. Bayoumi, "A dyadic wavelet affine invariant function for 2D shape recognition," *IEEE Trans. Pattern Analysis and Machine Intelligence*, vol. 25(10), pp. 1152-1164, 2001.

G. Chen and T. D. Bui, "Invariant fourier-wavelet descriptor for pattern recognition," *Pattern Recognition*, vol. 32, pp. 1083-1088, 1999.

J. Ricard, D. Coeurjolly, and A. Baskurt, "Generalizations of angular radial transform for 2D and 3D shape retrieval," *Pattern Recognition Letters*, vol. 26(14), 2005.

S.-M. Lee, A. L. Abbott, N. A. Clark, and P. A. Araman, "A shape representation for planar curves by shape signature harmonic embedding," in *Proc. IEEE Computer Society Conference on Computer Vision and Pattern Recognition*, 2006.

S. Tabbone, L. Wendling, and J.-P. Salmon, "A new shape descriptor defined on the radon transform," *Computer Vision and Image Understanding*, vol. 102(1), pp. 42-51, 2006.

G. Borgefors, "Distance transformations in digital images," in *Computer Vision, Graphics, and Image Processing*, June 1986, pp. 344-371.

G. S. di Baja and E. Thiel, "Skeletonization algorithm running on path-based distance maps," *Image Vision Computer*, vol. 14, pp. 47-57, 1996.

A. Dubinskiy and S. C. Zhu, "A multi-scale generative model for animate shapes and parts," in *Proc. Ninth IEEE International Conference on Computer Vision (ICCV)*, 2003.

4

Computational Intelligence Approaches to Brain Signal Pattern Recognition

Pawel Herman, Girijesh Prasad and Thomas Martin McGinnity

Intelligent Systems Research Centre, University of Ulster

Northern Ireland

1. Introduction

Analysis of electrophysiological brain activity has long been considered as one of indispensable tools enabling clinicians and scientists to investigate various aspects of cognitive brain functionality and its underlying neurophysiological structure. The relevance of electroencephalogram (EEG) in particular, due to its inexpensive and most importantly, non-invasive acquisition procedure, has been reflected in the abundance of clinical applications and the diversity of areas of research studies it has contributed to. These studies lie within the realm of brain science understood nowadays in a broad sense embracing and linking interdisciplinary fields of neuroimaging, cognitive psychology and neurophysiology among others. In medical practice, EEG is used more pragmatically to support clinicians in their effort to establish the presence, severity and cerebral distribution of neurological disorders. Epilepsy diagnostic serves as a prime example in this regard (Fisch, 1999). The complex nature of brain signals and the intricacies of the measurement process involved (Fisch, 1999; Niedermeyer & Lopes da Silva, 2004), particularly in the case of EEG, render their analysis and interpretation challenging (Kaiser, 2005). Historically, these signals used to be examined only qualitatively based on routine visual inspection and the experience of responsible technicians or practitioners. With the advent of the era of digital biosignal recordings, computerised quantitative electroencephalography gained notable popularity as a supplementary tool enhancing objectiveness of analysis (Kaiser, 2005). The fast pace of technological advancement, considerable progress in neuroscience and neuroengineering along with growing investments in medical and health sectors among others have opened up new possibilities for automated EEG analysis systems. A continually growing scope for their applications set dominant design trends and imposed requirements regarding their functionality that prevail in today's practice and research. One of the key points in this regard is the need for the increased independence, autonomy and thus the improved reliability of such systems. This has led to a more comprehensive formulation of a computational problem of brain signal analysis within the realm of pattern recognition, which facilitates a more generic description of existing approaches, and development or re-use of suitable pattern recognition methods. In consequence, the notion of brain signal pattern recognition has been introduced to refer to the underlying concept of processing raw data with the aim of acting upon its category (Niedermeyer & Lopes da Silva, 2004; Duda et al., 2001). The objective is to identify patterns in electrophysiological brain activity that are indicative of various cognitive brain states (Niedermeyer & Lopes da Silva, 2004). The demanding nature of this task is here emphasised due to the spatio-temporal complexity of brain signal dynamics and low signal-to-noise ratio, particularly in the case of EEG. In order to ensure robust recognition of relevant brain signal correlates, as required in automated brain signal analysis, the major challenges should be identified. One of the most urgent needs is to robustly account for uncertain information inherent to biological data sources. The uncertainty effects arise mainly out of stochastic nature of signal acquisition processes and nondeterministic characteristics of the underlying neurophysiological phenomena, which cannot be accurately explained by any biologically plausible model but are attributed to the existence of a general biological tendency to undergo changes and transitions (Fisch, 1999; Wolpaw et al., 2002). In this regard, the multitude of behavioural, cognitive and psycho-emotional or physiological factors play a substantial contributory role. The resultant uncertainty manifestations are rarely dealt with in an explicit and effective manner. It should be realised though that ignoring them or adopting simplistic assumptions may undermine the concept of robust brain signal analysis.

This chapter is concentrated on a particular instance of brain signal pattern recognition, where uncertainty and variability effects manifest themselves with relatively high intensity. More precisely, the problem of classification of spontaneous electrophysiological brain activity when the subject is voluntarily performing specific cognitive tasks is examined. This deliberate control of thoughts provides a scope for a communication channel between the brain and the external environment with brain signals being the carrier of information. Such an alternative form of communication, independent of peripheral nerves and muscles, underpins the concept of the so-called brain-computer interface (BCI). Thus, the outcome of the study reported in this chapter bears direct relevance and has intrinsic implications for a broad area of BCI. This work follows the prevailing trends in BCI and is focused on the discrimination between self-induced imaginations of right and left hand movements, referred to as motor imagery (MI), based on analysis of the associated EEG correlates. The essence of uncertainty manifestations in this challenging brain signal pattern recognition problem and a range of existing approaches adopted to minimise the associated detrimental effects on BCI performance are discussed in section 2. Then, in section 3 a computational intelligence methodology is briefly introduced with emphasis on fuzzy logic (FL) paradigms in the context of pattern recognition under uncertainty. Section 4 describes methods developed and employed in this work to address a given MI-based brain signal pattern recognition problem. It also reveals the details of a BCI experimental procedure allowing for MI related EEG data acquisition. A comparative analysis of the results obtained with novel approaches introduced in this chapter and with more conventional BCI techniques is reported in section 5. Final conclusions and summary of the chapter are included in section 6. The key directions for further work are also suggested.

2. Uncertainty effects in EEG-based BCI

Uncertainty as an inseparable feature of BCI operation needs to be properly addressed in order to develop practical and robust systems (Wolpaw et al., 2002). Effective handling of uncertainty effects, strongly reflected in EEG signals, has been recognised as a key challenge in BCI (Vaughan et al., 2003). These effects have been traditionally associated with inherent changes in the underlying brain dynamics and varying physical characteristics of the signal measurement environment (Wolpaw et al., 2002; Vaughan et al., 2003; Millán et al., 2003).

There are a number of behavioural and neurophysiological factors that determine the character of transitions between cognitive brain states. Consequently, electrophysiological signals display a degree of inconsistency due to a varying level of subject's awareness, mental focus, motivation and fatigue among others (Wolpaw et al., 2002). In addition, the brain plasticity harnessed by the mechanism of neurofeedback involved in BCI operation[*] inevitably produces changes in the brain's behaviour. With regard to signal recording environment, it has been reported that inter-session changes in EEG cap placement (McFarland et al., 1997) or in the impedance of scalp-electrode interface (Sykacek et al., 2004) may affect BCI performance.

Uncertainty in the space of brain state categories poses another challenge in BCI. It arises out of intrinsic ambiguity and vagueness in interpretation of different brain states correlated with specific cognitive tasks, no matter how well they are defined. It is hard to assume that there is a crisp unequivocal association between characteristic patterns of brain's electrophysiological activity and classes of particular mental tasks. As suggested in (Yang et al., 2007), a mixture of some residual correlates of different cognitive processes should always be expected. This facct of uncertainty related to brain state class assignments is perceived as an inherent feature of brain signal pattern recognition.

Regardless of the sources of variability in BCI, it is predominantly reflected in electrophysiological brain signals, particularly in EEG, in the form of nonstationarity effects at different temporal levels. Their manifestations are present in any low-dimensional EEG feature space and are difficult to model analytically due to limitations in today's understanding of the underlying brain phenomena. Thus, their handling is considered as a challenging task and poses an urgent objective in the presence of numerous literature reports on a detrimental impact of EEG nonstationarities on the performance of BCI systems. In (Cheng et al., 2004), significant discrepancies in the distribution of EEG power features, extracted from data sets acquired at different times than the original training data set, were observed to result in a relatively poor accuracy of linear classifiers employed in an MI-based BCI. A similar inter-session deterioration of the performance of a linear discriminant analysis (LDA) classifier was reported in (Obermaier et al., 2001). The authors concluded that the LDA method did not provide capabilities to generalise MI induced spatio-temporal patterns in EEGs. In (Townsend et al., 2006), special attention was paid to inconsistencies in machine learning-based selection of the most relevant discriminative EEG feature components within the same BCI data set. Analogous incoherence in the localisation of optimal electrodes and in the identification of the most reactive EEG rhythms providing the maximum distinguishability of MI related EEG signals was described in (Pregenzer & Pfurtscheller, 1999). The changes were particularly noticeable in feedback sessions. Shenoy et al. (2006) and Vidaurre et al. (2006) made an attempt to graphically illustrate session-to-session nonstationarities in different EEG feature spaces by performing their two-dimensional projections. Although the projection approaches adopted in (Shenoy et al.,

---

[*] In the context of EEG-based BCI, subjects receive mostly visual, auditory or haptic feedback information about their brain activity reflected in the EEG. It conveys the degree of success in voluntary control of the brain activity. Thus, the feedback signal has an important motivational role as it facilitates higher attention levels or otherwise causes frustration and confusion if it is unreliable (McFarland et al., 1998).

2006) and (Vidaurre et al., 2006) were distinct, the conclusions were the same. Namely, inter-session discrepancies between clusters of the features representing the classes of associated MIs were clearly identified. Schlögl et al. (2005) analysed several types of EEG nonstationarities in BCI experiments using the state-of-the-art adaptive autoregressive (AR) features and an LDA classifier. The effect of both short- and long-term variability of the EEG dynamics was reflected in the considerable inconsistency of BCI performance.

There has been some empirical evidence gathered (Millán et al., 2002; Pfurtscheller et al., 2000; Guger et al., 2001; Pfurtscheller & Neuper, 2001) that in the face of the problem of session-to-session performance transfer it is beneficial to update or re-train a BCI classifier on a regular basis using the most recent data from one or a few past sessions. Still, the effectiveness of this method is limited as presented in (Shenoy et al., 2006; Guger et al., 2001) using linear classification approaches. In addition, it appears rather impractical considering the automated nature of BCI systems. The burden associated with their frequent re-calibration can be partly mitigated by computationally efficient algorithms for BCI prototyping and incorporating necessary modifications, as suggested in (Guger et al., 2001). Despite the shortcomings discussed here, this practice of regular BCI update has been a traditional approach to the problem of inter-session variability in BCI and it is still widely utilised.

There has also been considerable research conducted on adaptive BCI classification (Sykacek et al., 2004; Vidaurre et al., 2006; Millán et al., 2003) in the spirit of Wolpaw's principle of adaptive human (brain)–machine interaction (Wolpaw et al., 2002). Unlike the approach involving frequent off-line BCI re-calibration, adaptive systems are updated nearly instantaneously in on-line mode. Some of them have demonstrated the enhanced potential in handling uncertainty effects and have thus led to improved BCI performance than regularly re-trained but static linear, quadratic and probabilistic classifiers (Sykacek et al., 2004; Vidaurre et al., 2006; Shenoy et al., 2006). It should be noted however that the focus of adaptive BCI has been on reducing the effect of spontaneous EEG variations, and thus on handling short-term within-session changes of the signal dynamics. In consequence, the concept of continuous on-line update (Vidaurre et al., 2006; Sykacek et al., 2004) is likely to result in undesirable excessive detuning of a BCI classifier under the conditions of acute variability when handling short-lived transients, as indicated in (Vaughan et al., 2003). Yet, it does not necessarily address the problem of long-term changes in the EEG dynamics, particularly in a session-to-session scenario. Moreover, on-line adaptive classifiers are generally developed under the assumption of a known type of the signal's feature distribution, which may not be satisfied increasing the risk of lower accuracy.

It has become clear that various manifestations of uncertainty inherent to brain signal pattern recognition constitute a serious challenge in BCI research. The problem of maintaining good BCI performance over a reasonably long period in spite of the presence of these effects has not yet been effectively addressed using classical signal processing techniques, statistical pattern recognition methods or machine learning approaches. In the next section, advantages of a different methodological paradigm referred to as computational intelligence, eg. (Gorzalczany, 2002), with emphasis on computing with fuzzy sets (FSs), in application to pattern recognition under uncertainty are outlined. Special attention is given to an emerging type-2 (T2) fuzzy logic (FL) methodology (Mendel, 2001) due to its enhanced uncertainty handling capabilities.

3. Computational intelligence in pattern recognition

As discussed earlier, the uncertainty effects inherent to brain signal pattern recognition have a multi-faceted nature. In the context of EEG-based BCI, nonstationarity of EEG dynamics reveals nondeterministic characteristics of the underlying data generation mechanism, and thus it is not suitable for analytical modelling. It is also difficult to make valid statistical inference about its probabilistic features. In the realm of uncertainty analysis, there appears a group of methods that have demonstrated true potential in dealing with complexity and uncertainty in numerical data without any underlying physical model of their generator. Such a model-free approach can be adopted using computational intelligence paradigms (Mendel, 2001; Gorzalczany, 2002). They allow for data-driven design of computational systems that are capable of generalising knowledge, performing abstract associations and inference using approximate reasoning even in the presence of vague, ambiguous or imprecise information in ill-structured environments, and thus providing robust low-cost solutions to real-world problems (Mendel, 2001). Pattern recognition naturally lends itself as an application domain for computational intelligence. When uncertainty is strongly manifested in a given class of problems, FL methodology and the related FS theory are of special relevance. With a suitable system framework, the transparency of inference methods and mechanisms, and the flexibility of available data-driven design methods, this computational intelligence tool offers considerable potential in the context of uncertainty management in brain signal pattern recognition.

Recently, new directions in FL development have been explored to further enhance uncertainty modelling apparatus of conventional type-1 (T1) FL systems (FLSs), eg. (Karnik et al., 1999; Mendel, 2001). As a result, the notion of an extended type-2 (T2) FS with an additional dimension of fuzziness has received growing research attention and the corresponding T2FL uncertainty calculus has been shown to outperform its classical T1 counterpart in practical applications (Mendel, 2001). Thus, T2FL methodology appears to be a promising approach to the challenging brain signal pattern recognition problem undertaken in this work. Below, fundamental concepts in the area of T2FL related to this work are briefly presented.

At the heart of T2FL lies the definition of a T2FS originally introduced by Zadeh (1975) as an extension or a fuzzy version of a classical T1FS. This additional level of fuzziness is associated with another dimension in the definition of a T2FS. As a result, instead of being two-dimensional, a T2FS $\tilde{A}$ is three-dimensional and the membership grade defined in (1) for any given $x^* \in U_X$ (U_X is a domain, also called a universe of discourse) is an ordinary FS with the membership function $\mu_{\tilde{A}}(x^*, u), u \in J_x \subseteq [0,1]$ (J_x is the primary membership of x), not a crisp number $\mu_A(x^*)$ in [0,1] as in a classical T1FS A (c.f. (2)):

$$\tilde{A} = \left\{ ((x,u), \mu_{\tilde{A}}(x,u)) \mid \forall x \in U_X, \forall u \in J_x \subseteq [0,1] \right\}. \tag{1}$$

$$A = \left\{ (x, \mu_A(x)) \mid \forall x \in U_X, \mu_A \in [0,1] \right\}. \tag{2}$$

The domain of support for membership functions in T2FS representation is two-dimensional and is often referred to as a foot of uncertainty (FOU) (Mendel, 2001). Since it is effectively the union of all $J_x, \forall x \in U_X$, the FOU allows for embedding a range of T1FSs. The resultant extra degrees of freedom facilitate capturing more information about the represented term than a single T1FS can and thus render FOU particularly important in handling inconsistently varying information content. This enhanced flexibility in modelling the associated uncertainty underlies the potential of T2FLSs to outperform their T1 counterparts in problems where classification or approximation is to be made under uncertain, variable conditions.

On the other hand, T2FLSs are more computationally expensive. This overhead can be reduced by exploiting the so-called interval T2FSs (IT2FSs) (Liang & Mendel, 2000). Their membership functions over the FOU are constant and equal one (Mendel, 2001). This substantially simplifies operations on FSs, which now amount to interval-type operations (Liang & Mendel, 2000; Gorzalczany, 1988) on the associated FOUs, and facilitates transparent flow of uncertainties through a T2FLS. Moreover, the use of IT2FSs has proven to be beneficial in practical applications (Mendel, 2001). FOUs of the two most common Gaussian IT2FS, with uncertain mean, m, but fixed standard deviation, σ, and with fixed mean and uncertain standard deviation, are depicted in Fig. 1a-b. Since they embed conventional T1FSs A_e, as mentioned earlier, these FOUs can be easily parameterised with T1 membership functions, respectively (with m_1, m_2, σ_1, σ_2 defining the ranges of parameter variations):

$$\mu_{A_e}(x) = \exp\left[\frac{(x-m)^2}{-2\sigma^2}\right], \quad m \in [m_1, m_2], \ \sigma \text{ fixed}, \tag{3a}$$

$$\mu_{A_e}(x) = \exp\left[\frac{(x-m)^2}{-2\sigma^2}\right], \quad \sigma \in [\sigma_1, \sigma_2], \ m \text{ fixed}. \tag{3b}$$

a)   b)

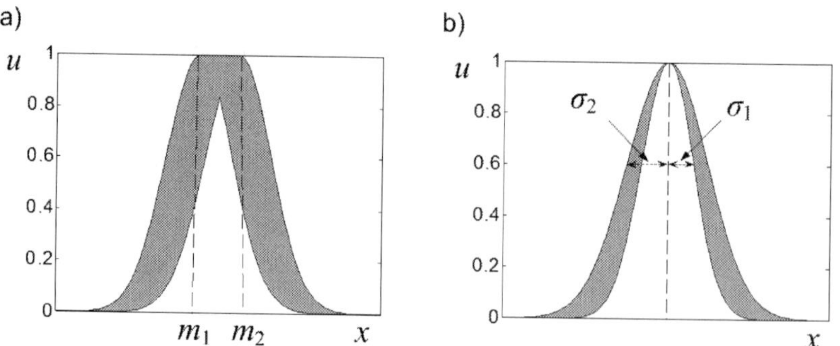

Fig. 1. An illustration of the FOUs of Gaussian T2FSs a) with uncertain mean and fixed standard deviation, b) with fixed mean and uncertain standard deviation.

Architecture of a T2FLS is analogous to that of its T1FLS counterpart with the difference in the type of FS representation in the antecedents and consequents of fuzzy rules, and in FS operators. In consequence, since the result of T2FL inference is a T2FS, the process of obtaining a crisp value from a final FLS output involves an additional step in T2FLSs when compared to T1FLSs. To this end, type reduction is applied to reduce a T2FS to a

T1FS before it is ultimately defuzzified using classical fuzzy methods. Type reduction constitutes the computational bottleneck in interval T2FLSs (IT2FLSs) (Mendel, 2001; Liang & Mendel, 2000). There are a number of type reduction approaches including approximate techniques reported in the fuzzy literature with centre-of-sets and centroid type reduction being the most popular (Karnik et al., 1999; Mendel, 2001). The entire process of information flow through a T2FLS can be summarised by the following sequence (c.f. Fig. 2):

1. Fuzzification (optional) – transforming a crisp input value to a T1FS or a T2FS.
2. Inference using a compositional rule (Mendel, 2001) involving the system input (fuzzified) and fuzzy rule base relations.
3. Aggregation of the resultant T2FSs obtained from different rules in the process of inference (in some cases, aggregation is considered as part of the inference process).
4. Type reduction, eg. by evaluating the centroid or the centre-of-sets of the aggregated output T2FS.
5. Defuzzification of the T1FS obtained in 4) (optional) to extract a crisp output.

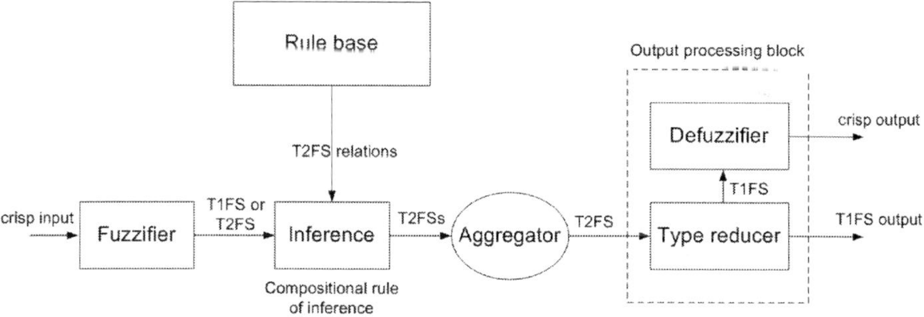

Fig. 2. T2FLS framework.

In the context of the brain signal pattern recognition problem considered in this chapter, it is expected that the increased flexibility of IT2FSs in modelling uncertainty can be effectively utilised to encapsulate the range of possible behaviours of brain signal dynamics correlated with MI and thus robustly account for the associated variability. Consequently, the central objective is to examine the potential of a novel IT2FLS-based approach to dichotomous classification of MI induced EEG patterns. The emphasis is on the classifier's capability to generalise well across a few data sets obtained at different times (exhibiting mainly long-term changes). At the same time, it should be realised that despite the early progress in the domain of applied T2FL, there has been rather limited research done on systematic approaches to data-driven design of IT2FLSs used in pattern recognition. This chapter also outlines some developments that address this emerging need and discusses key issues related to the effective exploitation of IT2FLS's uncertainty handling apparatus in the given instance of brain signal pattern recognition. Automation of the fuzzy classifier design process is intended and to this end, its computationally efficient implementation is proposed. A detailed description of the BCI experimental setup and the pattern recognition methods devised and employed in this work are presented in the next section.

4. Methods and experimental work

4.1 Experimental setup and data acquisition

In the presented work, EEG data acquired in BCI experiments in two different labs were utilised. The first data set was obtained from the Institute of Human–Computer Interfaces, Graz University of Technology. The EEG signals were recorded from three healthy subjects (S1, S2 and S3) in a timed experimental recording procedure where the subjects were instructed to imagine moving the left and the right hand in accordance with a directional cue displayed on a computer monitor (Fig. 3a). Each trial was 8 s in length. A fixation cross was displayed from $t = 0$ s to $t = 3$ s. The beginning of a trial was marked by acoustic stimulus at $t = 2$ s. Next, an arrow (left or right) was displayed as a cue at $t = 3$ s. Therefore the segment of the data recorded after $t = 3$ s of each trial was considered as event related and was used for off-line analysis. The recordings were made with a g.tec amplifier (http://www.gtec.at) and AgCl electrodes over two consecutive sessions, each session consisting of 140 trials for S1 and 160 trials for S2 and S3 with equal number of trials representing two MI classes (Wang et al., 2004). Two bipolar EEG channels were measured over C3 and C4 locations (two electrodes placed 2.5 cm anterior and posterior to positions C3 and C4) according to the international standard nomenclature (10/20 system) (Niedermeyer & Lopes da Silva, 2004). The EEGs were then sampled at a frequency of 128 Hz and band-pass filtered in the frequency range 0.5–30 Hz.

The second EEG data set was acquired at the Intelligent Systems Research Centre (ISRC), University of Ulster using the same g.tec equipment and the location of two bipolar channel electrodes as that used by the Graz BCI group. The EEG data were recorded from six healthy subjects (S_I–S_{VIII}) over ten 160-trial (balanced) sessions with a sampling frequency of 125 Hz. Depending on the subject, first one or two sessions were conducted without neurofeedback, and to this end, a directional cue following a fixation cross was displayed in the form of an arrow pointing to left or right to instruct a subject which MI should be carried out, as in the Graz paradigm. In the subsequent feedback sessions, the game-like basket paradigm was employed. In each trial of 7 s duration, two baskets were displayed at $t = 3$ s at the bottom of the screen in the form of bars – the target basket in green and the non-target one in red. Subjects were asked to perform MI that allowed them through the BCI to direct a ball falling from the top of the screen for the last 3 s of a trial to the target basket. The ball movement was continuously (in real-time) controlled in a horizontal direction from $t = 4$ s to $t = 7$ s utilising the proposed fuzzy classifier's output signal, which served as BCI feedback. The timing and a graph illustrating the concept of this paradigm are presented in Fig. 3b.

Although the EEG data sets under consideration were originally recorded in on-line BCI paradigms with continuous classification, they were also exploited in the context of off-line discrete classification of entire trials. As a result, two separate BCI study cases were investigated in this work, with continuous on-line (only on the ISRC data set) and discrete off-line application of an IT2FLS classifier. Still, it should be emphasised that they share similar characteristics of MI related brain signal pattern recognition with slightly different aspects of the uncertainty effects being exposed in each case (see section 5 for more discussion). From the perspective of a signal processing methodology, the major difference lies in the way that temporal information is handled at the feature extraction stage (c.f. section 4.2). Moreover, on-line verification of BCI classification performance raises additional issues related to instantaneous neurofeedback delivery, which are not taken into account in a post-hoc off-line simulation. They are given more attention in section 4.3.3.

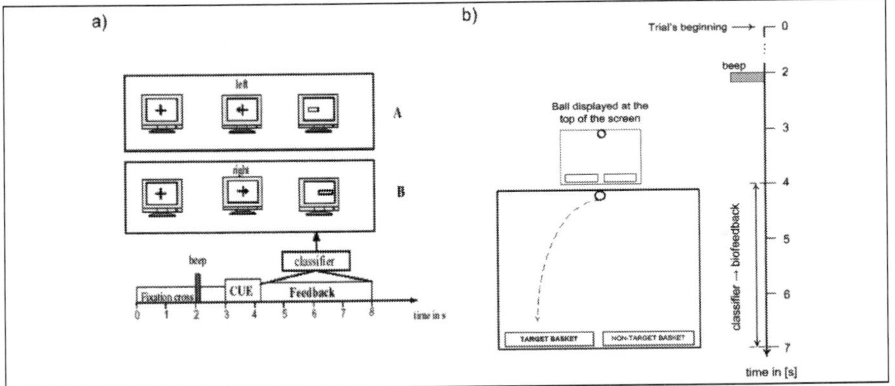

Fig. 3. Data recording in a) Graz BCI paradigm (Haselsteiner & Pfurtscheller, 2000) and b) BCI basket paradigm (Wang et al., 2004).

It should also be mentioned that only a few final sessions when individual subjects acquired an acceptable level of BCI control were closely examined and evaluated in the study reported in this chapter. The data gathered during earlier training sessions were exploited in most cases to pre-calibrate BCI methods and conduct preliminary off-line analyses.

4.2 EEG feature extraction and analysis

Sensorimotor rhythms represent the most discernible and reliable category of EEG correlates of MI induced brain phenomena (Vaughan et al., 2003; McFarland et al., 1997). Thus, brain signal patterns considered in this work are derived from mu (μ) and beta (β) rhythms of spontaneous EEG activity over the specified sensorimotor areas (C3 and C4 locations, c.f. section 4.1). In particular, the imagination of hand movement causes activation of the brain's motor cortex that is usually manifested in the interplay between contralateral attenuation of the μ rhythm and ipsilateral enhancement of the central β oscillations in different phases of MI. These processes occur due to the neurophysiological mechanisms of the so-called event-related desynchronization (ERD) and event-related synchronization (ERS) (Niedermeyer & Lopes da Silva, 2004). The exact sensorimotor EEG patterns and the most reactive frequency bands of ERS and ERD vary from subject to subject. Preliminary analysis performed in this work confirmed that overall, ERD manifestations in the μ range could be observed on the contralateral side and a slight ERS in the central β rhythm on the ipsilateral hemisphere. This hemispheric lateralisation of the oscillatory brain signal patterns underlies discrimination between the left and right MIs. In consequence, methods of spectral analysis played a dominant role in the process of EEG quantification conducted in this work to extract discriminative signal features.

As mentioned in section 4.1, the problem of MI related brain signal pattern recognition was addressed in two modes – with discrete classification of entire EEG trials and instantaneous discrimination within a trial. The main difference between these two BCI approaches lies in the temporal characteristics of a feature extraction protocol. Consequently, handling and quantification of the relevant spatio-temporal EEG patterns requires distinct approaches. They are described in two subsequent sections.

4.2.1 Off-line analysis of spectral EEG patterns

In off-line discrete classification each EEG trial is represented as a single feature vector. To this end, the event-related segment (starting from $t = 3$ s) of length $N = 5*128 = 640$ samples for the Graz data set and $N = 4*125 = 500$ samples for the ISRC data set was divided into rectangular windows depending on the settings of two parameters: window length, *win_len*, and the amount of overlap, *ovl*. Next, the frequency-related information was independently extracted from each of n_{win} windows (c.f. (5)) and the relevant spectral correlates of ERD and ERS phenomena were quantified. In particular, the μ and β bandpower components were merged within each window to constitute a feature vector element, r_i^j ($i=1,..,n_{win}$) given two recording channels, $j \in \{C3, C4\}$. The entire feature vector r representing an EEG trial was composed of $2n_{win}$ such components:

$$r = \left(r_1^{C3}, r_2^{C3}, ..., r_{n_{win}}^{C3}, r_1^{C4}, r_2^{C4}, ..., r_{n_{win}}^{C4} \right),$$

(4)

where:

$$n_{win} = \left\lfloor \frac{N - ovl}{win\_len - ovl} \right\rfloor.$$

(5)

In the preliminary analysis reported in (Herman et al., 2008a), a wide range of spectral methods such as power spectral density (PSD) estimation techniques (Stoica & Moses, 1997), atomic decompositions including short-time Fourier transform (STFT) (Stoica & Moses, 1997) and S-transform (Assous et al., 2006), quadratic time-frequency energy distributions and wavelet-based methods (Akay, 1997) were thoroughly examined in the given brain signal pattern recognition problem. They were all employed within the same window-based feature extraction framework to obtain signal's bandpower components in the μ and central β ranges. The resultant low-dimension feature representations (c.f. (4)) were assessed in terms of their discriminative properties quantified using the classification accuracy (CA) rate obtained with popular linear and nonlinear BCI classifiers (c.f. section 4.3.2). Since PSD approaches were demonstrated overall to deliver consistently superior performance in within-session and inter-session classification scenarios, this category of spectral quantification methods was exploited in this work. In particular, nonparametric periodogram (Stoica & Moses, 1997) and parametric PSD estimate using Yule-Walker algorithm (Haykin, 1996) were applied depending on the subject. The exact frequency bands within the μ and central β ranges, from which bandpower components were extracted, were tuned individually for each subject to maximise linear separability between the resultant feature vectors representing two-class MI related EEG trials. To this end, linear discriminative analysis (LDA) (Bishop, 1995) was conducted on the initial calibration data within a cross-validation (CV) framework.

In order to demonstrate the problem of variability in BCI, discussed in section 2, session-to-session changes in the distribution of class-specific EEG features acquired from one of the subjects under consideration are presented in Fig. 4. In particular, the feature space was projected on the principal components (PC) axes. PC analysis (PCA) was performed with one session (I) as the reference and the data in the other session (II) were transformed according to this new set of directions of the largest variance. For illustrative purposes, only the first two components accounting for over 70% of the total variance are shown. Apart from the projected two-dimensional feature samples, their means and standard deviations, estimated in each class after removing the most noticeable outliers, are depicted. The standard deviations presented in the form of ellipses centred at the corresponding means were scaled down to enhance the clarity of the illustrations.

Several relevant observations can be made based on the proposed analysis. Firstly, largely overlapping regions of the projected feature space corresponding to different MI classes are evident. Secondly, the inter-session shifts of the class means for both left MI and right MI groups are strongly manifested in the given data set (c.f. 4a-b). They are indicative of the variability effects inherent to BCI as discussed in section 2. Since there is no underlying model of these changes and due to their inconsistent nature, reported in a multi-session analysis, the issue of uncertainty arises and renders this brain signal pattern recognition problem particularly challenging.

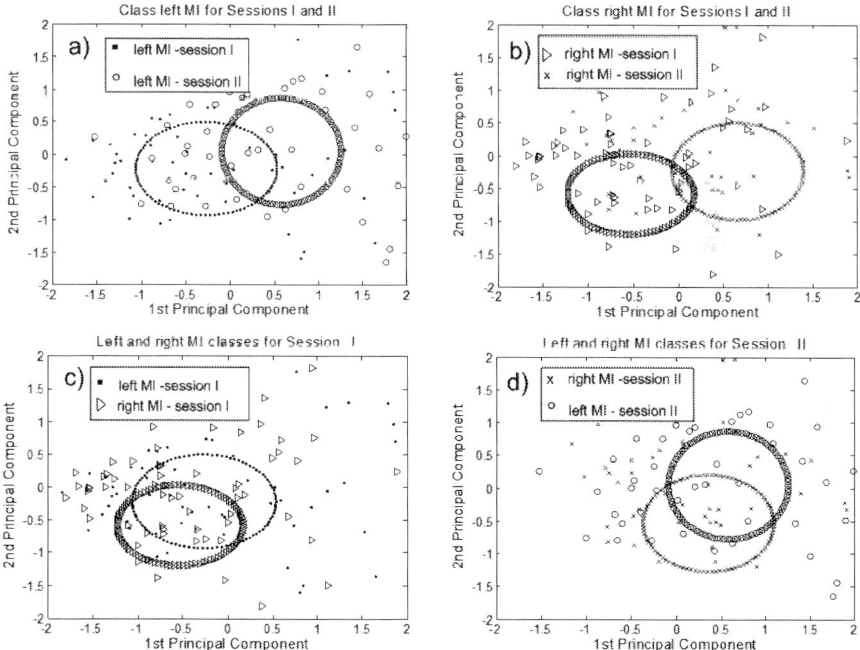

Fig. 4. The distribution of spectral EEG features in two-dimensional normalised PCs' space with their corresponding class means and scaled standard deviations: a) left and b) right MI features in sessions I and II plus within-session feature distribution: c) session I and d) session II.

4.2.2 Feature extraction for on-line BCI

As discussed in section 4.2, on-line BCI was implemented in continuous mode. In other words, EEG features were extracted and classified instantaneously within a trial, which led to as many classifications per trial as the number of its even-related data samples (considering that the length of the event-related part of a trial in a basket paradigm was 4 s, there were $4 * 125 = 500$ relevant applications of a feature extractor and a classifier). To this end, a sliding window approach was adopted within a causal framework. In consequence, the window acts as a buffer and introduces a delay with respect to the temporal occurrence of relevant MI correlates in the signal examined. The window sizes used in this work were identified with a view to compromising the time resolution of BCI control (reactivity) and the MI related content of spontaneous EEG activity. The delay was found to be acceptable in on-line operation and its effect could only be felt at the trial's onset.

Three alternative techniques of spectral analysis were utilised in this study to suit individual cases. Similarly as in the earlier study involving discrete classification of entire trials, PSD approaches, Welch periodogram and Yule-Walker's parametric PSD estimation in particular, were found to facilitate consistent and robust BCI performance. Additionally, for a small proportion of subjects, STFT was demonstrated in off-line preliminary analyses to lead to higher CA rates than those reported with PSD techniques. Therefore, the identification of an optimal feature type extractor for the on-line use was subject specific.

The spectral methods just mentioned were employed to extract bandpower information from EEGs in the frequency ranges related to the ERD/ERS phenomena. Due to distinct temporal scales of signal representation in continuous feature extraction and in a discrete approach (with an entire trial being represented as a feature vector), the relation between the quantified oscillatory components in the μ and β bands had different characteristics in both cases. Although spectral contributions from the two relevant frequency ranges were proven in the study reported in section 4.2.1 to provide more discriminative feature representation when merged together, in the preliminary off-line simulation of continuous BCI it was demonstrated that treating these ERD and ERS correlates separately, as independent feature components, led in the clear majority of cases to better classification results. Moreover, it was concluded that normalizing the resultant feature vector r (c.f. (5)), extracted on a sample-by-sample basis (the window was shifted at the sampling rate, i.e. every 8 ms), by its Euclidean length facilitated handling the variance of the signal's energy.

$$ r = \left(r_\mu^{C3}, r_\beta^{C3}, r_\mu^{C4}, r_\beta^{C4} \right), \tag{5} $$

where $r_{\mu(\beta)}^{C3(C4)}$ corresponds to the spectral feature component extracted from the adjusted μ (or β band) from the EEG channel C3 (or C4). The instantaneous feature extraction procedure is schematically illustrated in Fig. 5.

4.3 Classification of EEG trials

Classification constitutes another phase of recognition of brain signal patterns allowing for a categorical interpretation of EEG relying on its feature representation. In the context of the work reported in this chapter, the aim of BCI classification is to assign signal trials to the classes of the associated mental tasks (MIs). This given instance of brain signal pattern recognition is dichotomous since an imagination of left hand movement is to be distinguished from an imagination of right hand movement. As discussed earlier, the problem is challenging mainly due to strong EEG nonstationarity effects manifested even in low-dimensional feature spaces. The resultant inter-session variability in the feature distributions was demonstrated in section 4.2.1. In consequence, the study on single trial classification in discrete mode was aimed at effective dealing with these long-term changes in

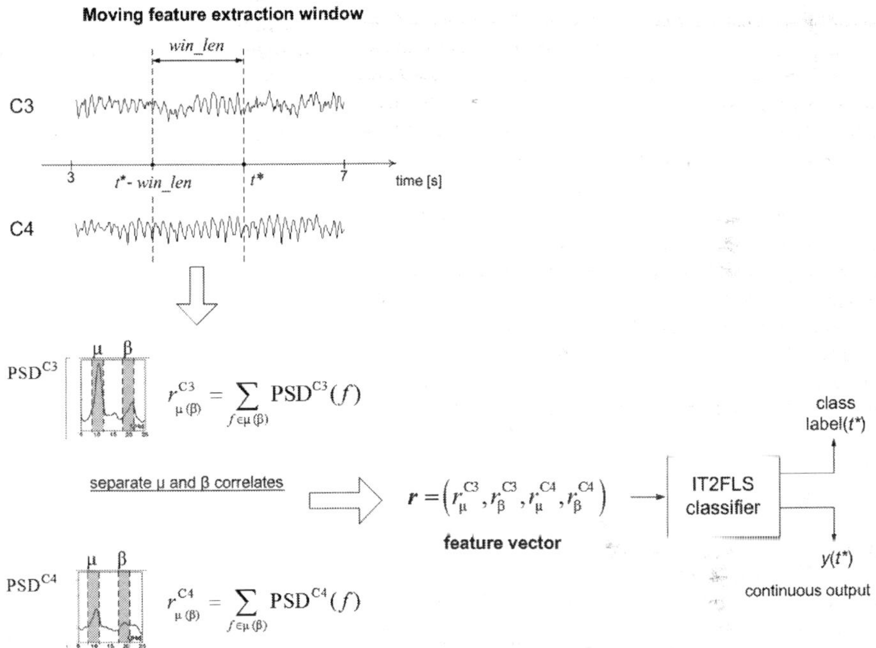

$$r^{C3}_{\mu(\beta)} = \sum_{f \in \mu(\beta)} PSD^{C3}(f)$$

$$r^{C4}_{\mu(\beta)} = \sum_{f \in \mu(\beta)} PSD^{C4}(f)$$

$$r = \left(r^{C3}_{\mu}, r^{C3}_{\beta}, r^{C4}_{\mu}, r^{C4}_{\beta} \right)$$

Fig. 5. Graph illustrating the proposed concept of instantaneous BCI feature extraction and classification.

EEG spectral patterns correlated with MI. A successful method is expected to maintain a satisfactory accuracy rate over a few sessions recorded with around one-week break in between without the need for frequent inter-session adjustments. The shorter-term within-trial manifestations are also reported difficult to handle in BCI experiments (Wolpaw et al., 2002; Vaughan et al., 2003; Sykacek et al., 2004). In this work, they could be observed in the study involving instantaneous BCI operation. The intrinsic characteristics of discrete and continuous BCI classification are discussed in section 4.3.3.

In conclusion, the concept of robust brain signal pattern recognition is linked to the key issue of uncertainty in a broader sense, as elaborated in section 2. The emphasis is on handling its multi-faceted manifestations at the classification stage. In order to address this urgent challenge, a novel fuzzy BCI classifier was proposed (c.f. section 4.3.1) and its inter-session performance was compared to that of more traditional BCI approaches: LDA and support vector machines (SVMs) (Cristianini & Shawe-Taylor, 2000) (c.f. section 4.3.2). The CA rate was used as an objective measure in this evaluation.

4.3.1 Fuzzy classification

As elaborated in section 3, T2FLS framework offers more flexibility in handling uncertain information content than its T1 counterpart. It should be emphasised however that in order to appropriately exploit the T2FL apparatus for handling uncertainty without sacrificing its generalisation capability, special care is required in T2FLS development. Therefore, considerable effort was devoted in this work to devise effective techniques for a fuzzy classifier design. For faster computations, IT2FSs were employed in the construction of a Mamdani-type rule base (Mendel, 2001) (c.f. section 2). The following template of a fuzzy rule was adopted:

$$\text{IF } X_1 \text{ is } \tilde{A}_1 \text{ AND...AND } X_n \text{ is } \tilde{A}_n \text{ THEN } class \text{ is } [c_{left}, c_{right}], \qquad (6)$$

where fuzzy variables $X_1,...,X_n$ correspond to the fuzzified components of an input feature vector $r=(r_1,...,r_n)$, n is their number and $\tilde{A}_1,..., \tilde{A}_n$ denote IT2FSs with uncertain means (c.f. Fig. 1a, section 3) that serve as the rule antecedents. C is the centroid of the consequent T2FS (in the form of a rectangular T1FS) representing the class that the input feature vector is assigned to. As a result, the rule base models uncertainty related to the variability of EEG features, as discussed in section 4.2.1 (c.f. Fig. 4), and the vagueness or ambiguity of a crisp MI label, i.e. left (associated with numerical value -1) versus right (value 1), c.f. section 2. When $\tilde{A}_i$'s are replaced by T1FSs and C becomes a crisp centroid of a T1FS, the T2 fuzzy rule reduces to the T1 rule format with limited capacity to account for the aforementioned types of uncertain information. The input features to both fuzzy classifiers are represented as T1FSs (fuzzification) to model stationary uniform noise present in the feature space (with standard deviation s_{fuzz_inp}). Gaussian type of FSs was used in the proposed design to facilitate gradient-based tuning. Fig. 6 illustratively juxtaposes the T1FL and T2FL rule pattern (for one-dimensional input) adopted in the reported study.

The IT2FLS classifier was developed in a two-stage procedure, inspired by general FLS design methodology. Firstly, an initial fuzzy rule base was identified and secondly, its parameters were tuned using a global optimisation approach. The design was conducted on a so-called calibration data set, split into a validation and a training subset. The final evaluation was performed on an unseen test data set. In most cases, the calibration and test data sets were taken from independent sessions.

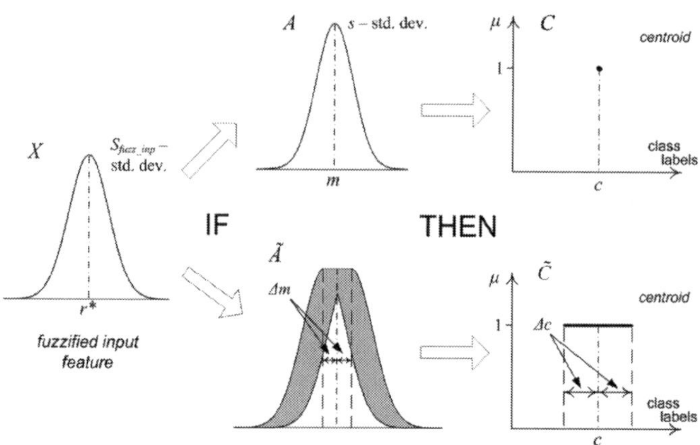

Fig. 6. Illustrative comparison of T1FL and T2FL rule patterns.

An initial fuzzy rule base was identified using a partitioning approach. In other words, the input space was divided into regions accounting for the underlying distribution of a training set of EEG features with the main objective to obtain a compact data representation that captures their salient characteristics and preserves the inherent input-output relationship (class assignments). Thus, a general clustering approach was adopted to construct a conventional prototype T1FLS rule base that could be extended to serve as an initial T2FLS framework (Herman et al., 2008c). Several clustering methods were examined to identify an optimal design strategy. To this end, a simple heuristic for their initial evaluation was developed. The resultant cluster validity index was primarily used as a criterion for selecting an optimal set of parameters for the initialisation schemes under consideration. It was based on the performance of a prototype (untrained) singleton T1FLS classifier derived directly from the given cluster structure on the calibration data set without any extra parameters, as described later in this section. A final comparative evaluation of the initialisation techniques was conducted within the entire design framework, i.e. in combination with a parameter tuning phase. In consequence, the CA rates obtained with fully trained T1FLSs and with T2FLSs in within-session CV and inter-session classification served as a final performance measure. The outcome of this analysis is discussed in section 5.1. Below, the fuzzy rule base initialisation methods investigated in this work are outlined.

Firstly, a mapping-constrained agglomerative (MCA) clustering algorithm was employed to reinforce the consistency in the mapping from the input to the output space. It has been proven to be robust in the presence of noise and outliers that can affect the input-output relationship (Wang & Lee, 2002). However, due to the excessive susceptibility of an original single-pass (sp) MCA to variations in the input data ordering, a heuristic modification was proposed to alleviate this problem. As a result, a multi-pass (mp) MCA algorithm was developed (Herman et al., 2008c). It relied on iterating the original spMCA several times (controlled by a parameter) with the core input data appended with the data points representing means of clusters found in the previous iteration. The core data were shuffled at each iteration. Moreover, for every iteration the record of the cluster validity index, reported on a separate validation set, serving as a performance measure of the given cluster structure was kept. The maximum of this measure determined the iteration that resulted in the selected cluster structure. The underlying concept of this approach is presented in the form of pseudocode in Fig. 7.

It is worth emphasising that the MCA provides information not only about the cluster position in the multi-dimensional input space (the cluster mean, m_{INP}) but also determines its spread in terms of the standard deviation estimate, s_{INP} (independently along different dimensions). Moreover, the assignment of a class label to each cluster is straightforward due to the consistency in the input-output mapping promoted by the algorithm.

Secondly, the well-established fuzzy c-means (FCM) clustering was examined in this work due to its wide applicability in fuzzy rule base identification (Bezdek, 1981). Although the algorithm requires the prior assumption of the number of clusters, its identification was automated using the above-mentioned cluster validity index as a selection criterion. The input data space was clustered resulting in the specified number of cluster centres m_{INP}. The clusters' width vectors, s_{INP}, were composed of the one-dimensional standard deviations, $s_{INP}^{(i)}$, $i = 1,\ldots, n$, calculated independently for each feature vector component over the subset of the input data points with the membership degree in the corresponding clusters above a certain threshold (controlled by a parameter). Since FCM does not explicitly enforce the consistency in mapping between the input and the output space, the class assignments were uniformly randomised in the interval corresponding to class labels, i.e. [-1,1].

Pseudocode of the mpMCA clustering

1. Divide an ordered data set $D=((r,y)_j)$ into a training D_{tr} and a validation subset D_{vld} (here the proportion of 80% to 20% was used). Iteration counter $l=0$.

2. Perform original spMCA clustering on D_{tr} and find the resultant cluster means $\boldsymbol{m}_{INP}$, their standard deviations s_{INP} and class assignments c.
Update iteration counter: $l=l+1$.

3. Initialise a prototype T1FLS based on the clusters found in 2 and use it for classification of the data set D_{vld}. Evaluate the CA rate as $CA_{vld}(l)$.

4. Shuffle D_{tr} and set $D'_{tr}=D_{tr}$:

$$D_{tr} \xrightarrow{\text{shuffle}} D'_{tr}$$

5. Update D_{tr} by appending the clusters' means to the beginning of the ordered set D'_{tr}:

$$D_{tr} = ((\boldsymbol{m}_{INP},c) \cup D'_{tr})$$

6. IF $l \leq N_{passes}$ THEN go back to 2.

7. Find an iteration where the CA_{vld} was maximum

$$l^* = \max_{1<l\leq N_{passes}} \arg CA_{vld}(l)$$

and restore the clusters means $\boldsymbol{m}_{INP}$ with their standard deviations s_{INP} and class assignments c that were identified at the l^*th iteration. They serve as the cluster output of the procedure.

Fig. 7. Pseudocode of the modified MCA algorithm – mpMCA.

Thirdly, subtractive clustering (Chiu et al., 1994) as a computationally effective implementation of mountain clustering, originally proposed by Yager and Filev (Yager & Filev, 1994), was employed in this study. The selection of cluster centres was based on the density of data points (feature vectors). The density-related measure assumed the form of an iterative combination (for subsequent clusters) of radial basis functions. Analogously to the FCM approach, a certain neighbourhood of each resultant cluster centre was specified to determine the membership status of the clustered data points and then to estimate the corresponding one-dimensional standard deviations. The size of the neighbourhood was controlled by an extra parameter, which facilitated adjustments of the size of overlap between the clusters. The output space assignments were made randomly for the same reasons as in the FCM-based scheme.

A prototype singleton T1FLS rule base was straightforwardly derived from the resultant clusters in the input space and their class assignments. To this end, each multi-dimensional cluster was projected on single input dimensions (feature vector components) to form a fuzzy rule. Its antecedents were modelled using Gaussian T1FSs, whose means, $m^{(i)}$, and widths, $s^{(i)}$, $i = 1,..,n$, were determined as the projections of the cluster's m_{INP} and s_{INP}, respectively. The consequent was defined in the output space as centroid centred at the associated class label. For the purpose of easy visualisation, an example of the projection of a two-dimensional cluster of data belonging to class c on the axes corresponding to respective feature vector components (r_j and r_k) and the resulting T1 fuzzy rule are illustrated in Fig. 8.

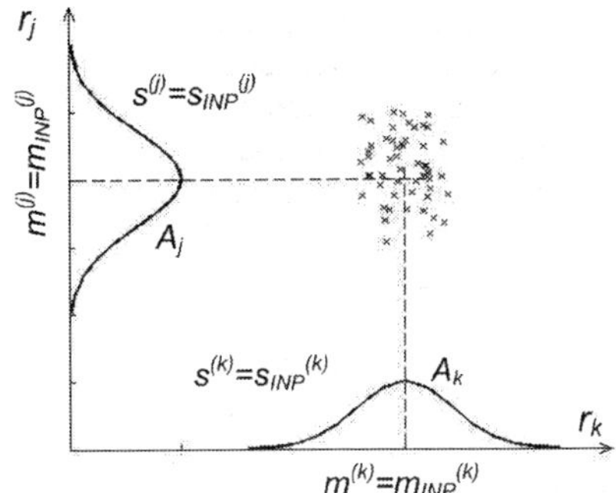

Fig. 8. A two-dimensional cluster in the feature space and the corresponding prototype T1 fuzzy rule.

After the identification of the prototype T1FLS, it was extended to serve as a framework for an IT2FLS. As presented above, each T1FL rule was described in terms of its antecedent FSs A_i (i=1, ,n), parameterised with vector m−($m^{(1)},...,m^{(n)}$) of their means and vector s=($s^{(1)},...,s^{(n)}$) of their standard deviations, and a crisp consequent, c. The uncertainty bounds of the FSs defining the antecedent and the consequent part of an IT2FL rule were expressed using additional quantities, Δm and Δc, respectively (c.f. Fig. 6). The resultant formulae for IT2FL rule induction from the classical T1FL rule prototype are as follows:

$$m_1 = m - \Delta m \qquad m_2 = m + \Delta m,$$
$$c_{left} = c - \Delta c \qquad c_{right} = c + \Delta c. \tag{7}$$

Vectors m_1 and m_2 refer to the lower and the upper bound of the uncertain means (c.f. Fig. 1a) in the antecedent IT2FSs and c_{left}, c_{right} define the consequent centroid. The standard deviations, s, of the prototype T1FSs were kept the same for the resultant IT2FSs. Furthermore, it was found that the constrained parameterization of Δm and s_{fuzz_inp} (used in the description of the fuzzified inputs, c.f. Fig. 6) with multiplicative factors dm and a in (8) and (9), respectively, led to a more computationally efficient parameter selection procedure.

$$\Delta m = dm\, s\ , \tag{8}$$

$$s_{fuzz\_inp} = a\, \sigma_r\,, \tag{9}$$

where σ_r is a vector of the standard deviations of the input features r in a training set.

The parameters dm, Δc and a, assumed to be homogeneous for the entire rule base, determined the initial bounds of the uncertainty captured in the system. They were selected in combination with a training process, described below, with the aim of maximising the performance of the resultant IT2FLS classifier evaluated using a CV approach on the selected calibration data set (within-session classification).

In the second stage of the IT2FLS classifier design, the quantities initialised in the earlier step, m_1, m_2, s, c_{left}, c_{right} and s_{fuzz_inp}, were tuned for every rule. A global nonlinear optimisation approach was adopted to this end. The learning algorithm was based on the concept of steepest gradient descent with the mean square error loss function, L, defined in (10). In the training phase, a continuous defuzzified output, y, of the fuzzy classifier was taken into account whereas in the recall process, simple thresholding was applied to obtain a dichotomous class label.

$$L = \frac{1}{M}\sum_{j=1}^{M}(y_j - label_j)^2 ,$$
(10)

where M is the number of training trials (feature vectors) and $label_j$ is the desired class label (-1 or 1) assigned to the j-th trial (feature vector).

A heuristic training strategy for IT2FLS classifiers was proposed in this work with a view to enhancing their generalisation properties and speeding up the convergence of nonlinear optimisation. It is composed of three stages and combines two approaches known in the domain of IT2FLSs: the conventional steepest gradient descent algorithm developed by Liang and Mendel (Liang & Mendel, 2000; Mendel, 2001), and the method based on the dynamic optimal rate theorem (Wang et al., 2004). This hybridisation was demonstrated to result in more robust and effective search for an optimal configuration of the system parameters than the conventional Liang and Mendel's approach in the given brain signal pattern recognition problem. The three stages were conducted as follows (Herman et al., 2008c):

Stage I)
The conventional steepest descent was applied with learning rates being reduced by a constant factor every 10 epochs. Identification of their initial values was found to play a significant role in the entire optimisation process and it was thus incorporated in the parameter selection scheme. A validation data set was utilised to implement an early stopping criterion. This facilitated an informed decision about terminating the optimisation process and led to the enhancement of the classifier's generalisation capabilities.

Stage II)
An algorithm based on the dynamic optimal rate theorem was applied to accelerate the optimisation of the parameters of the fuzzy rule consequents. In particular, the combination of sample-by-sample training of the standard deviations s_{fuzz_inp} and the antecedent parameters m_1, m_2 and s with a batch update of the consequents c_{left} and c_{right} was adopted. This parameter learning phase was terminated based on the same early stopping criterion as in the first stage.

Stage III)
The T2FLS's parameters were fine tuned using an algorithm similar to that of the first stage with far lower learning rates and the reduced number of epochs. The updated system parameters were accepted only if the classifier's performance in terms of the CA rate improved in comparison with the outcome of the second stage. Otherwise, the parameter configuration was rolled back.

In order to conduct a fair comparative analysis, an analogous learning algorithm was developed for T1FLS classifiers. As mentioned earlier, the results of the examination of the presented design variants are summarised in section 5.1.

4.3.2 Popular BCI classifiers

In a comparative evaluation, more conventional binary classifiers widely used in EEG-based BCI were verified. In the first place, parameter-less LDA, which is Bayes optimal classifier for normally distributed features in each of two classes with the same covariance matrix (Bishop, 1995), was employed. Although the condition mentioned is often violated (it was not met for any of the data sets considered in this study), LDA is commonly perceived as an effective, easy to use and computationally cheap classification method in BCI work (Vaughan et al., 2003; McFarland et al., 1997). In consequence, it has been proven to perform well even with relatively small data sets. SVM classifiers adopt a different approach to identifying a class separating hyperplane in dichotomous problems. Unlike in LDA, where the discriminative boundary is determined as a result of maximising the ratio of inter-class variance to the intra-class variance, SVM hyperplane provides the largest margin between classes without taking any second-order statistics into account (Cristianini & Shawe-Taylor, 2000). This intuitively facilitates generalisation and from an algorithmic perspective, it requires solving a quadratic programming problem with a unique solution. A soft version of SVM (Kecman, 2001) is more popular in real world problems involving discrimination in feature spaces with overlapping class specific regions. It allows for misclassification of a proportion of data points in a certain neighbourhood of the decision boundary, where overlapping is likely to occur. The size of the neighbourhood is controlled by a corresponding regularisation parameter that decides the trade-off between the training error and the size of the margin between classes. The core assets of SVM classifiers stem from their generalisation power, wide availability of computationally effective approaches to quadratic programming even in the presence of large data sets, and a kernel machine-based structure allowing for straightforward transformation of inherently linear classifiers into nonlinear ones. This latter property, which arises out of implicit nonlinear mapping determined by the so-called kernel function (Cristianini & Shawe-Taylor, 2000), is often exploited in practical applications. In this study, a Gaussian kernel with homogeneous variance was examined due to its successful application in other BCI studies, eg. (Garrett et al., 2005). For clarity, linear SVM (without a nonlinear kernel) is referred to throughout this chapter as SVM_{lin} whereas SVM with the Gaussian kernel – SVM_{Gauss}. Finally, the relevance of parameter selection for optimal SVM performance should be emphasised. In this work, the regularisation constant for SVM_{lin} and the kernel parameter with the regularisation constant for SVM_{Gauss} were identified in a simple off-line grid search based on the performance of the resultant classifiers. It was assessed using a CV estimate of the generalisation error, which was proven reliable in previous studies, eg. (Herman et al., 2008a).

4.3.3 Discrete vs. continuous classification

As emphasised in section 4.2, the main methodological difference between discrete and continuous classification of MI related EEG spectral patterns lies in the design of a feature extraction unit. The classification framework remains essentially the same with the structure determined by the format of a feature vector and the parameter setup reflecting the temporal characteristics of the features to be discriminated. In discrete mode, the number of classifier's inputs was dependent on the number of feature extraction windows, n_{win} (c.f. (4) and (5) in section 4.2.1). Since a feature vector described an entire signal trial, off-line handling of the resultant training data set was rather straightforward. This is more intricate in continuous classification mode. The dimensionality of the feature space and thus of the classifier's input was set to four at every time point (separate correlates of μ and β for C3 and C4 channels, c.f. section 4.2.2) within an event-related part of the trial. Consequently, in off-line calibration of the continuous BCI classifiers, there were as many data sets as many data points within a trial (a data set is defined here as a collection of feature vectors for all trials). In other words, there could be a new classifier set up at each time point. Since it was not considered to be a practical option, a single classifier to be applied in subsequent BCI sessions was derived using the most separable set of training features extracted at the so-called optimum classification time point (c.f. Fig. 9a). It was expected that the classifier's generalisation capability should secure robust performance over the entire trial's length. Discriminative properties of the given feature sets were quantified based on the average CA obtained in CV analysis. The trained BCI classifier was then continuously applied at every sample point in trials in the following sessions.

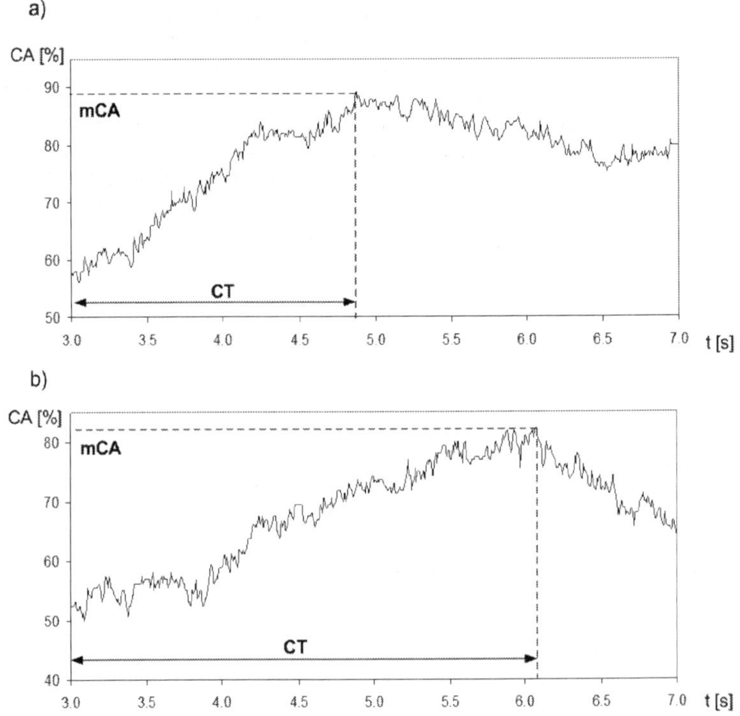

Fig. 9. Instance CA time courses obtained in a) off-line training and b) on-line BCI evaluation for subject S_{III}. Maximum CA and the optimum classification time within the event-related part of the trial are marked as mCA and CT, respectively.

Instantaneous mode also renders the evaluation process and performance assessment more complex than in discrete classification of entire EEG trials. Application of a continuous classifier in an experimental session does not result in a single CA rate but allows for

generating a CA time course. There are several measures commonly employed in the quantification of performance of continuous BCIs such as information transfer rate or mutual information (Wolpaw et al., 2002). Here, the focus is on a pattern recognition aspect and thus CA plays a key role. In particular, the resultant CA time course was quantified by the maximum CA (mCA) rate within the event-related segment of a trial. An example pair of CA time courses, the first one obtained in the CV-based evaluation on a training session and the other one reported on-line in the subsequent test session is depicted in Fig. 9a-b.
With regard to evaluation of an on-line BCI system it is important to realise that any comparative study has to involve retrospective off-line simulation of alternative BCIs since only one closed-feedback system (neurofeedback provider) can be used on-line at a time. To this end, the data recorded during on-line experiments with the original BCI (configured with an IT2FLS classifier) was exploited in the post-hoc examination of other BCI classifiers (c.f. section 4.3.2) in the way that ensured full correspondence in terms of the data handling strategy. Still, it should be noted that a comparative analysis of methods tested on-line and off-line has intrinsic limitations. An on-line BCI is part of a closed feedback loop and is thus coupled with the changes in the on-going MI related EEG activity due to the brain plasticity phenomenon (Herman et al., 2008b). This interaction renders on-line BCI classification particularly challenging. In short-term perspective, especially for subjects with little or no prior BCI experience, on-line BCI systems can either benefit from a facilitatory role of feedback in subject's learning or suffer from inhibitory feedback effects (Herman et al., 2008b). A retrospective off-line examination of BCI methods does not allow for such demanding verification. In spite of that, off-line evaluation still provides a valuable indicator of the potential of the methods being scrutinised to deal with a range of problems inherent to BCI. In this work, it served as the reference for demonstrating uncertainty handling capabilities of the proposed on-line T2FLS classification framework.

5. Results and discussion

5.1 Evaluation of fuzzy classifier design variants

The aim of the extensive examination of several different design variants for T1FLS and IT2FLS was to identify an effective strategy for devising robust fuzzy classifiers with strong uncertainty handling and generalisation capabilities needed in BCI applications. Due to the pattern recognition focus of the presented work and dichotomous nature of the BCI classification, CA was meant to serve as the key comparative criterion. Other aspects such as computational time or sensitivity to initial parameters were assessed qualitatively and were also taken into account. The analysis involving all possible combinations of the proposed clustering-based initialisation methods and the learning algorithms (c.f. section 4.3.1), conventional steepest descent and the enhanced hybrid learning scheme, was performed off-line in discrete classification mode on arbitrarily chosen initial calibration data sets (c.f. section 4.2). In particular, FLSs were set up using each of the design strategies and verified in two types of experimental tests. Firstly, within-session CV (five-fold) study was conducted to illustrate generalisation properties of the developed classifiers and secondly, session-to-session performance transfer was examined, i.e. the classifiers were calibrated including selection of design parameters (c.f. section 4.3.1) on data from one session and tested in single pass on unseen data from the other subsequent one. The inter-session classification helped to gain insight into the issue of dealing with long-term variability effects, highlighted in this chapter.

Despite rather insignificant differences in the classification performance reported with all the design schemes, the comparative evaluation still allowed for several valuable observations to be made. They motivated the final selection of an optimal approach to devising IT2FLS classifiers utilised in this work and were less informative in the case of T1FLS.

In the beginning, the proposed mpMCA-based initialisation was examined with the two parameter tuning approaches. As expected, it significantly alleviated the problem of inconsistency in the cluster structure due to random input data ordering, which manifested itself when the original spMCA was applied. The mpMCA heuristic also led to the improved classification performance of the resultant classifier, particularly IT2FLS in the session-to-session setup. As far as a training algorithm is considered, faster and steadier convergence was reported with the proposed heuristic learning strategy when the fuzzy rule base was initialised using mpMCA (Herman et al., 2008c).

In the next stage, the mpMCA approach was juxtaposed with the other fuzzy structure identification approaches under consideration. At first, a paramount role of the three-stage parameter tuning algorithm was reported in the development of FLSs initialised with the FCM-based technique. This heuristic optimisation approach stimulated a considerable increase of the inter-session CA rates obtained with the resultant classifiers and demonstrated the improved convergence when compared to the conventional steepest descent method. Less pronounced effects of its application were observed when the subtractive clustering-based initialisation was employed. Still, both FCM and subtractive clustering approaches rendered the IT2FLS's performance comparable (insignificantly worse) to that reported with the mpMCA-based fuzzy rule base identification. The differences were even more negligible in the domain of T1FLS. However, what turned out to play a decisive role was the fact that the mpMCA initialisation contributed to the faster convergence of the enhanced gradient descent training, and from the perspective of the derived FLS, mpMCA was found to be less susceptible to its initial parameters, especially considering the strong reliance of FCM upon the number of clusters to be found. In consequence, the combination of the mpMCA initialisation scheme and the proposed three-stage gradient descent-based learning algorithm was identified in this study as the most robust approach to fuzzy classifier design, IT2FLS in particular (Herman et al., 2008c). It was employed in the full evaluation of the proposed fuzzy pattern recognition methods on multi-session EEG data sets in discrete (section 5.2) and continuous (section 5.3) BCI classification.

5.2 Discrete classification

The same types of experimental tests were conducted to analyse the performance of BCI classification frameworks in discrete mode as in the examination of the proposed FLS design variants (c.f. section 5.1). At first, within-session CV was carried out on training sets to estimate the overall efficacy of the classifiers and to select optimal configurations of the system parameters. The main objective of the analysis however was to study the IT2FLS classifier's performance over longer periods across different recording sessions (they were obtained with one-week gaps in between), which were expected to reflect a broad range of non-stationary variability effects in the underlying EEG. To this end, four consecutive sessions were arbitrarily selected for each subject, except for the Graz data set including only two-session recordings, and a strategy for multi-session comparative evaluation involving single-pass tests was devised. In particular, using the initial parameters identified in the CV analysis the classifiers were calibrated on a training session data set and tested in one pass over multiple subsequent sessions. The overall results in the single pass training-test experimental setup were grouped into three main categories reflecting a temporal relationship between the training and the test session. Next, they were averaged within these categories resulting in three mean CAs for every subject. The first category was generated from three training-test pairs, session I–II, II–III and III–IV. The second one consisted of the test CAs from experiments involving session pairs: I–III and II–IV, and the third category with the largest temporal gap between the training and the test data sets was composed of one CA result obtained with a classifier trained on session I and tested on session IV. This configuration of training-test session pairs is conceptually illustrated in Fig. 10. These collective CAs were then averaged within each category over subjects. The inter-subject means and their standard deviations are presented in Table 1 for every classifier examined in this study, i.e. IT2FLS, T1FLS, LDA, SVM_{lin} and SVM_{Gauss}. In addition, the CV results averaged over three training sessions and subjects are also included in Table 1, in the column 'CV'.

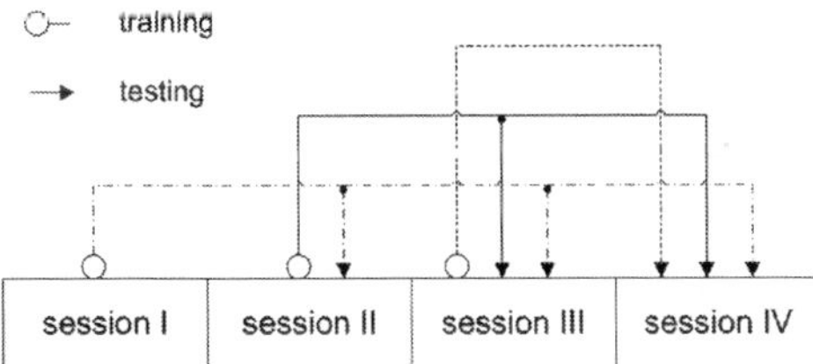

Fig. 10. An illustrative description of the multi-session experimental design for four-session data (lines connect training sessions with the corresponding test sessions).

Classifier	Training Session	Test-Cat. I	Test-Cat. II	Test-Cat. III
	mean CA ± std.dev. [%]			
	CV	*Single pass training-test evaluation*		
IT2FLS	71.2 ± 8.4	**73.4 ± 9.0**	**64.8 ± 6.7**	**65.4 ± 6.7**
T1FLS	70.4 ± 8.3	71.8 ± 9.1	63.6 ± 6.3	63.9 ± 7.5
LDA	71.5 ± 8.4	67.5 ± 9.3	61.8 ± 8.0	60.7 ± 7.1
SVM_{lin}	71.1 ± 9.3	69.8 ± 9.9	61.7 ± 7.5	60.3 ± 6.4
SVM_{Gauss}	71.0 ± 9.3	69.7 ± 9.8	61.8 ± 7.0	60.4 ± 6.9

Table 1. Comparative analysis of the fuzzy rule based classifiers, i.e. T1FLS and IT2FLS, LDA and SVMs: linear (SVM_{lin}) and with Gaussian kernel (SVM_{Gauss}) in terms of the mean CA rates obtained off-line in the multi-session setup with discrete classification. The mean values were calculated across subjects and averaged within given test categories. The standard deviations reflect inter-subject variability (Herman et al., 2008c).

The results in Table I were analysed using one-way ANOVA with repeated measures to test the significance of the differences in the classifiers' performance independently in each category. The null hypothesis could not be rejected for CV results so the focus was on the single pass test CA rates, which reflect the capability of the classifiers to effectively handle the inherent inter-session variability of the MI induced EEG patterns. The ANOVA test carried out on these sets of results revealed statistically significant ($p<0.05$) differences in the classifiers' performances. The post test comparison was conducted using Tukey's honestly significant difference criterion (at the significance level of $\alpha=0.05$) (Maxwell & Delaney, 2004). It showed that IT2FLS outperformed LDA and SVM in every test category, from I to III, whereas T1FLS delivered significantly higher CA rates than LDA only in the first category, i.e. when the classifiers were trained on the session directly preceding the test session.

Although the difference between the mean CA rates obtained with IT2FLS and T1FLS was not found statistically significant, the superior trend of the IT2FLS-based approach was observed consistently for every category of the presented results across all subjects considered in this work. Overall, the analysis demonstrated the potential of the designed IT2FLS in offering enhanced robustness against the inter-session uncertainty effects in MI induced brain phenomena reflected in EEG, especially when compared to common BCI methods.

5.3 Continuous classification and on-line BCI

As discussed in section 4.3.3, the evaluation of the real-time performance of the IT2FLS classifier embedded in the on-line BCI system was accompanied by a comparative off-line study involving other BCI classifiers applied post hoc in continuous mode. The original on-line study was conducted on six subjects performing MI tasks in the ISRC BCI setup over ten sessions (see section 4.1). Still, only four or five sessions when particular subjects showed some reasonable level of BCI control via neurofeedback mechanism are reported here. A strategy for off-line calibration and selection of a reliable BCI system configuration for on-line application was devised individually for each subject. The objective was to maintain a given on-line BCI setup, particularly the IT2FLS in use, over the longest possible time provided that its real-time performance was satisfactory. Otherwise, the classifier was re-trained and an optimal model was selected off-line using the most recent session data as a design (training) data set in the way described in section 4.3.3 (involving within-session CV-based estimate of generalisation error and the identification of the optimal classification time within a trial). This procedure of occasional (every few sessions) calibration of the BCI, with emphasis on the embedded IT2FLS classifier, was aimed at delivering the best possible on-line BCI performance (Herman et al., 2008b). More specifically, the maximum recognition rate in each session was of main concern (c.f. Fig. 9 and section 4.3.3) as it was directly relevant to the desirable effect of the biofeedback facilitating real-time BCI operation and enhancing the consistency of the EEG patterns correlated with the brain activity underlying MI generation.

With regard to the retrospective simulation of a continuous BCI with the other classifiers including T1FLS and the classical methods described in section 4.3.2, the combination of training and test data sets was made analogous to that adopted individually for each subject in on-line experiments. The performance was assessed based on the examination of the resultant CA time courses, as described in section 4.3.3 (c.f. Fig. 9b). In consequence, depending on the subject, four or five mCA rates are considered here as a result of single-pass test evaluation (on-line for IT2FLS and off-line for the rest of the classifiers). Their average is illustrated for every subject in Fig. 11. The mean values across all six subjects are then presented in Table 2.

Classifier	Average performance in test sessions
	mean mCA ± std.dev. [%]
IT2FLS (online)	**69.2 ± 4.6**
T1FLS	66.9 ± 4.3
LDA	66.0 ± 4.4
SVM$_{lin}$	66.8 ± 4.9
SVM$_{Gauss}$	67.1 ± 4.5

Table 2. The average mCA rates obtained in the comparative study with the classifiers evaluated off-line, i.e. T1FLS, LDA, SVM$_{lin}$, SVM$_{Gauss}$, and IT2FLSs applied on-line. The mean values were calculated across all subjects and respective test sessions. The standard deviations reflect inter-subject variability (Herman et al., 2008b).

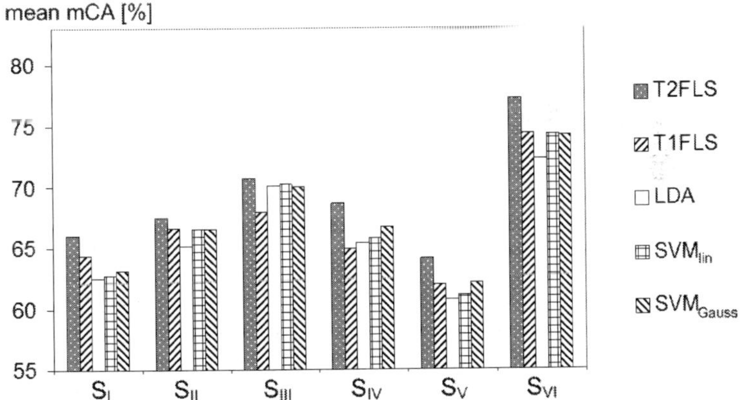

Fig. 11. The average mCA rates (maximum values in the CA time courses) obtained for every subject across BCI test sessions with LDA, SVM$_{lin}$, SVM$_{Gauss}$, T1FLS in off-line and with IT2FLS in on-line mode (Herman et al., 2008b).

Similarly as in the study on discrete classification of MI induced EEG spectral patterns, the experimental results were analysed in the framework of one-way ANOVA with repeated measures. It facilitated accounting for the inter-subject variability. The test conducted at a significance level of α=0.05 allowed for rejecting the null hypothesis about the equality of the grand average of the mCAs reported with different classifiers. The Tukey-Kramer post-ANOVA multiple comparison test demonstrated that the IT2FLS classifier produced overall better classification performance than the other classifiers except SVM$_{Gauss}$, which is generally known for its robustness in the presence of incoherency, noise and nonlinearity effects in the feature space (Cristianini & Shawe-Taylor, 2000; Kecman, 2001). Still, a complementary planned pair-wise comparison between IT2FLS and SVM$_{Gauss}$ with t-statistic and the Bonferroni adjustment helped in manifesting the statistically significant difference between the two mCA means. Fig. 11 illustrates the consistency of the IT2FLS approach across different subjects in delivering superior mCA rates even if the overall degree of the enhancement was rather modest. Despite the limitations of such comparative evaluation of

BCI methods applied on-line and those simulated off-line, as discussed in section 4.3.3, the results obtained in this study reinforce the conclusions drawn in the previous section regarding the potential of the IT2FLS-based classification framework to account for intrinsic uncertainty manifestations more effectively than the other more common BCI classifiers. It should be noted that unlike discrete single trial classification, continuous within trial analysis allows for examining BCI performance at different temporal scales – not only in the presence of inter-session variability effects.

With regard to the juxtaposition of a conventional T1FLS and a new IT2FLS, it should be reminded that the observed superiority trends of the latter method could not be proven statistically in the earlier study reported in section 5.2. However, in continuous recognition of MI induced EEG spectral patterns, the ANOVA test demonstrated a significant advantage of IT2FLS in terms of the average mCA rate. This outcome substantiates the fact that a conventional T1 uncertainty handling framework, unlike the enhanced IT2FLS, does not provide a sufficiently flexible mechanism to account for a range of variability effects observed in MI related EEG at various temporal levels. At the same time, the computational time involved in the IT2FLS optimisation was comparable to that of the T1FLS classifier due to rather small rule base sizes being used.

6. Summary, conclusions and future work

The major theme of this chapter has been centred on the demanding nature of brain signal pattern recognition in the presence of uncertain information intrinsically associated with the biological data source. Specifically, the problem of classification of EEG correlates of MI related brain phenomena has been studied in detail due to its direct relevance to the fast growing field of BCI. Uncertainty effects in EEG-based BCI pose a particularly serious challenge due to their strong manifestations and multi-faceted characteristics. As suggested in the BCI literature and confirmed in the work reported in this chapter, these effects are reflected in the nonstationary changes in the underlying spatio-temporal dynamics of the spectral EEG correlates. Long-term variability have been the main focus of this research due to its particularly adverse influence on inter-session classification performance. In consequence, the research efforts have been concentrated on creating a robust pattern recognition framework capable of more effective handling of the uncertainty manifestations to perform reliable brain signal analysis for BCI purposes. Two instances of a general MI related EEG classification problem have been examined in this chapter – firstly, discrete (single) classification of entire trials and secondly, continuous discrimination of MI induced EEG patterns in a multi-session setup for multiple subjects. The nature of relevant spectral EEG correlates is similar in both cases as they arise out of the same neurophysiological phenomena. However, feature extraction approaches were devised to suit different temporal characteristics of the given problem instances.

A fuzzy rule base classifier proposed here constitutes the core of the developed framework for robust brain signal pattern recognition. The emphasis in this chapter has been put on T2FLS methodology recently enjoying a considerably surge of interest. The extended definition of T2FSs provides more flexibility in modelling inherently uncertain phenomena. In order to effectively exploit this enhanced framework for handling variability effects and boost its generalisation capability, the need to devise a suitable design strategy has been identified and addressed in this chapter. In particular, incremental modifications and hybridisation of existing initialisation and optimisation techniques have resulted in an effective design scheme for IT2FLS classifiers.

The outcome of both empirical studies, conducted with discrete and continuous pattern recognition framework, has led to the overall conclusion that the proposed IT2FLS method lends itself as a more robust alternative to the state-of-the-art BCI classification approaches in the presence of intrinsic variability of the spectral EEG correlates of MI at different temporal scales. The IT2FLS classifier's capacity to embrace inter-trial variations in the EEG feature patterns over a training session and encapsulate them within the FOU for use on subsequent test sessions is considered to be of particular relevance in this regard (Herman et al., 2008c). It should be noted that the applicability of the proposed classification framework in real-world BCI situations was successfully verified in demanding on-line tests, which reflected the potential of IT2FLS in generating consistent and contingent real-time neurofeedback responses correlated with subjects' motor imaginations (Herman et al., 2008b). Consequently, the IT2FLS-based BCI has recently been used in a preliminary study on post-stroke rehabilitation.

In addition, it is worth mentioning that the inherent transparency of a fuzzy inference system was exploited in original work in an attempt to enhance the understanding of MI classification rules derived from the underlying data. Due to a purely qualitative nature of these investigations, they are not reported in this chapter. It suffices to say that they led to the identification of subject specific discriminative trends in spectro-spatio-temporal EEG patterns characteristic of each of the MI classes under consideration. This interpretative approach is still in its early stage. It is aimed to constrain the rule base analysis to gain valuable insight into more general (for a population of subjects) electrophysiological correlates of MI induced brain phenomena through the prism of the qualitative knowledge extracted in the classifier induction process. This may add a new dimension to machine learning-based BCI studies.

The work presented in this chapter is by no means completed. It marks a crucial development and experimental stage, still leaving room for further advancements. In the first place, it is suggested that a general problem of initialising uncertainty bounds for antecedents and consequents of IT2FLSs based on a priori knowledge, if available, could be investigated. In this work, where the fuzzy classifier was applied to MI induced brain signal pattern recognition problems, these bounds were adjusted to account for the inter-trial variability within a BCI session granted that uncertainty associated with session-to-session transfer was in the corresponding range. In this regard, a more systematic approach to quantifying or estimating the effective scope of T2FL uncertainty in data would be more beneficial. In a broader perspective, it could be paired with investigations into alternative methods of an initial IT2FLS structure identification. Research efforts should be then concentrated on the development of new clustering algorithms in the T2FL domain, which would also facilitate the initialisation process of the IT2FLS's uncertainty bounds.

From a more theoretical perspective, it is felt that more insight into the formalism of the underlying T2FL apparatus in comparison with well-established probabilistic approaches is needed. Investigations along these lines would pave the way for a more specific description and quantification of uncertainty effects and thus facilitate more informed IT2FLS design. This work could be inspired by the existing links between a probabilistic and a possibilistic perspective of modelling uncertain information.

In the longer perspective it is envisaged that an application of a generalised T2FLS (unlike simplified IT2FLS methodology employed in this work) in MI related EEG pattern recognition can result in further performance enhancement. It should be realised however that design of generalised T2FLSs involves several serious challenges, starting from a selection of initial rule bases expressed in terms of generalised T2FSs and ending with heuristic approaches to parameter optimisation. In addition, real-time feasibility is expected to be problematic when the resultant T2FLS classifier is applied within a BCI framework. Approximate algorithms may be needed in this regard. The starting point and inspiration for this work should be the remarkable contribution to the area of generalised T2FL made by the research team led by John, e.g. see a review in (John & Coupland, 2007).

In a broader context, it is envisaged that the integrated framework devised in this work to contend with a specific brain signal pattern recognition problem can address a range of complex nonstationary biological and physical signals with uncertain spatio-temporal characteristics that cannot be handled using a rigorous analytical modelling apparatus. In the presence of such highly variable components exhibiting nondeterministic behaviour, T2FLS methodology would appear particularly advantageous over other more conventional approaches. The proposed data driven design approach would promote then the development of a model-free, yet qualitatively interpretable, system for automated analysis with a classification output.

7. References

Akay, M. (ed.) (1997). *Time Frequency and Wavelets in Biomedical Signal Processing*. IEEE Press Series in Biomedical Engineering, New York.

Assous, S.; Humeau, A.; Tartas, M.; Abraham, P. & L'Huillier, J.-P. (2006). S transform applied to laser Doppler flowmetry reactive hyperemia signals. *IEEE Transactions on Biomedical Engineering*, vol. 53, pp.1032–1037.

Bezdek, J.C. (1981). *Pattern recognition with fuzzy objective function algorithms*, Plenum Press, New York.

Bishop, C. (1995). *Neural Networks for Pattern Recognition*, Oxford University Press, Oxford.

Cheng M.; Jia, W.; Gao, X.; Gao, S. & Yang, F. (2004). Mu rhythm-based cursor control: an offline analysis. *Clinical Neurophysiology*, vol. 115, pp. 745–751.

Chiu, S.L. (1994). Fuzzy model identification based on cluster estimation. *Journal of Intelligent and Fuzzy Systems*, vol. 2, pp. 267–278.

Cristianini, N. & Shawe-Taylor, J. (2000). *An Introduction to Support Vector Machines and Other Kernel-based Learning Methods*, Cambridge University Press.

Duda, R.O.; Hart, P.E. & Stork, D.G. (2001). *Pattern Classification*, Wiley, New York.

Fisch, B.J. (1999). *Fisch and Spehlmann's EEG Primer: Basic principles of Digital and Analog EEG*, Elsevier, Amsterdam.

Garrett, D.; Peterson, D.A.; Anderson, C.W. & Thaut, M.H. (2005). Comparison of Linear, Nonlinear, and Feature Selection Methods for EEG Signal Classification. *IEEE Transactions on Neural Systems and Rehabilitation Engineering*, vol. 11, no. 2, pp.141–144.

Gorzalczany, M.B. (1988). Interval-valued fuzzy controller based on verbal model of object. *Fuzzy Sets and Systems*, vol. 28, pp. 45–53.

Gorzalczany, M.B. (2002). *Computational Intelligence Systems and Applications: Neuro-Fuzzy and Fuzzy Neural Synergisms*. Physica-Verlag, Springer-Verlag, Heidelberg, Germany.

Guger, C; Schlögl, A.; Neuper, C., Walterspacher, D.; Strein, T. & Pfurtscheller, G. (2001). Rapid Prototyping of an EEG-Based Brain–Computer Interface (BCI). *IEEE Transactions on Neural Systems and Rehabilitation Engineering*, vol. 9, pp. 49–58.

Haselsteiner, E. & Pfurtscheller, G. (2000). Using Time-Dependent Neural Networks for EEG Classification. *IEEE Transactions on Rehabilitation Engineering*, vol. 8, pp. 457–463.

Haykin, S. (1996). *Adaptive Filter Theory*, Prentice Hall, 3rd edition.

Herman, P.; Prasad, G.; McGinnity, T.M. & Coyle, D. (2008a). Comparative analysis of spectral approaches to feature extraction for EEG-based motor imagery classification. *IEEE Transactions on Neural Systems and Rehabilitation Engineering*, vol. 16, no. 4, pp. 317–326, August 2008.

Herman, P.; Prasad, G. & McGinnity, T.M. (2008b). Design and On-line Evaluation of Type-2 Fuzzy Logic System-based Framework for Handling Uncertainties in BCI Classification. *Proc. of the 30th International IEEE Conference of Engineering in Medicine and Biology Society*, Vancouver, Canada, August 2008.

Herman, P.; Prasad, G. & McGinnity, T.M. (2008c). Designing a Robust Type-2 Fuzzy Logic Classifier for Non-stationary Systems with Application in Brain-Computer Interfacing. *Proc. of the 2008 IEEE International Conference on Systems, Man, and Cybernetics*, Singapore, October 2008.

John, R. & Coupland, S. (2007). Type-2 Fuzzy Logic: A Historical View. *IEEE Computational Intelligence Magazine*, vol. 2, no. 1, pp. 57–62.

Kaiser, D.A. (2005). Basic Principles of Quantitative EEG. *Journal of Adult Development*, vol. 12, pp. 99–104.

Karnik, N.N.; Mendel, J.M. & Liang, Q. (1999). Type-2 Fuzzy Logic Systems. *IEEE Transactions on Fuzzy Systems*, vol. 7, no. 6, pp. 643–658.

Kecman, V (2001). *Learning and Soft Computing*. Cambridge: MIT Press.

Liang, Q. & Mendel, J.M. (2000). Interval type-2 Fuzzy Logic Systems: Theory and Design. *IEEE Transactions on Fuzzy Systems*, vol. 8, pp. 535–550.

Maxwell, S.E. & Delaney, H.D. (2004). *Designing Experiments and Analyzing Data: A Model Comparison Perspective*. Lawrence Erlbaum, New Yersey.

McFarland, D.J.; McCane, L.M.; David, S.V. & Wolpaw, J.R. (1997). Spatial filter selection for EEG-based communication. *Electroencephalography and Clinical Neurophysiology*, vol. 103, pp. 386–394.

McFarland, D.J.; McCane, L.M. & Wolpaw, J.R. (1998). EEG-Based Communication and Control: Short-Term Role of Feedback. *IEEE Transactions on Neural Systems and Rehabilitation Engineering*, vol. 6, pp. 7–11.

Mendel, J.M (2001). *Uncertain Rule-Based Fuzzy Logic Systems: Introduction and New Directions*, Prentice-Hall, New York.

Millán, J. del R.; Mouriño, J.; Franzé, M.; Cincotti, F.; Varsta, M.; Heikkonen, J. & Babiloni, F. (2002). A local neural classifier for the recognition of EEG patterns associated to mental tasks. *IEEE Transactions on Neural Networks*, vol. 13, pp. 678–686.

Millán, J. del R. & Mouriño, J. (2003), Asynchronous BCI and Local Neural Classifiers: An Overview of the Adaptive Brain Interface Project. *IEEE Transactions on Neural Systems and Rehabilitation Engineering*, vol. 11, pp. 159–161.

Niedermeyer, E. & Lopes da Silva, F. (2004). *Electroencephalography: Basic principles, clinical applications, and related fields*, 5th ed., Williams & Wilkins, Baltimore.

B. Obermaier, C. Guger, C. Neuper, G. Pfurtscheller, (2001). Hidden Markov models for online classification of single trial EEG data. *Pattern Recognition Letters*, vol. 22, pp. 1299–1309.

Pfurtscheller, G.; Neuper, C.; Guger, C.; Harkam W.; Ramoser, H.; Schlögl, A.; Obermaier, B. & Pregenzer, M. (2000). Current trends in Graz Brain-Computer Interface (BCI) research. *IEEE Transactions on Rehabilitation Engineering*, vol. 8, no. 2, pp.216–219.

Pfurtscheller, G. & Neuper, C. (2001). Motor Imagery and Direct Brain-Computer Communication. *Proc. of the IEEE*, vol. 89, no. 7, pp. 1123-1134.

Pregenzer, M. & Pfurtscheller, G. (1999). Frequency Component Selection for an EEG-based Brain to Computer Interface. *IEEE Transactions on Rehabilitation Engineering*, vol. 7, no. 4, pp. 413–419.

Schlögl, A.; Vidaurre, C. & Pfurtscheller, G. (2005). Assessing non-stationarities in BCI data. *BCI 2005 Workshop*, Rensellarville, NY, USA, 14-19 June 2005.

Shenoy, P.; Krauledat, M.; Blankertz, B.; Rao, R.P.N. & Müller, K.-R. (2006). Towards adaptive classification for BCI. *Journal of Neural Engineering*, vol. 3, pp. 13–23.

Stoica, P. & Moses, R.L. (1997). *Introduction to Spectral Analysis*, Englewood Cliffs, USA, Prentice-Hall.

Sykacek, P.; Roberts, S.J. & Stokes, M. (2004). Adaptive BCI based on variational Bayesian Kalman filtering: an empirical evaluation. *IEEE Transactions on Rehabilitation Engineering*, vol. 51, no. 5, pp. 719–727.

Townsend, G.; Grainmann, B. & Pfurtscheller, P. (2006). A Comparison of Common Spatial Patterns With Complex Band Power Features in a Four-Class BCI Experiment. *IEEE Transactions on Biomedical Engineering*, vol. 53, no. 4, pp. 642–651.

Wang, C.H.; Cheng, C.S. & Lee, T.T. (2004). Dynamical optimal training for interval type-2 fuzzy neural network (T2FNN). *IEEE Transactions on Systems, Man and Cybernetics*, vol. 34, pp. 1462–1477.

Wang, J.-S. & Lee, C.S.G. (2002). Self-Adaptive Neuro-fuzzy inference systems for classification applications. *IEEE Transactions on Fuzzy Systems*, vol.10, pp.790–802.

Wolpaw, J.R.; Birbaumer, N.; McFarland, D.J.; Pfurtscheller, G. & Vaughan, T.M. (2002). Brain-computer interfaces for communication and control. *Clinical Neurophysiology*, vol. 113, pp. 767–791.

Vaughan, T.M.; Heetderks, W.J.; Trejo, L.J.; Rymer, W.Z.; Weinrich, M.; Moore, M.M.; Kübler, A.; Dobkin, B.H.; Birbaumer, N.; Donchin, E.; Wolpaw, E.W. & Wolpaw, J.R. (2003). Brain-Computer Interface Technology: a Review of the Second International Meeting. *IEEE Transactions on Neural Systems and Rehabilitation Engineering*, vol. 11, pp. 94–109.

Vidaurre, C.; Schlögl, A.; Cabeza, R.; Scherer, R. & Pfurtscheller, G. (2006). A Fully On-line Adaptive BCI. *IEEE Transactions on Biomedical Engineering*, vol. 53, no. 6, pp. 1214–1219.

Yager, R. & Filev, D. (1994). Approximate clustering by the mountain clustering. *IEEE Transactions on Systems, Man and Cybernetics*, vol. 24, no. 8, pp. 338–358.

Yang, B.-H.; Yan, G.-Z.; Wu, T. & Yan, R.-G. (2007). Subject-based feature extraction using fuzzy wavelet packet in brain-computer interfaces. *Signal Processing*, vol. 87, pp. 1569–1574.

Zadeh, L.A. (1975). The concept of a linguistic variable and its application to approximate reasoning-1. *Information Sciences*, vol.8, pp.199–249.

http://www.gtec.at (accessed on 10.08.2008).

5

Automatic Calibration of Hybrid Dynamic Vision System for High Resolution Object Tracking

Julie Badri[1,2], Christophe Tilmant[1], Jean-Marc Lavest[1],
Patrick Sayd[2] and Quoc Cuong Pham[2]
[1]*LASMEA, Blaise Pascal University, 24 avenue des Landais, Aubiere, F-63411*
[2] *CEA LIST, Boîte Courrier 94, Gif-sur-Yvette, F-91191*
France

1. Introduction

Visual object recognition and tracking require a good resolution of the object to accurately model its appearance. In addition, tracking systems must be able to robustly recover moving target trajectory, and possibly cope with fast motion and large displacements. Wide angle static cameras capture a global view of the scene but they suffer from a lack of resolution in the case of a large distance between the objects and the sensor. On the contrary, dynamic sensors such as Pan-Tilt-Zoom (PTZ) cameras are controlled to focus on a 3D point in the scene and give access to high resolution images by adapting their zoom level. However, when a PTZ camera focuses on a target, its very limited field of view makes the tracking difficult. To overcome these limitations, hybrid sensor systems composed of a wide angle static camera and a dynamic camera can be used. Coupling these two types of sensors enables the exploitation of their complementary desired properties while limiting their respective drawbacks.

Calibration is required to enable information exchange between the two sensors to produce collaborative algorithms. The calibration of our system is difficult because of changes of both intrinsic (focal length, central point, distortion) and extrinsic (position, orientation) parameters of the dynamic sensor during system exploitation. Two approaches for dynamic stereo sensor calibration are possible:

- **Strong calibration** involves a complete modeling of the system. Intrinsic parameters of each camera and extrinsic parameters are estimated. This approach enables the projection of 3D points, expressed in the world frame, in 2D points expressed in each image frame.
- **Weak calibration** does not target to estimate intrinsic or extrinsic parameters. The objective is only to estimate the direct relation between pixels of the different sensors. From a pixel in the first camera, which is the projection of a given 3D point, the calibration gives the projection of the same 3D point to the second camera. In this approach, the recovery of 3D point coordinates is not more difficult.

1.1 The strong calibration approach

Our system is composed of two cameras observing the same scene (see Fig. 1). We denote:

- P_w a 3D point of the scene. The 3D coordinates of P_w are expressed in the world reference frame R_w.

- P_{I_s} the projection of P_w in the image I_s from the static sensor. The 2D coordinates of P_{I_s} are expressed in the image frame R_{I_s}

- P_{I_d} the projection of P_w in the image I_d from the dynamic sensor. The 2D coordinates of P_{I_d} are expressed in the image frame R_{I_d}.

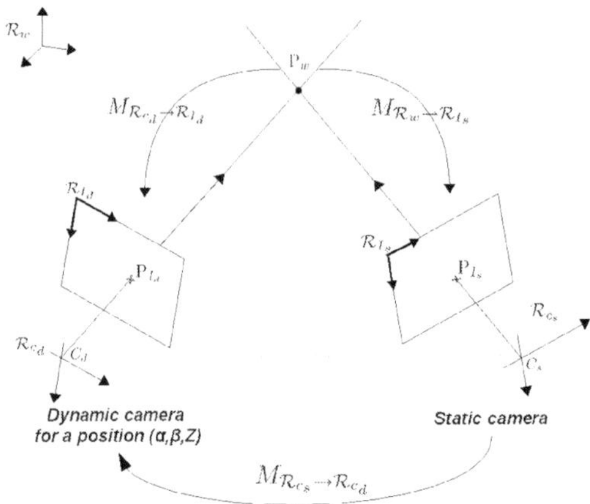

Fig. 1. Vision system and geometric relations.

The strong calibration enables the computation of the coordinates of P_{I_s} and P_{I_d} from the 3D coordinates of P_w. Reciprocally, the 3D coordinates of P_w can be inferred from the coordinates of P_{I_s} and P_{I_d} (triangulation). The calibration process consists in estimating the transformation matrices $M_{R_w\to R_{I_s}}$ from the world frame R_w to the image frame R_{I_s} of the static sensor and $M_{R_w\to R_{I_d}}$ from the world frame R_w to the image frame R_{I_d} of the dynamic sensor.

In the next section, we present methods for the calibration of the static sensor. Then, we present the calibration of the dynamic sensor following the same objectives as the static sensor calibration, but with its specific constraint. The third section is dedicated to solutions to gather the two sensors in the same world frame.

Static camera calibration

The pin-hole camera model is a usually used to represent image formation for standard camera. This model supposes that all light rays converge through a point C_s called the optical center (see Fig. 2). The focal length f represents the distance from the optical center to the image plane. The optical axis is defined by the point C_s and is orthogonal to the image plane. The principal point O is defined as the intersection of the optical axis with the image plane. The 3D world is projected on the image plane following a perspective transformation.

The calibration of the static sensor consists in estimating the transformation matrix $M_{R_w \to R_{I_s}}$ which is composed of the extrinsic transformation $M_{R_w \to R_{C_s}}$ from the world frame to the camera frame R_{C_s} and the intrinsic transformation from the camera frame R_{C_s} to the image frame R_{I_s} .

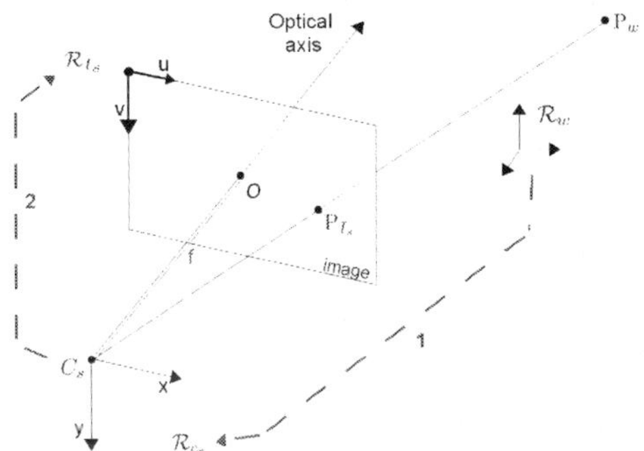

Fig. 2. The pinhole camera model for image formation.

$M_{R_w \to R_{I_s}}$ is composed of a rotation, denoted R , and a translation, denoted t . The transformation between P_w and P_{cs} is described as follows:

$$P_{C_s} = M_{R_w \to R_{C_s}} P_w = \begin{pmatrix} r_{11} & r_{12} & r_{13} & t_x \\ r_{21} & r_{22} & r_{23} & t_y \\ r_{31} & r_{32} & r_{33} & t_z \\ 0 & 0 & 0 & 1 \end{pmatrix} P_w = \begin{pmatrix} R & t \\ 0^t & 1 \end{pmatrix} P_w \qquad (1)$$

As proposed in (Horaud & Monga, 1995), the transformation $M_{R_{Cs} \to R_{Is}}$ is expressed as follows:

$$P_{I_s} = M_{R_{C_s} \to R_{I_s}} P_w = \begin{pmatrix} f & 0 & 0 & 0 \\ 0 & f & 0 & 0 \\ 0 & 0 & 1 & 0 \end{pmatrix} \begin{pmatrix} k_u & 0 & u_0 \\ 0 & k_v & v_0 \\ 0 & 0 & 1 \end{pmatrix} P_{C_s} \qquad (2)$$

It supposes that rows and columns of the sensors are orthogonal. The parameters k_u and k_v are respectively horizontal and vertical scale factors (expressed in pixels per length unit), u_0 and v_0 are the coordinates of the principal point O . These parameters are called intrinsic parameters.

$$P_{I_s} = M_{R_w \to R_{I_s}} P_w$$

$$P_{I_s} = \begin{pmatrix} k_u f & 0 & u_0 & 0 \\ 0 & k_v f & v_0 & 0 \\ 0 & 0 & 1 & 0 \end{pmatrix} \begin{pmatrix} R & t \\ 0^t & 1 \end{pmatrix} P_w \qquad (3)$$

Furthermore, optical distortions must be taken into account with real cameras. With standard cameras, two parameters are required to model radial and tangential distortion by polynomial functions (Lavest & Rives, 2003).

A standard approach to solve equation (3) consists in estimating both intrinsic and extrinsic camera parameters from the position of a known pattern (see Fig. 3). The first step of the calibration procedure deals with the accurate detection of pattern features on the calibration pattern. Several types of features can be used: cross (Peuchot, 1994), center of ellipse (Lavest et al., 1998; Brand & Mohr, 1994) and other techniques (Blaszka & Deriche, 1995). The extracted features serve as inputs of a non linear optimization process where the criterion to minimize is generally the sum of quadratic errors measured between the pattern features and their re-projection using the estimated camera model.

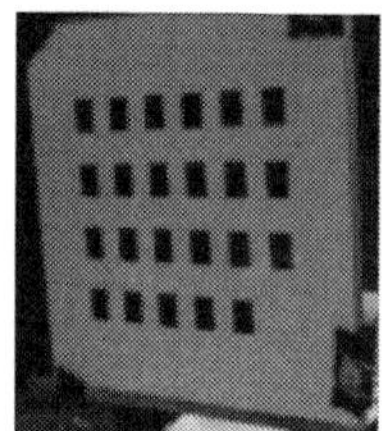
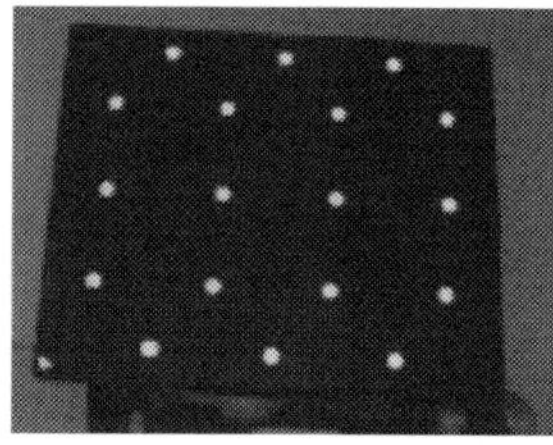
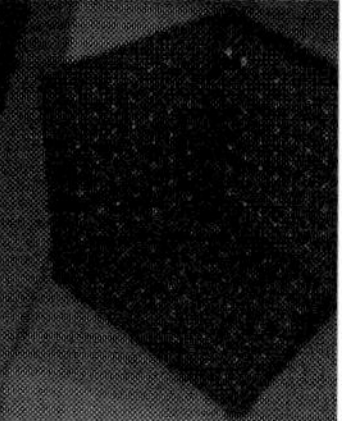

Fig. 3. Examples of calibration patterns.

Dynamic camera calibration

Geometric calibration of a dynamic sensor is much more complex than a standard camera one. Indeed, most of the proposed methods suppose a simple cinematic model (Fig. 4) where the rotation axes are orthogonal and centered on the optical axis (Barreto et al., 1999; Basu & Ravi, 1997; Collins & Tsin, 1999; Fry et al., 2000; Horaud et al., 2006; Woo & Capson, 2000).

Under this assumption, the camera geometric model can be represented by the following equation:

$$P_{I_d} = M_{R_{C_d} \to R_{I_d}} R_y R_x M_{R_w \to R_{C_d}} P_w \tag{4}$$

where R_x represents the pan rotation matrix and R_y the tilt rotation matrix.

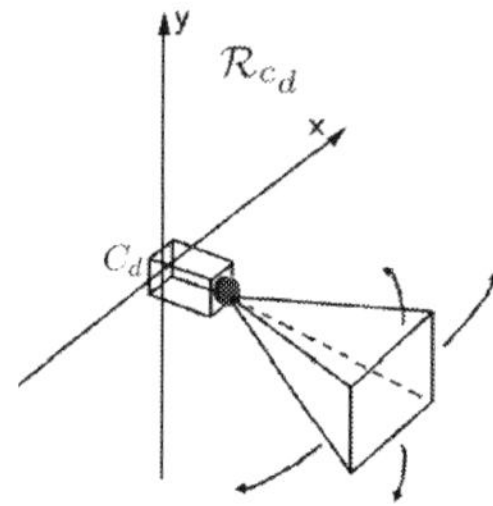

Fig. 4. Simplified cinematic model of a dynamic camera (Davis & Chen, 2003). The rotation axes (pan and tilt) are centered on the optical axis.

Standard dynamic cameras do not respect the constraint of rotation axes centered on the optical center because it is not compliant with low cost mechanic production. Indeed, rotation mechanisms are independent for pan and tilt. Furthermore, there is the motion of the optical center during zoom changes which makes this assumption unrealistic.

The modeling of standard mechanisms requires the introduction of an additive degree of freedom in the command equation (5). Davis and Chen (Davis & Chen, 2003) proposed a general formulation for this equation, which was extended later in (Jain et al., 2006).

$$P_{I_d} = M_{R_{C_d} \to R_{I_d}} t_y^{-1} R_y t_y t_x^{-1} R_x t_x M_{R_w \to R_{C_d}} P_w$$
$$P_{I_d} = M_{R_w \to R_{I_d}} (\Lambda, x, y) P_w$$

(5)

where R_x (resp. R_y) represents the rotation matrix in pan (resp. tilt), t_x (resp. t_y) represents the horizontal (resp. vertical) translation of the optical center. Λ represents the intrinsic and extrinsic parameters of the dynamic camera.

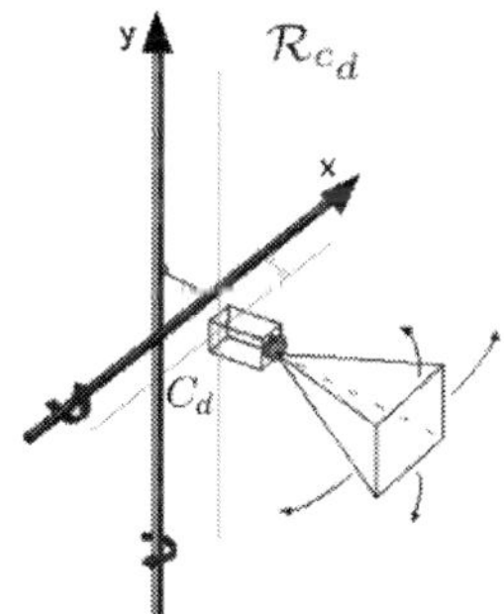

Fig. 5. Generalized cinematic model of the dynamic camera (Davis & Chen, 2003). Pan and tilt motions are represented by arrows and modeled as a rotation around a random 3D direction.

To determine $M_{R_w \to R_{I_d}} (\Lambda, x, y)$, a finite set of angle pairs (α_i, β_i) is regularly sampled in the range of the dynamic sensor motion. For each couple (α_i, β_i), the dynamic camera is considered as a static camera and it is calibrated with standard techniques. A set of correspondences between 3D points and their 2D projection in the image is built. Camera parameters are estimated by minimizing the differences between the projection of 3D points and their associated observations. Instead of using a passive calibration pattern, the authors use an active pattern composed of LEDs (Light-Emitting Diodes) in order to cover the complete field of view of the dynamic camera.

In (Jain et al., 2006), in addition to the calibration of rotation axes in position and orientation, correspondences between the camera command angles and the real observed angles are searched for. The extended method includes the following complementary steps:

1. Construction with interpolation of the expressions $\hat{\alpha} = g(\alpha)$ and $\hat{\beta} = g(\beta)$, which link the required angles α and β with the real ones $\hat{\alpha}$ and $\hat{\beta}$.

2. Construction by interpolation of transformations t_x and t_y with respect to zoom: for a given number of zoom values, the relative position of the optical center and the rotation axis are recorded.

A common reference frame
When the static and the dynamic cameras are calibrated, a common reference frame definition is required. As shown in Fig. 1, the following equations can be derived:

$$P_{C_s} = M_{R_w \to R_{C_s}} P_w$$
$$P_{C_d} = M_{R_w \to R_{C_d}} P_w \qquad (6)$$
$$P_{C_d} = M_{R_{C_s} \to R_{C_d}} P_{C_s}$$

The three transformations are dependent:

$$M_{R_w \to R_{C_s}} = M^{-1}_{R_{C_s} \to R_{C_d}} M_{R_w \to R_{C_d}}$$
$$M_{R_w \to R_{C_d}} = M_{R_{C_s} \to R_{C_d}} M_{R_w \to R_{C_s}} \qquad (7)$$
$$M_{R_{C_s} \to R_{C_d}} = M_{R_w \to R_{C_s}} M^{-1}_{R_w \to R_{C_d}}$$

The matrix $M_{R_{C_s} \to R_{C_d}}$ is easily determined from the calibration of each sensor, and can be written:

$$M_{R_{C_s} \to R_{C_d}} = \begin{pmatrix} r_{11} & r_{12} & r_{13} & b_x \\ r_{21} & r_{22} & r_{23} & b_y \\ r_{31} & r_{32} & r_{33} & b_z \\ 0 & 0 & 0 & 1 \end{pmatrix} \qquad (8)$$

where the vector $\mathbf{b} = \begin{pmatrix} b_x & b_y & b_z \end{pmatrix}^t$ is the translation between the optical centers of the static camera and the dynamic camera.

Conclusion on strong calibration
Strong calibration gives a complete geometric modeling of the pair of sensors. Knowing the projection model for each sensor and the spatial relation between the sensors, coordinates of 3D points can be inferred from their observations in images. This property is fundamental to recover 3D information for reconstruction purpose. Large orientation angles between the two sensors reduce the uncertainty on 3D reconstruction even if it complicates data matching between images.

These methods are based on the use of calibration patterns, and require human intervention. This constraint is not compatible with the objective to obtain a system able to adapt itself to environment changes, implying automatic re-calibration.

1.2 Weak calibration of the dynamic stereo sensor

In many computer vision applications such as object tracking and recognition, a pair of cameras with close points of view, make visual information matching possible (see Fig. 6). However, in this case, it was shown that the estimation of motion parameters become difficult, particularly for small angles in the dynamic sensor (Gardel, 2004). Weak calibration solves this problem, because it enables the estimation of the dynamic camera command from visual information extracted in static images, without analytic modeling of the vision system. The basic idea is to find a mapping between pixels coordinates in the static camera and rotation angles of the dynamic sensor, at a given zoom value. Moreover, weak calibration avoids explicit modeling of optical distortions. This approach also implicitly encodes the 3D structure of the observed scene.

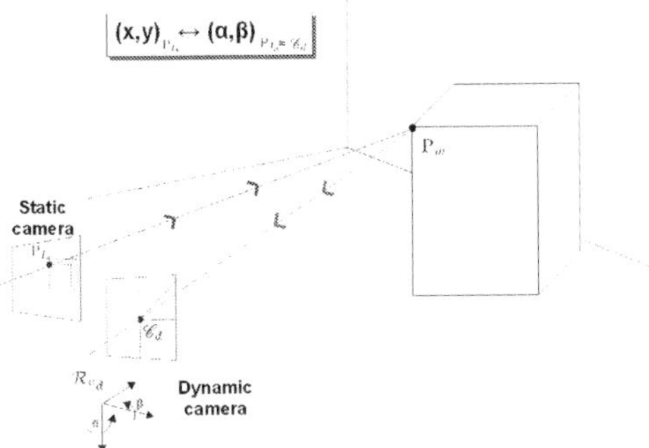

Fig. 6. Weak calibration of a pair of sensors.

Zhou et al. (Zhou et al., 2003) proposed an implementation of this method. A *lookup table* (LUT) linking a pixel of the static camera with the pan and tilt angles centering the dynamic sensor on the corresponding 3D point is built. The LUT is created in two steps:

- **Creation of an LUT for a set of points** P_{I_s} **in the static sensor:** for each point $P_{I_s}^k$, the dynamic sensor is manually commanded to set the center of the dynamic image on the corresponding point P_w^k of the real scene. The $P_{I_s}^k$ coordinates and pan-tilt angles (α_i, β_i) are recorded in the LUT.

- **Interpolation for all the pixels of the static sensor:** a linear interpolation is done between the pixels of the initial set. This linear interpolation is not adapted to handling optical distortions and nonlinear 3D geometry variations. The precision is acceptable to initialize a person tracking and so set up the PTZ camera, as the object is in the field of view, but not to perform pixel matching for intensive sensor collaboration. A denser initial set of points could lead to better accuracy, but it would require a considerable amount of intervention of the supervisor to control the PTZ.

More recently, Senior et al. (Senior et al., 2005) presented a calibration system applied to people tracking where the slave camera is steered to a pan/tilt position calculated using a sequence of transformations, as shown in Fig. 7. Each transformation is learned from unlabelled training data, generated by synchronized video tracking of people in each camera. The method is based on the assumption that people move on a plane and a homography is sufficient to map ground plane points (the location of the feet) in the master camera into points in the second camera. The homography H is learned using the approach described in (Stauffer & Tieu, 2003), and the transformation T inferred from the learned mapping between pan-tilt angles (α, β) generated on a spiral and the motion of the optical center in the dynamic camera compared to the known home position (x_0, y_0) where the camera correspondence homography was trained. Then, T is estimated by solving a least-squares linear system $\Theta = TX$ where Θ represents all couples (α, β), and X all coordinates $(x_i - x_0, y_i - y_0)$ corresponding to (α, β).

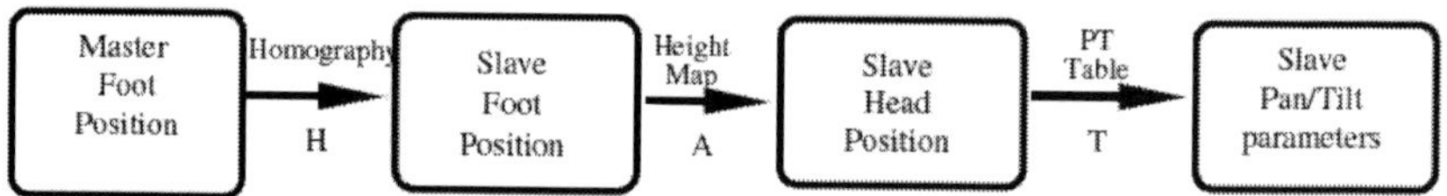

Fig. 7. Calibration approach proposed in (Senior et al., 2005): sequence of transformations to control the PTZ camera PTZ using tracking results in the static image.

1.3 Discussion on the choice of the calibration method for our vision system

Our objective is to develop information fusion between the two sensors. We chose to set cameras close to each other to facilitate image matching. This option led us to consider weak calibration (excluding 3D triangulation possibility). This choice is reinforced by material consideration. The low-cost PTZ camera makes strong calibration approach difficult (focal length management).

Weak calibration methods (Zhou et al., 2003; Senior et al., 2005) are manual or require expert skill contribution to elaborate learning bases. These constraints are not compatible with an autonomous and self calibrating system. We propose in the following a weak calibration method that requires no human intervention. Our contribution concerns the two main objectives:

- **Automatism and autonomy:** the proposed method is based on the construction of an LUT which associates pixels of the static sensor with pan-tilt angles to center the dynamic sensor on the corresponding scene point. Our approach exploits natural information, without using a calibration pattern or any supervised learning base. This automatic approach makes re-calibration possible during the system's life and thus drastically reduces the requirement on human intervention.
- **Precision:** the approach uses an interpolation function to get a correspondence for all pixels of the static image. This approach also takes into account distortions in images.

2. Learning-based calibration of the hybrid dynamic sensor system

2.1 Overview of the system

The hybrid dynamic vision system is composed of a static wide angle camera and a dynamic (Pan-Tilt-Zoom) camera. In the following, the images of the static and the PTZ cameras are respectively denoted I_s and $I_d(\alpha,\beta,Z)$. The parameters (α,β,Z) represent the pan, tilt, and zoom parameters of the PTZ camera.

The proposed calibration method can be considered as a registration process by visual servoing. It consists in learning the mapping ζ, for any zoom level Z, between the pixel coordinates (x_s,y_s) of a point P_{I_s} of the static camera and the pan-tilt command angles (α_Z,β_Z) to be applied to center the dynamic camera on the corresponding point P_{I_d} :

$$(\alpha_Z,\beta_Z) = \zeta(x_s,y_s,Z) \tag{9}$$

The data registration relies on the extraction of interest points in regions of interest, which are visually matched in the two images. The basic assumption for interest point matching is that there is locally enough texture information in the image. Moreover, in order to speed up the calibration procedure, the mapping between the two cameras is not computed for all pixels

P_{I_s} in the static camera. Thus, correspondences are searched for in a subset of pixels $\Gamma\{P_{I_s}\}$.

The complete mapping is then estimated by interpolation and coded in the LUT.

The learning of the mapping ζ is performed in two main steps:

1. Automatic sub area registration of the two cameras views for a subset of pre-defined positions $\Gamma\{P_{I_s}\}$ by visual servoing, at different zoom values $Z_{j=0,1,\cdots,m}$ (see Fig. 8)

    a. Learn the mapping ζ at the minimum zoom level, denoted Z_0, for pixels in $\Gamma\{P_{I_s}\}$

    b. Learn the mapping ζ at sampled zoom values $Z_{j=0,1,\cdots,m}$, for pixels in $\Gamma\{P_{I_s}\}$.

2. Automatic global area matching by interpolation for all pixels of I_S and all values of the zoom.

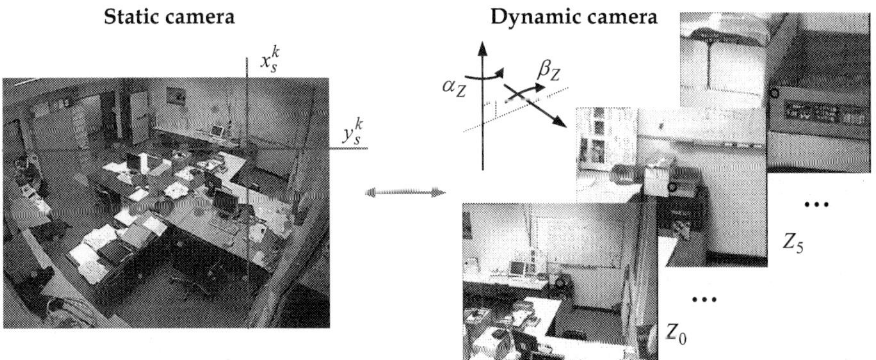

Fig. 8. Learning of the mapping ζ between a pixel (x_s, y_s) in the static camera and the pan-tilt angles (α_Z, β_Z) to be applied in the PTZ camera, at a given zoom level Z by visual servoing. The learning is performed for a subset of pre-defined points.

2.2 Calibrating the hybrid dynamic sensor system at Z_0

The proposed calibration method can be compared to the *Iterative Closest Point* (ICP) algorithm. The ICP was first presented by Chen and Medioni (Chen & Medioni, 1991) and Besl and McKay (Besl & McKay, 1992). This simple algorithm iteratively registers two points sets by finding the best rigid transform between the two datasets in the least squares sense.

In our calibration approach, points sets are registered such that the angular parameters of the PTZ camera are optimal, e.g. the point P_{I_d} corresponding to a considered point P_{I_s} is moved to the center C_d of the dynamic camera image.

The algorithm for registering the camera sub areas for points in $\Gamma\{P_{I_s}\}$ at Z_0 is summarized below:

1. Start with point $P_{I_s}^0$

2. For each point $P_{I_s}^k$ of the selected points subset $\Gamma\{P_{I_s}\}$

    a. Selection of images I_s and $I_d(\alpha, \beta, Z)$ to be compared

   b.   Detection and robust matching of interest points between a region of interest I'_s of I_s around $P^k_{I_s}$ and $I_d(\alpha,\beta,Z)$

   c.   Estimation of the homography H between interest points of I'_s and $I_d(\alpha,\beta,Z)$

   d.   Computation of $P^k_{I_d}$ coordinates in $I_d(\alpha,\beta,Z)$ by $P^k_{I_d} = H \times P^k_{I_s}$

   e.   Command of the dynamic camera in order to $P^k_{I_d}$ catch up with C_d

   f.   Process $P^k_{I_s}$ until the condition $\left| P^k_{I_d} - C_d \right| < \varepsilon$ is reached. Otherwise, the algorithm stops after n iterations.

3.   Go to step (2) to process the next point $P^{k+1}_{I_s}$.

The main difficulty for registering images from a hybrid camera system resides in the heterogeneity of image resolutions and a potentially variable visual appearance of objects in the two sensors in terms of contrast and color levels for instance.

The registration procedure thus requires a method for detecting and matching visual features robust to scale, rotation, viewpoint, and lightning. In (Mikolajczyk & Schmidt, 2005), the performance of state-of-the art feature matching methods is evaluated. The *Scale-Invariant Feature Transform* (SIFT) (Lowe, 1999) exhibits great performance regarding these constraints.

Because the field of view of the dynamic camera is smaller than that of the static camera, interest points are detected in a region of interest I'_s of I_s around the point $P^k_{I_s}$ such that I'_s approximately corresponds to the view of the dynamic camera. The estimated registration error is taken as the distance in pixels between P_{I_d} and C_d. Consequently, we must be able to calculate the coordinates of P_{I_d} and the transform between a point in the static camera and its corresponding point in the dynamic camera. We make the assumption that interest points in I'_s and $I_d(\alpha,\beta,Z)$ are linked by a homography H, which means that interest points are supposed to locally lie in a plane in the 3-D scene. Moreover, the distortion in the static camera is considered locally insignificant. The homography H is robustly computed with a RANSAC algorithm (Fischler & Bolles, 1981).

In order to ensure the convergence of P_{I_d} to C_d, we use a proportional controller based on the error between the coordinates of P_{I_d} and the coordinates of C_d so that it minimizes the criterion of step (2.f). Assuming that the pan-tilt axes and the coordinate axes are collocated for small displacements, we can write:

$$\begin{pmatrix} \alpha \\ \beta \end{pmatrix} = \begin{pmatrix} K_{x \to \alpha} & 0 \\ 0 & K_{x \to \beta} \end{pmatrix} \begin{pmatrix} \Delta x \\ \Delta y \end{pmatrix} \tag{10}$$

$$\text{where } \begin{pmatrix} \Delta x & \Delta y \end{pmatrix}^T = P_{I_d} - C_d$$

During the learning stage, the 3-D scene is assumed to be invariant. As the calibration procedure is an off-line process, there is no temporal constraint on the speed of the PTZ command. As system accuracy depends mainly on the mechanics of the dynamic camera, a proportional controller is sufficient for calibration purpose.

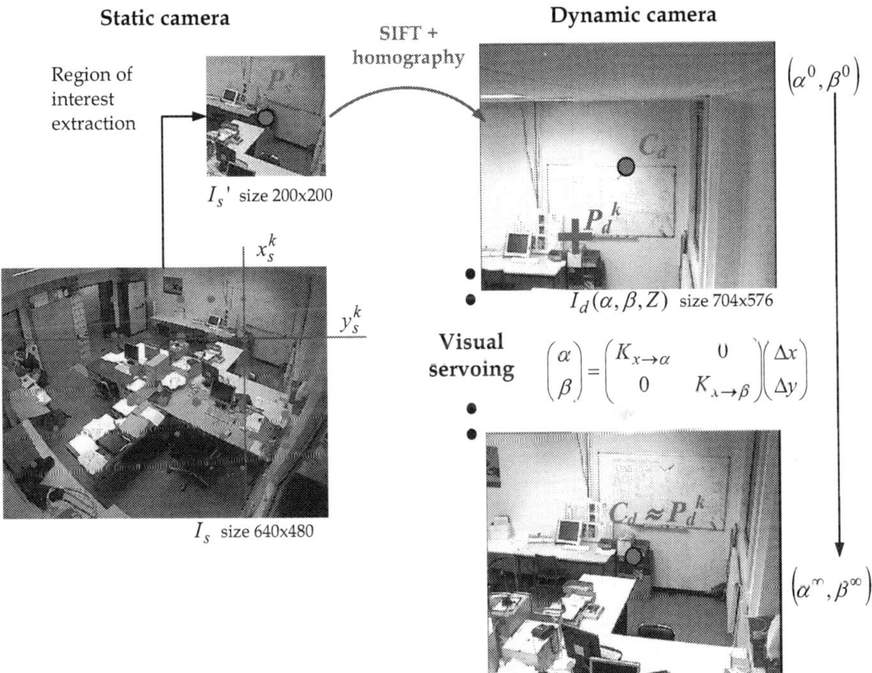

Fig. 9. Calibration of the hybrid sensor system at zoom Z_0 by visual servoing on a subset of pre-defined points.

2.3 Initialization of the dynamic camera for a given learning point P_{I_s}

Case of the initial point $P_{I_s}^0$

The objective of the initialization stage is to obtain a pair of pan-tilt angles such that the projection of $P_{I_s}^0$ and its neighborhood in the dynamic camera are visible in the image I_d.

Starting from the obtained configuration, the dynamic camera parameters are optimized through the visual servoing iterations. The initialization algorithm is given here.

Let $P_{I_s}^{C_d}$ be the projection of C_d in I_s.

Repeat until $P_{I_s}^{C_d}$ falls in the neighborhood of $P_{I_s}^0$:

1. Random generation of a pair of (α, β) values
2. Selection of current images I_s and $I_d(\alpha, \beta, Z)$ to be compared
3. Detection and robust matching of interest points between I_s and $I_d(\alpha, \beta, Z)$

4.   Computation of homography H between matched interest points in I_s and $I_d(\alpha,\beta,Z)$

5.   Computation of C_d coordinates in I_s by $P_{I_s}^{C_d} = H \times C_d$

Case of pre-defined $P_{I_s}^k$ points

Let us assume that m grid points $\left\{P_{I_s}^k\right\}_{k=1,\cdots,m}$ are already learned. To move the dynamic camera in the neighborhood of $P_{I_s}^{m+1}$, we estimate the command parameters $(\alpha^{m+1},\beta^{m+1})$ from previously learned positions. For each independent direction, the closest point to $P_{I_s}^{m+1}$ is searched for in the learning base, and serves as an initialization for the calibration on the current point.

2.4 Calibrating the hybrid dynamic sensor system at other zoom values

The presented learning algorithm for the system calibration at the initial zoom Z_0 and for a subset of pre-defined grid points can be applied at other zoom levels. The only difference is the selection of the reference image. At zoom Z_0, the image from the static camera is compared to the image in the dynamic camera. For other zoom values, the images to be registered come from the dynamic sensor at two different zoom levels $Z_k < Z_j$.

Instead of taking $k = j - 1$, which would incrementally cause an accumulation of calibration errors, we select Z_k as the minimum zoom value so that the two images can be registered. The main steps of the method are:

1.   For each point $P_{I_s}^k$

    a.   Initialize the dynamic camera at a reference zoom Z_{ref} (initially set to Z_0) using the previous learned command (α,β)

    b.   Select the current image in the dynamic camera, denoted I_d^{ref}

    c.   For each zoom value Z_j so that $Z_j < Z_{max}$

        i.   Apply the zoom Z_j

        ii.   Detect and match SIFT interest points between I_d^{ref} and I_d^j

        iii.   Estimate the homography H between interest points in I_d^{ref} and I_d^j

        iv.   Calculate the center C_d of I_d^{ref} in I_d^j by $P_{I_d^j}^k = H \times C_d$

        v.   Command the dynamic camera to minimize the distance between c_d and $P_{I_d^j}^k$ until $\left|P_{I_d^j}^k - C_d\right| < \varepsilon$

    d.   If the previous step fails, consider $Z_{ref} \leftarrow Z_{ref} + 1$, and go to (1.a)

2.   Go to (1) to process $P_{I_s}^{k+1}$ with $Z_{ref} = Z_0$.

2.5 Sampling grid

The calibration process involves the matching of interest points extracted with the SIFT algorithm. A regular sampling of the image in the static sensor does not take into consideration the structure information of the 3D scene. Some of the points of the sampling grid might fall in homogeneous regions, with poor texture information, and cause errors in estimating the homography between the images. To better exploit the 3D scene structure and increase confidence in the learning points, we propose an adaptive sampling strategy which selects more points in textured areas while in homogeneous regions, the mapping will be interpolated from neighboring grid nodes. For a given image I_s, SIFT points are detected. Then, a probability density estimated by Parzen windowing (Parzen, 1962) from extracted SIFT interest points is associated to every pixel in I_s .(see Fig. 10). The size of the window is taken to be equal to the size of the region of interest used for calibrating at zoom Z_0. Two additional constraints are introduced in the sampling method: (i) pixels near the image borders are rejected, (ii) the selected learning nodes must be distributed over the whole image.

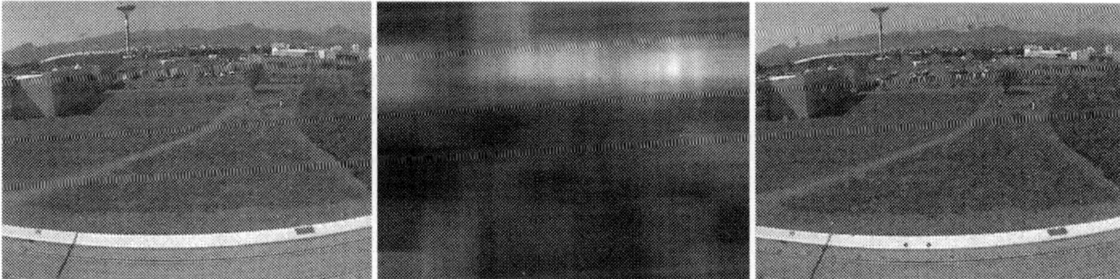

Fig. 10. Adaptive grid sampling of the 3-D scene. Left: the source image, middle: image representing the probability density of interest points using the Parzen windowing technique, right: the obtained sampling grid. The size of red circles represents the probability of the node.

2.6 Extending the LUT by Thin Plate Spline (TPS) interpolation

The previous learning method enables the determination of a sparse mapping between pixel coordinates in the static camera and angular parameters in the dynamic camera, at a limited number of grid nodes. In order to extend the LUT to all pixels in I_s, an approximation is made by using an interpolation function. Thin-Plate-Spline (TPS) interpolation functions, first presented by Bookstein (Bookstein, 1989) are a popular solution to interpolating problems because they give similar results to direct polynomial interpolation, while implicating lower degree polynomials. They also avoid Runge's phenomenon for higher degrees (oscillation between the interpolate points with a large variation).

3. Results and discussion

The presented calibration method finds a relation between the coordinates (x_s, y_s) of the point P_{I_s} of I_s and pan-tilt angles such that P_{I_d} coincides with C_d. In order to evaluate the accuracy of the method, we seek to estimate the error between the actual position of P_w in I_d and the sought position, e.g. C_d. Because the approach is a weak calibration of the camera pair, we have no access to the 3D coordinates of a point in the scene. Consequently, we used a calibration pattern to estimate the exact coordinates of a point. The pattern is a black ellipse on a white background which is seen in the two cameras (Fig. 11) and easily detectable. The coordinates of the center of gravity of the ellipse was estimated with a subpixellic detector after adaptive thresholding.

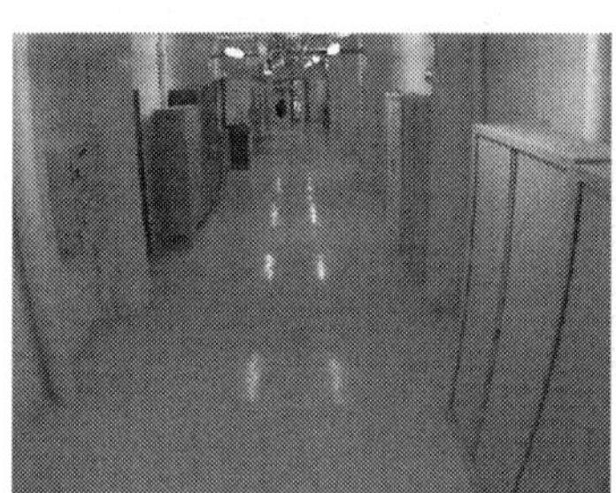

Fig. 11. Illustration of the elliptic calibration pattern (surrounded by red) used to evaluate the accuracy of the method of calibration. Left: in the static camera, right: in the dynamic camera.

This calibration method makes a distinction between points learned during the first stage of calibration and interpolated points after the second stage. The learned points serve as a basis for the interpolation function. We present here and evaluation showing, firstly, the accuracy obtained on the learning points, then, taking into account the interpolation stage, the accuracy obtained on any point of the scene observed in the static camera.

3.1 Accuracy of learning stage

In order to evaluate the accuracy of the visual servoing process during the calibration, we position the elliptic pattern on a number of nodes on the grid so that its center of gravity coincides with a selected node, and focus the dynamic camera with the learned command parameters. The coordinates of the center of gravity of the ellipse in I_d are determined.

Finally, the spatial error between this center of gravity and C_d is estimated and converted to an angular error.

Two dynamic cameras were tested:

- AXIS PTZ 213 network camera, 26x optical zoom, coverage: pan 340°, tilt 100°
- AXIS 233D high-end network dome camera, 35x optical zoom, coverage: pan 360° endless, tilt 180°.

Results for AXIS 233D dome camera

The grid points that are considered for evaluation are the points surrounded by black in Fig. 12. The points are sorted in a list, according to their probability density. The initial grid contains 124 nodes. As an example, node 3, 7 and 13 are points where SIFT points density is high. Nodes 43 and 61 present a medium density. The point 93 has a very low density.

One can note (Fig. 13)that the neighborhood of points 3 and 7 represents a region of the scene that exhibits large variations in the 3D geometry in terms of depth (about ten meters). The neighborhood of nodes 13 and 43 presents a greater homogeneity of the 3D geometry of the scene (a depth of several meters). The neighborhood of points 61 and 93 is mainly composed of a single plane.

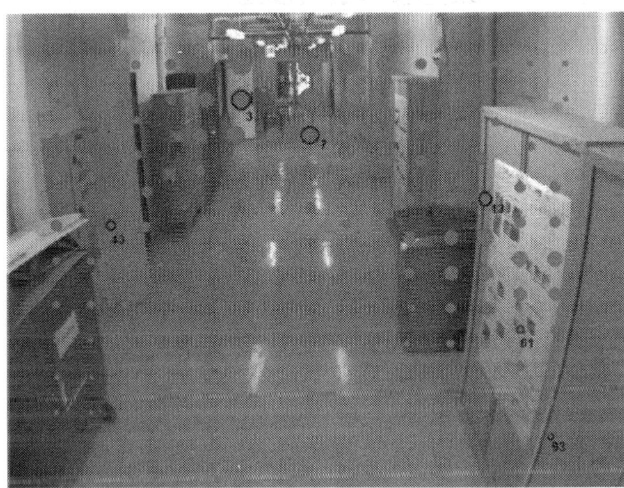

Fig. 12. Learning grid for calibration. The points surrounded by black are used in the discussion on the accuracy of the calibration. The size of the circles represents the probability density of detected SIFT points.

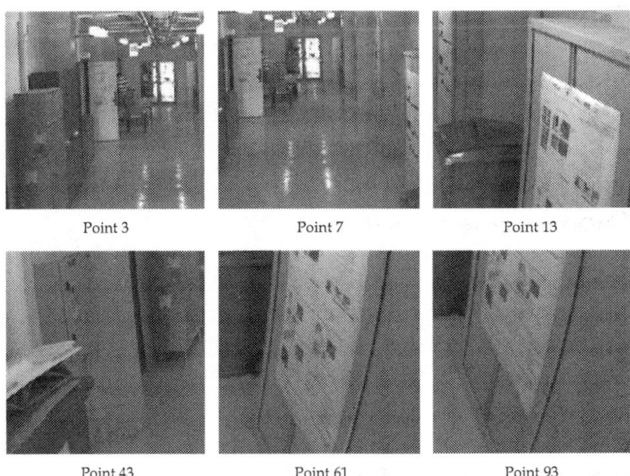

Fig. 13. Neighborhood of six points in I_s selected for evaluation and corresponding to the points surrounded by black in Fig. 12.

The results of the experiments are presented in Table 1.

	Point 3	Point 7	Point 13	Point 43	Point 61	Point 93
Angular error in pan (degrees)	0.54°	0.13°	0.13°	0.28°	0.09°	0.6°
Angular error in tilt (degrees)	0.02°	0.3°	0.16°	0.29°	0.08°	0.32°

Table 1. Angular errors made in the learning stage of the calibration method.

The method is based on the mapping of interest points that are used to estimate the coordinates of the projected grid point in I_d.

The accuracy of the projection estimate depends upon (i) the number of detected and matched SIFT points and (ii) the number of points that verify the homography assumption. It could be expected that the accuracy of the first points of the grid will be better than the last points because of their higher probability values. The neighborhood of points 13 and 43 and points 61 and 93 are visually similar (Fig.13). The notable difference between the two cases is the SIFT point density in the area of interest. One can notice that the accuracy for points 43 and 93 is lower than for 13 points and 61 although the environment is similar. This result shows the dependence of the calibration accuracy on the 3D scene structure and confirms the interest of this adaptive grid sampling.

However, the accuracy obtained for the points 3 and 7 is much lower than that obtained for items 61, while 3 and 7 own a high probability density. The neighborhood of points 3 and 7 presents sharp disparities in terms of 3D geometry, while the region around point 61 can be better approximated by a plane. This second observation is related to the homography approximation between 3D points of the scene and images in the two sensors.

The corridor is somehow an extreme case because of the large depth variation in the scene, contrary to an office environment for example. Its specific geometry invalidates in some cases the assumption that the learning points locally lie on a plane. Nevertheless, the accuracy achieved with our automatic calibration method remains acceptable in the context of visual surveillance application such as people tracking.

Results for AXIS 213 PTZ camera
The deviation due to zoom in this PTZ camera is very important. This means that at a high zoom, a pointed object is no longer entirely visible. For this type of equipment, it is therefore necessary to implement the step size for different zooms. Fig. 14 shows the average error committed at different zooms for a set of points of the learning grid and its associated deviation. One can remark that the errors due to calibration (0.2°-0.3°) are smaller than errors inherent to the zoom mechanism of the PTZ camera (0.6°-0.8°). Our calibration method therefore enables the compensation of the inaccuracy of the camera mechanism.

3.2 Accuracy of the interpolation stage
We evaluate here the overall accuracy of the calibration system, including the interpolation step. A number of points distributed over the image and not corresponding to learning points are selected (Fig. 15). The points labelled *a*, *b* and *c* are sampled in the middle of learned points. The points labelled *d* and *e* are chosen in an area with very few learned points because of its homogeneity (ground).
The results of experiments are presented in Table 2.

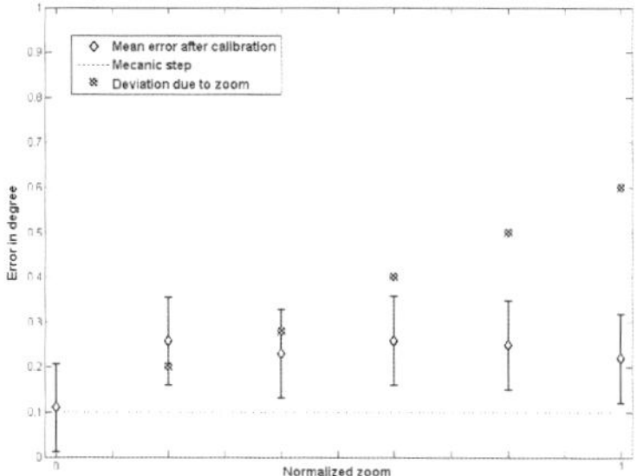
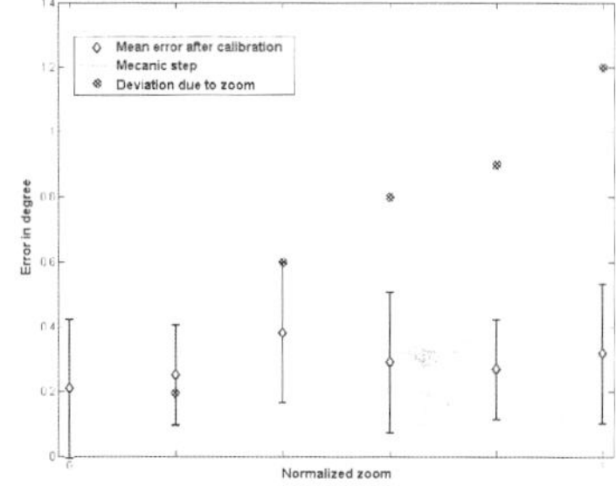

Fig. 14. Results for the accuracy of the method relative to the zoom parameter for the PTZ camera. The errors are represented by their mean and standard deviation, the red dots stand for the observed deviation due to the zoom mechanism. Left: error in degrees of the estimated pan angle, right: error in degrees on the estimated tilt angle.

	Point *a*	Point *b*	Point *c*	Point *d*	Point *e*
Angular error in pan (degrees)	0.12°	0.26°	0.13°	0.07°	0.5°
Angular error in tilt (degrees)	0.11°	0.02°	0.16°	0.34°	0.5°

Table 2. Angular errors for interpolated points.

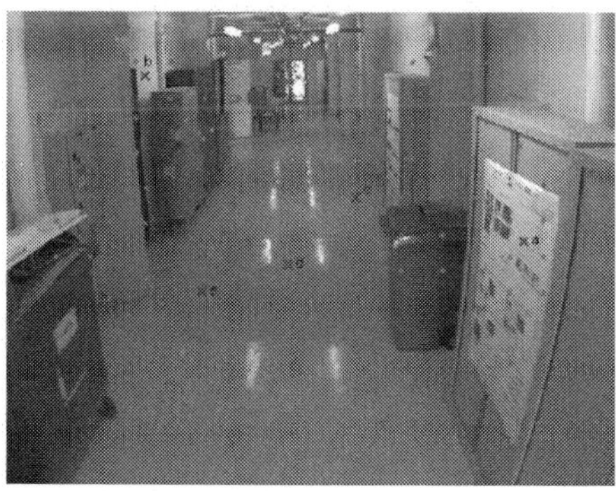

Fig. 15. Points where the error is measured (blue cross). These points do not belong to the learning grid represented by red dots.

Point *a* shows the best obtained accuracy, since its neighborhood corresponds to a 3D plane. The accuracy of point *b* and *c* is lower. In contrast to point *a*, their neighborhood cannot be easily approximated by a plane. As it was previously shown, the planar constraint affects the obtained accuracy. This influence is also observable at interpolated points. As expected, the accuracy obtained for points taken outside the learning grid (points *d* and *e*) is lower. But it is still acceptable for people tracking applications.

A solution to limit errors due to interpolation could be to increase the number of learning nodes either by using a finer sampling grid or by artificially enriching the scene with textured objects during the off-line calibration process, as shown in Fig. 16.

Fig. 16. Sampling grid in the case of calibration in a corridor. The first row shows the scene observed by the static camera. The second row represents the estimate of the probability density of SIFT points using Parzen windows. The last row shows the obtained sampling grid (the circles size is related to the probability density of the interest point).

4. Application to high resolution tracking

An immediate application of our calibration method is to use the pair of cameras as a master-slave system. An object is designated in the static camera and the dynamic camera is commanded to focus on it in order to obtain a higher resolution image. Fig. 17 illustrates the focalization of the dynamic camera using the LUT obtained by the calibration algorithm, for both indoor and outdoor environments. In the outdoor sample, the person and the blue car represent approximately 7x7 pixels in the static camera whereas in the PTZ image, they occupy 300x270 pixels. The object resolution obtained in the PTZ image is suitable for recognition tasks such as gesture recognition, license plate reading or people identification.

Fig. 17. Examples illustrating the direct application of our generic calibration method: indoor (first row) and outdoor (second row) scenes. The images obtained with the dynamic camera (right column) can be used for recognition applications.

We implemented a more elaborate system to automatically detect and track people in the static camera and focus on a particular individual in the dynamic sensor. The detection is carried out by robust and efficient statistical background modelling in the static camera, based on the approach described in (Chen et al., 2007). Detected blobs are then tracked with a Kalman Filter and a simple first order dynamic model, to reinforce spatial coherence of blob/target associations over time. Fig. 18 shows a result of tracking a person along a corridor with our calibrated hybrid dynamic vision system.

5. Conclusion

We have proposed a fast and fully automatic learning-based calibration method that determines a complete mapping between the static camera pixels and the command parameters of the dynamic camera, for all values of the zoom. The method encodes in an LUT the following relations:

- $(\alpha_Z, \beta_Z) = \zeta(x_s, y_s)$, for any pixel (x_s, y_s), at a given zoom Z,

- $(x_s, y_s) = \zeta^{-1}(\alpha_Z, \beta_Z)$, for any pair (α_Z, β_Z), at a given zoom Z.

The only requirement is that the observed scene presents sufficient texture information as the methods is based on visual features matching. The obtained results in the corridor

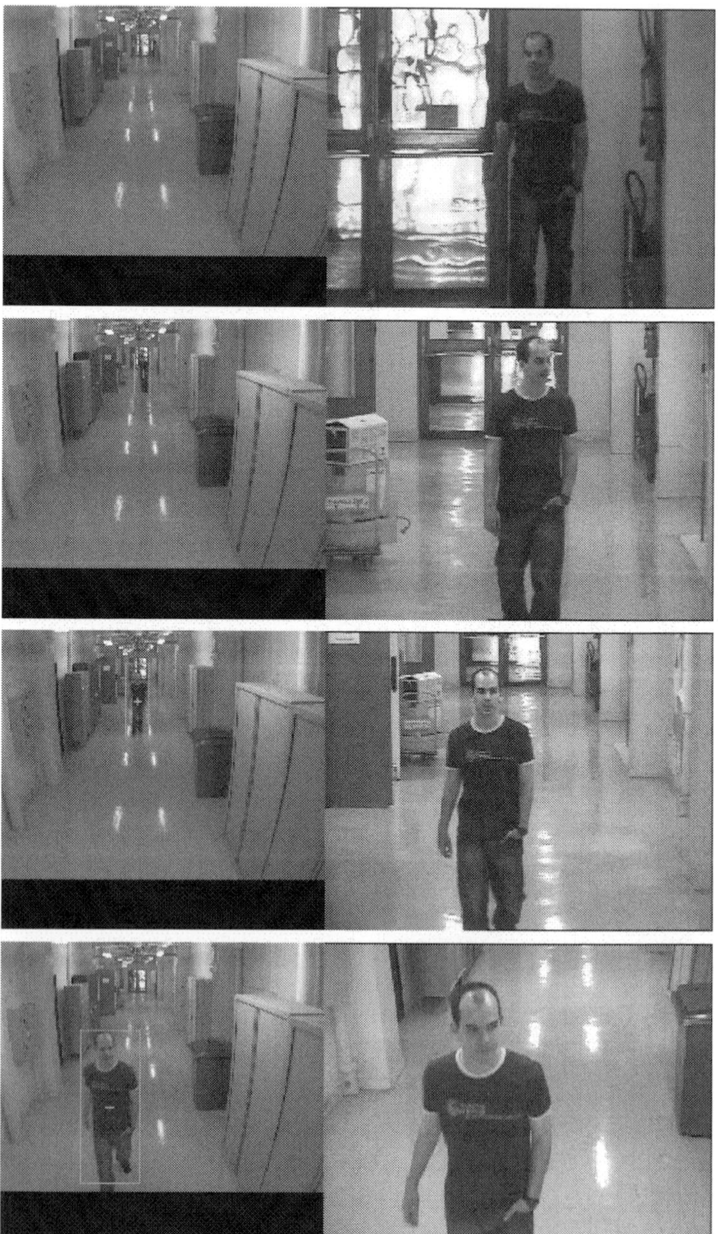

Fig. 18. Tracking a person walking in a corridor with a calibrated hybrid dynamic sensor system.

showed a good accuracy even in the case of high variations of depth in the scene. The knowledge of the complete mapping $\left(\zeta,\zeta^{-1}\right)$ relating the two sensors opens new perspectives for high resolution tracking and pattern recognition in wide areas by collaborative algorithms.

6. References

Barreto, J.; Peixoto, P.; Batista, J. & Araujo, H. (1999). Tracking multiple objects in 3D, *Proceedings of IEEE/RSJ International Conference on Intelligent Robots and Systems*, vol. 1, pp. 210–215, ISBN: 0-7803-5184-3, Kyongju, South Korea, October 1999, IEEE Computer Society Washington, DC, USA.

Basu, A. & Ravi, K. (1997). Active camera calibration using pan, tilt and roll. *IEEE Transactions on Systems, Man, and Cybernetics, Part B (Cybernetics)*, Vol. 27, No. 3, (June 1997) pp. 559–566, ISSN: 1083-4419.

Besl, P. J. & McKay, N. D. (1992). A method for registration of 3-D shapes. *IEEE Transactions on Pattern Analysis and Machine Intelligence*, Vol. 14, No. 2, (February 1992) pp. 239–256, ISSN:0162-8828.

Blaszka, T. & Deriche, R. (1995). A Model Based Method for Characterization and Location of Curved Image Features, *Proceedings of the 8th International Conference on Image Analysis and Processing*, pp. 77-82, ISBN: 3-540-60298-4, San Remo, Italy, September 1995, Lecture Notes in Computer Science, Springer.

Bookstein, F. L. (1989). Principal warps: Thin-Plate Splines and the decomposition of deformations. *IEEE Transactions Pattern Analysis Machine Intelligence*, Vol. 11, No. 6, (June 1989) pp. 567–585, ISSN:0162-8828.

Brand, P. & Mohr, R. (1994). Accuracy in image measure, in *Proceedings of the SPIE Conference on Videometrics III*, Vol. 2350, pp. 218- 228, S.F. El-Hakim (Ed.). Boston, Massachusetts, USA.

Chen, Y. & Medioni, G. (1991). Object modelling by registration of multiple range images, *Proceedings of the IEEE International Conference on Robotics and Automation*, Vol. 3, pp. 2724-2729, ISBN: 0-8186-2163-X, Sacramento, CA, USA, April 1991, IEEE Computer Society Washington, DC, USA.

Chen, Y.-T.; Chen, C.-S.; Huang, C.-R. & Hung, Y.-P. (2007). Efficient hierarchical method for background subtraction. *Pattern Recognition*, Vol. 40, No. 10, (October 2007) pp. 2706-2715, ISSN:0031-3203, Elsevier Science Inc., New York, NY, USA.

Collins, R. & Tsin, Y. (1999). Calibration of an outdoor active camera system, *Proceedings of the IEEE Computer Society Conference on Computer Vision and Pattern Recognition*, Vol. 1, pp. 528–534, ISBN: 0-7695-0149-4 , Fort Collins, CO, USA, June 1999, IEEE Computer Society Washington, DC, USA.

Davis, J. & Chen, X. (2003). Calibrating pan-tilt cameras in wide-area surveillance networks, *Proceedings of the IEEE International Conference on Computer Vision*, Vol. 1, pp. 144–149, ISBN: 0-7695-1950-4, Nice, France, October 2003, IEEE Computer Society Washington, DC, USA.

Fischler, M. A. & Bolles, R. C. (1981). Random sample consensus: a paradigm for model fitting with applications to image analysis and automated cartography. *Communications of the ACM*, Vol. 24, No. 6, (June 1981) pp. 381–395, ISSN: 0001-0782.

Fry, S. N.; Bichsel, M.; Muller, P. & Robert, D. (2000). Tracking of flying insects using pan-tilt cameras. *Journal of Neuroscience Methods*, Vol. 101, No. 1, (August 2000) pp. 59–67, ISSN: 0165 0270.

Gardel, A. (2004). Calibration of a zoom lens camera with pan & tilt movement for robotics. *PhD Thesis*, Université Blaise Pascal, Clermont-Ferrand.

Hartley, R. & Zisserman, A. (2000). *Multiple View Geometry in Computer Vision*, Cambridge University Press, ISBN: 0521623049, New York, NY, USA.

Horaud, R.; Knossow, D. & Michaelis, M. (2006). Camera cooperation for achieving visual attention. *Machine Vision Application*, Vol. 16, No. 6 (February 2006) pp. 1–2, ISSN:0932-8092.

Horaud, R. & Monga, O. (1995). *Vision par ordinateur: outils fondamentaux*, chapter *Géométrie et calibration des caméras*, pp. 139–186, Hermes Science Publications, ISBN: 2-86601-481-2, Paris, France.

Jain, A.; Kopell, D.; Kakligian, K. & Wang, Y.-F. (2006). Using stationary-dynamic camera assemblies for wide-area video surveillance and selective attention, *Proceedings of the IEEE Computer Society Conference on Computer Vision and Pattern Recognition*, Vol. 1, pp. 537–544, ISBN ~ ISSN:1063-6919 , 0-7695-2597-0, New York, NY, USA, June 2006, IEEE Computer Society Washington, DC, USA.

Lavest, J.-M. & Rives, G. (2003). *Perception visuelle par imagerie vidéo*, chapter *Etalonnage des capteurs de vision*, pp. 23–58, ISBN: 978-2-7462-0662-5, Hermes Science Publications.

Lavest, J.-M.; Viala, M. & Dhome, M. (1998). Do we really need an accurate calibration pattern to achieve a reliable camera calibration?, *Proceedings of the 5th European Conference on Computer Vision*, Vol. 1, pp. 158-174, ISBN: 3-540-64569-1, Freiburg, Germany, June 1998, Lecture Notes in Computer Science , Springer.

Lowe, D. G. (1999). Object recognition from local scale-invariant features, *Proceedings of the IEEE International Conference on Computer Vision*, Vol. 2, p. 1150, , September 1999, Kerkyra, Corfu, Greece, ISBN:0-7695-0164-8, IEEE Computer Society Washington, DC, USA.

Mikolajczyk, K. & Schmid, C. (2005). A performance evaluation of local descriptors. *IEEE Transactions on Pattern Analysis and Machine Intelligence*, Vol. 27, No. 10, (June 2003) pp. 1615–1630, ISSN: 1063-6919.

Otsu, N. (1979). A threshold selection method from grey scale histogram. *IEEE Transactions on Systems Man and Cybernetics*, Vol. 9, No. 1, (January 1979) pp. 62-66, ISSN: 0018-9472.

Parzen, E. (1962). On the estimation of a probability density function and mode. *Annals of Mathematical Statistics*, Vol. 33, pp. 1065–1076.

Peuchot, B. (1992). Accurate subpixel detectors, *Proceedings of the Annual International Conference of the IEEE Engineering in Medicine and Biology Society*, Vol. 14, pp.1958-1959, ISBN: 0-7803-0785-2, October 1992, IEEE Computer Society Washington, DC, USA.

Senior, A. W.; Hampapur, A. & Lu, M. (2005). Acquiring multi-scale images by pan-tilt-zoom control and automatic multi-camera calibration, *Proceedings of seventh IEEE Workshops on Application of Computer Vision*, Vol. 1, pp. 433–438, ISBN:0-7695-2271-8-1, Breckenridge, CO, USA, January 2005, IEEE Computer Society Washington, DC, USA.

Stauffer, C. & Tieu, K. (2003). Automated multi-camera planar tracking correspondence modelling, *Proceedings of the IEEE Computer Society Conference on Computer Vision and Pattern Recognition*, Vol. 1, pp. 259-266, ISBN: 0-7695-1900-8, Madison, Wisconsin, USA, June 2005, IEEE Computer Society Washington, DC, USA.

Woo, D. & Capson, D. (2000). 3D visual tracking using a network of low-cost pan/tilt cameras, *Proceedings of the Canadian Conference on Electrical and Computer Engineering*, Vol. 2, pp. 884–889, ISBN: 0-7803-5957-7, Halifax, NS, Canada, October 2000, IEEE Computer Society Washington, DC, USA.

Zhou, X.; Collins, R. T.; Kanade, T. & Metes, P. (2003). A master-slave system to acquire biometric imagery of humans at distance, *Proceedings of the ACM international workshop on video surveillance*, pp. 113–120, ISBN:1-58113-780-X, Berkeley, California, USA, ACM New York, NY, USA.

6

Image Representation Using Fuzzy Morphological Wavelet

Chin-Pan Huang

Department of computer and communication engineering,
Ming Chuan University
Taiwan, ROC

1. Introduction

Multiresolution techniques for image processing have grown very rapidly in the last few years (Burt & Adelson, 1983, Heijmans & Goutsias, 2000, Goutsias & Heijmans, 2000). The bank-of-filters implementation method, based on the discrete wavelet transform (Heijmans & Goutsias, 2000, Mallat, 1989), has been very significant. However, in general, such an implementation has limitations due to intensive computation, sequential implementation and lack of the geometrical information in the processing. Moreover, the theoretical extension from one-dimension to two-dimension is complex (Vaidyanathan, 1993). In this paper, we propose a technique based on fuzzy mathematical morphology (Sinha & Dougherty, 1992) to implement the multiresolution analysis, which is analogous to discrete wavelet transformation, in one- and two-dimensions. Fuzzy morphological operators, similar to conventional morphological operators (Sternberg, 1983, Haralick et al., 1987), are non-linear well suited for efficient implementation using parallel computing. Moreover, they have the ability to extract geometrical information in signals by appropriate transformations. Furthermore, our method can be easily extended to two-dimension.

Rcently, Mallat et al. (Heijmans & Goutsias, 2000, Mallat, 1989) have developed a hierarchical structure to decompose and reconstruct a signal based on one-dimensional wavelet orthogonal bases. Haralick et al. (Haralick et al., 1989) and Heijmans (Heijmans & Toet, 1991) have developed a morphological sampling theory that gives a theoretical basis to reconstruct sampled signals. Its application is constrained by sampling conditions. Toet (Heijmans & Toet, 1991) has proposed morphological approach using many scales but identical shape as structuring function. This approach has some computational benefits due to using the morphological filter instead of the linear filter. Although this method takes care of the geometrical information of the processing signal it uses only a single identical shape of structure in each scale. This decomposition structure is actually same as Burt and Adelsons' (Burt & Adelson, 1983) work which has the problem of 4/3 redundant for a sample representation (Kronander). Cha (Cha & Chaparro, 1999) has proposed a morphological wavelet transform which uses conventional morphology and is suitable for positive signals. Our objective is to develop a representation taking the advantage of the methods reviewed above while overcome some problems they have.

In new paper, we propose a fuzzy morphological approach to represent one- and two-dimensional signals, that extends the geometrical decomposition (Pitas & Venetsanopoulos, 1990, Pitas, 1991, Pitas & Venetsanopoulos, 1991) of signals using multiple structuring functions (Song & Delp, 1990) into the fuzzy morphological frame. We will develop a fuzzy morphological interpolator (FMI) which along with a hierarchical pyramid-like structure yields a multiresolution signal representation called fuzzy morphological wavelet (FMW). Our algorithm is illustrated by means of experiment to one- and two-dimensional signals for signal and image analysis and shape recognition.

In section 2, we briefly review fuzzy mathematical morphology. In section 3, we develop the one-dimensional FMW representation. A one-dimensional FMI algorithm is formulated first. We consider then fast pyramid implementation for the first and second order interpolators. In section 4, we extend our algorithm to two-dimensions. We discuss a two dimensional FMI. We then develop a two-dimensional FMW representation based on one-dimensional FMI and the two-dimensional FMI. A fast two-dimensional pyramid implementation is also derived. In section 5, we apply our representation to data compression and shape recognition, demonstrating the advantage of our representation over the commonly used Daubechies' wavelet and Fourier descriptor methods. Finally, concluding remarks are given in section 6.

2. Fuzzy mathematical morphology

Recently, Sinha and Dougherty (Sinha & Dougherty, 1992) proposed to consider fuzzy set theory (Zadeh, 1965) instead of the classical set theory to develop mathematical morphology. They have in fact, obtained a new approach that considers simultaneously binary and multilevel morphology. The concept of "umbra" is not longer needed to develop the multilevel case. Morphological operations are then developed on the "fuzzy" fitting so that for crisp sets the fitting still remains characterized as either 0 or 1, but fuzzy or no-crisp sets it is possible to have a fitting characterized by a value between 0 and 1. The closer to unity, the better the fitting of the structuring element. As in the classical morphology, fuzzy morphology (Sinha & Dougherty, 1992) also consists in transforming a fuzzy set into another. Such a transformation is performed by means of a fuzzy structuring set containing the desired geometric structure.

If we let X be the universe of discourse and x be its generic element, the difference between crisp and fuzzy sets is the characteristic function of a crisp set C is defined as $\mu C{:}X \rightarrow \{0,1\}$ while the membership function $\mu F{:}X \rightarrow [0,1]$ of a fuzzy set F is defined so that $\mu F(x)$ denotes the degree to which x *belongs* to the set F. Among the different operations on fuzzy sets (Dubois & Prade, 1980), the following are important that operations will be used later:

a.   Complement operation:

$$\mu F^c(x) = 1 - \mu F(x)$$

b.   Translation of a fuzzy set F by a vector $v \in X$:

$$\mu T(F;v)(x) = \mu F(x - v)$$

c.   Reflection of a set F :

$$\mu - F(x) = \mu F(-x)$$

d. Bold union of two sets F and G :

$$\mu F \Delta G(x) = min[1, \mu F(x) + \mu G(x)] \tag{1}$$

e. Bold intersection $F \nabla G$:

$$\mu F \nabla G(x) = max[0, \mu F(x) + \mu G(x) - 1] \tag{2}$$

The degree of fitting of a set A into a set B is measured by an inclusion grade operator

$$I(A,B) = \inf_{x \in X} \mu A^c \Delta B(x)$$

$$= 1 + min\left\{0, \inf_{x \in X}[\mu B(x) - \mu A(x)]\right\} \tag{3}$$

where Δ is the bold union operator. According to the above index the degree of subsethood of two crisp sets A, B is either 0 or 1, while for fuzzy sets C and D $I(C,D) \in [0,1]$. Moreover, if $C \subseteq D$ then $I(C,D) = 1$ and in general $0 \le I(C,D) \le 1$. Using such an index (Sinha & Dougherty, 1992) has shown the erosion operation can be defined, and from it the dilation, opening and closing operators are obtained. In fact, if $f(n)$ is a multilevel and $k(n)$ is a structuring element with supports F and K and membership function $\mu f(n)$ and $\mu k(n)$ then we have

Erosion:
$$\mu f \ominus k(n) = I(T(k;n), f)$$
$$= \min_{i \in K}\{min[1, 1 - \mu k(i) + \mu f(n+i)]\} \tag{4}$$

Dilation:
$$\mu f \oplus k(n) = \mu(f^c \ominus -k)^c(n)$$
$$= \max_{i \in K}\{max[0, \mu k(i) + \mu f(n-i) - 1]\} \tag{5}$$

Opening:
$$\mu f \circ k(n) = \mu(f \ominus k) \oplus k(n)$$

Closing:
$$\mu f \bullet k(n) = \mu(f \oplus k) \ominus k(n)$$

3. Fuzzy Morphological Wavelet (FMW) representation

This representation is analogous to the multiresolution decomposition (Heijmans & Goutsias, 2000, Mallat, 1989) and the morphological wavelet transform (Cha & Chaparro, 1999). We first introduce a fuzzy morphological interpolation (FMI) and then develop the FMW representation

3.1 Fuzzy morphological interpolation

In (Haralick et al., 1989, Heijmans & Toet, 1991), it is shown that under special conditions a morphological sampling theorem permits the reconstruction of sampled signals. We show in this section, that under general conditions one can develop an interpolation algorithm to reconstruct sampled membership functions by adapting the fuzzy structuring functions. Furthermore, fast computation algorithms can be obtained.

Let $F = \{n \mid 0 \le n \le M-1\}$ be the domain of the given signal $f(n)$ and its membership function $\mu f(n)$, and let $K = \{n \mid 0 \le n \le N-1\}$ be the domain of the fuzzy structuring function $\mu k_i(n)$ and the window function $W(n)$. Assuming $M \gg N$ and $K \subset F$ we then let $S = \{m \mid m = nQ, 0 \le n \le (N-1)/Q\}$ be the sampling domain where Q is the sampling rate. Choosing the sampling rate Q and the window length N appropriately, $Q < N$, we then define the positive integer $\theta = (N-1)/Q$ as the order of the interpolator.

Assuming there is no a-priori information about the geometrical structure of the membership function, a set of fuzzy structuring functions based on ordered normalized orthogonal polynomials (e.g., the NDLO (Neuman & Schonbach, 1974)) can be used for the interpolation.

For a windowed membership function $\mu z(n)$, $n \in K$, the sampled membership function in a window is defined as

$$\mu z \big|_s (n) = \begin{cases} \mu z(n) & n \in K \cap S \\ undefined & n \in K \cap \overline{S} \end{cases} \qquad (6)$$

Thus, $\mu z \big|_s (n)$ is equal to $\mu z(n)$ every Q sample but is undefined at other samples in the window. The sampled membership function with 0 for $n \in K \cap \overline{S}$, denoted as $\mu z \big|_s^0 (n), n \in K$ is defined as

$$\mu z \big|_s (n) = \begin{cases} \mu z(n) & n \in K \cap S \\ 0 & n \in K \cap \overline{S} \end{cases} \qquad (7)$$

The function $\mu z \big|_s^0 (n)$ is equal to $\mu z(n)$ every Q sample but is 0 at other samples in the window.

Just as in (Haralick et al., 1989) we can obtain a minimum approximation (fitting from below), denoted as $\mu^v f_{min}(n)$, and a maximum approximation (fitting from above), denoted as $\mu^v f_{max}(n)$, in a window $[0, N-1]$ by considering the approximation of the signal membership function $\mu^v z_0(n), n \in K$.

3.2 General interpolation algorithm

The following algorithm provides a way to interpolate the given samples of a signal membership function in a window. It basically obtains an adaptive approximation of the windowed membership function in a recursive way. This geometric decomposition permit us, just as in the fuzzy morphological polynomial representation(Huang & Chaparro, 1995), to obtain the adaptation coefficients as well as minimum and maximum reconstructions of the membership function. Our fuzzy morphological interpolation algorithm in a window v is as follows:

1.   Frame definition:

$$\mu^v x_0 \big|_s (n) = \mu f \big|_s (n) \times W(n - vN)$$

2.   Membership function selection (min and/or max approximation)

$$\mu^v z_0 \big|_s (n) = \mu^v x_0 \big|_s (n) \ \text{and/or} \ \mu^v z_0 \big|_s (n) = \mu^v x_0^c \big|_s (n) = 1 - \mu^v x_0 \big|_s (n).$$

3.   Adaptation:

$$\mu^v z_i \big|_s \circ a_i k_i \big|_s (n) = a_i \mu k_i \big|_s (n)$$

$$\mu^v \widetilde{f}_i(n) = a_i \mu k_i(n) \tag{8}$$

4.   Residual calculation:

$$\mu^v z_{i+1} \big|_s (n) = \mu^v z_i \big|_s (n) - \mu^v \widetilde{f}_i \big|_s (n) \tag{9}$$

5.   Termination criterion: For frame v if $i = 0$ stop and consider next frame; otherwise increment i and go to step 3. If all frames are done then stop. Consider both the minimum (i.e., when $\mu^v z_0 \big|_s (n) = \mu^v x_0 \big|_s (n)$) and the maximum (i.e., when $\mu^v z_0 \big|_s (n) = 1 - \mu^v x_0 \big|_s (n)$) interpolations.

In the above, $\circ$ stands for fuzzy morphological opening, and $\mu\, y_i \big|_s$ is a sampled membership function. The minimum and maximum reconstruction interpolated membership functions in a frame, are found to be equal

$$\mu^v f_{min}(n) = \sum_{i=0}^{\theta} \mu^v \widetilde{f}_i(n) = \sum_{i=0}^{\theta} a_i \mu k_i(n) \tag{10}$$

$$\mu^v f_{max}^c(n) = \sum_{i=0}^{\theta} \mu^v \widetilde{f}_i(n) = \sum_{i=0}^{\theta} a_i \mu k_i(n) \tag{11}$$

$$\mu^v f_{max}(n) = 1 - \mu^v f_{max}^c(n) \tag{12}$$

Whether to choose a minimum or a maximum reconstruction in the vth frame is determined by comparing the corresponding error. The error of the minimum interpolations at the given sampled pixel is defined as

$$\mu^v e_{min}(n) = \left| \mu^v x_0 \big|_s^0 (n) - \mu^v f_{min} \big|_s^0 (n) \right| \tag{13}$$

The error of the maximum interpolations at the given sampled pixel is defined as

$$\mu^v e_{max}(n) = \left| \mu^v x_0 \big|_s^0 (n) - \mu^v f_{max} \big|_s^0 (n) \right| \tag{14}$$

where $\mu^v x_0(n)$ is the given membership function, $\mu^v f_{min}(n)$ and $\mu^v f_{max}(n)$ are the minimum and maximum interpolation membership functions, respectively. The reconstruction error for the minimum ($\mu^v e_{tmi}$) and maximum ($\mu^v e_{tma}$) interpolation in a window is defined as

$$\mu^v e_{tmi} = \sum_{n=0}^{N-1} \left| \mu^v x_0(n) - \mu^v f_{min}(n) \right| \tag{15}$$

$$\mu^v e_{tma} = \sum_{n=0}^{N-1} \left| \mu^v x_0(n) - \mu^v f_{max}(n) \right| \tag{16}$$

where the $\mu^v x_0(n)$ is the given membership function, $\mu^v f_{min}(n)$ and $\mu^v f_{max}(n)$ are the minimum and maximum interpolation membership functions, respectively.

3.3 Properties

The following propositions will give insight on how the FMI works and how to calculate the adaptive coefficients $\{a_i\}$. Here, we work on a frame signal only, and thus the superscript v can be omitted.

Proposition 1. Given $\mu^v z_i(n)$, $\mu^v k_i(n)$, $n \in K \cap S$, $a_i \in [0,1]$ then

$$\mu^v z_i \mid \circ a_i k_i(n) = max[0, a_i \mu k_i(n) + \mu_c - 1], \; n \in K \cap S \tag{17}$$

where $\mu_c = 1 + min\{0, min_\ell [\mu z_i(\ell) - a_i \mu k_i(\ell)]\}, \; \ell \in K \cap S$

Proposition 2. If $\mu^v z_i(n)$, $\mu^v k_i(n)$, $n \in K \cap S$, then there exists an optimum $a_i \in [0,1]$ such that $\mu^v z_i \mid \circ a_i k_i(n) = a_i \mu k_i(n)$, for $n \in K \cap S$, if and only if the following *optimum* condition is satisfied

$$\min_{\ell \in K \cap S} [\mu z_i(\ell) - a_i \mu k_i(\ell)] \mu_c = 0 \tag{18}$$

Proposition 3. If *optimum* condition is met then:

i. $\left\{ a_i = \min\limits_{\substack{\ell \in K \cap S \\ \mu k_i(\ell) \neq 0}} \left\{ \dfrac{\mu z_i(\ell)}{\mu k_i(\ell)} \right\} \right\}$

ii. $a_0 = \min\limits_{\ell \in K \cap S} [\mu z_0(\ell)]$

iii. $0 \leq a_i \leq \min\limits_{\ell \in K \cap S} \mu z_i(\ell) \leq 1$

iv. $0 \leq \mu z_{i+1}(\ell) \leq \mu z_i(\ell) \leq 1, \; \ell \in K \cap S$

According to the above properties, a_i can be computed uniquely. When using orthogonal polynomials to generate the structuring functions, we need to consider the shifted and normalized orthogonal polynomials $\mu g_i(n)$ and their complements $\mu g_i^c(n)$. To determine either $\mu g_i(n)$ or $\mu g_i^c(n)$ is to be chosen as $\mu k_i(n)$ in the representation, we calculate the corresponding reconstruction errors using equation (15) or (16) and choose the one that gives the smaller error.

3.4 First and second orderinterpolation

The first-order or linear interpolator ($\theta = 1$, $N = 3$, $Q = 2$) keeps the sampled points and provides interpolated values in between using either the minimum or maximum interpolation. The second-order or quadratic interpolator ($\theta = 2$, $N = 5$, $Q = 2$) performs similarly with an additional condition on convexity. Convexity is tested by simply checking that the middle sample of the membership function is greater than or equal to the average of the other two points. For both interpolators it is possible to develop a closed form formula for calculating the interpolated points. The following propositions provide theoretical basis for the fast computation algorithms to be discussed later. Proofs are easily obtained by following the above interpolation algorithm.

Proposition 4. For a first order interpolator the windowed sampled membership function is

$$\mu x_0 \big|_s (n) = \{ \mu f(0), *, \mu f(2) \}.$$

Using either minimum or maximum reconstruction the interpolation results is

$$\mu \overline{f}(n) = \{ \mu f(0), 0.5[\mu f(0) + \mu f(2)], \mu f(2) \}.$$

Proposition 5. For a second order interpolator the windowed sampled membership function is

$$\mu x_0 \big|_s (n) = \{ \mu f(0), *, \mu f(2), *, \mu f(4) \}.$$

Using the minimum interpolation under convexity conditions or the maximum interpolation under concavity condition the interpolation result is

$$\mu \overline{f}(n) = \{ \mu f(0), \mu \widetilde{f}(1), \mu f(2), \mu \widetilde{f}(3), \mu f(4) \} \tag{19}$$

where $\mu \widetilde{f}(1) = 0.375 \mu f(0) + 0.75 \mu f(2) - 0.125 \mu f(4)$ and
$\mu \widetilde{f}(3) = -0.125 \mu f(0) + 0.75 \mu f(2) + 0.375 \mu f(4)$.

3.5 Higher order interpolation

When the order is greater than two, we do not have the assurance that the sampled points are kept, which as we will see is very important for the FMW representation. As a solution, we use the following algorithm to select the minimum or maximum interpolation and to correct the sampled points whenever necessary. In the case when the errors $\mu^v e_{min}(n) = 0$, $\mu^v e_{max}(n) = 0$ (see equations (13) and (14) then the interpolated membership function of the vth frame be

$$\mu^v \overline{f}(n) = \mu^v f_{min}(n) \tag{20}$$

$$\mu^v \overline{f}(n) = \mu^v f_{max}(n) \tag{21}$$

In this case the given sample points are preserved. Otherwise we would have that either be $\mu^v e_{min}(n) \leq \mu^v e_{max}(n)$ in which case the interpolated membership function at the vth frame is given by

$$\mu^v \overline{f}(n) = \mu^v x_0 \big|_s^0 (n) + \mu^v f_{min} \big|_0^s (n) \tag{22}$$

or

$$\mu^V \overline{f}(n) = \mu^V x_0 \big|_s^0 (n) + \mu^V f_{max} \big|_0^s (n) \tag{23}$$

when $\mu^V e_{min}(n) > \mu^V e_{max}(n)$ and where $\mu^V x \big|_0^s (n)$ is defined as

$$\mu^V x \big|_0^s (n) = \mu^V x(n) - \mu^V x \big|_s^0 (n) = \begin{cases} 0 & n \in K \cap S \\ \mu^V x(n) & n \in K \cap \overline{S} \end{cases}$$

where the set $\overline{S}$ is a complement of set S. This will guarantee that the given samples remain unchanged and the other values are interpolated. Knowing which of these situations occurred will allow us to proceed accordingly in the synthesis. In the case third or higher order interpolation both minimum and maximum interpolation need to be done simultaneously and the comparing the errors $\mu^V e_{min}(n)$ and $\mu^V e_{max}(n)$ and decide which of (20) to (23) to use. This algorithm guarantees perfect reconstruction.

4. Fuzzy morphological wavelet implementation

The wavelet representation (Heijmans & Goutsias, 2000, Mallat, 1989) has received a great deal of attention in image processing. Its implementation is done with a bank of filters. In this section, we show a realization of the basic idea behind the wavelet representation using the FMI algorithm presented before. Our implementation involves no phase in the output and allows perfect reconstruction. We first present the FMW representation using the first and second order interpolation and then present the representation using higher order interpolators.

Let $f_0(n) = f(n)$ be the input signal and $f_i(n)$ be the ith level signal. Let $d_i(n)$ be the ith error signal corresponding to the difference between the ith level signal and its fuzzy morphological interpolated signal. Let **L** be the linear fuzzifier and **D** be the linear defuzzifier described before. Let **H** be the interpolator described in the last section. Let $\downarrow, \uparrow$ correspond to decimation and expansion, respectively.

4.1 Fast implementation case

In Figs. 1, 2, we display the analysis and synthesis procedures based on the first and second order interpolation. In the analysis, the signal $f_i(n)$ is sampled and then linearly fuzzified to get its membership function $\mu f_i \big|_s (n)$, fuzzy morphological interpolation give us $\mu \overline{f}_i(n)$ which is then linearly defuzzified to get its interpolated signal $\overline{f}_i(n)$. Decimation is then used to get the next level signal $f_{i+1}(n)$ which has the sampled points of the original signal, while $d_i(n) \downarrow$ has the error of the interpolated values. If we denote the linear fuzzifier (**L**), the membership interpolator (**H**) and linear defuzzifier (**D**) as Π_f (i.e.,

$\Pi_f(f_i \big|_s (n)) = D\{H[L(f_i \big|_s (n))]\} = \overline{f}_i(n))$ then $f_{i+1}(n) = \Pi_f(f_i \big|_s (n)) \downarrow$ where $i = 0,1,2,\cdots$. The $d_i(n)$ is the error signal of the interpolation i.e., $d_i(n) = f_i(n) - \Pi_f(f_i \big|_s (n))$

In the synthesis, we proceed in an inverse fashion. The signal $f_{i+1}(n)$ is expanded and linearly fuzzified to get $\mu f_{i+1} \uparrow (n)$, then interpolated to get $\mu \overline{f}_{i+1} \uparrow (n)$, and finally linear defuzzified to get the interpolated signal $\Pi_f(f_{i+1}(n)\uparrow) = \overline{f}_i(n)$. The synthesis signal is

$\hat{f}_i(n) = \Pi_f(f_{i+1}(n) \uparrow) + d_i(n) = f_i(n)$ indicating perfect reconstruction.

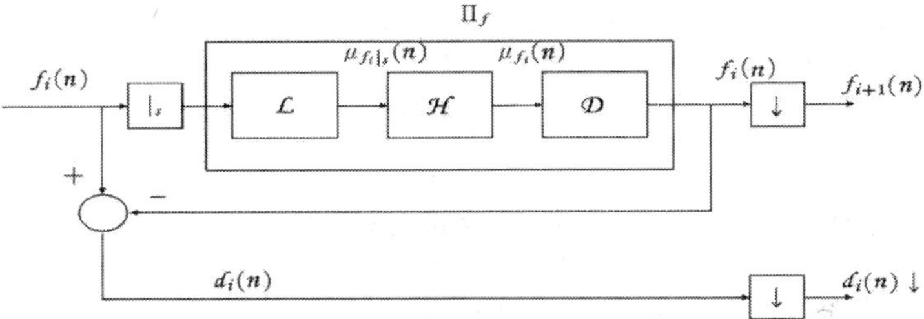

Fig.1. First and second order fuzzy morphological wavelet analysis

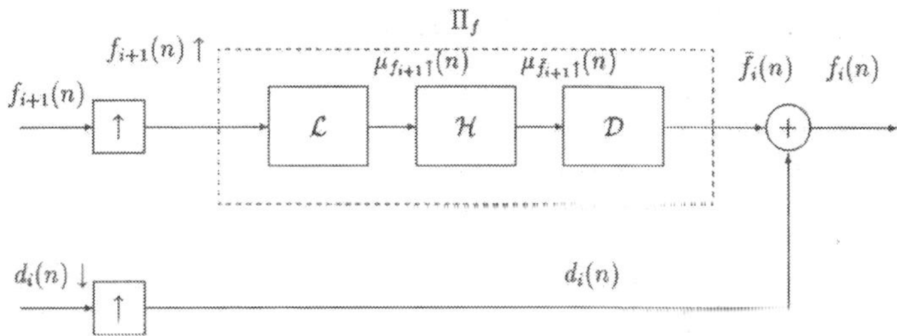

Fig. 2. First and second order fuzzy morphological wavelet synthesis

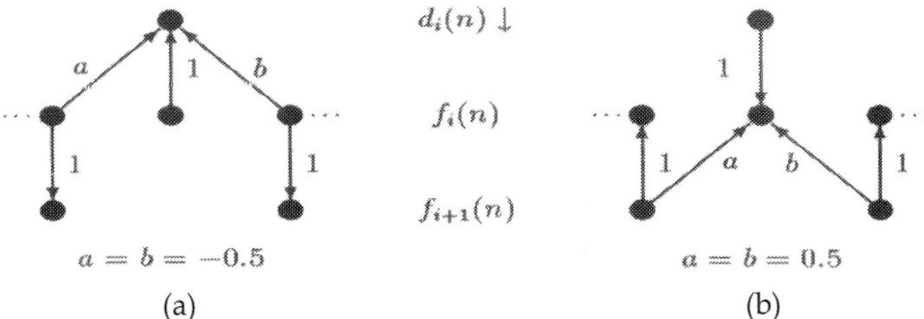

Fig. 3. FMW pyramid implementation for first-order interpolator (a) analysis (b) synthesis.

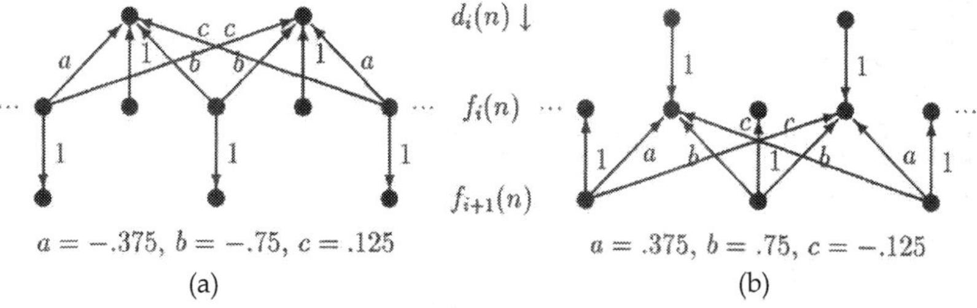

Fig. 4. FMW pyramid implementation for second-order interpolator (a) analysis (b) synthesis.

A pyramid implementation for FMW representation using first order and second order interpolators in a window is shown in Figs. 3, 4, respectively. The FMW representation can be implemented very fast.

We further derive close formulas to get the smooth and detail signal of any level from the original signal when using first- and second-order interpolator. The usefulness of these properties will be clear when the representation is applied to the shape recognition.

Proposition 6. The pyramidal components of the FMW representation using a first-order interpolator has the following properties for $n = 0,1,\cdots; i = 0,1,\cdots$.

i. $f_i(n) = f_0(2^i n);$

ii. $d_i(n) = f_0(2^i(2n+1)) - \dfrac{f_0(2^{i+1}n) + f_0(2^{i+1}(n+1))}{2};$

Proposition 7. The pyramidal components of the FMW representation using a second-order interpolator has the following properties for $n = 0,1,\cdots; i = 0,1,\cdots$.

i. $f_i(n) = f_0(2^i n);$

ii. $d_i(2n) = f_0(2^i(4n+1)) - 0.375 f_0(2^{i+1}2n) - 0.75 f_0(2^{i+1}(2n+1)) + 0.125 f_0(2^{i+1}(2n+2));$

 $d_i(2n+1) = f_0(2^i(4n+3)) + 0.125 f_0(2^{i+1}2n) - 0.75 f_0(2^{i+1}(2n+1)) - 0.375 f_0(2^{i+1}(2n+2));$

These propositions show that our smooth and detail signal of each level for the FMW representation can be obtained from the original signals and the number of pixels in the high level is smaller than that of the lower level. Notice that the first point of the smooth signal in every level is same as the first point in the original signal i.e. $f_i(0) = f_0(0), \forall i.$

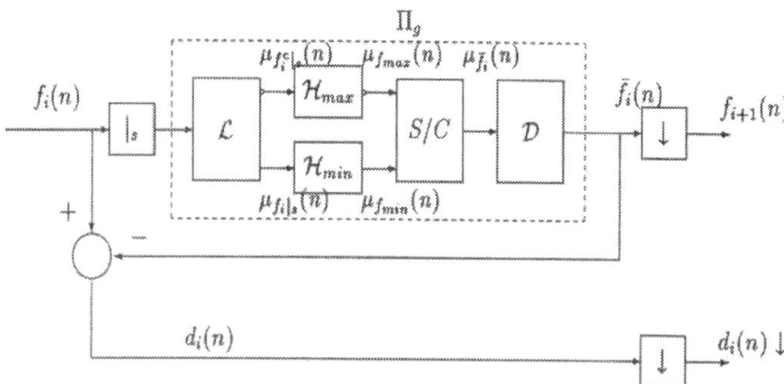

Fig. 5. Fuzzy morphological wavelet analysis (general)

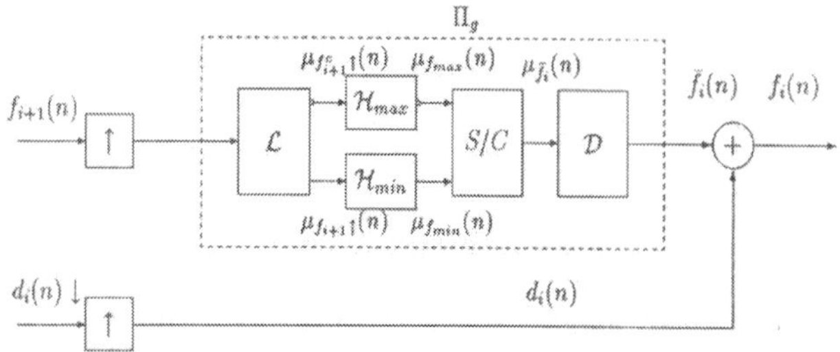

Fig. 6. Fuzzy morphological wavelet synthesis (general)

4.2 A general implementation case

When the order θ is three or more, the FMW analysis and synthesis blocks are shown in Fig. 5, 6, respectively. Perfect reconstruction is still possible as indicated before.

The interpolations are done using both minimum and maximum reconstruction, denoted as H_{max} and H_{min}, respectively. The block denoted as S/C is a selection and correction box, which is designed for choosing the maximum or minimum reconstruction as our interpolation output and correcting the error at sampled points. (see equation (20)-(23)).

5. Two-dimensional fuzzy morphological wavelet representation

The practical advantage of FMW becomes more evident in two-dimensions. The wavelet representation theory is much more complex in two-dimension than in one due to the difficulty of defining bivariate wavelets. Besides, the multirate methods in two-dimensions are more complex than in one-dimension to choose the sampling, decimation/expansion procedures. Although one-dimensional procedures can be applied when using separable two-dimensional filters, more appropriate non-separable filters make the procedure much more complex. The two-dimensional fuzzy morphological implementation is much simpler as it will be shown in the section.

5.1 Two-dimensional FMI

Unlike the one-dimensional case, there is no unique way to sample in two-dimension (Vaidyanathan, 1993). For simplicity, we consider two commonly used procedures: row/column sampling and quincunx sampling. Let $F = \{(m,n)\,|\,0 \le m \le M-1, 0 \le n \le N-1\}$ be domain of the given signal $f(m,n)$ and $S = \{(m_1,m_2)\,|\,[m_1,m_2]^T = V[n_1,n_2]^T\}$ be the sampling domain, where V is a sampling matrix in lattice transform (Vaidyanathan, 1993) and $[\cdot]^T$ is transpose operator. For a given image $f(m,n), (m,n) \in F$ the sampling signal $f\big|_s (m,n)$ is defined as

$$f\big|_s (m,n) = \begin{cases} f(m,n) & (m,n) \in F \cap S \\ undefined & (m,n) \in F \cap \overline{S} \end{cases} \tag{24}$$

where the set $\overline{S}$ is a complement of set S. In lattice transform, the row sampling matrix (Vaidyanathan, 1993) is defined as

$$V_r = \begin{bmatrix} 1 & 0 \\ 0 & 2 \end{bmatrix} \tag{25}$$

So that for a given image $f(m,n)$, the row sampling $f\big|_s (m,n)$ yields

$$\begin{pmatrix} f(0,0) & * & f(0,2) & * & f(0,4) & \cdots & f(0,N-1) \\ f(1,0) & * & f(1,2) & * & f(1,4) & \cdots & f(1,N-1) \\ \vdots & \vdots & \vdots & \vdots & \vdots & \ddots & \vdots \\ f(M-1,0) & * & f(M-1,2) & * & f(M-1,4) & \cdots & f(M-1,N-1) \end{pmatrix}$$

where * corresponds to undefined samples. Similarly, for the column sampling matrix. The quincunx sampling matrix (Vaidyanathan, 1993) is defined as

$$V_q = \begin{bmatrix} 1 & -1 \\ 1 & 1 \end{bmatrix} \qquad (26)$$

The quincunx sampling $f\downharpoonright_s (m,n)$ for the given image $f(m,n)$ is

$$\begin{pmatrix} f(0,0) & * & f(0,2) & * & f(0,4) & \cdots & f(0,N-1) \\ * & f(1,1) & * & f(1,3) & * & \cdots & * \\ f(0,0) & * & f(2,2) & * & f(2,4) & \cdots & f(0,N-1) \\ * & f(3,1) & * & f(3,3) & * & \cdots & * \\ \vdots & \vdots & \vdots & \vdots & \vdots & \ddots & \vdots \\ f(M-1,0) & * & f(M-1,2) & * & f(M-1,4) & \cdots & f(M-1,N-1) \end{pmatrix}$$

where * stands for undefined samples.

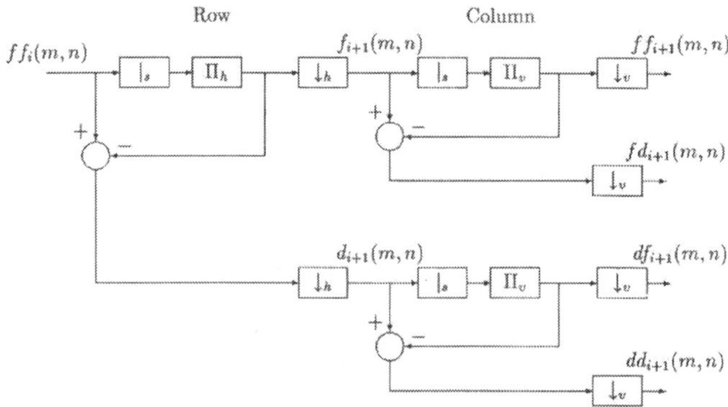

Fig. 7. FMW analysis block diagram for two-dimensional signals

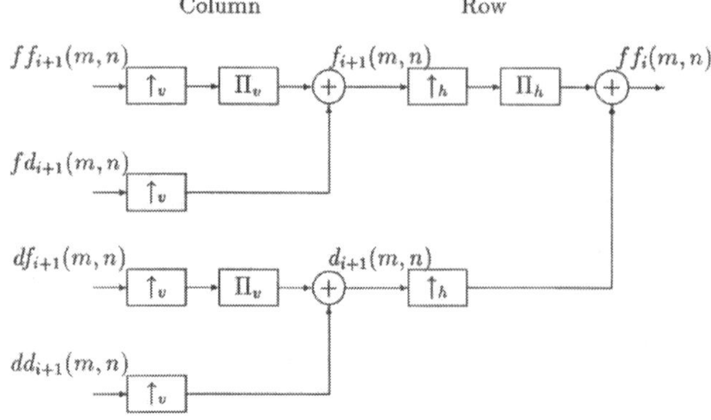

Fig. 8. FMW synthesis block diagram for two-dimensional signals

The interpolation in the row/column sampling can be done using the one-dimensional FMI discussed before. In the quincunx sampling case we extend the one-dimensional FMI algorithm using bivariate structuring functions. The structuring functions are generated as the product of one-dimensional ones. The structuring index ordering method in (Huang 1996) may be used to order these functions in two-dimensional space.

5.2 Two-dimensional FMW implementation

Figs. 7, 8 show the analysis and synthesis steps of the FMW representation using the row/column sampling. If the one-dimensional interpolator Π_x is first order we obtain the following relationship among the components for the analysis

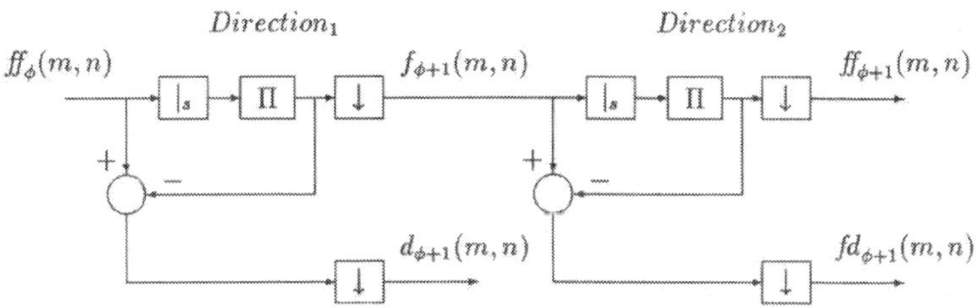

Fig. 9. TDFMW analysis block diagram with quincunx sampling

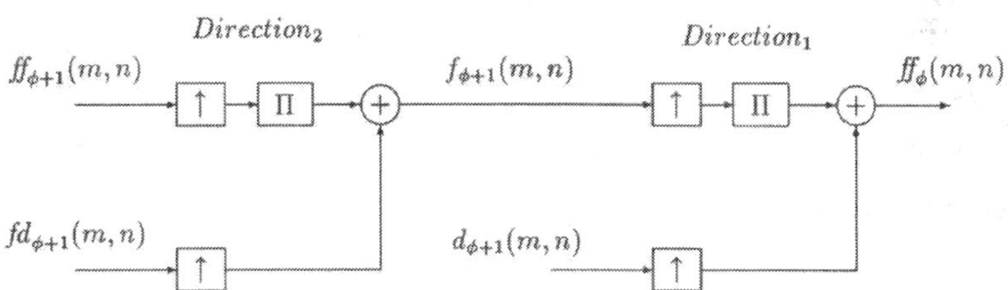

Fig. 10. TDFMW synthesis block diagram with quincunx sampling

1. $ff_{i+1}(m/2,n/2) = ff_i(m,n)$ m, n even

2. $fd_{i+1}((m-1)/2,n/2) = ff_i(m,n) - 0.5[ff_i(m-1,n) + ff_i(m+1,n)]$ m odd, n even

3. $df_{i+1}(m/2,(n-1)/2) = ff_i(m,n) - 0.5[ff_i(m,n-1) + ff_i(m,n+1)]$ m even, n odd

4.

$$df_{i+1}((m-1)/2,(n-1)/2) = ff_i(m,n) - 0.5[ff_i(m,n-1) + ff_i(m,n+1) + ff_i(m-1,n) + ff_i(m+1,n)]$$
$$+ 0.25[ff_i(m-1,n-1) + ff_i(m-1,n+1) + ff_i(m+1,n-1) + ff_i(m+1,n+1)]$$

m, n odd and for the synthesis we get that

1. $ff_i(2m,2n) = ff_{i+1}(m,n)$

2. $ff_i(2m,2n+1) = fd_{i+1}(m,n) + 0.5[ff_{i+1}(m,n) + ff_i(m,n+1)]$

3. $ff_i(2m+1,2n) = df_{i+1}(m,n) + 0.5[ff_{i+1}(m,n) + ff_{i+1}(m+1,n)]$

4.

$$ff_i(2m+1,2n+1) = dd_{i+1}(m,n) + 0.5[fd_{i+1}(m,n) + fd_{i+1}(m+1,n) + df_{i+1}(m,n) + df_{i+1}(m,n+1)]$$
$$+ 0.25[ff_{i+1}(m,n) + ff_{i+1}(m,n+1) + ff_{i+1}(m+1,n) + ff_{i+1}(m+1,n+1)]$$

Notice that if we use column/row instead of row/column sampling the signals $ff_{i+1}(m,n)$ and $dd_{i+1}(m,n)$ remain the same while $fd_{i+1}(m,n)$ and $df_{i+1}(m,n)$ are interchanged.

When the quincunx sampling is used, the Π is a TDFMI. The image is processed block by block. The structures of the analysis and synthesis are shown in Fig. 9, 10, respectively.

		Piles			Pepper		
stage		1	2	3	1	2	3
FMW	r/c	0.689	0.552	0.503	0.703	0.562	0.512
	q	0.697	0.565	0.519	0.708	0.584	0.531
WT	r/c	0.642	0.501	0.469	0.658	0.509	0.476

Table 1. Compression ratio for two-dimensional signal

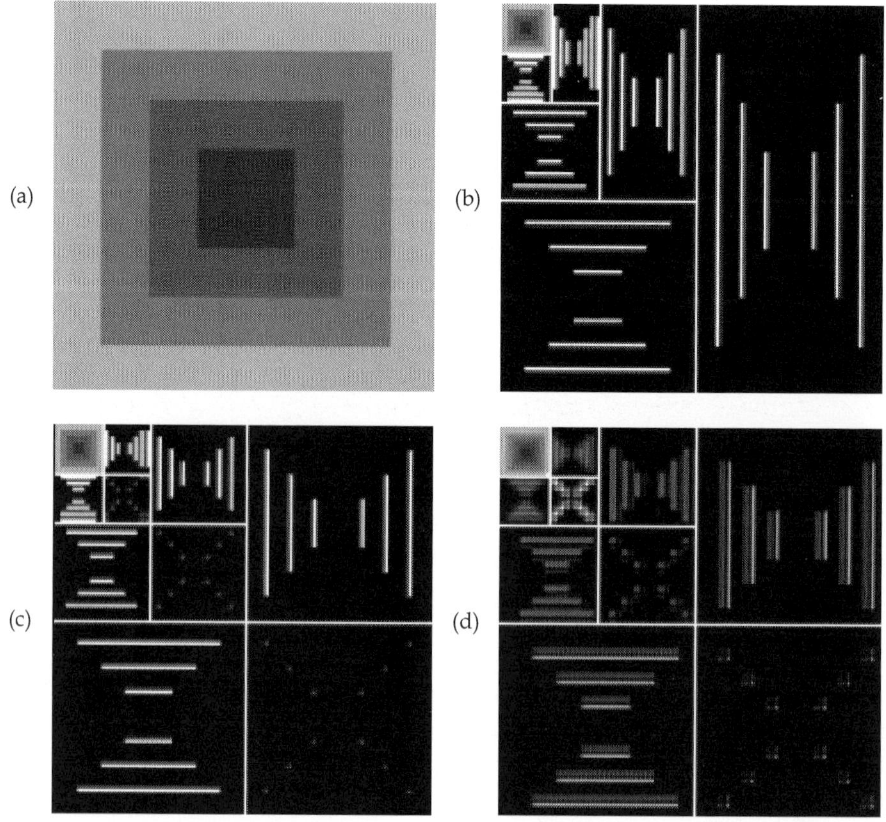

Fig. 11. Two-dimensional FMW and WT representation for artificial image: (a) original image, (b) TDFMW using quincunx sampling, (c) TDFMW using row/column sampling, (d) WT using row/column sampling.

6. Applications

To illustrate our representation, we show how it can be applied to data compression and shape recognition. We compare the data compression results with those using Daubechies' wavelet transform (Daubechies, 1988) and the shape recognition results with Fourier descriptor method (Gonzales & Woods, 2002, Persoon & Fu, 1977).

6.1 Data compression

The application of FMW representation for data compression is achieved by encoding the lowest resolution smoothed image and the detailed image. The performance of our representation is evaluated by the entropy-based compression ratio (ECR) defined as

$$\text{ECR} = \frac{\sum_{i=0}^{N-1} M_i \ell_i}{M_T \ell_T} \tag{27}$$

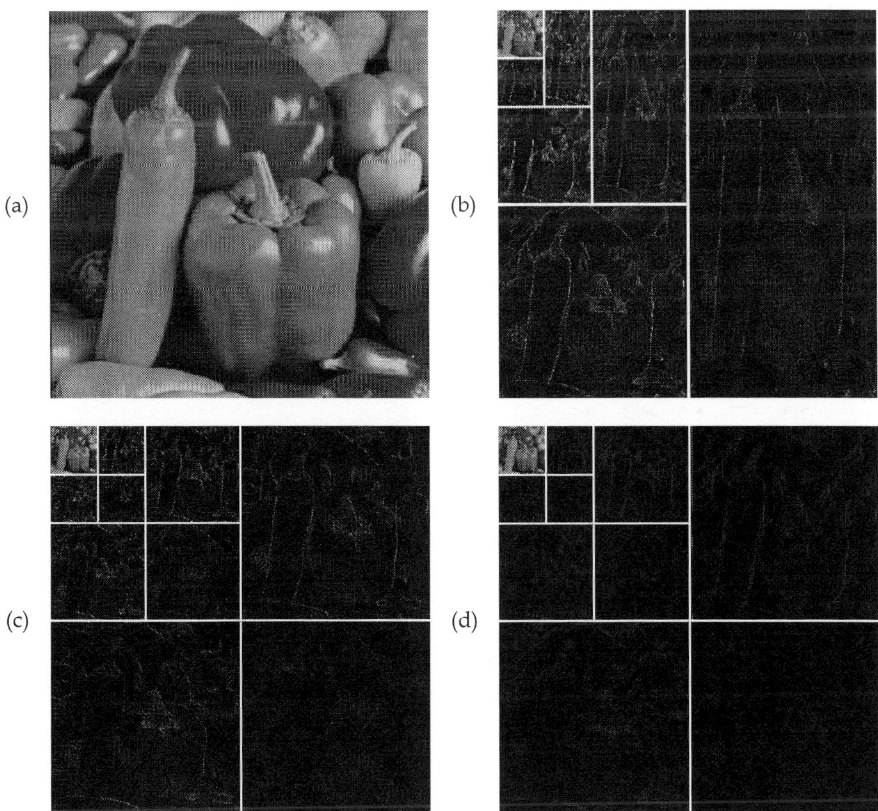

Fig. 12 Two-dimensional FMW and WT representation for pepper image

where N is the number of subblock signals, M_i is the number of samples of the subblock i, ℓ_i is the bits/sample required to code subblock i, ℓ_T is the bits/sample required for the original signal, M_T is the total number of samples of the original signal. The average bits/sample ℓ_i required to code a subblock signal is defined by entropy as:

$$\ell_i = -\sum_{j=0}^{G-1} p_j \, log_2 \, p_j \tag{28}$$

where p_j is a probability of a sample with amplitude j, G is the greatest amplitude of the signal.

The TDFMW representation is used to process the artificial (piles) and real (pepper) images. The TDFMW pyramid representations for piles image in Fig. 11 (a) are shown in Fig. 11 (b) and (c) using quincunx and row/column sampling with frame size of 3×3, respectively. For comparison, the result of WT using Daubechies' wavelet of length 8 is shown in Fig. 11 (d) using row/column sampling. The TDFMW pyramid representation for pepper image in Fig. 12 (a) are shown in Fig. 12 (b) and (c) using qucunx and row/column sampling with window size of 3×3, respectively. For comparison, the WT using Daubechies' wavelet of length 8 and row/column sampling method is shown in Fig. 12 (d). The data compression results for FMW and WT are shown in Table 1 for three stages.

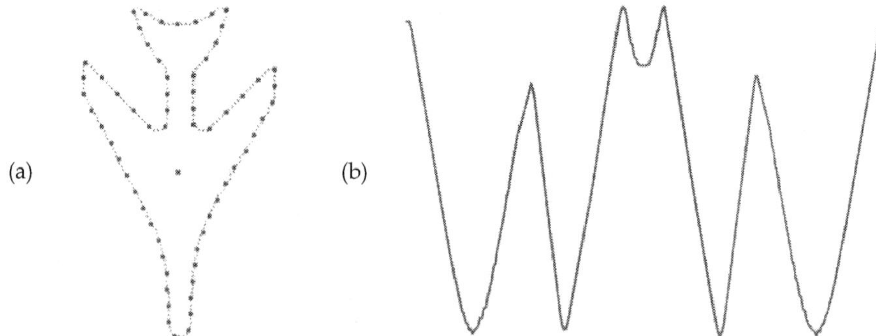

Fig. 13. Signature extraction: (a) shape sampling (b) signature

6.2 Aircraft shape recognition

In this section, we apply our FMW representation to aircraft shape recognition. The shapes are nonoverlapping, simply connected and closed planar contours, each represented by a set of boundary coordinates $\{(x(n),y(n)),n = 0,1,2,\cdots,N-1\}$. Due to closeness of the contour, the resulting observations are periodic i.e., $x(n) = x(n+N)$ and $y(n) = y(n+N)$. We compute the centroid, sample the boundary at equidistant points to calculate corresponding radii $\{r(n),n = 0,1,2,\cdots,M-1\}$ where M is usually less than N (Fig. 13(a)). These radii $\{r(n),n \in [0,M-1]\}$ form a one-dimensional signature (Fig. 13(b)) of the two-dimensional contour, which is invariant to translation, but it does depend on rotation and scaling [26].

In order to use the signature signal for shape recognition we need to overcome this dependence. When applying the FMW representations of the template and the test shapes, the linear fuzzification obviates the scaling dependence. The rotation of the object generates a signature that is shifted in a periodic way with respect to the template signature. To find a reference point we will then apply proposition 6 or 7 to do so. Basically these propositions establish that $\{f_0(0) = f_i(0), \forall i\}$, that is that at every stage in the FMW the first point is the same for every stage in the representation. By working from the lowest to highest resolution of the FMW representation, we then try to match the template signature with the test signature. The matchness is determined by the nearest-neighbor rule (Schalkoff, 1992) using the Euclidean distance between template and test signatures. This can be done by initiating the lowest resolution template signature with a known maximum and then sequentially shifting the lowest resolution test signature until either a match or a mismatch situation is encountered. If a match is obtained then we verify that it is a good match and stop, or consider the next higher resolution and repeat this process. The verification uses the detail signals of the FMW of the template and test signature.

60 test shapes used in the experiment are obtained by scaling, rotating the template shapes in Fig. 14, 10 scales from 1.0 with 0.15 increase in each step and 10 rotations from 0 with 15 degree increase in each step and then sample them to get the test signatures. As an example of the resulting test shapes is shown in Fig. 15. The shapes are all discriminated at the 6th level which contains 4 pixels. These results verify that using our FMW representation can effectively solve the scaling and rotation variant problem.

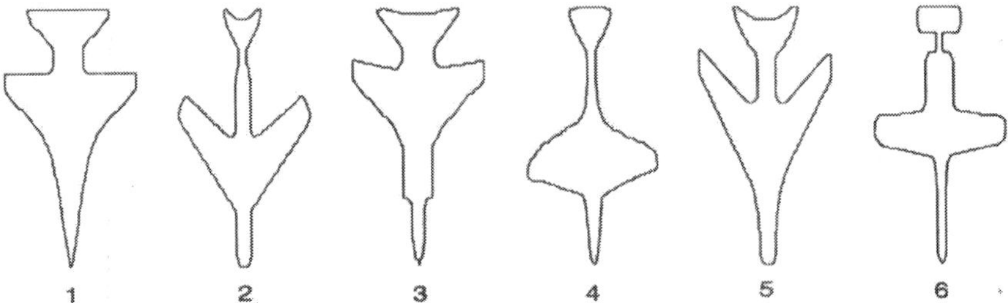

Fig. 14. Template aircraft shapes

For comparison purpose, the Fourier descriptor is used to do the same experiment. The nearest-neighbor rule is used to classify the shapes by Euclidean distance between the Fourier coefficients of the template and test shape. The results are that only the shapes without scaling and rotation is correctly classified surely when coefficients is greater than 4. The correctly classified shapes when using 16 coefficients are only 17 out of 60 (28 percent). The discrimination performance can be improved to recognize around 90 percent by the Fourier descriptor using optimal matching algorithm, however, the computation complexity will increase up to 94 times as described in (Persoon & Fu, 1977). These results show that our recognition method has better performance over the Fourier descriptor in recognizing the aircraft shapes.

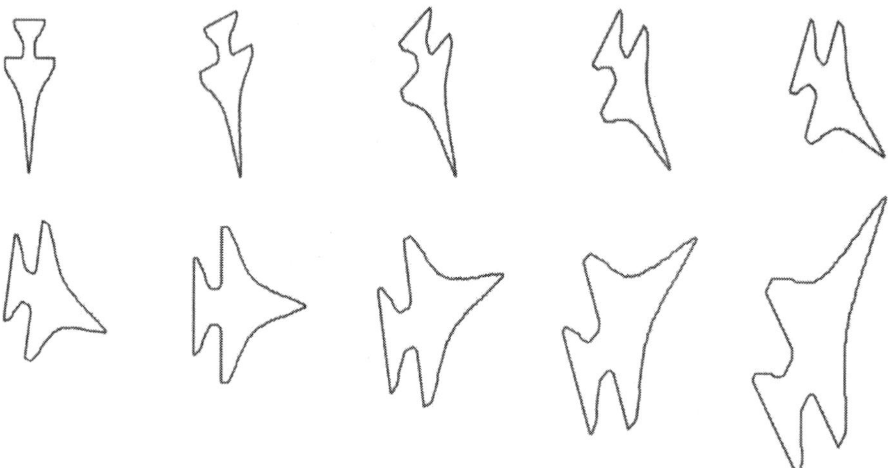

Fig. 15. Test aircraft shapes example

7. Conclusion

A novel image representation using fuzzy morphological approach has been presented in this paper. Using the fuzzy morphological operators and the minimum and maximum reconstruction we develop the fuzzy morphological interpolation (FMI) algorithm. Based on FMI and the hierarchical pyramid structure, we formulate the analysis and synthesis procedure, similar to those given by wavelet transform. Through using the fuzzy morphological approach, a signal can be efficiently represented with several additional advantages, such as lower computation complexity and easily extend to two dimensions. Furthermore, our representation can be implemented very fast by parallel. We successfully use the fuzzy mathematical morphology approach to extend the work of the Pitas and Venetsanopoulos and of Song and Delp on morphological signal representation. We have applied our representation to image analysis and shape recognition, the experimental results have shown the advantage of using our FMW representation as compare with the WT (Daubechies, 1988) and Fourier descriptor (Persoon & Fu, 1977) methods.

8. References

Bandemer, H. & Nather, W. (1992) *Fuzzy Data Analysis.* Kluwer Academic Publishers.
Burt, P. J. & Adelson, E. (1983) Laplacian pyramid as a compact image code, *IEEE Trans. on Communication*, Vol. COM-31, pp. 532-540.
Cha, H. & Chaparro, L. F. (1998) Adaptive morphological representation of signals: polynomial and wavelet methods, *Multidimensional Systems and Signal Processing.*
Daubechies, I. (1988) Orthonormal bases of compactly supported wavelets, *Comm. on Pure and Applied Math.*, vol. 41, pp. 909-996.
Dubois, D. & Prade, H. (1980)*Fuzzy Sets and systems theory and applications.* Academic Press.

Gonzales, R. & Woods, R. E. *Digital image processing.* Prentice-Hall, 2002.

Goutsias, J. & Heijmans, H. J. A. M. (2000) Nonlinear multiresolution signal decomposition schemes—PartI: Morphological pyramids, *IEEE Trans. on Image Processing,* vol. 9, pp. 1862-1876.

Haralick, R. M. Sternberg, S. R. & Zhuang, X. (1987) Image analysis using mathematical morphology, *IEEE Trans. on Pattern Analysis and Machine Intelligence.,* vol. PAMI-9, no. 4, pp. 532-550,.

Haralick, R. M. Zhuang, X. Lin, C. & Lee, J. (1989) The digital morphological sampling theorem, *IEEE Trans. Acoustics, Speech, and Signal Processing,* vol. 37, no. 12, pp. 2067-2090, 1989.

Heijmans, H. J. & Toet, A. (1991) Morphological sampling, *CVGIP-Image understanding,* vol. 54, no. 3, pp. 384-400.

Heijmans, H. J. A. M. & Goutsias, J. (2000) Nonlinear multiresolution signal decomposition schemes—PartII: morphological wavelet, *IEEE Trans. on Image Processing,* Vol. 9, 1897-1913.

Huang, C. P & Chaparro, L. F. (1995) Signal representation using fuzzy morphology, *Proc. ISUMA-NAFIPS (IEEE Computer Press 1995),* pp. 607-612.

Huang, C. P. (1996) *Signal representation using fuzzy morphology and its applications,* Ph.D. Dissertation, University of Pittsburgh, Pittsburgh, PA.

Kronander, T. (1987) Sampling of bandpass pyramid, *IEEE Trans. on Communication.,* vol. COM-35, no. 1, pp. 125-127.

Mallat, S. G.(1989) Multifrequency channel decompositions of images and wavelet models, *IEEE Trans. Acoustics, Speech, and Signal Processing,* vol. 17(12) , pp. 2091-2110.

Neuman, C. P. & Schonbach, D. I. (1974) Discrete (legendre) orthogonal polynomials – a survey, International Journal for Numerical Methods in Engineering, vol. 8, pp. 743-770.

Persoon, E. and Fu, K. S. (1977) Shape discrimination using fourier descriptors, *IEEE Trans. on Systems, Man, and Cybernatics,* vol. SMC-7, no. 3, pp. 170-179.

Pitas, I. & Venetsanopoulos, A. N. (1990) Morphological shape decomposition, *IEEE Trans. Pattern Analysis Machine Intell.,* vol. 12, pp. 38-45,

Pitas, I. & Venetsanopoulos, A. N. (1991) Morphological shape representation, in *Proc. IEEE Inter. Conf. on ASSP,* (Toronto, Canada), pp. 2381-2384.

Pitas, I. (1990) Morphological signal decomposition, in *Proc. IEEE Inter. Conf. on ASSP,* (New Mexico), pp. 2169-2172.

Schalkoff, R. (1992) *Pattern Recognition Statistical, Structural and Neural Approaches.* John Wiley and Sons.

Serra, J. (1982) *Image Analysis and Mathematical Morphology.* New York: Academic.

Sinha, D. & Dougherty, E. R. (1992) Fuzzy mathematical morphology, *Journel of Visual Communication and Image Processing,* pp. 286-302.

Song, J. & Delp, E. J. (1990) The analysis of morphological filters with multiple structuring elements," Computer Vision, Graphics, and Image Processing, vol. 50, pp. 308--328.

Sternberg, S. R. (1983) Biomedical image processing, *IEEE Computer Mag.,* vol. 16, pp. 22-34.

Vaidyanathan, P. (1993) *Multirate Systems and Filter Banks,* Prentice Hall.

Zadeh, L. A. & Fu, K. S. & et al., ed. (1975) *Fuzzy Sets and Their Applications to Cognitive and Decision Processes*. Academic Press,Inc..

Zadeh, L. A. (1965) Fuzzy sets, *Information and Control*, vol. 8, pp. 338--353.

7

Multidimensional Texture Analysis for Unsupervised Pattern Classification

K. Hammouche[1] and J.-G. Postaire[2]
[1]Université Mouloud Mammeri, Département d'Automatique Tizi Ouzou
[2]Université des Sciences et Technologies de Lille –
LAGIS 59655 VILLENEUVE D'ASCQ Cedex
[1]Algeria
[2] France

1. Introduction

Clustering techniques aim to regroup a set of multidimensional observations, represented as data points scattered through a N-dimensional data space, into groups, or clusters, according to their similarities or dissimilarities. Each point corresponds to a vector of observed features measured on the objects to be classified. Among the different approaches that have been developed for cluster analysis [Jain et al., 1999; Theodoridis & Koutroumbas, 2003; Tran et al., 2005; Xu & Wunsch, 2005; Filipone et al., 2008], we consider the statistical approach [Devijver & Kittler, 1983]. In this framework, many clustering procedures have been proposed, based on the analysis of the underlying probability density function (pdf). The high density of data points within the clusters gives rise to modal regions corresponding to the modes of the pdf that are separated by valleys of low densities [Parzen, 1962].

Independently from cluster analysis, a large amount of research effort is devoted to image segmentation. Starting from an unstructured collection of pixels, we generally agree about the different regions constituting an image due to our visual grouping capabilities. The most important factors that lead to this perceptual grouping are similarity, proximity and connectedness. More precisely, segmentation can be considered as a partitioning scheme such that:

- Every pixel of the image must belong to a region,
- The regions must be composed of contiguous pixels,
- The pixels constituting a region must share a given property of similarity.

These three conditions can be easily adapted to the clustering process. Indeed, each data point must be assigned to a cluster, and the clusters must be composed of neighbouring data points since the points assigned to the same cluster must share some properties of similarity. Considering this analogy between segmentation and clustering, several image segmentation procedures based on the gray-level function analysis have been successfully adapted to detect the modes or to seek the valleys of the pdf for pattern classification purpose [Botte-Lecocq et al., 2007].

In this framework, the underlying pdf is generally estimated on a regular discrete array of sampling points [Postaire & Vasseur, 1982]. The idea of using a pdf estimation for mode seeking is not new [Parzen, 1962] and in very simple situations, the modes can be detected by thresholding the pdf at an appropriate level, using a procedure similar to image binarization [Weszka, 1978]. A "mode" label is associated with each point where the underlying pdf is above the threshold. Otherwise, the corresponding point is assigned a "valley" label.

However, in practical situations, it can be difficult, or even impossible, to select an appropriate global threshold to detect the significant modes. A solution for improving this simple scheme is to consider the spatial relationships among the sampling points where the underlying pdf is estimated, rather than making a decision at each point independently of the decisions at other points. Probabilistic labeling, or relaxation, is a formalism through which object labels are iteratively updated according to a compatibility measure defined among the neighboring labels. This approach, which has been successfully applied to image processing [Dankner, 1981], has been adapted to cluster analysis to reduce local ambiguities in the mode/valley discrimination process [Touzani & Postaire, 1988].

The segmentation of an image can also be considered as a problem of edge detection [Davis, 1975]. Similarly, in the clustering context, a mode boundary can be localized at important local changes in the pdf. It can be detected by means of generalized gradient operators designed to perform a discrete spatial differentiation of the estimated pdf [Touzani & Postaire, 1989]. Although these spatial operators enhance substantially the discontinuities that delineate the modes, a relaxation labeling process, similar to the one used for thresholding, can be necessary for mode boundary extraction [Postaire & Touzani, 1989].

Beside procedures based on the concepts of similarity and discontinuity, mathematical morphology has proven to be a valuable approach for image segmentation. This theory has been adapted to cluster analysis by considering the sets of multidimensional observations as mathematical discrete binary sets [Postaire et al., 1993]. Binary erosions and dilations of these discrete sets eliminate irrelevant details in the shapes of the clusters without geometric distortions [Botte-Lecocq & Postaire, 1991]. Multivalue morphological operations, such as numerical erosions, dilations and homotopic thinnings have also been defined for processing multidimensional pdf using the umbra concept [Sbihi & Postaire, 1995]. With these operators, the clusters are delineated by means of the watershed transform [Benslimane et al., 1996].

Modeling spatial relationships between pixels by means of Markov random fields has proved to be relevant to the image segmentation problem [Manjunath & Chellappa, 1991; Panjwani & Healey, 1995]. The Markovian approach has been adapted to the mode detection problem in cluster analysis. The hidden field containing the "mode" and the "valley" labels is derived from the observable field representing the data set by means of the estimation-maximisation algorithm combined with the maximum a posteriori mode criterion [Sbihi et al., 2000; Moussa et al., 2008] .

All the above-mentioned clustering methods tend to generalize bi-dimensional procedures initially developed for image processing purpose. But, even though texture properties have been intensively used to solve image segmentation problems, they have not been extended to pattern classification problems. Following the main idea of adapting image processing techniques to cluster analysis, the objective of this chapter is to show how the texture concept can be used in the framework of clustering. The basic idea behind this new approach is the characterization of the local spatial distribution of the data points in the multidimensional data space in terms of textures [Hammouche et al., 2006].

Similarly to texture segmentation, the approach consists first in selecting a set of texture features that characterize the local multidimensional texture around each sampling point of the data space. These multidimensional textures, which reflect the spatial arrangement of the data points, are then classified on the basis of these features. The data points with similar local textures are aggregated in the data space to define compact connected components of homogeneous textures. Some of these multidimensional domains of uniform texture are finally considered as the cores of the clusters.

The chapter is organized as follows. We first describe the discretization process of the input data that yields an array of sampling points well conditioned for multidimensional texture analysis (Section 2). We then introduce the multidimensional texture concept itself, as an alternative to describe the spatial distribution of observations through the data space (Section 3). Such textures are locally characterized by a number of parameters that can be extracted from co-occurrence matrices or from sum and difference histograms, defined as straightforward generalizations of the tools used in textured image processing.

The mode detection strategy is based on the assumption that the texture is homogeneous within the modes of the data distribution, and different from the texture in the valleys between the clusters. Hence, similarly to segmentation of textured images, the sampling points where the local underlying texture is evaluated are classified into different texture classes in order to partition the data space into domains with homogeneous texture properties (Section 4). The determination of the set of the most discriminating texture parameters among all those that are available is based on a performance-dependent feature selection scheme (Section 5).

Many examples are presented to demonstrate the efficiency of this clustering strategy based on multidimensional texture analysis (Section 6). As the computational load could to be prohibitive for data sets of high dimensionality and large size, a specific attention is devoted to the implementation of the clustering procedure in order to improve the computation speed (Section 7).

2. Discretization of the data set

In order to adapt texture analysis tools to clustering, it is necessary to introduce a discrete array of sampling points [Postaire & Vasseur, 1982]. Let us consider Q observations $X_q = [x_{q,1}, x_{q,2}, ..., x_{q,n}, ..., x_{q,N}]$, $q=1, 2, ..., Q$, where $x_{q,1}, x_{q,2}, ..., x_{q,n}, ..., x_{q,N}$ are the N coordinates of the observation X_q in the data space. The range of variation of each component of the multivariate observations is normalized to the interval $[0,S]$, where S is an integer, by means of the transformation:

$$x'_{q,n} = S \frac{x_{q,n} - \min\limits_{q=1}^{q=Q}\left\{x_{q,n}\right\}}{\max\limits_{q=1}^{q=Q}\left\{x_{q,n}\right\} - \min\limits_{q=1}^{q=Q}\left\{x_{q,n}\right\}}.$$

Let $X'_q = [x'_{q,1}, x'_{q,2}, ..., x'_{q,n}, ..., x'_{q,N}]^T$, $q=1, 2, ..., Q$,be the Q new observations in the normalized data space. Each axis of this space is partitioned into S exclusive and adjacent intervals of unit width. This discretization defines an array of S^N hypercubes of unit side length. The centers of these hypercubes constitute a regular lattice of sampling points denoted P_r , $r = 1, 2, ..., S^N$. The unit hypercubic cell centered at point P_r is denoted $H(P_r)$. It is defined by its coordinates $h_{r,1}, h_{r,2}, ..., h_{r,n}, ..., h_{r,N}$, which are the integer parts of the coordinates of its center P_r . The qth normalized observation X'_q falls into the unit cell $H(P_r)$ of coordinates $h_{r,n} = \mathrm{int}(x'_{q,n})$, $n = 1, 2, ..., N$, where $\mathrm{int}(x'_{q,n})$ denotes the integer part of the real number $x'_{q,n}$.

Taking the integer parts of the coordinates of all the available normalized observations yields the list of the non-empty cells whose coordinates are defined on the set Z^{+N} . If several observations fall into the same cell, this one appears many times in the list of non-empty cells. It is easy to determine the number $q[H(P_r)]$ of observations that fall into the hypercubic cell of center P_r by counting the number of times the cell $H(P_r)$ appears in that list. As this number can be considered as proportional to a rough estimate of the local density of observations, it will be referred as the "density" $W(P_r) = q[H(P_r)]$ associated to the point P_r in what follows. Subsequently, the distribution of the data points can be approximated on the discrete multi-dimensional array of points P_r . The result of this sampling procedure is a multidimensional regular array of discrete integers in the range $[0, G]$, where G is the maximum value of $W(P_r)$, $r = 1, 2, ..., S^N$, that is well conditioned for multidimensional texture analysis. Fig. 1 shows a raw data set of bi-dimensional observations (cf. Fig 1(a)) and the corresponding array of discrete densities obtained for $S = 25$ (cf. Fig 1(b)).

3. Multidimensional texture characterization

To illustrate the basic ideas behind the proposed approach, let us consider the bi- and three-dimensional uniform random distributions of data points of Fig. 2. A close visual attention to this figure shows that the arrangement of the observations appears to be more or less coarse and more or less sparse, depending on the density of data points in the bi- or the three-dimensional data spaces. Thanks to the capacities of perception of the human visual system, it is easy to distinguish various random textures associated with these distributions. These considerations led to consider the texture as a property of the data points distribution. In this chapter, it is assumed that the texture tends to be uniform within the core associated with each cluster, so that these cores can be searched as domains of the data space characterized by a relative homogeneity of suitable texture descriptors.

When considering the examples of Fig. 2, it is clear that structural models based on primitive placement rules cannot satisfactorily describe the texture of the distribution of the data points. Therefore, one is led to consider the textural properties in terms of statistical models and the main difficulty is the selection of a set of relevant features to describe the properties of the spatial distribution of the data. A number of textural parameters have been proposed in the image processing literature, derived from autoregressive models [Comer & Delp, 1999], Markov random fields models [Cross & Jain, 1983], Gabor filters [Jain & Farrokhnia, 1991], wavelet coefficients [Porter & Canagarajah, 1996], fractal geometry [Keller & Crownover, 1989] and spatial gray-level dependence analysis [Haralick, 1978]. We have chosen to generalize the concepts of co-occurrence matrices and of sum and difference

4. Cluster core extraction

4.1 Texture classification

Similarly to image segmentation, it is expected that sampling points with similar texture properties could be aggregated in the data space to detect the clusters in the data.

When the sampling points are characterized by a set of texture features, they can be represented as feature vectors in a multidimensional feature space. Texture classification consists in assigning the sampling points of the discrete data space to different texture classes defined in the feature space. This is an unsupervised classification problem since no *a priori* knowledge about the feature vectors associated with the textures to be identified is available. A simple solution is to use the basic K-means algorithm where the desired number of classes of feature vectors has to be specified [Macqueen, 1967]. The ability of varying the number of expected classes makes it possible to give some insight into the significance of the clusters that can be identified within the data.

Fig. 5 shows the domains of homogeneous textures associated with the discrete data set of Fig.1(b) when the K-means algorithm requires 2, 3 and 4 classes of different textures characterized by means of co-occurrence matrices. The texture discrimination is performed in a 2-dimensional feature space defined by two features, namely the homogeneity f_3 and the correlation f_4 of table 1, with $S=25$. When two classes are required, the two domains correspond to the cluster cores and the valleys, respectively (cf. Fig. 5(a)). When the sampling points are assigned to 3 classes of textures, one of them corresponds to the cores; the second to their boundaries and the last one to the valleys (cf. Fig. 5(b)). In the case of 4 classes, Fig. 5(c) shows that the cores are surrounded by concentric domains corresponding to different distribution characteristics that are obviously linked to the local data point densities.

We have kept the parameter S and the two texture features unchanged in order to show the influence of the required number of texture classes on the resulting domains of homogeneous textures. A procedure to optimize the value of S, to select an appropriate set of texture features and to determine the number of texture classes will be presented in section 5.

4.2 Core extraction

Under the assumption that the cluster cores are multidimensional domains with homogeneous textures, it is expected that the hypercubes centered on the sampling points assigned to the same class of texture give rise to connected components in the data space. These components can be extracted by means of an aggregation procedure where two hypercubes whose centers belong to the same class of texture are assigned to the same component if they have at least one point in common. Small components resulting from this aggregation procedure may correspond to non significant domains with only a few data points. Therefore any domain containing less than 5% of the total number Q of observations is discarded.

Among the remaining components, those corresponding to the cores of the clusters are expected to be more compact than those corresponding to their boundaries or to the valleys between them. Hence, they can be discriminated from other components by analyzing their compactness defined as:

$$C = \frac{\left[\text{total number of hypercubes}\right]}{\left[\text{number of boundary hypercubes}\right]^N}$$

This compactness, which is as much as high as the component is compact, depends mainly on the dimensionality and on the structure of the data. In practice, the selection of the domains with a compactness higher than 50% of the highest compactness value among all the detected domains has proved to be a good strategy to identify the cluster cores [Hammouche et al., 2006].

Table 3 indicates the compactness of the domains resulting from the aggregation of the connected sampling points of Fig. 5. It is clear that the cluster cores are much more compact than the other domains. Cluster core detection is straightforward by simple thresholding of the compactness. Fig. 6 shows the cores identified among the domains of homogeneous texture of Fig. 5.

Due to irregularities in the distribution of the data points, especially for small data sets, the boundaries of the selected domains may present irrelevant details. In such situations, multidimensional binary morphology has proved to be an efficient solution to eliminate details in the data structure without changing the global shape of unsuppressed domains [Botte-Lecocq & Postaire, 1991]. A classical closing-opening operation, using a hypercubic structuring element of side length equal to 3, generally yields regularly shaped cluster cores.

Finally, many supervised classification procedures can be used to assign the observations to the clusters attached to the detected cores. One solution is to use the observations falling into the cores as prototypes. The remaining observations are assigned to the cluster attached to their nearest neighbor among these prototypes. They are assigned one by one to the clusters in a specific order depending on their distances to the prototypes. At each step of this procedure, we consider the distances between all the unassigned observations and all the prototypes. The smallest among these distances indicates the specific observation that must be assigned to the cluster attached to its nearest neighbor. It is integrated within the set of prototypes defining this cluster. This updating rule is iterated until all the observations are classified [Botte-Lecocq & Postaire, 1994].

5. Algorithm tuning and feature selection

The performance of the above described algorithm depends mainly on the adjustment of the discretization parameter S and on the relevance of the chosen texture features.

5.1 Discretization tuning

Let us first consider the effect of the resolution of the discretization process. In fact, the adjustment of S depends on the sample size Q, on the dimensionality N of the data and on the structure of the distribution of the observations. It can be expected that, when true clusters exist, stable connected subsets of data points with similar texture properties appear for a wide range of values of S. Based on this assumption, the adjustment of S can be governed by the concept of cluster stability [Eigen et al., 1974]. Choosing such a parameter in the middle of the largest range where the number of detected clusters remains constant, and different from one, has proved to be a good procedure to optimize a number of clustering algorithms when nothing is *a priori* known about the structure of the distribution of the observations [Postaire & Vasseur, 1981]. Note that the larger the range, the more reliable is the tuning procedure.

5.2 Feature selection

In the framework of multidimensional texture analysis, the key problem is the selection of a set of suitable texture features. For choosing relevant features while reducing the dimensionality of the texture classification problem, we propose a performance-dependent feature selection scheme which is directly related to the above mentioned concept of cluster stability. The effectiveness of a subset of features is evaluated by means of the width of the largest range of values of the discretization parameter S leading to the appropriate number of detected cluster cores. As mentioned at the end of § 5.1, the larger this range, the more reliable is the number of detected cores. This criterion is used to select a set of relevant features among the available ones by means of a sequential forward selection technique [Siedlecki & Sklansky, 1988].

To evaluate the relative relevance of M features $f_1, ..., f_m, ..., f_M$, we consider the feature subspaces $R^1, ..., R^m, ..., R^M$, taking into consideration an increasing number of texture features, from one to M. The algorithm starts with the M possible R^1 spaces. The feature which maximizes the range of values of S corresponding to a stable number of detected cores, different from one, is the first selected feature. This feature is combined, in a R^2 feature space, with each of the $M-1$ remaining ones. The corresponding $M-1$ lengths of the stable ranges for S are then determined and the pair of features that maximizes the length is kept.

When m features out of M have been chosen, the algorithm proceeds in the R^{m+1} feature space of $m+1$ dimensions to select the $(m+1)^{th}$ feature that maximizes the length of the range of S when combined with the m previously chosen features. This procedure is iterated until the M features have been ordered by diminishing relevance. The sequence $L(m)$ of length values thus obtained allows selecting a subset of relevant features within the set of M features. These salient features are those that correspond to the starting increasing phase of the length values in the sequence $L(m)$. All the features that follow the first decrease in the sequence $L(m)$ are discarded.

To demonstrate the efficiency of the proposed feature selection technique, we use the bi-dimensional data set of Fig. 1 constituted of three Gaussian clusters. The length $L(m)$ of the longest range of values of S where the same number of cluster cores is detected by the clustering procedure is plotted against the number m of selected features (cf. Fig. 7). The feature selected at each step is indicated at the corresponding point of the plot. The series $(f_4, f_5, f_1, f_3, f_6, f_2, f_7)$, $(f_5, f_1, f_2, f_4, f_7, f_3, f_6)$ and $(f_5, f_2, f_6, f_4, f_3, f_1, f_7)$ represent the 7 first selected features among the 13 computed from the co-occurrence matrices, ordered by decreasing relevance when 2, 3 and 4 classes of textures are required by the K-means algorithm, respectively. As expected, the number of required classes influences the feature selection. When 2 classes are required, the selected features are f_4, f_5 and f_1 since $L(m)$ begins to decrease when f_3 is selected (cf. Fig. 7(a-1)). With 3 classes of textures, the plot of Fig. 7(b-1) shows that the two first features f_5 and f_1 are selected for detecting the 3 clusters. When 4 classes of textures are used, it appears that only the first feature f_5 is selected for detecting the 3 clusters (cf. Fig. 7(c-1)). Fig. 7(a-2), 7(b-2) and 7(c-2) show the ordered features extracted from density sum and difference histograms when 2, 3 and 4 classes of textures are required by the K-means algorithm, respectively.

5.3 Number of texture classes

The next parameter that remains to be adjusted is the number of texture classes required by the K-means algorithm. This number is not determined automatically by the basic, but well controlled, version of the algorithm used in this work. In fact, the concept of cluster stability allows specifying this number by selecting the number of texture classes that leads to the longest range of variation of S where the number of detected cores remains constant. Fig. 7 shows that this wider range is reached when the textures are assigned to two classes with the three features f_4, f_5 and f_1 extracted from the COM and with the five features f_9, f_3, f_6, f_1 and f_4 extracted from the density SDH.

5.4 Hypercubic neighborhood size

The neighborhoods used to determine the local values of the texture features have been defined as hypercubes of side length equal to 3 (cf. § 2.2). But we could have used larger neighborhoods constituted of $(2h+1)^N$ unit cells centered at the sampling points. We have analyzed the effect of the parameter h on the behavior of the algorithm. For each neighborhood size varying from h =1 to h =4, we have selected the relevant texture features as explained in § 5.2 to classify the bi-dimensional data of figure 1(a), asking always for two texture classes. Table 4 indicates the largest ranges of the discretization parameter S where the numbers of detected clusters remain constant for each neighborhood size. It appears that the largest of these ranges are obtained for h =1 . Furthermore, beside being the best choice in terms of reliability of the results, the choice of the minimal neighborhood size (h =1) reduces the computation time while improving the sensitivity of the procedure to local texture properties.

6. Experimental results

The following examples have been chosen to provide some insight into the behavior of the proposed texture based clustering procedure and to demonstrate the interest of this approach for pattern classification.

6.1 Example 1

The first example illustrates all the steps of the algorithm and demonstrates the ability of the procedure to detect clusters of unequal weights. The data set is presented in Fig. 8(a). It is composed of 950 bidimensional observations drawn from the four normal distributions of unequal weights specified in table 5.

The local texture features are computed from the co-occurrence matrices, and, for comparison, from the density sum and difference histograms. In order to tune the algorithm, the number of required texture classes is varied from 2 to 4. In the two cases, the largest range where the number of detected clusters remains constant appears for two classes of textures. It corresponds to a partition of the data set into four clusters (cf. Figs. 8(c-1) and 8(c-2)). With the density SDH based texture features, the largest range of S where the number of detected cores remains constant is [13-38] (Fig. 8(c-2)). It is slightly larger than that obtained with the COM texture features, which is [26-50] (Fig. 8(c-1)).

Figs. 8(d-1) and 8(d-2) show the discrete data sets obtained for S = 38, which is the middle of the range associated with the co-occurrence features, and for S = 26 when the features are extracted from density sum and difference histograms, respectively. The four cores, detected as domains of homogeneous textures, are displayed in Fig. 8(e-1) and 8(e-2). The texture features extracted from the COM are f_1, f_4, f_3 and those extracted from the density SDH are f_1, f_9, f_5 .

The result of the classification is shown in Fig. 8(b). Table 5 summarizes the statistics of the four detected clusters. The performance of the classifier is measured by the classification error-rate, estimated as the ratio of the number of misclassified observations to the total number of observations. The error-rates obtained with the two proposed algorithms are identical and equal to 3.15% . In this example, the classes do not overlap too much and the actual error-rate is very close to the theoretical minimum error-rate achieved by use of the Bayes decision rule associated with the true statistics of the data set, which is equal to 2.63%. The difference between these two error-rates corresponds to only five observations misclassified out of over 950.

6.2 Example 2

The major difficulties in cluster analysis are with non spherical clusters, bridges between clusters and non linearly separable clusters. The bivariate data set of Fig. 9(a) has been generated keeping these well-known difficulties in mind. It is composed of three populations of 1000 data points each drawn as:

$$x_1 = A_1 \cos \Theta + B_1$$

$$x_2 = A_2 \cos \Theta + B_2$$

where Θ is a normal random variable with mean m and standard deviation s, and where B_1 and B_2 are normal random variables with means μ and variances σ (cf. Table 6).

For this example, the largest range of S where the three clusters have been identified is [24-50] when the co-occurrence features are used (cf. Fig. 9(c-1)), while it is [24-46] for the features extracted from density SDH (cf. Fig. 9(c-2)). Figs. 9(d-1) and 9(d-2) show the discrete data sets obtained for $S=37$ and $S=35$ respectively, i.e. the middles of these ranges that are very similar.

The three detected cores are displayed in Fig. 9(e-1) and 9(e-2). Two texture features, namely f_2 and f_6 , have been extracted from the COM to obtain the two cores shown in Fig. 9(e-1) and four texture features extracted from density SDH, namely f_6, f_3, f_1 and f_2 , have been selected to obtain the two cores shown in Fig. 9(e-2). The classification results achieved with the two algorithms are identical. They are shown in Fig. 9(b). The error-rate obtained with the texture clustering procedures is 1.12%, whereas it reaches 6.3% with the ISODATA algorithm [Ball & Hall, 1965]. This example shows that when central points cannot represent the clusters globally, the texture based approach, which takes into account the local properties of the distribution of the input data, performs much better than algorithms dedicated to globular clusters.

6.3 Example 3

We now present a multidimensional case, which demonstrates the ability of the procedure to identify interlaced clusters for data of higher dimensionality. The data shown in Fig. 10(a) consists of two clusters generated as circular torus formed by the rotation of a plane circular Gaussian distribution about an axis in the plane of that distribution. These two torus are interlaced as the rings of a chain.

The cluster cores detected by the clustering procedure based on the selected co-occurrence features f_3 and f_4 with two texture classes and with $S=34$, which is the middle of the [17-50] largest range where the number of detected clusters remains constant, are presented in Fig. 10(c). Figure 10(d) shows the two cluster cores detected with the features f_9, f_6, f_1, and f_8 extracted from the density sum and difference histograms with two texture classes and with $S=32$, i.e. the middle of the [14-50] largest range where the number of detected clusters remains constant. The classification results achieved with the two algorithms are identical. They are shown in Fig. 10(b). The error-rate associated with the two texture clustering procedures is 0.1% whereas it reaches 12.17% with the ISODATA algorithm. This result demonstrates the effectiveness of the approach in a non trivial situation.

7. Computational load

The proposed texture clustering algorithms are based on the same 3 steps scheme:
1. Data conditioning
2. Texture characterization
3. Clustering based on texture properties.

In the first data conditioning step, the distribution of the data points is approximated by the discrete multi-dimensional histogram constituted of S^N cells. Thanks to the fast algorithm proposed in [Postaire & Vasseur, 1982], the number of elementary operations required by this procedure is NQ.

In the last clustering step, the sampling points where the local underlying texture is evaluated are first assigned to different texture classes using the K-means algorithm that requires RKt operations, where R is the number of non-empty hypercubes, K is the number of texture classes and t is the number of iterations necessary for the algorithm to converge.

Then, the connected components are extracted by means of an aggregation procedure where two hypercubes that belong to the same class of texture are assigned to the same component if they have at least one point in common. As $(3^N - 1)$ adjacent neighbors of each sampling point are considered, $R3^N$ operations are required by the connected components extraction procedure.

The core extraction procedure requires the determination of the compactness of all the detected connected components, involving also $R3^N$ elementary operations. Using a hypercubic structuring element of side length equal to 3, the classical closing-opening morphological filtering process requires $4R3^N$ operations.

We now focus our attention on the complexity of the second step since the first and third steps are independent of the texture features extraction process. This second step, which consists in the characterization of the distributions in terms of texture, is split into two phases. The co-occurrence matrices or the density sum and difference histograms are generated in a first one, while the texture features are extracted from the matrices or from the histograms in a second phase.

The computational loads associated with the generation of the COM and the density SDH for each non-empty hypercube are similar, and depend on the number of the couples of adjacent sampling points encountered within a hypercubic neighborhood of size length $(2h+1)$. As there are $(3^N - 1)$ adjacent sampling points for each of the

$(2h+1)^N$ sampling points falling in the hypercubic neighborhood, $(3^N -1)(2h+1)^N$ couples of sampling points are considered to compute the co-occurrence matrix or the density sum and difference histogram at each sampling point of the discrete multidimensional histogram. As h is set to 1 (cf. § 5.4), the number of elementary operations is approximately equal to $(3^N)\times(3^N -1) \approx 9^N$. Hence, the determination of all the co-occurrence matrices or the density sum and difference histograms requires $R9^N$ operations.

The second phase is significantly different for the COM based and the density SDH based algorithms. It deserves a particular attention to avoid computational burden.

7.1 Complexity of the co-occurrence matrix based algorithm

In the case of the COM, each matrix must be looped through once or twice depending on the feature to be extracted. $(G+1)^2$ operations are necessary to explore the matrix so that the total complexity of the texture characterization using the co-occurrence matrices for R non-empty hypercubes is equal to:

$$O\left(R\left((9)^N +(\alpha + \beta)(G+1)^2\right)\right).$$

where α and β are the numbers of features using 1 and 2 loops, respectively.

When the quantization level G of the density and/or when the dimension N are large, the computation cost for computing the features becomes prohibitive. Several algorithms have been proposed in the texture analysis literature to overcome this problem. Some solutions are the reduction of the quantization level G [Clausi, 2002], the updating the features determined in a hypercubic neighborhood from those obtained in the adjacent neighborhoods [Argenti et al., 1990] or the storage of only the non-zero co-occurring density values [Clausi & Jernigan, 1998; Clausi & Zhao, 2002]. This last solution is well-adapted for large quantization levels G, i.e. when the co-occurrence matrices become large and sparse. We have used a hybrid data structure which combines a linked list and hash tables [Clausi & Zhao, 2002] to avoid the storage of the pairs of values of the co-occurrence matrices that have zero probability. This data structure is called hereafter the Hybrid Co-occurrence Matrix (HCM).

Each node of that linked list is a structure containing one of the pairs of co-occurring values effectively encountered in the hypercubic neighborhood, its probability of co-occurrence for neighboring sampling points and a link to the next node in the list. To include a new pair in a linked list, a node having the same pair of density values is searched. If such a node is found, then its probability is incremented. Otherwise, a new node is added at the end of the list. However, the search of a particular node is time consuming. To avoid this drawback, we use a hash table with the same size than the co-occurrence matrix, in order to give a direct access to each node of the linked list. The access to the hash table is provided by the pair of density values (i,j). Each entry in the hash table contains a pointer. If the pointer is null, then the particular co-occurring pair of density value (i,j) does not have a representative node on the linked list. In this case, a new node is created and inserted at the end of the linked list. If the pointer is not null, then it points to the existing corresponding node in the linked list and its probability is incremented.

The length L of the linked list is equal to the number of distinct pairs of values found in the considered hypercubic neighborhood. A total of $R\left((9)^D +(\alpha + \beta)L\right)$ operations are required to calculate the texture features for all the sampling points. The value of L, depends on the data structure, on the dimension N and on the discretization parameter S. As L is generally significantly smaller than $(G+1)^2$, the computational load to determine the texture features can be greatly reduced by means of the HCM.

7.2 Complexity of the density sum and difference histogram based algorithm

Let us now consider the algorithm based on the density sum and difference histograms that must be looped through once or twice to extract one feature. As the histograms are one-dimensional structures, they are explored in $(2G+1)$ operations and the resulting complexity of the whole characterization procedure is equal to:

$$O\left(R\left((9)^D + (\alpha + \beta)(2G+1)\right)\right).$$

As $(2G+1) \prec (G+1)^2$, it appears that the complexity of the density SDH based algorithm is significantly smaller than that of the COM based algorithm, especially for high values of G. However, the comparison between the complexities of the density SDH and HCM based algorithms is not easy since the value of L depends on many parameters. The complexity of the density SDH based algorithm is smaller than that of the HCM based algorithm only if $(2G+1) \prec L$.

7.3 Processing times comparison

In order to compare the processing speeds produced by the feature extraction procedures based on the COM, the HCM and the density SDH , we use data sets constituted of two well separated Gaussian distributions of observations with means μ =[2, 2, 2,..., 2]^T and μ =[-2, -2, -2,..., -2]^T and with unit covariance matrices $\Sigma_1 = \Sigma_2 = I_N$. For N-dimensional data, μ_1 and μ_2 are N-dimensional vectors, while Σ_1 and Σ_2 are $N \times N$ unit covariance matrices.

Since the main purpose of these simulations is to compare the computation times of the texture characterization procedures, the tuning of these algorithms is not optimized as proposed in section 5. On the contrary, all runs are made with $S = 10$ and with the largest number of available texture features for each algorithm. This strategy allows running the feature extraction procedures under comparable conditions for different dimensionalities N of the data and different sample sizes Q. For the density SDH based algorithm, we compute the 9 available features of table 2. For a fair comparison, we have selected the 9 most discriminatory features among the 13 that can be extracted from the COM and HCM (Table 1).

As the number of non-empty hypercubes depends on the structure of the data distribution, we have determined the average computation time per non-empty hypercube. Table 7 indicates these computation times for twelve data sets obtained with three different sample sizes (Q=1000, 5000 and 10 000) and for N varying from 2 to 5, using a Pentium M processor 715A/ 1.5GHz PC with 512 Moctets memory. Although the running times are computer dependent, they give an idea of the computation time improvement in a non trivial case.

We indicate, for each data set, the number R of non-empty hypercubes and the maximum value G of the densities. As the number of sampling points increases with the dimensionality N, the number of non-empty hypercubes is an increasing function of N for a given number Q of data points. As a consequence, the number of data points in each non-empty hypercube tends to decrease with increasing values of N, so that G is a decreasing function of N. The mean value of the lengths L of the linked lists produced by the HCM based procedure is also indicated in table 7. This mean value is denoted $\overline{L}$.

As expected, the processing times for the generation of the COM and the density SDH are similar. They increase with the dimensionality N and are independent of the number Q of data points.

Table 7 allows to compare the processing times of the feature extraction process from the COM, the HCM and the density SDH for different couples of values of Q and N.

The procedure based on the HCM is always faster than that based on the COM. The speed improvement is important when the value G is high and the mean value $\overline{L}$ of the lengths of the linked lists is low. For example, with Q =10 000 and with the lower dimension N =2, G reaches the value 869, $\overline{L}$ is equal to 63 and the extraction of the features from the HCM is more than 6000 times faster than the extraction from the COM. On the opposite, the improvement of the processing times is less significant for lower values of G and higher values of $\overline{L}$. For the same number Q =10 000 and a higher dimension (N =5), the maximum value G is equal to 61 and $\overline{L}$ reaches the value 804. In this case, the speed with the HCM is only twice faster than that with the COM (cf. table 7).

The procedure based on the density SDH is also always faster than that based on the COM. The larger the maximum value G, the more important is the speed improvement. For example, the extraction of the features from the density SDH is more than 400 times faster than the extraction from the COM when G reaches the value 869, i.e. with Q =10 000 and with the lower dimension N =2. For the same number Q =10 000 and a higher dimension (N =3), the maximum value G is equal to 415 and the speed with the density SDH is only 100 times faster. But, even for G=61, a significantly lower value corresponding to N=5, the speed remains more than 10 times faster with the feature extraction procedure based on the density SDH than that based on the COM.

If we compare the density SDH with the HCM based procedures, we can show that these two procedures provide comparable computation times. When the average value $\overline{L}$ of the lengths of the linked lists is smaller than the size $(2G+1)$ of the SDH, the extraction of the features from the HCM becomes faster than the extraction from the density SDH. For example, with Q=10 000, and with the dimension N =2, the extraction of the features from the HCM is more than 10 times faster than the extraction from the density SDH. On the contrary, for the same example and a higher dimension (N =5), the density SDH is more than 5 times faster than the HCM based procedure.

8. Conclusion

After a series of adaptations of classical image processing tools to cluster analysis such as thresholding, edge detection, relaxation, Markov field models and mathematical morphology, this chapter shows how texture analysis concepts can be introduced in the field of pattern classification. A general-purpose clustering procedure has been presented, based on multidimensional texture analysis. The basic idea behind this approach is the characterization of the local distribution of the data points in the multidimensional data space in terms of textures. A set of texture features extracted from co-occurrence matrices or density sum and difference histograms that accumulate spatial and statistical information is used to evaluate locally the multidimensional textures that characterize the data distributions. The clustering scheme is based on the classification of texture feature vectors rather than on a direct processing of the observations themselves in the data space. Experimental results show that the density SDH and the COM based clustering algorithms are nearly as accurate in terms of error rates. However, the processing time using the COM tends to be prohibitive, especially for large data sets. This time processing can be greatly reduced by means of an hybrid structure including a linked list associated with hash tables. The main advantage of sum and difference histograms for clustering is a substantial reduction in computation time and memory requirement without any loss of accuracy of the results.

When the texture based clustering procedures are compared with classical classification schemes for globular clusters detection, they perform comparably well. However, the new procedures are much more efficient in difficult clustering situations such as non spherical or non linearly separable clusters since they are sensitive to the local characteristics of the observation distributions.

9. References

Argenti, F. Alparone, L., Benelli, G., 1990. Fast algorithms for texture analysis using co-occurrence matrices, IEE Proc. 137 Pt. F, 6, 443-448.

Ball, G.H., Hall, D.J., 1965. ISODATA, a novel method of data analysis and pattern classification. NTIS rep. AD699 616 Stanford Res. Inst. Stanford CA.

Benslimane, R., Botte-Lecocq, C., Postaire, J.-G., 1996. A watershed algorithm for cluster analysis by mode detection. J. Européen des Systèmes Automatisés, RAIRO-APII series, 30, 9, 1169–1200.

Botte-Lecocq, C., Postaire, J.-G., 1991. Iterations of morphological transformations for cluster separation in pattern recognition. Symbolic-Numeric Data Analysis and Learning, Nova Science Pub., New-York, pp. 173-185.

Botte-Lecocq, C., Postaire, J.-G., 1994. Mode detection and valley seeking by binary morphological analysis of connectivity for pattern classification, in: Schade, M., Bertrand, P.,

Botte-Lecocq, C., Hammouche, K., Moussa, A. Postaire, J.-G., Sbihi, A. and Touzani A., 2007. Image processing techniques for unsupervised pattern classification. In Vision Systems : Scene Reconstruction, Pose Estimation and Tracking, Rustam Stolkin Eds., I-Tech, Vienna, Austria, Chap. 25, pp. 358-378.

Clausi, D.A., Jernigan, M.E., 1998. A fast method to determine co-occurrence texture features. IEEE Trans. Geosci. Remote Sensing, 36, 1, 298-300.

Clausi, D.A., Zhao, Y., 2002. Rapid co-occurrence texture features extraction using a hybrid data structure. Computers and Geosciences, 28, 6, 763-774.

Clausi, D. A., 2002. An analysis of co-occurrence texture statistics as a function of grey level quantization. Can. J. Remote Sensing, 28, 45-61.

Clausi, D. A., Zhao, Y., 2003. Grey level co-occurrence integrated algorithm (GLCIA): A superior computation method to rapidly determine co-occurrence probability texture features. Computer & Geosciences, 29, 837-850.

Comer, M.L., Delp, E.J., 1999. Segmentation of textured images using a multiresolution Gaussian autoregressive model. IEEE Trans. Image Process., 8, 408-420.

Cover, T.M., Hart, P.E., 1967. Nearest neighbor pattern classification. IEEE Info. Theory., 13, 1, 21-27.

Cross, G., Jain, A., 1983. Markov random fields texture models, IEEE Trans. Pattern Anal. Machine. Intell., 5, 25-39.

Dankner, A.J., Rosenfeld, A., 1981. Blob detection by relaxation, IEEE Trans. Pattern Anal. Machine. Intell., 3, 79-82.

Davis, L.S., 1975. A survey of edge detection techniques, Comput. Graphics Image Process., 4, 248-270.

Devijver, P.A., Kittler J., 1982. Pattern Recognition: A statistical Approach, Prentice-Hall, Englewood Cliffs, NJ.

Diday, E., Le Chevallier, Y., Burschy, B. (Eds.), New Approaches in Classification and Data Analysis, Springer-Verlag, pp. 194–203.

Eigen, D.J., Fromm, F.R., Northouse, R. A., 1974. Cluster Analysis based on dimensional information with applications to feature selection and classification. IEEE Trans. Syst. Man. Cybern., 284-294.

Filippone, M., Camastra, F., Masulli, F., Rovetta S., 2008. A survey of kernel and spectral methods for clustering, Pattern recognition, 41, 176-190.

Hammouche, K., Diaf, M., Postaire J.-G., 2006. Clustering method based on multidimensional texture analysis. Pattern Recognition, 39, 1265-1277.

Haralick, R. M., Shanmugam, K., Dinstein, I., 1973. Texture features for image classification. IEEE Trans. Syst. Man. Cybern. 3, 6, 610-621.

Haralick, R.M., 1978. Statistical and structural approaches to texture, Proc. 4th IJCPR, 45-60.

Jain, A. K., Farrokhnia, F., 1991. Unsupervised texture segmentation using Gabor filters. Pattern Recognition. 24, 1167-1186.

Jain, A.K., Murty, M.N., Flynn, P.J., 1999. Data clustering: A review. ACM Computer Surveys, 31, 265–323.

Keller, J. M., Crownover, R. M., 1989. Texture description and segmentation through fractal geometry. CVGIP: Graphical Models and Image Process., 45, 150-166.

Macqueen, J., 1967. Some methods for classification and analysis of multivariate observations. Proc. 5th Symp. Math. Stat. Prob., 281-297.

Manjunath, B. S., Chellappa, R., 1991. Unsupervised texture segmentation using Markov random field models. IEEE Trans. Pattern Anal. Machine. Intell., 13, 478-482.

Moussa, A., Sbihi, A., Postaire, J.-G., 2008. A Markov random field model for mode detection in cluster analysis. Pattern Recognition Letters, 29, 9, 1197-2008.

Panjwani, D.K., Healey, G., 1995. Markov random field models for unsupervised segmentation of texture color images. IEEE Trans. Pattern Anal. Machine. Intell., 17, 939-954.

Parzen, E. 1962. On estimation of a probability density function and mode, Ann. Math. Statist., 33, 1065-1076.

Porter, R., Canagarajah, N., 1996. A robust automatic clustering scheme for image segmentation using wavelets. IEEE Trans. Image Process., 5, 662-665.

Postaire, J.-G., Vasseur, C., 1981. An approximate solution to normal mixture identification with application to unsupervised classification. IEEE Trans. Pattern Anal. Machine Intell., 3, 2, 163–179.

Postaire, J.-G., Vasseur, C., 1982. A fast algorithm for non parametric density estimation. IEEE Trans. Pattern Anal. Machine Intell., 4, 6, 663–666.

Postaire, J.-G., Touzani, A., 1989. Mode boundary detection by relaxation for cluster analysis. Pattern Recognition Letters, 22, 5, 477–490.

Postaire, J.-G., Zhang, R.D., Botte-Lecocq, C., 1993. Cluster analysis by binary morphology. IEEE Trans. Pattern Anal. Machine Intell., 15, 2, 170–180.

Reed, T. R., Hans du Buf, J. M., 1993. A review of recent texture segmentation and feature extraction techniques. CVGIP: Image Understanding, 57, 359-372.

Sbihi, A., Postaire, J.-G., 1995. Mode extraction by multivalue morphology for cluster analysis, in: Gaul, W., Pfeifer, D. (Eds.), Data to Knowledge: Theoretical and Practical Aspect of Classification, Springer, Berlin, pp. 212–221.

Sbihi, A., Moussa, A., Benmiloud, B., Postaire, J.-G., 2000. A markovian approach to unsupervised multidimensionnal pattern classification, in: Groenen, P.J.F., Kiers, H.A.L., Rasson, J.P., Scheder, M., (Eds.), Data Analysis Classification Related Methods, Springer, Berlin, pp. 247–254.

Siedlecki, W., Sklansky, J., 1988. On automatic feature selection. Int. J. of Pattern Recognition and Artificial Intelligence, 2, 2, 197-220.

Theodoridis S and Koutroumbas K., 2003. Pattern recognition, Elsevier Academic Press.

Touzani, A., Postaire, J.-G., 1988. Mode detection by relaxation. IEEE Trans. Pattern Anal. Machine Intell., 10, 6, 970–978.

Touzani, A., Postaire, J.-G., 1989. Clustering by mode boundary detection. Pattern Recognition Letters, 9, 1, 1–12.

Tran, T. N., Wehrens, R., Buydens, L. M. C., 2005. Clustering multispectral images: A tutorial. Chemometrics and Intelligent Laboratory Systems, 77, 3-17.

Unser, M., 1986. Sum and difference histograms for texture classification, IEEE Trans. Pattern Anal. Machine Intell., 8, 118–125.

Weszka, J. S., 1978. A survey of threshold selection techniques, Comput. Graphics Image Process. 7, 259-265.

Xu, R., Wunsch, D., 2005. Survey of clustering algorithms. IEEE Trans. on Neuronal Network, 16, 645–678.

Figure captions

Fig. 1. Discretization of a data set

   (a) Raw data set   (b) Discrete multidimensional array of "densities" with $S = 25$

Fig. 2. Random textures synthesized as uniform bi- and tree- dimensional distributions of Q data points. (a) and (e) Q =200; (b) and (f) Q =600; (c) and (g) Q =1000; and (d) and (h) Q =1600

Fig. 3. Spatial variations of the 7 local texture features of table 1 for the data set of Fig.1. (The range of variation of each feature is normalized between 0 and 1)

(a) f_1: Uniformity - 1 (b) f_2: Uniformity – 2 (c) f_3: Homogeneity (d) f_4: Correlation (e) f_5: Energy (f) f_6: Entropy (g) f_7: Inertia

Fig. 4. Spatial variations of the 8 local texture features of table 2 for the data set of Fig.1

(The range of variation of each feature is normalized between 0 and 1)

(a) f_1: Dissimilarity (b) f_2: Inverse Difference (c) f_3: Inverse Difference Moment

(d) f_4: Cluster Shade (e) f_5: Cluster Prominence (f) f_6: Energy (g) f_7: Variance

(h) f_8: Correlation

Fig. 5. Domains of homogeneous textures associated with the data set of Fig. 1 when different numbers of texture classes are required by the K-means algorithm

(a) 2 classes of textures   (b) 3 classes of textures   (c) 4 classes of textures

x : cluster cores   + : valleys   o : core boundaries   * : core surrounding

Fig. 6. Compact cores resulting from the compactness thresholding of the domains of Fig. 5

(a) 2 classes of textures   (b) 3 classes of textures   (c) 4 classes of textures

Fig. 7. Plots of the lengths $L(m)$ of the largest ranges of S where the number of detected cores remains constant.

(a-i)* 2 classes of textures   (b-i)* 3 classes of textures   (c-i)* 4 classes of textures

* i=1 for the COM based texture features, i=2 for the density SDH based texture features

Fig. 8. Cluster analysis for the bi-dimensional data set of example 1

(a)   Raw data set (for statistical parameters, see table 6)
(b)   Result of clustering

(c-i)*   Effect of the parameter S on the number of detected cores

(d-i)*   Discrete multidimensional histogram

(e-i)*   The four detected cluster cores

* i=1 for the COM based texture features, i=2 for the density SDH based texture features

Fig. 9. Cluster analysis for the bi-dimensional data set of example 2

(a)   Raw data set (for statistical parameters, see table 6)
(b)   Result of clustering

(c-i)*   Effect of the parameter S on the number of detected cores

(d-i)*   Discrete multidimensional histogram

(e-i)*   The three detected cluster cores

* i=1 for the COM based texture features, i=2 for the density SDH based texture features

Fig. 10. Cluster analysis for the three-dimensional data set of example 3.

(a)   Raw data set

(b)   Result of clustering

(c) Detected cluster cores with the COM based texture features

(d) Detected cluster cores with the density SDH based texture features

Table captions

Table 1. Statistical texture features extracted from co-occurrence matrices

$$(\ N_c = \sum_{i=0}^{L}\sum_{j=0}^{L} T(i,j) \ \text{ is a normalizing parameter })$$

Table 2. Statistical texture features extracted from sum and difference histograms

$$(\ N_c = \sum_{i=0}^{2G} h_\Sigma(i) = \sum_{j=-G}^{G} h_\Delta(j) \ \text{ is a normalizing parameter }).$$

Table 3. Compactness of the different domains of Fig. 3 when 2, 3 and 4 texture classes are required by the K-means algorithm.

(In bold, compactness's higher than 50% of the highest compactness value among all the detected domains)

Table 4. Largest ranges of S where the number of detected cores remains constant for different neighborhood sizes

Table 5. Statistical parameters of the two bi-dimensional distributions from which are drawn the observations of example 1 and statistical parameters of the detected clusters

Table 6. Statistical parameters of the two bi-dimensional distributions from which are drawn the observations of example 2

Table 7. Processing times, in ms, of the texture characterization procedures.

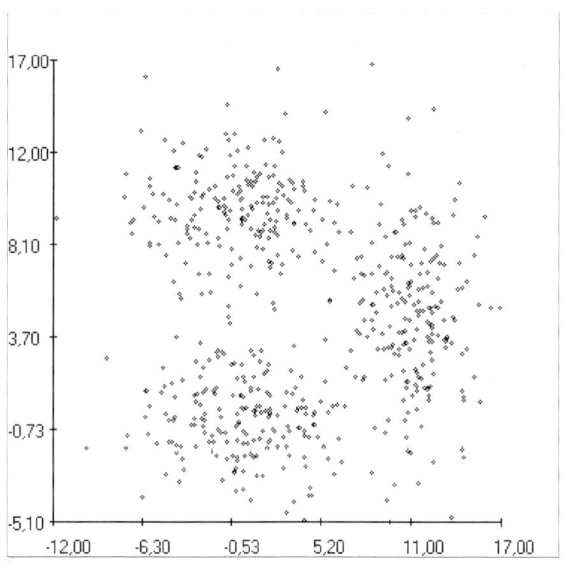

(a)

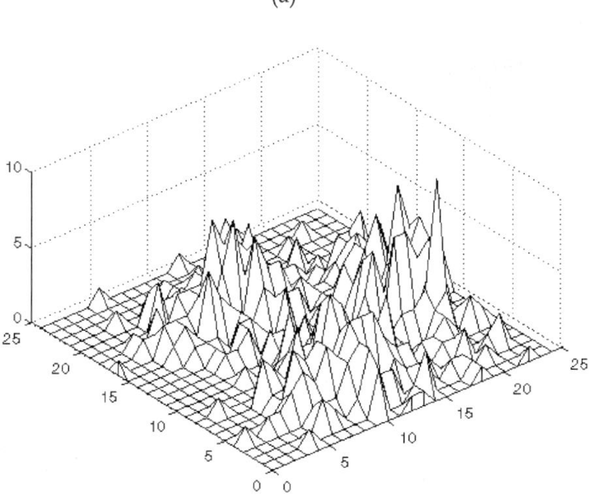

(b)

Fig. 1

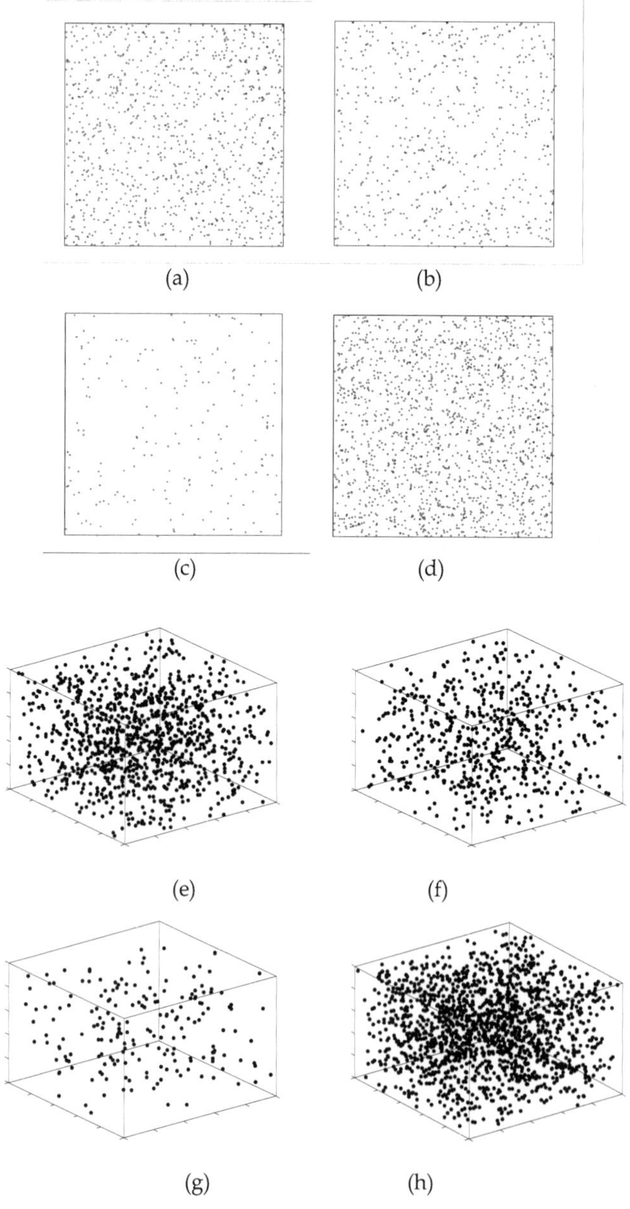

Fig. 2

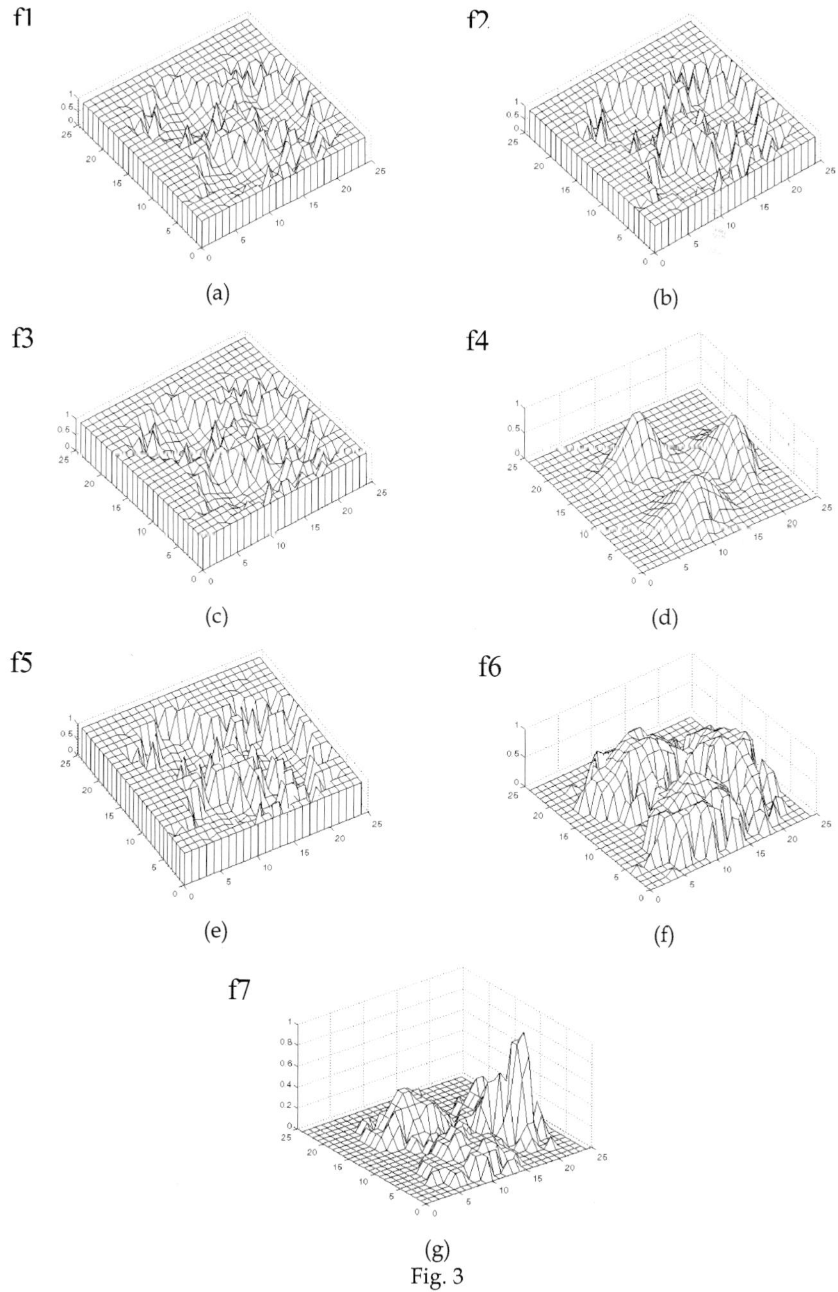

(a)

(b)

(c)

(d)

(e)

(f)

(g)

Fig. 3

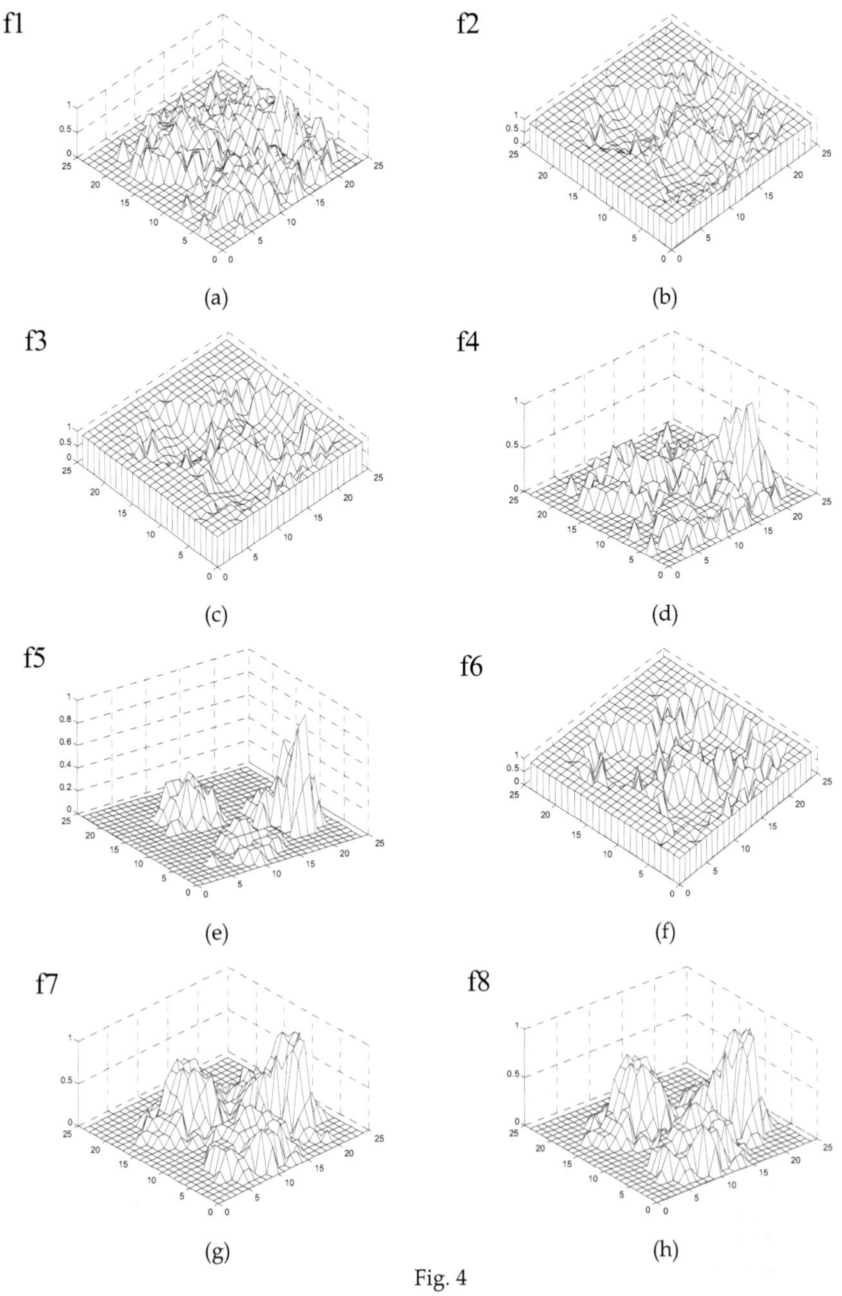

Fig. 4

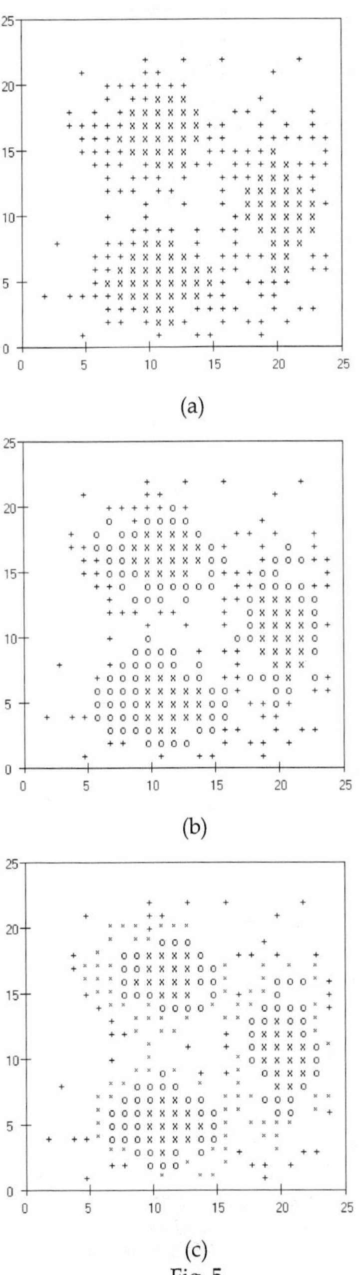

(a)

(b)

(c)

Fig. 5

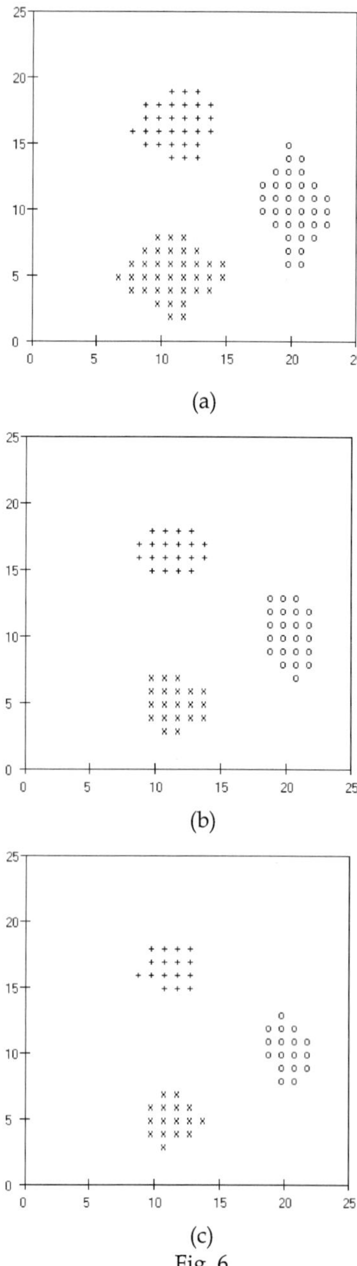

(a)

(b)

(c)

Fig. 6

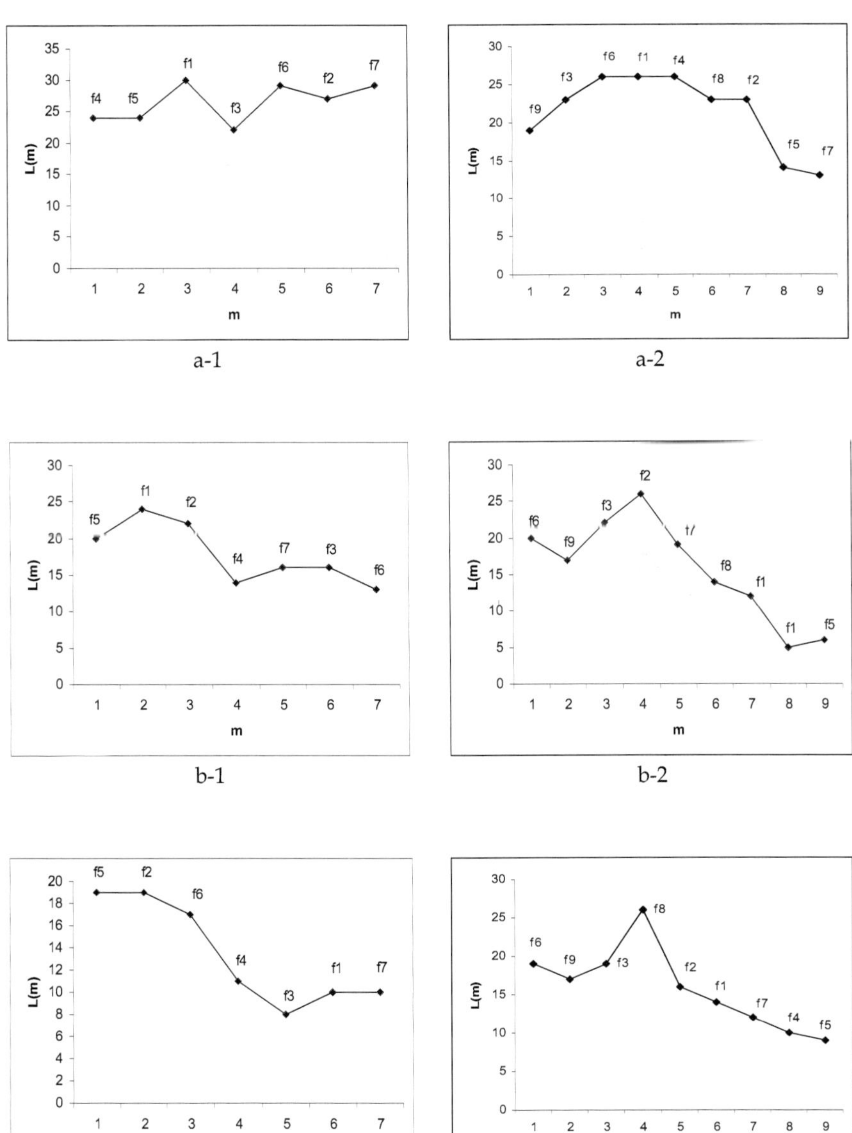

Fig. 7

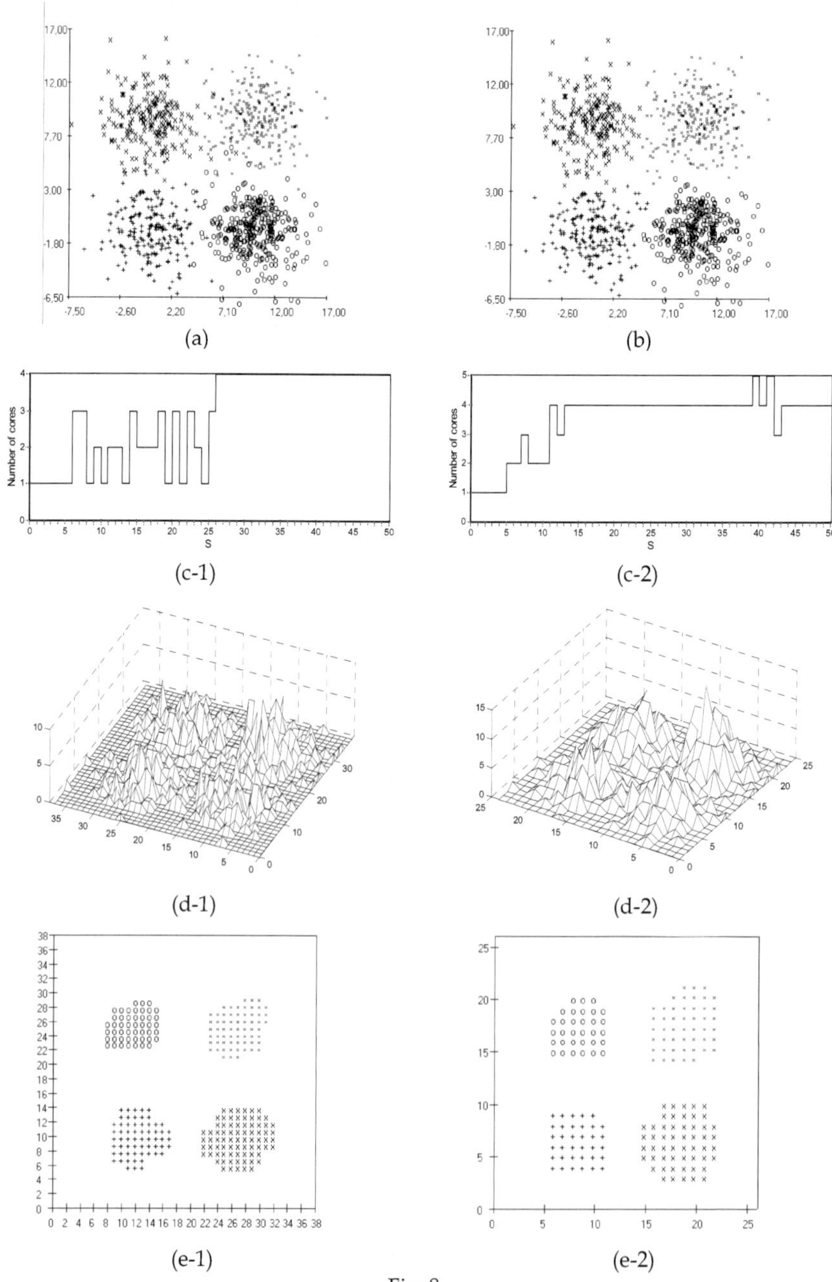

Fig. 8

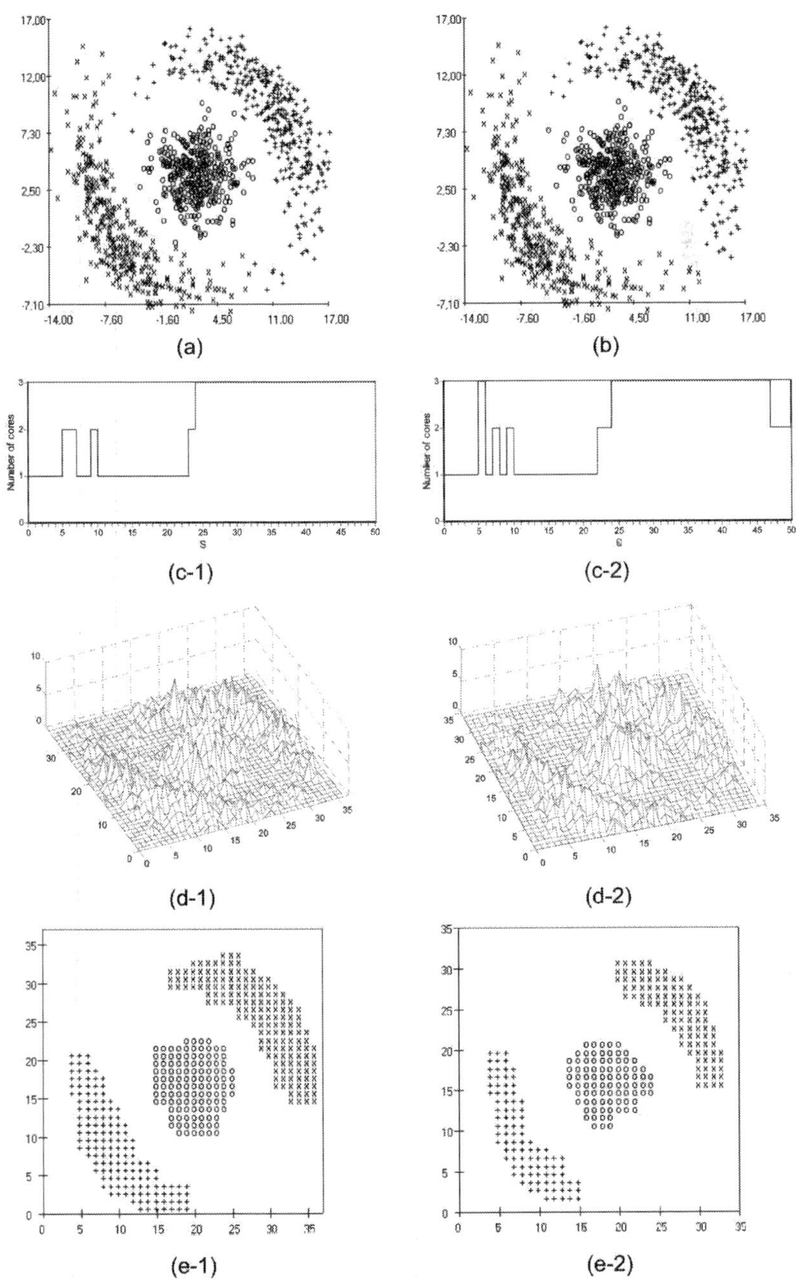

Fig. 9

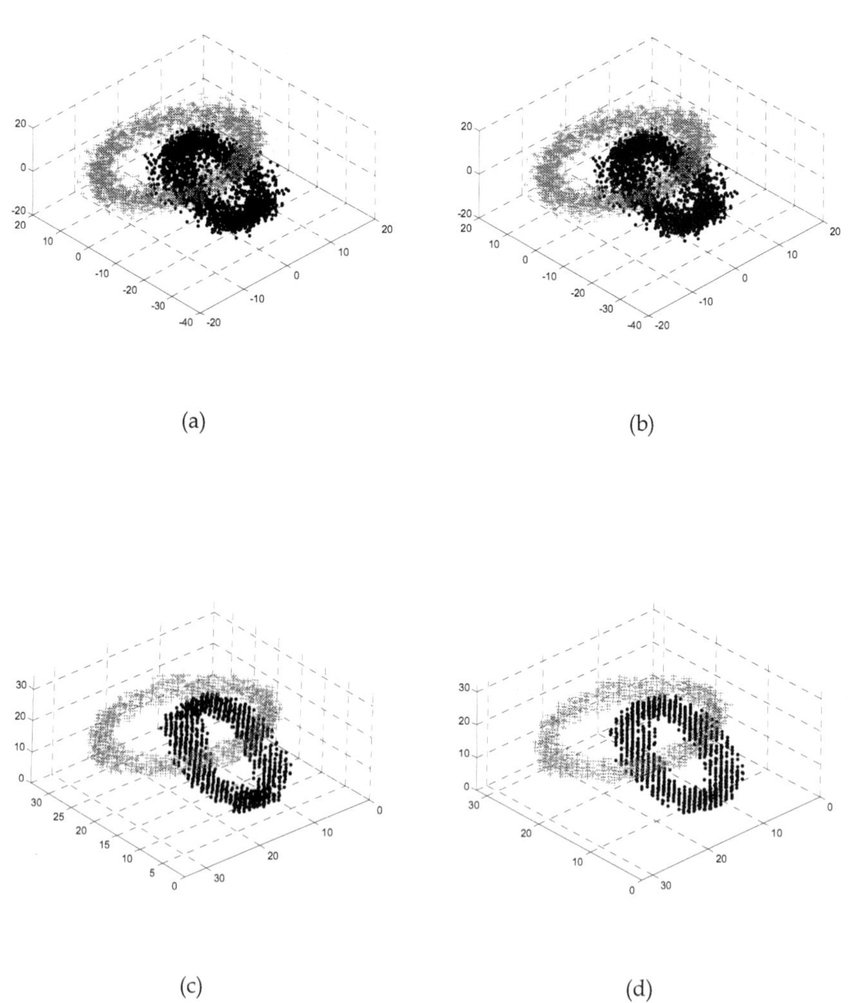

(a)   (b)

(c)   (d)

Fig. 10

Uniformity-1 (1st order)	$f_1 = \dfrac{1}{N_c} \sum\limits_{i=0}^{L} T(i,i)$
Uniformity-2 (2nd order)	$f_2 = \dfrac{1}{N_c^2} \sum\limits_{i=0}^{L} T(i,i)^2$
Homogeneity	$f_3 = \dfrac{1}{N_c} \sum\limits_{i=0}^{L} \sum\limits_{j=0}^{L} \dfrac{T(i,j)}{1+(i-j)^2}$
Correlation	$f_4 = \dfrac{1}{N_c} \sum\limits_{i=0}^{L} \sum\limits_{j=0}^{L} ij T(i,j)$
Energy	$f_5 = \dfrac{1}{N_c^2} \sum\limits_{i=0}^{L} \sum\limits_{j=0}^{L} T(i,j)^2$
Entropy	$f_6 = -\dfrac{1}{N_c} \sum\limits_{i=0}^{L} \sum\limits_{j=0}^{L} T(i,j) \log\left(T(i,j) \big/ N_c \right)$
Inertia	$f_7 = \dfrac{1}{N_c} \sum\limits_{i=0}^{L} \sum\limits_{j=0}^{L} (i-j)^2 T(i,j)$
Means	$f_8 = \dfrac{1}{N_c} \sum\limits_{i=0}^{L} \sum\limits_{j=0}^{L} i * T(i,j) \qquad f_9 = \dfrac{1}{N_c} \sum\limits_{i=0}^{L} \sum\limits_{j=0}^{L} j * T(i,j)$
Covariance	$f_{10} = \dfrac{1}{N_c} \sum\limits_{i=0}^{L} \sum\limits_{j=0}^{L} (i-f_8)(j-f_9) T(i,j)$
Cluster shade	$f_{11} = \dfrac{1}{N_c} \sum\limits_{i=0}^{L} \sum\limits_{j=0}^{L} \left((i-f_8)+(j-f_9)\right)^3 T(i,j)$
Cluster prominence	$f_{12} = \dfrac{1}{N_c} \sum\limits_{i=0}^{L} \sum\limits_{j=0}^{L} \left((i-f_8)+(j-f_9)\right)^4 T(i,j)$
Absolute value	$f_{13} = \dfrac{1}{N_c} \sum\limits_{i=0}^{L} \sum\limits_{j=0}^{L} |i-j| \, T(i,j)$

Table 1.

Dissimilarity	$f_1 = \sum_{j=-G}^{G} j \dfrac{h_\Delta(j)}{N_c}$
Inverse Difference	$f_2 = \sum_{j=-G}^{G} \dfrac{h_\Delta(j)}{(1+j)N_c}$
Inverse Difference Moment	$f_3 = \sum_{j=-G}^{G} \dfrac{h_\Delta(j)}{(1+j^2)N_c}$
Cluster Shade	$f_4 = \sum_{i=0}^{2G} (1-2\mu)^3 \dfrac{h_\Sigma(i)}{N_c} s \qquad \text{with} \qquad \mu = \dfrac{1}{2}\sum_{i=0}^{2G} i\dfrac{h_\Sigma(i)}{N_c}$
Cluster Prominence	$f_5 = \sum_{i=0}^{2G} (1-2\mu)^4 \dfrac{h_\Sigma(i)}{N_c}$
Energy	$f_6 = \sum_{i=0}^{2G} \dfrac{h_\Sigma^2(i)}{N_c^2} \sum_{j=-G}^{G} \dfrac{h_\Delta^2(j)}{N_c^2}$
Variance	$f_7 = \dfrac{1}{4}\left[\sum_{i=0}^{2G}(1-2\mu)^2 \dfrac{h_\Sigma(i)}{N_c} + \sum_{j=-G}^{G} j^2 \dfrac{h_\Delta(j)}{N_c} \right]$
Correlation	$f_8 = \dfrac{1}{4f_3}\left[\sum_{i=0}^{2G}(1-2\mu)^2 \dfrac{h_\Sigma(i)}{N_c} - \sum_{j=-G}^{G} j^2 \dfrac{h_\Delta(j)}{N_c} \right]$
Entropy	$f_9 = \sum_{i=0}^{2G} \dfrac{h_\Sigma(i)}{N_c}\log\!\left(\dfrac{h_\Sigma(i)}{N_c}\right) - \sum_{j=-G}^{G} \dfrac{h_\Delta(j)}{N_c}\log\!\left(\dfrac{h_\Delta(i)}{N_c}\right)$

Table 2

domain number	1	2	3	4	5	6	7	8
2 classes of textures	0.0026	**0.0333**	**0.0270**	**0.0285**				
3 classes of textures	0.0118	0.0083	**0.0347**	**0.0347**	0.0099	**0.0340**		
4 classes of textures	0.0052	0.0110	0.0099	**0.0330**	**0.0277**	0.0092	0.0082	**0.0295**

Table 3

	Most relevant features	Largest range of S
Co-occurrence matrices	For $h=1$: f_4, f_5 and f_1	30
	For $h=2$: f_6, f_3, f_1, f_2 and f_4	27
	For $h=3$: f_6	22
	For $h=4$: f_6, f_3 and f_2	18
Density sum and difference histograms	For $h=1$: f_9, f_3, f_6, f_1 and f_4	26
	For $h=2$: f_9, f_3	24
	For $h=3$: f_3, f_9, f_1	22
	For $h=4$: f_9, f_1	19

Table 4

	Generated data			Results of clustering		
	Number of data points	Mean vector	Covariance matrix	Number of data points	Mean vector	Covariance matrix
Population 1	200	$\begin{bmatrix} 0.11 \\ -0.14 \end{bmatrix}$	$\begin{bmatrix} 4.60 & -0.32 \\ -0.32 & 4.69 \end{bmatrix}$	197	$\begin{bmatrix} 0.14 \\ -0.23 \end{bmatrix}$	$\begin{bmatrix} 4.72 & -0.03 \\ -0.03 & 4.05 \end{bmatrix}$
Population 2	200	$\begin{bmatrix} -0.04 \\ 9.73 \end{bmatrix}$	$\begin{bmatrix} 5.23 & -0.29 \\ -0.29 & 5.02 \end{bmatrix}$	200	$\begin{bmatrix} -0.18 \\ 9.65 \end{bmatrix}$	$\begin{bmatrix} 4.32 & -0.15 \\ -0.15 & 4.05 \end{bmatrix}$
Population 3	300	$\begin{bmatrix} 9.87 \\ 0.03 \end{bmatrix}$	$\begin{bmatrix} 4.84 & -0.57 \\ -0.57 & 5.00 \end{bmatrix}$	292	$\begin{bmatrix} 9.96 \\ -0.13 \end{bmatrix}$	$\begin{bmatrix} 4.53 & -0.14 \\ -0.14 & 4.14 \end{bmatrix}$
Population 4	250	$\begin{bmatrix} 10.08 \\ 9.70 \end{bmatrix}$	$\begin{bmatrix} 5.13 & 0.07 \\ 0.07 & 4.83 \end{bmatrix}$	261	$\begin{bmatrix} 9.94 \\ 9.61 \end{bmatrix}$	$\begin{bmatrix} 5.44 & 0.39 \\ 0.39 & 4.87 \end{bmatrix}$

Table 5

	Θ	B_1	B_2	A_1	A_2
Population 1	$m=45°$ $s=30°$	$\mu_1=2$ $\sigma_1=2$	$\mu_2=2$ $\sigma_2=2$	$A_1=12$	$A_1=12$
Population 2	$m=225°$ $s=30°$	$\mu_1=2$ $\sigma_1=2$	$\mu_2=7$ $\sigma_2=2$	$A_1=12$	$A_1=12$
Population 3	$m=0°$ $s=30°$	$\mu_1=2$ $\sigma_1=5$	$\mu_2=4.5$ $\sigma_2=5$	$A_1=0$	$A_1=0$

Table 6

Q	Method	Dimension			
		2	3	4	5
	Generation times of COM, HCM or density SDH	0.01	0.06	0.40	2.77
1 000	Number of non-empty hypercubes (R)	61	209	466	736
	Maximum density (G)	65	28	11	6
	Computation times for feature extraction from COM	1.48	0.30	0.07	0.03
	Computation times for feature extraction from density SDH	0.10	0.06	0.02	0.01
	Computation times for feature extraction from HCM	0.04	0.12	0.06	0.02
	Mean values of the lengths of the linked lists $(\overline{L})$	53	140	91	35
5 000	Number of non-empty hypercubes (R)	67	329	857	1804
	Maximum density (G)	440	123	72	32
	Computation times for feature extraction from COM	57.79	5.05	1.92	0.54
	Computation times for feature extraction from density SDH	0.38	0.21	0.13	0.06
	Computation times for feature extraction from HCM	0.04	0.22	0.45	0.32
	Mean values of the lengths of the linked lists $(\overline{L})$	61	273	515	358
10 000	Number of non-empty hypercubes (R)	70	288	994	2489
	Maximum density (G)	869	415	141	61
	Computation times for feature extraction from COM	246	49.8	6.00	1.67
	Computation times for feature extraction from density SDH	0.58	0.40	0.22	0.13
	Computation times for feature extraction from HCM	0.05	0.25	0.73	0.70
	Mean values of the lengths of the linked lists $(\overline{L})$	63	322	855	804

Table 7

8

Rock Particle Image Segmentation and Systems

Weixing Wang

Collage of Computer Science and Technology, Hubei University of Technology,
Wuhan, Hubei,
China

1. Introduction

As known, most important, and the hard part of pattern recognition for rock particles, is image segmentation. Segmentation can be divided into two steps, one is segmentation based on gray levels (called image binarization, sometimes) in which a gray level image is processed and converted into a binary image. Another is segmentation based on rock particle shapes in a binary image, in which overlapping and touching particles will be split, and over-segmented particles will be merged based on some prior knowledge such as shape and size etc.

Segmentation algorithms for monochrome (gray level) images generally are based on one of two basic properties of gray-level values: similarity and discontinuity. The principal approaches in the first category are based on thresholding, region growing, and region splitting and merging. In the second category, the approach is to partition an image based on abrupt changes in gray level. The principal areas of interest within this category are detection of isolated points and detection of lines and edges in an image.

The choice of segmentation of rock particle images based on similarity or discontinuity of the gray-level values depends on both developed sub-algorithms and applications.

Rock particle images have their own characteristics compared to other particle images. Generally speaking, under the frontlighting illumination condition which is common case, rock particle images have the characteristics: (1) uneven background and foreground for which a simple thresholding algorithm cannot be applied to segment the images; (2) each rock particle may possess a textured surface and multiple faces, which often causes an over-segmentation problem; (3) rock particle overlapping each other, which hides parts of a particle, or causes breaks of the boundaries of rock particles; (4) touching rock particles forming a large cluster; (5) rain, snow, or much fine material making rock particle images clump together.

Rock particles may be densely packed or be separated mostly on a background. The former case is more difficult to process than the latter. As well known, most systems for rock particle images were developed based on simple thresholding algorithms (some of them combined with morphological segmentation algorithm) and boundary detection algorithms. The segmentation algorithm designing is application (here, the type of rock particle images) dependent. In this chapter, the author summarize own segmentation approaches for rock particle images, they are: (1) an algorithm based on edge detection; (2) an algorithm based on region split-and-merge; (3) an adaptive thresholding algorithm; and (4) an algorithm for splitting touching particles in a binary image.

The size, shape and texture of rock particles are very important characteristics of the physical properties for the geology research and rock particle production industry and mining industry. In mining, the size and shape distributions of fragments affect not only rock blasting, but also the whole mining production sequence. In the quarry manufacture, the size, shape and texture of rock particles must fit the requirements of customers, such as high way and rail way construction companies, the different companies in the building industries, etc. In geology, the size, shape and texture of gravel and sedimentary deposits are often used for analyzing and describing local geological properties in a certain region. Hence, rock particle size, shape and texture are widely applied and studied in both industries and research organizations.

Mechanical and manual measurement methods are traditional methods. Mechanical methods such as screens and classifiers will often separate rock particles according to their shapes, as well as density and size. In the laboratory, sieving of dry material is possible at sizes as fine as 0.05 mm and classification would not be applied to sizes greater than 0.1 mm. In industrial practices, it is impractical for screening the material sized below 3 mm, when the moisture is up to 3-10% by weight. These devices physically separate particles and often characterize the distribution of size in a limited size of a particle sample. The form of rock particle is often manually measured in a laboratory, in this way, three or more parameters such as the rock particle length, width, and thickness are often measured respectively for every individual particle. However, sieving and manual measurement methods are manpower and time consuming methods, in which the size of a sample is limited, and the measuring results are only suitable for the simple shape such as cube and cuboid. The results measured by different persons will be different in manual measurement [1]. In order to increase accuracy and speed of measurement, reduce manpower consuming, and enlarge sample size, new measurement methods are needed to be developed based on currently developed techniques. The image analysis method is one of these relatively new methods in engineering geology. For developing this kind of measurement methods or systems, the knowledge of geology or mining engineering, the techniques of image analysis and computer vision, as well as the skills of computer software development are needed.

As computers are widely used today, the cost of an image system is often relatively low, and rock particle size, shape and texture analysis can thereby be handled easily and quickly. Image analysis is a subset of the wider field computer vision, which aims at imitating biological or human vision performance. Identifying and separating overlapping objects from each other, is something that human vision can do with surprising (uncanny) ease. It is still an open question how to achieve this algorithmically in computer vision..

2. Literature review

The earliest image analysis system for rock particles was developed by Gallagher [2] in 1976. In his PHD study, he set up a system aimed to measure fragment size parameters on a conveyor belt. The camera was mounted above the particle stream with its optical axis aligned normal to the moving bed of particles. The size distribution of the fragments was then computed by finding the spacing of edges with a chord sizing method. Nyberg (1982) [3] presented an image system scanning chord size on an edge image of fragments in a rockpile. During the past fifteen years, image analysis for rock particles has become a hot topic of research, and a number of image systems have been developed for measuring rock particles in different applications such as gravitational flows, conveyor belts, rockpiles, and laboratories, and some of them are under development. The researches and developments have been and are carried out in many countries such as Sweden, Germany, France, England, Australia, Canada, United States, China, South Africa, and Spain etc.[4-11].

Generally speaking, a system consists of three parts: image acquisition, image segmentation and particle size and shape measurement. Image acquisition is about how to set up an image acquisition system to acquire rock particle images of good quality under different work conditions, which is often strongly application dependent. Image segmentation is an important part in the whole system. The design of an image segmentation algorithm depends on the characteristics of rock particle images. The image segmentation results affect the accuracy of measurement of size, shape and texture of rock particle particles. The basic requirement for size, shape and texture measurement is that the measurement results should be reproducible, and should reflect as much information as possible.

According to algorithms or methods of image segmentation, the existing systems could be classified into at least four classes. They are: (1) thresholding on histogram of gray levels [12-18]; (2) boundary tracing or edge detection [2-3, 7-8, 19-33]; (3) region growing or merge & split [9-10, 34-37]; and (4) thresholding and granulometry (= morphology segmentation on a binary image) [38-41].

Systems based on thresholding of histogram of gray levels were applied in some applications in which rock particle images have a uniform background, and rock particle possessing less surface texture. The typical application is measuring rock particles in a gravitational flow. Recently, such systems are used both in laboratories and for conveyor belts in the field [15-18]. The system uses backlighting illumination (a special lighting condition is constructed) to acquire rock particle images from a free falling rock particle stream, the acquired images being almost binarised ones. Therefore, a simple threshold can separate rock particles and background easily.

There is a number of systems developed based on boundary tracing or edge detection algorithms. The early systems mentioned before [2-3], used a difference operator to obtain a gradient magnitude image from a gray level image, then binarised the gradient magnitude image. The binarised image is the image with contours of particles. In most cases, the segmentation results are not satisfactory due to the fact that the contours of particles are not closed curves, and false edges exist. In order to overcome the problems, some recent systems include procedures (sub-algorithms) for gap linking, false edge elimination and curve closing. Some typical examples are summarized below.

In Lin, Yen and Miller's system (1995) [31], an image of overlapped rock fragments, taken from a moving conveyor belt, is first smoothed with an edge preserving filter, secondly detected by an edge detection operator (Canny's algorithm), then processed by edge linking and edge gap filling, finally followed by segment connection. Transforming the intensity function of the processed image for the desired intensity regions smooths the original image. The Canny edge detector is used with a so-called hysteresis thresholding algorithm to extract edges from the smoothed image. Supplementary to edge detection, edge linking and gap filling functions are added in the algorithm.

Kemeny et al. [24-27] system has been used in many cases. The system enhances an image by equalizing histogram of gray levels, then thresholds the enhanced image to separate void spaces among particles (non-particle regions), so-called shadows, from particles. Meanwhile a gradient magnitude image is obtained by using a Sobel difference operator. Particles are delineated by searching for large gradient paths ahead of sharp convexities of the shadows to separate clusters of touching rock particles. Using a morphological segmentation algorithm splits the remaining touching particles.

Norbert, Tom and Franklin [21-22 setup a system since 1988]: The work sequence of the segmentation algorithm is similar to Kemeny's one. It includes two steps. The first step is to segment particles by use of several conventional image processing techniques, including the use of thresholding and gradient operators. In this step, the faint shadows between adjacent particles are detected, and the work step is available for clean images with lightly textured rock surfaces. The second step uses a number of reconstruction techniques to further delineate particles which are only partly outlined during the first step. In the second step, the algorithm is just for closing particle contours. Bedair 1996 in his Ph.D. study, developed a similar particle contour closing algorithm, the detail description can be found in [32-33].

In morphological segmentation of rock particle images, the thresholded binary image is the objective. Two kinds of algorithms have been used in the image analysis systems for rock particles: one is granulometry, the other is Watershed algorithm.

The general idea of the Granulometry algorithm is that in order to simulate the sieving analysis, one can generate a series of squares (a maximum square inside of an particle) to obtain size distribution. In this algorithm, the complex segmentation is avoided. The ideal case is that particles have some regular shape (e.g. circle, square, or diamond). It is mainly based on the functions of opening and closing with a certain structure element, and distance transformation. The systems applying the algorithm can be found in [39-41].

Yen, Lin and Miller's method (1994) [38] - a derivative of the Watershed segmentation: It includes seven steps: (1) "Edge Preserving Smoothing" technique is applied to the overlapped fragment image to eliminate the fluctuation of highs and lows on the particle surface as much as possible but preserve the edge points; (2) the Sobel edge detector is used to find the edges on the smoothed particle image; (3) A median filter is utilized to eliminate the noise on the edge image; (4) the smoothed edge image is subtracted from the original image to construct an "edge cutted" (EC) image; (5) a gray scale morphology erosion is applied to shrink EC particle image to an extent such that no overlap occurs; (6) the "Otsu" thresholding algorithm [74] is used to shrunk, non-overlapped image and a labeling procedure used to identify each mark; (7) Once these inside markers have been located the "Odered Queue Watershed" algorithm can then be applied to the original particle image to separate the overlapped particles. The segmentation result is not very satisfactory even to well sorted particles with a good background.

The segmentation algorithms of region growing or merge & split for rock particle images [9-10, 34-37] were and are mainly developed by the author. The chapter will discuss that segmentation algorithm. All the four kinds of segmentation algorithms have been developed more or less in the study. The different developed algorithms have been chosen for different applications. The developed algorithms are described and compared too.

3. Image segmentation algorithm for rock particles

As mentioned before, most important, and the hard part of computer vision for rock particles, is segmentation. Segmentation can be divided into two steps, one is segmentation based on gray levels (called image binarization, sometimes) in which a gray level image is processed and converted into a binary image. Another is segmentation based on particle shapes in a binary image, in which overlapping and touching particles will be split, and oversegmented particles will be merged based on some prior knowledge such as shape and size etc.

3.1 The algorithms based on edge detection
3.1.1 Crucial algorithm edge detection

As most developed segmentation algorithms in the existing systems for rock particle images, an algorithm based on edge detection was also developed in this study. The main parts of the algorithm are (1) image smoothing; (2) edge detection by an edge operator; (3) thresholding on the obtained gradient magnitude image; and (4) noise edge deleting and edge gap linking.

After image smoothing (e.g. Gaussian smoothing), the Canny edge detector [59] is applied on the smoothed image. The gradient magnitude image obtained by Canny's operator, is thresholded by the P-tile thresholding algorithm, the value of the P-tile is chosen according to characteristics of rock particle images. Before noise edges deleting and edge gap linking, the thresholded image is thinned by a thinning function. After this operation, all the end points of edges (lines or curves) are detected, and small gaps between two edges are linked, where some end points disappear. All the edges of the end points are eroded from the end points within a certain length L_E(a number of pixels), the short edges of length $< L_E$, are removed. The remaining edges are then dilated to recover their original states. Finally, the gaps (e.g. the length of a gap is less than 20 pixels) between edges are linked.

As examples, two densely packed rock particle images are segmented by the algorithm (see Fig. 1). In the present stage, the algorithm can not provide closed curve for each individual particle, but the segmentation result can be used for estimation of average size of densely packed rock particle particles.

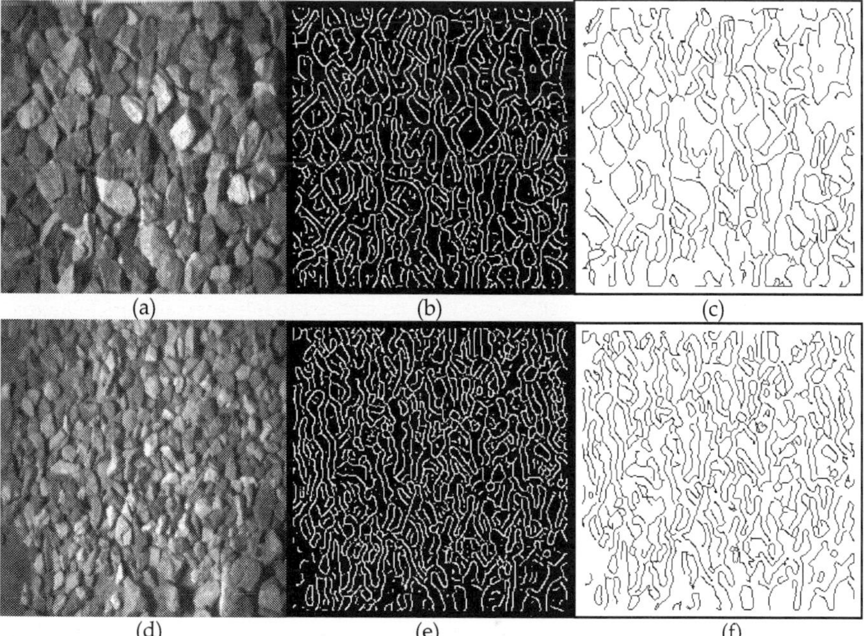

Fig. 1. Segmentation based on edge detection. (a) Original image #1. (b) Image after Canny operation on (a). (c) Image after deleting noise edges and gap linking on (b). (d) Original image #2. (e) Image after Canny operation on (d). (f) Image after noise edges deleting and gap linking on (e).

3.1.2 The algorithm of one-pass boundary detection

The goal of edge detection in our case is to quickly and clearly detect the boundaries of particles, it is not necessary to close every particle's boundary (it is too hard), but it should produce less gaps on boundaries and less noise edges on the particles. To reach this goal, we tested several widely used edge detection algorithms for a typical particle image; in Fig. 2, (a) original image (150x240x8 bits), (b) Sobel edge detection result that includes too much white noise, (c) Robert edge detection result that is mass, (d) Laplacian edge detection result that miss boundaries much, (e) Prewitt edge detection result that is similar to (a), (f) and (g) Canny edge detection results which are thresholding value dependent, and (h) the result from our developed one-pass boundary detection algorithm. By comparing results from the seven tests, the new algorithm gives the best edge (boundary) detection result. Our algorithm [53] is actually a kind of ridge detector (or line detector).

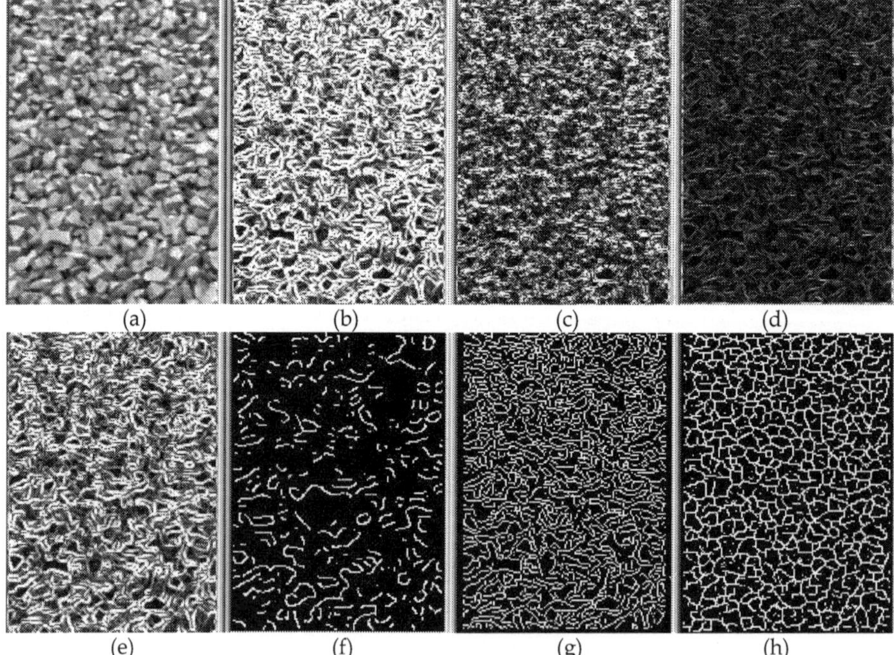

Fig. 2. Testing of edge detection algorithms: (a) Original image; (b) Sobel detection; (c) Robert detection; (d) Laplacian detection; (e) Prewitt detection; (f) Canny detection with a high threshold; (g) Canny detection with a low threshold; and (h) Boundary detection result by the new algorithm.

To overcome the disadvantages of the above first six edge detection algorithms, we studied a new boundary detection algorithm (Fig. 2 (h)) based on ridge (or valley) information. We use the word valley as an abbreviation of negative ridge. The algorithm is briefly described as follows:

A simple edge detector uses differences in two directions: $\Delta_x = f(x+1,y) - f(x,y)$ and $\Delta_y = f(x,y+1) - f(x,y)$, where $f(x,y)$ is a grey scale image.

In our valley detector, we use four directions. Obviously, in many situations, the horizontal and vertical grey value differences do not characterize a point, such as P (in Fig. 3), well.

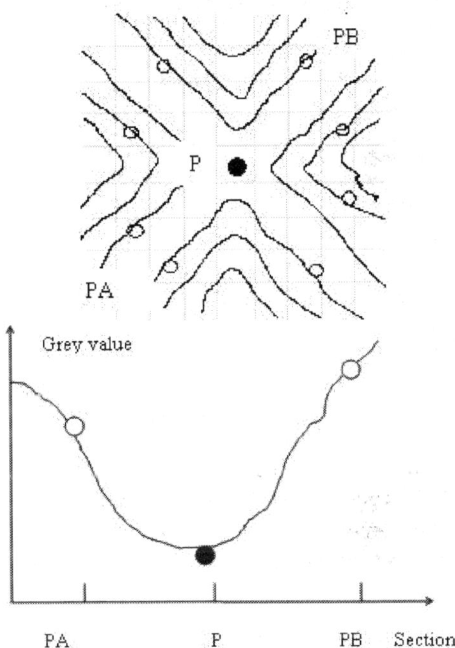

Fig. 3. Examine the point P, determining if it is a valley pixel, or not. Circles in the sparse (i, j)-grid. It moves for each P ∈ (x, y)-grid. (a) A grey value landscape over layered with a sample point grid. (b) PA-PB section.

In Fig. 3, we see that P is surrounded by strong negative and positive differences in the diagonal directions:

$\nabla_{45} < 0$, and $\Delta_{45} > 0$, $\nabla_{135} < 0$, and $\Delta_{135} > 0$, whereas, $\nabla_0 \approx 0$, and $\Delta_0 \geq 0$, $\nabla_{90} \approx 0$, and $\Delta_{90} \approx 0$, where Δ are forward differences: $\Delta_{45} = f(i+1, j+1) - f(i, j)$, and ∇ are backward differences: $\nabla_{45} = f(i, j) - f(i-1, j-1)$ etc. for other directions. We use $\max(\Delta_\alpha - \nabla_\alpha)$ as a measure of the strength of an edge point. It should be noted that we use sampled grid coordinates, which are much more sparse than the pixel grid $0 \leq x \leq n$, $0 \leq y \leq m$. f is the original gray value image after slight smoothing.

What should be stressed about the valley edge detector is:

a. It uses four instead of two directions;

b. It studies value differences of well separated points: the sparse $i \pm 1$ corresponds to $x \pm L$ and $j \pm 1$ corresponds to $y \pm L$, where $L \gg 1$, in our case, $3 \leq L \leq 7$. In applications, if there are closely packed particles of area > 400 pixels, images should be shrunk to be suitable for this choice of L. Section 3 deals with average size estimation, which can guide choice of L;

c.   It is nonlinear: only the most valley-like directional response $\left(\Delta_\alpha - \nabla_\alpha\right)$ is used. By valley-like, we mean $\left(\Delta_\alpha - \nabla_\alpha\right)$ value. To manage valley detection in cases of broader valleys, there is a slight modification whereby weighted averages of $\left(\Delta_\alpha - \nabla_\alpha\right)$- expressions are used.

$$w_1\Delta_\alpha\left(P_B\right)+w_2\Delta_\alpha\left(P_A\right)-w_2\nabla_\alpha\left(P_B\right)-w_1\nabla_\alpha\left(P_A\right),$$ where, P_A and P_B are shown in Fig. 3.

For example, w_1=2 and w_2=3 are in our experiments.

d.   It is one-pass edge detection algorithm; the detected image is a binary image, no need for further thresholding.

e.   Since each edge point is detected through four different directions, hence in the local part, edge width is one pixel wide (if average particle area is greater than 200 pixels, a thinning operation follows boundary detection operation);

f.   It is not sensitive to illumination variations, as shown in Fig. 4, an egg sequence image. On the image, illumination (or egg color) varies from place to place, for which, some traditional edge detectors (Sobel and Canny etc.) are sensitive, but the new edge detector can give a stable and clear edge detection result comparable to manual drawing result.

The algorithm has been tested for a number of images. It works satisfactory in several kinds of applications, and the testing results are shown in Figs. 5 -8.

In Fig. 5, the froth is very small, say, 43 pixels per bubble on average, it is hard to delineate by using a common image segmentation algorithm.

The image in Fig. 6 is different from the image in Fig. 5: the bubble size varies much; the white spots can clearly be seen on relative large bubbles. The ordinary edge detector may just detect the edges of the white spots, which are not the boundaries of the bubbles.

The image in Fig. 7 includes a mass of rough surface particles (average area is about 45 pixels), the new algorithm works well even for this kind of images.

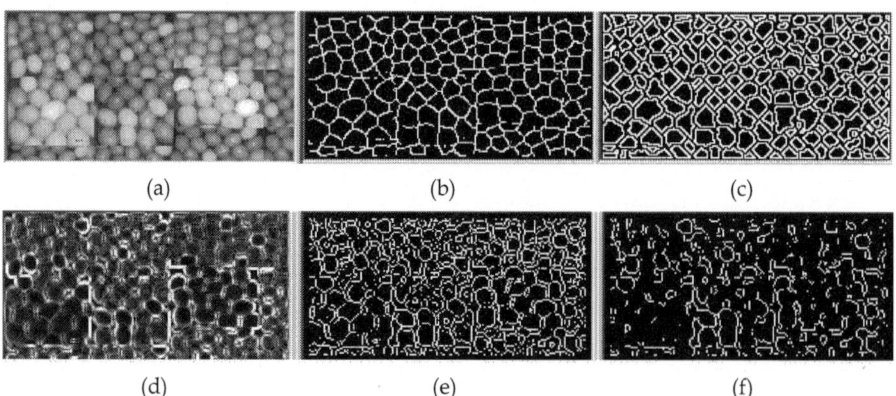

Fig. 4. Egg image test: (a) original image (400x200 pixels), (b) new algorithm result, (c) manual drawing result (180 eggs), (d) Sobel edge detection result, and (e) and (f) Canny edge detection results with different thresholds.

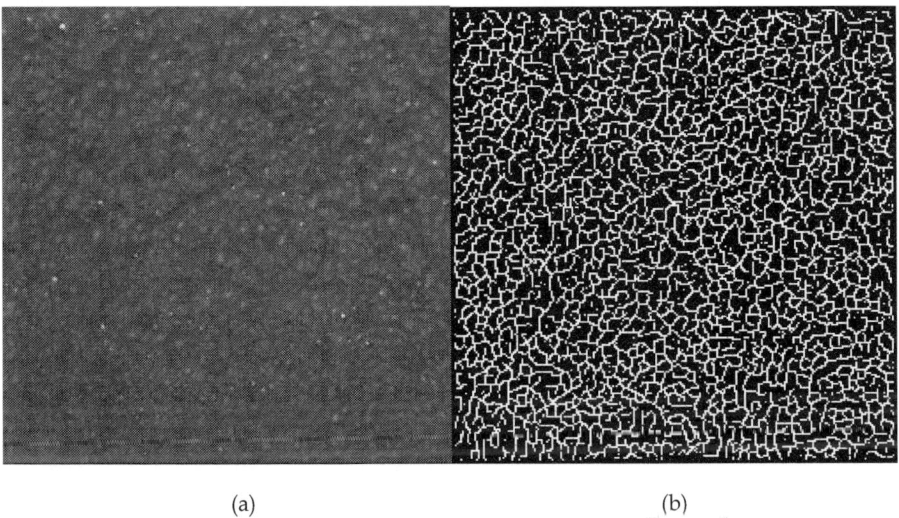

(a)   (b)

Fig. 5. Froth image of well sorted bubbles (image size 256x256, about 1516 bubbles): (a) Original image, (b) Boundary detection result.

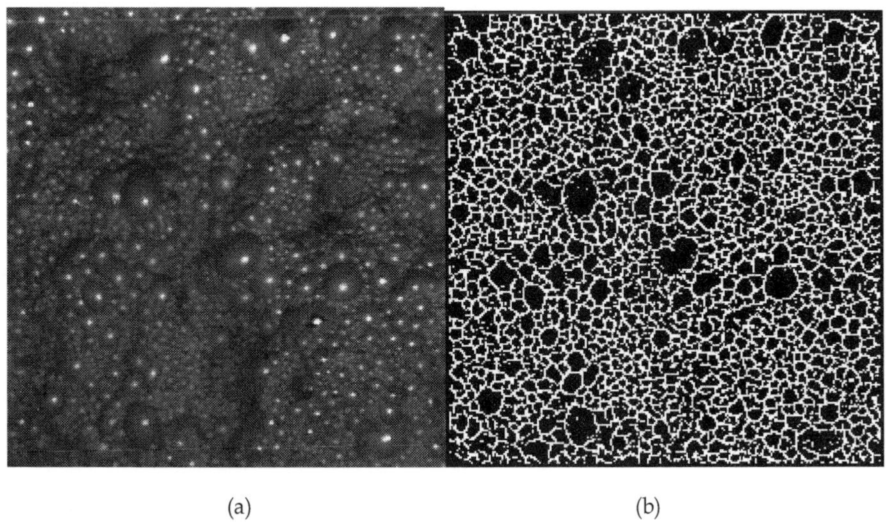

(a)   (b)

Fig. 6. Froth image of non-well sorted bubbles (image size 256x256, about 1421 bubbles): (a) Original image, (b) Boundary detection result.

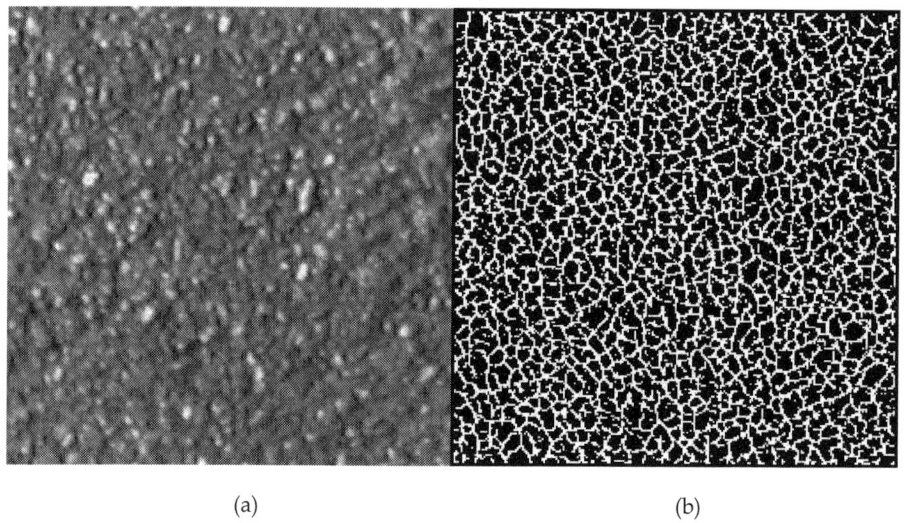

(a)   (b)

Fig. 7. Soil image of well sorted particles (image size 256x256, about 1445 particles): (a) Original image (particle surface is very rough), (b) Boundary detection result.

In Fig. 8, the image consists of a number of crushed aggregate particles, 47 pixels per aggregate particle on average. Even for the non-smooth (non-rounded) surface particles, the new edge detection algorithm can give a good detection result.

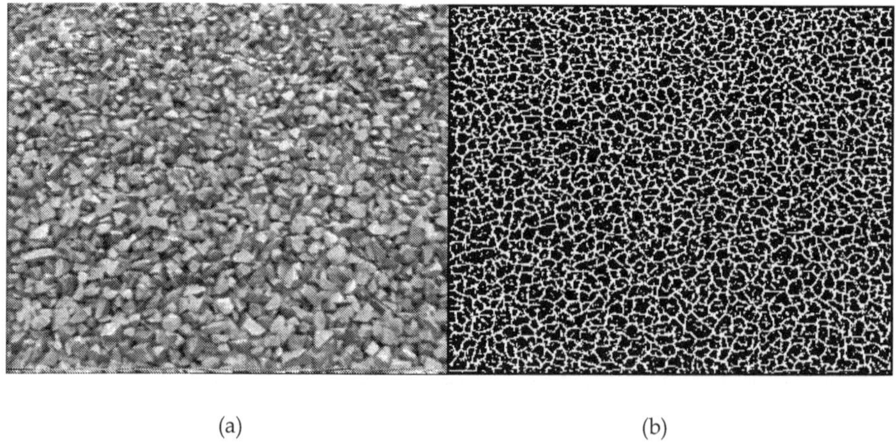

(a)   (b)

Fig. 8. Crushed aggregate image of well sorted particles (image size 356x288, about 2173 particles): (a) Original image, (b) Boundary detection result.

The new algorithm includes only some kind of differentiation - one of the three operations (differentiation, smoothing and labeling) by comparing to ordinary edge detectors. It is a kind of line detection algorithm, but detecting lines in four directions.

After boundary detection, the edge density will be counted and converted to particle size, the next section presents our particle size estimation algorithm.

3.2 The algorithm based on split-and-merge

For the images of densely packed rock particle particles, the above segmentation algorithm can provide average size rather than size distribution of particles. To meet the requirement of obtaining a size distribution of rock particle particles, a segmentation algorithm based on region split-and-merge was developed. The algorithm consists of three parts: (1) Suk & Chung algorithm-Single-pass split-and-merge [60]; (2) merging small regions into their adjacent large regions; (3) background split and regions merge based on shape of rock particle particles.

For a rock particle image, the Suk & Chung algorithm [60] is first applied to segment the rock particle image into small regions. However, this segmentation based on gray values, yields a number of the small regions amounting to tens up to hundreds times the real number of particles in an image. In order to reduce the number of the small regions, a merge procedure was developed, in which the two steps are included: (1) Find the small regions R_s ($< T_3$, T_3 is a threshold value); (2) Among R_j (j =1,2, ...), all the neighboring regions of R_s , find R_m ($j = m$) for which the common edges between R_s and R_j is maximal, and then merge R_s and R_m.

Sometimes, the whole rock particle image is not fully occupied by the particles. Parts of the non-particles regions or void spaces tend to be dark. To eliminate regions belonging to dark background, one may let regions of average gray value below a pre-defined threshold be re-classified as background, so-called "background split". The use of a pre-defined threshold is partly enabled by the normalization pre-processing procedure.

When the background is split from the image (i.e. the image is converted into a binary image), over-segmentation problem still exists in the binarized image. To overcome this problem, a procedure for merging regions based on shape of rock particle particles was constructed. In the merge procedure, three basic merge criteria were considered for two neighboring regions (or objects), they are: (1) their common boundary length is relatively long; (2) the gray value difference between two objects is not too large; and (3) if two objects are merged, the two junction points should not be concave points.

The whole algorithm work sequence is illustrated in the following Figures. An original rock particle image (from pavement) is shown in Fig. 9(a). In the first processing step, the image is merged and split into many small regions, each of them has an uniform gray intensity (see Fig. 9(b)). After merging small regions into their adjacent large regions, the result image is shown in Fig. 9(c), where the over-segmentation problem still exists. To reduce this kind of problem, in the last step, the merge procedure on a binary image, is used, and the result is shown in Fig. 9(d).

When a rock particle image is complex as shown in Fig. 10(a), one extra pre-processing algorithm has to be used before the segmentation algorithm is applied. The image pre-processing algorithm was designed to: (i) strengthen the edges among the rock particles; (ii) delete or decrease bright spots noises (= noise or irrelevant detail) in a rock particle image; and (iii) remove slowly varying intensity variations in a rock particle image. (i) is crucial because the contrast between touching or overlapping particle edges may be quite low, causing great difficulties for image segmentation. (ii) is very important for removing spots noise (e.g. fine material) and smooth particles. (iii) is of interest, since by making the image more homogeneous, eliminating some slowly sloping regions, segmentation is expected to work more efficiently. One example is shown in Fig. 10, to illustrate the usefulness of the

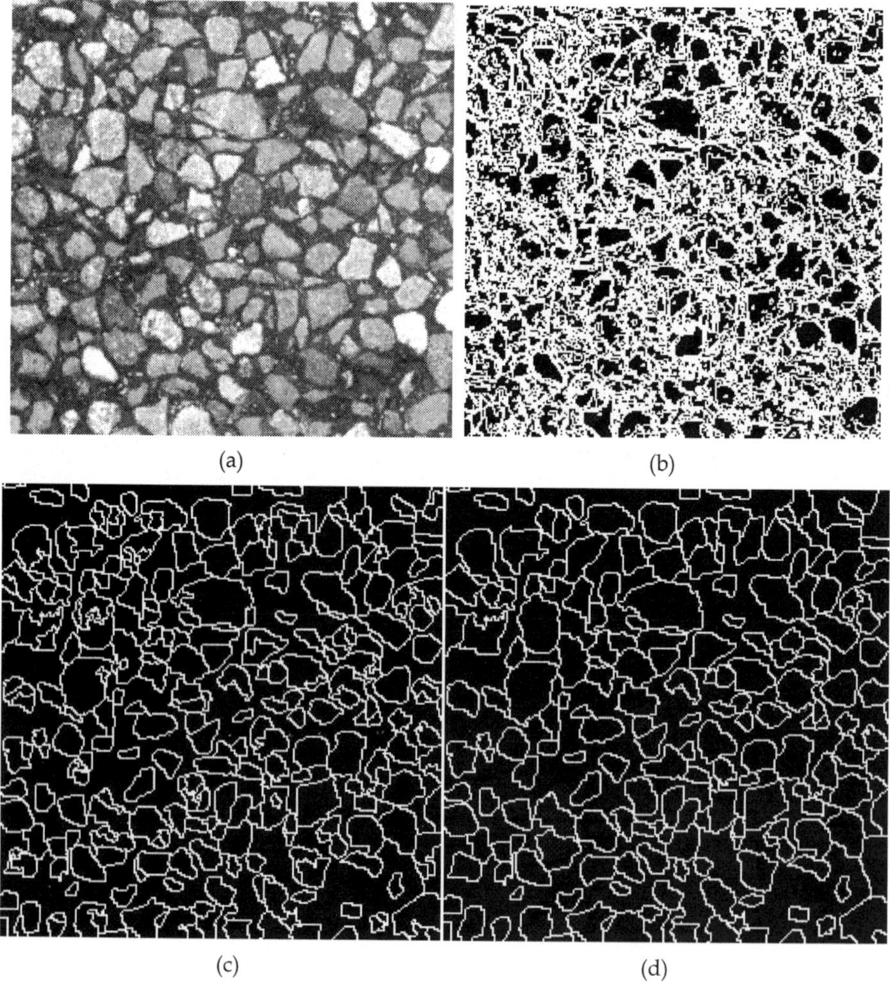

(a)   (b)

(c)   (d)

Fig. 9. Image segmentation based on split-and-merge. (a) Original image. (b) Result of split-and-merge. (c) Result after merging small regions into their adjacent large regions. (d) Image after regions merge based on shapes of rock particle particles.

image pre-processing algorithm. The segmentation result is not satisfactory because of without using the preprocessing procedure before segment the image.

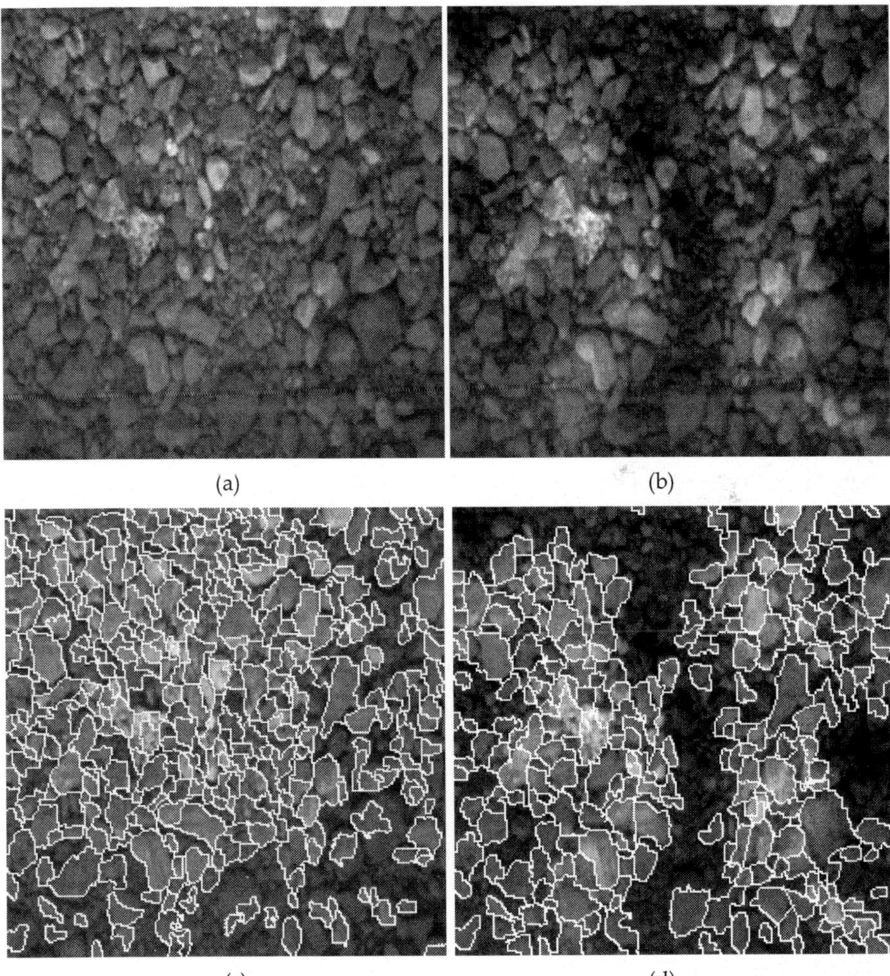

(a)   (b)

(c)   (d)

Fig. 10. Comparison between two segmentation results by using the segmentation algorithm described in the following section. (a) Original image. (b) Image after the pre-processing. (c) Segmented result on the image in (a). (d) Segmented result on the image in (b).

Before the above procedure, a preprocessing step is operated. as the follows.

The principal objective of image pre-processing is to process an image so that the result is more suitable than the original image for a specific segmentation algorithm. For the ceramic surface image segmentation, in order to make images more suitable for segmentation, we use our pre-processing program to reduce image noises in three steps: (1) strengthen the edges among the ceramic grains; (2) delete or decrease bright spots noises (= noise or irrelevant detail) in a ceramic image, and (3) remove slowly varying intensity variations in a ceramic image. Item (1) is crucial because the contrast between touching or overlapping grain edges may be quite low, causing great difficulties for image segmentation. Item (2) we have already discussed. Item (3) is of interest, since by making the image more homogeneous, eliminating some slowly sloping regions, segmentation is expected to work more efficiently.

We strengthen the edges by subtracting a gradient image (using Robert's difference operator) times a factor λ from fo, the original ceramic image, Eq. (1). We obtain a new image fn with more contrast along edges.

$$f_n(x,y) = f_o(x,y) - \lambda M(X,Y) \tag{1}$$

In Eq. (1), fn(x, y) is ceramic image after edge strengthening, fo(x, y) the original ceramic image, M(x, y) the magnitude image (based on fo) and λ a parameter, say $\lambda = 0.5$.

Next, a curved normalization surface T(x, y) is constructed, for which, a normalization value is assigned to each pixel, given by Eq. (2). In Eq. (2), $\mu 0$ and $d0$ are global mean grey value and standard deviation of fn, respectively, and μ and d are local mean grey value and standard deviation of fn (e.g. 16x16 window),

$$T = \mu - 0.2(d - d_0) - 0.5(\mu - \mu_0) \tag{2}$$

The image elements for which grey values are larger than T(x, y), (Here, T is used for grey value slicing, for finding bright regions. In Eq. (3), it is used for normalization.), will be processed through shrinking and expanding, so-called morphological operations, causing regions of width around 2 - 3 pixels, say narrow bright thin lines or bright spots, to vanish. In this case, the function T is used for detecting narrow or small bright regions.

$$f_N(x,y) = f_n(x,y) - T(x,y) + Const. \tag{3}$$

Narrow dark regions cannot be removed in this way since we then may destroy void space separating two grains. Slowly varying grey values can, locally, causes extra "shadows" in a grain, which makes segmentation difficult, for example, when separating away the background or when selecting threshold values for region merging and splitting, see the follows For that reason, the edge enhanced grey-level image fn is normalized by subtracting T, see Eq. (3), yielding fN.

By applying the procedures, the complicated images can be processed satisfactorily; the following figures show the results (Fig. 11).

3.3 The algorithms based on thresholding

When an rock particle image has a uniform background, or particles' gray intensity differs to their surrounding regions (local background regions), a segmentation algorithm based on thresholding is applicable. There is a number of thresholding algorithms published in literature [55]. They can be classified into global and local (adaptive) ones. In order to evaluate the existing global thresholding algorithms with respect to rock particle images, a comparison study has been carried out [55]. The comparison results show that for a rock particle image with a uniform background or a global background which can be distinguished from rock particles by human vision, the algorithms Optimal threshold (OPT), Between class variance (BCV), are the best choices for performing global threshold. One example is shown in Fig. 12. The original image was taken from a laboratory, and comprised of sand particles (of sizes 1 - 4 mm), the background gray value range is 130 - 250, and the range of gray values of particles is 10 -120. The BCV thresholding is presented in Fig. 12(b). The split algorithm summarized in next section split the touching particles.

Fig. 11. Image without clear edges, particle surface is rough, non-uniform background

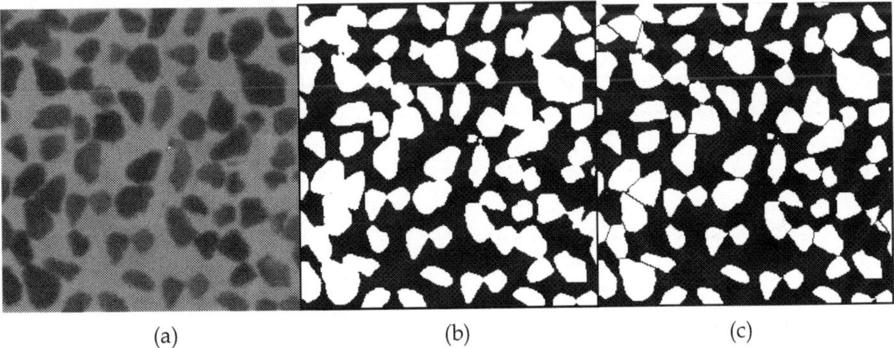

(a)   (b)   (c)

Fig. 12. Segmentation based on BCV global thresholding algorithm. (a) Original sand particle image. (b) Binarization result. (c) Touching particles were split by the split algorithm summarized in next section.

When the background gray level changes from part to part, and the gray level in some part of background is similar to that in some particle regions, the global thresholding cannot be used. In one case, when every particle region is surrounded by background, and the gray level of the local background is quite different to that of the surrounding particle region, an adaptive thresholding algorithm can be used. One special adaptive thresholding algorithm, a so-called recursive BCV algorithm, was developed for the rock particle images in this case. The developed algorithm assumes that the grey levels of *local* background are significantly higher than those of the particles (note that an object may consist of several particles touching each other to form a cluster); and that the range of the grey values in a particle is not too large. In practice the new algorithm processing sequence is: (1) the BCV algorithm is applied to the whole image for the initial thresholding round. Then, (2) for area A, a shape factor S and the range of grey levels Δf for *each* object is calculated. (3) For one object, if the area is too large, or the shape is 'strange' and the range of gray levels in the object is large enough, perform BCV thresholding in the object region. (4) Repeat the above step until no further object can be thresholded, according to these rules. Before formally presenting the algorithm, we will discuss data characteristics.

Characterization of data of one application example

Apart from the fact that the particles are locally brighter than the background, there are some characteristics of the grey value variation in the interior of the particles, which, generally-speaking, are fairly moderate. The images are taken with the sky as background. The sky, whether overcast or clear, is quite bright in comparison with the particles. A statistical analysis covering thousands of particles in long image sequences in our application (falling aggregate particles) shows that in most particles, the range of grey levels is less than 50. Some particles have a range around 80, often due to brighter spots around the edge of the particle, or, illumination differences on either side of interior edges separating two or more faces of a particle. Roughly speaking, there are three categories of imaged particles. For images of normal brightness the global threshold yields some kind of medium grey (around 128), and all objects have, by definition, grey values below this threshold. The first category are those particles for which grey values are in the range 40 to 85, and they are in a clear majority. The second category covers many fewer particles, and they tend to have a grey value range [40,85], except for 1-10% of the pixels in each particle. The third category may have up to half of the pixel grey values outside the range [40,85], and the other half within that range. When thresholding for the second class, this will result in the "loss" of some interior parts of the particle, or, of the particles appearing to break up into several pieces. To overcome this problem, we *define* Δf as the range when excluding 10% of the pixels, namely those with grey values from 0 to the value at which the *P-tile* is 5%, and the tail from the value at which the *P-tile* is 95% up to 255, *where P-tile* refers to the relative grey value histogram of the object, (The object can be a particle, or, a cluster of particles, or, a mix of background and particles.)

Formal algorithm description of an example

Let H_i be the local gray value histogram of object i, $i \in L^{(t)}$.

Define A_i (area in pixels), $S_i = P_i / 4\pi A_i$ and $\Delta f_i = 95\% tile\left(H_i\right) - 5\% tile\left(H_i\right)$.

Let BCV (region) denote BCV applied to a region.

Let $L^{(t)}$ be the list of numbered objects in iteration t, t = 1,2,...

BCV (whole image)

loop: { calculate A_i, S_i, Δf_i for $i \ni L^{(t)}$

       $\forall$ $i \ni L^{(t)}$ {

             if $A_i > 6400$ and $\Delta f_i > 50$ do {

                BCV ($object_i$), obtaining $L^{(t+1)}$

$$goto\ loop$$
$$\}\ else$$
$$if\ 1225 < A_i < 6400\ and\ \Delta f_i > 50\ do\ \{$$
$$if\ S_i > 2.8\ do\ \{$$
$$BCV\ (object_i\ ),\ obtaining\ L^{(t+1)}$$
$$goto\ loop$$
$$\}$$
$$\}$$
$$\}$$
$$\}$$

Fig. 13. Pseudo-code of Algorithm.

When formulating the algorithm below, we let the range test $\Delta f > 50$, where 50 is a *range threshold*, be a basic criterion determining whether to go on with recursive thresholding in current objects or not. For large objects consisting of both background and particles, the range of grey levels need to be large, $\Delta f > 50$. For touching particles, forming an object (without background), the range (as defined by Δf) is often, but not always, small. For small particles (below 35 mm) the range criterion is normally not applicable (bright spots around the edge of the particle). This is an example of the third category mentioned in the previous paragraph.

Hence, after global BCV thresholding, each of the objects is labeled and area A and perimeter P are calculated. Provided the grey value range is sufficiently large (e.g. $\Delta f > 50$), BCV thresholding is applied to an object if it is really large, $A > 6400$ pixels, or, if it is sufficiently large, i.e. $1225 < A < 6400$ and of 'complex shape', where we use a simple shape factor $S = P^2 / 4\pi A$ [if more detail shape information is needed, the least squares oriented Feret box algorithm can be used], defining $S > 2.8$ as complex shape (from experience, about hundred images were tested visually and using an interactive program).

Examples

Figure 14 and Table 1 show one example, where Figure 14A illustrates an original image. After global BCV thresholding, the binarized image is given in Figure 14B. The largest white object is given a label number 0. Because the object no. 0 has an area greater than 6400 and the range of grey levels is 116, the algorithm does BCV thresholding in the corresponding area of the original image, and the binarized image is shown in Figure 14C. In Figure 14C object nos. 1,2, 6, and 9 have an area greater than 1225 pixels. Expect for the object no. 9, the other three objects had a shape factor $S > 2.8$, and where selected for further processing and tests. Out of these three objects, nos. and 2 had a range of gray levels over 50. At the end of the whole sequence, the algorithm performed BCV thresholding both for object nos. 1 and 2 in the original image, and the final result is displayed in Figure 14D. To see if the new algorithm works better than some standard local / adaptive thresholding techniques, in the next section we will compare two widely-used thresholding algorithms.

particle No.	area (square mm)	shape factor	range of gray level	threshold
0, Figure. 5B	over 6400		154 - 38 = 116	128
1, Figure. 5C	1804	9.266	122 - 38 = 84	90
2, Figure. 5C	1489	3.442	122 - 49 = 73	93
6, Figure. 5C	1470	3.172	128 - 93 = 35	
9, Figure. 5C	2458	2.385	119 - 83 = 36	

Table 1. The area, shape and the range of gray levels in the five detected objects.

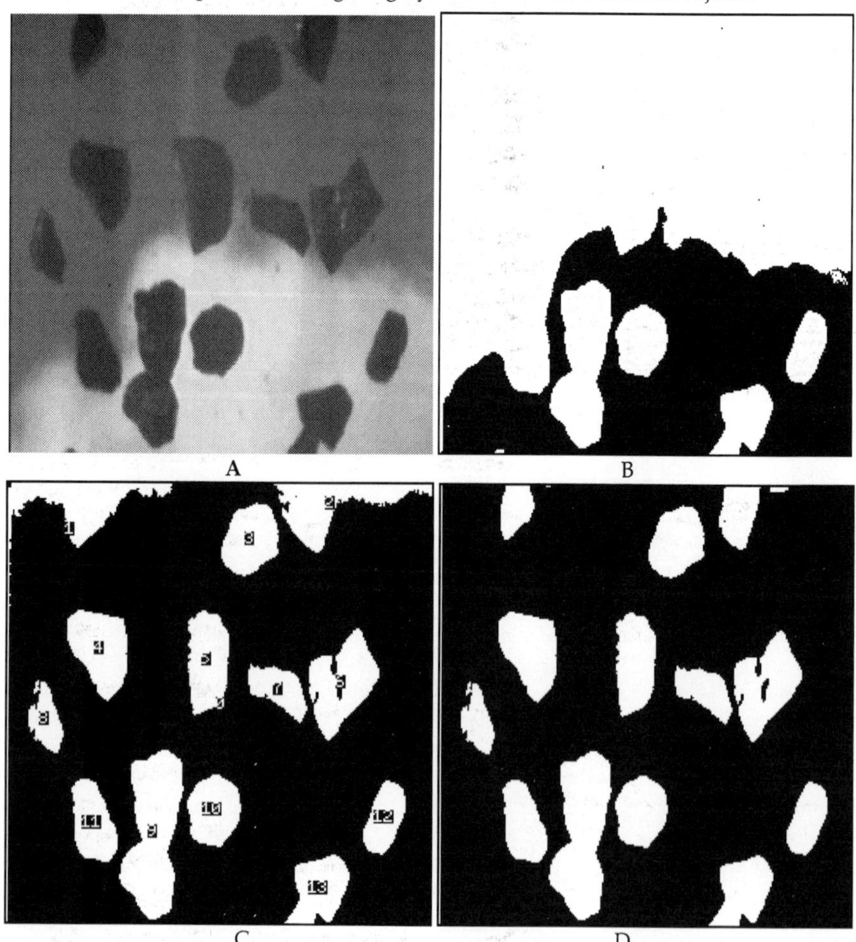

Fig.14. One example of recursive BCV thresholding performance (see Table 1). A — Original image. B — After global BCV thresholding. C — After thresholding of object No. 1 in B. D — Final thresholding result.

When the surface of a particle in an image is non-uniform (e.g. three dimensional geometry property shows up), the particle "loses" part of its area when the algorithm is applied, as Figure 15 shown. This is often caused by directional lighting. To avoid this problem, better to use diffuse lighting.

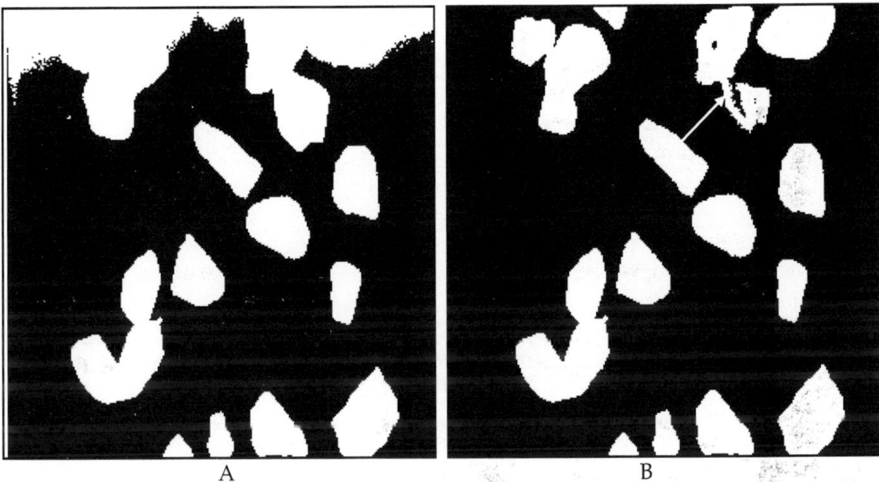

A   B

Fig. 15. An example of recursive BCV thresholding performance on an image. A — After global BCV thresholding. B — After thresholding of the largest object in A, the arrows indicate that the two particles "lost" more than 25% of their area.

3.4 The algorithm for splitting touching particles in a binary image
3.4.1 The algorithm for splitting touching particles
It is normal that when a rock particle image is segmented based on its gray level information, the resulting binary image has often an under-segmentation problem. Therefore, after image segmentation based on gray-level, an intelligent algorithm is, by necessity, developed for splitting touching particles in a binary image. The algorithm has been developed mainly based on shape analysis of rock particles. The split algorithm is a heuristic search algorithm.

In the past, there were a number of existing algorithms for splitting touching particles, but not for touching rock particle particles. In general, the existing algorithms first try to find a pair of cut points on the boundary of a particle (start and end points), and then detect an optimal cut path or synonymously, split path by using a cost function. To find a pair of cut points, one may use curvature information around a particle boundary, or ridge information of a particle, or partial gray level intensity (e.g. strength of local gradient magnitude or flatness). An optimal path could be detected by using distances, local intensity of gray levels, or local shape information or combinations thereof.

The existing algorithms cannot be applied for splitting touching rock particles, because the boundaries of rock particles are rough, the touching parts of rock particles have less local gray level information, and the touching situations are complex [62].

In the new algorithm for splitting touching rock particles, the main steps are:

Polygonal approximation for each object (touching particles): the advantages in this step are (1) smooth boundary to eliminate concave points caused by boundary roughness; (2) easier and more accurate calculation of perimeter of a particle, based on detected vertices after polygonal approximation; (3) in a concave part of an object, only the deepest concave point in a concave region is detected after polygonal approximation; (4) the degree or classes of concave points can be determined by both   angle and lengths of the intersected lines at a detecting point; and (5) the opposite direction cone at a concave point is easily and robustly constructed.

Classification of concavities: the classification of concave points (or concavities) is quite important for judging if one object is formed by touching particles, and if a hole in an object should be opened. It is also used for detecting the touching situations, start and end cut points. Split large clusters into simple clusters: the degrees of touching situations are classified into (1) two or three touching particles - a simple cluster, (2) multiple touching particles and (3) multiple touching particles with holes - a large cluster. For the situation (3), the new algorithm opens holes in some optimal paths, to convert the touching situation (3) to the touching situation (2) The touching situation (2) then becomes the situation (1) through an optimal split routine.

Supplementary cost functions for two or three touching particles: when two or three particles touch and form a cluster, a split path is difficult to correctly search, a simple rule or criterion easily leads to a wrong split path. The variables such as the shortest distance, the shortest relative distance, minimum number of unmatched concave points, "opposite direction", classes of concavities, area and maximum ratio between two split parts in terms of areas, are applied for construction of the supplementary cost functions in the new algorithm.

The algorithm has been tested in an on-line system for measuring crushed rock particles in a gravitational flow, in which, normally two or three rock particles touching together. In addition to this, it has also been tested for other different particle images (e.g. crushed rock particles, natural and rounded rock particles, and potatoes) in which particles touch in a complicated fashion. The test results show that the algorithm works in a promising way. A typical example is shown in Fig. 16. In this example, the image binarization is not satisfactory (Fig. 16(b), but the split result (Fig. 16(c)) is rather good.

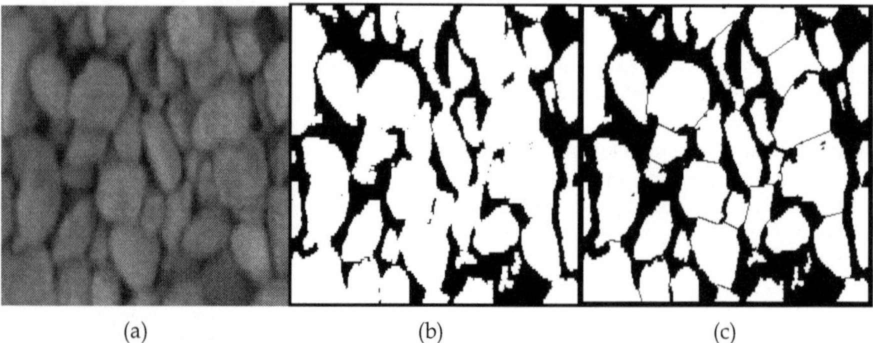

(a)   (b)   (c)

Fig. 16. Example of splitting touching rock particle particles: (a) original image; (b) binarized image; (c) splitting result.

3.4.2 Discussion of the split algorithm

The split algorithm consists of three different "treatments" or procedures in a certain order, namely (1) for holes prevailing inside an object; (2) for multiple touching particles; and (3) for two or three touching particles. All the three treatments are important for performance of the whole algorithm. If we do not consider procedures (1) and (2), the split result will be as shown in Fig. 17(a). Some split paths cross holes or background area.

If one opens holes by using an erosion procedure instead (say, repeating three times), then uses procedure (2) and (3) to split particles, the split result (Fig. 17(b)) is better than that of Fig. 17(a). However, in Fig. 17(b), some particles result from split, including new concave parts, and some touching particles are still not split completely or over-split. This takes place because erosion with a fixed number of iterations is not flexible enough. Note that parallel dilation after erosion cannot preserve the shape of particle.

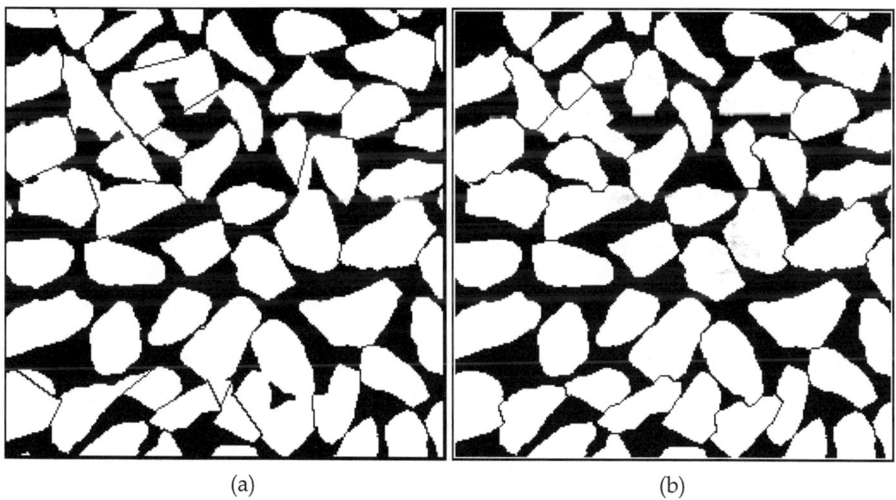

(a)   (b)

Fig. 17. Two split results on the image in Fig. 19 (a): (a) split result without hole opening and without the procedure for multiple touching particles; (b) split result after opening holes by erosion of objects three times followed by split and parallel dilation, of objects.

In the algorithm, one principal part is procedure (3), based on polygonal approximation. *Without polygonal approximation*, the classification and the detection of concave points *are difficult to* carry out. As described before, in most previous algorithms, a concave point is detected by the use of an angle or a curvature threshold. The angle is constructed by two chord lines with equally number of pixels, are usually determined by experience.. The following figures show an angle calculated by using two chord lines, each of them crossed 4 pixels (Fig. 18(a)); and an angle calculated by using two chord lines, each of them crossed 8-19 pixels (Fig. 18(b)), where the number of pixels on a chord line increases as the perimeter of the object increases. In both cases, the threshold for detecting a significant concave point is 64 degrees (angle $\alpha \le 64^0$). The images in Fig. 18 (white points are detected significant concave points) show that short chord lines give a rather precise detection of concave points, but, however, many scattered irrelevant candidates for the cut points (start and end points) are obtained (Fig. 18(a)). On the other hand, long chord lines are good in signalling significant concave part (Fig. 18(b)), but there are too many adjacent candidates of cut points (fragmented and non-fragmented) located closely to the true significant concave point. In these cases, one has to develop special procedures to search for start and end points for candidates of split paths.

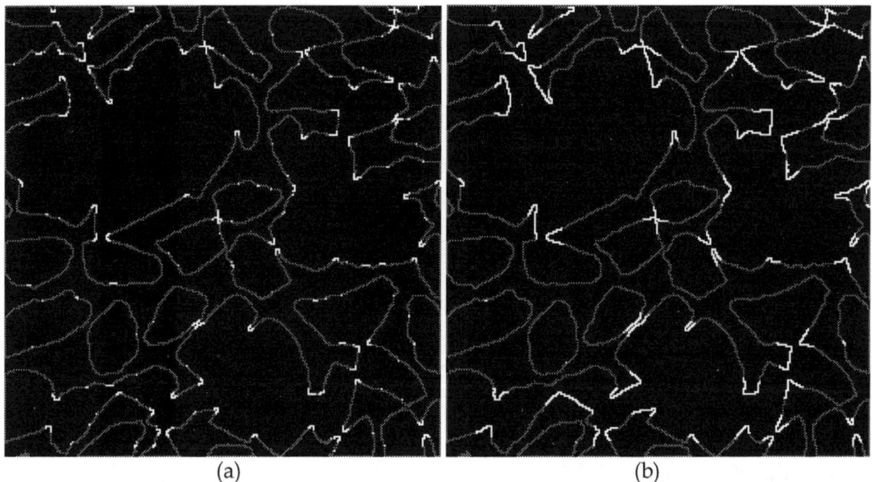

(a)   (b)

Fig. 18. Significant concave points detected by using two chord lines, each of them crossed the same number of pixels (angle $\alpha \leq 64^{0}$): (a) each of the two chord lines crosses 4 pixels; (b) each of the two chord lines crosses a q pixel, where $q \in [8,19]$ depending on object size (e.g. area or perimeter).

Figure 18 illustrates that the angle obtained in reference, so-called k-curvature, is quite sensitive to choice of lengths of 2-vertex lines (chords).

3.4.3 Test results of the algorithm

The new split algorithm has been tested for aggregate images from muckpiles, laboratories, conveyor belts and gravity flows. The test results show that it works in a promising way.

In a quarry of central Sweden (Västerås), an on-line system for the analysis of size and shape of aggregates in a gravitational flow, i.e. falling particles, was set-up. An interlaced CCD camera acquires aggregate images from a gravity flow at a speed of 25 frames per second. The odd-lines images were transferred into a PC computer with a resolution 256x256x8 bits. The system first checks the image quality (if the image is qualified for further processing or not, e.g. blurry or empty images cannot be chosen for further processing). When an image passes this checkpoint, image binarisation is performed. After this, investigating 1000 particles in 52 binary images, on average, there are 40% particles with a touching problem, and normally two or three particles touch together, and just a few clusters consist of 5-6 particles without holes. In order to resolve this kind of touching problem, a procedure of the split algorithm described in this article, for splitting two or three touching particles, is applied to all the binarised images, and finally size and shape of aggregates are analysed.

The system has been tested for about two months. It takes about ten minutes to process twenty images as one analysis data set, yielding size or shape distributions. Traditional sieving analysis results show that there is 5-10% of aggregate for which the size is over 64 mm. Performed image analysis also yields the same results, which indicates that either there are no touching problems or the new split algorithm works.

In order to clarify the issue, two hundred images were randomly picked up from all data. Out of all the images, only 21 of them had no touching problem. The number of clusters in the other 179 images was about 1602. A comparison between before and after splitting has been carried out by human vision; 90% of the clusters have been completely split by using the new splitting procedure for two or three touching particles. In the other 10% of clusters, 4% are over-split due to concavity errors caused by noise, and 6% are under-split due to omission of some existing concavities not very significant for the algorithm. These two opposite situations may be related to concavity classification in the algorithm. The detail results are listed in Table 2. Split results from two example images are shown in Figs. 19-20.

No. of images	No. of particles	No. of clusters	Over-split clusters	Under-split clusters	Fully split clusters
200	3815	1602	63	91	1448

Table 2. Test results in an on-line system

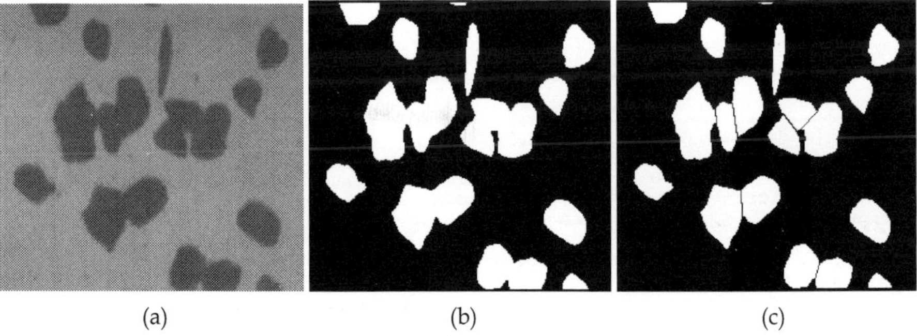

(a)   (b)   (c)

Fig. 19. Example #1 of split result of aggregate images from a gravitational flow: (a) original image; (b) binary image; (c) split result, used thresholds:

$$(L_1, L_2, L_3, \alpha_1, \alpha_2) = (6, 0.5, 0.6, 100^0, 60^0).$$

We have tested the algorithm on a number of rock particle images with different situations of touching particles. The following examples illustrate the power of the split algorithm on realistic data for images of packed particles. The following figures show examples of split results from our split algorithm consisting of three main procedures: filling and opening holes, splitting multiply touching particles, and splitting two or three touching particles, which has been applied in an on-line system. Different grey shades in binary images are for different clusters (one object = one cluster) before split.

In Fig. 21(a), the image is a binarised image, and the original image is taken from a laboratory, of crushed aggregate particles of different sizes. The image includes two large clusters and one single particle, and the split result image (Fig. 21(c)) shows that two large clusters were completely split into 54 particles.

In Fig. 22(a), an original aggregate (natural) image is presented, taken from a conveyor belt in the laboratory. Although manual binarisation result (Fig. 22(b)) is not very satisfactory, the split result is quite promising.

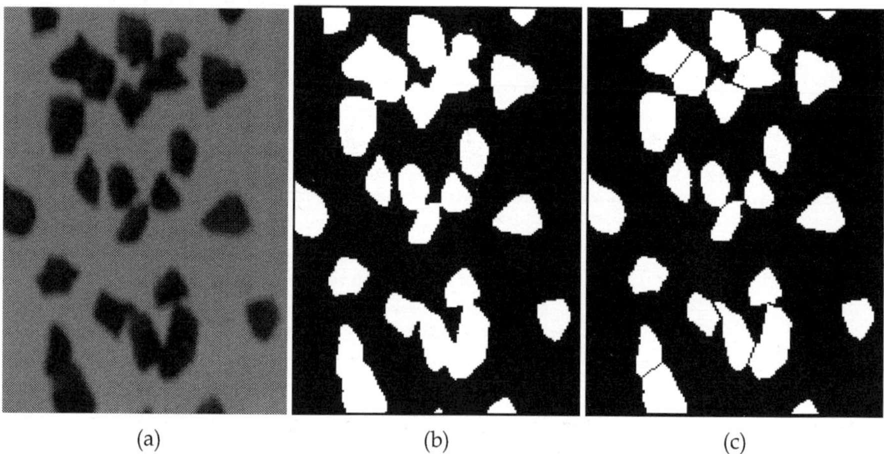

(a)   (b)   (c)

Fig. 20. Example #2 of split result of aggregate images from a gravitational flow: (a) original image; (b) binary image; (c) split result, used thresholds:

$$(L_1, L_2, L_3, \alpha_1, \alpha_2) = (6, 0.5, 0.6, 100^0, 60^0) .$$

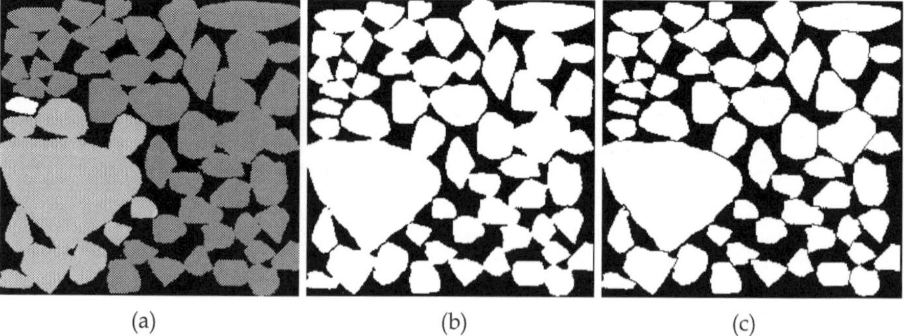

(a)   (b)   (c)

Fig. 21. Split result of touching particles of crushed aggregates: (a) a binary image taken with the illumination of backlighting, consisting of two clusters and one single particle; (b) the image after hole treatment; (c) the image after split, consisting of 55 particles.

The new algorithm for splitting touching rock particles is developed based on polygonal approximation. It includes classification of concavities and analysis of supplementary cost functions. The whole procedure consists of three major steps: (1) two or three touching particles; (2) multiple touching particles; and (3) holes prevailing inside an object. The algorithm can be applicable not only to crushed rock particle images, but also to other particle images, e.g. cells or chromosomes, or cytological, histological, metallurgical or agricultural images.

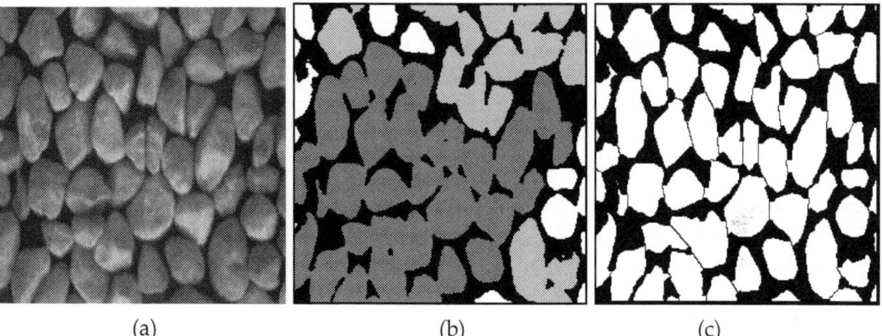

(a)   (b)   (c)

Fig. 22. Split result of touching particles of natural aggregates: (a) an original image taken with the illumination of frontlighting; (b) the image after binarisation, is made up of four clusters and thirteen particles; (c) the image after split, consisting of 59 particles.

The new algorithm has some advantages over the existing algorithms, and is capable of decomposing touching rock particles. The test results show that the un-split touching particles only have concave points with degrees of concavity below 3, which indicates that the classification of degree of concavity is quite important. The split algorithm yields data suitable for analysis of aggregate size and shape, which will be reported elsewhere. Polygonal approximation and classification of concavity, based on polygons, substantially enhanced the robustness of the algorithm.

4. Discussion and conclusion of segmentation algorithms

Rock particle image segmentation is typically the first and most difficult task [59]. All subsequent interpretation tasks, including particle size, shape and texture analysis, rely heavily on the quality of the segmentation results. Since rock particle images vary from one to another, it is difficult or impossible to design and develop one segmentation algorithm for all kinds of rock particle images. The presented segmentation algorithms were developed for just several types of rock particle images with a certain characteristics with respect to segmentation.

In general, both two steps of rock particle image segmentation, i.e. segmentation based on gray level and segmentation based on shape and size of rock particle particles, are needed in most cases of rock particle application. The thresholding algorithms are for images where particles or particle clusters differ everywhere in intensity from the background. The thresholding algorithms are not sensitive to texture on particles, and have normally a low cost for processing. When particles are densely packed, and particles are surrounded by particles and some void spaces (background), the algorithm based on split-and-merge can be applied for the image.

The algorithm based on split-and-merge has the advantage of producing higher level primitives, but the region so extracted may not correspond to actual particles, and the boundary of the extracted region is rough. The algorithm based on edge detection is suitable for the images without too much texture on the surface of particles. It has the disadvantage of producing low-level primitives (segments) even after considerable processing. As one example, the two algorithms are compared in Fig. 23. In Fig. 23(a), the original image is a fragments image taken from a rockpile. Where, fragments show multiple faces in the image, and natural light caused illumination non-uniform. The two algorithms were used for segmenting the original image without any preprocessing. The image in Fig. 23(c) is a thresholded edge image without doing noise edge deleting and gap linking. The algorithm based on edge detection is very sensitive to this kind of image. The algorithm based on split-and-merge can not exactly extract every individual fragment.

(a)   (b)   (c)

Fig. 23. Comparison between two segmentation algorithms. (a) Original fragment image from a rockpile. (b) Image segmented by the algorithm based on split-and-merge. (c) Edge image processed by Canny's edge detector.

The algorithm for splitting touching particles in a binary image is important for overcoming the problem of over-segmentation in a gray level image. In most cases, as discussed before, any single one of the gray level segmentation algorithms cannot segment a gray level image completely. As a supplementary procedure, the segmentation algorithms based on rock particle shapes should be used for further segmentation.

In conclusions, segmentation algorithm selection is based on the types of rock particle images and requirement of measuring rock particles. If one needs a crude segmentation result for densely packed rock particle image, the algorithm based on edge detection will be very useful. The algorithm based on thresholding often lead to an under-segmentation problem, which can be resolved by using the split algorithm for touching particles. The algorithm based on split-and-merge is a combination of segmentation on gray level and segmentation based on shape of rock particles. The algorithm includes several techniques such as image pre-processing, region split-and-merge, thresholding, binary image segmentation. Combinations of the mentioned segmentation algorithms are more powerful than the individual procedures by themselves.

5. References

Wang, W.X. and Fernlund, J., Shape Analysis of Rock particles. KTH-BALLAST Report no. 2, KTH, Stockholm, Sweden (1994).

Gallagher, E., Optoelectronic coarse particle size analysis for industrial measurement and control. Ph.D. thesis, University of Queensland, Dept. of Mining and Metallurgical Engineering (1976).

Nyberg, L., Carlsson, O., Schmidtbauer, B., Estimation of the size distribution of fragmented rock in ore mining through automatic image processing. Proc. IMEKO 9th World Congress, May, Vol. V/III (1982), pp. 293 - 301.

Hunter, G.C., et al., A review of image analysis techniques for measuring blast fragmentation. Mining Science and Technology, 11 (1990) 19-36.

Franklin, J.A, Kemeny J.M. and Girdner, K.K., Evolution of measuring systems: A review. Measurement of Blast Fragmentation, Ed by J.A. Franklin and T. Katsabanis, Rotterdam: Balkema (1996), 47-52.

Wang, W.X. and Dahlhielm, S., Evaluation of image methods for the size distribution of rock fragments after blasting. Report no. 1 on the project within the Swedish-Sino cooperation in metallic materials and mining, Luleå, Sweden, October (1989).

Lange, T., Real-time measurement of the size distribution of rocks on a conveyor belt. Int. Fed. Automatic control, Workshop on applied Measurements in Mineral and Metal Processing, Johannesburg (1989).

Lang, T.B., Measurement of the size distribution of rock on a conveyor belt using machine vision. Ph.D. thesis, the Faculty of Engineering, University of the Witwatersrand, Johannesburg (1990).

Zeng, S., Wang, Y. and Wang, W.X., Study on the techniques of photo -image analysis for rock fragmentation by blasting. Proc. for third period of Sino-Swedish joint research on science and technology of metallurgy, Publishing House of Metallurgical Industry, China (1992), pp. 103-115.

Wang, Y., Zeng, S. and Wang, W.X., Study on the image analysis system of photographic film. Proc. for third period of Sino-Swedish joint research on science and technology of metallurgy, Publishing House of Metallurgical Industry, China (1992), pp. 116-126.

Montoro, J.J. and Gonzalez, E., New analytical techniques to evaluate fragmentation based on image analysis by computer methods. 4th Int. Symp. Rock Fragmentation by Blasting, Keystone, Vienna, Austria (1993), pp. 309 -316.

McDermott, C., Hunter, G.C. and Miles, N.J., The application of image analysis to the measurement of blast fragmentation. Symp. Surface Mining-Future Concepts, Nottingham University, Marylebone Press, Manchester (1989), pp. 103-108.

Ord, A., Real time image analysis of size and shape distributions of rock fragments. Proc. Aust. Int. Min. Metall., 294, 1 (1989).

Lin, C.L and Miller, J.D., The Development of a PC Image-Based On-line Particle Size Analyzer. Minerals & Metallurgical Processing, No. 2 (1993) 29-35.

Von Hodenberg, M., Monitoring crusher gap adjustment using an automatic particle size analyzer, Mineral process, Vol. 37, (1996) 432-437 (Germany).

HAVER CPA, Computerized particle analyzer, User's Guide :CPA - 3, Printed by HAVER & BOECKER, Drahtweberei, Ennigerloher Straße 64, D-59302 OELDE Westfalen, (1996).

Blot, G. and Nissoux, J.-L., Les nouveaux outils de controle de la granulométrie et de la forme (New tools for controlling size and shape of rock particles), Mines et carrières, Les Techniques V/94, SUPPL.-Déc., Vol. 96, (1994) (France).

J. Schleifer and B. Tessier, Fragmentation Assessment using the FragScan System: Quality of a Blast, Fragblast, Volume 6, Numbers 3-4 / December 2002, pp. 321 - 331, Publisher: Taylor & Francis.

Grannes, S.G., Determine size distribution of moving pellets by computer image processing, 19th Application of Computers and Operations Reaserch in Mineral Industry(editor, R.V. Ramani), Soc. Mining Engineers, Inc. (1986), pp. 545-551.

Donald, C. and Kettunen, B.E., On-line size analysis for the measurement of blast fragmentation. Measurement of Blast Fragmentation , Ed by J.A. Franklin and T. Katsabanis. Rotterdam: Balkema, (1996) 175-177.

Norbert H Maerz, Tom W, Palangio. Post-Muckpile, Pre-Primary Crusher, Automated Optical Blast Fragmentation Sizing, Fragblast, Volume 8, Number 2 / June 2004, pp. 119 – 136, Publisher: Taylor & Francis.

Norbert H. Maerz and Wei Zhou , Calibration of optical digital fragmentation measuring systems, Fragblast, Volume 4, Number 2 / June 2000, pp. 126 - 138, Publisher: Taylor & Francis..

Paley, N., Lyman, G..J. and Kavetsky, A., Optical blast fragmentation assessment, Proc. 3rd Int. Symp. Rock Fragmentation by Blasting, Australian IMM, Brisbane, Australia (1990), pp. 291-301.

Wu, X., and Kemeny, J.M., A segmentation method for multiconnected particle delineation, Proc. of the IEEE Workshop on Applications of Computer vision, IEEE Computer Society Press, Los Alamitos, CA (1992) 240-247.

Kemeny J, Mofya E, Kaunda R, Lever P. Improvements in Blast Fragmentation Models Using Digital Image Processing, Fragblast, Volume 6, Numbers 3-4 / December 2002, pp. 311 - 320, Publisher: Taylor & Francis.

.Kemeny, J., A practical technique for determining the size distribution of blasted benches, waste dumps, and heap-leach sites, Mining Engineering, Vol. 46, No. 11 (1994), 1281-1284.

Girdner, K.K., Kemeny, J..M., Srikant, A. and McGill, R., The split system for analyzing the size distribution of fragmented rock. Measurement of Blast Fragmentation, Ed by J.A. Franklin & T. Katsabanis. Rotterdam: Balkema (1996), pp. 101-108.

Vogt, W. and Aßbrock, Digital image processing as an instrument to evaluate rock fragmentation by blasting in open pit mines, 4th Int. Symp. Rock fragmentation by Blasting, Keystone, Vienna, Austria (1993), 317-324.

Havermann, T. and Vogt, W., TUCIPS. A system for the estimation of fragmentation after production blasts, Measurement of Blast Fragmentation, Ed by J.A. Franklin and T. Katsabanis. Rotterdam: Balkema (1996), pp. 67-71.

Rholl, S.A., et al., Photographic assessment of the fragmentation distribution of rock quarry muckpiles, 4th Int. Symp. Rock Fragmentation by Blasting, Vienna, Austria (1993), pp. 501-506.

Lin, C.L, Yen, Y.K. and Miller, J.D. , On-line coarse particle size measurement -industrial testing. SME Annual Meeting, March 6-9, Denver, Colorado, USA, (1995).

Bedair A., Daneshmend L.K. and Hendricks C.F.B. Comparative performance of a novel automated technique for identification of muck pile fragment boundaries. Measurement of Blast Fragmentation, Ed by J.A. Franklin & T. Katsabanis. Rotterdam: Balkema, (1996) 157-166.

Bedair, A., Digital image analysis of rock fragmentation from blasting. Ph.D. thesis, Department of Mining and Metallurgical Engineering, McGill University, Montreal, Quebec (1996).

Wang, W.X. and Dahlhielm, S., An algorithm for automatic recognition of rock fragmentation through digitizing photo images, Report no. 5 on the project within the Swedish-Sino cooperation in metallic materials and mining, July (1990).

Stephansson, O., Wang, W.X. and Dahlhielm, S., Automatic image processing of rock particles, ISRM Symposium: EUROCK '92, Chester, UK, 14-17 September, British Geotechnical Society, London, UK (1992), pp. 31-35.

Wang, W. X., Automatic Image Analysis of Rock particles from A Moving Conveyor Belt. Licentiate Thesis. Dept. of Civil and Environmental Engineering, Royal Institute of Technology, Stockholm, Sweden (1995).

Dahlhielm, S., Industrial applications of image analysis. The IPACS system. Measurement of Blast Fragmentation, Ed by J.A. Franklin & T. Katsabanis. Rotterdam: Balkema (1996), pp. 59-65.

Yen, Y. K., Lin, C. L. and Miller, J. D., The overlap problem in on-line coarse size measurement - segmentation and transformation, SME Annual Meeting, February 14-17, Albuquerque, New Mexico, US. (1994), Preprint No. 94-177.

Schleifer, J. and Tessier, B., FRAGSCAN: A tool to measure fragmentation of blasted rock. Measurement of Blast Fragmentation, Ed by J.A. Franklin and T. Katsabanis. Rotterdam: Balkema (1996), pp. 73-78.

Cheimanoff, N.M., Chavez, R. and Schleifer, J., FRAGMENTATION: A scanning tool for fragmentation after blasting, 4th Int. Symp. Rock Fragmentation by Blasting, Keystone, Vienna, Austria (1993), pp. 325-330.

Chung S.H., Experience in fragmentation control. Measurement of Blast Fragmentation, Ed by J.A. Franklin & T. Katsabanis. Rotterdam: Balkema (1996), pp. 247-252.

LIN, C.L., Miller, J.D., Luttrell, G.H. and Adel, G.T., On-line washability analysis for the control of coarse coal cleaning circuits, SME/AIME, Editor S.K. Kawatra (1995), pp. 369-378.

Fua, P. and Leclerc, Y.G., Object-centered surface reconstruction: Combining multi-image stereo and shading. International Journal of Computer Vision, Vo. 16, No. 1 (1995), 35-56.

Parkin, R.M., Calkin, D.W. and Jackson, M.R., Roadstone rock particle: An intelligent opto-mechatronic product classifier for sizing and grading. Mechanics Vol. 5, No. 5, Printed in Great Britain (1995), 461-467.

Cheung, C.C. and Ord, A., An on line fragment size analyzer using image processing techniques, 3rd Int. Symp. Rock Fragmentation by Blasting, Brisbane, August 26 -31 (1990), pp. 233-238.

Liang, J., Intelligent splitting the chromosome domain, Pattern Recognition, Vol. 22, No. 5 (1989), pp. 519-532.

Yeo, X.C., Jin, S.H., Ong, Jayasooriah and R. Sinniah, Clump splitting through concavity analysis, Pattern Recognition Lett. 15, (1994), pp. 1013-1018.

Otsu, N., A threshold selection method from gray-level histogram, IEEE Trans. Systems Man Cybernet, SMC-9 (1979), pp. 62-66.

Tor, N., Sven, H., Wang, W.X. and Dahlhielm, S., System för bildtolking av kornstorleksfördelning i naturmaterial och förädlat material, BDa-raport 1, March (1991), (for vägverket in Luleå).

Tor, N., Sven, H., Wang, W.X. and Dahlhielm, S., System för bildtolking av kornstorleksfördelning i naturmaterial och förädlat material, BDa-raport 2, October (1991), (for vägverket in both Borlänge and Luleå).

Jansson, M. and Muhr, T., A study of geometric form of ballast material (in Swedish). Ms. thesis. Dept. of Civil and Environmental Engineering, Royal Institute of Technology, Stockholm, Sweden, EX-1995-002 (1995).

Wang, W.X., 2006, Image analysis of particles by modified Ferret method – best-fit rectangle, International Journal: Powder Technology, Vol. 165, Issue 1, pp. 1-10.

Wang, W.X., 2008, Fragment Size Estimation without Image Segmentation, International Journal: Imaging Science Journal, Vol. 56, p.91-96, April, 2008

Wang, W.X. and Bergholm, F., On edge density for automatic size inspection, Theory and Applications of Image Analysis II, Ed by Gunilla Borgefors, publisher World Scientific Publishing Co. Pte. Ltd. Singapore (1995), pp. 393-406.

Weixing Wang, 2007, An Image Classification and Segmentation for Densely Packed Aggregates, LNAI, Vol. 4426, pp.887-894.

Norbert, H. M., Image sampling techniques and requirements for automated image analysis of rock fragmentation. Measurement of Blast Fragmentation, Ed by J.A. Franklin and T. Katsabanis. Rotterdam: Balkema (1996), pp. 47-52.

Michael, W. B., Image Acquisition, (handbook of machine vision engineering volume I), Printed in Great Britain at The Alden Press, Oxford. ISBN 0 412 47920 6., Published by Chapman & Hall, 2-6 Boundary Row, London SE1 8HN, UK., (1996), pp. 1, 109-126, 127-136, 169, 229-239.

Bir, B. and Sungkee, L., Genetic Learning for Adaptive Image Segmentation, Kluwer Academic Publishers, USA.(1994), pp. 2-4.

Cany, J.F., A computational approach to edge detection, IEEE Trans. Pattern Analysis. March. Intell. 8 (1986), pp. 679-698.

Suk, M., and Chung, S.M., A new image segmentation technique based on partition mode test. Pattern Recognition Vol. 16, No. 5. (1983), pp. 469-480.

Wang, W.X., 1998, Binary image segmentation of aggregates based on polygonal approximation and classification of concavities. International Journal: Pattern Recognition, 31(10), 1503-1524..

Wang, W.X., 1999, Image analysis of aggregates, International Journal: Computers & Geosciences 25, 71-81..

Jansson, M. and Muhr, T., Field tests of an image analysis system for ballast on a conveyor belt in three quarries in Sweden (in Swedish). Technical Report. KTH-Ballast, Stockholm, Sweden. ISNN 1400-1306 (1995).

Cunningham, C.V.B., Fragmentation estimates and the Kuz-Ram model four years on. 2nd Int. Symp. on Rock Fragmentation by Blasting, Keystone, USA (1987), pp. 475-487.

9

Unsupervised Texture Segmentation

Michal Haindl and Stanislav Mikeš
Institute of Information Theory and Automation of the ASCR
Czech Republic

1. Introduction

Segmentation is the fundamental process which partitions a data space into meaningful salient regions. Image segmentation essentially affects the overall performance of any automated image analysis system thus its quality is of the utmost importance. Image regions, homogeneous with respect to some usually textural or colour measure, which result from a segmentation algorithm are analysed in subsequent interpretation steps. Texture-based image segmentation is area of intense research activity in the past thirty years and many algorithms were published in consequence of all this effort, starting from simple thresholding methods up to the most sophisticated random field type methods. Unsupervised methods which do not assume any prior scene knowledge which can be learned to help segmentation process are obviously more challenging than the supervised ones.

Segmentation methods are usually categorized (Reed et al., 1993) as region-based, boundary-based, or as a hybrid of the two. Different published methods are difficult to compare because of lack of a comprehensive analysis together with accessible experimental data, however available results indicate that the ill-defined texture segmentation problem is still far from being satisfactorily solved. The clustering approach resulted in agglomerative and divisive algorithms which were modified for image segmentation as region-based merge and split algorithms. Spatial interaction models and especially Markov random field-based models are increasingly popular for texture representation (Kashyap, 1986; Reed et al., 1993; Haindl, 1991), etc. Several researchers dealt with the difficult problem of unsupervised segmentation using these models see for example (Panjwani et al., 1995; Manjunath et al., 1991; Andrey et al., 1998; Haindl, 1999) or (Haindl et al., 2004, 2005, 2006a). In this chapter we assume constant illumination and viewing angles for all scene textures, or alternatively that the Lambert law holds for all scene surfaces. If this assumption cannot be assumed than all textures have to be treated either as Bidirectional Texture Functions (BTFs) or some illumination invariant features (Haindl et al., 2006b; Vacha et al., 2007) have too be used.

2. Texture segmentation methods

Segmentation methods are based on some pixel or region similarity measure in relation to their local neighbourhood. Boundary-based methods search for the most dissimilar pixels which represent discontinuities in the image, while region based methods on the contrary search for the most similar areas. These similarity measures in texture segmentation methods use some textural spatial-spectral-temporal features such as Markov random field statistics (MRF) (Haindl et al., 2004, 2005, 2006a), cooccurrence matrix based features, Gabor features, local binary pattern (LBP) (Ojala et al., 1999), autocorrelation features and many others. Segmentation methods can be categorized using various criteria, e.g. region / boundary based, MAP / clustering methods, graph theoretic methods, etc.

2.1 Region growing

The basic approach of a region growing algorithm (Pal et al., 1993; Belongie et al., 1998; Deng et al., 2001, 2004; Scarpa et al., 2006, 2007) is to start from a seed regions (mostly one or few pixels) that are assumed to be inside the object to be segmented. The neighbouring pixels to every seed region are evaluated to decide if they should be considered part of the object or not. If they are recognized as similar, they are added to the region and the process continues as long as any undecided pixels remain. Region growing algorithms vary depending on the similarity criteria, seed region selection, the type connectivity used to determine neighbours, and the strategy used to visit neighbouring pixels.

The JSEG method (Deng et al., 2001) consists of two independent steps: colour quantization and region growing spatial segmentation on multiscale thematic maps from the first step.

The Blobworld scheme aims to transform images into a small set of regions which are coherent in colour and texture (Belongie et al., 1998). This is achieved by clustering pixels in a joint colour-texture-position eight-dimensional feature space using the EM algorithm. The feature vector is represented by a Gaussian mixture model.

2.2 Split and merge

Split and merge techniques (Pal et al., 1993) start with recursive splitting image into smaller regions until they do not satisfy some homogeneity criterion. The second merging step merges adjacent regions with similar attributes.

2.3 Watershed

Watershed segmentation (Shafarenko et al., 1997) classifies pixels into regions using gradient descent on image features and analysis of weak points along region boundaries. The image feature space is treated, using a suitable mapping, as a topological surface where higher values indicate the presence of boundaries in the original image data. It uses analogy with water gradually filling low lying landscape basins. The size of the basins grow with increasing amounts of water until they spill into one another. Small basins (regions) gradually merge together into larger basins. Regions are formed by using local geometric structure to associate the image domain features with local extremes measurement. Watershed techniques produce a hierarchy of segmentations, thus the resulting segmentation has to be selected using either some prior knowledge or manually. These methods are well suited for different measurements fusion and they are less sensitive to user defined thresholds.

2.4 Level set segmentation

The paradigm of the level set (Brox et al., 2006) is that it is a numerical method for tracking the evolution of contours and surfaces. Instead of manipulating the contour directly, the contour is embedded as the zero level set of a higher dimensional function called the level-set function. The level-set function is evolved under the control of a differential equation using some image-based features. At any time, the evolving contour can be obtained by extracting the zero level-set from the output. Level sets allow to model arbitrarily complex shapes and topological changes such as merging and splitting are handled implicitly.

2.5 Mean shift segmentation

Edison (Christoudias et al., 2002) is a mean shift based image segmentation with embedded edge information. Its first filtering step uses the mean shift (Comaniciu et al., 2002) segmenter in the combined colour $L^*u^*v^*$ and coordinate feature space. The mean shift weights are derived from the edge confidence measure. The second fusion step recursively fuses the basins of attraction of the modes. The method requires six segmentation parameters to be tuned.

2.6 Graph-theoretic segmentation

These methods (Felzenszwalb et al., 1998; Shi et al., 2000; Boykov et al., 2003; Galun et al., 2003; Barbu et al., 2004; Estrada et al., 2005) use graph representation for image pixels or regions where usually small neighbourhood elements are mutually connected with weighted graph edges. These weights indicate pairwise elements similarities. The segmentation is based on finding groups of nodes that are strongly connected to each other, but weakly with the remaining nodes in the graph.

3. GMRF-GM segmenter

The adequate representation of general static Lambertian multispectral textures requires three dimensional models. Although full 3D models allows unrestricted spatial-spectral correlation description its main drawback is large amount of parameters to be estimated and in the case of Markov random field based models (MRF) also the necessity to estimate all these parameters simultaneously. Alternatively, it is possible to factorize the 3D static texture space into several (equal to the number d of spectral bands) 2D subspaces. A combination of several simpler 2D data models with less parameters per model allows more compact texture representation and faster estimation algorithms. Natural measured texture data space can be decorrelated only approximately thus the independent spectral component representation suffers with some loss of image information. However, because the segmentation is less demanding application than the texture synthesis, it is sufficient if such a representation maintains discriminative power of the full model even if its visual modeling strength is slightly compromised. The GMRF-GM segmenter (Haindl et al., 2004) uses such 2D generative Gaussian Markov representation.

3.1 Spectral factorization

Spectral factorization using the Karhunen-Loeve expansion transforms the original centered data space θ defined on the rectangular $M{\times}N$ finite lattice I into a new data space with K-L coordinate axes $\tilde{Y}$. This new basis vectors are the eigenvectors of the second-order statistical moments matrix

$$\Phi = E\{\tilde{Y}_r \tilde{Y}_r^T\} \tag{1}$$

where the multiindex r has two components $r = [r_1, r_2]$, the first component is row and the second one column index, respectively. The projection of the centered random vector $\tilde{Y}_r$ onto the K-L coordinate system uses the transformation matrix $T = [u_1^T, u_2^T, \ldots u_d^T]^T$ which has single rows u_j that are eigenvectors of the matrix Φ.

$$\bar{Y}_r = T\tilde{Y}_r \tag{2}$$

Components of the transformed vector $\bar{Y}_r$ (2) are mutually uncorrelated. If we assume further on Gaussian vectors $\bar{Y}_r$ then they are also independent, i.e.,

$$p(\bar{Y}_r) = \prod_{k=1}^{d} p(\bar{Y}_{r,k})$$

and single monospectral random fields can be modeled independently.

3.2 GMRF texture model

We assume that single monospectral texture factors $(Y_r = \bar{Y}_{r,k})$ can be modeled using a Gaussian Markov random field model (GMRF). This model is obtained if the local conditional density of the MRF model is Gaussian:

$$p(Y_r \mid Y_{r-s} \; \forall s \in I_r) = (2\pi\sigma^2)^{-\frac{1}{2}} e^{-\frac{1}{2}\sigma^{-2}(Y_r - \mu_r)^2} ,$$

where the mean value is

$$E\{Y_r \mid Y_{r-s} \; \forall s \in I_r\} = \tilde{\mu}_r = \mu_r + \sum_{s \in I_r} a_s(Y_{r-s} - \mu_{r-s}) \tag{3}$$

and σ, $a_s \; \forall s \in I_r$ are unknown parameters.

The 2D GMRF model can be expressed as a stationary non-causal correlated noise driven 2D autoregressive process:

$$Y_r = \sum_{s \in I_r} a_s Y_{r-s} + e_r \tag{4}$$

where the noise e_r is random variable with zero mean $E\{e_r\} = 0$. The e_r noise variables are mutually correlated

$$R_e = E\{e_r e_{r-s}\} = \begin{cases} \sigma^2 & \text{if } s = (0,0), \\ -\sigma^2 a_s & \text{if } s \in I_r, \\ 0 & \text{otherwise.} \end{cases} \tag{5}$$

Correlation functions have the symmetry property $E\{e_r e_{r+s}\} = E\{e_r e_{r-s}\}$ hence the neighbourhood support set I_r and its associated coefficients have to be symmetric, i.e., $s \in I_r \Rightarrow -s \in I_r$ and $a_s = a_{-s}$.

The selection of an appropriate GMRF model support is important to obtain good results in modeling of a given random field. If the contextual neighbourhood is too small it can not capture all details of the random field. Inclusion of the unnecessary neighbours on the other hand add to the computational burden and can potentially degrade the performance of the model as an additional source of noise. We use hierarchical neighbourhood system I_r, e.g., the first-order neighbourhood is $I_r = \{-(0, 1),+(0, 1),-(1, 0),+(1, 0)\}$, etc. An optimal neighbourhood is detected using the correlation method (Haindl et al., 1997) favoring neighbours locations corresponding to large correlations over those with small correlations. Parameter estimation of a MRF model is complicated by the difficulty associated with computing the normalization constant. Fortunately the GMRF model is an exception where the normalization constant is easy obtainable however either Bayesian or ML estimate requires iterative minimization of a nonlinear function. Therefore we use the pseudo-likelihood estimator which is computationally simple although not efficient. The pseudo-likelihood estimate for a_s parameters evaluated for a sublattice $J_r \subset I$ and $J_r = \{s : |\, r_1 - s_1| \le m \wedge |\, r_2 - s_2| \le n\}$ centered on the r index. The pseudo-likelihood estimate for a_s parameters has the form

$$\gamma_r = [a_s \quad \forall s \in I_r] = \left[\sum_{\forall s \in J_r} X_s^T X_s \right]^{-1} \sum_{\forall s \in J_r} X_s^T Y_s \, , \tag{6}$$

where $X_s = [Y_{s+t} \quad \forall t \in I_s]$.

3.3 Mixture model based segmentation

Multi-spectral texture segmentation is done by clustering in the GMRF parameter space $\Theta \in \mathbb{R}^n$ defined on the lattice I where

$$\Theta_r = [\gamma_{r,1}, \zeta_{r,1}, \gamma_{r,2}, \zeta_{r,2}, \dots \gamma_{r,d}, \zeta_{r,d}]^T \, . \tag{7}$$

$\gamma_{r,i}$ is the parameter vector (6) computed for the i-th transformed spectral band for the lattice location r and $\zeta_{r,i}$ is the average local spectral value. We assume that this parametric space can be represented using the Gaussian mixture model with diagonal covariance matrices. Hence the GMRF parametric space is first decorrelated using the Karhunen-Loeve transformation (analogously to (1)-(2)). The Gaussian mixture model for GMRF parametric representation is as follows:

$$p(\Theta_r) = \sum_{i=1}^{K} p_i \, p(\Theta_r \,|\, v_i, \Sigma_i) \tag{8}$$

$$p(\Theta_r \,|\, v_i, \Sigma_i) = \frac{|\Sigma_i|^{-\frac{1}{2}}}{(2\pi)^{\frac{n}{2}}} e^{-\frac{(\Theta_r - v_i)^T \Sigma_i^{-1} (\Theta_r - v_i)}{2}} \, . \tag{9}$$

The mixture equations (8),(9) are solved using the modified EM algorithm. The algorithm is initialized using v_i, Σ_i statistics estimated from the corresponding rectangular subimages obtained by regular division of the input texture mosaic. An alternative initialization can be random choice of these statistics. For each possible couple of rectangles the Kullback Leibler divergence

$$D\left(p(\Theta_r \,|\, v_i, \Sigma_i) \,\|\, p(\Theta_r \,|\, v_j, \Sigma_j)\right) = \int_\Omega p(\Theta_r \,|\, v_i, \Sigma_i) \log\left(\frac{p(\Theta_r \,|\, v_i, \Sigma_i)}{p(\Theta_r \,|\, v_j, \Sigma_j)}\right) d\Theta_r \tag{10}$$

is evaluated and the most similar rectangles, i.e.,

$$\{i,j\} = \arg\min_{k,l} D\left(p(\Theta_r \mid v_l, \Sigma_l) \,\|\, p(\Theta_r \mid v_k, \Sigma_k)\right)$$

are merged together in each step. This initialization results in K_{ini} subimages and recomputed statistics v_i, Σ_i. $K_{ini} > K$ where K is the optimal number of textured segments to be found by the algorithm. After initialization two steps of the EM algorithm are repeating:

$$E: \quad p^{(t)}(\omega_i \mid \Theta_r) = \frac{p_i\, p(\Theta_r \mid v_i, \Sigma_i)}{\sum_{j=1}^{K} p_j\, p(\Theta_r \mid v_j, \Sigma_j)}$$

$$M: \qquad\qquad\qquad\qquad \forall j = 1, \dots, K$$

$$p_j^{(t+1)} = \frac{1}{|I|} \sum_{\forall \Theta_r} p^{(t)}(\omega_j \mid \Theta_r)$$

$$v_j^{(t+1)} = \frac{\sum_{\forall \Theta_r} \Theta_r\, p^{(t)}(\omega_j \mid \Theta_r)}{\sum_{\forall \Theta_r} p^{(t)}(\omega_j \mid \Theta_r)}$$

$$\Sigma_j^{(t+1)} = \frac{\sum_{\forall \Theta_r} p(\omega_j \mid \Theta_r)\left(\Theta_r - v_j^{(t+1)}\right)\left(\Theta_r - v_j^{(t+1)}\right)^T}{\sum_{\forall \Theta_r} p^{(t)}(\omega_j \mid \Theta_r)} \,. \tag{11}$$

The components with smaller weights $p_j < \xi$ than a given threshold are eliminated. For every pair of components we estimate their Kullback Leibler divergence (10). From the most similar couple, the component with the weight smaller than the threshold is merged to its stronger partner and all statistics are actualized using the EM algorithm. The algorithm stops when either the likelihood function has negligible increase ($\mathcal{L}_t - \mathcal{L}_{t-1} < 0.05$) or the maximum iteration number threshold is reached.

The parametric vectors representing texture mosaic pixels are assigned to the clusters according to the highest component probabilities, i.e., Y_r is assigned to the cluster ω_j if

$$\arg\max_j \sum_{s \in Neigh} weight(s)\, p(\Theta_{r-s} \mid v_j, \Sigma_j) \tag{12}$$

$$p(\Theta_r \mid v_j, \Sigma_j) > p(\Theta_r \mid v_i, \Sigma_i) \; \forall i \neq j \,.$$

The area of single cluster blobs is evaluated in the post-processing thematic map filtration step. Thematic map blobs with area smaller than a given threshold are attached to its neighbour with the highest similarity value. If there is no similar neighbour the blob is eliminated. After all blobs are processed remaining blobs are expanded.

4. AR3D-GM segmenter

If we do not like to lose spectral information due to the spectral decorrelation step, we have to use three dimensional models for adequate representation. One of few 3D models which does not require any approximation and can be treated analytically is the 3D simultaneous causal autoregressive random field model (CAR) used in the AR3D-GM segmenter (Haindl et al., 2006a).

We assume that single multispectral textures can be locally modeled using the CAR model. This model can be expressed as a stationary causal uncorrelated noise driven 3D autoregressive process (Haindl et al., 1992):

$$Y_r = \gamma X_r + e_r \; , \tag{13}$$

where

$$\gamma = [A_1, \ldots, A_\eta]$$

is the $d \times d\eta$ parameter matrix, d is the number of spectral bands, I_r^c is a causal neighbourhood index set with $\eta = \mathrm{card}(I_r^c)$ and e_r is a white Gaussian noise vector with zero mean and a constant but unknown covariance, X_r is a corresponding vector of the contextual neighbours Y_{r-s} and $r, r-1, \ldots$ is a chosen direction of movement on the image index lattice I. The selection of an appropriate CAR model support (I_r^c) is important to obtain good texture representation but less important for segmentation. The optimal neighbourhood as well as the Bayesian parameters estimation of a CAR model can be found analytically under few additional and acceptable assumptions using the Bayesian approach (Haindl et al., 1992). The recursive Bayesian parameter estimation of the CAR model is (Haindl et al., 1992):

$$\hat{\gamma}_{r-1}^T = \hat{\gamma}_{r-2}^T + \frac{V_{x(r-2)}^{-1} X_{r-1} (Y_{r-1} - \hat{\gamma}_{r-2} X_{r-1})^T}{(1 + X_{r-1}^T V_{x(r-2)}^{-1} X_{r-1})} \; , \tag{14}$$

where $V_{x(r-1)} = \sum_{k=1}^{r-1} X_k X_k^T + V_{x(0)}$. Local texture for each pixel is represented by four parametric vectors. Each vector contains local estimations of the CAR model parameters. These models have identical contextual neighbourhood I_r^c but they differ in their major movement direction (top-down, bottom-up, rightward, leftward), i.e.,

$$\tilde{\gamma}_r^T = \{\hat{\gamma}_r^t, \hat{\gamma}_r^b, \hat{\gamma}_r^r, \hat{\gamma}_r^l\}^T \; . \tag{15}$$

The parametric space $\tilde{\gamma}$ is subsequently smooth out, rearranged into a vector and its dimensionality is reduced using the Karhunen-Loeve feature extraction ($\bar{\gamma}$). Finally we add the average local spectral values ζ_r to the resulting feature vector (Θ_r).

4.1 AR2D-GM segmenter

The AR2D-GM segmenter (Haindl et al., 2005) uses the 2D simultaneous causal autoregressive random field model and thus it requires the spectral decorrelation described in section 3.1. If we stack single decorrelated mono spectral pixel components into $d \times 1$ vectors Y_r, the model can be formalized using the same equations as the AR3D model, i.e. (13)-(15). The AR2D models differ in having diagonal parameter matrices A_s and a diagonal white noise covariance matrix.

4.2 Mixture based segmentation

Multi-spectral texture segmentation is done by clustering in the CAR parameter space Θ defined on the lattice I where

$$\Theta_r = [\bar{\gamma}_r, \zeta_r]^T$$

is the modified parameter vector (15) computed for the lattice location r. We assume that this parametric space can be represented using the Gaussian mixture model (GM) with diagonal covariance matrices due to the previous CAR parametric space decorrelation. The Gaussian mixture model for CAR parametric representation is again (8),(9) and can be solved similarly as (10)-(12).

5. Evaluation methodology

Unsupervised or supervised texture segmentation is the prerequisite for successful content-based image retrieval, scene analysis, automatic acquisition of virtual models, quality control, security, medical applications and many others. Although more than 1000 different methods were already published (Zhang, 1997), this problem is still far from being solved. This is among others due to missing reliable performance comparison between different techniques because very limited effort was spent to develop suitable quantitative measures of segmentation quality that can be used to evaluate and compare segmentation algorithms. Rather than advancing the most promising image segmentation approaches novel algorithms are often satisfied just being sufficiently different from the previously published ones and tested only on a few carefully selected positive examples. The optimal alternative to check several variants of a developed method and to carefully compare results with state-of-theart in this area is practically impossible because most methods are too complicated and insufficiently described to be implemented in the acceptable time. Because there is no available benchmark fully supporting segmentation method development, we implemented a solution in the form of web based data generator and benchmark software. Proper testing and robust learning of performance characteristics require large test sets and objective ground truth which is unfeasible for natural images. Thus, inevitably all such image sets such as the Berkeley benchmark (Martin et al., 2001) share the same drawbacks - subjectively generated ground truth regions and limited extent which is very difficult and expensive to enlarge. These problems motivated our preference for random mosaics with randomly filled textures even if they only approximate natural image scenes. The profitable feature of this compromise is the unlimited number of different test images with corresponding objective and free ground truth map available for each of them.

The segmentation results can be judged (Zhang, 1997) either by using manually segmented images as reference (Lee et al., 1990), or visually by comparing to the original images (Pal et al., 1993), or just by applying quality measures corresponding to human intuition (Sahoo et al., 1988; Lee et al., 1990; Pal et al., 1993). However it is difficult to avoid subjective ranking conclusions by using either of above approaches on limited test databases.

A prior work on the segmentation benchmark is the Berkeley benchmark presented by Martin et al. (Martin et al., 2001). This benchmark contains more than 1000 various natural images (300 in its public version) from the Corel database, each of which is manually processed by a group of people to get the ground-truth segmentation in the form of partitioning of the image into a set of disjoint segments. Without any special guidance, such manual segmentations reflect the subjective human perception and therefore, different people usually construct different ground truths on the same image. The Berkeley benchmark suffers from several drawbacks. Apart from subjective ground truth, also its performance criteria a global consistency error (GCE) and a local consistency error (LCE) tolerate unreasonable refinement of the ground truth. Over-segmented machine segmentations have always zero consistency error, i.e., they wrongly suggest an ideal segmentation. The benchmark comparison is based on region borders hence different border localization from the human based drawing can handicap otherwise correct scene segmentation.

Another segmentation benchmark Minerva (Sharma et al., 2001) contains 448 colour and grey scale images of natural scenes which are segmented using four different segmenters, segmented regions are manually labelled and different textural features can be learned from these regions and subsequently used by the kNN supervised classifier. This approach suffers from erroneous ground truth resulting from an imperfect segmenter, manual labelling and inadequate textural feature learning from small regions.

Outex Texture Database (Ojala et al., 2002) provides a public repository for three types of empirical texture evaluation test suites. It contains 14 classification test suites, while one unsupervised segmentation test set is formed by 100 texture mosaics all using the same regular ground truth template and finally one texture retrieval test set. The test suites are publicly available on the website (http://www.outex.oulu.fi), which allows searching, browsing and downloading of the test image databases. Outex currently provides limited test repository but does not allow results evaluation or algorithms ranking.

A psycho-visual evaluation of segmentation algorithms using human observers was proposed in (Shaffrey et al., 2002). The test was designed to visually compare two segmentations in each step and to answer if any consensus of the best segmentation exists. While such human judgement certainly allows meaningful evaluation, this approach is too demanding to be applicable in image segmentation research.

5.1 Prague texture segmentation benchmark

The Prague texture segmentation data-generator and benchmark Fig.1 is web based service (http://mosaic.utia.cas.cz) developed as a part of EU NoE no. 507752 MUSCLE project. The goal of the benchmark is to produce score, performance and quality measures for an algorithm's performance for two main reasons: So that different algorithms can be compared to each other, and so that progress toward human-level segmentation performance can be tracked and measured over time. A good experimental evaluation should allow comparison of the current algorithm to several leading alternative algorithms, using as many test images as possible and employing several evaluation measures for comparison (in the absence of one clearly optimal measure). Our benchmark possesses all these features.

Single textures as well as the mosaics generation approach were chosen on purpose to produce unusually difficult tests to allow an improvement space for future better segmentation algorithms.

The benchmark operates either in full mode for registered users (unrestricted mode - U) or in a restricted mode. The major differences between both working modes are that the restricted operational mode does not permanently store visitor's data (results, algorithm details, etc.) into its online database and does not allow custom mosaics creation. To be able to use full-unrestricted benchmark functionalities the user is required to be registered (registration page).

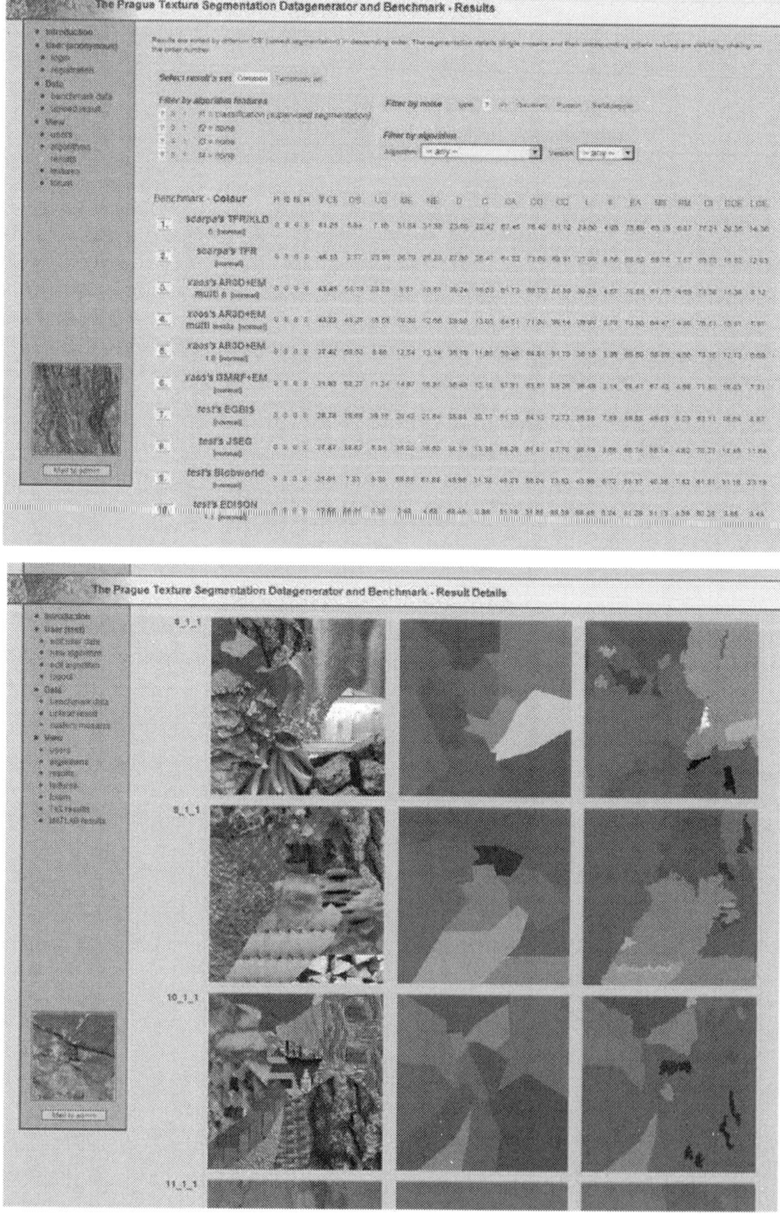

Fig. 1. Benchmark interfaces, the comparison table (top) and detailed method's evaluation on benchmark test mosaics.

The benchmark allows:

- To obtain customized experimental texture mosaics and their corresponding ground truth (U),
- To obtain the benchmark texture mosaic sets with their corresponding ground truth,
- To evaluate visitor's working segmentation results and compare them (Fig.1- top) with state-of-the-art algorithms,
- To update the benchmark database (U) with an algorithm (reference, abstract, benchmark results) and use it for subsequent other algorithms benchmarking,
- To grade noise endurance of an algorithm,
- To check single mosaics evaluation details (criteria values and resulted thematic maps),
- To rank segmentation algorithms according to the most common benchmark criteria,
- To obtain LaTeX or MATLAB coded resulting criteria tables (U).

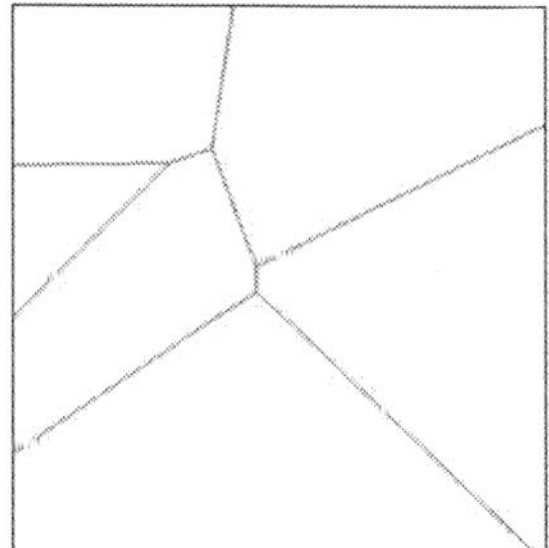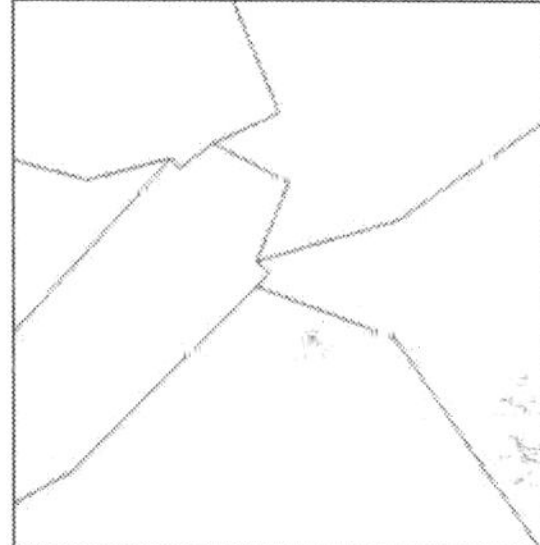

Fig. 2. Voronoi (left) and modified (right) mosaic polygons.

5.2 Benchmark generation

Benchmark datasets are computer generated 512 ×512 random mosaics filled with randomly selected textures. The random mosaics are generated by using the Voronoi polygon random generator (Shewchuk, 1996). It creates firstly a Delaunay triangulation, secondly determines the circumcircle centres of its triangles, and thirdly connects these points according to the neighbourhood relations between the triangles. Resulting Voronoi polygons can further be modified, (see Fig.2), if required by inserting additional border points into each polygon line. We exploit the fact that segmenting smaller and irregular objects is more difficult than segmenting bigger and regular objects such as squares or circles.

5.3 Performance criteria

The submitted benchmark results are evaluated and stored (U) in the server database and used for the algorithm ranking according to a chosen criterion. We have implemented the twenty seven most frequented evaluation criteria categorized into four groups: region-based (5+5), pixel-wise (12), consistency measures (2) and clustering comparison criteria (3). The performance criteria mutually compare ground truth image regions with the corresponding machine segmented regions. Symbols ↑ / ↓ further denote required increase or decrease of the corresponding criterion. The basic region-based criteria available are correct, over-segmentation, undersegmentation, missed and noise. All these criteria are available either for a single threshold parameter setting or as the performance curves (e.g. Fig.3) and their integrals. Our pixel-wise criteria group contains the most frequented classification criteria such as the omission and commission errors, class accuracy, recall, precision, mapping score, etc. The consistency criteria group incorporates the global and local consistency errors. Finally, the last criterion set contains three clustering comparison measures. By clicking on a required criterion the evaluation table is reordered, according to this chosen criterion.

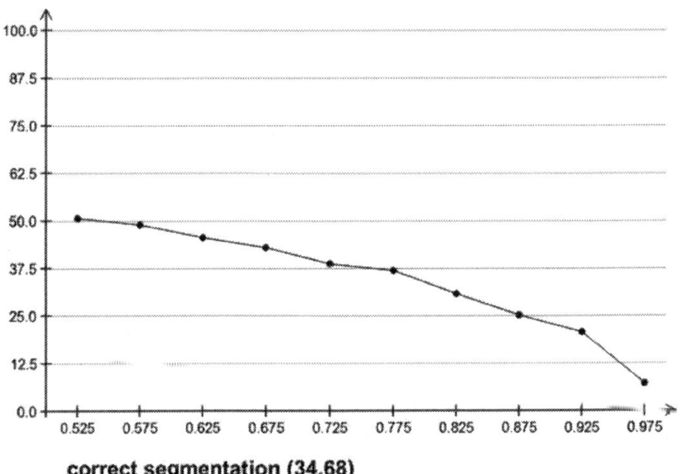

Fig. 3. The correct segmentation sensitivity (performance) curve and its integral for the AR3D-GM segmenter.

6. Results

Our algorithms were tested on natural colour textures mosaics from the Prague Texture Segmentation Data-Generator and Benchmark (Mikeš et al., 2006; Haindl et al., 2008). The benchmark test mosaics layouts and each cell texture membership are randomly generated and filled with colour textures from the large (more than 1000 high resolution colour textures) Prague colour texture database. The benchmark ranks segmentation algorithms according to a chosen criterion.

Tab.1 compares the overall benchmark performance of our algorithms (segmentation time 7 min/img on the Athlon 2GHz processor) with the Blobworld (Carson et al., 1999) (30 min/img), JSEG (Deng et al., 2001) (30 s/img), Edison (Christoudias et al., 2002) (10 s/img), respectively. These results demonstrate very good pixel-wise, correct region segmentation and low undersegmentation properties of both our methods while the oversegmentation results are only average. For all the pixel-wise criteria or the consistency measures our methods are either the best ones or the next best with marginal difference from the best one. Fig.4 shows four selected 512×512 experimental benchmark mosaics created from five to eleven natural colour textures. The last four columns demonstrate comparative results from the four alternative algorithms. Hard natural textures were chosen rather than synthesized (for example using Markov random field models) ones because they are expected to be more difficult for the underlying segmentation model. The third column demonstrates robust

	Benchmark – Colour				
	AR3D-GM	GMRF-GM	JSEG	Blobworld	EDISON
↑ CS	**37.42**	31.93	27.47	21.01	12.68
↓ OS	59.53	53.27	38.62	**7.33**	86.91
↓ US	8.86	11.24	5.04	9.30	**0.00**
↓ ME	12.55	14.97	35.00	59.55	**2.48**
↓ NE	13.14	16.91	35.50	61.68	**4.68**
↓ O	**34.32**	33.61	37.94	41.45	73.17
↓ C	100.00	100.00	92.77	**58.94**	100.00
↑ CA	**59.46**	57.91	55.29	46.23	31.19
↑ CO	**64.81**	63.51	61.81	56.04	31.55
↑ CC	91.79	89.26	87.70	73.62	**98.09**
↓ I.	**35.19**	36.49	38.19	43.96	68.45
↓ II.	3.39	3.14	3.66	6.72	**0.24**
↑ EA	**69.60**	68.41	66.74	58.37	41.29
↑ MS	**58.89**	57.42	55.14	40.36	31.13
↓ RM	4.88	4.86	4.96	7.96	**3.21**
↑ CI	**73.15**	71.80	70.27	61.31	50.29
↓ GCE	**12.13**	16.03	18.45	31.16	3.54
↓ LCE	6.69	7.31	11.64	23.19	**3.44**
↓ dM	15.43	15.27	**15.19**	20.03	16.84
↓ dD	**19.76**	20.63	23.38	31.11	35.37
↓ dVI	17.10	17.32	17.37	**15.84**	25.65
↑ $\overline{CS}$	**34.68**	31.04	29.13	19.10	12.95
↓ $\overline{OS}$	53.32	49.74	37.70	**10.81**	76.35
↓ $\overline{US}$	9.24	11.33	6.38	8.35	**0.00**
↓ $\overline{ME}$	19.90	21.92	34.72	58.54	**13.91**
↓ $\overline{NE}$	20.80	23.59	35.38	61.24	**15.29**
↑ $\overline{F}$	**72.08**	70.79	69.23	60.46	47.42

Table 1. Benchmark criteria (×100): CS = correct segmentation; OS = oversegmentation; US = under-segmentation; ME = missed error; NE = noise error; O = omission error; C = commission error; CA = class accuracy; CO = recall – correct assignment; CC = precision - object accuracy; I. = type I error; II. = type II error; EA = mean class accuracy estimate; MS = mapping score; RM = root mean square proportion estimation error; CI = comparison index; GCE = Global Consistency Error; LCE = Local Consistency Error;

behaviour of our GMRF-GM algorithm but also infrequent algorithm failures producing the oversegmented thematic map for some textures. Such failures can be reduced by a more elaborate postprocessing step. The JSEG (Deng et al., 2001), Blobworld (Carson et al., 1999) and Edison (Christoudias et al., 2002) algorithms on these data performed steadily worse as can be seen in the last two columns of Fig.4, some areas are undersegmented while other parts of the mosaics are oversegmented. The GMRF GM (Haindl et al., 2004) method is slower and its results are surprisingly also slightly worse than the AR3D-GM results. Resulting segmentation results are promising however comparison with all state-of-the-art algorithms is difficult because of lack of sound experimental evaluation results in this area. Our results can be further improved by an appropriate postprocessing.

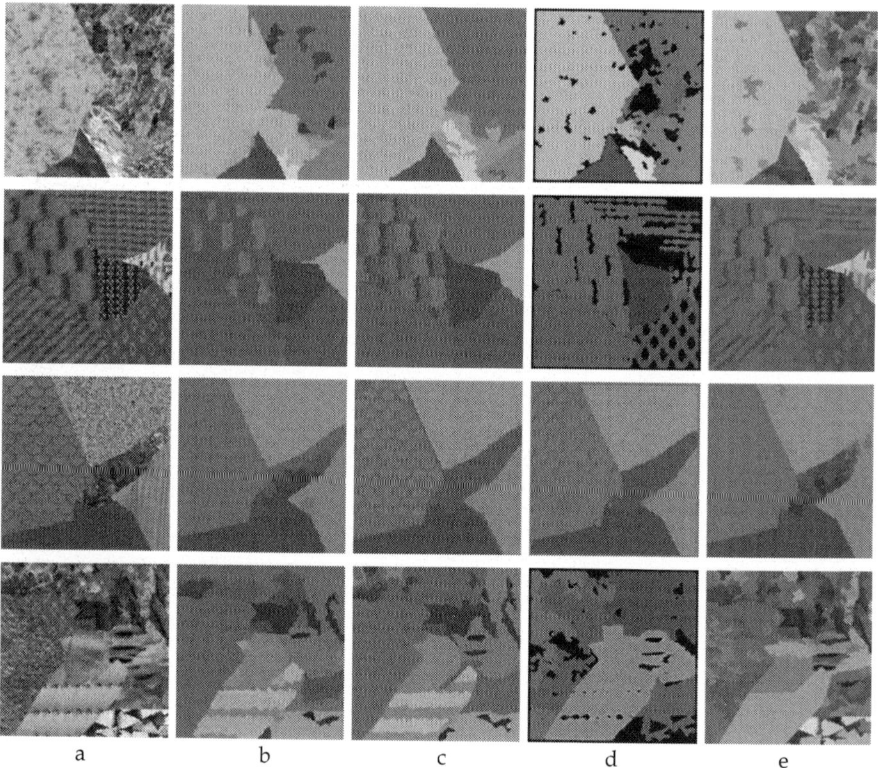

Fig. 4. Selected benchmark texture mosaics (a), AR3D-GM (b), GMRF-GM (c), Blobworld (d), and Edison segmentation results (e), respectively.

6.1 Mammography

Breast cancer is the leading cause of death (Tweed et al., 2002; Qi et al., 2003) among all cancers for middle-aged women in most developed countries. Current effort is focused on cancer prevention and early detection which can significantly reduce the mortality rate. X-ray screening mammography is the most frequented method for breast cancer early detection although not without problems (Qi et al., 2003) such as rather large minimum detectable tumor size, higher mammogram sensitivity for older women or radiation exposition. Automatic mammogram analysis is still difficult task due to wide variation of breast anatomy, nevertheless a computer-aided diagnosis system can successfully assist a radiologist, and can be used as a second opinion. The first step in a such system is detection of suspicious potentially cancerous regions of interest . Several approaches to detect these regions of interest (ROI) were published (Tweed et al., 2002), mostly based on supervised learning. We propose an unsupervised segmentation method for fast automatic mammogram segmentation into the regions of interest (ROI) using a statistical random field based texture representation.

The presented method detects the fibroglandular tissue regions from either craniocaudal (CC) or mediolateral oblique (MLO) views and thus can help focus a radiologist to this most important breast region.

Breast Detector The method starts with automatic breast area detection because it can be cheaply computed and simplifies the subsequent fibroglandular tissue region detection. This is performed using simple histogram thresholding with an automatically selected threshold. In this step the method also recognizes several label areas on a mammogram. We compute their areas and all but the largest one are discarded and merged with the

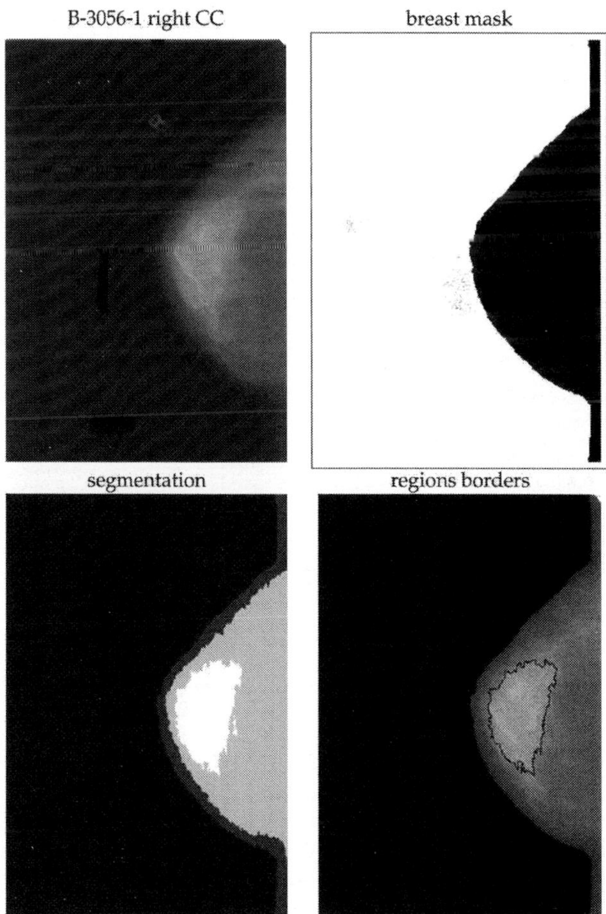

Fig. 5. Normal right breast mammogram (patient age 58, but with a cancerous lesion in the left breast), the detected breast area, segmentation result and detected regions of interest, respectively.

background. In this stage the algorithm also decides the breast orientation on the mammogram (left or right). Fig. 5 - breast mask show resulting detected breast area (in inverted grey levels). The following detection of regions of interest is performed only in the breast region ignoring the background area set in the mask template.

Breast Tissue Texture Model Our method segments pseudo-colour multiresolution mammograms each created from the original greyscale mammogram and its two nonlinear gamma transformations. We assume to down-sample input image Y into $M = 3$ different resolutions $Y^{(m)} = \downarrow^{\iota_m} Y$ with sampling factors ι_m $m = 1, \ldots, M$ identical for both directions and $Y^{(1)} = Y$. Local texture for each pixel $Y_r^{(m)}$ is represented using the 3D CAR model parameter space $\Theta_r^{(m)}$. The concept of decision fusion (Kittler et al., 1997) for high-performance pattern recognition is well known and widely accepted in the area of supervised classification where (often very diverse) classification technologies, each providing complementary sources of information about class membership, can be integrated to provide more accurate, robust and reliable classification decisions than the single

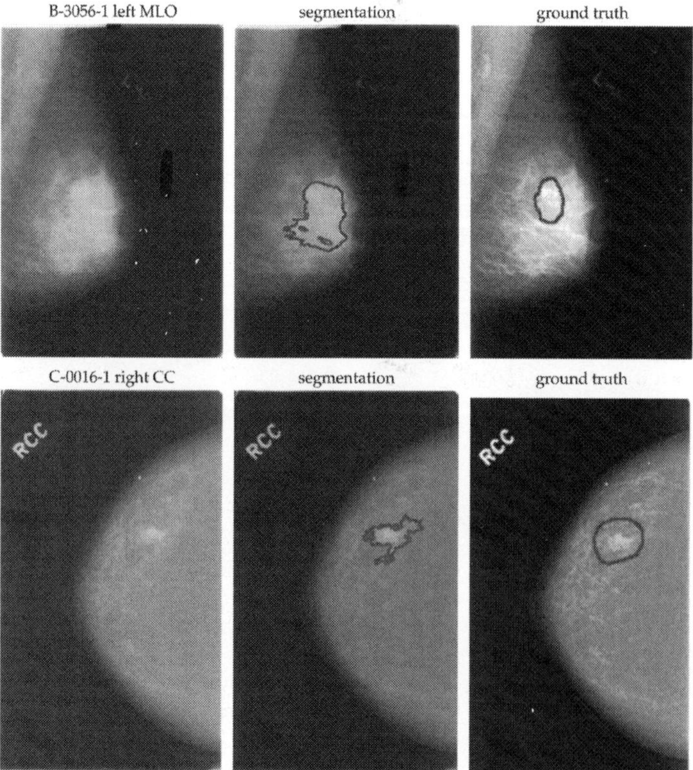

Fig. 6. Cancerous mammograms (patients age 58 (top) and 80 (bottom)), radiologist associated ground truth and detected regions of interest using the multiple segmenter approach, respectively.

classifier applications. The proposed method circumvents the problem of multiple unsupervised segmenters combination (Haindl et al., 2007) by fusing multiple-processed measurements into a single segmenter feature vector.

Experimental Results The algorithm was tested on mammograms from the Digital Database for Screening Mammography (DDSM) from the University of South Florida (Heath et al., 2000). This database contains 2620 four view (left and right craniocaudal (CC) and mediolateral oblique (MLO)) mammograms in different resolutions. Single mammograms cases are divided into normal, benign, benign without callback volumes and cancer. All our experiments are done with three resolutions (M=3) using sampling factors $\iota_1 = 2, \iota_2 = 4, \iota_3 = 8$ and the causal neighbourhood with fourteen neighbours (η= 14). Fig. 6-top show left MLO mammogram of a patient age 58 with detected malignant asymmetric lesion and the right CC mammogram (Fig. 6-bottom) of a patient age 80 with detected irregular, spiculated malignant lesion type. The segmenter correctly found the region of interest with the cancer lesion on both mammograms. The detected region of interest results Figs. 5-6 demonstrate very good region segmentation and low oversegmentation properties of our method.

6.2 Remote sensing

Segmentation of remote sensing imagery for various applications (e.g. agriculture, geological survey, military and security, weather forecast, terrain classification, astronomy, the detection of changes and anomalies, etc.) is challenging task due to huge amounts of data measured by satellite or airborne sensors. Large remote sensing images suffer not only with geometric and radiometric distortions problems but also with various challenges due to the high heterogeneity both within and across classes. The within class heterogeneity is due to the difference of acquisition process, orientation, and intrinsic appearance (Fauqueur et al., 2005).

We modified our unsupervised segmentation methods (sections 3,4) to be able to handle large aerial images (up to 8000 × 8000) distributed by the British National Space Centre (BNSC) as a CDROM called "Window On The UK". These aerial images (Fig.7) cover both urban and rural areas of the United Kingdom. The parametric space Θ (7) build over large images from this set requires efficient memory handling and distance based region class merging to avoid expensive memory swapping during the segmentation. Segmentation results illustrated on Fig.7-bottom do not use any prior information except the minimal region area. This parameter can be easily determined from the image resolution and the intended thematic map application.

7. Conclusions

We discussed three efficient and robust methods for unsupervised texture segmentation with unknown number of classes based on the underlying Markovian and GM texture models and their modifications for medical mammographics and remote sensing applications, respectively. Although these algorithm use the random field type models they are fast because they use efficient recursive or pseudo-likelihood parameter estimation of the underlying texture models and therefore they are much faster than the usual Markov

Fig. 7. Aerial Lmw 4800 × 4800 image (top left), its detail (top right), the corresponding unsupervised segmentation (bottom left) and parrac 8000 × 8000 image segmentation result, respectively.

chain Monte Carlo estimation approach. Usual handicap of segmentation methods is their lot of application dependent parameters to be experimentally estimated. Our methods require only a contextual neighbourhood selection and two additional thresholds. Their performance is demonstrated on the extensive benchmark tests on natural texture mosaics. They perform favorably compared with four alternative segmentation algorithms. The AR-GM methods are faster than the GMRF-GM method. These segmenters allow to build efficient methods for completely automatic unsupervised detection of mammogram fibroglandular tissue regions of interest which can assist a radiologist, and can be used as a second opinion. Alternatively our segmenters can be used to detect meaningful areas in large remote sensing images and in various other image segmentation applications.

8. Acknowledgements

This research was supported by the projects GAČR 102/08/0593, 1ET400750407 of the Grant Agency of the Academy of Sciences CR and partially by the MŠMT grants 1M0572, 2C06019.

9. References

Andrey, P. & Tarroux, P. (1998). Unsupervised segmentation of markov random field modeled textured images using selectionist relaxation. *IEEE Transactions on Pattern Analysis and Machine Intelligence*, 20(3), 252–262.

Barbu, A. & Zhu, S. C. (2004). Multigrid and multi-level swendsen-wang cuts for hierarchic graph partition. In *CVPR (2)*, volume 2 pp. 731–738.

Belongie, S.; Carson, C.; Greenspan, H., & Malik, J. (1998). Color and texture-based image segmentation using em and its application to content-based image retrieval. In *International Conference on Computer Vision*: IEEE.

Boykov, Y. & Kolmogorov, V. (2003). Computing geodesics and minimal surfaces via graph cuts. In *ICCV03* pp. 26–33. Nice, France.

Brox, T. & Weickert, J. (2006). Level set segmentation with multiple regions. *IEEE Trans. Image Processing*, 15(10), 3213–3218.

Carson, C.; Thomas, M.; Belongie, S.; Hellerstein, J. M., & Malik, J. (1999). Blobworld: A system for region-based image indexing and retrieval. In *Third International Conference on Visual Information Systems*: Springer.

Christoudias, C.; Georgescu, B., & Meer, P. (2002). Synergism in low level vision. In R. Kasturi, D. Laurendeau, & C. Suen (Eds.), *Proceedings of the 16th International Conference on Pattern Recognition*, volume 4 pp. 150–155. Los Alamitos: IEEE Computer Society.

Comaniciu, D. & Meer, P. (2002). Mean shift: A robust approach toward feature space analysis. *IEEE Transactions on Pattern Analysis and Machine Intelligence*, 24(5), 603–619.

Deng, H. & Clausi, D. A. (2004). Unsupervised image segmentation using A simple MRF model with A new implementation scheme. *Pattern Recognition*, pp. 2323–2335.

Deng, Y. & Manjunath, B. (2001). Unsupervised segmentation of color-texture regions in images and video. *IEEE Transactions on Pattern Analysis and Machine Intelligence*, 23(8), 800–810.

Estrada, F. & Jepson, A. (2005). Quantitative evaluation of a novel image segmentation algorithm. In *CVPR*, volume II pp. 1132–1139.: IEEE.

Fauqueur, J.; Kingsbury, N. G., & Anderson, R. (2005). Semantic discriminant mapping for classification and browsing of remote sensing textures and objects. In *ICIP (2)* pp. 846–849.

Felzenszwalb, P. & Huttenlocher, D. (1998). Image segmentation using local variation. In *CVPR* pp. 98–104.: IEEE.

Galun, M.; Sharon, E.; Basri, R., & Brandt, A. (2003). Texture segmentation by multiscale aggregation of filter responses and shape elements. In *International Conference on Computer Vision* pp. 716–723.

Haindl, M. (1991). Texture synthesis. *CWI Quarterly*, 4(4), 305–331.

Haindl, M. (1999). Texture segmentation using recursive markov random field parameter estimation. In K. Bjarne & J. Peter (Eds.), *Proceedings of the 11th Scandinavian Conference on Image Analysis* pp. 771–776. Lyngby, Denmark: Pattern Recognition Society of Denmark.

Haindl, M. & Havlíček, V. (1997). *Prototype Implementation of the Texture Analysis Objects.* Technical Report 1939, ÚTIA AV Č R, Praha, Czech Republic.

Haindl, M. & Mikeš, S. (2005). Colour texture segmentation using modelling approach. *Lecture Notes in Computer Science,* (3687), 484–491.

Haindl, M. & Mikeš, S. (2006a). Unsupervised texture segmentation using multispectral modelling approach. In Y. Tang, S.Wang, D. Yeung, H. Yan, & G. Lorette (Eds.), *Proceedings of the 18th International Conference on Pattern Recognition, ICPR 2006,* volume II pp. 203–206. Los Alamitos: IEEE Computer Society.

Haindl, M. & Mikeš, S. (2007). Unsupervised texture segmentation using multiple segmenters strategy. In M. Haindl, J. Kittler, & F. Roli (Eds.), *MCS 2007,* volume 4472 of *Lecture Notes in Computer Science* pp. 210–219.: Springer.

Haindl, M. & Mikeš, S. (2008). Texture segmentation benchmark. In B. Lovell, D. Laurendeau, & R. Duin (Eds.), *Proceedings of the 19th International Conference on Pattern Recognition, ICPR 2008* pp. accepted. Los Alamitos: IEEE Computer Society.

Haindl, M. & Mikeš, S. (2004). Model-based texture segmentation. *Lecture Notes in Computer Science,* (3212), 306 – 313.

Haindl, M. & Šimberová, S. (1992). *Theory & Applications of Image Analysis,* chapter A Multispectral Image Line Reconstruction Method, pp. 306–315. World Scientific Publishing Co.: Singapore.

Haindl, M. & Vácha, P. (2006b). Illumination invariant texture retrieval. In Y. Tang, S. Wang, D. Yeung, H. Yan, & G. Lorette (Eds.), *Proceedings of the 18th International Conference on Pattern Recognition, ICPR 2006,* volume III pp. 276–279. Los Alamitos: IEEE Computer Society.

Heath, M.; Bowyer, K.; Kopans, D.; Moore, R., & Kegelmeyer, P. (2000). The digital database for screening mammography. In *Proc. of the 5th Int. Workshop on Digital Mammography:* Medical Physics Publishing.

Kashyap, R. (1986). Image models. In K. F. T.Y. Young (Ed.), *Handbook of Pattern Recognition and Image Processing.* New York: Academic Press.

Kittler, J.; Hojjatoleslami, A., & Windeatt, T. (1997). Weighting factors in multiple expert fusion. In *Proc. BMVC* pp. 41–50.: BMVA BMVA.

Lee, S. U.; Chung, S. Y., & Park, R. H. (1990). A comparitive performance study of several global thresholding techniques for segmentation. *Computer Vision, Graphics, and Image Processing,* 52, 171–190.

Manjunath, B. & Chellapa, R. (1991). Unsupervised texture segmentation using markov random field models. *IEEE Transactions on Pattern Analysis and Machine Intelligence,* 13, 478–482.

Martin, D.; Fowlkes, C.; Tal, D., & Malik, J. (2001). A database of human segmented natural images and its application to evaluating segmentation algorithms and measuring ecological statistics. In *Proc. 8th Int. Conf. Computer Vision,* volume 2 pp. 416–423.

Mikeš, S. & Haindl, M. (2006). Prague texture segmentation data generator and benchmark. *ERCIM News*, (64), 67–68.

Ojala, T.; Maenpaa, T.; Pietikainen, M.; Viertola, J.; Kyllonen, J., & Huovinen, S. (2002). Outex: New framework for empirical evaluation of texture analysis algorithms. In *International Conference on Pattern Recognition* pp. I: 701–706.

Ojala, T. & Pietikainen, M. (1999). Unsupervised texture segmentation using feature distributions. *Pattern Recognition*, 32(477-486).

Pal, N. & Pal, S. (1993). A review on image segmentation techniques. *Pattern Recognition*, 26(9), 1277–1294.

Panjwani, D. & Healey, G. (1995). Markov random field models for unsupervised segmentation of textured color images. *IEEE Transactions on Pattern Analysis and Machine Intelligence*, 17(10), 939–954.

Qi, H. & Diakides, N. A. (2003). Thermal infrared imaging in early breast cancer detection - a survey of recent research. In *25th Annual Int. Conference of the IEEE EMBS* pp. 448–452.

Reed, T. R. & du Buf, J. M. H. (1993). A review of recent texture segmentation and feature extraction techniques. *CVGIP–Image Understanding*, 57(3), 359–372.

Sahoo, P. K.; Soltani, S., & Wong, A. K. C. (1988). Survey of thresholding techniques. *Computer Vision, Graphics and Image Processing*, 41(2), 233–260.

Scarpa, G. & Haindl, M. (2006). Unsupervised texture segmentation by spectralspatial-independent clustering. In Y. Tang, S. Wang, D. Yeung, H. Yan, & G. Lorette (Eds.), *Proceedings of the 18th International Conference on Pattern Recognition, ICPR 2006*, volume II pp. 151–154. Los Alamitos: IEEE Computer Society.

Scarpa, G.; Haindl, M., & Zerubia, J. (2007). A hierarchical texture model for unsupervised segmentation of remotely sensed images. *Lecture Notes in Computer Science*, 4522, 303–312.

Shafarenko, L.; Petrou, M., & Kittler, J. (1997). Automatic watershed segmentation of randomly textured color images. *IEEE Trans. on Image Processing*, 6(11), 1530–1544.

Shaffrey, C. W.; Jermyn, I. H., & Kingsbury, N. G. (2002). Psychovisual evaluation of image segmentation algorithms. In *ACIVS 2002*.

Sharma, M. & Singh, S. (2001). Minerva scene analysis benchmark. In *Seventh Australian and New Zealand Intelligent Information Systems Conference* pp. 231–235.: IEEE.

Shewchuk, J. R. (1996). Triangle: Engineering a 2D Quality Mesh Generator and Delaunay Triangulator. In M. C. Lin & D. Manocha (Eds.), *Applied Computational Geometry: Towards Geometric Engineering*, volume 1148 of *Lecture Notes in Computer Science* pp. 203–222. Springer-Verlag. From the First ACMWorkshop on Applied Computational Geometry.

Shi, J. & Malik, J. (2000). Normalized cuts and image segmentation. *IEEE Trans. Pattern Anal. Mach. Intell.*, 22(8), 888–905.

Tweed, T. & Miguet, S. (2002). Automatic detection of regions of interest in mammographies based on a combined analysis of texture and histogram. In *ICPR*, volume 02 pp. 448–452. Los Alamitos, CA, USA: IEEE Computer Society.

Vacha, P. & Haindl, M. (2007). Image retrieval measures based on illumination invariant textural mrf features. In *CIVR '07: Proceedings of the 6th ACM international conference on Image and video retrieval* pp. 448–454. New York, NY, USA: ACM Press.

Zhang, Y. J. (1997). Evaluation and comparison of different segmentation algorithms. *Pattern Recognition Letters*, 18, 963–974.

10

Optimization of Goal Function Pseudogradient in the Problem of Interframe Geometrical Deformations Estimation

A.G. Tashlinskii

Ulyanovsk State Technical University

Russia

1. Introduction

The systems of information extraction that include spatial apertures of signal sensors are widely used in robotics, for the remote exploration of Earth, in medicine, geology and in other fields. Such sensors generate dynamic arrays of data which are characterized by space-time correlation and represent the sequence of framed of image to be changed (Gonzalez & Woods, 2002). Interframe geometrical deformations can be described by mathematical models of deformations of grids, on which images are specified.

Estimation of variable parameters of interframe deformations is required when solving a lot of problems, for example, at automate search of fragment on the image, navigation tracking of mobile object in the conditions of limited visibility, registration of multiregion images at remote investigations of Earth, in medical investigations. A large number of calls for papers are devoted to different problems of interframe deformations estimation (the bibliography is presented for example in (Tashlinskii, 2000)). This chapter is devoted to one of approaches, where the problems of optimization of quality goal function pseudogradient in pseudogradient procedures of interframe geometrical deformations parameters estimation are considered.

Let the model of deformations is determined with accuracy to a parameters vector $\bar{\alpha}$, frames $\mathbf{Z}^{(1)} = \left\{ z_{\bar{j}}^{(1)} : \bar{j} \in \Omega \right\}$ and $\mathbf{Z}^{(2)} = \left\{ z_{\bar{j}}^{(2)} : \bar{j} \in \Omega \right\}$ to be studied of images are specified on the regular sample grid $\Omega = \left\{ \bar{j} = \left(j_x, j_y \right) \right\}$, and a goal function of estimation quality is formed in terms of finding extremum of some functional $J(\bar{\alpha})$. However, it is impossible to find optimal parameters in the mentioned sense because of incompleteness of image observations description. But we can estimate parameters $\bar{\alpha}$ on the basis of analysis of specific images $\mathbf{Z}^{(1)}$ and $\mathbf{Z}^{(2)}$ realizations, between of which geometrical deformations are estimated. At that it is of interest to estimate $\bar{\alpha}$ directly on values $J\left(\hat{\bar{\alpha}}, \mathbf{Z}^{(1)}, \mathbf{Z}^{(2)}\right)$ (Polyak & Tsypkin, 1984):

$$\hat{\bar{\alpha}}_t = \hat{\bar{\alpha}}_{t-1} - \mathbf{\Lambda}_t \nabla J\left(\hat{\bar{\alpha}}, \mathbf{Z}^{(1)}, \mathbf{Z}^{(2)}\right), \tag{1}$$

where $\hat{\overline{\alpha}}_t$ - the next after $\hat{\overline{\alpha}}_{t-1}$ approximation of the extremum point of $J(\hat{\overline{\alpha}}, \mathbf{Z}^{(1)}, \mathbf{Z}^{(2)})$; Λ_t - positively determined matrix, specifying a value of estimates change at the t-th iteration; $\nabla J(\cdot)$ - gradient of functional $J((\cdot))$. The necessity of multiple and cumbrous calculations of gradient opposes to imply the procedure (1) in the image processing. We can significantly reduce computational costs if at each iteration instead of $J(\hat{\overline{\alpha}}, \mathbf{Z}^{(1)}, \mathbf{Z}^{(2)})$ we use its reduction $\nabla \hat{J}(\hat{\overline{\alpha}}_{t-1}, Z_t)$ on some part Z_t of realization which we call the local sample

$$Z_t = \left\{ z_{jt}^{(2)}, \tilde{z}_{jt}^{(1)} \right\}, \quad z_{jt}^{(2)} \in \mathbf{Z}^{(2)}, \quad \tilde{z}_{jt}^{(1)} = \tilde{z}^{(1)}(\bar{j}_t, \hat{\overline{\alpha}}_{t-1}) \in \tilde{Z}, \tag{2}$$

where $z_{jt}^{(2)}$ – samples of a deformed image $\mathbf{Z}^{(2)}$, chosen to the local sample at the t-th iteration; $\tilde{z}_{jt}^{(1)}$ – sample of a continuous image $\tilde{Z}^{(1)}$ (obtained from $\mathbf{Z}^{(1)}$ by means of some interpolation), the coordinates of which correspond to the current estimate of sample $z_{jl}^{(2)} \in \mathbf{Z}^{(2)}$; $\bar{j}_t \in \Omega_t \in \Omega$ – coordinates of samples $z_{jt}^{(2)}$; Ω_t – plan of the local sample at the t-th iteration. Let us call the number of samples $\left\{ z_{jt}^{(2)} \right\}$ in Z_t through the local sample size and denote through μ.

At large image sizes pseudogradient procedures (Polyak & Tsypkin, 1973; Tashlinskii, 2005) give a solution satisfying to requirements of simplicity, rapid convergence and availability in different real situations.

For considered problem the pseudogradient $\overline{\beta}_t$ is any random vector in the parameters space, for which the condition $\left[\nabla J(\hat{\overline{\alpha}}_{t-1}, Z_t) \right]^T M\{\overline{\beta}_t\} \geq 0$ is fulfilled, где T - sign of transposition; $M\{\cdot\}$ - symbol of the mathematical expectation.

Then pseudogradient procedure is (Tzypkin, 1995) :

$$\hat{\overline{\alpha}}_t = \hat{\overline{\alpha}}_{t-1} - \Lambda_t \overline{\beta}_t, \tag{3}$$

where $t = \overline{0,T}$ - iteration number; T - total number of iterations.

Procedure (3) own indubitable advantages. It is applicable to image processing in the conditions of a priory uncertainty, supposes not large computational costs, does not require preliminary estimation of parameters of images to be estimated. The formed estimates are immune to pulse interferences and converge to true values under rather weak conditions. The processing of the image samples can be performed in an arbitrary order, for example, in order of scanning with decimation that is determined by the hardware speed, which facilitates obtaining a tradeoff between image entering rate and the speed of the available hardware (Tashlinskii, 2003).

However, pseudogradient procedures have disadvantages, in particular, the presence of local extremums of the goal function estimate at real image processing, that significantly reduces the convergence rate of parameters estimates. To the second disadvantage we can refer relatively not large effective range, where effective convergence of estimates is ensured. This disadvantage depends on the autocorrelation function of images to be estimated. A posteriori optimization of the local sample (Minkina et al., 2005; Samojlov et al., 2007; Tashlinskii et al., 2005), assuming synthesis of estimation procedures, when sample size automatically adapted at each iteration for some condition fulfillment is directed on the struggle with the first one. Relatively second disadvantage it is necessary to note that for increasing speed of procedures we tend to decrease local sample size, which directly influences on the convergence rate of parameters to be estimated to optimal values: as μ is larger, the convergence rate is higher. However on the another hand the increase of μ inevitably leads to increase of computational costs, that is not always acceptable. Let us note that at different errors of parameters estimates from optimal values at the same value of sample size the samples chosen in different regions of image ensure different estimate convergence rate. Thus, the problems of optimization of size and plan of local sample of samples used for goal function pseudogradient finding are urgent. The papers (Samojlov, 2006; Tashlinskii @ Samojlov, 2005; Dikarina et al., 2007) are devoted to solution of the problem of a priory optimization of local sample, in particular, on criteria of computational expenses minimum The problems of optimization of a plan of local sample samples choice are investigated weakly, that has determined the goal of this work.

Pseudogradient estimation of parameters (3) is recurrent, thus as a result of iteration the estimate $\hat{\alpha}_{i,t}$ of the parameter α_i changes discretely: $\hat{\bar{\alpha}}_t = \hat{\bar{\alpha}}_{t-1} + \Delta\hat{\bar{\alpha}}_t$. At that the following events are possible:

- If $\mathrm{sign}(\varepsilon_{i,t-1}) = \mathrm{sign}\Delta\alpha_{i,t}$, then change of the estimate $\hat{\bar{\alpha}}_t$ is directed backward from the optimal value α_i^*, where $\varepsilon_{i,t} = \hat{\alpha}_{i,t} - \alpha_i^*$ – the error of its optimal value of the parameter α_i^* and its estimate, $i = \overline{1, m}$. In accordance with (Tashlinskii & Tikhonov, 2001) let us denote the probability of such an event through $\rho_i^-(\bar{\varepsilon}_t)$.

- At $\Delta\alpha_{i,t} = 0$ the estimate $\hat{\bar{\alpha}}_t$ does not change with probability $\rho_i^0(\bar{\varepsilon}_t)$.

- If $-\mathrm{sign}(\varepsilon_{i,t-1}) = \mathrm{sign}\Delta\alpha_{i,t}$, the change of the estimate $\hat{\bar{\alpha}}_t$ is directed towards the optimal value of the estimate with some probability $\rho_i^+(\bar{\varepsilon}_t)$.

Let us note, that the probabilities $\rho_i^+(\bar{\varepsilon}_t)$, $\rho_i^0(\bar{\varepsilon}_{t-1})$ and $\rho_i^-(\bar{\varepsilon}_t)$ depend on the current errors $\bar{\varepsilon}_t = (\varepsilon_{1,t}, \varepsilon_{2,t}, \ldots, \varepsilon_{m,t})^T$ of other parameters to be estimated, but because of divisible group of events we have $\rho_i^+(\bar{\varepsilon}_t) + \rho_i^-(\bar{\varepsilon}_t) = 1 - \rho_i^0(\bar{\varepsilon}_t)$. If the goal function is maximized and $\varepsilon_{i,t} > 0$, then $\rho_i^+(\bar{\varepsilon}_t)$ is the probability of the fact that projection β_i of the pseudogradient on the parameters α_i axes will be negative, and $\rho_i^-(\bar{\varepsilon}_t)$ – positive:

$$\rho_i^+(\bar{\varepsilon}_t) = P\{\beta_i < 0\} = \int_{-\infty}^{0} w(\beta_i)d\beta_i, \quad \rho_i^-(\bar{\varepsilon}_t) = P\{\beta_i > 0\} = \int_{0}^{\infty} w(\beta_i)d\beta_i, \tag{4}$$

where $w(\beta_i)$ – probability density function of the projection β_i on the axes α_i.

Probabilities $\rho_i^+(\bar{\varepsilon}_t)$, $\rho_i^0(\bar{\varepsilon}_t)$ and $\rho_i^-(\bar{\varepsilon}_t)$ will be used below for finding optimal region of local sample samples choice on some criterion.

2. Finding goal functions pseudorgadients with usage of finite differences

In the papers (Vasiliev & Tashlinskii, 1998; Vasiliev &Krasheninikov, 2007) it is shown, that when pseudogradient estimating of interframe deformations parameters as a goal function it is reasonable to use interframe difference mean square and interframe correlation coefficient. Pseudogradients of the mentioned functions are found through a local sample Z_t and estimates $\hat{\bar{\alpha}}_{t-1}$ of deformations parameters at the pervious iteration:

$$\bar{\beta}_t = \sum_{\bar{j}_t \in \Omega_t} \frac{\partial \widetilde{z}_{\bar{j},t}^{(1)}}{\partial \bar{\alpha}} \left(\widetilde{z}_{\bar{j},t}^{(1)} - z_{\bar{j},t}^{(2)} \right) \Bigg|_{\bar{\alpha} = \hat{\bar{\alpha}}_{t-1}} \quad \text{and} \quad \bar{\beta}_t = - \sum_{\bar{j}_t \in \Omega_{\bar{j},t}} \frac{\partial \widetilde{z}_{\bar{j},t}^{(1)}}{\partial \bar{\alpha}} z_{\bar{j}t}^{(2)} \Bigg|_{\bar{\alpha} = \hat{\bar{\alpha}}_{t-1}} .$$

However the direct usage of the obtained expressions for images, specified by discrete sample grids, is impossible, because they include analytic derivatives. Thus let us briefly consider approaches for goal functions pseudogradients calculation.

At the explicitly given function its estimate $\hat{J}$ at the current iteration can be found, using estimates $\hat{\bar{\alpha}}$ of deformations parameters, obtained by this iteration, information about brightness z and coordinates (x,y) of samples of the local sample, formed at the current iteration, and accepted deformations model. Thus the dependence of the goal function on parameters can be represented directly:

$$\hat{J} = f(\bar{\alpha}) , \tag{5}$$

and through intermediate brightness functions:

$$\hat{J} = f(z(\bar{\alpha})) , \quad z = u(\bar{\alpha}) \tag{6}$$

and coordinates:

$$\hat{J} = f(x(\bar{\alpha}), y(\bar{\alpha})) , \quad x = v_x(\bar{\alpha}) , \quad y = v_y(\bar{\alpha}) . \tag{7}$$

In accordance with rules of partial derivatives calculation different approaches of pseudogradient calculation correspond to the expressions (5)–(7):
for relation (5)

$$\bar{\beta} = \frac{\partial \hat{J}}{\partial \bar{\alpha}} = \frac{\partial f}{\partial \bar{\alpha}} ; \tag{8}$$

for relation (6)

$$\bar{\beta} = \frac{df}{dz} \frac{\partial z}{\partial \bar{\alpha}} ; \tag{9}$$

for relation (7)

$$\bar{\beta} = \frac{\partial f}{\partial x} \frac{\partial x}{\partial \bar{\alpha}} + \frac{\partial f}{\partial y} \frac{\partial y}{\partial \bar{\alpha}} . \tag{10}$$

Let us analysis the possibilities of finding derivatives $\dfrac{\partial f}{\partial \bar{\alpha}}$, $\dfrac{df}{dz}$, $\dfrac{\partial z}{\partial \bar{\alpha}}$, $\dfrac{\partial x}{\partial \bar{\alpha}}$ and $\dfrac{\partial y}{\partial \bar{\alpha}}$. Since the sample grid is discrete then the true finding of derivative $\dfrac{\partial f}{\partial \bar{\alpha}}$ is impossible. We can find its estimate by means of finite differences of the goal function. At that each component β_i of the pseudogradient $\overline{\beta}$ is determined separately through increments $\Delta_{\alpha i}$ of the relative i-th parameter:

$$\beta_i = \frac{\partial f}{\partial \alpha_i} \approx \frac{\hat{J}(Z_t, \hat{\alpha}_1, \ldots, \hat{\alpha}_i + \Delta_{\alpha i}, \ldots, \hat{\alpha}_m) - \hat{J}(Z_t, \hat{\alpha}_1, \ldots, \hat{\alpha}_i - \Delta_{\alpha i}, \ldots, \hat{\alpha}_{m,})}{2\Delta_{\alpha i}}, \quad i = \overline{1, m} \tag{11}$$

where Z_t – the local sample. Let us note, that for forming elements $\tilde{z}_{jt}^{(1)}$ of the local sample (2) it is necessary to specify the deformations model and the kind of the reference image interpolation. However the requirements to their first derivatives existence are not laid.

If the derivative of the goal function on variable z exists, then the derivative $\dfrac{df}{dz}$ can be found analytically (or calculated by numerous methods) for explicit and implicit representation of the function. The partial derivative $\dfrac{\partial z}{\partial \overline{\alpha}}$ can not be found analytically, because the sample grid of images is discrete. We can estimate it in coordinates of each sample $\tilde{z}_{jt}^{(1)}$, $\bar{j}_t \in \Omega_t$, through increments $\Delta_{\alpha i}$ of the corresponding i-th deformation parameter. Then in accordance with (9):

$$\beta_i \approx \frac{df}{dz} \frac{\sum\limits_{\Omega_t}\left(\hat{s}\left(\bar{j}_t, \hat{\alpha}_1, \ldots, \hat{\alpha}_i + \Delta_{\alpha i}, \ldots, \hat{\alpha}_m\right) - \hat{s}\left(\bar{j}_t, \hat{\alpha}_1, \ldots, \hat{\alpha}_i - \Delta_{\alpha i}, \ldots, \hat{\alpha}_{m,}\right)\right)}{2\Delta_{\alpha i}}. \tag{12}$$

Another approach for finding the derivative estimate $\dfrac{\partial z}{\partial \overline{\alpha}}$ is the representation of z in the combined functional form $z = s(x(\overline{\alpha}), y(\overline{\alpha}))$, then (9) is:

$$\overline{\beta} = \frac{df}{dz}\left(\frac{\partial z}{\partial x}\frac{\partial x}{\partial \overline{\alpha}} + \frac{\partial z}{\partial y}\frac{\partial y}{\partial \overline{\alpha}}\right). \tag{13}$$

If for the given deformations model the requirements to its first derivatives on parameters existence are fulfilled then the partial derivatives $\dfrac{\partial x}{\partial \overline{\alpha}}$ and $\dfrac{\partial y}{\partial \overline{\alpha}}$ can be found analytically, and derivatives $\dfrac{\partial z}{\partial x}$ and $\dfrac{\partial z}{\partial y}$ can be estimated through finite differences of samples brightness (Minkina et al., 2007).

In the expression (10) there are derivatives $\dfrac{\partial x}{\partial \overline{\alpha}}$ and $\dfrac{\partial y}{\partial \overline{\alpha}}$, which were considered above, and also derivatives $\dfrac{\partial f}{\partial x}$ and $\dfrac{\partial f}{\partial y}$, their estimates can be found through finite differences on coordinate axes. Then:

$$\overline{\beta} = \frac{\hat{J}\left(Z_t(x+\Delta_x), \hat{\overline{\alpha}}_{t-1}\right) - \hat{J}\left(Z_t(x-\Delta_x), \hat{\overline{\alpha}}_{t-1}\right)}{2\Delta_x}\frac{\partial x}{\partial \overline{\alpha}} + \frac{\hat{J}\left(Z_t(y+\Delta_y), \hat{\overline{\alpha}}_{t-1}\right) - \hat{J}\left(Z_t(y-\Delta_y), \hat{\overline{\alpha}}_{t-1}\right)}{2\Delta_y}\frac{\partial y}{\partial \overline{\alpha}}. \tag{14}$$

where $Z_t(x \pm \Delta_x)$ – the local sample, the samples $\{\tilde{z}^{(1)}_{jt}\}$ coordinates of which are shifted on the axis x by a value Δ_x, $\bar{j}_t \in \Omega_t$. As well as estimates of derivatives $\dfrac{\partial z}{\partial x}$ and $\dfrac{\partial z}{\partial y}$, they are identical for all parameters to be estimated.

Thus, four approaches to calculate pseudogradient of the goal function, which are defined by expressions (11), (12), (13) and (14), are possible. Let us note, when usage of different approaches different requirements are laid to features of the goal function and deformations model.

We can obtain the estimate of interframe difference mean square at the next iteration, using local sample (2) and estimates $\hat{\bar{\alpha}}_{t-1}$ of parameters to be estimated, obtained at the previous iteration:

$$\hat{J}_t = \frac{1}{\mu} \sum_{l=1}^{\mu} \left(\tilde{z}^{(1)}_{jl} - z^{(2)}_{jl} \right)^2 . \tag{15}$$

The estimate of interframe correlation coefficient is determined by equation of sample correlation coefficient calculation:

$$\hat{J}_t = \frac{1}{\mu \hat{\sigma}_{\tilde{z}1} \hat{\sigma}_{z2}} \left(\sum_{l=1}^{\mu} \tilde{z}^{(1)}_{jl} z^{(2)}_{jl} - \mu \tilde{z}^{(1)}_{av} \tilde{z}^{(2)}_{av} \right), \tag{16}$$

where $\hat{\sigma}^2_{\tilde{z}1}, \hat{\sigma}^2_{z2}$ и $\tilde{z}^{(1)}_{av}$, $z^{(2)}_{av}$ - estimates of variances and mean values of $z^{(2)}_{jt}$ and $\tilde{z}^{(1)}_{jt}$, $\bar{j}_t \in \Omega_t$.

As an example let us find design expressions for calculation of the pseudogradient of interframe difference mean square through finite differences. At that for definition let us suppose, that the affine deformations model, containing parameters of rotation angle φ, scale coefficient κ and parallel shift $\bar{h} = (h_x, h_y)$ is used. Then coordinates (x, y) of the point on the image $\mathbf{Z}^{(1)}$ at vector $\bar{\alpha} = (h_x, h_y, \varphi, \kappa)^T$ of deformations transform to coordinates:

$$\left(\tilde{x} = x_0 + \kappa((x - x_0)\cos\varphi - (y - y_0)\sin\varphi) + h_x, \ \tilde{y} = y_0 + \kappa((x - x_0)\sin\varphi + (y - y_0)\cos\varphi) + h_y \right), \tag{17}$$

where (x_0, y_0) – rotation center coordinates. We use bilinear interpolation for a forecast of brightness in the point $(\tilde{x}, \tilde{y})$ from the image $\tilde{Z}^{(1)}$. Subject to accepted limitations let us concretize the methods for pseudogradient calculation. Let us note that these limitations are introduced for concretization of the obtained expressions and do not reduce consideration generality.

The first method. It is the least laborious way in calculus, where differentiation of the deformations model and the goal function is not used. The component β_{it} of the pseudogradient is calculated as normalized difference of two estimates of the goal function:

$$\beta_{it} = \frac{\sum\limits_{l=1}^{\mu} \left(\tilde{z}^{(1)}_{jl}(\hat{\alpha}_{i,t-1} + \Delta_{\alpha i}) - z^{(2)}_{jl} \right)^2 - \sum\limits_{l=1}^{\mu} \left(\tilde{z}^{(1)}_{jl}(\hat{\alpha}_{i,t-1} - \Delta_{\alpha i}) - z^{(2)}_{jl} \right)^2}{2\mu \Delta_{\alpha i}}, \tag{18}$$

where $\tilde{z}_{jl}^{(1)}(\hat{\alpha}_{i,t-1}\pm\Delta_{\alpha i})\in Z_t$ - brightness of the interpolated image in the point with coordinates $(\tilde{x}_l,\tilde{y}_l)$, determined by deformations model and current parameters estimates $\hat{\bar{\alpha}}_{t-1}$; $\bar{j}_l\in\Omega_t$ - samples coordinates $z_{jl}^{(2)}$; $\Delta_{\alpha i}$ - increment of a parameter α_i to be estimated. In particular, for affine model (17) for shifts on the axis x, y, scale coefficient and rotation angle we obtain correspondingly:

$$
\begin{aligned}
\tilde{x}_l &= x_0 + \hat{\kappa}_{t-1}((x_l - x_0)\cos\hat{\varphi}_{t-1} - (y_l - y_0)\sin\hat{\varphi}_{t-1}) + \hat{h}_{x,t-1} + \Delta_h, \\
\tilde{y}_l &= y_0 + \hat{\kappa}_{t-1}((x_l - x_0)\sin\hat{\varphi}_{t-1} + (y_l - y_0)\cos\hat{\varphi}_{t-1}) + \hat{h}_{y,t-1}, \\
\tilde{x}_l &= x_0 + \hat{\kappa}_{t-1}((x_l - x_0)\cos\hat{\varphi}_{t-1} - (y_l - y_0)\sin\hat{\varphi}_{t-1}) + \hat{h}_{x,t-1}, \\
\tilde{y}_l &= y_0 + \hat{\kappa}_{t-1}((x_l - x_0)\sin\hat{\varphi}_{t-1} + (y_l - y_0)\cos\hat{\varphi}_{t-1}) + \hat{h}_{y,t-1} + \Delta_h, \\
\tilde{x}_l &= x_0 + (\hat{\kappa}_{t-1} + \Delta_\kappa)((x_l - x_0)\cos\hat{\varphi}_{t-1} - (y_l - y_0)\sin\hat{\varphi}_{t-1}) + \hat{h}_{x,t-1}, \\
\tilde{y}_l &= y_0 + (\hat{\kappa}_{t-1} + \Delta_\kappa)((x_l - x_0)\sin\hat{\varphi}_{t-1} + (y_l - y_0)\cos\hat{\varphi}_{t-1}) + \hat{h}_{y,t-1}, \\
\tilde{x}_l &= x_0 + \hat{\kappa}_{t-1}((x_l - x_0)\cos(\hat{\varphi}_{t-1} + \Delta_\varphi) - (y_l - y_0)\sin(\hat{\varphi}_{t-1} + \Delta_\varphi)) + \hat{h}_{x,t-1}, \\
\tilde{y}_l &= y_0 + \hat{\kappa}_{t-1}((x_l - x_0)\sin(\hat{\varphi}_{t-1} + \Delta_\varphi) + (y_l - y_0)\cos(\hat{\varphi}_{t-1} + \Delta_\varphi)) + \hat{h}_{y,t-1}.
\end{aligned}
\tag{19}
$$

Brightness of the sample $\tilde{z}_{jl}^{(1)}(\hat{\alpha}_{i,t-1}\pm\Delta_{\alpha i})$ in the point $(\tilde{x}_l,\tilde{y}_l)$ is found, for example, by means of bilinear interpolation:

$$
\begin{aligned}
\tilde{z}_{\tilde{x}_l,\tilde{y}_l}^{(1)} &= z_{jx-,jy-}^{(1)} + (\tilde{x}_l - j_{x-})(z_{jx+,jy-}^{(1)} - z_{jx-,jy-}^{(1)}) + (\tilde{y}_l - j_{y-})(z_{jx-,jy+}^{(1)} - z_{jx-,jy-}^{(1)}) + \\
&\quad + (\tilde{x}_l - j_{x-})(\tilde{y}_l - j_{y-})(z_{jx+,jy+}^{(1)} + z_{jx-,jy-}^{(1)} - z_{jx+,jy-}^{(1)} - z_{jx-,jy+}^{(1)}).
\end{aligned}
\tag{20}
$$

where $j_{x-} = \operatorname{int}\tilde{x}_l$, $j_{x+} = j_{x-} + 1$, $j_{y-} = \operatorname{int}\tilde{y}_l$, $j_{y+} = j_{y-} + 1$ - coordinates of nodes of the image $\mathbf{Z}^{(1)}$, nearby to the point $(\tilde{x}_l,\tilde{y}_l)$; $z_{jx\pm,jy\pm}^{(1)}$ - brightness in the corresponding nodes of thesample grid. Let us note that the expression (18) can be written in more handy form for calculations.

The second method is based on the analytical finding of derivative $\dfrac{df}{dz}$ and estimation through limited differences of derivative $\dfrac{\partial z}{\partial\bar{\alpha}}$. Subject to (12) and (15) we obtain:

$$
\beta_{it} \approx \frac{\sum_{l=1}^{\mu}(\tilde{z}_{jl}^{(1)}(\hat{\alpha}_{i,t-1}) - z_{jl}^{(2)})(\tilde{z}_{jl}^{(1)}(\hat{\alpha}_{i,t-1} + \Delta_{\alpha i}) - \tilde{z}_{jl}^{(1)}(\hat{\alpha}_{i,t-1} - \Delta_{\alpha i}))}{\mu\Delta_{\alpha i}},
$$

where coordinates of interpolated samples $\tilde{z}_{jl}^{(1)}(\hat{\alpha}_{i,t-1}\pm\Delta_{\alpha i})$ are found on the equations (19), and their brightness at bilinear interpolation - on the equation (20).

The third method assumes the existence derivative $\dfrac{df}{dz}$ and particular derivatives $\dfrac{\partial x}{\partial \alpha}$ and $\dfrac{\partial y}{\partial \alpha}$. Derivatives of brightness $\dfrac{\partial z}{\partial x}$ and $\dfrac{\partial z}{\partial y}$ on the base axis are estimated through finite differences. Then in accordance with (13):

$$\overline{\beta}_{it} \approx \frac{1}{\mu}\sum_{l=1}^{\mu}\left(\widetilde{z}_{jl}^{(1)} - z_{jl}^{(2)}\right)\left(\frac{\widetilde{z}_{\widetilde{x}l+\Delta x,\,\widetilde{y}l}^{(1)} - \widetilde{z}_{\widetilde{x}l-\Delta x,\,\widetilde{y}l}^{(1)}}{\Delta_x}\frac{\partial x}{\partial \alpha_i} + \frac{\widetilde{z}_{\widetilde{x}l,\,\widetilde{y}l+\Delta y}^{(1)} - \widetilde{z}_{\widetilde{x}l,\,\widetilde{y}l-\Delta y}^{(1)}}{\Delta_y}\frac{\partial y}{\partial \alpha_i}\right), \qquad (21)$$

where coordinates of samples $\widetilde{z}_{\widetilde{x}l\pm\Delta x,\,\widetilde{y}l}^{(1)}$, $\widetilde{z}_{\widetilde{x}l,\,\widetilde{y}l\pm\Delta y}^{(1)}$ are found in points $(\widetilde{x}_l \pm \Delta_x, \widetilde{y}_l)$, $(\widetilde{x}_l, \widetilde{y}_l \pm \Delta_y)$ of the image $\widetilde{Z}^{(1)}$. Derivatives $\dfrac{\partial x}{\partial \alpha}$ and $\dfrac{\partial y}{\partial \alpha}$ depend on the accepted deformations model. At affine model in the point $(\widetilde{x}_l, \widetilde{y}_l)$:

$$\frac{\partial \widetilde{x}_l}{\partial h_x} = 1, \ \frac{\partial \widetilde{y}_l}{\partial h_x} = 0; \ \frac{\partial \widetilde{x}_l}{\partial h_y} = 0, \ \frac{\partial \widetilde{y}_l}{\partial h_y} = 1;$$

$$\frac{\partial \widetilde{x}_l}{\partial \varphi} = \hat{\kappa}_{t-1}\left((x_l - x_0)\sin\hat{\varphi}_{t-1} - (y_l - y_0)\cos\hat{\varphi}_{t-1}\right),$$

$$\frac{\partial \widetilde{y}_l}{\partial \varphi} = \hat{\kappa}_{t-1}\left((x_l - x_0)\cos\hat{\varphi}_{t-1} + (y_l - y_0)\sin\hat{\varphi}_{t-1}\right); \qquad (22)$$

$$\frac{\partial \widetilde{x}_l}{\partial \kappa} = (x_l - x_0)\cos\hat{\varphi}_{t-1} - (y_l - y_0)\sin\hat{\varphi}_{t-1},$$

$$\frac{\partial \widetilde{y}_l}{\partial \kappa} = (x_l - x_0)\sin\hat{\varphi}_{t-1} + (y_l - y_0)\cos\hat{\varphi}_{t-1}.$$

Having introduced denotations $\dfrac{\partial \widetilde{x}_l}{\partial \alpha_i} = c_{il}$ and $\dfrac{\partial \widetilde{y}_l}{\partial \alpha_i} = d_{il}$, for the i-th component of pseudogradient we can write:

$$\beta_{it} = \frac{1}{\mu}\sum_{l=1}^{\mu}\left(\widetilde{z}_{jl}^{(1)} - z_{jl}^{(2)}\right)\left(\frac{\widetilde{z}_{\widetilde{x}l+\Delta x,\,\widetilde{y}l}^{(1)} - \widetilde{z}_{\widetilde{x}l-\Delta x,\,\widetilde{y}l}^{(1)}}{\Delta_x}c_{il} + \frac{\widetilde{z}_{\widetilde{x}l,\,\widetilde{y}l+\Delta y}^{(1)} - \widetilde{z}_{\widetilde{x}l,\,\widetilde{y}l-\Delta y}^{(1)}}{\Delta_y}d_{il}\right). \qquad (23)$$

In the case if increments on coordinates are equal to the step of sample grid $\Delta_x = \Delta_y = 1$, then (23) takes a form

$$\beta_{it} = \frac{1}{\mu}\sum_{l=1}^{\mu}\left(\widetilde{z}_{jl}^{(1)} - z_{jl}^{(2)}\right)\left(\left(\widetilde{z}_{\widetilde{x}l+1,\,\widetilde{y}l}^{(1)} - \widetilde{z}_{\widetilde{x}l-1,\,\widetilde{y}l}^{(1)}\right)c_{il} + \left(\widetilde{z}_{\widetilde{x}l,\,\widetilde{y}l+1}^{(1)} - \widetilde{z}_{\widetilde{x}l,\,\widetilde{y}l-1}^{(1)}\right)d_{il}\right).$$

Let us note, that the number of computational operations in the last expression can be reduced in the assumption of equality of derivatives on coordinates for the sample $\widetilde{z}_{jl}^{(1)}$ of the image $\widetilde{Z}^{(1)}$ and the sample $z_{jl}^{(2)}$ of the image $\mathbf{Z}^{(2)}$. This assumption is approximately fulfilled at small deviations $\hat{\alpha}$ from the optimal value $\overline{\alpha}$. Тогда :

$$\beta_{it} = \frac{1}{\mu} \sum_{l=1}^{\mu} \left(\tilde{z}_{jl}^{(1)} - z_{jl}^{(2)} \right) \left(\left(z_{jxl+1,\,jyl}^{(2)} - z_{jxl-1,\,jyl}^{(2)} \right) c_{il} + \left(z_{jxl,\,jyl+1}^{(2)} - z_{jxl,\,jyl-1}^{(2)} \right) d_{il} \right).$$

The fourth method is based on the estimation of derivatives $\dfrac{\partial f}{\partial x}$ and $\dfrac{\partial f}{\partial y}$ through finite differences at analytic finding derivatives $\dfrac{\partial x}{\partial \alpha}$ and $\dfrac{\partial y}{\partial \alpha}$:

$$\beta_{it} = \frac{1}{2\mu} \left[\frac{1}{\Delta_x} \sum_{l=1}^{\mu} \left(\left(\tilde{z}_{\tilde{x}l+\Delta x,\,\tilde{y}l}^{(1)} - z_{jl}^{(2)} \right)^2 - \left(\tilde{z}_{\tilde{x}l-\Delta x,\,\tilde{y}l}^{(1)} - z_{jl}^{(2)} \right)^2 \right) \frac{\partial x}{\partial \alpha_i} + \frac{1}{\Delta_y} \sum_{l=1}^{\mu} \left(\left(\tilde{z}_{\tilde{x}l,\,\tilde{y}l+\Delta y}^{(1)} - z_{jl}^{(2)} \right)^2 - \left(\tilde{z}_{\tilde{x}l,\,\tilde{y}l-\Delta y}^{(1)} - z_{jl}^{(2)} \right)^2 \right) \frac{\partial y}{\partial \alpha_i} \right].$$

3. Improvement coefficient of parameters estimates

The convergence of parameters estimates of interframe deformations depends on a large number of influencing factors. We can divide them into a priory factors, which can be defined by probability density functions and autocorrelation functions of images and interfering noises, and a posteriori factors, determined by procedure (3) characteristics: pseudogradient calculation method, the kind of a gain matrix and number of iterations. As a rule, we can refer a goal function to the first group. For analysis it is desirable to describe the influence of the factors from the first group by a small number of values as far as possible. In the papers (Tashlinskii & Tikhonov, 2001) as such values it is proposed to use probabilities (4) of estimates change in parameters space. On their basis in the paper (Samojlov, 2006) a coefficient characterizing probabilistic characteristics of parameters change in the process of convergence is proposed. Let us consider it in details. If a value of parameter estimate at the $(t-1)$-th iteration is $\hat{\alpha}_{i,t-1}$, then the mathematical expectation of the estimate at the t-th iteration can be expressed through probabilities $\rho^+(\bar{\varepsilon})$ and $\rho^-(\bar{\varepsilon})$:

$$\mathrm{M}[\hat{\alpha}_{i,t}] = \hat{\alpha}_{i,t-1} - \lambda_{i,t} \left(\rho^+(\bar{\varepsilon}_{t-1}) - \rho^-(\bar{\varepsilon}_{t-1}) \right).$$

If $\rho^+(\bar{\varepsilon}_{t-1}) > \rho^-(\bar{\varepsilon}_{t-1})$, then the estimate is improved, if not – is deteriorated. Thus the characteristic

$$\mathfrak{R}_i = \rho_i^+(\bar{\varepsilon}) - \rho_i^-(\bar{\varepsilon}) \tag{24}$$

let us call the estimate improvement coefficient. The range of its change is from –1 to +1. At that a value +1 means that the mathematical expectation $\mathrm{M}[\hat{\alpha}_{i,t}]$ of the estimate is improved at the t-th iteration by $\lambda_{i,t}$.
The improvement coefficient can be the generalized characteristic of images to be estimated, effecting noises and also chosen goal function. Having used for its calculation the equations (4), we obtain

$$\mathfrak{R}_i = \int_{-\infty}^{0} w(\beta_i)\,d\beta_i - \int_{0}^{\infty} w(\beta_i)\,d\beta_i . \tag{25}$$

Let us analyze possibilities for improvement coefficient calculation for the cases of usage as a goal function interframe difference mean square and interframe correlation coefficient. At that let us assume that $\rho_i^0(\overline{\varepsilon}) = 0$. The last assumption is true at unquantified samples of images to be studied. Subject to divisible group of events $\rho_i^+(\overline{\varepsilon}) = 1 - \rho_i^-(\overline{\varepsilon})$, then

$$\Re_i = 2\rho_i^+(\overline{\varepsilon}) - 1 = 2 \int_{-\infty}^{0} w(\beta_i)d\beta_i - 1 \ .$$

Interframe difference mean square

The estimate of interframe difference mean square at each iteration of estimation can be found on the relation (15). Let us assume the images to be studied have Gaussian distribution of brightness with zero mean and unquantified samples and the model of images $\widetilde{Z}^{(1)}$ and $Z^{(2)}$ is additive :

$$Z^{(1)} = \widetilde{S}^{(1)} + \Theta^{(1)}, \quad Z^{(2)} = S^{(2)} + \Theta^{(2)} \ ,$$

where $\widetilde{S}^{(1)} = \left\{\widetilde{s}_j^{(1)}\right\}$, $S^{(2)} = \left\{s_j^{(2)}\right\}$ – desired random fields with identical variances σ_s^2, at that the field $\left\{s_j^{(2)}\right\}$ has autocorrelation function $R(\ell)$; $\Theta^{(1)} = \left\{\theta_j^{(1)}\right\}$, $\Theta^{(2)} = \left\{\theta_j^{(2)}\right\}$ – independent Gaussian random fields with zero mean and equal variances σ_θ^2. Let us accept the affine model of deformations (17): $\overline{\alpha} = \left(h_x, h_y, \varphi, \kappa\right)^T$.

In accordance with (25) for calculation of the estimate improvement coefficient $\Re_i$ it is necessary to find probability density function $w(\beta_i)$ of projection β_i of pseudogradient $\overline{\beta}$ on the parameter α_i axis. For this purpose let us use the third way (21) for interframe difference mean square pseudogradient calculation.

Analytic finding probability distribution (23) as a function of σ_s^2, σ_θ^2 and $R(\ell)$ is a difficult problem. However the approximate solution can be found (Tashlinskii & Tikhonov, 2001), if we use the circumstance, that as μ increases the component β_i normalizes quickly. At $\mu = 1$ (23) includes from four to eight similar summands, at $\mu = 2$ – from eight to sixteen, etc. Thus the distribution of probabilities β_i can be assumed to be close to Gaussian. Then:

$$\Re_i(\overline{\varepsilon}) = 2F\left(\frac{M[\beta_i]}{\sigma[\beta_i]}\right) - 1, \ i = \overline{1, m} \ , \tag{26}$$

where $F(\cdot)$ – Laplace function; $M[\beta_i]$ and $\sigma[\beta_i]$ – mathematical expectation and standard deviation of the component β_i . Thus the problem can be reduced to finding the mathematical expectation and variance of β_i . For relation (23) we obtain:

$$M[\beta_i] = -\sigma_s^2 \sum_{i=1}^{\mu} \left(\left(R\left(\ell_{a-1,b}^{(l)}\right) - \ell_{a+1,b}^{(l)} \right) c_{il} + \left(R\left(\ell_{a,b-1}^{(l)}\right) - R\left(\ell_{a,b+1}^{(l)}\right) \right) d_{il} \right); \tag{27}$$

$$\sigma^2[\beta_i] = \sigma_s^4 \sum_{l=1}^{\mu} \left(4 \left(\left(c_{il}^2 + d_{il}^2\right)\left(1 - R\left(\ell_{a,b}^{(l)}\right)\right)\left(1 - R(2)\right) + g^{-1}\left(2 - R\left(\ell_{a,b}^{(l)}\right) - R(2) + g^{-1}\right)\right) + $$

$$+ \left(c_{il}\left(R\left(\ell_{a-1,b}^{(l)}\right) - R\left(\ell_{a+1,b}^{(l)}\right)\right) + d_{il}\left(R\left(\ell_{a,b-1}^{(l)}\right) - R\left(\ell_{a,b+1}^{(l)}\right)\right)\right)^2 \right), \tag{28}$$

where $\ell_{a,b}^{(l)}$ – Euclidian distance between point with coordinates (a_l, b_l) and point with coordinates (x_l, y_l), $l = \overline{1, \mu}$; $R(\ell_{a,b})$ – normalized autocorrelation function of the image; c_{il} and d_{il} – functions c and d for the i-ro parameter in the point (a_l, b_l) (Tashlinskii @ Minkina, 2006). For finding $\Re_i$ it is necessary to substitute (27) and (28) into (26).

As it is seen from (27) and (28) $\Re_i$ does not depend only on σ_s^2, σ_θ^2 and $R(\ell)$, it also depends on a plan of the local sample Z_t, namely on reciprocal location of samples (a_l, b_l), of the deformed image which are in the local sample at the t-th iteration.

In Fig. 1,a as an example the plots of the improvement coefficient for rotation angle ($\Re_\varphi$) as a function of error $\varepsilon_\varphi = \hat{\varphi} - \varphi^*$, where φ^* is the sought value of parameter are presented. The results are obtained for images with Gaussian autocorrelation function with correlation radius equal to 5 at signal/noise ration $g = 20$ and local sample size $\mu = 3$. At that it is supposed that coordinates of points of the local sample are chosen on the circle with radius $L = 20$ (curve 1) and $L = 30$ (curve 2) with the center, coinciding with rotation center.

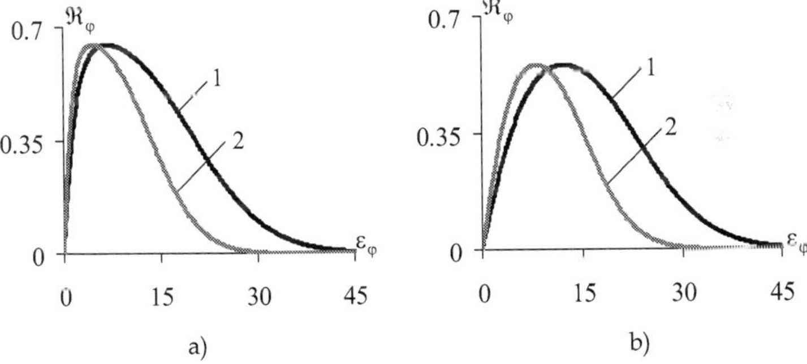

Fig. 1. The dependence of estimate improvement coefficient of rotation angle versus error

Interframe correlation sample coefficient
When choosing as a goal function interframe correlation coefficient its estimate at each iteration can be found on the relation (16). Having accepted for image to be studied the same assumptions as in the previous case for finding $w(\beta_i)$ let us use the expression:

$$\beta_{it} = \frac{1}{2\mu^2 \hat{\sigma}_{z1}^3 \hat{\sigma}_{z2}} \left[\mu \hat{\sigma}_{z1}^2 \left(\sum_{l=1}^{\mu} \left(z_{jl}^{(2)} - z_{cp}^{(2)} \right) \times \right. \right.$$

$$\times \left(\frac{\tilde{z}_{\tilde{x}l+\Delta x, \tilde{y}l}^{(1)} - \tilde{z}_{\tilde{x}l-\Delta x, \tilde{y}l}^{(1)}}{\Delta_x} \frac{\partial \tilde{x}}{\partial \alpha_i} + \frac{\tilde{z}_{\tilde{x}l, \tilde{y}l+\Delta y}^{(1)} - \tilde{z}_{\tilde{x}l, \tilde{y}l-\Delta y}^{(1)}}{\Delta_y} \frac{\partial \tilde{y}}{\partial \alpha_i} \right) \right) -$$

$$- \left(\sum_{l=1}^{\mu} \left(z_{jl}^{(2)} - z_{cp}^{(2)} \right) \tilde{z}_{\tilde{x}l, \tilde{y}l}^{(1)} \right) \sum_{l=1}^{\mu} \left(\tilde{z}_{\tilde{x}l, \tilde{y}l}^{(1)} - \frac{1}{\mu-1} \sum_{k=1, k \neq l}^{\mu} \tilde{z}_{\tilde{x}k, \tilde{y}k}^{(1)} \right) \times$$

$$\times \left(\frac{\tilde{z}_{\tilde{x}l+\Delta x, \tilde{y}l}^{(1)} - \tilde{z}_{\tilde{x}l-\Delta x, \tilde{y}l}^{(1)}}{\Delta_x} \frac{\partial \tilde{x}}{\partial \alpha_i} + \frac{\tilde{z}_{\tilde{x}l, \tilde{y}l+\Delta y}^{(1)} - \tilde{z}_{\tilde{x}l, \tilde{y}l-\Delta y}^{(1)}}{\Delta_y} \frac{\partial \tilde{y}}{\partial \alpha_i} \right) \right],$$

$$(29)$$

where coordinates and brightness of samples $\tilde{z}^{(1)}_{\tilde{x}l\pm\Delta x,\,\tilde{y}l}$, $\tilde{z}^{(1)}_{\tilde{x}l,\,\tilde{y}l\pm\Delta y}$ are determined by equations (19) and (20) correspondingly. The derivatives $\dfrac{\partial\tilde{x}}{\partial\alpha_i}$ and $\dfrac{\partial\tilde{y}}{\partial\alpha_i}$ can be found on equations (22).

Let us consider several cases. At first let us suppose that mean values $z^{(2)}_{av}$ and $\tilde{z}^{(1)}_{av}$ are equal to zero, and estimates of standard deviation $\hat{\sigma}_{z1}$ and $\hat{\sigma}_{z2}$ are known a priory. In this case pseudogradient of interframe correlation coefficient differs from pseudogradient of covariation estimate of images $\mathbf{Z}^{(1)}$ and $\mathbf{Z}^{(2)}$ only by constant factor $(\sigma_{z1}\sigma_{z2})^{-1}$, and $M[\beta_i]$ from expression (27) – by factor $-(2\mu\sigma_s^2)^{-1}$. The variance of β_i :

$$\sigma^2[\beta_i]=\frac{1}{\mu^2}\sum_{l=1}^{\mu}\left(\frac{1}{2}\left(c_{il}^2+d_{il}^2\right)\left(1+g_1^{-1}\right)\left(1-R(2)+g_2^{-1}\right)+\right.$$
$$\left.+\frac{1}{4}\left(c_{il}\left(R\left(\ell^{(l)}_{a-1,b}\right)-R\left(\ell^{(l)}_{a+1,b}\right)\right)+d_{il}\left(R\left(\ell^{(l)}_{a,b-1}\right)-R\left(\ell^{(l)}_{a,b+1}\right)\right)\right)^2\right),$$

where $g_1=\sigma_{s1}^2/\sigma_{\theta1}^2$, $g_2=\sigma_{s2}^2/\sigma_{\theta2}^2$ – signal/noise ratio for images $\tilde{Z}^{(1)}$ and $\mathbf{Z}^{(2)}$ correspondingly.

If only variances σ_{z1}^2, σ_{z2}^2 are known a priory, then

$$\beta_i=\frac{1}{\mu\sigma_{z1}\sigma_{z2}}\sum_{l=1}^{\mu}\frac{\partial z^{(1)}_{\tilde{x}l,\tilde{y}l}}{\partial\alpha_i}\left(\frac{\mu-1}{\mu}z^{(2)}_{\tilde{j}l}-\frac{1}{\mu}\sum_{k=1,k\neq l}^{\mu}z^{(2)}_{\tilde{j}k}\right).$$

For simplification of finding the mathematical expectation and the variance of β_i summands in the sum $\displaystyle\sum_{k=1,k\neq l}^{\mu}z^{(2)}_{\tilde{j}k}$ let us assume to be noncorrelated with a value $z^{(2)}_{\tilde{j}l}$. The assumption aboud noncorrelatedness of $z^{(2)}_{\tilde{j}k}$, $k=\overline{1,\mu}$, $k\neq l$ and $z^{(2)}_{\tilde{j}l}$ is not rigid, because samples to the local sample are chosen as a rule to be weakly correlated (Tashlinskii @ Minkina, 2006). Then:

$$M[\beta_i]=\frac{1}{2\mu}\left(1-\frac{1}{\mu}\right)\sum_{l=1}^{\mu}\left(c_{il}\left(R\left(\ell^{(l)}_{a-1,b}\right)-R\left(\ell^{(l)}_{a+1,b}\right)\right)+d_{il}\left(R\left(\ell^{(l)}_{a,b-1}\right)-R\left(\ell^{(l)}_{a,b+1}\right)\right)\right), \tag{30}$$

$$\sigma^2[\beta_i]=\frac{1}{\mu^2}\sum_{l=1}^{\mu}\left(\frac{1}{2}\left(c_{il}^2+d_{il}^2\right)\left(\left(1-\frac{1}{\mu}\right)(1-R(2))+g_1^{-1}\left(1-R(2)+g_2^{-1}\right)+g_2^{-1}\right)+\right.$$
$$\left.+\frac{1}{4}\left(1-\frac{1}{\mu}\right)^2\left(c_{il}\left(R\left(\ell^{(l)}_{a-1,b}\right)-R\left(\ell^{(l)}_{a+1,b}\right)\right)+d_{il}\left(R\left(\ell^{(l)}_{a,b-1}\right)-R\left(\ell^{(l)}_{a,b+1}\right)\right)\right)^2\right). \tag{31}$$

As an example in Fig. 1,b the plots of the improvement coefficient for rotation angle ($\Re_\varphi$) as the function of errors ε_φ are presented. Image parameters, signal/noise ration and sample size correspond to the example (Fig. 1,a). From the plot it is seen, that at similar conditions $\Re_\varphi$ for interframe correlation coefficient is less, than for interframe difference mean square.

Similarly the case when σ_{z1}^2, σ_{z2}^2 of $z_{av}^{(2)}$ and $\tilde{z}_{av}^{(1)}$ are a priory known can be considered.

4. Optimization of samples choice region on criterion of estimate improvement coefficient maximum

Let one parameter is estimated. Then for finding optimal region of samples of a local sample we can use results, obtained in the previous part, choosing the estimate improvement coefficient maximum of a parameter to be estimated as an optimality criterion. At the affine deformations model the improvement coefficient for parameters h_x and h_y depends only on their errors from optimal values and does not depend on the location of samples of the local sample. Thus when estimating parallel shift parameters it is impossible to improve estimates convergence at the expense of choice of samples of the local sample. For parameters of rotation φ and scale κ the improvement coefficient depends on the samples coordinates. Correspondingly, the region of image, where the improvement coefficient maximum is ensured, can be found.

As an example let us find the image region at the known error ε_φ of rotation angle ψ. It is not difficult to show, that initial region at the given image parameters is determined by the distance L_{op} from the rotation centre (x_0, y_0). At that for each error ε_φ a value L_{op} will be individual. In Fig. 2 for $\varepsilon_\varphi = 5^o$ the dependences of $\Re_\varphi$ as the function versus distance L from the rotation centre when using as the goal function interframe difference mean square (рис. 2,a) and interframe correlation coefficient (рис. 2,b), calculated by equations (26), (28) and (30), (31) correspondingly. The image was assumed to be Gaussian with autocorrelation function with correlation radius equal to 13 steps of the sample grid and signal/noise ratio $g = 50$. From the plot it is seen that for interframe difference mean square maximum of estimation coefficient attainess at $L_{op} = 58$, for interframe correlation coefficient- at $L_{op} = 126.7$.

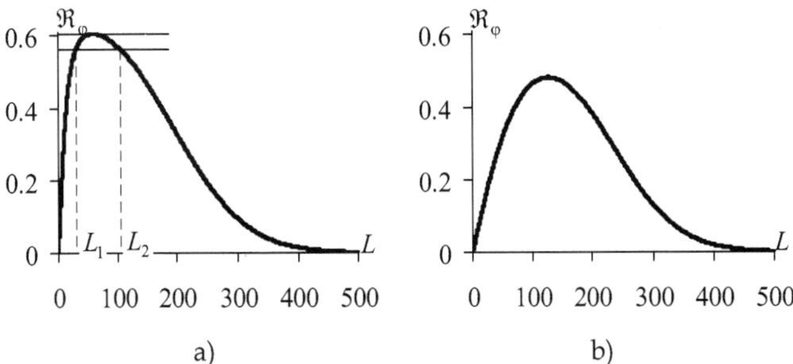

Fig. 2. The dependence of estimate improvement coefficient of rotation angle versus the distance from rotation center

If we know the dependence of ε_φ change versus the number of iterations, we can find L_{op} for each iteration. The rule of forming the dependence ε_φ on the number of iterations can be different and can depend on conditions of the problem to be solved. For instance, if we use a minimax approach, then it is enough to find the dependence beginning from maximum possible parameter error (for the worst situation), and to find the number of iterations which is necessary for the given accuracy attainment. In the sequel the obtained rule of L_{op} change on the number of iterations is applied for any initial parameter error, ensuring the estimation accuracy which is not worse than the given one. At that the dependence of change of error ε_φ versus the number of iterations can be found either theoretically for the given autocorrelation function and probability density function of image brightness by the method of pseudogradient procedures simulation at finite number of iterations (Tashlinskii & Tikhonov, 2001), or experimentally on the current estimates, averaged on the given realizations assemblage. At the last approach the following algorithm can be used.

1^0. To specify the initial error $\varepsilon_{\varphi 0}$ of rotation angle.

2^0. To find L_{op1} for the first iteration.

3^0. To perform the iteration u times. On the obtained estimates to find the average error $\varepsilon_{\varphi 1} = \dfrac{1}{u}\sum_{r=1}^{u}\varepsilon_{\varphi 0,r}$, where u – given number of realizations.

4^0. For obtained $\varepsilon_{\varphi 1}$ to repeat operators 1^0–3^0 T times until the next $\varepsilon_{\varphi T}$ is less the required estimation error ε_{nop}, T – total number of iterations.

Let us notice, that for digital images the circle with radius L_{op} can be considered as an optimal region only conditionally, because the probability of its intersection with nodes of sample grid is too small. To obtain the suboptimal region we can specify some range of acceptable values for the improvement coefficient from $\gamma\Re_{max}$ to $\Re_{max}$ (Fig. 2,a), where γ – threshold coefficient. Then values L_1 and L_2 specify region bounds, where the improvement coefficient does not differ from maximum more than, for example, 10%. At that the suboptimal region is ring. As an example in Fig. 3 the dependences L_{op} versus error ε_φ for interframe difference mean square (curve 1) and interframe correlation coefficient (curve 2) are shown. From figure it is seen that values of L_{op} for correlation coefficient exceed values of L_{op} for difference mean square.

In Fig. 4 the dependence ε_φ versus the number of iterations (curve 1), obtained at usage of pseudogradient procedure with parameter $\lambda_\varphi = 0.15^o$, initial error $\varepsilon_{\varphi 0} = 45^o$ and choice of samples of the local sample from 10 % suboptimal region on the image of size 1024×1024 pixels are presented. On the same figure the dependences for $\varepsilon_{\varphi 0} = 25^o$ (curve 2) and $\varepsilon_{\varphi 0} = 15^o$ (curve 3), obtained at the same rule of suboptimal region change and dependence obtained for $\varepsilon_{\varphi 0} = 45^o$ without optimization (curve 4) are shown. All curves are averaged on 200 realizations. It is seen that optimization increases the convergence rate of rotation angle about several times. At initial errors which are less the maximum errors(curves 2 and 3), the convergence rate of estimate is a little less, than at maximum one, but the number of iterations which is necessary for the given error attainment does not exceed the number of iterations at maximum error. The behavior of estimates for scale coefficient estimation is similar.

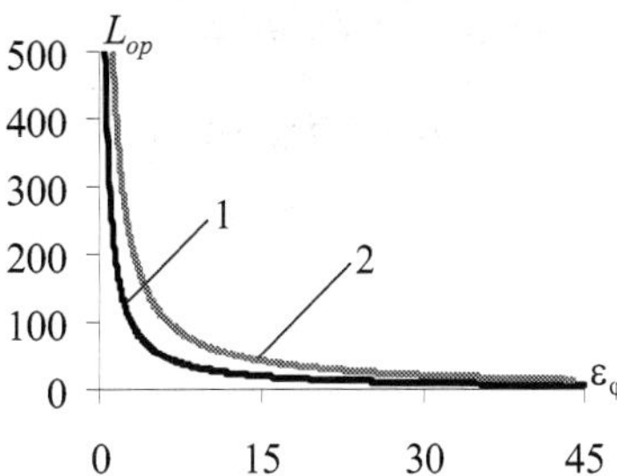

Fig. 3. The dependence of L_{op} versus ε_φ

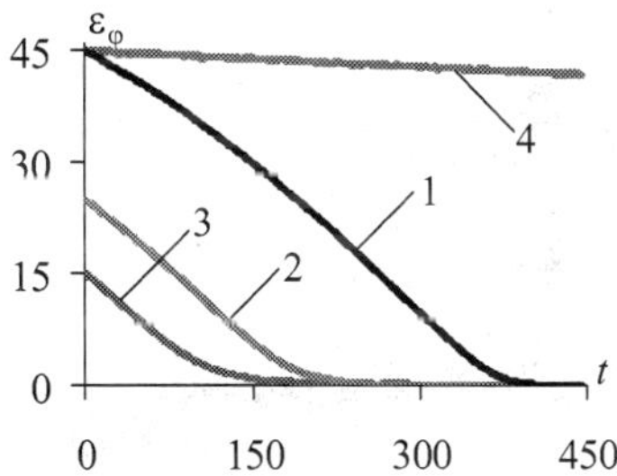

Fig. 4. The dependence of ε_φ versus the number of iterations

Let us note, that the considered method of optimization of the local sample samples choice region is unacceptable when estimating a parameters vector. It is due to the fact that the improvement coefficient of parameters vector can not be found on estimates improvement coefficient of separate parameters. Thus let us consider another approach for the case when estimating a vector of parameters.

5. Optimal Euclidian error distance of deformations parameters estimates

For any set of deformations model parameters as a result of the next iteration performing for the sample $z_{jk}^{(2)}$ with coordinates $\left(j_{xk}, j_{yk}\right)$ its estimate $\tilde{z}_k^{(1)}$ is found on the reference image with coordinates $\left(\tilde{x}_k, \tilde{y}_k\right)$. At that the location of the point $\left(\tilde{x}_k, \tilde{y}_k\right)$ relatively the point $\left(j_{xk}, j_{yk}\right)$ can be defined through Euclidian error distance (EED) $\mathfrak{R} = \sqrt{\left(j_{xk} - \tilde{x}_k\right)^2 + \left(j_{yk} - \tilde{y}_k\right)^2}$ and angle $\phi = \arg tg \dfrac{j_{yk} - \tilde{y}_k}{j_{xk} - \tilde{x}_k}$ (Fig. 5). It can be shown that if only rotation angle is estimated then in different regions maximum EED attains at different values of estimate error, but at the same EED value. It is explained in Fig. 6. What is more when estimating any another parameter (scale, shift on one of the axis) or their set maximum EED attains at the same EED. We can suppose, that this optimal value of EED depends only on the goal function and characteristics of images to be studied and does not depend on the model of deformations.

On the other hand the optimal value of EED at the known error of parameters estimates determines the optimal region of samples for the local sample. Thus the solution of the problem of finding of optimal (suboptimal) region of samples of local sample can be divided into two steps:

1) finding for the chosen goal function of estimation quality optimal EED as a function of image parameters (probability density function of brightness, autocorrelation function of desired image and signal/noise ratio);

2) determining on the deformations model and a vector of parameters estimates error the optimal region of choice of samples of the local sample as a region in which the optimal EED is ensured.

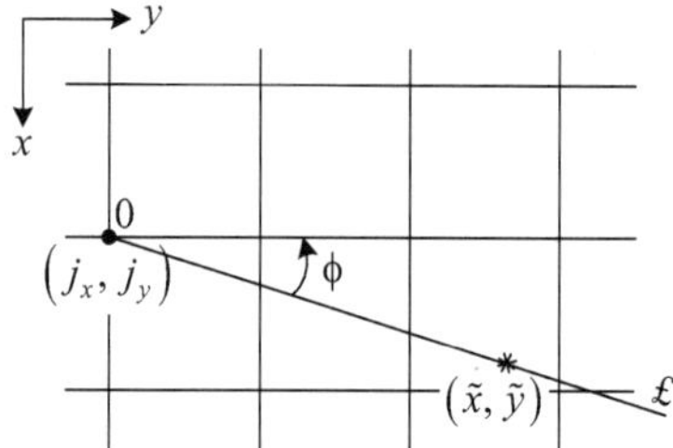

Fig. 5. Illustration of points $\left(j_x, j_y\right)$ and $(\tilde{x}, \tilde{y})$ location

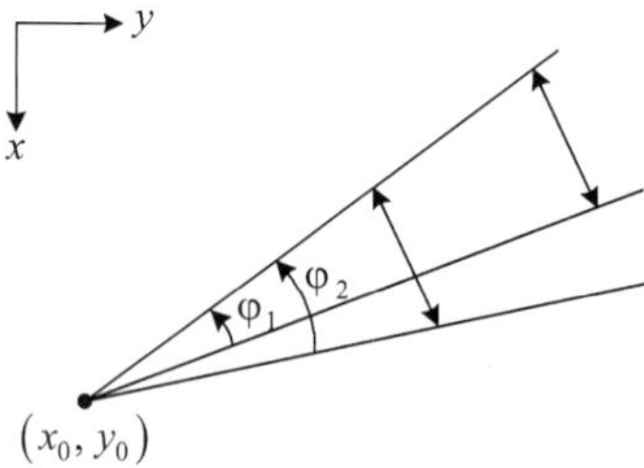

Fig. 6. Location of optimal EED in dependence on rotation angle

Let us consider the solution of the first mentioned problems. Let us the goal function of estimation quality is given. It is required to find value of EED, when maximum information about reciprocal deformation of images $\mathbf{Z}^{(1)}$ and $\mathbf{Z}^{(2)}$ is extracted. Let us understand the quantity of information in the sense of information, contained in one random value respectively another random value.

The estimate of the goal function gradient is calculated on the local sample, containing μ samples pairs. Each pair of samples $z_{jk}^{(2)}$ and $\tilde{z}_k^{(1)}$, $k = \overline{1, \mu}$, of the local sample has desired information about contact degree of these samples. At that all pairs of samples are equal on average, thus bellow we will consider one pair.

Assuming the image to be isotropic, for simplification of analysis of influence of distance between samples $z_{jk}^{(2)}$ and $\tilde{z}_k^{(1)}$ on the features of the goal function estimate it is reasonable to amount the problem to one-dimensional problem. For that it is enough to specify the coordinate axis $0-l$, passing through coordinates of samples with the centre in the point $\left(j_{xk}, j_{yk}\right)$ (Fig. 5). Correspondingly the literal notations for samples are simplified: $z = z_{jk}^{(2)}$, $\widetilde{z}_k^{(1)} = \widetilde{z}_\pounds$, where $\pounds$ – the distance between samples.

As it was already noticed, the information about contact degree of samples z and $\widetilde{z}_\pounds$ is noisy. For the additive model of image observations: $z = s + \theta$, $\widetilde{z}_\pounds = \widetilde{s}_\pounds + \widetilde{\theta}_\pounds$, the noise component is caused by two factors: additive noises θ, $\widetilde{\theta}_\pounds$ and sample correlatedness. The influence of noncorrelated noises is equal for any sample location. As the distance between them increases the random component increases too. Thus the noise component is minimum if the coordinates of samples coincide, correspondingly in this case the correlatedness is maximum. Actually, let us assume that variances of the samples $z = s + \theta$ and $\widetilde{z} = \widetilde{s} + \widetilde{\theta}$ are equal, and

$$\sigma_s^2 = \sigma_{\widetilde{s}}^2 , \quad \sigma_\theta^2 = \sigma_{\widetilde{\theta}}^2 , \tag{32}$$

for the mathematical expectation and variance of difference $z - \widetilde{z}_\pounds$ square we obtain:

$$M\left[(z - \widetilde{z}_\pounds)^2\right] = M\left[(s + \theta - \widetilde{s}_\pounds - \widetilde{\theta}_\pounds)^2\right] = 2\sigma_s^2\left(1 - R(\pounds) + g^{-1}\right),$$

$$D\left[(z - \widetilde{z}_\pounds)^2\right] = M\left[(z - \widetilde{z}_\pounds)^4\right] - M^2\left[(z - \widetilde{z}_\pounds)^2\right] = 8\sigma_s^4\left(1 - R(\pounds) + g^{-1}\right)^2,$$

where $R(\pounds)$ – normalized autocorrelation function of images to be studied; $g - \dfrac{\sigma_s^2}{\sigma_\theta^2}$ – signal/noise ratio. The plots normalized to σ_s^2 for the mathematical expectation and the mean-square distance of $(z - \widetilde{z}_\pounds)^2$ as the function of $\pounds$ at $g = 20$ and Gaussian $R(\pounds)$ with correlation radius, equal to 5 steps of the sample grid, are given in Fig. 7 and Fig. 8 correspondingly.

For the mathematical expectation and variance of the product $z\widetilde{z}_\pounds$ correspondingly we obtain:

$$M[z\widetilde{z}_l] = \mathrm{cov}\left[(s + \theta)(\widetilde{s}_\pounds + \widetilde{\theta}_\pounds)\right] = \sigma_s^2 R(\pounds) ,$$

$$D[z\widetilde{z}_\pounds] = \sigma_s^4\left((1 + g^{-1})^2 + R^2(\pounds)\right) .$$

The normalized plots of covariation and mean-square distance $(z\widetilde{z}_\pounds)$ as a function of $\pounds$ at the same image parameters are shown in Fig. 9 and Fig. 10 correspondingly. Let us notice that according to the assumptions (32) the normalized covariation, namely the correlation coefficient between samples z and $\widetilde{z}$, is determined by the expression:

$$r(\pounds) = \frac{\mathrm{cov}\left[(s + \theta)(\widetilde{s}_\pounds + \widetilde{\theta}_\pounds)\right]}{D[s + \theta]} = \frac{R(\pounds)}{1 + g} .$$

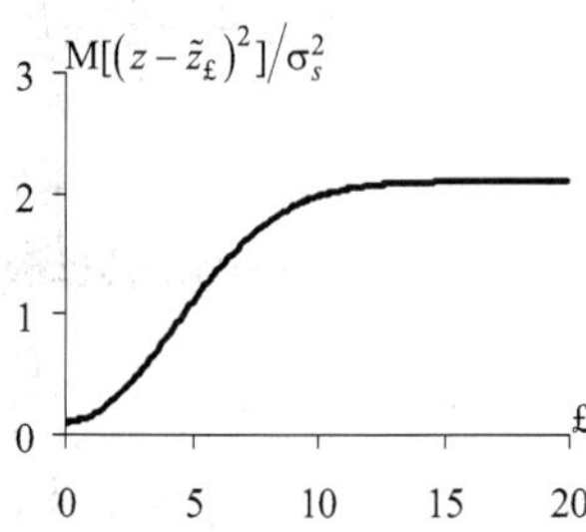

Fig. 7. Normalized mathematical expectation of $(z - \tilde{z}_\pounds)^2$

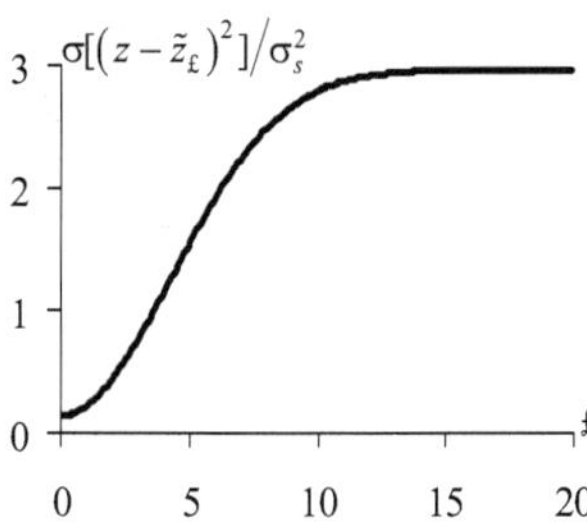

Fig. 8. Normalized standard deviation of $(z - \tilde{z}_\pounds)^2$

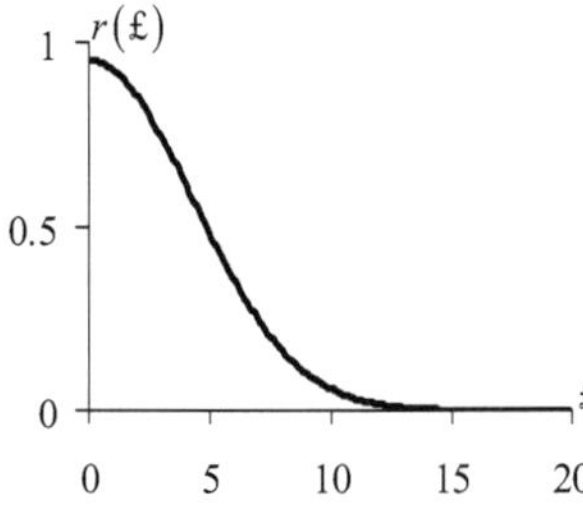

Fig. 9. Correlation coefficient for z and $\tilde{z}_\pounds$

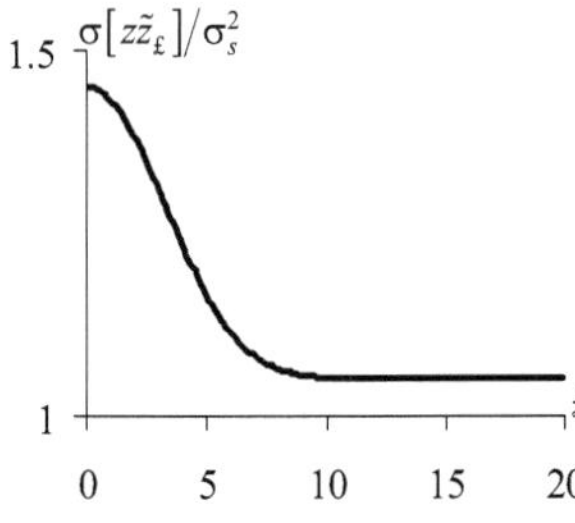

Fig. 10. Normalized standard deviation of $(z\tilde{z}_\pounds)$

However when pseudogradient estimating interframe deformations parameters we are interested in the contact degree of samples z and $\tilde{z}_{\pounds}$, containing in the goal function pseudogradient. As it was already noticed, this information is noisy. Thus let us consider the influence of the noise component on the information, which we are interested in, about goal function gradient. The gradient of the goal function in the given direction can be found either accordingly to the relation (8): $\beta = \dfrac{\partial \hat{J}}{\partial \pounds}$, or, if the first derivative on the variable z exists, – in accordance with the relation (9): $\overline{\beta} = \dfrac{df}{dz}\dfrac{\partial z}{\partial \pounds}$. Taking into account that the both methods imply the approximation of derivatives with finite differences we obtain

$$\beta \approx \frac{\hat{J}(\pounds+\Delta_\pounds)-\hat{J}(\pounds-\Delta_\pounds)}{2\Delta_\pounds} \tag{33}$$

for (8) and

$$\beta \approx \frac{df}{dz}\frac{\left(\tilde{z}_{\pounds+\Delta_\pounds}-\tilde{z}_{\pounds-\Delta_\pounds}\right)}{2\Delta_\pounds} \tag{34}$$

for (9).

Let us specify the expressions (33) and (34) for interframe difference mean square, covariation and sample correlation coefficient.

Mean square of samples brightness

In this case accordingly to (33) and (34) for the pseudogradient of the difference $z-\tilde{z}_{\pounds}$ we obtain the expressions relatively:

$$\beta_{\text{IDMS}} \approx \frac{\left(z-\tilde{z}_{\pounds+\Delta_\pounds}\right)^2-\left(z-\tilde{z}_{\pounds-\Delta_\pounds}\right)^2}{2\Delta_\pounds}, \tag{35}$$

$$\beta_{\text{IDMS}} \approx -\frac{\left(z-\tilde{z}_{\pounds}\right)\left(\tilde{z}_{\pounds+\Delta_l}-\tilde{z}_{\pounds-\Delta_\pounds}\right)}{\Delta_\pounds}, \tag{36}$$

where $\Delta_\pounds$ – the increment of the coordinate $\pounds$. Analysis of (35) and (36) shows, that at $\pounds \to 0$ and $\pounds \to \infty$ the mathematical expectation $M[\beta_{\text{IDMS}}]$ of the pseudogradient β_{IDMS} tends to zero and does not have any information, which we could use for deformation parameters change. At some value of $\pounds$, corresponding to maximum steepness of the goal function, the module of $M[\beta_{\text{IDMS}}]$ attains maximum value. Actually if we assume the model (35) and suppose validity of the assumption (32), we obtain that the mathematical expectation of β_{IDMS} is determined by the expression:

$$M[\beta_{\text{IDMS}}] = M\left[\frac{\left(z-\tilde{z}_{\pounds+\Delta_\pounds}\right)^2-\left(z-\tilde{z}_{\pounds-\Delta_\pounds}\right)^2}{2\Delta_\pounds}\right] = -\frac{\sigma_s^2}{\Delta_\pounds}(R(\pounds+\Delta_\pounds)-R(\pounds-\Delta_\pounds)), \tag{37}$$

where $R(\pounds)$ –normalized autocorrelation function of the image. Let us note that a similar relation is obtained for (36). From the plot in Fig. 11 that maximum module of $M[\beta_{\text{IDMS}}]$ attains at $\pounds \approx 4.3$.

As it was noticed information about gradient is extracted in noise conditions. At the assumed model of images the noise component is caused by additive noises θ and correlatedness of samples z and $\tilde{z}$. Let us characterize a value of the noise component by its variance. For finding a variance $D[\beta_{\text{IDMS}}]$ let us make use of the expression (36). Then, on the assumption of (32), we obtain

$$D[\beta_{\text{IDMS}}] = \frac{\sigma_s^4}{(\Delta_\pounds)^2}\left(4\left((1-R(\pounds))(1-R(2\Delta_\pounds)) + \right.\right.$$
$$\left.\left. + g^{-1}\left(2-R(\pounds)-R(2\Delta_\pounds)+g^{-1}\right)\right) + (R(\pounds+\Delta_\pounds)-R(\pounds-\Delta_\pounds))^2\right), \tag{38}$$

where g – signal/noise ration. The plots of the normalized mean-square distance $\sigma[\beta_{\text{IDMS}}]$ as a function of $\pounds$ at the same $R(\pounds)$ and signal/noise ratio $g = 500$ (curve 1), 10 (curve 2) and 5 (curve 3) are given in Fig. 12.

Let us find the condition when the information about contact degree of the samples s and $\tilde{s}$, extracted from the gradient of $(z-\tilde{z}_\pounds)^2$, is maximum on average. Since in accordance with (37) the mathematical expectation of the noise component is equal to zero, as such a condition maximum of module of mathematical expectation-to-mean-square distance ratio can be:

$$\max\left|\frac{M[\beta]}{\sigma[\beta]}\right|. \tag{39}$$

Having substituted the expression (37) and (38) in (39) we obtain the condition, from which we can find the distance $\pounds_{op}$ between samples, ensuring extraction of maximum information for pseudogradient parameters estimation when choosing as the goal function interframe difference mean square:

$$\max\left|\frac{R(\pounds+\Delta_\pounds)-R(\pounds-\Delta_\pounds)}{\sqrt{4\left((1-R(\pounds))(1-R(2\Delta_\pounds))+g^{-1}\left(2-R(\pounds)-R(2\Delta_\pounds)+g^{-1}\right)\right)+(R(\pounds+\Delta_\pounds)-R(\pounds-\Delta_\pounds))^2}}\right|. \tag{40}$$

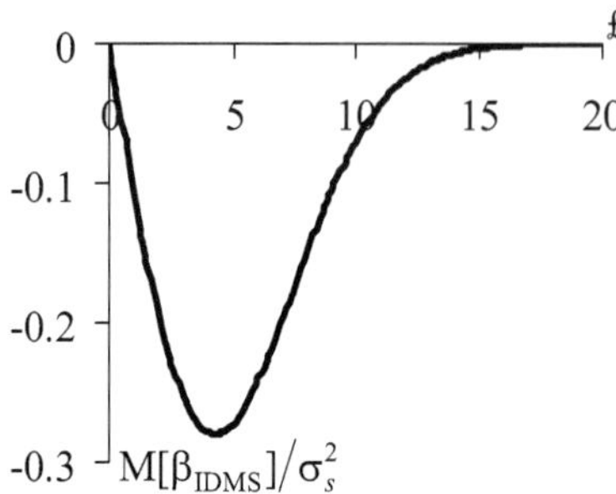

Fig. 11. Normalized mathematical expectation of β_{IDMS}

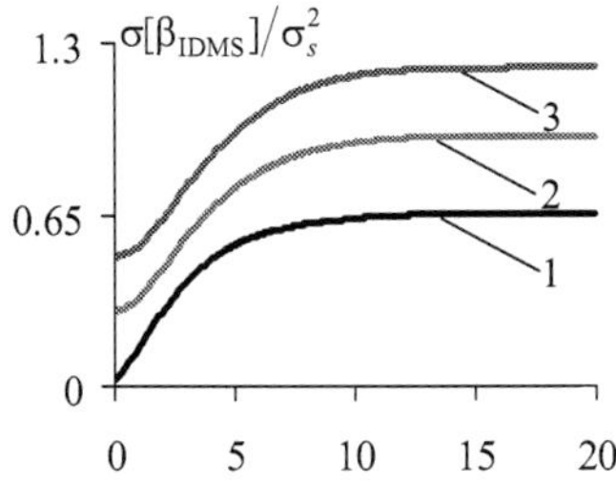

Fig. 12. Normalized standard deviation of β_{IDMS}

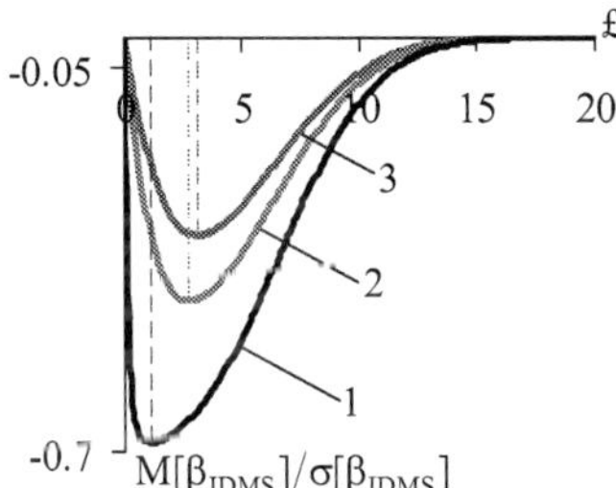

Fig. 13. Mathematical expectation of β_{IDMS} -to- its standard deviation ratio

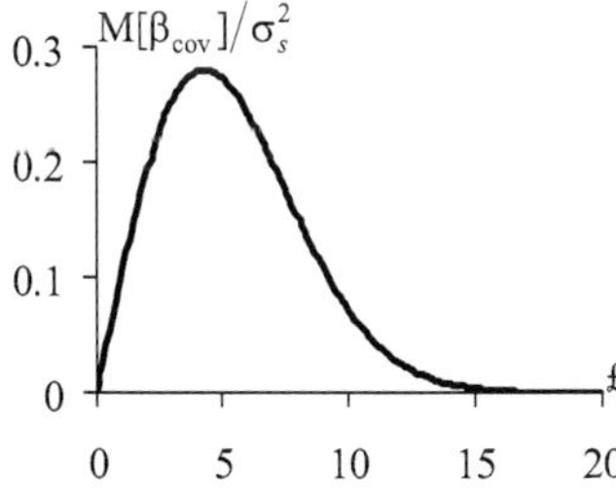

Fig. 14. Normalized mathematical expectation of β_{cov}

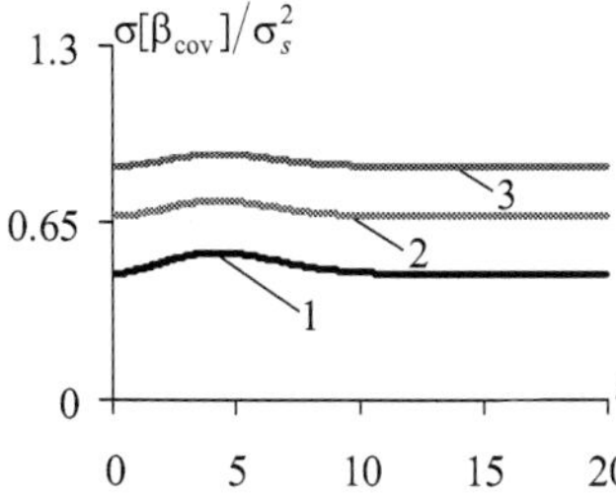

Fig. 15. Normalized standard deviation of β_{cov}

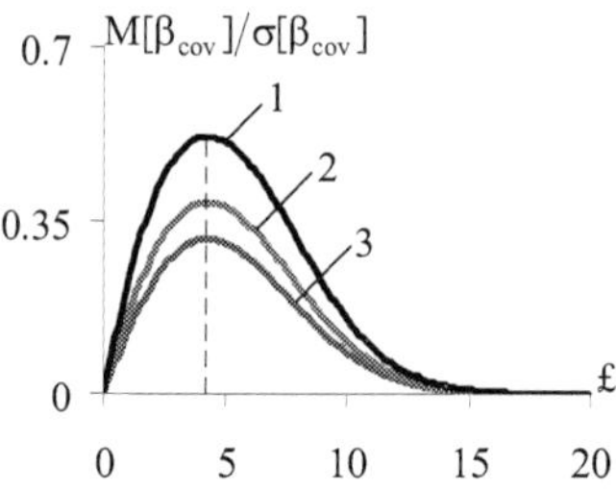

Fig. 16. Mathematical expectation of β_{cov} -to-its standard deviation ratio

Let us call this distance the optimal EED $£_{op}$. The plots of ratio $M[\beta_{\mathrm{IDMS}}]/\sigma[\beta_{\mathrm{IDMS}}]$ as the function of $£$ at $g = 500$ (curve 1), 10 (curve 2) and 5 (curve 3) are presented in Fig. 13. The distance $£_{op}$ can be found by traditional method by means of equating of the first derivative to zero

$$\frac{d}{d£}\left(\frac{M[\beta_{\mathrm{IDMS}}]}{\sqrt{D[\beta_{\mathrm{IDMS}}]}}\right) = \frac{1}{(D[\beta_{\mathrm{CKMP}}])^{3/2}}\left(4(R'(£+\Delta_£)-R'(£-\Delta_£))[(1-R(£))(1-R(2\Delta_£))+\right.$$

$$\left.+ g^{-1}(2-R(£)-R(2\Delta_£)+g^{-1})]+2(R(£+\Delta_£)-R(£-\Delta_£))R'(£)[1-R(2\Delta_£)+g^{-1}]\right).$$

We obtain the implicit equation for finding $£_{op}$:

$$\left(\frac{[\beta_{\mathrm{IDMS}}]}{\sigma[\beta_{\mathrm{IDMS}}]}\right) = 2(R'(£+\Delta_£)-R'(£-\Delta_£))[(1-R(£))(1-R(2\Delta_£))+$$

$$+ g^{-1}(2-R(£)-R(2\Delta_£)+g^{-1})]+(R(£+\Delta_£)-R(£-\Delta_£))R'(l)[1-R(2\Delta_£)+g^{-1}]=0.$$

In particular, for Gaussian $R(£)=\exp\left(-(£/a)^2\right)$ correlation function of images:

$$\left(\frac{[\beta_{\mathrm{IDMS}}]}{\sigma[\beta_{\mathrm{IDMS}}]}\right) = -\frac{4}{a^2}\left((£+\Delta_£)e^{-\left(\frac{£+\Delta_£}{a}\right)^2}-(£-\Delta_£)e^{-\left(\frac{£-\Delta_£}{a}\right)^2}\right)\times$$

$$\times\left[\left(1-e^{-\left(\frac{£}{a}\right)^2}\right)\left(1-e^{-\left(\frac{2\Delta_£}{a}\right)^2}\right)+g^{-1}\left(2-e^{-\left(\frac{£}{a}\right)^2}e^{-\left(\frac{2\Delta_£}{a}\right)^2}+g^{-1}\right)\right]- \tag{41}$$

$$-\frac{2£}{a^2}e^{-\left(\frac{£}{a}\right)^2}\left(e^{-\left(\frac{£+\Delta_£}{a}\right)^2}-e^{-\left(\frac{£-\Delta_£}{a}\right)^2}\right)\left[1-e^{-\left(\frac{2\Delta_£}{a}\right)^2}+g^{-1}\right]=0.$$

As noise increases the distance, when maximum of the relation (40) attains, increases too. For instance, for the correlation function with correlation radius equal to 5 at $g = 500$ we obtain $£_{op} = 1.14$, at $g = 10$ – $£_{op} = 2.75$ and at $g = 5$ – $£_{op} = 3.11$ (Fig. 13).

Thus in the situation when as the goal function interframe difference mean square of images $\widetilde{Z}^{(1)}$ and $Z^{(2)}$ is used for finding $£_{op}$ it is necessary to know the autocorrelation function of the mage $\widetilde{S}^{(1)}$, variances of images $\widetilde{S}^{(1)}$ and $S^{(2)}$ and variance of additive noises Θ. Value $£_{op}$ as the function of mentioned factors is found from the condition (40).

Samples covariation

Let us consider the mathematical expectation and the variance of pseudogradient of product $z\tilde{z}_{£}$. In accordance with relations (33) and (34) we can write:

$$\beta_{cov} = \frac{\partial(z\tilde{z}_{£})}{\partial £} = \frac{\partial(z\tilde{z})}{\partial z}\frac{\partial z}{\partial £} \approx \frac{z\tilde{z}_{£+\Delta_{£}} - z\tilde{z}_{£-\Delta_{£}}}{2\Delta_{£}}, \tag{41}$$

where $\Delta_{£}$ – increment of coordinate $£$. Appling to (41) the same reasoning as well as to expressions (35) and (36), we obtain that the mathematical expectation of β_{cov} is determined by simple expression:

$$M[\beta_{cov}] = \frac{\sigma_s^2}{2\Delta_{£}}(R(£+\Delta_{£}) - R(£-\Delta_{£})) .$$

The plot of the normalized $M[\beta_{cov}]$ as the function of $£$ is given in Fig. 14. Maximum of module of $M[\beta_{cov}]$ attains at $£ \approx 4.3$.

Let us find the variance $D[\beta_{cov}]$ on the assumption of (32):

$$D[\beta_{cov}] = \frac{\sigma_s^4}{4(\Delta_{£})^2}\left(2(1 - R(2\Delta_{£})) + (R(£+\Delta_{£}) - R(£-\Delta_{£}))^2 + 2g^{-1}\left(1 - R(2\Delta_{£}) + g^{-1}\right)\right).$$

The examples of plots for the normalized $\sigma[\beta_{cov}]$ as the function of $£$ at signal\noise ration $g = 500$ (curve 1), 10 (curve 2) и 5 (curve 3) are presented in Fig. 15. As it is seen from the figure, $\sigma[\beta_{cov}]$ has maximum, which does not depend on signal/noise ratio and attains at the same $£_{op}$, as well as maximum of $M[\beta_{cov}]$. Plots for of $M[\beta_{cov}]$-to-$\sigma[\beta_{cov}]$ ratio confirm the same fact(Fig. 16).

Using (38) we obtain the condition when information about degree of samples s and $\tilde{s}$, which is extracted from pseudogradient of the product $(z\tilde{z}_{£})$, is maximum on average:

$$\max\left|\frac{R(£+\Delta_{£}) - R(£-\Delta_{£})}{\sqrt{2(1 - R(2\Delta_{£})) + (R(£+\Delta_{£}) - R(£-\Delta_{£}))^2 + 2g^{-1}\left(1 - R(2\Delta_{£}) + g^{-1}\right)}}\right| . \tag{42}$$

Let us note that maximum of (42) attains at maximum of the numerator, because extremums of numerator and denominator coincide. It is easy to show if we represent (42) in the form

$$\left(\sqrt{1 + 2\frac{(1 - R(2\Delta_{£}))\left(1 + g^{-1}\right) + g^{-2}}{(R(£+\Delta_{£}) - R(£-\Delta_{£}))^2}}\right)^{-1} .$$

Then we get implicit equation for finding $£_{op}$

$$\frac{d}{d£}R(£_{op} - \Delta£) = \frac{d}{d£}R(£_{op} + \Delta£) . \tag{43}$$

For Gaussian correlation function of images:

$$(£_{op} - \Delta_{£})\exp\left(-\left(\frac{£_{op} - \Delta_{£}}{a}\right)^2\right) = (£_{op} + \Delta_{£})\exp\left(-\left(\frac{£_{op} + \Delta_{£}}{a}\right)^2\right) .$$

In particular at the correlation radius equal to 5 independently on a value of the noise we obtain $£_{op} = 4.28$.

Thus in the situation when as the goal function is samples covariation of images $\widetilde{Z}^{(1)}$ and $Z^{(2)}$ for finding $£_{op}$ it is enough to know only autocorrelation function of the image $\widetilde{S}^{(1)}$.

Samples correlation coefficient

It is not difficult to show that the mathematical expectation and the variance of pseudogradient of interframe correlation sample coefficient

$$\frac{\sum\limits_{k=1}^{\mu} z_£ \, \widetilde{z}_{£k}}{\mu \sigma_z \sigma_{\widetilde{z}}} = \frac{\sum\limits_{k=1}^{\mu} z_£ \, \widetilde{z}_{£k}}{\mu\left(1 + g^{-1}\right)\sigma_s^2}$$

is determined by expressions:

$$M[\beta_{\mathrm{ICC}}] = \frac{1}{2\Delta_£(1 + g^{-1})}(R(£_k + \Delta_£) - R(£_k - \Delta_£)) ,$$

$$D[\beta_{\mathrm{ICC}}] = \frac{1}{2(\Delta£)^2 \mu\left(1 + g^{-1}\right)^2}\left((1 + g^{-1})(1 - R(2\Delta_£) + g^{-1}) + \frac{1}{2}(R(£ + \Delta_£) - R(£ - \Delta_£))^2\right),$$

where $j_{£k}$ – coordinates on the axis $£$ of samples of the local sample, $k = \overline{1, \mu}$; $£_k$ – coordinates of estimates of corresponding samples; μ – local sample size; g – signal/noise ratio. Then the condition, when information about degree of samples s and $\widetilde{s}$, which is extracted from pseudogradient of the correlation coefficient, is maximum on average is:

$$\max\left|\frac{\mu(R(£ + \Delta_£) - R(£ - \Delta_£))}{\sqrt{\left(2(1 + g^{-1})(1 - R(2\Delta_£) + g^{-1}) + (R(£ + \Delta_£) - R(£ - \Delta_£))^2\right)}}\right| . \tag{44}$$

Let us note that the condition (44) attains at the same distance $£_{op}$, as well as the condition (42). Thus, when choosing as the goal function interframe correlation coefficient for finding $£_{op}$, as in the previous case it is enough to know only autocorrelation function of the image $\widetilde{S}^{(1)}$. At that $£_{op}$ is found from the condition (43).

6. Finding optimal region of samples of the local sample when estimating vector of parameters

Let us consider the second step of solution of samples choice suboptimal region finding, which consists in finding on the base of the model of deformations and parameters estimates error vector imager region, in which suboptimal value of EED is ensured. For definition let us assume that the model of deformations is affine (17).

Choice of initial estimates approximation

Since the convergence of parameters $\overline{\alpha}$ estimates depends on their initial approximation $\hat{\overline{\alpha}}_0$, let us specify the rule of choice $\hat{\overline{\alpha}}_0$ from the condition of minimum of EED mathematical expectation, which is induced by the initial approximation of each parameter.

Let us the definition domain $\Omega_{\overline{\alpha}}$ of possible parameters values is:

$$\Omega_{\overline{\alpha}} : \left\{ h_{x\min} \div h_{x\max}, h_{y\min} \div h_{y\max}, \varphi_{\min} \div \varphi_{\max}, \kappa_{\min} \div \kappa_{\max} \right\}.$$

In order to provide the accepted condition the initial approximation of each parameter has to give a EED component, which is equal to the mathematical expectation of Euclidian distances which are induced by all possible values of this parameter:

$$M[\pounds] = \int_{\alpha\min}^{\alpha\max} \sqrt{\left(\tilde{x}(\alpha) - x^*\right)^2 + \left(\tilde{y}(\alpha) - y^*\right)^2}\; w(\alpha)d\alpha,$$

where $(\tilde{x}(\alpha), \tilde{y}(\alpha))$ – the current estimate of the point (x^*, y^*) coordinates (x^*, y^*), obtained after substitution the true parameters value into the model (17); $w(\alpha)$ – probability density function of possible values of the parameter α. In particular, on the assumption of $w(\alpha)$ is uniform, for parameters of shift and rotation angle we obtain

$$\hat{h}_{x0} = \frac{h_{x\min} + h_{x\max}}{2},\; \hat{h}_{y0} = \frac{h_{y\min} + h_{y\max}}{2},\; \varphi_0 = \frac{\varphi_{\min} + \varphi_{\max}}{2}.$$

For scale coefficient $\tilde{x} = x_0 + \kappa(x - x_0),\; \tilde{y} = y_0 + \kappa(y - y_0)$, then

$$M[\pounds] = \left(1 - \frac{\kappa_{\max} + \kappa_{\min}}{2}\right)\sqrt{(x - x_0)^2 + (y - y_0)^2},$$

i. e. for the initial approximation of κ we obtain: $\kappa_0 = \dfrac{\kappa_{\max} + \kappa_{\min}}{2}.$

Suboptimal region forming at the given vector of estimates error
As the reference point for suboptimal region forming let us choose the rotation centre coordinates (x_0, y_0). For a random point $(\tilde{x}, \tilde{y})$ EED (distance to the point (x^*, y^*)) is determined by all parameters to be estimated. At that the module $\Delta\pounds_h$ and the argument ϕ_h of contribution of parameters h_x and h_y in EED does not depend on the point location on the image:

$$\Delta\pounds_h = \sqrt{(\varepsilon_x)^2 + (\varepsilon_y)^2},\quad \phi_h = \arg tg\,\frac{\varepsilon_y}{\varepsilon_x},$$

where ε_x and ε_y – errors of estimates $\hat{h}_x$ and $\hat{h}_y$ from the optimal values of parameters h_x^* and h_y^*.

The contribution of parameters φ and κ depends on the distance L from the rotation centre. If the error of angle estimate $\hat{\varphi}$ from the optimal value φ^* is equal to ε_φ, then it ensures the contribution in EED

$$\Delta\pounds_\varphi = 2L\sin\frac{\varepsilon_\varphi}{2},$$

where $L = \sqrt{(\tilde{x} - x_0)^2 + (\tilde{y} - y_0)^2}$; $\Delta\pounds_\varphi$ – the module of the contribution vector, the argument

of which is equal to $\phi_\varphi = \arg tg \dfrac{\tilde{y} - y_0 - (\tilde{x} - x_0)\sin\varepsilon_\varphi - (\tilde{y} - y_0)\cos\varepsilon_\varphi}{\tilde{x} - x_0 - (\tilde{x} - x_0)\cos\varepsilon_\varphi + (\tilde{y} - y_0)\sin\varepsilon_\varphi}$. The error ε_κ of scale

coefficient estimate from the optimal value κ^* specifies the contribution:

$$\Delta\pounds_\kappa = L(1 + \varepsilon_\kappa), \quad \phi_\kappa = \arg tg \frac{\tilde{y} - y_0}{\tilde{x} - x_0} .$$

The above-mentioned reasonings are illustrated in Fig. 17.

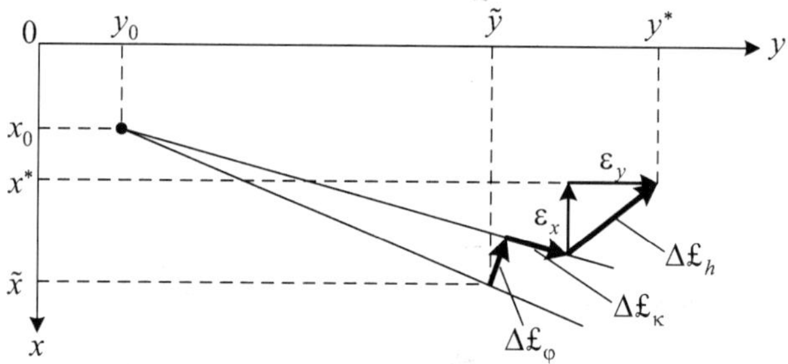

Fig. 17. Dependence of EED versus a vector of parameters estimates error

For the assemblage of shift and scale parameters:

$$\Delta\pounds_{\varphi,\kappa} = L\sqrt{1 + ((1 + \varepsilon_\kappa))^2 - 2(1 + \varepsilon_\kappa)\cos\varepsilon_\varphi} .$$

At that $\Delta\pounds_{\varphi,\kappa}$ does not depend on the direction of the segment L . Taking into account the error of shift we obtain:

$$\pounds = \sqrt{L^2\left(1 + (\varepsilon_\kappa)^2 - 2(1 + \varepsilon_\kappa)\cos\varepsilon_\varphi\right) + (\varepsilon_x)^2 + (\varepsilon_y)^2 -}$$
$$\overline{- 2L(\varepsilon_x(\cos\gamma - (1 + \varepsilon_\kappa)\cos(\gamma + \varepsilon_\varphi)) + \varepsilon_y(\sin\gamma - (1 + \varepsilon_\kappa)\sin(\gamma + \varepsilon_\varphi)))},$$

where $\gamma = \arg\sin \dfrac{\tilde{y} - y_0}{L}$ – an angle, determining the direction of L relatively the basic

image axis $(0 - x)$.

At the known values of $\pounds_{op}$ and vector $\bar{\varepsilon} = (\varepsilon_x, \varepsilon_y \varepsilon_\varphi, \varepsilon_\kappa)^T$ the expression (45) enables to find

the optimal value L_{op} as a function of angle γ . At the given angle γ the optimal distance

L_{op} can be obtained for example as the solution $L_{op} = a + \sqrt{a^2 - b}$ of quadratic equation

$L_{op}^2 - 2aL_{op} + b = 0$,   where $b = \dfrac{(\varepsilon_x)^2 + (\varepsilon_y)^2 - (\pounds_{op})^2}{1 + (1 + \varepsilon_\kappa)^2 - 2(1 + \varepsilon_\kappa)\cos\varepsilon_\varphi}$;

$a = \dfrac{(\varepsilon_x(\cos\gamma - (1 + \varepsilon_\kappa)\cos(\gamma + \varepsilon_\varphi)) + \varepsilon_y(\sin\gamma - (1 + \varepsilon_\kappa)\sin(\gamma + \varepsilon_\varphi)))}{1 + (1 + \varepsilon_\kappa)^2 - 2(1 + \varepsilon_\kappa)\cos\varepsilon_\varphi}$. The solution can also be obtained by means of other methods. For instance, it is not difficult to show that at the affine model of deformations the geometrical location of points for which EED is equal to $£_{op}$, represents the circle $(x - c)^2 + (y - d)^2 = r^2$ with centre in the point

$$\left(c = \frac{\varepsilon_x - (1 + \varepsilon_k)(\varepsilon_x \cos\varepsilon_\varphi + \varepsilon_y \sin\varepsilon_\varphi)}{1 + (1 + \varepsilon_k)^2 - 2(1 + \varepsilon_k)\cos\varepsilon_\varphi} , \; b = \frac{\varepsilon_y - (1 + \varepsilon_k)(\varepsilon_y \cos\varepsilon_\varphi - \varepsilon_x \sin\varepsilon_\varphi)}{1 + (1 + \varepsilon_k)^2 - 2(1 + \varepsilon_k)\cos\varepsilon_\varphi} \right)$$

and radius $\; r = \dfrac{(£_{op})^2 - (\varepsilon_x)^2 - (\varepsilon_y)^2}{1 + (1 + \varepsilon_k)^2 - 2(1 + \varepsilon_k)\cos\varepsilon_\varphi} + c^2 + d^2$.

Forming the estimates error vector

In order to obtain the suboptimal region it is required to find two values L_1 and L_2, corresponding to the range of EED from $£_1$ to $£_2$, where either EED does not differ from optimal value more than the given value or bounds are chosen from the condition: $£_1 = £_{op} - \Delta_£$, $£_2 = £_{op} + \Delta_£$, where $\Delta_£$ – some deviation which is calculated experimentally.

The dependence of estimates error vector versus the number of iterations can be formed by different methods and in general case depends on the conditions of the problem to be solved. For example, for ensuring the best convergence on average we can propose the following algorithm.

1^0. To specify the initial approximation $\bar{\varepsilon}$ of the parameters estimates vector $\bar{\varepsilon}$.

2^0. To find the mathematical expectation for each estimate.

3^0. Using (45) to find bounds L_1 and L_2 of suboptimal region of samples local sample.

4^0. To simulate the performing of the next iteration by pseudogradient procedure for calculation of the density of distribution of parameters estimates (for this purpose the method of calculation at finite number of iterations can be used (Tashlinskii & Tikhonov, 2001)).

5^0. To repeat operators 2^0–4^0 to attain the given estimation accuracy.

However more of practical interest represents a minimax approach, when the dependence of suboptimal region versus the number of iterations for the initial approximation, corresponding to the highest possible parameters error (for the worst case) is found. The number of iterations, which is necessary to reach the given estimation accuracy, is determined. In the sequel the obtained rule of suboptimal region change is applied for any initial approximation of parameters, ensuring the estimation accuracy, which is not worse than the given one. At that for the given image class (for the given autocorrelation function and probability density function of image brightness) the rule of suboptimal region change can be found analytically with usage of probabilistic simulation and one of methods of suboptimal region construction, considered above. Another method for finding bounds L_1 and L_2 of the suboptimal region is to find at each iteration EED on the parameters estimates error, obtained experimentally and averaged on the given realizations assemblage.

It is necessary to note that for parameters of angle and scale under the assumption about quite large image size theoretically it is always possible to find suboptimal region. The error on shift is invariant for any point of the image (this statement is true, if only parallel shift is specified) and can significantly exceed $£_1$ and $£_2$, specially on the initial stage of estimation. In this case we can specify the base region on some criterion, where samples of the local sample are chosen until the error increase on shift enables to form suboptimal region.

As an example in Fig. 18 suboptimal regions of samples local sample on the image of size 1024×1024 with Gaussian autocorrelation function with correlation radius equal to 13 and signal/noise ratio $g = 50$ are shown. As thr goal function interframe deformations mean square is used. Optimization is carried out for the pseudogradient procedure with parameters of the diagonal gain matrix $\lambda_x = 0.1$, $\lambda_y = 0.1$, $\lambda_\varphi = 0{,}15^o$, $\lambda_\kappa = 0.01$. The initial error of the parameters vector is $\bar{\varepsilon} = \left(\varepsilon_x = 10,\ \varepsilon_y = 10,\ \varepsilon_\varphi = 25^o,\ \varepsilon_\kappa = 0.5\right)^T$. The size of the base region is 64×64. Suboptimal region is formed according to the rule: $L_1 = L_{op} - 12$, $L_2 = L_{op} + 12$. The value L_{op} is calculated by means of the relation (45). Estimates errors vector is determined in accordance with a minimax approach of statistic simulation. In figure suboptimal regions for 1, 200, 400 and 600 iterations, which correspond to errors: at $t = 200$ – $\varepsilon_x = 4.9,\ \varepsilon_y = 7.9,\ \varepsilon_\varphi = 15.4^o,\ \varepsilon_\kappa = 0.33$; at $t = 400$ – $\varepsilon_x = 0.8,\ \varepsilon_y = 2.7,\ \varepsilon_\varphi = 2.9^o,\ \varepsilon_\kappa = 0.03$; at $t = 600$ – $\varepsilon_x = 0.02,\ \varepsilon_y = 0.21,\ \varepsilon_\varphi = 0.04^o,\ \varepsilon_\kappa = 0.008$ are given. In Fig. 19 the plots of parameters estimates error versus the number of iterations with usage of suboptimal region of samples choice (curves 1) and without it (curves 2), averaged on 100 realizations are presented.

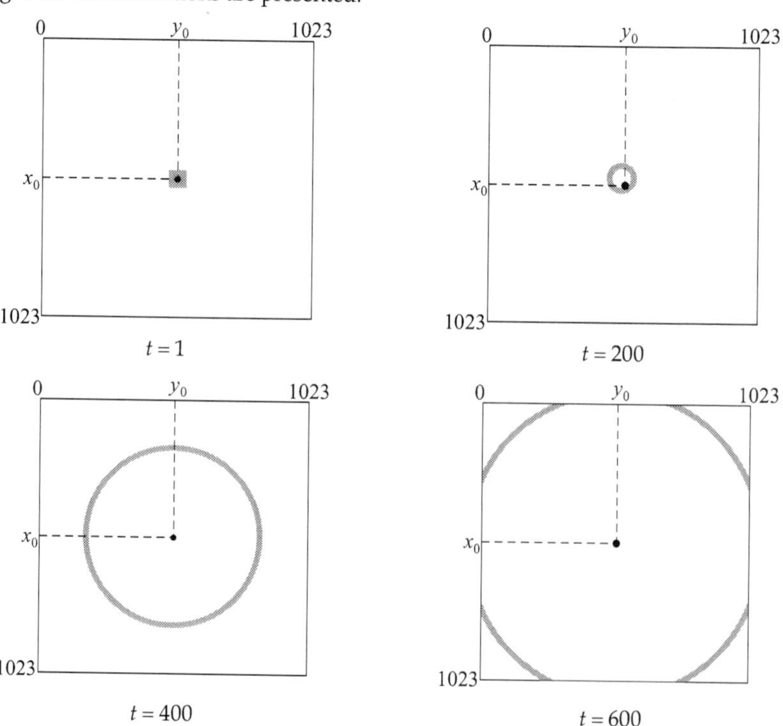

Fig. 18. Suboptimal region of samples choice for different iterations

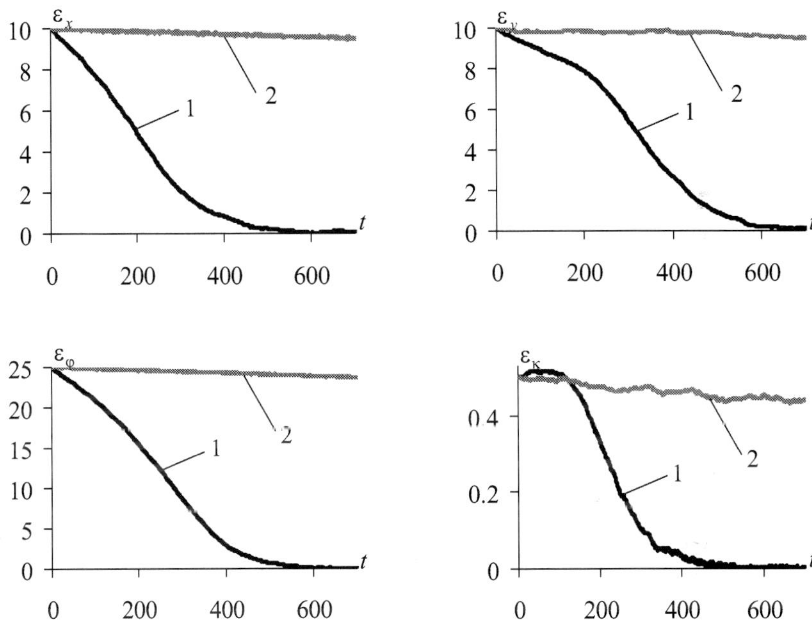

Fig. 19. Estimates convergence (1 – at region optimization; 2 – without optimization)

In Fig. 20 the dependence of EED (at $L = 20$) for the mentioned experiment is shown. It is seen, roughly to the 120-th iteration, while samples of the local sample are chosen from the base region, the convergence rate of EED is a little lower, because the conditions of optimality are not ensured. The decrease of the convergence rate is also observed at small values of EED, that is caused by suboptimal region spillover of image sizes. It is confirmed by Fig. 21, where the dependence of L_{op} versus the number of iterations is presented.

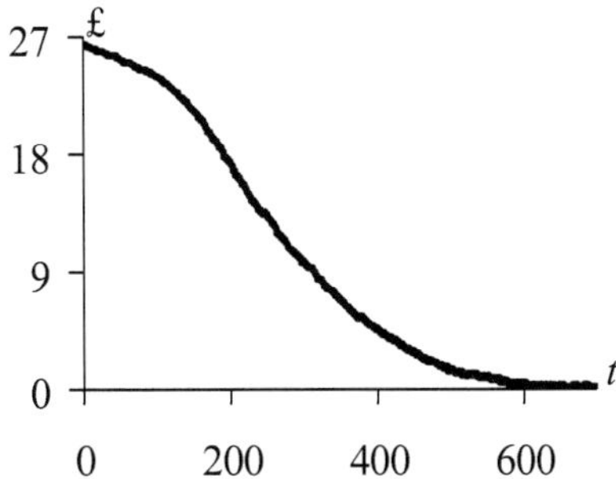

Fig. 20. EED convergence

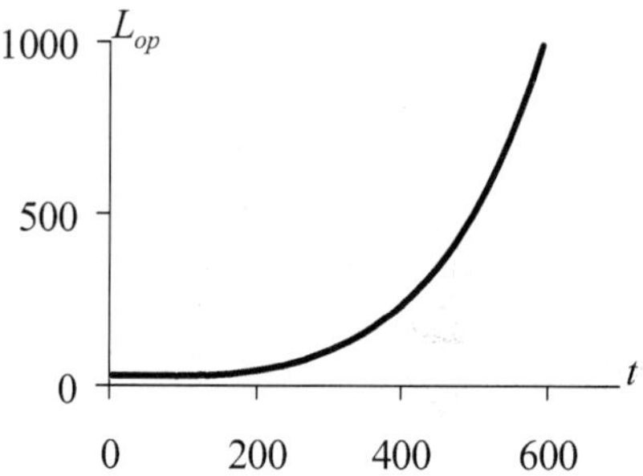

Fig. 21. Dependence of L_{op} versus the number of iterations

Thus optimization of image samples choice region enables to reduce computational costs significantly (about of dozens times) for the same parameters estimation accuracy attainment. In particular a value of EED=0.5 ($L = 20$) at optimization attains on average to 600 iterations and without it– to 14000 iterations, that corresponds to the gain in speed of about 24 times.

7. Conclusion

The discreteness of digital images amounts to estimation of derivatives through limited differences. Analysis of approaches to calculation of pseudogradient of a goal function on the local sample and current estimates of parameters to be measured exposed four possible methods for pseudogradient calculation:
-   in the first method components of pseudogradient are calculated as a normalized difference of two estimates of a goal function (at that the differentiation of deformations model and goal function is not used);
-   the second method is based on the analytic finding derivative of estimate of a goal function on brightness and estimation of brightness derivative on parameters through finite differences;
-   the third one assumes the possibility of analytic finding derivative of goal function estimate and partial derivatives of deformations model on parameters (brightness derivative on the base axis are estimated through finite differences) ;
-   the fourth methods is based on the estimation of derivatives of goal function on the base axis of image through finite differences and analytic finding derivatives of deformations model on parameters to be estimated.

When estimating interframe geometrical deformations parameters plan of the local sample of samples, used for finding pseudogradient of the goal function, significantly influences on the parameters estimates convergence character. The estimates convergence character depends also on brightness distribution and autocorrelation functions of images and interference noises and also on the chosen kind of the goal function. For description of mentioned factors influence on the probabilistic features of estimate in the process of its convergence it is handy to use estimate improvement coefficient, which is equal to difference of probabilities of estimate movement to optimal and from optimal value.

On the basis of estimate improvement coefficient maximization we can realize the method of fining optimal (suboptimal) region of local sample samples choice. However this method is effective only at one parameter estimation, because at its usage for parameters vector insuperable mathematical difficulties arise.

For a case of parameters vector estimation finding optimal region can be based on optimization of EED (the distance between true coordinates of a point at current estimate of its location). At that maximum of ratio of mathematical expectation of goal function estimate gradient to its variance corresponds to the optimal EED. Let us denote, that at usage of interframe difference mean square EED depends on signal/noise ratio and autocorrelation function of images. At that it increases when variance of noises increases. At usage of covariation and correlation coefficient optimal value determined by only image autocorrelation function.

On the deformations model and parameters estimates error vector it is not difficult to find calculated expressions for optimal region. At that the dependence of estimates error vector versus the number of iterations can be found theoretically on the given autocorrelation function and image brightness distribution and experimentally on the current estimates averaged on the assemblage of realizations.

8. References

Dikarina, G. V., Minkina, G. L., Repin, A. I. & Tashlinskii, A. G. (2007). Pseudogradient optimization in the problem of image interframe geometrical deformations estimation. *8-th International Conference PRIA-8-2007*, Vol. I, pp. 72–74, ISBN 978-5-8158-0577-4, Yoshkar-Ola, October, 2007, MarGTU, Yoshkar-Ola

Gonzalez, R. C. & Woods, R. E. (2002). *Digital Image Processing*. Prentice Hall, New Jersey, ISBN 0-201-18075-8

Minkina, G. L., Samojlov, M. U. @ Tashlinskii, A. G. (2005). Choice of values, characterizing estimates convergence at pseudogradient estimation of image interframe deformations parameters. *Vestnik UlGTU [Herald of the UlSTU]*, No. 4, pp. 32–37, ISSN 1674-7016, UlGTU, Uljanovsk [in Russian]

Minkina, G. L.; Samojlov, M. U. & Tashlinskii, A. G. (2007). Choice of The Objective Function for Pseudogradient Measurement of Image Parameters. *Pattern Recognition and Image Analysis*, Vol. 17, No. 1, pp. 136–139, ISSN 1054-6618

Polyak, B. T. & Tsypkin, Ya. Z. (1973). Pseudogradient Algorithms of Adaptation and Education. *Avtomatika i telemechanika [Automation and Telemechanics]*, No. 3, pp. 45–68, ISSN 0005-2310 [in Russian]

Polyak, B. T. & Tsypkin, Ya. Z. (1984). Criterion Algorithms of Stochastic Optimization. *Avtomatika i telemechanika [Automation and Telemechanics]*, No. 6, pp. 95–104, ISSN 0005-2310 [in Russian]

Samojlov, M. U. (2006). Procedure Optimization of Image Interfarme Geometrical Deformation Parameter Pseudogradient Estimation. *Radiolocation, Navigation, Connection: Proc. of The XII Inter. Sci.-Tech. Conf.*, Vol. 1, pp. 162–167, ISBN 5-9900094-8-8, Voronezh, March, 2006, Sakvoee, Voronezh

Samojlov, M. U., Minkina, G. L. @ Dikarina, G. V. (2007). Optimization of pseudogradient in the problem of pseudogradient estimation of image interframe geometrical deformations. *Mathematical Methods of Pattern Recognition: Proceedings of the 13-th Inter. Conf.*, pp. 363–366, ISBN 978-5-317-02060-6, Max-press, Moskow [in Russian]

Tashlinskii, A. G. (2000). *Otsenivanie parametrov prostranstvennih deformatsii posledovatelnostei izobrazhenii [Image Sequence Spatial Deformation Parameters Estimation]*, UlGTU, ISBN 5-89146-204-4, Uljanovsk [in Russian]

Tashlinskii, A. G. & Tikhonov, V. O. (2001). The Method of Multidimensional Process Parameter Pseudogradient Measuring Error Analysis. *Izvestija Vuzov: Radioelektronika, [Proceedings of institutes of higher education: Radio Electronics]*, Vol. 44, No. 9, pp. 75–80, ISSN 0021-3470 [in Russian]

Tashlinskii, Alexandr (2003). Computational Expenditure Reduction in Pseudo-Gradient Image Parameter Estimation. *Computational Science*, Vol. 2658, No. 2, pp. 456-462, ISSN 0302-9743

Tashlinskii, A.G. (2005). Structural optimization of image interframe geometrical deformation measurement recurrent algorithms. *Automation, Control, and Information Technology: Signal and Image Processing - A Publication of The International Association of Science and Technology for Development - IASTED*, pp. 98-102, ISBN 0-88986-461-6, ACTA Press, Anaheim-Calgary-Zurich

Tashlinskii, A. G. @ Samojlov, M. U. (2005). Minimization of computational costs in algorithms of pseudogradient estimation of image parameters. *Electronnaya technika: mezhvuzovskii sbornik nauchnych trudov [Electronic Technique: Interuneversity Collection of Scientific Proceedings]*, pp. 13–17, ISBN 5-89146-401-2, UlGTU, Uljanovsk [in Russian]

Tashlinskii, A. G., Minkina, G. L., & Dikarina, G. V. (2006). Adaptive forming of local sample size in pseudogradient procedures of image interframe geometrical deformations estimation. *Vestnik UlGTU [Herald of the UlSTU]*, No. 3, pp. 53–58, ISSN 1674-7016, UlGTU, Uljanovsk [in Russian]

Tashlinskii, A. G. @ Minkina, G. L. (2006). Probabilistic characteristics of convergence of image interframe geometrical deformations parameters estimates at pseudogradient estimation. *LXI Nauchnaya Sessiya, Posvyaschennaya Dnyu Radio [LXI Scientific Session, Devoted to Radio Day]*, pp. 428–432, ISBN 978-5-9795-0023-2, Infomizdat, Moscow [in Russian]

Taslinskii, A. G. (2007). Pseudogradient Estimation of Digital Images Interframe Geometrical Deformations. *Vision Systems: Segmentation & Pattern Recognition*. I-Tech Education and Publishing, Vienna, pp. 465-494. – ISBN 978-3-902613-05-9

Tsypkin, Ya. Z. (1995). *Informatsionnaya teoriya identifikatsii [Information theory of Identification]*, Nauka/ Fizmatlit, ISBN 5-02-015071-1, Moskow [in Russian]

Vasiliev, K. K. & Tashlinskii, A. G. (1998). Estimation of Deformation Parameters of Multidimensional Images to Be Observed on The Background of Interference. *Pattern Recognition and Image Analysis: New Information Technologies, Proceedings of the IV Inter. Conf.*, Vol. 1, pp. 261–264, Novosibirsk, June, 1998, SO RAN, Novosibirsk, ISBN 5-89896-189-5

Vasiliev, K. K. &Krasheninikov, V. R. (2007). *Statisticheskii analiz mnogomernyh izobrazhenii [Statistical Analysis of Multidimensional Images]*. UlGTU, Uljanovsk , ISBN 978-5-9795-0119-2 [in Russian]

11

New Digital Approach to CNN On-chip Implementation for Pattern Recognition

Daniela Durackova
Slovak University of Technology, Bratislava
Slovakia

1. Introduction

There are many cases where image processing is performed using the neural network. The content of this Chapter is implementation of CNN (Cellular Neural Network) on a chip in a new original digital approach. First, testing of some features of the proposed cell of the neural network is evaluated. Then the design of the basic circuit containing the cell for the CNN will be introduced. The idea is to use it for a more complex chip with image processing application.

CNN have been extensively used in various image processing applications.

One of the most important problems in signal processing is noise removal. The input signals mostly arrive from the real world and therefore they contain relatively high amounts of noise. The CNN circuits are capable of removing this noise partly. The possibility of noise removing depends on the template (weight) coefficients between the cells.

CNN networks are based on relatively simple principles, very similar to biological neurons. The input signals are multiplied by appropriate weights, the weight matrix being given intuitively, as it is typical for CNN networks. Then they are added and multiplied by the transfer function. We describe also the settings of weights coefficients. CNN have been extensively used in various image processing applications (Matsumoto & Yokohama, 1990) or (Szirányi & Csicsvári, 1993).

The main problem of CNN implementations on a chip is the chip area consumption. The most area is reserved for the multiplexer, so we looked for alternative multiplications. We describe the achieved results with the designed chip. During the creation of the chip architecture we proposed and introduced special original coding for the weight coefficients. After simulations we recognized that the results were better with rounding than without it, but we found that the rounding during multiplication was not as important as we previously expected. Therefore we decided – instead of a hardware multiplexer – to use multiplication realized by simple gate timing of the special signal.

The circuit was designed as a digital synchronized circuit. For the design and simulation we used the Xilinx tool. The cell is based on sub-circuits as it will be shown in detail.

The Chapter describes the designed circuit. We introduce also our novel simulator for the CNN using the program tool Visual Basic for Application, and its algorithm which was based on the same principle as the planned designed circuit. The network can process the patterns with 400 points of recognition.

The aim of our work is an original approach to the designed digital chip architecture using special coding of the weights coefficients. This implementation of the CNN on a chip widens the family of the previous designed circuits.

2. Some notes to using CNN for image processing

The modern world needs image processing very often. There exist various methods for image processing, among them the methods based on the principle of neural networks are also useful. The advantage of the neural network is parallel processing and the implementation on the chip is designed as an analogue or digital circuit, however, the principle for both approaches is similar. According to the theory it is based on the sequences of single inputs (x1... x9) multiplied by weights (w1....w9), then the conversion through the transfer function (as we see in Fig. 1) prepares the signal for the next processing.

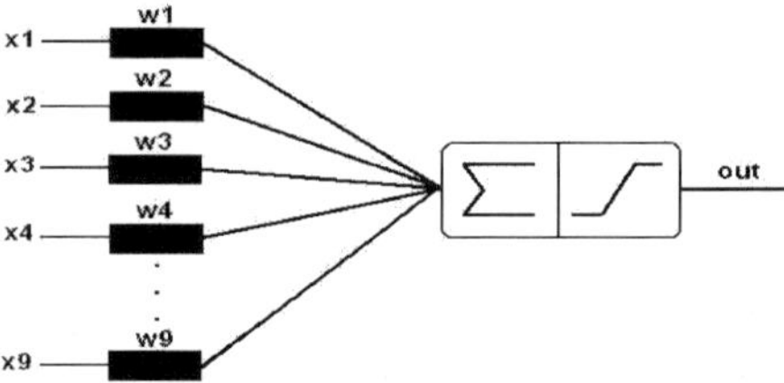

Fig. 1. Graphic representation of the cell.

There exist various transfer functions, as for example the sigmoid function, hard-limiter function or threshold logic function. For image processing the sigmoid function is commonly used. The properties of the network, as for example noise removing, depend on correct choices of the weight matrix. Every image is characterized by its weight matrix. We skip here the basic details well known from the classical theory introduced by Prof. L.O.Chua (Chua & Yang, 1988a; 1988b). As we will see in the next parts of the Chapter, according to the theory of CNN networks the weight matrix is set intuitively.

3. The Novel simulator of CNN

The basic circuit of the neural network is called the cell. The network contains cells connected together according to the proposed rule. The cellular neural network used neighbourhood 1, which means that each cell is connected with only the nearest neighbours. For the theoretical results we first created a simulator for CNN programmed as a macro in Visual Basic for Application. The results from the simulator were first used for evaluation of CNN behaviour, then to compare the results with those obtained from the designed chip. The results of simulations were achieved in matrix and graphical representations. The input and output values are in the range from –15 to + 15 and the graphical form is represented using spectra of two colours, as shown in Fig. 2.

Fig. 2. The spectra of used colours.

In the first row there is a red colour scale which represents positive numbers, the blue colour in the second row represents negative numbers.
Our first simulator contained 16 cells. We tested some features of the neuron network, as e.g. detection of vertical lines (see Fig. 3) or filling of the picture (Fig. 4).

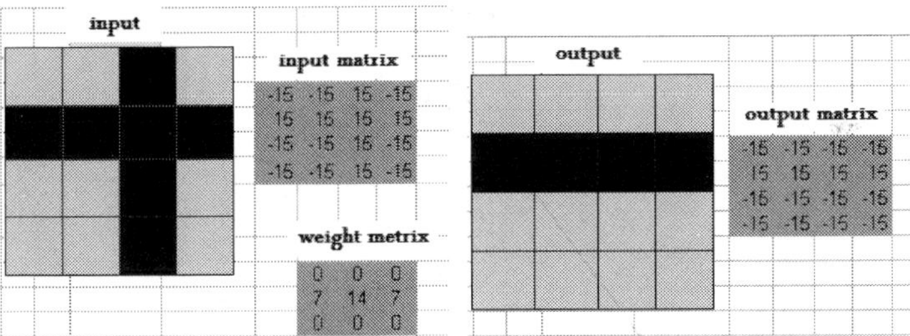

Fig. 3. Filling of the lines for the given pattern.

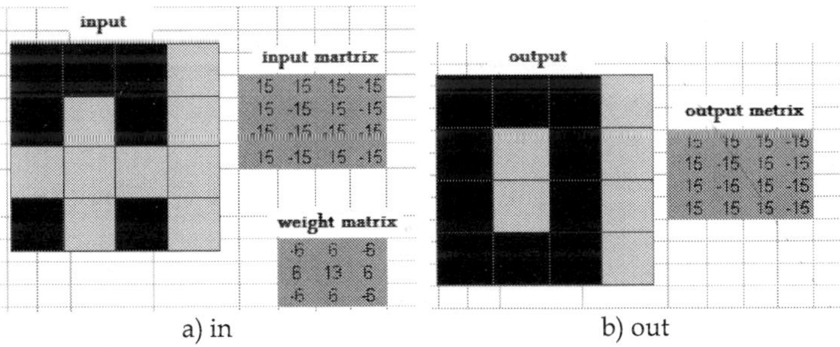

a) in   b) out

Fig. 4. Completing rectangle rims

These figures illustrate the simple tasks for image processing. The left parts show the pattern input, the right parts are the output results.
From this pattern we can recognize that the network is able to satisfy the given conditions. For more complicated image processing we need to widen the network to 400 cells. As the input matrix we use the 20×20 input values and a 3×3 input weight matrix. During the simulations we can change the slope of the sigmoid function, to fix the number of iterations, or to finish it automatically. The simulator gives the results with rounding, or without it. The results were mostly similar, however, the proposed rounding gave more precise results. The next experiment was focused on noise filtering. As an input we used letter "E", with the random noise (around 35 %). The results are in Fig. 5. The quality of the results was dependent on the weight matrix and the position of the fault information. The weight matrix was given intuitively, as it is typical for CNN networks. In the first example (Fig. 5b), five points are not removed because we chose an incorrect weight matrix. Figure 5c shows perfect noise removal.
The weight matrices for Figs. 5b and 5c are as follows:

$$\text{For figure } b: \begin{bmatrix} -4 & 6 & -4 \\ 6 & 7 & 6 \\ -4 & 6 & -4 \end{bmatrix} \quad \text{and for figure } c: \begin{bmatrix} -3 & 6 & -3 \\ 6 & 7 & 6 \\ -3 & 6 & -3 \end{bmatrix}$$

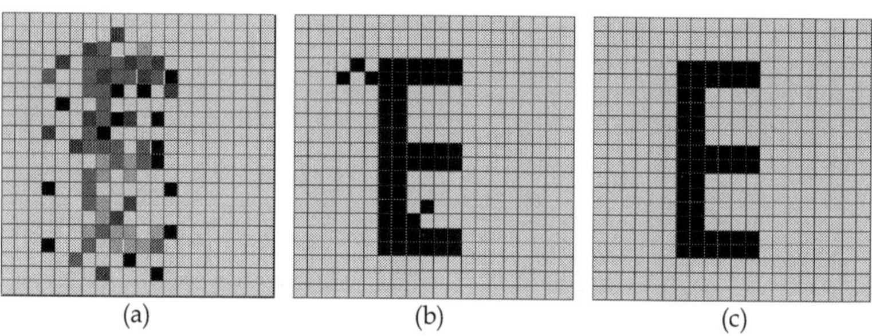

(a)   (b)   (c)

Fig. 5. Noise filtering

a) input to the network

b) output after the use of an inappropriate weight matrix

c) output after perfect noise removing

We have developed a novel simulator for the CNN using the program tool Visual Basic for Application, and its algorithm was based on the same principle as the planned designed circuit. The network can process the patterns with the recognition of 400 points. The created universal simulator can change various simulation parameters.

We have found that rounding by multiplication is not as important as we previously expected. On the basis of the simulations we have design a novel digital CNN cell. This will be used for CNN consisting of 400 cells which will be used for image processing in the future. The circuit contains some service signals. For the cells connected into a CNN network it is inevitable to design a control circuit which will control synchronization.

4. The design of the digital CNN cell

After the simulations we started to design our digital approach for CNN implementation on a chip. The proposed circuit was designed as a digital synchronized circuit. For the design and simulation we used the Xilinx tool. The cell is based on sub-circuits as schematically shown in Fig. 6.

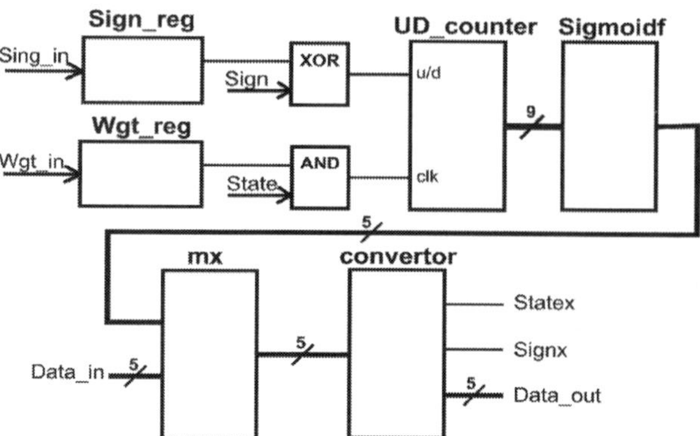

Fig. 6. The block diagram of the digital CNN cell

CNN networks are based on relatively simple principles, very similar to biological neurons. The input signals are multiplied by appropriate weights, then they are added and multiplied by the transfer function. The main problem of the CNN implementations on a chip is the chip area consumption. Most of the area is reserved for the multiplexer, so we looked for alternative multiplications. After the simulations we recognized that the results were almost the same with rounding and without it.

As an input   we set *Wgt_reg*, then the sign 9 bit serial register *sign_reg* and input values State from the neighbour cells. Then we included also their sign and the input of the cells themselves because in the CNN theory the cell is the neighbour also to itself.

The inputs from each cell are multiplexed by the input multiplexer. The input has information about the sign of the state of the next cell. These inputs are multiplexed by the weight register in the AND gate, and the inputs are compared with the gate XOR. The weights have to be specially timed, so by timing we can perform multiplication.

Then the results are added in the *Ud_counter* and sequentially transferred through block *sigmoidf* . Function hard limiter (hl) has the values true or false, while functions threshold logic(tl) and sigmoid function(sf) could have values also between these extreme values true and false. We decided that function (sf) is the best as it has ist derivative in the whole range, while function (tl) has no derivative in points –1 and +1. This behaviour is important for neural networks which are able to learn. The plot of function (sf) for various slopes is in Fig. 7.

The results are passing through the block *sigmoidf*, which realized the sigmoid function. The block *converter* transfers value output on the time interval, which sends nearest neighbors and contains register, where is the result storing.

According to Fig. 6. the inputs from each cell are multiplexed by the input multiplexer. The block converter contains a register, where the result is stored.

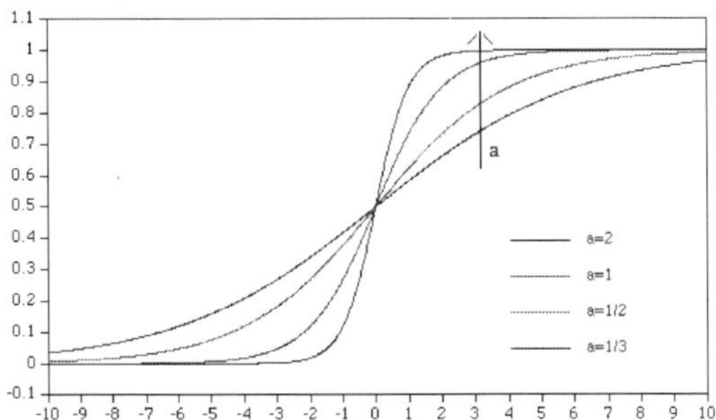

Fig. 7. The sigmoid function

5. Multiplication of signals using the AND gate

The method of multiplication is based on the fact that at multiplication the input value must be converted to the time signal and the weight value has to be special picked, so multiplication starts by timing. We proposed special coding for the weights.

We used a special system of 15parts, e.g., one cycle is divided into 15 parts. In Fig. 8 we see the first 15 weights and their original coding.

An example of special rounding and coding of the weights is shown in Fig. 9. The real value of the multiplication is x.w=0.293 and the result after Fig. 9. is 4/15=0.26. We used the simulator to recognize that we can neglect this rounding.

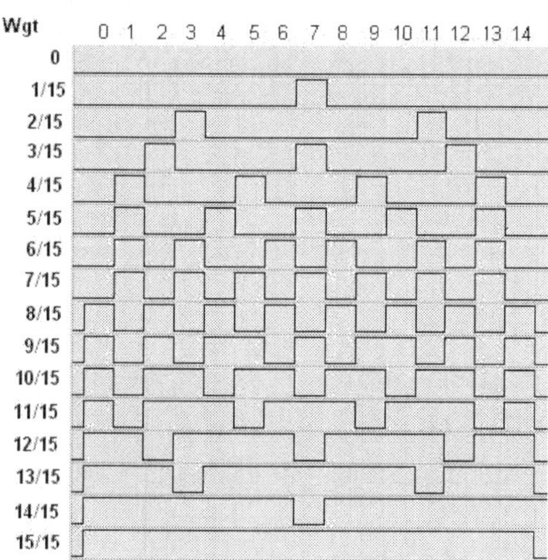

Fig. 8. The first fifteen weights in the proposed system

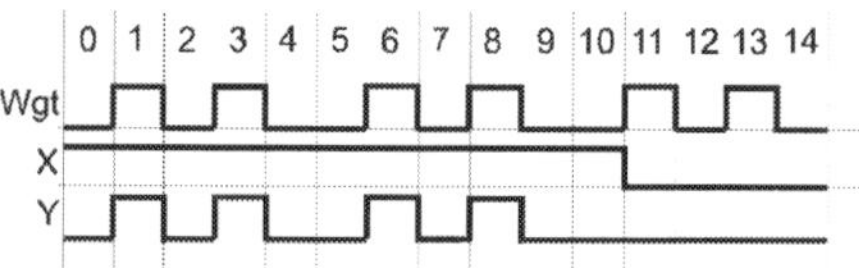

Fig. 9. An example of evaluation for weight wgt=6/15 and input x=11/15

6. The results of the simulations of the designed CNN cell

After creating the architecture of our implemented CNN we made some simulations on the circuit. In Fig. 10 we can see the filling of the lines for the given pattern. At the input a) we see the corners of the input pattern. After 15 iterations we get the result as we see in Fig. 10b.

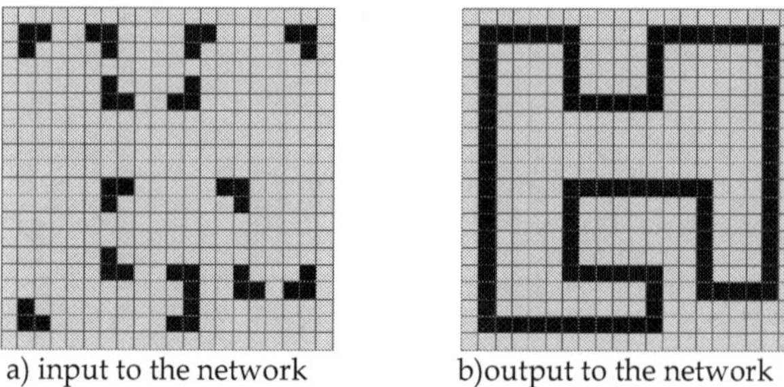

a) input to the network   b)output to the network

Fig. 10. The network completes the corners into a continuous line

The next experiment was focused on noise filtering. As an input we used letter "A" with random noise (around 10 %). Figure 11b shows the noise filtering output after the 3rd iteration. The quality of the results was dependent on the weight matrix and the position of the fault information. For the noise filtering of letter "A" we use the following weight matrix: $\begin{bmatrix} -1 & 2 & -1 \\ 2 & 8 & 2 \\ -1 & 2 & -1 \end{bmatrix}$

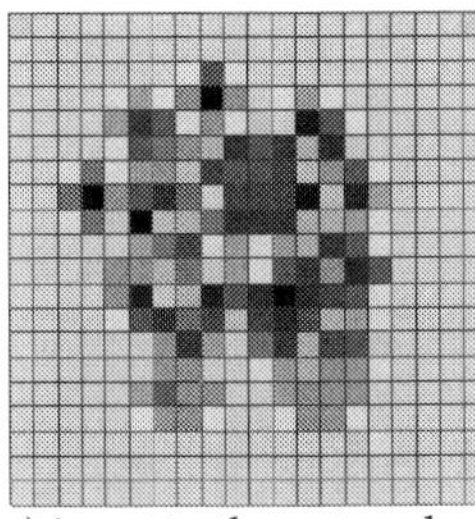

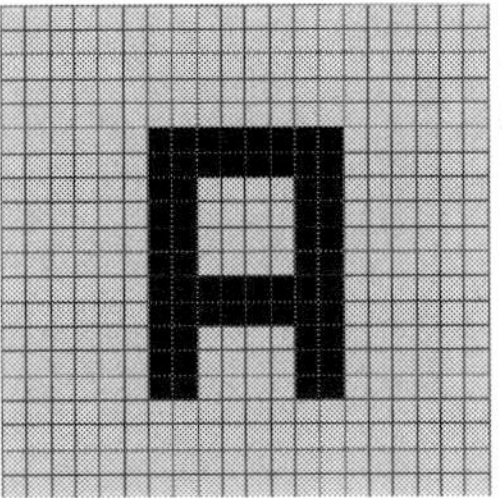

a) input to the network   b) output the network

Fig. 11. Filtering of the noise from the letter.

The weight (wgt-out) is timed so that we can multiply it with the input. The result (here denoted as (sucin)) after multiplication with the sigmoid function and converting to the time interval is stored in (statex) multiplied with the sign (signx). In Fig. 12 we see the result after 15 tacts from the beginning.

7. Conclusion

We developed a novel simulator for the CNN using the program tool Visual Basic for Application. Its algorithm is based on the same principle as the planned designed circuit. The network can process the patterns with 400 point recognition. The created universal simulator can change various simulation parameters.

We found that the rounding at multiplication is not as important as we previously expected. On the basis of the simulations we designed a novel digital CNN cell implemented on a chip. This will be used for the CNN consisting of 400 cells. The architecture of the designed digital chip is cascadable, so we can create various capacity of CNN networks.

We expect the applications of the designed chip in CNN for interactive education of the deaf (particularly children) trying to learn how to use the dactyl alphabet.

The new experiment with the Data sensor glove used for this purpose is the topics of our present research.

8. References

Chua, L.O. & Yang.L. (1988). Cellular neural networks: Theory, IEEE Trans. On Circuits and Systems, Vol. 35, No. 10, (1988). Pp.1257-1272

Chua, L.O. & Yang.L. (1988). Cellular neural networks: Applications, IEEE Trans. On Circuits and Systems, Vol. 35, No. 10, (1988). Pp.1273-1290

Durackova, D & Raschman, E. (2007). Pattern recognition for the letters of dactyl alphabet by using a novel neural network simulator, Proceedings of the 5th IEEE Conference on Computational Cybernetics, 19-21 October 2007, Gammarth, Tunisia, pp. 97-99.

Matsumoto, T., Yokohama,T., Suzuki, H., Furukawa, (1990). Several image processing examples by cnn, Proceedings of IEEE International Workshop on Cellular Neural Networks and their Applications, Budapest

Szirányi, T.; & Csicsvári, J. (1993). High speed character recognition using a dual cellular neural network architecture (cnnd), Analog and Digital Signal Processing, Vol. 40, No. 3, pp. 223-231.

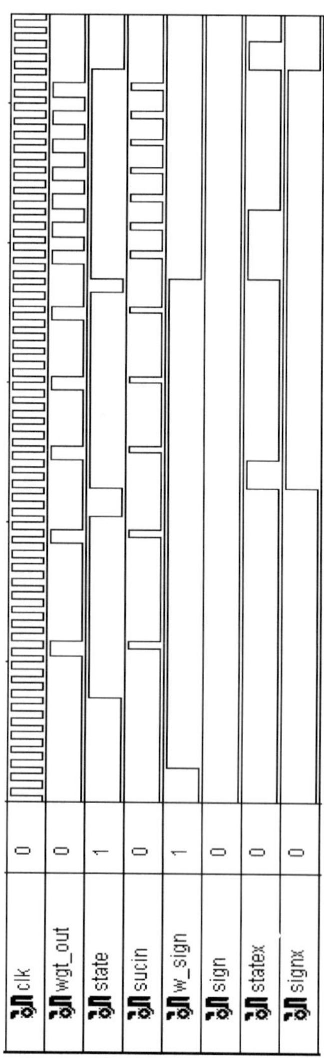

Figure 12. The output results from the Xilinx simulations

12

Distortion-Invariant Pattern Recognition with Adaptive Correlation Filters

Vitaly Kober[1] and Erika M. Ramos-Michel[2]
[1]Computer Science Department, CICESE,
[2]Faculty of Telematic, University of Colima,
Mexico

1. Introduction

Pattern recognition based on correlation is one of the most useful techniques for many applications. Since the pioneer work of VanderLugt (1964), correlation filters have gained popularity thanks to their shift-invariance property, good mathematical basis, and easy implementation by means of digital, optical or hybrid optical/digital systems. However, conventional correlation filters are sensitive to intensity signal degradations (blurring and noise) as well as to geometrical distortions of an object of interest. Basically, blurring is owing to image formation process, and it can be produced by imperfection of capturing devices, relative motion between a camera and an input scene, propagation environment, etc. An observed input scene always contains noise produced by an imaging system (i.c. imperfection of imaging sensors) or by a recording medium (i.e. quantization errors) (Bertero & Boccacci, 1998; Perry et al., 2002). On the other hand, geometric distortions change the information content and, therefore, affect the accuracy of recognition techniques. Two types of geometric distortions are distinguished: internal and external distortions. The internal distortions are produced by the geometrics of a sensor; they are systematic and can be corrected by a calibration. External distortions affect the sensor position or the object shape; they are unpredictable (Starck et al., 1998).

This chapter treats the problem of distortion-invariant pattern recognition based on adaptive composite correlation filters. The distinctive feature of the described methods is the use of an adaptive approach to the filters design (Diaz-Ramirez et al., 2006; González-Fraga et al., 2006). According to this concept, we are interested in a filter with good performance characteristics for a given observed scene, i.e., with a fixed set of patterns or a fixed background to be rejected, rather than in a filter with average performance parameters over an ensemble of images. Specifically, we treat two problems: reliable recognition of degraded objects embedded into a linearly degraded and noisy scene (Ramos-Michel & Kober, 2007) and adaptive recognition of geometrically distorted objects in blurred and noisy scenes (Ramos-Michel & Kober, 2008).

The first problem concerns with the design of optimum generalized filters to improve the recognition of a distorted object embedded into a nonoverlapping background noise when the input scene is degraded with a linear system and noise. The obtained filters take into account explicitly information about an object to be recognized, background noise, linear system degradation, linear target distortion, and sensor noise. For the filter design, it is assumed that this information is available or can be estimated from the nature of degradations. Therefore, the proposed filters establish upper bounds of patterns recognition quality among correlation filters with respect to the used criteria when the input scene and the target are degraded. The second problem is to decide on presence or absence of a geometrically distorted object embedded on a degraded and noisy scene. Since the performance of conventional correlation filters degrades rapidly with object distortions, one of the first attempts to overcome the problem was the introduction of synthetic discriminant functions (SDFs) (Casasent, 1984). However, conventional SDF filters often posses a low discrimination capability. New adaptive SDF filters for reliable recognition of a reference in a cluttered background designed on the base of optimum generalized filters are presented. The information about an object to be recognized, false objects, and background to be rejected is utilized in the proposed iterative training procedure. The designed correlation filter has a prespecified value of discrimination capability. The synthesis of adaptive filters also takes into account additive sensor noise by training with a noise realization. Therefore, the adaptive filters may possess a good robustness to the noise. Computer simulation results obtained with the proposed filters are compared with those of various correlation filters in terms of recognition performance.

2. Generalized correlation filters for pattern recognition in degraded scenes

In pattern recognition two different tasks are distinguished: detection of objects and estimation of their exact positions (localization) in images. Using a correlation filter, these tasks can be done in two steps. First, the detection is carried out by searching the highest correlation peak at the filter output, then, this coordinate is taken as the position estimation of a target in the input scene. The quality of detection and localization of a target may be limited by: (i) presence of additive and disjoint background noise in observed scenes, (ii) scene intensity degradations owing to image formation process, and (iii) geometric distortions of a target. Next, we design generalized optimum filters which are tolerant to intensity degradations of input scenes.

2.1 Design of generalized optimum filters

The detection ability of correlation filters can be quantitatively expressed in terms of several criteria, such as probability of detection errors, signal-to-noise ratio, peak sharpness, and discrimination capability (Vijaya-Kumar & Hassebrook, 1990). Optimization of these criteria leads to reducing false recognition errors. After the detection task has been solved, we still are faced with small errors of target position estimation that are due to distortions of the object by noise. The coordinate estimations lie in the vicinity of their actual values. Therefore the accuracy of the target location can be characterized by the variance of measurement errors along coordinates (Kober & Campos, 1996; Yaroslavsky, 1993). The variance minimization depends on a mathematical model of the input scene. Basically, two models are considered: overlapping and nonoverlapping models. Many correlation filters were proposed. For instance, if an input scene contains a reference object corrupted by additive noise (overlapping model), the matched spatial filter (MSF) (VanderLugt, 1964) is optimal with respect to the signal-to-noise ratio. Horner and Gianino (1984) suggested the phase-only filter (POF) that maximizes the light efficiency. For the overlapping model, the optimal filter (OF) was proposed by minimizing the probability of anomalous errors (false alarms) (Yaroslavsky, 1993). If an input scene contains a reference object embedded into a disjoint background (nonoverlapping model) and additive noise, the following correlation filters were derived: the generalized matched filter (GMF) maximizes the ratio of the expected value of the squared correlation peak to the average output variance (Javidi & Wang, 1994), the generalized phase-only filter (GPOF) maximizes the light efficiency (Kober et al., 2000), and the generalized optimum filter (GOF) maximizes the ratio of the expected value of the squared correlation peak to the average expected value of the output signal energy (POE) (Javidi & Wang, 1994). Other generalized filters were also introduced (Goudail & Réfrégier, 1997; Javidi et al., 1996; Réfrégier, 1999; Réfrégier et al., 1993; Towghi & Javidi, 2001). Conventional filters are sensitive to intensity signal degradations. So particular cases of the degradations were taken into account in the filter design (Campos et al., 1994; Carnicer et al., 1996; Navarro et al., 2004; Vargas et al., 2003). However, it appears that the problem of detection and localization with correlation filters has not been solved when the target and the input scene are degraded with linear systems. In this section, we derive generalized filters which are tolerant to the degradations. The POE criterion is defined as the ratio of the square of the expected value of the correlation peak to the expected value of the output signal energy (Javidi & Wang, 1994):

$$\text{POE} = \left| E\{y(x_0, x_0)\} \right|^2 / \overline{E\{y(x, x_0)\}^2}, \tag{1}$$

where $y(x, x_0)$ is the filter output when the target is located at the position x_0 in the input scene. $E\{.\}$ denotes statistical averaging, and the overbar symbol in the denominator denotes statistical averaging over x.

The second used criterion is referred to as the peak-to-average output variance (SNR). It is defined as the ratio of the square of the expected value of the correlation peak to the average output variance (Javidi & Wang, 1994):

$$\text{SNR} = \left| E\{y(x_0, x_0)\} \right|^2 / \overline{\text{Var}\{y(x, x_0)\}}, \tag{2}$$

where $\text{Var}\{.\}$ denotes the variance. The light efficiency (Horner & Gianino, 1984) is important in optical pattern recognition. For the nonoverlapping model of the input scene, it can be expressed as

$$\eta_H = \int \left| E\{y(x, x_0)\} \right|^2 \, dx / \int \left| E\{s(x, x_0)\} \right|^2 \, dx, \tag{3}$$

where $s(x)$ represents the input scene.

Next, we derive three generalized optimum filters by maximizing the criteria. For simplicity, one-dimensional notation is used. Integrals are taken between infinite limits. The same notation for a random process and its realization is used.

A. Generalized correlation filters for object recognition in a noisy scene degraded by a linear system

Let us consider the nonoverlapping signal model. The input scene $s(x)$ is degraded by a linear system $h_{LD}(x)$ and corrupted by additive sensor noise $n(x)$, and contains a target $t(x)$ located at unknown coordinate x_0 (random variable) and a spatially disjoint background noise $b(x, x_0)$:

$$s(x, x_0) = \left[t(x - x_0) \right] + b(x, x_0) \bullet h_{LD}(x) + n(x), \tag{4}$$

where "•" denotes the convolution operation, and $\int h_{LD}(x)dx = 1$. The following notations and assumptions are used.

1. The nonoverlapping background signal $b(x,x_0)$ is regarded as a product of a realization $b(x)$ from a stationary random process (with expected value μ_b) and an inverse support function of the target $w(x)$ defined as zero within the target area and unity elsewhere:

$$b(x,x_0) = b(x)w(x-x_0). \tag{5}$$

2. $B_0(\omega)$ is the power spectral density of $b_0(x)=b(x)-\mu_b$.
3. $n(x)$ is a realization from a stationary process with zero-mean and the power spectral density $N(\omega)$.
4. $T(\omega)$, $W(\omega)$, and $H_{LD}(\omega)$ are the Fourier transforms of $t(x)$, $w(x)$, and $h_{LD}(x)$, respectively.
5. The filter output $y(x)$ is given by $y(x,x_0)=s(x,x_0)\bullet h(x)$, where $h(x)$ is the real impulse response of a filter to be designed.
6. The stationary processes and the random target location x_0 are statistically independent of each other.

Next, we derive optimum correlation filters. These filters are modified versions of the following generalized correlation filters: the GOF (Javidi & Wang, 1994), GMF (Javidi & Wang, 1994), and GPOF (Kober et al., 2000). The transfer functions of the designed filters are referred to as GOF$_{LD}$, GMF$_{LD}$, and GPOF$_{LD}$, which are optimal with respect to the POE, the SNR, and the light efficiency, respectively (Ramos-Michel & Kober, 2007).

1. *Generalized Optimum Filter (GOF$_{LD}$)*

The filter GOF$_{LD}$ maximizes the POE given in Eq. (1). From Eq. (4) the expected value of the filter output $E\{y(x,x_0)\}$ can be expressed as

$$E\{y(x,x_0)\} = \frac{1}{2\pi}\int[T(\omega)+\mu_b W(\omega)]H_{LD}(\omega)H(\omega)\exp[j\omega(x-x_0)]d\omega. \tag{6}$$

The square of the expected value of the output peak can be written as

$$\left|E\{y(x_0,x_0)\}\right|^2 = \frac{1}{4\pi^2}\left|\int[T(\omega)+\mu_b W(\omega)]H_{LD}(\omega)H(\omega)d\omega\right|^2. \tag{7}$$

The denominator of the POE can computed as

$$\overline{E\left\{[y(x,x_0)]^2\right\}} = \overline{\mathrm{Var}\{y(x,x_0)\}}+\overline{\left|E\{y(x,x_0)\}\right|^2}. \tag{8}$$

Here, the spatial averaging converts a nonstationary process at the filter output to a stationary process. It is supposed that the output-signal energy is finite (for instance, spatial extend of the filter output is L (Javidi & Wang, 1994)). The expressions for the average of the output-signal variance $\overline{\mathrm{Var}\{y(x,x_0)\}}$ and the average energy of the expected value of the filter output $\overline{\left|E\{y(x,x_0)\}\right|^2}$ are given, respectively, by

$$\overline{\mathrm{Var}\{y(x,x_0)\}} = \frac{1}{2\pi}\int\left\{\left[\frac{\alpha}{2\pi}B_0(\omega)\bullet|W(\omega)|^2\right]|H_{LD}(\omega)|^2+N(\omega)\right\}|H(\omega)|^2d\omega, \tag{9}$$

and

$$\overline{\left|E\{y(x,x_0)\}\right|^2} = \frac{1}{2\pi}\int \alpha\left|T(\omega)+\mu_b W(\omega)\right|^2 \left|H_{\mathrm{LD}}(\omega)\right|^2 \left|H(\omega)\right|^2 d\omega, \tag{10}$$

where $\alpha=1/L$ is a normalizing constant (Kober & Campos, 1996). Substituting Eqs. (9) and (10) into Eq. (8), we obtain the average output energy:

$$\overline{E\{y[(x,x_0)]^2\}} = \frac{1}{2\pi}\int \left\{\alpha\left[\left|T(\omega)+\mu_b W(\omega)\right|^2 + \frac{1}{2\pi}B_0(\omega)\bullet\left|W(\omega)\right|^2\right]\left|H_{\mathrm{LD}}(\omega)\right|^2\right.$$
$$\left.+N(\omega)\right\}\left|H(\omega)\right|^2 d\omega. \tag{11}$$

Using Eqs. (7) and (11) the POE can be written as

$$\mathrm{POE} = \frac{(2\pi)^{-1}\left|\int[T(\omega)+\mu_b W(\omega)]H_{\mathrm{LD}}(\omega)H(\omega)d\omega\right|^2}{\int\left\{\alpha\left[\left|T(\omega)+\mu_b W(\omega)\right|^2 + \frac{1}{2\pi}B_0(\omega)\bullet\left|W(\omega)\right|^2\right]\left|H_{\mathrm{LD}}(\omega)\right|^2 + N(\omega)\right\}\left|H(\omega)\right|^2 d\omega}. \tag{12}$$

Applying the Schwarz inequality, we obtain the optimum filter:

$$\mathrm{GOF}_{\mathrm{LD}}(\omega) = \frac{\left\{[T(\omega)+\mu_b W(\omega)]H_{\mathrm{LD}}(\omega)\right\}^*}{\alpha\left[\left|T(\omega)+\mu_b W(\omega)\right|^2 + \frac{1}{2\pi}B_0(\omega)\bullet\left|W(\omega)\right|^2\right]\left|H_{\mathrm{LD}}(\omega)\right|^2 + N(\omega)}, \tag{13}$$

where the asterisk denotes the complex conjugate. Note that the filter takes into account information about a linear image degradation and additive noise by means of $H_{\mathrm{LD}}(\omega)$ and $N(\omega)$, respectively. Besides, the transfer function of the filter contains $T(\omega)+\mu_b W(\omega)$, which defines a new target to be detected. Therefore, the information about the target support function and the mean value of a background is important as well as the target signal itself.

2. *Generalized Matched Filter (GMF$_{LD}$)*

This filter maximizes SNR given in Eq. (2). Using Eqs. (7) and (9), the SNR can be expressed as follows:

$$\mathrm{SNR} = \frac{(2\pi)^{-1}\left|\int[T(\omega)+\mu_b W(\omega)]H_{\mathrm{LD}}(\omega)H(\omega)d\omega\right|^2}{\int\left\{\left[\frac{\alpha}{2\pi}B_0(\omega)\bullet\left|W(\omega)\right|^2\right]\left|H_{\mathrm{LD}}(\omega)\right|^2 + N(\omega)\right\}\left|H(\omega)\right|^2 d\omega}. \tag{14}$$

Applying the Schwartz inequality, the optimum correlation filter is obtained:

$$\mathrm{GMF}_{\mathrm{LD}}(\omega) = \frac{\left\{[T(\omega)+\mu_b W(\omega)]H_{\mathrm{LD}}(\omega)\right\}^*}{\left[\frac{\alpha}{2\pi}B_0(\omega)\bullet\left|W(\omega)\right|^2\right]\left|H_{\mathrm{LD}}(\omega)\right|^2 + N(\omega)}. \tag{15}$$

One can observe that the filter contains information about the linear degradation system and additive noise.

3.   *Generalized Phase Optimum Filter (GPOF$_{LD}$)*

Using Eq. (4), the light efficiency given by Eq. (3) can be expressed as

$$\eta_H = \frac{\int \left| \left[T(\omega) + \mu_b W(\omega) \right] H_{LD}(\omega) \right|^2 \left| H(\omega) \right|^2 d\omega}{\int \left| \left[T(\omega) + \mu_b W(\omega) \right] H_{LD}(\omega) \right|^2 d\omega} . \tag{16}$$

Thus, the optimum correlation filter is given by

$$GPOF_{LD}(\omega) = \frac{\left[T(\omega) + \mu_b W(\omega) \right]^*}{\left| T(\omega) + \mu_b W(\omega) \right|} \exp \left[-j\theta_{H_{LD}}(\omega) \right], \tag{17}$$

where $\theta_{H_{LD}}(\omega)$ is the phase distribution of the linear degradation. It can be seen that the GPOF$_{LD}$ does not take into account the degradation by additive noise. Therefore, it is expected that this filter will be sensitive to the noise.

B. Generalized correlation filters for recognition of a linearly degraded object in a noisy scene degraded by a linear system

The input scene contains a linearly degraded target located at unknown coordinate x_0 and a spatially disjoint background $b(x,x_0)$. The scene is additionally degraded with a linear system and corrupted by additive noise $n(x)$:

$$s(x,x_0) = \left[t(x - x_0) \bullet h_{TD}(x) + b(x) w_{TD}(x - x_0) \right] \bullet h_{LD}(x) + n(x), \tag{18}$$

where $h_{TD}(x)$ is a real impulse response of target degradation, $\int h_{TD}(x) dx = 1$, $w_{TD}(x - x_0) = 1 - w_T(x - x_0) \bullet h_{TD}(x)$, $w_T(x)$ is a support function of the target (with unity within the target area and zero elsewhere). It is assumed that linear degradations of the target and the scene do not affect each other. In a similar manner, three generalized correlation filters are derived. The transfer functions of these filters are referred to as GOF$_{LD_TD}$, GMF$_{LD_TD}$, and GPOF$_{LD_TD}$. They maximize the POE, the SNR, and the light efficiency, respectively (Ramos-Michel & Kober, 2007).

1.   *Generalized Optimum Filter (GOF$_{LD_TD}$)*

From the model of the input scene given in Eq. (18), the expected value of the filter output is

$$E\{y(x,x_0)\} = \frac{1}{2\pi} \int \left[T(\omega) H_{TD}(\omega) + \mu_b W_{TD}(\omega) \right] H_{LD}(\omega) H(\omega) \exp \left[j\omega(x - x_0) \right] d\omega, \tag{19}$$

where $H_{TD}(\omega)$ and $W_{TD}(\omega)$ are the Fourier transforms of $h_{TD}(\omega)$ and $w_{TD}(\omega)$, respectively. The intensity correlation peak can be computed as follows:

$$\left| E\{y(x_0,x_0)\} \right|^2 = \frac{1}{4\pi^2} \left| \int \left[T(\omega) H_{TD}(\omega) + \mu_b W_{TD}(\omega) \right] H_{LD}(\omega) H(\omega) d\omega \right|^2 . \tag{20}$$

$\overline{Var\{y(x,x_0)\}}$ and $\overline{\left| E\{y(x,x_0)\} \right|^2}$ can be obtained, respectively, as

$$\overline{Var\{y(x,x_0)\}} = \frac{1}{2\pi} \int \left\{ \left[\frac{\alpha}{2\pi} B_0(\omega) \bullet \left| W_{TD}(\omega) \right|^2 \right] \left| H_{LD}(\omega) \right|^2 + N(\omega) \right\} \left| H(\omega) \right|^2 d\omega, \tag{21}$$

and

$$\overline{\left|E\{y(x,x_0)\}\right|^2} = \frac{1}{2\pi}\int\alpha\left|T(\omega)H_{TD}(\omega)+\mu_b W_{TD}(\omega)\right|^2\left|H_{LD}(\omega)\right|^2\left|H(\omega)\right|^2 d\omega. \qquad (22)$$

With the help of Eqs. (1), (8), and (20)-(22), the POE is given by

$$\text{POE} = \frac{(2\pi)^{-1}\left|\int[T(\omega)H_{TD}(\omega)+\mu_b W_{TD}(\omega)]H_{LD}(\omega)H(\omega)d\omega\right|^2}{\int\left\{\alpha\left[\left|T(\omega)H_{TD}(\omega)+\mu_b W_{TD}(\omega)\right|^2+\dfrac{1}{2\pi}B_0(\omega)\bullet\left|W_{TD}(\omega)\right|^2\right]\left|H_{LD}(\omega)\right|^2+N(\omega)\right\}\left|H(\omega)\right|^2 d\omega}. \qquad (23)$$

Applying the Schwarz inequality, a generalized optimum filter is derived:

$$\text{GOF}_{LD\_TD}(\omega) = \frac{\left\{[T(\omega)H_{TD}(\omega)+\mu_b W_{TD}(\omega)]H_{LD}(\omega)\right\}^*}{\alpha\left[\left|T(\omega)H_{TD}(\omega)+\mu_b W_{TD}(\omega)\right|^2+\dfrac{1}{2\pi}B_0(\omega)\bullet\left|W(\omega)\right|^2\right]\left|H_{LD}(\omega)\right|^2+N(\omega)}. \qquad (24)$$

2.   *Generalized Matched Filter (GMF$_{LD_TD}$)*
From Eqs. (2), (20), and (21), the SNR can be expressed as

$$\text{SNR} = \frac{(2\pi)^{-1}\left|\int[T(\omega)H_{TD}(\omega)+\mu_b W_{TD}(\omega)]H_{LD}(\omega)H(\omega)d\omega\right|^2}{\int\left\{\left[\dfrac{\alpha}{2\pi}B_0(\omega)\bullet\left|W_{TD}(\omega)\right|^2\right]\left|H_{LD}(\omega)\right|^2+N(\omega)\right\}\left|H(\omega)\right|^2 d\omega}. \qquad (25)$$

Applying the Schwartz inequality, the optimum correlation filter is given by

$$\text{GMF}_{LD\_TD}(\omega) = \frac{\left\{[T(\omega)H_{TD}(\omega)+\mu_b W_{TD}(\omega)]H_{LD}(\omega)\right\}^*}{\left[\dfrac{\alpha}{2\pi}B_0(\omega)\bullet\left|W_{TD}(\omega)\right|^2\right]\left|H_{LD}(\omega)\right|^2+N(\omega)}. \qquad (26)$$

We see that the filter contains information about the linear system and additive noise.
3.   *Generalized Phase Optimum Filter (GPOF$_{LD_TD}$)*
By maximizing the light efficiency given in Eq. (3), the transfer function of the GPOF can be written as

$$\text{GPOF}_{LD\_TD}(\omega) = \frac{[T(\omega)H_{TD}(\omega)+\mu_b W_{TD}(\omega)]^*}{\left|T(\omega)H_{TD}(\omega)+\mu_b W_{TD}(\omega)\right|}\exp\left[-j\theta_{H_{LD}}(\omega)\right]. \qquad (27)$$

The filter does not take into account the degradation by additive noise. Therefore, it is expected that this filter will be sensitive to the noise.

2.2 Performance of optimum generalized filters
In this section the performance of the MSF (VanderLugt, 1964), the POF (Horner & Gianino, 1984), the OF (Yaroslavsky, 1993), the GMF (Javidi & Wang, 1994), the GOF (Javidi & Wang, 1994), the GPOF (Kober et al., 2000) and the proposed generalized filters is presented. The recognition of either a target or a moving object embedded into degraded test scenes is

evaluated in terms of discrimination capability (DC) and location accuracy. The DC is defined as the ability of a filter to distinguish a target from other different objects. If a target is embedded into a background that contains false objects, the DC can be expressed as

$$DC = 1 - \frac{\left|C^B(0)\right|^2}{\left|C^T(0)\right|^2},$$ (28)

where $\left|C^B\right|$ is the maximum in the correlation plane over the background area to be rejected, and $\left|C^T\right|$ is the maximum in the correlation plane over the area of target position. The area of the actual position is determined in the close vicinity of the actual target location. The background area is complementary to the area of target position. In our computer simulations the area of target position is chosen as the target area. Negative values of the DC indicate that a tested filter fails to recognize the target. The location accuracy can be characterized by means of the location errors (LE) defined as

$$LE = \sqrt{\left(x_T - \tilde{x}_T\right)^2 + \left(y_T - \tilde{y}_T\right)^2},$$ (29)

where $\left(x_T, y_T\right)$ and $y\left(\tilde{x}_T, \tilde{y}_T\right)$ are the coordinates of the target exact position and the coordinates of the correlation peak taken as a target position estimation, respectively.

(a)   (b)

Fig. 1. (a) Test input scene, (b) objects used in experiments.

All correlation filters were implemented with the fast Fourier transform. To guarantee statistically correct results, 30 statistical trials of each experiment for different positions of a target and 20 realizations of random processes were carried out. The size of images used in experiments is 256×256. The signal range is [0-1]. Figure 1(a) shows a test input scene. The scene contains two objects with a similar shape and size (approximately 44×28 pixels) but with different gray-level contents. The target (upper butterfly) and the false object are shown in Fig. 1(b). The mean value and the standard deviation over the target area are 0.42 and 0.2, respectively. The spatially inhomogeneous background has a mean value and a standard deviation of 0.37 and 0.19, respectively.

Two scenarios of the object recognition are considered: (a) detection of a target in linearly degraded and noisy scenes, and (b) detection of a moving target in linearly degraded and noisy scenes.

A. Recognition of a target in linearly degraded and noisy scenes

First, the test input scene is homogenously degraded with a linear system. An example of the linear degradation is a uniform image defocusing by a camera.

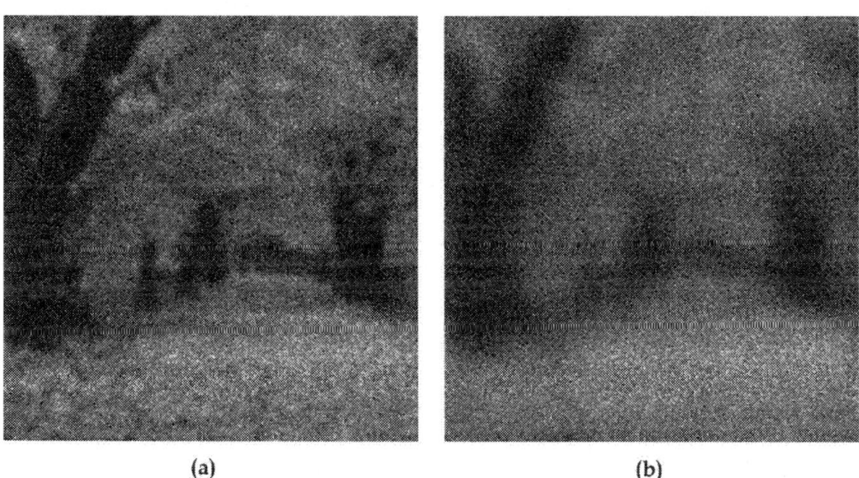

(a)   (b)

Fig. 2. Test scenes corrupted by additive noise with σ_n=0.12 and defocused with: (a) D=7, and (b) D=23 pixels.

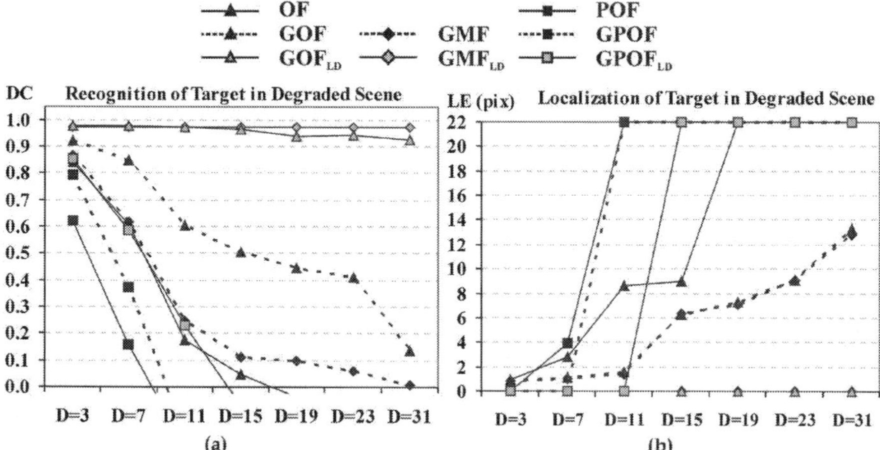

Fig. 3. Performance of correlation filters when the input scene is defocused with different values of D: (a) DC versus D, (b) LE versus D.

Assume that the impulse response of the blurring is an impulse disk with a diameter D. The values of D used in the experiments are 3, 7, 11, 15, 19, 23, and 31 pixels. Since additive sensor noise is always present, the test scene is additionally corrupted by additive zero-mean white Gaussian noise with the standard deviation σ_n. The values of σ_n are equal to 0.02, 0.04, 0.08, 0.12, 0.16, and 0.17. Figures 2(a) and 2(b) show examples of the test scene linearly degraded with $D=7$ and 23 pixels, respectively, and corrupted by overlapping noise with $\sigma_n=0.12$. Figures 3(a) and 3(b) show the performance of the tested correlation filters with respect to the DC and the LE when the input is defocused with different values of D. It can be seen that the proposed filters GOF$_{LD}$ and GMF$_{LD}$ are always able to detect and localize exactly the target, whereas the GPOF$_{LD}$ is sensitive to the linear degradation. The performance of the other filters decreases as a function of D. The conventional GOF is able to detect the target; however, it yields large location errors. The MSF filter fails to recognize the target.

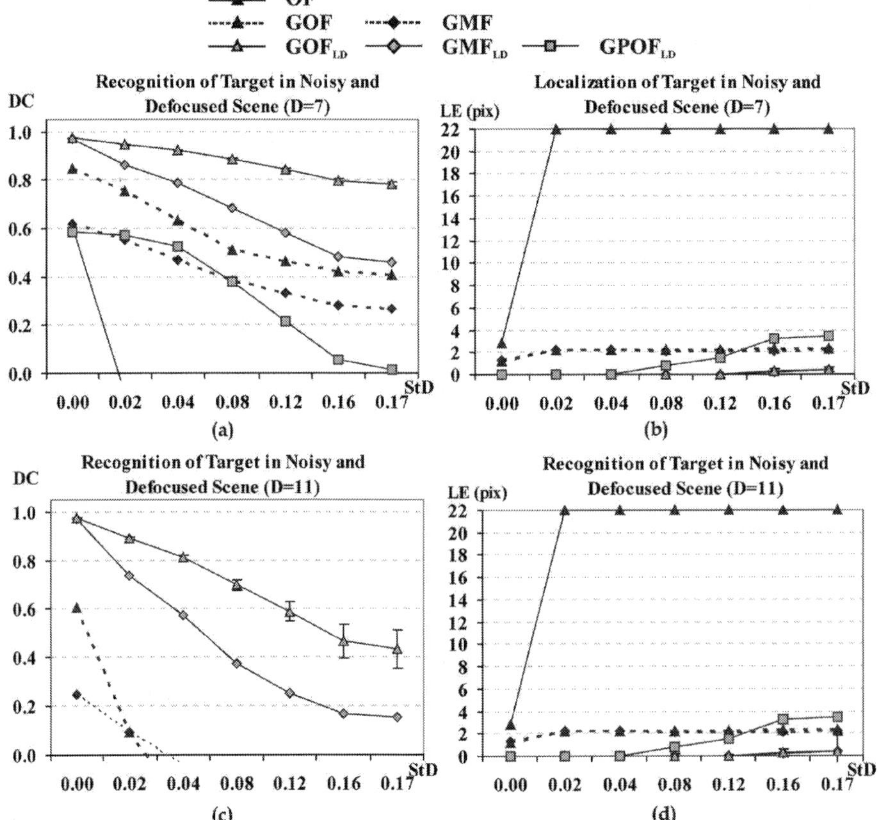

Fig. 4. Tolerance to noise of correlation filters for pattern recognition in blurred scenes: (a) DC versus σ_n with $D=7$, (b) LE versus σ_n with $D=7$, (c) DC versus σ_n with $D=11$, (d) LE versus σ_n with $D=11$.

Now we illustrate robustness of the filters to additive noise. Figure 4 shows the performance of the filters for pattern recognition in blurred (with $D=7$ and $D=11$) and noisy test scenes when the standard deviation of additive noise is varied. One can observe that the proposed filters GOF_{LD} and GMF_{LD} are always able to detect and to localize the object with small location errors, whereas the performance of the rest of the filters worsens rapidly as a function of D and σ_n. 95% confidence intervals in the performance of the GOF_{LD} are shown in Figs. 4 (c) and 4(d).

B. Recognition of a moving target in linearly degraded and noisy scenes

Let us consider a uniform target motion across a fixed background. For clarity and simplicity, we assume that the object moves from left to right with a constant velocity V during a time capture interval of $[0, T]$. The impulse response of the target degradation can be expressed as follows (Biemond et al., 1990):

$$h_{\text{TM}}(x) = \begin{cases} 1/M, & \text{if } 0 \le x \le M = VT \\ 0, & \text{otherwise} \end{cases} \tag{30}$$

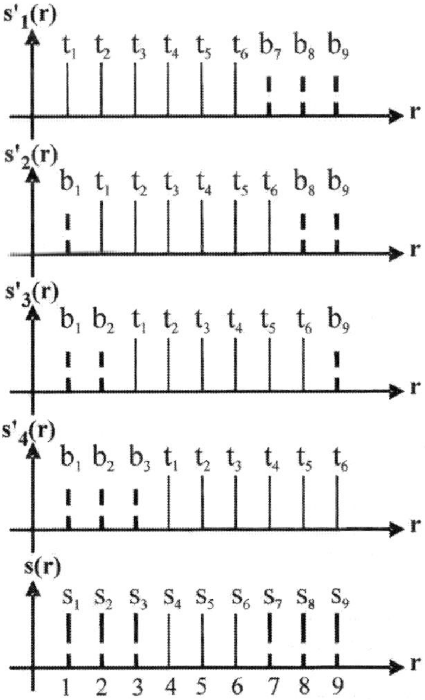

$$s(1) = \frac{3b_1 + t_1}{4}$$

$$s(2) = \frac{2b_2 + t_1 + t_2}{4}$$

$$s(3) = \frac{b_3 + t_1 + t_2 + t_3}{4}$$

$$s(4) = \frac{t_1 + t_2 + t_3 + t_4}{4}$$

$$s(5) = \frac{t_2 + t_3 + t_4 + t_5}{4}$$

$$s(6) = \frac{t_3 + t_4 + t_5 + t_6}{4}$$

$$s(7) = \frac{b_7 + t_4 + t_5 + t_6}{4}$$

$$s(8) = \frac{2b_8 + t_5 + t_6}{4}$$

$$s(9) = \frac{3b_9 + t_6}{4}$$

Fig. 5. Illustration of a linear degradation by a uniform target motion in 3 pixels from left to right.

The target motion leads to a partial (inhomogeneous) blur of the input scene. Figure 5, illustrates this degradation when a target and a background are one-dimensional discrete signals $(t_1,...,t_6)$ and $(b_1,...,b_9)$, respectively, and the target moves in 3 pixels from left to right. The input signal $s(r)$ is formed as the average of intermediate sequences $s'(r)$. In experiments, a uniform target motion from left to right on M pixels in test scenes is considered. The values of M used in our experiments are 3, 5, 7, 9, 11, and 15 pixels. The test

(a)   (b)

Fig. 6. Test scene shown in Fig. 1(a) corrupted by: (a) target motion ($M=9$) and scene degradation ($D=7$), (b) target motion ($M=9$), scene degradation ($D=7$), and additive noise ($\sigma_n=0.12$).

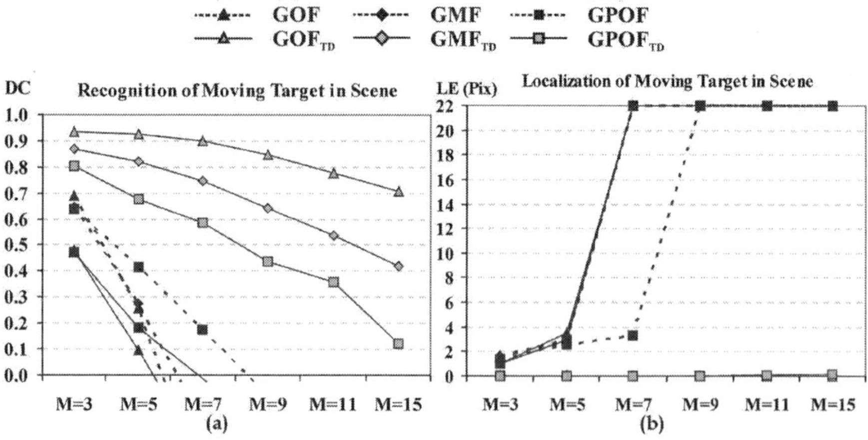

Fig. 7. Performance of correlation filters for recognition of a moving target: (a) DC versus M, (b) LE versus M for the scene.

scene containing the moving target may be homogeneously degraded by a linear system with the parameter D. The values of D used in our experiments are 3, 7, 9, 15, 19, and 23 pixels. Fig. 6(a) shows the test scene degraded with $M=9$ and $D=7$. Fig. 6(b) shows the degraded scene with $M=9$ and $D=7$, which is additionally corrupted by overlapping noise with $\sigma_n=0.12$.

Let us analyze the performance of the tested filters for recognition of a moving object in the still undistorted background. In this case, generalized optimum filters referred to as GMF_{TD}, GOF_{TD}, and $GPOF_{TD}$ can be obtained from Eqs. (24), (26), and (27), respectively, by substituting into these equations $H_{LD}(\omega)=1$. Figures 7(a) and 7(b) show the performance of the correlation filters with respect to the DC and the LE when the input scene in Fig. 1(a) contains a moving target with different values of M.

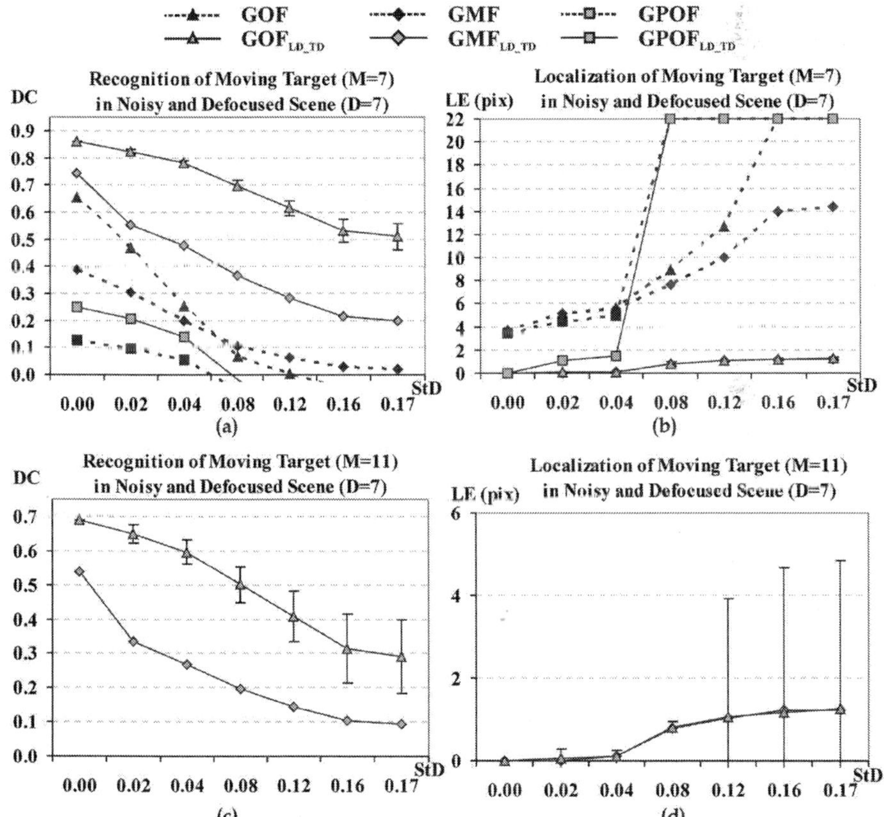

Fig. 8. Recognition of a moving object in defocused with $D=7$ and noisy test scene: (a) DC versus σ_n with $M=7$, (b) LE versus σ_n with $M=7$, (c) DC versus σ_n with $M=11$, (b) LE versus σ_n with $M=11$.

Note that the proposed filters the GOF_{TD}, the GMF_{TD}, and the $GPOF_{TD}$ are able to detect the target without location errors. On the other hand, one can see that the performance of the rest of the filters rapidly deteriorates in terms of the DC and the LE when the target displacement increases.

Next, the filters are tested for recognition of a moving object in defocused and noisy test scenes. The performance of the filters for $M=7$, 11, and $D=7$ in terms of the DC and the LE as a function of the standard deviation of additive noise is shown in Fig. 8. Under these degradation conditions, the OF, the MSF, and the POF yield a poor performance. The GMF_{LD_TD} is always able to detect and to localize the moving object for any tested values of M, D, and σ_n. However, it yields low values of the DC. The GOF_{LD_TD} provides the best performance in terms of the DC and the LE when the scene is corrupted by additive noise with $\sigma_n \leq 0.12$ and the target moves by $M \leq 15$ pixels.

3. Adaptive composite filters for recognition of geometrically distorted objects

3.1 Design of adaptive composite filters

In this section, we consider the task of recognition of geometrically distorted targets in input scenes degraded with a linear system and corrupted by noise. Various composite optimum correlation filters for recognition of geometrically distorted objects embedded in a nonoverlapping background have been proposed (Chan et al., 2000; Sjöberg & Noharet, 1998). However, there are no correlation-based methods for detection and localization of geometrically distorted objects in blurred and noisy scenes. We use *a priori* information about an object to be recognized, false objects, background noise, linear degradations of the input scene and target, geometrical distortions of the target, and additive sensor noise.

An attractive approach to geometrical distortion-invariant pattern recognition is based on SDF filters (Casasent, 1984; Mahalanobis et al., 1987; Vijaya-Kumar, 1986). Basically, a conventional SDF filter uses a set of training images to generate a filter that yields prespecified central correlation outputs in the response to training images. It is able to control only one point at the correlation plane for each training image. This is why SDF filters often have a low discrimination capability. We are interested in a filter which is able to recognize geometrically distorted objects in a set of observed degraded scenes, i.e., with a fixed set of patterns and backgrounds to be rejected (Ramos-Michel & Kober, 2008), rather than in a filter with average performance parameters over an ensemble of images (Chan et al., 2000). The impulse response of the obtained filter is a linear combination of correlation filters optimized with respect to the peak-to-output energy and common matched filters. The optimum generalized filters are derived from a set of training images, whereas the matched filters are designed from the background to be rejected. With the help of an iterative training procedure, an adaptive composite filter is generated. The filter ensures high correlation peaks corresponding to versions of the target while suppressing possible false peaks. The proposed algorithm of the filter design requires knowledge of the background image. The background can be described either deterministically (typical picture) or stochastically (realization of a stochastic process).

Suppose that an input scene is homogenously degraded by a linear system and corrupted by additive noise. It contains geometrically distorted targets. For each object to be recognized, a generalized optimum filter (GOF_{LD}) is designed [see Eq. (13)]. Each filter takes into account *a priori* information about the corresponding reference, background noise, linear degradation of the input scene, geometrical target distortions, and additive sensor noise. Let $\{t_i(x),\ i=1,2,...,N\}$ be a set of target images (linearly independent), each with d pixels. This set is called the *true class* of objects. The set includes geometrically distorted versions of the references. For the i'th image the transfer function of the GOF_{LD} filter is given by

$$\text{GOF}_i^{\text{LD}}(\omega) = \frac{\left\{\left[T_i(\omega) + \mu_b W_i(\omega)\right] H_{\text{LD}}(\omega)\right\}^*}{\alpha\left[\left|T_i(\omega) + \mu_b W_i(\omega)\right|^2 + \dfrac{1}{2\pi} B_0(\omega) \bullet \left|W_i(\omega)\right|^2\right]\left|H_{\text{LD}}(\omega)\right|^2 + N(\omega)},$$ (31)

where $T_i(\omega)$ and $W_i(\omega)$ are the Fourier transforms of the i'th training object $t_i(x)$ and its inverse support function $w_i(x)$, respectively. We use the same notation and assumptions as in Section 2. Let $h_i^G(x)$ be the inverse Fourier transform of the complex-conjugate frequency response of the generalized optimum filter for the i'th pattern. A linear combination of $\{h_i^G(x),\ i=1,2,...,N\}$ can form a SDF filter for intraclass distortion-invariant pattern recognition. In this case the coefficients of a linear combination must satisfy a set of constraints on the filter output requiring a prespecified value for each training pattern.

Assume that there are various classes of objects to be rejected. For simplicity, a two-class recognition problem is considered. Thus, we are looking for a filter to recognize training images from one class and to reject images from another class, called the false class. Suppose that there are M training images from the false class $\{p_i(x),\ i=1,2,...,M\}$. Let us denote a set of training images formed from the input patterns as $\mathbf{S}=\{t_1(x),...,\ t_N(x),p_1(x),...,\ p_M(x)\}$, and a new combined set of training images is defined as $\mathbf{S}_N=\{h_1^G(x),...,h_N^G(x),\ p_1(x),...,\ p_M(x)\}$. According to the SDF approach (Casasent, 1984), the composite image is computed as a linear combination of training images belonging to $\mathbf{S}_N$, i.e.,

$$h_{\text{SDF}}(x) = \sum_{i=1}^{N} a_i h_i^G(x) + \sum_{i=N+1}^{M+N} a_i p_i(x).$$ (32)

Let $\mathbf{R}$ denote a matrix with $N+M$ columns and d rows, whose i'th column is given by the vector version of the i'th element of $\mathbf{S}_N$. Using vector-matrix notation, Eq. (32) can be rewritten as

$$\mathbf{h}_{\text{SDF}} = \mathbf{R}\mathbf{a},$$ (33)

where $\mathbf{a}$ represents the column vector of weighting coefficients $\{a_i,\ i=1,...,M+N\}$. We can set the filter output $\{u_i=1,\ i=1,...,N\}$ for the true class objects and $\{u_i=0,\ i=N+1,\ N+2,...,N+M\}$ for the false class objects, i.e. $\mathbf{u}=[1\ 1\ 1\ \cdots 0\ 0\ \cdots 0]^T$. Here superscript T denotes the transpose. Let $\mathbf{Q}$ be a matrix with $N+M$ columns and d rows, whose i'th column is the vector version of the i'th element of $\mathbf{S}$. The weighting coefficients are chosen to satisfy the following condition:

$$\mathbf{u} = \mathbf{Q}^+ \mathbf{h}_{\text{SDF}},$$ (34)

where superscript + means conjugate transpose. From Eqs. (33) and (34) we obtain

$$\mathbf{h}_{\text{SDF}} = \mathbf{R}\left[\mathbf{Q}^+ \mathbf{R}\right]^{-1} \mathbf{u}.$$ (35)

Using the filter given in Eq. (35), we expect that the central correlation peaks will be close to unity for all targets and it will be close to zero for false objects. It is important to note that this procedure lacks control over the full correlation output, because we are able to control only the output at the location of cross-correlation peaks. Therefore, other sidelobes may appear everywhere on the correlation plane. To achieve a good recognition, a modified iterative algorithm (Diaz-Ramirez et al., 2006; González-Fraga et al., 2006) is proposed. At each iteration, the algorithm suppresses the highest sidelobe peak, and therefore the value of discrimination capability monotonically increases until a prespecified value is reached.

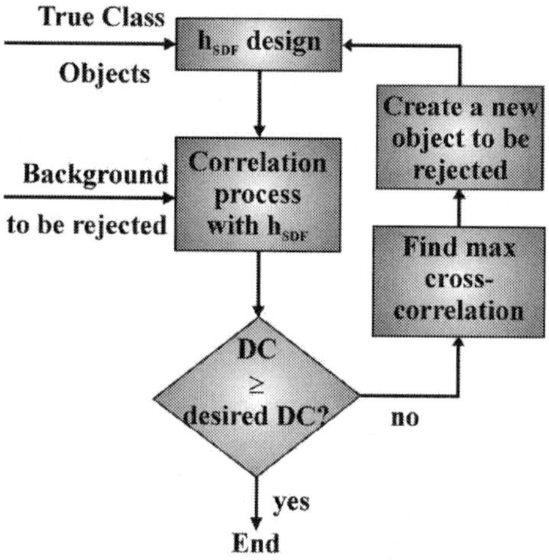

Fig. 9. Block diagram of the iterative algorithm for the filter design.

The first step of the iterative algorithm is to carry out a correlation between a background (deterministic or stochastic) and the SDF filter given in Eq. (35). This filter is initially trained only with available versions of targets and known false objects. Next, the maximum of the filter output is set as the origin, and around the origin we form a new object to be rejected from the background. This object has a region of support equal to the union of those of all targets. The created object is added to the false class of objects. Now, the two-class recognition problem is utilized to design a new SDF filter. The described iterative procedure is repeated till a specified value of the DC is obtained. A block diagram of the procedure is shown in Fig. 9. The proposed algorithm consists of the following steps:

1. Design a basic SDF filter using available distorted versions of targets and known false objects [see Eq. (35)].
2. Carry out the correlation between a background and the filter, and calculate the DC using Eq. (28).
3. If the value of the DC is greater or equal to a desired value, then the filter design procedure is finished, else go to the next step.
4. Create a new object to be rejected from the background. The origin of the object is at the highest sidelobe position in the correlation plane. The region of support of the object is the union of the region of supports of all targets. The created object is added to the false class of objects.
5. Design a new SDF filter using Eq. (35) with the same true class and the extended false class of objects. Go to step 2.

As a result of this procedure, the adaptive composite filter is synthesized. The performance of this filter in the recognition process is expected to be close to that in the synthesis process.

3.2 Performance of adaptive composite filters

Now, we analyze the performance of the generalized optimum filter for pattern recognition in a linearly distorted scene (GOF$_{LD}$) [given by Eq. (13)], the adaptive SDF filter (AMSF) (González-Fraga et al., 2006), the distortion-invariant minimum-mean-squared-error (MMSE) filter (Chan et al., 2000), and the proposed adaptive filter (AGOF) in terms of discrimination capability and location accuracy.

(a)   (b)

Fig. 10. Test scene (degraded by motion blur with M=5 and additive noise with σ_n=0.08) contains the target: (a) rotated by 5 degree and scaled by factor of 0.8, (b) rotated by 10 degree and scaled by factor of 1.2.

We carried out experiments for recognition of scaled and rotated targets in blurred and noisy scenes. It is assumed that a camera moves from right to left on M=5 pixels. So, the input scene is degraded by the uniform motion blur given in Eq. (30). The scene also contains sensor noise with σ_n=0.08. Figures 10(a) and 10(b) show two examples of input scenes used in the experiment. To guarantee statistically correct results, 30 statistical trials for different positions of a target and 20 realizations of random processes were performed. For the filter design of the tested composite filters (AGOF, AMSF and MMSE) we used the same set of training images. The set contains versions of the target scaled by factors 0.8, 0.85, 0.9, 1.1, and rotated by 0, 3, 6, and 9 degrees (see Fig. 11). Besides, for the synthesis of the adaptive filters we used the background shown in Fig. 1(a) degraded with M=5 and σ_n=0.08.

Figure 12 shows the performance of the filters with respect to the DC and the LE when the target is scaled and rotated by 5 and 10 degrees. One can see that the proposed filter AGOF possesses the best average performance in terms of both criteria. The AMSF fails to recognize the distorted object when the target is scaled by a factor lower than 1.2. It is important to say that the number of iterations during the design process of the AGOF depends on a background and true and false objects. In our case, after 9 iterations in the design process the filter yields DC=0.93.

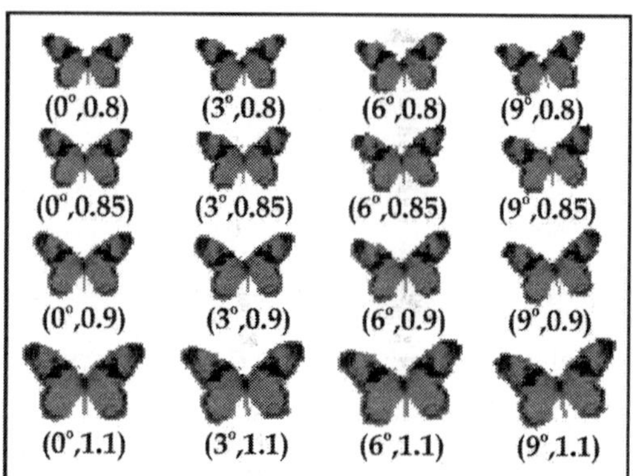

Fig. 11. Versions of the target distorted by rotation and scaling.

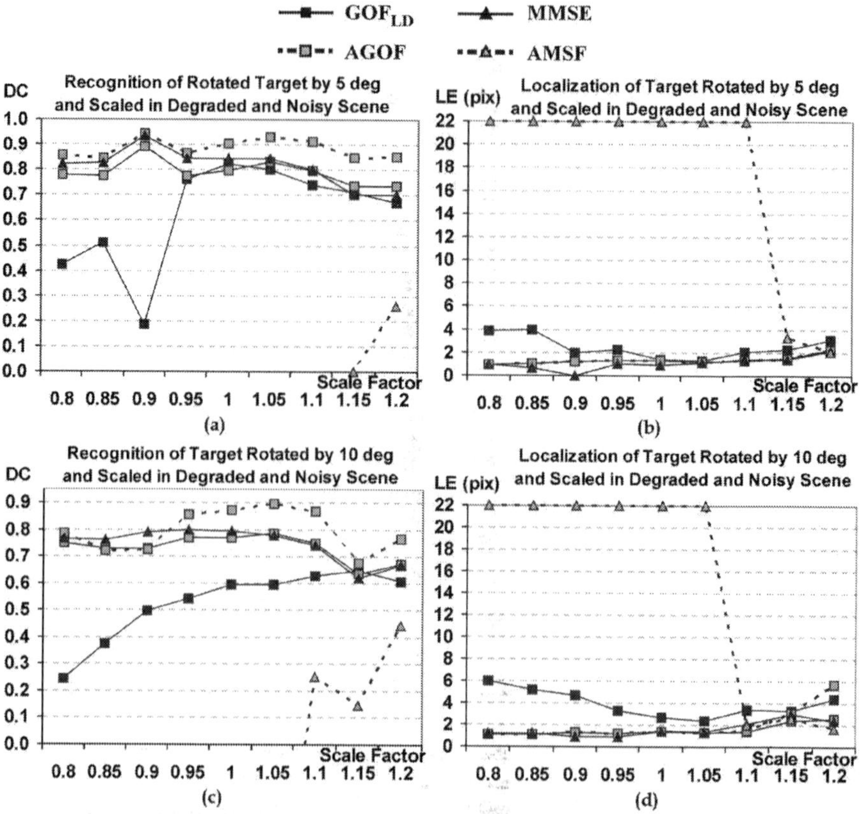

Fig. 12. Performance of correlation filters for recognition of rotated and scaled objects.

4. Conclusion

In this chapter we treated the problem of distortion-invariant pattern recognition based on adaptive composite correlation filters. First, we proposed optimum generalized filters to improve recognition of a linearly distorted object embedded into a nonoverlapping background noise when the input scene is degraded with a linear system and noise. The obtained filters take into account explicitly information about an object to be recognized, disjoint background noise, linear system degradation, linear target distortion and sensor noise. For the filter design, it is assumed that this information is available or can be estimated from the nature of degradations. Next, adaptive composite correlation filters for recognition of geometrically distorted objects embedded into degraded input scenes were proposed. The filters are a linear combination of generalized optimum filters and matched spatial filters. The information about an object to be recognized, false objects, and a background to be rejected is utilized in iterative training procedure to design a correlation filter with a prespecified value of discrimination capability. Computer simulation results obtained with the proposed filters are compared with those of various correlation filters in terms of recognition performance.

5. References

Bertero, M. & Boccacci, P. (1998). *Introduction to Inverse Problems in Imaging*, Institute of Physics Publishing, ISBN 0-7503-0435-9, Bristol.

Biemond, J., Lagendijk, R. L. & Mersereau, R. M. (1990). Iterative methods for image deblurring. *Proc. IEEE.* Vol. 78, No. 5, (May 1990) (856-883), ISSN 0018-9219.

Campos, J., Bosch, S., Sallent, J. & Berzal, A. (1994). Experimental implementation of correlation filters for optical pattern recognition in defocused images. *J. Opt.* Vol. 25, No. 1, (January 1994) (25-31), ISSN 0150-536X.

Carnicer, A., Vallmitjana, S., de F. Moneo, J. R. & Juvells, I. (1996). Implementation of an algorithm for detecting patterns in defocused scenes using binary joint transform correlation. *Opt. Commun.* Vol. 130, No. 4-6, (October 1996) (327-336), ISSN 0030-4018.

Casasent, D. (1984). Unified synthetic discriminant function computational formulation. *Appl. Opt.* Vol. 23, No. 10, (May 1984) (1620-1627), ISSN 0003-6935.

Chan, F., Towghi, N., Pan, L. & Javidi, B. (2000). Distortion-tolerant minimum-mean-squared-error filter for detecting noisy targets in environmental degradation. *Opt. Eng.* Vol. 39, No. 8, (August 2000) (2092-2100), ISSN 0091-3286.

Diaz-Ramirez, V. H., Kober, V. & Alvarez-Borrego, J. (2006). Pattern recognition with an adaptive joint transform correlator. *Appl. Opt.* Vol. 45, No. 23, (August 2006) (5929-5941), ISSN 0003-6935.

González-Fraga, J. A., Kober, V. & Álvarez-Borrego, J. (2006). Adaptive synthetic discriminant function filters for pattern recognition. *Opt. Eng.* Vol. 45, No. 5, (May 2006) (0570051-05700510), ISSN 0091-3286.

Goudail, F. & Réfrégier, P. (1997). Optimal target tracking on image sequences with a deterministic background. *J. Opt. Soc. Am. A.* Vol. 14, No. 12, (December 1997) (3197-3207), ISSN 1084-7529 (print), 1520-8532 (online).

Horner, J. L. & Gianino, P. D. (1984). Phase-only matched filtering. *Appl. Opt.* Vol. 23, No. 6, (March 1984) (812-816), ISSN 0003-6935.

Javidi, B. & Wang, J. (1994). Design of filters to detect a noisy target in nonoverlapping background noise. *J. Opt. Soc. Am. A.* Vol. 11, No. 10, (October 1994) (2604-2612), ISSN 1084-7529 (print), 1520-8532 (online).

Javidi, B., Parchekani, F. & Zhang, G. (1996). Minimum-mean-square-error filters for detecting a noisy target in background noise. *Appl. Opt.* Vol. 35, No. 35, (December 1996) (6964-6975), ISSN 0003-6935.

Kober, V. & Campos, J. (1996). Accuracy of location measurement of a noisy target in a nonoverlapping background. *J. Opt. Soc. Am. A.* Vol. 13, No. 8, (August 1996) (1653-1666), ISSN 1084-7529 (print), 1520-8532 (online).

Kober, V., Seong, Y. K., Choi, T. S. & Ovseyevich, I. A. (2000). Trade-off filters for optical pattern recognition with nonoverlapping target and scene noise. *Pattern Recog. Image Anal.* Vol. 10, No. 1, (February 2000) (149-151), ISSN 1054-6618 (print), 1555-6212 (online).

Mahalanobis, A., Vijaya Kumar, B. V. K. & Casasent, D. (1987). Minimum average correlation energy filters. *Appl. Opt.* Vol. 26, No. 17, (September 1987) (3633-3640), ISSN 0003-6935.

Navarro, R., Nestares, O. & Valles, J. J. (2004). Bayesian pattern recognition in optically degraded noisy images. *J. Opt. A.: Pure Appl. Opt.* Vol. 6, (January 2004) (36-42), ISSN 0963-9659 (print), 1361-6617 (online).

Perry, S. W., Wong, H. S. & Guan, L. (2002). *Adaptive image processing. A computational intelligence perspective*, CRC, ISBN 0-8493-0283-8, Boca Raton.

Ramos-Michel, E. M. & Kober, V. (2007). Design of correlation filters for recognition of linearly distorted objects in linearly degraded scenes. *J. Opt. Soc. Am. A.* Vol. 24, No. 11, (November 2007) (3403-3417), ISSN 1084-7529 (print), 1520-8532 (online).

Ramos-Michel, E. M. & Kober, V. (2008). Adaptive composite filters for pattern recognition in linearly degraded and noisy scenes. *Opt. Eng.* Vol. 47, No. 4, (April 2008) (047204(1-7)), ISSN 0091-3286.

Réfrégier, P. (1999). Bayesian theory for target location in noise with unknown spectral density. *J. Opt. Soc. Am. A.* Vol. 16, No. 2, (February 1999) (276-283), ISSN 1084-7529 (print), 1520-8532 (online).

Réfrégier, P., Javidi, B. & Zhang, G. (1993). Minimum mean square error filter for pattern recognition with spatially disjoint signal and scene noise. *Opt. Lett.* Vol. 18, No. 17, (September 1993) (1453-1455), ISSN 0146-9592 (print), 1539-4794 (online).

Sjöberg, H. & Noharet, B. (1998). Distortion-invariant filter for nonoverlapping noise. *Appl. Opt.* Vol. 37, No. 29, (October 1998) (6922-6930), ISSN 0003-6935.

Starck, J. L., Murtagh, F. & Bijaoui, A. (1998). *Image processing and data analysis: the multiscale approach*, Cambridge University Press, ISBN 0521590841, Cambridge, U.K.

Towghi, N. & Javidi, B. (2001). Optimum receivers for pattern recognition in the presence of Gaussian noise with unknown statistics. *J. Opt. Soc. Am. A.* Vol. 18, No. 8, (August 2001) (1844-1852), ISSN 1084-7529 (print), 1520-8532 (online).

VanderLugt, A. B. (1964). Signal detection by complex filtering. *IEEE Trans. Inf. Theory.* Vol. 10, No. 2, (April 1964) (139-145), ISSN 0018-9448.

Vargas, A., Campos, J., Martin, C. S. & Vera, N. (2003). Filter design of composite trade-off filter with support regions to obtain invariant pattern recognition with defocused images. *Opt. Laser Eng.* Vol. 40, No. 1-2, (July-August 2003) (67-79), ISSN 0143-8166.

Vijaya-Kumar, B. V. K. (1986). Minimum variance synthetic discriminant functions. *J. Opt. Soc. Am. A.* Vol. 3, No. 10, (October 1986) (1579-1584), ISSN 1084-7529 (print), 1520-8532 (online).

Vijaya-Kumar, B. V. K. & Hassebrook, L. (1990). Performance measures for correlation filters. *Appl. Opt.* Vol. 29, No. 20, (July 1990) (2997-3006), ISSN 0003-6935.

Yaroslavsky, L. P. (1993). The theory of optimal methods for localization of objects in pictures. In: *Progress in Optics XXXII*, E. Wolf, (Ed.), (145-201), Elsevier Science, North-Holland.

13

Manifold Matching for High-Dimensional Pattern Recognition

Seiji Hotta
Tokyo University of Agriculture and Technology
Japan

1. Introduction

In pattern recognition, a kind of classical classifier called *k-nearest neighbor rule* (kNN) has been applied to many real-life problems because of its good performance and simple algorithm. In kNN, a test sample is classified by a majority vote of its k-closest training samples. This approach has the following advantages: (1) It was proved that the error rate of kNN approaches the Bayes error when both the number of training samples and the value of k are infinite (Duda et al., 2001). (2) kNN performs well even if different classes overlap each other. (3) It is easy to implement kNN due to its simple algorithm. However, kNN does not perform well when the dimensionality of feature vectors is large. As an example, Fig. 1 shows a test sample (belonging to class 5) of the MNIST dataset (LeCun et al., 1998) and its five closest training samples selected by using Euclidean distance. Because the selected five training samples include the three samples belonging to class 8, the test sample is misclassified into class 8. Such misclassification is often yielded by kNN in high-dimensional pattern classification such as character and face recognition. Moreover, kNN requires a large number of training samples for high accuracy because kNN is a kind of memory-based classifiers. Consequently, the classification cost and memory requirement of kNN tend to be high.

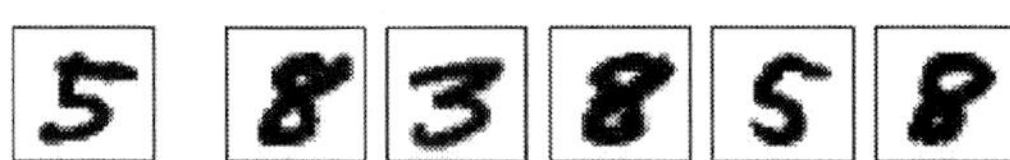

Fig. 1. An example of a test sample (leftmost). The others are five training samples closest to the test sample.

For overcoming these difficulties, classifiers using subspaces or linear manifolds (affine subspace) are used for real-life problems such as face recognition. Linear manifold-based classifiers can represent various artificial patterns by linear combinations of the small number of bases. As an example, a two-dimensional linear manifold spanned by three handwritten digit images '4' is shown in Fig. 2. Each of the corners of the triangle represents pure training samples, whereas the images in between are linear combinations of them. These intermediate images can be used as artificial training samples for classification. Due to this property, manifold-based classifiers tend to outperform kNN in high-dimensional pattern classification. In addition, we can reduce the classification cost and memory requirement of manifold-based classifiers easily compared to kNN. However, bases of linear manifolds have an effect on classification accuracy significantly, so we have to select them carefully. Generally, orthonormal bases obtained with *principal component analysis* (PCA) are used for forming linear manifolds, but there is no guarantee that they are the best ones for achieving high accuracy.

Fig. 2. A two-dimensional linear manifold spanned by three handwritten digit images '4' in the corners.

In this chapter, we consider about achieving high accuracy in high-dimensional pattern classification using linear manifolds. Henceforth, classification using linear manifolds is called *manifold matching* for short. In manifold matching, a test sample is classified into the class that minimizes the residual length from a test sample to a manifold spanned by training samples. This classification rule can be derived from optimization for reconstructing a test sample from training samples of each class. Hence, we start with describing square error minimization between a test sample and a linear combination of training samples. Using the solutions of this minimization, we can define the classification rule for manifold matching easily. Next, this idea is extended to the distance between two linear manifolds. This distance is useful for incorporating transform-invariance into image classification. After that, accuracy improvement through kernel mapping and transform-invariance is adopted to manifold matching. Finally, learning rules for manifold matching are proposed for reducing classification cost and memory requirement without accuracy deterioration. In this chapter, we deal with handwritten digit images as an example of high-dimensional patterns. Experimental results on handwritten digit datasets show that manifold-based classification performs as well or better than state-of-the-art such as a support vector machine.

2. Manifold matching

In general, linear manifold-based classifiers are derived with *principal component analysis* (PCA). However, in this section, we start with square error minimization between a test sample and a linear combination of training samples. In pattern recognition, we should not compute the distance between two patterns until we had transformed them to be as similar to one another as possible (Duda et al., 2001). From this point of view, measuring of a distance between a test point and each class is formalized as a square error minimization problem in this section.

Let us consider a classifier that classifies a test sample into the class to which the most similar linear combination of training samples belongs. Suppose that a d-dimensional training sample $\boldsymbol{x}_i^j = (x_{i1}^j \cdots x_{id}^j)^{\top} \in \mathbb{R}^d$ $(i = 1, ..., n_j)$ belonging to class j $(j = 1, ...,C)$, where n_j and C are the numbers of classes and training samples in class j, respectively. The notation $\top$ denotes the transpose of a matrix or vector. Let $\mathbf{X}_j = (\boldsymbol{x}_1^j | \boldsymbol{x}_2^j | \cdots | \boldsymbol{x}_{n_j}^j) \in \mathbb{R}^{d \times n_j}$ be the matrix of training samples in class j. If these training samples are linear independent, they are not necessary to be orthogonal each other.

Given a test sample $\boldsymbol{q} = (q_1 \ldots q_d)^{\top} \in \mathbb{R}^d$, we first construct linear combinations of training samples from individual classes by minimizing the cost for reconstructing a test sample from $\mathbf{X}_j$ before classification. For this purpose, the reconstruction error is measured by the following square error:

$$\min_{\boldsymbol{b}_j} \|\boldsymbol{q} - \mathbf{X}_j \boldsymbol{b}_j\|^2 = \left\| \boldsymbol{q} - \sum_{i=1}^{n_j} b_i^j \boldsymbol{x}_i^j \right\|^2 \tag{1}$$
$$\text{s.t.} \qquad \boldsymbol{b}_j^{\top} \mathbf{1}_{n_j} = \sum_{i=1}^{n_j} b_i^j = 1,$$

where $\boldsymbol{b}_j = (b_1^j \cdots b_{n_j}^j)^{\top} \in \mathbb{R}^{n_j}$ is a weight vector for the linear combination of training samples from class j, and $\mathbf{1}_{n_j} = (1 \cdots 1)^{\top} \in \mathbb{R}^{n_j}$ is a vector of which all elements are 1. The same cost function can be found in the first step of locally linear embedding (Roweis & Saul, 2000). The optimal weights subject to sum-to-one are found by solving a least-squares problem. Note that the above cost function is equivalent to $\|(\mathbf{Q}-\mathbf{X}_j)\boldsymbol{b}_j\|^2$ with $\mathbf{Q} = (\boldsymbol{q} | \boldsymbol{q} | \cdots | \boldsymbol{q}) \in \mathbb{R}^{d \times n_j}$ due to the constraint $\boldsymbol{b}_j^{\top} \mathbf{1}_{n_j} = 1$. Let us define $\mathbf{C}_j = (\mathbf{Q} - \mathbf{X}_j)^{\top}(\mathbf{Q} - \mathbf{X}_j)$, and by using it, Eq. (1) becomes

$$\min_{\boldsymbol{b}_j} \quad \boldsymbol{b}_j^{\top} \mathbf{C}_j \boldsymbol{b}_j$$
$$\text{s.t.} \ \boldsymbol{b}_j^{\top} \mathbf{1}_{n_j} = 1. \tag{2}$$

The solution of the above constrained minimization problem can be given in closed form by using Lagrange multipliers. The corresponding Lagrangian function is given as

$$J_L(\boldsymbol{b}_j) = \frac{1}{2}\boldsymbol{b}_j^{\top} \mathbf{C}_j \boldsymbol{b}_j + \lambda(\boldsymbol{b}_j^{\top} \mathbf{1}_{n_j} - 1), \tag{3}$$

where λ is the Lagrange multiplier. Setting the derivative of Eq. (3) to zero and substituting the constraint $\boldsymbol{b}_j^{\top} \mathbf{1}_{n_j} = 1$ into the derivative, the following optimal weight is given:

$$\boldsymbol{b}_j = \frac{\mathbf{C}_j^{-1} \mathbf{1}_{n_j}}{\mathbf{1}_{n_j}^{\top} \mathbf{C}_j^{-1} \mathbf{1}_{n_j}}. \tag{4}$$

Regularization is applied to $\mathbf{C}_j$ before inversion for avoiding over fitting or if $n_j > d$ using a regularization parameter $\alpha > 0$ and an identity matrix $\mathbf{I}_{n_j} \in \mathbb{R}^{n_j \times n_j}$ such as $\mathbf{C}_j + \alpha \mathbf{I}_{n_j}$.

In the above optimization problem, we can get rid of the constraint $\boldsymbol{b}_j^\top \mathbf{1}_{n_j} = 1$ by transforming the cost function from $\|\boldsymbol{q} - \mathbf{X}_j \boldsymbol{b}_j\|^2$ to $\|\boldsymbol{q} - (\boldsymbol{m}_j + \bar{\mathbf{X}}_j \boldsymbol{b}_j)\|^2$, where $\boldsymbol{m}_j$ is the centroid of class j, i.e., $\boldsymbol{m}_j = \sum_{i=1}^{n_j} \boldsymbol{x}_i^j / n_j$, and $\bar{\mathbf{X}}_j = (\boldsymbol{x}_1^j - \boldsymbol{m}_j | \cdots | \boldsymbol{x}_{n_j}^j - \boldsymbol{m}_j) \in \mathbb{R}^{d \times n_j}$, respectively. By this transformation, Eq. (1) becomes

$$\min_{\boldsymbol{b}_j} \|\boldsymbol{q} - (\boldsymbol{m}_j + \bar{\mathbf{X}}_j \boldsymbol{b}_j)\|^2. \tag{5}$$

By setting the derivative of Eq. (5) to zero, the optimal weight is given as follows:

$$\boldsymbol{b}_j = (\bar{\mathbf{X}}_j^\top \bar{\mathbf{X}}_j)^{-1} \bar{\mathbf{X}}_j^\top (\boldsymbol{q} - \boldsymbol{m}_j). \tag{6}$$

Consequently, the distance between $\boldsymbol{q}$ and the linear combination of class j is measured by

$$\begin{aligned}
d_j &= \|\boldsymbol{q} - (\boldsymbol{m}_j + \bar{\mathbf{X}}_j \boldsymbol{b}_j)\|^2 \\
&= \|\boldsymbol{q} - \boldsymbol{m}_j\|^2 - 2(\boldsymbol{q} - \boldsymbol{m}_j)^\top \bar{\mathbf{X}}_j \boldsymbol{b}_j + \boldsymbol{b}_j^\top \bar{\mathbf{X}}_j^\top \bar{\mathbf{X}}_j \boldsymbol{b}_j \\
&= \|\boldsymbol{q} - \boldsymbol{m}_j\|^2 - (\boldsymbol{q} - \boldsymbol{m}_j)^\top \bar{\mathbf{X}}_j (\bar{\mathbf{X}}_j^\top \bar{\mathbf{X}}_j)^{-1} \bar{\mathbf{X}}_j (\boldsymbol{q} - \boldsymbol{m}_j) \\
&= \|\boldsymbol{q} - \boldsymbol{m}_j\|^2 - \|\mathbf{V}_j^\top (\boldsymbol{q} - \boldsymbol{m}_j)\|^2,
\end{aligned} \tag{7}$$

where $\mathbf{V}_j \in \mathbb{R}^{d \times r}$ is the eigenvectors of $\bar{\mathbf{X}}_j \bar{\mathbf{X}}_j^\top \in \mathbb{R}^{d \times d}$, where r is the rank of $\bar{\mathbf{X}}_j \bar{\mathbf{X}}_j^\top$. This equality means that the distance d_j is given as a residual length from $\boldsymbol{q}$ to a r-dimensional linear manifold (affine subspace) of which origin is $\boldsymbol{m}_j$ (cf. Fig. 3). In this chapter, a manifold spanned by training samples is called *training manifold*.

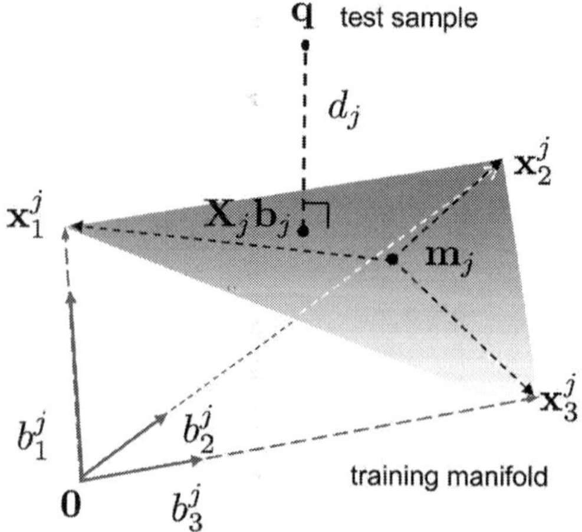

Fig. 3. Concept of the shortest distance between $\boldsymbol{q}$ and the linear combination of training samples that exists on a training manifold.

In a classification phase, the test sample $\boldsymbol{q}$ is classified into the class that has the shortes distance from $\boldsymbol{q}$ to the linear combination existing on the linear manifold. That is we define the distance between q and class j as $d_j = \|q - X_j b_j\|^2$ or $d_j = \|q - (m_j + \bar{X}_j b_j)\|^2$, test sample's class (denoted by ω) is determined by the following classification rule:

$$\omega = \arg\min_j d_j. \tag{8}$$

The above classification rule is called with different names according to the way of selection the set of training samples X_j. When we select the k-closest training samples of q from each class, and use them as X_j, the classification rule is called *local subspace classifier* (LSC) (Laaksonen, 1997; Vincent & Bengio, 2002). When all elements of b_j in LSC are equal to $1/k$, LSC is called local-mean based classifier (Mitani & Hamamoto, 2006). In addition, if we use an image and its tangent vector as m_j and $\bar{X}_j$ respectively in Eq. (7), the distance is called *one-sided tangent distance* (1S-TD) (Simard et al., 1993). These classifier and distance are described again in the next section. Finally, when we use the $r' \ll r$ eigenvectors corresponding to the r' largest eigenvalues of $\bar{X}_j \bar{X}_j^\top$ as V_j, the rule is called *projection distance method* (PDM) (Ikeda et al., 1983) that is a kind of subspace classifiers. In this chapter, classification using the distance between a test sample and a training manifold is called *one-sided manifold matching* (1S-MM).

2.1 Distance between two linear manifolds

In this section, we assume that a test sample is given by the set of vector. In this case the dissimilarity between test and training data is measured by the distance between two linear manifolds. Let $Q = (q_1 \mid q_2 \mid \ldots \mid q_m) \in \mathbb{R}^{d \times m}$ be the set of m test vectors, where $q_i = (q_{i1} \cdots q_{id})^\top$ $\in \mathbb{R}^d$ $(i - 1, \ldots, m)$ is the ith test vector. If these test vectors are linear independent, they are not necessary to be orthogonal each other. Let $a = (a_1 \ldots a_m)^\top \in \mathbb{R}^m$ is a weight vector for a linear combination of test vectors.

By developing Eq. (1) to the reconstruction error between two linear combinations, the following optimization problem can be formalized:

$$\min_{a,b} \quad \|Qa - Xb\|^2$$
$$\text{s.t. } a^\top 1_m = 1, \ b^\top 1_n = 1, \tag{9}$$

The solutions of the above optimization problem can be given in closed form by using Lagrange multipliers. However, they have complex structures, so we get rid of the two constraints $a^\top 1_m = 1$ and $b^\top 1_n = 1$ by transformating the cost function from $\|Qa - Xb\|^2$ to $\|(m_q + \bar{Q}a) - (m_j + \bar{X}_j b_j)\|^2$, where m_q and $\bar{Q}$ are the centroid of test vectors (i.e., $m_q = \sum_{i=1}^m q_i/m$) and $\bar{Q} = (q_1 - m_q \mid \ldots \mid q_m - m_q) \in \mathbb{R}^{d \times m}$, respectively. By this transformation, Eq. (9) becomes

$$\min_{a,b} \|(m_q + \bar{Q}a) - (m_j + \bar{X}_j b)\|^2. \tag{10}$$

The above minimization problem can be regarded as the distance between two manifolds (cf. Fig. 4). In this chapter, a linear manifold spanned by test samples is called *test manifold*.

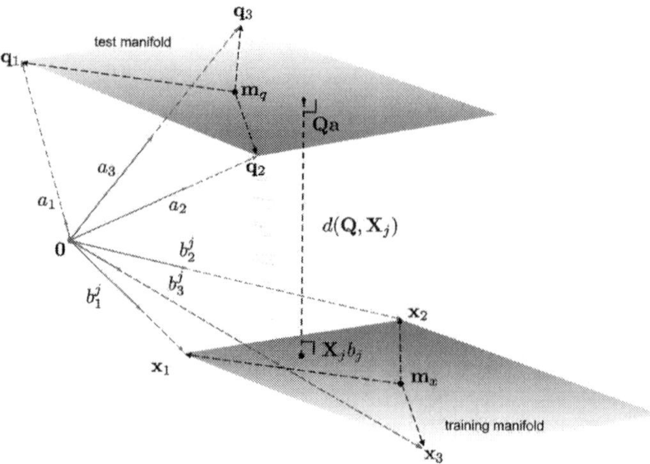

Fig. 4. Concept of the shortest distance between a test manifold and a training manifold.

The solutions of Eq. (10) are given by setting the derivative of Eq. (10) to zero. Consequently, the optimal weights are given as follows:

$$a = (\mathbf{Q}_1 - \mathbf{Q}_2\mathbf{X}_1^{-1}\mathbf{X}_2)^{-1}(\mathbf{Q}_2\mathbf{X}_1^{-1}\bar{\mathbf{X}}_j^\top - \bar{\mathbf{Q}}^\top)(\boldsymbol{m}_q - \boldsymbol{m}_j), \tag{11}$$

$$b = (\mathbf{X}_1 - \mathbf{X}_2\mathbf{Q}_1^{-1}\mathbf{Q}_2)^{-1}(\bar{\mathbf{X}}_j^\top - \mathbf{X}_2\mathbf{Q}_1^{-1}\bar{\mathbf{Q}}^\top)(\boldsymbol{m}_q - \boldsymbol{m}_j), \tag{12}$$

where

$$\mathbf{Q}_1 = \bar{\mathbf{Q}}^\top\bar{\mathbf{Q}}, \ \mathbf{X}_1 = \bar{\mathbf{X}}_j^\top\bar{\mathbf{X}}_j, \tag{13}$$

$$\mathbf{Q}_2 = \bar{\mathbf{Q}}^\top\bar{\mathbf{X}}_j, \ \mathbf{X}_2 = \bar{\mathbf{X}}_j^\top\bar{\mathbf{Q}}. \tag{14}$$

If necessary, regularization is applied to $\mathbf{Q}_1$ and $\mathbf{X}_1$ before inversion using regularization parameters $\alpha_1, \alpha_2 > 0$ and identity matrices $\mathbf{I}_m \in \mathbb{R}^{m \times m}$ and $\mathbf{I}_{n_j} \in \mathbb{R}^{n_j \times n_j}$ such as $\mathbf{Q}_1 + \alpha_1\mathbf{I}_m$ and $\mathbf{X}_1 + \alpha_2\mathbf{I}_{n_j}$.

In a classification phase, the test vectors $\mathbf{Q}$ is classified into the class that has the shortest distance from $\mathbf{Q}a$ to the $\mathbf{X}_jb_j$. That is we define the distance between a test manifold and a training manifold as $d(\mathbf{Q}, \mathbf{X}_j) = \|(\boldsymbol{m}_q + \bar{\mathbf{Q}}a) - (\boldsymbol{m}_j + \bar{\mathbf{X}}_jb_j)\|^2$, and the class of the test manifold (denoted by ω) is determined by the following classification rule:

$$\omega = \arg\min_j d(\mathbf{Q}, \mathbf{X}_j). \tag{15}$$

The above classification rule is also called by different names according to the way of selecting the sets of test and training, i.e., $\mathbf{Q}$ and $\mathbf{X}_j$. When two linear manifolds are represented by orthonormal bases obtained with PCA, the classification rule of Eq. (15) is called inter-subspace distance (Chen et al., 2004). When $\boldsymbol{m}_q$, $\boldsymbol{m}_j$ are bitmap images and $\bar{\mathbf{Q}}$, $\bar{\mathbf{X}}_j$ are their tangent vectors, the distance $d(\mathbf{Q}, \mathbf{X}_j)$ is called *two-sided tangent distance* (2S-TD) (Simard et al.,

1993). In this chapter, classification using the distance between two linear manifolds is called *two-sided manifold matching* (2S-MM).

3. Accuracy improvement

We encounter different types of geometric transformations in image classification. Hence, it is important to incorporate transform-invariance into classification rules for achieving high accuracy. Distance-based classifiers such as kNN often rely on simple distances such as Euclidean distance, thus they suffer a high sensitivity to geometric transformations of images such as shifts, scaling and others. Distances in manifold-matching are measured based on a square error, so they are also not robust against geometric transformations. In this section, two approaches of incorporating transform-invariance into manifold matching are introduced. The first is to adopt kernel mapping (Schölkopf & Smola, 2002) to manifold matching. The second is combining *tangent distance* (TD) (Simard et al., 1993) and manifold matching.

3.1 Kernel manifold matching

First, let us consider adopting kernel mapping to 1S-MM. The extension from a linear classifier to nonlinear one can be achieved by a kernel trick $\Phi(x)^{\mathsf{T}}\Phi(y) = K(x, y)$ for mapping samples from an input space to a feature space $\mathbb{R}^{d} \mapsto \mathcal{F}$ (Schölkopf & Smola, 2002). By applying kernel mapping to Eq. (1), the optimization problem becomes

$$\min_{b_j} \|(\mathbf{Q}^{\Phi} - \mathbf{X}_j^{\Phi})b_j\|^2$$
$$\text{s.t.} \quad b_j^{\mathsf{T}}\mathbf{1}_{n_j} = 1, \tag{16}$$

where $\mathbf{Q}^{\Phi}$ and $\mathbf{X}_j^{\Phi}$ are defined as $\mathbf{Q}^{\Phi} = (\Phi(q)|\cdots|\Phi(q))$ and $\mathbf{X}_j^{\Phi} = (\Phi(x_1^j)|\cdots|\Phi(x_{n_j}^j))$, respectively. By using the kernel trick and Lagrange multipliers, the optimal weight is given by the following:

$$b_j = \frac{\mathbf{K}_j^{-1}\mathbf{1}_{n_j}}{\mathbf{1}_{n_j}^{\mathsf{T}}\mathbf{K}_j^{-1}\mathbf{1}_{n_j}}, \tag{17}$$

where $\mathbf{K}_j \in \mathbb{R}^{n_j \times n_j}$ is a kernel matrix of which the (k, l)-element is given as

$$(\mathbf{K}_j)_{kl} = K(q, q) - K(q, x_l^j) - K(x_k^j, q) + K(x_k^j, x_l^j). \tag{18}$$

When applying kernel mapping to Eq. (5), kernel PCA (Schölkopf et al., 1998) is needed for obtaining orthonormal bases in $\mathcal{F}$. Refer to (Maeda & Murase, 2002) or (Hotta, 2008a) for more details.

Next, let us consider adopting kernel mapping to 2S-MM. By applying kernel mapping to Eq. (10), the optimization problem becomes

$$\min_{a,b} \left\| \Phi(m_q) + \bar{\mathbf{Q}}^{\Phi}a - (\Phi(m_x) + \bar{\mathbf{X}}_j^{\Phi}b) \right\|^2, \tag{19}$$

where $\Phi(m_q)$, $\Phi(m_x)$, $\bar{\mathbf{Q}}^{\Phi}$, and $\bar{\mathbf{X}}_j^{\Phi}$ are given as follows:

$$\Phi(\boldsymbol{m}_q) = \frac{1}{m}\sum_{k=1}^{m}\Phi(\boldsymbol{q}_k), \ \Phi(\boldsymbol{m}_x) = \frac{1}{n_j}\sum_{l=1}^{n_j}\Phi(\boldsymbol{x}_l^j), \tag{20}$$

$$\bar{\mathbf{Q}}^{\Phi} = \left(\Phi(\boldsymbol{q}_1) - \Phi(\boldsymbol{m}_q)|\Phi(\boldsymbol{q}_2) - \Phi(\boldsymbol{m}_q)|\cdots|\Phi(\boldsymbol{q}_m) - \Phi(\boldsymbol{m}_q)\right), \tag{21}$$

$$\bar{\mathbf{X}}_j^{\Phi} = \left(\Phi(\boldsymbol{x}_1^j) - \Phi(\boldsymbol{m}_x)|\Phi(\boldsymbol{x}_2^j) - \Phi(\boldsymbol{m}_x)|\cdots|\Phi(\boldsymbol{x}_{n_j}^j) - \Phi(\boldsymbol{m}_x)\right). \tag{22}$$

By setting the derivative of Eq. (19) to zero and using the kernel trick, the optimal weights are given as follows:

$$\boldsymbol{a} = (\mathbf{K}_{QQ} - \mathbf{K}_{QX}\mathbf{K}_{XX}^{-1}\mathbf{K}_{XQ})^{-1}(\mathbf{K}_{QX}\mathbf{K}_{XX}^{-1}\boldsymbol{k}_X - \boldsymbol{k}_Q), \tag{23}$$

$$\boldsymbol{b} = (\mathbf{K}_{XQ}\mathbf{K}_{QQ}^{-1}\mathbf{K}_{QX} - \mathbf{K}_{XX})^{-1}(\mathbf{K}_{XQ}\mathbf{K}_{QQ}^{-1}\boldsymbol{k}_Q - \boldsymbol{k}_X), \tag{24}$$

where $\mathbf{K}_{QQ} \in \mathbb{R}^{m\times m}$, $\mathbf{K}_{XX} \in \mathbb{R}^{n_j\times n_j}$, $\mathbf{K}_{QX} \in \mathbb{R}^{m\times n_j}$, $\mathbf{K}_{XQ} \in \mathbb{R}^{n_j\times m}$, $\boldsymbol{k}_Q \in \mathbb{R}^m$, and $\boldsymbol{k}_X$ $\in \mathbb{R}^{n_j}$ of which the $(k,\ l)$-elements of matrices and the lth element of vectors are given by

$$\begin{aligned}(\mathbf{K}_{QQ})_{kl} = {} & K(\boldsymbol{q}_k, \boldsymbol{q}_l) - \frac{1}{m}\sum_{t=1}^{m}K(\boldsymbol{q}_k, \boldsymbol{q}_t) \\ & - \frac{1}{m}\sum_{s=1}^{m}K(\boldsymbol{q}_s, \boldsymbol{q}_l) + \frac{1}{m^2}\sum_{s=1}^{m}\sum_{t=1}^{m}K(\boldsymbol{q}_s, \boldsymbol{q}_t),\end{aligned} \tag{25}$$

$$\begin{aligned}(\mathbf{K}_{XX})_{kl} = {} & K(\boldsymbol{x}_k^j, \boldsymbol{x}_l^j) - \frac{1}{n_j}\sum_{t=1}^{n_j}K(\boldsymbol{x}_k^j, \boldsymbol{x}_t^j) \\ & - \frac{1}{n_j}\sum_{s=1}^{n_j}K(\boldsymbol{x}_s^j, \boldsymbol{x}_l^j) + \frac{1}{n_j^2}\sum_{s=1}^{n_j}\sum_{t=1}^{n_j}K(\boldsymbol{x}_s^j, \boldsymbol{x}_t^j),\end{aligned} \tag{26}$$

$$\begin{aligned}(\mathbf{K}_{QX})_{kl} = {} & K(\boldsymbol{q}_k, \boldsymbol{x}_l^j) - \frac{1}{n_j}\sum_{t=1}^{n_j}K(\boldsymbol{q}_k, \boldsymbol{x}_t^j) \\ & - \frac{1}{m}\sum_{s=1}^{m}K(\boldsymbol{q}_s, \boldsymbol{x}_l^j) + \frac{1}{mn_j}\sum_{s=1}^{m}\sum_{t=1}^{n_j}K(\boldsymbol{q}_s, \boldsymbol{x}_t^j),\end{aligned} \tag{27}$$

$$\begin{aligned}(\mathbf{K}_{XQ})_{kl} = {} & K(\boldsymbol{x}_k^j, \boldsymbol{q}_l) - \frac{1}{m}\sum_{s=1}^{m}K(\boldsymbol{x}_k^j, \boldsymbol{q}_s) \\ & - \frac{1}{n_j}\sum_{t=1}^{n_j}K(\boldsymbol{x}_t^j, \boldsymbol{q}_l) + \frac{1}{mn_j}\sum_{t=1}^{n_j}\sum_{s=1}^{m}K(\boldsymbol{x}_t^j, \boldsymbol{q}_s),\end{aligned} \tag{28}$$

$$\begin{aligned}(\boldsymbol{k}_Q)_l = {} & \frac{1}{m}\sum_{s=1}^{m}K(\boldsymbol{q}_l, \boldsymbol{q}_s) - \frac{1}{n_j}\sum_{t=1}^{n_j}K(\boldsymbol{q}_l, \boldsymbol{x}_t^j) \\ & - \frac{1}{m^2}\sum_{s=1}^{m}\sum_{t=1}^{m}K(\boldsymbol{q}_s, \boldsymbol{q}_t) + \frac{1}{mn_j}\sum_{s=1}^{m}\sum_{t=1}^{n_j}K(\boldsymbol{q}_s, \boldsymbol{x}_t^j),\end{aligned} \tag{29}$$

$$(\boldsymbol{k}_X)_l = \frac{1}{m} \sum_{s=1}^{m} K(\boldsymbol{x}_l^j, \boldsymbol{q}_s) - \frac{1}{n_j} \sum_{t=1}^{n_j} K(\boldsymbol{x}_l^j, \boldsymbol{x}_t^j)$$
$$- \frac{1}{mn_j} \sum_{t=1}^{n_j} \sum_{s=1}^{m} K(\boldsymbol{x}_t^j, \boldsymbol{q}_s) + \frac{1}{n_j^2} \sum_{s=1}^{n_j} \sum_{t=1}^{n_j} K(\boldsymbol{x}_s^j, \boldsymbol{x}_t^j). \tag{30}$$

In addition, Euclidean distance between $\Phi(\boldsymbol{m}_q)$ and $\Phi(\boldsymbol{m}_x)$ in $\mathcal{F}$ is given by

$$d_{qx}^{\Phi} = \|\Phi(\boldsymbol{m}_q) - \Phi(\boldsymbol{m}_x)\|^2$$
$$= \frac{1}{m^2} \sum_{k=1}^{m} \sum_{s=1}^{m} K(\boldsymbol{q}_k, \boldsymbol{q}_s) - \frac{1}{mn_j} \sum_{k=1}^{m} \sum_{l=1}^{n_j} K(\boldsymbol{q}_k, \boldsymbol{x}_l^j)$$
$$- \frac{1}{mn_j} \sum_{l=1}^{n_j} \sum_{k=1}^{m} K(\boldsymbol{x}_l^j, \boldsymbol{q}_k) + \frac{1}{n_j^2} \sum_{l=1}^{n_j} \sum_{t=1}^{n_j} K(\boldsymbol{x}_l^j, \boldsymbol{x}_t^j). \tag{31}$$

Hence, the distance between a test manifold and a training manifold of class j in $\mathcal{F}$ is measured by

$$d(\mathbf{Q}, \mathbf{X}_j)^{\Phi} =$$
$$d_{qx}^{\Phi} + 2\boldsymbol{k}_Q^{\top}\boldsymbol{a} - 2\boldsymbol{k}_X^{\top}\boldsymbol{b} + \boldsymbol{u}^{\top}\mathbf{K}_{QQ}\boldsymbol{a} - \boldsymbol{a}^{\top}\mathbf{K}_{QX}\boldsymbol{b} - \boldsymbol{b}^{\top}\mathbf{K}_{XQ}\boldsymbol{a} + \boldsymbol{b}^{\top}\mathbf{K}_{XX}\boldsymbol{b}. \tag{32}$$

If necessary, regularization is applied to $\mathbf{K}_{QQ}$ and $\mathbf{K}_{XX}$ such as $\mathbf{K}_{QQ} + \alpha_1 \mathbf{I}_m$, $\mathbf{K}_{XX} + \alpha_2 \mathbf{I}_{n_j}$.

For incorporating transform-invariance into kernel classifiers for digit classification, some kernels have been proposed in the past (Decoste & Sch"olkopf, 2002; Haasdonk & Keysers, 2002). Here, we focus on a *tangent distance kernel* (TDK) because of its simplicity. TDK is defined by replacing Euclidean distance with a tangent distance in arbitrary distance-based kernels. For example, if we modify the following radial basis function (RBF) kernel

$$K(\boldsymbol{x}, \boldsymbol{y}) = \exp(-\beta\|\boldsymbol{x} - \boldsymbol{y}\|^2) \tag{33}$$

by replacing Euclidean distance with 2S-TD, we then obtain the kernel called *two sided TD kernel* (cf. Eq.(36)):

$$K(\boldsymbol{x}, \boldsymbol{y}) = \exp(-\beta \times d_{2S}(\boldsymbol{x}, \boldsymbol{y})). \tag{34}$$

We can achieve higher accuracy by this simple modification than the use of the original RBF kernel (Haasdonk & Keysers, 2002). In addition, the above modification is adequate for kernel setting because of its natural definition and symmetric property.

3.2 Combination of manifold matching and tangent distance
Let us start with a brief review of tangent distance before introducing the way of combining manifold matching and tangent distance.

When an image q is transformed with small rotations that depend on one parameter α, and so the set of all the transformed images is given as a one-dimensional curve S_q (i.e., a nonlinear manifold) in a pixel space (see from top to middle in Fig. 5). Similarly, assume that the set of all the transformed images of another image x is given as a one-dimensional curve S_x. In this situation, we can regard the distance between manifolds S_q and S_x as an adequate dissimilarity for two images q and x. For computational issue, we measure the distance between the corresponding tangent planes instead of measuring the strict distance between their nonlinear manifolds (cf. Fig. 6). The manifold S_q is approximated linearly by its tangent hyperplane at a point q:

$$S_q \simeq q + \sum_{i=1}^{r} \alpha_i^q t_i^q = q + \mathbf{T}_q \boldsymbol{\alpha}_q, \tag{35}$$

where t_i^q is the ith d-dimensional *tangent vector* (TV) that spans the r-dimensional tangent hyperplane (i.e., the number of considered geometric transformations is r) at a point q and the α_i^q is its corresponding parameter. The notations $\mathbf{T}_q$ and $\boldsymbol{\alpha}_q$ denote $\mathbf{T}_q = (t_1^q \ldots t_r^q)$ and $\boldsymbol{\alpha}_q = (\alpha_1^q \ldots \alpha_r^q)^\top$, respectively.

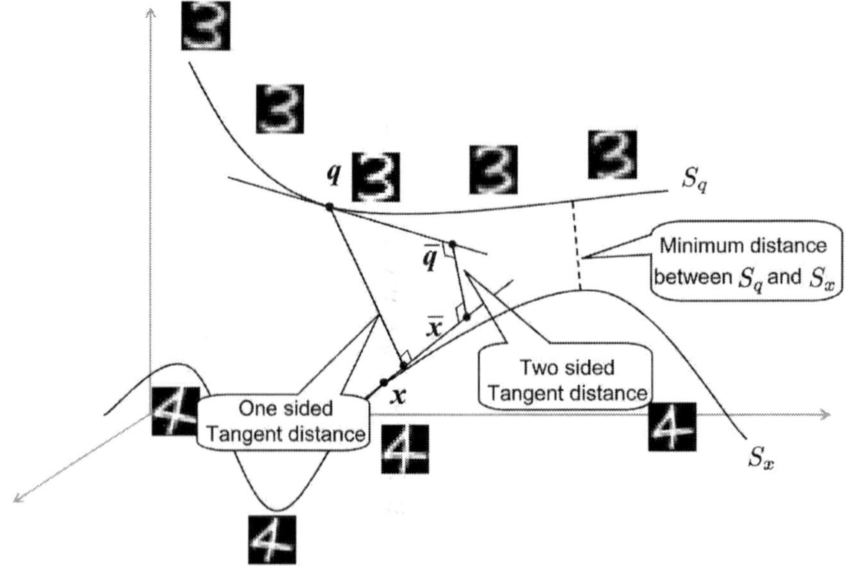

Fig. 6. Illustration of Euclidean distance and tangent distance between q and x. Black dots denote the transformed-images on tangent hyperplanes that minimize 2S-TD.

For approximating S_q, we need to calculate TVs in advance by using finite difference. For instance, the seven TVs for the image depicted in Fig. 5 are shown in Fig. 7. These TVs are derived from the Lie group theory (thickness deformation is an exceptional case), so we can deal with seven geometric transformations (cf. Simard et al., 2001 for more details). By using these TVs, geometric transformations of q can be approximated by a linear combination of the original image q and its TVs. For example, the linear combinations with different amounts of α of the TV for rotation are shown in the bottom in Fig. 5.

test sample

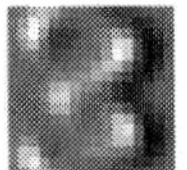   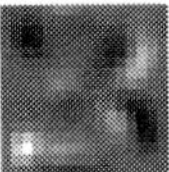 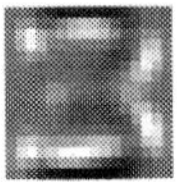  

Fig. 7. Tangent vectors t_i for the image depicted in Fig. 3. Fromleft to right, they correspond to x-translation, y-translation, scaling, rotation, axis deformation, diagonal deformation and thickness deformation, respectively.

When measuring the distance between two points on tangent planes, we can use the following distance called *two sided TD* (2S-TD):

$$d_{2S}(\boldsymbol{q}, \boldsymbol{x}) = \|\boldsymbol{q} + \mathbf{T}_q \boldsymbol{\alpha}_q - (\boldsymbol{x} + \mathbf{T}_x \boldsymbol{\alpha}_x)\|^2 . \tag{36}$$

The above distance is the same as 2S-MM, so the solutions of $\boldsymbol{\alpha}_q$ and $\boldsymbol{\alpha}_x$ can be given by using Eq. (11) and Eq. (12). Experimental results on handwritten digit recognition showed that kNN with TD achieves higher accuracy than the use of Euclidean distance (Simard et al., 1993).

Next, a combination of manifold matching and TD for handwritten digit classification is introduced. In manifold matching, we uncritically use a square error between a test sample and training manifolds, so there is a possibility that manifold matching classifies a test sample by using the training samples that are not similar to the test sample. On the other hand, Simard *et al.* investigated the performance of TD using kNN, but the recognition rate of kNN deteriorates when the dimensionality of feature vectors is large. Hence, manifold matching and TD are combined to overcome each of the difficulty. Here, we use the k-closest neighbors to a test sample for manifold matching for achieving high accuracy, thus the algorithm of the combination method is described as follows:

Step1: Find k-closest training samples x_1^j, ..., x_k^j to a test sample from class j according to d_{2S}.

Step2: Store the geometric transformed images of the k-closest neighbors existing on their tangent planes as $\mathbf{X}_j = (\bar{x}_1^j | \cdots | \bar{x}_k^j)$, where $\bar{x}_i^j$ is calculated using the optimal weight $\boldsymbol{\alpha}_{x_i}^j$ as follows:

$$\bar{x}_i^j = x_i^j + \mathbf{T}_{x_i}^j \boldsymbol{\alpha}_{x_i}^j \ (i = 1, ..., k). \tag{37}$$

Step3: Also store the k geometric transformed images of the test sample used for selecting the k-closest neighbors x_i^j using 2S-TD as $\mathbf{Q} = (\bar{q}_1 | ... | \bar{q}_k)$, where $\bar{q}_i$ is calculated using the optimal weight $\boldsymbol{\alpha}_i^j$ as follows:

$$\bar{q}_i^j = q + \mathbf{T}_q \boldsymbol{\alpha}_i^j \ (i = 1, ..., k). \tag{38}$$

Step4: Classify $\mathbf{Q}$ with 2S-MM using $\mathbf{X}_j$.

The two approaches described in this section can improve accuracy of manifold matching easily. However, classification cost and memory requirement of them tend to be large. This fact is showed by experiments.

4. Learning rules for manifold matching

For reducing memory requirement and classification cost without deterioration of accuracy, several schemes such as learning vector quantization (Kohonen, 1995; Sato & Yamada, 1995) were proposed in the past. In those schemes, vectors called codebooks are trained by a steepest descent method that minimizes a cost function defined with a training error criterion. However, they were not designed for manifold-based matching. In this section, we adopt *generalized learning vector quantization* (GLVQ) (Sato & Yamada, 1995) to manifold matching for reducing memory requirement and classification cost as small as possible.

Let us consider that we apply GLVQ to 1S-MM. Given a labelled sample $q \in \mathbb{R}^d$ for training (not a test sample), then measure a distance between q and a training manifold of class j by $d_j = \|q - X_j b_j\|^2$ using the optimal weights obtained with Eq. (4). Let $X_1 \in \mathbb{R}^{d \times n_1}$ be the set of codebooks belonging to the same class as q. In contrast, let $X_2 \in \mathbb{R}^{d \times n_2}$ be the set of codebooks belonging to the nearest different class from q. Let us consider the relative distance difference $\mu(q)$ defined as follows:

$$\mu(q) = \frac{d_1 - d_2}{d_1 + d_2},\tag{39}$$

where d_1 and d_2 represent distances from q to $X_1 b_1$ and $X_2 b_2$, respectively. The above $\mu(q)$ satisfies $-1 < \mu(q) < 1$. If $\mu(q)$ is negative, q is classified correctly; otherwise, q is misclassified. For improving accuracy, we should minimize the following cost function:

$$S = \sum_{i=1}^{N} f(\mu(q_i)),\tag{40}$$

where N is the total number of labelled samples for training, and $f(\mu)$ is a monotonically increasing function. To minimize S, a steepest descent method with a small positive constant ϵ $(0 < \epsilon < 1)$ is adopted to each X_j:

$$X_j \leftarrow X_j - \epsilon \frac{\partial S}{\partial X_j}, \ (j = 1, 2).\tag{41}$$

Now $\partial S / \partial X_j$ is derived as

$$\begin{aligned}\frac{\partial S}{\partial X_j} &= \frac{\partial S}{\partial \mu}\frac{\partial \mu}{\partial d_j}\frac{\partial d_j}{\partial X_j}\\ &= (-1)^j \frac{\partial f}{\partial \mu}\frac{4d_{3-j}}{(d_1 + d_2)^2}(q - X_j b_j)b_j^\top \ (j = 1, 2).\end{aligned}\tag{42}$$

Consequently, the learning rule can be written as follows:

$$X_j \leftarrow X_j + \delta_j(q - X_j b_j)b_j^\top \ (j = 1, 2),\tag{43}$$

where $\delta_j = (-1)^j \epsilon \frac{\partial f}{\partial \mu} \frac{d_{3-j}}{(d_1+d_2)}$ $(j = 1, 2)$. If we use $d_j = \|q - (m_j + \bar{X}_j b_j)\|^2$ as the distance, the learning rule becomes

$$m_j \leftarrow m_j - \delta_j(q - (m_j + \bar{X}_j b_j)),$$
$$\bar{X}_j \leftarrow \bar{X}_j - \delta_j(q - (m_j + \bar{X}_j b_j))b_j^\top . \tag{44}$$

Similarly, we can apply a learning rule to 2S-MM. Suppose that a labelled manifold for training is given by the set of m vectors $\mathbf{Q} = (q_1 \,|\, q_2 \,|\, \ldots \,|\, q_m)$ (not a test manifold). Given this $\mathbf{Q}$, a distance between $\mathbf{Q}$ and $\mathbf{X}_j$ is measured as $d(\mathbf{Q}, \mathbf{X}_j) = \|m_q + \bar{\mathbf{Q}}a - (m_j + \bar{X}_j b_j)\|^2$ using the optimal weights obtained with Eq. (11) and Eq. (12). Let $\mathbf{X}_1$ be the set of codebooks belonging to the same class as $\mathbf{Q}$. In contrast, let $\mathbf{X}_2$ be the set of codebooks belonging to the nearest different class from $\mathbf{Q}$. By applying the same manner mentioned above to 2S-MM, the learning rule can be derive as follows:

$$m_j \leftarrow m_j - \delta_j(m_q + \bar{\mathbf{Q}}a - (m_j + \bar{X}_j b_j)),$$
$$\bar{X}_j \leftarrow \bar{X}_j - \delta_j(m_q + \bar{\mathbf{Q}}a - (m_j + \bar{X}_j b_j))b_j^\top , \tag{45}$$

where $\delta_j = (-1)^j \epsilon \frac{\partial f}{\partial \mu} \frac{d(\mathbf{Q}, \mathbf{X}_{3-j})}{(d(\mathbf{Q}, \mathbf{X}_1)+d(\mathbf{Q}, \mathbf{X}_2))}$ $(j = 1, 2)$.

In the above learning rules, we change $d_j/(d_1 + d_2)^2$ into $d_j/(d_1 + d_2)$ for setting ϵ easily. However, this change dose not affect the convergence condition (Sato & Yamada, 1995). As the monotonically increasing function, a sigmoid function $f(\mu, t) = 1/(1 - e^{\mu t})$ is often used in experiments, where t is learning time. Hence, we use $f(\mu, t)\{1 - f(\mu, t)\}$ as $\partial f/\partial \mu$ in practice.

classifier	parameter (ϵ)
one sided manifold matching (1S-MM)	# dimension of manifolds r'
two sided manifold matching (2S-MM)	# dimension of training manifolds r'
Local Subspace Classifier (LSC)	# neighbor training samples k
Kernelized 1S-MM (K1S-MM, cf. Section 3)	# dimension of training manifolds r' in $\mathcal{F}$ parameters for kernel function
2S-MM with 2S-TD (2S-MM with 2S-TD, cf. Section 3)	# neighbors k
kNN with Euclidean Distance (kNN)	# neighbor training samples k
kNN with 2S-TD (kNN+2S-TD)	# neighbor training samples k
Support Vector Machine (SVM)	Soft margin constant and parameters for kernel function

Table 1. Summary of classifiers used in experiments

In this case, $\partial f/\partial \mu$ has a single peak at $\mu = 0$, and the peak width becomes narrower as t increases. After the above training, q and $\mathbf{Q}$ are classified by the classification rules Eq. (8) and Eq. (15) respectively using trained codebooks. In the learning rule of Eq. (43), if the all elements of b_j are equal to $1/\sqrt{n_j}$, this rule is equivalent to GLVQ. Hence, Eq. (43) can be regarded as a natural extension of GLVQ. In addition, if $\mathbf{X}_j$ is defined by k-closest training samples to q, the rule can be regarded as a learning rule for LSC (Hotta, 2008b).

5. Experiments

For comparison, experimental results on handwritten digit datasets MNIST (LeCun et al., 1998) and USPS (LeCun et al., 1989) are shown in this section. The MNIST dataset consists of

60,000 training and 10,000 test images. In experiments, the intensity of each 28×28 pixels image was reversed to represent the background of images with black. The USPS dataset consists of 7,291 training and 2,007 test images. The size of images of USPS is 16×16 pixels. The number of training samples of USPS is fewer than that of MNIST, so this dataset is more difficult to recognize than MNIST. In experiments, intensities of images were directly used for classification.

The classifiers used in experiments and their parameters are summarized in Table 1. In 1SMM, a training manifold of each class was formed by its centroid and r' eigenvectors corresponding to the r' largest eigenvalues obtained with PCA. In LSC, k-closest training samples to a test sample were selected from each class, and they were used as X_j. In 2S-MM, a test manifold was spanned by an original test image (m_q) and its seven tangent vectors ($\overline{X}_j$) such as shown in Fig. 7. In contrast, a training manifold of each class was formed by using PCA. In K1S-MM, kernel PCA with TDK (cf. Eq. 34) was used for representing training manifolds in $\mathcal{F}$. All methods were implemented with MATLAB on a standard PC that has Pentium 1.86GHz CPU and 2GB RAM. In implementation, program performance optimization techniques such as mex files were not used. For SVM, the SVM package called LIBSVM (Chang & Lin, 2001) was used for experiments.

5.1 Test error rate, classification time, and memory size

In the first experiment, test error rates, classification time per test sample, and a memory size of each classifier were evaluated. Here, a memory size means the size of a matrix for storing training samples (manifolds) for classification. The parameters of individual classifiers were tuned on a separate validation set (50000 training samples and 10000 validation samples for MNIST; meanwhile, 5000 training samples and 2000 validation samples for USPS).

Table 2 and Table 3 show results on MNIST and USPS, respectively. Due to out of memory, the results of SVM and K1S-MM in MNIST were not obtained with my PC. Hence, the result of SVM was referred to (Decoste & Schölkopf, 2002). As shown in Table 2, 2S-MM outperformed 1S-MM but the error rate of it was higher than those of other manifold matching such as LSC. However, classification cost of the classifiers other than 1S-MM and 2S-MM was very high. Similar results can be found in the results of USPS. However, the error rate of 2S-MM was lower than that of SVM in USPS. In addition, manifold matching using accuracy improvement described in section 3 outperformed other classifiers. However, classification cost and memory requirement of them were very high.

classifier	test error [%]	time [sec.]	memory size for classification
1S-MM ($r' = 30$)	4.3	0.003	784×310
2S-MM ($r' = 20$)	3.1	0.03	784×210
LSC ($k = 26$)	1.4	1	784×60000
K1S-MM	–	–	out of memory
2S-MM+2S-TD ($k = 23$)	0.7	1.9	784×60000
kNN ($k = 3$)	2.9	0.3	784×60000
kNN+2S-TD ($k = 1$)	1.4	0.6	784×60000
SVM (Polynomial kernel) with 1-pixel translation	1.2	–	$784 \times$ ca. 30000 (# support vectors)

Table 2. Test error rates, classification time per test sample, and memory size on MNIST.

classifier	test error [%]	time [sec.]	memory size for classification
1S-MM ($r' = 30$)	5.1	0.001	256×310
2S-MM ($r' = 20$)	4.2	0.01	256×210
LSC (k=11)	3.9	0.05	256×7291
K1S-MM ($r' = 10$)	3.3	1.6	$256 \times 7291 + 729 \times 10 \times 10$
2S-MM+2S-TD ($k = 7$)	2.2	1.2	256×7291
kNN ($k = 1$)	5.3	0.2	256×7291
kNN+2S-TD	2.4	0.13	256×7291
SVM (RBF kernel)	4.6	0.005	256×3220 (# support vectors)

Table 3. Test error rates, classification time per test sample, and memory size on USPS.

5.2 Effectiveness of learning

Next, the effectiveness of learning for manifold matching was evaluated by experiments. In general, handwritten patterns include various geometric transformations such as rotation, so it is difficult to reduce memory sizes without accuracy deterioration. In this section, learning for 1S-MM using Eq. (44) is called *learning 1S-MM* (L1S-MM). The initial training manifolds were formed by PCA as shown in the left side of Fig. 8. Similarly, learning for 2S-MM using Eq. (45) is called *learning 2S-MM* (L2S-MM). The initial training manifolds were also determined by PCA. In contrast, a manifold for training and a test manifold were spanned by an original image and its seven tangent vectors. The numbers of dimension for training manifolds of L1S-MM and L2S-MM were the same as those of 1S-MM and 2S-MM in the previous experiments, respectively. Hence, their classification time and memory size did not change. Learning rate ϵ was set to $\epsilon = 10^{-7}$ empirically. Batch type learning was applied to L1S-MM and L2S-MM to remove the effect of the order which training vectors or manifolds were presented to them. The right side of Fig. 8 shows the trained bases of each class using MNIST. As shown in this, learning enhanced the difference of patterns between similar classes.

method	test error [%]	training time [s]	memory size for training
L1S-MM ($r' = 30$)	2.3	109680	784×60000
L2S-MM ($r' = 20$)	1.8	71909	784×60000
GLVQ	10.4	536	784×60000
SVM	1.2	–	60000×60000

Table 4. Test error rates, training time, and memory size for training on MNIST.

method	test error [%]	training time [s]	memory size for training
L1S-MM ($r' = 30$)	4.9	2789	256×7291
L2S-MM ($r' = 20$)	3.7	3437	256×7291
GLVQ	8.7	37	256×7291
SVM	4.6	34.9	7291×7291

Table 5. Test error rate and training time on USPS.

Figure 9 shows training error rates of L1S-MM and L2S-MM in MNIST with respect to the number of iteration. As shown in this figure, the training error rates decreased with time. This means that the learning rules described in this chapter converge stably based on the convergence property of GLVQ. Also 50 iteration was enough for learning, so the maximum number of iteration was fixed to 50 for experiments. Table 4 and Table 5 show test error rates, training time, and memory size for training on MNIST and USPS, respectively. For comparison, the results obtained with GLVQ were also shown. As shown in these tables, accuracy of 1S-MM and 2S-MM was improved satisfactorily by learning without increasing of classification time and memory sizes. The right side of Fig. 8 shows the bases obtained with L2S-MM on MNIST. As shown in this, the learning rule enhanced the difference of patterns between similar classes. It can be considered that this phenomenon helped to improve accuracy. However, training cost for manifold matching was very high by comparison to those of GLVQ and SVM.

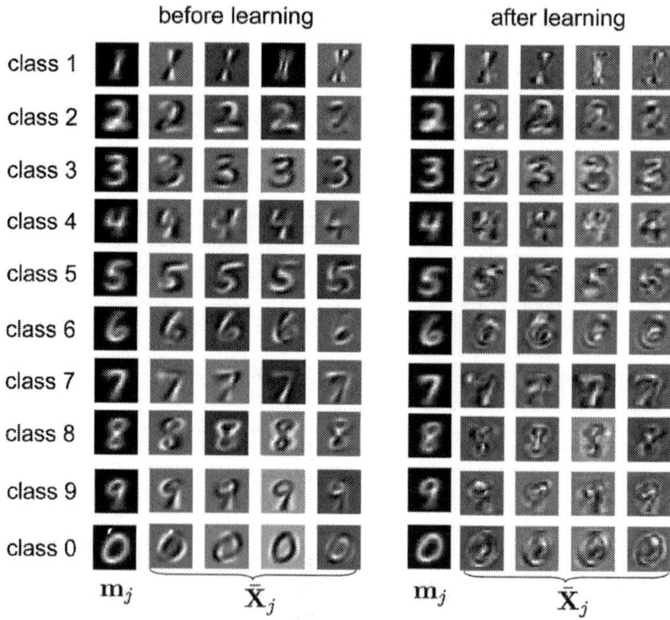

Fig. 8. Left: Origins (m_j) and orthonormal bases $\mathbf{X}_j$ of individual classes obtained with PCA (initial components for training manifolds). Right: Origins and bases obtained with L2S-MM (components for training manifolds obtained with learning).

6. Conclusion

In this chapter manifold matching for high-dimensional pattern classification was described. The topics described in this chapter were summarized as follows:
- The meaning and effectiveness of manifold matching
- The similarity between various classifiers from the point of view of manifold matching
- Accuracy improvement for manifold matching
- Learning rules for manifold matching

Experimental results on handwritten digit datasets showed that manifold matching achieved lower error rates than other classifiers such as SVM. In addition, learning improved accuracy and reduced memory requirement of manifold-based classifiers.

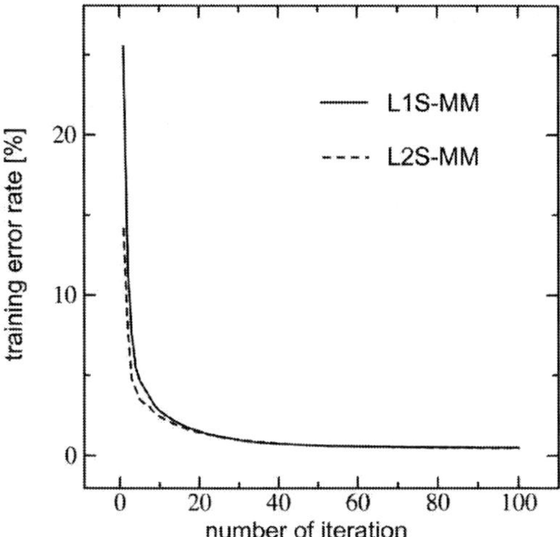

Fig. 9. Training error rates with respect to the number of iteration.

The advantages of manifold matching are summarized as follows:
- Wide range of application (e.g., movie classification)
- Small memory requirement
- We can adjust memory size easily (impossible for SVM)
- Suitable for multi-class classification (not a binary classifier)

However, training cost for manifold matching is high. Future work will be dedicated to speed up a training phase and improve accuracy using prior knowledge.

7. References

Chang, C.C. and Lin, C. J. (2001), LIBSVM: A library for support vector machines. Software available at http://www.csie.ntu.edu.tw/~cjlin/libsvm

Chen, J.H., Yeh, S.L., and Chen, C.S. (2004), Inter-subspace distance: A new method for face recognition withmultiple samples," *The 17th Int'l Conf. on Pattern Recognition ICPR (2004)*, Vol. 3, pp. 140–143

Duda, R.O., Hart, P.E., & Stork, D.G. (2001). Pattern classification. 2nd edition, John Wiley & Sons.

Decoste, D. and Sch¨olkopf, B. (2002). Training invariant support vector machines. *Machine Learning*, Vol. 46, pp. 161–190

Haasdonk, B. & Keysers, D. (2002), Tangent distance kernels for support vector machines. *The 16th Int'l Conf. on Pattern Recognition ICPR (2002)*, Vol. 2, pp. 864–868

Hotta, S. (2008a). Local subspace classifier with transform-invariance for image classification. *IEICE Trans. on Info. & Sys.*, Vol. E91-D, No. 6, pp. 1756–1763

Hotta, S. (2008b). Learning vector quantization with local subspace classifier. *The 19th Int'l Conf. on Pattern Recognition ICPR (2008)*, to appear

Ikeda, K., Tanaka, H., and Motooka, T. (1983). Projection distance method for recognition of hand-written characters. J. IPS. Japan, Vol. 24, No. 1, pp. 106–112

Kohonen., T. (1995). Self-Organizingmaps. 2nd Ed., Springer-Verlag, Heidelberg

Laaksonen, J. (1997). Subspace classifiers in recognition of handwritten digits. *PhD thesis, Helsinki University of Technology*

LeCun, Y., Boser, B., Denker, J.S., Henderson, D., Howard, R.E., Hubbard, W., & Jackel, L.D. (1989). Backpropagation applied to handwritten zip code recognition. *Neural Computation*, Vol. 1, No. 4, pp. 541–551

LeCun, Y., Bottou, L., Bengio, Y., & Haffner, P. (1998). Gradient-based learning applied to document recognition. *Proc. of the IEEE*, Vol. 86, No. 11, pp. 2278-2324

Maeda, E. and Murase, H. (1999). Multi-category classification by kernel based nonlinear subspace method. *Proc. of ICASSP*, Vol. 2, pp. 1025–1028

Mitani, Y. & Hamamoto, Y. (2006). A local mean-based nonparametric classifier. *Patt. Recog. Lett.*, Vol. 27, No. 10, pp. 1151–1159

Roweis, S.T. & Saul, L.K. (2000). Nonlinear dimensionality reduction by locally linear embedding. *Science*, Vol. 290–5500, pp. 2323–2326

Sato,A. and Yamada, K. (1995). Generalized learning vector quantization. *Prop. of NIPS*, Vol. 7, pp. 423–429

Schölkopf, B., Smola, A.J., and M¨uller, K.R. (1998). Nonlinear component analysis as a kernel eigenvalue problem. *Neural Computation*, Vol. 10, pp. 1299–1319

Schölkopf, B. and Smola, A.J. (2002). Learning with kernels. *MIT press*

Simard, P.Y., LeCun, Y., & Denker, J.S. (1993). Efficient pattern recognition using a new transformation distance. *Neural Information Processing Systems*, No. 5, pp. 50–58

Simard, P.Y., LeCun, Y., Denker, J.S., & Victorri, B. (2001). Transformation invariance in pattern recognition – tangent distance and tangent propagation. *Int'l J. of Imaging Systems and Technology*, Vol. 11, No 3

Vincent, P. and Bengio, Y. (2002). K-local hyperplane and convex distance nearest neighbor algorithms. *Neural Information Processing Systems*

14

Output Coding Methods: Review and Experimental Comparison

Nicolás García-Pedrajas and Aida de Haro García
University of Cordoba,
Spain

1. Introduction

Classification is one of the ubiquitous problems in Artificial Intelligence. It is present in almost any application where Machine Learning is used. That is the reason why it is one of the Machine Learning issues that has received more research attention from the first works in the field. The intuitive statement of the problem is simple, depending on our application we define a number of different classes that are meaningful to us. The classes can be different diseases in some patients, the letters in an optical character recognition application, or different functional parts in a genetic sequence. Usually, we are also provided with a set of patterns whose class membership is known, and we want to use the knowledge carried on these patterns to classify new patterns whose class is unknown.

The theory of classification is easier to develop for two class problems, where the patterns belong to one of only two classes. Thus, the major part of the theory on classification is devoted to two class problems. Furthermore, many of the available classification algorithms are either specifically designed for two class problems or work better in two class problems.

However, most of the real world classification tasks are multiclass problems. When facing a multiclass problem there are two main alternatives: developing a multiclass version of the classification algorithm we are using, or developing a method to transform the multiclass problem into many two class problems. The second choice is a must when no multiclass version of the classification algorithm can be devised. But, even when such a version is available, the transformation of the multiclass problem into several two class problems may be advantageous for the performance of our classifier. This chapter presents a review of the methods for converting a multiclass problem into several two class problems and shows a series of experiments to test the usefulness of this approach and the different available methods.

This chapter is organized as follows: Section 2 states the definition of the problem; Section 3 presents a detailed description of the methods; Section 4 reviews the comparison of the different methods performed so far; Section 5 shows an experimental comparison; and Section 6 shows the conclusions of this chapter and some open research fields.

2. Converting a multiclass problem to several two class problems

A classification problem of K classes and n training observations consists of a set of patterns whose class membership is known. Let $T = \{(x_1, y_1), (x_2, y_2), ..., (x_n, y_n)\}$ be a set of n training samples where each pattern x_i belongs to a domain X. Each label is an integer from the set $Y = \{1, …, K\}$. A multiclass classifier is a function $f: X \rightarrow Y$ that maps a pattern x to an element of Y. The task is to find a definition for the unknown function, $f(x)$, given the set of training patterns. Although many real world problems are multiclass problems, $K > 2$, many of the most popular classifiers work best when facing two class problems, $K = 2$. Indeed many algorithms are specially designed for binary problems, such as Support Vector Machines (SVM) (Boser et al., 1992). A class binarization (Fürnkranz, 2002) is a mapping of a multiclass problem onto several two-class problems in a way that allows the derivation of a prediction for the multi-class problem from the predictions of the two-class classifiers. The two-class classifier is usually referred to as the *binary classifier* or *base learner*.

In this way, we usually have two steps in any class binarization scheme. First, we must define the way the multiclass problem is decomposed into several two class problems and train the corresponding binary classifier. Second, we must describe the way the binary classifiers are used to obtain the class of a given query pattern. In this section we show briefly the main current approaches of converting a multiclass problem into several two class problems. In the next section a more detailed description is presented, showing their pros and cons. Finally, in the experimental section several practical issues are addressed.

Among the proposed methods for approaching multi-class problems as many, possibly simpler, two-class problems, we can make a rough classification into three groups: one-vs-all, one-vs-one, and error correcting output codes based methods:

- One-vs-one (*ovo*): This method, proposed in Knerr et al. (1990), constructs $K(K-1)/2$ classifiers. Classifier ij, named f_{ij}, is trained using all the patterns from class i as positive patterns, all the patterns from class j as negative patterns, and disregarding the rest. There are different methods of combining the obtained classifiers, the most common is a simple voting scheme. When classifying a new pattern each one of the base classifiers casts a vote for one of the two classes used in its training. The pattern is classified into the most voted class.

- One-vs-all (*ova*): This method has been proposed independently by several authors (Clark & Boswell, 1991; Anand et al., 1992). *ova* method constructs K binary classifiers. Classifier i-th, f_i, is trained using all the patterns of class i as positive patterns and the patterns of the other classes as negative patterns. An example is classified in the class whose corresponding classifier has the highest output. This method has the advantage of simplicity, although it has been argued by many researchers that its performance is inferior to the other methods.

- Error correcting output codes (*ecoc*): Dieterich & Bakiri (1995) suggested the use of error correcting codes for multiclass classification. This method uses a matrix M of $\{-1, 1\}$ values of size $K \times L$, where L is the number of binary classifiers. The j-th column of the matrix induces a partition of the classes into two *metaclasses*. Pattern x belonging to class i is a positive pattern for j-th classifier if and only if $M_{ij} = 1$. If we designate f_j as the sign of the j-th classifier, the decision implemented by this method, $f(x)$, using the Hamming distance between each row of the matrix M and the output of the L classifiers is given by:

$$f(x) = argmin_{r \in 1,2,…K} \sum_{i=1}^{L} \left(\frac{1 - sign\left(M_{ri} f_i(x) \right)}{2} \right) \tag{1}$$

These three methods comprehend all the alternatives we have to transform a multiclass problem into many binary problems. In this chapter we will discuss these three methods in depth, showing the most relevant theoretical and experimental results.

Although there are differences, class binarization methods can be considered as another form of ensembling classifiers, as different learners are combined to solve a given problem. An advantage that is shared by all class binarization methods is the possibility of parallel implementation. The multiclass problem is broken into several *independent* two-class problems that can be solved in parallel. In problems with large amounts of data and many classes, this may be a very interesting advantage over monolithic multiclass methods. This is a very interesting feature, as the most common alternative for dealing with complex multiclass problems, ensembles of classifiers constructed by boosting method, is inherently a sequential algorithm (Bauer & Kohavi, 1999).

3. Class binarization methods

This section describes more profoundly the three methods mentioned above with a special interest on theoretical considerations. Experimental facts are dealt with in the next section.

3.1 One-vs-one

The definition of one-vs-one (*ovo*) method is the following: *ovo* method constructs, for a problem of K classes, $K(K-1)/2$ binary classifiers[1], f_{ij}, $i = 1, ..., K-1$, $j = i+1, ..., K$. The classifier f_{ij} is trained using patterns from class i as positive patterns and patterns from class j as negative patterns. The rest of patterns are ignored. This method is also known as *round-robin classification*, *all-pairs* and *all-against-all*.

Once we have the trained classifiers, we must develop a method for predicting the class of a test pattern x. The most straightforward and simple way is using a voting scheme, we evaluate every classifier, $f_{ij}(x)$, which casts a vote for either class i or class j. The most voted class is assigned to the test pattern. Ties are solved randomly or assigning the pattern to the most frequent class among the tied ones. However, this method has a problem. For every pattern there are several classifiers that are forced to cast an erroneous vote. If we have a test pattern from class k, all the classifiers that are not trained using class k must also cast a vote, which cannot be accurate as k is not among the two alternatives of the classifier. For instance, if we have $K = 10$ classes, we will have 45 binary classifiers. For a pattern of class 1, there are 9 classifiers that can cast a correct vote, but 36 that cannot. In practice, if the classes are independent, we should expect that these classifiers would not largely agree on the same wrong class. However, in some problems whose classes are hierarchical or have similarities between them, this problem can be a source for incorrect classification. In fact, it has been shown that it is the main source of failure of *ovo* in real world applications (García-Pedrajas & Ortiz-Boyer, 2006).

This problem is usually termed as the problem of the *incompetent classifiers* (Kim & Park, 2003). As it has been pointed out by several researchers, it is an inherent problem of the method, and it is not likely that a solution can be found. Anyway, it does not prevent the usefulness of *ovo* method.

---

1 This definition assumes that the base learner used is class-symmetric, that is, distinguishing class i from class j is the same task as distinguishing class j from class i, as this is the most common situation.

Regarding the causes of the good performance of *ovo*, Fürnkranz (2002) hypothesized that *ovo* is just another ensemble method. The basis of this assumption is that *ovo* tends to perform well in problems where ensemble methods, such as bagging or boosting, also perform well. Additionally, other works have shown that the combination of *ovo* and ADABOOST boosting method do not produce improvements in the testing error (Schapire, 1997; Allwein et al, 2000), supporting the idea that they perform a similar work.

One of the disadvantages of *ovo* appears in classification time. For predicting the class of a test pattern we need to evaluate $K(K-1)/2$ classifiers, which can be a time consuming task if we have many classes. In order to avoid this problem, Platt et al. (2000) proposed a variant of *ovo* method based on using a directed acyclic graph for evaluating the class of a testing pattern. The method is identical to *ovo* at training time and differs from it at testing time. The method is usually referred to as the Decision Directed Acyclic Graph (*DDAG*). The method constructs a rooted binary acyclic graph using the classifiers. The nodes are arranged in a triangle with the root node at the top, two nodes in the second layer, four in the third layer, and so on. In order to evaluate a *DDAG* on input pattern **x**, starting at the root node the binary function is evaluated, and the next node visited depends upon the results of this evaluation. The final answer is the class assigned by the leaf node visited at the final step. The root node can be assigned randomly. The testing error reported using *ovo* and *DDAG* are very similar, the latter having the advantage of a faster classification time.

Hastie & Tibshirani (1998) gave a statistical perspective of this method, estimating class probabilities for each pair of classes and then coupling the estimates together to get a decision rule.

3.2 One-vs-all

One-vs-all (*ova*) method is the most intuitive of the three discussed options. Thus, it has been proposed independently by many researchers. As we have explained above, the method constructs K classifiers for K classes. Classifier f_i is trained to distinguish between class i and all other classes. In classification time all the classifiers are evaluated and the query pattern is assigned to the class whose corresponding classifier has the highest output.

This method has the advantage of training a smaller number of classifiers than the other two methods. However, it has been theoretically shown (Fürnkranz, 2002) that the training of these classifiers is more complex than the training of *ovo* classifiers. However, this theoretical analysis does not consider the time associated with the repeated execution of an actual program, and also assumes that the execution time is linear with the number of patterns. In fact, in the experiments reported here the execution time of *ova* is usually shorter than the time spent by *ovo* and *ecoc*.

The main advantage of *ova* approach is its simplicity. If a class binarization must be performed, it is perhaps the first method one thinks of. In fact, some multiclass methods, such as the one used in multiclass multilayer Perceptron, are based on the idea of separating each class from all the rest of classes.

Among its drawbacks several authors argue (Fürnkranz, 2002) that separating a class from all the rest is a harder task than separating classes in pairs. However, in practice the situation depends on another issue. The task of separating classes in pairs may be simple, but also, there are fewer available patterns to learn the classifiers. In many cases the classifiers that learned to distinguish between two classes have large generalization errors due to the small number of patterns used in their training process. These large errors undermine the performance of *ovo* in favor of *ova* in several problems.

3.3 Error-correcting output codes

This method was proposed by Dietterich & Bakiri (1995). They use a "coding matrix" $M \in \{-1, +1\}^{KxL}$ which has a row for each class and a number of columns, L, defined by the user. Each row codifies a class, and each column represents a binary problem, where the patterns of the classes whose corresponding row has a +1 are considered as positive samples, and the patterns whose corresponding row has a -1 as negative samples. So, after training we have a set of L binary classifiers, $\{f_1, f_2, ..., f_L\}$. In order to predict the class of an unknown test sample $\mathbf{x}$, we obtain the output of each classifier and classify the pattern in the class whose coding row is *closest* to the output of the binary classifiers $(f_1(\mathbf{x}), f_2(\mathbf{x}), ..., f_L(\mathbf{x}))$. There are many different ways of obtaining the closest row. The simplest one is using Hamming distance, breaking the ties with a certain criterion. However, this method loses information, as the actual output of each classifier can be considered a measure of the probability of the bit to be 1. In this way, L^1 norm can be used instead of Hamming distance. The L^1 distance between a codeword M_i and the output of the classifiers $F = \{f_1, f_2, ..., f_L\}$ is defined by:

$$L^1\left(M_i, F\right) = \sum_{j=0}^{L} \left| M_{ij} - f_j \right| \qquad (2)$$

The L^1 norm is preferred over Hamming distance for its better performance and as it has also been proven that *ecoc* method is able to produce reliable probability estimates. Windeatt & Ghaderi (2003) tested several decoding strategies, showing that none of them was able to improve the performance of L^1 norm significantly. Several other decoding methods have been proposed (Passerini et al., 2004) but only with a marginal advantage over L^1 norm.

This approach was pioneered by Sejnowski & Rosenberg (1987) who defined manual codewords for the NETtalk system. In that work, the codewords were chosen taking into account different features of each class. The contribution of Dietterich & Bakiri was considering the principles of error-correcting codes design for constructing the codewords.

The idea is considering the classification problem similar to the problem of transmitting a string of bits over a parallel channel. As a bit can be transmitted incorrectly due to a failure of the channel, we can consider that a classifier that does not predict accurately the class of a sample is like a bit transmitted over an unreliable channel. In this case the channel consists of the input features, the training patterns and the learning process. In the same way as an error-correcting code can recover from the failure of some of the transmitted bits, *ecoc* codes might be able to recover from the failure of some of the classifiers.

However, this argumentation has a very important issue, error-correcting codes rely on the independent transmission of the bits. If the errors are correlated, the error-correcting capabilities are seriously damaged. In a pattern recognition task, it is debatable whether the different binary classifiers are independent. If we consider that the input features, the learning process and the training patterns are the same, although the learning task is different, the independence among the classifiers is not an expected result.

Using the formulation of *ecoc* codes, Allwein et al. (2000) presented a unifying approach, using coding matrices of three values, *{-1, 0, 1}*, 0 meaning "don't care". Using this approach, *ova* method can be represented with a matrix of 1's in the main diagonal and -1 in the remaining places, and *ovo* with a matrix of $K(K-1)/2$ columns, each one with a +1, a -1 and the remaining places in the column set to 0. Allwein et al. also presented training and generalization error bounds for output codes when loss based decoding is used. However, the generalization bounds are not tight, and they should be seemed more as a way of considering the qualitative effect of each of the factors that have an impact on the generalization error. In general, these theoretical studies have recognized shortcomings and the bounds on the error are too loose for practical purposes. In the same way, the studies on the effect of *ecoc* on bias/variance have the problem of estimating these components of the error in classification problems (James, 2003).

As an additional advantage, Dietterich & Bakiri (1995) showed, using rejection curves, that *ecoc* are good estimators of the confidence of the multiclass classifier. The performance of *ecoc* codes has been explained in terms of reducing bias/variance and by interpreting them as large margin classifiers (Masulli & Valentini, 2003). However, a generally accepted explanation is still lacking as many theoretical issues are open.

In fact, several issues concerning *ecoc* method remain debatable. One of the most important is the relationship between the error correcting capabilities and the generalization error. These two aspects are also closely related to the independence of the dichotomizers. Masulli & Valentini (2003) performed a study using 3 real-world problems without finding any clear trend.

3.3.1 Error-correcting output codes design

Once we have stated that the use of codewords designed by their error-correcting capabilities may be a way of improving the performance of the multiclass classifier, we must face the design of such codes.

The design of error-correcting codes is aimed at obtaining codes whose separation, in terms of Hamming distance, is maximized. If we have a code whose minimum separation between codewords is d, then the code can correct at least $\lfloor (d-1)/2 \rfloor$ bits. Thus, the first objective is maximizing minimum row separation. However, there is another objective in designing *ecoc* codes, we must enforce a low correlation between the binary classifiers induced by each column. In order to accomplish this, we maximize the distance between each column and all other columns. As we are dealing with class symmetric classifiers, we must also maximize the distance between each column and the complement of all other columns. The underlying idea is that if the columns are similar (or complementary) the binary classifiers learned from those columns will be similar and tend to make correlated mistakes.

These two objectives make the task of designing the matrix of codewords for *ecoc* method more difficult than the designing of error-correcting codes. For a problem with K classes, we have $2^{k-1} - 1$ possible choices for the columns. For small values of K, we can construct exhaustive codes, evaluating all the possible matrices for a given number of columns. However, for larger values of K the designing of the coding matrix is an open problem.

The designing of a coding matrix is then an optimization problem that can only be solved using an iterative optimization algorithm. Dietterich & Bakiri (1995) proposed several methods, including randomized hill-climbing and BCH codes. BCH algorithm is used for designing error correcting codes. However, its application to *ecoc* design is problematic, among other factors because it does not take into account column separation, as it is not needed for error-correcting codes. Other authors have used general purpose optimization algorithms such as evolutionary computation (García-Pedrajas & Fyfe, 2008).

More recently, methods for obtaining the coding matrix taking into account the problem to be solved have been proposed. Pujol et al. (2006) proposed *Discriminant ECOC*, a heuristic method based on a hierarchical partition of the class space that maximizes a certain discriminative criterion. García-Pedrajas & Fyfe (2008) coupled the design of the codes with the learning of the classifiers, designing the coding matrix using an evolutionary algorithm.

4. Comparison of the different methods

The usual question when we face a multiclass problem and decide to use a class binarization method is which is the best method for my problem. Unfortunately, this is an open question which generates much controversy among the researchers.

One of the advantages of *ovo* is that the binary problems generated are simpler, as only a subset of the whole set of patterns is used. Furthermore, it is common in real world problems that the classes are pairwise separable (Knerr et al., 1992), a situation that is not so common for *ova* and *ecoc* methods.

In principle, it may be argued that replacing a K classes problem by $K(K-1)/2$ problems should significantly increase the computational cost of the task. However, Fürnkranz (2002) presented theoretical arguments showing that *ovo* has less computational complexity than *ova*. The basis underlying the argumentation is that, although *ovo* needs to train more classifiers, each classifier is simpler as it only focuses on a certain pair of classes disregarding the remaining patterns. In that work an experimental comparison is also performed using as base learner Ripper algorithm (Cohen, 1995). The experiments showed that *ovo* is about 2 times faster than *ova* using Ripper as base learner. However, the situation depends on the base learner used. In many cases there is an overhead associated with the application of the base learner which is independent of the complexity of the learning task. Furthermore, if the base learner needs some kind of parameters estimation, using cross-validation or any other method for parameters setting, the situation may be worse. In fact, in the experiments reported in Section 5, using powerful base learners, the complexity of *ovo* was usually greater than the complexity of *ova*.

There are many works devoted to the comparison of the different methods. Hsu & Lin (2002) compared *ovo*, *ova* and two native multiclass methods using a SVM. They concluded that *ova* was worse than the other methods, which showed a similar performance. In fact, most of the previous works agree on the inferior performance of *ova*. However, the consensus about the inferior performance of *ova* has been challenged recently (Rifkin & Klautau, 2004). In an extensive discussion of previous work, they concluded that the differences reported were mostly the product of either using too simple base learners or poorly tuned classifiers. As it is well known, the combination of weak learners can take advantage of the independence of the errors they make, while combining powerful learners is less profitable due to their more correlated errors. In that paper, the authors concluded that *ova* method is very difficult to be outperformed if a powerful enough base learner is chosen and the parameters are set using a sound method.

5. Experimental comparison

As we have shown in the previous section, there is no general agreement on which one of the presented methods shows the best performance. Thus, in this experimental section we will test several of the issues that are relevant for the researcher, as a help for choosing the most appropriate method for a given problem.

For the comparison of the different models, we selected 41 datasets from the UCI Machine Learning Repository which are shown in Table 1. The estimation of the error is made using 10-fold cross-validation. The datasets were selected considering problems of at least 6 classes for *ecoc* codes (27 datasets), and problems with at least 3 classes for the other methods. We will use as main base learner a C4.5 decision tree (Quinlan, 1993), because it is a powerful widely used classification algorithm and has a native multiclass method that can be compared with class binarization algorithms. In some experiments we will also show results with other base learners for the sake of completeness. It is interesting to note that this set of problems is considerably larger than the used in the comparison studies cited along the paper.

When the differences between two algorithms must be statistically assessed we use a Wilcoxon test for several reasons. Wilcoxon test assumes limited commensurability. It is safer than parametric tests since it does not assume normal distributions or homogeneity of variance. Thus, it can be applied to error ratios. Furthermore, empirical results show that it is also stronger than other tests (Demšar, 2006).

Dataset	Cases	Inputs	Classes	Binary classifiers		
				Dense ecoc	*Sparse ecoc*	*One-vs-one*
Abalone	4177	10	29	2.68e+8	3.43e+13	406
Anneal	898	59	5	15	90	10
Arrhythmia	452	279	13	4095	7.88e+5	78
Audiology	226	93	24	8.38e+6	1.41e+11	276
Autos	205	72	6	31	301	15
Balance	625	4	3	3	6	3
Car	1728	16	4	7	25	6
Dermatology	366	34	6	31	301	15
Ecoli	336	7	8	127	3025	28
Gene	3175	120	3	3	6	3
Glass	214	9	6	31	301	15
Horse	364	58	3	3	6	3
Hypo	3772	29	4	7	25	6
Iris	150	4	3	3	6	3
Isolet	7797	617	26	3.35e+7	1.27e+12	325
Krkopt	28056	6	6	1.31e+5	1.93e+8	153
Led24	200	24	10	511	28501	45
Letter	20000	16	26	3.35e+7	1.27e+12	325
Lrs	531	101	10	511	28501	45
Lymph	148	38	4	7	25	6
Mfeat-fou	2000	76	10	511	28501	45
Mfeat-kar	2000	64	10	511	28501	45
Mfeat-mor	2000	6	10	511	28501	45

Dataset	Cases	Inputs	Classes	Binary classifiers		
				Dense ecoc	Sparse ecoc	One-vs-one
Mfeat-zer	2000	47	10	511	28501	45
New-thyroid	215	5	3	3	6	3
Nursery	12960	23	5	15	90	10
Optdigits	5620	64	10	511	28501	45
Page-blocks	5473	10	5	15	90	10
Pendigits	10992	16	10	511	28501	45
Primary	339	23	22	2.09e+6	1.56e+10	231
Satimage	6435	36	6	31	301	15
Segment	2310	19	7	63	966	21
Soybean	683	82	19	2.62e+5	5.80e+8	171
Texture	5500	40	11	1023	86526	55
Vehicle	846	18	4	7	25	6
Vowel	990	10	11	1023	86526	55
Waveform	5000	40	3	3	6	3
Wine	178	13	3	3	6	3
Yeast	1484	8	10	511	28501	45
Zip	9298	256	10	511	28501	45
Zoo	101	16	7	63	966	21

Table 1. Summary of datasets used in the experiments.

The first set of experiments is devoted to studying the behavior of *ecoc* codes. First, we test the influence of the size of codewords on the performance of *ecoc* method. We also test whether the use of codes designed by their error correcting capabilities are better than codes randomly designed. For the first experiment we use codes of 30, 50, 100 and 200 bits.

In many previous studies it has been shown that, in general, the advantage of using codes designed for their error correcting capabilities over random codes is only marginal. We construct random codes just generating the coding matrix randomly with the only post-processing of removing repeated columns or rows. In order to construct error-correcting codes, we must take into account two different objectives, as mentioned above, column and row separation. Error-correcting design algorithm are only concerned with row separation so their use must be coupled with another method for ensuring column separation. Furthermore, many of these algorithms are too complex and difficult to scale for long codes. So, instead of these methods, we have used an evolutionary computation method, a genetic algorithm to construct our coding matrix.

Evolutionary computation (EC) (Ortiz-Boyer at al., 2005) is a set of global optimization techniques that have been widely used over the last years for almost every problem within the field of Artificial Intelligence. In evolutionary computation a population (set) of individuals (solutions to the problem faced) are codified following a code similar to the genetic code of plants and animals. This population of solutions is evolved (modified) over a certain number of generations (iterations) until the defined stop criterion is fulfilled. Each individual is assigned a real value that measures its ability to solve the problem, which is called its *fitness*.

In each iteration, new solutions are obtained combining two or more individuals (crossover operator) or randomly modifying one individual (mutation operator). After applying these two operators a subset of individuals is selected to survive to the next generation, either by sampling the current individuals with a probability proportional to their fitness, or by selecting the best ones (elitism). The repeated processes of crossover, mutation and selection are able to obtain increasingly better solutions for many problems of Artificial Intelligence. For the evolution of the population, we have used the CHC algorithm. The algorithm optimizes row and columns separation. We will refer to these codes as CHC codes throughout the paper for brevity's sake.

This method is able to achieve very good matrices in terms of our two objectives, and also showed better results than other optimization algorithms we tried. Figure 1 shows the results for the four sizes of code length and both types of codes, random and CHC. For problems with few classes, the experiments are done up to the maximum length available. For instance, glass dataset has 6 classes, which means that for dense codes we have 31 different columns, so for this problem only codes of 30 bits are available and it is not included in this comparison.

The figure shows two interesting results. Firstly, we can see that the increment in the size of the codewords has the effect of improving the accuracy of the classifier. However, the effect is less marked as the codeword is longer. In fact, there is almost no differences between a codeword of 100 bits and a codeword of 200 bits. Secondly, regarding the effect of error correcting capabilities, there is a general advantage of CHC codes, but the differences are not very marked. In general, we can consider that a code of 100 bits is enough, as the improvement of the error using 200 bits is hardly significant, and the added complexity important.

Allwein et al. (2000) proposed sparse *ecoc* codes, where 0's are allowed in the columns, meaning "don't care". It is interesting to show whether the same pattern observed for dense codes, is also present in sparse codes. In order to test the behavior of sparse codes, we have performed the same experiment as for dense codes, that is, random and CHC codes of 30, 50, 100 and 200 bits and C.45 as base learner. Figure 2 shows the testing error results. For sparse codes we have more columns available (see Table 1), so all the datasets with 6 classes or more are included in the experiments.

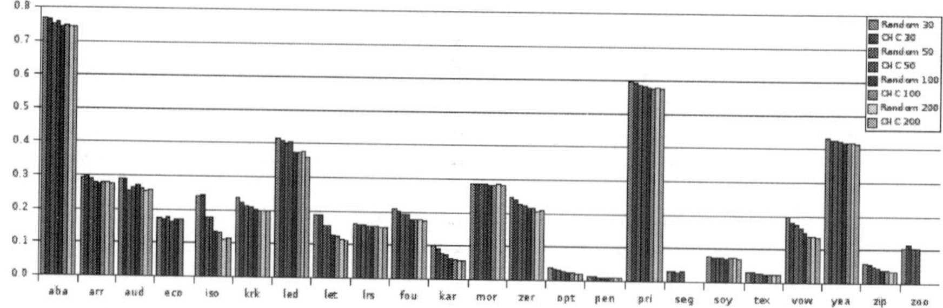

Fig. 1. Error values for *ecoc* dense codes using codewords of 30, 50, 100 and 200 bits and a C4.5 tree as base learner.

As a general rule, the results are similar, with the difference that the improvement of large codes, 100 and 200 bits, over small codes, 30 and 50 bits, is more marked than for dense codes. The figure also shows that the performance of both kind of codes, dense and sparse, is very similar. It is interesting to note that Allwein et al. (2000) suggested codes of $\lfloor 10\log_2(K)\rfloor$ bits for dense codes and of $\lfloor 15\log_2(K)\rfloor$ bits for sparse codes, being K the number of classes. However, in our experiments it is shown that these values are too small, as longer codes are able to improve the results of codewords of that length.

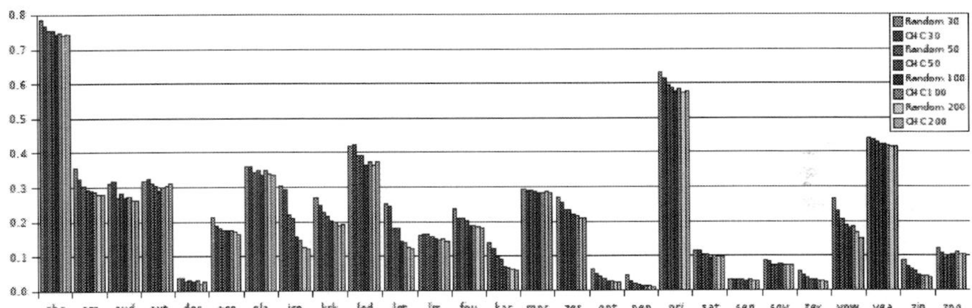

Fig. 2. Error values for *ecoc* sparse codes using codewords of 30, 50, 100 and 200 bits and a C4.5 tree as base learner.

We measure the independence of the classifiers using Yule's Q statistic. Classifiers that recognize the same patterns will have positive values of Q, and classifiers that tend to make mistakes in different patterns will have negative values of Q. For independent classifiers the expectation of Q is 0. For a set of L classifiers we use an average value Q_{av}:

$$Q_{av} = \frac{2}{L(L-1)}\sum_{i=1}^{L-1}\sum_{k=i+1}^{L} q_{i,k},$$

(3)

where $q_{i,j}$ is the value of Q statistic between i and j classifiers which is given by:

$$q_{i,j} = \frac{N^{11}N^{00} - N^{01}N^{10}}{N^{11}N^{00} + N^{01}N^{10}},$$

(4)

where N^{11} means both classifiers agree and are correct, N^{00} means both classifiers agree and are wrong, N^{01} means classifier i is wrong and classifier j is right, and N^{10} means classifiers i is right and classifier j is wrong. In this experiment, we test whether constructing codewords with higher Hamming distances improves independence of the classifiers.

After these previous experiments, we consider that a CHC code of 100 bits can be considered representative of *ecoc* codes, as the improvement obtained with longer codes is not significant.

It is generally assumed that codes designed by their error correcting capabilities should improve the independence of the errors between the classifiers. In this way, their failure to improve the performance of random codes is attributed to the fact that more difficult dichotomies are induced. However, whether the obtained classifiers are more independent is not an established fact. In this experiment we study if this assumption of independent errors is justified.

For this experiment, we have used three base learners, C4.5 decision trees, neural networks and support vector machines. Figure 3 shows the average values of Q statistic for all the 27 datasets for dense and sparse codes using random and CHC codes in both cases. For dense codes, we found a very interesting result. Both types of codes achieve very similar results in terms of independence of errors, and CHC codes are not able to improve the independence of errors of random codes, which is probably one of the reasons why CHC codes are no better than random codes. This is in contrast with the general belief, showing that some of the assumed behavior of *ecoc* codes must be further experimentally tested.

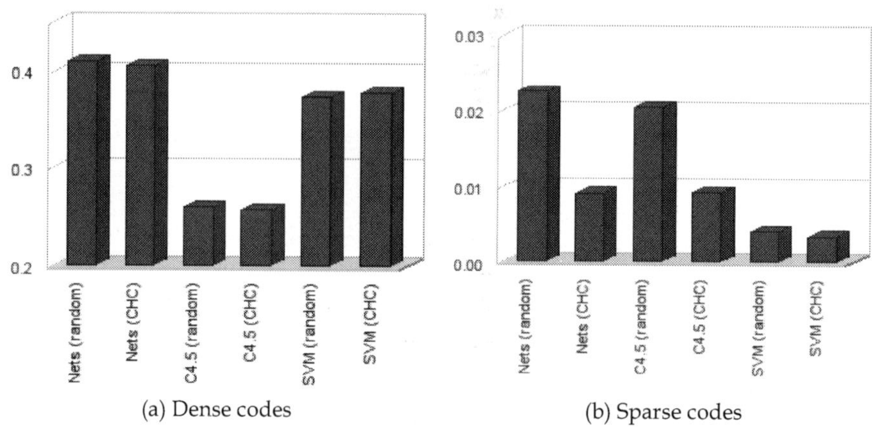

(a) Dense codes   (b) Sparse codes

Fig. 3. Average Q value for dense and sparse codes using three different base learners

The case for sparse codes is different. For these types of codes, CHC codes are significantly more independent for neural networks and C4.5. For SVM, CHC codes are also more independent although the differences are not statistically significant. The reason may be found in the differences between both types of codes. For dense codes, all the binary classifiers are trained using all the data, so although the dichotomies are different, it is more difficult to obtain independent classifiers as all classifiers are trained using the same data. On the other hand, sparse codes disregard the patterns of the classes which have a 0 in the corresponding column representing the dichotomy. CHC algorithm enforces column separation, which means that the columns have less overlapping. Thus, the binary classifiers induced by CHC matrices are trained using datasets that have less overlapping and can be less dependent.

So far we have studied *ecoc* method. The following experiment is devoted to the study of the other two methods: *ovo* and *ova*. The differences in performance between *ovo* and *ova* is a matter of discussion. We have stated that most works agree on a general advantage of *ovo*, but a careful study performed by Rifkin & Klautau (2004) has shown that most of the reported differences are not significant. In the works studied in that paper, the base learner was a support vector machine (SVM). As we are using a C4.5 algorithm, it is interesting to show whether the same conclusions can be extracted from our experiments. Figure 4 shows a comparison of results for the 41 tested datasets of the two methods. The figure shows for each dataset a point which reflects in the *x*-axis the testing error of *ovo* method, and in the *y*-axis the testing error of *ova* method. A point above the main diagonal means that *ovo* is performing better than *ova*, and vice versa. The figures shows a clear advantage of *ovo* method, which performs better than *ova* in 31 of the 41 datasets. The differences are also marked for many problems, as it is shown in the figure by the large separation of the points from the main diagonal. As C4.5 has no relevant parameters, the hypothesis of Rifkin & Klautau of a poor parameter setting is not applicable.

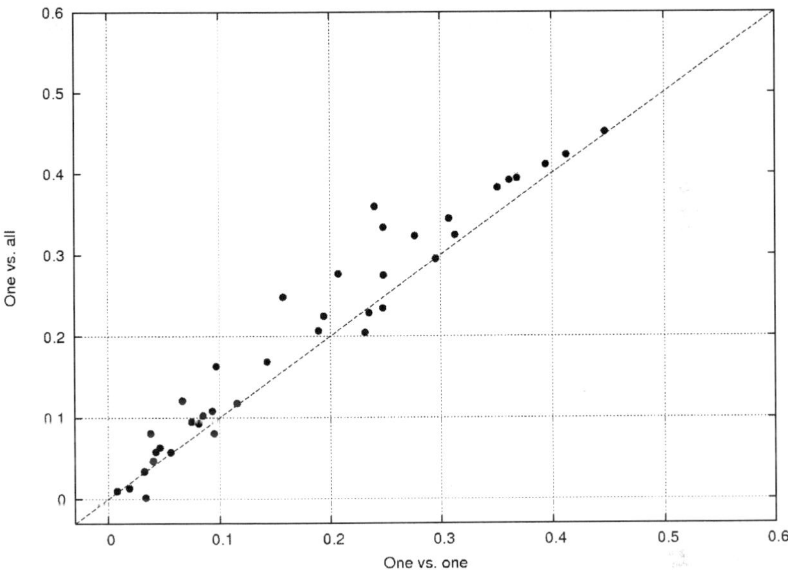

Fig. 4. Comparison of *ovo* and *ova* methods in terms of testing error.

In the previous experiments, we have studied the behavior of the different class binarization methods. However, there is still an important question that remains unanswered. There are many classification algorithms that can be directly applied to multiclass problems, so the obvious question is whether the use of *ova*, *ovo* or *ecoc* methods can be useful when a "native" multiclass approach is available. For instance, for C4.5 *ecoc* codes are more complex than the native multiclass method, so we must get an improvement from *ecoc* codes to overcome this added complexity. In fact, this situation is common with most classification methods, as a general rule class binarization is a more complex approach than the available native multiclass methods.

We have performed a comparison of *ecoc* codes using a CHC code of 100 *bits*, *ovo* and *ova* methods and the native multiclass method provided with C4.5 algorithm. The results are shown in Figure 5, for the 41 datasets.

The results in Figure 5 show that *ecoc* and *ovo* methods are able to improve native C4.5 multiclass method most of the times. In fact, *ecoc* method is better than the native method in all the 27 datasets. *ovo* is better than the native method in 31 out of 41 datasets. On the other hand, *ova* is not able to regularly improve the results of the native multiclass method. These results show that *ecoc* and *ovo* methods are useful, even if we have a native multiclass method for the classification algorithm we are using.

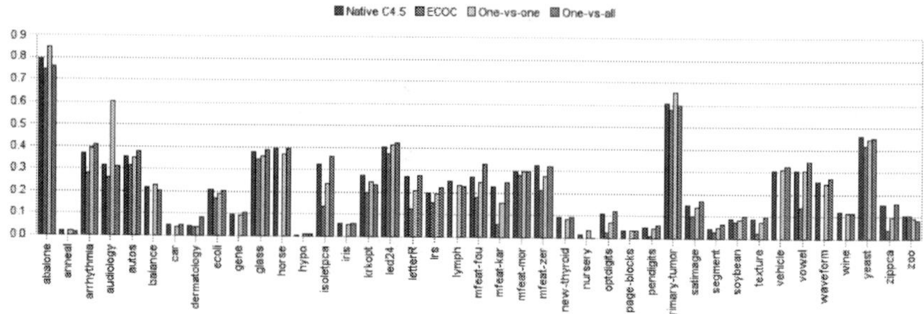

Fig. 5. Error values for *ovo*, *ova* and *ecoc* dense codes obtained with a CHC algorithm using codewords of 100 bits (or the longest available) and a C4.5 tree as base learner, and the native C4.5 multiclass algorithm.

Several authors have hypothesized that the lack of improvement when using codes designed by their error correcting capabilities over random ones may be due to the fact that some of the induced dichotomies could be more difficult to learn. In this way, the improvement due to a larger Hamming distance may be undermined by more difficult problems. In the same way, it has been said that *ovo* binary problems are easier to solve than *ova* binary problems. These two statements must be corroborated by the experiments.

Figure 6 shows the average generalization binary testing error of all the base learners for each dataset for random and CHC codes. As in previous figures a point is drawn for each

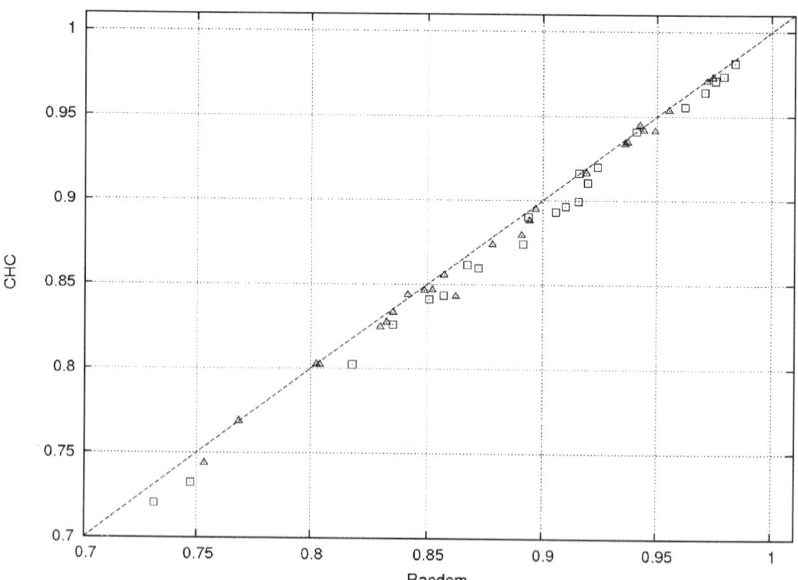

Fig. 6. Average generalization binary testing error of all the base learners for each dataset for random and CHC codes, using a C4.5 decision tree. Errors for dense codes (triangles) and sparse codes (squares).

dataset, with error for random codes in x-axis and error for CHC codes in y-axis. The figure shows the error for both dense and sparse codes. The results strongly support the hypothesis that the binary problems induced by codes designed by their error correcting capabilities are more difficult. Almost all the points are below the main diagonal, showing a general advantage of random codes. As the previous experiments failed to show a clear improvement of CHC codes over random ones, it is clear that the fact that the binary performance of the former is worse may be one of the reasons.

In order to assure the differences shown in the figure we performed a Wilcoxon test. The test showed that the differences are significant for both, dense and sparse codes, as a significance level of 99%.

In the same way we have compared the binary performance of *ovo* and *ova* methods. First, we must take into account that this comparison must be cautiously taken, as we are comparing the error of problems that are different. The results are shown in Figure 7, for a C4.5 decision tree, a support vector machine and a neural network as base learners.

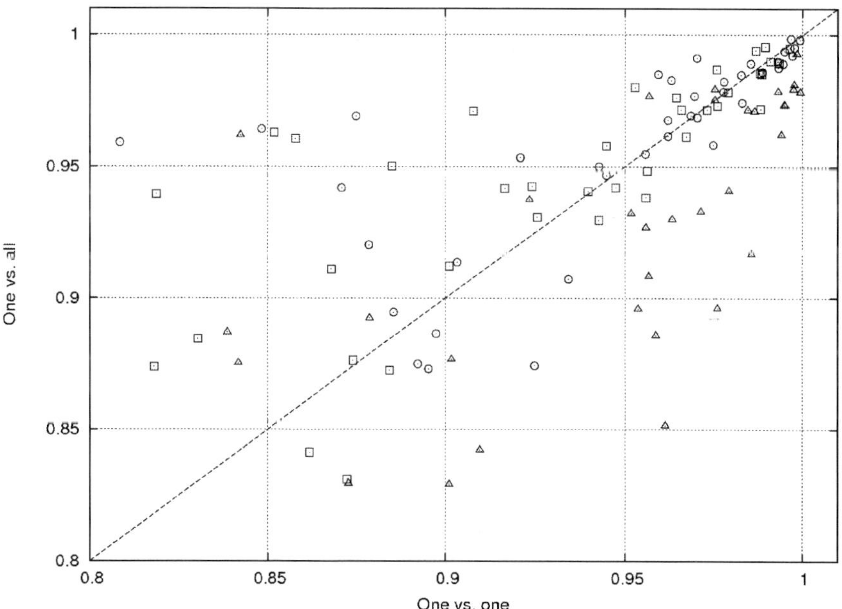

Fig. 7. Average generalization binary testing error of all the base learners for each dataset for *ovo* and *ova* methods, using a C4.5 decision tree (triangles), a support vector machine (squares) and a neural network (circles).

In this case, the results depend on the base learner used. For C4.5 and support vector machines, there are no differences, as it is shown in the figure and corroborated by Wilcoxon test. However, for neural networks the figure shows a clear smaller error of *ovo* method. The difference is statistically significant for Wilcoxon test at a significance level of 99%.

We must take into account that, although separating two classes may be easier than separating a class for all the remaining classes, the number of available patterns for the former problem is also lower than the number of available patterns for the latter. In this way, this last problem is more susceptible to over-fitting. As a matter of fact, binary classifiers training accuracy is always better for one-vs-one method. However, this problem does not appear when using a neural network, where one-vs-one is able to beat one-vs-all in terms of binary classifier testing error. As in previous experiments, C4.5 seems to suffer most from small training sets.

It is noticeable that for some problems, namely abalone, arrhythmia, audiology, and primary-tumor, the minimum testing accuracy of the binary classifiers for one-vs-one method is very low. A closer look at the results shows that this problem appears in datasets with many classes. For some pairs, the number of patterns belonging to any of the two classes is very low, yielding to poorly trained binary classifiers. These classifiers might also have a harmful effect on the overall accuracy of the classifier. This problem does not arise in one-vs-all methods, as all binary classifiers are trained with all the data.

7. Conclusions

In this chapter, we have shown the available methods to convert a k class problem into several two class problems. These methods are the only alternative when we use classification algorithms, such as support vector machines, which are specially designed for two class problems. But, even if we are dealing with a method that can directly solve multiclass problems, we have shown that a class binarization can be able to improve the performance of the native multiclass method of the classifier.

Many research lines are still open, both in the theoretical and practical fields. After some recent works on the topic (García-Pedrajas & Fyfe, 2008) (Escalera et al., 2008) it has been shown that the design of the *ecoc* codes and the training of the classifiers should be coupled to obtain a better performance. Regarding the comparison among the different approaches, there are still many open questions, one of the most interesting is the relationship between the relative performance of each method and the base learner used, as contradictory results have been presented depending on the binary classifier.

8. References

Allwein, E. L., Schapire, R. E. & Singer, Y (2000). Reducing multiclass to binary: A unifying approach for margin classifiers, *Journal of Machine Learning Research*, vol. 1, pp. 113-141.

Anand, R., Mehrotra, K. G., Mohan, C. K. & Ranka, S. (1992). Efficient classification for multiclass problems using modular neural networks, *IEEE Trans. Neural Networks*, vol. 6, pp. 117-124.

Bauer, E. & Kohavi, R. (1999). An Empirical Comparison of Voting Classification Algorithms: Bagging, Boosting, and Variants, *Machine Learning*, vol. 36, pp. 105-139.

Boser, B. E., Guyon, I. M. & Vapnik, V. N. (1992). A training algorithm for optimal margin classifiers, *Proceedings of the 5th Annual ACM Workshop on COLT*, pp. 144-152, D. Haussler, Ed.

Clark, P. & Boswell, R. (1991). Rule induction with CN2: Some recent improvements, *Proceedings of the 5th European Working Session on Learning (EWSL-91)*, pp. 151-163, Porto, Portugal, Spinger-Verlag.

Cohen, W. W. (1995). Fast effective rule induction, In: *Proceedings of the 12th International Conference on Machine Learning (ML-95)*, Prieditis A. & Russell, S. Eds., pp. 115-123, Lake Tahoe, CA, USA, 1995, Morgan Kaufmann.

Dietterich, T. G. & Bakiri, G. (1995). Solving multiclass learning problems via error-correcting output codes, *Journal of Artificial Intelligence Research*, vol. 2, pp. 263-286.

Demšar, J. (2006). Statistical Comparisons of Classifiers over Multiple Data Sets, *Journal of Machine Learning Research*, vol. 7, pp. 1-30.

Escalera, S., Tax, D. M. J., Pujol, O., Radeva, P. & Duin, R. P. W. (2008). Subclass Problem-Dependent Design for Error-Correcting Output Codes, *IEEE Trans. Pattern Analysis and Machine Intyelligence*, vol. 30, no. 6, pp. 1041-1054.

Fürnkranz, J. (2002). Round robin classification, *Journal of Machine Learning Research*, vol. 2, pp. 721-747.

García-Pedrajas, N. & Fyfe, C. (2008). Evolving output codes for multiclass problems, *IEEE Trans. Evolutionary Computation*, vol. 12, no. 1, pp. 93-106.

García-Pedrajas, N. & Ortiz-Boyer, D. (2006). Improving multiclass pattern recognition by the combination of two strategies, *IEEE Trans. Pattern Analysis and Machine Intelligence*, vol. 28, no. 6, pp. 1001-1006.

Hastie, T. & Tibshirani, R. (1998). Classification by pairwise coupling, *The Annals of Statistics*, vol. 26, no. 2. pp. 451-471.

Hsu, Ch.-W. & Lin, Ch.-J. (2002). A Comparison of methods for support vector machines, *IEEE Trans. Neural Networks*, vol. 13, no. 2, pp. 415-425.

James, G. M. (2003). Variance and bias for general loss functions, *Machine Learning*, vol. 51, no. 2, 115-135.

Kim, H. & Park, H. (2003). Protein secondary structure prediction based on an improved support vector machines approach, *Protein Engineering*, vol. 16, no. 8, pp. 553-560.

Knerr, S., Personnaz, L. & Dreyfus, G. (1990). Single-layer learning revisited: A stepwise procedure for building and training a neural network, In: *Neurocomputing: Algorithms, Architectures and Applications*, Fogelman, J. Ed., Springer-Verlag, New York.

Knerr, S., Personnaz, L. & Dreyfus, G. (1992). Handwritten digit recognition by neural networks with single-layer training, *IEEE Trans. Neural Networks*, vol. 3, no. 6, pp. 962-968.

Masulli, F. & Valentini, G. (2003). Effectiveness of error correcting output coding methods in ensemble and monolithic learning machines, *Pattern Analysis and Applications*, vol. 6, pp. 285-300.

Ortiz-Boyer, D., Hervás-Martínez, C. & García-Pedrajas, N. (2005). CIXL2: A crossover operator for evolutionary algorithms based on population features, *Journal of Artificial Intelligence Research*, vol. 24, pp. 33-80.

Passerini, A., Pontil, M. & Frasconi, P. (2004). New results on error correcting output codes of kernel machines, *IEEE Trans. Neural Networks*, vol. 15, no. 1, pp. 45-54.

Platt, J. C., Cristianini, N. & Shawe-Taylor, J. (2000). Large margin DAGs for multiclass classification, In: *Advances in Neural Information Processing Systems 12 (NIPS-99)*, Solla, S. A., Leen, T. K. & Müller, K.-R. Eds., pp. 547-553, MIT Press.

Pujol, O., Radeva, P. & Vitriá, J. (2006). Discriminant ECOC: A heuristic method for application dependent design of error correcting output codes, *IEEE Trans. Pattern Analysis and Machine Intelligence*, vol. 28, no. 6, pp. 1007- 1012.

Quinlan, J. R. (1993). *C4.5: Programs for Machine Learning*, Morgan Kaufmann, San Mateo, CA, USA.

Rifkin, R. & Klautau, A. (2004). In defense of one-vs-all classification, *Journal of Machine Learning Research*, vol. 5, pp. 101-141.

Schapire, R. E. (1997). Using output codes to boost multiclass learning problems, In: *Proceedings of the 14th International Conference on Machine Learning (ICML-97)*, Fisher, D. H. Ed., pp. 313-321, Nashville, TN, USA, 1997, Morgan Kaufmann.

Sejnowski, T. J. & Rosenberg, C. R. (1987). Parallel networks that learn to pronounce English text, *Journal of Complex Systems*, vol. 1, no. 1, pp. 145-168.

Windeatt, T. & Ghaderi, R. (2003). Coding and decoding strategies for multi-class problems, *Information Fusion*, vol. 4, pp. 11-21.

15

Activity Recognition Using Probabilistic Timed Automata

Lucjan Pelc[1] and Bogdan Kwolek[2]
[1]*State Higher Vocational School in Jarosław,*
[2]*Rzeszów University of Technology*
Poland

1. Introduction

Activity recognition focuses on what is happening in the scene. It endeavors to recognize the actions and goals of one or more actors from a sequence of observations both on the actor actions and the environmental conditions. Automated recognition of human activity is essential ability that may be used in the surveillance to provide security in indoor as well as outdoor environments. Understanding human activity is also important for human-computer-interaction systems including tele-conferencing and for content-based retrieval of video from digital repositories.

The main technique utilized in activity recognition is computer vision. In vision-based activity recognition, a great deal of work has already been done. This is partially due to increasing computational power that allows huge amount of video to be processed and stored, but also due to the large number of potential applications. In vision-based activity recognition, we can distinguish four steps, namely human detection, human tracking, human activity recognition and then a high-level activity evaluation.

A method of (Viola et al., 2003) detects a moving pedestrian in a temporal sequence of images. A linear combination of filters is applied to compute motion and appearance features that are then summed to determine a cumulative score, employed afterwards in a classification of the detection window as including the moving object. For vision based activity recognition, tracking is the fundamental component. The entity must be first tracked before the recognition can take place. Briefly, the goal of visual tracking is to find and describe the relative position change of the moving object from one frame to another in the whole sequence, while the task of action recognition is to classify the person's action given the person's location, recent appearance, etc. Kalman filters (Crowley & Berard, 1997; Kwolek, 2003) and particle filtering–based algorithms (Nait-Charif & McKenna, 2003) are utilized extensively for object tracking in this domain. These algorithms generally involve an object state transition model and an observation model, which reflect both motion and appearance of the object (Haykin & de Freitas, 2004). After tracking of the moving objects the action recognition stage occurs, where Dynamic Time Warping (Myers et al., 1980; Myers & Rabiner, 1981) and Hidden Markov Models (Brand & Kettnaker, 2000) are employed very often at this stage. Sophisticated stochastic models such as Dynamic Bayesian Networks (Albrecht et al., 1997; Ghahramani, 1997), Stochastic Context Free

Grammar (Pynadath et al., 1998), Probabilistic State Dependent Grammars (Pynadath et al., 2000), Abstract Hidden Markow Models (Bui et al., 2002), among others, were elaborated in order to represent high-level behaviors.

In this chapter, we focus on recognition of student activities during a computer-based examination where some knowledge about the layout of the scene is known. One characteristic of such activities is that they exhibit some specific motion patterns. The recognition is done on the basis of coordinates of the tracked heads, the activated activity areas and the probabilistic timed automata.

2. Relevant work

In the past decade, there has been intensive research in designing algorithms for tracking humans and recognizing their actions. An overview of work related to modeling and recognizing people's behaviors, particularly largely structured behaviors, can be found in work (Aggarwal & Cai, 1999). A more recent survey on recognizing of behaviors in surveillance images can be found in (Hu et al., 2004). There is now a rich literature on vision based action recognition. In this section, we focus on approaches and applications that are closely related to our work.

In work of (Rota & Thonnat, 2003), the video interpretation encompasses incremental recognition of scene states, scenarios and behaviors, which are described in a declarative manner. A classical constraint satisfaction algorithm called Arc Consistency-4 or AC4, is utilized to reduce the computation time for the process of recognizing such activities. The system described in work (Madabhushi & Aggarwal, 2000) is capable to recognize activities using head movement. The system is able to recognize 12 activities based on nearest neighbor classification. The activities include: standing up, sitting down, bending down, getting up, etc. A recognition rate about of 80% has been reported in this work.

The Finite State Machine (FSM) to model high-level activities has been used in work (Ayers & Shah, 2001). However, the approach presented in the mentioned work does not account for uncertainty in the model. State machine-based representations of behaviors have also been utilized in work (Bremond & Medioni, 1998), where deterministic automata in order to recognize airborne surveillance scenarios with vehicle behaviors in aerial imagery have been employed. Non-deterministic finite automaton has been employed in work (Wada & Matsuyama, 2000) as a sequence analyzer. An approach for multi-object activity recognition based on activity driven selective attention has been proposed. Bayesian networks and probabilistic finite-state automata were used to describe single-actor activities in work (Hongeng et al. 2004). The activities are recognized on the basis of the characteristics of the trajectory and the shape of the moving blob of the actor. The interaction between multiple actors was modeled by an event graph.

Recognition of mutual interactions between two pedestrians at blob level has been described in work (Sato & Aggarval, 2004). Most of the research connected with recognition of human interactions considers multiple-person interactions in remote scenes at a coarse level, where each person is represented as a single moving box. An extension of Hidden Markov Models, called Behavior Hidden Markov Models (BHMMs) has been presented in work (Han & Veloso, 1999) in order to describe behaviors and interactions in a robot system. Using such a representation an algorithm for automatically recognizing behaviors of single robots has been described too.

Hidden Markow Models (HMMs) are popular state-based models. In practice, only the observation sequence is known, while the underlying state sequence is hidden, which is why they are called Hidden Markov Models. HMMs have been widely employed to represent temporal trajectories and they are especially known for their application in temporal pattern recognition. A HMM is a kind of stochastic state machines (Brand et al., 1997), which changes its state once *every* time unit. However, unlike finite state machines, they are not deterministic. A finite state machine emits a deterministic symbol in a given state. It then deterministically transitions to another state. HMMs do neither deterministically, rather they both transition and emit under a probabilistic model. Its use consists in two stages, namely, training and recognition. HMM training stage involves maximizing the observed probabilities for examples belonging to a class. In the recognition stage, the probability with which a particular HMM emits the test symbol sequence corresponding to the observations is computed. However, the amount of data that is required to train a HMM is typically very large. In addition, the number of states and transitions can be found using a guess or trial and error and in particular, there is no general way to determine this. Furthermore, the states and transitions depend on the class being learnt. Despite such shortcomings the HMMs are one of the most popular algorithms employed in recognition of actions.

In our previous work related to action recognition, we presented a timed automata based approach for recognition of actions in meeting videos (Pelc & Kwolek, 2006). Timed automata are finite state machines extended about possibility for modelling of the behavior of real-time systems over time (Alur & Dill, 1994). A declarative knowledge provided graphically by the user together with person positions extracted by a tracking algorithm were used to generate the data for recognition of actions. The actions were formally specified as well as recognized using the timed automata.

In this chapter, we present a system for recognition of high-level behaviors of people in complex laboratory environments. The novelty of the presented approach is in the use of probabilistic timed automata (PTA). The probabilistic timed automata can model state-dependent behaviors, and with the support of time, probabilistic inference of high-level behaviors from low-level data. The PTA-based recognition module of behaviors takes sequences of coordinates of observed heads that are determined by the tracking module. Some declarative knowledge that has been specified graphically in advance by the system supervisor together with such coordinates is utilized to prepare the input data for the automata recognizing behaviors under uncertainty. The system also recognizes person-to-person interactions, which in our student examination scenario are perceived as not allowed behaviors.

3. Vision-based person tracking

Vision-based recognition of human activities involves extraction of relevant visual information, representation that information from the point of view of learning and recognition, and finally interpretation and evaluation of activities to be recognized. Image sequences consist of huge quantity of data in which the most relevant information for activity recognition is contained. Thus, the first step in activity recognition is to extract the relevant information in the form of movement primitives. Typically, this is achieved through vision-based object detection and tracking.

Tracking and activity recognition are closely related problems. A time series, which has been extracted by an object tracker provides a descriptor that can be used in a general recognition framework. Robust detection and tracking of moving objects from an image sequence is a substantial key for reliable activity recognition. Much tracking methods can be applied in scenarios with simple backgrounds and constant lighting conditions. Unfortunately, in real scenarios only occasionally do such situations arise. Typically, tracking requires consideration of complicated environments with difficult visual scenarios, under varying lighting conditions.

The shape of the head is one of the most effortlessly recognizable human parts and can be sufficiently well approximated by an ellipse. Its shape undergoes relatively little changes in comparison to changes of the human silhouette. In our scenario the position of the head is very useful because on the basis of its location we can recognize the actions consisting in looking at the terminal of a neighboring student. Moreover, on the basis of the location of the head we can determine the person's movement through the scene and in consequence we can recognize several actions like entering the scene, leaving the scene, standing up, sitting down, using a computer terminal, and so on.

The participant undergoing tracking can make rotations of both his/her body and head and thus the actions should be identified in either the frontal and lateral view. This implies that the usage of only color information for person tracking in long image sequences can be infeasible. In work (Kwolek, 2004) it has been demonstrated a tracker that has proven to be very useful in long-term tracking of people attending a meeting. This particle filter based tracker is built on gradient, color and stereovision. Human face is rich both in details and texture and consequently the depth map covering a face region is usually dense. The algorithm can track a person's head with no user intervention required. More importantly, this algorithm is efficient enough to allow real-time tracking on typical 850 MHz personal computer with PIII. It can accurately track in real-time multiple subjects in most situations. The detection of person entrance has also been done on the basis of the head. The entering and leaving the scene by participants of the exam is detected in entry and exit zones on the basis of method described in (Kwolek, 2005). Assuming that the person's head is relatively flat and that the entrance should be done at some distance from the camera we can suppress pixels not belonging to the person.

4. Activity recognition using probabilistic timed automata

4.1 The problem

The aim of the system is to recognize activities as well as to detect abnormal activities (suspicious and forbidden) that can take place during examination of the students. During the exam the students solve individually some tasks using computers and the collaboration between students is not permitted. In other words, each student should solve his/her task one-self, without looking into the computer screen of the neighbor. During the unaided work the student must not change workplace and take an empty workplace, and particularly, crib another student's solution from the computer screen, if such a student temporally left his/her workplace in order to pass the oral part of the exam in another part of the laboratory or lecturer's room. Additionally, the system should recognize the start as well as the end of the activities in order to record the corresponding key-frames.

Figure 1 depicts a scene that has been shot in a typical laboratory environment. The rectangles that are overlaid on the image are employed in detection of activity areas in order to pre-segment low-level data for recognition. In work (Pelc & Kwolek, 2006) the timed automata were used in action recognition and a person was required to continuously occupy positions within rectangular activity areas for specified in advance time intervals. It this work, the probabilistic timed automata are employed to model state-dependent activities, and with the support of time, to perform probabilistic inference of high-level behaviors from low-level data. The activity recognition under uncertainty is done on the basis of sequences of head coordinates. Some declarative knowledge in form of rectangular areas that can be activated together with such coordinates is utilized to pre-segment the input data for the automata. The system recognizes also person-to-person interactions, which in our student examination scenario are perceived as not allowed behaviors.

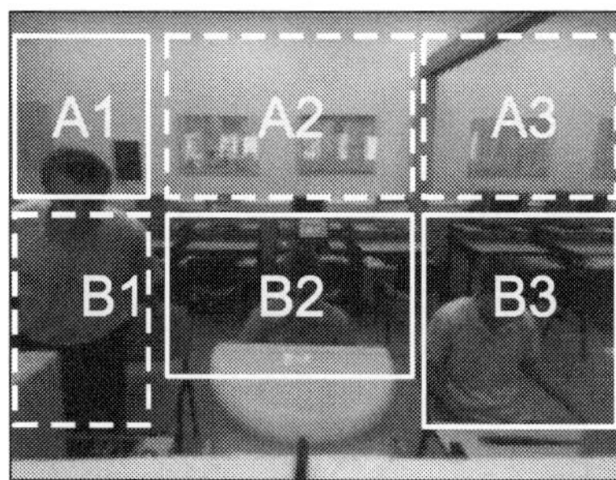

Fig. 1. A view of the scene from the camera

Using probabilistic timed automata the system recognizes the following activities:
- A_Work – work of the examined student,
- A_PartialC – partial collaboration of two students,
- A_FullC – full collaboration of two students,
- A_Suspicious – suspicious action of a student,
- A_Forbidden – forbidden action of a student.

As we already mentioned above, the system determines also both the start and the end of such activities in order to record some important key-frames. A more precise explanation of actions to be recognized will be given in the remaining subsections in coherence with description of automata.

4.2 Probabilistic timed automata

A description of probabilistic timed automata can be found in (Alur and Dill, 1994; Kwiatkowska et al., 2004). It is worth to note that the probabilistic timed automaton can be represented via a directed graph. In such a graph-based representation the nodes stand for the states, whereas the edges are labeled by actions. Time domain is represented by positive integer values. The variables of such a type are called clocks. They are employed to formulate state invariants and guards for the edges. After transition along an edge the clocks can be reset. In order to express probabilities the edges can be forked and they can connect more than two states. The state that will be reached by the automata after performing the action connected with the edges depends on the probability (assuming positive real values) of the given transition. Figure 2. depicts an example of elementary probabilistic timed automaton. This automaton consists of:
- two states: State0 and State1, and one clock t,
- two state invariants: $t \leq T$ and true, respectively, where T is some integer parameter assuming positive values, whereas true means that the invariant is always satisfied,

- one action: a,
- one guard of the action: $t{\geq}T$,
- reset function of the clock, $t{:=}0$,
- probabilities of the transitions: p and $1{-}p$.

At the beginning the automaton is in the state State0 and it can occupy this state for a period of time not longer than T. If in a period of time T an action a occurs, then automaton may change its state. The moment of the transition is determined by the guard $t{\geq}T$, which together with the initial state invariant determines the moment of the transition. The automaton makes the transition that has been caused by the action a and resets the clock t. The automaton may transit to State1, what occurs with probability equal to p or remain in the state State0, what occurs with the probability $1{-}p$.

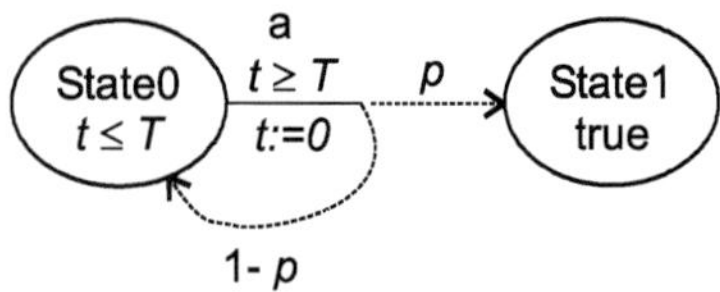

Fig. 2. Example of an elementary probabilistic timed automaton

It is worth to note that the passage of time is an action itself.

4.3 PTA-based action recognition

The PTA-based action recognition is done on the basis of four different concurrent automata, which synchronize themselves if needed. The aim of the automata is to recognize the following actions:

- PTA_ElementaryActionPx - recognition of an elementary action of the person Px,
- PTA_ActionWorkPx – recognition of action A_Work of person Px,
- PTA_Interact – recognition of collaboration between persons and recognition of actions not allowed: A_PartialC, A_FullC, A_Suspicious, A_Forbidden,
- PTA_StartEnd – determination of the start, the end as well as persistence of the actions undergoing recognition.

For each person the system activates separate instances of the automaton PTA__ElementaryActionPx, where x assumes values 1, 2 and 3.

In description of the PTA-based action recognition that follows in four subsequent subsections we utilize the following notation:

- names of the automata begin with PTA_, for example PTA_Interact,
- actions recognized by the system begin with A_, for example, action work is denoted as A_Work,
- actions moving an automaton from one state to another are denoted by names, which begin with a_, for example, the action connected with a step of computation is denoted by a_step,
- names of the states of the automata begin with S_, for example, in case of recognition of the action A_Work the state of the automaton PTA_ActionWorkPx is denoted as S_Work.

The system recognizes 48 actions, including actions listed in Section 4.2. Such a set of actions consists of 8 basic actions, 8 elementary actions and 4 auxiliary actions for each basic action, see Table 1.

Type of action	Denotation	Description
Basic actions	A_NWork	no work
	A_PWork	probable work
	A_Work	work
	A_NoC	no collaboration
	A_PartialC	partial collaboration
	A_FullC	full collaboration
	A_Suspicious	suspicious action
	A_Forbidden	forbidden action
Elementary actions	A_Desk1, ..., A_Desk3	Standing at workplace 1, 2, 3, respectively
	A_Outside	Person is outside of the camera's field of view
	A_Chair1, ..., A_Chair3	Seating at workplace 1, 2, 3, respectively
	A_Move	Moving between workplaces
Auxiliary actions	A_Start_A_NWork, ... A_Start_A_Forbidden	Start of basic action A_NWork, ..., A_Forbidden, respectively
	A_During_A_NWork, ... A_During_A_Forbidden	Persistence of basic action A_NWork, ..., A_Forbidden, respectively
	A_End_A_NWork, ... A_End_A_Forbidden	End of basic action A_NWork, ..., A_Forbidden, respectively
	A_No_A_NWork, ... A_No_A_Forbidden	Lack of basic action A_NWork, ..., A_Forbidden, respectively

Table 1. Statement of actions that are recognized by the system

4.3.1 Automaton PTA_ElementaryActionPx

The automaton PTA_ElementaryActionPx is designated for recogniton of elementary actions, which are listed in Table 1. It is depicted in a simplified form in Fig. 3.

The detection of an elementary action is connected with reaching by the automaton of the suitable state. The states, except the states S_Outside and S_Move, are connected with the presence of the person in the suitable rectangular area depicted in Fig. 1. Table 2 lists the connections between the active areas, the states of the automaton PTA_ElementaryActionPx, and the recognized elementary actions.

The state S_Move reflects the absence of a person in the assumed activity areas of the scene, see Fig. 1. In such a situation we assume that a person moves between the workplaces. The state S_Outside is reached when a person is out of the camera's field of view.

From the analysis of the automaton shown in Fig. 3 we can notice that the PTA-based activity recognizer detects entry and exit to/from the activity areas of the scene depicted in Fig. 1. For example, the entry event into the area A1 in the Fig. 1, and then exit from this area is connected with action (edge) a_dk1_on, which transits the automaton to state S_Desk1, and after that the action a_dk1_off deriving the automaton from that state, see Fig. 3. Analogously, for the area A2 it would be a_dk2_on and a_dk2_off, whereas for the area B1 (S_Chair1 in automaton) a_ch1_on and a_ch1_off, and so on.

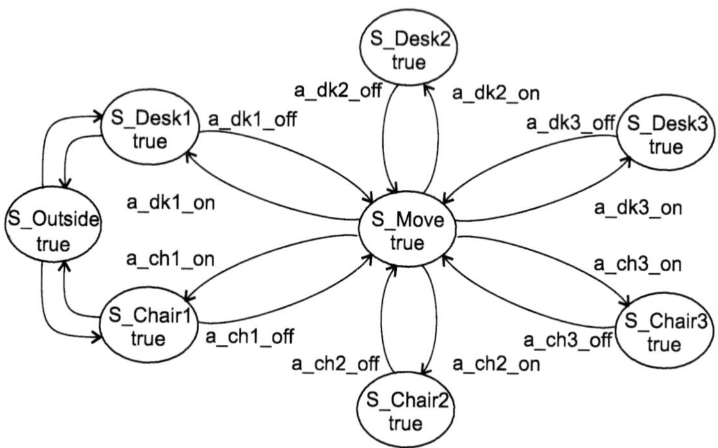

Fig. 3. The automaton for recognition of elementary actions

Area of scene	State of the automaton PTA_ElementaryActionPx	The recognized elementary actions
A1	S_Desk1	A_Desk1
A2	S_Desk2	A_Desk2
A3	S_Desk3	A_Desk3
B1	S_Chair1	A_Chair1
B2	S_Chair2	A_Chair2
B3	S_Chair3	A_Chair3

Table 2. Connections between the active areas, the states of the automaton PTA_ElementaryActionPx, and the recognized elementary actions

4.3.2 Automaton PTA_ActionWorkPx

The action A_Work can be recognized with some likelihood. The system activates separate instances of the automaton PTA_ActionWorkPx for each person Px. Let us consider the person P1 acting in front of the area B1. The smaller number of times the area B1 has been left by the person in time Tw, and at the same time, the smaller was his/her total time of staying outside B1, the greater the likelihood is, that the person P1 is working. Time Tw stands for minimal time that should elapse between the entry and the exit of the workplace to indicate that activity relying on work has been started.

The automaton PTA_ActionWorkPx is shown at Fig. 4 (for clarity of presentation some less important details have been omitted). It consists of the following states:

S_NWork – the considered person is not working,

S_PWork – it is possible that the considered person is working,

S_Work – the considered person is working.

In case the automaton PTA_ActionWorkPx has synchronized with the suitable automata, then attaining by it the state S_NWork is equivalent with recognition by the system the action A_NWork. Analogous relationship is between S_PWork and A_PWork, S_Work and A_Work, see also Tab. 1.

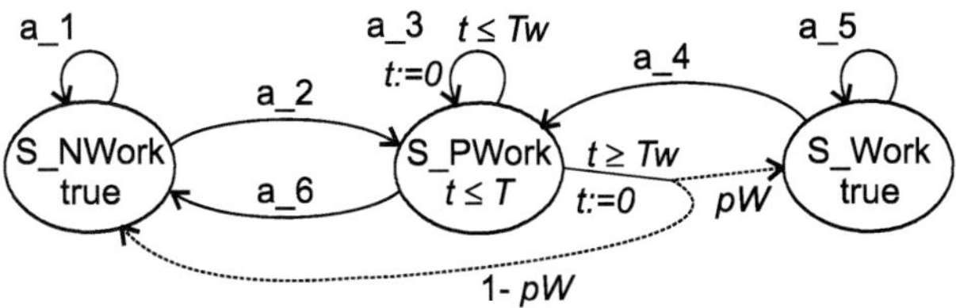

Fig. 4. Automaton PTA_ActionWorkPx

Let us assume, that the person P1 is doing alternately the actions A_Chair1 (area B1 in Fig. 1) and A_Move (outside B1). Such a probable work will be recognized as action A_PWork. In dependence of how the transitions frequent are, as well as how long they appeared in total according to time Tw, the person P1 may in consequence either work with the probability pW, what exemplifies the action A_Work, or may not work, what exemplifies the action A_NWork with probability 1-pW.

The probability pW has been determined as follows:

$$pW = w \cdot pWt + (1 - w) \cdot pWn \qquad (1)$$

where w denotes a weight that can assume values between 0 and 1.0, pWt stands for probability resulting from the summed time of temporal absences in the area Bx, see Fig. 1, pWn is a probability resulting from the number of the mentioned above absences in period of time Tw.

Figure 5a illustrates the method of determining the probability pWt. Let us denote by tn the summed time of the absence in the period of time Tw. Then

$$pWt = \begin{cases} 1\text{-}(1/Tmax) \cdot tn & \text{for } 0 \leq tn \leq Tmax \\ 0 & \text{for } tn > Tmax \end{cases} \qquad (2)$$

where $Tmax$ denotes maximal admissible sum of temporal absences at the workplace. The value of time $Tmax$ must be less than the value Tw.

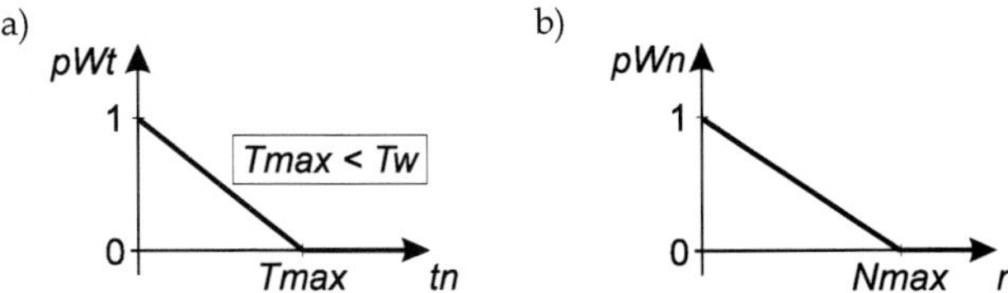

Fig. 5. The probability functions: a) pWt, b) pWn

Figure 5b illustrates the method of computation of the probability pWn. Let us denote by n the number of absences at workplace in the period of time Tw. Then

$$pWn = \begin{cases} 1\text{-}(1/Nmax)\cdot n & \text{for } 0 \leq n \leq Nmax \\ 0 & \text{for } n > Nmax \end{cases} \tag{3}$$

where $Nmax$ stands for maximal admissible number of absences in the workplace during time period equal to Tw.

In the sequel we explain actions of the automaton PTA_ActionWorkPx in the context of the remaining automata. The meaning of actions a_1, ..., a_6 depicted in Fig. 4, under assumption that they were done by person P1, is as follows:

- a_1 – will occur, if at the moment of occurrence of action a_step the automaton PTA_ElementaryActionPx is in other state than S_Chair1, what means that the considered person P1 is not seating at his/her workplace,
- a_2 – will occur, if at the moment of occurrence of action a_step the automaton PTA_ElementaryActionPx is in state S_Chair1, what means that the considered person is seating at his/her workplace,
- a_3 – will take place, if at the moment of occurrence of action a_step the automaton PTA_ElementaryActionPx is in the state S_Chair1 or S_Move, in other words, the considered person seats at his/her workplace, and from time to time the person lefts it temporary. Because of the guard $t<Tw$, the mentioned behavior can only take time shorter than Tw.
- a_4 – analogously to the action a_1, likewise, the action a_5 is analogous to action a_2,
- a_6 – will occur, if the action a_step is occurring and the automaton PTA_ElementaryActionPx is not neither in the state S_Chair1 nor S_Move,
- $t{\geq}Tw$ – action connected with passage of time.

4.3.3 Automaton PTA_Interact

As we already mentioned in Section 4.1 the system should recognize the activity A_Work as well as the following activities:

- Partial collaboration – A_PartialC,
- Full collaboration – A_FullC,
- Suspicious action – A_Suspicious,
- Forbidden action – A_Forbidden.

Below is a more detailed description of assumed conditions that are used in process of the recognition of the listed above activities.

1. If two persons work, then with the probability of 10% they collaborate each other and in consequence the action A_PartialC takes place.
2. If A_PartialC took place and the considered persons still work together, then the probability of persistence of the collaboration is 50%.
3. If the neighboring persons collaborate each other and one of them looks at the screen of one of the neighbors, then with the probability of 90% the action A_FullC occurs.
4. If a person is not present at his/her workplace, and another person Px is present at his/her workplace, then Px makes the suspicious action denoted as A_Suspicious.
5. If the action A_Suspicious extends in time, for time not longer than some assumed value ta, then the person Px makes forbidden action denoted as A_Forbidden.

Figure 6 illustrates a part of the automaton PTA_Interact for recognition of collaboration between P1 and P2. The state S_NoC stands for no collaboration.

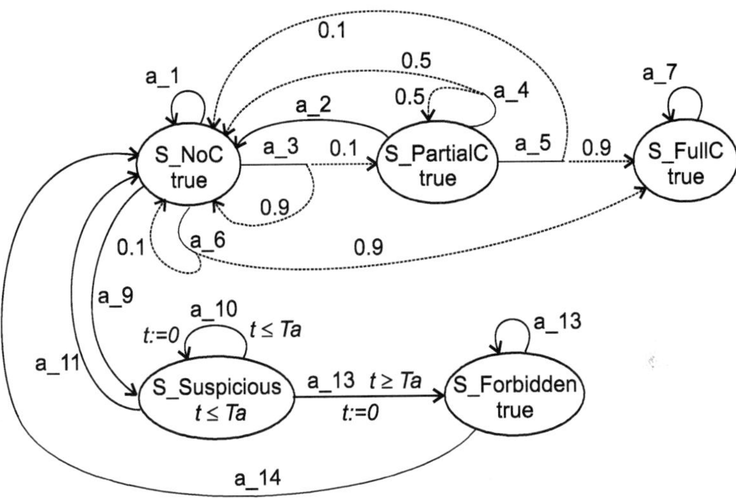

Fig. 6. Automaton PTA_Interact

The meaning of actions depicted in Fig. 6 is as follows:

- a_1 – the automata PTA_ActionWorkP1 and PTA_ActionWorkP2 are not simultaneously in the states S_Work,
- a_2, a_8 – similar meaning with a_1,
- a_3 – the automata PTA_ActionWorkP1 and PTA_ActionWorkP2 are simultaneously in the states S_Work,
- a_4, a_7 – similar meaning with a_3,
- a_5 – the automata PTA_ActionWorkP1 and PTA_ActionWorkP2 are simultaneously in the states S_Work, and additionally, the automaton PTA_ElementaryActionP1 is in the state S_Char2 or the automaton PTA_ElementaryActionP2 is in the state S_Char1,
- a_6 – similar meaning with a_5,
- a_9 – the automaton PTA_ElementaryActionP1 is in the state S_Char2, whereas the automaton PTA_ElementaryActionP2 is in the state S_Outside,
- a_10 – similarly to a_9, but the time of being in the state S_Suspicious is shorter than an assumed value Ta,
- a_11, a_14 – have a sense similar with the negation of the action a_9,
- a_12 – similarly to a_10, but time Ta elapsed,
- a_13 – similar meaning with a_9.

For the remaining persons the rest of the automaton will be analogous.

4.3.4 Automaton PTA_SartEnd

The automaton consists of four states for each basic action recognized by the system, see also Tab. 1. The first state is reached when the suitable action begins, the second one is when the action is in progress, the third one is reached when the action ends, whereas the fourth state exemplifies no action. The transitions between the mentioned states depend on the suitable states. The discussed automaton is employed in recording of the key-frames of the video.

4.4 Realization of the activity recognizer in PRISM

PRISM (Kwiatkowska et al., 2006) is a verifier of probabilistic, stochastic and non-deterministic automata. This tool has no built-in support for expressing the elapse of time in the probabilistic automata, i.e. it has no support for constructing probabilistic timed automata. In our PTA-based based system for activity recognition an event-based approach has been used to express the elapse of time. This allowed us to code the reachability graphs of our PTA-based activity recognizer for proper period of time. Such PRISM-based realization of the recognizer has been tested both on real data, i.e. from our tracker and on data obtained form a module modeling selected person activities. The module responsible for modeling the person activities is described below.

4.5 Simulations

For practical test of the formal model as well as simulation purposes we prepared models of the activities to be recognized. Such models of the person activities have a form of deterministic timed automata. The aim of the automata is to express real activities that can happen in our scenario. They are employed to generate the input data for the probabilistic timed automata responsible for activity recognition. Such an approach permits the analysis of the correctness of the recognition for typical activities. Furthermore, the simulation was helpful in tuning of the system through setting the values of parameters. In particular, owing to simulation experiments we chosen the following values of the parameters:

- the number and location of the activity areas,
- $Tmax$ - maximal admissible sum of temporal absences at the workplace,
- Tw - minimal time of being in workplace, that allows us to draw a conclusion that the person might begin his/her work,
- $Nmax$ - maximal admissible number of absences in the workplace during time period equal to Tw,
- w – weight in (1),
- Ta – minimal admissible time of being in another than the assigned workplace.

Our simulation experiments demonstrated that practical difficulties related to too small activity areas can be compensated through larger values of $Nmax$ and smaller values of the parameter w. Good choice of the mentioned parameters guarantees high recognition rate despite smaller activity areas. In case of not suspicious actions, a decrease of the size of activity areas leads to smaller efficiency of the recognition.

5. Experiments

The system for activity recognition has been tested both on simulated as well as real data that were provided by the person tracking module. The experiments demonstrated that the system correctly recognizes the activities described previously. Figure 7 shows example images with visualization of the recognition process. The dotted line illustrates the activity zones in which no person attendance (no head) has been recognized, solid line marks the activity zones in which presence of a person has been recognized, double line informs about attendance of two persons in a single activity zone, whereas the crossed zone notifies about a forbidden action.

At Fig. 7a we can observe person P1 inclining to person's P2 side. Because this activity persisted over sufficiently long time, the system recognized the full collaboration A_FullC between the person P1 and the person P2, what has been depicted via double line overlaid on the zone B2. At Fig. 7b a full collaboration between P2 and P3 has been depicted in a similar manner. Figure 7c illustrates a situation where the person P3, who should occupy only the workplace number 3 in the zone B3, changed workplace during absence of the person P2 and now occupies his/her workplace in zone B2. Because this action was sufficiently long the system recognized the action A_Forbidden, what has been visualized via crossing the zone B2.

a)   b)   c)

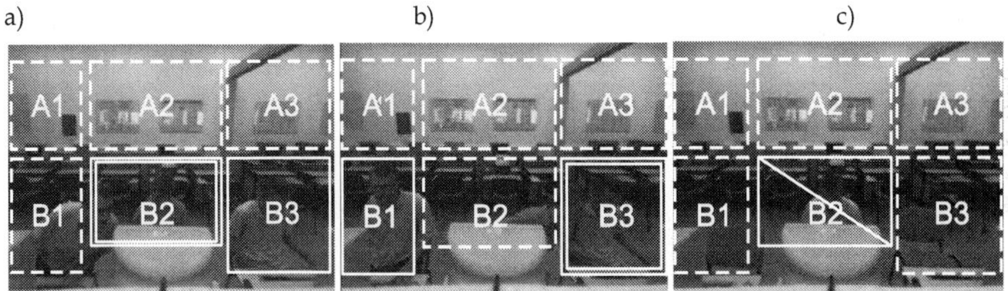

Fig. 7. Recognition of student activities during an exam, action A_FullC between P1 and P2 (a), and P2 and P3 (b), action A_Forbidden done by person P3 at workplace number 2 (c)

The images used in this work are 320 x 240 in size. They were acquired by commercial binocular Megapixel Stereo Head (Konolige, 1997). The stereo head is designed to operate with SRI's stereo engine for fast range determination on standard PC hardware. It delivers range and color images at frame rates 30 Hz with a PIII 750 MHz. Range is interpolated to 1/16 pixel, texture and consistency filters eliminate ambiguous areas in the range images. We decided to utilize stereo information in our head detection and tracking algorithm because of its usefulness in varying illumination conditions. Using it in the tracking algorithm we determine the length of the ellipse's minor axis approximating the oval shape of the head. The stereo information serves also as constraint region both in head detection and tracking.

By employing shape, color, stereovision as well as elliptical shape features our particle filter based tracker (Kwolek, 2004) can estimate the location of the person's head reliably. It is able to track the heads of persons over the whole image sequences of typical exam. Its robustness with respect to full 360-degree out-of-plane rotation, considerable head tilting, substantial but short in time head occlusions, moving people in background, as well as varying illumination conditions play very important role in the process of activity recognition without user intervention.

To test the activity recognition system, we have conducted several experiments in circumstances occurring naturally in laboratory. The aim of the experiments was to automatically detect the entrance of students into the exam, and then to track the heads. The videos as well as the 3D locations of the heads with the corresponding ellipse sizes were stored in files for further analysis. The activity recognition as well as visualization are done on the basis of such data.

6. Conclusions

We have developed a system for recognizing and monitoring human behaviors. It recognizes both single- and multiple actor activities. The approach is based upon probabilistic timed automata. The input data for the probabilistic timed automata are extracted via person's head tracker. By employing depth, color, as well as elliptical shape features the utilized particle filter tracks a head over a sequence of images and generates the trajectories of the head. Experimental results demonstrate the ability of the system to provide monitoring of high level behaviors in the student exam scenario. Given workplace - specific constraints, the system enabled the actions of working, collaborating, doing forbidden actions to be recognized. Although we only showed example in the context of the student exam, our system is capable to monitor a wide variety of events. One of the advantages of the presented approach is that it does not require a large amount of training data for recognition of activities at acceptable level.

7. References

Aggarwal, J. K., Cai, Q. (1999). Human motion analysis: A review, *Computer Vision and Image Understanding*, vol. 73, no. 3., pp. 428-440.

Albrecht, D., Zukerman, I., Nicholson, A. (1997). Bayesian models for keyhole plan recognition in an adventure game. *User Modelling and User-Adapted Interaction*, vol. 8, no. 1-2, pp. 5-47.

Alur, R., Dill, D. (1994). A theory of timed automata, *Theoretical Computer Science*, vol. 126, no. 2, pp. 183-235.

Ayers, D., Shah, M. (2001). Monitoring human behavior from video taken in an office environment, *Image and Vision Computing*, vol. 19, no. 12, pp. 833-846.

Brand, M., Oliver, N., Pentland, A. (1997). Coupled hidden Markov models for complex action recognition, In Proc. IEEE Conf. on Computer Vision and Pattern Rec., pp. 994-999.

Brand, M., Kettnaker, V. (2000). Discovery and segmentation of activities in video, *IEEE Trans. on Pattern Anal. Machine Intell.*, vol. 22, pp. 844-851.

Bremond, F., Medioni, G. (1998). Scenario recognition in airborne video imagery, In Proc. Int. Workshop on Interpretation of Visual Motion, pp. 57-64.

Bui, H. H., Venkatesh, S., West, G. (2002). Policy recognition in the Abstract Hidden Markov Model, *Journal of Artificial Intelligence Research*, vol. 17, pp. 451-499.

Crowley, J. L., Berard, F. (1997). Multi-modal tracking of faces for video communications, IEEE Conf. on Comp. Vision and Pattern Recognition, Puerto Rico, pp. 640-645.

Ghahramani, Z. (1997). Learning Dynamic Bayesian Networks, Lecture Notes in Computer Science, vol. 1387, pp. 168-197.

Han, K., Veloso, M. (2000). Automated robot behavior recognition applied to robotic soccer. In: J. Hollerbach and D. Koditschek (eds.), Robotics Research: the Ninth Int. Symposium, Springer-Verlag, pp. 199-204.

Hongeng, S., Nevatia, R., Bremond, F. (2004). Video-based event recognition: activity representation and probabilistic recognition methods, *Computer Vision and Image Understanding*, vol. 96, no. 2, pp. 129-162.

Hu, W., Tan, T., Wang, L., Maybank, S. (2004). A survey on visual surveillance of object motion and behaviors, *IEEE Trans. on Systems, Man, and Cybernetics*, Part C, vol. 34, no. 3, pp. 334-352.

Haykin, S., de Freitas, N. (eds.) (2004). Special Issue on Sequential State Estimation. *Proceedings of the IEEE*, vol. 92, no. 3, pp. 399-574.

Konolige, K. (1997). Small Vision System: Hardware and implementation, Proc. of Int. Symp. on Robotics Research, pp. 111-116.

Kwiatkowska, M., Norman, G., Sproston, J., Wang, F. (2004). Symbolic model checking for probabilistic timed automata, Joint Conf. on Formal Modelling and Analysis of Timed Systems (FORMATS) and Formal Techniques in Real-Time and Fault Tolerant Systems (FTRTFT), vol. 3253, Lectures Notes in Computer Science, Springer-Verlag, pp. 293-308.

Kwiatkowska, M., Norman, G., Parker, D. (2006). Performance analysis of probabilistic timed automata using digital clocks, *Formal Methods in System Design*, Springer, vol. 29, pp. 33-78.

Kwolek, B. (2003). Visual system for tracking and interpreting selected human actions, *Journal of WSCG*, vol. 11, no. 2, pp. 274-281

Kwolek, B. (2004). Stereovision-based head tracking using color and ellipse fitting in a particle filter, European Conf. on Comp. Vision, LNCS, vol. 3691, Springer, 2004, pp. 192–204.

Kwolek, B. (2005). Action recognition in meeting videos using head trajectories and fuzzy histogram, *Informatica*, Special Issue on Soft Computing in Multimedia Processing, vol. 29, pp. 281-289.

Madabhushi, A., Aggarwal, J. K. (2000). Using head movement to recognize activity, In Proc. of 15th Int. Conf. on Pattern Recognition, pp. 698-701.

Myers, C. S., Rabinier, L. R., Rosenberg, A. (1980). Performance tradeoffs in dynamic time warping algorithms for isolated word recognition, *IEEE Trans. on Acoustics, Speech, and Signal Processing*, vol. 28, no. 6, pp. 623-635.

Myers, C. S., Rabiner, L. R. (1981). A comparative study of several dynamic time-warping algorithms for connected word recognition, *The Bell System Technical Journal*, vol. 60, no. 7, pp. 1389-1409.

Nait-Charif, H., McKenna, S. J. (2003). Head tracking and action recognition in a smart meeting room, the IEEE Int. Workshop on Performance Evaluation of Tracking and Surveillance, Graz, Austria, pp. 24-31.

Pelc, L., Kwolek, B. (2006). Recognition of actions in meeting videos using timed-automata, *Machine Graphics and Vision*, vol. 15, no. 3-4, pp. 577-584

Pynadath, D. V., Wellman, M. P. (1998). Generalized queries on probabilistic context-free grammars. *IEEE Trans. on Pattern Analysis and Machine Intelligence*, vol. 20, no. 1, pp. 65–77.

Pynadath, D. V., Wellman, M. P. (2000). Probabilistic statedependent grammars for plan recognition. In Proc. of the 16th Annual Conf. on Uncertainty in Artificial Intelligence, San Francisco, CA, pp. 507–514.

Rota, N. A., Thonnat, M. (2002). Activity recognition from video sequences using declarative models, Proc. European Conf. on Artificial Intelligence, pp. 673-680.

Sato, K., Aggarval, J. K. (2004). Temporal spatio-velocity transform and its application to tracking and interaction, *Computer Vision and Image Understanding*, vol. 96, no. 2, pp. 100-128.

Viola, P., Jones, M., Snow, D. (2003). Detecting pedestrians using patterns of motion and appearance, *Int. J. of Computer Vision*, vol. 63, no. 2, pp. 153-161.

Wada, T., Matsuyama, T. (2000). Multi-object behavior recognition by event driven selective attention method, *IEEE Trans. on Pattern Anal. Machine Intelligence*, vol. 22, pp. 873-887.

16

Load Time-Series Classification Based on Pattern Recognition Methods

George J. Tsekouras[1-2], Anastasios D. Salis[2],
Maria A. Tsaroucha[2] and Irene S. Karanasiou[2]
[1]Hellenic Naval Academy,
[2]School of Electrical and Computer Engineering, National Technical University of Athens,
Greece

1. Introduction

1.1 Introduction to load time series classification

The formation of typical chronological load curves is an important tool of resolution of many problems in power systems, such as the short-term and medium-term load forecasting, the adaptation of customers' tariffs and the classification of electricity customers.

Classical indexes, like maximum power or load factor, can not describe the electricity behaviour of a customer or a power system thoroughly, as it can be comprehended from the example of Fig 1.1, where the customer of Fig 1.1(a) fatigues the power system's generators less than the customer of Fig 1.1(b) for the same peak load, load factor and power factor, because the number of the load demand changes are fewer. If an energy storage system is used, the second customer will need smaller battery system than the first one. These inferences cannot be drawn without the customers' load profiles.

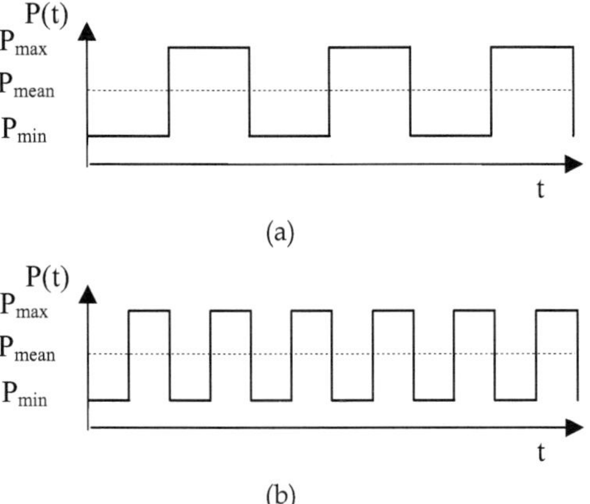

Fig. 1.1. Indicative load curves of electricity consumers with the same max load, load factor and power factor

In the case of short-term load forecasting the use of the typical days decreases the mean absolute percentage error, especially for anomalous days (i.e. holiday periods) (Chicco et al., 2001; Lamedica et al., 1996). Through this segmentation the load forecasting models are not misled by the respective load curves of last days in which more weight is usually given. Similarly the formation of typical chronological load curves and the corresponding diachronic development can be used for medium-term load forecasting (Al - Hamadi & Soliman, 2005), so that the maintenance of the units and electric network, the fuel supply, the electrical energy imports/exports and the exploitation of the water reserves for hydrothermal scheduling can be implemented.

In a deregulated electricity market, each supplier wishes to identify his customers' electricity behaviour accurately, in order to provide them with satisfactory services at a low cost, recovering the energy and power cost and having a fair profit. So the classification of electricity customers is a necessary stage. At the same time, each consumer wants to know his electricity behaviour, in order to select the proper tariff or to apply energy efficiency measures successfully. Taking into consideration the demand-side bidding in competitive markets (Task VIII of IEA, 2002) the accurate estimation of the next day's load profile is a fundamental requirement for each large customer, so that it can find the way to minimize its electricity bill.

During the last years, a significant research effort has been focused on load curves classification regarding the short-term load forecasting of anomalous days and the clustering of the customers of the power systems. The clustering methods have been used so far are:

- the "modified follow the leader" (Chicco et al., 2003a; -,2003b; -, 2004; -, 2006),
- the self-organizing map (Beccali et al., 2004; Chicco et al., 2004; -, 2006 ; Figueiredo et al., 2003; Lamedica et al. 1996; Verdu et al., 2003),
- the k-means (Chicco et al., 2006; Figueiredo et al., 2003),
- the average and Ward hierarchical methods (Chicco et al., 2004; -, 2006; Gerber et al., 2003) and
- the fuzzy k-means (Chicco et al., 2004; -, 2006; Gerber et al., 2003; -, 2004; -, 2005).

All the above methods generally belong to pattern recognition techniques (Theodoridis & Koutroumbas, 1999). Alternatively, classification problem can be solved by using data mining (Kitayama et al., 2003; Figueiredo et al., 2005), wavelet packet transformation (Petrescu & Scutariu, 2002), frequency-domain data (Carpaneto et al., 2006), stratified sampling (Chen et al., 1997). For the reduction of the size of the clustering input data set Sammon map, principal component analysis and curvilinear component analysis have been proposed (Chicco et al., 2006).

The respective adequacy measures that are commonly used are:

- the mean index adequacy (Chicco et al., 2003a; -, 2003b; -, 2004),
- the clustering dispersion indicator (Chicco et al., 2003a; -, 2003b; -, 2004; -, 2006),
- the similarity matrix indicator (Chicco et al., 2004),
- the Davies-Bouldin indicator (Beccali et al., 2004; Chicco et al., 2003; -, 2006; Gerbec et al., 2004; -, 2005),
- the modified Dunn index (Chicco et al., 2006),
- the scatter index (Chicco et al., 2006) and
- the mean square error (Gerbec et al., 2003; -, 2004; -, 2005).

In all cases analytical chronological load curves are required, which have resulted via suitable measurements or load surveys. The use of classification methods allow us to compress data information implementing the fundamental concepts of data mining and pattern recognition.

1.2 Why should load time-series classification be realized using unsupervised pattern recognition methods? What kind of problems are we going to meet?

According to R.O.Duda, P.E. Hart, D. G. Stock (Duda et al., 2001), it is known that *"pattern recognition"* is the act of taking in raw data and making an action based on the category of the pattern. Generally any method that incorporates information from training samples in the design of a classifier employs learning. There are three kinds of learning:

- *Supervised learning*, in which a category label or cost for each pattern is provided in a training set and the sum of these patterns should be minimized using methods based on Bayesian decision theory, maximum likelihood and Bayesian parameter estimation, multilayer neural networks, probabilistic neural network etc.
- *Unsupervised learning* or clustering, where there are no any a priori category labels for patterns and the pattern recognition system forms clusters - sets of the input patterns. Different clustering algorithms, such as self organizing map, adaptive vector quantization etc, lead to different clusters.
- *Reinforcement learning*, where no desired category signal is given, but the only feedback is that the specified category is right or wrong, without saying why it is wrong.

In our case the clusters of the load time-series are unknown. We do not know either the clusters, or their number. The danger of an inappropriate representation is big. In order to realize the categorization of the load time-series and to select the proper number of clusters we are going to study the behaviour of the adequacy measures, which show us when the proper number of clusters is determined. Other basic notions in our approach are the following:

- the modification of the clustering techniques for this kind of classification problem, such as the appropriate weights initialization for the k-means and fuzzy k-means;
- the proper parameters calibration, such as the training rate of mono-dimensional SOM, in order to fit the classification needs;
- the comparison of the performance of the clustering algorithms for each one of the adequacy measures;
- the introduction of the ratio of within cluster sum of squares to between cluster variation, which is first presented for this kind of classification.

1.3 Mathematical modeling of clustering methods and adequacy measures
1.3.1 General introduction

We assume that the classification of daily load curves is necessary using the proper pattern recognition method. Generally N is defined as the population of the input vectors, which are going to be clustered. The ℓ-th input vector is symbolized as follows:

$$\vec{x}_\ell = \left(x_{\ell 1}, x_{\ell 2}, \ldots x_{\ell i}, \ldots x_{\ell d} \right)^T \tag{1.1}$$

where d is its dimension, which equals to 96 or 24, if the load measurements are taken every 15 minutes or every hour respectively. The corresponding set of vectors is given by:

$$X = \left\{ \vec{x}_\ell : \ell = 1, ..., N \right\} \tag{1.2}$$

It is worth mentioning that $x_{\ell i}$ are normalized using the upper and lower values of all elements of the original input patterns set, aiming the achievement of the best possible results after the application of clustering methods.

Each classification process makes a partition of the initial N input vectors to M clusters, which can be the typical days of the under study customer (first example) or the customer classes (second example - the second stage of the proposed methodology of (Tsekouras et al., 2007)) or the typical days of the power system (third example). The j-th cluster has a representative, which is the respective load profile and is represented by the vector of d dimension:

$$\vec{w}_j = \left(w_{j1}, w_{j2}, ... w_{ji}, ... w_{jd} \right)^T \tag{1.3}$$

The last vector also expresses the cluster's centre or the weight vector of neuron, if a clustering artificial neural network is used. In our case it is also called the j-th *class representative load diagram*. The corresponding set is the classes' set, which is defined by:

$$W = \left\{ \vec{w}_k, k = 1, ... M \right\} \tag{1.4}$$

The subset of input vectors $\vec{x}_\ell$, which belong to the j-th cluster, is Ω_j and the respective population of load diagrams is N_j. More specifically Ω_j is determined as follows:

$$\Omega_j = \left\{ \vec{x}_\ell, \ell = 1, ... N \ \& \ \arg\min_{\forall k'} f\left(\vec{x}_\ell, \vec{w}_{k'} \right) \to j \right\} \tag{1.5}$$

where $\Omega_j \subseteq X$ and $\arg\min_{\forall k'} f\left(\vec{x}_\ell, \vec{w}_{k'} \right)$ the corresponding criterion of classification of the l-th vector in the j-th cluster.

For the study and evaluation of classification algorithms the following distances' forms are defined:

1. the Euclidean distance between ℓ_1, ℓ_2 input vectors of the set X:

$$d\left(\vec{x}_{\ell_1}, \vec{x}_{\ell_2} \right) = \sqrt{ \frac{1}{d} \sum_{i=1}^{d} \left(x_{\ell_1 i} - x_{\ell_2 i} \right)^2 } \tag{1.6}$$

2. the distance between the representative vector $\vec{w}_j$ of j-th cluster and the subset Ω_j, calculated as the geometric mean of the Euclidean distances between $\vec{w}_j$ and each member of Ω_j:

$$d\left(\vec{w}_k, \Omega_k \right) = \sqrt{ \frac{1}{N_k} \sum_{\vec{x}_\ell \in \Omega_k} d^2\left(\vec{w}_k, \vec{x}_\ell \right) } \tag{1.7}$$

3. the infra-set mean distance of a set, defined as the geometric mean of the inter-distances between the members of the set, i.e. for the subset Ω_j and for the subset W:

$$\hat{d}(\Omega_k) = \sqrt{\frac{1}{2N_k} \sum_{\vec{x}_\ell \in \Omega_k} d^2\left(\vec{x}_\ell, \Omega_k\right)} \tag{1.8}$$

$$\hat{d}(W) = \sqrt{\frac{1}{2M} \sum_{k=1}^{M} d^2\left(\vec{w}_k, W\right)} \tag{1.9}$$

1.3.2 Adequacy measures

In order to evaluate the performance of the clustering algorithms and to compare them with each other, six different adequacy measures are applied. Their purpose is to obtain well-separated and compact clusters to make the load diagrams self explanatory. The definitions of these measures are the following:

1. *Mean square error or error function (J)* (Gerber et al., 2003), which expresses the distance of each vector from its cluster's centre with the same value of weight:

$$J = \frac{1}{N} \sum_{\ell=1}^{N} d^2\left(\vec{x}_\ell, \vec{w}_{k:\vec{x}_\ell \in \Omega_k}\right) \tag{1.10}$$

2. *Mean index adequacy (MIA)* (Chicco et al., 2003a), which is defined as the average of the distances between each input vector assigned to the cluster and its centre:

$$MIA = \sqrt{\frac{1}{M} \sum_{k=1}^{M} d^2\left(\vec{w}_k, \Omega_k\right)} \tag{1.11}$$

3. *Clustering dispersion indicator (CDI)* (Chicco et al., 2003a), which depends on the mean infra-set distance between the input vectors in the same cluster and inversely on the infra-set distance between the class representative load curves:

$$CDI = \frac{1}{\hat{d}(W)} \sqrt{\frac{1}{M} \sum_{k=1}^{M} \hat{d}^2\left(\Omega_k\right)} \tag{1.12}$$

4. *Similarity matrix indicator (SMI)* (Chicco et al., 2003b), which is defined as the maximum off-diagonal element of the symmetrical similarity matrix, whose terms are calculated by using a logarithmic function of the Euclidean distance between any kind of class representative load curves:

$$SMI = \max_{p \rangle q}\left\{\left(1 - \frac{1}{\ln\left[d\left(\vec{w}_p, \vec{w}_q\right)\right]}\right)^{-1}\right\} : p, q = 1, \ldots, M \tag{1.13}$$

5. *Davies-Bouldin indicator (DBI)* (Davies & Bouldin., 1979), which represents the system-wide average of the similarity measures of each cluster with its most similar cluster:

$$DBI = \frac{1}{M} \sum_{k=1}^{M} \max_{p \neq q} \left\{ \frac{\hat{d}\left(\Omega_p\right) + \hat{d}\left(\Omega_q\right)}{d\left(\vec{w}_p, \vec{w}_q\right)} \right\} : p, q = 1, \ldots, M \tag{1.14}$$

6. *Ratio of within cluster sum of squares to between cluster variation (WCBCR)* (Hand et al., 2001), which depends on the sum of the distance's square between each input vector and its cluster's representative vector, as well as the similarity of the clusters' centres:

$$WCBCR = \frac{\displaystyle\sum_{k=1}^{M} \sum_{\vec{x}_\ell \in \Omega_k} d^2\left(\vec{w}_k, \vec{x}_\ell\right)}{\displaystyle\sum_{1 \leq q < p}^{M} d^2\left(\vec{w}_p, \vec{w}_q\right)} \tag{1.15}$$

The success of the different algorithms for the same final number of clusters is expressed by having small values of the adequacy measures. By increasing the number of clusters all the measures decrease, except of the similarity matrix indicator. An additional adequacy measure could be the number of the *dead* clusters, for which the sets are empty. It is intended to minimize this number. It is noted that in eq. (1.10)-(1.15), M is the number of the clusters without the dead ones.

1.3.3 K-means

The k-means method is the simplest hard clustering method, which gives satisfactory results for compact clusters (Duda et al., 2001). The k-means clustering method groups the set of the N input vectors to M clusters using an iterative procedure. The respective steps of the algorithm are the follows:

a. Initialization of the weights of M clusters is determined. In the classic model a random choice among the input vectors is used (Chicco et al., 2006; Figueiredo et al., 2003). In the developed algorithm the w_{ji} of the j-th centre is initialized as:

$$w_{ji}^{(0)} = a + b \cdot (j-1)/(M-1) \tag{1.16}$$

where a and b are properly calibrated parameters. Alternatively the w_{ji} is initialized as:

$$w_{ji}^{(0)} = a_i + b_i \cdot (j-1)/(M-1) \tag{1.17}$$

where $a_i = \min_{\forall j}\left(x_{ji}\right)$ and $b_i = \max_{\forall j}\left(x_{ji}\right)$.

b. During epoch t for each training vector $\vec{x}_\ell$ its Euclidean distances $d\left(\vec{x}_\ell, \vec{w}_j\right)$ are calculated for all centres. The ℓ-th input vector is put in the set $\Omega_j^{(t)}$, for which the distance between $\vec{x}_\ell$ and the respective centre is minimum, which means:

$$d\left(\vec{x}_\ell, \vec{w}_k\right) = \min_{\forall j} d\left(\vec{x}_\ell, \vec{w}_j\right) \tag{1.18}$$

c. When the entire training set is formed, the new weights of each centre are calculated as:

$$\vec{w}_j^{(t+1)} = \frac{1}{N_j^{(t)}} \sum_{\vec{x}_\ell \in \Omega_j^{(t)}} \vec{x}_\ell \qquad (1.19)$$

where $N_j^{(t)}$ is the population of the respective set $\Omega_j^{(t)}$ during epoch t.

d. Next, the number of the epochs is increased by one. This process is repeated (return to step b) until the maximum number of epochs is used or weights do not significantly change ($\left|\vec{w}_j^{(t)} - \vec{w}_j^{(t+1)}\right| < \varepsilon$, where ε is the upper limit of weight change between sequential iterations). The algorithm's main purpose is to minimize the appropriate error function J. The main difference with the classic model is that the process is repeated for various pairs of (a,b). The best results for each adequacy measure are recorded for various pairs (a,b).

At the end of the execution of the algorithm the six adequacy measures are calculated, which are used for comparison reasons with the other clustering methods. The core of algorithm is executed from M_1 to M_2 neurons, because the necessary number of clusters is not known a priori, as it depends on the time period which is examined and the available number of patterns.

1.3.4 Kohonen adaptive vector quantization - AVQ

This algorithm is a variation of the k-means method, which belongs to the unsupervised competitive one-layer neural networks. It classifies input vectors into clusters by using a competitive layer with a constant number of neurons. Practically in each step all clusters compete each other for the winning of a pattern. The winning cluster moves its centre to the direction of the pattern, while the rest clusters move their centres to the opposite direction (supervised classification) or remain stable (unsupervised classification).

Here, we will use the last unsupervised classification algorithm. The respective steps are the following:

a. Initialization of the weights of M clusters is determined, where the weights of all clusters are equal to 0.5, that is $w_{ji}^{(0)} = 0.5, \forall j, i$.

b. During epoch t each input vector $\vec{x}_\ell$ is randomly presented and its respective Euclidean distances from every neuron are calculated. In the case of existence of bias factor λ, the respective minimization function is:

$$f_{winner\_neuron}(\vec{x}_\ell) = j : \min_{\forall j}\left(d(\vec{x}_\ell, \vec{w}_j) + \lambda \cdot N_j / N\right) \qquad (1.20)$$

where N_j is the population of the respective set Ω_j during epoch t-1.

The weights of the winning neuron (with the smallest distance) are updated as:

$$\vec{w}_j^{(t)}(n+1) = \vec{w}_j^{(t)}(n) + \eta(t) \cdot \left(\vec{x}_\ell - \vec{w}_j^{(t)}(n)\right) \qquad (1.21)$$

where n is the number of input vectors, which have been presented during the current epoch, and $\eta(t)$ is the learning rate according to:

$$\eta(t) = \eta_0 \cdot \exp\left(-\frac{t}{T_{\eta 0}}\right) > \eta_{\min} \qquad (1.22)$$

where η_0, $\eta_{\min}$ and $T_{\eta 0}$ are the initial value, the minimum value and the time parameter respectively. The remaining neurons are unchangeable for $\vec{x}_\ell$, as introduced by the Kohonen winner-take-all learning rule (Kohonen, 1989; Haykin, 1994).

c. Next, the number of the epochs is increased by one. This process is repeated (return to step b) until either the maximum number of epochs is reached or the weights converge or the error function J does not improve, which means:

$$\left|\frac{J^{(t)} - J^{(t+1)}}{J^{(t)}}\right| < \varepsilon' \text{ for } t \geq T_{in} \qquad (1.23)$$

where ε' is the upper limit of error function change between sequential iterations and the respective criterion is activated after T_{in} epochs.

The core of algorithm is executed for specific number of neurons and the respective parameters η_0, $\eta_{\min}$ and $T_{\eta 0}$ are optimized for each adequacy measure separately. This process is repeated from M_1 to M_2 neurons.

1.3.5 Fuzzy k-means

During the application of the k-mean or the adaptive vector quantization algorithm each pattern is assumed to be in exactly one cluster (hard clustering). In many cases the areas of two neighbour clusters are overlapped, so that there are not any valid qualitative results.

If we want to relax the condition of exclusive partition of an input pattern to one cluster, we should use fuzzy clustering techniques. Specifically, each input vector $\vec{x}_\ell$ does not belong to only one cluster, but it participates to every j-th cluster by a membership factor $u_{\ell j}$, where:

$$\sum_{j=1}^{M} u_{\ell j} = 1 \ \& \ 0 \leq u_{\ell j} \leq 1, \forall j \qquad (1.24)$$

Theoretically, the membership factor gives more flexibility in the vector's distribution. During the iterations the following objective function is minimized:

$$J_{fuzzy} = \frac{1}{N}\sum_{j=1}^{M}\sum_{\ell=1}^{N} u_{\ell j} \cdot d^2\left(\vec{x}_\ell, \vec{w}_j\right) \qquad (1.25)$$

The simplest algorithm is the fuzzy k-means clustering one, in which the respective steps are the following:

a. Initialization of the weights of M clusters is determined. In the classic model a random choice among the input vectors is used (Chicco et al., 2006; Figueiredo et al., 2003). In the developed algorithm the w_{ji} of the j-th centre is initialized by eq. (1.16) or eq. (1.17).

b. During epoch t for each training vector $\vec{x}_\ell$ the membership factors are calculated for every cluster:

$$u_{\ell j}^{(t+1)} = \frac{1}{\sum\limits_{k=1}^{M} \dfrac{d\left(\vec{x}_\ell, \vec{w}_j^{(t)}\right)}{d\left(\vec{x}_\ell, \vec{w}_k^{(t)}\right)}}$$ (1.26)

c. Afterwards the new weights of each centre are calculated as:

$$\vec{w}_j^{(t+1)} = \frac{\sum\limits_{\ell=1}^{N}\left(u_{\ell j}^{(t+1)}\right)^q \cdot \vec{x}_\ell}{\sum\limits_{\ell=1}^{N}\left(u_{\ell j}^{(t+1)}\right)^q}$$ (1.27)

where q is the *amount of fuzziness* in the range $(1, \infty)$ which increases as fuzziness reduces.

d. Next, the number of the epochs is increased by one. This process is repeated (return to step b) until the maximum number of epochs is used or weights do not significantly change.

This process is repeated for different pairs of (a,b) and for different amounts of fuzziness. The best results for each adequacy measure are recorded for different pairs (a,b) and q.

1.3.6 Self-organizing map - SOM

The Kohonen SOM (Kohonen, 1989; SOM Toolbox for MATLAB 5, 2000; Thang et al., 2003) is a topologically unsupervised neural network that projects a d-dimensional input data set into a reduced dimensional space (usually a mono-dimensional or bi-dimensional map). It is composed of a predefined grid containing $M_1 \times M_2$ d-dimensional neurons $\vec{w}_k$, which are calculated by a competitive learning algorithm that updates not only the weights of the winning neuron, but also the weights of its neighbour units in inverse proportion of their distance. The neighbourhood size of each neuron shrinks progressively during the training process, starting with nearly the whole map and ending with the single neuron.

The process of algorithm is described by the following stages:

- *Initialization stage.* The weights of the neural network are initialized connecting the neurons of the input layer with the map neurons.
- *Competition stage.* For each input pattern the map neurons calculate the corresponding value of the competition function, where the neuron with the biggest value is the winner.
- *Collaboration stage.* The winner neuron determines the territorial area of topological neighbourhood, providing the subbase for the collaboration between the neighbouring neurons.
- *Weights' adaptation stage.* The neurons that belong in the winning neighbourhood adapt their weights of winner-neuron, so that its response will be strengthened during the presentation of a training input pattern.

The training of SOM is divided to two phases:

- *rough ordering,* with high initial learning rate, large radius and small number of epochs, so that neurons are arranged into a structure which approximately displays the inherent characteristics of the input data,

- *fine tuning*, with small initial learning rate, small radius and higher number of training epochs, in order to tune the final structure of the SOM.

The transition of the rough ordering phase to the fine tuning one is happened after T_{s0} epochs.

More analytically, the respective steps of the SOM algorithm are the following:

a. The shape and the number of neurons of the SOM's grid are defined and the initialization of the respective weights is determined. Specifically, in the case of the mono-dimensional SOM the weights can be given by (a) $w_{ki} = 0.5, \forall k, i$, (b) the random initialization of each neuron's weight, (c) the random choice of the input vectors for each neuron. In the case of the bi-dimensional SOM the additional issues that must be solved, are the shape, the population of neurons and their respective arrangement. The rectangular shape of the map is defined by rectangular or hexagonal arrangement of neurons, as it is presented in Fig. 1.2. The population of the neurons is recommended to be $5 \times \sqrt{N}$ to $20 \times \sqrt{N}$ (Chicco et al., 2004; SOM Toolbox for MATLAB 5, 2000; Thang et al., 2003;). The height/width ratio M_1/M_2 of the rectangular grid can be calculated as the ratio between the two major eigenvalues λ_1, λ_2 of the covariance matrix of the input vectors set (with $\lambda_1 > \lambda_2$). The initialization of the neurons can be a linear combination of the respective eigenvectors $\vec{e}_1$ and $\vec{e}_2$ of the two major eigenvalues or can be equal to 0.5. It is reminded that the element s_{k_1,k_2} of the covariance matrix of the input vectors set is given by:

$$s_{k_1,k_2} = \sum_{\ell=1}^{N}\left(x_{k_1\ell} - \overline{x}_{k_1}\right)\cdot\left(x_{k_2\ell} - \overline{x}_{k_2}\right)\Big/\left(N-1\right) \tag{1.28}$$

where $\overline{x}_{k_1}$ is the mean value of the respective k_1 dimension of all input patterns.

b. The SOM training commences by first choosing an input vector $\vec{x}_\ell$, at t epoch, randomly from the input vectors' set. The Euclidean distances between the n-th presented input pattern $\vec{x}_\ell$ and all $\vec{w}_k$ are calculated, so as to determine the winning neuron i' that is closest to $\vec{x}_\ell$ (competition stage). The j-th reference vector is updated (weights' adaptation stage) according to:

$$\vec{w}_j^{(t)}\left(n+1\right) = \vec{w}_j^{(t)}\left(n\right) + \eta\left(t\right)\cdot h_{i'j}\left(t\right)\cdot\left(\vec{x}_\ell - \vec{w}_j^{(t)}\left(n\right)\right) \tag{1.29}$$

where $\eta\left(t\right)$ is the learning rate according to:

$$\eta\left(t\right) = \eta_0 \cdot \exp\left(-\frac{t}{T_{\eta_0}}\right) > \eta_{min} \tag{1.30}$$

with η_0, η_{min} and T_{η_0} representing the initial value, the minimum value and the time parameter respectively. During the rough ordering phase $\eta_r, T_{\eta 0}$ are the initial value

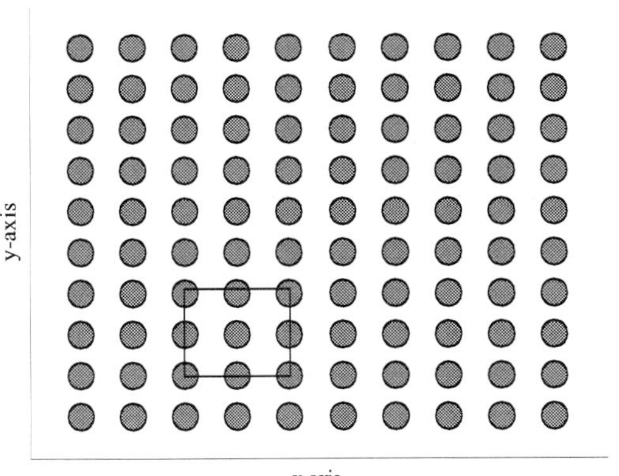

a. Rectangular arrangement

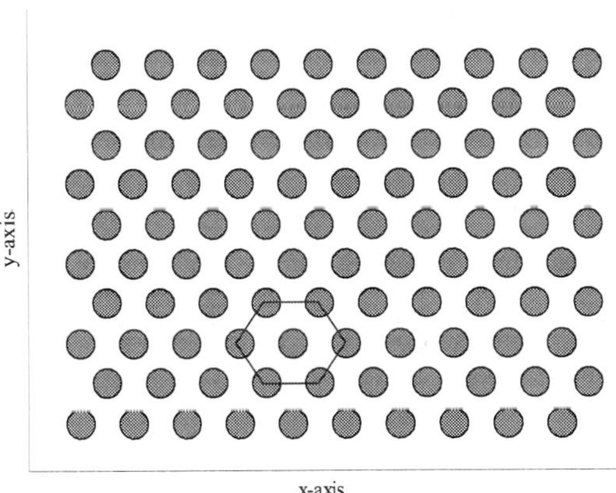

b. Hexagonal arrangement

Fig. 1.2. Arrangement of bi-dimensional self-organized map 10x10

and the time parameter respectively, while during the fine tuning phase the respective values are $\eta_f, T_{\eta 0}$. The $h_{i'j}(t)$ is the neighbourhood symmetrical function, that will activate the j neurons that are topologically close to the winning neuron i', according to their geometrical distance, who will learn from the same $\vec{x}_\ell$ (collaboration stage). In this case the Gauss function is proposed:

$$h_{i'j}(t) = \exp\left[-\frac{d_{i'j}^2}{2 \cdot \sigma^2(t)}\right] \tag{1.31}$$

where $d_{i'j} = \left\| \vec{r}_{i'} - \vec{r}_j \right\|$ is the respective distance between i' and j neurons, $\vec{r}_j = \left(x_j, y_j \right)$ are the respective co-ordinates in the grid, $\sigma(t) = \sigma_0 \cdot \exp\left(-t/T_{\sigma_0} \right)$ is the decreasing neighbourhood radius function where σ_0 and T_{σ_0} are the respective initial value and time parameter of the radius respectively.

c. Next, the number of the epochs is increased by one. This process is repeated (return to step b) until either the maximum number of epochs is reached or the index I_s gets the minimum value (SOM Toolbox for MATLAB 5, 2000):

$$I_s(t) = J(t) + ADM(t) + TE(t) \tag{1.32}$$

where the quality measures of the optimum SOM are based on the quantization error J - given by (1.10)-, the topographic error TE and the average distortion measure ADM. The topographic error measures the distortion of the map as the percentage of input vectors for which the first i_1' and second i_2' winning neuron are not neighbouring map units:

$$TE = \sum_{\ell=1}^{N} neighb\left(i_1', i_2' \right) \bigg/ N \tag{1.33}$$

where, for each input vector, $neighb\left(i_1', i_2' \right)$ equals to 1, if i_1' and i_2' neurons are not neighbours, either 0. The average distortion measure is given for the t epoch by:

$$ADM(t) = \sum_{\ell=1}^{N} \sum_{j=1}^{M} h_{i' \to \vec{x}_\ell, j}(t) \cdot d^2\left(\vec{x}_\ell, \vec{w}_j \right) \bigg/ N \tag{1.34}$$

This process is repeated for different parameters of $\sigma_0, \eta_f, \eta_r, T_{\eta 0}, T_{\sigma 0}$ and T_{s_0}. Alternatively, the multiplicative factors ϕ and ξ are introduced -without decreasing the generalization ability of the parameters' calibration:

$$T_{s_0} = \phi \cdot T_{\eta_0} \tag{1.35}$$

$$T_{\sigma_0} = \xi \cdot T_{\eta_0} \big/ \ln \sigma_0 \tag{1.36}$$

The best results for each adequacy measure are recorded for different parameters $\sigma_0, \eta_f, \eta_r, T_{\eta 0}, \phi$ and ξ.

In the case of the bi-dimensional map, the immediate exploitation of the respective clusters is not a simple problem. We can exploit the map either through human vision or applying a second simple clustering method. According to Chicco et al., (2002), the simple k-mean method was used, while, here, the proposed k-mean method with initialization by eq. (1.16) is used. Practically, the neurons of the map sustain a new data compression from which the final classification of the input patterns is concluded.

1.3.7 Hierarchical agglomerative algorithms

Hierarchical algorithms have a different philosophy compared to the aforementioned algorithms. Instead of producing a single clustering, they produce a hierarchy of clustering.

Agglomerative algorithms are based on matrix theory (Theodoridis & Koutroumbas, 1999). The input is the $N \times N$ dissimilarity matrix P_0. At each level t, when two clusters are merged into one, the size of the dissimilarity matrix P_t becomes $(N-t) \times (N-t)$. Matrix P_t is obtained from P_{t-1} by deleting the two rows and columns that correspond to the merged clusters and adding a new row and a new column that contain the distances between the newly formed cluster and the old ones. The distance between the newly formed cluster C_q (the result of merging C_i and C_j) and an old cluster C_s is determined as:

$$d(C_q, C_s) = f\left(d(C_i, C_s), d(C_j, C_s), d(C_i, C_j)\right) \tag{1.37}$$

Alternatively eq. (1.37) is written as:

$$d(C_q, C_s) = a_i \cdot d(C_i, C_s) + a_j \cdot d(C_j, C_s) + b \cdot d(C_i, C_j) + c \cdot \left| d(C_i, C_s) - d(C_j, C_s) \right| \tag{1.38}$$

where a_i, a_j, b and c correspond to different choices of the dissimilarity measure.
The basic algorithms, which are going to be used in our case, are:

*   the *single link* algorithm (SL) -it is obtained from (1.38) for $a_i{=}a_j{=}0.5$, $b{=}0$ and $c = -0.5$:

$$d(C_q, C_s) = \min\left\{ d(C_i, C_s), d(C_j, C_s) \right\} - \frac{1}{2} \cdot d(C_i, C_s) + \frac{1}{2} \cdot d(C_j, C_s) - \frac{1}{2} \cdot \left| d(C_i, C_s) - d(C_j, C_s) \right| \tag{1.39}$$

*   the *complete link* algorithm (CL) -it is obtained from (1.38) for $a_i{=}a_j{=}0.5$, $b{=}0$ and $c = 0.5$:

$$d(C_q, C_s) = \max\left\{ d(C_i, C_s), d(C_j, C_s) \right\} = \frac{1}{2} \cdot d(C_i, C_s) + \frac{1}{2} \cdot d(C_j, C_s) + \frac{1}{2} \cdot \left| d(C_i, C_s) - d(C_j, C_s) \right| \tag{1.40}$$

*   the *unweighted pair group method average* algorithm (UPGMA):

$$d(C_q, C_s) = \frac{n_i \cdot d(C_i, C_s) + n_j \cdot d(C_j, C_s)}{n_i + n_j} \tag{1.50}$$

where n_i and n_j - are the respective members' populations of clusters C_i and C_j.

*   the *weighted pair group method average* algorithm (WPGMA):

$$d(C_q, C_s) = \frac{1}{2} \cdot \left\{ d(C_i, C_s) + d(C_j, C_s) \right\} \tag{1.42}$$

*   the *unweighted pair group method centroid* algorithm (UPGMC):

$$d^{(1)}(C_q, C_s) = \frac{\left(n_i \cdot d^{(1)}(C_i, C_s) + n_j \cdot d^{(1)}(C_j, C_s) \right)}{\left(n_i + n_j \right)} - n_i \cdot n_j \cdot \frac{d^{(1)}(C_i, C_j)}{\left(n_i + n_j \right)^2} \tag{1.43}$$

where $d^{(1)}(C_q, C_s) = \left\| \vec{w}_q - \vec{w}_s \right\|^2$ and $\vec{w}_q$ is the representative centre of the q-th cluster according to the following equation (which is similar to (1.39)):

$$\vec{w}_q = \frac{1}{n_q} \cdot \sum_{\vec{x}_v \in C_q} \vec{x}_v \tag{1.44}$$

- the *weighted pair group method centroid* algorithm (WPGMC):

$$d^{(1)}\left(C_q, C_s\right) = \frac{1}{2} \cdot \left(d^{(1)}\left(C_i, C_s\right) + d^{(1)}\left(C_j, C_s\right)\right) - \frac{1}{4} \cdot d^{(1)}\left(C_i, C_j\right) \tag{1.45}$$

- the *Ward or minimum variance* algorithm (WARD):

$$d^{(2)}\left(C_q, C_s\right) = \frac{\left(n_i + n_s\right) \cdot d^{(2)}\left(C_i, C_s\right) + \left(n_j + n_s\right) \cdot d^{(2)}\left(C_j, C_s\right) - n_s \cdot d^{(2)}\left(C_i, C_j\right)}{\left(n_i + n_j + n_s\right)} \tag{1.46}$$

where:

$$d^{(2)}\left(C_i, C_j\right) = \frac{n_i \cdot n_j}{n_i + n_j} \cdot d^{(1)}\left(C_i, C_j\right) \tag{1.47}$$

It is noted that in each level t the respective representative vectors are calculated by eq.(1.44).

The respective steps of each algorithm are the following:

a.   *Initialization*: The set of the remaining patterns $\Re_0$ for zero level ($t = 0$) is the set of the input vectors X. The similarity matrix $P_0 = P\left(X\right)$ is determined. Afterwards t increases by one ($t=t+1$).

b.   During level t clusters C_i and C_j are found, for which the minimization criterion is satisfied $d\left(C_i, C_j\right) = \min_{r,s=1,\dots,N, r \neq s} d\left(C_r, C_s\right)$.

c.   Then clusters C_i and C_j are merged into a single cluster C_q and the set of the remaining patterns $\Re_t$ is formed as: $\Re_t = \left(\Re_{t-1} - \left\{C_i, C_j\right\}\right) \cup \left\{C_q\right\}$.

d.   The construction of the dissimilarity matrix P_t from P_{t-1} is realized by applying eq.(1.37).

e.   Next, the number of the levels is increased by one. This process is repeated (return to step b) until the remaining patterns $\Re_{N-1}$ is formed and all input vectors are in the same and unique cluster.

It is mentioned that the number of iterations is determined from the beginning and it equals to the number of input vectors decreased by 1 (N-1).

1.4 A pattern recognition methodology for evaluation of load profiles and typical days of large electricity customers

1.4.1 General description of the proposed methodology

The classification of daily chronological load curves of one customer is achieved by means of the pattern recognition methodology, as shown in Fig. 1.3.

The main steps are the following (Tsekouras et al., 2008):

a. *Data and features selection*: Using electronic meters, the active and reactive energy values are registered (in kWh and kvarh) for each time period in steps of 15 minutes, 1 hour, etc. The daily chronological load curves are determined for the study period.

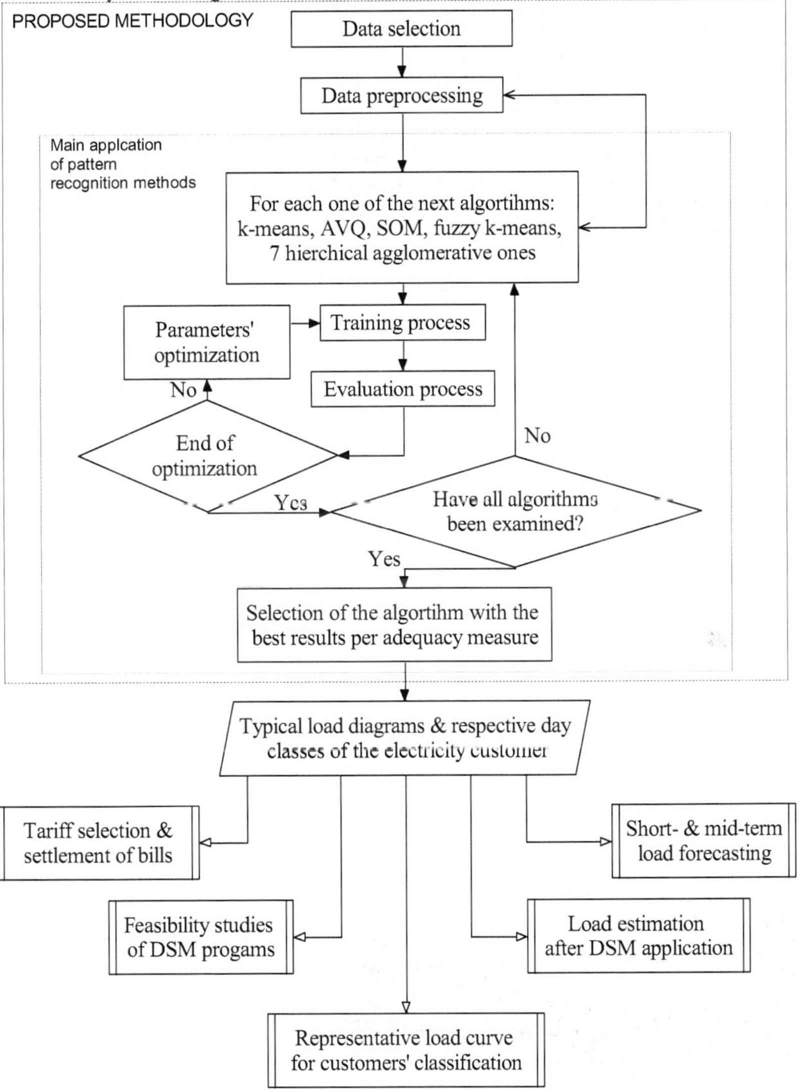

Fig. 1.3. Flow diagram of pattern recognition methodology for the classification of daily chronological load curves of one large electricity customer

b. *Data preprocessing:* The load diagrams of the customer are examined for normality, in order to modify or delete the values that are obviously wrong (*noise suppression*). If it is necessary, a preliminary execution of a pattern recognition algorithm is carried out, in order to track bad measurements or networks faults, which will reduce the number of the useful typical days for a constant number of clusters, if they remain uncorrected. In future, a filtering step can be added using principal component analysis, Sammon map, and curvilinear component analysis (Chicco et al., 2006), for the reduction of the load diagrams dimensions.

c.   *Main application of pattern recognition methods*: For the load diagrams of the customer, a number of clustering algorithms (k-means, adaptive vector quantization, self organized map, fuzzy k-means and hierarchical clustering) is applied. Each algorithm is trained for the set of load diagrams and evaluated according to six adequacy measures. The parameters of the algorithms are optimized, if it is necessary. The developed methodology uses the clustering methods that provide the most satisfactory results. It should be noted that conventional methods, like statistical tools, supervised techniques, etc., cannot be used, because the classification of the typical days must be already known.

1.4.2 Application of the proposed methodology to a medium voltage customer

1.4.2.1 General

The developed methodology was analytically applied on one medium voltage industrial paper mill customer of the Greek distribution system. The data used are 15 minutes load values for a period of ten months in 2003. The respective set of the daily chronological curves has 301 members. Nine curves were rejected through data pre-processing, while the remaining 292 diagrams were used by the aforementioned clustering methods. The last diagrams are registered in Fig. 1.4 and Fig. 1.5, in which the load variability is also presented. The load behaviour is significantly decreased during holiday time. The mean load demand is 6656 kW and the peak load demand is 9469 kW during the period under study.

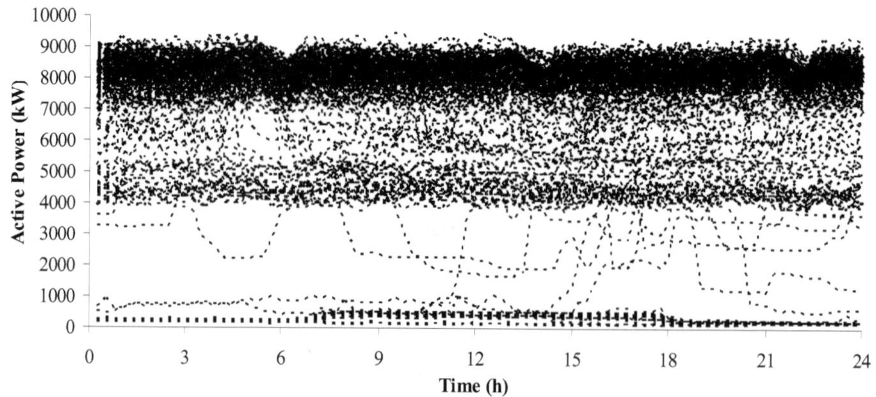

Fig. 1.4. Daily chronological 15-minutes load diagrams for a set of 292 days for the industrial medium voltage customer for each day (February – November 2003)

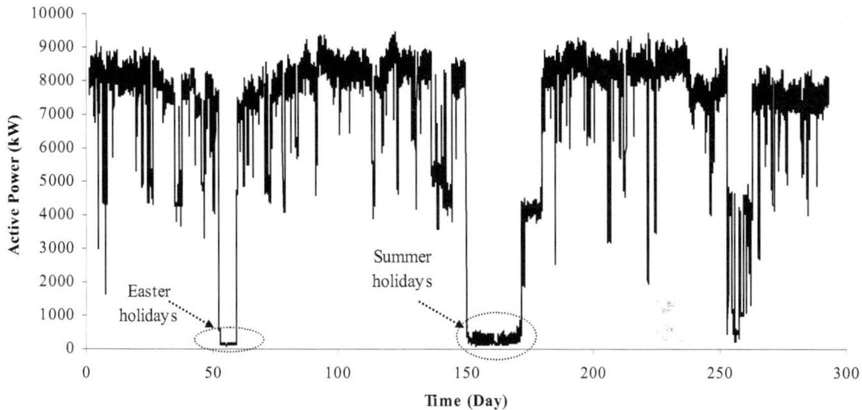

Fig. 1.5. Chronological 15-minutes load diagram for a set of 292 days for the industrial medium voltage customer for the time period under study (February-November 2003)

The main goal of the application of this methodology is the representation of the load behaviour of the customer with typical daily load chronological diagrams. This is achieved through the following steps:

- The calibration of the parameters of each clustering method is realized for every adequacy measure separately and the performance for different number of clusters is registered.
- The clustering models are compared to each other using the six adequacy measures, the behaviour of these measures is studied and the appropriate number of the clusters is defined.

The representative daily load chronological diagrams of the customer are calculated for the best clustering techniques and the proposed number of clusters.

1.4.2.2 Application of the k-means

The proposed model of the k-means method (k-means-scenario 1 with the weights initialization based on eq.(1.16)) is executed for different pairs (a,b) from 2 to 25 clusters, where $a=\{0.1,0.11,\ldots,0.45\}$ and $a+b=\{0.54,0.55,\ldots,0.9\}$. For each cluster, 1332 different pairs (a,b) are checked. The best results for the 6 adequacy measures do not refer to the same pair (a,b). The second model of the k-means method (k-means-scenario 2) is based on eq. (1.17) for the weights initialization. The third model (k-means-scenario 3) is the classic one with the random choice of the input vectors during the centres' initialization. For the classic k-means model, 100 executions are carried out and the best results for each index are registered. In Fig. 1.6, it is obvious that the proposed k-means is superior to the other two scenarios of k-means. The superiority of the proposed model applies in all cases of neurons.

A second advantage comprises the convergence to the same results for the respective pairs (a,b), which cannot be reached using the classic model.

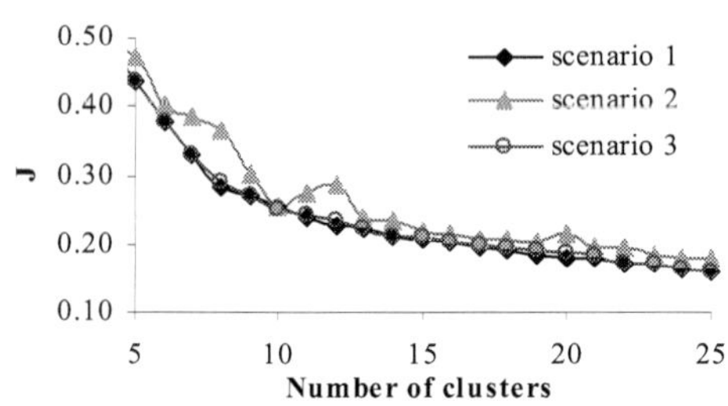

a. *J* indicator

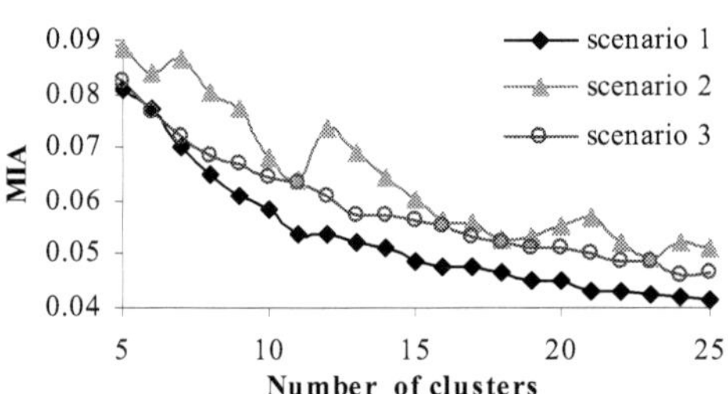

b. *MIA* indicator

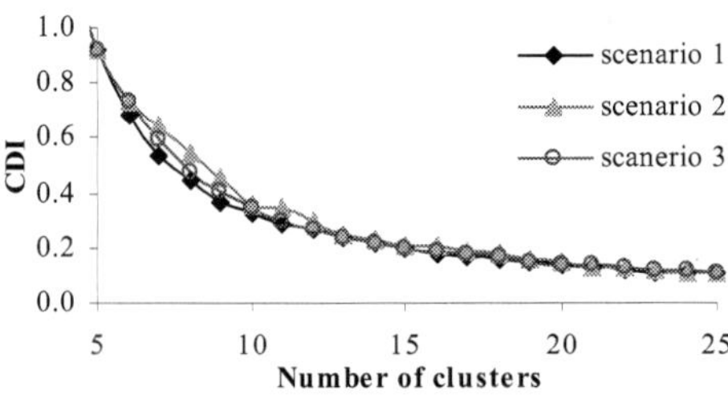

c. *CDI* indicator

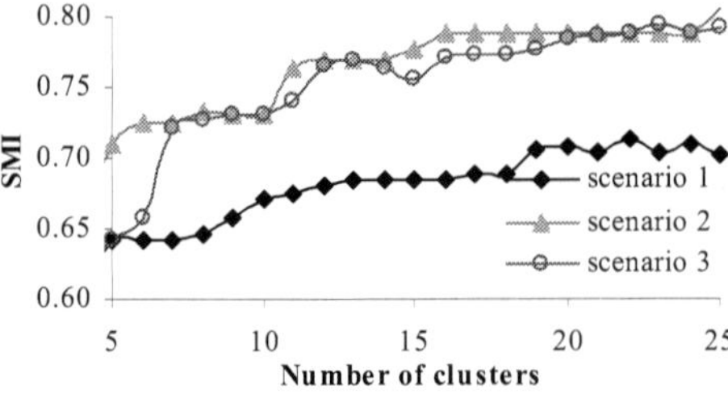

d. *SMI* indicator

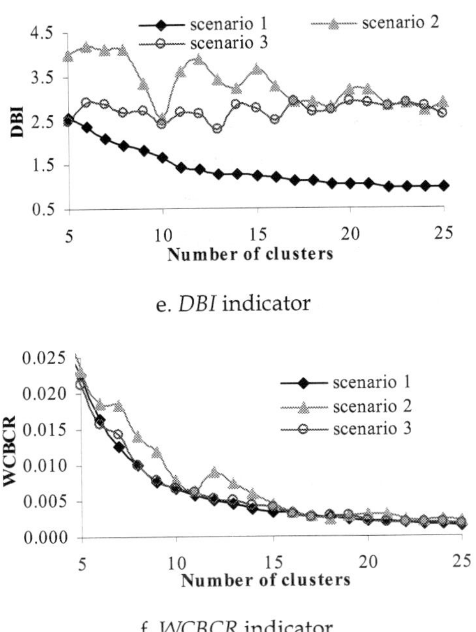

e. *DBI* indicator

f. *WCBCR* indicator

Fig. 1.6. Adequacy measures for the k-means method for a set of 292 training patterns for 5 to 25 clusters (scenario 1: proposed method – weights initialization based on eq. (1.16)-, scenario 2: alternative method – weights initialization based on eq. (1.17)-, scenario 3: classic method)

In Fig. 1.7 the dead clusters for the proposed k-means method are presented for the six different adequacy measures. It is obvious that *WCBCR* presents the best behaviour, because the first dead cluster is presented when 23 clusters are required, while all other measures present dead clusters for smaller required clusters.

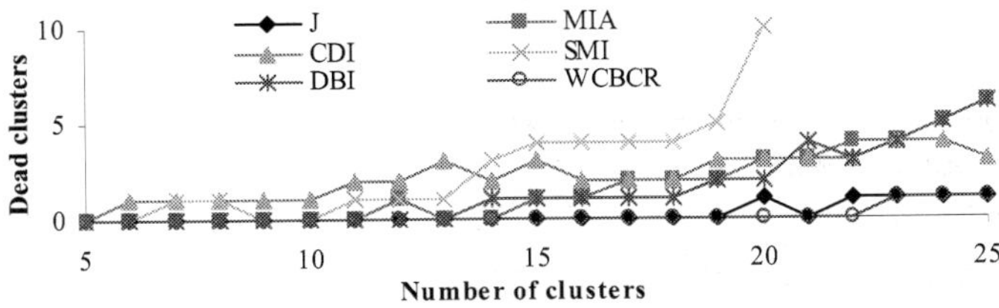

Fig. 1.7. Dead clusters for the proposed k-means method for the six different adequacy measures for a set of 292 training patterns for 5 to 25 clusters

It is mentioned that the maximum number of epochs is 200 for the three scenarios, the upper limit of the weight change between sequential iterations ε is 10^{-4}. Practically the algorithm is always converged after at most 20-30 iterations.

1.4.2.3 Application of the adaptive vector quantization

During the application of the AVQ method with serial presentation and without bias factor the parameters η_0, $\eta_{\min}$ and $T_{\eta 0}$ should be optimized. Specifically, the model is executed for $\eta_0 = \{0.05, 0.1, ..., 0.9\}$ and $T_{\eta 0} = \{500, 1000, ..., 5000\}$ from 2 to 25 clusters with $\eta_{\min}$ stable ($=10^{-5}$). Indicatively the adequacy measures of the AVQ method for 10 clusters are presented in Fig. 1.8, where the best results for each adequacy measure are presented for different areas of η_0 and $T_{\eta 0}$.

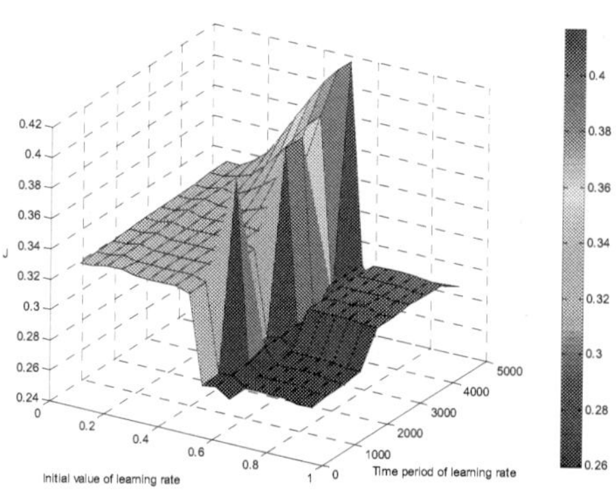

a. *J* indicator

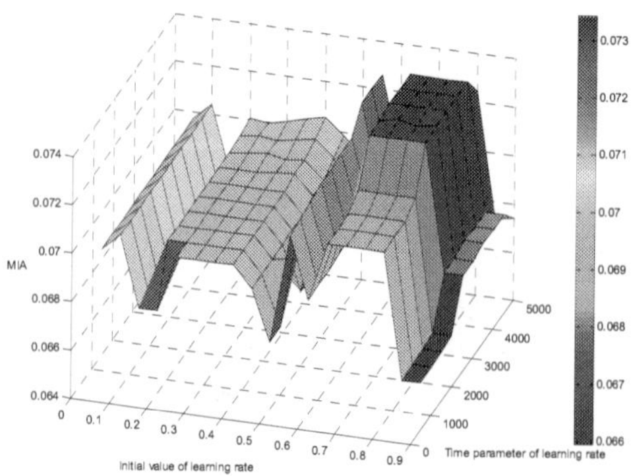

b. *MIA* indicator

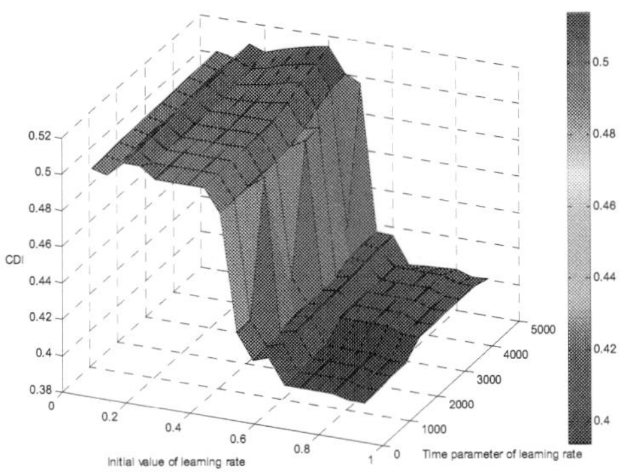

c. *CDI* indicator

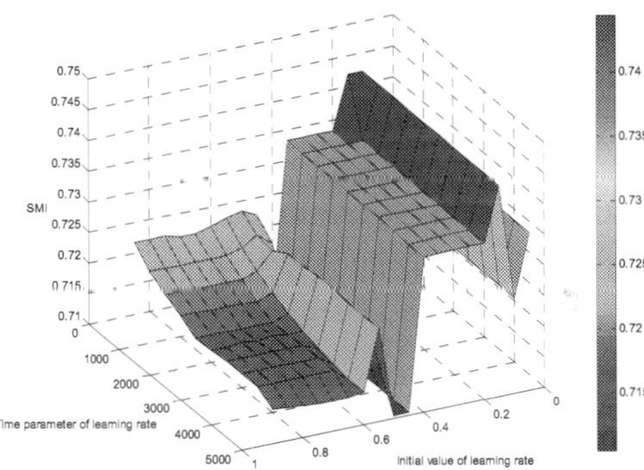

d. *SMI* indicator

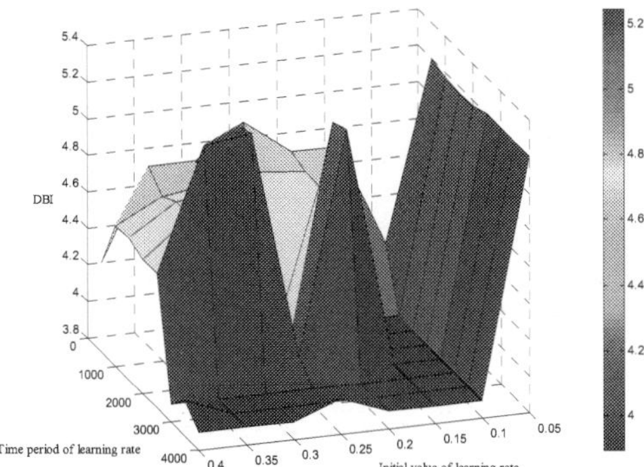

e. *DBI* indicator

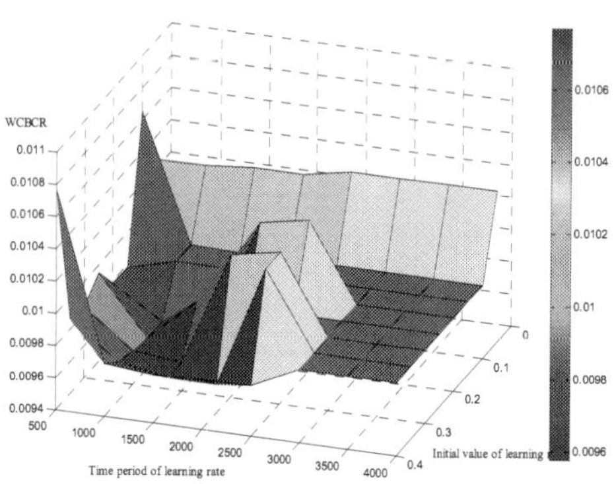

f. *WCBCR* indicator

Fig. 1.8. Adequacy measures for the AVQ method (with serial presentation and without bias factor) for a set of 292 training patterns for 10 clusters, η_0={0.05, 0.1,..., 0.9}, $T_{\eta 0}$={500, 1000, ..., 5000}

The *J* indicator presents the best results for $\eta_0 > 0.45$ and $T_{\eta 0} \leq 2000$, while the *CDI* indicator has similar behaviour to the *J* one. The *MIA* and *WCBCR* indicators present their best results for $\eta_0 > 0.85$ and $T_{\eta 0} \leq 2000$, *DBI* and *SMI* indicators for $\eta_0 \approx 0.45$, $\forall$ $T_{\eta 0}$. For different number of clusters the pairs ($\eta_0, T_{\eta 0}$) for the best results are not the same, but the greater areas are similar, as it is presented for the *J* indicator for 8 and 15 clusters in Fig. 1.9 indicatively. Generally, as the number of clusters increases, so the respective behaviour of ($\eta_0, T_{\eta 0}$) is stabilized. The value of the parameter $\eta_{\min}$ is not significant, but it helps towards the algorithm's convergence for a big number of epochs with the condition $\eta_{\min}$ not having zero value. In this problem the proper values of this parameter are between 10^{-4} and 10^{-6}.

During the application of the AVQ method with random presentation and without bias factor the respective results are improved against the serial presentation having two disadvantages:

♦ the computing time increases by 10% and

♦ the convergence areas for pairs (η_0, $T_{\eta 0}$) have more unstable shape.

Indicatively, *J* and *WCBCR* measures are presented for 10 clusters in Fig. 1.10 improving the respective values in comparison to serial presentation from 0.259 to 0.250 and from 0.0083 to 0.0068 respectively.

If the bias factor is used with values between 10^{-3} and 10, the respective results are not practically improved (there is a slight improvement of the forth significant digit for each adequacy measure). Since the computing time is increased by 50%, we propose not to use the bias factor.

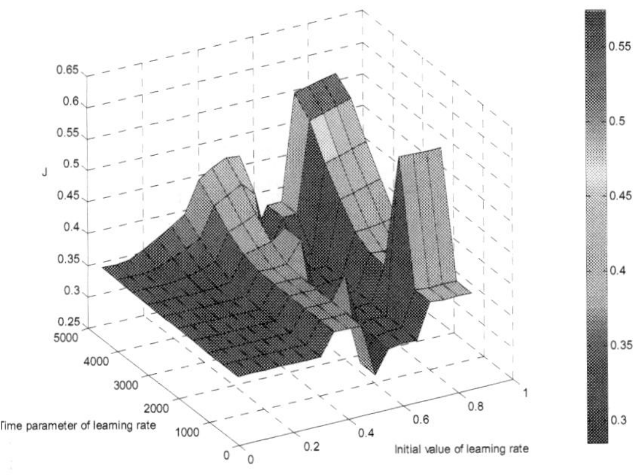

a. *J* indicator - 8 clusters

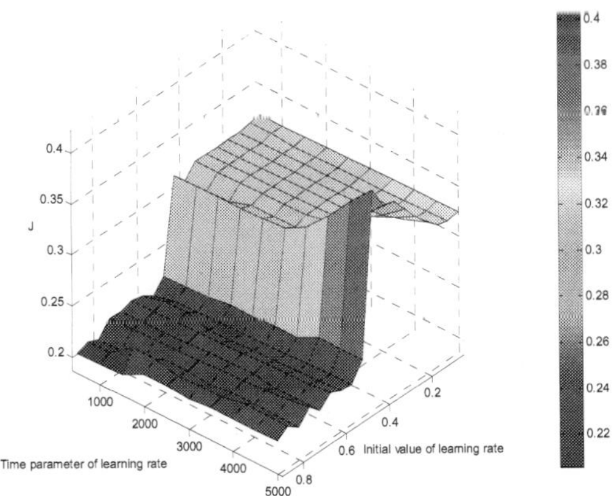

b. *J* indicator - 15 clusters

Fig. 1.9. *J* adequacy measures for the AVQ method (with serial presentation and without bias factor) for a set of 292 training patterns for 8 clusters and 15 clusters, η_0={0.05, 0.1,..., 0.9}, $T_{\eta 0}$={500, 1000, ..., 5000}

It is mentioned that the maximum number of epochs is 10000, the upper limit of the weight change between sequential iterations ε and the upper limit of the error function change between sequential iterations ε' are 10^{-4}. The algorithm usually converges after a few hundreds epochs after $T_{\eta 0}$ epochs.

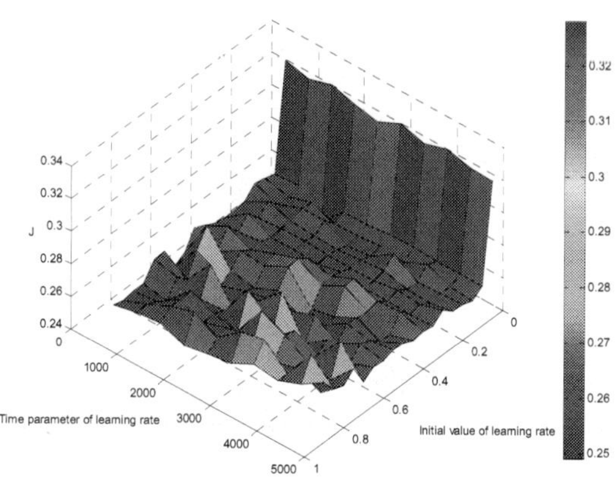

a. J indicator

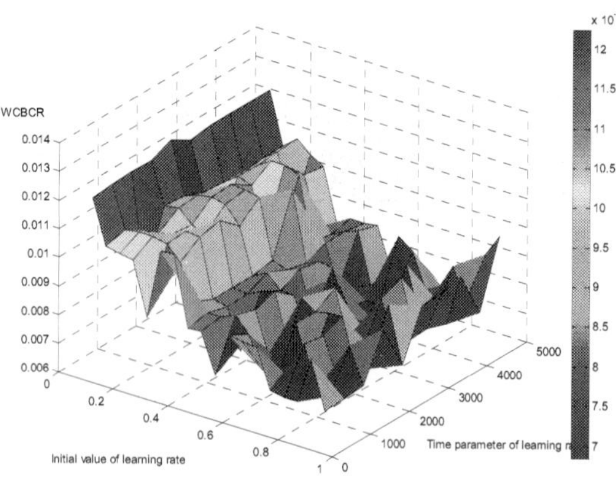

b. *WCBCR* indicator

Fig. 1.10. *J* and WCBCR adequacy measures for the AVQ method (with random presentation, without bias factor) for a set of 292 training patterns for 10 clusters, η_0={0.05, 0.1,..., 0.9}, $T_{\eta 0}$={500, 1000, ..., 5000}

In Fig. 1.11 the two basic scenarios of the AVQ method (serial and random presentation without the bias factor) are presented for all adequacy measures. The method with the random presentation is slightly superior to the other one for all adequacy measures for 9 clusters and above, except the *SMI* and *DBI* indicators.

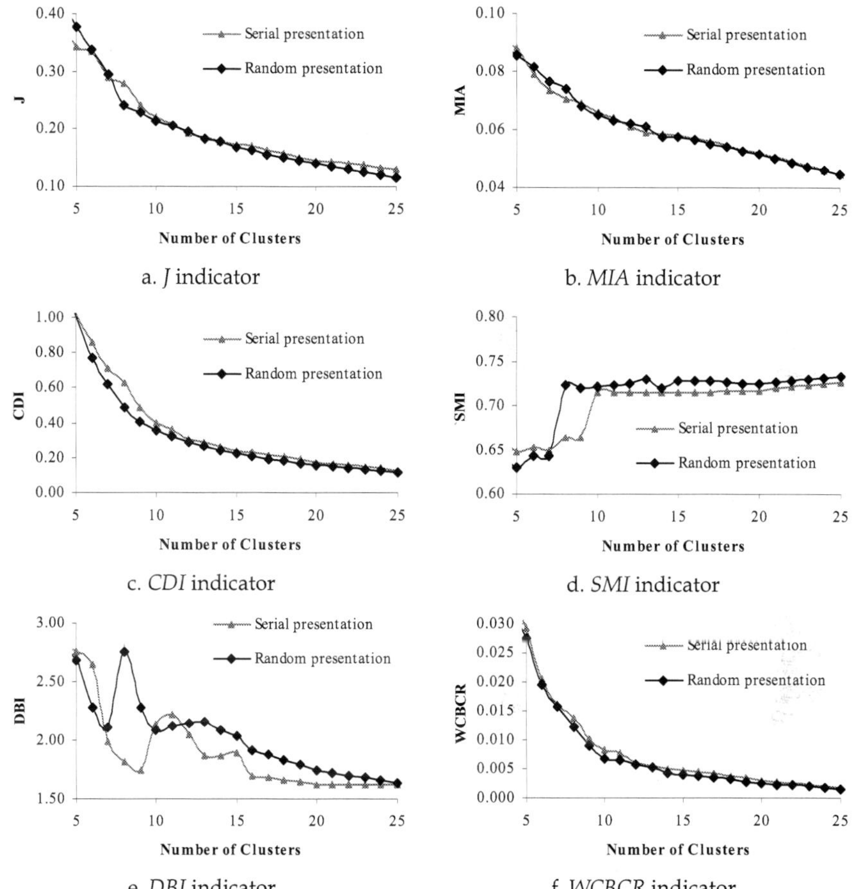

a. *J* indicator

b. *MIA* indicator

c. *CDI* indicator

d. *SMI* indicator

e. *DBI* indicator

f. *WCBCR* indicator

Fig. 1.11. Adequacy measures for the AVQ method for a set of 292 training patterns for 5 to 25 clusters (serial presentation and random presentation without bias factor)

The use of the AVQ algorithm with random presentation without the bias factor is proposed, even if there is a small computing time increment against the algorithm with serial presentation.

1.4.2.4 *Application of the fuzzy k-means*

In the fuzzy k-means algorithm the results of all adequacy measures (except *J*) improve as the amount of fuzziness increases, as shown in Fig. 1.12, where the six adequacy measures are presented for different number of clusters and for three cases of $q=\{2,4,6\}$.

It is noted that the initialization of the respective weights is similar to the proposed k-means. The maximum number of epochs is 500 for the three scenarios and the upper limit of the weight change between sequential iterations ε is 10^{-4}. Practically the algorithm is always converged after at most 400 iterations.

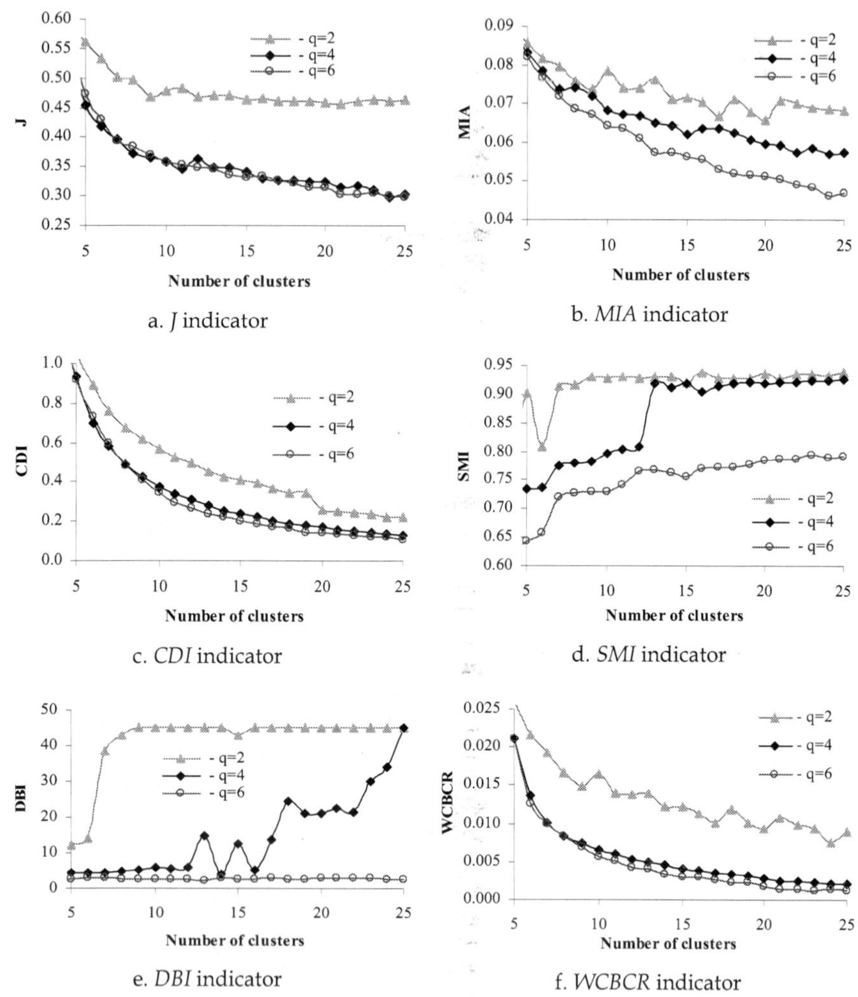

a. J indicator b. MIA indicator

c. CDI indicator d. SMI indicator

e. DBI indicator f. $WCBCR$ indicator

Fig. 1.12. Adequacy measures for the fuzzy k-means method for a set of 292 training patterns, for 5 to 25 clusters and q=2, 4, 6

1.4.2.5 Application of hierarchical agglomerative algorithms

In the case of the seven hierarchical models the best results are given by the *WARD* model for *J* and *CDI* adequacy measures and by the *UPGMA* model for *MIA, SMI, WCBCR* indicators. For the *Davies-Bouldin* indicator there are significant variances, according to Fig.1.13. It should be mentioned that there are not any other parameters for calibration, such as maximum number of iterations etc.

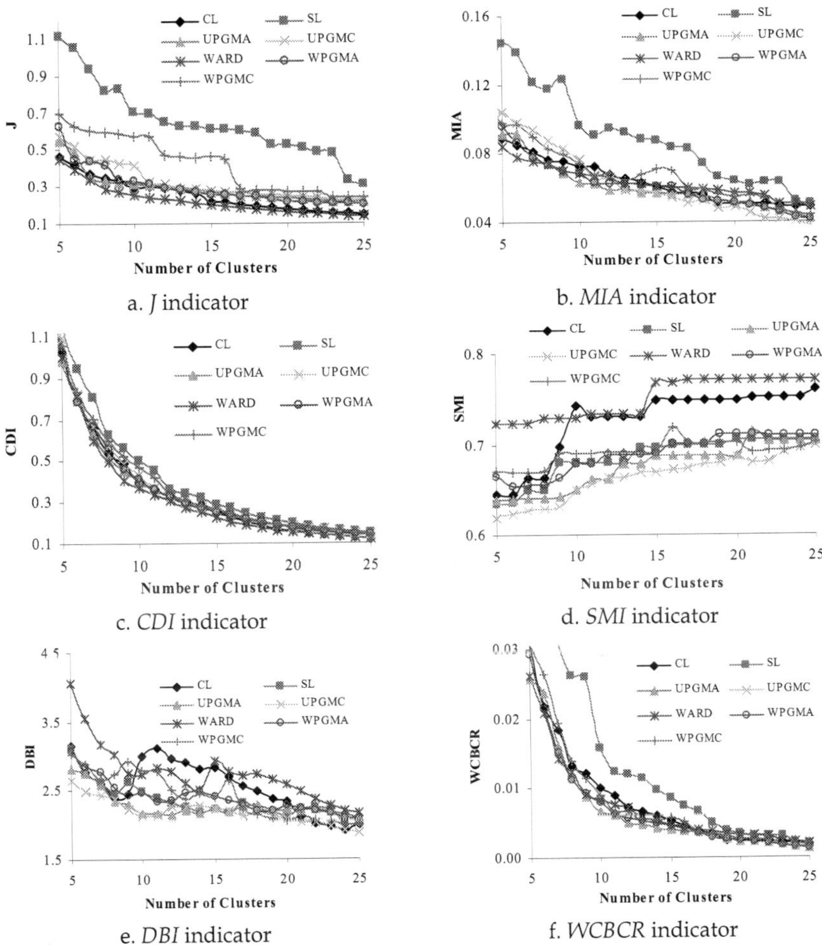

a. *J* indicator

b. *MIA* indicator

c. *CDI* indicator

d. *SMI* indicator

e. *DBI* indicator

f. *WCBCR* indicator

Fig. 1.13. Adequacy measures for the 7 hierarchical clustering algorithms for a set of 292 training patterns for 5 to 25 clusters

1.4.2.6 Application of mono-dimensional self-organizing maps

Although the SOM algorithm is theoretically well defined, there are several issues that need to be solved for the effective training of SOM. The major problems are:

- to stop the training process of the optimum SOM. In this case the target is to minimize the index *Is* (eq.(1.32)), which combines the quality measures of the quantization error given by eq.(1.4), the topographic error given by eq. (1.33) and the average distortion measure error given by eq.(1.34). In Fig. 1.14, the normalized values of these four indices are registered for the case of a 10x1 SOM for the chronological load curves of the industrial customer under study. Generally, it is noticed that the convergence is completed after $0.5 \div 2.0 \cdot T_{\eta_0}$ epochs during fine tuning phase, when T_{η_0} has big values (≥ 1000 epochs).

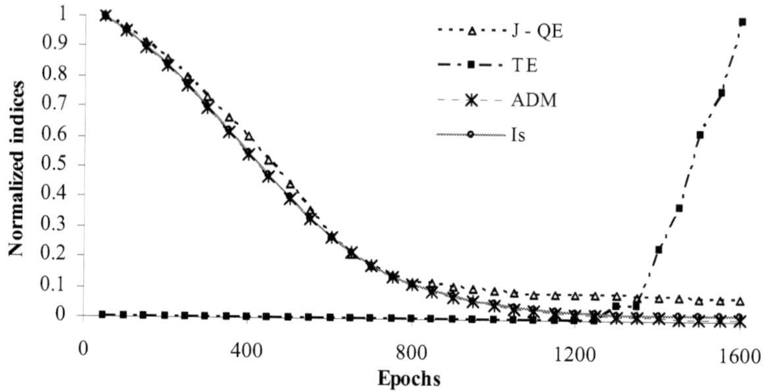

Fig. 1.14. Quality normalized measures of the quantization error (QE), the topographic error (TE), the average distortion measure error (ADM) and the index (Is) for the mono-dimensional SOM with 10 clusters, $\eta_r = 0.1$, $\eta_f = 0.001$, $T_{\eta_0} = 1000$, $\sigma_0 = 10$, $T_{s_0} = T_{\eta_0}$, $T_{\sigma 0} = T_{\eta_0} / \ln \sigma_0$ in the case of a set of 292 training patterns of the industrial customer under study

- the proper initial value of the neighbourhood radius σ_0. The radius follows the decreasing power of the neighbourhood radius function $\sigma(t) = \sigma_0 \cdot \exp(-t / T_{\sigma 0})$, which has the advantage to act on all neurons of the map with decreasing weights according to the respective distances of the winning neuron. On the contrary, the linear radius function does not change the weights of those neurons with distances from the winning neuron larger than $\sigma(t)$. The computational time of the last one is significantly smaller than the power function. In Fig. 1.15 the effects of the initial radius σ_0 on the adequacy measures are registered. It is noticed that the neural network's performance is improved, if the initial radius is increased σ_0, especially for $T_{\eta_0} \leq 2000$.

- the proper values of the multiplicative factor ϕ between T_{s_0} (epochs of the rough ordering phase) and T_{η_0} (time parameter of learning rate). In Fig. 1.16 the adequacy measures with respect to ϕ and T_{η_0} are presented as indicative examples, from which it is concluded that the best behaviour of *J, CDI, SMI, DBI* indicators is registered for $T_\eta \geq$ 800 and $\phi = 1$, while of *MIA, WCBCR* ones for $\phi = 2$ respectively.

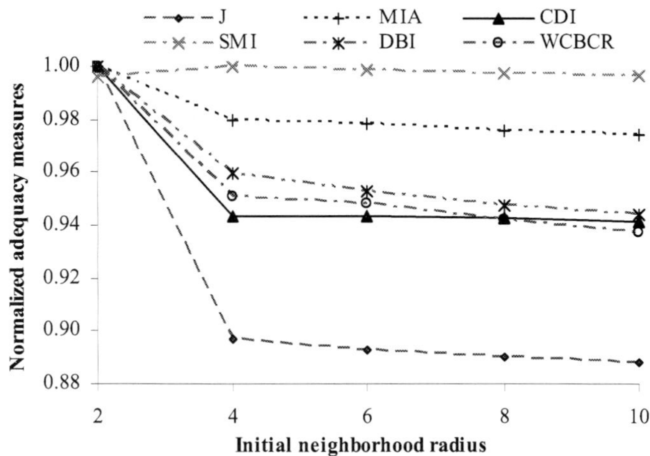

Fig. 1.15. Normalized adequacy measures with respect to the initial radius σ_0 for the mono-dimensional SOM with 10 clusters, $\eta_r = 0.1$, $\eta_f = 0.001$, $T_{\eta_0} = 1000$, $T_{s_0} = T_{\eta_0}$, $T_{\sigma 0} = T_{\eta_0} / \ln \sigma_0$ in the case of a set of 292 training patterns of the industrial customer under study

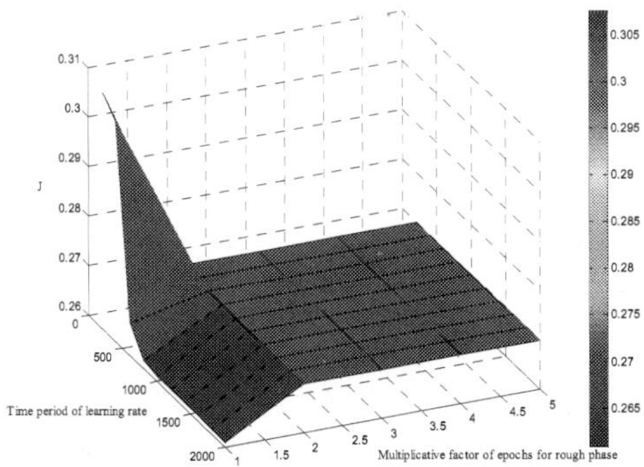

a. *J* indicator

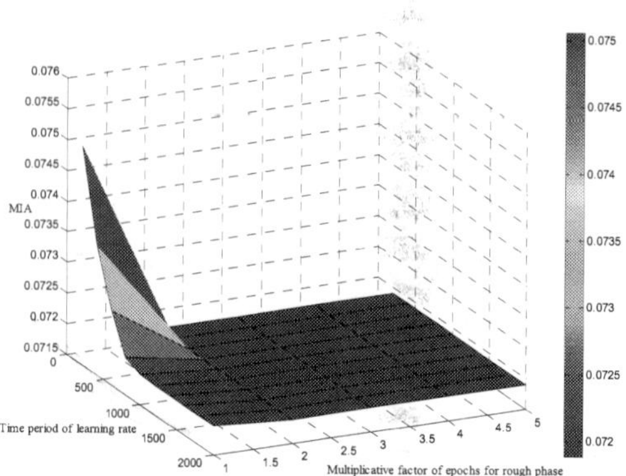

b. *MIA* indicator

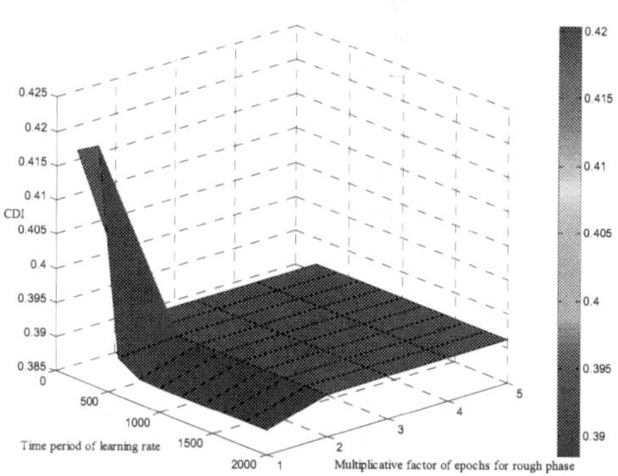

c. *CDI* indicator

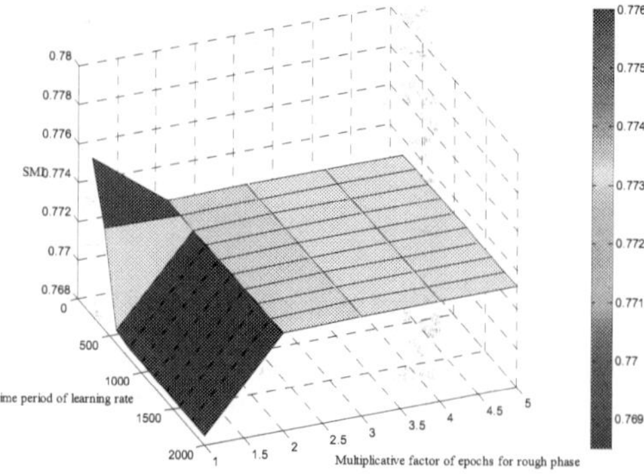

d. *SMI* indicator

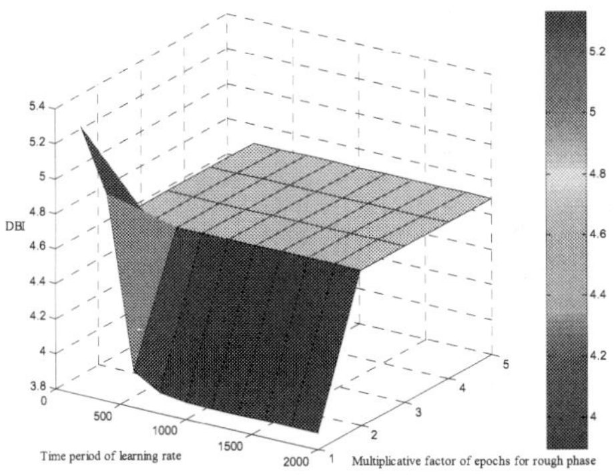

e. *DBI* indicator

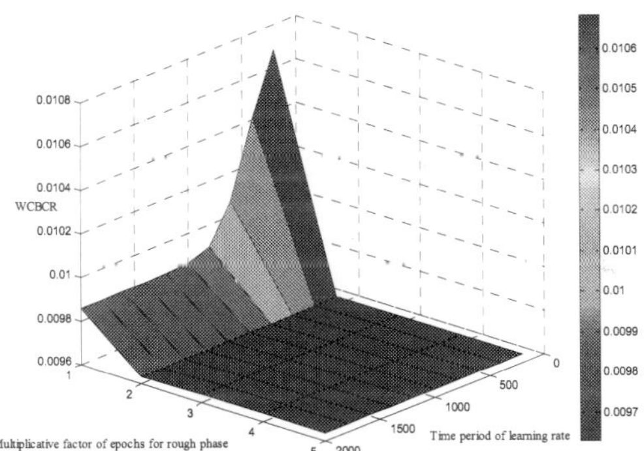

f. *WCBCR* indicator

Fig. 1.16. Adequacy measures with respect to $\phi = \{1,2,3,4,5\}$ and $T_{\eta_0} = \{200,400, ..., 2000\}$ for the mono-dimensional SOM with 10 clusters, $\eta_r = 0.1$, $\eta_f = 0.001$, $\sigma_0 = 10$, $T_{\sigma_0} = T_{\eta_0} / \ln \sigma_0$ in the case of a set of 292 training patterns for the industrial customer under study

- the proper values of the multiplicative factor ξ between T_{σ_0} (time parameter of neighbourhood radius) and T_{η_0}. In Fig. 1.17 the adequacy measures with respect to ξ and T_{η_0} are presented as indicative examples, from which it is concluded that the best behaviour of *J*, *CDI* indicators is registered for $T_\eta \geq 1000$ and $\xi = \{0.2,...,1\}$, of *SMI*, *DBI* ones for $T_\eta \geq 1000$ and $\xi = 0.6$, of *MIA*, *WCBCR* ones for $T_\eta \geq 1000$ and $\xi = \{0.2,0.4\}$ respectively.

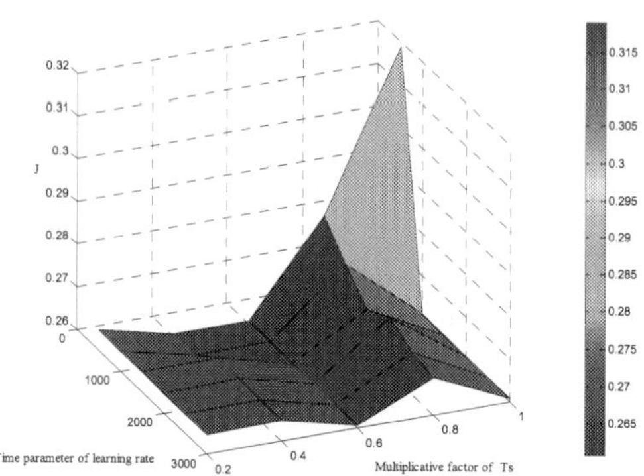

a. *J* indicator

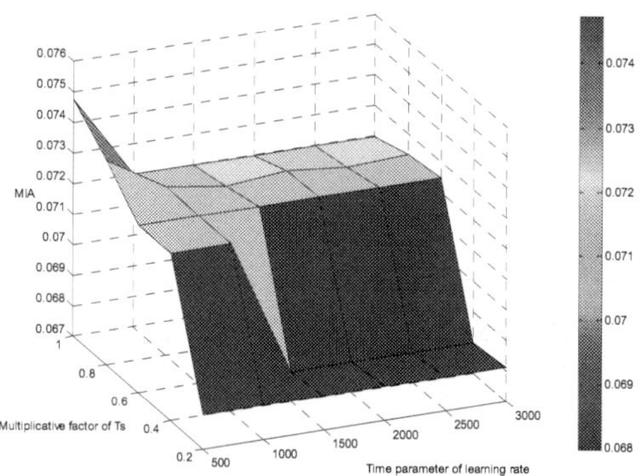

b. *MIA* indicator

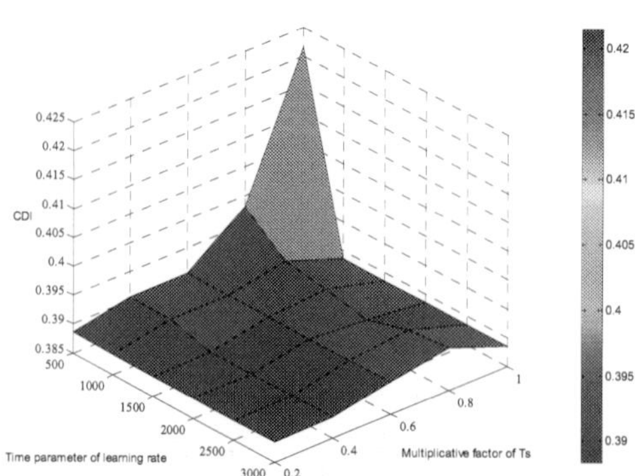

c. *CDI* indicator

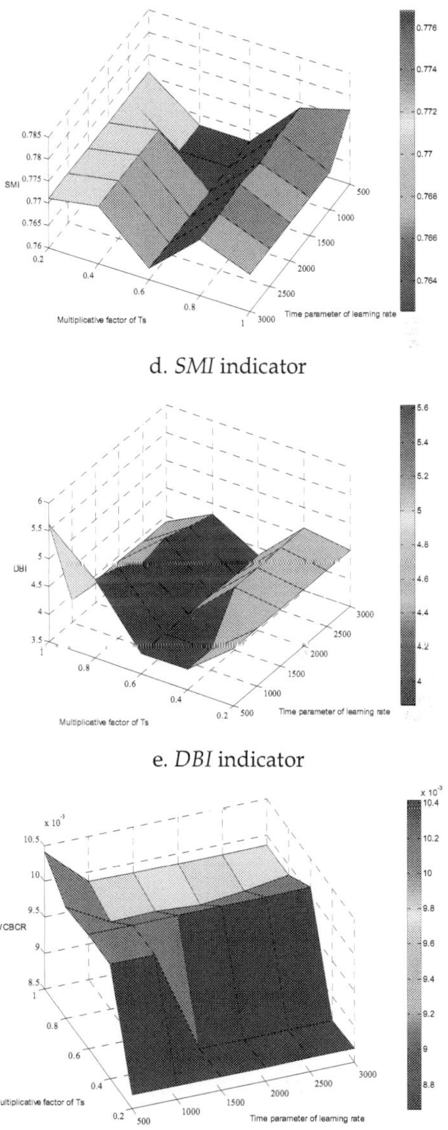

d. *SMI* indicator

e. *DBI* indicator

f. *WCBCR* indicator

Fig. 1.17. Adequacy measures with respect to $\xi = \{0.2,0.4,...,1.0\}$ and $T_{\eta_0} = \{500,1000, ..., 3000\}$ for the mono-dimensional SOM with 10 clusters, $\eta_r=0.1$, $\eta_f = 0.001$, $\sigma_0=10$, $T_{\sigma_0} = T_{\eta_0} / \ln \sigma_0$ in the case of a set of 292 training patterns for the industrial customer under study

- the proper values of the learning rate η_r during the rough ordering phase. In Fig. 1.18 the adequacy measures with respect to η_r and T_{η_0} are presented as indicative examples, from which it is concluded that the best behaviour for all indicators is registered for $T_\eta \geq$ 1000 and $0.1 \leq \eta_0 \leq 0.15$. Especially for *MIA, WCBCR* indicators the best results are succeeded for $1000 \leq T_\eta \leq 1500$ and $0.2 \leq \eta_0 \leq 0.4$ with big variations.

- the learning rate η_f during the fine tuning phase. From the results of the performed study, it is derived that the proper value of the parameter η_f must be smaller than 20% of the initial value of the learning rate η_r and between 10^{-3} and 10^{-4}. If η_f is increased, the behaviour of *J, CDI, SMI, DBI, WCBCR* indicators is improved whereas that of *MIA* is worsened.

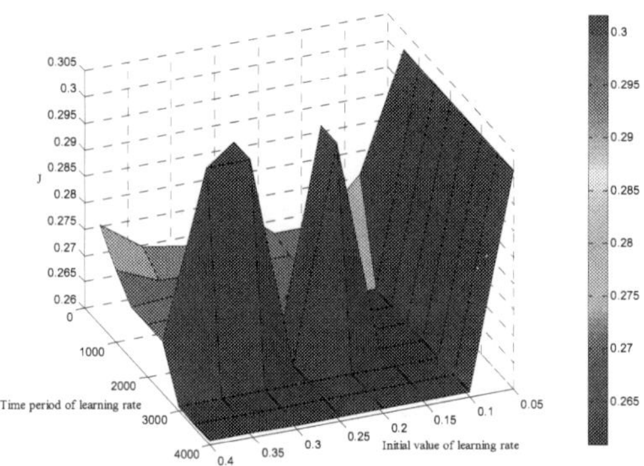

a. *J* indicator

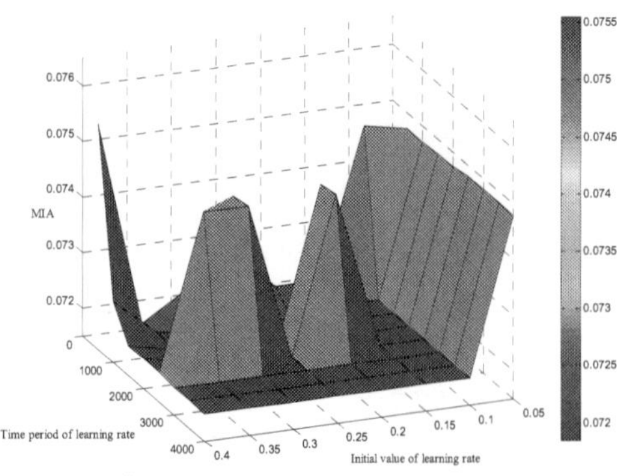

b. *MIA* indicator

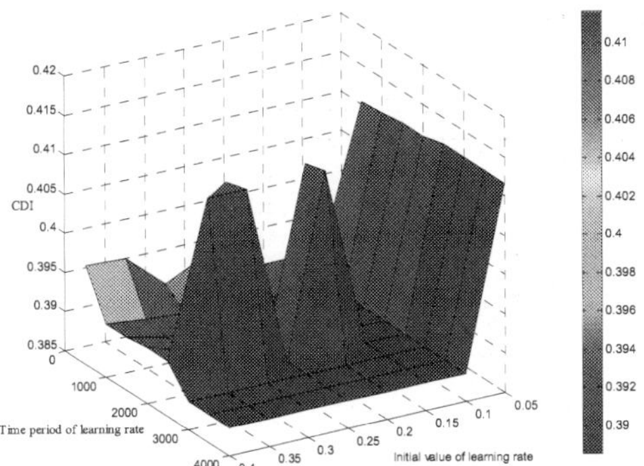

c. *CDI* indicator

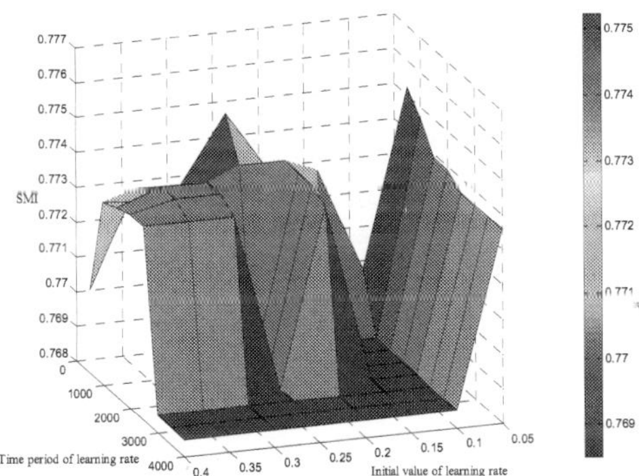

d. *SMI* indicator

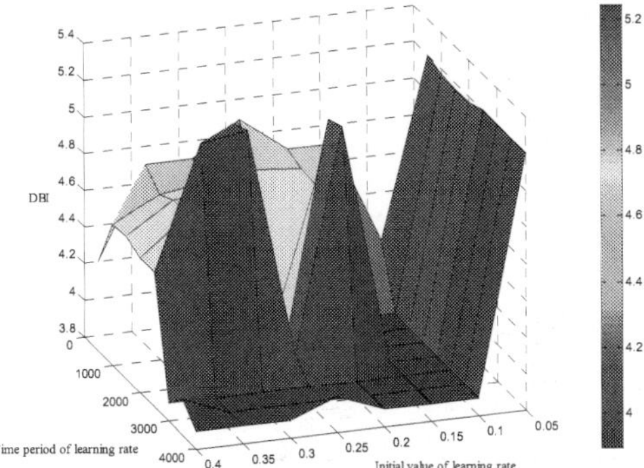

e. *DBI* indicator

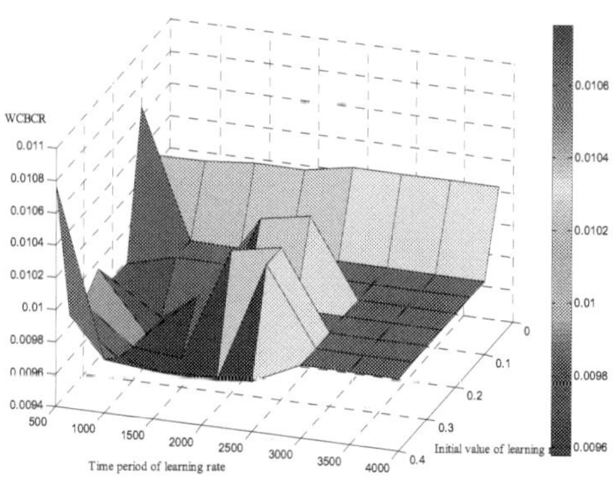

f. *WCBCR* indicator

Fig. 1.18. Adequacy measures with respect to $\eta_r = \{0.05, 0.10, ..., 0.4\}$ and $T_{\eta_0} = \{500, 1000, ..., 4000\}$ for the mono-dimensional SOM with 10 clusters, $\eta_f = 0.001$, $\sigma_0 = 10$, $T_{s_0} = T_{\eta_0}$, $T_{\sigma_0} = T_{\eta_0} / \ln \sigma_0$ in the case of a set of 292 training patterns for the industrial customer under study

- the initialization of the weights of the neurons. Three cases were examined: (a) $w_{ki} = 0.5, \forall k, i$, (b) the random initialization of each neuron's weight, (c) the random choice of the input vectors for each neuron. The best training behaviour was presented in case (a).

The optimization process for the mono-dimensional SOM parameters is repeated for any population of clusters.

1.4.2.7 Application of bi-dimensional self-organizing maps

In the case of the bi-dimensional SOM, the shape, the population of neurons and their respective arrangement are issues to be solved –beyond the optimization of parameters, which is considered during the training process of the mono-dimensional SOM.

The rectangular shape of the map is defined with rectangular or hexagonal arrangement of neurons. The population of the last ones is recommended to be $5 \times \sqrt{N}$ to $20 \times \sqrt{N}$ (SOM Toolbox for MATLAB 5, 2000; Thang et al., 2003; Chicco et al., 2004). In the case of the industrial customer, a set of 292 vectors was given. The map can have 85 ($\cong 5 \times \sqrt{292}$) to 342 ($\cong 20 \times \sqrt{292}$) neurons. The respective square maps can be 9x9 to 19x19. Using the ratio between the two major eigenvalues, the respective ratio is 27.31 (=4.399/0.161) and the proposed grids can be 55x2 and 82x3. In Table 1.1 the quality indices are presented for different grids, arrangements of neurons, weights' initialization. The best result for the index *Is* is given for the square grid 19x19. It is noted that the initialization of the neurons can be a linear combination of the respective eigenvectors of the two major eigenvalues (scenario of initialization 1) or can be equal to 0.5 (scenario of initialization 2).

2D SOM-neurons population	Arrangement - weights initialization	Total epochs - t	$Is(t)$	$ADM(t)$	$TE(t)$	$J(t)$	Calibration of $T_\eta - \xi - \phi - \eta_r - \eta_f - \sigma_0$
9x9=81	Rect. –(2)	3600	0.2832	0.08853	0.10616	0.08853	1500-0.4-2-0.15-0.001-9
9x9=81	Hex. –(2)	2400	0.3245	0.08372	0.15753	0.08372	1000-1.0-2-0.20-0.001-9
10x10=100	Rect. –(2)	3600	0.2208	0.06757	0.08562	0.06757	1500-0.6-2-0.40-0.001-10
10x10=100	Hex. –(2)	2400	0.2354	0.07147	0.09247	0.07147	1000-1.0-2-0.25-0.001-10
12x12=144	Rect. –(2)	1100	0.2371	0.05176	0.13356	0.05176	500-1.0-2-0.15-0.001-12
12x12=144	Hex. –(2)	4400	0.2679	0.05003	0.16781	0.05003	2000-1.0-2-0.05-0.001-12
14x14=196	Rect. –(2)	3600	0.2306	0.04167	0.14726	0.04167	1500-1.0-2-0.05-0.001-14
14x14=196	Hex. –(2)	2200	0.2245	0.03521	0.15410	0.03521	500-1.0-2-0.05-0.001-16
16x16=256	Rect. –(2)	2200	0.1356	0.02840	0.07877	0.02840	1000-1.0-2-0.10-0.001-16
16x16=256	Hex. –(2)	3300	0.1678	0.02909	0.10959	0.02909	1500-1.0-2-0.10-0.001-16
19x19=361	Rect. –(2)	4400	0.0970	0.01254	0.07192	0.01254	2000-1.0-2-0.15-0.001-19
19x19=361	Hex. –(2)	4400	0.1267	0.01538	0.09589	0.01538	2000-1.0-2-0.05-0.001-19
55x2=110	Rect. –(2)	1200	0.3504	0.05532	0.23973	0.05532	500-1.0-2-0.15-0.001-55
55x2=110	Rect. –(1)	1200	0.3503	0.05532	0.23973	0.05532	500-1.0-2-0.15-0.001-55
82x3=246	Rect. –(2)	1100	0.2040	0.01982	0.16438	0.01982	500-1.0-2-0.30-0.001-82

Table 1.1. Quality Indices for Different Cases of Bi-Dimensional SOM

The type of the arrangement and the weights initialization do not affect the respective results significantly. Practically, the clusters of the bi-dimensional map cannot be directly exploited because of the size and the location of the neurons into the grid, as shown in Fig. 1.19. This problem is solved through the application of a basic classification method (e.g. the

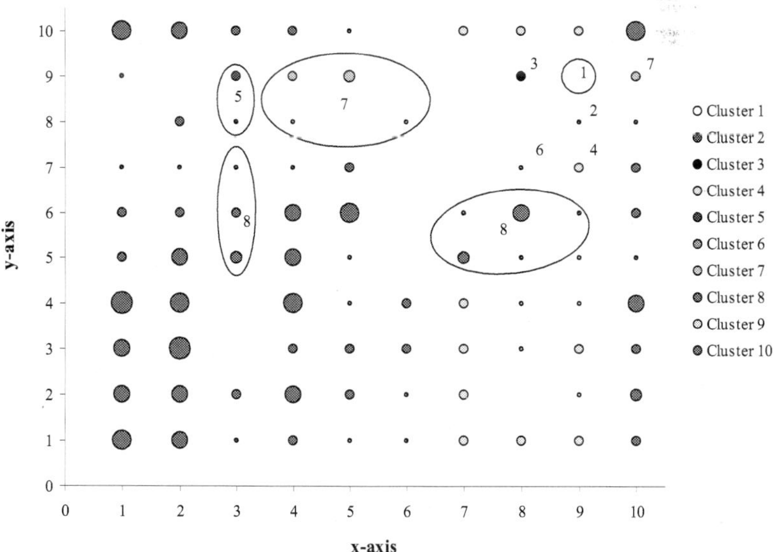

a. Bi-dimensional SOM 10x10 with rectangular arrangement

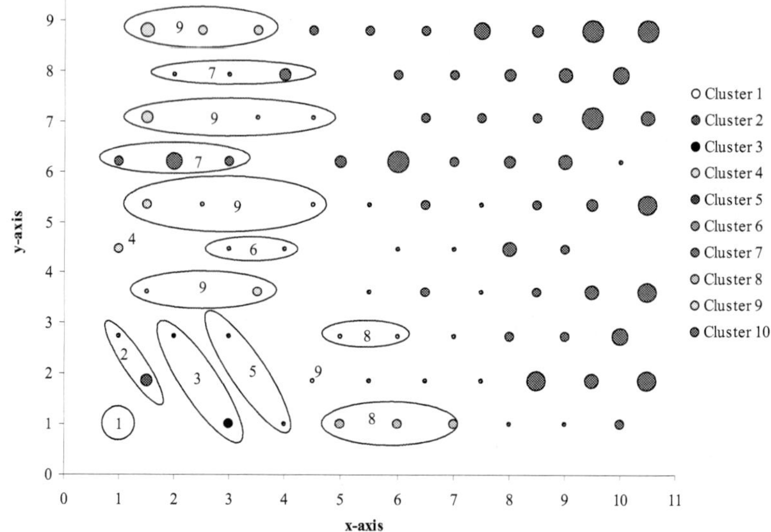

a. Bi-dimensional SOM 10x10 with hexagonal arrangement

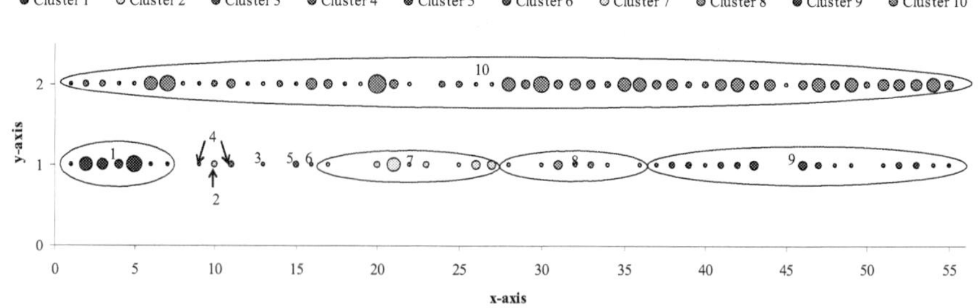

b. Bi-dimensional SOM 55x2 with rectangular arrangement

Fig. 1.19. Different cases of bi-dimensional SOM after the application of the proposed k-means method at the neurons of SOM

proposed k-means) for the neurons of the bi-dimensional SOM (Chicco et al., 2004). The adequacy measures are calculated using the load daily chronological curves of the neurons which form the respective clusters of the basic classification method. In Table 1.2, the adequacy measures of the aforementioned maps are presented, using the proposed k-means method for 10 final clusters.

For the industrial customer, the best results of the application of the k-means method to the neurons of the SOM are given for the maps with the ratio between the two major eigenvalues of the covariance matrix of the input vectors set (see Table 1.2). The respective clusters are also more compact than the ones of the square maps, as it can be seen in Fig. 1.19.

2D SOM-neurons population	Arrangement –weights initialization	Adequacy Measure					
		J	MIA	CDI	SMI	DBI	WCBCR $(*10^{-3})$
9x9=81	Rect. – (2)	0.309430	0.064420	0.365331	0.668309	2.01767	8.4570
9x9=81	Hex. – (2)	0.284911	0.064730	0.358870	0.666259	1.91128	9.1605
10x10=100	Rect. – (2)	0.269351	0.066746	0.358512	0.661059	1.76758	8.7586
10x10=100	Hex. – (2)	0.285281	0.062488	0.369192	0.682404	1.81237	8.4091
12x12=144	Rect. – (2)	0.267056	0.065584	0.353097	0.671649	1.74857	9.2029
12x12=144	Hex. – (2)	0.268810	0.070409	0.351914	0.661194	1.85451	9.4168
14x14=196	Rect. – (2)	0.272213	0.066418	0.360227	0.662015	1.68854	8.8566
14x14=196	Hex. – (2)	0.273781	0.069001	0.361199	0.666046	1.75621	10.0756
16x16=256	Rect. – (2)	0.267521	0.066970	0.349423	0.669469	1.88224	9.2304
16x16=256	Hex. – (2)	0.268528	0.068710	0.364127	0.660511	1.69430	9.4152
19x19=361	Rect. – (2)	0.266128	0.065389	0.351903	0.682931	1.85560	8.5386
19x19=361	Hex. – (2)	0.267087	0.067618	0.343808	0.660950	1.70171	8.8486
55x2=110	Rect. – (2)	0.262634	0.060581	0.345677	0.654891	1.68728	7.7872
82x3=246	Rect. – (2)	0.258002	0.063284	0.334516	0.681566	1.75790	8.1426

Table 1.2. Adequacy Indices for 10 Clusters – Typical Load Chronological Curves of the Industrial Customer Using Proposed K-Means Method at the Second Classification Level for Different Cases of Bi-Dimensional SOM

1.4.2.8 Comparison of clustering models & adequacy indicators

In Fig. 1.20, the best results for each clustering method (proposed k-means, fuzzy k-means, adaptive vector quantization, self-organized maps and hierarchical algorithms) are depicted. The proposed k-means model has the smallest values for the *MIA, CDI, DBI* and *WCBCR* indicators. The *WARD* algorithm presents the best behaviour for the mean square error *J*, the unweighted pair group method average algorithm (*UPGMA*) and the bi-dimensional SOM (with the application of the proposed k-means at the second level) for the *SMI* indicator. The proposed k-means model has similar behaviour to the *WARD* algorithm for the *J* indicator and to the *UPGMA* algorithm for the *WCBCR*. All indicators -except DBI-exhibit improved performance, as the number of clusters is increased.

In Table 1.3 the results of the best clustering methods are presented for 10 clusters with the respective parameters, which is the finally proposed size of the typical days for that customer. The optimized parameters for the mono- dimensional and bi- dimensional self-organized maps have been analyzed in §1.4.2.5 and §1.4.2.6 respectively. The proposed k-means method gives the best results for the *MIA, CDI, DBI* and *WCBCR* indicators (for different pairs of (a,b)), while the adaptive vector quantization should be used for *J* indicator and the bi-dimensional self organized map using proposed k-means for classification in a second level for *SMI* indicator.

Observing the number of dead clusters for the under study models (Fig. 1.20.g) the behaviour of *DBI* and *SMI* indicators for bi-dimensional SOM and k-means emerges a significant variability. For the above reasons the proposed indicators are *MIA* and *WCBCR*. Studying the number of dead clusters for the proposed k-means model (Fig. 1.7), it is obvious that the use of *WCBCR* indicator is slightly superior to the use of *MIA* and *J* indicators. It is also noted, that the basic theoretical advantage of the *WCBCR* indicator is the fact that it combines the distances of the input vectors from the representative clusters and the distances between clusters, covering also the *J* and *CDI* characteristics.

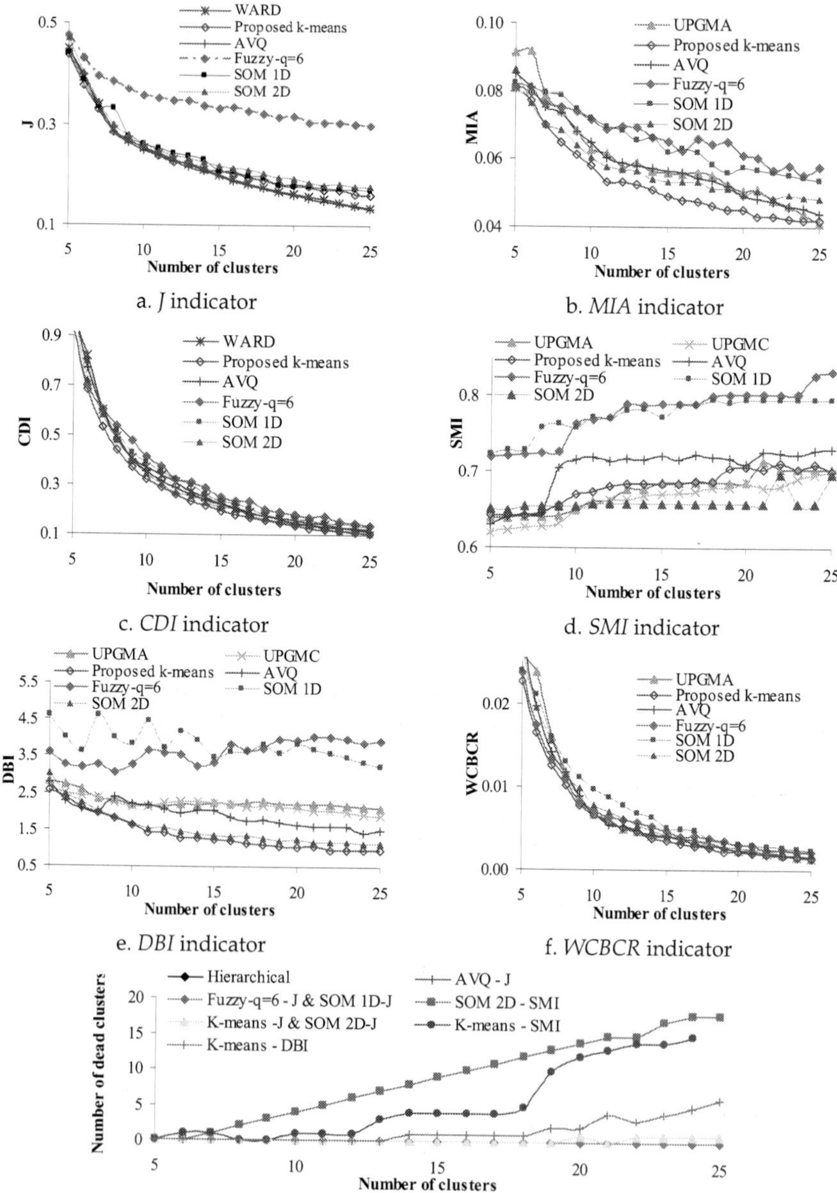

a. *J* indicator

b. *MIA* indicator

c. *CDI* indicator

d. *SMI* indicator

e. *DBI* indicator

f. *WCBCR* indicator

g. Dead clusters for the basic clustering methods

Fig. 1.20. The best results of each clustering method for the set of 292 training patterns of a medium voltage industrial customer for 5 to 25 clusters

The improvement of the adequacy indicators is significant for the first 10 clusters. After this point, the behaviour of the most indicators is gradually stabilized. It can also be estimated graphically by using the rule of the "knee" (Gerbec et al., 2004; -, 2005), as shown in Fig. 1.21. If this knee is not clearly shown, the tangents are drawn estimating the knee for 10 clusters for the current case study.

After having taken into consideration that the ratio of the computational training time for the under study methods is 0.05:1:22:24:36:50 (hierarchical: proposed k-means: adaptive vector quantization: mono-dimensional SOM: fuzzy k-means for q=6: bi-dimensional SOM), the use of the hierarchical and k-means models is proposed. It is mentioned that the necessary computational training time for the proposed k-means method is approximately one hour for Pentium 4, 1.7 GHz, 768 MB.

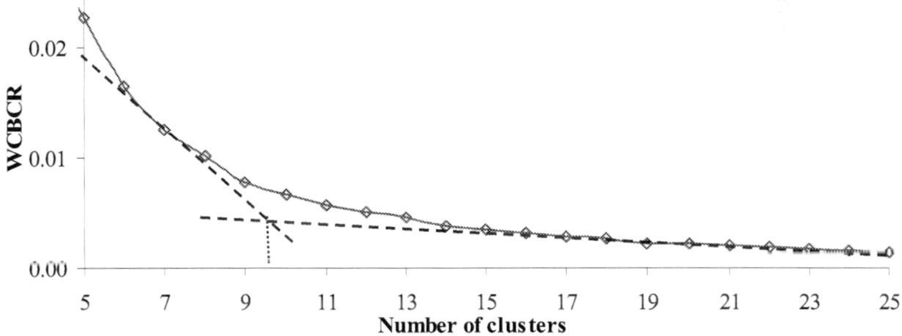

Fig. 1.21. Indicative estimation of the necessary clusters for the typical load daily chronological curves of a medium voltage industrial customer, using the proposed k-means model with the *WCBCR* adequacy measure

Consequently, the proposed k-means model with *WCBCR* adequacy measure is suggested for the description of the load behaviour of the analyzed paper-mill medium voltage customer. More generally, the *WCBCR* indicator should be used because of its aforementioned basic theoretical advantage. But for completeness reasons we will examine all adequacy measures for all models for other 93 customers in §1.4.2.10. Before this step the results for the analyzed paper-mill medium voltage customer will be presented.

1.4.2.9 Representative daily load chronological diagrams of a paper-mill medium voltage customer

The results of the respective clustering for 10 clusters using the proposed k-means model with the optimization of the *WCBCR* indicator are presented in Tables 1.4 and in Fig. 1.22. This number of clusters is qualitatively satisfied.

The retailer and the head engineer of the under study industry can observe the customer's daily demand behaviour during the year based on the respective load curves. Specifically, cluster 1 represents holidays, clusters 2 and 4 the days of the re-operation of the industry, cluster 3 the days of stopping the operation of the industry, cluster 5 a day with partial internal power fault, cluster 6 the workdays with one of the two lines for production in operation, clusters 7 and 8 the workdays for which one of the two lines for production is out of operation for few hours, clusters 9 and 10 the usual workdays, where every 8 hours there is a small variance because of the workers' change.

Methods -Parameters	Adequacy Measure					
	J	MIA	CDI	SMI	DBI	WCBCR
Proposed k-means (scenario 1)	0.2527	0.05828	0.3239	0.6711	1.6515	0.006679
a parameter	0.10	0.19	0.35	0.17	0.18	0.11
b parameter	0.77	0.35	0.55	0.48	0.37	0.60
K-means (scenario 2)	0.2537	0.06782	0.3601	0.7311	2.5603	0.007760
Classic k-means (scenario 3)	0.2538	0.06435	0.3419	0.7306	2.4173	0.006716
AVQ	0.2496	0.06472	0.3537	0.7160	2.1884	0.006886
η_0 parameter	0.80	0.85	0.85	0.75	0.60	0.70
$T_{\eta 0}$ parameter	500	1500	500	2000	500	500
Fuzzy k-means (q=6)	0.3575	0.07144	0.3697	0.7635	3.2559	0.007153
a parameter	0.31	0.27	0.18	0.13	0.10	0.10
b parameter	0.49	0.31	0.36	0.54	0.59	0.46
CL	0.2973	0.07271	0.3977	0.7427	2.9928	0.010052
SL	0.7027	0.09644	0.5049	0.6798	2.4855	0.015696
UPGMA	0.3127	0.06297	0.4008	0.6494	2.1714	0.006684
UPGMC	0.4147	0.07656	0.4346	0.6494	2.1198	0.009908
WARD	0.2538	0.06804	0.3723	0.7296	2.7334	0.008399
WPGMA	0.3296	0.06807	0.4112	0.6781	2.4764	0.007991
WPGMC	0.5747	0.07386	0.4665	0.6900	2.7903	0.008884
Mono-dimensional SOM	0.2607	0.07189	0.3903	0.7588	3.8325	0.009631
Bi-dimensional SOM 55x2 using proposed k-means for classification in a second level	0.2623	0.06059	0.3456	0.6549	1.6873	0.007787
a parameter of k-means	0.15	0.24	0.36	0.44	0.22	0.22
b parameter of k-means	0.69	0.28	0.51	0.11	0.30	0.30

Table 1.3. Comparison of the Best Clustering Models for 10 Clusters for the Medium Voltage Industrial Customer

Load cluster	Day (1 for Monday, 2 for Tuesday etc.)							Days per cluster
	1	2	3	4	5	6	7	
1	4	4	4	4	3	4	4	27
2	1	0	0	0	2	0	0	3
3	1	0	0	0	0	1	0	2
4	0	1	1	0	0	0	0	2
5	0	1	0	0	0	0	0	1
6	4	2	4	4	3	2	2	21
7	6	4	3	4	4	2	0	23
8	2	1	1	1	2	2	1	10
9	9	11	16	11	11	11	13	82
10	14	17	12	18	16	21	22	120
Total number of days under study								292

Table 1.4. Results of the Proposed k-means Model with optimization to WCBCR Adequacy Measure for 10 clusters for the Medium Voltage Industrial Customer

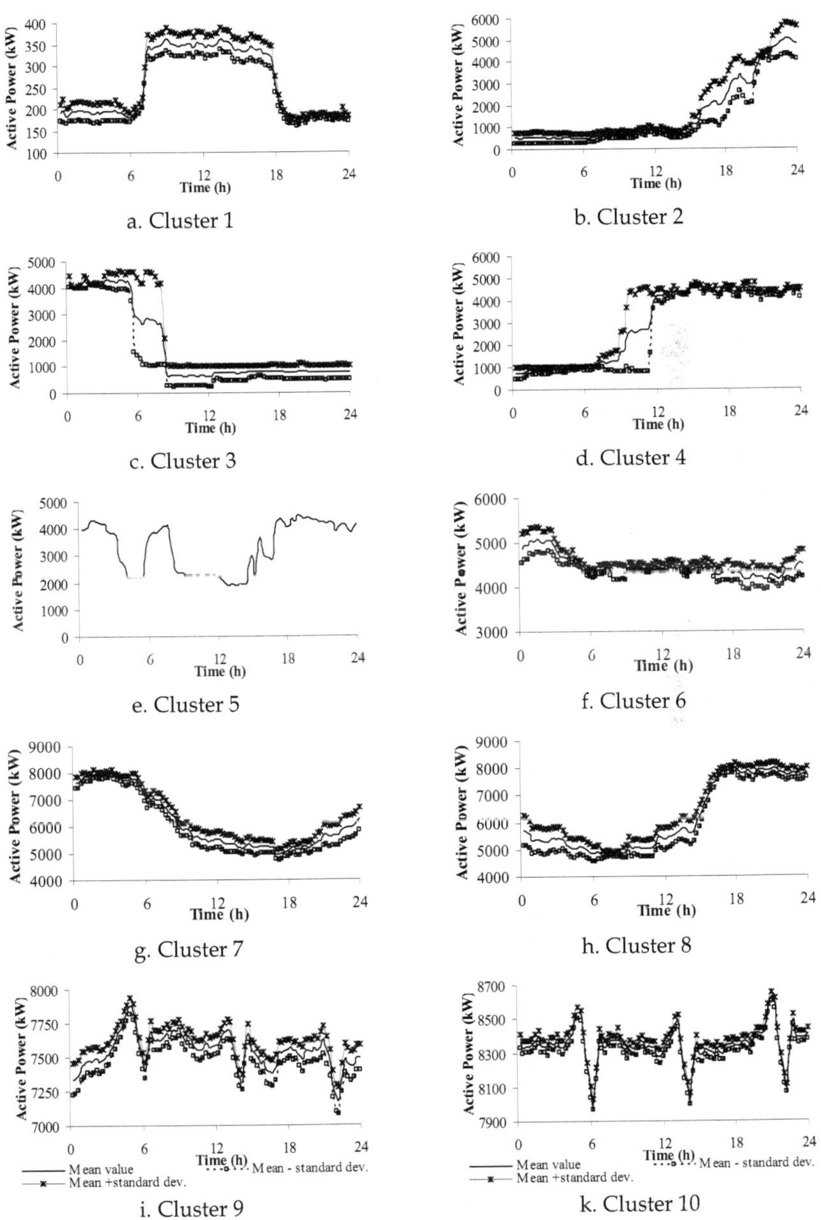

Fig. 1.22. Typical daily chronological load curves for the medium voltage industrial customer using proposed k-means model with optimization to *WCBCR* adequacy measure

The daily load diagrams are well identified using the k-means clustering method and the *WCBCR* indicator, as it is indicatively presented in Fig. 1.23, where the typical load curve of cluster 10 (which represents the most populated day and the day with peak load simultaneously) along with the 120 measured clustered load curves are shown. It is obvious from table 1.4 that the number of the days for each representative cluster of this customer is not influenced by the day of the week.

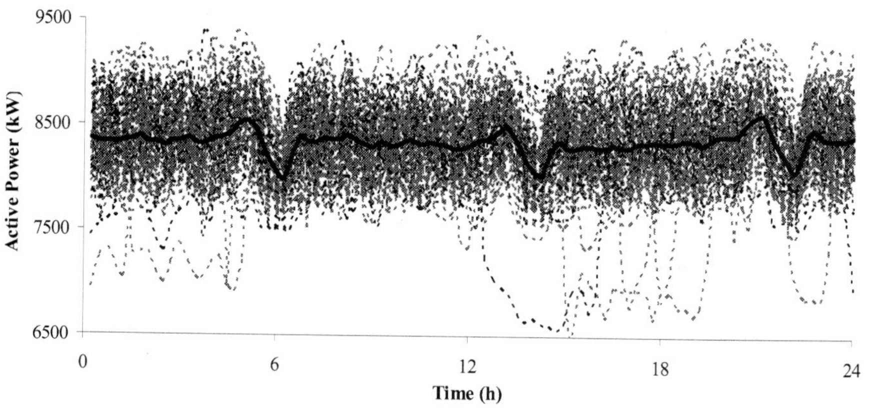

Fig. 1.23. Daily chronological load curve of cluster 10 for the MV industrial customer (bold line) along with its 120 clustered measured curves (thin lines) using the proposed k-means clustering method and the *WCBCR* indicator

1.4.2.10 Application of the Proposed Methodology to a Set of Medium Voltage Customers

The same process was repeated for 93 more medium voltage customers of the Greek power distribution system, with load curves qualitatively described by using 8-12 clusters for each customer. The scope of this application is the representation of the comparison of the clustering algorithms and the adequacy measures for more than one customer. The performance of these methods is presented in Table 1.5 and in Fig. 1.24, through the indication of the number of customers which achieves the best value of adequacy measure.

It is evident, by observing Fig. 1.24, in which a comparison of the algorithms is depicted, that the developed k-means method achieves a better performance for *MIA*, *CDI* and *WCBCR* measures, the bi-dimensional SOM model using proposed k-means for classification in a second level for *J* measure and the adaptive vector quantization for *SMI*, *DBI* indicators. It can be noticed that the other two k-means models show the worst performance in adequacy measures.

Methods	Adequacy Measure					
	J	MIA	CDI	SMI	DBI	WCBCR
Proposed k-means (scenario 1)	6	28	85	16	13	37
K-means (scenario 2)	0	0	0	0	0	0
Classic k-means (scenario 3)	0	0	0	0	0	0
AVQ	2	2	0	32	47	1
Fuzzy k-means (q=6)	0	0	0	0	1	6
CL	0	1	0	0	0	0
SL	0	5	0	2	4	4
UPGMA	0	15	0	3	7	12
UPGMC	0	20	0	22	6	18
WARD	16	0	0	0	0	1
WPGMA	0	13	0	0	3	8
WPGMC	0	6	0	2	1	7
Mono-dimensional SOM	5	1	0	0	0	0
Bi-dimensional SOM using proposed k-means for classification in a second level	65	3	9	17	12	0

Table 1.5. Comparison of the Clustering Models for the Set of 94 MV Customers for 10 clusters

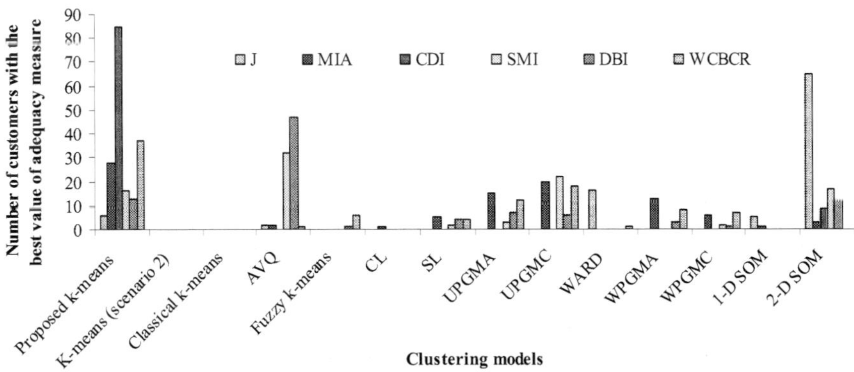

Fig. 1.24. Population of customers with the best value of adequacy measure, with respect to different clustering models for the set of the 94 medium voltage customers of the Greek Power Distribution System

In practice, the proposed k-means model and hierarchical ones should be used, as they lead to the best results compared to the other models, especially for the *WCBCR* indicator.

1.4.3 Usefulness of the application of the proposed methodology

The results of the developed methodology can be used for:

- the proper selection of an adequate tariff by the customer or the recommendation of a tariff from the supplier,
- the settlement of the customer's bills in the case of energy and power bought from more than one suppliers,
- the feasibility studies of the energy efficiency and demand side management measures, which are proper for the customer,
- the customer's short-term and mid-term load forecasting, load estimation after the application of demand side management programs, in which the customer as well as the suppliers are interested,
- the selection of the representative chronological load diagram of the customer by choosing the type of typical day (such as the most populated day, the day with the peak demand load or with the maximum demand energy, etc), which will be used for the customers' classification by the suppliers.

1.5 A two-stage pattern recognition of load curves for classification of electricity customers

1.5.1 General description of the proposed two-stage methodology

Based on the pattern recognition methodology for the classification of the daily load curves of a customer a two-stage methodology, which has been developed for the classification of electricity customers, is presented by Tsekouras et al., 2007. In the first stage, typical chronological load curves of various customers are estimated using pattern recognition methods and their results are compared using the six adequacy measures, as in the case of the first paradigm. In the second stage, classification of customers is performed by the same methods and measures, along with the representative load patterns of customers being obtained from the first stage. The flow chart of the proposed methodology is shown in Fig. 1.25, while its basic steps are the following:

a. *Data and features selection* (same to (*a*) step of the methodology of §1.4).

b. *Customers' clustering using a priori indices*: Customers can be characterized by their geographical region, voltage level (high, medium, low), economic activity, installed power, contracted energy, power factor, etc. These indices are not necessarily related to the load curves according to the experience of the power distribution company. They can be used however for the pre-classification of customers. It is mentioned that the load curves of each customer are normalized using the respective minimum and maximum loads of the period under study.

c. *Data preprocessing* (same to (*b*) step of the methodology of §1.4).

d. *Typical load curves clustering for each customer –First stage application of pattern recognition methods*: For each customer, a number of clustering algorithms (k-means, adaptive vector quantization, fuzzy k-means, self-organized maps and hierarchical clustering) is applied. Each algorithm is trained for the set of load curves and evaluated according to six adequacy measures. The parameters of the algorithms are optimized, if necessary. The developed methodology uses the clustering methods that provide the most satisfactory results. This process is repeated for the total set of customers under study. Special customers, such as seasonal ones (e.g. oil-press industry, small seaside hotels) are identified. Practically, it is the (c) step of the main application of the pattern recognition methods of the methodology of §1.4.

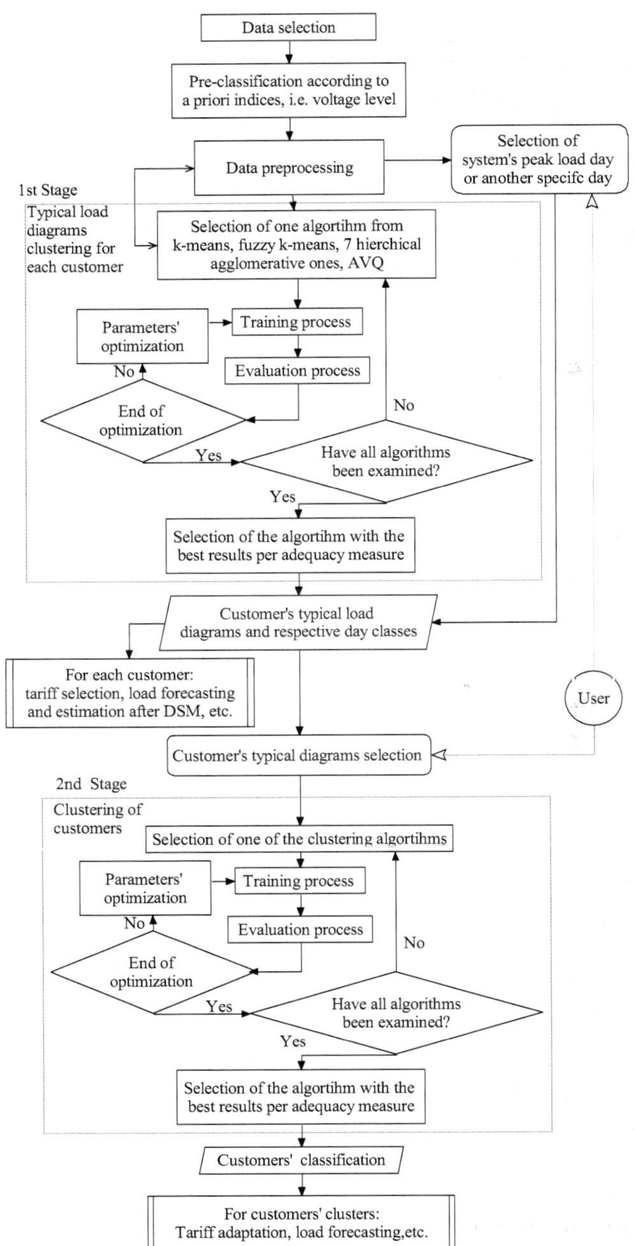

Fig. 1.25. Flow chart of two stage pattern recognition methodology for the classification of customers

e.   *Selection of typical chronological load curves for customers*: The typical load curves of customers that will be used for the final clustering are selected by choosing the type of typical day (such as the most populated day, the day with the peak demand load or with the maximum demand energy, etc). It is possible to omit the customer's typical load curves clustering, if the user wishes to compare the customer's behaviour in specific days, such as the day of system peak load, the mean July workday, etc. However, the customers' behaviour is not entirely representative for the period under study. It is noticed that special customers can be handled separately.

f.   *Clustering of customers - Second stage application of pattern recognition methods*: The clustering methods are applied for the set of the customer's representative load curves. After algorithms' calibration, the clusters of customers and the respective classes representative load curves are formed.

1.5.2 Application of the two-stage methodology to a set of medium voltage customers

1.5.2.1 General

For the application of the proposed methodology a set of 94 medium voltage customers of the Greek power distribution system is used. It should be noticed that larger customer sets coming from different power distribution systems can be handled applying the same procedure and the expected results might be better. However, only the set of 94 customers is available.

Firstly, the first stage of the proposed methodology is realized, which has been already presented in § 1.4.2.1 - § 1.4.2.9 (analytically for one customer) and § 1.4.2.10 (synoptically for the set of the 94 medium voltage customers). Next, the second stage is implemented. The characteristic customer's typical day can be either the most populated day of the customer or the day with the peak load demand (independently of the best number of clusters for each individual customer). Here, two case studies are presented: the first with the most populated day of each customer and the second with the peak load demand. In both cases the representative load curve for each customer is obtained by the clustering method that shows the best results for the adequacy measure being used (here is *WCBCR*). The clustering methods are applied for the set of the representative load curve for each customer using *WCBCR* as adequacy measure because of its theoretical advantage (see §1.4.2.8).

1.5.2.2 Case study I: the most populated day of each customer

For this case study the most populated day of each customer is used. For example the respective cluster is the 10th one for the industrial customer in Table 1.2. Fig. 1.26 shows the best results of each clustering method by using the *WCBCR* measure. The developed k-means and UPGMC models are proved to be the best ones, as it is also registered in Table 1.6. The respective number of clusters is determined by using the rule of the "knee" (see §1.4.2.8) finding that the necessary number of clusters is 12.

The results of clustering for 12 clusters using the UPGMC model with the optimization of the *WCBCR* measure are presented in Table 1.7 and in Fig. 1.27. Practically eighty-nine customers form seven main clusters (it is proposed empirically the number of the clusters to be between 2 and $\sqrt{89} \approx 9$ (Figueiredo et al., 2005)), while the remaining five customers show specific unique characteristics among the members of the set of the 94 customers (respective individual clusters 2, 4, 5, 9, 10).

Each customer class presents its separate behaviour. Specifically, customers of cluster 1 have stable load demand equal to approximately 10% of the respective normalized peak load

(=1.0). Similarly customers of cluster 7 and cluster 12 have stable load demand equal to approximately 45% and 80% of the respective normalized peak load respectively. Cluster 3 has the most customers (40 from 94), whose load behaviour is characteristic: gradual load increment from 18% to 45% of normalized peak load from 6:00 to 10:00, a small variation at 12:00, afterwards a slow load reduction from 14:00 to 24:00.

Load demand of customers of cluster 8 has a rapid increment at 8:00 (from 40% to 70% of normalized peak load), it remains stable until 20:00, then it has a slow reduction until 23:00 (receiving 40% of normalized peak load). This cluster has mainly industrial and commercial customers. On the contrary, cluster 11 has only industrial customers with similar load behaviour (load demand has a rapid increment at 6:00 from 50% to 80% of maximum peak load, it remains stable until 22:00, then it has a rapid reduction to 50% of maximum peak load, while it is obvious that there is a small variation approximately at 14:00). The separate customers of clusters 4, 5 and 9 have similar load behaviour with the customers of clusters 8 and 11, but they have some special characteristics, such as different hours of load increment etc.

The two commercial customers of cluster 6 and the separate customer of cluster 2 have maximum load demand during early night hours (completely opposite behaviour from the other customers).

The obtained representative curves provide useful information about the load demand of the customers' clusters throughout the year. It is obvious that the a priori index of customer's activity is not representative for load curves, which is also confirmed by (Chicco et al., 2003a; -, 2003b; -, 2004; -, 2006; Figueiredo et al., 2003). This can not be generalized since it may vary within countries and distribution companies depending on the respective data of customers (Gerbec et al., 2003; -, 2004; -, 2005). But the proposed methodology can be applied directly to the respective set of customers, in order to study their respective load behaviour. The same process can be repeated for all other adequacy measures. The number of the clusters being used can also be selected according to the desirable precision and the relative improvement of the respective measure.

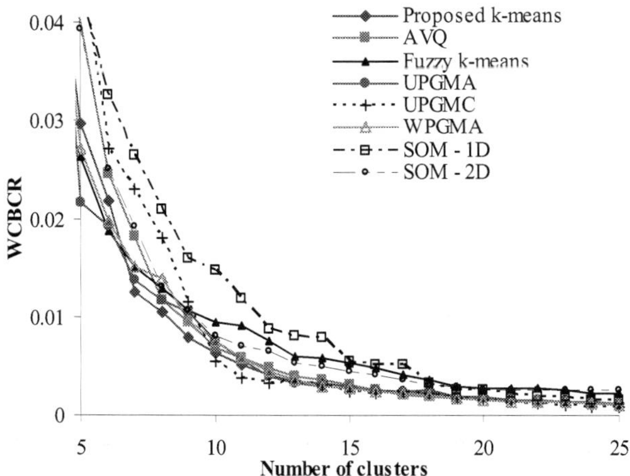

Fig. 1.26. *WCBCR* measure of the best fitting clustering methods for 5 to 25 neurons for the training patterns set of 94 medium voltage customers for the most populated day

Methods -Parameters	Adequacy Measure					
	J	*MIA*	*CDI*	*SMI*	*DBI*	*WCBCR*
Proposed k-means	0.3840	0.04950	*0.2064*	0.6732	1.6694	0.004100
AVQ	0.3601	0.05453	0.2215	0.6736	*1.2345*	0.004877
Fuzzy k-means (q=6)	0.5751	0.06559	0.2656	0.7411	2.1210	0.007577
CL	0.4058	0.05484	0.2291	0.7010	1.7056	0.004926
SL	1.2718	0.08737	0.3421	0.7050	2.7942	0.011694
UPGMA	0.4956	0.05070	0.2442	0.6664	1.6341	0.004008
UPGMC	0.5462	*0.04696*	0.2528	*0.6593*	1.8610	*0.003315*
WARD	0.3728	0.05369	0.2349	0.6984	1.7817	0.005258
WPGMA	0.4573	0.05367	0.2288	0.6768	1.6965	0.004452
WPGMC	0.4617	0.05579	0.2301	0.6752	1.6779	0.004712
Mono-dimensional SOM	0.4163	0.06330	0.2694	0.7184	2.0013	0.008752
Bi-dimensional SOM 14x3 using proposed k-means for classification in a second level	*0.3265*	0.05920	0.2157	0.6676	1.7604	0.006599

Table 1.6. Comparison of the Best Clustering Models for 12 Clusters for the set of 94 medium voltage customers using the most populated day based on WCBCR adequacy measure of the 1st stage

Load cluster	Activity of customer (1: commercial, 2: industrial, 3: public services, 4:traction)				Customers per cluster
	1	2	3	4	
1	12	6	3	1	22
2	1	0	0	0	1
3	26	9	3	2	40
4	0	1	0	0	1
5	1	0	0	0	1
6	2	0	0	0	2
7	5	3	1	0	9
8	6	2	0	0	8
9	0	1	0	0	1
10	0	1	0	0	1
11	0	3	0	0	3
12	0	5	0	0	5
Total	53	31	7	3	94

Table 1.7. Results of the UPGMC Model with optimization to WCBCR measure for 12 clusters for a set of 94 Customers using the most populated day

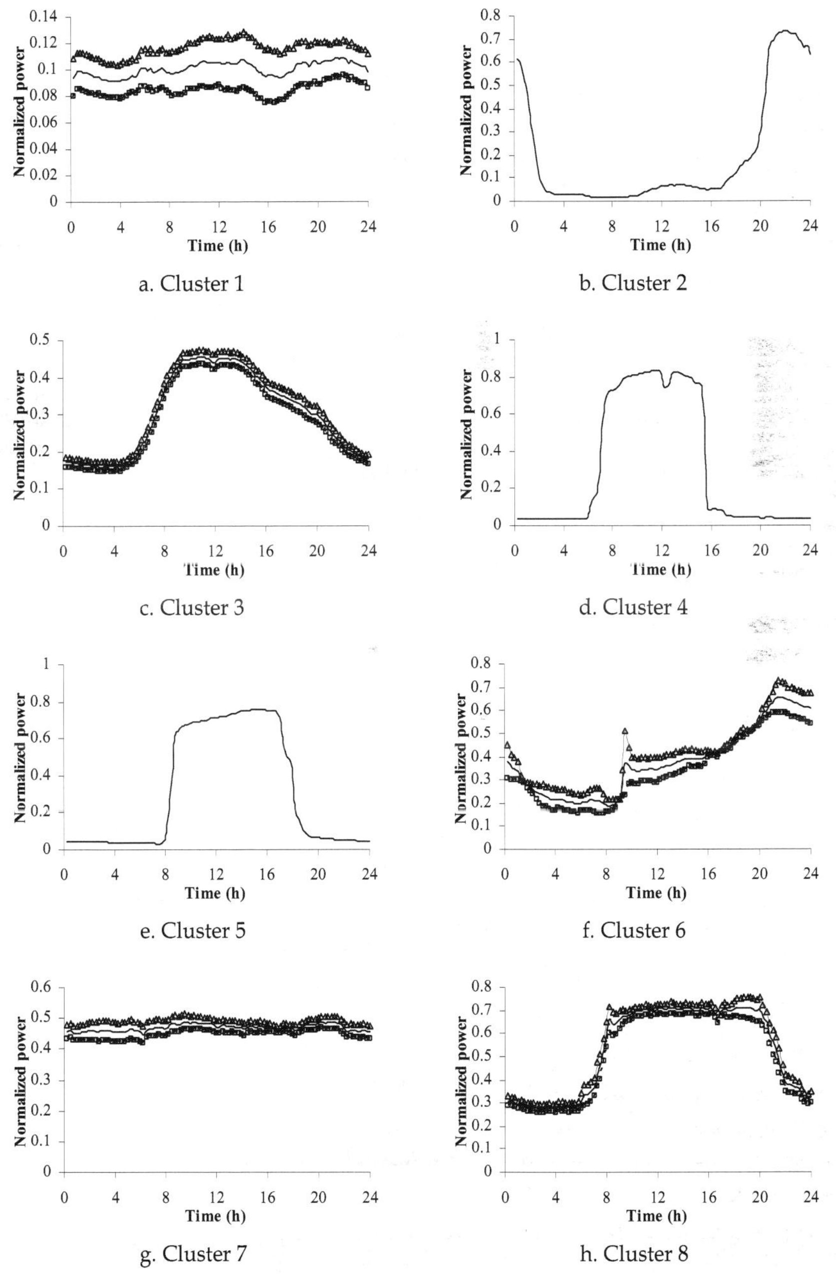

a. Cluster 1

b. Cluster 2

c. Cluster 3

d. Cluster 4

e. Cluster 5

f. Cluster 6

g. Cluster 7

h. Cluster 8

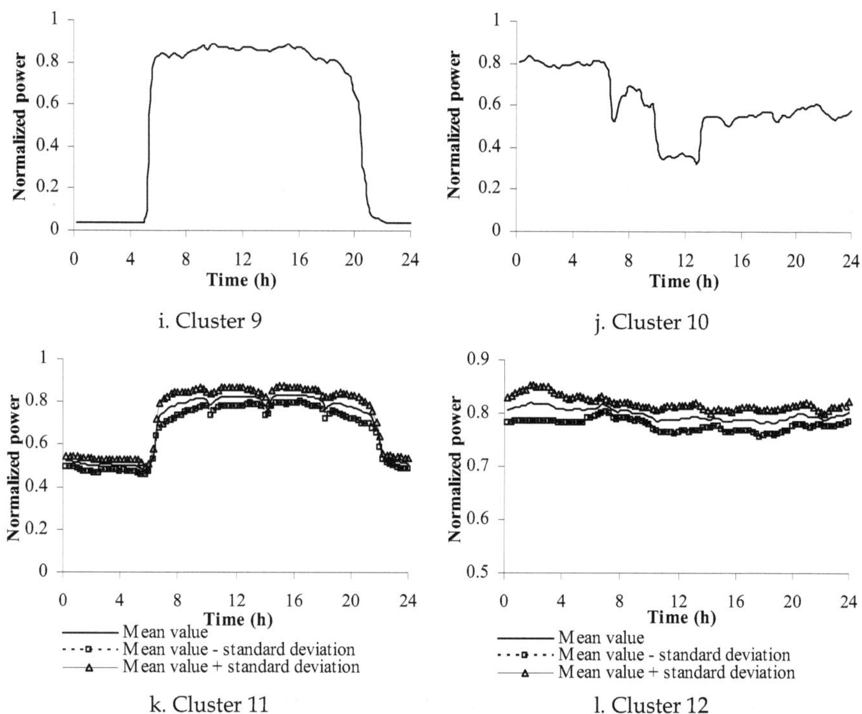

i. Cluster 9

j. Cluster 10

k. Cluster 11

l. Cluster 12

Fig. 1.27. Normalized representative chronological load curves of typical classes from the classification of a set of 94 medium voltage customers (as derived from the load curves of the most populated typical day of each customer) for the Greek power distribution system to 12 clusters using UPGMC model with the optimization of the WCBCR measure

1.5.2.3 Case study II: the day with peak load demand

For this case study the day with the respective peak load demand of each customer is used. For example the respective cluster is the 10th one for the industrial customer (see Fig. 1.22), which is also characterised by the most populated day (this congruency rarely happens).

Fig. 1.28 shows the best results of each clustering method by using the WCBCR measure. The WPGMA and UPGMC models are proved to be the best ones, as it is also registered in Table 1.8. Using the rule of the "knee" the necessary number of clusters is between 9 and 15 choosing finally 12 (the position of the knee is not clear).

The results of clustering for 12 clusters using the WPGMA model with the optimization of the WCBCR measure are presented in Table 1.9 and in Fig. 1.29. Practically eighty-nine customers form seven main clusters, as it has been already happened for the most populated day, but it is an accidental occasion. The respective representative load curves are more abrupt and sharp than the ones of the most populated day.

Specifically, customers of cluster 11 (with 20 customers from 94) have stable load demand equal to approximately 80% of the respective normalized peak load. The load behaviour of cluster 10, which has the most customers (36 from 94), presents a gradual load increment from 30% to 85% of normalized peak load from 6:00 to 11:00, afterwards a slow load reduction from 13:00 to 24:00. Both of these clusters present small variations.

The load behaviour of clusters 3, 4, 8 and 9 presents larger variations than the respective one of clusters 10 and 11. Customers of cluster 3 have a gradual load increment from 10% to 70% of normalized peak load from 6:00 to 15:00, afterwards a slow load reduction from 15:00 to 24:00. Customers of cluster 4 have a rapid load increment from 10% to 90% of normalized peak load at 8:00, then their load remains stable practically until 16:00, afterwards their load reduces sharply at 16:00. Load demand of customers' cluster 9 has a gradual increment from 10% to 90% of normalized peak load from 8:00 to 13:00, it remains stable until 20:00, then it has a rapid reduction until 24:00.

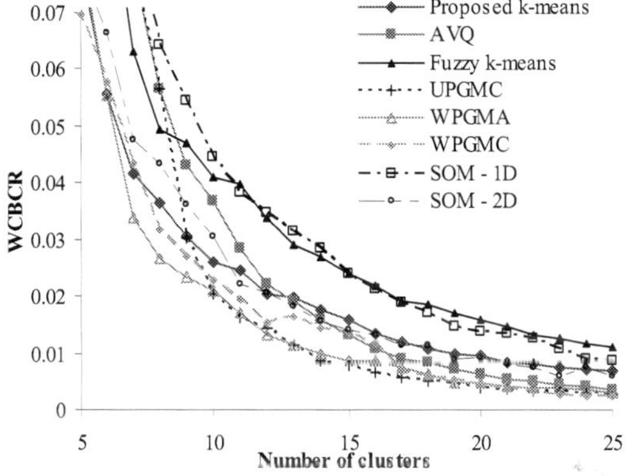

Fig. 1.28. *WCBCR* measure of the best fitting clustering methods for 5 to 25 neurons for the training patterns set of 94 medium voltage customers for the day with the peak load demand

Methods -Parameters	Adequacy Measure					
	J	*MIA*	*CDI*	*SMI*	*DBI*	*WCBCR*
Proposed k-means	1.1754	0.1043	*0.3434*	0.6591	2.1421	0.02033
AVQ	1.1304	0.1043	0.4389	0.6557	*2.0546*	0.02222
Fuzzy k-means (q=6)	1.6999	0.1282	0.4963	0.7073	3.3089	0.03387
CL	1.2138	0.1105	0.4663	0.6752	2.7041	0.02702
SL	2.5647	0.1256	0.5420	0.6373	3.3553	0.02870
UPGMA	1.3303	0.0989	0.4219	0.6584	2.5309	0.01657
UPGMC	1.6186	*0.0951*	0.4435	*0.6223*	2.7116	0.01430
WARD	1.1696	0.1145	0.4739	0.6828	2.7926	0.03122
WPGMA	1.4141	0.0953	0.4031	0.6377	2.5680	*0.01327*
WPGMC	1.7250	0.1040	0.4274	0.6303	2.9650	0.01536
Mono-dimensional SOM	1.1682	0.1139	0.4981	0.6788	2.7897	0.03480
Bi-dimensional SOM 14x3 using proposed k-means for classification in a second level	*1.0373*	0.1023	0.3475	0.6500	2.1731	0.02067

Table 1.8. Comparison of the Best Clustering Models for 12 Clusters for the set of 94 medium voltage customers using the day with the peak load demand based on WCBCR adequacy measure of the 1st stage

Load cluster	Activity of customer (1: commercial, 2: industrial, 3: public services, 4:traction)				Customers per cluster
	1	2	3	4	
1	0	1	0	0	1
2	1	0	1	0	2
3	8	1	1	3	13
4	3	4	0	0	7
5	0	1	0	0	1
6	0	1	0	0	1
7	0	1	0	0	1
8	6	0	0	0	6
9	2	2	1	0	5
10	25	8	3	0	36
11	8	11	1	0	20
12	0	1	0	0	1
Total	53	31	7	3	94

Table 1.9. Results of the UPGMC Model with optimization to WCBCR measure for 12 clusters for a set of 94 Customers using the day with the peak load demand

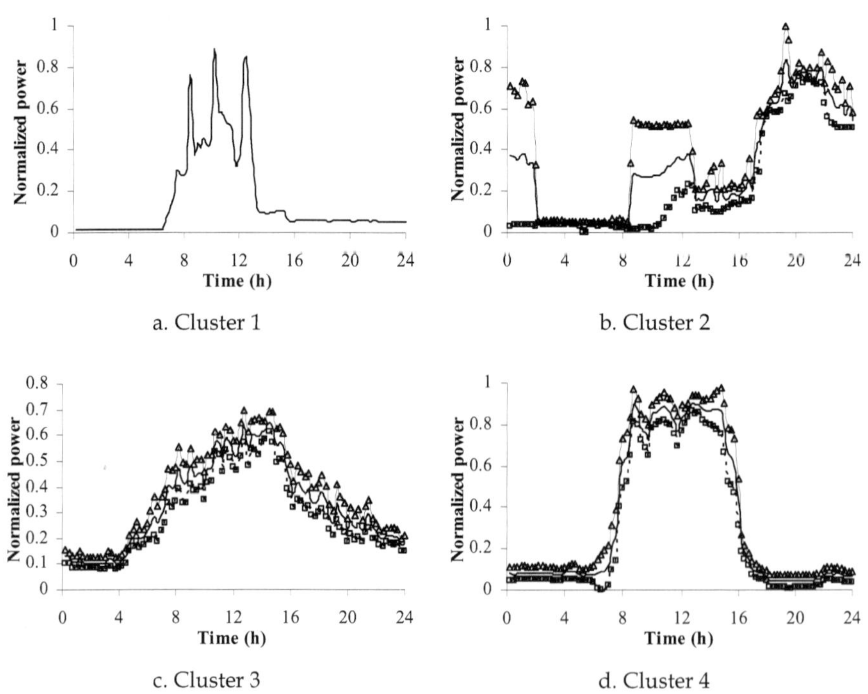

a. Cluster 1

b. Cluster 2

c. Cluster 3

d. Cluster 4

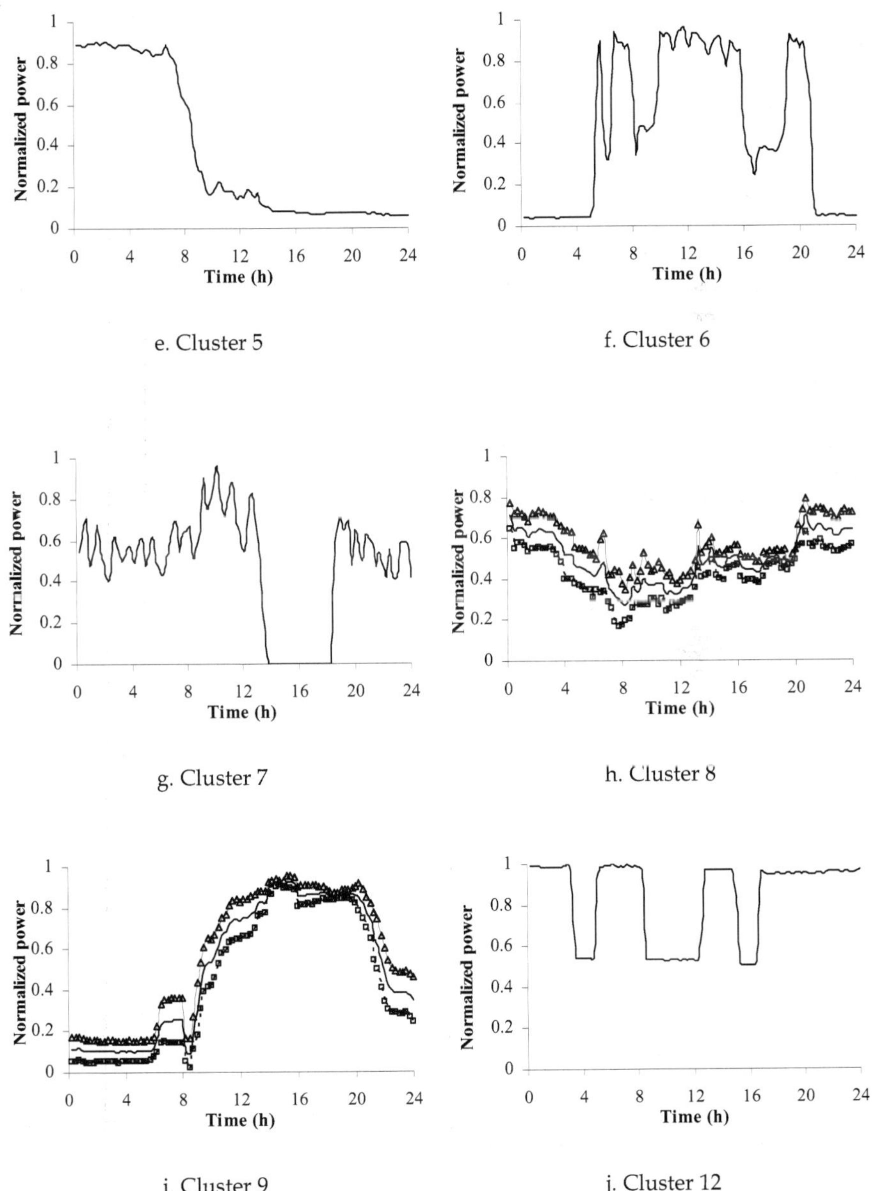

e. Cluster 5

f. Cluster 6

g. Cluster 7

h. Cluster 8

i. Cluster 9

j. Cluster 12

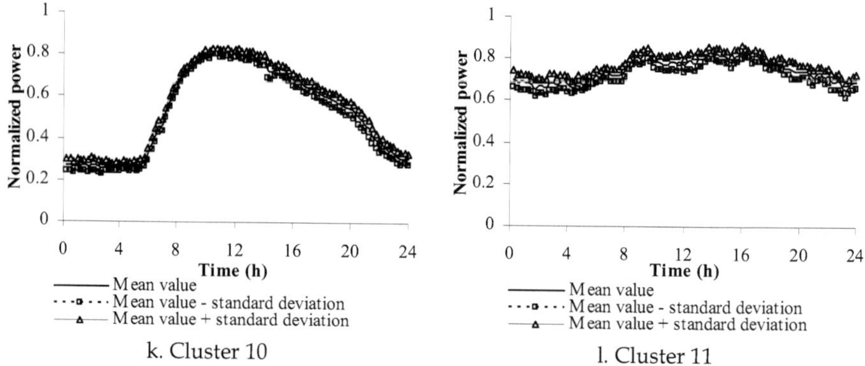

k. Cluster 10   l. Cluster 11

Fig. 1.29. Normalized representative chronological load curves of typical classes from the classification of a set of 94 medium voltage customers (as derived from the load curves of the days with the peak load of each customer) for the Greek power distribution system to 12 clusters using WPGMA model with the optimization of the $WCBCR$ measure

Cluster 8 presents an opposite load behaviour against clusters 3, 4 and 9, because the maximum load demand is achieved during early night hours (70% of peak load), while during the rest day load varies from 30% to 50% of peak load.

The rest seven customers are represented by six clusters (the clusters 1, 5, 6, 7, 12 contain one customer each and the cluster 2 contains two ones), where its customer presents unique characteristics for its chronological typical load curve.

It is mentioned that the type of typical day (such as the most populated day etc) is defined by the user according to his needs.

1.5.3 Usefulness of the application of the proposed two-stage methodology

The results of the developed methodology can be used either for each customer separately or for a set of customers. The results of the first stage are the respective ones of the typical chronological load curves of each customer of §1.4.3.

The results of the second stage can be used as important input information for:

- the adaptation of tariffs for each customer class from the suppliers,
- the adaptation of tariffs for ancillary services of the reactive demand on behalf of the distribution or transmission operator, if the respective representative curves of reactive load are calculated,
- the feasibility studies of the energy efficiency and demand side management measures, which are proper for each customer class (extraordinary useful for the suppliers, in order to smooth their respective daily load demand curve),
- the short-term and mid-term load forecasting for the customer classes, for which the suppliers, the system operator and the regulatory energy authority are interested.

1.6 A pattern recognition methodology for power system load profiles for applications of demand side management programs

1.6.1 General description of the proposed methodology

Based on the pattern recognition methodology for the classification of the daily load curves of a customer a similar pattern recognition methodology can be used for the classification of daily chronological load curves of power system, as shown in Fig. 1.30. The main steps are the following:

a. *Data and features selection* (same to (*a*) step of the methodology of §1.4). The active and reactive energy values are registered (in MWh and Mvarh) for each time period in steps of 1 hour.

b. *Data pre-processing* (same to (*b*) step of the methodology of §1.4).

c. *Main application of pattern recognition methods* (same to (c) step of the methodology of §1.4).

As we can see this methodology is quite similar to one of §1.4. This can lead us to propose the extension of the application of this methodology for the classification of similar time-series curves, such as daily chronological temperatures curves, etc (Tsekouras, 2006).

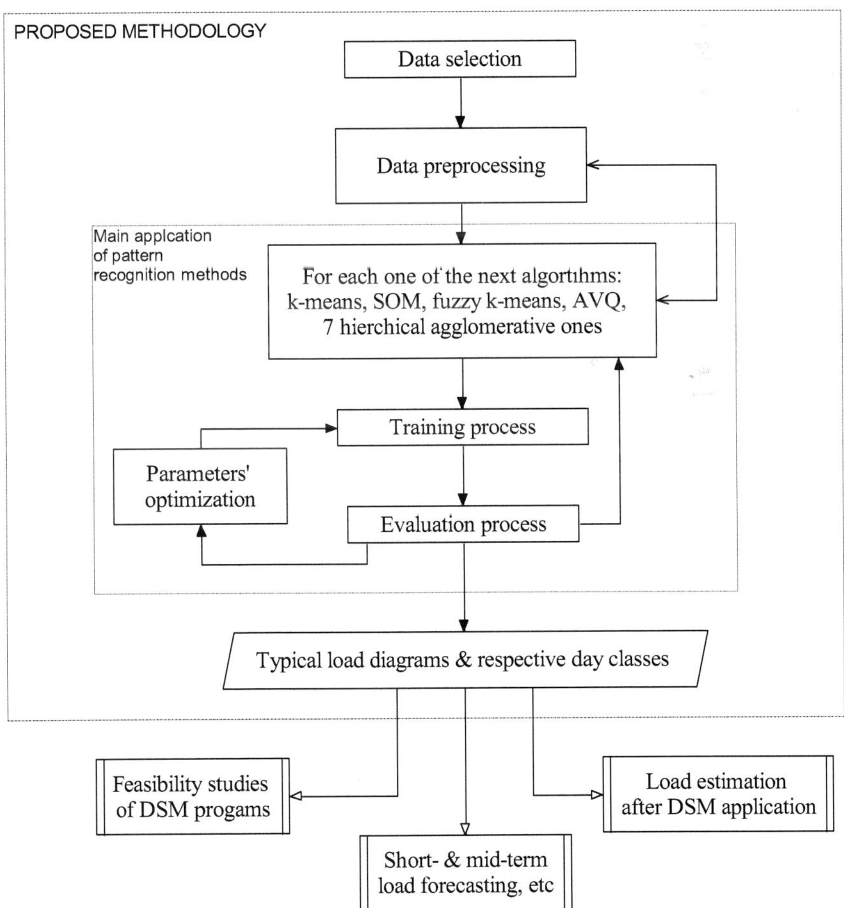

Fig. 1.30. Flow diagram of pattern recognition methodology for the classification of daily chronological load curves of power system

1.6.2 Application of the Greek power system

1.6.2.1 General

The developed methodology is applied on the Greek power system, analytically for the summer of the year 2000 and concisely for the period of years 1985-2002 per epoch and per year. The data used are hourly load values for the respective period, which is divided into two epochs: summer (from April to September) and winter (from October to March of the next year).

In the case of the summer of the year 2000, the respective set of the daily chronological curves has 183 members, from which none is rejected through data pre-processing. In the following next paragraphs the application of each clustering method is analyzed.

1.6.2.2 Application of the k-means

The proposed model of the k-means method is executed for different pairs (a,b) from 2 to 25 clusters, where a={0.1,0.11,…,0.45} and a+b={0.54,0.55,…,0.9}, as in the case of § 1.4.2.2. The best results for the six adequacy measures do not refer to the same pair (a,b) –as it is presented in Table 1.10 for 10 clusters. The alternative model is the classic one with the random choice of the input vectors during the centres' initialization. For the classic k-means model 100 executions are carried out and the best results for each index are registered. The superiority of the proposed model is the fact that applies in all above cases of neurons and that it converges to the same results for the respective pairs (a,b), which can not be achieved using the classic model.

1.6.2.3 Application of the adaptive vector quantization

The initial value η_0, the minimum value η_{min} and the time parameter $T_{\eta 0}$ of learning rate are properly calibrated. The best results of the adequacy measures are given for different pairs of (η_0, $T_{\eta 0}$), according to the results of Table 1.10 for 10 clusters. The η_{min} value does not practically improve the neural network's behaviour assuming that it ranges between 10^{-5} and 10^{-6}.

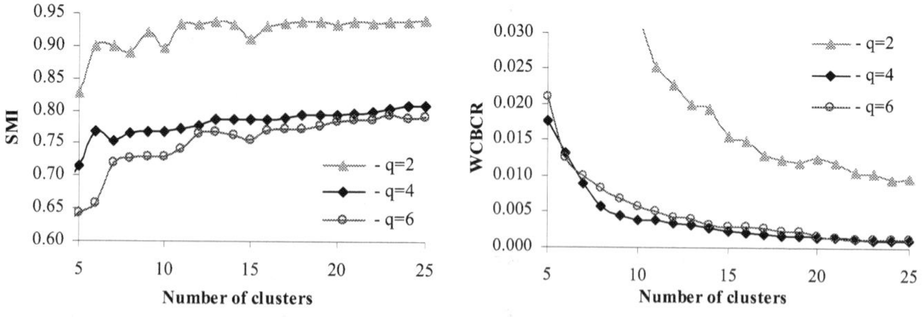

a. *SMI* indicator (similar to *DBI*)   b. *WCBCR* indicator (similar to *J, MIA & CDI*)

Fig. 1.31. *SMI* and *WCBCR* for the fuzzy k-means method for the set of 183 load curves of the summer of the year 2000 for the Greek power system with *q*=2, 4, 6 for 5 to 25 clusters

1.6.2.4 Application of the fuzzy k-means

In the fuzzy k-means algorithm the results of the adequacy measures depend on the amount of fuzziness increment. In Fig. 1.31 *SMI* and *WCBCR* adequacy measures are indicatively presented for different number of clusters for three cases of $q=\{2,4,6\}$. The best results are given by $q=4$ for J, MIA, CDI and $WCBCR$ adequacy measures, by $q=6$ for SMI and DBI indicators. It is noted that the initialization of the respective weights is similar to the proposed k-means.

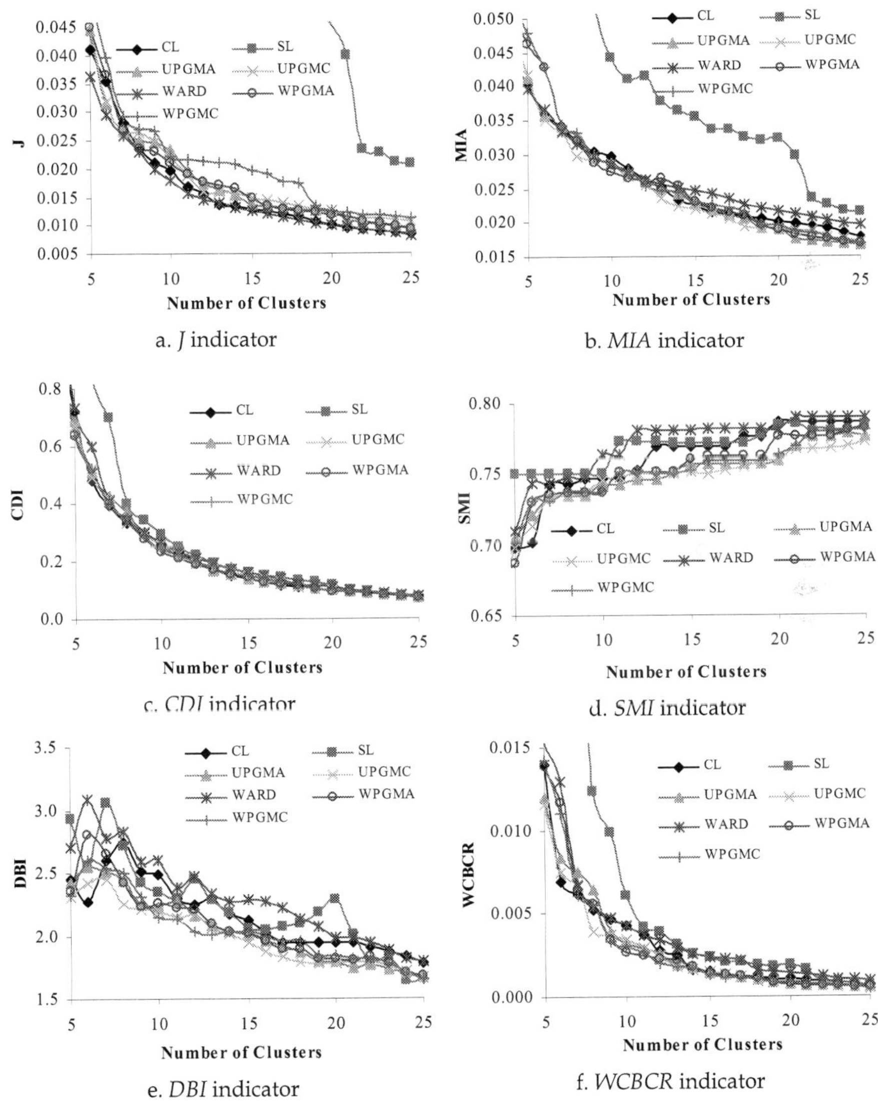

a. *J* indicator

b. *MIA* indicator

c. *CDI* indicator

d. *SMI* indicator

e. *DBI* indicator

f. *WCBCR* indicator

Fig. 1.32. Adequacy measures for the 7 hierarchical clustering algorithms for the set of 183 load curves of the summer of the year 2000 for the Greek power system for 5 to 25 clusters

1.6.2.5 Application of hierarchical agglomerative algorithms

In the case of the seven hierarchical models the best results are given by the WARD model for *J*, by the UPGMC model for *MIA*, by the WPGMA model for *CDI*, by the UPGMC and UPGMA models for *SMI*, by the UPGMC and WPGMC models for *DBI*, by the UPGMC, UPGMA, WPGMC and WPGMA models for *WCBCR* adequacy measure, according to Fig. 1.32.

1.6.2.6 Application of mono-dimensional self-organizing maps

The main problems during the training of the mono-dimensional SOM are:
- the proper termination of the SOM's training process, which is solved by minimizing the index I_s (eq.(1.32)),
- the proper calibration of (a) the initial value of the neighbourhood radius σ_0, (b) the multiplicative factor ϕ between T_{s_0} (epochs of the rough ordering phase) and T_{η_0} (time parameter of learning rate), (c) the multiplicative factor ξ between T_{σ_0} (time parameter of neighbourhood radius) and T_{η_0}, (d) the proper initial values of the learning rate η_r and η_f during the rough ordering phase and the fine tuning phase respectively.
- the proper initialization of the weights of the neurons.

The optimization process for the mono-dimensional SOM parameters is similar to that one of §1.4.2.6 and it is repeated for any population of clusters

1.6.2.7 Application of bi-dimensional self-organizing maps

In the case of the bi-dimensional SOM the additional issues that must be solved, are the shape, the population of neurons and their respective arrangement. In the case of the set of 183 load curves for the summer of the year 2000 the map can have 67 ($\cong 5 \times \sqrt{183}$) to 270 ($\cong 20 \times \sqrt{183}$) neurons. Using the ratio between the two major eigenvalues the respective value is 22.739 (=0.26423/0.01162) and the proposed grids can be 46x2 (see Fig. 1.33) and 68x3.

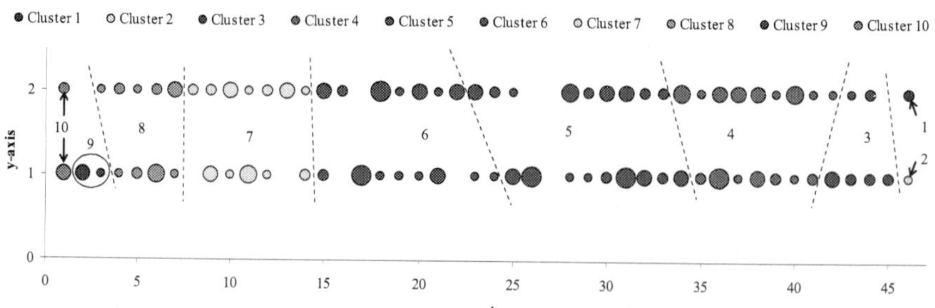

Fig. 1.33. 46x2 SOM after the application of the proposed k-means method at the neurons of SOM for the set of 183 load curves of the summer of the year 2000 for the Greek power system for 10 neurons

Because of the size and the location of the neurons in the grid, the clusters of the bi-dimensional map cannot be directly exploited and the proposed k-means is applied for the neurons of the bi-dimensional SOM, as it has already happened in §1.4.2.7. The adequacy measures are calculated using the load curves of the neurons which form the respective clusters of the proposed k-means method and the best results are given by the 46x2 grid for all adequacy measures for different pairs (a,b) of the k-means method.

1.6.2.8 Comparison of clustering models & adequacy indicators

In Fig. 1.34 the best results achieved by each clustering method are depicted. The proposed k-means model has the smallest values for the *MIA* and *WCBCR* indicators, the bi-dimensional SOM (with the application of the proposed k-means at the second level) for the *J* and *SMI* indicator and the adaptive vector quantization for *DBI* indicator. The proposed k-means model and the bi-dimensional SOM give equivalent results for the *CDI* indicator.

By observing the number of dead clusters for the proposed k-means model (Fig. 1.34.h) it is obvious that the use of *WCBCR* indicator is slightly superior to *MIA* and *J* indicators. Taking into consideration the basic theoretical advantage of the *WCBCR* indicator and the significant variability of the behaviour of *DBI* and *SMI* indicators for different clustering techniques the *WCBCR* indicator is proposed to be used.

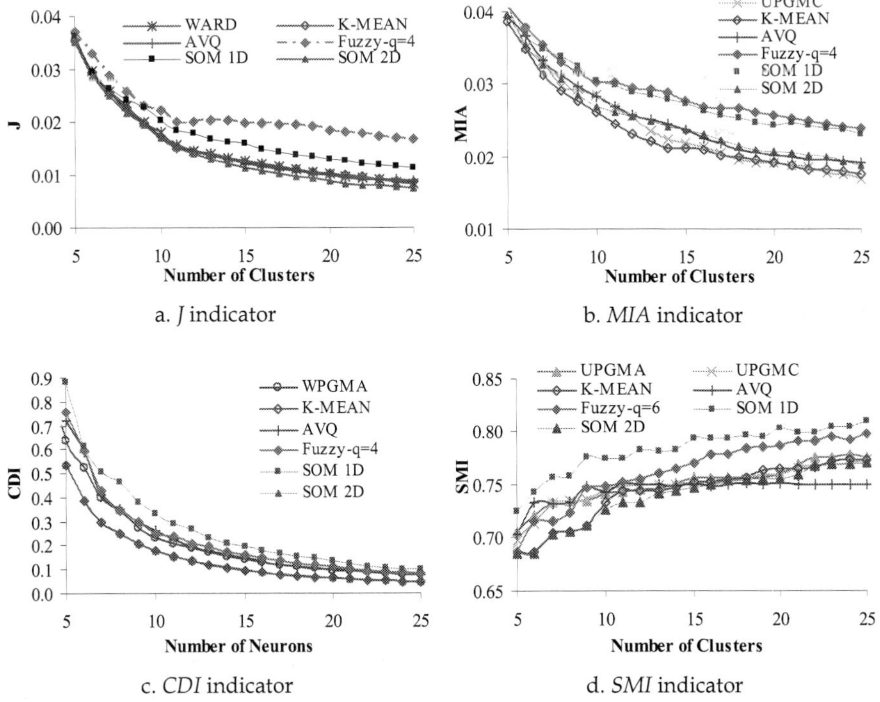

a. *J* indicator

b. *MIA* indicator

c. *CDI* indicator

d. *SMI* indicator

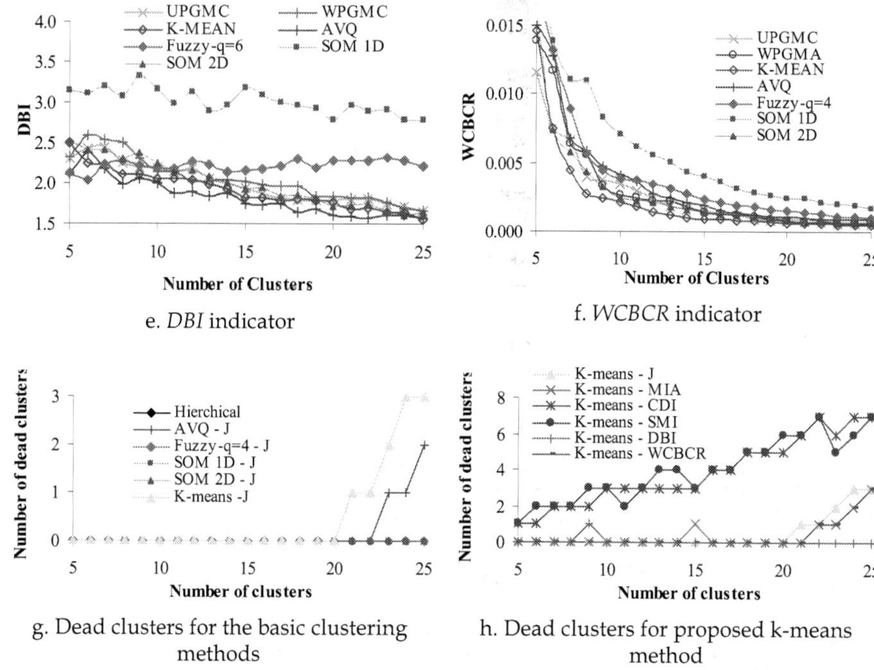

e. *DBI* indicator

f. *WCBCR* indicator

g. Dead clusters for the basic clustering methods

h. Dead clusters for proposed k-means method

Fig. 1.34. The best results of each clustering method for the set of 183 load curves of the summer of the year 2000 for the Greek power system for 5 to 25 clusters

The improvement of the adequacy indicators is significant until 10 clusters. After this value the behaviour of the most indicators is gradually stabilized. It can also be estimated graphically by using the rule of the "knee", which gives values between 8 to 10 clusters (see Fig. 1.35). In Table 1.10 the results of the best clustering methods are presented for 10 clusters, which is the finally proposed size of the typical days for this case.

Taking into consideration that the ratio of the computational training time for the under study methods is 0.05:1:24:28:36:50 (hierarchical: proposed k-means: mono-dimensional SOM: AVQ: fuzzy k-means: bi-dimensional SOM), the use of the hierarchical and k-means models is proposed. It is mentioned that the computational training time for the proposed k-means method is approximately 20 minutes for a Pentium 4, 1.7 GHz, 768 MB.

For this case study (load daily chronological curves of the summer of the year 2000 for the Greek power system) the proposed k-means model with the *WCBCR* adequacy indicator is going to be used.

1.6.2.9 Representative daily load curves of the summer of the year 2000 for the Greek power system

The results of the respective clustering for 10 clusters using the proposed k-means model with the optimization of the *WCBCR* indicator are presented in Table 1.11 and in Fig. 1.36 respectively.

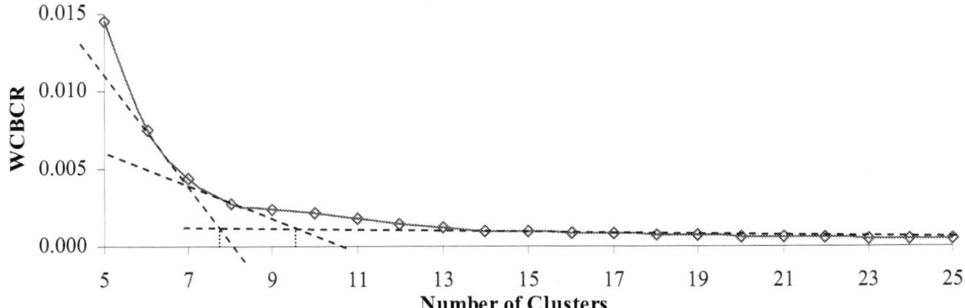

Fig. 1.35. Indicative estimation of the necessary clusters for the typical load daily chronological curves of the summer of the year 2000 for the Greek power system for the WCBCR adequacy indicator

Methods -Parameters	Adequacy Measure					
	J	MIA	CDI	SMI	DBI	WCBCR
Proposed k-means	0.01729	0.02262	0.1778	0.7331	2.0606	0.002142
a- b parameters	0.26 – 0.39	0.15-0.44	0.45-0.45	0.10-0.78	0.15-0.43	0.14-0.61
Classic k-means	0.01934	0.02434	0.1935	0.7549	2.7517	0.002346
AVQ	0.01723	0.02819	0.2615	0.7431	1.9973	0.004145
$\eta_0 - \eta_{min} - T_{\eta_0}$ parameters	0.5-5x10-7-1000	0.4-5x10-7-4000	0.5-5x10-7-5000	0.4-5x10-7-2000	0.8-5x10-7-1000	0.4-5x10-7-4000
Fuzzy k-means	0.02208	0.03036	0.25328	0.7182	2.1936	0.003894
q- a- b parameters	4-0.22-0.46	4-0.18-0.62	4-0.18-0.70	6-0.12-0.62	6-0.14-0.74	4-0.18-0.62
CL	0.01960	0.02974	0.2636	0.7465	2.4849	0.004233
SL	0.06249	0.04435	0.2950	0.7503	2.3509	0.006103
UPGMA	0.02334	0.02885	0.2544	0.7423	2.2401	0.003186
UPGMC	0.02200	0.02847	0.2603	0.7455	2.1934	0.003412
WARD	0.01801	0.02858	0.2645	0.7635	2.5964	0.004227
WPGMA	0.02094	0.02743	0.2330	0.7373	2.2638	0.002619
WPGMC	0.02227	0.02863	0.2418	0.7378	2.1498	0.003008
Mono-dimensional SOM	0.02024	0.03043	0.3366	0.7752	3.1656	0.007126
$\sigma_0 - \phi - \xi - \eta_f - \eta_r - T_{\eta_0}$ parameters	10-1.0-0.6-0.15-10-3-1500	10-2.0-0.2-0.10-10-3-1750	10-1.0-0.6-0.15-10-3-1500	10-1.0-0.6-0.15-10-3-1500	10-1.0-0.6-0.10-10-3-1500	10-2.0-0.2-0.10-10-3-1750
2D SOM 46x2 using proposed k-means for classification in a 2nd level	0.01685	0.02697	0.1785	0.7271	2.2572	0.002459
$\sigma_0 - \phi - \xi - \eta_f - \eta_r - T_{\eta_0}$ -a- b parameters	46-1.0-1.0-0.30-10-3-500-0.28-0.36	46-1.0-1.0-0.30-10-3-500-0.15-0.58	46-1.0-1.0-0.30-10-3-500-0.44-0.46	46-1.0-0.2-0.20-10-3-500-0.10-0.77	46-1.0-0.2-0.20-10-3-500-0.44-0.25	46-1.0-1.0-0.30-10-3-500-0.15-0.58

Table 1.10. Comparison of the Best Clustering Models for 10 Clusters for the Set of 183 Load Curves of the Summer of the Year 2000 for the Greek Power System

Load cluster	Day (1 for Monday, 2 for Tuesday etc.)							Days per cluster
	1	2	3	4	5	6	7	
1	0	0	0	0	0	0	1	1
2	1	0	0	0	1	0	0	2
3	0	1	0	0	0	2	13	16
4	9	8	9	8	7	12	2	55
5	4	3	2	3	4	4	8	28
6	4	6	6	4	3	7	1	31
7	4	3	4	6	6	0	1	24
8	4	3	2	3	3	2	0	17
9	0	2	3	1	2	0	0	8
10	0	0	0	1	0	0	0	1

Table 1.11. Results of the Proposed k-means Model with optimization to WCBCR for 10 clusters for a Set of 183 Load Curves of the summer of the year 2000 for the Greek Power system

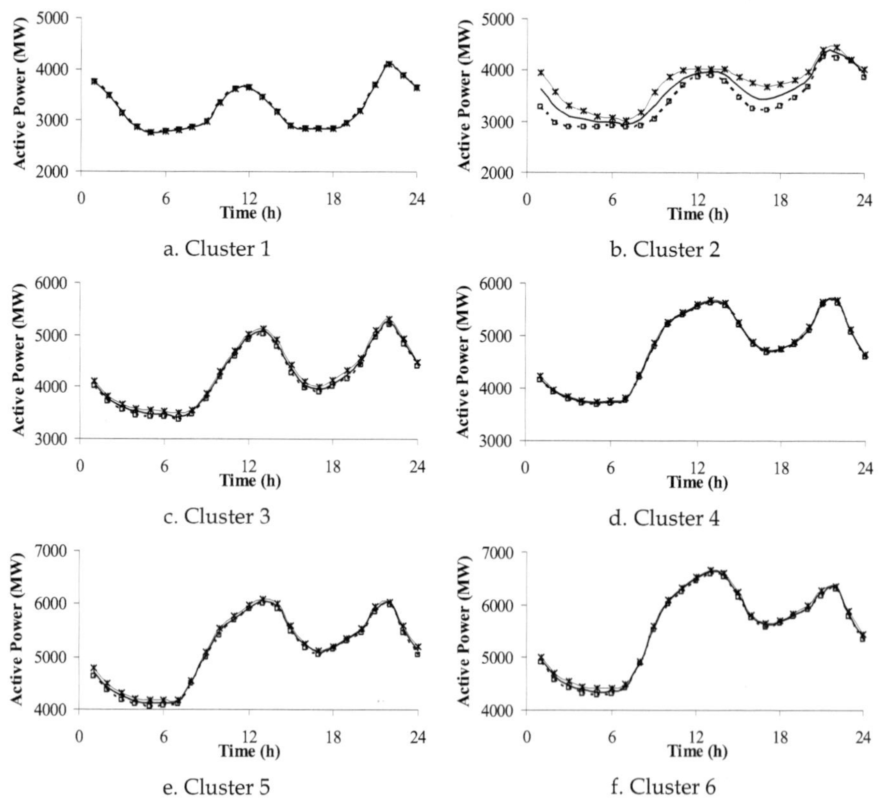

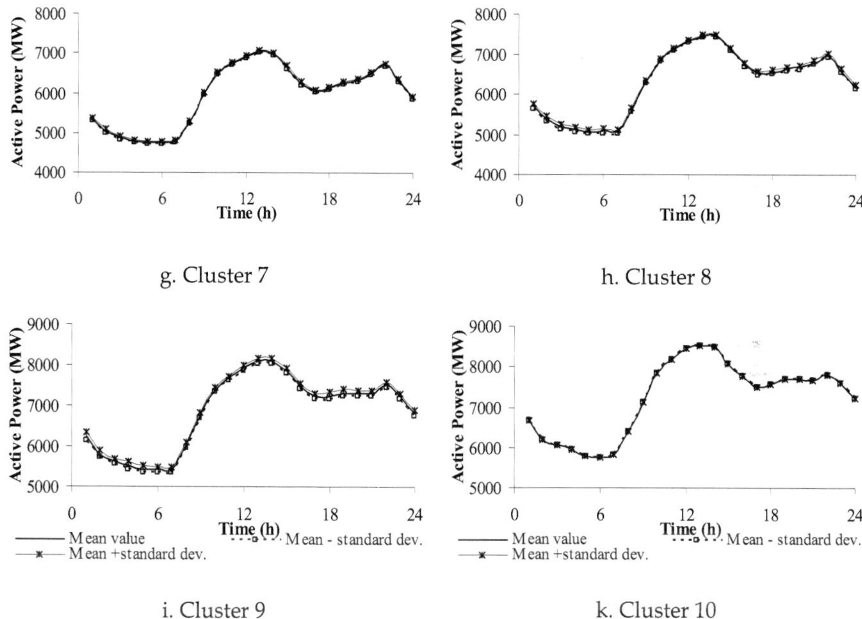

g. Cluster 7   h. Cluster 8

i. Cluster 9   k. Cluster 10

Fig. 1.36. Typical daily chronological load curves for the set of 183 curves of the summer of the year 2000 for the Greek power system using proposed k-means model with optimization to *WCBCR*

Specifically, cluster 1 represents Easter, cluster 2 Holy Friday and Monday after Easter, cluster 3 the Sundays of April, May, early June and September, Holy Saturday and Labour day. Cluster 4 contains the workdays of very low demand (during April, early May and September) with normal temperatures (22-28°C) and Saturdays of April, May, early June and September, while cluster 5 includes the workdays of low demand and Sundays of high peak load demand during the hot summer days. Cluster 6 represents the workdays of medium peak load demand and Saturdays of high peak load demand, while clusters 7 to 10 mainly involves workdays with gradually increasing peak load demand.

As we can notice the separation between work days and non-work days for each season is not so much descriptive for the load behaviour of a power system, as we have proved that 8 to 10 clusters are needed.

1.6.2.10 Application of the Proposed Methodology for the Greek Power System Per Seasons and Per Years for the time period 1985-2002

The same process is repeated for the summer (April–September) and the winter (October-March) periods for the years between 1985 and 2002. The load curves of each season are qualitatively described by using 8-10 clusters. The performance of these methods is presented in Table 1.12 by indicating the number of seasons that achieves the best value of adequacy measure respectively.

Methods	Adequacy Measure					
	J	MIA	CDI	SMI	DBI	WCBCR
Proposed k-means	1	24	31	7	12	29
Classic k-means	0	0	0	0	0	0
AVQ	2	0	0	7	16	0
Fuzzy k-means	0	0	0	0	0	1
CL	0	0	0	0	0	0
SL	0	0	0	0	0	0
UPGMA	0	3	0	0	0	1
UPGMC	0	7	0	2	5	3
WARD	0	0	0	0	0	0
WPGMA	0	0	0	0	1	0
WPGMC	0	3	0	0	2	2
Mono-dimensional SOM	0	0	0	0	0	0
Bi-dimensional SOM using proposed k-means for classification in a second level	34	0	6	21	1	1

Table 1.12. Comparison of the Clustering Models for the Sets of Load Curves of the Greek Power System per Season for the time period 1985-2002

The comparison of the algorithms shows that the developed k-means method achieves a better performance for *MIA, CDI* and *WCBCR* measures, the bi-dimensional SOM model using proposed k-means for classification in a second level for *J* and *SMI* indicators and the adaptive vector quantization for *DBI* adequacy measure.

The methodology is also applied for each year during the period 1985-2002, where the load curves are qualitatively described by using 15-20 clusters. The respective performance is presented in Table 1.13 by indicating the number of years which achieves the best value of adequacy measure respectively. The comparison of the algorithms shows that the developed k-means method achieves a better performance for *MIA, CDI, DBI* and *WCBCR* measures, the bi-dimensional SOM model using proposed k-means for classification in a second level for *J* indicator and the UPGMC algorithm for *SMI* index.

The main disadvantage of the load curves classification per year is that each cluster does not contain the same family of days during the time period under study. I.e. if 20 clusters are selected to represent the load demand behaviour of the Greek power system per year, the 20th cluster will contain the workdays with the highest peak load demand of the winter for the years 1985-1992 and that of summer for the rest years. In order to avoid this problem, the classification per season is proposed.

1.6.3 Usefulness of the application of the proposed methodology

The results of the second stage can be used as important input information for:

- power system short-term and mid-term load forecasting,
- energy trades,
- techno-economic studies of the energy efficiency and demand side management programs and
- the respective load estimation after the application of these programs.

Methods	Adequacy Measure					
	J	MIA	CDI	SMI	DBI	$WCBCR$
Proposed k-means	0	8	18	0	13	14
Classic k-means	0	0	0	0	0	0
AVQ	1	0	0	1	3	0
Fuzzy k-means	0	0	0	0	0	0
CL	0	0	0	0	0	0
SL	0	0	0	0	0	0
UPGMA	0	1	0	0	0	0
UPGMC	0	6	0	14	1	2
WARD	0	0	0	0	0	0
WPGMA	0	1	0	0	0	0
WPGMC	0	1	0	0	0	2
Mono-dimensional SOM	0	0	0	0	0	0
Bi-dimensional SOM using proposed k-means for classification in a second level	17	1	0	3	1	0

Table 1.13. Comparison of the Clustering Models for the Sets of Load Curves of the Greek Power System per Year for the time period 1985-2002

1.7 Conclusions

In this chapter pattern recognition methodologies for the study of the load time series were presented. Specifically, the first methodology deals with the classification of the daily chronological load curves of each large electricity customer, in order to estimate his typical days and his respective representative daily load profiles. It is based on classical pattern recognition methods, such as k-means, hierarchical agglomerative clustering, Kohonen adaptive vector quantization, mono-dimensional and bi-dimensional self-organized maps and fuzzy k-means. The parameters of each clustering method are properly selected by an optimization process, which is separately applied for each one of six adequacy measures. The latter are the mean square error, the mean index adequacy, the clustering dispersion indicator, the similarity matrix, the Davies-Bouldin indicator and the ratio of within cluster sum of squares to between cluster variation. Some pattern recognition methods, such as k-means, were properly modified, in order to achieve better values for the adequacy measures. The results can be used for the load forecasting of each consumer, the choice of the proper tariffs and the feasibility studies of demand side management programs. This methodology is in detail applied for one medium voltage paper mill industrial customer and synoptically for a set of 94 medium voltage customers of the Greek power distribution system, although it is applicable to any power system. From this execution the basic conclusions are:

- The daily chronological load of each large customer for a year can be classified to 8÷12 clusters satisfactorily (in the special case of seasonal customers, like small seaside hotels, oil-press industry, less clusters are needed).

- The ratio of within cluster sum of squares to between cluster variation (*WCBCR*) is proposed as the most suitable adequacy measure, because of (a) the presentation of the minimum dead clusters with respect to the desired number of clusters against the other adequacy measures and (b) its basic theoretical advantage, which is the combination of the distances of the input vectors from the representative clusters and the distances between clusters, covering the characteristics of the mean square error (*J*) and the mean index adequacy (*CDI*) simultaneously.

- The proposed k-means method and the hierarchical agglomerative methods (especially the unweighted pair group method average (*UPGMA*) & the unweighted pair group method centroid (*UPGMC*)) present the best results for the set of 94 medium voltage customers of the Greek power distribution system with respect to the *WCBCR* adequacy measure taking into consideration the computational training time.

Secondly, a two-stage methodology developed for the classification of electricity customers is presented. In the first stage, typical chronological load curves of various customers are estimated using pattern recognition methods and their results are compared using six adequacy measures, as it has already happened in the first case. In the second stage, classification of customers is performed by the same methods and measures, together with the representative load patterns of customers being obtained from the first stage. The basic contribution of this methodology is that its first stage enables the modification of the representative day, such as the most populated day, and avoids the a priori definition of a single day or the "mean" day of a specific time period (as it is suggested by previously published methodologies (Chicco et al., 2002 ; -,2003a; -,2003b; -, 2004; -,2006; Figueiredo et al., 2003; -, 2005; Gerbec et al., 2003 ;-,2004;-,2005)). The results of the second stage provide valuable information for electricity suppliers in competitive energy markets. The developed methodology was applied on the aforementioned set of 94 customers. From this execution the basic conclusions are:

- The representative clusters of the customers classes can be approximately 10÷15 for a set of 94 customers.

- The ratio of within cluster sum of squares to between cluster variation (*WCBCR*) is proposed as the most suitable adequacy measure for the same reasons for which it was also proposed in the first stage.

- The proposed k-means method and the hierarchical agglomerative methods (especially the weighted pair group method average (*WPGMA*) & the unweighted pair group method centroid (*UPGMC*)) present the best results for the classification of the second stage with respect to the *WCBCR* adequacy measure independently from the kind of the typical day which was examined (the most populated one and the day with the peak load).

- The a priori index of customer's activity is not representative for the classification of the load curves, which is also confirmed by (Chicco et al., 2002 ; -,2003a; -,2003b; -, 2004; -,2006; Figueiredo et al., 2003; -, 2005). This can not be generalized since it may vary within countries and distribution companies, depending on the respective data of customers (Gerbec et al., 2003 ;-,2004;-,2005).

Finally, the pattern recognition methodology for the classification of the daily chronological load curves of the Greek power system is presented, in order to estimate their respective representative daily load profiles, which can be used for load forecasting and the feasibility studies of demand side management programs. Practically it is the same one with the first methodology or with the first stage of the two-stage methodology. It has been applied for the Greek power system for the period of years 1985-2002 per season (summer & winter) and per year, and from its execution the main conclusions are:

- The daily chronological load curves of the Greek power system for a season can be classified to 8÷10 clusters, which proves that the separation to workdays and no-workdays is not satisfactory. For a year the necessary clusters should be 15÷20.

- The ratio of within cluster sum of squares to between cluster variation (*WCBCR*) is proposed as the most suitable adequacy measure for the same reasons for which it was also proposed in the first methodology.

- The proposed k-means method and the hierarchical agglomerative methods (especially the weighted pair group method centroid (*WPGMC*) & the unweighted pair group method centroid (*UPGMC*)) present the best results for the classification of the load curves with respect to the *WCBCR* adequacy measure.

At the end, it should be mentioned that the basic contributions of the aforementioned methodologies are:

- The use of a set of pattern recognition methods, whose parameters are optimized properly for each adequacy measure separately, in order to use that method which gives the best results for the respective adequacy measure.

- The use of the ratio of within cluster sum of squares to between cluster variation (*WCBCR*) for this kind of methodologies for the first time.

These pattern recognition methodologies can be used for the classification of similar time-series curves, such as daily chronological temperatures curves, etc (Tsekouras, 2006).

1.8 References

Al-Hamadi, H. M. & Soliman, S.A. (2006). Long-term/mid-term electric load forecasting based on short-term correlation and annual growth. *Electric Power Systems Research*, Vol. 74, 2005, pp.353-361.

Beccali, M.; Cellura, M.; Lo Brano, V. & Marvuglia, A. (2004). Forecasting daily urban electric load profiles using artificial neural networks. *Energy Conversion and Management*, Vol. 45, 2004, pp. 2879-2900.

Carpaneto, E.; Chicco, G.; Napoli, R. & Scutariu, M. (2006). Electricity customer classification using frequency-domain load pattern data. *Electrical Power and Energy Systems*, Vol. 28, 2006, pp. 13-20.

Chen, C. S.; Hwang, J. C. & Huang, C. W. (1997). Application of load survey systems to proper tariff design. *IEEE Transactions on Power Systems*, Vol. 12, No. 4, November 1997, pp. 1746-1751.

Chicco, G.; Napoli, R. & Piglione, F. (2001). Load pattern clustering for short-term load forecasting of anomalous days. *IEEE Porto Power Tech Conference*, September 10-13, 2001, Porto, Portugal, p.6.

Chicco, G.; Napoli, R.; Piglione, F.; Scutariu, M.; Postolache, P. & Toader, C. (2002). Options to classify electricity customers. *Med Power 2002*, November 4-6, 2002, Athens, Greece.

Chicco, G.; Napoli, R.; Postolache, P.; Scutariu, M. & Toader, C. (2003a). Customer characterization for improving the tariff offer. *IEEE Transactions on Power Systems*, Vol. 18, No. 1, February 2003, pp. 381-387.

Chicco, G.; Napoli, R. & Piglione, F. (2003b). Application of clustering algorithms and self organising maps to classify electricity customers. *IEEE Power Tech Conference*, June 23-26, 2003, Bologna, Italy.

Chicco, G.; Napoli, R.; Piglione, F.; Postolache, P.; Scutariu, M. & Toader, C. (2004). Load pattern-based classification of electricity customers. *IEEE Transactions on Power Systems*, Vol. 19, No. 2, May 2004, pp. 1232-1239.

Chicco, G.; Napoli, R. & Piglione, F. (2006). Comparisons among clustering techniques for electricity customer classification. *IEEE Transactions on Power Systems*, Vol. 21, No. 2, May 2006, pp. 933-940.

Davies, D.L. & Bouldin, D.W. (1979). A cluster separation measure. *IEEE Transactions on Pattern Analysis and Machine Intelligence*, Vol. 2, April 1979, pp. 224-227.

Duda, R.O.; Hart, P.E. & Stork, D.G.(2001). *Pattern Classification*. A Wiley-Interscience Publication, 1st edition.

Figueiredo, V.; Duarte, F. J.; Rodrigues, F.; Vale, Z.; Ramos, C. & Gouveia, J. B.(2003). Electric customer characterization by clustering. *ISAP 2003*, Lemnos, Greece, August 2003.

Figueiredo, V.; Rodrigues, F.; Vale, Z. & Gouveia, J. B.(2005). An electric energy consumer characterization framework based on data mining techniques. *IEEE Transactions on Power Systems*, Vol. 20, No. 2, May 2005, pp. 596-602.

Gerbec, D.; Gasperic, S. & Gubina, F. (2003). Determination and allocation of typical load profiles to the eligible consumers. *IEEE Power Tech Conference*, Bologna, Italy, June 23-26, 2003.

Gerbec, D.; Gasperic, S.; Smon, I. & Gubina, F. (2004). Determining the load profiles of consumers based on fuzzy logic and probability neural networks, *IEE*

Proceedings on Generation, Transmission & Distribution, Vol. 151, May 2004, pp. 395-400.

Gerbec, D.; Gasperic, S.; Smon, I. & Gubina, F. (2005). Allocation of the load profiles to consumers using probabilistic neural networks. *IEEE Transactions on Power Systems*, Vol. 20, No. 2, May 2005, pp. 548-555.

Hand, D.; Manilla, H. & Smyth, P.(2001). *Principles of data mining*. The M.I.T. Press, Cambridge, Massachusetts, London, England.

Haykin, S. (1994). *Neural Networks, A Comprehensive Foundation*. Englewood Cliffs, NJ: Prentice Hall.

Kitayama, M.; Matsubara, R. & Izui, Y. (2002). Application of data mining to customer profile analysis in the power electric industry. *IEEE PES Winter Meeting 2002*, New York, USA.

Kohonen, T. (1989). *Self–organization and Associative Memory*. New York: Springer-Verlag, 3nd edition.

Lamedica, R.; Prudenzi, A.; Sforna, M.; Caciotta, M. & Orsolini Cencelli, V (1996). A neural network based technique for short-term forecasting of anomalous load periods. *IEEE Transactions on Power Systems*, Vol. 11, No. 4, November 1996, pp. 1749-1756.

Petrescu, M. & Scutariu, M. (2002). Load diagram characterization by means of wavelet packet transformation. *2nd Balkan Conference*, Belgrade, Yugoslavia, June 2002, pp. 15-19.

SOM Toolbox for MATLAB 5 (2000). Helsinki, Finland: Helsinki Univ. Technology.

Task VIII of International Energy Agency (2002). Demand-Side Bidding in a Competitive Electricity Market. *Research Report*, No. 1, Ver. 2, January 2002, with title *Market participants' views towards and experiences with Demand Side Bidding*.

Thang, K. F.; Aggarwal, R. K.; McGrail, A. J. & Esp, D. G.(2003). Analysis of power transformer dissolved gas data using the self-organizing map. *IEEE Transactions on Power Delivery*. Vol. 18, No. 4, October 2003, pp. 1241-1248.

Theodoridis, S. & Koutroumbas, K. (1999). *Pattern Recognition*, Academic Press, New York, 1st edition,.

Tsekouras, G. J. (2006). *Contribution to short-term and mid-term load and energy forecasting for power systems based on pattern recognition methods*. Ph.D. Thesis, School of Electrical and Computer Engineering, NTUA, Greece, July 2006 (in Greek).

Tsekouras, G. J.; Hatziargyriou, N.D. & Dialynas, E.N. (2007). Two-Stage Pattern Recognition of Load Curves for Classification of Electricity Customers. *IEEE Transactions on Power Systems*, Vol. 22, No. 3, August 2007, pp. 1120-1128.

Tsekouras, G. J.; Kotoulas, P. B.; Tsirekis, C.D.; Dialynas, E.N. & Hatziargyriou, N.D. (2008). A pattern recognition methodology for evaluation of load profiles and typical days of large electricity customers. *Electric Power Systems Research*, Vol.78, 2008, pp.1491-1510.

Verdu, S. V.; Garcia, M. O.; Senabre, C.; Marin, A. G. & Garcia Franco F. J. (2003). Classification, filtering, and identification of electrical customer load patterns through the use of self-organizing maps. *IEEE Transactions on Power Systems*, Vol. 18, No. 1, February 2003, pp. 381-387.

17

Theory of Cognitive Pattern Recognition

Youguo Pi, Wenzhi Liao, Mingyou Liu and Jianping Lu
School of Automation Science and Engineering, South China University of Technology
Guangzhou, Guangdong,
China

1. Basis of cognitive psychology related to pattern recognition

1.1 Perception and its constancy

Born and developed in the middle of 1970's, cognitive science is a kind of intersectional and integrative science aiming to study both the working principle and the developing mechanism of human brain and psyche. It is a product from the processes of intersection, infiltration and aggregation of such sciences as psychology, computer science, neurology, linguistics, anthropology, philosophy, and so on.

As one of the important parts of cognitive science, cognitive psychology[1-6], developed in the middle of 1950's, is a kind of psychology making the view of information processing as the core, thus also named information processing psychology, and a kind of science studying the processes of transforming, processing, storing, recovering, extracting and using information through sense.

Perception has always been an important studying field of psychology. Cognitive psychology treats perception as the organization and explanation of sense information, and the process of acquiring the meanings of sense information. Correspondingly, this process is treated as a series of consecutive information processing, and the ability of the process depends on the past knowledge and experience.

We can cover a building far away by just a finger, it means that the image of finger formed on the retina is bigger than that of the building. But if we move away the finger and first look at the building then the finger, we will feel the building is much bigger than the finger anyway, that indicating a very important feature of perception-constancy. The constancy of perception refers to perception keeps constant when the condition of perception changes in a certain range [7]. In the real world, various forms of energy are changed while reaching our sense organs, even the same object reaching our sense organs. Constancy in size and shape keeps our lives normal in this daedal world. Although an object sometimes seems smaller or bigger, we can recognize it. Constancy is the basis of stable perception of human to the outside. For instance, students can always recognize their own schoolbag, no matter far away (assuming it is visible) or close, overlooking or upward viewing, or looking in the front or sides. Although the images formed in the retina under the different conditions mentioned above are different from each other student's perceptions of this object are the same schoolbag.

Constancy in size and shape are two main types of the perception constancy. Perception constancy in size means that although the size of object images shot on the retina change, human perception of the size of object keeps constant. The size of image on the human retina directly depends on the distance between the object and our eyes.

For example, a man is coming toward you from far away, but after you recognize who he is, although his image on your retina is growing bigger and bigger as he is getting closer and closer to you, your perception of the coming person has nearly no change but just that guy. This perception, of course, has boundary, the farthest boundary are where you can recognize the person. Is there any nearest boundary? Suppose a very tall man, which is double or triple of you, gets close to you, you can only see his leg, at this time you can not recognize who he is. When he returns back facing you, as the distance between you and him increases, the image you have is closer and closer to his panorama, then you can recognize him. Therefore we may interpret the size constancy of perception as this: in the condition that image information is enough to recognize the pattern, the size of the image doesn't affect human's perception.

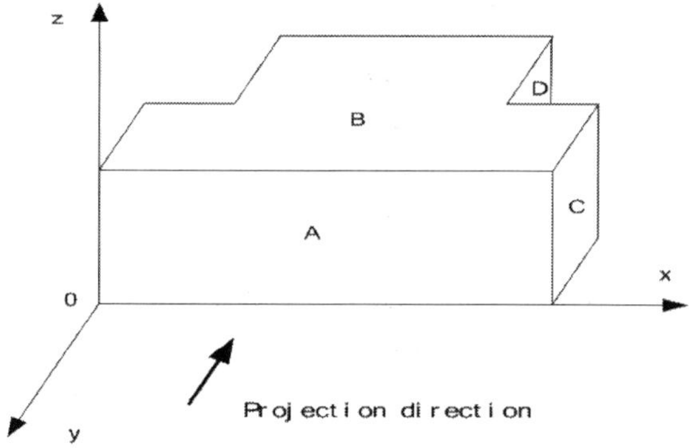

Fig. 1. The constancy of the perception

The shape constancy of perception means that in perception, although the shape of the object image shot on retina changes, people's perception of the shape of object stays constant. The shape of image on human retina directly depends on the angle of view between the object and eyes. As shown in figure 1, when the object is projected in the normal direction of plane A, we can only see plane A without the whole shape of this object. When we move the direction of view along the positive way of x and z axis, and can see plane A, B, C, and D. No matter what the size and proportion of these four planes, we can still recognize the object. This is shape constancy of perception. We now can interpret it as follows: when image information is enough to recognize the pattern, the changes of image shape don't affect human perception of the object.

1.2 Pattern recognition

Pattern recognition is one of the fundamental core problems in the field of cognitive psychology. Pattern recognition is the fundamental human cognition or intelligence, which stands heavily in various human activities. Tightly linking with such psychological processes as sense, memory, study, and thinking, pattern recognition is one of important windows through which we can get a perspective view on human psychological activities.

Human pattern recognition can be considered as a typical perception process which depends on knowledge and experience people already have. Generally, pattern recognition refers to a process of inputting stimulating (pattern) information and matching with the information in long-term memory, then recognizing the category which the stimulation belongs to. Therefore, pattern recognition depends on people's knowledge and experience. Without involving individual's knowledge and experience, people cannot understand the meanings of the stimulating information pattern inputted, then neither possible to recognize the patterns, which means to recognize the objects. The process which a person distinguishes a pattern he percepts with others and identifies what it is means pattern recognition. Current cognitive psychology has proposed such theoretical models or hypothesis as the Theory of Template (Model of Template Matching), the Theory of Prototype (Model of Prototype Matching), the Theory of Feature (Model of Feature Analysis), and so on.

(1) The Theory of Template

As the simplest theoretical hypothesis in pattern recognition, the Theory of Template mainly considers that people store various mini copies of exterior patterns formed in the past in the long-term memory. These copies, named templates, correspond with the exterior stimulation patterns one by one. When a simulation acts on people's sense organs, the simulating information is first coded, compared and matched with pattern stored in brain, then identified as one certain pattern in brain which matches best. thus the pattern recognition effect is produced, otherwise the stimulation can not be distinguished and recognized. Because every template relates to a certain meanings and some other information, the pattern recognized then will be explained and processed in other ways. In daily life we can also find out some examples of template matching. Comparing with template, machine can recognize the seals on paychecks rapidly.

Although it can explains some human pattern recognition, the Theory of Template, meanwhile, has some obvious restrictions. According to the Theory of Template, people have to store an appropriate template before recognize a pattern. Although pre-processing course is added, these templates are still numerous, not only bringing heavy burden to memory but also leading pattern recognition less flexible and stiffer. The Theory of Template doesn't entirely explain the process of human pattern recognition, but the template and template matching cannot be entirely denied. As one aspect or link in the process of human pattern recognition, the template still works anyway. In some other models of pattern recognition, some mechanisms which are similar to template matching will also come out.

(2) The Theory of Prototype

The Theory of Prototype, also named the Theory of Prototype Matching, has the outstanding characteristic that memory is not storing templates which matches one-by-one with outside patterns but prototypes. The prototype, rather than an inside copy of a certain pattern, is considered as inside attribute of one kind of objects, which means abstractive characteristics of all individuals in one certain type or category. This theory reveals basic features of one type of objects. For instances, people know various kinds of airplanes, but a long cylinder with two wings can be the prototype of airplane. Therefore, according to the Theory of Prototype, in the process of pattern recognition, outside simulation only needs to be compared with the prototype, and the sense to objects comes from the matching between input information and prototype[5]. Once outside simulating information matches best with a certain prototype in brain, the information can be ranged in the category of that prototype and recognized. In a certain extent the template matching is covered in the Theory of Prototype, which appears more flexible and more elastic. However, this model also has some drawbacks, only having up-down processing but no bottom-up processing, which is sometimes more important for the prototype matching in human perceptional process.

Biederman(1987,1990) proposed the theory of Recognition-By-Components, whose core assumption is that, object is constituted by some basic shapes or components, or say geometries which includes block, cylinder, sphere, arc, and wedge. Although the number of components seems not enough for us to recognize all objects, these geometries can be used to describe efficiently, for the various spatial relations of all geometries can constitute countless assembles. The Step one of Biederman's Recognition-By-Components process is extracting edges, and the Step two divides a visible object into some segments to establish the components or geometries constituting the object. The other key is that the edge information has invariant properties, based on which the components and geometries of the visible object are established.

(3) The Theory of Feature

The Theory of Feature is other theory explaining pattern perception and shape perception. According to this theory, people try to match the features of pattern with those stored in memory, rather than the entire pattern with template or prototype. This model is the most attractive one currently, the Model of Feature Analysis has been applied widely in computer pattern recognition. However, it is just a bottom-up processing model, lacking up-down processing. Therefore, it still has some drawbacks.

1.3 Memory

First、 The Description of memory

Memory is a reflection of the past experience in human brain, and, in cognitive psychology, a process of information coding, storing, and extracting in a certain condition in future. Having a big effect on human history and individual person development, memory is a gift from the nature to individual life, and also a power with which individual keeps and uses the achieved stimulating information, knowledge and experience

As a necessary condition of the intellect development, memory is the root of all intelligence. People keep past experience into their brain by memory, and then, based on experience recovering, have thinking and imagination, whose results are kept again in brain as the basis of further thinking and imagining.

Memory, in cognitive psychology, can be seen as a process of information inputting, coding, storing, and extracting, therefore, it can be separated as instantaneous memory, short-term memory, and long-term memory according to the time of storage. Recent years, more and more researchers propose to view memory as multiple memory form with different property functions formed with various forms, systems or types (Schacter 1985).

Second、 The model of memory system

In 1960's, relying on the deep research of short-term and long-term memory, researchers on cognitive psychology gradually proposed and built some memorial theory and related memorial models. Among them, the Multiple Mnemonic Model proposed by Atkinson and Shiffrin in 1968 is the most attractive one, as shown in figure 2.

In this model, memory is described by 3 kinds of memory storages: ①sensory store, limited number and very short time for the information keeping; ②short-term store, longer time of storage but still limited number to keep;③long-term store, powerful power of storage, and able to keep for a long time, or maybe even forever. However, recently cognitive psychologists usually describe these 3 kinds of storages as sensory memory, short-term memory, and long-term memory. In this model, outside information first input into sensory registration, which has various kinds of information but probably disappears very soon. Then the information will be transferred into short-term memory, in which the information is organized by hearing, language or spoken language acknowledgement, and is stored longer than that in sensory storage. If processed meticulously, repeated, and transferring acknowledged, the information will be input into long-term memory, or else will decline or disappear.

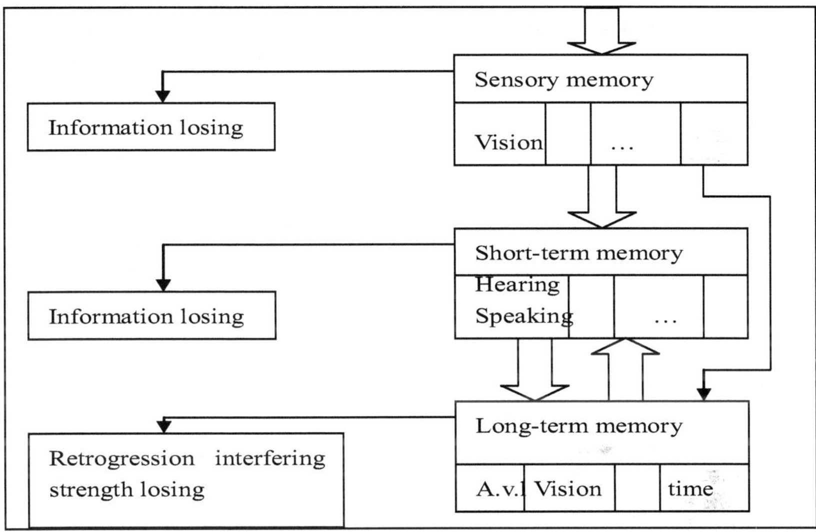

Fig. 2. The model of memory system

1.4 The expression and organization of knowledge

Human has transcendental imagination. If imagination is produced by experience and knowledge, then human's knowledge must be organized by a certain way. Cognitive psychology describes inside knowledge attribution of individual through establishing cognitive model, which has 3 hypothetical models.

First, Hypothesis of symbol-net model

This model can comparatively indicate how every part of knowledge in human brain arrays and interacts with each other in a certain connecting mode.

In symbol-net model, conceptions are usually described as "node", which links each other with a arrowed line, and therefore the two concepts are connected by a certain mode. In symbol-net model, we describe this relation with "up and down level", adding with arrowed line. What needs to be attended is the arrow direction, which has some theoretical meanings in symbol-net model, as figure 3 showing.

The fundamental assumption of symbol-net model is a reflection of people's knowledge organization, which is similar to searching among the network nodes. The search is performed one node by another along the direction of the arrows according to the form of cognitive process series, until reach the nearest node and search out the knowledge. If the knowledge in the nearest node can answer the certain question, the search will cease, otherwise the search will continue till finding out answer or giving up.

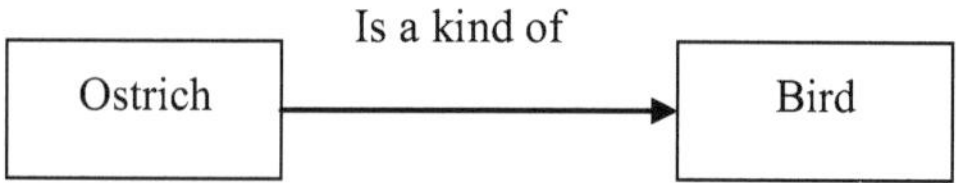

Fig. 3. The Symbol-net model

Second、Level-semantics-net model
The Level-semantics-net Model, proposed by Collins and Quillian, is a net connecting with various elements, the node represents a concept and the arrowed line reflects the affiliation of concepts. This model indicates that every concept or node has two relationships, one is that every concept is subject to other concepts, which deciding the type of knowledge attribution and describing the affiliation with "is a kind of" relation; the other is that every concept has one or more characteristics, meaning the "have" relation of concept, as figure 4 showing.

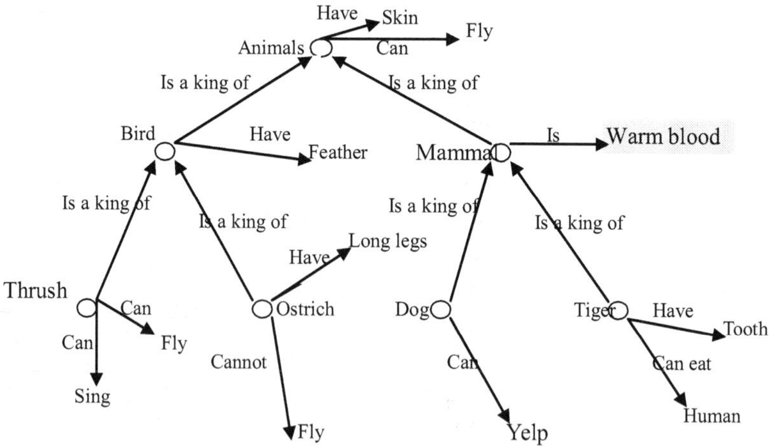

Fig. 4. The Level-semantics-net model

According to this model, the organized knowledge attribution is a level dendriform view, in which lines link nodes denoting concepts of each grade, actually in a certain extent has some imagining function. In this model, because concepts form a net according to "up-and-down" grades, every concept and characteristic locates in a specific position in the network, and the meaning of a concept depends on connecting links. According to the cognitive economic principle, the Level-semantics-net model maximizes the effective storage capability while minimizes the redundancy.
Third、The activation-diffusion model

The core of Level-semantics-net model is the network established by the logical relations of noun concepts. This features the model clean and clear, but also causes some problems, which mainly appears that the model explains human knowledge organization and attribution assuming on logics rather than psychology. Therefore, Collins and Loftus modified the original model and proposed a new one, which is the activation-diffusion model. Giving up the level structure of the concepts,, the new model organizes concepts by the connection or similarity of semantics.

In activation-diffusion model, the knowledge stored in individual's knowledge structure is a big network of concepts, between which certain connection is established, namely some knowledge is contained in advance. Therefore, activation-diffusion model is also a kind of pre-storing model, as shown in figure 5.

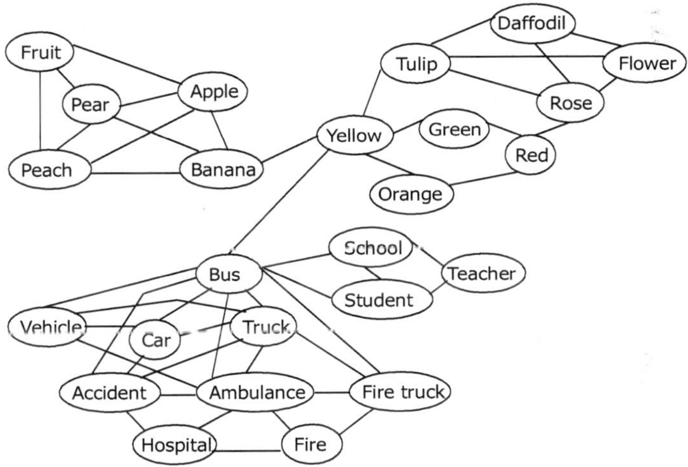

Fig. 5. The activation-diffusion model

The activation-diffusion model has two assumptions related to knowledge structure: first, the line between concepts reveals their relation, the shorter the line, the tighter their relation, and the more similar their features, for instance, "car" having tight relation with "truck", rather with "teacher", second, the intension of concept of the model is decided by other related concepts, especially the tight ones, but the features of concept is unnecessary to be stored in different grades.

1.5 The theory of topological vision

Lin Chen, involving topology into visual perception study, proposed The theory of topological vision [7]. The topology study of perceptual organization is based on a core idea and composed by two aspects. The core idea is that, perceptual organization should be interpreted in the angle of transformation and its invariance perception. One aspect emphasizes the topological structure in shape perception, which means that the global characteristic of perceptual organization can be described by topological invariance. The other aspect further emphasizes the early topological characteristic perception, which means that, topological characteristic perception priors to the partial characteristic perception. The word "prior" has two rigid meanings: the entire organization decided by topological characteristics are basis of the perception of partial geometric characters, and topological characteristics perception of physical connectivity is ahead of perception of partly geometric characteristics.

2. Brief commentary of machine pattern recognition

Machine pattern recognition developed rapidly in the beginning of 1960's and became a new science, then has been in rapid development and successfully applied in weather forecasting, satellite aerochart explanation, industrial products measurement, character recognition, voice recognition, fingerprint recognition, medical image analysis and so on.

By now Machine pattern recognition (pattern recognition for short) mainly has two basic methods: statistics pattern recognition and structure (syntax) pattern recognition. Structure pattern recognition, based on image features of structure, accomplishes pattern recognition by using dendriform information of the layered structure of pattern and subschema. Statistics pattern recognition, which has wider application, is based on the type probability density function of samples in feature space and separates pattern statistics into types, which means pattern recognition integrated with Bayesian decision in proportion statistics, is also called decision theory recognition method.

In statistics pattern recognition, some knowledge and experience can decide the principle of classification, which means the rules of judgment. According to appropriate rules of judgment, we can separate the samples of feature space into different types and thus change feature space to type space. We separate feature space into type space while we classify the patterns. Statistics pattern recognition is based on the type probability density function of samples in feature space, and the rule of judgment of multiple statistics pattern recognition is Bayesian decision theory, aiming to minimize the expected risk of prior probability and lost function. Because nonlinear classification can be transferred into linear classification, the fact is searching the hyper plane of optimal decision. Although Bayesian decision rules solve the problem of engineering the optimal classifier, the implement has to be first settled with the more difficult problem of probability density distribution, thus research develops surrounding decision rules and probability density distribution. For the former, Rueda L G and Oommen B J's researches in recent years indicate that the normal distribution and other criteria functions with the covariance matrix unequal are linear and their classifiers is optimal[9]; Liu J N K, Li B N L, and Dillon T S improved Bayesian classifier with genetic algorithm when choosing input feature subset in classification problem[10]; Ferland G and Yeap T, studying the math structure of RTANN method, identified the condition of achieving optimal Bayesian classification with such method[11]. For the issue of probability density distribution, usual assuming density is a model with parameters like multiple normal distribution, while the parameters are estimated by the training sample. When the sample is not enough, the estimated error which is contained by distribution function will affect the precision of recognition. In order to improve the precision of recognition, Ujiie H et al transformed the reference data closer to normal distribution, no matter what the distribution of original data, and found the optimal transformation in theory [12]. The emergence of statistic learning and supporting vector machine bring theoretical and methodological supplement for the transformation. Core function which satisfy the Mercer condition realizes the design of the nonlinear classifier without knowing the specific form of nonlinear transformation[13]. Fisher judgment and principal component analysis are traditional linear methods which widely applied in pattern classification and feature extraction. The Fisher judgment [14-15]and principal component analysis[16] in recent years both based on the core function are their linear widespread. One-dimensional parameter search and recursion Fisher method can get better training result than normal Fisher judgment. Using Mercer core, we can generalize these two methods into nonlinear decision plane[17]. There are also some reports of improving the function of classifier by declining pattern overlapping with fuzzy cluster analysis[18].

Therefore, there are two main problems need to be solved in pattern recognition:

1. Because of the requirement of sample amount, statistics pattern recognition cannot function well in small sample recognition.
2. so far, the pattern recognition is mainly based on the classification mechanism of the recognized objects, rather than on the perception mechanism. In "recognition", namely in the aspect of acknowledge of objects (study), there is large difference between human perception process and limited learning ability.

3. Theory of cognitive pattern recognition

3.1 Perceptive constancy and topological invariance

In the first chapter, we generally express perceptive constancy as: in the condition that the image information of the object is sufficient to determine its pattern, the geometry changing in the size and shape does not affect people's perception for the object.

The above questions refer to a special kind of geometric properties of geometry, which involve the property of the geometric overall structure, named the topological property. Obviously, these topological properties are not related to such aspects of the geometry as the size, the shape and the straight or curved of lines and so on, which means that they can not be dealt with by ordinary geometric methods. Topology is to study the invariable property when geometry makes elastic deformation, the same as the perceptive constancy that changing in size and shape of the geometry do not affect people's perception for the objcct.

Now let's make a further analysis to the topological property. As mentioned above, topology embodies the overall structure of geometric features, that any changes in shapes (such as squeezing, stretching or distorting, etc), as long as the geometry is neither torn nor adhered, will not destroy its overall structure and the topological properties remain the same. The above deformations are called the topological transformation, so the topological invariability is the property keeping the same when the geometry transforms topologically. The topological property can be accurately described by the set and mapping language. The changing of the geometry M to M' (both can be regarded as a set of topological feature points) is a one-to-one mapping (therefore the overlap phenomenon will not appear, moreover new points will not be created) $f : M \rightarrow M'$, where f is continuous (that means

no conglutination). Generally speaking, if both f and f^{-1} are continuous, the one-to-one mapping f, which changes M to M', can be regarded as a topological transformation from M to M', also f and f^{-1} are the mapping of homeomorphism. Therefore, topological property is common in the homeomorphous geometries. The geometries of homeomorphism have no differentiation in topology because their topological properties are the same.

3.2 Perceptive constancy and pattern invariance

From above discussion, we can regard the perceptive constancy as the topological invariance. As the size constancy, changing the size of geometry is actually compressing and expanding the geometry during which the topological properties of the geometry do not change. And the shape constancy means to carry unequal proportional compression and expansion on geometries. As shown in figure 1, when we make projection on the normal direction of plane A, which creates conglutination between plane A and plane B, C, D, geometric topology has been changed, so the object can not be perceived. When the projection points move along the x-axis and z-axis, we can observe that conglutination has not been created among plane A, B, C, D, the topological structure has not been changed, so the object can be perceived.

Furthermore, we will discuss perceptive constancy by using the theory of topology.

First, size constancy :

As mentioned above, as the distance between human eyes and the object changes the image sizes of geometry on the retina change, but in our minds we perceive the images of different sizes as an object, we call this kind of information processing size constancy. The explanation of size constancy is shown in figure 7. In the figure, as the distance between the eyes and the object changes, the images are named a, b, c and d respectively. In image a, the distance between the eyes and object is so near that the image of the object cannot be seen entirely, thus unable to be recognized. As the distance between the eyes and object becomes farther and farther, the images of the object on the retina become smaller and smaller, as shown in figure b, c and d. In the figure d, the distance to the eyes is too far and the image of the object is too small to recognize.

Sequence images of the object are generated on the retina as the distance between the eyes and an object X changes. Now suppose Y is the image generated on the retina at a certain distance from eyes within the human visual range, the topological information set (such as connection, holes, nodes, branches and so on)of the image Y can be expressed as $Y = \{y_1, y_2, \cdots, y_m\}$, where any element of Y can be obtained by the compression and expansion of the corresponding element of object X (in order to discuss conveniently, every set is supposed to have m elements, but that not means different sets have the same number of the elements). The topological information set of the object X is expressed as $X = \{x_1, x_2, \cdots, x_m\}$.

Suppose the power set of Y(the collection containing all subsets of Y)is Ψ_Y

$$\begin{aligned}
\Psi_Y = \{ &\{y_1\}, \{y_1, y_2\}, \cdots, \{y_1, y_2, \cdots, y_{m-1}\}, \\
&\{y_2\}, \{y_2, y_3\}, \cdots, \{y_2, \cdots, y_m\}, \\
&\{y_3\}, \{y_3, y_4\}, \cdots, \{y_3, \cdots, y_m\}, \\
&\cdots, \{y_{m-1}, y_m\}, Y, \varnothing\}
\end{aligned}$$

Suppose the power set of X is Ψ_X

$$\Psi_X = \{\{x_1\}, \{x_1, x_2\}, \cdots, \{x_1, \cdots, x_{m-1}\},$$
$$\{x_2\}, \{x_2, x_3\}, \cdots, \{x_2, \cdots x_m\},$$
$$\{x_3\}, \{x_3, x_4\}, \cdots, \{x_3, \cdots, x_m\},$$
$$\cdots, \{x_{m-1}, x_m\}, X, \varnothing\}$$

Proposition 3.1: Ψ_Y is the topology of the topological information set of the image Y, then (Y, Ψ_Y) constitutes a discrete topological space.

Proof: Because Ψ_Y, the power set of **Y**, contains all subsets of **Y**, obviously Ψ_Y satisfies three topological theorems as follows:

1. Both **Y** and $\varnothing$ are in Ψ_Y;

2. The union of random number of any subcollection of Ψ_Y is in Ψ_Y;

3. The intersection of limited number of subcollection of Ψ_Y is in Ψ_Y.

Therefore, Ψ_Y is the topology of the topological information set of the image **Y**, and (**Y**, Ψ_Y) constitutes a discrete topological space, thus the proposition is proved and established.

Similarly, (**X**, Ψ_X) also constitutes a discrete topological space which denotes the topological space of the topological information set of the object **X**.

People can not only see the whole object, but also a part of it, thus the elements of **Y** can combine into any different subset which means the whole information of the image, the whole information of a partial image, the whole information of certain feature of the image (Although the integration of features in image is not separated, the combination among the elements of **Y** still can be characterized)

Proposition 3.2: When other conditions remain unchanged relatively, as the distance between the eyes and the object changes, the topological space of the topological information set of the image (Y, Ψ_Y) and (X, Ψ_X) which is the topological space of the topological information set of the object X have the same homeomorphism.

Proof: Y is the image of the object X generated on the retina, the topological space (X, Ψ_X) of the object X is the direct foundation of the topological space of the image Y. (**Y**, Ψ_Y) is the result of (**X**, Ψ_X) converted by human visual perception system. When Other conditions remains relatively unchanged and in the range of human visual perception, as the distance between the eyes and object changes, the image Y is just the compression or expansion of the object X, but the topology of it has not changed. As shown in Fig 6, for any element (that is topological properties, such as connectivity, the number of "hole" and so on)in the image **Y** there is a unique corresponding element in the object **X**. For example the elements y_1 and y_m of the image **Y** respectively corresponds to the elements x_1 and x_m of the object **X**.

Therefore, there exists a bijective correspondence between the object **X** and the image **Y**

$f: \mathbf{X} \rightarrow \mathbf{Y}$

The mapping direction indicates the relationship between the reason and the result. Whereas, there also exists a bijective correspondence from the topological information set of the image **Y** to the topological information set of the object **X**

$$f^{-1}: \mathbf{Y} \rightarrow \mathbf{X}$$

Moreover, f and f^{-1} are continuous. According to the definition of the homeomorphism in topology, f is the mapping of homeomorphism. As a result, the topological space $(\mathbf{Y}, \; \Psi_Y)$ of the image **Y** and $(\mathbf{X}, \; \Psi_X)$ which is the topological space of the object **X** have the same homeomorphism. So the proposition is proved and established.

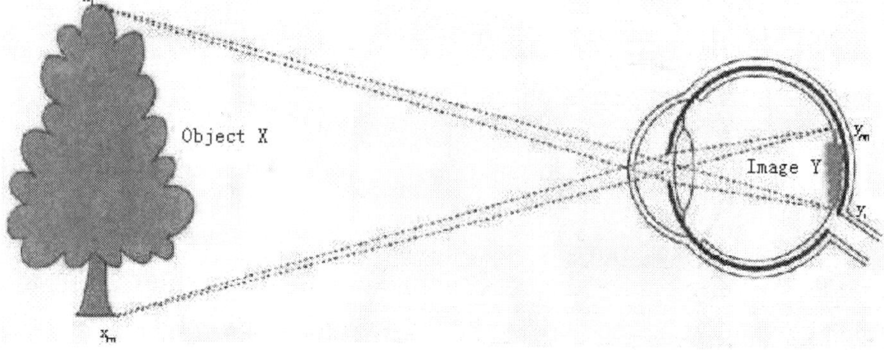

Fig. 6. The relationship between the object and its image

Proposition 3.3: The size constancy of visual perception has the property of topological invariance.

Proof: suppose the smallest distinguishable image (image of object X generated on retina from the farthest distance) is the topological space Y1 (proved in Proposition 3.1 and corresponding to the of Figure 7(c)), as the distance between the eyes and the object changes, different topological spaces $\mathbf{Y_2}$, $\mathbf{Y_3}$, ..., $\mathbf{Y_i}$, ..., are generated on the retina, $\mathbf{Y_n}$ is the topological space of the biggest image (as shown in Fig 7(b)). From proposition 3.2, when other conditions remain relatively unchanged, as the distance between the eyes and the object changes, the topological spaces of the images have the same homeomorphism as the topological space of the object **X**. So $\forall i \in \{1, \cdots, n\}$, $\mathbf{Y_i}$ and **X** have the same homeomorphism, which means $\mathbf{Y_i} \cong \mathbf{X}$. Also because the property of homeomorphism has the transitivity, every $\mathbf{Y_i}$ is has the same homeomorphism with each other, which means for $\forall i, j \in \{1, \cdots, n\}$ all satisfies $\mathbf{Y_i} \cong \mathbf{Y_j}$. Thus the topological spaces $\mathbf{Y_1}$, $\mathbf{Y_2}$, ..., $\mathbf{Y_i}$, ..., $\mathbf{Y_n}$ have the same homeomorphism, indicating that the size constancy of visual perception has the property of topological invariance.

In figure 7, the above are the images and below are the topological structures corresponding to its image. From the figure, (b) and (c) can be perceived as a cuboid because they have the same topology. For image (a), the size of the image is expanded seriously, only a few partial information about the object can be seen, therefore the object cannot be recognized for not enough information available; in figure (d), the image is compressed so excessively that we are not sure whether it is a cuboid, cylinder or a small piece of others. There does not exist a bijective correspondence between the topological spaces of the (a), (d) and the topological spaces of the (b), (c), therefore, they do not have the same homeomorphism as the topological spaces of the (b) and (c).

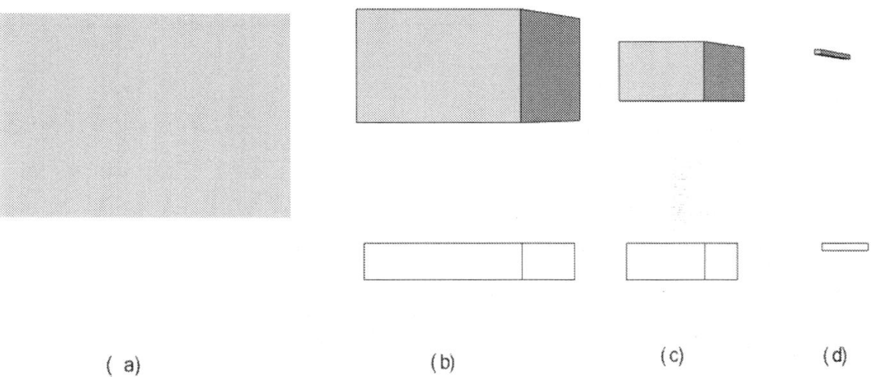

(a)   (b)   (c)   (d)

Fig. 7. The Size constancy

Thus, it is concluded that when the sizes of the images change, as long as the topology of the images has not been changed, people can perceive them as the same object, that is to say, the size constancy can perceive the objects which make the topological transformation as the same object.

Second, shape constancy :

As mentioned above, shape constancy is a kind of information procession which mainly as the angles between the eyes and the object change, the shapes of the images on the retina change, but in our minds we perceive different shapes of images as the same object.

The explanation of the shape constancy is shown in Figure 8.

Suppose Y_1 is the topological space of the distinguishable image(the image generated on the retina when the eyes are at the bottom of the object), different topological spaces Y_2, Y_3, ..., Y_i, ...of the images are generated as the angles between the eyes and object change, Y_n is the topological space of the image generated on the retina when the eyes are at the top of the object. Obviously the relationship between the topological spaces the images of Y_1 and Y_i (i=2, ..., n) are squeeze and stretch. As the angles between the eyes and the object changes, part of the object are squeezed, while other part of the object are stretched, as shown in the figure 8. But as constancy, which means that, at the range of the human visual perception, each side and each part of the object keep the original characteristics well, without adhesion or tearing. Therefore the topological spaces Y_1, Y_2, ..., Y_i, ..., Y_n have the same homeomorphism, namely the shape constancy of the human visual perception has the property of the topological invariance, the method of the proof is just the same as that of the size constancy.

In Fig 8, the above row are the images and below are the topological structures corresponding to its image. From the figure, (a), (b) and (c) can be perceived as a cuboid, because they have the same topology. (b) and (f) have the same topology different with others, we cannot perceived them as a cuboid, maybe we will perceived them as folded piece of a rectangle. We may perceive (g) as a piece papper.

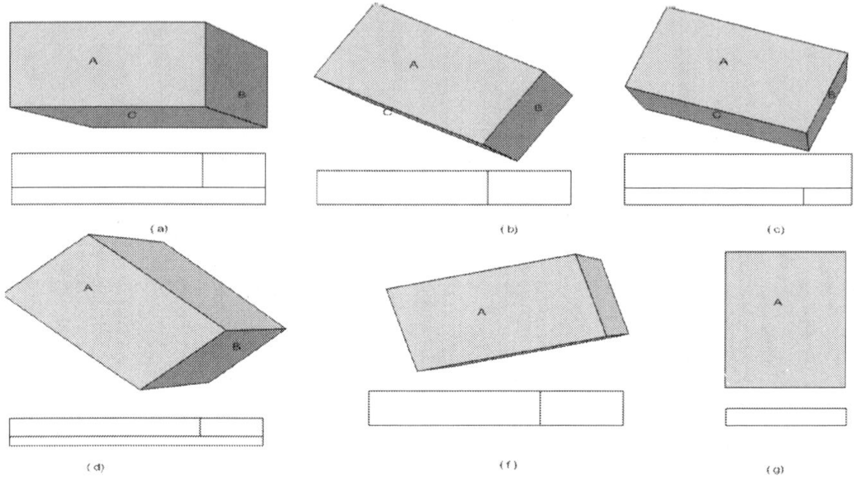

Fig. 8. The shape constancy

Therefore, it can be concluded that when the images' shapes of the object change, as long as the topology of the images has not been changed, we can perceive them as the same object, in other words, the shape constancy can perceive the objects making topological transformation as the same object.

From the above analysis, we can see that the constancy in size and shape of the visual perception can be described by topological invariance. As long as the topology of the images keeps unchanged, we can perceive the images that make topological transformation as the same object at the range of the human visual perception.

In conclusion, we can believe that the constancy of the human visual perception can be described by the topology invariance, that is, people can perceive the objects which are changed by topological transformation as the same object.

3.3 Composition of patterns

From the theory of the component recognition, the principle which the components constitute objects in the real world can be understood like this: there are countless type of materials in the world, but the types of the chemical elements composing the materials are just a little more than 100. Various colors in the world can be composed by the three colors of red, green and blue. All buildings, no matter how grand and splendid they are, are composed by the foundation, beams, column doors, walls, floors and the ceilings. A variety of delicious food can be cooked by just a few spices of the oil, salt, sugar, vinegar, soy sauce and so on.

Music is wonderful, and countless musical works are composed by the seven notes of 1,2,3,4,5,6,7 and their changeable sound. The number of the English words is very huge, moreover in the rapid development, but they are just composed by the 52 letters including

26 uppercase and 26 lowercase letters. As we know the number of figures in various aspects of the world is endless, but in the decimal system these figures are constituted by 0 to 9 altogether ten figures; in the hexadecimal 0 to 9 ten figures and A to F six letters are needed; in the binary only two symbols 0 and 1 are needed.

Therefore we can take it that Biederman's theory of the components recognition reveals the pattern of the real world's construction: all the objects of the world are composed by a few components, that is to say, all the objects can be decomposed into certain components.

Biederman's theory holds that the limited components have almost infinite combination, thus compose almost unlimited objects. This conforms to Chinese philosophy of "one lives two, two lives three, and three lives everything". In terms of the geometry, the objects can be fully described by the geometries, because various spatial relationships among the geometries have infinite combination. The same components can form different objects through different combination. The English words "on" and "no", "dear" and "dare", "hear" and "hare" respectively have the same letters, but when combination is different, the words composed are completely different.

We call such a combination of the objects structures, which is a very important concept in pattern recognition. The definition of the structure is the organization of each part of the object[19].

In pattern recognition, the structure is the combinational relations between the object and its' components, and the combination of their components. For example, the English word "structure" is composed by s, t, r, u, c, e six letters, the order of the arrangement is s-t-r-u-c-t-u-r-e. In organic chemistry, Methane (CH_4) is composed by the two elements of Carbon(C) and Hydrogen(H), and the structure of the CH_4 is a regular tetrahedron, that the carbon atom is in the center of the tetrahedron, while four hydrogen atoms are in the vertices of the tetrahedron, as shown in Fig 9.

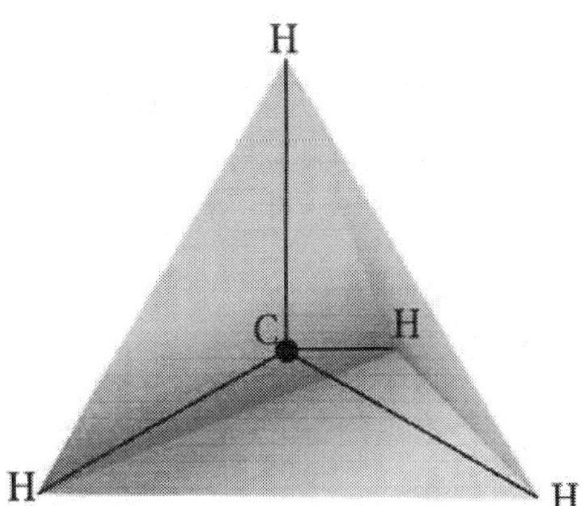

Fig. 9. The structure of the methane

The structure of objects, has its own laws, which cannot be constructed arbitrarily. In English, the letters have certain regulations of arrangement to construct the words, for example we cannot arrange w, v, u and some other letters together repeatedly. In appearance of the human face, there are not more than two eyes, only one nose and only one mouth, moreover the distribution of them is that the eyes are at the top of the face, the nose in the middle, and the mouth at the bottom.

Now we use the theory of set to describe the construction of the object:

Definition 3.1 The objects which have the same characteristics in some aspects compose a set, denoted as O.

Definition 3.2 The elements in the object set O are called object or pattern, denoted as m, that is $m \in O$.

Definition 3.3 For any $m \in O$, we can decompose it to one or several components according to a certain regulations, then the components form a set which is recorded as C_i (i is the natural number)

Definition 3.4 For any $m \in O$, we call the mutual relationship of the components structure which can be denoted as S or S $(C_1, C_2, ..., C_n)$.

For example, with a certain structure the word "study" is composed by the letters "s, t, u, d, y", which can be denoted as follow:

$$Study = S(s,t,u,d,y).$$

All patterns in the object set can be decomposed into a component or more according to a certain structure, that is, all the objects in the set can be composed by the several components according to a certain structure.

3.4 The relationship between the prototype and the components of objects

The theory of prototype believes that the storage in the long-term memory is the prototypes, rather than the templates corresponding to the external patterns. What is the prototype after all? Prototype is the internal characteristic of a class of objects and also the general characteristic of all individuals of a class of objects, but not the internal copy of a specific model. It is considered by component recognition that objects are composed by a number of basic shapes or components, that is to say, are composed by the geometries.

From the above two theories, it appears that there is a difference in the content of their researches: the theory of the prototype matching is to study the human brain for perceiving the outside world, while the theory of the component recognition is to study the composition of the objects. However, the two theories are to study human's pattern recognition, is there any relationship between them?

Prototype, the general characteristic of all individuals in a category or area, reflects a class of the objects' basic characteristics, is the generalization and abstraction of the object's characteristics. As analyzed in the preceding chapter, an object is constituted by some elements that are concrete and determined under its structure. Therefore, there exists a process from general to determine and from abstract to concrete between the prototypes and the components.

We might understand prototype like this: for an object set of English word, and for any word in the object set, all of them are constituted by one or more of 52 symbols which has 26 uppercase and 26 lowercase letters. With 26 uppercase and 26 lowercase letters, the 52 symbols are the generalization and abstraction of the components of all the English words. No matter how many English words and various fonts there are, they can be constituted by some letters changing in size and shape. Therefore, English words' uppercase and lowercase letters are the prototypes of this object of English words. The sizes and shapes of prototypes are fixed, the matches between them and the components with various size and shape can be realized by topological mapping. The deduction of the concept is shown in Figure 10.

In Fig 10, the prototype set P has 52 elements including 26 uppercase and 26 lowercase letters, while all the English words compose the set of the objects. The elements in the set of the objects are specific English words *"Pattern Recognition* PATTERN RECOGNITION", which are composed by elements of the prototypes "R, P, A, T, E, N, C, O, I, G, e, c, o, g, n, I, t". The elements' size and font in the prototype set are fixed, the prototypes can match each kind size and font of the components through the topological transformation.

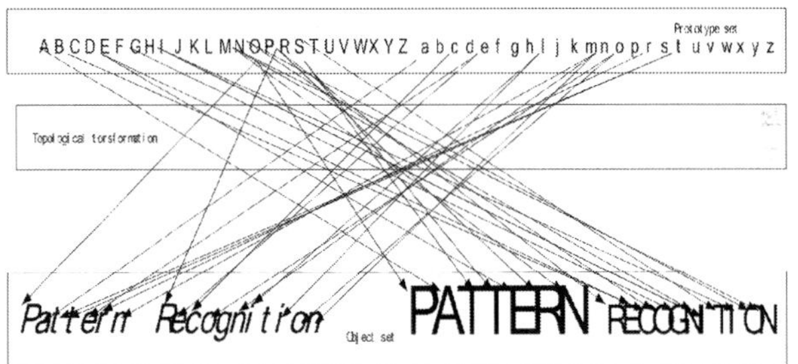

Fig. 10. The relationship between the prototypes and the components of objects

It can be described from the perspective of topology:

Definition 3.5 A set without any repeated elements abstracted from the component collection C of all the objects M in a kind of object O, is called the prototype of this kind of object O, denoted as P,

From the definition 3.3 and 3.5, all objects M in every class of object O can be decomposed, under a certain rule, into some components C, from which a set abstracted without any repeated elements becomes prototype P, as shown in Fig 11.

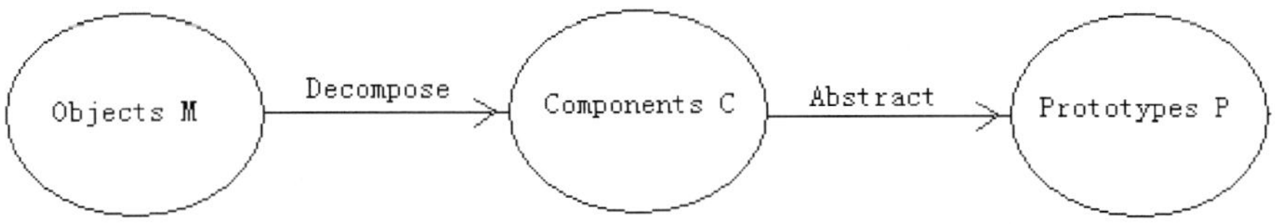

Fig. 11. Objects-Components-Prototypes

In the example above the specific objects are the following English words *"Pattern, Recognition,* PATTERN, RECOGNITION", if set M={*Pattern, Recognition,* PATTERN, RECOGNITION }, then M can be decomposed into the component collection C={{*P, a, t, t, e, r, n*}, {*R, e, c, o, g, n, i, t, i, o, n*}, {P, A, T, T, E, R, N}, {R, E, C, O, G, N, I, T, I, O, N}}. The differences of the components among the *R*, R and R are only size and shape, there is no difference on topology among these three elements, so these three elements can be abstracted as a prototype R. Therefore, the prototype set P can be abstracted from the component collection C, that is the prototype set P = (R, P, A, T, E, N, C, O, I, G, e, c, o, g, n, i, t).

Further expatiation on topological theory is following.

Suppose M=$\{m_1, m_2, \cdots, m_n\}$ is the set of all the objects in O, each element in it denotes an object; $C_i = \{c_{i1}, c_{i2}, \cdots, c_{im}\}$ (i=1,…,n) denotes the components of the ith object in M, C=$\{C_1, C_2, \cdots, C_n\}$ denotes the collection of all components sets; P=$\{p_1, p_2, \cdots, p_r\}$ denotes the set of all the prototypes which is abstracted from the component collection C of all the objects M in O.

Suppose Γ_P is the power set of the prototypes P, Γ_{C_i} is the power set of C_i, Γ_M is the power set of M.

Proposition 3.4 Γ_P is a topology of the prototype set P, (P, Γ_P) constitutes a discrete topological space.

The method of proof is the same as that of the proposition 3.1.

Similarly, it can be proved that (M, Γ_M) and (C_i, Γ_{C_i}) also constitute discrete topological spaces.

Proposition 3.5 The collection C=$\{C_1, C_2, \cdots, C_n\}$ is a basis of the prototypes' topological space (P, Γ_P) .

Proof: P is the unions of the component set C_i, that is P=$\bigcup\limits_{i=1}^{n} C_i$, so C is a subcollection of the (P, Γ_P) . Each element in Γ_P can be denoted by the union of some elements in C, satisfying the definition of basis[20] in topological space, therefore, the collection C=$\{C_1, C_2, \cdots, C_n\}$ constitutes a basis of the prototypes' topological space (P, Γ_P) .

From another perspective, (P, Γ_P) is a discrete topological space, moreover any discrete topological space has a simplest basis (of course, there may be more than one basis for any topology), which is composed by all single-point subset of it. The single-point subset of the topological space (P, Γ_P) is $C_1, C_2, \cdots, C_n$, therefore the collection C=$\{C_1, C_2, \cdots, C_n\}$ constitutes a basis of the prototypes' topological space (P, Γ_P) .

So any prototypes in the prototype set P are abstracted from the component collection C of all the objects M in O.

Proposition 3.6 If f is the mapping from the topological space of the components C to the topological space of the prototypes P, then f is surjective.

Proof: P is the set of the prototypes abstracted from the components collection C of all the objects M in O, that is P=$\bigcup\limits_{i=1}^{n} C_i$, thus there exist topological mappings $f(f_1, f_2, \cdots, f_r)$, and $f_i(f_{i1}, f_{i2}, \cdots, f_{im})$ (i=1,2,…,r) , which make

$$f_i(C_1, C_2, \cdots, C_n) = p_i,$$

The prototypes P abstracted from the components C, have not changed the topology of the component c_{ij} of the objects, just make a small change in the size or the shape of the component c_{ij}, thus

$$f_{ij}(c_{ij}) = p_i,$$

which is a homeomorphism, therefore

$$f(C) = P.$$

thus f is surjective.

For example in English words, if M={*Pattern, Recognition*, PATTERN, RECOGNITION }, then M can be decomposed into components C_1={*P, a, t, t, e, r, n*}, C_2={*R, e, c, o, g, n, i, t, i, o, n*}, C_3={P, A, T, T, E, R, N}, C_4={R, E, C, O, G, N, I, T, I, O, N}, namely, C = (C1, C2, C3, C4), and the prototype set P={R, P, A, T, E, N, C, O, I, G, e, c, o, g, n, i, t} which is abstracted from the component collection C of all the objects in M, that is,

$$f_1(R, \mathbf{R}, R) = R = p_{1\circ}$$

$$f_{11}(R) = R = p_1,$$

$$f_{12}(\mathbf{R}) = R = p_1,$$

$$f_{13}(R) = R = p_1,$$

$$f_2(P, \mathbf{P}) = P = p_{2\circ}$$

$$f_{21}(P) = P = p_2,$$

$$f_{22}(\mathbf{P}) = P = p_2,$$

$$\cdots$$

$$f_i(f_{i1}, f_{i2}, \cdots, f_{im}) = p_i$$

$$\cdots$$

Where each mapping f_{ij} is a homeomorphism, so $f(f_1, f_2, \cdots, f_r)$ which can makes

$$f : C \rightarrow P$$

is surjective.

With topological transformation, any object m in the set M can be constituted by certain elements in the prototype set P, that is, the elements in the prototype set P firstly change into the elements of the components throughout topological transformation, and then compose the objects according to a certain structure. Therefore the mathematical model, which expresses the course that the components compose the objects, is shown in Fig 12 and equation (3.1), the process and the plan are contrary to Fig 11.

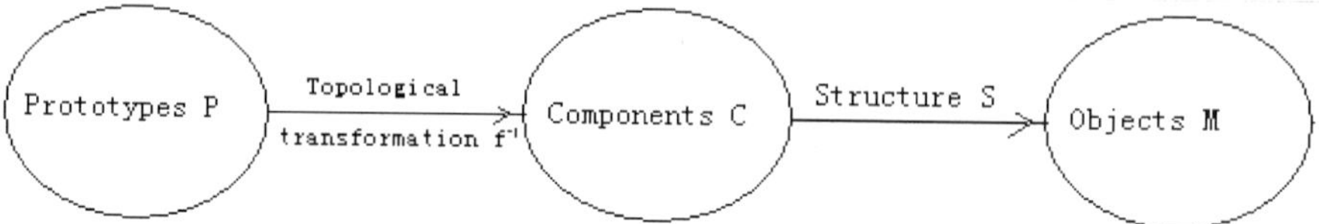

Fig.12. The components compose the objects

$$M = S\ (C)\ = S\ (f^{-1} : P \to C)\tag{3.1}$$

For example, as shown in 10, the word PATTERN can be obtained like this: with the topological transformation the elements A, E, N, P, R, T in the prototype set P change into the components A, E, N, P, R, T, and then according to certain structure the word is constituted by the components, that is

$$\text{PATTERN} = S(A, E, N, P, R, T)_\circ$$

The model of composing object based on the theory of prototype matching can be described like this:

There exists a set of the prototypes, which are abstracted from the components of all objects. Each object can be constituted by one or more elements in the prototype set through the topological transformation.

3.5 Matching and coverage

As discussed above that the power set Γ_p of the prototype set P is a topology of P, according to the theory of the prototype, there exist prototype set $P = \bigcup\limits_{i \in \{1,2,\cdots,n\}} C_i$, thus Γ_p is a coverage of P. It is known in the theory of prototype matching that, all objects are constituted by a limited prototypes, that is there are limited members in coverage Γ_p, so Γ_p is the limited coverage of P. The following are proving it in the theory of topology.

Proposition 3.7: The topological space Γ_p of the prototype set P is compact.

Proof: As (P, Γ_p) is a discrete topological space, and it is known by the theory of prototype that all of the objects M in a class of object O are constituted by limited prototypes, that Γ_p is limited and the discrete topological space is a compact topological space as long as its' elements are limited [21]. The proposition is proved and established.

Proposition 3.8: The prototype topological space (P, Γ_p) can satisfy the second countable axiom.

Proof: From the proposition above that $\mathbf{C}=\{C_1,C_2,\cdots,C_n\}$ is a basis of $(P,\ \Gamma_p)$, the prototypes decomposed by all the objects in M are limited, that is, the number of the elements in collection $C = \{C_1,C_2,\cdots,C_n\}$ is numerable, so $(P,\ \Gamma_p)$ has a numerable basis- --- $\mathbf{C}=\{C_1,C_2,\cdots,C_n\}$, that satisfies the definition of the second countable axiom[22], therefore, the prototype topological space $(P,\ \Gamma_p)$ can satisfy the second countable axiom and it is the space of A2, the proposition is proved and established.

Proposition 3.9: The prototype topological space $(P,\ \Gamma_p)$ can satisfy the first countable axiom.

Proof: From the proposition above that $\mathbf{C}=\{C_1,C_2,\cdots,C_n\}$ is a numerable basis of $(\mathbf{P},\ \Gamma_p)$, for $\forall p \in P, \Gamma_{P_c} = \{C' \in \Gamma_P \mid p \in C'\}$ is a neighborhood of p, which is a sub-collection of C and is numerable collection, so P has a numerable neighborhood basis Γ_{P_C} at the point p, that satisfies the definition of the first countable axiom of the topological space[23], so the prototype topological space $(P,\ \Gamma_p)$ can satisfy the first countable axiom and it is the space of A1, the proposition is proved and established.

Proposition 3.10: The prototype topological space $(P,\ \Gamma_p)$ can satisfy any axiom of separability.

Proof: $(\mathbf{P},\ \Gamma_p)$ is a discrete topological space, and the discrete topological space is the space which meets all the properties of the spaces stated by the separability axiom [24], which includes T1 space, T2 space (also called Hausdorff space), T3 space, T3.5 space (also called Tychonoff Space), T4 space, regular space and so on. Therefore, as a discrete topological space, the prototype topological space $(P,\ \Gamma_p)$ can satisfy any axiom of separability, the proposition is proved and established.

From Proposition 3.7, the prototype P is compact, so the open coverage must have limited sub-coverage in prototype P. In other words, the process of the prototype matching is to use the topological transformation of one or more elements in prototype set to cover the components of the pattern.

3.6 The evaluation of matching

The multi-value problem of matching extent between prototype and pattern's components changes into the yes-or-no problems that whether matching or not matching. There is a decision-making process and a evaluation criteria. The evaluation method of the traditional machine pattern recognition is Bayesian decision theorem, the final judgement is the threshold. The threshold is the value of domain, if higher than the threshold, it pass; otherwise it fails. In pattern recognition, the threshold is established artificially by people's hard working, the higher the threshold is, the higher the rate of rejecting identifier and the lower that of wrong identifier are, Otherwise, the lower the rate of rejecting identifier and the higher that of wrong identifier are.

In fact, the method of threshold is derived from a way of information solving or data processing in statistic, rather than a law of nature.

In a condition of large sample, by using the method of threshold, the workload of data processing can be greatly reduced. For example, the scores of exam which entering school by students, uses a threshold to differentiate. Matriculating the students whose scores are higher than the threshold, and rejecting the students whose scores are lower than the threshold.For instance, a product has a qualified threshold, higher that is eligible, lower is not.

In fact, the students who get higher scores at one exam not actually learn well than the one who gets lower scores. While the groups of student who get higher scores learn well than the groups of students who get lower scores.

The people whose ages are over 60 are elders, while the others whose ages are 59 and 11 months are not elders. Even though all are 60 years old, the psychology and physiology are diverse. Therefore, the threshold is the method of handling problem but not a natural law.

However, in some situations, we cannot adopt the method of threshold. For instance, the voting may fail if we set a threshold, that is, there exist some possibilities that the threshold is so high that nobody can reach it or the threshold is so low that lots of people can reach it.

It seems that there is an orientation to pursue "best" around our world. Most people hope his or her room bigger at home. However, in the earthquake areas having happened in china in May 12th 2008, the temporary movable rooms are only tens of square meters, but people also live well, even they live in the several -square -meters tents. People always hope the bed can be bigger, it is surprise that two meters beds can be brought nowadays. It is a fashionable that people sleep in big beds, so people almost want to buy the big bed. While the sleepers are only 60cm wide in the trains, which is less than the 1/3 of the big beds, people also can sleep very well. But we can observe that people on the train are changing the posture frequently when they are sleeping. Whether or not the example above can prove that people have the orientation to pursue the "best" under a certain restricted condition?

There is a similar situation in the natural world. We have observed that the trees grow under the stones, the advantage of them is that they can break through the huge stone and grow up under great resistance. Groups of bamboos can grow up highly and straightly, while the single trees or bamboos which grow on the wide area are short and bended, they are Looking for a best developing direction when they are restricted by the surrounding environment, can it be explained that the plants which grow in the natural world also have the orientation to pursue the "best" under a certain restricted condition?

These exists a extreme point at mathematics, which means the function can get the extreme value at this point or at the boundary points of the interval.

In human pattern recognition, which is researched by cognition psychology, once the external stimulating information has the nearest matching with certain prototype in brain, it can be added into the category of this prototype and then recognized. The nearest means the best matching among them, obviously, it is not enough to satisfy one threshold.

Actually, sometimes these twos are combined to use. The modern people like to obtain the projects or business contracts by bid. The process of bid can be viewed as the recognition for suppliers or contractors. The first condition in the bid process is the qualification, also call the threshold. Only the people who meet the qualification of bid can submit a bid. However, the best method is to summarize the elements of the quality, price, service etc, and then choose the winner among several qualified bidder who meet the tenderee's profit.

We can take the same idea used to solve public bidding problem to deal with the problem of estimating the discriminating result in recognition. The threshold method and the extreme method are always introduced in the estimation: we choose the most nearest matching from those whom satisfy the very condition of threshold.

3.7 Processing method

The theory of prototype matching adopts up-down processing method, which is the fault of this matching theory. The work of human's pattern recognition is complex. Take the image recognition as an example, recognizing the plant, animal, all kinds of objects which are man-made, image, character even all the objects in the world are very complex. Just because the objects that people facing are so complex that we can not forecast the properties of them, so it can not prepare the corresponding matching information to build up the up-down processing method. In fact, if possible, people often use the up-down processing method or combine them when recognition, for example, when someone has heard that some relative will come to visit, they will adopt up-down processing method to recognize the coming person, of course they will make mistake by up-down process.

The work of recognition is more easily for the system in machine pattern recognition, which is a special recognition system that usually aims to a class of objects. For example, character recognition aims to character, while face recognition aims to face, fingerprint recognition aims to fingerprint, and glass inspecting recognition aims to glass. The ability of machine pattern recognition is much weaker than people's. Just because we can build up a systemic knowledge by using of the special knowledge of special system to achieve or partly achieve the combination of up-down process method and bottom-up process method. For example, "0" is recognized as a number in number recognition system but recognized as a character in character recognition system. For the images of visual perception, especially for the images' topology, the topology of them is the same. And it settles the shortage of up-down processing method to a certain extent.

3.8 Memory

In machine pattern recognition, because knowledge and prototype must be memorized, the memory mechanism of cognition psychology must be used. But in machine pattern recognition, sensory memory need not be considered. Figure 13 is the memory model.

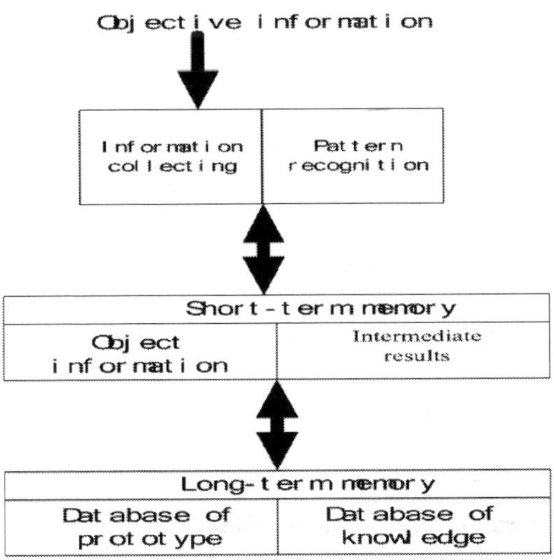

Fig. 13.

In the model, the short-term memory seems to a work memory, used for memorizing the correlative knowledge extracted form the prototype database and the knowledge database in the long-term memory, which is necessary for analyzing the input data. The operation itself has characteristics of the up-down processing method, and then calculate it according to prototype pattern recognition. Add the prototype and knowledge which are needed to their corresponding database.

3.9 The organization of knowledge

In most of person's free imagination, it can be shown their knowledge is organized. As for how to organize, it is the content of cognition psychology.

The above chapters have introduced that the achievement we have got in cognition psychology are three hypothetic models: symbol-net model, level-semantics-net model and activation-diffusion model.

In the researching of cognitive pattern recognition, we can research the level-semantics-net model firstly, the reason is that this model is proposed according to language understanding of computer simulation. This hypothetic model explains the organization and expression of the human knowledge by logic not psychology. It is much easily realized in computers, though has a suspicion to take a shortcut, it is a good method.

4. The systemic construction of cognitive pattern recognition

4.1 The systemic construction of traditional pattern recognition

From the perspective of technique, pattern recognition experiences the whole course which is from the mode space to the feature space, then to the type space. So, the system of pattern recognition must have some essential functions such as pattern collection, feature extraction/selection, pattern classification and so on, the systemic framework of machine pattern recognition can be showed as the figure 14.

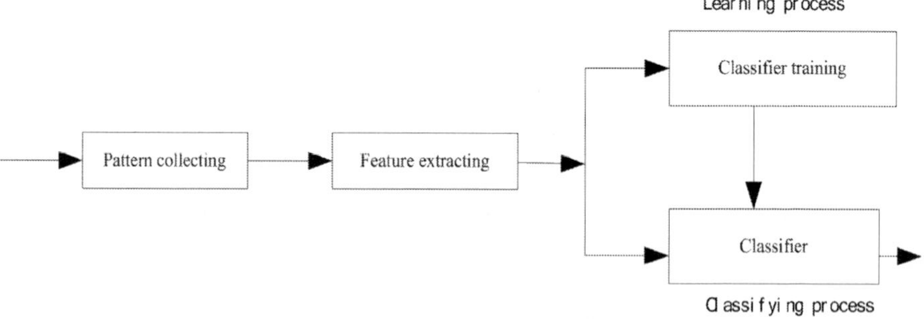

Fig. 14. The systemic framework of machine pattern recognition

According to the object for recognition, the process of pattern collection can choose every kind of sensors such as metrical devices, image collecting devices and some other devices used for conversion, filter, enhancement, reducing noise, correcting distortion. Feature extraction is realized by transforming mode space to feature space, which compress dimensions effectively. The classifier can classify those samples with unknown property. In order to design the classifier, we should confirm its evaluated rules and train it firstly. Then, the classifier can work effectively.

4.2 The framework of cognitive pattern recognition

In the traditional machine pattern recognition, the template approach has been used; however, the feature theory has been used widely. We believe that there is no essentially difference among the template theory, the prototype theory and the feature theory. They are all a description of the object in the application of machine recognition. We believe that the prototype is a method which describes feature, is the component templates of the object. In other words, we can believe that the feature is a method used to describe the prototype, and the template is also a describing method of the feature. These are controversies of different academic attitudes in cognitive psychology. We do not want to join these arguments, but just to meet targets of the description of requirements. In order to facilitate the handling, the following discussion will consider the feature/prototype, that is, integrating the template into the discussion of the prototype.

4.3 The application of the memory principle

Cognitive psychology believes that the process of memory can be divided into three stages, that is, feeling memory→short-term memory→long-term memory. Accordingly, in the process of machine recognition, there are only two stages, one stage can acquire information of the outside world through a sensor, another stage can store the objects recognized in the computer for a short time. The knowledge stored in long-term memory is features and the prototypes as well as knowledge and rules, then the databases can be created to store the corresponding features, prototypes and the knowledge and rules. In the traditional pattern recognition, the rejection conclusions will be obtained, when it can not be matched in the short-term memory. While in the pattern recognition, if the appropriate patterns can not be found in the databases of the feature or the prototype, then the corresponding patterns will be added to the appropriate databases. If no relations, structures, methods or other knowledge can be found in the databases of the knowledge and the rule, then they will be added to the corresponding databases, in order to simulate human's learning ability better.

Cognitive psychology proposes two information processing modes of the top-down and bottom-up, while in machine pattern recognition the processing mode mainly used is the data-driven process supported with the top-down process, and the partial knowledge can be used to predict. The processing method of that global features processed before local features is adopted in the global and local aspect.

Cognitive psychology suggests that in the process of pattern recognition if the background information related with the object is stored in the long-term memory, it may have an important impact on decision through the so-called superiority effect. In the process of recognition, computer must deal with the problems of the overall and partial, topology, the superiority effect and so on, and carry on effective imagination. These can be integrated into the scope of knowledge.

Based on the above analysis, we can get the framework of cognitive pattern recognition, as shown in Figure 15. The process of pattern collection is as the same of that in traditional pattern recognition, that is, we can choose various sensors such as metrical devices, image collecting devices, and other devices used for conversion, filter, enhancement, reducing noise, correcting distortion and so on according to the object to be recognized. The functions of the pattern analysis processing are a little stronger than that of traditional pattern recognition, it can analyze the simulating signal collecting from the real world, including feature extraction, prototype analysis, topological judgment, description for the organization and structure of the features or prototypes, as well as the background description and so on, preparing for further works including knowledge searching, character/prototype searching, and matching

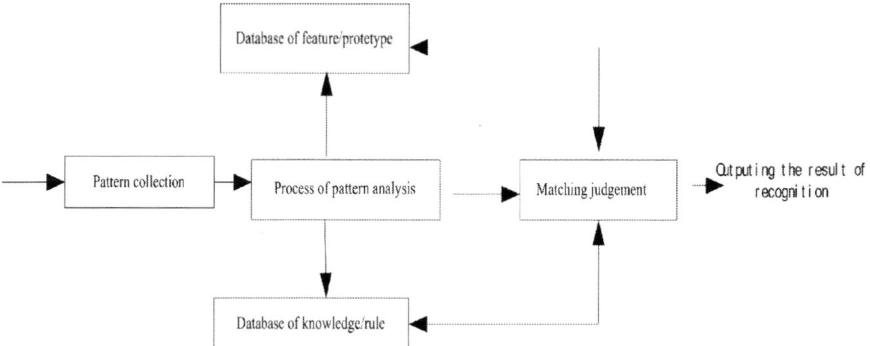

Fig. 15. The framework of cognitive pattern recognition

decision-making.The database of the character/prototype, which stores the features of the external objects and the prototypes that constitute of them, only contains a part of human's long-term memory. This database have extended the ability which is able to append new character/prototype into it. The database of the feature/prototype together with the database of knowledge/rule which stores transcendent knowledge, rules of prototype combining, feature relation knowledge and so on, responds to human's long-term memory. The section of matching decision-making is combing the result of pattern analysis, first searching the feature /prototype and the knowledge/rule from the corresponding database, and then matching them and evaluating the result with some rules, in the end outputting the results of the recognition. If the matching fails, the system will add those new items to their databases correspondingly, In this way, the system can learn and memorize new things.

5. Example application of cognition pattern recognition to Chinese character intelligent formation

Combined with the tradition theory of Chinese character formation with prototype theory in cognition psychology, Chinese character intelligent formation is formed basing on cognition mechanism and can be expressed as follows:
The Chinese character is a combination of either single hieroglyphic or self-explanatory symbol, or the combination of several of them based on meaning and *echoism* rules. The hieroglyphic and self-explanatory symbols of the all components in Chinese character set are Chinese character prototype. In other words, the hieroglyphic and self-explanatory symbols are the basic unit of Chinese character, so they are called basic elements. The components of the Chinese character are the basic elements with the topological mapping on the structure of the Chinese character. The relationship between the entire character and the basic elements, and the basic elements themselves which constitute the character, constitutes the hierarchical structure of the Chinese character. According to the

mathematical model of the prototype structure object in equation (3.1), we can build a mathematical model of Chinese character intelligent formation, which can be defined as

$$M = S\ (C)\ = S\ (\,g : P \to C\,) \qquad\qquad (4.1)$$

Where M is the Chinese character set, S is the structure set, P is the basic element set, C is the Chinese character component set, and g is the topological mapping from basic element to Chinese character component.

5.1 Systemic structure of the Chinese character intelligent formation

According to 4.1, the Chinese character is composed of mapping from basic elements of Chinese character to structure of Chinese character. The principle of Chinese character intelligent formation according to the research above is shown in figure 16.

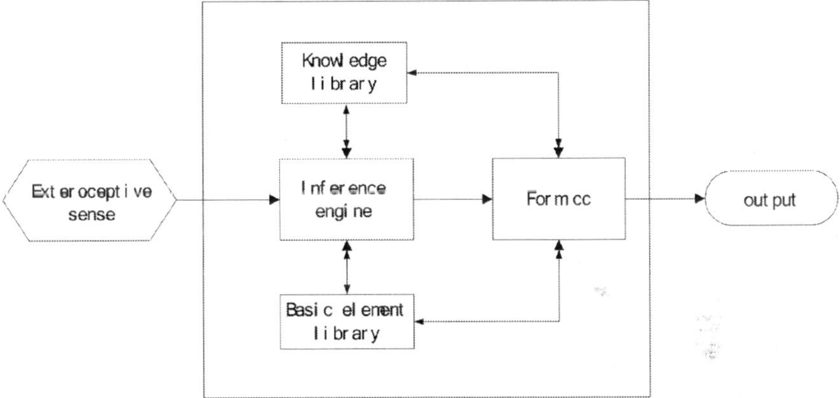

Fig. 16. The principle of Chinese character intelligent formation

In figure 16, we can see that the Chinese character intelligent formation is composed of the Chinese character basic element database, the Chinese character knowledge database, the inference machine and the Chinese character intelligent formation models, which are stated separately as follows:

(1) Basic element database

Basic element database, one kind of long-term memory, stores basic elements. As argued above, the Chinese character contains hieroglyphic and self-explanatory symbols and their combinations, which embodies the ideographic characteristic of the Chinese character because each basic element which constitutes the character has its own meaning. Therefore, the Chinese character is, currently, the only remained ideographic character. From the above analysis, the hieroglyphic and self-explanatory symbols are basic elements. The Chinese character, whose basic elements mainly manifest the meaning of Chinese character, is a combination of the shape, sound and meaning.

(2) Knowledge database

Knowledge database, another kind of long-term memory, stores the knowledge of structure and mapping. The Chinese character being a kind of structured character, is also a combination of the shape, sound and meaning. The "shape" embodies the structure of the

Chinese character, which is the combination relationship between the entire character and the basic elements, and between the basic elements themselves which constitute the character. Moreover, the structure, which can describe the position, the size and the shape of the basic elements in the Chinese character, is also the combination rules in Chinese character intelligent formation. With the structure of Chinese character, the unceasingly developing Chinese character can be formed by some limited basic elements. As the long history of Chinese character, there already have many research results of structure of Chinese character, so determining the structure of Chinese character, as well as determining the basic element, has double tasks of inheriting culture and realizing high efficiency of computer processing.

The basic element, as an abstract, is the most basic and representative characteristic of Chinese character. The conversion from the basic element to the components of Chinese character is called topological transformation. The Chinese character has its concrete form, which is composed by the concrete basic elements distributed in a character plain based on the structure of Chinese character. The process from the basic elements to the specific component of Chinese character is a mapping from abstract to concrete object maintaining the topological invariance.

(3) Inference machine

The inference machine perceives the input information, and then explains the meaning of the information, such as what is the structure of the Chinese character, how many levels are there in the structures, what is the basic elements in each level of the structure. Next, according to the result, the corresponding basic elements can be searched out from the basic element database, and the corresponding topology mapping knowledge can also be searched out according to the structure.

(4) Chinese character intelligent formation model

The principle of Chinese character intelligent formation model can be described as follows: first, extracting the corresponding basic element form the basic element library, then, according to the knowledge of basic element mapping, mapping the basic element to the structure of Chinese character, and finally after accomplishing all the mapping of the components, a Chinese character is formed, as shown in figure 17 and 18.

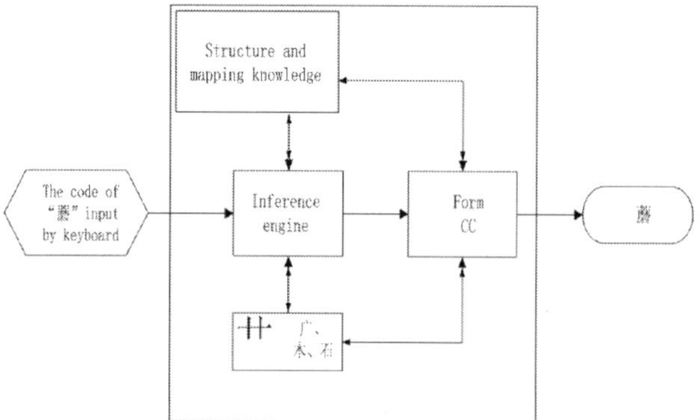

Fig. 17. The process of Chinese character intelligent formation

The basic elements corresponding to some prototypes don't constitute integral structure of the Chinese character directly, which is exactly constituted by some compounds from the basic elements after one or more times changes, such a character has the multistage structures. According to the compound number of times, it is called second-level structure, third-level structure, and fourth-level structure. Taking "蘑" for example, the analysis process of the hierarchical structure of Chinese character is shown in Figure 19.

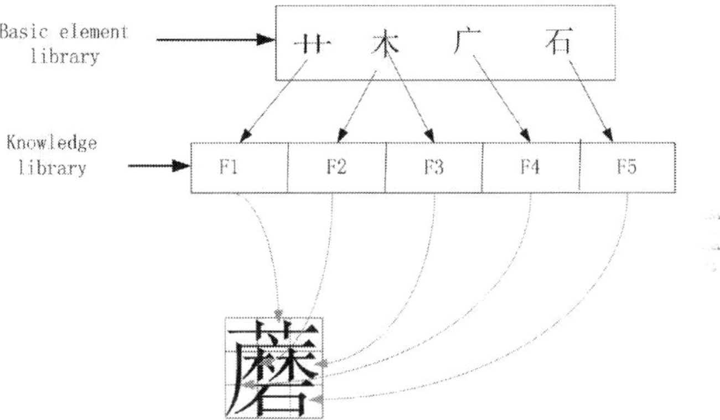

Fig. 18. Sketch of Chinese character intelligent formation

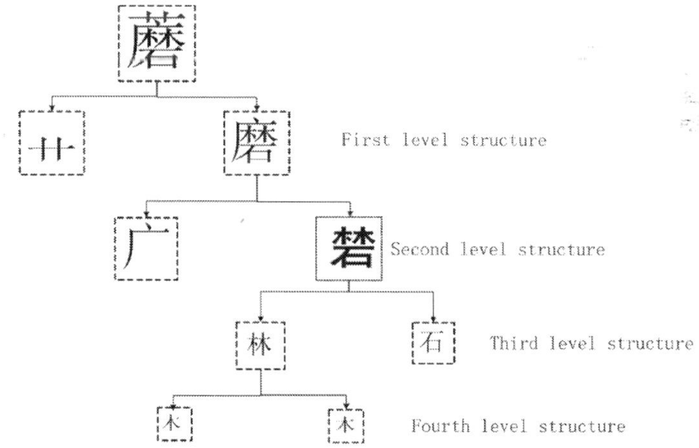

Fig. 19. Analysis of the structure of Chinese character

6. References

Anderson JR, Cognitive Psychology and Its Implication . New York: Freeman 1990
Ausubel DP. Education Psychology: A cognitive View. New York: Holt, Rinebart & Winston, 1968
Briars DJ, Larkin JH. An Integrated Model of Skill in Solving Elementary Word Problems. Cognition and Instruction,1984,1:245-269

Gagne RM. The Conditions of Learning. New York, NY: Holt, Rinehart and Winston,1965

Robert L. Solso, M. Kimberly MacLin, Otto H.MacLin. Cognitive Psychology[M]. Seventh Edition. BeiJing: PeKing university press,2005: 104-139.

Fang Junming. THE DEVELOPMENT OF AND CHALLENGES TO COGNITIVE PSYCHOLOGY OF INFORMATION PROCESSING. PSYCHOLOGICAL SCIENCE[J].1998;6(21):481-484.

邵志芳.认知心理学——理论、实践和应用.上海出版社 2006.12,p79-113.

Jain A.K, Duin, R.P.W, Jianchang Mao. statistical pattern recognition a review. Pattern Analysis and Machine Intelligence, IEEE TRANSACTIONS ON, 2000;22(1):4-37.

Rueda L G, Oommen B J. On optimal pairwise linear classifiers for normal distributions: the two−dimensional case. Pattern Analysis and Machine Intelligence, IEEE Transactions on , 2002; 24(2): 274-280.

Liu J N K, Li B N L, Dillon T S. An improved naive Bayesian classifier technique coupled with a novel input solution method [infall prediction]. Systems, Man and Cybernetics, Part C, IEEE Transactions on,2001; 31(2):249-256.

Ferland G, Yeap T. Achieving optimal Bayesian classification performance using a novel approach: the'race to the attractor'neural network model. Virtual and Intelligent Measurement Systems, 2001. IEEE International Workshop on. VIMS 2001; Vol.1: 115-120.

Ujiie H, Omachi S, Aso H. A discriminant function considering normality improvement of the distribution. Pattern Recognition, 2002. Proceedings. 16th International Conference on, 2002; Vol.2: 224-227.

ZHANG Xuegong. introduction to statistical learning theory and support vector machines. acta automatica sinica[j]. 2000; 26(1): p32-42.

LUO Gong liang. Kernel-based methods(B). Metallurgical Industry Automation[J]. 2002; 26(4): p1-4.

Guttman O, Meir R. Nonlinear Fisher discriminant using kernels. Electrical and Electronic Engineers in Israel, 2000. The 21st IEEE Convention of the, 2000; vol.1: 257-260.

LUO Gong liang. Kernel-based methods(A). Metallurgical Industry Automation[J]. 2002;26(3): p1-4.

Cooke T. Two variations on Fisher's linear discriminant for pattern recognition. Pattern Analysis and Machine Intelligence, IEEE Transactions on, 2002; 24(2):268-273.

WANG Shou-jue. Bionic (Topological) Pattern Recognition−A New Model of Pattern Recognition Theory and Its Applications. Acta Electronica Sinica[J]. 2002; 30(10): 1417-1420.

《新华词典》商务印书馆 北京 1987 年 3 月北京第十次印刷。

孙克宽,郭驼英等.拓扑学.华中师范大学出版社:7.

孙克宽,郭驼英等.拓扑学.华中师范大学出版社:59.

陈霖.拓扑性质知觉----计算理论的一朵可能的乌云.钱学森主编,关于思维科学.上海人民出版社.1986:250-301.

熊金城.点集拓扑讲义(第三版).高等教育出版社:141-142

熊金城.点集拓扑讲义(第三版).高等教育出版社:178-214

18

Parametric Circle Approximation Using Genetic Algorithms

Victor Ayala-Ramirez, Raul E. Sanchez-Yanez,
Jose A. Gasca-Martinez and Sergio A. Mota-Gutierrez
Universidad de Guanajuato FIMEE
Salamanca, Mexico

1. Introduction

Pattern recognition is one of the main research areas in the computer vision community. The basic problem consists in detecting and recognizing one or several known patterns in a data stream. Patterns can be specified in the raw data space or in any feature space suitable for the analysis of the input data. In particular, visual pattern recognition deals with applications where the pattern description is specified in terms of visual information and where input data comes from any kind of visual sensor (Chen & Wang, 2005). A common classification scheme divides pattern recognition according to the way the pattern is defined. There are then structural and statistical techniques. With respect to the problem solving approach, object location techniques are divided into two types of methods: i) deterministic methods like Hough transform, e.g. (Yuen et al., 1990), geometric hashing and template or model matching, e.g. (Iivarinen et al., 1997; Jones et al., 1990) and ii) stochastic techniques, including RANSAC (Fischer & Bolles, 1981), simulated annealing and genetic algorithms (Roth & Levine, 1994).

Geometric shapes are very useful in a number of tasks because they are often present in human-made environments. They are also widely used as a part of man-designed symbols. To recognize this kind of shapes, many methods have been developed. In particular, circle and ellipse detection problems have been widely studied in the shape recognition community. Most approaches use Hough transform-based techniques. For instance, Lam and Yuen (Lam & Yuen, 1996) have proposed to use a hypothesis filtering approach to a Hough transform to detect circles in images. Yuen and Lo (Yuen & Lo, 1994) have posed the circle detection problem as a multi-resolution problem for the Hough transform. A traffic sign detector proposed by Mainzer uses a circle detector (Mainzer, 2002a,b). Shape classification using a soft computing approach is addressed by Rosin and Nyongesa (Rosin & Nyongesa, 2000).

Genetic Algorithms (GA), proposed by Holland (Holland, 1975) in the 60s, are a family of algorithms where we apply an artificial evolution process. The purpose of the evolution is to produce a computational individual which is the best fitted to solve a specific problem. GA have been extensively used to solve optimization problems. Genetic Algorithms (GA) have been already used for several pattern classification tasks. In order to apply them to a pattern recognition problem, we need to pose the pattern recognition problem as an optimization problem. We need then to associate key elements in both approaches. Bandyopadhay

(Bandyopadhay et al., 1995) have proposed a GA-based method to classify patterns by selecting the position of the decision boundaries in an N-dimensional feature space. They place H hyper planes in order to minimize misclassification of the sample points. They have also developed some methods to remove the redundant hyper planes originated by the overestimation of H (Pal, et al., 1998). Decision boundaries selected by the GA-based pattern classification method will approach those found by the Bayes maximum likelihood classification (Murthy, et al., 1996). Van Hove and Verschoren (van Hové & Verschoren, 1996) have also applied a GA-based method in the recognition of binary trees that represent bitmap images. They propose to use a two dimensional GA (2DGA) as a model to use GA in image processing tasks. Buckles et al. (Buckles, et al., 1996) apply a GA to label mesoscale features arising from satellite images. They use a combination between semantic nets and fuzzy predicates to improve labeling of satellite images.

We are interested in the problem of interacting with a computer by using graphical sketches to simplify its use by novice users. Sketch understanding is a research field where shape recognition plays a role to complete successfully the task (Notowidigdo & Miller, 2004). Hand-drawn input has been already used in a number of human-computer interface applications.

In this application context, we are interested in approximating geometrical shapes drawn by a human user to parametric ones to be handled by a computer user interface. As a first example, we show how to approximate circles drawn by a human user to ideal circles by using a GA-based approach. Using GAs to detect shapes in an image involves mainly the making of design choices for the solution elements in a genetic algorithms framework. We work on images containing one or several circles. The circles are searched through the edge image resulting from an image pre-processing step. A classical Sobel edge detector was used for this purpose. Our algorithm can detect one or many circles present in the image under analysis and estimate shape parameters for them. Parametric estimation is achieved with sub-pixel accuracy. In the rest of this paper, we will show how to pose the circle detection problem in terms of a genetic algorithm approach. Section 2 presents an overview of GA. We show how GA can be used to solve a circle detection task in Section 3. The test protocol and the performance evaluation results for the proposed approach are shown in Section 4. Conclusions arising from these results are presented in Section 5. Some extensions to this work are also depicted in this section.

2. Genetic algorithms

Genetic algorithms are a pseudo-random optimization technique that mimics natural evolution to find the solution of the problem being solved. The block diagram of the Simple Genetic Algorithm (SGA) is shown in Figure 1. As described by this diagram, to use a SGA, we need to initialize a population of candidate solutions. Each potential solution is represented as a computational individual where the genetic material is encoded in the form of on and off bits. We name computational chromosome to such a string of bits. There is also an encoding and decoding function that let us go both ways from the solution space to the chromosome space. Every computational individual is evaluated in order to find the best solutions among the population. We need to define the so called fitness function in order to assign a fitness value to each potential solution. The fitness value encodes the knowledge we have about the characteristics of the best solution and tries to reward potential solutions that best fit these features. Best solutions are kept and they are given the privilege of mating to generate a new population that will be analyzed in the same way, until a stopping condition is fulfilled. Genetic operators like mating and mutation operate directly on the bit string representing the parent individuals in order to generate bit patterns that represent best-fitted solutions to the problem being solved.

Main advantage of such stochastic optimization is the possibility of escaping from local minima through the mutation, selection and mating operations. Main drawback is the need of definition of a good fitness function that reflects how well any bit pattern performs in the solution space. For the sake of completeness, we are going to present an overview of the key elements of a GA.

2.1 Encoding mechanism

The encoding scheme used in a GA has the function of representing in a unique way each solution in the problem search space by using one or several computational chromosomes. We understand by computational chromosome a concatenated string of symbols, where the symbols are chosen from a particular alphabet. Most often used representations are based in a binary alphabet. That is, every potential solution is represented as a string of bits. We can use binary strings to encode candidates in almost any optimization problem with good results. Many optimization problems require using real precision values as the computer implementation data type. We can use integer representations to simplify computational handling of the information. However, we use a mapping function to decode the integer index of the candidate into a real value.

2.2 Population initialization

GA work on an initial population searching for best fitted individuals. Each individual corresponds to a potential solution of the optimization problem. We can use any a priori procedure to populate the GA. Such initialization schemes could exploit a priori knowledge on the specific problem to be solved. Nevertheless, and as a mean of providing diversity to the GA population, this step is done by randomly selecting a number of individuals from the search space.

2.3 Fitness evaluation

We need to evaluate how well each candidate solution performs. To do this, we use a function $f(x)$ that is optimized when x assumes the value that solves the problem. In this function, we need to encode all the knowledge about the problem being solved. For each potential solution, this function returns a fitness score used to rank potential solutions. In this step, the bit string representing the solution (also called the genotype) is decoded to get the features associated to such a bit string (also called the phenotype). These parameters are used by the fitness function to compute the fitness score. Fitness function complexity can vary depending on the problem being solved. The fitness score is always the key to decide which individuals remain being part of the GA population.

2.4 Selection mechanism

The selection mechanism let us set up survival strategies in the evolutionary framework. One of the simplest survival strategies to be considered is the best fitted survival. In this method, individuals which have the better fitness score are kept to participate with its genetic code to the next iteration of the GA population. We need to define how many parent individuals will be selected to mate among them in order to generate a new population for the GA, and how much will each of them contribute to the next generation of the GA.

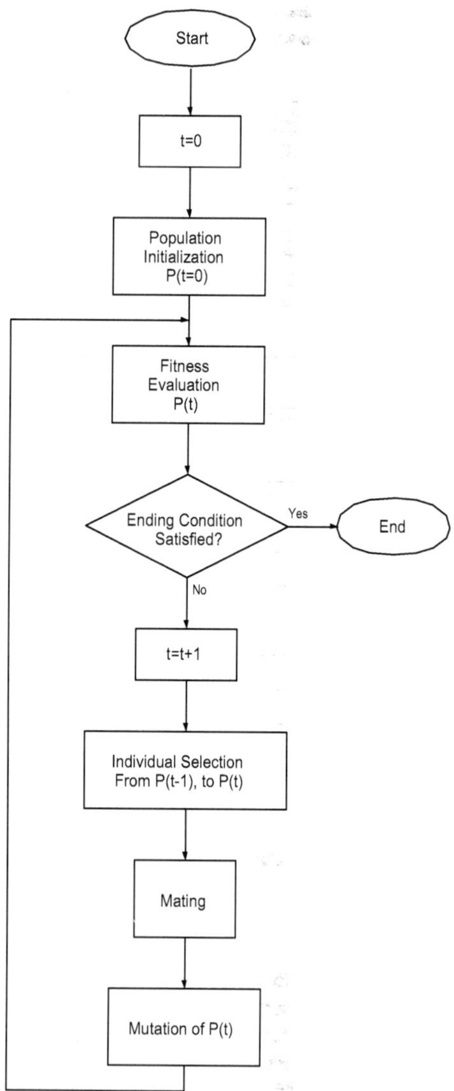

Fig. 1. A block diagram of the operations involved in a SGA.

2.5 Mating procedure

In order to generate a new population of candidate solutions, a mating operator is used. We choose the parents to be mated and how they will exchange genetic material to generate new individuals. We need to specify a crossover rate that defines the probability of a genetic code exchange to occur. At each generation, there are a number of individuals that are kept as elite individuals. They possess the best fitness scores among the genotype population currently being analyzed, and they are kept for the fitness function to follow a monotonic behavior in its temporal evolution.

2.6 Mutation operator

The mutation operator is a random perturbation operator used to change in a slightly sort the genetic material of the computational chromosomes. The application of such an operator is intended to maintain the population diversity and to avoid the premature convergence of the algorithm in a local optimum. The operator is represented by a mutation probability value. This value is proportional to the easiness of a random change in each bit in the genotype. It is recommended to use small values for this probability.

3. Circle approximation using genetic algorithms

3.1 Related work

Chakraborty and Deb (Chakraborty & Deb, 1998) have proposed to use a GA in combination with the Randomized Hough Transform (RHT) to detect analytic curves in images. In their work, they extract straight lines from an image. They use GA to guide the random search associated to the RHT. Roth and Levine (Roth & Levine, 1994) have proposed to use minimal point subsets to define geometric primitives. Lutton and Martinez (Lutton & Martinez, 1994) have improved the shape parameters to reduce redundancy in the primitive representation. They show an implementation to detect several shapes in images including segments, circles and ellipses in synthetic and real images. Yuen and Ma (Yuen & Ma, 2000) have proposed to use a GA to detect shape templates in images. They detect shapes with up to 6 degrees of freedom using a multi-modal GA. A multi-population GA is used by Yao et al. (Yao et al., 2004) to detect ellipses in images. They use the coordinates of five points as the genes of the computational individuals. In the work by Ayala et al. (Ayala et al., 2006), it is proposed to arrange all the edge points in an array and to use only the index of the point in this array as the encoding value of the point. Their approach reduces dimensionality of the search space. A recent application (Moreno et al., 2008) uses a variant of the former approach for depth estimation of micro-sized particles. They use a SGA to identify the minimal intensity ring on an image generated by the diffraction of the light of a laser beam when micro-sized particles are illuminated. As said before, the characteristics of that ring (namely the central spot size, CSS) identify the depth of the small particle in a microscopic test setup. In order to apply a SGA to the CSS measurement problem, they have used a fitness function that concurrently optimizes the existence of low- intensity pixel points along the circumference of the candidate solution and the low intensity average of the individual under test.

3.2 Our approach

Our method uses the following steps:

i. Firstly, a binary image is acquired as input. We consider this image as figure-background edge image. Such an image can contain any number of shapes; however, at this time we are only interested in detecting circles.

ii. We create a vector by considering only the figure points in the image under analysis. To decide which points are the figure points, we need to consider the application context.

According to the acquisition system convention, figure points could be black or white points in the input image.

iii. We set up a simple genetic algorithm to search for the best circle in the image under analysis. Circles are encoded as three integer vector indexes in the GA chromosome. These indexes define a circle in a continuous parametric space (x, y, r). Circle optimality is defined by using a fitness function that validates if the candidate circle is actually present in the test image. Presence of the candidate circle is verified in a set of points along the circumference of the candidate.

iv. The search procedure in the reduced sub-space leads to a circle finding algorithm fast enough to identify a circle in an input image. The best individual of the genetic population is considered as the best solution to generate the approximated circle. In the case of multiple circles present in the input image, the best circle is deleted from the input image and steps iii) and iv) are repeated.

3.1 GA design

Using GAs to detect shapes in an image involves mainly the making of design choices for the solution elements in a genetic algorithms framework. We work on images containing one or several circles. The circles are searched through the edge image obtained from an image pre-processing step. A classical Sobel edge detector is used for this purpose. In the following paragraphs we show how to pose the circle detection problem in terms of a genetic algorithm approach as stated by (Ayala et al., 2006).

3.2 Individual representation

Each individual C uses three edge points as chromosomes. Edge points are represented by their relative index in a list V of all the edge points resulting from the edge extraction step. Each individual represents then a feasible circle where their (x_0, y_0, r) parameters are defined as follows:

$$(x - x_0)^2 + (y - y_0)^2 = r^2 \tag{1}$$

with:

$$x_0 = \frac{\begin{vmatrix} x_j^2 + y_j^2 - (x_i^2 + y_i^2) & 2(y_j - y_i) \\ x_k^2 + y_k^2 - (x_i^2 + y_i^2) & 2(y_k - y_i) \end{vmatrix}}{4((x_j - x_i)(y_k - y_i) - (x_k - x_i)(y_j - y_i))} \tag{2}$$

$$y_0 = \frac{\begin{vmatrix} 2(x_j - x_i) & x_j^2 + y_j^2 - (x_i^2 + y_i^2) \\ 2(x_k - x_i) & x_k^2 + y_k^2 - (x_i^2 + y_i^2) \end{vmatrix}}{4((x_j - x_i)(y_k - y_i) - (x_k - x_i)(y_j - y_i))} \tag{3}$$

and

$$r = \sqrt{(x - x_0)^2 + (y - y_0)^2}$$ (4)

We can then represent the shape parameters (for the circle, [x_0, y_0, r]) as a transformation T of the edge vector indexes i, j, k.

$$[x_0, y_0, r] = T(i, j, k)$$ (5)

This approach enables us to sweep a continuous space for the shape parameters while keeping a binary string for the GA individual. We can then reduce the search space by eliminating unfeasible solutions.

3.3 Fitness evaluation

Each individual has a fitness value proportional to the number of actual edge points matching the locus generated by the parameters of the shape (x_0, y_0, r). In our practical implementation, we can not test for every point in the feasible circle so we perform a uniform sampling along the circumference. If we take N_s points, we construct an array of points $S_i = (x_i, y_i)$. Their coordinates are given by:

$$x_i = x_0 + r \cdot \cos \frac{2\pi i}{N_S}$$ (6)

$$y_i = y_0 + r \cdot \sin \frac{2\pi i}{N_S}$$ (7)

Fitness function $F(C)$ accumulates the number of expected edge points (i.e. the points in the set S) that actually are present in the edge image $E(x_i, y_i)$. That is:

$$F(C) = \frac{\sum_{i=0}^{N_s - 1} E(x_i, y_i)}{N_S}$$ (8)

We also use some other factors to favour the context of specific applications for detection, including completeness of the circumference or a given size for the circles.

4. Tests and results

We present tests on images containing a single circle on several images. Our test set contains synthetic and hand-drawn images. Our method presents a good qualitative approximation over a set of test images.

4.1 Test protocol

Given that hand-drawn shapes cannot be standardized to some measure, we propose to measure the accuracy of our approach by using the following two quantitative tests: i) We have generated synthetic circles having a sinusoidal undulation effect along its circumference, and ii) We have also generated synthetic circles corrupted by additive Gaussian noise in the radius parameter. Figure 2 shows examples for both types of synthetic images. In both cases, we know the parameters of the perturbation functions and our goal is to measure how the results of our approach are related to the ground truth information.

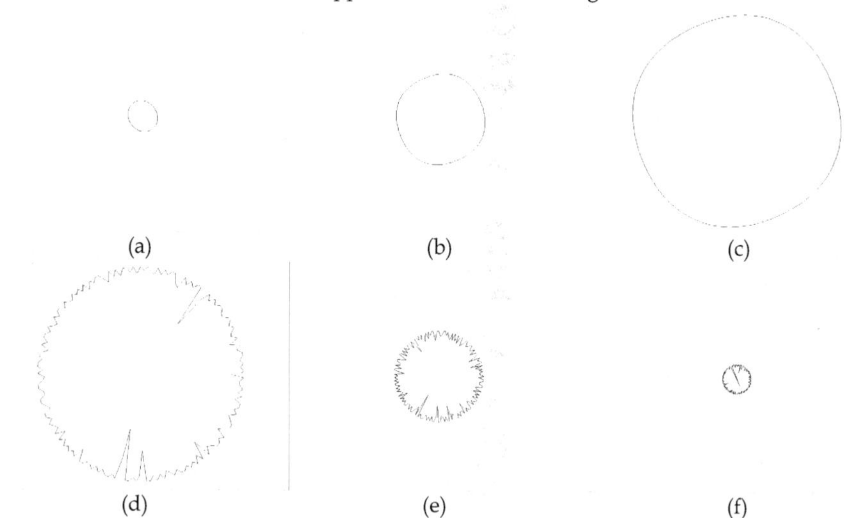

(a)   (b)   (c)

(d)   (e)   (f)

Fig. 2. Sample deformed circles: showing sinusoidal undulations along the circumference (a-c) and corrupted with noise in the radius parameter (d-f).

Circles perturbed by a sinusoidal undulation are described by the following equation in the polar plane (ρ, θ) :

$$\rho = k + n \cdot sen\left(m\theta\right) \tag{9}$$

Where n is the amplitude of the sinusoidal perturbation and m is the number of periods that it will traverse along the circumference of the circle.

Noisy circles are constructed by computing a set of points modified with additive Gaussian noise in the radius parameter along the circumference of the circle. In the polar plane (ρ, θ) , we have:

$$\rho = k + \eta\left(\mu, \sigma\right) \tag{10}$$

With μ being the mean value of the Gaussian pdf $\eta\left(\bullet\right)$ and σ being the standard deviation value for the noise pdf. In our tests, we have used $\mu=0$ in order to avoid biasing estimation. Synthetic images were computed using VGA resolution (640×480pixels). Without loss of generality, we have placed the circle in the middle of the image.

A qualitative test was also performed, we have presented the systems with real human user drawn circles, and we have subjectively analyzed the results to gain insight on the advantages and inconveniences of the proposed method.

4.2 Test results
4.2.1 Circles corrupted by undulating sinusoids

A circle for each combination of the Cartesian product $k \times n \times m$, has been created, using k=32, 96, 160, 224; n=2, 4; and m=2, 4, 8, according to Equation 9. For each image, series of 30 estimations of the center (x,y) and radius (k) are performed and then the mean and standard deviation of such parameters are compared against those used for the ground truth construction. Just for comparison purposes, the circles estimated in one execution of the algorithm over those images in Figures 2 a-c, are shown as light gray overlays in Figures 3 a-c. Note in Figure 3a the circle detected for a figure containing two periods of the oscillating perturbation.

Results for the estimation of parameter k are given in Table 1. Here, each row corresponds to a *30* execution series. Mean and standard deviation values should be compared against the n value, which controls the deformation in the circles. We can see a small relative error of the estimated radius against the ground truth data except for some cases. In particular, let us consider the cases where $n=4$, $m=2, 4$. In these cases, the perturbed circle has lost its circular appearance, and it seems like a rounded rectangle. Our method tries to adjust the best circle in the image. So it gets in a random manner a circle inscribed on one of the four corners as the best result.

Parameters	k	μ_k	σ_k	e_k
$n = 2$, $m = 2$	32	29.1750	0.2711	2.8250
$n = 2$, $m = 4$	32	33.3615	0.8627	1.3615
$n = 2$, $m = 8$	32	33.3034	0.0761	1.3034
$n = 4$, $m = 2$	32	26.2145	0.1842	5.7855
$n = 4$, $m = 4$	32	29.4962	0.0661	2.5038
$n = 4$, $m = 8$	32	35.6446	0.0443	3.6446
$n = 2$, $m = 2$	96	92.5663	0.2959	3.4337
$n = 2$, $m = 4$	96	93.8680	0.1385	2.1320
$n = 2$, $m = 8$	96	97.7291	0.0577	1.7291
$n = 4$, $m = 2$	96	88.3233	0.3180	7.6767
$n = 4$, $m = 4$	96	67.4882	4.7472	28.5118
$n = 4$, $m = 8$	96	92.5621	0.0783	3.4379
$n = 2$, $m = 2$	160	156.5334	0.1239	3.4666
$n = 2$, $m = 4$	160	158.3205	0.0449	1.6795
$n = 2$, $m = 8$	160	161.6845	0.0413	1.6845
$n = 4$, $m = 2$	160	151.4321	0.3150	8.5679
$n = 4$, $m = 4$	160	155.5221	0.2715	4.4779
$n = 4$, $m = 8$	160	163.7453	0.0371	3.7453
$n = 2$, $m = 2$	224	220.2067	0.1070	3.7933
$n = 2$, $m = 4$	224	225.5948	0.0490	1.5948
$n = 2$, $m = 8$	224	222.5754	0.0719	1.4246
$n = 4$, $m = 2$	224	217.0377	0.1371	6.9623
$n = 4$, $m = 4$	224	227.4639	1.3441	3.4639
$n = 4$, $m = 8$	224	227.3497	0.0446	3.3497

Table 1. Results for the estimated radius.

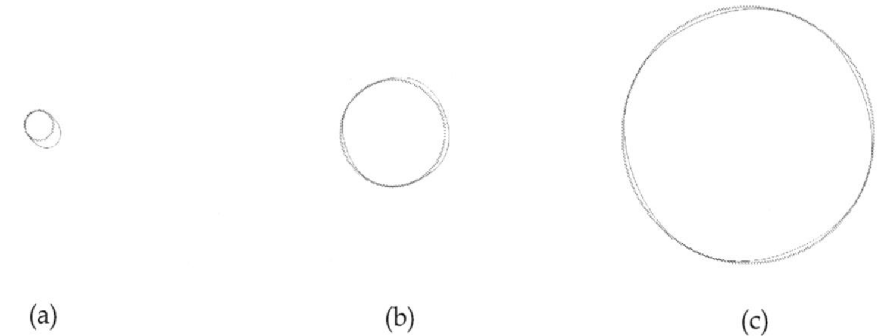

(a)   (b)   (c)

Fig. 3. Deformed circles in Figure 2 a-c and the circles estimated using a GA.

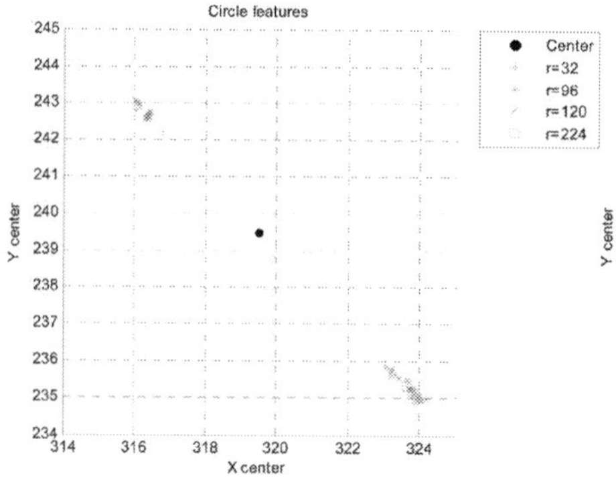

(a)

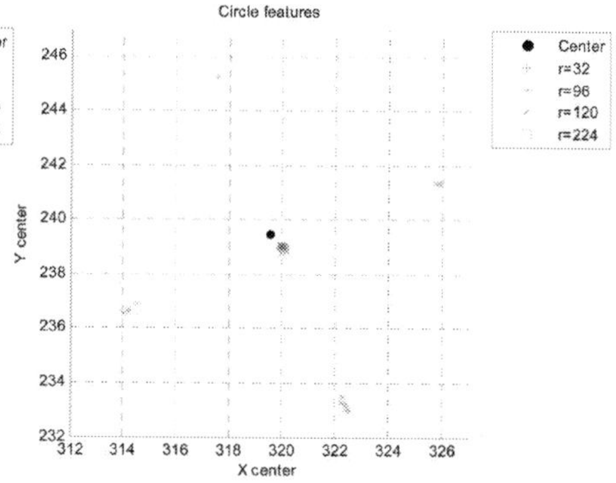

(b)

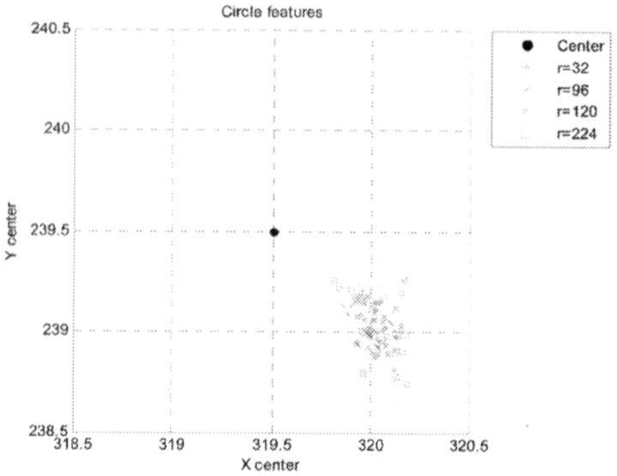

(c)

Fig. 4. Center of circles estimations for $k=2$ and $m=2$ in (a), $m=4$ in (b), and $m=8$ in (c).

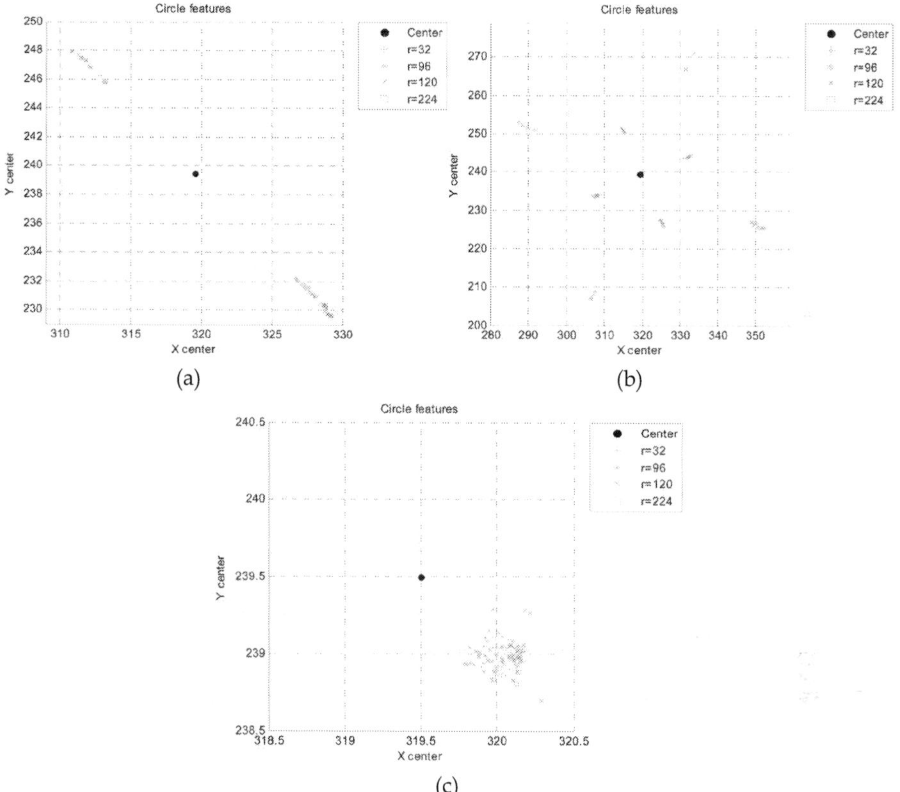

Fig. 5. Center of circles estimations for *k=4* and *m=2* in (a), *m=4* in (b), and *m=8* in (c).

Results for the center of circles estimations are given in Figures 4a-c for *k=2*, while Figures 5a-c show results for *k=4*. Observe in Figures 4a-b and 5a-b, the oscilating nature of the center estimation when we have *m=2* and *m=4* periods of the sinusoidal perturbation along the circumference of the circle.

We can observe on both figures, the cyclic nature of the estimated position of the center of the circle. As explained before, the center shift is provoked by the round polygon appearance of the perturbed circles. A difference with this trend is shown in Figures 4c and 5c, where the center estimation shows a sub-pixellic error (lower than 0.5 pixels). In this case, the perturbed circle seems more like a circle because of the low amplitude of the sinusoidal perturbation.

4.2.2 Circles corrupted by additive gaussian noise

A circle for each combination of the Cartesian product $k \times \sigma$, has been created, using k=*32, 96, 160, 224*, and σ=*4 ,8, 16*, for the additive Gaussian noise perturbation, defined in Equation 10.

As for the circles distorted with sinusoidal waves, series of *30* estimations of the center *(x,y)* and radius *(k)* are performed for each image, and then the mean and standard deviation of such parameters are compared agaist those used for the ground truth construction.

Circles estimated in one execution of the algorithm over those images in Figures 2 d-f, are shown in Figures 6 a-c, in a light gray overlay. Note here that circle accuracy is higher than for the undulating distortion case. That happens because the distorted points follow a normal distribution in the radius coordinate in the polar plane.

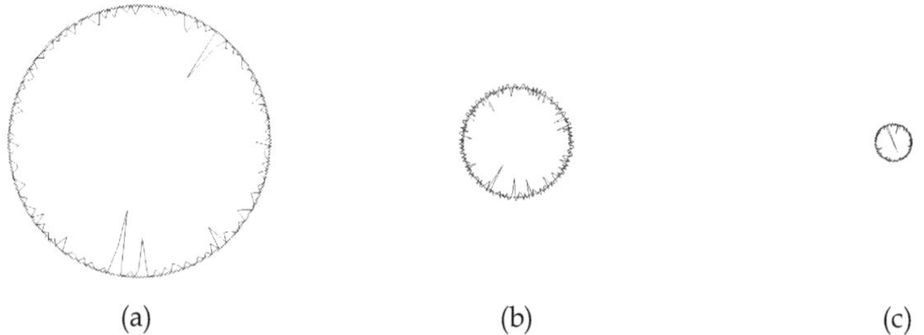

(a)   (b)   (c)

Fig. 6. Deformed circles in Figure 2 d-f and their corresponding circles estimated using a GA.

Results for the estimation of parameter k are given in Table 2, each row corresponding to a *30* execution series. Compare these results with those given previously in Table 1. In this kind of tests, error bound is lowered, as expected, with respect to the undulating circles.

Parameters	k	μ_k	σ_k	e_k
$\sigma = 4$	32	31.6944	0.1056	0.3056
$\sigma = 8$	32	30.4204	0.0813	1.5796
$\sigma = 16$	32	24.9730	0.4624	7.0270
$\sigma = 4$	96	95.7740	0.0293	0.2260
$\sigma = 8$	96	95.1253	0.1399	0.8747
$\sigma = 16$	96	91.0716	1.3534	4.9284
$\sigma = 4$	160	159.6619	0.0189	0.3381
$\sigma = 8$	160	159.2446	0.1209	0.7554
$\sigma = 16$	160	159.7199	0.4473	0.2801
$\sigma = 4$	224	223.6464	0.0277	0.3536
$\sigma = 8$	224	222.8001	0.1105	1.1999
$\sigma = 16$	224	223.6822	0.2805	0.3178

Table 2. Results for the estimated radius of noisy circles.

Plots of centers of circles estimated on tests are given in Figure 7. Note the high accuracy on parameter determination, yielding errors less than *1* pixel in magnitude.

4.2.3 Hand drawn circle approximation

Qualitative testing of our algorithm has been made by using as input images, circles drawn by a human user on a computer drawing program. Figure 8 shows eight hand-drawn circles by human users. A lighter gray overlay shows the best circle approximating the graphical sketch. As we can see in Figure 8, our approach results in good circle approximation. The parametric circle found using our approach follows very closely the graphical sketch. As we can see in the results, the approximated circle sticks to the longer circular arcs present in the hand-drawn shape.

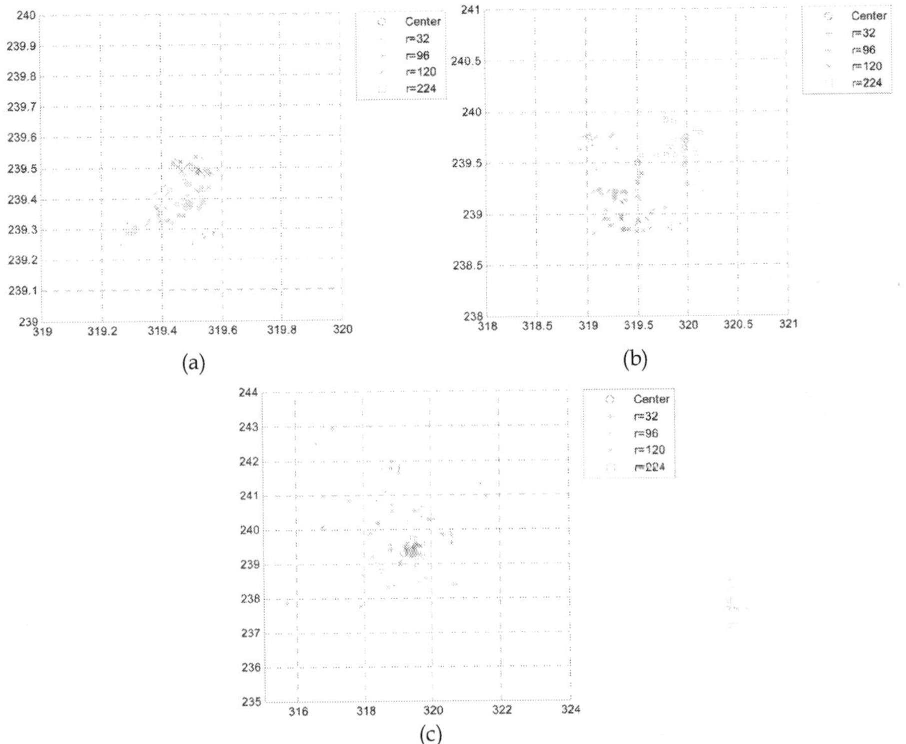

Fig. 7. Center of circles estimations for σ =4, 8,16 are shown in (a), (b), and (c), respectively.

4.3 Analysis and discussion

Tests have shown a good performance of our algorithm in both syntethic and real images using quantitative and qualitative tests. The undulation perturbation tests present to the algorithm smooth curves to be approximated by a circle. As expected, there is a bias in center position originated by the rounded corner effect generated by the sinusoidal waveform mounted on the circumference of the circle being detected. This effect is attenuated when the amplitude of the perturbating waveform is kept as a small fraction of the radius of the circle. That represents a more common case for circles drawn by human users.

With respect to the Gaussian noise test, we get accuracies in the sub-pixellic range because outlier points along the circumference generate candidate circles that are not supported by evidence. This leads the GA to choose as the best solution a circle bound by points in the ring where there is a larger density of points. In our case, the ring with the ground truth radius is very close to the found parameter.

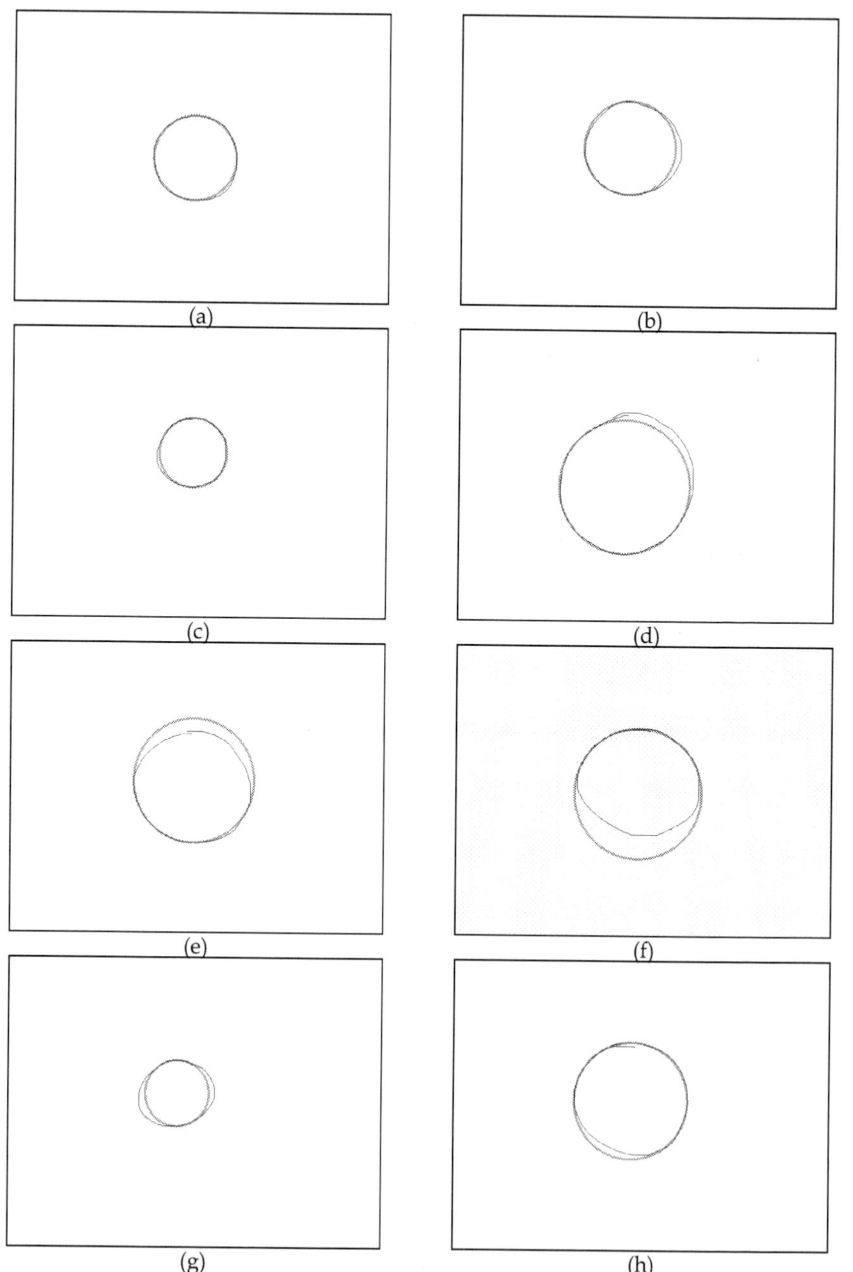

Fig. 8. Results for the circle detection using hand drawn shapes by human users.

5. Conclusions and perspectives

We have presented an algorithm that approximates circles by using a GA-based approach. Also, we have presented a brief overview of GA-based techniques and we have shown how to pose a pattern recognition problem to use GA for solving it. To know, we solve a circle approximation task.

We have executed two quantitative tests to evaluate the performance of the proposed method. We have also performed a subjective qualitative test over hand-drawn images. As a result, we have found in one hand, a high accuracy algorithm performance on circles corrupted by Gaussian noise. In the other hand, sinusoidal perturbations are better recognized if the amplitude of the perturbation is small with respect to the circle radius. For any other case, our algorithm will try to fit a circle to one of the rounded corners of the perturbed circle. We have also shown the result of a number of qualitative tests on human input. The results are promising enough to consider this as a building block for graphical sketch recognition.

We are developing at this moment other modules to recognize more geometrical shapes that can be expressed in parametric terms. We are developing modules to recognize ellipses, quadrilaterals and polygons in general.

6. Acknowledgements

This work has been partially supported by the CONCYTEG project GTO-2005-C04-18605 "Herramientas Mecatrónicas para la Implementación de Entornos Virtuales".

7. References

Ayala-Ramirez, V.; Garcia-Capulin, C.H; Perez-Garcia, A. & Sanchez-Yanez, R.E. (2006). Circle detection on images using genetic algorithms, Pattern Recognition Letters, (27) pp. 652-657.

Bandyopadhyay, S.; Murthy, C.A. & Pal, S.K. (1995). Pattern classification Using Genetic Algorithm, Pattern Recognition Letters, 16(8), pp. 801-808.

Buckles, B.P.; Petry, F.E.; Prabhu, D. & Lybanon, M. (1996). Mesoscale Feature Labeling from Satellite Images, in Genetic Algorithms for Pattern Recognition, Pal, S.K. & P.P. Wang (Eds.), CRC Press, Boca Raton, FL., pp. 167-178.

Chakraborty, S. & Deb, K. (1998). Analytic Curve Detection from a Noisy Binary Edge Map Using Genetic Algorithm. 5th PPSN, Amsterdam, The Netherlands, LNCS (1498), pp. 129-138.

Chen, C.H. & Wang, P.S.P. (2005), Handbook of Pattern Recognition and Computer Vision, 3rd Ed., World Scientific, Singapore.

Fischer, M., Bolles, R., (1981) Random sample consensus: A paradigm to model fitting with applications to image analysis and automated cartography, Comm. ACM, Vol. 24, No. 6, pp. 381–395.

Holland, J. (1975). Adaptation in Natural and Artificial Systems, University of Michigan Press, Ann Arbor, MI.

Iivarinen, J.; Peura, M.; Sarela,J. & Visa, A. (1997). Comparison of combined shape descriptors for irregular objects, Proc. 8th British Machine Vision Conf., pp. 430–439.

Yuen, H.; Princen, J.; Illingworth, J. & Kittler, J. (1990). Comparative study of Hough transform methods for circle finding, *Image Vision Comput.*, Vol. 8, No. 1, pp. 71–77.

Jones, G.; Princen, J.; Illingworth, J. & Kittler, J. (1990). Robust estimation of shape parameters. *Proc. British Machine Vision Conf.*, pp. 43–48.

Lam, W. & Yuen, S. (1996). Efficient techniques for circle detection using hypothesis filtering and Hough transform, IEEE Proc. Visual Image Processing, 143(5), pp.292-300.

Lutton, E. & Martinez, P. (1992). A Genetic algorithm for detection of 2D geometric primitives in images. Proc. of the IEEE Int. Conf. on Pattern Recognition (ICPR), (1) pp. 526-528.

Mainzer, T., (2002). Genetic algorithm for shape detection, Tech. Report DCSE/TR-2002-06, University of West Bohemia in Pilsen, Pilsen, Czech Republic.

Mainzer, T., (2002). Genetic algorithms for traffic sign detection, Proc. Int. Conf. on Applied Electronics, Pilsen, Czech Republic, pp. 129-132.

Moreno-Hernandez, D.; Ayala-Ramirez, V. & Guerrero-Viramontes, J.A. (2008) 3D positioning of micro-spherical particles by using genetic algorithms, Proc. LEOS Symposium on Photonics in Mexico (SPIM).

Murthy, C.A.; Bandyopadhyay, S. & Pal, S.K. (1996). Genetic algorithm-based pattern classification: relationship with bayes classifier, in genetic algorithms for pattern recognition, Pal, S.K. & P.P. Wang (Eds.), CRC Press, Boca Raton, FL., pp. 127-144.

Notowidigdo, N. & Miller, R.C. (2004) Off-line sketch interpretation. Proc. of AAAI Fall Symp. On Making Pen-Based Interaction Intelligent and Natural, pp. 120-126.

Pal, S.K.; Bandyophadyay, S. & Murthy, C.A. (1998), Genetic algorithm for generation of class boundaries. IEEE Trans. On Systems, Man and Cybernetics B, 28(6), pp. 816-828.

Rosin, P.L. and Nyongesa, H.O., (2000), Combining evolutionary, connectionist, and fuzzy classification algorithms for shape analysis, In Proc. EvoIASP, Real World Applications of Evolutionary Computing. pp. 87-96.

Roth, G. & Levine, M.D. (1994). Geometric primitive extraction using a genetic algorithm., *IEEE Trans. Pattern Anal. Mach. Intell.*, Vol. 16, No. 9, pp. 901–905.

Van Hove, H. & Verschoren A., (1996). Genetic Algorithms and Recognition Problems, in Genetic Algorithms for Pattern Recognition, Pal, S.K. & P.P. Wang (Eds.), CRC Press, Boca Raton, FL., pp. 167-178.

Yuen, K.S. and Lo, E.K. (1994). A coarse-to-fine approach for circle detection, in Proc. Int. Symp. On Speech, Image Processing and Neural Networks, Hong Kong, HK. pp. 523-526.

Yuen, S. Y. & Ma, C. H. (2000). Genetic algorithm with competitive image labelling and least square. Pattern Recognition 33(12), pp. 1949-1966.

19

Registration of Point Patterns Using Modern Evolutionary Algorithms

Peng-Yeng Yin

Department of Information Management, National Chi Nan University
Taiwan

1. Introduction

Registration of point patterns is a fundamental process prior to many applications such as image alignment, object recognition, and pattern retrieval. When two images are aligned, people prefer to deal with sets of local features (for example, dominant points) instead of pixel arrays to increase the accuracy and save the computational time. Given two point patterns, the aim of point pattern registration (PPR) problem is to find an optimal geometric transformation which transforms one point pattern by reference to the other such that a dissimilarity measure between them is minimized.

PPRs can be classified into various categories according to two features, *completeness* and *label*. Complete registration stipulates that the two registered patterns should have exactly the same number of points and there exists a one-to-one correspondence mapping between the members of the two point sets. While the incomplete registration deals with patterns with missing and spurious points, a mapping between subsets of the point patterns is thus sought. On the other hand, labeled registration is conducted using the *a priori* information (e.g., point order, intensity, gradient, etc.) as well as the point coordinates. While unlabeled registration determines the point correspondences based on the coordinates information of the data points only. Conspicuously, incomplete unlabeled registration is the hardest category of all the PPR classifications.

The PPR considered in this chapter is confined by the affine transformation consisting of rotation, scaling, and translation. Let $A = \{a_i \mid i = 1,\ 2,\ ...,\ n\}$ and $B = \{b_i \mid i = 1,\ 2,\ ...,\ m\}$ be two point patterns in R^2 and they are affinely-dependent under a transformation $T = (\theta, s, t_x, t_y)$ where θ denotes the rotation angle, s is the scale factor, and t_x and t_y are the translation offsets along the directions of x- and y-axis. Also let (a_i, b_j) be one of the pair-wise point mappings with T, and denote by $a_i = [x_{a_i}\ \ y_{a_i}]^T$ and $b_j = [x_{b_j}\ \ y_{b_j}]^T$ the corresponding coordinates, we have the following affine relation.

$$T(a_i) = s \begin{bmatrix} \cos\theta & -\sin\theta \\ \sin\theta & \cos\theta \end{bmatrix} \begin{bmatrix} x_{a_i} \\ y_{a_i} \end{bmatrix} + \begin{bmatrix} t_x \\ t_y \end{bmatrix} = \begin{bmatrix} x_{b_j} \\ y_{b_j} \end{bmatrix} = b_j \tag{1}$$

Nevertheless, the ideal transformation (1) usually does not hold under many real situations such as the existence of missing and spurious points and the distortion of patterns, resulting in a registration error. Two error dissimilarity measures between two aligning point patterns are broadly used in the literature to assess the quality of the registration result.

- *Agrawal's Heuristic Dissimilarity* (AHD) *Measure*   Let Ω be the set of point correspondences between the two patterns with $|\Omega| \leq \min(n, m)$. The registration error of Ω with respect to transformation T can be evaluated using the integral squared error defined as

$$\varepsilon^2 = \sum_{(a_i, b_j) \in \Omega} \left\| T(a_i) - b_j \right\|^2 \tag{2}$$

where $\left\| \bullet \right\|$ indicates the vector length in the Euclidean space. Agrawal *et al.* (1994) proposed an overall registration dissimilarity measure as

$$AHD(A, B) = \begin{cases} \dfrac{\varepsilon^2}{s|\Omega|} \left(1 + \left(\dfrac{m-2}{|\Omega|-2} \right) \log_2 \left(\dfrac{m-2}{|\Omega|-2} \right) \right) & |\Omega| \geq 3 \\ \infty & |\Omega| = 0,\ 1,\ 2 \end{cases} \tag{3}$$

The AHD measure is normalized with the scale factor s and includes a penalty term for the unregistered points in the searched pattern.

- *Partial Hausdorff Distance* (PHD) Huttenlocher *et al.* (1993) used the directed partial Hausdorff distance from A to B as

$$DPHD_k(A, B) = K^{th}_{a_i \in A} \min_{b_j \in B} \left\| T(a_i) - b_j \right\| \tag{4}$$

where K^{th} returns the kth smallest value of $\min_{b_j \in B} \left\| T(a_i) - b_j \right\|$ for all $a_i \in A$. The directed partial Hausdorff distance from B to A can be analogously defined as

$$DPHD_k(B, A) = K^{th}_{b_j \in B} \min_{a_i \in A} \left\| b_j - T(a_i) \right\| \tag{5}$$

Finally, the partial Hausdorff distance from both patterns is given by

$$PHD_k(A, B) = \max\left(DPHD_k(A, B),\ DPHD_k(B, A) \right) \tag{6}$$

In contrast to AHD, the PHD measure only takes into account the registered points such that the situation of incomplete registration can be accommodated.

Many approaches have been proposed for tackling various PPR problems. According to our recent survey, there was a departure in the PPR approaches in 1990s. Traditional approaches take advantage of the geometric properties involved with the point patterns to improve the search efficiency and effectiveness. More recently, some evolutionary algorithms were proposed to evolve the optimal transformation between the given point sets. The conceptions of existing methods are summarized as follows.

- *Clustering* The technique (Chang et al., 1997; Goshtasby & Stockman, 1985; Umeyama, 1991; Wang & Chen, 1997; Yuen, 1993) calculates the registration transformation parameters θ, s, t_x and t_y for each pair of points contained in both patterns and increases the frequency count of the corresponding cell (θ, s, t_x, t_y) in an accumulator. The clusters of the cells with respect to the frequencies are detected. The peak of the cluster with the maximum frequency corresponds to the optimal transformation parameters. Clustering methods are computationally intensive due to the large number of combinations of point pairs and the dimensionality of the parameter space.

- *Parameter decomposition* The method (Griffin & Alexopoulos, 1991; Huttenlocher et al., 1993; Olson & Huttenlocher, 1997) divides the parameter estimation process into multiple phases. At the first phase, a selected parameter is estimated based on the domain knowledge such as the geometric invariant constraints. Then, at each of the following phases, one or more of the remaining parameters are estimated by reference to the partial parameters values previously determined, hence, the number of possible combinations between values of separate parameters is greatly reduced. However, the inaccuracy of parameter estimation could be magnified due to successive propagation through various phases.

- *Relaxation* The technique (Ogawa, 1984; Ranade & Rosenfeld, 1980; Ton and Jain, 1989) iteratively updates the merit score of every point mapping (a_i, b_j) from both patterns given the merit scores of the other interacting point mappings. The interacting point mappings are those that are mutually constrained for registration due to geometry properties. The algorithm converges when those merit values become consistent (or hardly changed) between consecutive iterations and the point mappings with the maximum merits are considered as the true transformation point correspondence.

- *Bounded alignment* Mount et al. (1999) proposed a geometric branch-and-bound search of the transformation space and used the point alignment information to bound the search. They specify an approximation factor to guarantee the accuracy of the final match and use point alignments when a significant number of point correspondences can be inferred to accelerate the search. The robustness of the algorithm has been demonstrated on registration of real satellite images.

- *Spectral graph analysis* Carcassoni and Hancock (2003) applied the spectral graph theory to compute the point correspondence. The global structural properties of the point pattern are ascribed by the eigenvalues and eigenvectors of the proximity weighting matrix. The influence of the contamination and drop-out in the point pattern is discounted via the EM algorithm so the accuracy of the registration is increased.

- *Genetic algorithms* Some researchers (Ansari et al., 1990; Zhang et al., 2003) have applied genetic algorithms to explore the search space of point mappings. The chromosomes encode instances of point mappings and evolve by performing genetic operators to reduce the AHD or PHD dissimilarity values, such that the optimal registration transformation can be obtained.

- *Simulated annealing* The authors of (Ansari et al., 1993; Starink & Backer, 1995) employed the simulated annealing technique to tackle the PPR problem. The identification of point correspondences between two point patterns is mathematically formulized as energy minimization. The registration error incurred by the current configuration of point correspondences is treated as the energy of that configuration. Simulated annealing rearranges the particles of configuration to reach thermal equilibrium at various temperature levels and finally converges to an optimum configuration as the system is frozen.

This chapter investigates the strengths and weaknesses of applying modern evolutionary algorithms, in particular, the particle swarm optimization and scatter search, to cope with the incomplete unlabeled PPR problem. The performance of the two algorithms is evaluated by competing with existing algorithms on synthetic datasets. The experimental results manifest that the modern evolutionary algorithms are superior and malleable against varying scenarios such as positional perturbations, contaminations and drop-outs from the point patterns.

The remainder of this chapter is organized as follows. Section 2 reviews the underlying modern evolutionary algorithms. Section 3 presents the proposed methods for the PPR problem. In Section 4, the experimental results are illustrated. Finally, a conclusion is given in Section 5.

2. Modern evolutionary algorithms

The notion of evolutionary algorithms has been introduced since 1960's and usually refers to a class of genome-inspired computation algorithms consisting of genetic algorithms, evolutionary programming, evolutionary strategy and genetic programming. These novel algorithms have exhibited great successes in many engineering and science applications. In the mid 1990's, another class of evolutionary algorithms emerged. These algorithms are bio-inspired and established on metaphors of socio-cognition. Typical examples in this class include culture algorithms, ant colony optimization, particle swarm optimization and scatter search. This chapter is focused on the application of particle swarm optimization and scatter search to the point pattern registration problem. In this section, we give a brief review of the two modern evolutionary algorithms.

2.1 Particle swarm optimization

Particle swarm optimization (PSO) is a new evolutionary algorithm proposed in (Kennedy & Eberhart, 1995). PSO is bio-inspired and it models the social dynamics of bird flocking. A large number of birds flock synchronously, change direction suddenly, scatter and regroup iteratively, and finally perch on a target. This form of social intelligence not only increases the success rate for food foraging but also expedites the process. The PSO algorithm facilitates simple rules simulating bird flocking and serves as an optimizer for continuous nonlinear functions. The general principles of the PSO algorithm can be outlined in the following features.

- *Particle representation*   The particle in the PSO is a candidate solution to the underlying problem and move iteratively and objectively in the solution space. The particle is represented as a real-valued vector rendering an instance of all parameters that characterize the optimization problem. We denote the ith particle by $P_i = \left(p_{i1}, p_{i2}, ..., p_{id} \right)^T \in R^d$, where d is the number of parameters.

- *Swarm*   The PSO explores the solution space by flying a number of particles, called swarm. The initial swarm is generated at random and the size of swarm is usually kept constant through iterations. At each iteration, the swarm of particles search for target optimal solution by referring to previous experiences.

- *Personal best experience and swarm's best experience*   The PSO enriches the swarm intelligence by storing the best positions visited so far by every particle. In particular, particle i remembers the best position among those it has visited, referred to as $pbest_i$, and the best position by its neighbors. There are two versions for keeping the neighbors' best position, namely $lbest$ and $gbest$. In the local version, each particle keeps track of the best position *lbest* attained by its local neighboring particles. For the global version, the best position *gbest* is determined by any particles in the entire swarm. Hence, the *gbest* model is a special case of the *lbest* model. It has been shown that the local version is often better, particularly the one using random topology neighborhood where each particle generates L links at random after each iteration if there has been no improvement i.e. if the best solution seen so far by the swarm is still the same. In our implementation, we set $L = 10$.

- *Particle movement*   The PSO is an iterative algorithm according to which a swarm of particles fly in the solution space until the stopping criterion is satisfied. At each iteration, particle i adjusts its velocity v_{ij} and position p_{ij} through each dimension j by reference to, with random multipliers, the personal best position ($pbest_{ij}$) and the swarm's best position ($lbest_{ij}$, if the local version is adopted) using Eqs. (7) and (8) as follows.

$$v_{ij} = K[v_{ij} + c_1 r_1(pbest_{ij} - p_{ij}) + c_2 r_2(lbest_{ij} - p_{ij})] \tag{7}$$

and

$$p_{ij} = p_{ij} + v_{ij} \tag{8}$$

where c_1 and c_2 are the cognitive coefficients and r_1 and r_2 are random real numbers drawn from $U(0, 1)$. Thus the particle flies toward *pbest* and *lbest* in a navigated way while still exploring new areas by the stochastic mechanism to escape from local optima. Clerc & Kennedy (2002) has pointed out that the use of the constriction factor K is needed to insure convergence of the algorithm and its value is determined by

$$K = \frac{2}{\left|2 - \varphi - \sqrt{\varphi^2 - 4\varphi}\right|} \tag{9}$$

where $\varphi = c_1 + c_2$, $\varphi > 4$. Typically, φ is set to 4.1 and K is thus 0.729.

- *Stopping criterion*   The PSO algorithm is terminated with a maximal number of iterations or the best particle position of the entire swarm cannot be improved further after a sufficiently large number of iterations.

PSO has received great successes in many applications including evolving weights and structure for artificial neural networks (Eberhart & Shi, 1998), manufacture end milling [21], state estimation for electric power distribution systems (Shigenori et al., 2003), and curve segmentation (Yin, 2004). The convergence and parameterization aspects of the PSO have been also discussed (Clerc & Kennedy, 2002; Trelea, 2003).

2.2 Scatter search

Scatter search (SS) is another new evolutionary algorithm proposed in (Glover, 1998), although its original proposal may appear in an earlier literature (Glover, 1977). SS operates on a set of diverse elite solutions, referred to as *reference set*, and typically consists of the following elementary components.

- *Diversification generation method* An arbitrary solution is used as a starting point (or seed) to generate a set of diverse trial solutions. There are a number of ways to implement this process such as using experimental design in statistics or taking advantage of the problem structure.

- *Improvement method* This method is concerned with solution improvement in two aspects: feasibility and quality. The improvement method generally incorporates a heuristic procedure to transform an infeasible solution into a feasible one, or to transform an existing feasible solution to a new one with a better objective value.
- *Reference set update method* A small reference set containing high quality and mutually diverse solutions is dynamically updated throughout the evolution process. Subsets of the reference set are used to produce new solutions that compete with the incumbent members of the reference set for inclusion as new members. A simple option to update the reference set is to include the best solution as the first member and then select the remaining members according to their solution quality relative to the objective value. However, the next solution to be selected must satisfy the minimum diversity criterion requesting that the minimum distance between this solution and the members currently in the reference set is greater than a specified threshold.
- *Subset generation method* Subsets from the reference set are successively generated as a basis for creating combined solutions. The simplest implementation is to generate all 2-element subsets consisting of exactly two reference solutions. Campos et al. (2001) have empirically shown that the subset generation method employing 2-element subsets can be quite effective, though systematic procedures for generating key subsets consisting of larger numbers of elements invite further investigation.
- *Solution combination method* Each subset produced by the subset generation method is used to create one or more combined solutions. The combination method for solutions represented by continuous variables employs linear combinations of subset elements, not restricted to convex combinations. The weights are systematically varied each time a combined solution is generated.

SS manifested a wealth of successful applications (Marti, 2006), ranging from resource assignment, flow shop scheduling, network routing, software testing, to bioinformatics.

3. The proposed methods

Next, we propose our methods for tackling PPR using PSO and SS, respectively.

3.1 PSO for PPR

This method is based on our previous work (Yin, 2006). To apply PSO for solving the PPR problem, we device specific features as follows.

Particle Coding Scheme

We encode the affine transformation parameters, namely, the rotation angle θ, the scale factor s, and the translation offsets t_x and t_y in the particle representation, i.e., the particle vector looks like

$$P = (\theta, s, t_x, t_y)^T \tag{10}$$

where each parameter value is a random real number and is restricted by an appropriate range. In particular, $0° \leq \theta \leq 360°$, $0 < s \leq 10$, and $-200 \leq t_x, t_y \leq 200$ are appropriate for a large number of applications. As such each particle encoded in this way corresponds to one set of affine transformation parameters to align the point patterns. During evolution, the particles are constrained to move in the same ranges as they are initialized. When the particles reach the boundary constraints, they are set to boundary values.

Fitness Evaluation and Bounding Criterion

In PSO, the solution quality, or *fitness*, delivered by each particle is evaluated. The two alternative registration distance measures, AHD and PHD, can be used for this purpose. Since these measures are error functions, a particle delivering a smaller AHD or PHD value is considered to be superior to the other particles with larger AHD or PHD values. As such the *pbest* and *lbest* can be determined according to the fitness values of all particles.

Here we propose a bounding criterion to speedup the computation for determining *pbest* and *lbest*. The formulae (7)-(9) of particle movement refer to representations of *pbest*, *lbest*, and the particle itself, not directly to their fitness values. We propose to use this property for saving computation time. Since the fitness value of a particle is only used for updating of *pbest* and *lbest*, we can use the fitness value of the incumbent *pbest$_i$* as an error upper bound to terminate the fitness computation of particle i. More precisely, the computation of AHD involves an error summation over point registration (see Eqs. (2) and (3)) and the computation of PHD is also resulted from the maximum of two sub-error measures (see Eq. (6)), both of which are a value-increasing computation. Hence, we can terminate the error computation for particle i upon the time the intermediate error value exceeds the fitness value of the incumbent *pbest$_i$*, and go directly to the fitness evaluation of the next particle. Also, only those *pbest$_i$* that have been updated at the current iteration need to be compared to associated *lbest* for its possible updating. The use of bounding criterion can save the computational time significantly.

The Algorithm

The proposed algorithm is summarized in Fig. 1. Initially, a swarm of particles are created at random and each of which is a vector corresponding to an instance of transformation parameters to the underlying problem. Then, the particle movement is repeated until a maximal number of iterations have been passed. During each iteration, the particle individual best and swarm's best positions are determined using the bounding criterion. The particle adjusts its position based on the individual experience (*pbest$_i$*) and the swarm intelligence (*lbest$_i$*). When the algorithm is terminated, the best of all *pbest$_i$* and the corresponding fitness value are output and considered as the optimal transformation parameters and the alignment error.

1. Initialize.
   1.1 Randomly generate M particles, $P_1, P_2, ..., P_M$, according to Eq. (10).
2. Repeat until a given maximal number of iterations is achieved.
   2.1 Determine *pbest$_i$* and *lbest$_i$*, $i = 1, 2, ..., M$ using the bounding criterion.
   2.2 Update velocities v_{ij} using Eqs. (7) and (9)
   2.3 Update particles' positions using Eq. (8).
3. Output the best of all *pbest$_i$* and the corresponding fitness value as the optimal transformation parameters and the alignment error.

Fig. 1. PSO algorithm for the PPR problem.

Unless specified, in all of the experiments presented in the next section we use a swarm of 20 particles, acceleration constants $c_1 = c_2 = 2.05$, and constriction factor K is equal to 0.729. These parameter values are determined empirically and conform to most settings in existing applications.

3.2 SS for PPR

Now we describe the implementation details of SS for solving the PPR problem.

Solution Coding Scheme and Improvement

The nature parameter coding scheme (10) can also be employed in SS to represent a candidate solution x, respecting the appropriate ranges of parameters. At this stage, the SS method generates a set of random solutions and improves their quality by perturbation. For each random solution, the improvement method sequentially selects each parameter in turn and alters its value by an arbitrary small deviation. If the fitness of the random solution is improved, the altered solution replaces the random solution. Otherwise, the random solution is restored. This process is repeatedly performed until the current solution cannot be further improved by examining all parameters once. As such, we obtain a set of local optimal solutions from the initial random solutions.

The initial reference set is built by selecting elements from the local optimal solutions based on the minimum diversity criterion. The best local optimal solution is firstly included in the reference set, the selection of the next best member, however, should satisfy the minimum diversity criterion, i.e., the minimum distance between the solution to be selected and all the members currently contained in the reference set is greater than a specified threshold. Therefore, the quality and diversity of the reference set are above a critical level.

Subset Generation and Solution Combination

Inspired by previous comparative researches, we implement 2-element subset generation and linear solution combination. In other words, every subset of reference set containing exactly two reference solutions is subject to linear solution combination. Given a subset containing two reference solutions x^1 and x^2, from which three new solutions x^3, x^4 and x^5 are generated as follows.

$$x^3 = x^1 - r(x^2 - x^1) \tag{11}$$

$$x^4 = x^1 + r(x^2 - x^1) \tag{12}$$

$$x^5 = x^2 + r(x^2 - x^1) \tag{13}$$

where $r \in (0, 1)$. Hence, the generated solutions x^3, x^4 and x^5 are located on the line determined by the two reference solutions x^1 and x^2 if r is constant. Nevertheless, we adopted different values of r along various parameter dimensions to expand the search beyond the line.

Bounding Criterion and Reference Set Update

The bounding criterion used in our PSO method is also enforced here to expedite the process. For each candidate solution produced by the solution combination method, we evaluate its fitness and use the worst fitness of current members in reference set as the upper bound. That is, the fitness evaluation of the candidate solution is terminated if the intermediate fitness value exceeds the upper bound and this candidate solution is abandoned.

Assume that k_1 feasible solutions (satisfying the bounding criterion) are produced by the solution combination method and the reference set contains k_2 solutions. Our reference set update method is conducted as follows. The best $k_2/2$ solutions in the pool of new solutions and the reference set are selected first into the new reference set. For each of the rest $k_1 + k_2/2$ solutions, the minimum distance to the current members in the new reference set is computed. Then, the solution with the maximum of these minimum distances is added to the new reference set. This max-min selection process is repeated until the new reference set contains k_2 solutions. Thus, both the quality and the diversity of the reference set members are guaranteed.

The Algorithm

Our SS algorithm proceeds as follows. The diversification generation method and improvement method are applied to create a set of random solutions that satisfy a critical level of diversity and quality. This set is used to produce the initial reference set. Every 2-element subset of the reference set is generated and used to produce three new solutions by the solution combination method. Only quality new solutions passing the bounding criterion are remained. The remained solutions are further improved by the improvement method. The reference set is then updated by comparing the new solutions to the solutions currently in the reference set according to the reference set update method. The process is repeated until the reference set cannot be further updated. The SS algorithm is summarized in Fig. 2.

1. Initialize.
    1.1 Create a set P of local optimal solutions obtained by altering a set of random solutions using the improvement method.
    1.2 Build the initial reference set, denoted by *RefSet*, by selecting members from P based on the minimum diversity criterion.
2. Repeat until *RefSet* cannot be further updated.
    2.1 Generate all 2-element subsets of *RefSet*.
    2.2 Use the members of each 2-element subset to generate three new solutions by applying Eqs. (11)-(13).
    2.3 Remain quality new solutions using the bounding criterion and improve them by the improvement method.
    2.4 Update *RefSet* by the max-min selection process.
3. Output the best member of *RefSet* and the corresponding fitness value as the optimal transformation parameters and the alignment error.

Fig. 2. SS algorithm for the PPR problem.

4. Experimental results

In this section, we present the experimental results and analyze the computational performance. The platform of the experiments is a PC with a 1.8 GHz CPU and 192 MB RAM. All programs are coded in C++ language.

4.1 Synthetic datasets

To evaluate the performance of competing algorithms, several synthetic datasets are prepared. Fig. 3(a) shows a typical point set, referred to as pattern A, consisting of 250 points generated at random. Four scenarios widely seen in real-world applications are used to generate testing patterns as shown in Figs. 3(b)-3(e) to match with pattern A.

- Scenario RST: A testing pattern is generated by applying to pattern A with an affine transformation consisting of rotation, scaling, and translation. In particular, the transformation parameters (θ, s, t_x, t_y) are set to $(30°, 1.5, 19.0, 42.0)$. The resulting testing pattern, referred to as pattern B, is shown in Fig. 3(b). It can be formulated by

$$\text{Pattern } B = T[\text{Pattern } A]$$

- Scenario RSTP: In addition to applying Scenario RST, a random perturbation quantity is added to the coordinates of each transformed data point. The random perturbation quantity is generated uniformly within one percent of the maximum positional span along every coordinate axis dimension and the resulting testing pattern is shown in Fig. 3(c). The formulation is as follows.

$$\text{Pattern } B = T[\text{Pattern } A] + \text{perturbation}$$

- Scenario RSTPA: Besides applying Scenario RSTP, we augment the size of the resulting point pattern by 20% by adding 50 spurious random points and thus yielding a 300-point pattern (see Fig. 3(d)), *viz.*,

$$\text{Pattern } B = T[\text{Pattern } A] + \text{perturbation} + 20\% \text{ points}$$

- Scenario RSTDA: First, Scenario RST is applied to pattern *A*. Then, randomly select 20% of the points and remove them. Generate the same number of spurious points and add them to the point pattern (see Fig. 3(e)). The formulation is as follows.

$$\text{Pattern } B = T[\text{Pattern } A] - 20\% \text{ points} + 20\% \text{ points}$$

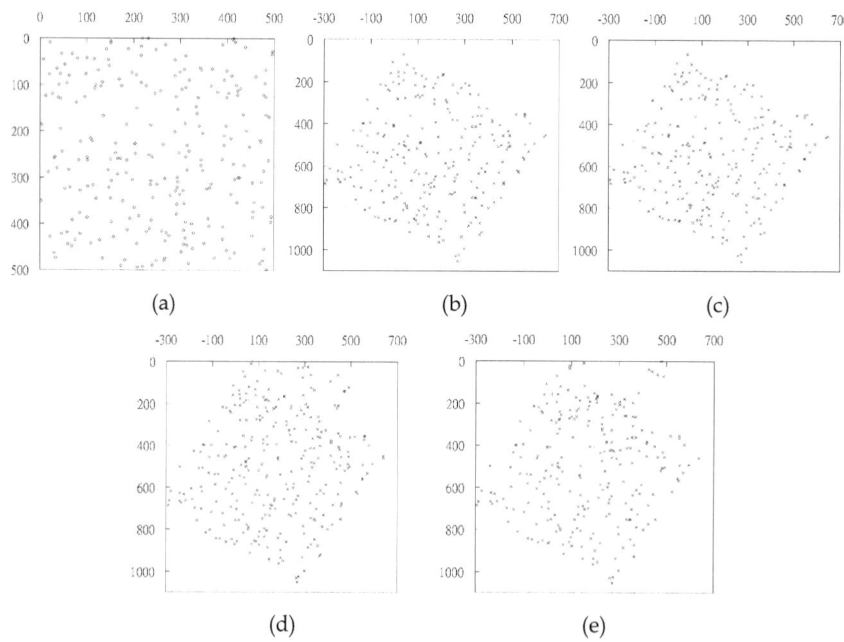

Fig. 3 Synthetic point patterns. (a) Pattern *A*, (b) a testing pattern generated by Scenario RST, (c) a testing pattern generated by Scenario RSTP, (d) a testing pattern generated by Scenario RSTPA, and (e) a testing pattern generated by Scenario RSTDA.

Following the protocol generating the previous dataset, we can create other datasets with different numbers of points (n), in particular, point patterns having 50, 250, and 500 points under the previously noted real scenarios are built.

4.2 Empirical study

The comparative performance of the proposed evolutionary algorithms is analyzed by comparing to competing algorithms under various testing scenarios. In particular, we have implemented two traditional evolutionary algorithms, namely, genetic algorithm (GA) and simulated annealing (SA). GA is a population-based evolutionary algorithm which explores the search space using a number of individual agents, called *chromosomes*. We implemented the GA with the same coding scheme, initialization ranges, and fitness evaluation as used to implement our proposed algorithms. In addition to the broadly used genetic operations, namely the selection, crossover, and mutation, we further emploied fitness scaling and elitist strategy (Goldberg, 1989) to enhance the performance of the GA. On the other hand, SA is an evolutionary algorithm based on perturbation of the current configuration (candidate solution) in order to reach an equilibrium state, simulating the thermal annealing process. The implemented SA also uses the same coding scheme, initialization ranges, and fitness function as used by our algorithms.

The comparative performance of competing algorithms is evaluated with different datasets containing various numbers of data points (n), in particular, $n = 50$, 250, and 500, respectively. For a fair comparison, all competing algorithms are terminated when they have consumed 4000 times of fitness evaluations because solution fitness is the most informative element and is also the most time consuming component. In all experiments, PSO is executed with 20 particles, SS maintains a reference set containing 20 elite solutions, and GA is conducted with 20 chromosomes. It is worth noting that SA is a single agent search algorithm instead of a population-based one, we thus let SA execute with 4000 iterations. The numerical results for each dataset are the mean value and the standard deviation (σ) from 30 independent runs and they are summarized in Tables 1 and 2 (the CPU times are evaluated in seconds) for AHD and PHD measures, respectively. We have the following observations.

- Overall, PSO and SS have the best performance among all the competing algorithms in terms of both dissimilarity measures (AHD and PHD) and computational time, SA is ranked at the middle place, and GA seems to be the worst of all.

- PSO and SS are also more stable than GA and SA, by producing consistent results with smaller standard deviation values.

- For all RST testing datasets, PSO does not yield any registration errors for both AHD and PHD measures because RST incurs a complete registration with no perturbation, SS produces negligible errors, while both GA and SA entail significant amount of errors and fail to find the optimal transformation.

- For all RSTDA testing datasets, PSO produces no registration errors for the PHD measure, which means the PSO algorithm is able to find the groundtruth transformation for incomplete registration without perturbation (PSO does not generate zero error with AHD measure because AHD penalizes an incomplete registration, however, the point correspondences are still correctly identified).

- At average, PSO consumes about 80% of the CPU time required by GA and about 91% of the CPU time required by SA. The average CPU time cost by SS is comparable to that cost by PSO, but the large value of standard deviation indicates that the individual CPU time spent by SS in each independent run varies a lot. This is because the CPU time consumed by SS depends on the number of times the reference set is updated and this number is determined by the time upon which good quality solutions are generated, which varies with different runs.

		PSO		SS		GA		SA	
n	Scenario	AHD (σ)	Time (σ)	AHD (σ)	Time (σ)	AHD (σ)	Time (σ)	AHD (σ)	Time (σ)
50	RST	0.0 (0.0)	8.8 (0.1)	0.1 (0.1)	8.8 (0.6)	9.2 (0.5)	11.5 (0.1)	0.3 (0.3)	9.9 (0.3)
	RSTP	11.2 (0.0)	8.6 (0.1)	11.2 (0.0)	7.6 (2.6)	14.3 (1.1)	10.8 (0.1)	11.6 (0.5)	9.7 (0.2)
	RSTPA	14.1 (0.0)	10.3 (0.1)	14.2 (0.0)	6.6 (1.6)	14.9 (1.2)	12.9 (0.2)	14.6 (0.3)	11.2 (0.1)
	RSTDA	204.2 (0.0)	8.7 (0.1)	204.4 (0.1)	6.2 (2.3)	211.4 (6.2)	10.9 (0.1)	205.9 (1.9)	9.5 (0.1)
250	RST	0.0 (0.0)	206.4 (3.0)	0.0 (0.0)	155.6 (2.6)	9.5 (0.7)	262.1 (2.5)	0.9 (1.3)	237.0 (2.6)
	RSTP	10.8 (0.0)	206.4 (1.6)	10.8 (0.1)	153.7 (1.3)	40.9 (2.4)	262.8 (1.6)	11.4 (0.5)	229.7 (1.9)
	RSTPA	13.0 (0.0)	245.4 (0.2)	13.5 (0.3)	189.7 (3.6)	29.5 (1.7)	309.4 (1.8)	16.1 (2.3)	271.1 (2.5)
	RSTDA	112.3 (0.0)	204.9 (0.2)	112.5 (0.2)	155.7 (4.3)	123.9 (3.6)	263.9 (2.4)	113.4 (1.1)	224.6 (1.5)
500	RST	0.0 (0.0)	821.2 (2.1)	0.1 (0.1)	612.0 (7.9)	15.1 (1.3)	1060.3 (8.6)	0.8 (0.6)	895.7 (1.9)
	RSTP	11.4 (0.0)	817.7 (1.8)	11.5 (0.1)	597.0 (11.2)	15.9 (1.1)	1059.0 (9.3)	13.1 (2.3)	895.7 (3.6)
	RSTPA	55.3 (0.0)	979.3 (2.4)	55.3 (0.0)	692.0 (6.1)	72.6 (3.4)	1249.5 (9.2)	60.7 (3.9)	1077.6 (13.1)
	RSTDA	53.9 (0.0)	816.6 (2.0)	53.9 (0.1)	570.8 (10.5)	62.8 (3.0)	1042.9 (10.4)	55.9 (0.8)	893.9 (2.3)

Table 1. Comparative performances of the PSO, SS, GA and SA algorithms with respect to the AHD measure and the used computational time (in seconds).

		PSO		SS		GA		SA	
n	Scenario	PHD (σ)	Time (σ)	PHD (σ)	Time (σ)	PHD (σ)	Time (σ)	PHD (σ)	Time (σ)
50	RST	0.0 (0.0)	12.1 (0.2)	0.2 (0.1)	11.7 (2.6)	20.4 (1.4)	14.1 (0.1)	2.0 (2.4)	13.0 (0.1)
	RSTP	16.6 (0.1)	11.8 (0.1)	17.4 (0.1)	14.1 (5.7)	24.5 (1.6)	14.3 (0.2)	20.3 (2.0)	12.9 (0.1)
	RSTPA	22.4 (0.6)	14.1 (0.1)	23.8 (0.6)	16.0 (2.1)	36.4 (2.2)	17.2 (0.3)	24.8 (1.8)	15.4 (0.1)
	RSTDA	0.0 (0.0)	11.8 (0.1)	0.1 (0.1)	12.3 (5.3)	29.5 (1.9)	16.9 (0.2)	1.4 (1.4)	12.9 (0.1)
250	RST	0.0 (0.0)	288.3 (1.8)	0.3 (0.2)	312.0 (5.3)	149.7 (4.8)	374.0 (2.1)	1.0 (1.1)	315.3 (1.3)
	RSTP	19.8 (0.1)	289.3 (1.7)	20.5 (0.2)	306.7 (2.2)	37.2 (2.1)	347.9 (2.3)	22.0 (1.0)	314.0 (0.3)
	RSTPA	24.1 (1.5)	341.6 (1.9)	25.8 (0.4)	369.6 (14.9)	168.9 (6.1)	427.9 (2.9)	30.4 (5.0)	376.8 (1.8)
	RSTDA	0.0 (0.0)	283.8 (0.2)	0.1 (0.0)	269.8 (7.6)	116.8 (3.9)	346.0 (1.9)	2.4 (2.6)	312.8 (1.4)
500	RST	0.0 (0.0)	1148.8 (2.2)	0.1 (0.1)	1132.3 (26.3)	9.7 (0.7)	1386.7 (6.2)	1.2 (1.0)	1259.0 (1.1)
	RSTP	18.4 (0.1)	1147.3 (2.7)	19.0 (0.1)	1215.4 (21.7)	24.5 (1.2)	1382.2 (8.1)	22.4 (2.4)	1259.3 (3.1)
	RSTPA	53.7 (2.1)	1385.5 (8.0)	56.6 (0.8)	1305.2 (35.8)	70.4 (4.5)	1656.1 (9.3)	71.7 (14.7)	1497.4 (2.2)
	RSTDA	0.0 (0.0)	1130.9 (2.7)	0.1 (0.1)	1090.8 (13.6)	76.2 (3.8)	1366.8 (8.6)	0.9 (0.9)	1234.7 (2.2)

Table 2. Comparative performances of the PSO, SS, GA and SA algorithms with respect to the PHD measure and the used computational time (in seconds).

Fig. 4 shows the registration results between pattern A and pattern B with all testing scenarios obtained using the proposed PSO method. The registration results obtained using the proposed SS method is very similar to that obtained by PSO, so we omit the illustration of SS for saving space. For each testing scenario, PSO is performed with AHD and PHD dissimilarity metrics, respectively. For the Scenario RST (see Figs. 4(a) and 4(b)) and the Scenario RSTP (see Figs. 4(c) and 4(d)), the PSO can find the complete registration between the two patterns and the one-to-one correspondence relationship is correctly identified. For the Scenario RSTPA (see Figs. 4(e) and 4(f)) and the Scenario RSTDA (see Figs. 4(g) and 4(h)), the PSO derives the incomplete registration. The point patterns are appropriately aligned for both scenarios and the groundtruth point registration correspondences are found. Note that in all testing scenarios both AHD and PHD measures work well with the proposed method.

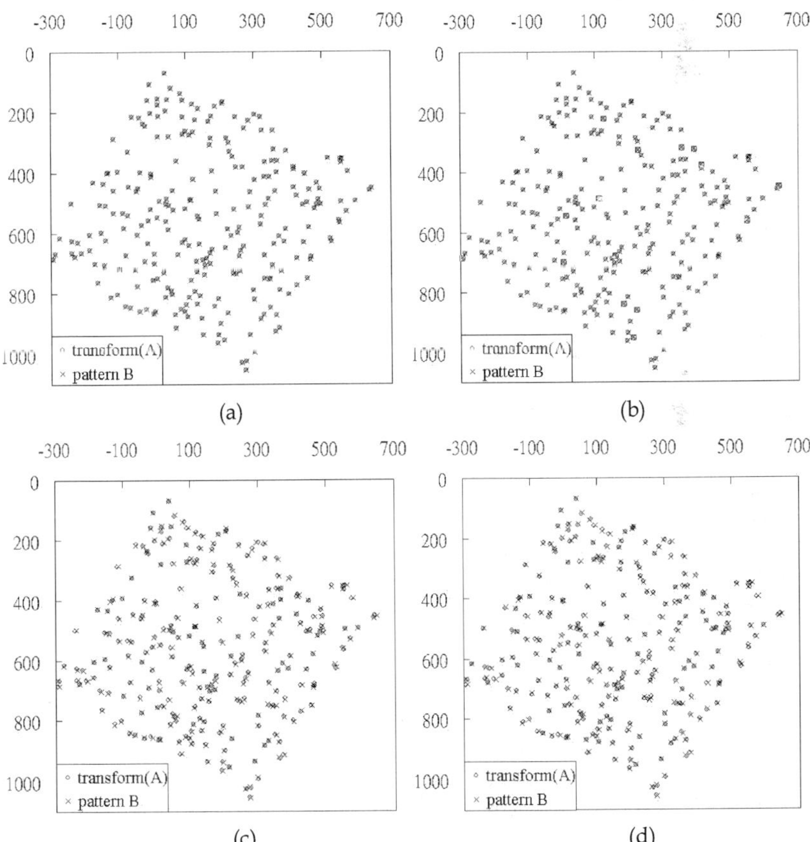

(a)   (b)

(c)   (d)

Fig. 4 Registration results obtained using the PSO method for all testing scenarios. (a) Scenario RST with AHD metric, (b) Scenario RST with PHD metric, (c) Scenario RSTP with AHD metric, (d) Scenario RSTP with PHD metric, (e) Scenario RSTPA with AHD metric, (f) Scenario RSTPA with PHD metric, (g) Scenario RSTDA with AHD metric, and (h) Scenario RSTDA with PHD metric.

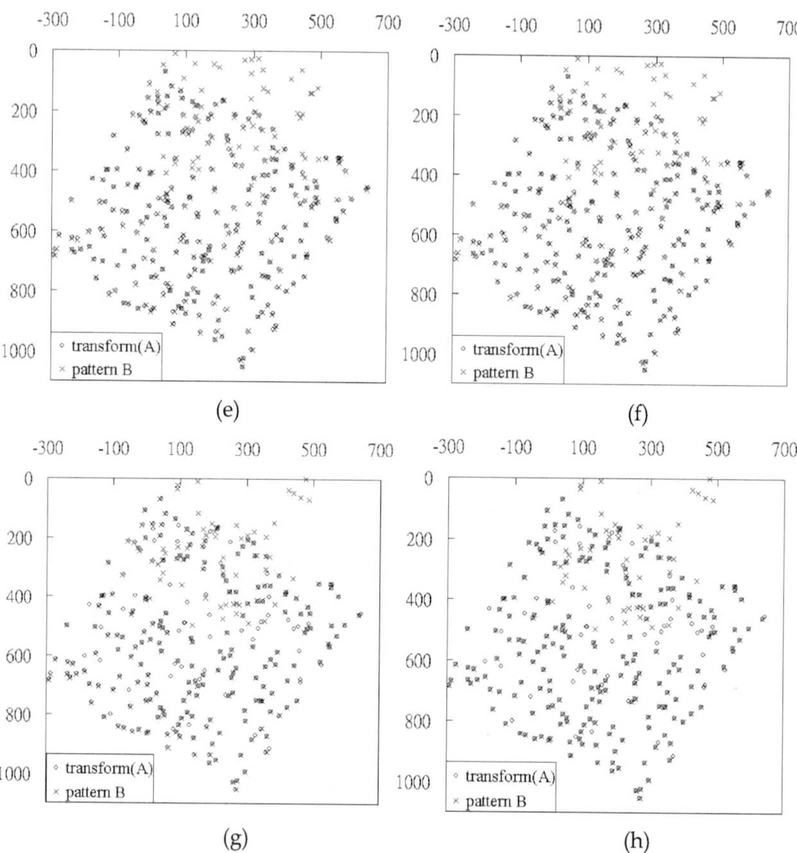

(e)   (f)

(g)   (h)

Fig. 4 Registration results obtained using the PSO method for all testing scenarios (continued.)

5. Conclusion

This chapter investigates the strengths and weaknesses of PPR approaches based on modern evolutionary algorithms, in particular, the particle swarm optimization (PSO) and scatter search (SS). The experimental results manifest that PSO and SS are malleable under varying scenarios such as positional perturbations, contaminations and drop-outs from the point patterns. PSO and SS are also more effective and efficient than the methods based on genetic algorithm (GA) and simulated annealing (SA) in minimizing the registration error. The advantage of our algorithms is due to the natural metaphor, stochastic move, adaptivity, and positive feedback. Our observations disclose the truism that modern evolutionary algorithms have competitive features that provide a chance to create a solution method which is both effective and efficient and is significantly different from that created by tradition evolutionary algorithms.

6. References

Agrawal, A.; Ansari, N. & Hou, E. (1994). Evolutionary programming for fast and robust point pattern matching, *Proceedings of IEEE International Conference on Neural Networks*, pp. 1777-1782.

Ansari, N.; Chen, M.H. & Hou, E. (1990). Point pattern matching by a genetic algorithm, *Proceedings of IEEE International Conference on Industrial Electronics*, II, pp. 1233-1238.

Ansari, N.; Hou, E. & Agrawal, A. (1993). Point pattern matching by simulated annealing, *Proceedings of IEEE Regional Conference on Control Systems*, pp. 215-218.

Campos, V.; Glover, F.; Laguna, M. & Martí, R. (2001). An experimental evaluation of a scatter search for the linear ordering problem, *Journal of Global Optimization*, Vol. 21, pp. 397-414.

Carcassoni, M. & Hancock, E.R. (2003). Spectral correspondence for point pattern matching, *Pattern Recognition*, Vol. 36, pp. 193-204.

Chang, S.H.; Cheng, F.H.; Hsu, W.H. & Wu, G.Z. (1997). Fast algorithm for point pattern matching: invariant to translations, rotations and scale changes, *Pattern Recognition*, Vol. 30, pp. 311-320.

Clerc, M. & Kennedy, J. (2002). The particle swarm explosion, stability, and convergence in a multidimensional complex space, *IEEE Transaction on Evolutionary Computation*, Vol. 6, pp. 58-73.

Eberhart, R.C. & Shi, Y. (1998). Evolving artificial neural networks, *Proceedings of International Conference on Neural Networks and Brain*, pp. 5-13.

Glover, F. (1977). Heuristics for integer programming using surrogate constraints, *Decision Sciences*, Vol. 8, pp. 156-166.

Glover, F. (1998). A template for scatter search and path relinking, *Artificial Evolution*, Lecture Notes in Computer Science 1363, pp. 13-54.

Goldberg, D.E. (1989). *Genetic Algorithms in Search, Optimization and Machine Learning*, Addison-Wesley, Reading, MA.

Goshtasby, A. & Stockman, G.C. (1985). Point pattern matching using convex hull edges, *IEEE Transaction on Systems, Man and Cybernetics*, Vol. 15, pp. 631-637.

Griffin, P.M. & Alexopoulos, C. (1991). Point pattern matching using centroid bounding, *IEEE Transaction on Systems, Man and Cybernetics*, Vol. 19, pp. 1274-1276.

Huttenlocher, D.P.; Klanderman, G.A. & Rucklidge, W.J. (1993). Comparing images using the Hausdorff distance, *IEEE Transactions on Pattern Analysis and Machine Intelligence*, Vol. 15, pp. 850-863.

Kennedy, J. & Eberhart, R.C. (1995). Particle swarm optimization, *Proceedings of IEEE International Conference on Neural Networks*, IV, pp. 1942-1948.

Marti, R. (2006). Scatter search – wellsprings and challenges, *European Journal of Operational Research*, Vol. 169, pp. 351-358.

Mount, D.M.; Netanyahu, N.S. & Moigne, J.L. (1999). Efficient algorithms for robust feature matching, *Pattern Recognition*, Vol. 32, pp. 17-38.

Ogawa, H. (1984). Labeled point pattern matching by fuzzy relaxation, *Pattern Recognition*, Vol. 17, pp. 569-573.

Olson, C.F. & Huttenlocher, D.P. (1997). Automatic target recognition by matching oriented edge pixels, *IEEE Transactions on Image Processing*, Vol. 6, pp. 103-113.

Ranade, S. & Rosenfeld, A. (1980). Point pattern matching by relaxation, *Pattern Recognition*, Vol. 12, pp. 269-275.

Shigenori, N.; Takamu, G.; Toshiku, Y. & Yoshikazu, F. (2003). A hybrid particle swarm optimization for distribution state estimation, *IEEE Transaction on Power Systems*, Vol. 18, pp. 60-68.

Starink, J.P. & Backer, E. (1995). Finding point correspondences using simulated annealing, *Pattern Recognition*, Vol. 28, pp. 231-240.

Tandon, V. (2000). Closing the gap between CAD/CAM and optimized CNC end milling, Master thesis, Purdue School of Engineering and Technology, Indiana University Purdue University Indianapolis.

Ton, J. & Jain, A.K. (1989). Registering Landsat images by point matching, *IEEE Transactions on Geoscience and Remote Sensing*, Vol. 27, pp. 642-651.

Trelea, I.C. (2003). The particle swarm optimization algorithm: convergence analysis and parameter selection, *Information Processing Letters*, Vol. 85, pp. 317-325.

Umeyama, S. (1991). Least-squares estimation of transformation parameters between two point patterns, *IEEE Transactions on Pattern Analysis and Machine Intelligence*, Vol. 13, pp. 376-380.

Wang, W.H. & Chen, Y.C. (1997). Point pattern matching by line segments and labels, *Electronic Letters*, Vol. 33, pp. 478-479.

Yin, P.Y. (2004). A discrete particle swarm algorithm for optimal polygonal approximation of digital curves, *Journal of Visual Communication and Image Representation*, Vol. 15, pp. 241-260.

Yin, P. Y. (2006). Particle swarm optimization for point pattern matching, *Journal of Visual Communication and Image Representation*, Vol. 17, pp. 143-162.

Yuen, P.C. (1993). Dominant point matching algorithm, *Electronic Letters*, Vol. 29, pp. 2023-2024.

Zhang, L.; Xu, W. & Chang, C. (2003). Genetic algorithm for affine point pattern matching, *Pattern Recognition Letters*, Vol. 24, pp. 9-19.

20

Investigation of a New Artificial Immune System Model Applied to Pattern Recognition

José Lima Alexandrino, Cleber Zanchettin, Edson C. de B. Carvalho Filho
Federal University of Pernambuco
Brazil

1. Introduction

The discovery of new functionalities through the study of human physiology has contributed toward the evolution of Artificial Immune Systems. In this chapter we can investigate a new architecture through observations of natural immunological behaviour, for which application to known algorithms contributed toward an improved performance. It considers a boarding where the antibodies are grouped in an organized way and from an evolutionary process the antibodies that belong to these groupings can improve the adaptive immune reply to a determined antigen. Thus, antibodies of the same class are in the same grouping. Others techniques were implemented such as Clonalg, MLP and K-NN to compare this new model.

2. Artificial immune systems

The Artificial Immune Systems (AIS) are a relatively new area of research with considerable potential in helping solve a myriad of difficulties. Its growth has allowed the proposal of new techniques and approaches for solving known problems.
The aim of this technology is to model defence mechanism characteristics and functionalities of living beings. The defence mechanism allows an organism to defend against invasion from foreign substances. The recognition of these substances is based on the key and lock analogy, in which the objective is to find antibodies that have the best immune response to the invading antigens (De Castro & Timmis, 2002).
The natural immune system stores the best antibodies in its genetic memory. These are later used to identify antigens that have previously invaded the organism, thereby obtaining a quicker, more efficient response.
New functionalities observed in the biological environment were studied for the modelling of this new immunological approach, principally the organization and clustering of similar antibodies (Ab) throughout the process. It is believed that these functionalities may improve the recognition capacity of artificial immune algorithms.

3. Hybrid architecture

There are a number of factors that motivate the hybridization of artificial immune algorithms with other techniques. Many complex problems can be decomposed into a number of parts, for some of which exact methods, or very good heuristics, may already be available. In these cases it makes sense to use a combination of the most appropriate methods for different sub problems.

In practice frequently, apply those algorithms and evolutionary algorithms (EAs) to a problem where there is a considerable amount of hard-won user experience and knowledge. In such cases performance benefits can often arise from utilizing this information in the form of specialist operators and/or good solutions. Provided that care is taken not to bias the search too much away from the generation of novel solutions. EAs are very good at rapidly identifying good areas of the search space (exploration) and they are less good at the "endgame" of fine-tuning solutions (exploitation) partly as a result of the stochastic nature of the variation operators.

An overall successful and efficient general problem solver, in fact, do not exist. It is commonly experienced that the combination of an evolutionary algorithm and a heuristic method (the hybrid EA) performs better than either of its "parents" algorithms alone (Eiben & Smith, 2003). For this reason, a Memetic Algorithm (Smith & Krasnogor, 2005) was developed based on features of natural immune systems. Memetic algorithms are characterized by the hybridization of Evolutionary Algorithms with the use of Local Searches at particular points of the algorithm (Alexandrino & Carvalho Filho, 2006; Oliveira et al., 2006; Eiben & Smith, 2003). The initialization method for the main population of antibodies is also a hybridization method, as it employs known solutions (Eiben & Smith, 2003).

The performance of this model was compared to other techniques found in the literature in order to assess the response quality of the algorithm. MLP (Multi-Layer Perceptron (Rumelhart et al., 1986)), K-NN (K-Nearest Neighbor (Duda & Hart, 2000)) and Clonalg (Clonal Selection Algorithm (De Castro & Von Zuben, 2000)) were used. Thus, it was possible to estimate the contribution this new model may have in research regarding artificial immune systems and pattern recognition.

4. Artificial immune functions

The discovery of new features from research into the physiology of the human body has contributed toward the evolution of the Artificial Immune System (Dasgupta, 2006). Such architecture has developed the organization and clustering of similar antibodies. The main features of this algorithm are hybridization with local search techniques, the heuristics of population construction, and uses of "intelligent" operators and the generational selection of survivors.

4.1 Antibody memory

Smith and Krasnogor (2005) suggest the use of information on previous populations through the retrieval of individuals from past generations. The aim of this technique is to recover genetic information that the algorithm has discarded, functioning as a kind of genetic memory bank to influence the search mechanisms of the algorithm.

This architecture was implemented using genetic memory to investigate the impact of this functionality on the performance of the algorithm.

4.2 Antibody clustering

The idea of evolving multiple populations in tandem is also known as island EAs, parallel EAs and more precisely coarse-grain parallel EAs (Eiben & Smith, 2003). The essential idea is to run multiple populations in parallel, in some kind of communication structure. After a (usually fixed) number of generations (known as an epoch), a number of individuals are selected from each population to be exchange with others from neighboring populations – this can be thought of as migration.

The original formulation of the GA as a trade-off between exploration of unexplored regions of the search space and exploitation of knowledge gained via search in the vicinity of known high quality solutions. The suggest that during the epochs between communication, when each subpopulation is evolving independently of the others, exploitation occurs, so that the subpopulations each explore the search space around the fitter solutions that they contain. When communication takes place, the injection of individuals of potentially high fitness, and with (possibly) radically different genotypes, facilitates exploration, particularly as recombination happens between the two different solutions.

Whilst extremely attractive in theory, and possessing the highly desirable quality of explicit parallelism, it is obvious that there are no guarantees per se that the different subpopulations are actually exploring different regions of the search space. One possibility is clearly to achieve a start at this through a careful initialization process, but even if this is used, there are a number of parameters that have been shown to affect the ability if this technique to explore different peaks and obtain good results even then when only a single solution is desired as the end result.

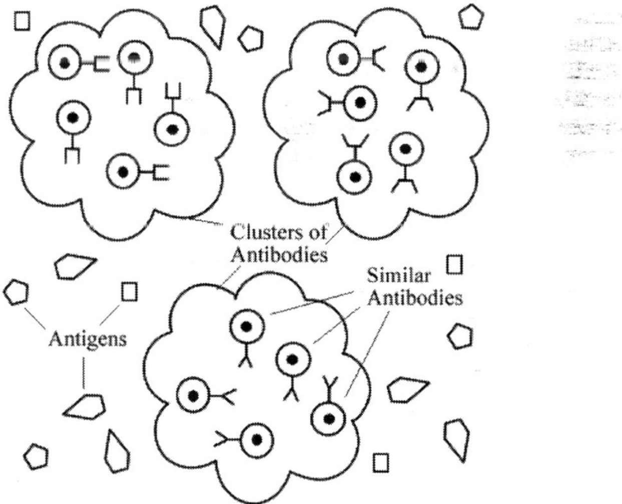

Fig. 1. Clusters with similar antibody

In this specific model, similar antibodies responsible for recognizing a class of antigens are organized into clusters (Fig. 1). With the presentation of an antigen from this class, the antibodies from this cluster multiply and differentiate by means of mutation in order to improve the immune response of the individuals to the antigen class presented. After recognition, the swarm of antibodies undergoes reduction back to its normal size, discarding less apt individuals. The best individuals remain in the swarm of antibodies to improve recognition during future events.

Genetic memory is organized as islands of evolution (Eiben & Smith, 2003). This suggests that clusters within sets of similar antibodies are maintained in separate evolution, which allows antibodies to be spatially organized into clusters of individuals in Fig. 1.

Separation allows the antibodies to evolve more quickly, which is different from the approach used in Clonalg (De Castro & Von Zuben, 2000), where the principal population of antibodies has individuals from a number of different classes. Thus, a more intuitive and better quality evolution is expected in the proposed approach, with antibodies that have a closer affinity to the antigens. This characteristics is important for multi-objective problems. Specifically for pattern recognition like handwritten digit problems.

The individuals of the genetic memory may be newly selected to once again compose the main antibody population, thereby participating in the evolution process. Thus, lost genetic filaments from previous generations can be recovered and reused in future generations.

5. Immunological model

This study uses an artificial immune algorithm based on the clonal selection theory and the hill climbing search algorithm (Russell & Norvig, 2003) as a local search method of the antibodies of the offspring population. The best individuals are stored in a structure based on the adaptive resonance theory.

In the model, similar antibodies responsible for recognizing a class of antigens are organized into clusters. With the presentation of an antigen from this class, the antibodies from this cluster multiply and differentiate by means of mutation in order to improve the immune response of the individuals to the antigen class presented. After recognition, the swarm of antibodies undergoes reduction back to its normal size, discarding less apt individuals. The best individuals remain in the swarm of antibodies to improve recognition during future events.

Genetic memory is organized as islands of evolution (Eiben & Smith, 2003). This concept suggests that clusters within sets of similar antibodies are maintained in separate evolution, which allows antibodies to be spatially organized into clusters of individuals.

Separation allows the antibodies to evolve more quickly, which is different from the approach used in Clonalg, where the principal population of antibodies has individuals from a number of different classes. Thus, a more intuitive and better quality evolution is expected in the proposed approach, with antibodies that have closer affinity to the antigens. The individuals from the genetic memory may be newly selected to once again compose the main antibody population, thereby participating in the evolution process. Thus, lost genetic filaments from previous generations can be recovered and reused in future generations.

5.1 Generation of the populations

In the present approach, it was determined that the main antibody population would be composed of $\lambda = 20$ individuals and the offspring population would have 40 individuals. The memory population is the same size as the training set and is generated from a selection of the best individuals.

At the beginning of the algorithm, the main population is generated randomly. With the next generation, the main population is composed of 50% random individuals and 50% individuals from the genetic memory of the antigen class that is being presented. This type of formation helps maintain the diversity of the main antibody population and allows the reuse of lost genetic material to initialize the main population with individuals of high affinity (Eiben & Smith, 2003).

Each individual of the offspring population is generated from a size-2 tournament selection (Eiben & Smith, 2003) of the antibodies in the main population. The antibody chosen undergoes the application of the mutation operators.

This type of main population generation seeks to model a biological generational characteristic in the human organism. When an antigen is presented, the multiplication of antibodies in that set occurs in order to find the antibody that has the best response to the antigen. This type of initialization of the main population allows the algorithm to retrieve individuals from the genetic memory bank that may have been discarded during a survival selection based on fitness (Eiben & Smith, 2003).

5.2 Memory population

De Castro & Von Zuben (2000) propose Clonalg using a selection of survivors proportional to fitness, in which only the most apt antibodies survive to the next generation. In the present study, the antibody population is generational (Eiben & Smith, 2003). This choice was made to avoid the premature convergence of the algorithm in regions of local minimums due to the highly elitist choice of antibodies used in Clonalg.

This point of the algorithm is determined by the add antibody to population memory Fig. 3 and constitutes the memory population, which is responsible for the learning of the training antigens. At each iteration, the best antibody in the principal and offspring populations is selected by the flow chart demonstrated in Fig. 3. This antibody is the candidate to integrate the memory population. If it possesses better fitness than an individual in the memory population, it will replace it. The added antibody is responsible for recognizing the antigen presented by the training population. There will be one antibody in the memory population associated to each antigen of the training population.

Following this step, the individual is added to the genetic memory of the class of training antigen that is being presented. There is a genetic memory for each class of the training set. This memory contains all the antibody candidates from the memory population that were selected during the execution of the algorithm. The set of antibodies will be used to compose the main population of upcoming generations.

5.3 Populevaluation

The quality of each antibody in the population is measured by the Hamming Distance DH (De Castro & Timmis, 2002) calculation between it and the antigen that is being presented, according to (1). Shorter distances equal greater quality.

Considering N the set of antigens (Ag) Ag_i, $i = 1,...,L (Ag_i \in N)$ to be recognized, and P the set of antibodies (Ab) Ab_i, $i = 1,...,L (Ab_i \in P)$ to be used as pattern recognizers. The antigens and antibodies have the same length L.

$$D_H = \sum_{i=1}^{L} \delta, \text{ where } \delta = \begin{cases} 1 \text{ if } Ag_i \neq Ab_i \\ 0 \text{ otherwise} \end{cases} \tag{1}$$

5.4 Mutation operators

Two mutation operators were employed in the present study: *simpleMutation* and *totalMutation*. With the first operator, one gene is chosen from all possible genes and only this gene will undergo mutation (Eiben & Smith, 2003).

With the second operator, all genes have a 30% likelihood of undergoing mutation (Eiben & Smith, 2003).

All antibodies have 30% likelihood of mutation application. This variable determines if an individual will undergo mutation or return to its copy.

5.5 Local search

The Hill Climbing (HC) Search Algorithm (Russell & Norvig, 2003) is a local search and is shown in Fig. 2. It is simply a loop that continually moves in direction of increasing quality value.

```
BEGIN
    WHILE ( TERMINITION CONDITIONAL is not satisfied ) DO
        newSolution ← neighbor( bestSolution );
        IF newSolution IS BETTER THAN actualSolution THEN
            bestSolution ← actualSolution;
        END IF
    END WHILE
END
```

Fig. 2. The general schema of a search in pseudocode

This architecture opts to implement the local search after the mutation operations and before the selection of survivors, as described in Fig. 3.

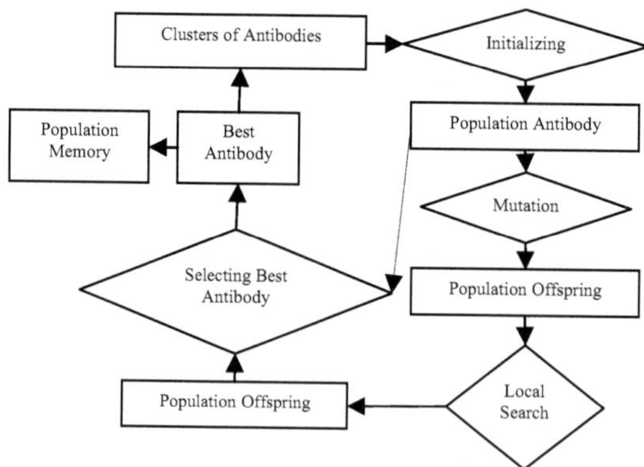

Fig. 3. Flow chart of the algorithm

5.6 Description of the algorithm

With each presentation of an antigen, a new main population is created. From this, a new offspring population is formed through the application of mutation operators. The best antibody found by the two populations is the candidate for incorporating the memory population of antibodies. This antibody will automatically be added to the genetic memory of the antigen class that is being added. At the end of the presentation of all the training patterns, a generation of the algorithm will be considered.

At the end of each generation, the classification rate in the test set is calculated in relation to the memory population of antibodies. The best configuration of the memory population is stored until the stopping criterion of the algorithm is satisfied. Only the maximum number of generations was considered in this implementation.

At the end of each generation, the classification rate in the test set is calculated in relation to the memory population of antibodies. The best configuration of the memory population is stored until the stopping criterion of the algorithm is satisfied. Only the maximum number of generations was considered in this implementation.

6. Recognition of handwritten digits

The analyzed patterns consist of binary images of handwritten digits from 0 to 9. The database used in this analyse corresponds to 8000 handwritten digit patterns divided into two sets of 6000 training patterns and 2000 test patterns. Each one of the ten classes had the same number of patterns.

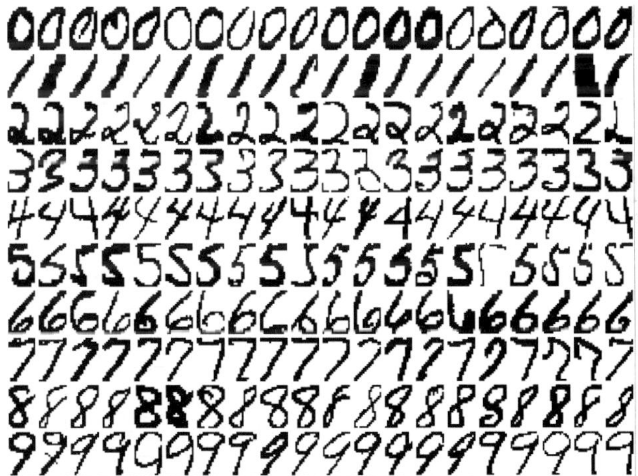

Fig. 4. Examples of patterns used

The patterns have 24x16 pixels and were transformed into binary matrices with 24 lines and 16 columns. An individual is composed of 24 genes, corresponding to a Size-24 vector that is the number of input features. Each element of the vector corresponds to each line of the binary matrices and one gene in the pattern. Each gene was formed by a number with binary form and size 16 that corresponds to a line of the binary matrix. This number was transformed into base 10.

7. Experiments and results

In the neural network training the aim is to achieve topologies with few connections and small error. In these tests, an MLP was used with only one intermediate layer and a Sigmoid Logistic Function. The MLP contains all possible connections of forward propagation (feedforward) between adjacent layers, without having connections that link the processing units of non-adjacent layers. In network training, considering N_C classes in the data set, the true class of the pattern x from the training set Pt is defined as:

$$\gamma(x) \in \{1, 2, ..., N_C\}, \forall x \in P_t \tag{2}$$

In the experiment, the winner-takes-all classification rule was used, in which the number of output units (N3) is equal to the number of classes (N_C).

As $o_k(x)$ is the output value of the output unit k for the pattern x, the class assigned to pattern x is defined as:

$$\varphi(x) = \text{argmax} o_k(x), \forall x \in P_t, k \in \{1, 2, ..., N_3\} \tag{3}$$

The network error for the pattern x is defined as follows:

$$\varepsilon(x) = \begin{cases} 1, & \text{if } \varphi(x) \neq \gamma(x). \\ 0, & \text{if } \varphi(x) = \gamma(x). \end{cases} \tag{4}$$

Therefore, the classification error for the training set Pt, which represents the percentage of incorrectly classified training patterns, can be defined as:

$$E(P_t) = \frac{100}{\#P_t} \sum_{x \in P_t} \varepsilon(x) \tag{5}$$

where #Pt is the number of patterns in the set Pt.
The percentage of connections used by the network is given by:

$$\psi(C) = \frac{100}{N_{max}} \sum_{i=1}^{N_{max}} c_i \tag{6}$$

The training process stops if: (1) the GL5 criterion defined in Proben1 (Prehelt, 1994) is met (based on the classification error or SEP of the validation set); or (2) the maximum number of iterations is reached. For the implementation of the GL5 criterion, the classification error or SEP for the validation set is evaluated at each IT iterations.

The GL5 criterion is a good approach for avoiding overfitting to the training set. The classification error for the validation set Pv is given by E(Pv), which is calculated according to Equation (5). Thus, using V(k) to denote the classification error E(Pv) at iteration $i = kI_T$, $k = 1, 2, ..., I_{max}/I_T$, the generalization loss parameter (GL) is defined as the relative increase in the validation error over the minimum-so-far. The GL5 criterion stops the execution when the parameter GL becomes higher than 10%.

$$GL(k) = \left(\frac{V(k)}{\min_{j \leq k} V_j} - 1 \right) \tag{7}$$

To choose a data set of training patterns for the K-NN was used uniform distribution with maximum size of training patterns (600). For each execution a new set of training is chosen. Liu et al., 2003 state that the quality of the K-NN classifier is directly influenced by the k number of its nearest neighbors. Therefore, all training patterns are used as prototypes in the present analysis.

#	Architecture	Clonalg	K-NN	MLP
1	[46.43, 47.57]	[38.44, 40.43]	[41,97, 43,03]	[87.36, 93.84]
2	[48.74, 49.73]	[39.00, 40.74]	[47,45, 48,22]	[88.24, 93.89]
4	[56.46, 57.41]	[42.82, 44.31]	[56,34, 57,40]	[88.77, 94.43]
8	[60.72, 61.81]	[44.73, 45.87]	[58,89, 60,04]	[90.94, 97.13]
16	[63.81, 64.73]	[47.92, 48.54]	[66,19, 67,47]	[90.63, 96.64]
32	[72.83, 73.50]	[52.65, 53.35]	[74,93, 75,74]	[91.68, 97.38]
64	[76.02, 77.11]	[53.62, 55.05]	[79,84, 80,90]	[90.02, 95.91]

Table 1. Analysis of algorithm performance in relation to aggregate training performance

Each algorithm was executed with the same training data, but of different sizes. This served to test the generalization capacity of each algorithm under situations of different quantities of training patterns and analyze their performance. Training sets of the following sizes were used: 1, 2, 4, 8, 16, 32 and 64 patterns per class. For all cases, the classes always have the same number of patterns. The test set has the same 100 patterns for each class. At the end of the training step, the classification rate is calculated for the four algorithms analyzed.

Each algorithm was executed 30 times to obtain the classification rate. Table 1 displays the confidence intervals of the samples for the four algorithms studied. These intervals serve for a grounded comparison between algorithms. The confidence level considered was 95%.

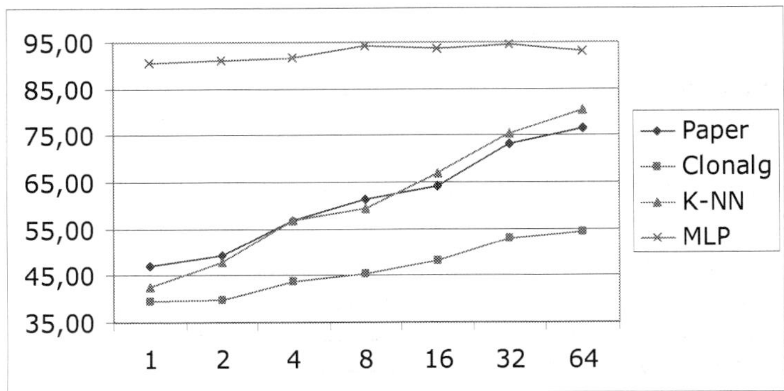

Fig. 5. Evolution of classification rate

The present study demonstrates that the new approach is both more biologically plausible and obtains better results than other AIS, such as clonalg.

Algorithm performance is measured through the classification rate in the data set of test patterns.

As Fig. 5 shows, the proposed algorithm obtained similar results to K-NN. This performance proximity between the proposed architecture and K-NN, with a comparison to Clonalg, suggests that the new approach makes a significant contribution toward improving the results. Considering the average value of the recognition rate, the algorithm proposed obtained a good performance. Analyzing the computational cost of the four algorithms, the MLP presented the best cost-benefit in providing training time when compared to the other algorithms. Despite having the best recognition rate, the architecture proposed had the longest training time of all the algorithms.

Depending on the type of problem studied, the time available for training can be a critical variable. Regarding the analysis of test patterns, this approach, Clonalg and MLP presented similar times. K-NN obtained the longest time of all due to its high computational cost.

8. Conclusions

This chapter describes an application based on Artificial Immune System (AIS) with biologically inspired characteristics, such as the grouping of similar antibodies and memory antibodies were studied to allow the evolution of the AIS. The focus of this chapter was to evaluate the quality of this model to recognize handwritten digits patterns and evolving its performance and comparing it to other technique.

This architecture combined different techniques to form a hybrid immune algorithm. It was biologically inspired, with the use of the Clonal selection principle as a method for propagating the genetic material of the individuals. Biological memory proved to be an efficient functionality for hybridization in the generation of the main population, thereby constituting a more biologically plausible evolutionary view.

The selection of generational survivors proved more biologically plausible, suggesting the organization of antibodies into clusters during the evolution process. This model allowed a more intuitive evolution of antibodies. All the antibodies created during the evolutionary process are stored in an antibody memory in order to avoid the loss of good individuals. It is possible to use good genetic material in the future by employing antibodies from past generations. The best antibodies are responsible for the recognition of the set of test antigens and these individuals will be organized into clusters.

The selection of generational survivors proved more biologically plausible, suggesting the organization of antibodies into clusters during the evolution process. This model allowed a more intuitive evolution of antibodies.

One advantage of this model is the possibility of adaptation to new patterns through the preservation of previously acquired knowledge while continuing to learn new knowledge.

This study offers a good contribution to the literature. It presents an efficient model in comparison to other artificial immune systems, thereby contributing significantly toward an improvement in the results.

9. Acknowledgment

The authors would like to thank CNPq and CAPES (Brazilian research agencies) for their financial support.

10. References

Alexandrino, J. L. & Carvalho Filho, E. C. B. (2006). Investigation of a new artificial immune system model applied to pattern recognition. *Proceedings of International Conference on Hybrid Intelligent Systems*, Auckland, New Zealand, December, 2006, pp. 16–20.

Alexandrino J. L. ; Zanchettin C. & Carvalho Filho, E. C. B. (2007) Artificial Immune System with ART Memory Hibridization. *Proceedings of International Conference on Hybrid Intelligent Systems*, Kaiserslautern, Germany, September, 2007, pp. 59-64.

Carpenter, G. A. & Grossberg, S. (1986). A massively parallel architecture for a self-organizing neural pattern recognition machine. Computer Vision, Graphics, and Image Processing, Vol 37, pp. 54-115.

Dasgupta, D. (2006). Advances in Artificial Immune Systems. *IEEE Computational Intelligence Magazine*.

De Castro, L. N. & Von Zuben, F. J. (2000). The Clonal Selection Algorithm with Engineering Applications, *Proceedings of Genetic and Evolutionary Computation Conference*, Las Vegas, Nevada, USA, July, 2000, pp 36-37.

De Castro, L. N. & Timmis, J. I. (2002). Artificial Immune Systems: A Novel Paradigm for Pattern Recognition, In : *Artificial Neural Networks in Pattern Recognition*, L. Alonso, J. Corchado, C. Fyfe, 67-84, University of Paisley.

Duda, R. O. & Hart, P. E. (2000). *Pattern Classification*, John Wiley and Sons, New York.

Eiben, E. & Smith, J. E. (2003). Introduction to Evolutionary Computing, In : *Natural Computing Series*, MIT Press, Springer, Berlin.

Liu, C. L. ; Nakashima, K. ; Sako, H. & Fujisawa, H. (2003) Handwritten Digit Recognition: Benchmarking of State-of-the-Art Techniques, *Pattern Recognition*, Vol. 36, No. 10, October 2003, 2271-2285.

Moscato, P. (1989) On evolution, search, optimization, GAs and martial arts: toward memetic algorithms, California Institute Technology., Pasadena, CA, Tech. Rep. Caltech Concurrent Comput. Prog. Rep. 826, (1989).

Oliveira, H. C. B. ; Alexandrino, J. L. & Souza M. M. Memetic and genetic algorithms: A comparison among different approaches to solve vehicle routing problem with time windows. *Proceedings of International Conference on Hybrid Intelligent Systems*, Auckland, New Zealand, December, 2006, pp. 55–60.

Ong, Y.-S.; Lim, M.-H.; Zhu, N. and Wong, K.-W. (2006) Classification of Adaptive Memetic Algorithms: A Comparative Study, *IEEE Transactions on Systems, Man, and Cybernetics – part B: Cybernetics*, Vol. 36, No. 1, February 2006.

Prehelt, L. (1994). Proben1 - a set of neural network benchmark problems and benchmarking rules. *Technical Report 21*, University of Karlsruhe.

Rumelhart, D. E.; Hinton, G. E. & Williams, R. J. (1986). Learning internal representations by error propagation, In : *Parallel Distributed Processing,* Vol. 1, pp. 318-362, Cambridge, MIT Press.

Russell, S. J. & Norvig, P. (2003) *Artificial Intelligence: A Modern Approach.* Prentice Hall.

Smith, J. & Krasnogor, N. (2005). A Tutorial for Competent Memetic Algorithms: Model, Taxonomy, and Design Issues. *IEEE Transactions on Evolutionary Computation,* Vol. 9, No. 5, October 2005, 474-488.

21

Designing a Pattern Recognition Neural Network with a Reject Output and Many Sets of Weights and Biases

Le Dung and Makoto Mizukawa
Shibaura Institute of Technology
Japan

1. Introduction

Most neural networks that have been designed to solve the problems of pattern recognition use a supervised training method with a training data set. This data set contains examples of input patterns together with the corresponding output results, and the neural network learns to infer the relationship between input patterns and output results through training.

In supervised training, we often try to find out a set of weights and biases for the neural network in order to classify all patterns in the training data set. In general, training with a larger training data set can reduce the recognizing error rate. However, it would be difficult to find out a good design of neural network that will be able to learn all patterns in a large training data set, because it usually contains some patterns that are difficult to classify. Even if network layers and neurons were added more, there are still some misclassified patterns after a long time training process. The number of these patterns will increase when the size of the training data set is enlarged. If the neural network has to recognize a pattern that approximates in shape to one of the misclassified patterns, the recognition result will be incorrect. Furthermore, if a new pattern is updated, which approximates in shape to one of the misclassified patterns in the old training data set, the neural network may not still classify it, and it will become a new misclassified; thus, the error rate will increase.

In this chapter, we introduce a new design of pattern recognition neural network that has a simple structure but is still able to classify almost all training patterns exactly. The neural network is designed with an especial output that is called "Reject output". With this output, a large training data set can be separated into some parts, and with a smaller number of patterns in each part, they can be classified by the neural network more easily using a distinct set of weights and biases. Additionally, we also design a training method with some phases, which helps the neural network with the reject output to find out not only one but many sets of weights and biases for classifying almost all the training patterns. All the sets of weights and biases have to be kept in the order that they have been received from the training process.

Moreover, the reject output is also used to control the updating process for new patterns more easily. With the reject output, the pattern recognition neural network can produce not only correct or incorrect results but also reject results; therefore, it can control the recognizing rejection and reduce the error rate.

On the other hand, with this design, the size of the neural network can be reduced to be implemented on a hardware-based platform in order to make fast classifiers.

2. Neural network with a reject output and many sets of weights and biases

In this session, the idea of designing a reject output for a pattern recognition neural network will be presented, and then the reason why this neural network uses many sets of weight and biases will be also explained.

2.1 Problems with a large training data set

Most pattern recognition neural networks have been designed with a supervised training algorithm, which uses the training data set to adjust the network's weights and bias so as to minimize an error function, such as the mean squared error function (MSE) (Martin et al., 1996), and try to classify all patterns in the training data set. The neural network can be considered a transfer function that changes a pattern space into an output space, in which each pattern class is clustered in a separate area. Figure 1 shows an example of handwritten digit pattern recognition for the above principle. After training, the neural network will have a set of weights and biases that will be used to recognize the new patterns.

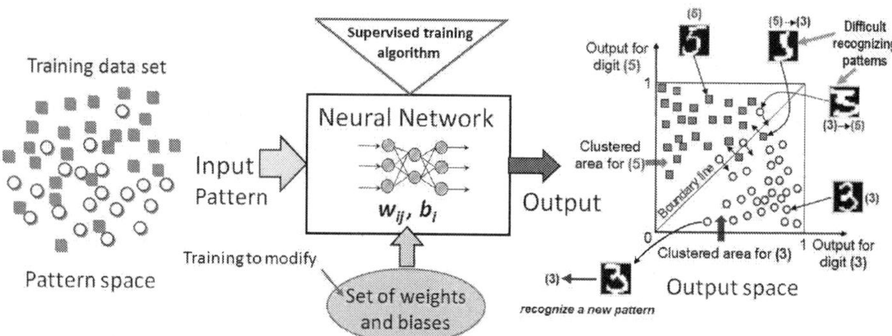

Fig. 1. Neural network is trained with a supervised training algorithm to cluster all training patterns from pattern space into output space.

In general, training neural network with a larger training data set can reduce the recognizing error rate, but there are some problems that we have to consider.

- Training neural network with a larger training data set, it requires more time to minimize the error function, especially when the data set contains some patterns that are difficult to classify correctly. Even though the neural network has been trained by many epochs (Martin et al., 1996), they are still clustered in a wrong area; hence, they are called the misclassified patterns (Gloger et al., 1997). These patterns keep some other patterns staying close to boundary line (Fig. 1); therefore, the error function reduces very slowly in training process.
- The number of the misclassified patterns will increase when the size of the training data set is enlarged. If the neural network has to recognize a pattern that approximates in shape to one of the above patterns, the recognition result will be incorrect.

- When some new patterns are updated to the training data set, the neural network must be trained with all old and new patterns, so it takes more time. Furthermore, if a new pattern approximates in shape to one of the misclassified patterns in the old data set, maybe it will become a new misclassified in the new data set.

- Adding more hidden layers and neurons to the neural network in some cases, it can classify more patterns in the large training data set. However, it is difficult to determine how many hidden layers and neurons we have to add. Moreover, with a large number of neurons and complex connections, the neural network definitely spends more time to bring out a recognition result.

2.2 The idea of reject output

To solve the above problems, we propose a new structure of pattern recognition neural network with an especial output that is called "Reject output", and build a training method corresponding to this structure. The name "Reject output" that means it is used to separate all difficult recognizing patterns (Fig.1) from the training data set. Hence, these patterns are called "Rejected patterns".

In order to explain the idea of the reject output straightforwardly, we will start with the single layer perceptron that was invented in 1957 by Frank Rosenblatt. The single layer perceptron with the perceptron learning rule is only capable to cluster linearly separable patterns (Frank, 1958). In the training pattern space, if there is not any hyperplane (or decision boundary) (Martin et al., 1996), which can separate all types of patterns perfectly, the training process of the perceptron is not guaranteed to converge. This was showed in a famous book entitled "Perceptrons" by Marvin Minsky and Seymour Papert in 1969 with the well-known problem that was called the exclusive-or (XOR) problem (Fig. 2).

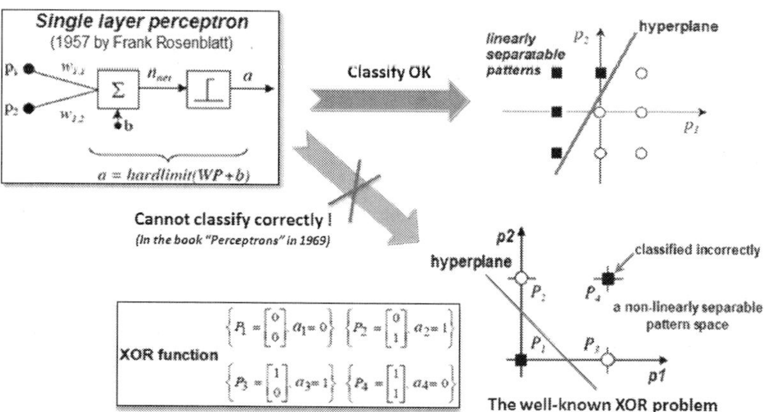

Fig. 2. The single layer perceptron and the XOR problem (Minsky & Papert, 1969).

Until the 1980s, the above limitation of the single layer perceptron was overcome with multilayer perceptron (Rumelhart et al., 1986) and back-propagation learning rule. Figure 3 illustrates the way that a multilayer perceptron with a hidden layer solves the XOR problem.

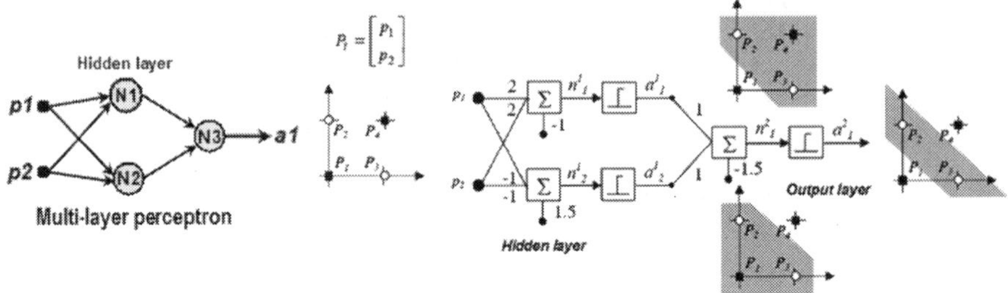

Fig. 3. A two-layer perceptron can solve the XOR problem (Martin et al., 1996).

We realized that adding a reject output to the single layer perceptron is also able to solve the XOR problem. In figure 2, the hyperplane separated the XOR patterns space into two areas for two types of the pattern, but the pattern – (P4) was classified incorrectly. Thus, (P4) is a misclassified pattern and (P1), (P2), (P3) are classified patterns, and now it can be considered as a new classifying problem with two classes: classified and misclassified. In this classifying problem, a hyperplane can be found out easily to separate perfectly misclassified pattern from classified patterns (Fig. 4). The reject output is added to the single layer perceptron to determine this hyperplane. Hence, (P4) will be masked as a rejected pattern and trained by the reject output. If the reject output (a2) is inactive, the normal output (a1) gives the correct result of the XOR function. If the reject output (a2) is active, the result given by the normal output (a1) is incorrect. In this two class problem, that means the inversion of this result (a1) is the correct result (Fig. 4).

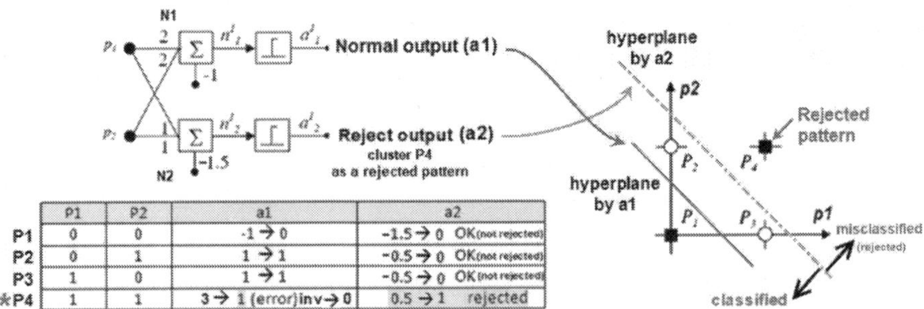

Fig. 4. Using the reject output to solve the XOR problem.

In brief, the reject output plays a role to separate all misclassified patterns from classified patterns. It can also be said that the reject output is used to reject all misclassified patterns from the training data set. However, it cannot be said that the reject output always rejects perfectly all misclassified patterns. The example pattern space in figure 5 shows that the reject output (a2) cannot reject perfectly two misclassified patterns (PA3) (PA4) from all classified patterns that have already classified by the normal output (a1). The reject output tried to separate 2 misclassified patterns (PA3) (PA4) from the others, but it also rejected 2 classified patterns (PB3) (PB4). However, this problem leaded us to the idea to extend the training process in order to find more sets of weight and biases to classify almost all training patterns.

2.3 Neural network uses many sets of weights and biases

After training, the perceptron (Fig 5) with the reject output (a2) and a set of weights and biases can reject four patterns, such as (PA3) (PA4) (PB3) and (PB4). They are thus called rejected patterns. These rejected patterns include both types of training patterns, such as (A) and (B). And now, we can consider them as a new training data set to train the perceptron. With this new training data set, the perceptron can classify easily, and then the second set of weights and biases will be found out from this extended training process.

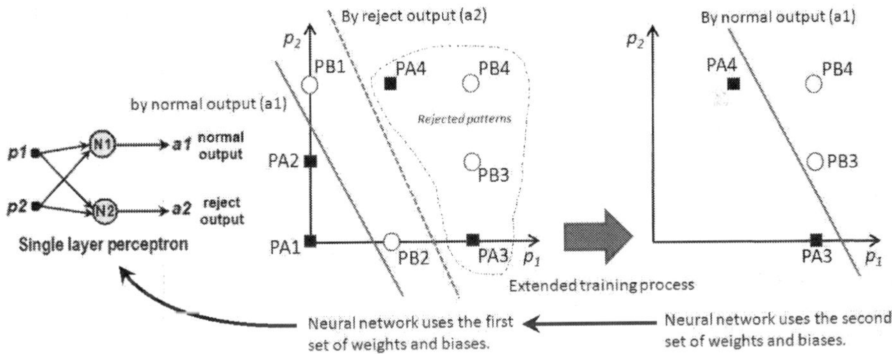

Fig. 5. Separate rejected patterns from training data set and then train them in the extended training process. The perceptron will use 2 sets of weights and biases to classify all patterns.

With a larger training data set, the number of the misclassified patterns will increase, that means the number of the rejected patterns that will be trained in the extended training process will also increase. If the normal output cannot classify all these patterns in the extended training process, the reject output will be used once more to separate misclassified patterns looks like the way in the previous training step. Therefore, we can receive more than 2 sets of weights and biases. The neural network will use all these sets of weights and biases to classify a new pattern in a fixed order. As a result, all the sets of weights and biases have to be kept in the order that we receive them from the training process. The training process can be divided into some phases.

2.4 Advantages and disadvantages

In principle, the pattern space in figure 2 can be clustered by 3 hyperplanes, it means that a multilayer perceptron with a hidden layer included 3 neurons can also cluster all patterns correctly. However, using the reject output and many sets of weights and biases still has some advantages in comparison with a multilayer perceptron without the reject output:

- With a simpler structure, the neural network will run faster. Moreover, this structure can be designed in parallel processing structure on a hardware-based platform; therefore the response time of the hardware-based neural network will be reduced.
- The neural network is designed with a reject output to separate the training data set into some parts, and with a smaller number of patterns in each part, they can be classified more easily.
- If a new training pattern is added to the training data set, maybe it would be a misclassified pattern when the neural network uses the first set of weights and biases,

but it is rejected by the reject output. In this case, we only have to train this pattern with other rejected patterns in the extended training process; thus, the neural network can learn this new pattern more easily.

- With the reject output, the reject rate of recognition can be controlled. We can increase the reject rate to reduce the error rate by changing a threshold at the reject output.

There are some disadvantages of this neural network:

- Because the training process has some phases, the training program is more complex.
- The data set of rejected patterns in the previous training process sometimes has a large number of patterns in the same class in comparison with the other classes; thus, training the neural network with this data set usually gives a not good set of weights and biases. Therefore, we have to select more patterns to add to this data set for training. How to select these patterns that is still a problem for studying.

3. Design of pattern recognition neural network with a reject output

The single layer perceptron with the reject output in the previous session is only a simple example to present basically our idea of neural network designed with a reject output and many sets of weights and biases. In order to interpret in detail the problems of this chapter, a design of neural network for recognizing handwritten digits patterns will be chosen as an illustrative example, because the handwritten digits recognition that is a typical application of pattern recognition neural network (Le & Mizukawa, 2006).

3.1 Structure of the pattern recognition neural network

There are many types of neural network that can be used for pattern recognition (Bishop et al., 1986). The convolutional neural network (CNN) is a famous type of pattern recognition neural network that has been successfully applied to handwritten character recognition (LeCun et al., 1995). The CNNs are designed to recognize visual patterns directly from pixel images with minimal pre-processing (LeCun et al., 1998). Thus, the convolutional structure was chosen for the design of pattern recognition neural network in this chapter. However, we intentionally designed a small and simple CNN, because we want to prove our small CNN can still classify almost all patterns in a large training data set by using the reject output and many sets of weights and biases. That is the main goal of this chapter.

Figure 6 illustrates our CNN designed for recognizing the handwritten digit pattern 16x16 pixels. Therefore, the input layer has 256 neurons arrange in a matrix 16x16. The CNN has only one convolutional layer and one sub-sampling (LeCun et al., 1998). The convolutional layer (C1) has only 2 non-symmetric feature maps of size 7x7 and 5x5. Each neuron in each feature map connects to the input layer in a matrix 4x4 neighbourhood type (LeCun et al., 1998). Moreover, this neighbourhood type is design with two unit overlap (Patrice et al., 2003) for the 7x7 feature map and one unit overlap for the 5x5 feature map. The sub-sampling layer (S1) has 2 feature maps of size 5x5 and 2 feature maps 3x3 using 3x3 neighbourhood type to connect to (C1) with two unit overlap. The neural networks for handwritten digits recognition have almost only 10 outputs corresponding to 10 digits (from 0 to 9); thus, our CNN also has 10 outputs that we called 10 normal outputs.

With this design, our CNN can be considered as a small CNN. We assert that it would be difficult to classify all patterns in a large training data set by the above CNN (without the reject output structure). In fact, we have already tried to train our CNN (without the reject output) with a training data set of 5000 patterns. After more 500 epochs, there are still 267 misclassified patterns. Adding more feature maps to the convolutional layer and sub-sampling layer will help the CNN to classify more patterns in the training data set. However, the size of the CNN will increase considerably and there are still some misclassified patterns. The consideration leads us to design the reject output for our CNN to cluster all misclassified patterns, and then they are extracted from the training data set in order to set up a new training data set for classifying in the extended process (Fig. 6).

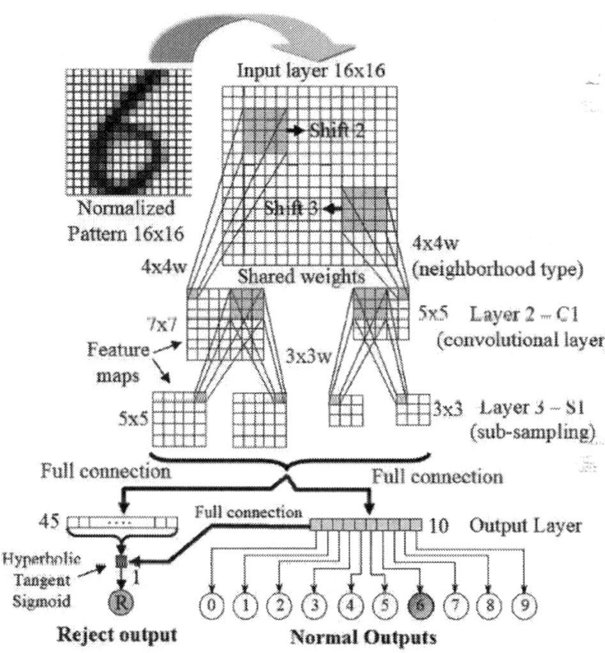

Fig. 6. A small convolutional neural network is designed with the reject output.

3.2 Design of the reject output

With the role of the reject output to classify all rejected patterns, which included all misclassified patterns and some classified patterns, the design of the reject output will be considered as a design of neural network. Therefore, we added to the CNN not only one neuron for the reject output but also a hidden layer before the reject output (Fig. 6). The hidden layer has 45 neurons corresponding to 45 areas between any two of ten directions in the patterns space. In fact, we have already tried to use 10, 25, 45, 55 and 100 neurons for this hidden layer and finally the hidden layer with 45 neurons is the best selection for the ability and speed of classification. All neurons of this hidden layer are fully connected to the sub-sampling layer (S1) of CNN. Especially, the reject output also connects to 10 normal outputs, because the values of 10 normal outputs are considered as important data for the rejection. Although 46 neurons are added to the CNN, it is still a small CNN in comparison with other CNN (LeCun et al., 1998) (Patrice et al., 2003). The activation function of the reject output neuron is Hyperbolic Tangent Sigmoid that differs from 10 normal outputs with Log-Sigmoid function. Therefore, the value of the reject output is in range between -1 and +1.

$$\text{Reject output value} = a \quad - \quad \frac{e^{n_{net}} \quad e^{n_{net}}}{e^{n_{net}} + e^{n_{net}}} \tag{1}$$

a> threshold → the input pattern is rejected
a≤ threshold → the input pattern is not rejected

The threshold value should be determined for the reject output in order to decide between rejected pattern and un-rejected pattern. We will discuss this problem in section 4.

4. The training method with the reject output

Our training method is designed for a training process with many phases. The number of phases depends on the training data set that is used in the training process. If the training data set is not so large, the training process is often performed in four basic phases. With a larger training data set, the training process needs more extend phases. On the other hand, the training method is also concerned with the case when there are some new patterns that should be update to the training data set. For training the CNN by minimizing the mean squared error function (MSE), we have chosen the back-propagation algorithm (Bishop et al., 1986), which is perhaps the most widely used training algorithm for multilayer feedforward networks (Martin et al., 1996).

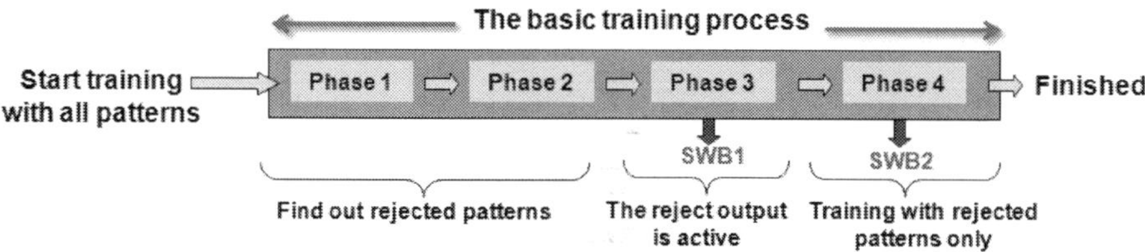

Fig. 7. The basic training process with four basic phases.

4.1 Four basic phases in the training process
- **The first phase**: the neural network is trained with all patterns in the training data set. The reject output is not active, that means the reject output neuron and 45 neurons in the hidden layer is not connected to the neural network. Back-propagation algorithm is used for 10 normal outputs. We use online-training method with 10 learning rates that are distributed for 10 outputs corresponding to their error values (Le & Mizukawa, 2006). In this phase, the biggest learning rate was used that is 0.5. This method makes the MSE to reduce faster. Our training software always tracks the decrease of MSE and the current total of misclassified patterns. Until two values reduce very slowly, we will switch to the second phase. After this phase, if there are some misclassified patterns, they will be marked as rejected patterns.
- **The second phase:** The neural network is still trained with all patterns but there is a small change. After the first phase, all misclassified patterns have already marked as rejected patterns, and the remains of training data set are classified patterns. To

separate all misclassified patterns from the classified patterns in the next phase more easily, in the second phase we train the neural network with all classified patterns in normal manner, but train all outputs with zero value for all rejected patterns. This training manner can push all rejected patterns toward the root (Fig. 8); thus, they will be clustered more easily in the third phase. However, in this phase, the reject output is still not active. The MSE usually continues to reduce in this phase, and we can increase the learning rate. Until MSE attains a low value, we will switch to the third phase. However, before doing the third phase, we should check all the rejected patterns and mark the rejected patterns again. In fact, some of the rejected patterns are classified correctly after the second phase; thus, they should be marked as the classified patterns.

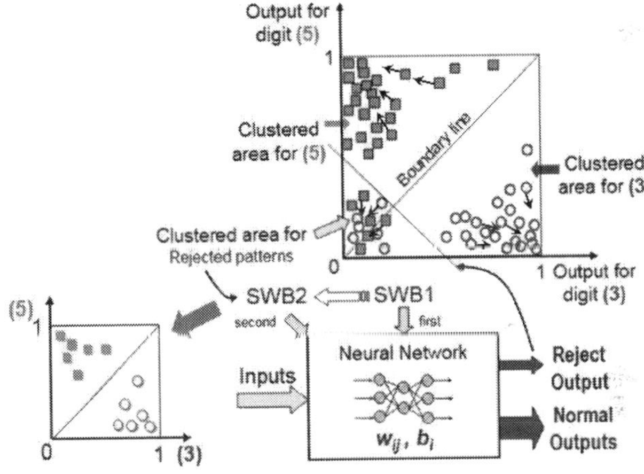

Fig. 8. Training the neural network with rejected patterns.

- **The third phase:** All patterns are used for training, and the reject output is active now to cluster all rejected patterns that were marked in the second phase. That is the most important phase in our training method.

In this phase, when a training pattern is placed into the input layer, the training program has already known the pattern is one of rejected or un-rejected pattern that correspond with misclassified or classified pattern in the second phase. If this pattern is one of rejected patterns, the neural network will be trained with value 0 for all ten normal outputs and value 1 for the reject output. If the pattern is an un-rejected pattern (or classified pattern), it will be classified by the corresponding normal output and the reject output is trained with value -1. In this manner, we want to continue clustering all rejected patterns in the area that is near the root point (Fig. 8).

We realize that the number of the rejected patterns is always smaller than the number of the un-rejected pattern, and if the neural network was trained with all rejected and un-rejected patterns in the original order of them in the training data set, the training process would take a long time to converge. Thus, the rejected patterns and the un-rejected patterns should be placed one after the other into the input layer of the neural network for training. The training software can do it very easy. As a result, the rejected patterns are used in rotation in each training epoch; thus, they usually are clustered by the reject output faster than the un-rejected patterns.

The reject output value is always in range from -1 to +1. The neural network uses the reject output to cluster for the rejected patterns with value 1 and for the un-rejected patterns with value -1. Therefore, a threshold value R has been determined for the reject output to separate all the rejected patterns from the un-rejected patterns (Fig. 9). That means the minimum value α of all the values of the reject output corresponding to all the rejected patterns must be higher than R, and the maximum value β of all the values of the reject output corresponding to all the un-rejected patterns must be lower than or equal R. The training software can track the α and β in this phase, and the neural network should be trained until $\alpha > \beta$. At that time, the reject output can separate all the rejected patterns from the un-rejected patterns by the threshold R = α.

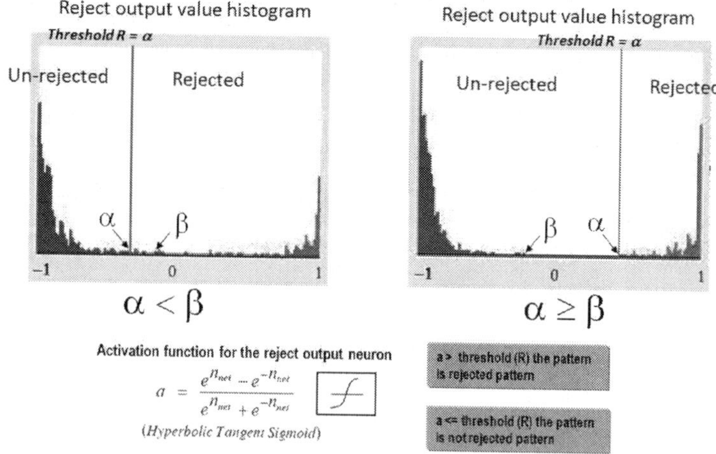

$$a = \frac{e^{n_{net}} - e^{-n_{net}}}{e^{n_{net}} + e^{-n_{net}}}$$

Fig. 9. Determine the threshold (R) for the reject output.

However, we do not need to wait until $\alpha > \beta$, because if $\alpha < \beta$ and R = α, all the rejected patterns are still clustered by the reject output, although some un-rejected patterns are classified as rejected patterns (Fig. 9). It is no problem, because these patterns will be classified again in the next phase. Thus, if α is still smaller than β after hundreds of epochs, we should check all the training patterns and mark the rejected patterns again. If a pattern has already clustered by the rejected output, it is still marked as a rejected pattern. If a pattern is not classified correctly by the normal outputs, it should be marked as a rejected pattern. As the result, the number of the patterns that were marked as the rejected patterns may be changed in this phase. In brief, the rejected patterns and un-rejected patterns are classified flexibly. The threshold value R can be used to control the reject rate of the neural network. After this phase, we have the first set of weights and biases (SWB1) and the threshold value R for the reject output separated the training data set into two parts.

- **The fourth phase:** We must reset all weights and biases in order to start training the neural network with only the rejected patterns that have been classified by the reject output in the third phase. The reject output is not active. If the number of the rejected patterns is not so large, the training process will converge in a short time. However, if the number of the rejected patterns is too small in comparison with the total of patterns in the training data set, or it includes a large number of patterns in the same class in comparison with the other classes, the set of weights and biases that we received in this phase is usually not good for recognizing. Therefore, we have to select more patterns to add to this training phase. In fact, we have had to use a smaller threshold value R to reject provisionally some patterns for this training phase. After this phase, the second set of weights and biases (SWB2) is determined. The training process is over and the neural network has two sets of weights and biases for recognizing.

4.2 Extended phases

If the number of the rejected pattern is large, the neural network might be not able to classify all of them in the fourth phase. Thus, the training process must be continued with some extended phases. The reject output will be used again to separate the set of the rejected patterns into 2 parts for classifying with the extend phases look like the third phase and the fourth phase (Fig. 10). In that way, we can separate a large training data set into more than two parts and use only one neural network with many sets of weights and biases to classify all patterns in each part. All the sets of weights and biases should be numbered in the order that we received them in the training process. If the size of neural network is reduced, the training process will require more extended phases, and the neural network will have many sets of weights and biases.

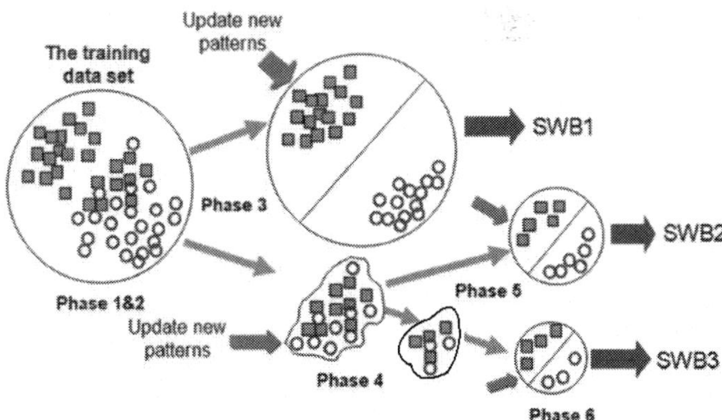

Fig. 10. With the reject output, a large training data set can be separated into more two parts to classify by using many sets of weights and biases (SWB).

4.3 Update new patterns to the training data set

First of all, we use the neural network to recognize all new patterns and check the recognition results. There are some cases of the recognizing result for each new pattern and the corresponding update method as follow:

- The new pattern is recognized incorrectly (misclassified) but the reject output does not reject this pattern. Thus, the pattern should be trained as an un-rejected pattern in the third phase. After some epochs, if the pattern cannot be classified correctly, it will be marked as a rejected pattern for training with the reject output. After the reject output can be able to reject this pattern, it will be used to train the neural network in forth phase.

- In the case of the recognizing result is not correct and the reject output rejects this pattern, this pattern should be trained in the fourth phase.
- If the new pattern is recognized correctly but the reject output rejects this pattern, we should try to train this pattern as an un-rejected pattern in the third phase. If it takes a long time, the updating process should stop and return to the starting point, and then training this pattern as a rejected pattern in the fourth phase.
- In the case of the recognizing result is correct and the reject output does not rejects this pattern, the pattern could be trained as an un-rejected pattern in the third phase.
- We realize that the third phase and the fourth phase sometimes can perform simultaneously; thus, the time that we spend for updating new patterns is reduced.

5. Experimental result

The goal of our experiments is to prove a not big neural network with the reject output can be able to classify almost all training patterns and the recognizing ability of the neural network is improved.

The patterns that we use for training and testing are from the well-known MNIST database of handwritten digits (http://yann.lecun.com/exdb/mnist). Our software extracts the patterns in the MNIST database (with 60000 training patterns) to build our own data sets, such as data sets of 600 patterns and 5000 patterns. We also built two testing data set with 200 patterns and 1000 patterns from the MNIST testing database (with 10000 testing patterns).

- **The first experiment**: The data set of 600 patterns was used to train the neural network. After 30 epochs of training in the first phase and second phase, 22 misclassified patterns were found out. They were masked as rejected patterns for training with the reject output in the third phase. In the third phase, 22 rejected patterns were separated easily from the training data set by the reject output with threshold R=0.76. With this threshold, these 22 patterns do not include any un-rejected patterns (we mean that is the case of $\alpha > \beta$). Then, these patterns were classified completely in the fourth phase. We received 2 sets of weights and biases (SWB1 and SWB2). Moreover, we also continuously tried to train the neural network in the first phase with hundreds of epochs but there were still 14 misclassified patterns. After this work, the neural network also has a set of weights and biases (SWB0) for testing. It is clear that the neural network with reject output and two 2 sets of weights and biases (SWB1 and SWB2) can classify all 600 training patterns correctly.

The recognizing ability of the neural network has been tested with 200 and 1000 testing patterns in some cases that were showed in Table 1.

From the testing results in Table I, we can see that the number of errors will be reduced if we use SWB1 and SWB2. If the neural network uses only SWB1 and the reject output is active, the number of errors is reduced more but we have to accept a number of rejected patterns, which may include some patterns that have been classified correctly by the normal outputs.

Testing data set	Use SWB0	Use SWB1 not use reject output	Use SWB1 with reject output	Use SWB1 and SWB2 with reject output
200 patterns	7 errors	11 errors	0 error 12 rejected	0 error
1000 patterns	166 errors	167 errors	138 errors 36 rejected	146 errors

Table 1. Testing results after training the neural network with 600 patterns.

We also tested the neural network with some values of threshold R. Table 2 illustrates the testing results when we use the threshold R=0, R=0.5, R=0.76 and R=0.85 for the reject output. The threshold R=0.76 is equal the minimum value α of 22 values of the reject output corresponding to 22 rejected patterns that were found out in the third phase. From table 2, we can see that the result is best with R=α.

Test	R=0.76 (=α)	R=0	R=0.5	R=0.9
1000 patterns	146 errors 36 rejected 8 errors with SWB2	158 errors 94 rejected 53 errors with SWB2	150 errors 66 rejected 30 errors with SWB2	163 errors 5 rejected 0 errors with SWB2

Table 2. Testing the reject output with some threshold values

- **The second experiment**: we use the data set of 5000 patterns for training. The number of patterns that were marked as the rejected patterns for the fourth phases is 426, but that included 159 un-rejected patterns (we mean that is the case $\alpha<\beta$). With R=0.59, there were still 11 rejected patterns that the reject output cannot classified correctly. After checking these patterns, we realize that they look like other patterns very much; thus, it is difficult to cluster them by the rejected output. They should be rejected from the training data set because they are bad patterns (Fig. 11).

In the fourth phase, we tried to classify the above 421 patterns, but after hundreds of epochs, there were still 36 rejected patterns classified not correctly. Thus, we had to continue with two extended phases. After these extended phases, we found out 2 sets of weights and biases, such as SWB2 and SWB3. As a result, the neural network uses three sets of weights and biases to classify the 5000 training patterns with only 11 errors. The neural network was also tested with the 1000 testing patterns. Table 3 shows that the error rate will be reduced, if the neural network uses many SBWs with the reject output.

	Wrong output	Right output	Reject output		Wrong output	Right output	Reject output
7 >>> 7	7 (0.9989)	3 (0.0067)	-0.993	5 >>> 9	9 (0.9820)	5 (0.9764)	-1.000
9 >>> 0	0 (0.9984)	9 (0.0000)	-0.997	4 >>> 5	5 (0.7182)	4 (0.5982)	-1.000

Fig. 11. Some bad patterns cannot be clustered by the reject output.

We also tried to train the neural network with 60000 patterns from the MNIST training database. That is really larger number for our small neural network. After the third phase, with SWB1 and R=0 the reject output separated 12159 rejected patterns from the 60000 patterns, and there are 5903 un-rejected patterns that were clustered by the reject output. The neural network was trained with only these rejected patterns in the fourth phase and we received the SWB2, but there are still 2445 misclassified patterns.

Testing data set	Use SWB1 not use reject output	Use SWB1 and SWB2 with reject output	Use SWB1,SWB2 and SWB3 with reject output
1000 patterns	119 errors	103 errors 85 rejected	97 errors

Table 3. Testing results after training the neural network with 5000 patterns

Table 4 illustrates the testing results when the neural network tries to classify 10000 testing patterns from the MNIST testing database. We also see that the error rate 8.7 % will be reduced to 5.4 %, if the neural network uses SBW1 and SWB2 with the reject output.

Testing data set	Use only SWB1	Use SWB1 with reject output	Use SWB1,SWB2 with reject output
10000 patterns	870 errors	225 errors and 1699 rejected	540 errors

Table 4. Testing results after training the neural network with 60000 patterns

6. Future work

The main objective of our research is to design a smart vision sensor for the robots. This sensor will be designed with pattern recognition neural networks that require a small response time. The design of reject output for pattern recognition neural network in this chapter can reduce the size of pattern recognition neural network; thus, it can be applied to design our smart vision sensor in the near future. The structure of neural network with reject output has already opened some abilities to design the neural network in parallel processing structure that will be implemented on FPGA to make the smart sensor run faster (Fig. 12).

The manner that the neural network using the reject output to update a new pattern is one of studying directions to make the smart sensor can enhance its ability after it is commissioned.

7. Conclusion

Adding the reject output to the pattern recognition neural network is an approach to help the neural network can classify almost all patterns of a training data set by using many sets of weights and biases, even if the neural network is small. With a smaller number of neurons, we can implement the neural network on a hardware-based platform more easily and also reduce the response time of it. With the reject output the neural network can produce not only right or wrong results but also reject results. It is significant, if we design a neural network to help a robot to interact with people. The reject results can be accepted by the robot in this interaction process. If the neural network rejected a pattern, the robot would ask people to make the pattern again that looks like we talk "Pardon me".

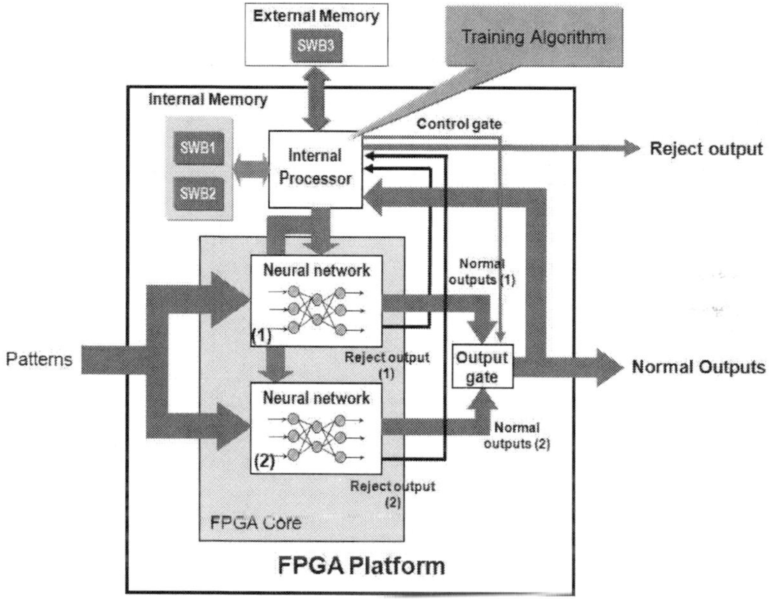

Fig. 12. Implement the neural network with the reject output on FPGA in parallel structure.

8. References

Bishop, C.M. (1995). *"Neural Networks for Pattern Recognition"*, Oxford University Press, USA

Frank Rosenblatt (1958), *"The Perceptron: A Probabilistic Model for Information Storage and Organization in the Brain"*, Cornell Aeronautical Laboratory, Psychological Review, v65, No. 6, pp. 386-408.

Gloger J. M., Kaltenmeier A., Mandler E., Andrews L.. (1997). "Reject Management in a Handwriting Recognition System", *Proceedings of the 4th International Conference on Document Analysis and Recognition*, pp: 556–559, ISBN: 0-8186-7898-4, IEEE Computer Society Washington, DC, USA

LeCun, Y., Bottou, L., Bengio, Y., Haffner, P. (1998). "Gradient-based learning applied to document recognition", *Proceedings of the IEEE*, vol. 86, pp. 2278--2324, ISSN: 0018-9219, November 1998

LeCun, Y., L. D. Jackel, L. Bottou, A. Brunot, C. Cortes, J. S. Denker, H. Drucker, I. Guyon, U. A. Muller, E. Sackinger, P. Simard, and V. Vapnik. (1995). "Comparison of learning algorithms for handwritten digit recognition," *International Conference on Artificial Neural Networks, (F. Fogelman and P. Gallinari, eds.)*, pp. 53-60, Paris

Le Dung, Makoto Mizukawa. (2006). "Automatic handwritten postcode reading system using image processing and neural network technology", *Proceedings of SICE System Integration Division Conference (SI2006)*, pp. 930-931, Hokkaido, December 2006.

Martin T. Hagan, Howard B. Demuth, Mark Beale. (1996). *"Neural Network Design"*, Thomson Learning, ISBN: 981-240-485-6

Minsky, Marvin and Seymour Papert (1969), *"Perceptrons: An introduction to Computational Geometry"*, MIT Press.

Patrice Y. Simard, Dave Steinkraus, John C. Platt. (2003). "Best Practices for Convolutional Neural Networks Applied to Visual Document Analysis", *International Conference on Document Analysis and Recognition (ICDAR)*, pp. 958-962, IEEE Computer Society, Los Alamitos, 2003

Rumelhart, David E., Hinton, Geoffrey E., Williams, Ronald J. (1986), *"Learning internal representations by error propagation"*, ISBN: 0-262-68053-X, MIT Press

22

A SIFT-Based Fingerprint Verification System Using Cellular Neural Networks

Giancarlo Iannizzotto and Francesco La Rosa
University of Messina (VisiLAB)
Italy

1. Introduction

Recently, with the increasing demand of high security, person identification has become more and more important in our everyday life. The purpose of establishing the identity is to ensure that only a legitimate user, and not anyone else, accesses the rendered services. The traditional identification methods are based on *"something that you possess"* and *"something that you know"* such as key, user-ID, password, PIN, etc. Examples of such applications include secure access to buildings, airports, computer systems, cellular phones and ATM machines. Another family of identification methods uses biometric characteristics. Biometric recognition, or simply *biometrics,* refers to the automatic recognition of individuals based on their physiological and/or behavioral characteristics. Biometrics allows us to confirm or establish an individual's identity based on *who she is*, rather than by *what she possesses* (e.g., an ID card) or *what she knows* (e.g., a password). Current biometric systems make use of identifiers such as fingerprints, hand geometry, iris, face and voice to establish an identity. Biometric systems also introduce an aspect of user convenience. For example, they alleviate the need for a user to remember multiple passwords associated with different applications.

Fingerprint characterization is the oldest and the prevalent member of the biometric family and has been extensively used for person identification in a number of commercial, civil and forensic applications.

The question that is being asked about biometric technologies in general and about fingerprints in particular is that whether these technologies can work all the time, everywhere, and in all contexts for reliable person identification and authentication.

One of the design criteria for building such completely automatic and reliable fingerprint identification (and verification) systems is that the underlying sensing, representation, and matching technologies must also be very robust.

In practice, due to variations in impression conditions, ridge configuration, skin conditions (aberrant formations of epidermal ridges of fingerprints, postnatal marks, occupational marks), acquisition devices and non-cooperative attitude of subjects a significant percentage of acquired fingerprint images is of poor quality. In order to ensure that the performance of a feature extraction algorithm will be robust with respect to the quality of input fingerprint images, an enhancement algorithm which can improve the clarity of the ridge structures is useful. Most of the fingerprint image enhancement methods (Gabor, directional or anisotropic filter based) use convolution to obtain the results. Another way to address these requirements of robust performance is to adopt robust representation schemes that capture the discriminatory information in fingerprint impressions.

Also, thanks to the increasing power of computers and to the substantial improvement in capture devices, the use of fingerprint for personal identification in portable applications is very significant.

For purpose of commercialization, a fingerprint verification system has to take the following four crucial factors into consideration: *processing speed, recognition rate, power consumption* and *size*. These approaches described are computationally very expensive tasks.

An alternative to the traditional approaches is provided by the *Cellular Neural Network* (CNN) paradigm, introduced by Prof. L.O. Chua in 1988 (Chua & Yang, 1988a; 1988b). A CNN consists of a network of first order nonlinear circuits, locally interconnected by linear (resistive) connections.

The rapidly growing field of Cellular Neural Networks (CNNs) and analogic cellular computing CNN-UM (Chua & Roska, 1993) has found a number of potential applications (Chua & Yang, 1988b), especially in image and video processing problems (Moreira-Tamayos & Gyvez, 1999; Iannizzotto et al., 2005, Costantini et al., 2004) where real-time signal processing is required. This architecture provides an efficient tool to explore the rich world of dynamical systems and makes possible to introduce new approaches for pattern recognition (Szirànyi & Csicsvàri, 1993; Theodoridis & Koutroumbas, 2006) and object classification (Milanova & Buker, 2000; Bálya, 2003), relevant problems in image processing.

CNNs can process information at very high speeds comparable to today's supercomputers. The regular lattice architecture of CNNs allows massive parallelism that makes it very suitable for performance-demanding applications in image processing.

Fingerprint-based identification (and verification) systems using CNNs are very promising for personal identification and in particular, if incorporated in a VLSI chip, for use in portable applications.

They have the potential to *realize a fingerprint-based identification (or verification) system on one chip* assuming that it is possible to incorporate a capacitive or optical sensor on the same chip.

Various approaches to implement real-time person verification and identification systems on CNNs have been proposed (Su et al., 2006; Gao et al., 2001; Gao & Moschytz, 2001; 2004). However in (Su et al., 2006) the level of accuracy and robustness of the fingerprint verification system was not investigated and in (Gao & Moschytz, 2004) are not used public domain fingerprint databases.

The most popular method for fingerprint representation is based on local landmarks called minutiae. The minutiae-based systems first locate the points, often referred as minutiae points, in fingerprint image where the fingerprint ridges either terminate or bifurcate (see fig. 1) and then match minutiae relative placement in a given finger and the stored template (Jain et al., 1997).

While minutiae-based fingerprint verification systems have shown to be fairly accurate, further improvements are needed for acceptable performance, especially in applications involving very large scale databases.

The aim of this chapter is to re-formulate an algorithm for fingerprint verification using Scale Invariant Feature Transform (SIFT) (Lowe 1999; Lowe, 2004; Park et al., 2008) in such a way to exploit the high degree of parallelism inherent in a single-layer CNN.

SIFT detects and describes local features in images. The SIFT features are local and based on the appearance of the object at particular interest points and are invariant to image scale and rotation. They are also robust to changes in illumination, noise, occlusion and minor changes in viewpoint. In addition, the SIFT features are discriminant and allow for correct object identification with low probability of mismatch and are easy to match against a (*large*) database of local features (Bicego et al., 2006).

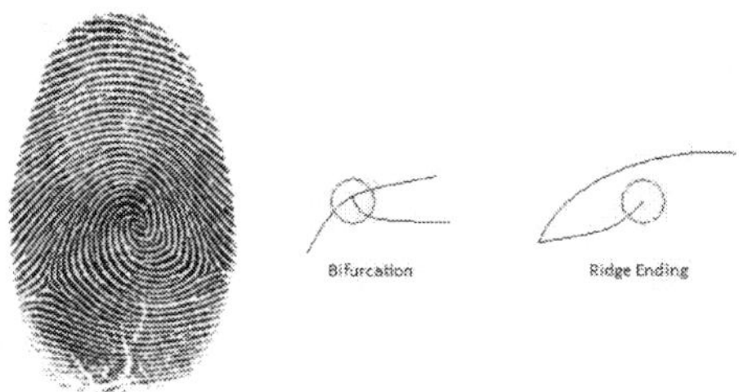

Fig. 1. An example of bifurcation and ridge ending in a fingerprint image

In our implementation we extract characteristic SIFT feature points in scale space and perform a matching based on the texture information around the feature points using the SIFT operator (Chikkerur, 2006).

The input to the system is a gray level fingerprint image where a number of feature points (*keypoints*) are located using a difference-of-Gaussian function in a scale space. A descriptor, representing each feature point and invariant to rotation, scale and change of lighting, is calculated.

In this chapter we describe the technique developed and present a set of experimental results. In the final section we draw our conclusions on the work carried out.

2. Scale invariant feature transform

There are three typical categories of fingerprint verification methods: i) minutiae, ii) correlation, and iii) ridge features. However, considering the types of information used, a method can be broadly categorized as minutiae based or texture based. While the minutiae based fingerprint verification systems have shown high accuracy (Jain et al., 1997; Ratha et al., 1996), they ignore the rich information in ridge patterns which can be useful to improve the matching accuracy. Most of the texture based matchers use the entire fingerprint image or local texture around minutiae points (Chikkerur et al., 2006). Using local texture is more desirable because the global texture will be more sensitive to non-linear and non-repeatable deformation of fingerprint images. When the local texture is collected based on the minutiae points, the texture based fingerprint representation is again limited and its performance depends upon the reliability of extracted minutiae points. It is not obvious how one could capture the rich discriminatory texture information in the fingerprints that is not critically dependent on finding minutiae points or core points.

For the purpose of extending characteristic feature points of fingerprint beyond minutiae points, we adopt Scale Invariant Feature Transform (SIFT) (Lowe, 2004). SIFT extracts repeatable characteristic feature points from an image and generates descriptors representing the texture around the feature points. In (Park, 2008) the authors have demonstrated the utility of SIFT representation for fingerprint-based identification. As the SIFT feature points have already demonstrated their efficacy in generic object recognition problems, in the same way this representation is also stable and reliable for many of the matching problems related to the fingerprint domain. Further, since SIFT feature points are based on texture analysis of the entire scale space, these feature points are probably robust to the fingerprint quality and deformation variation.

The features are selected to be invariant to image scale and rotation, and to provide robust matching across a substantial range of affine distortion, addition of noise and partial change in lighting.

The features are highly distinctive, in the sense that a single feature can be correctly matched with high probability against a large database of features from many images, providing a basis for object and scene recognition. In the original implementation, the recognition proceeds by matching individual features to a database of features from known objects using a fast nearest-neighbour algorithm, followed by a generalized Hough transform to identify clusters belonging to a single object, and finally performing verification through least-squares solution for consistent pose parameters.

Following are the major stages of computation used to generate the set of image features:

- **Scale-space extrema detection:** to identify potential interest points invariant to scale it's used a difference-of-Gaussian function (see fig.2).
- **Keypoint localization:** at each candidate location, a detailed model is fit to determine location and scale. Keypoints are selected based on measures of their stability.
- **Orientation assignment:** one or more orientations are assigned to each keypoint location based on local image gradient directions. All future operations are performed on image data that has been transformed relative to the assigned orientation (providing invariance to these transformations).
- **Keypoint descriptor:** the local image gradients are measured at the selected scale in the region around each keypoint. These are transformed into a representation that allows for significant levels of local shape distortion and change in illumination.

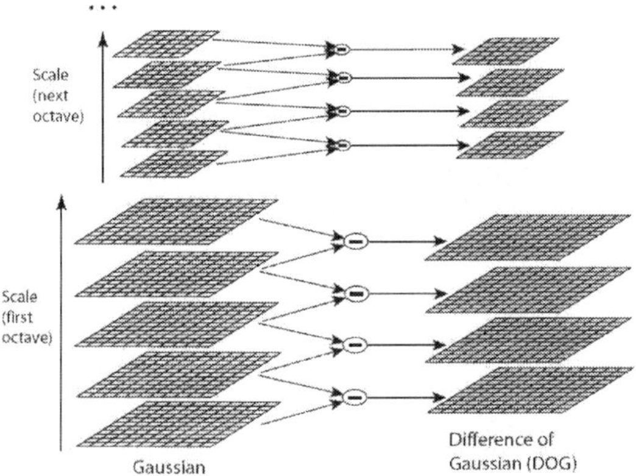

Fig. 2. Scale-space extrema detection

This approach has been named Scale Invariant Feature Transform (**SIFT**), as it transforms image data into scale-invariant coordinates relative to local features.

An important property of this approach is that it generates large numbers of features that densely cover the image over the full range of scales and locations. A typical image of size 500x500 pixels will give rise to about 2000 stable features (although this number depends on both image content and choices for various parameters). The quantity of features is particularly important for object recognition, where the ability to detect small objects in cluttered backgrounds requires that at least 3 features be correctly matched from each object for reliable identification.

For image matching and recognition, SIFT features are first extracted from a set of reference images and stored in a database. A new image is matched by individually comparing each feature from the new image to this previous database. In seminal work of Lowe (Lowe, 1999) the finding candidate matching features is based on Euclidean distance of their feature vectors. Specifically, a fast nearest-neighbour algorithm is used to perform this computation rapidly against large databases. In our implementation, we have evaluated two different metrics: the Lowe and Szatmári (Szatmári, 2006) metrics.

3. Cellular Neural Network

As stated in the introduction, a CNN consists of an array of non-linear, locally interconnected, first order circuits. As connections are local, each cell is connected only to the cells belonging to its neighbourhood, as it is shown in fig.3.

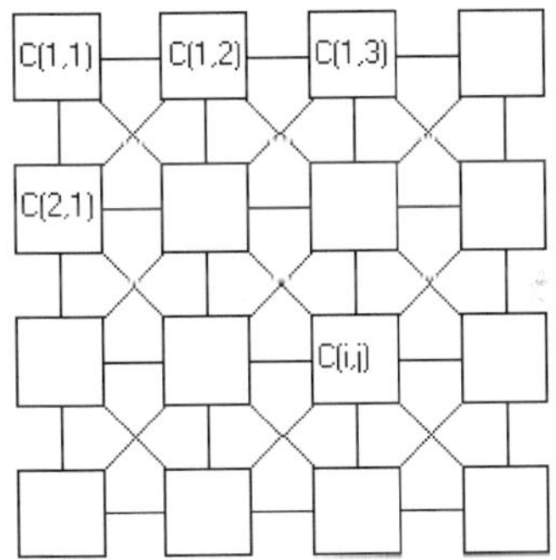

Fig. 3. Architecture of a CNN

If we call the generic cell in the MxN array as C_{ij} (the cell on the i-th row and the j-th column of the array), a formal definition of the neighbourhood of radius r of the cell Cij, $N_{r(i,j)}$, is given by:

$$N_r(i,j) = \left\{ C_{kl} : max\left\{ (k-i(,(l-j(\right\} \leq r, 1 \leq k \leq M, 1 \leq l \leq N \right\} \tag{1}$$

An MxN CNN, with MxN cells arranged in M rows and N columns, is entirely characterized by a set of MxN non-linear differential equations, associated with each cell. The generic cell x_{ij} is described by the following relations:

$$C\frac{dv_{x_{ij}}(t)}{dt} = -R^{-1}v_{x_{ij}}(t) + \sum_{kl \in N_r} A_{ij,kl} v_{y_{kl}}(t) + \sum_{kl \in N_r} B_{ij,kl} v_{u_{kl}}(t) + I_{ij}$$

$$+ \sum_{kl \in N_r} A1_{ij,kl}\left(\Delta v_{yy}\right) + \sum_{kl \in N_r} B1_{ij,kl}\left(\Delta v_{uu}\right) + \sum_{kl \in N_r} D_{ij,kl}\left(\Delta v\right) \tag{2}$$

$$v_{y_{ij}}(t) = f\left(v_{y_{ij}}(t)\right) = 0.5\left(\left(v_{x_{ij}}(t)+1\left(-\left(v_{x_{ij}}(t)-1\left(\right)\right.\right.\right.$$

where:

$$\Delta v_{yy} = v_{y_{kl}}(t) - v_{y_{ij}}(t)$$

$$\Delta v_{uu} = v_{u_{kl}} - v_{u_{ij}}$$

$$\Delta v = v_{u,x,y_{kl}}(t) - v_{u,x,y_{ij}}(t) \tag{3}$$

$$\left(v_{x_{ij}}(t) \right| \le 1, \left(v_{u_{ij}} \right| \le 1, \left(I_{ij} \right| \le v_{max}$$

$$1 \le i \le M, 1 \le j \le N$$

where $v_{x_{ij}}$, $v_{u_{ij}}$, $v_{y_{ij}}$ are respectively the state, input and output voltage of the CNN cell.

The state and output vary in time, whereas the input is kept constant. The indexes ij refer to the position of the cell in the 2D grid, while $kl \in N_r$ is a grid point in the neighborhood within the radius r of the cell ij. Matrices A, B, $A1$, $B1$, D, called *templates*, describe the interaction of the cell with its neighbourhood and regulate the evolution of the CNN state and output vectors. Template connections can be realised by voltage-driven current generators.

$A_{ij,kl}$ is called linear feedback template, $B_{ij,kl}$ the linear control template, I_{ij} is a current bias in the cell. $A1_{ij,kl}$, $B1_{ij,kl}$ and $D_{ij,kl}$ are non-linear templates respectively applied to Δv_{yy}, Δv_{uu} and Δv. $A1_{ij,kl}$ is called difference controlled nonlinear feedback template, $B1_{ij,kl}$ is the difference controlled non-linear control template, $D_{ij,kl}$ is the generalized non-linear generator. The output characteristic f adopted is a sigmoid-type piecewise-linear function.

CNNs are exploited for image processing by associating each pixel of the image to the input or initial state of a single cell. Subsequently, both the state and output of the CNN matrix evolve to reach an equilibrium state. The evolution of the CNN is governed by the choice of the template. A lot of templates have already been defined in order to perform basic image processing operations, like gradient computation, smoothing, hole detection, line deletion, isolated pixel extraction and deletion, and so on. Simple operations can be performed just by using the basic templates A, B, and the bias I, whereas more complicated processing requires the use of the nonlinear templates $A1$, $B1$, and the generalized nonlinear generator D. The proposed algorithm can be totally implemented onto a *"CNN Universal Machine"* (CNN-UM), an hardware structure able to implement CNNs (Chua & Roska, 1993).

The main advantage of using CNNs in image processing is related to the increasing of throughput due to the massive parallelism of the structure, joined to the similar way of signal processing, typical of CNNs. In fact they are able to perform a complete image processing analysis in time of order of 10^{-6} s (by using a CNN hardware implementation), this in form of sequences of simple tasks like array target segmentation, background intensity extraction, target detection and target intensity extraction.

Depending on the type of neurons that are basic elements of the network, it is possible to distinguish continuous-time CNN (CTCNN), discrete-time CNN (DTCNN) (oriented especially on binary image processing), CNN based on multi-valued neurons (CNN-MVN) and CNN based on universal binary neurons (CNN-UBN). CNN-MVN makes possible processing, which is defined by some multiple-valued threshold functions, and CNN-UBN allows processing defined not only by threshold, but also by arbitrary boolean function.

4. The fingerprint verification system

Scale Invariant Feature Transform (SIFT) (Lowe, 2004) was originally developed for general purpose object recognition. SIFT detects stable feature points in an image and performs matching based on the descriptor representing each feature point.

Even though SIFT was originally developed for general purpose object recognition and does not require image preprocessing, we have performed a few preprocessing steps on fingerprint images to obtain better matching performance. The preprocessing is performed in two steps: i) adjusting the graylevel distribution (Csapodi & Roska, 1996) ii) defining a bounding box search area to filter the boundary points of fingerprint. When the fingerprint images show similar texture, the performance is expected to be improved because SIFT uses texture information both for extracting feature points and matching. First, to overcome some apparent differences in gray level distributions, we consider the "image intensity" and adjust the histogram. Second, the boundary area of a fingerprint always causes some feature points to be detected because they are local extrema.

However, the boundary region is different for every fingerprint impression even for the same finger. Therefore, feature points on the fingerprint boundary usually result in false matches. We construct a binary mask that includes only the inner part of a fingerprint and use it to prevent any noisy feature points from being detected on the boundary. In fig.4 is shown a schematic representation of the our algorithm.

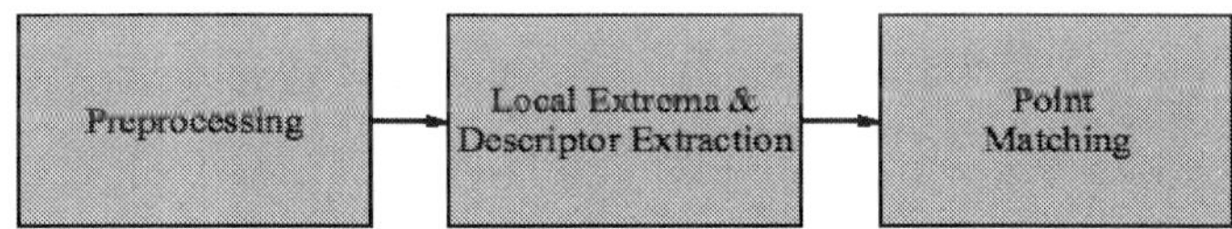

Fig. 4. Flow chart of fingerprint matching using SIFT operator

The feature points are detected using a cascade filtering approach to identify candidate locations that are then examined in further detail. The first stage of keypoint detection is to identify locations and scales that can be assigned under differing "views" of the same object. Detecting locations that are invariant to scale change of the image can be accomplished by searching for stable features using a continuous function of scale known as scale space (Witkin, 1983).

To obtain a scale space (see fig. 2) the initial image is incrementally convolved with Gaussians to produce images separated by a constant factor k in scale space, shown stacked in the left column of fig. 2. Adjacent image scales are subtracted to produce the difference-of-Gaussian images (DOG) shown on the right of fig. 2. The set of Gaussian-smoothed images and DOG images are called an octave. Once a complete octave has been processed, we resample the Gaussian image that has twice the initial value of σ by taking every second pixel in each row and column. As stated in (Park, 2008) a typical number of scales and octaves for SIFT operation is 5 and 6, respectively.

In a CNN, an implementation of the Gaussian filter with aperture σ can be obtained using the *Heat Diffusion* template (Rekeczky et al., 1998; 1999) with *ad hoc* diffusion coefficient (Roska, 1999). As pointed out by Witkin (Witkin, 1983), convolution of the original signal with Gaussians at each scale is equivalent to solving the heat equation with the original image as initial condition.

An example of Heat Diffusion template is as follow:

$$A = \begin{bmatrix} 0.1 & 0.15 & 0.1 \\ 0.15 & 0 & 0.15 \\ 0.1 & 0.15 & 0.1 \end{bmatrix} \quad B = \begin{bmatrix} 0 & 0 & 0 \\ 0 & 0 & 0 \\ 0 & 0 & 0 \end{bmatrix} \quad z = \boxed{0} \qquad (4)$$

where z is the central element of the matrix I (see eq. 2).

In fig. 5 is shown the obtained results applying the Heat Diffusion template on an image of example.

Fig. 5. An example of use of the *Heat Diffusion* template

The standard deviation of the Gaussian filter depend on the a_{ij} matrix elements.

Also, to obtain a difference image it's possible to use the technology described in (Sadeghi-Emamchaie, 1998), where a locally connected analog cellular neural networks (CNNs) is used to implement digital arithmetic arrays; the arithmetic is implemented using a Double-Base Number System (DBNS). Specifically, a CNN array, using a simple non-linear feedback template, with hysteresis, can perform arbitrary length arithmetic with good performance in terms of stability and robustness.

In according to (Lowe, 2004), to obtain a number of feature points we detect the local maxima and minima of the DOG images; each sample point is compared to its eight neighbours in the current image and nine neighbours in the scale above and below (see fig. 2). A feature point is selected only if it is larger than all of these neighbours or smaller than all of them. Then, the same technique is applied for the higher (and lower) octave.

If the first octave is sampled at the same rate as the input image, the highest spatial frequencies will be ignored. This is due to the initial smoothing, which is needed to provide separation of peaks for robust detection.

Therefore, we expand the input image by a factor of 2, using an algorithm of interpolation, prior to building the scale space. In a CNN, an implementation of an algorithm of interpolation (Roska, 1999) can be obtained using the following template:

$$A = \begin{bmatrix} 0 & 0 & -2 & 0 & 0 \\ 0 & -4 & 16 & -4 & 0 \\ -2 & 16 & -39 & 16 & -2 \\ 0 & -4 & 16 & -4 & 0 \\ 0 & 0 & -2 & 0 & 0 \end{bmatrix} \quad B = \begin{bmatrix} 0 & 0 & 0 & 0 & 0 \\ 0 & 0 & 0 & 0 & 0 \\ 0 & 0 & 0 & 0 & 0 \\ 0 & 0 & 0 & 0 & 0 \\ 0 & 0 & 0 & 0 & 0 \end{bmatrix} \quad z = \boxed{0} \qquad (5)$$

In fig. 6 we show an example of interpolation obtained with this template.

The local maximum (and minimum) in a given neighbourhood (see fig. 7) can be computed using a single layer CNN through a difference-controlled template (**Local maxima detector** *template*), as described in (Chua et al., 1993). Each local minimum can also be detected if the input image is inverted. However an improvement of the performances can be obtained using a local maxima detector based on multi-layer CNN (Roska & Chua, 1993).

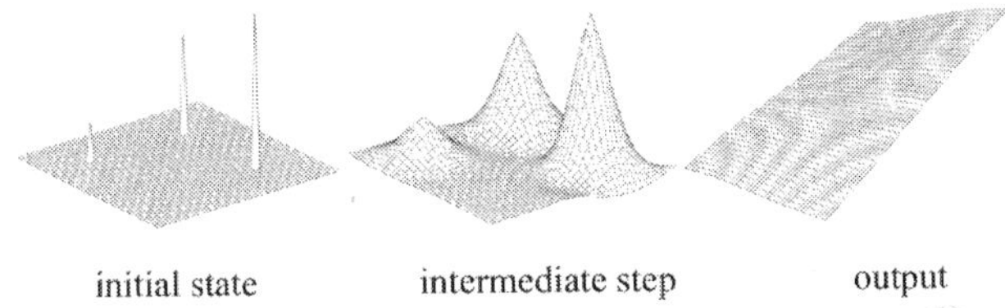

Fig. 6. Fitting a surface on three given points. Image size: 80x80.

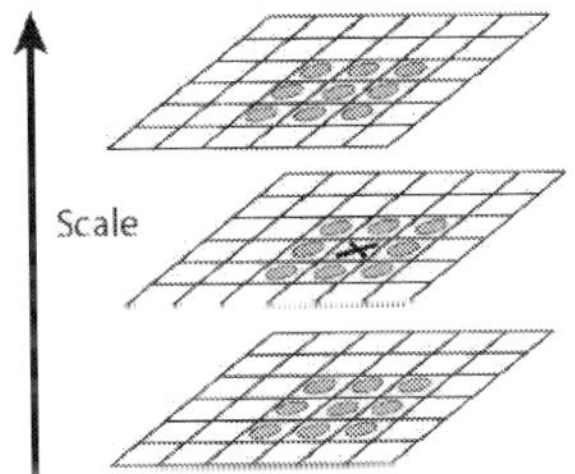

Fig. 7. Maxima and minima of the difference-of-Gaussian images are detected by comparing a pixel (marked with X) to its 26 neighbours in 3x3 regions at the current and adjacent scales (marked with circles).

A local extrema is observed if its derivative in scale space is stable and if it is on an apparent edge. If an extremum is decided as unstable or is placed on an edge, it is removed because it can not be reliably detected again with small deformations or lighting changes.

To remove the extremum placed on an edge we use a mask image obtained processing the input image with an edge-detector described in (Roska, 1999). Then, the next step is to reject the points that have low contrast (and are therefore sensitive to noise).

In order to reject the points that have low contrast we use a mask image obtained processing the input image with the technique introduced in (Cserey et al., 2003). In this approach a parallel histogram modification technique based on embedded morphological pre-processing is formulated in terms of non-linear partial differential equations (PDE).

Now, to characterize the image at each key location (keypoint), the first smoothed image at each octave of the pyramid is processed to extract image gradients and orientations.

In a CNN, the estimation of the gradient intensity in a local neighbourhood can be obtained using the following template:

$$\mathbf{A} = \begin{array}{|c|c|c|} \hline 0 & 0 & 0 \\ \hline 0 & 0 & 0 \\ \hline 0 & 0 & 0 \\ \hline \end{array} \qquad \mathbf{B} = \begin{array}{|c|c|c|} \hline b & b & b \\ \hline b & 0 & b \\ \hline b & b & b \\ \hline \end{array} \qquad z = \boxed{0} \tag{6}$$

where $b = |\,vuij - vukl\,|\,/8$.

To each key location is assigned a "canonical orientation", so that the image descriptors are invariant to rotation. This orientation is estimated by the gradient orientations of sample points within a region around the keypoints. To make the descriptor stable against lighting or contrast changes, the orientation is determined as follow:

- we estimate the gradient orientation of the pixels, within a region around the keypoint, applying a grayscale line detector template (8 *templates* for 8 *directions*) presented in (Roska, 1999);
- we add the 8 *maps* obtained (*SUM* – to each pixel of the image we have an estimate of its orientation);
- we obtain an image *mask* applying the mathematical morphology operator dilation (Roska, 1999) on an image that contains only keypoints (*keypoints mask*). The mask locates the points that will contribute to the estimate of the *keypoints orientation*;
- we calculate the local mean (neighbourhood – 3x3) of the image *SUM* (Moreira-Tamayos & Gyvez, 1999) on the points "selected" by the mask image.

The orientations estimated correspond to dominant directions of local gradients. Given a stable location, scale, and orientation for each key, it is now possible to describe the local image region in a manner invariant to these transformations. In addition, it is desirable to make this representation robust against change in lighting and small shifts in local geometry, such as arise from affine.

One obvious approach would be to sample the local image intensities around the keypoint at the appropriate scale, and to match these using a normalized correlation measure. However, simple correlation of image patches is highly sensitive to changes that cause misregistration of samples, such as affine or non-rigid deformations.

In according to (Park, 2008), now we generate a map of gradient orientations around each local extremum and then to make the descriptor orientation invariant, all gradient orientations are rotated respect to the major orientation (*keypoints orientation*) of the local extremum.

To obtain a *local map* of gradient orientation we proceed as follow:

- we calculate the gradient intensity of the fingerprint image;
- we use the grayscale line detector templates (8 orientation images, applied only on the keypoints neighbourhood – size: 16x16);
- we add the 8 orientation images to obtain a *local gradient orientation image*;
- we calculate the difference (**SUB**) between the local gradient orientation image and the keypoints orientation image (*canonical orientation of the keypoints*), the **SUB** image contains the gradient orientations rotated respect to the keypoints orientation;
- we calculate a weighted mean (Moreira-Tamayos & Gyvez, 1999) of the **intensity gradient image** and of the "rotated" **local gradient orientation image**.

In the original implementation (Lowe, 1999) of SIFT the best candidate match for each keypoint is found by identifying its nearest neighbour in the database of keypoints from training images. The nearest neighbour is defined as the keypoint with minimum Euclidean distance for the invariant descriptor vector. To obtain more details on matching process read (Lowe, 2004).

In our tests we used two metrics:

- the original solution described in (Lowe, 1999);
- the metric described in (Szatmári, 2006).

The first solution is more accurate (see Section 5) but it's not implemented on a CNN. The second metric though implemented on CNN, indeed, is less accurate, reliable and robust.

In (Szatmári, 2006) the author investigated PDE-based dynamic phenomena for comparing objects and introduced a spatio-temporal non-linear wave metric. This metric is capable of comparing both binary and gray-scale object pairs in a parallel way. Spatio-temporal waves are controlled to explore the quantitative properties of objects. In addition to spatial data time related information is also extracted and used for evaluating differences and similarities. The detailed analysis of the proposed metric shows that this wave-based approach can outperform well-known metrics such as Hausdorff and Hamming metrics in selectivity and sensitivity.

5. Experimental results

In according to (Park, 2008), the performances of the proposed SIFT based fingerprint verification has been evaluated on FVC2002 DB1 and DB2 fingerprint databases (Maio, 2002). Both the databases contain images of 100 different fingers with 8 impressions for each finger. In FVC2002 project, a total of ninety students (20 years old on the average) enrolled in the first two years of a Computer Science degree program agreed to act as volunteers for providing fingerprints. The volunteers were randomly partitioned into different groups, each group was associated to a DB and therefore to a different fingerprint scanner. Forefinger and middle finger of both the hands (four fingers total) of each volunteer were acquired by interleaving the acquisition of the different fingers to increase differences in finger placement. The top-ten quality fingers were removed from each database since they do not constitute an interesting case study. The remaining 110 fingers were split into set A (100 fingers - evaluation set) and set B (10 fingers - training set). To make set B representative of the whole database, the 110 collected fingers were ordered by quality. During a session, fingers were alternatively dried and moistened.
Some characteristics of these two databases are summarized in table 1.

	Sensor Type	Image Size	Images	Resolution
DB1	Optical Sensor	388x374	100x8	500 dpi
DB2	Optical Sensor	296x560	100x8	569 dpi

Table 1. Description of FVC 2002 DB1 and DB2 databases

The performance of the whole system, was evaluated by the Equal Error Rate (EER) for each metric used (see table 2). At Equal Error Rate, FAR=FRR. As the name implies, the FAR (False Acceptance Rate) describes the ability of the system to reject fingerprints which are not allowed to access the system, while the FRR (False Rejection Rate) describes the ability of the system to accept fingerprints which belong to the system users.

	EER1	EER2
DB1	9.30%	9.67%
DB2	11.65%	12.36%

Table 2. Description of the experimental results. EER1 and EER2 are, respectively, the equal error rate with the Lowe's metric and the Szatmári's metric.

As stated in section 4, the first metric is more accurate but it's not implemented on CNNs (*therefore with a lower matching speed*).

6. Conclusion

In this chapter we re-formulate an algorithm for fingerprint verification using the Scale Invariant Feature Transform (SIFT) (Lowe, 2004; Park et al., 2008) in such a way to exploit the high degree of parallelism inherent in a single-layer CNN. In our implementation we extract characteristic SIFT feature points in scale space and perform a matching based on the texture information around the feature points using the SIFT operator (Chikkerur, 2006). Experimental measures of the accuracy of the our fingerprint verification system were carried out.

7. References

Bálya, D. (2003). CNN universal machine as classification platform: an art-like clustering algorithm. *Int. J. Neural Syst.*, Vol. 13, No. 6, December 2003, pp. 415-425.

Bicego, M.; Lagorio, A.; Grosso, E. & Tistarelli, M. (2006). On the Use of SIFT Features for Face Authentication, *Proceedings of CVPRW'06*, pp. 35, 0-7695-2646-2, IEEE Computer Society, New York, NY.

Chikkerur, S.; Pankanti, S.; Jea, A.; Ratha, N. & Bolle, R. (2006). Fingerprint Representation Using Localized Texture Features. *Proceedings of ICPR 2006*, pp. 521-524, 1051-4651, August 2006, IEEE Computer Society, Hong Kong, China.

Chua, L. & Yang, L. (1988). Cellular neural networks: Theory, *IEEE Trans. on Circuits and Systems*, Vol. 35, No. 10, pp. 1257-1272.

Chua, L. & Yang, L. (1988). Cellular neural networks: Applications, *IEEE Trans. on Circuits and Systems*, Vol. 35, No. 10, pp. 1273-1290.

Chua, L.O.; Roska, T.; Kozek, T. & Zarándy, Á. (1993). The CNN Paradigm − A Short Tutorial, *Int. J. Circuit Theory and Applications*, Cellular Neural Networks Special Issue, 1993, pp. 1-14, 0-471-93836-X.

Costantini, G.; Casali, D.; Carota, M. & Perfetti, R. (2004). Translation and Rotation of Grey-Scale Images by means of Analogic Cellular Neural Network. *Proceedings of the IEEE International Workshop on Cellular Neural Networks and their Applications (CNNA'2004)*, pp. 213-218, 963-311-357-1, IEEE Computer Society, Budapest, Hungary.

Csapodi, M. & Roska, T. (1996). Adaptive histogram equalization with Cellular Neural Networks. *Proceedings of CNNA'96*, pp. 81-86, 0-7803-3261-X, , Seville, Spain.

Cserey, G.; Rekeczky, C. & Földesy, P. (2003). PDE Based Histogram Modification With Embedded Morphological Processing of the Level-Sets, *Journal of Circuits, System and Computers*, Vol. 12, No. 4, August 2003, pp. 519-538.

Gao, Q.; Förster, P.; Möbus, K.R. & Moschytz, G.S. (2001). Fingerprint Recognition Using CNNs: Fingerprint Preprocessing, *Proceedings of IEEE International Symposium on Circuits and Systems*, pp. 433-436, 0-7803-6685-9, May 2001, IEEE Computer Society, Sydney, Australia.

Gao, Q. & Moschytz, G.S. (2001). Fingerprint Feature Extraction Using CNNs, *Proceedings of European Conference on Circuit Theory and Design*, pp. 97-100, 9-5122-6337-8, August 2001, Espoo, Finland.

Gao, Q. &. Moschytz, G.S (2004). Fingerprint Feature Matching Using CNNs, *Proceedings of ISCAS'04*, pp. 73-76, 0-7803-8251-X, May 2004, IEEE Computer Society, Vancouver, Canada.

Huttenlocher, D.; Klanderman, G. & Rucklidge, A. (1993). Comparing images using the hausdorff distance, *IEEE Transactions on Pattern Analysis and Machine Intelligence*, Vol. 15, No. 9, (September 1993),pp. 850–863.

Iannizzotto, G.; Lanzafame, P. & La Rosa, F. (2005). A CNN-based Framework for 2D Still-image Segmentation, *Proceedings of CAMP05*, pp. 210-215, 0769522556, Terrasini, July 2005, IEEE Computer Society, Palermo, Italy.

Jain, A.K.; Hong, L. & Bolle, R. (1997). On-line fingerprint verification, *IEEE Transactions on Pattern Analysis and Machine Intelligence*, Vol. 19, April 1997, pp. 302-314, 0162-8828.

Lowe, D. (2004). Distinctive image features from scale-invariant key points. *International Journal of Computer Vision*, Vol. 60, No. 2, pp. 91-110.

Lowe, D. (1999). Object Recognition from Local Scale-Invariant Features. *Proceedings of ICCV'99*, pp. 1150-1157, 0-7695-0164-8, IEEE Computer Society, Kerkyra, Greece.

Maio, D.; Maltoni, D.; R. Cappelli; Wayman, J.L. & Jain, A.K. (2002). FVC2002: Second Fingerprint Verification Competition. *Proceedings of ICPR'02*, pp., 0-7695-1695-X, IEEE Computer Society, Quebec City, Canada.

Milanova, M. & Buker, U. (2000). Object recognition in image sequences with cellular neural networks, *Neurocomputing*, Vol. 31, No. 1-4, March 2000, pp. 125–141.

Moreira-Tamayos, O. & Gyvez, J. P. D. (1999). Subband coding and image compression using cnn, *International Journal of Circuit Theory and Applications*, Vol. 27, No. 1, March 1999, pp. 135–151, 0098-9886.

Park, U.; Pankanti, S. & Jain, A.K. (2008). Fingerprint Verification Using SIFT Features. *Proceedings of SPIE Defense and Security Symposium*, 0277-786X, SPIE, Orlando, Florida.

Ratha, N. K.; Karu, K. ; Chen, S. & Jain, A. K. (1996). A Real-Time Matching System for Large Fingerprint Databases, *IEEE Transactions on Pattern Analysis and Machine Intelligence*, Vol. 18, No. 8, August 1996, pp. 799–813, 0162-8828.

Rekeczky, C.; Tahy, A.; Vegh, Z. & Roska, T. (1999). CNN based spatio-temporal nonlinear filtering and endocardial boundary detection in echocardiography. *International Journal of Circuit Theory and Applications*, Vol. 27, No. 1, March 1999, pp. 171 – 207, 0098-9886.

Roska, T. & Chua, L.O. (1993). The CNN universal machine: an analogic array computer. *IEEE Transactions on Circuits and Systems II: Analog and Digital Signal Processing*, Vol. 40, No. 3, March 1993, pp. 163 – 173.

Roska, T.; Kek, L. ; Nemes, L.; Zarandy, A. & Szolgay, P. (1999). CNN Software Library (templates and algorithms), vers. 7.3. Tech. Rep. DNS-CADET-15. Analogical & Neural Computing Laboratory. Computer and Automation Research Institute, Hungarian Academy of Sciences.

Rekeczky, C.; Roska, T. & Ushida A. (1998). CNN-based difference-controlled adaptive nonlinear image filters. *International Journal of Circuit Theory and Applications*, Vol. 26, July-August 1998, pp. 375-423.

Sadeghi-Emamchaie, S.; Jullien, G.A.; Dimitrov, V. & Miller, W.C. (1998). Digital Arithmetic Using Analog Arrays. *Proceedins of the Great Lakes Symposium on VLSI '98*, p. 202, 0-8186-8409-7, IEEE Computer Society, Lafayette, LA, USA.

Szatmári, I. (2006). Object comparison using PDE-based wave metric on cellular neural networks. *International Journal of Circuit Theory and Applications, Vol. 34, No. 4, June 2006, pp. 359 – 382.*

Su, T.; Du, Y.; Cheng, Y. & Su, Y. (2005). A Fingerprint Recognition System Using Cellular Neural Networks. *Proceedings of Int'l Workshop on Cellular Neural Networks and Their Applications,* pp. 170-173, 0-7803-9185-3, IEEE Computer Society, Istanbul, Turkey.

Szirànyi, T. & Csicsvàri, J. (1993). High-speed character recognition using a dual cellular neural network architecture (cnnd), *IEEE Transactions on Circuits and Systems II: Analog and Digital Signal Processing,* Vol. 40, No. 3, March 1993, pp. 223–231, 1057-7130.

Theodoridis, S. & Koutroumbas, K. (2006). Pattern Recognition. Academic Press, 0-12-369531-7.

Witkin, A.P. (1983). Scale-space filtering. *Proceedings of International Joint Conference on Artificial Intelligence,* pp. 1019-1022, Karlsruhe, Germany.

23

The Fourth Biometric - Vein Recognition

Li Xueyan and Guo Shuxu
College of Electronic Science and Engineering, Jilin University,
Changchun 130012, P. R. China

1 . Introduction

A reliable biometric system, which is essentially a pattern-recognition that recognizes a person based on physiological or behavioral characteristic [1], is an indispensable element in several areas, including ecommerce(e.g. online banking), various forms of access control security(e.g. PC login), and so on. Nowadays, security has been important for privacy protection and country in many situations, and the biometric technology is becoming the base approach to solve the increasing crime.

As the significant advances in computer processing, the automated authentication techniques using various biometric features have become available over the last few decades. Biometric characteristics include fingerprint, face, hand/finger geometry, iris, retina, signature, gait, voice, hand vein, odor or the DNA information [2], while fingerprint, face, iris and signature are considered as traditional ones.

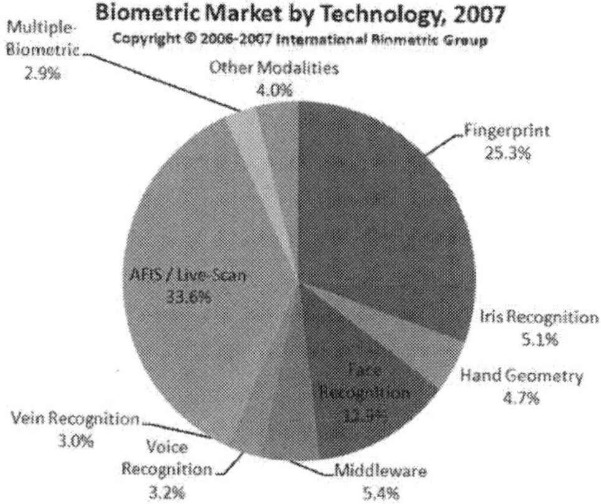

Fig. 1. IBG Biometric Market by Technology [3]

Due to each biometric technology has its merits and shortcoming, it is difficult to make a comparison directly. Jain et al. have identified seven factors [4], which are (1) universality, (2) uniqueness, (3) permanence, (4) measurability, (5) performance, (6) acceptability, (7) circumvention, to determine the suitability of a trait to be used in a biometric application.

Vein pattern is the network of blood vessels beneath person's skin. The idea using vein patterns as a form of biometric technology was first proposed in 1992, while researches only paid attentions to vein authentication in last ten years. Vein patterns are sufficiently different across individuals, and they are stable unaffected by ageing and no significant changed in adults by observing. It is believed that the patterns of blood vein are unique to every individual, even among twins.

Contrasting with other biometric traits, such as face or fingerprint, vein patterns provide a really specific that they are hidden inside of human body distinguishing them from other forms, which are captured externally. Veins are internal, thus this characteristic makes the systems highly secure, and they are not been affected by the situation of the outer skin (e.g. dirty hand).

At the same time, vein patterns can be acquired by infrared devices by two ways, non-contact type and contact type. In the case of non-contact method, there is no need to touch the device, and therefore it is friendly to individuals in the target population who utilize the systems. In the contact type, the collection type is the same as fingerprint which has already been accepted by most people.

From the customer's point of view, the authentication system is not only high accuracy level for security but also easy to enroll. Vein patterns serve as a high secure form of personal authentication as iris recognition (Iris is known for high accurate rates of authentication, but it is regarded unfriendly by users due to the direct application of light into their eyes), and serve as a convenient form as fingerprint recognition.

On account of the several advantages, vein authentication is not only interested in lab researchers but also in industries, and the products perform well in tests of the International Biometric Group (IBG) [5]. Recently, vein recognition appears to be making real headway in the market, and considered as one of the more 'novel' biometric, which is called 'the Fourth Biometric'.

2. Vein pattern recognition

Nearly any part of vein in human body (such as retinal vein, facial vein, veins in hand) could be used for personal identification, but veins in hand are always preferred [6]. It is usually an uncovered part. Veins in hand are closer to the surface than other organizes, so the traits can be easier detected by low-resolution cameras. In this paper, vein in hand is involved, finger vein, palm vein, wrist vein and dorsal hand vein, and each of them offers stable and unique biometric features.

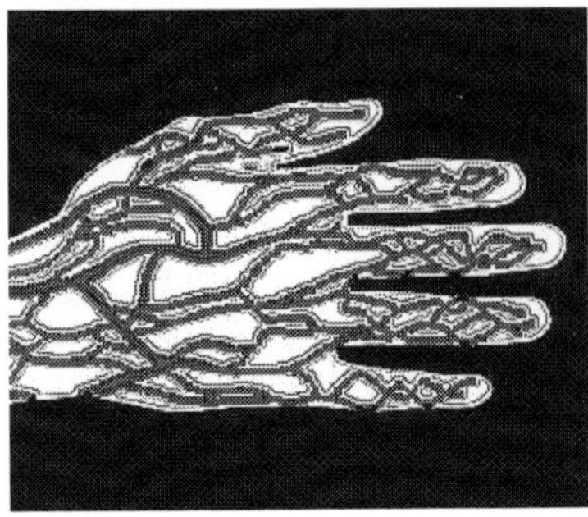

Fig. 2. the venous plexus of the hand

Category	Traits	Univer sality	Uniqu eness	Perma nence	Measura bility	Perfor mance	Accepta bility	Circum vention
Conventi onal	Face	H	L	M	H	L	H	H
	FP	M	H	H	M	H	M	M
	Vein	M	M	M	M	M	M	L
	Iris	H	H	H	M	H	L	H
	Voice	M	L	L	M	L	H	L

H: High   M: Medium   L:Low

Table 1. Comparison of Various Biometric Technologies at Seven Factors [7]

Category	Traits	Anti-Forgery	Accuracy	Speed	Enrollment Rates	Resistance	Cost
Conventional	Face	M	L	M	M	H	L
	Fingerprint	L	M	M	L	L	M
	Vein	H	H	H	M	M	M
	Iris	M	II	M	M	H	H
	Voice	M	L	M	M	H	M

H: High   M: Medium   L:Low

Table 2. Comparison of Various Biometric Methods [8]

3. Imaging principle

As veins are internal, their structure cannot be discerned in visible light. Based on the kinds of light of acquisition, a vein image can be classified as X-ray scanning, ultrasonic scanning and infrared scanning. X-ray and ultrasonic are used to capture vein images in medical treatment, but they are not used in identification due to the health case. Until now, researchers used infrared imaging for personal identification.

Infrared (IR) is electromagnetic radiation whose wavelength is longer than that of visible light, and Infrared light has a range of wavelengths lies between about 750nm and 1mm, just like visible light has wavelengths that range from red light to violet. Infrared is commonly divided into 3 spectral regions: near, mid and far-infrared light, but the boundaries between them are not agreed upon.

There are two choices that focuses on imaging of vein patterns in hand by infrared light, the far-infrared (FIR) imaging and the near-infrared (NIR) imaging, which are suitable to capture human bodies images in a non-harmful way.

Some papers had discussed the principle of the FIR and NIR imaging methods. In the FIR method, superficial human veins have higher temperature than the surrounding tissues. For NIR light method, the principle could be explained by photobiology. In biology, there is a "medical spectral window", which extends approximately from about 740 to 1100 nm. The light in this window could penetrate deeply into tissues. Because blood and surrounding tissues have different effect on the NIR light, we could use a CCD camera with an attached IR filter to capture images in which vein appears darker.

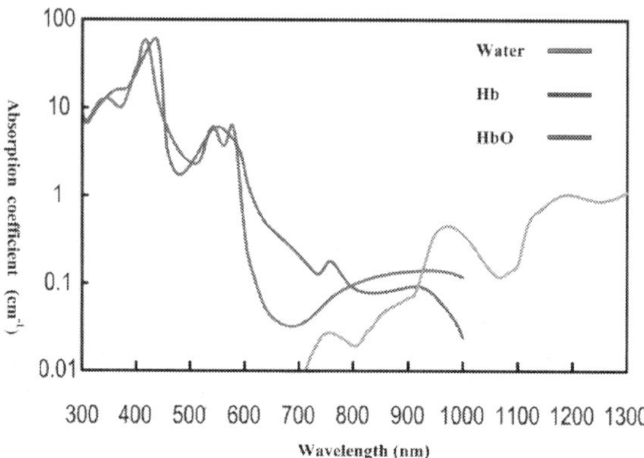

Fig. 3. the venous plexus of the hand

3.1 FIR Way

The human body temperature is about 36.85°C, and the temperature of surface of human veins is higher than that of the surrounding parts. Therefore when the FIR light irradiates hand, the hand vein structure is thermally mapped by an infrared camera at room temperature. The captured image shows a gradient of temperature between surrounding tissues and the back-of-hand veins.

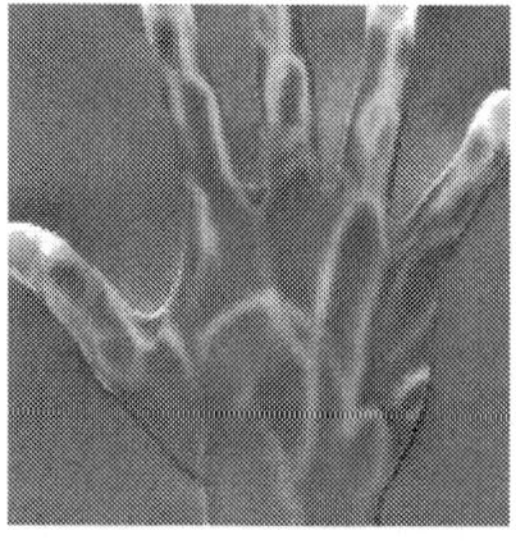
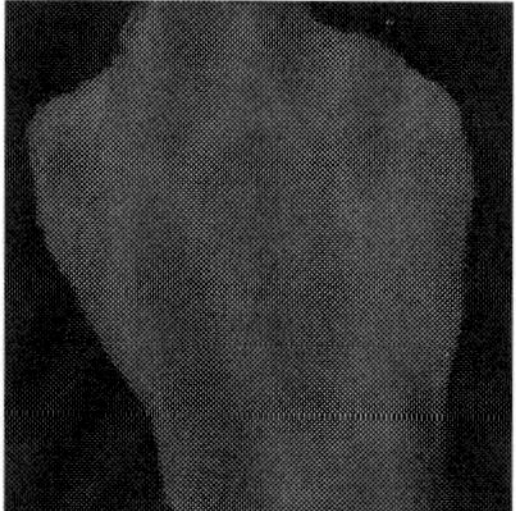

Fig. 4. FIR images of dorsal hand vein

In literature [9], it is proved that the captured FIR image of the back of hand has good quality, which means containing more useful information, but FIR vein image at palm and wrist have poor quality. Whilst this method deeply affects by the humidity and temperature of surrounding, as well as the users' perspiration does.

3.2 NIR Way

Near infrared wavelength is between about 700 nm to 1400 nm, and we can use the same observing methods as that used for visible light, except for observation by eye. The NIR light is not thermal. NIR scanning device cannot penetrate very deep under the skin therefore the device will recognize the superficial veins and rarely the deep veins.

In the NIR way, the light of specific wavelength is almost completely absorbed by the deoxidized hemoglobin in vein while almost penetrated the oxidized hemoglobin in the arteries. Oxygenated and deoxygenated hemoglobin absorb light equally at 800 nm, whereas at 760 nm absorption is primarily from deoxygenated hemoglobin [10]. Then the veins appear as dark areas in an image taken by a CCD camera. Near-infrared (NIR) spectroscopy is a noninvasive technique that uses the differential absorption properties of hemoglobin to evaluate skeletal muscle oxygenation.

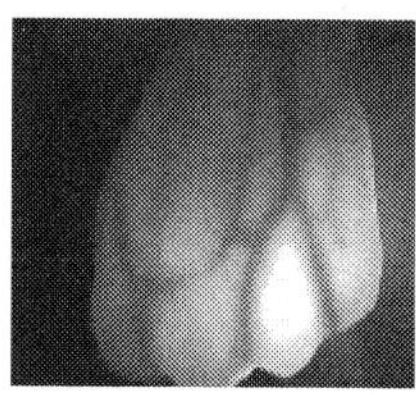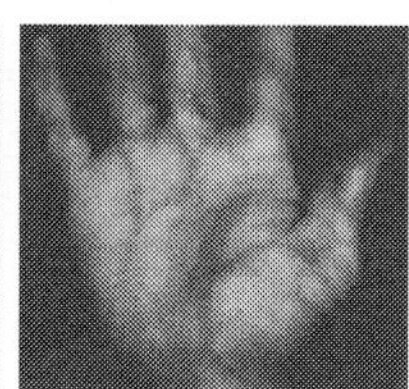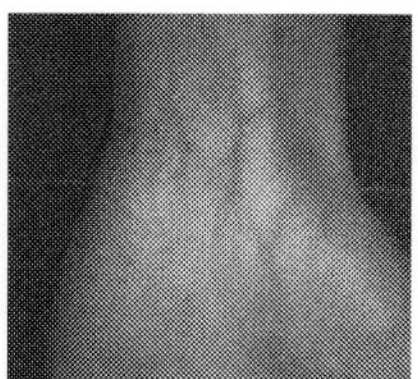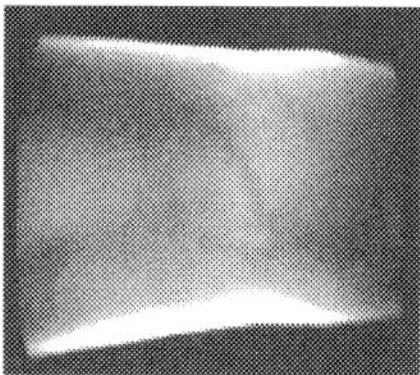

Fig. 5. NIR images of hand vein of four different parts, dorsal hand, palm, wrist, and finger vein.

NIR method is not a temperature based technique since normal body temperature or surrounding temperature cannot interfere with this method. The FIR method is often used in hand-dorsa vein imaging, and NIR method can be used in all veins imaging in hand. In order to benefit the processing, the captured images are always the grayscale image.

4. Vein pattern extraction

Because the temperature, illumination, locus and angle vary each collection, the captured digital picture varies each time. In order to provide 'better' input for automated image processing and realize a robust system against some fluctuation, some form of normalization should to be done aforehand. Conventional preprocessing algorithms can do this work. Then the vein patterns are extracted after noise reduction and normalization.
Several algorithms have been carried out to separate the vein patterns from the image background. The captured images contain shading, noise and vein patterns, moreover, the vein patterns are not salient. The more the information of veins is extracted and preserved, the better the accuracy is. So the appropriate processing extracting the vein patterns is important for the authentication system. Recently vein of hand extraction algorithm has been widely studied.
Wherever the veins are, in finger, wrist, palm or the back of hand, the various forms of vein patterns extracting algorithms usually fall into four broad categories: tracking-based, transform-based, matched filter method and thresholding method. Here we will describe some work on each of these areas.

4.1 Tracking-based
The tracing algorithm is based on repeated line tracking the vein from initial seed-point in the captured NIR image, moving pixel by pixel along the dark line in the cross sectional profiles [11]. In figure6, there is a certain position 's', and the left is its cross sectional intensity profile of finger vein image. Tracking direction is determined by the position of deepest point in the cross sectional. This method can extract vein patterns from low quality NIR images, but it is sharply affected by the temporal change of widths of veins.

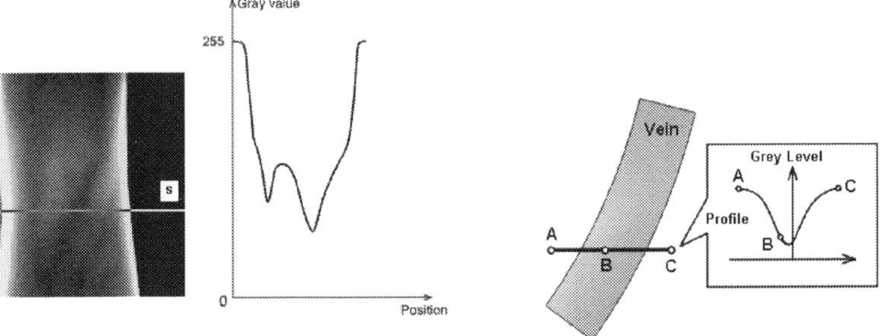

Fig. 6. cross sectional intensity profile of finger vein image

4.2 Transform-based methods

The captured image always has low contrast and contains noise, so contrast enhancement and noise reduction are crucial in ensuring the quality of the subsequent steps. Transform-based methods can convert image to a certain domain in which it is more suitable for extracting the patterns. Wavelet, which supports multi-resolution analysis, is one of the appropriate methods for vein structure and feature extracting. The wavelet multi-resolution approach employs a wavelet basis to analyze at different resolutions and increase resolution from coarse to fine, so the content of image in each scale can be understood. Vein patterns are well structured objects consisting of line-like veins and areas in between. The wider veins can be analyzed in the lower resolution, and the thinner veins can be analyzed in the higher resolution.

In paper [12], dyadic wavelet transform is adopted to extract finger vein patterns from background. Image is transformed from spatial domain to wavelet domain, and the grayscale image is changed into wavelet coefficients, which contain vein patterns wavelet coefficients and noise wavelet coefficients. The vein pattern variance of coefficients is larger than that of noise, and with the increasing of wavelet scale, the noise variance decreases.

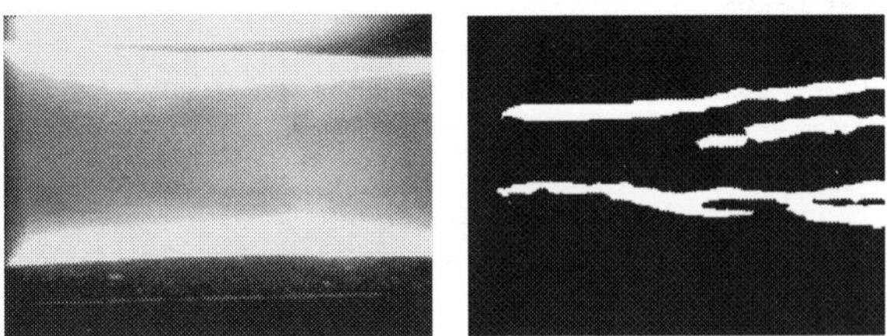

Fig. 7. extracted vein pattern by transform-based method

4.3 Matched filter method

By observing the cross sectional profiles of vein patterns, some researchers proposed an intensity profile model to detect vein patterns. Several models have been presented to describe the cross sectional profile of vessel [13-15]. The gray-level profile of the cross section is approximated a Gaussian shaped curve, which is prevalent used, whilst the matched filter is utilized to detect vein patterns. Since vein patterns may appear in any orientation, a set of cross sectional profiles in equiangular rotations is employed as a filter bank.

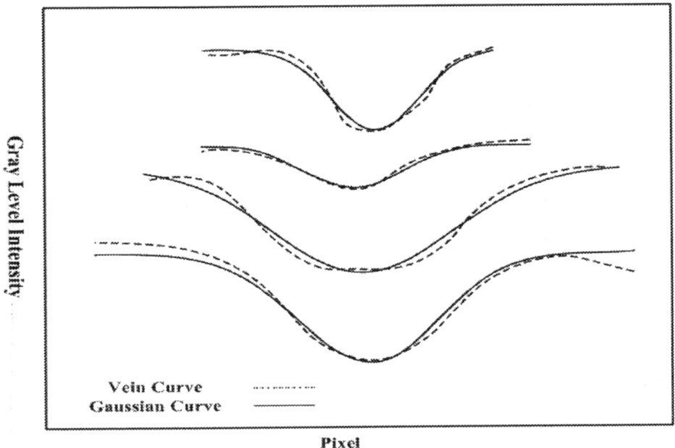

Fig. 8. the cross sectional profiles and the fitted Gaussian curves

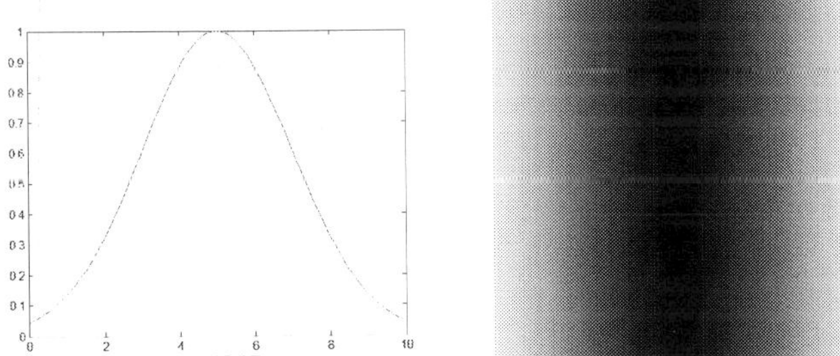

Fig. 9. the matching filter in 1-D and 2-D

4.4 Thresholding method

Intensity thresholding is usually utilized to obtain a better representation of shapes of the vein patterns. In the IR image the different location has different intensity values of the veins. Hence applying a single global thresholding is inappropriate. Via adaptively adjusting local thresholding, we can choose different threshold values for every pixel in the image based on the analysis of its surrounding neighbors [9], then, separate the vein patterns from the background, after that the desired vein image is extracted.

5. Pattern matching

The extracted vein patterns of the input image can directly be compared with the templates. A certain distance is defined to calculate the similarity between the template and the input patterns. But when the template is not small, the comparing time lasts long.

After pattern extracting process, most systems are interesting in eliciting skeletonisation of the vein patterns. Then Vessels can be represented by the number of intersections, the total segment length, the longest segment, and the angles found in the image, the distribution of the vein, and other statistical features. Hausdorff distance, SVM, and nearest neighbor are adopted as matching algorithm by researchers.

6. Database

Recently, significant work is continuously being done in vein recognition algorithms both in academy and industry. However, the conclusion of each work is usually achieved on their own databases but not the sharable databases. Large sharable vein databases are required to evaluate and compare various algorithms.

Vein pattern data collection is an expensive and time-consuming work. There are some inconveniences in large databases collection [16]. Firstly, it is expensive both in terms of money and time; secondly, it is tedious for both the technicians and for the volunteers; thirdly, due to privacy information, it is difficult to share data with others. Though the real images cannot be replaced, the synthetic vein images have proven to be a valid substitute for real vein for design, benchmarking and evaluation of vein recognition systems. A synthetic like-vein image method is requested.

Based on the cross sectional profiles of vein patterns, the vein pattern can be synthesized in semiautomatic way as figure10. Firstly, lines which look like vein patterns were drawn by hand [17]. Secondly, according to the different cross sectional profile models, the like-vein patterns can generation by programs.

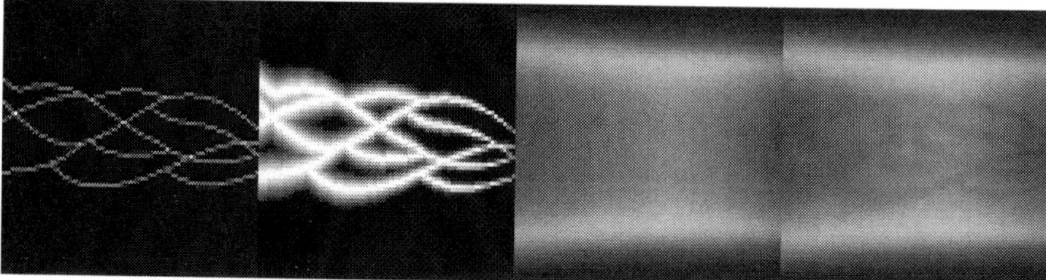

Fig. 10. synthesis finger vein image of normal pattern

7. Application of vein recognition system and future work

Vein recognition technology has some fundamental advantages over fingerprint systems. Vein patterns in hand are biometric characteristics that are not left behind unintentionally in everyday activities. Vein patterns of inanimate bodily parts become useless after a few minutes. Hence, nowadays, vein recognition system is regarded a mainstream technology. IBG expects it to play a larger role and comprise more than 10% of the biometric market [18]. Nearly all major vein authentications are manufactured in Japan and Korea, and the application of these manufactures are used in Asia. In Japan and some other countries, such products spread particularly in the financial sector.

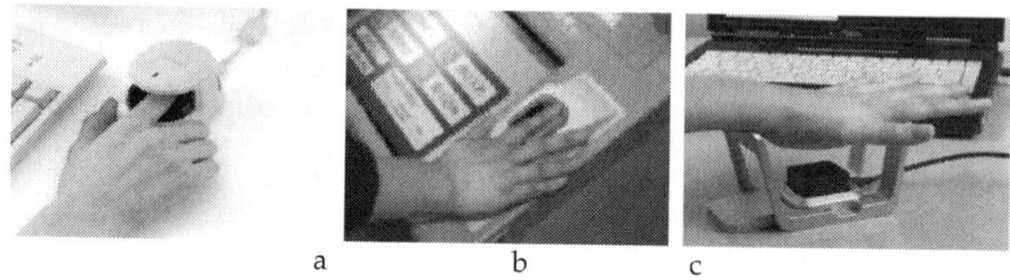

Fig. 11. a) Hitachi's Finger Vein device; b) Hitachi's Finger Vein ATM; c) PalmSecure by Fujitsu

The recent launch of vein recognition technology is successful. Nevertheless, some research issues need to be addressed in future. For one thing, work continued across the vein imaging device to make it cheaper, more accurate and robust. For another thing, the quality of vein IR image is affected by the relationship of intensity between the IR light and the ambient light, as well as the ambient temperature. Moreover, the sharable large databases should be founded for a thorough evaluation on the efficacy of different vein recognition algorithms. Lastly, vein trait is able to conjunct with other biometrics in a multi-modal system.

8. Reference

S. Prabhakar, S. Pankanti, and A. K. Jain, "Biometric Recognition: Security and Privacy Concerns", IEEE Security and Privacy, 2003.1(2), pp. 33-42.

J. L. Wayman, A. K. Jain, D. Maltoni, and D. Maio, "Biometric Systems: Technology, Design and Performance Evaluation", 2005, Springer.

International Biometric Group, "Biometrics Market and Industry Report 2007-2012", 2007.

A. K. Jain, R. Bolle, and S. Pankanti, "Biometrics: Personal Identification in Networked Society", 1999, Kluwer Academic Publishers.

Michael Thieme, "New· Vein performs well in tests", Biometric Technology Today, 2006.14(10), pp. 4.

S. Crisan, l. G. Tarnovan, and T. E. Crisan, "A Low Cost Vein Detection System Using Near Infrared Radiation", IEEE Sensors Applications Symposium 2007, San Diego, California USA, 2007.

A. K. Jain, A. Ross, and S. Prabhakar, "An Introduction to Biometric Recognition", IEEE Trans. on Circuits and Systems for Video Technology, 2004.14(1), pp. 4-19.

J. Hashimoto, "Finger Vein Authentication Technology and its Future", VLSI Circuits, 2006. Digest of Technical Papers. 2006 Symposium on, 2006, pp. 5-8.

L. Wang, G. Leedham and S. Y. Cho, "Infrared imaging of hand vein patterns for biometric purposes", The Institution of Engineering and Technology 2007 IET Comput Vis., 2007, pp. 113–122.

D. M. Mancini, L. Bolinger, H. Li, K. Kendrick, B. Chance and J. R. Wilson, "Validation of near-infrared spectroscopy in humans", Journal of Applied Physiology, 1994. 77(6), pp. 2740-2747.

Miura, N., A. Nagasaka, and T. Miyatake, "Feature extraction of finger-vein patterns based on repeated line tracking and its application to personal identification", Machine Vision and Applications, 2004.15(4), pp. 194-203.

Li, Xueyan, Guo, Shuxu, Gao, Fengli, and Li, Ye, "Vein Pattern Recognitions by Moment Invariants", The 1st International Conference on Bioinformatics and Biomedical Engineering, 2007, pp. 612-615.

A. Hoover, V. Kouznetsova, and M. Goldbaum, "Locating blood vessels in retinal images by piece-wise threshold probing of a matched filter response", IEEE Trans. on Medical Imaging, 2000.19(3), pp. 203–210.

L. Gang, O. Chutatape, and S. M. Krishnan, "Detection and Measurement of Retinal Vessels in Fundus Images Using Amplitude Modified Second-Order Gaussian Filter", IEEE Trans on Biomedical Engineering, 2003. 49(2), 168-172.

S. Chaudhuri, S. Chatterjee, N. Katz, M. Nelson, and M. Goldbaum, "Detection of blood vessels in retinal images using two-dimensional matched filters", IEEE Trans. on Medical Imaging, 1989.8(3), pp. 263–269.

D. Maltoni, D. Maio, A. K. Jain, and S. Prabhakar, "Handbook of Fingerprint Recognition", 2003, Springer.

Naoto MIURA, Akio NAGASAKA, and Takafumi MIYATAKE, "Extraction of Finger-Vein Patterns Using Maximum Curvature Points in Image Profiles", The Institute of Electronics, Information and Communication Engineers, 2007. 90(8), pp. 1185-1194.

Wendy Atkins, "Industry squares up to multiple opportunities", Biometric Technology Today, 2007, pp. 8-10.

24

A Hybrid Pattern Recognition Architecture for Cutting Tool Condition Monitoring

Pan Fu[1] and A. D. Hope[2]
[1]*Mechanical Engineering Faculty, Southwest JiaoTong University, ChengDu 610031,*
[2]*Systems Engineering Faculty, Southampton Institute, Southampton SO14 OYN,*
[1]*China*
[2]*U.K.*

1. Introduction

One of the important developments in modern manufacturing industry has been the trend towards cost savings through stuff reductions whilst simultaneously improving the product quality. Traditional tool change strategies are based on very conservative estimates of tool life from past tool data and this leads to a higher tool change frequency and higher production costs. Intelligent sensor based manufacturing provides a solution to this problem by coupling various transducers with intelligent data processing techniques to deliver improved information relating to tool condition. This makes optimization and control of the machining process possible.

Many researchers have published results in the area of automatic tool condition monitoring. The research work of Scheffer C. etc. showed that proper features for a wear monitoring model could be generated from the cutting force signal, after investigating numerous features. An approach was developed to use feed force measurements to obtain information about tool wear in lathe turning (Balazinski M. etc.). An analytical method was developed for the use of three mutually perpendicular components of the cutting forces and vibration signature measurements (Dimla D. E. etc.). A tool condition monitoring system was then established for cutting tool-state classification (Dimla D. E. etc.). In another study, the input features were derived from measurements of acoustic emission during machining and topography of the machined surfaces (Wilkinson P. Etc.). Li, X etc. showed that the frequency distribution of vibration changes as the tool wears (Li X. etc.). Tool breakage and wear conditions were monitored in real time according to the measured spindle and feed motor currents, respectively (LI X. L. Etc.).

Advanced signal processing techniques and artificial intelligence play a key role in the development of tool condition monitoring systems. Sensor fusion is also found attractive since loss of sensitivity of one of the sensors can be compensated by other sensors. A new on-line fuzzy neural network (FNN) model with four parts was developed (Chungchoo C. etc.). They have the functions of classifying tool wear by using fuzzy logic; normalizing the inputs; using modified least-square back propagation neural network to estimate flank and crater wear. A new approach for online and indirect tool wear estimation in turning using neural networks was developed, using a physical process model describing the influence of cutting conditions on measured process parameters (Sick B.). Two methods using Hidden

Markov models, as well as several other methods that directly use force and power data were used to establish the health of a drilling tool (Ertunc H. M.).

In this study, a new fuzzy neural hybrid pattern recognition algorithm was developed to accomplish multi-sensor information integration and tool wear states classification. The technique shows some remarkable characteristics by imitating the thinking and judging modes of human being. It has shown that definite mathematical relationships between tool wear states and sensor information are not necessarily needed and that the effects caused by experimental noise can also be decreased greatly. The monitoring system that has been developed provided accurate and reliable tool wear classification results over a range of cutting conditions.

2. Tool condition monitoring system

The tool wear monitoring system is composed of four types of sensors, signal amplifying and collecting devices and the main computer, as shown in Fig. 1. The power consumption, cutting force (in three perpendicular directions), acoustic emission (AE) and vibration sensors chosen were found to provide healthy time domain signals for tool condition monitoring.

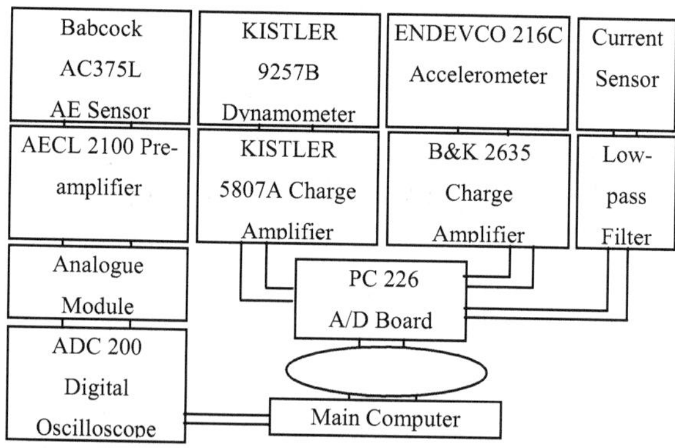

Fig. 1. The tool condition monitoring system

The experiments were carried out on a Cincinnati Milacron Sabre 500 machining centre. Like many other modern machine tools, it delivers a motor current signal that is proportional too torque, which at a constant spindle speed, corresponds to the actual power consumption. A KISTLER 9257B force dynamometer was used to measure cutting forces in three mutually perpendicular directions. The dynamometer has a measuring range of 5000 (N) in each direction, linearity of 1%, stiffness of 350 N/µm in the Z direction and 1000N/µm in the X and Y directions and a resonant frequency of 4kHz.

The acoustic emission (AE) measuring apparatus includes an AE sensor and a signal processing device. The AE sensor has a measuring frequency range of 100KHz - 2MHz. The 60dB pre-amplifier connects the AE sensor to the AE output instrument and has a 113KHz - 1.1 MHz built-in filter. An analogue module receives the input from the pre-amplifier and provides outputs of both amplified AE analogue signals and AE RMS signals. An accelerometer was mounted in the feed direction. The sensor has a frequency response of 5 - 33 kHz, mounted resonant frequency 50 kHz. Fig.2 shows the power consumption, cutting force (in the cutting direction), vibration and acoustic emission signals collected in milling process. The entry and exit of an insert in relation to the workpiece can be easily recognized. From those healthy signals many tool wear relevant features can be extracted for the future pattern recognition process.

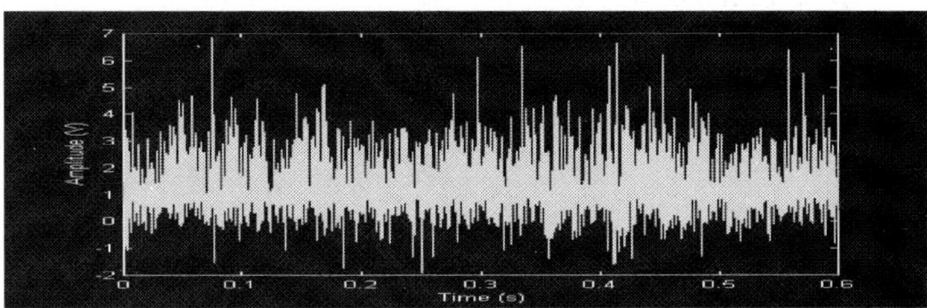

(a)The power consumption signal

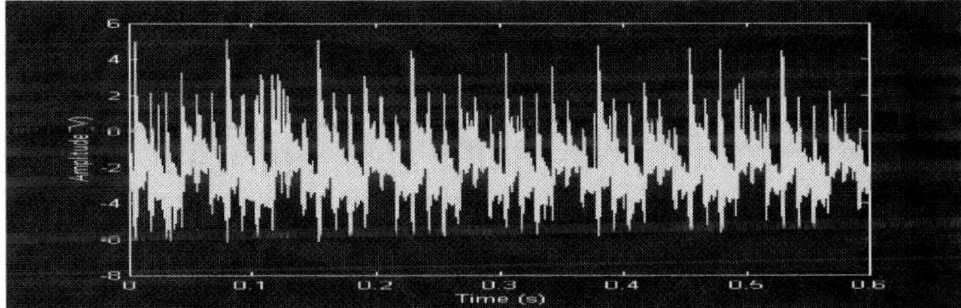

(b)The cutting force signal

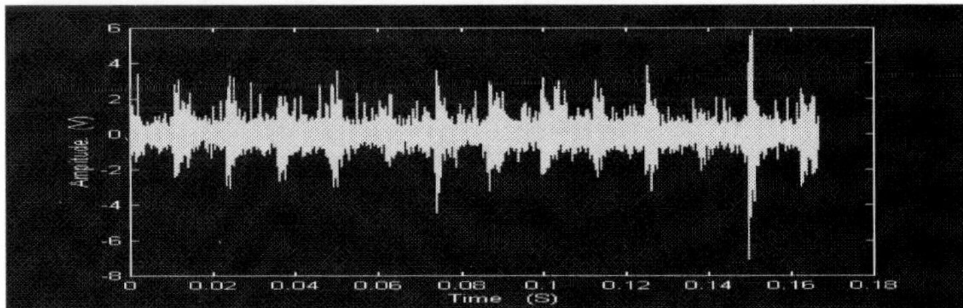

(c)The vibration signal

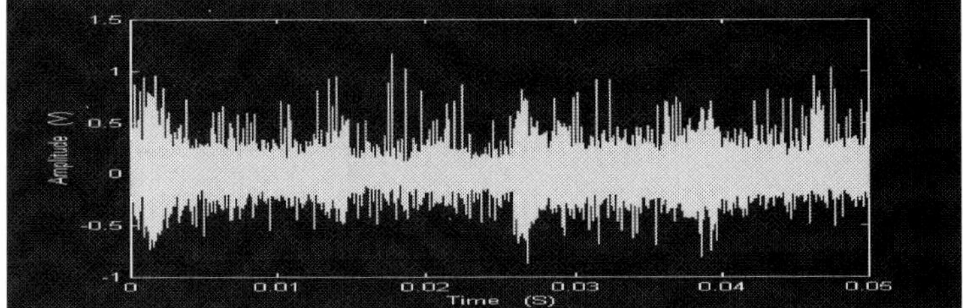

(d)The Acoustic emission signal

Fig. 2. Tool condition monitoring sensor signals

3. Feature extraction

The original signals have large dimensions and can not be directly used to estimate tool wear value. The purpose of feature extraction is to greatly reduce the dimension of the raw signal but at the same time maintain the tool condition relevant information in the extracted features. This step is the foundation for the pattern recognition process.

In the time domain the mean value and the standard deviation are simple but effective features. Power spectrum density (PSD) analysis in the frequency domain can provide very useful information and experimental results show that for force, AE and vibration signals, the spectrum distribution changes with tool wear.

A typical group of features extracted from the time domain and frequency domain for the further pattern recognition are as follows. Power consumption signal: mean value; AE-RMS signal: mean value, skew and kutorsis; Cutting force, AE and vibration : mean value, standard deviation and the mean power in 10 frequency ranges. Fig. 3 shows several features (under cutting condition 1*) in time and frequency doorman. It can be seen that both the amplitude and the distribution pattern represent the development of tool flank wear (VB).

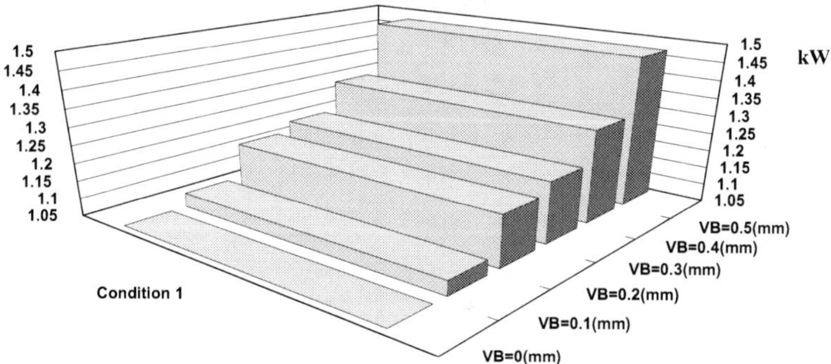

(a) Mean value of the power consumption signal

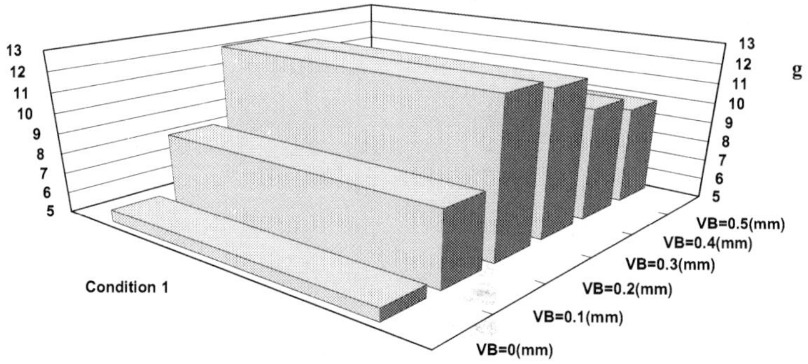

(b) Standard deviation of the vibration signal

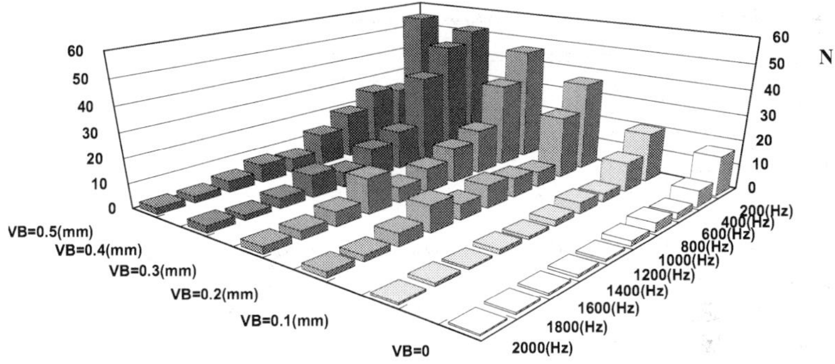

(c)Frequency spectra of cutting force (F_x) signal

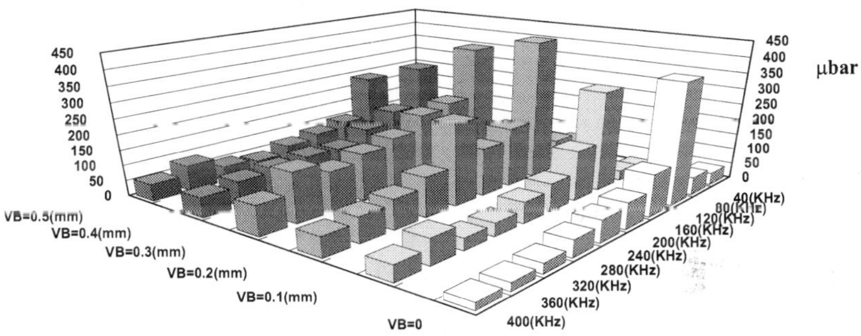

(d) Frequency spectra of the AE signal

Fig. 3. Features extracted from different sensor signals

4. Fuzzy driven neural network

4.1 Fuzzy membership function

The features of sensor signals can reflect the tool wear states. Theoretical analysis and experimental results show that these features can be regarded as normal distribution fuzzy sets. The membership function of the fuzzy set A_i can be represented as:

$$A_i(x) = 1 - \frac{(x - a_i)^2}{2\sigma_i^2} \quad a_i - \sqrt{2}\sigma_i \le x \le a_i + \sqrt{2}\sigma_i$$

$$= 0, \qquad \text{for all others}$$

(1)

where a and σ are mean value and standard deviation.

4.2 Fuzzy approaching degree

Fuzzy approaching degree is an index that represents the fuzzy distance between two fuzzy sets (A and B). Assume that $\Im$ (X) is the fuzzy power set of a universal set X and the map,

N: $\mathfrak{I}(X) \times \mathfrak{I}(X) \rightarrow [0,1]$ satisfies: (1). $\forall A \in \mathfrak{I}(X)$, $N(A,A)=1$ (2). $\forall A, B \in \mathfrak{I}(X)$, $N(A,B)=N(B,A)$ (3). If $A,B,C \in \mathfrak{I}(X)$ satisfies $|A(x)-C(x)| \geq |A(x)-B(x)|$ $(\forall x \in X)$ then $N(A,C) \leq N(A,B)$, so the map N is the approaching degree in $\mathfrak{I}(X)$ and $N(A,B)$ is called the approaching degree of A and B. Approaching degree can be calculated by using different methods. Here the inner and outer products are used.

If $A,B \in \mathfrak{I}(X)$, $A \bullet B = \vee \{A(x) \wedge B(x) : x \in X\}$ is defined as the inner product of A and B and $A \oplus B = \wedge \{A(x) \vee B(x) : x \in X\}$ is defined as the outer product of A and B. Finally, in the map $N : \mathfrak{I}(X) \times \mathfrak{I}(X) \rightarrow [0,1]$, $N(A,B)$ is the approaching degree of A and B.

$$N(A,B) = (A \bullet B) \wedge (A \oplus B)^c \qquad (2)$$

Using conventional fuzzy pattern recognition methods, the fuzzy approaching degrees between corresponding features of the object to be recognized and different models are calculated to determine the fuzzy similarity between a given object and different models. The method can be further improved by assigning suitable weights to different features in order to reflect their specific influences in the pattern recognition process. ANNs have the ability to continuously classify the inputs and also update classifications. In this study, ANNs are connected with a fuzzy logic system to establish a fuzzy driven neural network pattern recognition system and its principle is shown by Fig. 4.

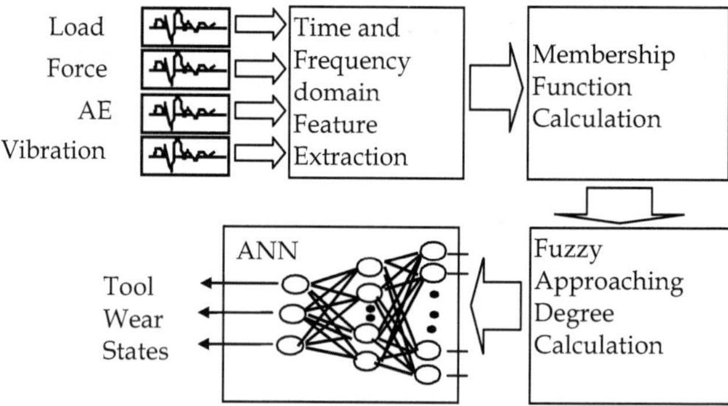

Fig. 4. The fuzzy driven neural network

Here a back propagation ANN is used to carry out tool wear classification. The approaching degree calculation results are the input of the ANN. The associated weights can be updated as: $w_i(new) = w_i(old) + \alpha \delta x_i$. Here α, δ, x_i are learning constant, associated error measure and input to the i-th neuron. In this updating process, the ANN recognizes the patterns of the features corresponding to certain tool wear state. So in practical machining process, the feature pattern can be accurately classified. In fact the ANN assigns each feature a proper synthesized weight and the outputs of the ANN are weighted approaching degrees. This enables the tool wear classification process be more reliable.

Altogether six standard tool wear values were selected as standard wear values, ranging from new to severe wear where the width of the flank wear area increased from 0 to 0.5 mm in steps of 0.1 mm. Cutting tools with standard wear values are used in milling operations and multi-channel sensor signals were collected. So, for all the models, the membership functions of all their features can be calculated and then stored in a library in the computer. ANNs can then be trained to recognize different tool wear states, under each specific cutting condition.

After the training the constructed frame and associated weights of the ANN can reflect the distinct importance of each individual feature for each model under specific cutting conditions. These feature weights will change, under different cutting conditions, to truely represent the practical situation. So the future tool wear classification results can be reliable and accurate. The determination of the membership functions of all the features for each model and the construction of ANNs for classification mark the end of the learning stage.

5. Algebraic neurofuzzy networks

A neural fuzzy system has both the transparent representation of a fuzzy system and the learning ability of neural networks. It processes information using fuzzy reasoning techniques, but it can be trained using neural type learning algorithms because it also has a multi-layer ANN structure. The combination of the rule based representation and adaptive numeric processing can lead to a robust modeling system. Various applications of fuzzy neural integrated systems may be cited (Blanz W. E. etc.) (Brown M. etc.) (Fukuda T. etc.). Many neurofuzzy systems use B-spline or Gaussian basis functions (Brown etc.). Gaussian representation is potentially more flexible, but it is harder to generate appropriate fuzzy algorithms. Adaptive B-spline based neurofuzzy system uses algebraic operators and B-spline fuzzy membership functions to simplify the overall system, produces more transparent models. It is also possible to use learning algorithms to extract neurofuzzy models directly from the input data.

5.1 B-spline fuzzy sets

As mentioned before, signal features can be treated as fuzzy sets, which can then be represented by fuzzy membership functions. Here, B-spline basis functions, piecewise polynomials of order k, are used to represent fuzzy membership functions. Fig. 5 shows the B-spline basis function of order 3. When the order k is changed, they can represent membership functions of different shapes.

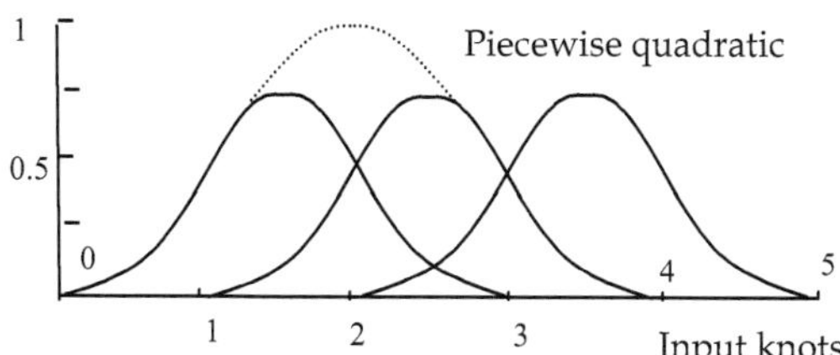

Fig. 5. B-spline fuzzy membership function

The order and the knot vector determine the smoothness and shape of the basis functions. The knots partition the input space into a series of intervals on which the basis functions are defined. Multivariate B-spline basis functions are formed by taking tensor production of n univariate basis functions, where only one univariate function is defined on each input axis. The multivariate basis functions are then defined on a lattice, which is generated from the projection of all the individual knot vectors parallel to the remaining input axes.

5.2 Fuzzy knowledge representation

The relation between signal features and tool wear values can be expressed by the description: if the power consumption is large and cutting force is medium and ... then the tool wear value is large. This can be represented:

$$r_{ij} : \text{IF} (x_1 = A_1^i \text{ AND } x_2 = A_2^i \text{ AND...AND } x_n = A_n^i) \text{ THEN } (y = B^j), (c_{ij}) \qquad (3)$$

where x_k and y are the input and output, r_{ij} is the fuzzy rule and c_{ij} is the rule confidence.

A_k^i is the univariate linguistic term and B^j is the output linguistic term.

The union (fuzzy OR) of a group of fuzzy rules is called a fuzzy algorithm in which the knowledge of a fuzzy system is stored. So the set of all the confidences c_{ij} (rule confidence matrix) illustrates the complex relation between the input and the output of the system. To fulfill the fuzzy rule set, functions must be chosen to implement the fuzzy logic functions, AND, OR, IF ( ), THEN (), etc. Recent research shows that the algebraic operators, sum and product, can produce smoother output than the traditional truncation operators, min and max [12].

5.3 The B-spline neurofuzzy system

The process of calculating the output of a fuzzy system includes fuzzification, inference and defuzzification. This involves representing the crisp input as fuzzy sets, pattern matching this with the rules stored in the rule base, combining each rule and mapping the resulting sets to crisp output. Here, B-splines are used to implement the fuzzy membership functions. Singleton fuzzy sets are used to represent the crisp input. Algebraic operators are chosen to accomplish the fuzzy logic functions and the diffuzzification is realized by using a centre of gravity algorithm, and the rule confidences are normalized. Thus the output of the neurofuzzy system can be given by:

$$y(X) = \sum_i \mu_{A^i}(X) w_i \qquad (4)$$

Where $\mu_{A^i}(X)$ is the i-th fuzzy membership function of a multivariate input X and w_i is the weight. The structure of the neurofuzzy system is shown in Fig. 6.

In Fig. 6, the multivariate fuzzy input sets (termed as basis functions) are defined on a lattice in the input space. The weight of a basis function is an estimate of the value of the network's output; given that the input lies within the set.

A weight can be fuzzified to produce a rule confidence vector which can then be defuzzified to produce the original weight. The output of the network is linearly dependent on the weight set. This network structure allows an efficient linear learning strategy, Conjugate Gradient, to be used to adapt the weights for optimal performance.

The neurofuzzy system can be a powerful tool for cutting tool condition monitoring. In the training process, for all the signal features of each model (cutting tool with standard wear value), a group of feature values are put into the neurofuzzy network as the training input. A fuzzy rule base is then established to describe the mapping between the systems input and output states. So in the practical condition monitoring process, it can recognize the incoming feature pattern and associate the pattern with different models with corresponding classification confidence.

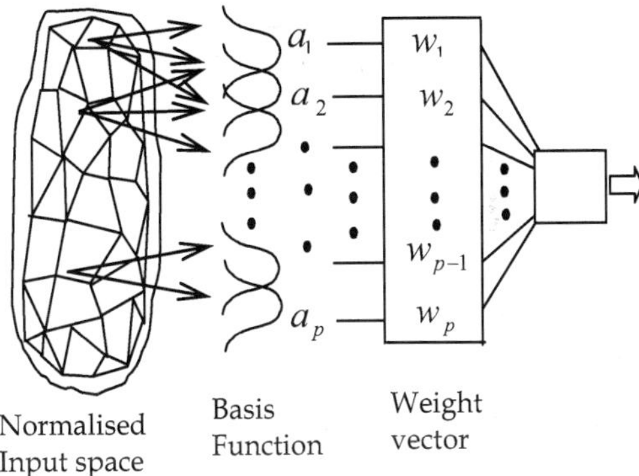

Fig. 6. Algebraic neurofuzzy network

6. Fusion on two levels

Tool wear is a very complex process and it is unlikely that tool condition monitoring could be reliably accomplished by using only one sensor and conventional signal processing strategies. Modern condition monitoring systems are based on the integration of multi-sensor information and the development of reliable intelligent signal classification routines.

To make the tool condition monitoring system more reliable, fusion on two levels is employed in this study. The first level is sensor fusion. The monitoring system is equipped with four kinds of sensors and multi-sensor signal features are fused by the intelligent data processing process. Different sensor signals can reflect the tool wear state from different aspects. Their functions are independent and mutually complementary. For example, the dynamometer, accelerometer and AE sensor work respectively in the frequency ranges from several hertz to 1 MHz and higher. The fused information describes the tool wear process more comprehensively.

The second fusion is on a higher level: the fusion of two pattern recognition algorithms. As stated before, both the fuzzy driven neural network and the algebraic neurofuzzy network can carry out intelligent pattern recognition. These methods are the modified and improved versions of the traditional fuzzy logic and neural network pattern recognition processes and experimental results have shown that they have better or at least the same good performance. But because of the extreme complexity of the tool wear mechanism, these algorithms still may not be completely reliable in a few exceptional cases.

It should be noticed that the two proposed algorithms have different characteristics and they can describe the tool wear process from different view points. The calculation of normal distribution type fuzzy membership functions is a statistical calculation process and this makes the results of the fuzzy driven neural network quite reliable. But in some cases the confidence of the classification may not be as high as it should. The algebraic neurofuzzy network works in a different way. It uses B-splines to represent the membership functions of the input sets and the relation between the signal features and the tool wear values are represented by a fuzzy rule base and the rule confidence matrix. This algorithm is quite accurate for most circumstances but exceptionally, where the rule base is not perfectly complete, the system may refuse to classify some individual objects.The authors of this paper argue that by combining the two algorithms to establish a fused pattern recognition process the tool wear classification results can be more reliable and this idea is supported by large amounts of experiment results.

7. Fuzzy neural hybrid pattern recognition system

The fuzzy neural hybrid pattern recognition system is established by the integration of the fuzzy driven neural network and the algebraic neurofuzzy network. The multi-sensor signals collected from the machining process are first processed to extract tool wear relevant features. Then the membership functions of the features and the fuzzy approaching degrees between the corresponding features of the object and different models can be calculated.

These features that have unstable value or only small change of value of approaching degree for different models should be removed. This step can filter out the redundant features and decrease the training time of the network greatly. The parameters of the determined membership functions can also help the neurofuzzy network to choose correct knots on each input axis.

Both the two systems provide the similarities between the object and different models and classify the object to the most similar model with a certain confidence value. These two confidence values are not necessarily equal, but combining them provides a more reliable and accurate result. A threshold is set by considering the difference between the classification confidence values and tool wear values of the two classification results. Should the two pattern recognition processes give different results, the system averages the results when the difference is within threshold and refuses to do the classification if the threshold is exceeded. The failure of the classification shows the incoming data is too noisy or the networks have not been fully trained and need to be improved. By doing this, the reliability of the classification process is improved.

Signals collected under 220 representative cutting conditions have been processed to verify the proposed fuzzy neural hybrid system (Experiments were partly carried out in the Advanced Manufacturing Lab. of Southampton Institute, U.K.). The system showed very good classification accuracy and reliability.y. Following is an example, fifteen tools with unknown flank wear value were used in milling operations and Fig.7 shows the classification results. It can be seen that all the tools were classified correctly with the confidence of higher than 80%. Experiments under other representative cutting conditions showed the similar results.

8. Conclusion

An intelligent tool condition monitoring system has been established. Tool wear classification is realized by applying a unique fuzzy neural hybrid pattern recognition system. On the basis of this investigation, the following conclusions can be made.

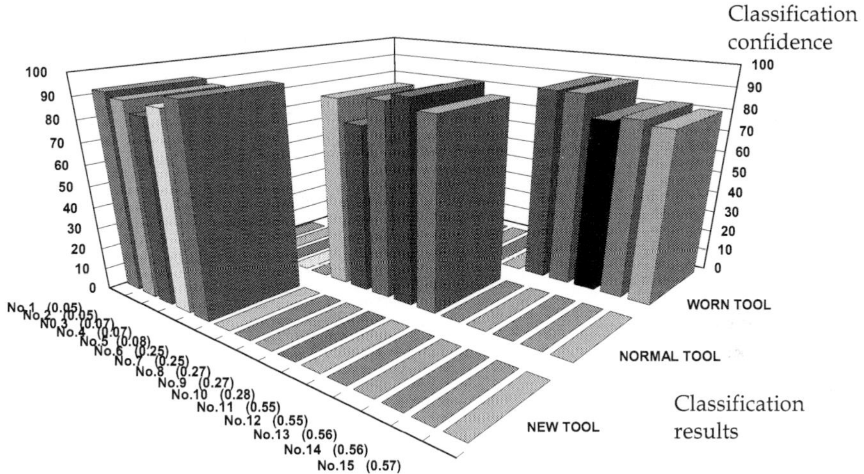

Fig. 7. A group of tool wear states classification results

1. Power consumption, vibration, AE and cutting force sensors are applicable for monitoring tool wear in metal cutting process. The healthy signals picked up by these sensors describe tool condition comprehensively.
2. Many features extracted from time and frequency domains are found to be relevant to the changes of tool wear state. This makes accurate and reliable pattern recognition possible.
3. The combination of ANNs and fuzzy logic system integrates the strong learning and classification ability of the former and the superb flexibility of the latter to express the distribution characteristics of signal features with vague boundaries. This methodology indirectly solves the weight assignment problem of the conventional fuzzy pattern recognition system and the resulting fuzzy driven neural network is more accurate and reliable.
4. B-splines that are defined on a lattice-type structure mean that a fuzzy representation of the network can be generated. The Fuzzy rule base established can well describe the mapping between the systems input and output states. A smoother defuzzification surface can be obtained by the use of algebraic operators. The developed neurofuzzy networks have a simplified structure and produces better and more transparent models than a general fuzzy system.
5. Armed with the advanced pattern recognition methodology, the established intelligent tool condition monitoring system has the advantages of being suitable for different machining conditions, robust to noise and tolerant to faults.

* Cutting condition 1(for milling operation): cutting speed - 600 rev/min, feed rate - 1 mm/rev, cutting depth - 0.6 mm, workpiece material - EN1A, cutting inserts -Stellram SDHT1204 AE TN-42.

Please read these instructions carefully. Prepare your manuscript exactly according to the instructions. That is the easiest and the most efficient way to have a good published manuscript.

9. References

Balazinski M., Czogala E. and Jemielniak K. Jan., (2002). Tool condition monitoring using artificial intelligence methods, *Engineering Application of Artificial Intelligence*, pp. 73-80,

Blanz W. E. and Gish S. L. (1990), A connectionist classifier architecture applied to image segmentation, *Proc. 10th Int. Conf. Pattern Recognition*, pp. 272-277.

Brown M. and Harris C. J. (1995), On the condition of adaptive neurofuzzy models, *Int. Conf. of the 4th Int. Conf. on Fuzzy Systems and the 2nd Int. Fuzzy Engineerig Symp., IEEE/IFES*, pp. 663-670.

Chungchoo C., and Saini D. (2002), On-line tool wear estimation in CNC turning operations using fuzzy neural network model, *Int. J. of Machine Tools and Manufacture*, pp. 29-40.

Dimla D. E. and Lister P. M, (2000). On-line metal cutting tool condition monitoring. I: force and vibration analyses, *Int. J. of Machine Tools and Manufacturing*, pp. 739-768, ,

Dimla D. E. and Lister P. M, May (2000), On-line metal cutting tool condition monitoring. II: tool-state classification using multi-layer perceptron neural networks, *Int. J. of Machine Tools and Manufacturing*, pp. 769-781,

Ertunc H. M., and Loparo K. A. (2001), A decision fusion algorithm for tool wear condition monitoring in drilling, *Int. J. of Machine Tools and Manufacture*, pp. 1347-1362.

Fukuda T., Shimojima K., etc. (1992), "Multi-sensor integration system with fuzzy inference and neural network", *Proc. Int. Joint Conf. Neural networks, vol. II*, pp. 757-762.

Li X., Dong S. and Venuvinod P. K. (2000), Hybrid learning for tool wear monitoring, *Int. J. of Advanced Manufacturing Technology*, pp. 303-307.

LI X. L., Tso S. K. and Wang J. (2000), Real-time tool condition monitoring using wavelet transforms and fuzzy techniques, *IEEE Transactions on Systems, Man and Cybernetics Part C: Applications and Reviews*, pp. 353-357.

Scheffer C. and Kratz H., May. (2003). Development of a tool wear-monitoring system for hard turning, *Int. J. of Machine Tools and Manufacturing*, pp. 973-985,

Sick B. (2001), Tool wear monitoring in turning: A neural network application, *Measurement and Control*, pp. 207-222.

Wilkinson P., Reuben R. L. and Jones J. D. C. et al. (1999), Tool wear prediction from acoustic emission and surface characteristics via an artificial neural network, *Mechanical Systems and Signal Processing*, pp. 955-966.

25

Mining Digital Music Score Collections: Melody Extraction and Genre Recognition

Pedro J. Ponce de León, José M. Iñesta and David Rizo
Department of Software and Computing Systems
University of Alicante,
Spain

1. Introduction

In the field of computer music, pattern recognition algorithms are very relevant for music information retrieval (MIR) applications. Two challenging tasks in this area are the automatic recognition of musical genre and melody extraction, having a number of applications like indexing and selecting musical databases.

One of the main references for music is its melody. In a practical environment of digital music score collections the information can be found in standard MIDI file format. Music is structured as a number of tracks in this file format, usually one of them containing the melodic line, while other tracks contain the accompaniment. Finding that melody track is very useful for a number of applications, like speeding up melody matching when searching in MIDI databases, extracting motifs for musicological analysis, building music thumbnails or extracting melodic ringtones from MIDI files.

In the first part of this chapter, musical content information is modeled by computing global statistical descriptors from track content. These descriptors are the input to a random forest classifier that assigns the probability of being a melodic line to each track. The track with the highest probability is then selected as the one containing the melodic line of the MIDI file. The first part of this chapter ends with a discussion on results obtained from a number of databases of different music genres.

The second part of the chapter deals with the problem of classifying such melodies in a collection of music genres. A slightly different approach is used for this task, first dividing a melody track in segments of fixed length. Statistical features are extracted for each segment and used to classify them as one of several genres. The proposed methodology is presented, covering the feature extraction, feature selection, and genre classification stages. Different supervised classification methods, like Bayesian classifier and nearest neighbors are applied. As a proof of concept, the performance of such algorithms against different description models and parameters is analyzed for two particular musical genres, like jazz and classical music.

2. Symbolic music information retrieval

Music information retrieval (MIR) is a field of research devoted to the extraction of meaningful information from the content of music sources. In the application of pattern recognition techniques to MIR, two main folds can be found in the literature: audio information retrieval and symbolic music information retrieval.

In the first case the raw digital audio signal is processed. Usually wav or MP3 files are the input to these systems. No explicit information about notes, voices or any musical symbol or tag is encoded in the signal. On the other hand, symbolic MIR is based on processing symbols with direct musical meaning: notes with pitch and duration, lyrics, tags, etc. The most common formats used as input for these systems are ASCII text files like kern, abc, MusicXML, or binary files containing note control information like MIDI files. In these formats input data contain information about what and how is to be played, instead of the rendered music itself like in the audio signal. The semantics of both approaches is different, at least in the first stage of information retrieval algorithms. In the case of symbolic processing, as musical information use to be found as input, most existing music information theory can be applied to the task. On the other hand, the use as raw audio lacks from the basic music information as notes or voices notes or voices. Signal processing techniques must be used to extract this musical data, thus introducing noise to the actual musical material found in the audio. Currently, some of the most active tasks in audio information retrieval have as objective the extraction of that musical information like note onsets, timbre or voices. With this preprocessing of the raw audio, many of the work lines that can be found in the symbolic music information retrieval can also be tackled, but with the drawback of the possibly ill musical data extracted.

The goals of symbolic music information retrieval can be said to be more close to the actual music theory or musicological analysis that those of audio information retrieval. Some of the most active work areas in the symbolic approach nowadays is listed below:

- *Genre and mood classification:* the objective in those two tasks is to tell the mood or musical genre a given input belongs to (McKay & Fujinaga, 2004; Zhu et al., 2004; Cruz et al., 2003; Buzzanca, 2002; Pérez-Sancho et al., 2004; Dannenberg et al., 1997; van Kranenburg & Backer, 2004; Ponce de León et al., 2004)
- *Similarity and retrieval:* the final target in this work line is to be able to perform a search in a music data base to get the most similar pieces to an input query (Typke et al., 2003; Lemstrom & Tarhio, 2000)
- *Cover song identification:* the detection of plagiarisms and variations of the same song is the main goal in this case (Grachten et al., 2004; Li & Sleep, 2004; Rizo et al., 2008)
- *Key finding:* Guess the tonality and key changes of the score given the notes (Rizo et al., 2006a; Temperley, 2004)
- *Melody identification:* to identify the melody line among several MIDI tracks or music staffs, in opposite to those that contain accompaniment (Rizo et al., 2006b)
- *Motive extraction:* to find motives (short note sequences) in a score that are the most repeated ones acting as the main themes of the song (Serrano & Iñesta, 2006)
- *Meter detection:* given the input song reconstruct the meter from the flow of notes (Temperley, 2004)
- *Score segmentation:* split the song in parts like musical phrases (Spevak et al., 2002)
- *Music analysis:* perform musicological analysis for teaching, automatic or computed assisted composition, automatic expressive performance, and build a musical model for other MIR tasks (Illescas et al., 2007)

3. Melody characterization

A huge number of digital music score can be found on the Internet or in multimedia digital libraries. These scores are stored in files conforming to a proprietary or open format, like MIDI or the various XML music formats available. Most of these files contain music organized in a way such that the leading part of the music, the melody, is stored separately from the rest of the musical content, which is often the accompaniment for the melody. In particular, a standard MIDI file is usually structured as a number of tracks, one for each voice in a music piece. One of them usually contains a melodic line or *melody*, specially in the case of modern popular music.

Melody is a somewhat elusive musical term that often refers to a central part of a music piece that catches most of the listener's attention, and which the rest of music parts are subordinated to. This is one of many definitions that can be found in many places, particularly music theory manuals. Most of these definitions share some melody traits, like 'sequential', 'monophonic', 'main reference', 'unity in diversity', 'lyrics related', 'culturally dependent', etc.

Our goal is to automatically find this melody track in a MIDI file using statistical properties of the musical content and pattern recognition techniques. The proposed methodology can be applied to other symbolic music file formats, because the information used to take decisions is based solely on how the notes are arranged within each voice of a digital score. Only the feature extraction front-end would need to be adapted for dealing with other formats.

The identification of the melody track is very useful for a number of applications. For example, in melody matching, when the query is either in symbolic format (Uitdenbogerd & Zobel, 1999) or in audio format (Ghias et al., 1995), the process can be speeded up if the melody track is known or if there is a way to know which tracks are most likely to contain the melody, because the query is almost always a melody fragment. Another useful application can be helping motif extraction systems to build music thumbnails of digital scores for music collection indexing.

3.1 Related works

To our best knowledge, the automatic description of a melody has not been tackled as a main objective in the literature. The most similar problem to the automatic melody definition is that of extracting a melody line from a polyphonic source. This problem has been approached from at least three different points of view with different understandings of what a melody is. The first approach is the extraction of melody from a polyphonic *audio* source. For this task it is important to describe the melody in order to leave out those notes that are not candidates to belong to the melody line (Eggink & Brown, 2004). In the second approach, a melody line (mainly monophonic) must be extracted from a *symbolic* polyphonic source where no notion of *track* is used (I.Karydis et al., 2007). With this approach, Uitdenbogerd and Zobel (Uitdenbogerd & Zobel, 1998) developed four algorithms for detecting the melodic line in polyphonic MIDI files, assuming that a melodic line is a monophonic sequence of notes. These algorithms are based mainly on note pitches; for example, keeping at every time the note of highest pitch from those that sound at that time (skyline algorithm).

Other works on this line focus on how to split a polyphonic source into a number of monophonic sequences by partitioning it into a set of melodies (Marsden, 1992). In general, these works are called monophonic reduction techniques (Lemstrom & Tarhio, 2000).

The last approach to melody characterization is to select one track containing the melody from a list of input tracks of symbolic polyphonic music (e.g. MIDI). This is, by the way, our own approach. Other authors, like (Ghias et al., 1995), built a system to process MIDI files extracting a sort of melodic line using simple heuristics. (Tang et al., 2000) presented a work where the aim was to propose candidate melody tracks, given a MIDI file. They take decisions based on single features derived from informal assumptions about what a melody track may be. (Madsen & Widmer, 2007) try to solve the problem by the use of several combination of the entropies of different melody properties like pitch classes, intervals, etc.

3.2 What's a melody?

Before focusing on the machine learning methodology to extract automatically the characterization of a *melody*, the musical concept ofmelody needs to be reviewed.

Melody is a concept that has been given many definitions, all of them complementary. The variability of the descriptions can give an idea on the difficulty of the task to extract a description automatically.

From the music theory point of view, Ernst Toch (Toch, 1997) defines it as *"a succession of different pitch sounds brighten up by the rhythm"*. He also writes *"a melody is a sound sequence with different pitches, in opposition to its simultaneous audition that constitutes what is named as chord"*. He distinguishes also the term 'melody' from the term 'theme'.

A music dictionary (Sadie & Grove, 1984) defines melody as: *"a combination of a pitch series and a rhythm having a clearly defined shape"*.

The music theory literature lacks works about melody in favour of works about counterpoint, harmony, or "form" (Selfridge-Field, 1998). Besides, the concept of melody is dependant on the genre or the cultural convention. The most interesting studies about melody have appeared in recent years, mainly influenced by new emerging models like generative grammars (Baroni, 1978), artificial intelligence (Cope, 1996), and Gestalt and cognitive psychology (Narmour, 1990). All these works place effort on understand the melody in order to generate it automatically.

The types of tracks and descriptions of *melody* versus *accompaniment* is posed in (Selfridge-Field, 1998). The author distinguishes:

- *compound* melodies where there is only a melodic line where some notes are principal, and others tend to accompany, being this case the most frequent in unaccompanied string music.
- *self-accompanying* melodies, where some pitches pertain both to the thematic idea and to the harmonic (or rhythmic) support
- *submerged* melodies consigned to inner voices
- *roving* melodies, in which the theme migrates from part to part
- *distributed* melodies, in which the defining notes are divided between parts and the prototype cannot be isolated in a single part.

From the audio processing community, several definitions can be found about what a melody is. Maybe, the most general definition is found in (Kim et al., 2000): *"melody is an auditory object that emerges from a series of transformations along the six dimensions: pitch, tempo, timbre, loudness, spatial location, and reverberant environment"*.

(Gomez et al., 2003) gave a list of mid and low-level features to describe melodies:

- Melodic attributes derived from numerical analysis of pitch information: number of notes, tessitura, interval distribution, melodic profile, melodic density.
- Melodic attributes derived from musical analysis of the pitch data: key information, scale type information, cadence information.
- Melodic attributes derived from a structural analysis: motive analysis, repetitions, patterns location, phrase segmentation.

Another attempt to describe a melody can be found in (Temperley, 2004). In that book, Temperley proposes a model of melody perception based on three principles:

- Melodies tend to remain within a narrow pitch range.
- Note-to-note intervals within a melody tend to be small.
- Notes tend to conform to a key profile (a distribution) that depends on the key.

All these different properties a melody should have can be used as a reference to build an automatic melody characterization system.

4. Melody track identification

As stated before, in this work the aim is to decide which of the tracks contains the main melody in a multitrack standard MIDI file. For this, we need to assume that the melody is indeed contained in a single track. This is the case for today's world music.

The features that should characterize melody and accompaniment voices must be defined in order to be able to select the melodic track. There are some features in a melody track that, at first sight, seem to be enough for identifying it, like the presence of higher pitches (Uitdenbogerd & Zobel, 1998) or being monophonic. Unfortunately, any empirical analysis will show that these hypotheses do not hold in general, and more sophisticated criteria need to be devised in order to take accurate decisions.

To overcome these problems, a classifier ensemble able to learn what is a melodic track from note distribution statistics has been used in this work. In order to setup and test the classifier, a number of data sets based on several music genres and consisting of multitrack standard MIDI files have been constructed. All tracks in such files are labeled either as melody or non-melody.

The classic methodology in the pattern recognition field has been used in this work. A vector of numeric descriptors is extracted from each track of a target midifile, and these descriptors are the input to a classifier that assigns to each track its probability of being a melody. This is the big picture of the method. The random forest classifier (Breiman, 2001) – an ensemble of decision trees– was chosen as the pattern recognition tool for this task. The WEKA (Witten & Frank, 1999) toolkit was used to implement the system.

4.1 MIDI track characterization

The content of each non-empty track[1] is characterized by a vector of descriptors based on descriptive statistics of note pitches and durations that summarize track content information. This kind of statistical description of musical content is sometimes referred to as *shallow structure description* (Pickens, 2001; Ponce de León et al., 2004b).

A set of descriptors has been defined, based on several categories of features that assess melodic and rhythmic properties of a music sequence, as well as track related properties. This set of descriptors is presented in Table 1. The left column indicates the category being analyzed, and the right one shows the kind of statistics describing properties from that category.

Four features were designed to describe the track as a whole and fifteen to describe particular aspects of its content. For these fifteen descriptors, both normalized and non-normalized versions have been computed. The former were calculated using the formula $(value_i - min)/(max - min)$, where $value_i$ is the descriptor to be normalized corresponding to

---

[1] tracks containing at least one note event. Empty tracks are discarded.

the i-th track, and *min* and *max* are, respectively, the minimum and maximum values for this descriptor for all the tracks of the target midifile. This allows to know these properties proportionally to the other tracks in the same file. This way, a total number of $4+15\times2 = 34$ descriptors were initially computed for each track.

Category	Descriptors
Track information	Normalized duration
	Number of notes
	Occupation rate
	Polyphony rate
Pitch	Highest
	Lowest
	Mean
	Standard deviation
Pitch intervals	Number of different intv.
	Largest
	Smallest
	Mean
	Mode
	Standard deviation
Note durations	Longest
	Shortest
	Mean
	Standard deviation
Syncopation	Number of Syncopated notes

Table 1. Track content descriptors

The track information descriptors are its normalized duration, number of notes, occupation rate (proportion of the track length occupied by notes), and the polyphony rate, defined as the ratio between the number of ticks in the track where two or more notes are active simultaneously and the track duration in ticks.

Pitch descriptors are measured using MIDI pitch values. The maximum possible MIDI pitch is 127 (note G_8) and the minimum is 0 (note C_{-2}). The interval descriptors summarize information about the difference in pitch between consecutive notes. The absolute pitch interval values were computed. Finally, note duration descriptors were computed in terms of beats, so they are independent from the MIDI file resolution.

4.2 Feature selection

The descriptors listed above are a complete list of computed features, but any pattern recognition system needs to explore which are those features that actually are able to separate the target classes.

Some descriptors show evidence of statistically significant differences when comparing their distributions for melody and non-melody tracks, while other descriptors do not. This property is implicitly observed by the classification technique utilized (see Section 4.3), that performs a selection of features in order to take decisions.

A view to the graphs in Figure 1 provides some hints on how a melody track could look like. This way, a melody track seems to have less notes than other non-melody tracks, an average mean pitch, it contains small intervals, and has not too long notes. When this sort of hints are combined by the classifier, a decision about the track "melodicity" is taken.

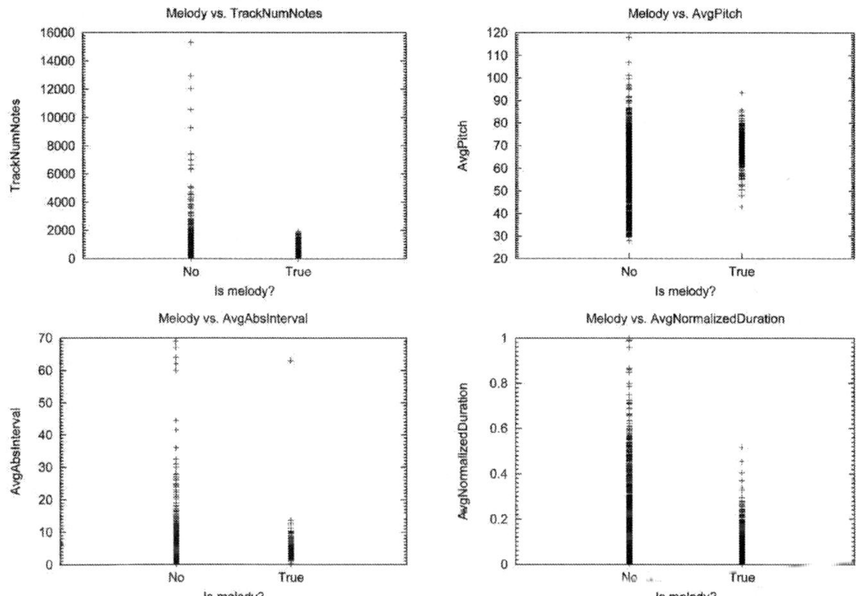

Fig. 1. Distribution of values for some descriptors: (top-left) number of notes, (top-right) mean pitch, (bottom-left) mean absolute interval, and (bottom-right) mean relative duration.

4.3 The random forest classifier

A number of classifiers were tested in an initial stage of this research and the random forest classifier yielded the best results among them, so it was chosen for the experiments presented in the next section.

Random forests (Breiman, 2001) are weighed combinations of decision trees that use a random selection of features to build the decision taken at each node. This classifier has shown good performance compared to other classifier ensembles with a high robustness with respect to noise. One forest consists of K trees. Each tree is built to maximum size using CART (Duda et al., 2000) methodology without pruning. Therefore, each leaf on the tree corresponds to a single class. The number F of randomly selected features to split on the training set at each node is fixed for all the trees. After the trees have grown, new samples are classified by each tree and their results are combined, giving as a result a membership probability for each class.

In our case, the membership for class "melody" is interpreted as the probability that a track will contain a melodic line.

4.4 Track selection procedure

There are MIDI files that contain more than one track which is suitable to be classified as melody: singing voice, instrument solos, melodic introductions, etc. On the other hand, as usually happens in classical music, some songs do not have an obvious melody, like in complex symphonies or single-track piano sequences. The algorithm proposed here can deal with the first case. For the second case, there are more suitable methods (Uitdenbogerd & Zobel, 1998) that perform melody extraction from polyphonic data.

In some of the experiments in the next section, at most one melody track per MIDI file is selected. However, a file can contain more than one melody track. Therefore, given a file, all its non-empty tracks are classified and their probabilities of being a melody are obtained. Then the track with the highest probability is selected as the melody track. If all tracks have near-zero probability (actually less than 0.01), no melody track is selected –that is, all tracks are considered as non-melody tracks.

In the first stages of this work, a probability threshold around 0.5 was established in order to discard tracks whose probability of being a melody was below that value. This resulted in some files in our test datasets being tagged as melody-less. However most of those files actually have a melody. In general, this produced systems with lower estimated accuracy than systems with a near-zero probability threshold.

4.5 Experiments

4.5.1 Datasets and tools

Six corpora (see Table 2) were created, due to the lack of existing databases for this task. The files were downloaded from a number of freely accessible Internet sites. First, three corpora (named JZ200, CL200, and KR200) were created to set up the system and to tune the parameter values. JZ200 contains jazz music files, CL200 has classical music pieces where there was a melody track, and KR200 contains popular music songs with a part to be sung (karaoke (.kar) format). All of them are made up of 200 files. Then, three other corpora (named JAZ, CLA, and KAR) from the same music genres were compiled from a number of different sources to validate our method. This dataset is available for research purposes on request to the authors.

Corpus ID	Genre	Files	Tracks	Melody tracks
CL200	Classical	200	687	197
JZ200	Jazz	200	769	197
KR200	Popular	200	1370	179
CLA	Classical	131	581	131
JAZ	Jazz	1023	4208	1037
KAR	Popular	1360	9253	1288

Table 2. Corpora used in the experiments, with identifier, music genre, number of files, total number of tracks, total number of melody tracks and baseline success ratio.

The main difficulty for building the data sets was to label the tracks in the MIDI files. Text tagging of MIDI tracks based on metadata such as the track name, is unreliable. Thus, a manual labeling approach was carried out. A musician listened to each one of the MIDI files playing all tracks simultaneously. For each file, tracks containing the perceived melody were identified and tagged as *melody*. The rest of tracks in the same file were tagged as *non-melody*. In particular, introduction passages, second voices or instrumental solo parts were tagged as *non-melody*.

Some songs had no tracks tagged as melody because either it was absent, or the song contained some kind of melody-less accompaniment, or it had a canon-like structure, where the melody moves constantly from one track to another. Other songs contained more than one melody track (e.g. duplicates, often with a different timbre) and all those tracks were tagged as *melody*.

The WEKA package was used to carry out the experiments described here. It was extended to compute the proposed track descriptors directly from MIDI files.

Four experiments have been carried out, as listed below:

- Melody vs. non-melody classification
- Melody track selection
- Genre specificity
- Training set specificity

The first one tries to assess the capability of random forests to classify melodic and non-melody tracks properly. In the second experiment, the aim is to evaluate how accurate the system is for identifying the melody track in a MIDI file. Finally, the specificity of the system with respect to both the music genre and the corpora utilized were tested.

4.5.2 Melody versus non-melody classification

As described before, our aim is to assess the capability of the classifier to discriminate melody from non-melody tracks. Therefore, given a set of tracks, this experiment classifies them either as melody or non-melody. The random forest classifier assigns a class membership probability to each test sample, so in this experiment a test track is assigned to the class with the highest membership probability.

As a proof of concept, three independent sub-experiments were carried out, using the three 200-file corpora (CL200, JZ200, and KR200). This way, 2826 tracks provided by these files were classified in two classes: *melody / non-melody* A ten-fold cross-validation scheme was used to estimate the accuracy of the method. The success results are shown in Table 3 and figure 2, along with the baseline ratio when considering a dumb classifier that always output the most frequent class (*non-melody* for all datasets). The remarkable success percentages obtained are due to the fact that the classifier was able to successfully map the input feature vector space to the class space. This shows that content statistics in combination with decision tree based learning can produce good results on the task at hand.

Also, precision (P), recall (R) and the F-measure (F) are shown for melody tracks. These standard information retrieval measures are based on the so-called *true-positive* (TP), *false-positive* (FP) and *false-negative* (FN) counts. For this experiment, TP is the number of melody tracks successfully classified, FP is the number of misclassified non-melody tracks, and finally, FN is the number of misclassified melody tracks. The precision, recall and F-measure are calculated as follows:

$$P = \frac{TP}{TP + FP}$$

$$R = \frac{TP}{TP + FN}$$

$$F = \frac{2 \times R \times P}{R + P}$$

These results have been obtained using $K = 10$ trees and $F = 5$ randomly selected features for the random forest trees. The same classifier structure was used in the rest of experiments presented in the next sections.

Corpus	Success	Std. dev.	Baseline	P	R	F
CL200	99.6%	0.7	71.3%	0.996	0.998	0.997
JZ200	98.3%	1.4	74.4%	0.981	0.996	0.989
KR200	96.8%	1.8	87.0%	0.971	0.994	0.982

Table 3. Melody versus non-melody classification results.

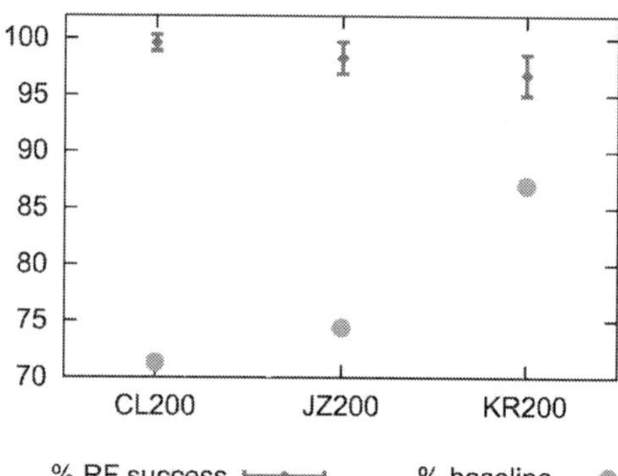

Fig. 2. Melody vs. non-melody classification success and baseline

4.5.3 Melodic track selection experiment

In this second experiment, the goal is to test wether the method selects the proper melody track from a MIDI file. For this experiment, the system was trained the same way as in the previous one, but now a test sample is not a single track but a MIDI file. Due to the limited number of samples available (200 per corpus), this experiment was performed using a leave-one-out scheme at the MIDI file level to estimate the classification accuracy. The classifier assigns a class membership probability to each track in a test file. For each file, the system outputs the track number that gets highest membership probability for class *melody*, except when all these probabilities are near-zero, in which case the system considers the file has no melody track.

The classifier answer for a givenMIDI file is considered correct if

1.   At least one track is tagged as *melody* and the selected track is one of them.
2.   There are no melody tracks and the classifier outputs no melody track number.

Results are shown in Table 4.

Corpus	Success
CL200	100.0%
JZ200	96.5%
KR200	72.3%

Table 4. Melody track selection results.

Note the high quality of the results for CL200 and JZ200. However, a lower success rate has been obtained for the karaoke files. This is due to the fact that 31 out of 200 files in this corpus were tagged by a human expert as having no actual melody track, but they have some portions of tracks that could be considered as melody (like short instrument solo parts), thus confusing the classifier as FP hits, therefore lowering the classifier precision for this corpus.

4.5.4 Genre specificity

This experiment was designed in order to evaluate the system robustness against different corpora. In particular, it is interesting to know how specific the classifier's inferred rules are with respect to the music genre of files considered for training. For it, two melody track selection sub-experiments, like the ones in the previous section, were performed: in the first one, the classifier was trained with a 200-file corpus of a given music genre, and tested with a different corpus of the same genre (see Table 5). For the second sub-experiment, the classifier was trained using data from two genres and then tested with files from the third genre dataset (see Table 6).

Train.	Test	Success
CL200	CLA	60.6%
JZ200	JAZ	96.5%
KR200	KAR	73.9%

Table 5. Melody track selection within genre.

Train.	Test	Success
KAR+JAZ	CLA	71.7%
CLA+KAR	JAZ	92.6%
CLA+JAZ	KAR	64.9%

Table 6. Melody track selection across genres.

The results in Table 5 show that the performance of the system degrades when more complex files are tested. The 200-file corpora are datasets that include MIDI files that were selected among many others for having an 'easily' (for a human) identifiable melody track. This holds also for the JAZ corpus, as most jazz music MIDI files have a lead voice (or instrument) track plus some accompaniment tracks like piano, bass and drums. However, it does not hold in general for the other two corpora. Classical music MIDI files (CLA corpus) come in very different structural layouts, due to both the way that the original score is organized and the idiosyncrasy of the MIDI file authors. This is also mostly true for the KAR corpus. Moreover, karaoke files tend to make intensive use of duplicate voices and dense pop arrangements with lots of tracks containing many ornamentation motifs. In addition, we have verified the presence of very short sequences for the CLAS corpus, causing less quality in the statistics that also degrades the classification results.

As both the training and test corpora contain samples of the same music genre, better results were expected. However, the CLA and KAR corpora are definitively harder to deal with, as it became clear in the second experiment presented in this section. So, it can be said that the difficulty of the task resides more on the particular internal organization of tracks in the MIDI files than on the file music genre, despite that the results in Table 5 seem to point out that genre makes a difference. The second experiment presented in Table 6 showed some evidence in that direction.

Most errors for the CLA test set were produce because a non-melody track was selected as melody (a kind of false positive). Same type of errors can be found for the KAR corpus, along with errors due to the classifier not finding any melody tracks in files with a melody tagged track (a kind of false-negative).

Results from the second sub-experiment show that performance is poorer (with respect to the first one) when no data from the test genre were used for training. This does not happen in classical music, probably due to effects related to the problems expressed above.

4.5.5 Training set specificity

To see how conditioned are these results by the particular training sets utilized, a generalization study was carried out building a new training set merging the three 200-files corpora (named *ALL200*), and then using the other corpora for test. The problem to solve is again the one discussed in section 4.5.3: selecting the proper melody track from a MIDI file. The results are detailed in Table 7.

This shows that, when using a multi-genre dataset, the performance of the system is somewhat improved (now the training set contains samples from the same genre as the test dataset). Note that the results are better despite that the size of the training set is smaller than the size of those used in Section 4.5.4.

Training	Test	Success
ALL200	CLA	73.8%
ALL200	JAZ	97.0%
ALL200	KAR	70.2%

Table 7. Melody track selection by genres when training with data from all the genres.

When combining all the success results, taking into account the different cardinalities of the test sets, the average successful melody track identification percentage is 81.2 %.

The method proposed here can be used as a tool for extracting the melody track in conjunction with a system for music genre recognition presented in the next section. This system is a melody based genre recognition system. It extracts information from melody tracks in order to recognize the melody genre. This way MIDI files need not to be preprocessed by an expert in order to identify the melody track.

5. Music genre recognition

One of the problems to solve in MIR is the modelization of music genre. The computer could be trained to recognise the main features that characterise music genres in order to look for that kind of music over large musical databases. The same scheme is suitable to learn stylistic features of composers or even model a musical taste for users. Other application of such a system can be its use in cooperation with automatic composition algorithms to guide this process according to a given stylistic profile.

A number of papers explore the capabilities of machine learning methods to recognise music genre. Pampalk et al. (Pampalk et al., 2003) use self-organising maps (SOM) to pose the problem of organising music digital libraries according to sound features of musical themes, in such a way that similar themes are clustered, performing a content-based classification of the sounds. (Whitman et al., 2001) present a system based on neural networks and support vector machines able to classify an audio fragment into a given list of sources or artists. Also, in (Soltau et al., 1998) a neural system to recognise music types from sound inputs is described. An *emergent* approach to genre classification is used in (Pachet et al., 2001), where a classification emerges from the data without any *a priori* given set of genres. The authors use co-ocurrence techniques to automatically extract musical similarity between titles or artists. The sources used for classification are radio programs and databases of compilation CDs.

Other works use music data in symbolic form (most MIDI data) to perform genre recognition. (Dannenberg et al., 1997) use a naive Bayes classifier, a linear classifier and neural networks to recognize up to eight moods (genres) of music, such as lyrical, frantic, etc. Thirteen statistical features derived from MIDI data are used for this genre discrimination. In (Tzanetakis et al., 2003), pitch features are extracted both from MIDI data and audio data and used separately to classify music within five genres. Pitch histograms regarding to the tonal pitch are used in (Thom, 2000) to describe blues fragments of the saxophonist Charlie Parker. Also pitch histograms and SOM are used in (Toiviainen & Eerola, 2001) for musicological analysis of folk songs. Other researchers use sequence processing techniques like Hidden Markov Models (Chai & Vercoe, 2001) and universal compression algorithms (Dubnov & Assayag, 2002) to classify musical sequences.

(Stamatatos & Widmer, 2002) use stylistic performance features and the discriminant analysis technique to obtain an ensemble of simple classifiers that work together to recognize the most likely music performer of a piece given a set of skilled candidate pianists. The input data are obtained from a computer-monitored piano, capable of measuring every key and pedal movement with high precision.

Compositions from five well known eighteenth-century composers are classified in (van Kranenburg & Backer, 2004) using several supervised learning methods and twenty genre features, most of them being counterpoint characteristics. This work offers some conclusions about the differences between composers discovered by the different learning methods.

In other work (Cruz et al., 2003), the authors show the ability of grammatical inference methods for modeling musical genre. A stochastic grammar for each musical genre is inferred from examples, and those grammars are used to parse and classify new melodies. The authors also discuss about the encoding schemes that can be used to achieve the best recognition result. Other approaches like multi-layer feed-forward neural networks (Buzzanca, 2002) have been used to classify musical genre from symbolic sources.

(McKay & Fujinaga, 2004, 2007a) use low and mid-level statistics of MIDI file content to perform music genre recognition by means of genetic algorithms and pattern recognition techniques. They have developed several tools for feature extraction from music symbolic sources (particularly MIDI files) or web sites (McKay & Fujinaga, 2006a, 2007b). In (McKay & Fujinaga, 2006b), the authors provide some insight on why is it worth continuing research in automatic music genre recognition, despite the fact that the ground-truth information available for research is often not too reliable, being subject to subjective tagging, market forces or being culture-dependent. Most of the classification problems detected seem to be related to the lack of reliable ground-truth, from the definition of realistic and diverse genre labels, to the need of combining features of different nature, like cultural, high- and low-level features. They also identify, in particular, the need for being able to label different sections of a music piece with different tags.

The system presented in this section share some features with the one developed by McKay, as the use of low level statistics and pattern recognition techniques but, while McKay extract features from the MIDI file as a whole, our system focus on melody tracks, using a *sliding window* technique to obtain melody segments that become instances to feed the pattern recognition tools. This allows to obtain partial decisions for a melody track that can offer the users sensible information for different parts of a music work. Also, this decisions can be combined to output a classification decision for a music piece.

5.1 An experimental framework for automatic music genre recognition

In this section a framework for experimenting on automatic music genre recognition from symbolic representation of melodies (digital scores) is presented. It is based on shallow structural features of melodic content, like melodic, harmonic, and rhythmic statistical descriptors. This framework involves all the usual stages in a pattern recognition system, like feature extraction, feature selection, and classification stages, in such a way that new features and corpora from different musical genres can be easily incorporated and tested.

Our working hypothesis is that melodies from a same musical genre may share some common low-level features, permitting a suitable pattern recognition system, based on statistical descriptors, to assign the proper musical genre to them.

Two well-defined music genres, like jazz and classical, have been chosen as a workbench for this research. The initial results have been encouraging (Ponce de León & Iñesta, 2003) but the method performance for different classification algorithms, descriptor models, and parameter values needed to be thoroughly tested. This way, a framework for musical genre recognition can be set up, where new features and new musical genres can be easily incorporated and tested.

This section presents the proposed methodology, describing the musical data, the descriptors, and the classifiers used. The initial set of descriptors will be analyzed to test their contribution to the musical genre separability. These procedures will permit us to build reduced models, discarding not useful descriptors. Then, the classification results obtained with each classifier and an analysis of them with respect to the different description parameters will be presented. Finally, conclusions and possible lines of further work are discussed.

5.2 Musical data

MIDI files from jazz and classical music, were collected. These genres were chosen due to the general agreement in the musicology community about their definition and limits. Classical melody samples were taken from works by Mozart, Bach, Schubert, Chopin, Grieg, Vivaldi, Schumann, Brahms, Beethoven, Dvorak, Haendel, Paganini and Mendelssohn. Jazz music samples were standard tunes from a variety of well known jazz authors including Charlie Parker, Duke Ellington, Bill Evans, Miles Davis, etc. The MIDI files are composed of several tracks, one of them being the melody track from which the input data are extracted[2]. The corpus is made up of a total of 110 MIDI files, 45 of them being classical music and 65 being jazz music. The length of the corpus is around 10000 bars (more than 6 hours of music). Table 8 summarizes the distribution of bars from each genre. This dataset is available for research purposes on request to the authors.

---

[2] All the melodies are written in 4/4 meter. Anyway, any other meter could be used because the measure structure is not use in any descriptor computation. All the melodies are monophonic sequences (at most one note is playing at any given time).

	Min.	Max.	Avg.	Total	% of total
JAZZ	16	203	73	4734	47.5%
CLAS	44	297	116	5227	52.5%

Table 8. Distribution of melody length in bars

This corpus has been manually checked for the presence and correctness of key, tempo and meter meta-events, as well as the presence of a monophonic melody track. The original conditions under which the MIDI files were created are unknown; They may be human performed tracks or sequenced tracks (i.e. generated fromscores) or even something of both worlds. Nevertheless, most of the MIDI files seem to fit a rather common scheme: a human-performed melody track with several sequenced accompaniment tracks.

The monophonic melodies consist of a sequence of musical events that can be either notes or silences. The pitch of each note can take a value from 0 to 127, encoded together with the MIDI note onset event. Each of these events at time t has a corresponding note off event at time $t + d$, being d the note duration measured in ticks[3]. Time gaps between a note off event and the next note onset event are silences.

5.3 Description scheme

A description scheme has been designed based on descriptive statistics that summaris the content of the melody in terms of pitches, intervals, durations, silences, harmonicity, rhythm, etc.

Each sample is a vector of musical descriptors computed from each melody segment available (See section 5.4 for a discussion about how these segments are obtained). Each vector is labeled with the genre of the melody which the segment belongs to. We have defined an initial set of descriptors based on a number of feature categories that assess the melodic, harmonic and rhythmic properties of a musical segment, respectively.

This initial model is made up of 28 descriptors summarized in table 9, and described next:

- Overall descriptors:
    - *Number of notes, number of significant silences, and number of not significant silences.* The adjective *significant* stands for silences explicitly written in the underlying score of the melody. In MIDI files, short gaps between consecutive notes may appear due to interpretation nuances like *stacatto*. These gaps (interpretation silences) are not considered significant silences since they should not appear in the score. To make a distinction between kinds of silence is not possible from the MIDI file and it has been made based on the definition of a silence duration threshold. This value has been empirically set to a duration of a sixteenth note. All silences with longer or equal duration than this threshold are considered significant.
- Pitch descriptors:
    - *Pitch range* (the difference in semitones between the highest and the lowest note in the melody segment), *average pitch* relative to the lowest pitch, and *standard deviation of pitches* (provides information about how the notes are distributed in the score).

---

[3] A *tick* is the basic unit of time in a MIDI file and is defined by the resolution of the file, measured in ticks per beat.

Category	Descriptors
Overall	Number of notes
	Number of significant silences
	Number of non-significant silences
Pitch	Pitch range
	Average pitch
	Dev. pitch
Note duration	Note duration range
	Avg. note duration
	Dev. note duration
Silence duration	Silence duration range
	Avg. silence duration
	Dev. silence duration
Inter Onset Interval	IOI range
	Avg. IOI
	Dev. IOI
Pitch interval	Interval range
	Avg. interval
	Dev. interval
Non-diatonic notes	Num. non-diatonic notes
	Avg. non-diatonic degrees
	Dev. non-diatonic degrees
Syncopation	Number of syncopes
Normality	Pitch distrib. normality
	Note duration distrib. normality
	Silence duration distrib. normality
	IOI distrib. normality
	Interval distrib. normality
	Non-diatonic degree distrib. normality

Table 9. Musical descriptors

- Note duration, silence duration and IOI[4] descriptors are measured in ticks and computed using a time resolution of $Q = 48$ ticks per bar [5]. Interval descriptors are computed as the difference in absolute value between the pitches of two consecutive notes.
- Harmonic descriptors:
    - *Number of non diatonic notes*. An indication of frequent excursions outside the song key (extracted from the MIDI file) or modulations.
    - *Average degree of non diatonic notes*. Describes the kind of excursions. This degree is a number between 0 and 4 that indexes the non diatonic notes of the diatonic scale of the tune key, that can be major or minor key[6]
    - *Standard deviation of degrees of non diatonic notes*. Indicates a higher variety in the non diatonic notes.

---

[4] An IOI is the distance, in ticks, between the onsets of two consecutive notes. Two notes are considered consecutive even in the presence of a silence between them.

[5] This is call quantisation. $Q = 48$ means that when a bar is composed of 4 beats, each beat can be divided, at most, into 12 ticks.

[6] Non diatonic degrees are: 0: ♭ II, 1: ♭ III (♮III for minor key), 2: ♭ V, 3: ♭ VI, 4: ♭ VII. The key is encoded at the beginning of the melody track. It has been manually checked for correctness in our data.

- Rhythmic descriptor:
  - *Number of syncopations*: notes that do not begin at measure beats but in some places between them (usually in the middle) and that extend across beats.
- Normality descriptors. They are computed using the D'Agostino statistic for assessing the distribution normality of the n values v_i in the segment for pitches, durations, intervals, etc. The test is performed using this equation:

$$D = \frac{\sum_i (i - \frac{n+1}{2}) v_i}{\sqrt{n^3 (\sum_i v_i^2 - \frac{1}{n} (\sum_i v_i)^2)}} \tag{1}$$

For pitch and interval properties, the range descriptors are computed as maximum minus minimum values, and the average-relative descriptors are computed as the average value minus the minimum value (only considering the notes in the segment). For durations (note duration, silence duration, and IOI descriptors) the range descriptors are computed as the ratio between the maximum and minimum values, and the average-relative descriptors are computed as the ratio between the average value and the minimum value.

This descriptive statistics is similar to histogram-based descriptions used by other authors (Thom, 2000; Toiviainen & Eerola, 2001) that also try to model the distribution of musical events in a music fragment. Computing the range, mean, and standard deviation from the distribution of musical properties, we reduce the number of features needed (each histogram may be made up of tens of features). Other authors have also used this sort of descriptors to classify music (Tzanetakis et al., 2003; Blackburn, 2000), mainly focusing on pitches.

5.4 Free parameter space

Given a melody track, the statistical descriptors presented above are computed from equal length segments extracted from the track, by defining a window of size ω measures. Once the descriptors of a segment have been extracted, the window is shifted δ measures forward to obtain the next segment to be described. Given a melody with $m > 0$ measures, the number of segments s of size $\omega > 0$ obtained from that melody is

$$s = \begin{cases} 1 & \text{if } \omega \geq m \\ 1 + \lceil \frac{m-\omega}{\delta} \rceil & \text{otherwise} \end{cases} \tag{2}$$

showing that at least one segment is extracted in any case (ω and s are positive integers; m and δ may be positive fractional numbers).

Taking ω and δ as free parameters in our methodology, different datasets of segments have been derived from a number of values for those parameters. The goal is to investigate how the combination of these parameters influences the segment classification results. The exploration space for this parameters will be referred to as $\omega\delta$-space. A point in this space is denoted as $\langle \omega, \delta \rangle$.

ω is the most important parameter in this framework, as it determines the amount of information available for the descriptor computations. Small values for ω would produce windows containing few notes, providing little reliable statistical descriptors. Large values for ω would lead to merge –probably different– parts of a melody into a single window and they also produce datasets with fewer samples for training the classifiers (see Eq. 2). The value of δ would affect mainly to the number of samples in a dataset. A small δ value combined with quite large values for ω may produce datasets with a large number of samples (see also Eq. 2). The details about the values used for these parameters can be found in section 5.7.

5.5 Feature selection procedure

The features described above have been designed according to those used in musicological studies, but there is no theoretical support for their genre classification capability. We have applied a selection procedure in order to keep those descriptors that better contribute to the classification. The method assumes feature independence, that is not true in general, but it tests the separability provided by each descriptor independently, and uses this separability to obtain a descriptor ranking.

Consider that the M descriptors are random variables $\{X_j\}_{j=1}^{M}$ whose N sample values are those of a dataset corresponding to a given $\omega\delta$-point. We drop the subindex j for clarity, because all the discussion applies to each descriptor. We split the set of N values for each descriptor into two subsets: $\{X_{C,i}\}_{i=1}^{N_C}$ are the descriptor values for classical samples and $\{X_{J,i}\}_{i=1}^{N_J}$ are those for the jazz samples, being N_C and N_J the number of classical and jazz samples, respectively. X_C and X_J are assumed to be independent random variables, since both sets of values are computed from different sets of melodies. We want to know whether these random variables belong to the same distribution or not. We have considered that both sets of values hold normality conditions, and assuming that the variances for X_C and X_J are different in general, the test contrasts the null hypothesis $H_0 \equiv \mu_C = \mu_J$ against $H_1 \equiv \mu_C \neq \mu_J$. If H_1 is concluded, it is an indication that there is a clear separation between the values of this descriptor for the two classes, so it is a good feature for genre classification. Otherwise, it does not seem to provide separability between the classes.

The following statistical for sample separation has been applied:

$$z = \frac{|\bar{X}_C - \bar{X}_J|}{\sqrt{\frac{s_C^2}{N_C} + \frac{s_J^2}{N_J}}} \quad , \tag{3}$$

where $\bar{X}_C$ and $\bar{X}_J$ are the means, and s_C^2 and s_J^2 the variances for the descriptor values for both classes. The greater the z value is, the wider the separation between both sets of values is for that descriptor. A threshold to decide when H_0 is more likely than H_1, that is to say, the descriptor passes the test for the given dataset, must be established. This threshold, computed from a t-student distribution with infinite degrees of freedom and a 99.7% confidence interval, is $z = 2.97$. Furthermore, the z value permits to arrange the descriptors according to their separation ability.

When this test is performed on a number of different $\omega\delta$-point datasets, a threshold on the number of passed tests can be set as a criterion to select descriptors. This threshold is expressed as a minimum percentage of tests passed. Once the descriptors are selected, a second criterion for grouping them permits to build several descriptor models incrementally. First, selected descriptors are ranked according to their z value averaged over all tests. Second, descriptors with similar z values in the ranking are grouped together. This way, several descriptor groups are formed, and new descriptor models can be formed by incrementally combining these groups. See the section 5.7.1 for the models that have been obtained.

5.6 Classifier implementation and tuning

Two algorithms from different classification paradigms have been used for genre recognition. They are fully supervised methods: The Bayesian classifier and the k-nearest neighbor (k-NN) classifier (Duda et al., 2000).

The Bayesian classifier is parametric and, when applied to a two-class problem, computes a discriminant function:

$$g(X) = log \frac{P(X \mid \omega_1)}{P(X \mid \omega_2)} + log \frac{\pi_1}{\pi_2} \tag{4}$$

for a test sample X where $P(X \mid \omega_i)$ is the conditional probability density function for class i and π_i are the priors of each class. Gaussian probability density functions for each genre are assumed for each descriptor. Means and variances are estimated separately for each class from the training data. The classifier assigns a sample to ω_1 if $g(X) > 0$, and to ω_2 otherwise. The decision boundaries, where $g(X) = 0$, are in general hyperquadrics in the feature space. The k-NN classifier uses an Euclidean metrics to compute the distance between the test sample and the training samples. The genre label is assigned to the test sample by a majority decision among the nearest k training samples (the k-neighborhood).

5.7 Experiments and results on music genre recognition
5.7.1 Feature selection results

The feature selection test presented in section 5.5 has been applied to datasets corresponding to 100 randomly selected points of the $\omega\delta$-space. This is motivated by the fact that the descriptor computation is different for each ω and the set of values is different for each δ, so the best descriptors may be different for different $\omega\delta$-points. Thus, by choosing a set of such points, the sensitivity of the classification to the feature selection procedure can be analysed. Being a random set of points is a good trade-off decision to minimise the risk of biasing this analysis.

The descriptors were sorted according to the average z value ($\bar{z}$) computed for the descriptors in the tests. The list of sorted descriptors is shown in table 10. The $\bar{z}$ values for all the tests and the percentage of passed tests for each descriptor are displayed. In order to select descriptors, a threshold on the number of passed tests has been set to 95%. This way, those descriptors which failed the separability hypothesis in more than a 5% of the experiments were discarded from the reduced models. Only 12 descriptors out of 28 were selected. In the right most column, the reduced models in which the descriptors were included are presented. Each model is denoted with the number of descriptors included in it.

Three reduced size models have been chosen, with 6, 10, and 12 descriptors. This models are built according to the $\bar{z}$ value as displayed in figure 3. The biggest gaps in the $\bar{z}$ values for the sorted descriptors led us to group the descriptors in these three reduced models. Note also that the values for $\bar{z}$ show a small deviation, showing that the descriptor separability is quite stable in the $\omega\delta$-space.

It is interesting to remark that at least one descriptor from each category of those defined in section 5.3 were selected for a reduced model. The best represented categories were pitches and intervals, suggesting that the pitches of the notes and the relation among them are the most influent features for this problem. From the statistical point of view, standard deviations were the most important features, since five from six possible ones were selected.

descriptor	$\bar{z}$	passed tests	models
Number of notes	22.5	100%	6,10,12
Average pitch	22.3	100%	6,10,12
Pitch range	22.2	100%	6,10,12
Interval range	20.3	100%	6,10,12
Syncopation	19.6	100%	6,10,12
Dev. pitch	18.7	100%	6,10,12
number of significant silences	14.2	100%	10,12
Interval distrib. normality	14.2	100%	10,12
Dev. interval	14.0	100%	10,12
Dev. IOI	13.2	97%	10,12
Dev. note duration	9.3	95%	12
Dev. non-diatonic degrees	9.1	100%	12
Dev. silence duration	6.3	94%	–
Silence duration range	6.1	87%	–
Note duration distrib. normality	6.0	89%	–
Avg. note duration	5.6	71%	–
Avg. silence duration	5.1	85%	–
Avg. non-diatonic degrees	4.9	66%	–
IOI range	4.7	53%	–
number of non-significant silences	4.5	76%	–
Silence duration distrib. normality	4.3	45%	–
Avg. IOI	4.2	53%	–
Non-diatonic degree distrib. normality	3.5	39%	–
Note duration range	3.3	34%	–
Pitch distrib. normality	2.6	25%	–
Num. non-diatonic notes	2.5	32%	–
IOI distrib. normality	2.2	20%	–
Avg. interval	1.7	14%	–

Table 10. Feature selection results

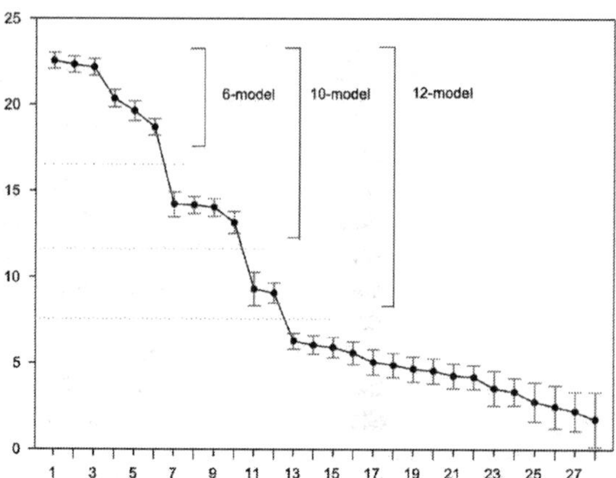

Fig. 3. Values for $\bar{z}$ for each descriptor as a function of their order numbers. The relative deviations for $\bar{z}$ in all the experiments are also displayed. The biggest gaps for $\bar{z}$ and the models are outlined.

5.7.2 The $\omega\delta$-space framework

The melodic segment parameter space has been established as follows:

$$\omega = 1, ..., 100 \qquad (5)$$

and, for each ω

$$\delta = \begin{cases} 1, ..., \omega & \text{if } \omega \leq 50 \\ 1, ..., 20 & \text{otherwise} \end{cases} \qquad (6)$$

The range for δ when $\omega > 50$ has been limited to 20 due to the very few number of samples obtained with large δ values for this ω range. This setup produces a total of 2275 points $\langle\omega,\delta\rangle$ in the $\omega\delta$-space. A number of experiments have been made for each of these points: one with each classifier (Bayes, NN) for each of the four description models discussed in section 5.7.1. Therefore, 12 different experiments for each $\omega\delta$-point have been made, denoted by $(\omega,\delta,\mu,\gamma)$, where $\mu \in \{6,10,12,28\}$ is the description model and $\gamma \in \{Bayes,NN\}$ the classifier used.
In order to obtain reliable results, a ten-fold crossvalidation scheme has been carried out for each of the $(\omega,\delta,\mu,\gamma)$ experiments, making 10 sub-experiments with about 10% of samples saved for test in each sub-experiment. The success rate for each $(\omega,\delta,\mu,\gamma)$ experiment is averaged for the 10 sub experiments.
The partitions were made at the MIDI file level, to make sure that training and test sets do not share segments from any common melody. Also the partitions were made in such a way that the relative number of measures for both genres were equal to those for the whole training set. This permits us to estimate the prior probabilities for both genres once and then use them for all the sub-experiments. Once the partitions have been made, segments of ω measures are extracted from the melody tracks, and labeled training and test datasets containing μ-dimensional descriptor vectors are constructed.
To summarise, 27300 experiments consisting of 10 sub-experiments each, have been carried out. The maximum number of segments extracted is $s = 9339$ for the $\omega\delta$-point $\langle3,1\rangle$. The maximum for s is not located at $\langle1,1\rangle$ as expected, due to the fact that segments not containing at least two notes are discarded. The minimum is $s = 203$ for $\langle100,20\rangle$. The average number of segments in the whole $\omega\delta$-space is 906. The average proportion of jazz segments is 36% of the total number of segments, with a standard deviation of about 4%. This is a consequence of the classical MIDI files having a greater length in average than jazz files, although there are less classical files than jazz files.

5.8 Classification results

Each $(\omega,\delta,\mu,\gamma)$ experiment has an average success rate, obtained from the crossvalidation scheme discussed in the previous section. The results presented here are based on those rates.

5.8.1 Bayes classifier

For one sub-experiment in a point in the $\omega\delta$-space, all the parameters needed to train the Bayesian classifier are estimated from the particular training set, except for the priors of each genre, that are estimated from the whole set, as explained above.
Figure 4 shows the classification results for the Bayesian classifier over the $\omega\delta$-space for the 12-descriptor model. This was one of the best combination of model and classifier (89.5% of success) in average for all the experiments. The best results for this classifier were found around $\langle58,1\rangle$, where a 93.2% average success was achieved.

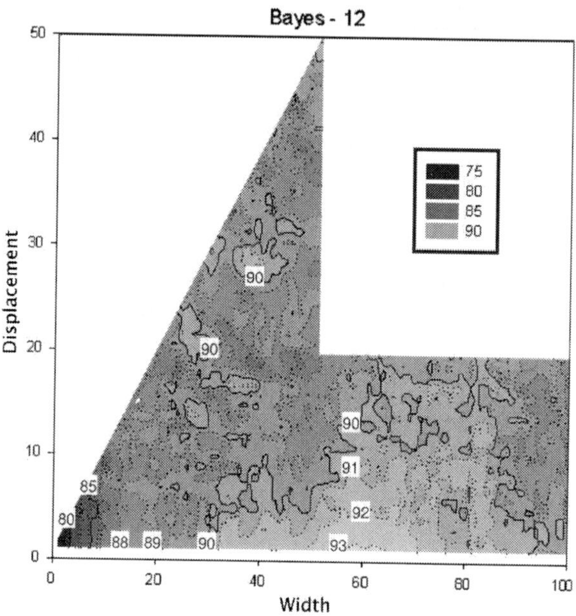

Fig. 4. Illustration of the recognition percentage in the $\omega\delta$-space for the Bayesian classifier with the 12-descriptor model. Numbers on top of level curves indicate the recognition percentage at places on the curve. The best results (around 93.2%) are found in the lighter area, with large widths and small displacements.

The best results for genre classification were expected to be found for moderate ω values, where enough musical events to calculate reliable statistical descriptors are contained in a segment, while musical events located in other parts of the melody are not mixed in a single segment. But the best results are generally obtained with a combination of large ω values and small δ. Experiments for $\omega = \infty$ (taking the whole melody as a single segment) are discussed in section 5.8.3.

The worst results occurred for small ω, due to the few musical events at hand when extracting a statistical description for such a small segment, leading to non reliable descriptors for the training samples.

All the three reduced models outperformed the 28-descriptor model (see Fig. 5 for a comparison between models for $\delta = 1$), except for $\omega \in [20,30]$, where the 28- descriptor model obtains similar results for small values of δ. For some reason, still unknown, the particular combination of ω and δ values in this range results in a distribution of descriptor values in the training sets that favours this classifier.

The overall best result (95.5% of average success) for the Bayesian classifier has been obtained with the 10-descriptor model in the point $\langle 98,1 \rangle$. See Table 11 for a summary of best results – indices represent the $\langle \omega, \delta \rangle$ values for which the best success rates were obtained. About 5% of the sub-experiments (4556 out of 91000) for all models yielded a 100% classification success.

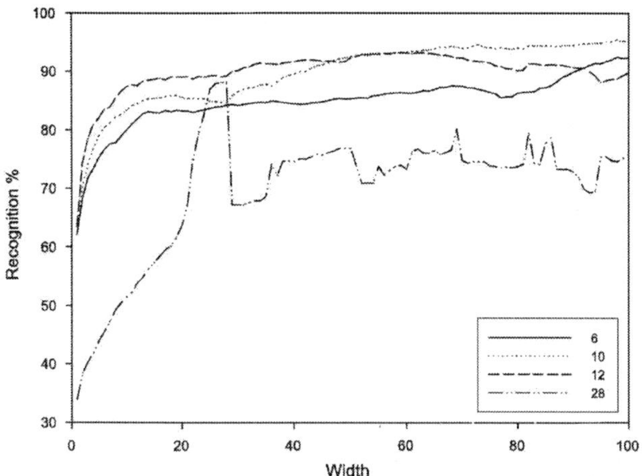

Fig. 5. Bayes recognition results for the differentmodels versus the windowwidth, with a fixed $\delta = 1$.

model	Bayes	NN
6	$93.2_{\langle 100,2\rangle}$	$94.0_{\langle 91,16\rangle}$
10	$95.5_{\langle 98,1\rangle}$	$92.6_{\langle 99,19\rangle}$
12	$93.2_{\langle 58,1\rangle}$	$92.6_{\langle 98,19\rangle}$
28	$89.5_{\langle 41,33\rangle}$	$96.4_{\langle 95,13\rangle}$

Table 11. Best success rates

5.8.2 k-NN classifier

Before performing the main experiments for this classifier, a study of the evolution of the classification as a function of k has been designed, in order to test the influence of this parameter in the classification task. The results are displayed in Fig. 6. Recognition percentage is averaged for all $\langle \omega,1\rangle$ points. Note that there is almost no variation in the recognition rate as k increases, except a small improvement for the 6-descriptor model. Thus, the simplest classifier was selected: $k = 1$, to avoid unnecessary time consumption due to the very large number of experiments to be performed.

Once the classifier has been set, the results for the different models were obtained and are displayed in Fig. 7 for $\delta = 1$. All models performed comparatively for $\omega \leq 35$. For $\omega > 35$, the 28-descriptor model begins to perform better than the reduced models. Its relatively high dimensionality and a greater dispersion in the samples (the larger the ω, the higher the probability of different musical parts to be contained in the same segment) causes larger distances among the samples, making the classification task easier for the k-NN.

The best results (96.4%) were obtained for the point $\langle 95,13\rangle$ with the 28-descriptor model. The best results for all the models have been consistently obtained with very large segment lengths (see Table 11). The percentage of perfect (100%) classification sub-experiments amounts to 18.7% (17060 out of 91000).

For the whole $\omega\delta$-space, the NN classifier obtained an 89.2% in average with the 28-descriptor model, while the other models yielded similar rates, around 87%. The behavior of the 10- and 12-descriptor models was almost identical over the parameter space (Fig. 7) and for the different tested values for k (Fig. 6).

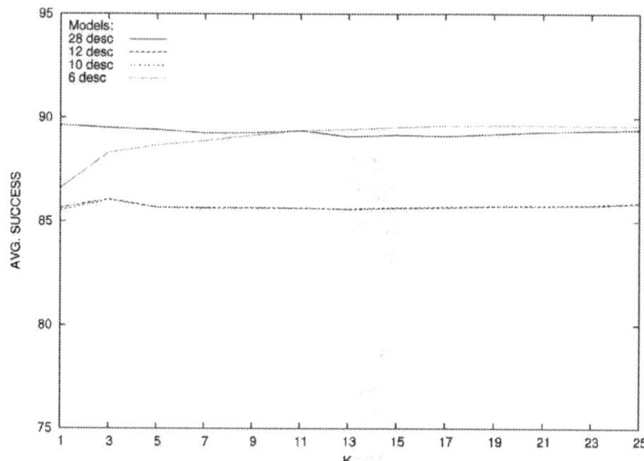

Fig. 6. Evolution of k-NN recognition for the different models against values of k.

model	Bayes	NN
6	84.2 ± 2.0	87.4 ± 2.9
10	88.5 ± 3.2	86.9 ± 2.5
12	89.5 ± 1.7	87.1 ± 2.5
28	71.1 ± 6.3	89.2 ± 4.5

Table 12. Averages and standard deviations of success rates

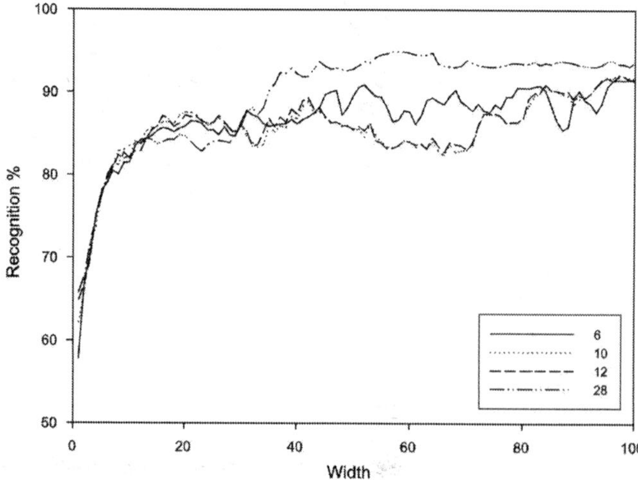

Fig. 7. NN recognition results for the different models versus the window width, with a fixed $\delta = 1$.

5.8.3 Whole melody segment classification

The good results obtained for large ω called our attention to the question of how good would be the results of classifying whole melodies, instead of fragments, as presented so far. The first problem is the small number of samples available this way (110 samples for training and test). The results of these experiments are displayed in Table 13. The same 10-fold cross-validation scheme described in section 5.7.2 was used here. The results are comparable or even better than the average in the $\omega\delta$-space for both classification paradigms.

model	Bayesian	NN
6	88.0	87.0
10	91.0	88.0
12	91.0	88.0
28	79.0	93.0

Table 13. Average success rates for whole melody segment length ($\omega = \infty$)

In spite of this good behavior for Bayes and k-NN, this approach has a number of disadvantages. Training is always more difficult due to the smaller number of samples. The classification cannot be performed *on-line* in a real-time system, because all the piece is needed in order to take the decision. There are also improvements to the presented methodology, like cooperative decisions using different segment classifications that can not be applied to the complete melody approach.

5.8.4 Results comparison

Bayesian and NN classifier performed comparatively. There were, in general, lower differences in average recognition percentages between models for NN than those found with the Bayesian classifier (see Table 12), probably due to its non-parametric nature.

An ANOVA test with Bonferroni procedure for multiple comparison statistics (Hancock & Klockars, 1996) was used to determine which combination of model and classifier gave the best classification results in average. According to this test, with the number of experiments performed, the required difference between any two recognition rates in Table 12 must be at least 0.45123 in order to be considered statistically different at the 95% confidence level. Thus, it can be stated that Bayes classifier with 12-descriptor model and NN classifier with 28-descriptor model perform comparatively well, and both outperform the rest of classifier and model combinations. The Bayes classifier has the advantage of using a reduced size description model.

In a recent work using the same data set (Pérez-Sancho et al., 2004), several text categorization algorithms have been used to perform genre recognition from whole melodies. In particular, a naive Bayes classifier with several multivariate Bernoulli and multinomial models are applied to binary vectors indicating the presence or absence of n-length words (sequences of n notes) in a melody. The work reported around 93% of success as the best performance. This is roughly the same best result reported here for the whole melody, although it is outperformed by the window classification results.

Results for the $\omega\delta$-space are hardly comparable with results by other authors, due to our use of segments instead of complete melodies, and mainly due to the different datasets put under study by different authors. Nevertheless a comparison attempt can be made with the results found in (Tzanetakis et al., 2003) for pair-wise genre classification. The authors use information from all the tracks on the MIDI files except tracks playing on the percussion channel. In that work, a 94% accuracy for Irish Folk music and Jazz identification is reported as the best result. Unfortunately, they did not use Classical samples. This accuracy percentage is similar to our results with whole melody length segments and the NN classifier (93%). A study on the classification accuracy as a function of the input data length is also reported, showing a behavior similar to the one reported here: classification accuracy using statistical information reaches its maximum for larger segment lengths, as they reported a maximum accuracy for five classes with 4 minute segment length. Our best results were obtained for $\omega > 90$ (see Table 11).

6. Some conclusions and future work

6.1 Conclusions on melody characterization

The method proposed here identifies the voice containing the melody in a multitrack digital score. It has been applied to standard MIDI files in which music is stored in several tracks, so the system determines whether a track is a melodic line or not. The track with the highest probability among the melodic tracks is finally labeled as the one containing the melody of that song.

The decisions are taken by a pattern recognition algorithm based on statistical descriptors (pitches, intervals, durations and lengths), extracted from each track of the target file. The classifier used for the experiments was a decision tree ensemble classifier named random forest. It was trained using MIDI tracks with the melody track previously labeled by a human expert.

The experiments yielded promising results using databases from different music genres, like jazz, classical, and popular music. Unfortunately, the results could not be compared to other systems because of the lack of similar works.

The results show that enough training data of each genre are needed in order to successfully characterize the melody track, due to the specificities of melody and accompaniment in each genre. Classical music is particularly hard for this task, because of the lack of a single track that corresponds to the whole melodic line in some files. In these files, melody moves from one track to another, as different instruments take the melody lead role. To overcome this problem, more sophisticated schemes oriented to melodic segmentation are needed.

The use of information about the layout of the tracks within a MIDI file is being investigated. We hope this would help to improve the performance of the system when dealing with particularly hard instances like the ones found in karaoke files. The extraction of human-readable rules from the trees in the random forest that help characterize melody tracks has been another topic of research that yielded some promising results. Several rule systems, including some fuzzy rule systems have been obtained (Ponce de León et al., 2007; Ponce de León et al., 2008). Being able to automatically obtain melody characterization rules that easily understandable by humans could be of interest for musicologists and would help building better tools for searching and indexing symbolically encoded music.

6.2 Conclusions on music genre recognition

Our main goal in this work has been to test the capability of melodic, harmonic, and rhythmic statistical descriptors to perform musical genre recognition. We have developed a framework for feature extraction, selection and classification experiments, where new corpora, description models, and classifiers can be easily incorporated and tested.

We have shown the ability of two classifiers, based on different paradigms, to map symbolic representations of melodic segments into a set of musical genres. Jazz and classical music have been used as an initial benchmark to test this ability. The experiments have been carried out over a parameter space defined by the size of segments extracted from melody tracks of MIDI files and the displacement between segments sequentially extracted from the same source. A total of 273000 classification sub-experiments have been performed.

From the feature selection stage, a number of interesting conclusions can be drawn. From the musical point of view, pitches and intervals have shown to be the most discriminant features. Other important features have been the number of notes and the rhythm syncopation. Although the former set of descriptors may be probably important in other genre classification problems, probably these latter two have found their importance in this particular problem of classical versus jazz. From the statistical point of view, standard deviations were very relevant, since five of them from six possible ones were selected.

The general behavior for all the models and classifiers against the values for ω was to have bad classification percentages (around 60%) for $\omega = 1$, rapidly increasing to an 80% for $\omega \approx 10$, and then keep stable around a 90% for $\omega > 30$. This general trend supports the importance of describing large melody segments to obtain good classification results. The preferred values for δ were small, because they provide a higher number of training data.

Bayes and NN performed comparatively. The parametric approach preferred the reduced models but NN performed well with all models. In particular, with the complete model, without feature selection, it achieved very good rates, probably favored by the large distances among prototypes obtained with such a high dimensionality. The best average recognition rate in the $\omega\delta$-space has been found with the Bayesian classifier and the 12-descriptor model (89.5%), although the best result was obtained with the NN, that reached a 96.4% with $\omega = 95$ and $\delta = 13$.

Also, whole melody classification experiments were carried out, removing the segment extraction and segment classification stage. This approach is simpler, faster, and provide comparative results even with few training samples, but has a number of disadvantages. It does not permit the use of on-line implementations where the system can input data and take decisions in real-time, since all the piece needs to be entered to the classifier in a single step. In addition, the segment classification approach permits to analyse a long theme by sections, performing local classifications.

An extension to this framework is under development, where a voting scheme for segments is used to collaborate in the classification of the whole melody. The framework permits the training of a large number of classifiers that, combined in a multi-classifier system, could produce even better results.

An experimental graphical user interface has been developed to facilitate working on the problem of music genre recognition. The main motivation for such a tool is to allow investigate why classification errors occur. A snapshot of the interface (actually in spanish) is shown in figure 8. The interface allows to select a model (ω,δ,μ,γ) for classifying selected tracks from MIDI files. The classification of each extracted window is shown in a row and encoded by colors. Each window content can be played individually and its description visualized.

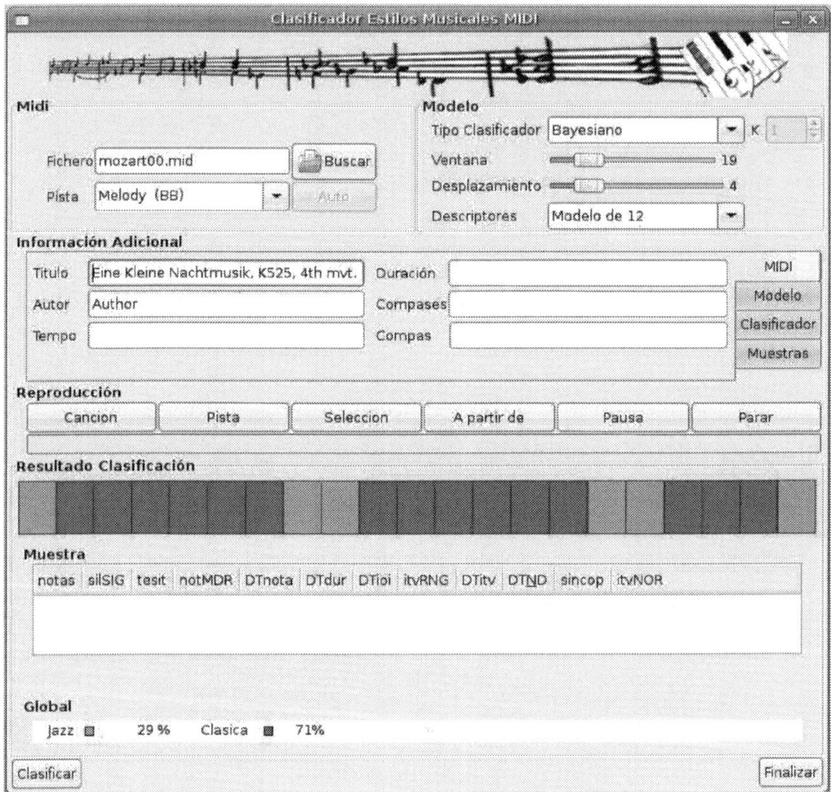

Fig. 8. Graphical user interface for automatic music genre recognition.

7. Acknowledgments

This work is supported by the spanish national projects: GV06/166 and CICyT TIN2006-14932-C02, partially supported by EU ERDF.

8. References

M. Baroni (1978). *Proposal for a Grammar of Melody: The Bach Chorales.* Les Presses de l'Université de Montréal.

S. G. Blackburn (2000). *Content Based Retrieval and Navigation of Music Using Melodic Pitch Contours.* PhD thesis, Department of Electronics and Computer Science, University of Southampton, UK.

L. Breiman (2001). Random forests. *Machine Learning*, 45(1):5–32.

G. Buzzanca (2002). A supervised learning approach to musical style recognition. In Music and Artificial Intelligence. Additional Proceedings of the Second International Conference, ICMAI 2002.

W. Chai and B. Vercoe (2001). Folk music classification using hidden Markov models. In *Proc. of the Int. Conf. on Artificial Intelligence*, Las Vegas, USA.

D. Cope (1996) *Experiments in Musical Intelligence.*, volume 2. Cambridge University Press, New York, NY, USA.

P. P. Cruz, E. Vidal, and J. C. Pérez-Cortes (2003) Musical style identification using grammatical inference: The encoding problem. In Alberto Sanfeliu and José Ruiz-Shulcloper, editors, *Proc. of CIARP 2003*, pages 375–382, La Habana, Cuba.

R. Dannenberg, B. Thom, and D. Watson (1997). A machine learning approach to musical style recognition. In *Proceedings of the International Computer Music Conference (ICMC'97)*, pages 344–347.

S. Dubnov and G. Assayag (2002). *Mathematics and Music*, chapter 9, pages 147–158. Springer.

R. O. Duda, P. E. Hart, and D. G. Stork (2000). *Pattern Classification*. John Wiley and Sons.

J. Eggink and G. J. Brown (2004). Extracting melody lines from complex audio. In *Intl. Conf. on Music Information Retrieval*.

A. Ghias, J. Logan, D. Chamberlin, and B. C. Smith (1995). Query by humming: Musical information retrieval in an audio database. In *Proc. of 3rd ACM Int. Conf. Multimedia*, pages 231–236.

A. E. Gómez, A. Klapuri and B.Meudic (2003). Melody description and extraction in the context of music content processing. *Journal of New Music Research*, 32-1.

M. Grachten, J. Ll. Arcos, and R. López deMántaras (2004). Melodic similarity: Looking for a good abstraction level. In *Proceedings of the 5th International Conference onMusic Information Retrieval*.

G. R. Hancock and A. J. Klockars (1996). The quest for alpha; developments in multiple comparison procedures in the quarter century since games (1971). *Review of Educational Research*, 66(3):269–306.

I. Karydis, A. Nanopoulos, A. Papadopoulos, E. Cambouropoulos, and Y. Manolopoulos (2007). Horizontal and vertical integration/segregation in auditory streaming: a voice separation algorithmfor symbolicmusical data. In *Proceedings 4th Sound and Music Computing Conference (SMC'2007)*, Lefkada.

Pl. R. Illescas, D. Rizo, and J. M. Iñesta (2007). Harmonic, melodic, and functional automatic analysis. In *Proceedings of the 2007 International Computer Music Conferrence*, volume I, pages 165–168.

Y. E. Kim, W. Chai, R. Garcia, and B. Vercoe (2000). Analysis of a contour-based representation for melody. In *ISMIR*.

K. Lemstrom and J. Tarhio (2000). Searching monophonic patterns within polyphonic sources. In *Proceedings of the RIAO Conference, volume 2*, pages 1261– 1278.

M. Li and R. Sleep (2004). Melody classification using a similarity metric based on kolmogorov complexity. In *Proc. Sound and Music Computing*.

S. T. Madsen and G. Widmer (2007). Towards a computational model of melody identification in polyphonic music. In *20th International Joint Conference on Artificial Intelligence (IJCAI 2007)*, pages 459–464.

A. Marsden (1992). Modelling the perception of musical voices: a case study in rulebased systems. In *Computer Representations and Models in Music*, pages 239–263. Academic Press.

C. McKay and I. Fujinaga (2004). Automatic genre classification using large high-level musical feature sets. In *Int. Conf. on Music Information Retrieval, ISMIR 2004*, pages 525–530.

C. McKay and I. Fujinaga (2006a). jSymbolic: A feature extractor for midi files. In *Proceedings of the International Computer Music Conference*, pages 302–305.

C. McKay and I. Fujinaga (2006b). Musical genre classification: Is it worth pursuing and how can it be improved? In *International Conference on Music Information Retrieval*, pages 101–106.

C.McKay and I. Fujinaga (2007a). Style-independent computer-assisted exploratory analysis of largemusic collections. *Journal of Interdisciplinary Music Studies*, 1(1): 63–85.

C. McKay and I. Fujinaga (2007b). jWebMiner: A web-based feature extractor. In *Proc. of the International Conference on Music Information Retrieval*, pages 113– 114.

E. Narmour (1990). The Analysis and Cognition of Basic Melodic Structures. University Of Chicago Press.

F. Pachet, G. Westermann, and D. Laigre (2001). Musical datamining for emd. In *Proceedings of the Wedelmusic Conference*.

E. Pampalk, S. Dixon, and G. Widmer (2003). Exploring music collections by browsing different views. In *Proceedings of the 4th International Conference on Music Information Retrieval (ISMIR'03)*, pages 201–208, Baltimore, USA.

C. Pérez-Sancho, J.M. Iñesta, and J. Calera-Rubio (2004). Style recognition through statistical event models. In *Proc. of the Sound and Music Computing Conference*.

J. Pickens (2001). A survey of feature selection techniques for music information retrieval. Technical report, Center for Intelligent Information Retrieval, Departament of Computer Science, University of Massachussetts.

P. J. Ponce de León and J. M. Iñesta (2003). Feature-driven recognition of music styles. In *1st Iberian Conference on Pattern Recognition and Image Analysis. LNCS, 2652*, pages 773–781.

P. J. Ponce de León, J. M. Iñesta, and C. Pérez-Sancho (2004). A shallow description framework formusical style recognition. *Lecture Notes in Computer Science - Lecture Notes in Artificial Intelligence*, 3138.

P. J. Ponce de León, D. Rizo, and J. M. Iñesta (2007). Towards a human-friendly melody characterization by automatically induced rules. In Simon Dixon, David Brainbridge, and Rainer Typke, editors, *Proceedings of the 8th International Conference on Music Information Retrieval*, pages 437–440, Vienna. Austrian Computer Society.

P. J. Ponce de León, D. Rizo, and R. Ramirez (2008). Melody characterization by a fuzzy rule system. In *Proccedings of theMusic and Machine Learning Workshop*.

D. Rizo, J.M. Iñesta, and P.J. Ponce de León (2006a). Tree model of symbolic music for tonality guessing. In *Proc. of the IASTED Int. Conf. on Artificial Intelligence and Applications, AIA 2006*, pages 299–304, Innsbruck, Austria. IASTED, Acta Press.

D. Rizo, K. Lemström, and J.M. Iñesta (2008). Tree structured and combined methods for comparing metered polyphonic music. In *Proc. Computer Music Modeling and Retrieval 2008 (CMMR'08)*, pages 263–278, Copenhagen, Denmark, Copenhagen, Denmark.

D. Rizo, P. J. Ponce de León, C. Pérez-Sancho, A. Pertusa, and J. M. Iñesta (2006b). A pattern recognition approach for melody track selection in midi files. In Tindale A. Dannenberg R., Lemström K., editor, *Proc. of the 7th Int. Symp. on Music Information Retrieval ISMIR 2006*, pages 61–66, Victoria, Canada.

S. Sadie and G. Grove (1984). The New Grove Dictionary of Music and Musicians. Macmillan.

E. Selfridge-Field (1998). *Conceptual and representational issues in melodic comparison*, volume 11 of *Computing in Musicology*, pages 3–64. Cambridge, Massachusetts: MIT Press.

J. F. Serrano and J. M. Iñesta (2006). Music information retrieval through melodic similarity using hanson intervallic analysis. *Research in Computing Science*, 20: 131–142.

H. Soltau, T. Schultz, M. Westphal, and A. Waibel (1998). Recognition of music types. In *Proc. IEEE International Conference on Acoustics, Speech, and Signal Processing (ICASSP-1998)*, pages 1137–1140.

C. Spevak, B. Thom, and K. Höthker (2002). Evaluating melodic segmentation. In *ICMAI '02: Proceedings of the Second International Conference on Music and Artificial Intelligence*, pages 168–182, London, UK. Springer-Verlag.

E. Stamatatos and G. Widmer (2002). Music performer recognition using an ensemble of simple classifiers. In *Proceedings of the European Conference on Artificial Intelligence (ECAI)*, pages 335–339.

M. Tang, C. L. Yip, and B. Kao (2000). Selection of melody lines for music databases. In *Proceedings of Annual Int. Computer Software and Applications Conf. COMPSAC*, pages 243–248.

D. Temperley (2004). The Cognition of Basic Musical Structures. The MIT Press.

B. Thom (2000). Unsupervised learning and interactive Jazz/Blues improvisation. In *Proceedings of the AAAI2000*, pages 652–657.

E. Toch (1997). La melodía (translation of 'Melodielehre', 1923). Span Press Universitaria.

P. Toiviainen and T. Eerola (2001). Method for comparative analysis of folk music based on musical feature extraction and neural networks. In *III International Conference on Cognitive Musicology*, pages 41–45.

R. Typke, P. Giannopoulos, R.C. Veltkamp, F. Wiering, and R. van Oostrum (2003). Using transportation distances for measuring melodic similarity. In *Proceedings of the 4th International Conference on Music Information Retrieval*.

G. Tzanetakis, A. Ermolinskyi, and P. Cook (2003). Pitch histograms in audio and symbolic music information retrieval. *Journal of New Music Research*, 32(2):143–152.

A. Uitdenbogerd and J. Zobel (1999). Melodic matching techniques for large music databases. In *Proceedings of the seventh ACM International Multimedia Conference (Part 1)*, pages 57–66. ACMPress.

A. L. Uitdenbogerd and J. Zobel (1998). Manipulation of music for melody matching. In *Proceedings of the sixth ACM International Multimedia Conference*, pages 235– 240. ACMPress.

P. van Kranenburg and E. Backer (2004). Musical style recognition - a quantitative approach. In *Proceedings of the Conference on Interdisciplinary Musicology (CIM)*, pages 106–107.

B. Whitman, G. Flake, and S. Lawrence (2001). Artist detection in music with minnowmatch. In *Proc. IEEE Workshop on Neural Networks for Signal Processing*, pages 559–568.

I. H. Witten and E. Frank (1999). *Data Mining: Practical Machine Learning Tools and Techniques*. Morgan Kaufmann Series in Data Management Systems. Morgan Kaufmann.

J. Zhu, X. Xue, and H. Lu (2004). Musical genre classification by instrumental features. In *Int. Computer Music Conference, ICMC 2004*, pages 580–583.

26

Application of Forward Error Correcting Algorithms to Positioning Systems

Nikos Petrellis, Fotios Gioulekas, Michael Birbas,
John Kikidis and Alex Birbas
Analogies S.A., Patras Scientific Park
Greece

1. Introduction

The indoor localisation of a mobile target is an important issue in many robotics, automation, virtual reality and pervasive computing environments. The most sophisticated method for indoor localisation is based on processing the images captured by cameras that are placed on the target in order to recognise familiar landmarks and their distance (Jin et al, 2004); (Porta & Krose, 2006); (Clerentin et al, 2005); (Tovar et al, 2006); (Se et al, 2002). Image processing in conjunction with other localisation approaches described below (Borenstein et al., 1996) is very popular in autonomous robotics applications making feasible the familiarisation of a robot with unknown areas. Stochastic processing is often applied in this case in order to evaluate an estimated position. Nevertheless, expensive sensors and processing units are required in order to support the high computational complexity of this approach.

More popular lower cost approaches are based either on measuring the round trip time of a reflected wave or the strength of a signal. In the first case, the cost is higher if optical or laser scanning is employed since very short time intervals have to be measured with high precision (Miura et al, 2006); (Clerentin et al, 2005); (Victorino et al, 2003); (Arras et al, 2001). Ultrasonic signals can offer a lower cost alternative to this approach since the sonar waves travel with much lower speed than light but their main drawback is that this type of signal is not directional enough (Smith & Zografos, 2005); (Minami et al, 2004); (Tardos et al, 2002); (Bicho et al, 2000); (Baskent & Barshan, 1999). Moreover, it is more difficult to isolate the sonar transmitter from the receiver in order to reassure that only the reflected signal will be received.

Measuring the signal strength of multiple transmitters (Ladd et al, 2005); (Flora et al, 2005) can also provide an indication about the target position. This technique has already been adopted in cellular phone, Wireless Local Access Network (WLAN) or Bluetooth applications. Although wide areas can be covered in these networks, the distance estimation error is usually higher than half a meter. Even magnetic fields have been used for the accurate non-contact control of tools and medical instruments (Schlageter et al, 2001); (Kosel et al, 2005). The distance measured in this approach cannot be longer than some tenths of centimetres although a distance estimation of up to 10m has been reported in (Prigge & How, 2004).

Infrared light has been employed using either passive or active sensors in order to avoid obstacles, estimate distance (Jin et al, 2004); (Bicho, 2000) or to profile the surface of an object by recognising its texture (Aytac & Barshan, 2004); (Benet et al, 2002); (Novotny & Ferrier, 1999).

A low cost infrared–based solution that relies on recognising digital patterns has been presented in (Petrellis et al, 2007a and 2007b). The reception quality of the patterns that are sent by at least two transmitters that are placed around the covered area is utilised for estimating the position of the receiver. A calibration procedure, that is carried out once, before real time operation, familiarises the target with the area. During this stage, the target visits predetermined positions and enumerates the recognised patterns in a period of time. Using several types of patterns, a position identity can be formed by the success rate of each pattern type. During real time operation, the current position identity is compared to the identities that were estimated during the calibration stage and the closer position is selected. Specific regression techniques can be employed in order to reach a more accurate estimation of the real target position.

The speed and accuracy of the position estimation method described above are strongly affected by instant noise that has not been taken into account during the calibration stage. The estimation speed can be improved by increasing the frequency of the carrier that is used for the pattern transmission. In this way, shorter patterns can be employed. Several rules can be applied to validate the results of the position estimation procedure and discard false results caused by instant noise. In this case, the estimation procedure should be repeated for the specific position (Petrellis et al, 2007b).

In the present work, we employ Forward Error Correction (FEC) techniques in order to reduce the effect of instant noise and speed up the estimation procedure. The interleaving process employed in Turbo decoding can minimize the effect of the burst errors caused by the instant noise (Schlegel & Perez, 2004); (Kschischang et al, 2001); (Hagenauer et al, 1996); (Gamal & Hammons, 2001) (Arzel et al, 2007). Instead of recognizing a large number of long patterns as the case was in our previous work, a small number of short signatures are used. These signatures are encoded in both interleaved and uninterleaved form at the side of the transmitter and the resulting bit stream is broadcast as an infrared signal. When the attenuated signal is received at the target, it is corrected by a decoder that can be implemented either in software or by dedicated hardware (Gioulekas et al, 2005); (Bickerstaff et al, 2003). Since our localisation approach is based on the quality of the received signal, the intension is to minimise the burst errors caused by instant noise through the selected FEC method rather than fully correct all the errors.

The control of the error rate margins can be based on the study of the behaviour of the specific infrared channel and its noise sources. Choosing "equalised" signatures can minimise some types of errors. The new sampling method employed at the side of the receiver increases significantly the estimation speed. The processing overhead of the error correction is small compared to the duration of the infrared signatures used. Besides the speed enhancement, the accuracy and the estimation reliability is also improved.

The architecture of the infrared transmitters and receivers of the present work as well as their topology is described in Section 2. The infrared channel features are studied and the decoding algorithms used are discussed in Section 3 and Section 4 respectively. The simulation results are presented in Section 5. The different experimental pattern structures that were tested are described in Section 6. Finally, the experimental results are presented in Section 7 along with some discussion on the advantages and the disadvantages of the various pattern structures.

2. System architecture and topology

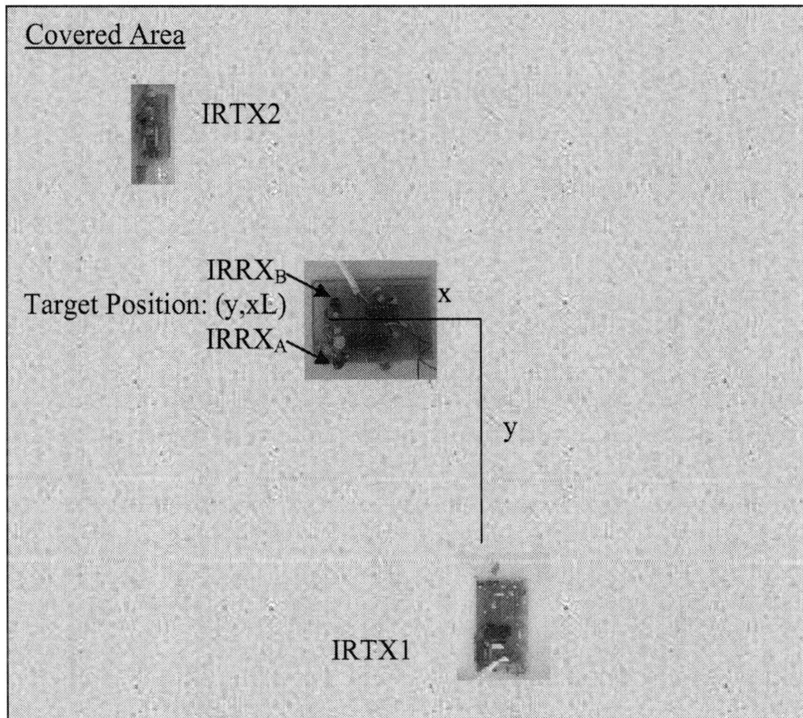

Fig. 1. The topology of the infrared transmitters and receivers

The Position Estimation System described in this work consists of 2 or more infrared transmitters (IRTX) positioned at the borders of the covered area as shown in Fig. 1. Each one of these transmitters is broadcasting a specific set of pattern types. The second IRTX device is basically used to break the symmetry between the right and the left side of the first IRTX device as well as to extend the covered area. Two infrared sensors are placed at the target facing opposite directions. The main transmitting device (IRTX1) is used as a reference for the position of the target. The coordinates of the target in Fig. 1, are (y,xL), meaning that the target has horizontal and vertical distance x and y respectively and is positioned at the left (L) side of the IRTX1.

The architecture of an infrared transmitter is shown in Fig. 2. The processing unit of the IRTX device is responsible for the generation of the supported infrared patterns. It is also responsible for the encoding and the interleaving of the transmitted information although the encoded and interleaved form of the original signatures may have been stored a priori in the memory of the IRTX device. The patterns are transmitted over a carrier that may also be generated by the processing unit of the transmitter in order to reduce external circuitry. The patterns and the carrier are mixed and amplified before the infrared emitting diode is driven. More than one infrared emitting diode may be connected in parallel and placed in circular arrangement in order to cover a wider area. In the present setup we used two diodes in parallel in both IRTX devices.

Different IRTX devices should be wired if they share the same processing unit. Independent IRTX devices may also be employed but this may have an impact on the estimation speed, accuracy and cost as will be discussed in Sections 6 and 7.

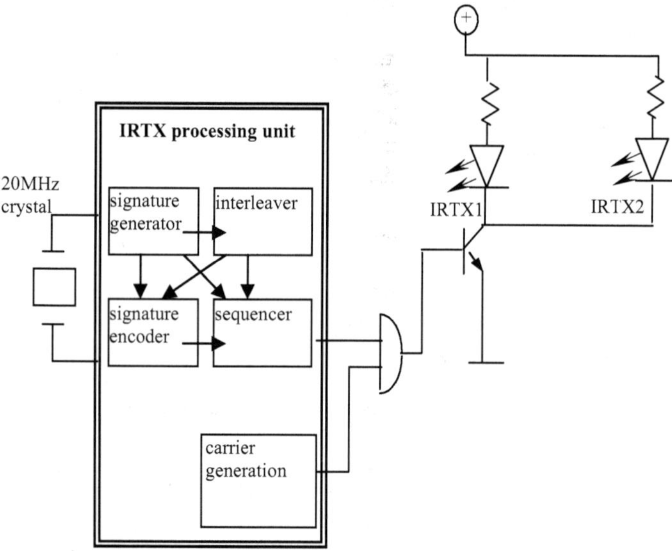

Fig. 2. Architecture of the IRTX device

The architecture of the receivers (IRRX devices) that are mounted on the target is presented in Fig. 3. An IRRX device accepts only the signals that were modulated on a specific carrier frequency. This is achieved through a bandpass filter and a carrier rejection circuitry that may be embedded in the infrared sensor if a standard carrier frequency is used. The use of the carrier protects from the interference of other infrared sources like the sunlight. The processing unit of the receiver is responsible for the sampling of the input signal and the recognition of the limits of the signatures, the encoded parity bits, etc. The received interleaved or uninterleaved signatures along with the parity bits are input to the Decoder and the Interleaver blocks. The corrected patterns are sent to a host computer that estimates the position of the target. The results of the position estimation could be utilised by other applications installed on the host computer. The decoding and error correction of the received signatures can be alternative performed by the host computer instead of the processing unit of the receiver. This is mandatory for a decoding algorithm that is based on complicated high precision arithmetic operations that cannot be handled by a low cost microcontroller.

The patterns transmitted by the IRTX devices in (Petrellis et al, 2007) are described in Fig. 4. The transmission starts with a preamble that is actually a long pause period. Then, a constant number of identical patterns are sent. These patterns are of the same type and each one consists of i pulses. These patterns are named MODi and are separated by a pause interval. Then, another set of MOD*j* patterns is transmitted with different number of pulses (*j*). In the example of Fig. 4, the preamble is followed by two MOD2 and one MOD4 pattern. The pulse width is not the same for different patterns types. More specifically, the pulse width in MOD*i* is chosen to be longer than the pulse width of MOD*j*, if *i*<*j*. In this way, MOD*i* patterns can be recognised with lower error rate than MOD*j* patterns. The number of MOD*i* patterns that are recognised at the receiver is the success rate of MOD*i*. The set of the success rates of all the supported pattern types forms an identity for a specific position. The receiver simply counts rising or falling edges between the pause intervals of the input signal, in order to recognise a pattern. Although the sampling is a simple procedure in this case, the pause intervals between the patterns lead to higher convergence times and lower estimation speed.

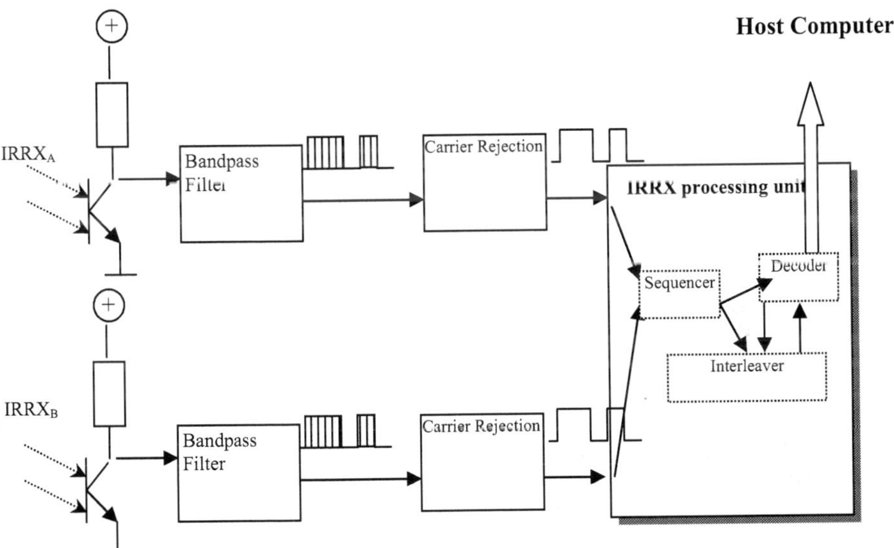

Fig. 3. Architecture of the IRRX devices

The sampling method described above cannot be applied if the transmitted patterns are not just a sequence of identical pulses. If more complicated signatures are transmitted, the receiver should sample the input signal at regular time intervals.

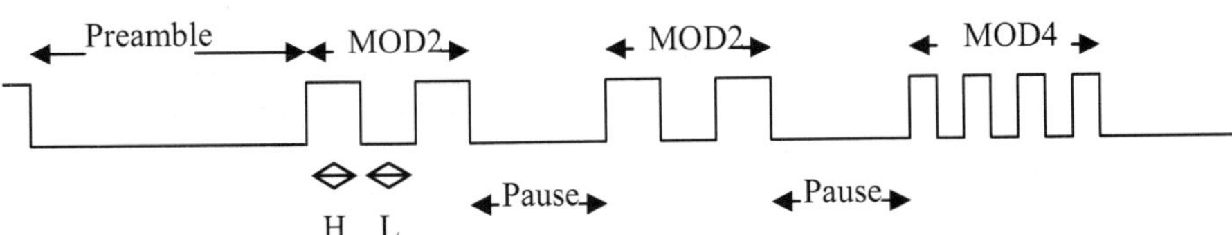

Fig. 4. The patterns transmitted in (Petrellis et al, 2007)

Consider for example the case where the signature 0x01 followed by the parity bytes 0x01 and 0x68 have to be transmitted as shown in Fig. 5a. The preamble in this case is again a long pause interval followed by a Start File Delimiter (SFD). As an SFD we selected the binary code 101. In general, the preamble is followed by the SFD, the original signature (SGN1), the parity bits of SGN1 (PA1) and the parity bits of the interleaved SGN1 (PB1) as shown in Fig. 5b. The code rate of this transmission is 1/3 if the PA1 and PB1 are considered as redundant information. Alternatively, the interleaved SGN1 can also be transmitted in order to increase the error correcting capability of the receiver (code rate 1/4).

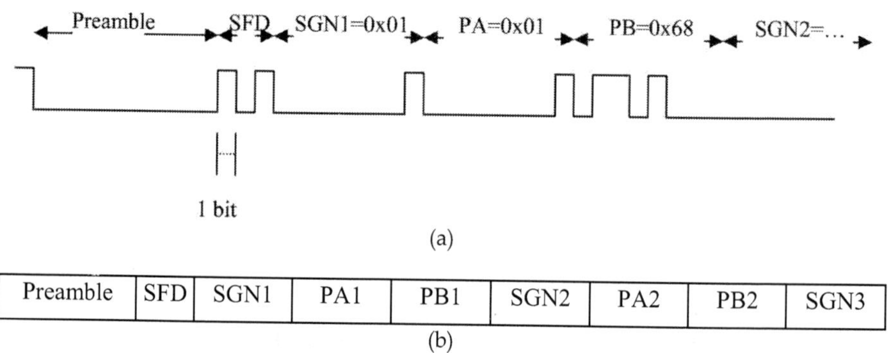

Preamble	SFD	SGN1	PA1	PB1	SGN2	PA2	PB2	SGN3

(b)

Fig. 5. Signature transmission in the present work

All the transmitted bits have the same width that is known to the receiver. The receiver has the option to sample the input signal sometime within the bit transmission period. If this single sampling occurs at a noisy time period the bit will not be recognised correctly. For this reason, we choose a different sampling scheme: if the bit period is T_b the input signal is sampled S_b times at regular time intervals of T_b/S_b. If more than $S_b/2$ of the samples are found to be logic '1', the specific bit is recognised as logic '1', otherwise as '0'. This procedure is shown in Fig. 6. Using the scheme described in Fig. 5 and Fig. 6, no pause intervals are necessary between the signatures and the parity info and hence, the position estimation speed is significantly improved.

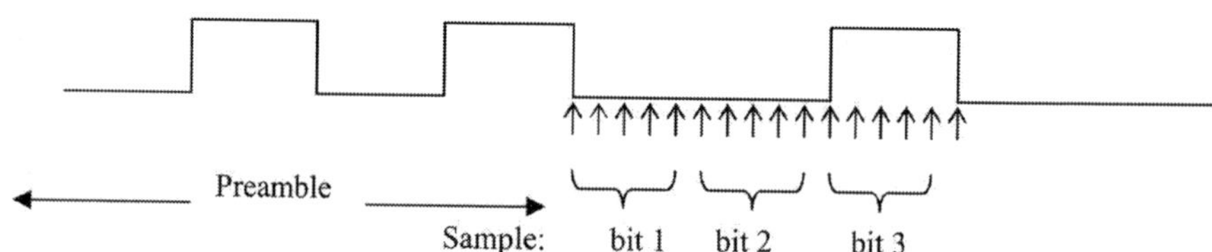

Fig. 6. Bit recognition based on the majority of samples

The retrieved signatures and parity bits are input to the interleaver and the decoder at the side of the receiver. These two modules are attempting to correct some error bits. Nevertheless, this is not always feasible due to the low Signal to Noise Ratio of the channel. The receiver may accept or ignore the results of the error correcting method since it is aware of the expected signature and parity bits. The matching degree of the received signatures with the expected ones forms an identity of the corresponding position.

Before the real time operation of the system, the target visits predetermined position in the covered area (e.g., the nodes of a virtual grid) and stores the matching degree of the various patterns that were retrieved at each node. During real time operation, the matching degrees estimated at the current target position are compared to the stored ones and the closer node is selected. The real target position can be further approximated if a two dimensional interpolation search is applied (Petrellis et al, 2007a).

3. Error sources in the specific infrared channel

The estimation of the distortion posed by the infrared channel in the transmitted signal is very important since the selection of the appropriate patterns and correction method can modify the bit error rate features of the reception. The experimental study of the errors that appear in the various patterns shows that we can distinguish five error sources: (a) reflections, (b) sampling method (c) scrambling of patterns transmitted by different IRTX devices, (d) signal attenuation and (e) random errors.

As already mentioned in the previous section, during the transmission of a logic '1', the IRTX device sends a high pulse modulated at the carrier frequency while nothing is sent during the transmission of a logic '0'. The infrared light transmitted when a '1' is sent reaches directly the receiver but is also reflected at the walls and the obstacles of the environment. Although the reflected infrared light fades soon, it is possible that the receiver will interpret a '10' transmission as a '11' since some additional samples can still be interpreted as '1' during the transmission of the second bit. Hence, the channel has memory due to the Inter-Symbol Interference (ISI) caused by the reflections since the currently received bit value depends on the previously transmitted one. If the environment favours reflections, the previous 2 bits that were transmitted may still affect the value of the current bit but their contribution is different in that case. By adopting the model used in the Partial Response channels of the magnetic storage media (Vasic & Kurtas, 2005), the reflections and the random errors of a channel are expressed as:

$$y(t) = \sum_{k=0}^{M_c} a_k x(t-k) + n(t) \tag{1}$$

$$\sum_{k=0}^{M_c} a_k^2 = 1 \tag{2}$$

$$\sigma^2 = {N_0}/{2}, \quad SNR = \frac{E_b}{2\sigma^2} = \frac{E_C}{2R\sigma^2} \tag{3}$$

$$A(D) \equiv \sum_{k=0}^{M_c} a_k D^k \tag{4}$$

The parameter x(t) is the transmitted bit while y(t) is the received one at the time point t. M_c is the memory of the channel i.e., the number of previous bits that affect the current one. The parameter n(t) expresses the Additive White Gaussian Noise (AWGN) of the channel with variance σ^2 (where E_c is the energy per coded bit, E_b is the energy per uncoded bit and $N_0/2$ is the (two-sided) noise power spectral density . If expression (2) is valid, then the Signal to

Noise Ratio (SNR) of the channel is estimated by (3). Fig. 7 shows the ISI of the current bit with the previous two bits.

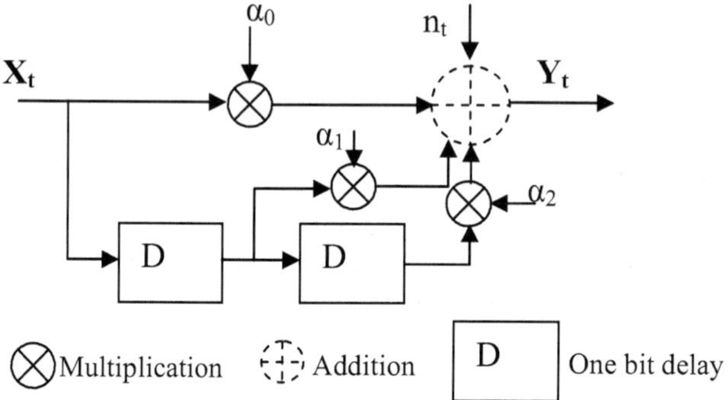

Fig. 7. Description of 2-bit interference scheme in the specific infrared channel

The sampling method described in the previous paragraph determines the value of the current bit from the majority of the samples retrieved in a period of time equal to the duration of the bit transmission. This method may lead to false recognition of a bit for two reasons: (a) the majority of the samples are noisy or (b) lack of synchronisation. The synchronisation is carried out when a preamble is sent. The lack of synchronisation may occur if a long bit sequence is transmitted and will usually affect the last bits of this sequence. It usually appears in the received pattern as an early recognised logic '1'. For example, the transmission of '01' may be recognised as '11' at the receiver.

The patterns transmitted concurrently by different IRTX devices are received by the two IRRX devices mounted on the target either directly or through reflections. For example, if IRTX1 is facing IRRX$_A$ and IRTX2 is facing IRRX$_B$, then if both IRTX devices transmit a logic '1', this bit will be probably recognised correctly by the two IRRX devices. Nevertheless, if the IRTX devices do not transmit the same bit value, both the IRRX devices may recognise a logic '1' due to the reflected signal of the IRTX device that transmits a logic '1'.

The signal of an IRTX device is attenuated if the target is positioned at a long distance from the transmitter. This is the main noise source that is responsible for the recognition of a transmitted logic '1' as a logic '0'. The errors caused by signal attenuation are considered to have been generated by a Rayleigh-like effect and expression (1) becomes:

$$y(t) = a_R(t) \sum_{k=0}^{M_c} a_k x(t-k) + n(t) \tag{5}$$

$$\Pr(a_R(t)) = 2l(t)e^{-l(t)^2} \, , \, a_R(t) > 0 \tag{6}$$

Equation (6) represents the probability density function for the Rayleigh parameter $a_R(t)$, while l(t) is the distance of the receiver from the transmitter.

All the noise sources described above can be combined in the pair of expressions that describe how each IRRX device is expected to receive the signals transmitted by the two IRTX devices:

$$y_A(t) = a_R(t) \sum_{k=-1}^{M_c} a_k x_1(t-k) + a_R(t) \sum_{k=-1}^{M_c} a'_k x_2(t-k) + n(t) \tag{7}$$

$$y_B(t) = a_R(t) \sum_{k=-1}^{M_c} a_k x_2(t-k) + a_R(t) \sum_{k=-1}^{M_c} a'_k x_1(t-k) + n(t) \tag{8}$$

The IRTX1 and IRTX2 devices transmit the input signals $x_1(t)$ and $x_2(t)$ respectively while IRRX$_A$ receives $y_A(t)$ and IRRX$_B$ receives $y_B(t)$. The summation starts from k=-1 in order to include the sampling errors. The parameter M_c is practically less or equal than 2. The second summation term at the right side of both (7) and (8) represents the reflected signal that is transmitted by the IRTX device that is not facing the specific IRRX sensor. Since the reflected signal is more attenuated compared to the signal that is received directly, it holds that:

$$a_k \geq a'_k, \forall k \tag{9}$$

Some of the error types described above are shown in the example of Fig. 8.

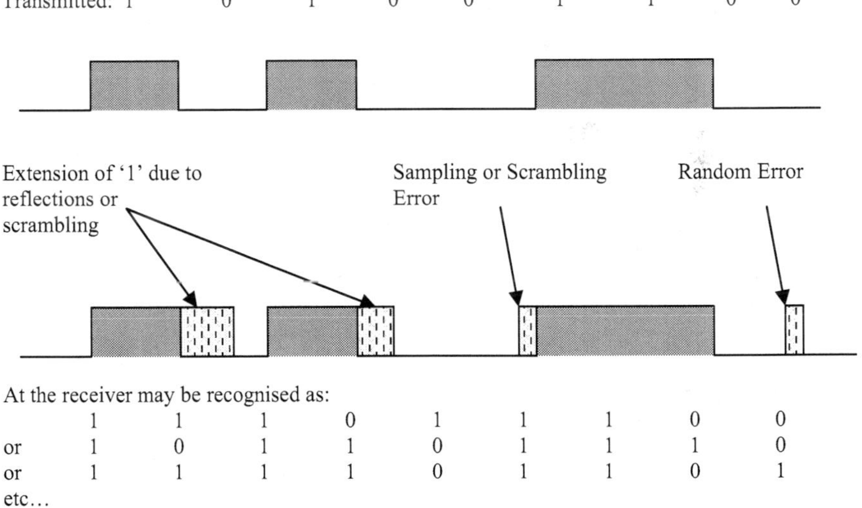

Fig. 8. Example errors during reception from the target

4. Decoding algorithms

The encoding of the signatures at the side of the transmitter is carried out through the well known Recursive Systematic Convolutional (RSC) encoder presented in Fig. 9 and described by the polynomial $(1+ D^2)/(1+D+D^2)$. If a signature is n-bits long, the encoded parity bits have also n-bits length. Each signature is interleaved and the interleaved signature bits are also encoded by the same RSC encoder. The n-bits of the original signature (SGN), its parity bits that are generated by the RSC encoder (PA) and the parity bits of the interleaved signature (PB) are transmitted by the Sequencer module of the IRTX device as shown in Fig. 5b (code rate: 1/3). It is also possible that the interleaved signature is also transmitted in order to enhance the error correction capability at the side of the receiver by providing more redundant information (code rate: 1/4).

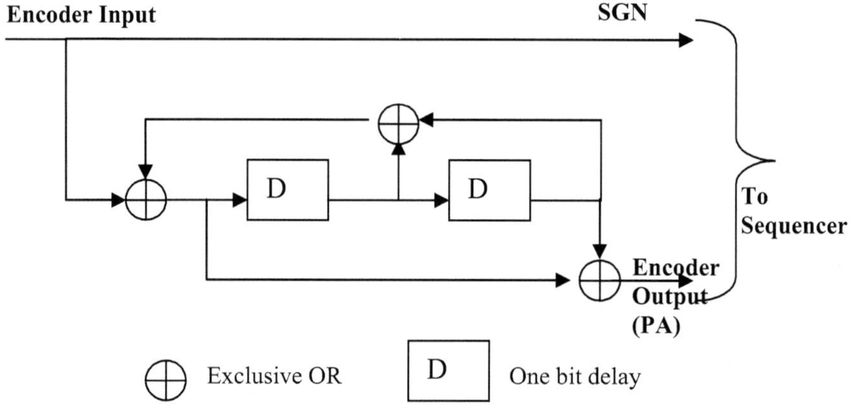

Fig. 9. Recursive Convolutional Encoder scheme employed

The encoding performed by the RSC state machine of Fig. 9 is also described by the state machine of Fig. 10 and the Trellis diagram of Fig. 11. The state names represent the output of the two Delay elements of the encoder. Each arrow in the state diagram is marked with the symbol i/o, where i is the input required for the state transition and o the resulting output of the RSC encoder.

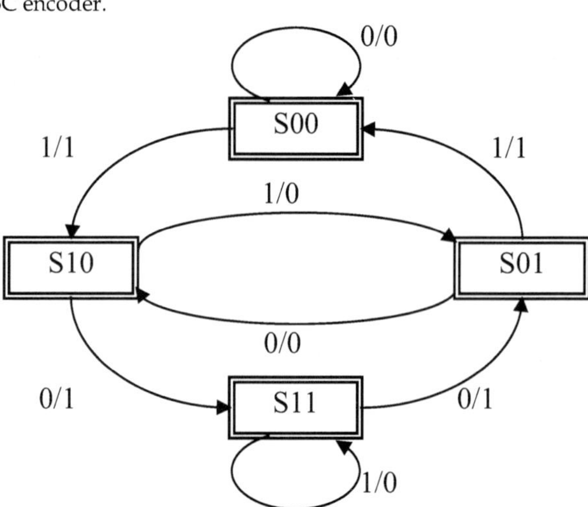

Fig. 9. The state diagram of the RSC encoder of Fig. 8

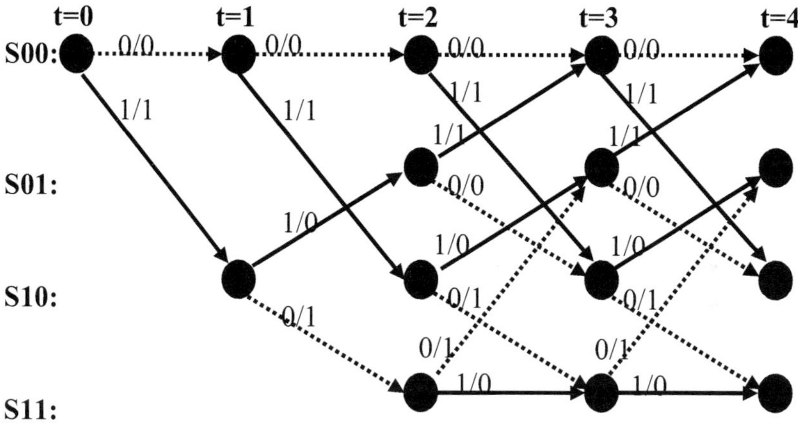

Fig. 10. The Trellis diagram of the RSC encoder of Fig. 8

The received signature and parity bits are input to the decoder. The decoder exploits the redundancy information of the parity bits in order to correct the error bits in the received signatures. The correction capability is strongly related to the SNR of the channel. If the SNR is too low, the decoder may not be able to correct all the error bits or it may even produce an output that has more error bits than its input. The decoder that we used is based on the Trellis diagram of Fig. 10. Every Trellis stage is implemented by the architectural blocks that are shown in Fig. 11.

The calculations performed at each one of the A-G blocks of Fig. 11 if a Sum-Product decoding algorithm is used (Hagenauer et al, 1996) are listed in Table 1. The input of each stage consists of: (a) the probabilities that $y_u(t)$ is received given that the transmitted data bit is 1 $(x_u(t)=1)$ or 0 $(x_u(t)=0)$, (b) the probabilities that $y_p(t)$ is received given that the transmitted parity bit is 1 $(x_p(t)=1)$ or 0 $(x_p(t)=0)$ respectively. Due to the conditional probabilities used as soft input, the decoder that is constructed by the blocks shown in Fig. 11 is called Soft In Soft Out decoder (SISO). In Turbo decoding, two SISO decoders need to be used in parallel as shown in Fig. 12 operating on either the interleaved or the uninterleaved received data. Each SISO decoder produces the extrinsic information (block F of Fig. 11) that is exploited by the complementary SISO decoder as intrinsic information (block B). The SISO decoders are activated in an iterative way i.e., SISO 1 uses the input and initial intrinsic information and produces extrinsic information that is interleaved and used along with the interleaved input by the SISO 2 decoder. The extrinsic information of SISO 2 is deinterleaved and provided as intrinsic info to SISO 1 that is activated next. This process is repeated for a specific number of iterations.

Blocks A and B of Fig. 11 estimate the branch metrics of the Trellis diagram from the data/parity input and the intrinsic information. Blocks C and D estimate the node metrics of the Trellis diagram which are propagating forwards (a_S) and backwards (b_S) through the Trellis. The blocks E, F and G combine the input, the node and the branch metrics in order to produce the output (block G) and the extrinsic information (block F).

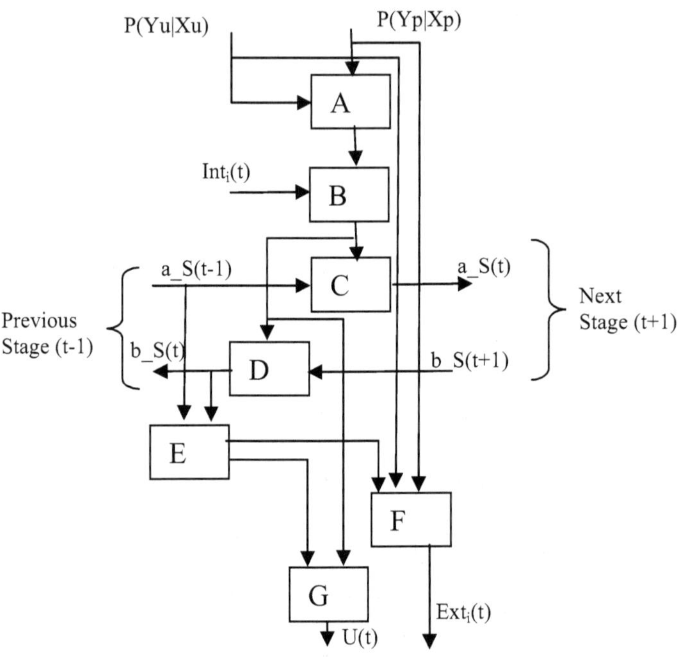

Fig. 11. Implementation of a Trellis decoder stage

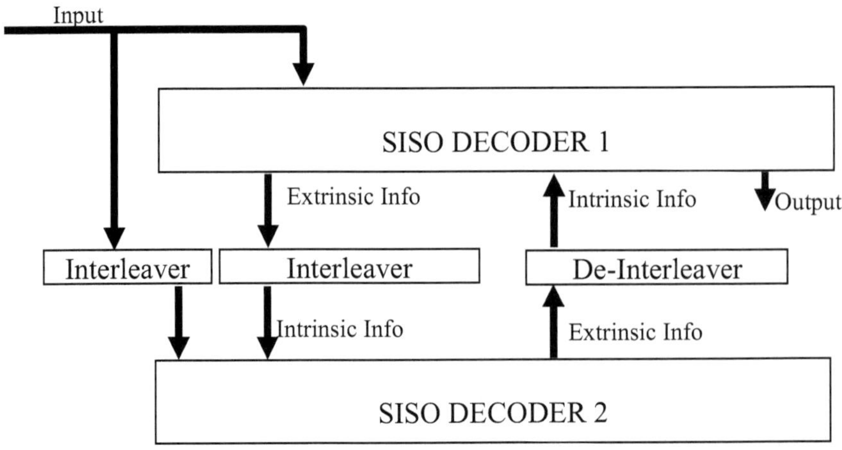

Fig. 12. A Turbo decoder

Block	Calculation
A	$\gamma'_{ij} = \Pr(y_u(t) \mid x_u(t) = i)\,\Pr(y_p(t) \mid x_p(t) = j)$, $i, j \in \{0,1\}$
B	$\gamma_{ij} = \gamma'_{ij}\,Int_i(t)$, $i, j \in \{0,1\}$
C	$a\_S(t) = \sum_{S'} a\_S'(t-1)\gamma_{S' \to S}$
D	$b\_S'(t) = \sum_{S} b\_S(t+1)\gamma_{S' \to S}$
E	$I_{ij} = \sum_{i/j, S' \to S} a\_S'(t-1)b\_S(t)$
F	$Ext_i(t) = \sum_{j} I_{ij}\,\Pr(y_p(t) \mid x_p(t) = j)$, $i \in \{0,1\}$
G	$U_i(t) = \sum_{j} I_{ij}\gamma_{ij}$, $i \in \{0,1\}$

Table 1. Calculations performed by the Sum-Product Algorithm

The operations listed in Table 1 are additions and multiplications. If the Sum-Product algorithm is implemented by the processing unit of the receiver of Fig. 2, then the processing unit should support multiplications of high accuracy. Lower cost processing units can be used if the Min-Sum or the Max-Log MAP algorithm is used instead of the Sum-Product. Specifically, by using the Andersen identity:

$$-\ln(e^{-x} + e^{-y}) = \min(x, y) - \ln(1 + e^{-|y-x|}) \tag{10}$$

and applying the $-\ln(x)$ function to the left and the right side of the expressions in the blocks A, B and C of Table 1 we get:

$$\gamma'_{ij} = \Pr(y_u(t) \mid x_u(t) = i)\,\Pr(y_p(t) \mid x_p(t) = j) \Rightarrow$$
$$-\ln(\gamma'_{ij}) = -\ln(\Pr(y_u(t) \mid x_u(t) = i)) - \ln(\Pr(y_p(t) \mid x_p(t) = j)) \Rightarrow \tag{11}$$
$$\gamma''_{ij} = \Pr^{MS}(y_u(t) \mid x_u(t) = i) + \Pr^{MS}(y_p(t) \mid x_p(t) = j)$$

$$\gamma_{ij} = \gamma'_{ij}\,Int_i(t) \Rightarrow$$
$$-\ln(\gamma_{ij}) = -\ln(\gamma'_{ij}) - \ln(Int_i(t)) \Rightarrow \tag{12}$$
$$\gamma_{ij}^{MS} = \gamma''_{ij} + Int_i^{MS}(t)$$

$$a\_S(t) = \sum_{S'} a\_S'(t-1)\gamma_{S' \to S}(t) \Rightarrow$$
$$-\ln(a\_S(t)) = -\ln(\sum_{S'} e^{-(-\ln(a\_S'(t-1)\gamma_{S' \to S}(t)))}) \Rightarrow \tag{13}$$
$$a\_S^{MS}(t) = \min_{S'}(a\_S'(t-1) + \gamma_{S' \to S}(t)) + CorrectionFactor$$

The correction factor appearing in (13) has the form of the second term at the right part of (10). If a similar transformation is applied to the rest of the blocks of Table 1 and the correction factor is omitted, then we get the expressions of the Min Sum Algorithm that are listed in Table 2.

Block	Calculation
A	$\gamma_{ij}'' = \mathrm{Pr}^{MS}(y_u(t) \mid x_u(t) = i) + \mathrm{Pr}^{MS}(y_p(t) \mid x_p(t) = j)\,,\ i,j \in \{0,1\}$
B	$\gamma_{ij}^{MS} = \gamma_{ij}'' + Int_i^{MS}(t)\,,\ i,j \in \{0,1\}$
C	$a\_S(t)^{MS} = \min_{S'}(a\_S'(t-1)^{MS} + \gamma_{S' \to S}^{MS})$
D	$b\_S'(t)^{MS} = \min_{S}(b\_S(t+1)^{MS} + \gamma_{S' \to S}^{MS})$
E	$I_{ij}^{MS} = \min_{i/j,S' \to S}(a\_S'(t-1)^{MS} + b\_S(t)^{MS})$
F	$Ext_i^{MS}(t) = \min_{j}(I_{ij}^{MS} + \mathrm{Pr}^{MS}(y_p(t) \mid x_p(t) = j))\,,\ i \in \{0,1\}$
G	$U_i^{MS}(t) = \min_{j}(I_{ij}^{MS} + \gamma_{ij}^{MS})\,,\ i \in \{0,1\}$

Table 2. Calculations performed by the Min-Sum algorithm

If (14) is used and ln(x) is applied instead of –ln(x) the expressions of the Max-Log MAP algorithm can be derived, but they are omitted since they are identical to the ones of Table 2 if *min* function is replaced with the *max* one.

$$\min(x, y) = -\max(-x, -y) \tag{14}$$

5. Simulation Results

The Sum-Product and the Min-Sum decoding algorithms described in the previous section have been simulated using as input the specific 160-bit signatures that are used in the localisation system of the present work and are listed in Table 3.

Non-equalised signatures		Equalised signatures	
IRTX1	IRTX2	IRTX1	IRTX2
0x01010101	0x66666666	0x88888484	0x89898c8c
0x11111111	0xaaaaaaaa	0x18181212	0x1c1c1313
0x15151515	0xa4a4a4a4	0xc8c8c4c4	0xc9c9cccc
0x55555555	0x44444444	0x38383232	0x3c3c3333
0x33333333	0x04040404	0xe3e3e7e7	0xe1e1f3f3

Table 3. The 160 bit signatures used

The non-equalised signatures consist of 5 parts where the frequency of the bit value 1 occurs is different in each one of these parts. Moreover, the transmission of 1's by IRTX1 is not overlapping with the transmission of 1's by IRTX2. Based on this fact, a lot of scrambling errors are expected during real time operation.

The definition of the equalised signatures is based on the use of signature parts by the two IRTX devices that differ in fewer bits than the non-equalised signatures in order to avoid scrambling. Moreover, the 1s are gathered together in order to reduce the errors caused by the reflections since less 1→0 transitions appear in the signatures as discussed in Section 3. The original signatures are transmitted along with the corresponding parity bits of the original and the interleaved signatures that are generated by the encoder. The techniques applied for reducing the scrambling and reflection errors in the equalised signatures do not have any effect in the parity bits since if for example less 1→0 transitions appear in the original signature, it is not guaranteed that fewer 1→0 transitions will also appear in the parity bits.

The only simulated noise is of AWGN type with the SNR being in the range of [-1dB..+2dB]. This SNR range has been experimentally determined by taking into consideration the total number of errors in the received patterns at various spots in the covered area.

Fig. 13 presents the simulated results for various Turbo iterations. The non-equalised signatures are tested with a Random Interleaver. The equalised signatures are tested with the same Random interleaver and with a 2-level interleaver as well that generates equalised interleaved signatures. The 2-level interleaver rotates to the right by 3 positions the 32-bit signature parts at the first level and then the internal 32-bits of each part are reversed. This type of interleaving is described in Fig. 14 for which the following expression holds:

$$Interleaver[32 \cdot i + j] = 32 \cdot ((i+3)\%5) + 31 - j , 0 \le i < 5,\ 0 \le j < 32 \tag{15}$$

Based on the diagrams of Fig. 13 it can be concluded that if the number of iterations is 10 or higher, the error correcting capability is not significantly improved. For this reason, the Turbo decoder at the position localisation system will use 10 iterations as the best trade off between decoder performance and speed.

The Min-Sum algorithm shows a 0.5dB penalty in its performance compared to the Sum-Product if the SNR is low due to the omission of the correction factor. If the SNR is high, these algorithms have the same performance. In our experimental setup the error correction algorithm is executed in the Host Computer. Hence, the Sum-Product algorithm is used in order to achieve a better error correcting performance.

The choice of a proper interleaver affects significantly the performance since the 2-level interleaver tested has 0.5dB penalty at low SNR and more than 1.5dB penalty if the SNR is higher than 1dB. Even if the interleaved signature is also transmitted (code rate 1/4), the final bit error rate of the corrected patterns will not be improved since although fewer errors will occur at the interleaved signature, the capability of correcting the rest of the errors is reduced. For this reason, for the position localisation system, the Random Interleaver is used with the equalised signatures that are transmitted along with the corresponding parity bits of the signatures (code rate 1/3).

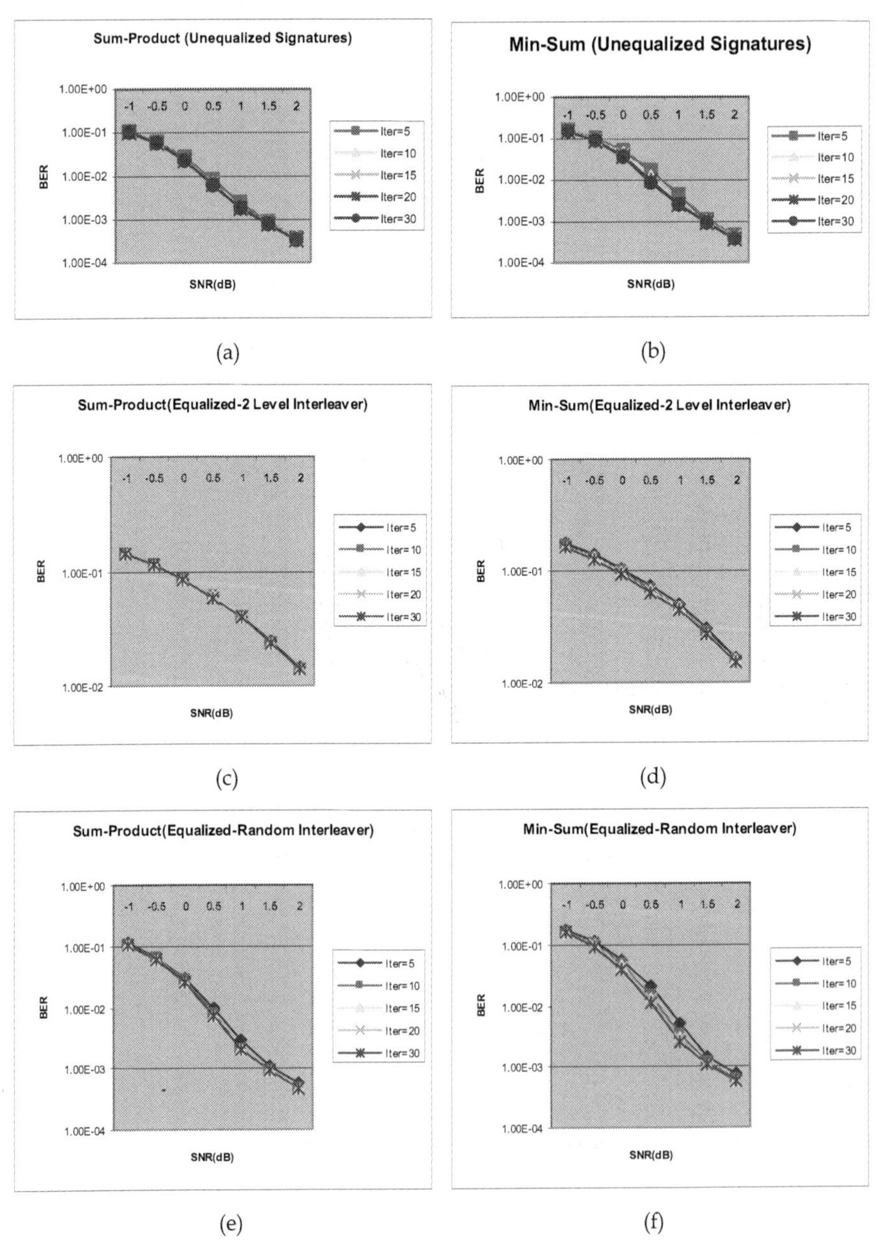

(a)

(b)

(c)

(d)

(e)

(f)

Fig. 13. Simulation results for the Sum-Product and the Min-Sum algorithms

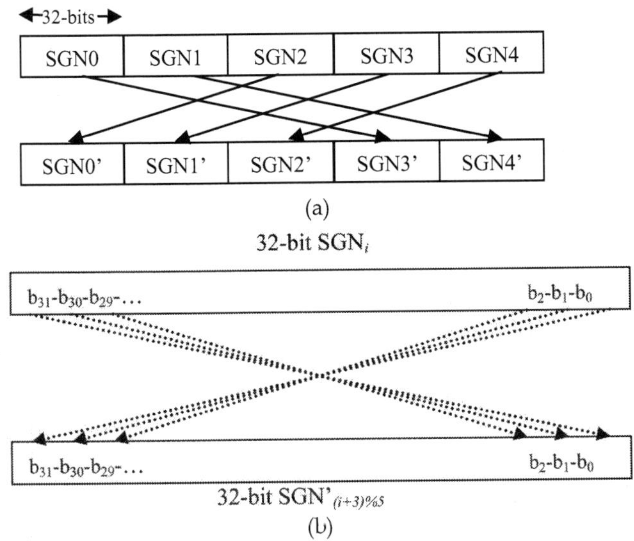

Fig. 14. A 2-level interleaver that generates equalised signatures

6. Experimental setup

The experimental setup beyond the signatures listed in Table 3 include also a number of short 8-bit signatures. The latter were not simulated in the previous section due to the fact that it is known that Turbo decoding has not considerable effect on data blocks with short length. We define the following signature structures that were experimentally tested:

6.1 Previous architecture (Setup1)

This is the previous setup described in (Petrellis et al, 2007). The patterns transmitted have the form of Fig. 4. The IRTX1 device transmits MOD2, MOD5, MOD6, MOD9 while IRTX2 transmits MOD3, MOD4, MOD7 and MOD8. The IRTX devices are independent and transmit concurrently. The number of the received pattern codes of each type is used as a multidimensional position identity. The time needed to transmit all the supported patterns between two preambles is:

$$T_{setup1} \propto 10\max(2T_2 + 5T_5 + 6T_6 + 9T_9,$$

$$3T_3 + 4T_4 + 7T_7 + 8T_8) \tag{16}$$

The parameter T_i is the duration of a pulse in MODi. If the time needed to transmit a bit in the rest of the setups is T_b, then the following values have been chosen for T_2-T_9: T_9=T_b, T_9<T_8<...< T_2. The pause interval between the successive patterns transmitted is $10T_b$.

6.2 Overlapping 8-bit signatures (Setup2)

The new architecture with a Sum-Product Turbo Decoder is used. Five short 8-bit signatures are transmitted along with their corresponding randomly interleaved signatures and their parity bits (code rate 1/4). The receiver tests alternatively the original or the interleaved signature bits as input to the decoder and uses the best results that are obtained. The two IRTX devices are independent and transmit concurrently. The set of signatures that are transmitted by IRTX1 is {0x85, 0x94, 0xa9, 0xd5, 0xbb} while IRTX2 transmits: {0x24, 0x4c, 0x5a, 0x3b, 0x6f}. These signatures have been selected so that each one of them differs in the number 1's. This is expected to force the receiver to recognise each one of these signatures with different error rate and hence, a multidimensional identity will be assigned to the specific position of the target. If s is the number of signatures, r is the code rate and b the number of bits per signature, then the time needed to transmit a set of signatures is:

$$T_{setup2} \propto \frac{s \cdot b \cdot T_b}{r} \tag{17}$$

6.3 Non-overlapping 8-bit signatures (Setup3)
Similar to Setup2 but the IRTX devices transmit in a non overlapping manner i.e., the IRTX1 does not transmit when IRTX2 does and vice versa. The signatures in this setup are received from the channel with lower bit error rate since scrambling is avoided. The time needed to transmit a set of signatures in this case is:

$$T_{setup3} \propto 2\frac{s \cdot b \cdot T_b}{r} \tag{18}$$

6.4 Overlapping 160-bit signatures (Setup4)
The non-equalised signatures of Table 3 are transmitted concurrently by the two IRTX devices. The interleaved signature bits are not transmitted (code rate 1/3). The time needed to transmit the signature and the parity bits is determined by (17).

6.5 160-bit signatures. One IRTX transmitting (Setup5)
Similar to the Setup4 but only one IRTX device is transmitting. The position identities are formed by 5 signature match degrees instead of 10 since the single IRTX device transmits a 160-bit signature with 5 parts. This setup is tested in order to see whether a second IRTX device is really necessary. The time needed to transmit the signature and the parity bits is determined again by (17).

6.6 Non-Overlapping 160-bit signatures (Setup6)
Similar to the Setup4 but the IRTX devices transmit in a non overlapping manner in order to avoid scrambling. The time needed to transmit the signature and the parity bits is determined by (18).

6.7 Equalised 160-bit signatures (Setup7)
The equalised signatures of Table 3 are used in order to let the IRTX devices transmit concurrently but achieve a lower bit error rate at the channel due to the structure of the signatures. The code rate is again 1/3 since the interleaved signatures are not transmitted. The time needed to transmit the signature and the parity bits is determined by (17).

7. Experimental results - discussion

The experiments for each of the aforementioned set-ups (described in the previous section) were performed with the IRTX1 and IRTX2 placed in 2.5m vertical distance and 60cm horizontal displacement as shown in Fig. 1. We focused in a region of 2.5mx1.5m between the two IRTX devices where the signal of both transmitters is strong. A virtual grid with 30cmx30cm squares is assumed to cover this region. The coordinates of a grid node or a real target position within this region are represented as (y,xD), where y is the vertical distance from IRTX1, x the horizontal displacement from IRTX1 and D denotes whether the target is on the Left (L) or the Right (R) of the IRTX1 device.

During the calibration stage that was carried out in each setup before real time operation, the target visited the nodes of the grid and stored the measured signature (parts) matching degrees. Then, during real time operation the target visited positions that were closer to each one of the grid nodes listed in Table 4. In each one of these positions, 5 localisation procedures were carried out repeatedly. The results of these localisation procedures are not all identical. If at least one of them finds the closer grid node or one of the other three neighbouring grid nodes, the position is marked as Successful (S), or Acceptable (A) respectively, otherwise it is marked as Fail (F). The exact results for each position are presented in Table 4.

In the first column the position coordinates are listed and the mark of the position appears in column C1. If a position is marked as Successful, the column C2 has a number that indicates how many of the 5 localisation procedures led to the closer grid node while column C3 indicates how many localisation procedures led to an acceptable grid node. Column C4 shows how many different grid nodes were selected in each position by the localisation procedures. The asterisk in Setup3-Setup7 marks a position in which the Turbo Decoding results were used. We do not have such an indication in Setup2 although Turbo Decoding was used in that case too, since in this setup the better results of Turbo Decoding on either the interleaved or the original signatures are always used.

Position	Setup 1				Setup 2				Setup 3				Setup 4				Setup 5				Setup 6				Setup 7			
	C1	C2	C3	C4	C1	C2	C3	C4	C1	C2	C3	C4	C1	C2	C3	C4	C1	C2	C3	C4	C1	C2	C3	C4	C1	C2	C3	C4
30,30L	A		2	2	F			1	F*			1	F			1	A*		3	2	A*		2	3	S	1	2	2
30,30R	S	2		2	A		2	2	F*			1	S	2	1	5	S*	1		1	S*	1	2	3	A		2	4
60,30L	S	3		2	A		5	2	F*			1	A*		2	2	A*		2	3	F*			1	F*			2
60,0	S	2	2	3	A		5	1	F*			1	F			1	S	2	2	4	A*		3	3	A		3	2
60,30R	A		2	2	S	5		1	F			1	A*		1	3	A*		2	5	S*	2	2	3	S	1	3	3
60,60R	S	1	3	3	F			2	A		5	1	A		2	5	F			1	F			3	S	2	1	4
90,60L	F			2	S	5		1	F			1	S*	5		1	F*			2	S*	5		1	A*		3	3
90,0	F			2	A		5	1	F			1	A		3	3	A		5	2	S	2		2	F			1
90,30R	F			2	S	5		1	F			1	S	1		4	A		5	3	A		2	3	S*	2	1	3
90,60R	S	2	1	4	A		5	1	F*			1	F			2	F			2	F			2	A		5	4
120,30L	F			4	F			5	F			1	A*		5	1	A*		3	4	A*		5	1	S	1	2	3
120,30R	F			3	A		4	2	F*			1	S	2	3	2	S	3		3	S	2	2	4	A		1	3
150,0	A		1	5	F			1	F			1	A		4	3	A		5	1	S	5		2	S	1	4	2
150,60R	F			1	S	5		1	A*		3	3	A		5	4	A*		1	3	S	2	2	4	S	5		1
180,30L	A		1	2	F			1	F			1	F			2	F*			2	A*		3	3	F			1
180,0	S	1	4	2	A		5	1	A		5	1	A		3	3	F			2	S	3	2	2	A		2	2
180,30R	A		4	2	S	3	2	2	A*		5	1	A		5	2	A		2	2	S	3	2	3	S*	1	2	4
210,0	S	4		2	S	5		1	A*		5	1	S	2		3	F*			3	S	5		1	F			1
210,60R	S	5		1	S	1		3	S*	1	4	2	S*	1	2	2	F*			1	A*		4	3	S	3		2
Totals	8S 5A 6F	20	20		7S 7A 5F	29	33		1S 5A 13F	1	27		6S 9A 3F	13	36		3S 9A 7F	6	30		10S 6A 3F	30	31		9S 6A 4F	17	31	

Table 4. The experiment results

Based on the results of Table 4 the accuracy and stability results can be obtained for each setup. Achieving a successful estimation is 3 times more important than an acceptable estimation since for a specific position there is only one successful node and three acceptable nodes among the ones of the whole grid. Using this fact the accuracy and stability results are compared in Fig. 15a and Fig. 15b. The speed of a localisation procedure in each setup is determined by the delay estimated by the expressions: (16)-(18). These expressions lead to the speed comparison of Fig. 15c.

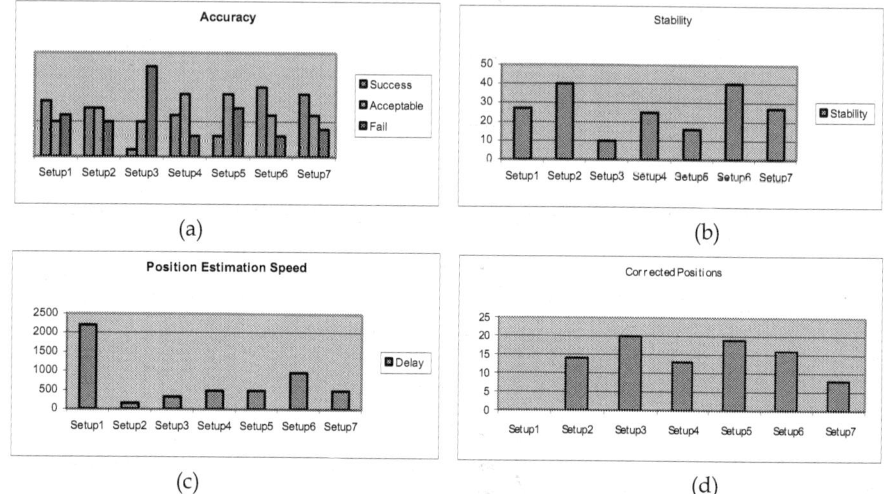

Fig. 15. Setup Comparison

Fig. 15d, presents the number of nodes where Turbo Decoding of the original signatures was exploited during the calibration stage, since error correction was achieved. Error correction could not be achieved in the rest positions due to the fact that the SNR is extremely low there.

The results with the best accuracy are obtained by Setup6 followed by Setup7 where non-overlapping or equalised signatures are used respectively. Nevertheless, Setup7 is twice as fast as Setup6. Setup2 is the fastest and the most stable setup, but produces results with moderate accuracy. This is due to the fact that short signatures are received with a small number of errors. Most of these few errors are further corrected by the Turbo Decoder. This leads to position identities that do not differ enough and may be easily confused with each other. This impact of this fact is worse in Setup3 where the signatures are transmitted in a non overlapping manner. Setup3 is twice slower than Setup2 and produces the worse accuracy results.

Besides the wider area coverage, the use of a second IRTX device improves the accuracy and the stability results of a localisation procedure since these features are not quite good in Setup5 where a single IRTX device was used.

Concluding, it can be said that all the new setup architectures tested are 2-13 times faster than our previous setup and most of them provide better accuracy and stability results. The use of equalised signatures in Setup7 seems to provide the best trade off between speed accuracy and stability.

8. Conclusions

Several new position estimation methods based on the error rate of received infrared patters were discussed in this chapter. The estimation of the features of the infrared channel of the positioning system allowed the selection of appropriate pattern structures and forward error correction methods that improve the speed, the accuracy and the stability of the localisation procedure. This is due to the fact that the impact of instant noise that cannot be taken into consideration during the calibration stage was limited.

Future work will focus on testing other pattern types as well as different forward correction techniques like Viterbi or LDPC. Moreover, different encoders with more delay elements will also be tested in order to correct more efficiently shorter patterns.

9. References

Arzel, M. Lahuec, C., Seguin, F., Gnaedig, D. & Jezequel, M. Semi-Iterative Analog Turbo Decoding. *IEEE Transactions on Circuits and Systems*. Vol. 54, No. 6, 2007, pp. 1305-1315

Arras, K., Tomatis, N., Jensen, B. & Siegward, R., Multisensor On-the-Fly Localisation : Precision and Reliability for Applications. *Elsevier Robotics and Autonomous Systems*, 43(2001), pp. 131-143.

Aytac, T. & Barshan, B., Simultaneous Extraction of Geometry and Surface Properties of Targets Using Simple Infrared Sensors. *Optical Engineering*, 43(10), Oct. 2004, pp. 2437-2447

Baskent, D. & Barshan, B. Surface Profile Determination from Multiple Sonar Data Using Morphological Processing. *Int. Journal of Robotics Research*. Vol .18, No. 8, 1999, pp. 788-808

Benet, G, Blanes, F., Simo, J. & Perez, P. Using Infrared Sensors for Distance Measurement in Mobile Robots. *Robot Autonomy Systems*, Vol. 30, 2002, pp. 255-266

Bicho, E., Mallet, P. & Schoner, G. Target Representation on an Autonomous Vehicle with Low Level Sensors, *Int. Journal of Robotics Research*, Vol. 19, No. 5, May 2000, pp. 424-447

Bickerstaff M.A., Garret D., Prokop T., Thomas C., Nicol C., A 24 Mb/s radix-4 logMAP Turbo decoder for 3GPP-HSDPA mobile wireless, *in Proc. IEEE Int. Solid-State Circuits Conf., San Francisco, pp.150-151, Feb. 2003.*

Borenstein, J. Everett, B. & Feng, L. (1996). *Navigating Mobile Robots: Systems and Techniques*, A.K. Peters Ltd Wellesley, MA

Clerentin A., Delahoche, A., Brassart, E. & Drocourt, C. Self Localisation: A New Uncertainty Propagation Architecture. *Elsevier Robotics and Autonomous Systems*, 51(2001), pp. 151-166

Flora, C., Ficco, M., Russo, S. & Vecchio, V. Indoor and Outdoor Location Based Services for Portable Wireless Devices. *Proceedings of 1st IEEE Int. Workshop on Services and Infrastructure for Ubiquitous and Mobile Internet*, pp. 244-250, June 2005, Columbus OH

Gamal, H. & Hammons, R. Analyzing the Turbo Decoder Using Gaussian Approximation. *IEEE Transactions on Information Theory*. Vol. 47, No. 2, 2001, pp. 671-686

Gioulekas, F., Birbas, M., Birbas, A., Bilionis, G: Analog Error-Correcting Decoders Using SiGe BiCMOS Technology. *International Journal of Analog Integrated Circuits and Signal Processing, Springer*, Vol. 52, No. 3 pp.117-132. October 16, 2007

Hagenauer, J. Offer, E. & Papke, L. Iterative Decoding of Binary Block and Convolutional Codes. *IEEE Transactions on Information Theory*. Vol. 42, No. 6, 1996, pp. 429-445

Jin, T., Lee, J. & Tso, S. A New Space and Time Sensor Fusion Method for Mobile Robot Navigation. *Wiley Journal of Robotics Systems*, 21(7), 2004, pp. 389-400

Kosel, J. Pfutzner, H., Mehnen, L., Kaniusas, E., Meydan, T., Vazquez, N., Rohn, M., Merlo, A. & Marquardt, B. Non Contact Detection of Magnetoelastic Position Sensors. *Elsevier Sensors and Actuators A*, 123-124 (2005), pp. 349-353

Kschischang, F., Frey, B. & Loeliger, H. Factor Graphs and the Sum-Product Algorithm. *IEEE Transactions on Information Theory*. Vol. 47, No. 2, 2001, pp. 498-519

Ladd, A., Bekiris, K., Rudys, A., Kavraki, L. & Wallach, D. Robotics Based Location Sensing Using Wireless Ethernet. *Wireless Networks*, Vol. 11, No. 1-2, Jan 2005, pp. 189-204

Minami, M., Fukuju, Y., Hirasawa, K., Yokoyama, S., Mizumachi, M., Morikawa, H. & Aoyama, T. Dolphin: A Practical Approach for Implementing a Fully Distributed Indoor Ultrasonic Positioning System. *Lect Not Comp Sci*, 3205, 2004, pp. 347-365

Miura, J., Negishi, Y. & Shirai, Y. Adaptive Robot Speed Control by Considering Map and Motion Uncertainty. *Elsevier Robotics and Autonomous Systems*, 54(2006), pp. 110-117

Novotny, P. & Ferrier, N. Using Infrared Sensors and the Phong Illumination Model to Measure Distances. *Proceedings of the IEEE Int. Conf. On Robotics and Automation*, pp. 1644-1649, 1999, Detroit MI

Petrellis, N. Konofaos, N. & Alexiou, G. A Sensors System for Indoor Localisation of A Moving Target Based on Infrared Pattern Recognition. *I-Tech Scene Reconstruction, Pose Estimation and Tracking*, Chapter 16 (2007), pp. 283-304

Petrellis, N. Konofaos, N. & Alexiou, G. Using Future Position Restriction Rules for Stabilizing the Results of a Noise-Sensitive Indoor Localization System. *Optical Engineering*, 46(6), 2007, pp. 067202-1-067202-11

Prigge, E. & How, J. Signal Architecture for Distributed Magnetic Local Positioning System. *IEEE Sensors Journal*. Vol. 4, No. 6, 2004, pp. 864-873

Schlageter, V., Besse, P., Popovic, R. & Kucera, P. Tracking System with 5deg of Freedom Using a 2D Array of Hall Sensors and a Permanent Magnet. *Elsevier Sensors and Actuators A*, 92, 2001, pp. 37-42

Schlegel, C. & Perez, L. Trellis and Turbo Coding, *IEEE Series on Digital & Mobile Communication*, Wiley Interscience (2004)

Se, S., Lowe, D. & Little, J. Mobile Robot Localisation and Mapping With Uncertainty Using Scale Invariant Visual Landmarks. *Int. Journal of Robotics Research*. Vol. 21, No. 8, 2002, pp. 735-758

Smith, P. & Zografos, K. Sonar for Recognizing the Texture of Pathways. *Robotics and Autonomous Systems*. Vol. 51, 2005, pp. 17-28

Tardos, J., Neira, J., Newmann, P. & Leonard, J. Robust Mapping and Localization In Indoor Environments Using Sonar Data. *Int joural of Robotics Research*. Vol 21, No. 8, 2002, pp. 311-330

Tovar, B., Gomez, L., Cid, R., Miranda, M., Monroy, R. & Hutchinson, S. Planning Exploration Strategies for Simultaneous Localisation and Mapping. *Elsevier Robotics and Autonomous Systems*. 54(2006), pp. 314-331

Vasic, B. & Kurtas, E. (2005) *Coding and Signal Processing for Magnetic Recording Systems*. CRC Press, NY

Victorino A., Rives, P. & Borelly, J. Safe Navigation for Indoor Mobile Robots Part II: Exploration, Self Localisation and Map Building. *Int. Journal of Robotics Research*. Vol. 22, No. 12, Dec 2003, pp. 1019-1039

27

Pattern Recognition in Time-Frequency Domain: Selective Regional Correlation and Its Applications

Ervin Sejdić[1] and Jin Jiang[2]
[1]Bloorview Research Institute and the Institute of Biomaterials and Biomedical Engineering, University of Toronto, Toronto, Ontario, M4G 1R8,
[2]Department of Electrical and Computer Engineering,
The University of Western Ontario, London, Ontario, N6A 5B9,
Canada

1. Introduction

Pattern recognition is a very powerful tool in automated data analysis and it is widely used in many different applications (Chou & Juang, 2003; Jiang,1994; Blue et al., 1994; Milosavljević, 1994; Moreels & Smrekar, 2003). However, the application of such a tool can be a difficult task in some cases. For example, in a correlation-type scheme, the basic idea is to correlate the signal being analyzed with a known template or templates (Shiavi, 1999; Scharf, 1991) and make decisions based on the magnitude of the correlation coefficients, which is between 0 and 1. In practice, these extreme values are seldom achieved due to corrupting signals/noise that can affect the accuracy of pattern matching and subsequently lead to errors in classification (Kil & Shin, 1996). The corrupting signals may also bear some resemblance to the template being matched. This is particularly true if the pattern of interest is a non-stationary transient signal. Furthermore, it is well known that traditional time domain correlation-based pattern recognition methods do not fully utilize the frequency characteristics of the template and the signal being analyzed. Hence, such methods perform poorly when applied to transient signals. To overcome these difficulties, a scheme known as selective regional correlation (SRC) has been developed (Sejdić & Jiang, 2007). It has been shown that if a template has bandlimited characteristics, significant improvement in the performance of pattern recognition can be readily made by a relatively simple pre-processing of the signal and the template in the time-frequency domain (Sejdić & Jiang, 2007). The redundant representation of a 1D signal in a 2D time-frequency domain can provide an additional degree of freedom for signal analysis. Such pre-processing effectively separates the intertwined time domain features of the signal, allowing the important characteristics to be exposed in the time-frequency domain, resulting in more effective pattern matching. Hence, correlation between the signal being analyzed and the template needs to be conducted only in selected regions of interest in the time-frequency domain.

An overview of the theoretical developments behind the SRC is provided in this chapter along with some recent results. The performance of the scheme is briefly reviewed and compared with that of the general correlation technique through the analysis of a set of synthetic short duration transients. The results have shown that the SRC enhances the resolution and accuracy for classification of transient signals significantly. The technique described herein may be of significance in many applications where correlation-based techniques have traditionally been used. The technique has already been applied to classification of heart sounds (Sejdić & Jiang, 2007), and to classification of a faulty machine tool positioning drive (Rehorn et al., 2006). In both cases, the SRC convincingly outperforms the general correlation based technique.

The theoretical background of the SRC is covered in Section 2, whereas Section 3 illustrates its performance using a set of synthetic signals. In Section 4, the application of SRC to heart sound analysis is reviewed, while in Section 5 the review of the application of SRC to detect a specific fault in a machine tool positioning drive is presented. Finally, conclusions are drawn in Section 6.

2. Mathematical developments behind SRC

The decision of a correlation-based pattern classifier depends on the output value of the correlator and thus its performance will be directly related to the quality of the correlation process. Hence, the essence of SRC is to represent a 1D time domain signal in a 2D time-frequency representation to reveal its true characteristics for more accurate pattern matching as depicted in Fig. 1.

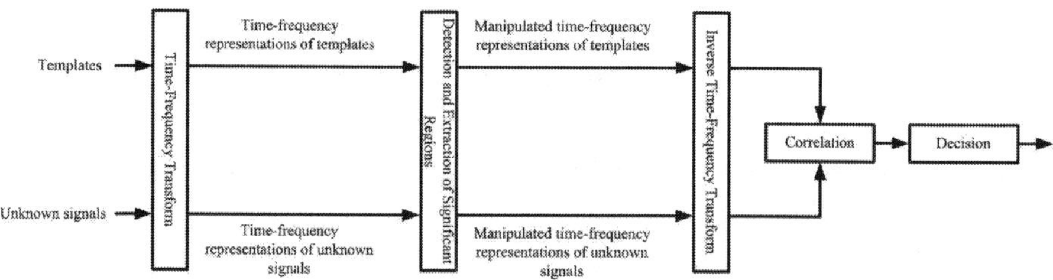

Fig. 1. A block diagram of SRC.

A time-frequency transform of a bandlimited template, $p(t)$, can be represented as:

$$Tp(t,\omega) = \int_{-\infty}^{+\infty} p(\tau)\phi_{t,\omega}(\tau)d\tau \tag{1}$$

and

$$Tp(t,\omega) \equiv 0 \quad \forall \quad t \notin [t_1, t_2] \quad \omega \notin [\omega_1, \omega_2] \tag{2}$$

where t_1 and t_2 are the lower and the upper limits of the time band, ω_1 and ω_2 are the lower and the upper limits of the frequency band and $\phi_{t,\omega} \in \mathbf{L}^2(\mathbb{R})$ (sometimes known as the time-frequency atom) is a well-concentrated function in time and frequency (Mallat, 1999). The time-frequency atoms considered in this chapter are given in Table 1.

Furthermore, assume that there exists a finite duration signal, $s(t)$, composed of elements that are similar to the template, $s^{(1)}(t)$, and elements different from the template, $s^{(2)}(t)$. Thus, the following signal decomposition is in order:

$$Ts(t,\omega) = Ts^{(1)}(t,\omega) \cup Ts^{(2)}(t,\omega) \tag{3}$$

Method	$\phi_{\tau,\omega}(t)$
Short-time Fourier transform (STFT) (Mallat, 1999)(Gröchenig, 2001)	$e^{-j\omega t}g(t-\tau)$ where g is a window function.
Continuous wavelet transform (CWT) (Mallat, 1999)(Daubechies, 1992)	$\frac{1}{\sqrt{s}}\psi\left(\frac{t-\tau}{s}\right)$ where ψ is a mother wavelet.
S-transform(Stockwell et all., 1996)(Pinnegar, 2001)	$e^{-j\omega t}g\left(\frac{t-\tau}{\omega}\right)$ where g is a Gaussian window.

Table 1. The time-frequency atoms in different transforms.

where

$$Ts^{(1)}(t,\omega) = Ts(t,\omega) \qquad t \in [t_1,t_2] \ \text{ and } \ \omega \in [\omega_1,\omega_2] \tag{4}$$

and

$$Ts^{(2)}(t,\omega) = \overline{Ts(t,\omega) \cap Ts^{(1)}(t,\omega)} \tag{5}$$

with $Ts^{(1)}(t,\omega)$ and $Ts^{(2)}(t,\omega)$ denoting time-frequency representations of $s^{(1)}(t)$ and $s^{(2)}(t)$, respectively. To effectively obtain $Ts^{(1)}(t,\omega)$ from $Ts(t,\omega)$, different 2D windows can be used (Sejdić & Jiang, 2007):

$$Ts^{(1)}(t,\omega) = Ts(t,\omega) \cdot W(t,\omega) \ \ t \in [t_1,t_2] \ \text{ and } \ \omega \in [\omega_1,\omega_2]. \tag{6}$$

where $W(t,\omega)$ is a 2D window in the time-frequency domain.

Assuming that $s^{(1)}(t)$ is similar to pattern $p(t)$, then the following statement is true:

$$\max\left[\left|corr(s^{(1)}(t),p(t))\right|\right] > \max\left[|corr(s(t),p(t))|\right] \tag{7}$$

where $\max\left[|corr(x(t),y(t))|\right]$ is defined as:

$$\max\left[|corr(x(t),y(t))|\right] = \max_{\tau}\left[\left|\frac{\int_{-\infty}^{\infty}x(t)y(t+\tau)dt}{\sqrt{\int_{-\infty}^{\infty}x(t)^2dt}\sqrt{\int_{-\infty}^{\infty}y(t)^2dt}}\right|\right] \tag{8}$$

and $x(t)$ and $y(t)$ are assumed to be zero-mean signals. This statement is possible due to the fact that $s^{(2)}(t)$ lies in the frequency and the time bands outside those of pattern $p(t)$. For a complete proof, please refer to (Sejdić & Jiang, 2007).

The concept of the SRC is also applicable to a multiple templates case, but the templates must be mutually exclusive. Hence, the templates $p_1(t)$, ..., $p_m(t)$ with the time-frequency representations $Tp_1(t,\omega)$, ..., $Tp_m(t,\omega)$ would have

$$Tp_1(t,\omega) \cap Tp_2(t,\omega) \cap Tp_3(t,\omega) \cap .... \cap Tp_m(t,\omega) = \emptyset \tag{9}$$

However, if

$$Tp_k(t,\omega) \cap Tp_l(t,\omega) \neq \emptyset \quad \text{ for } \quad k \neq l \tag{10}$$

for some k and l, it is necessary to introduce a mutually exclusive template in order to reduce the peak correlation coefficient when the signal does not match the template. This exclusivity is represented in the time-frequency domain as:

$$Tp_k^{(1)}(t,\omega) = Tp_k(t,\omega) - (Tp_k(t,\omega) \cap Tp_l(t,\omega)) \tag{11}$$

and the corresponding template can be found by multiplying a time-frequency decomposition of the template $Tp_k^{(1)}(t,\omega)$ with a 2D window, $W_k(t,\omega)$, with appropriate time and frequency bands, and inverting back to the time domain.

Based on (9)-(11), it can be stated that any template can be expressed as a sum of mutually exclusive terms, $p^{(1)}(t)$, and $p^{(2)}(t)$, that is,

$$p(t) = p^{(1)}(t) + p^{(2)}(t) \tag{12}$$

where $p^{(2)}(t)$ would be zero for disjoint templates. Therefore, if the signal $z(t)$ does not contain the template $p(t)$, the SRC using $p^{(1)}(t)$ will produce a smaller correlation coefficient, namely,

$$\max\left[\|corr(z(t),p(t))\|\right] > \max\left[\left\|corr(z(t),p^{(1)}(t))\right\|\right] \tag{13}$$

where $\max\left[\|corr(x(t),y(t))\|\right]$ is as defined in (8). In addition, it is necessary to have the following constraint:

$$\int_{-\infty}^{\infty}\int_{-\infty}^{\infty}\left|Tp^{(1)}(t,\omega)\right|d\tau d\omega \gg \int_{-\infty}^{\infty}\int_{-\infty}^{\infty}\left|Tp^{(2)}(t,\omega)\right|d\tau d\omega \tag{14}$$

For a complete proof, please refer to (Sejdić & Jiang, 2007).

The mutual exclusivity of the templates is the main reason why SRC is a superior pattern matching technique to general correlation-based approaches. The exclusivity of the templates is only possible by introducing a redundant representation of the signal, such as the one in time-frequency domain.

3. Comparative performance evaluation of SRC using synthetic test signals

In this section, the performance of the SRC compared to general correlation is reviewed through a set of test signals. Having this objective in mind, it is prudent to understand that most of the real-world patterns are not limited to a single frequency, but rather are often a sum of transients containing different frequencies. These frequencies can vary with time and are often within a certain frequency band. Therefore, in order mimic practical conditions, the following templates and signals have been selected in this evaluation:

$$p_1(t) = \begin{cases} p_o(t) + \sin(2\pi 95t) + \sin(2\pi 102t) \\ \qquad\quad + \sin(2\pi 105t) + \sin(2\pi 110t) & 0.4 \leq t \leq 0.6 \\ p_o(t) & \text{otherwise} \end{cases} \tag{15}$$

$$p_2(t) = \begin{cases} p_o(t) + \sin(2\pi 60t) + \sin(2\pi 67t) \\ \qquad\quad + \sin(2\pi 70t) + \sin(2\pi 75t) & 0.58 \leq t \leq 0.74 \\ p_o(t) & \text{otherwise} \end{cases} \tag{16}$$

$$s_{1_i}(t) = \begin{cases} p_o(t) + \sum_{k=1}^{k=6} \sin(\lfloor 2\pi 250R \rfloor\, t) & 0.04 + \frac{\lfloor 30R \rfloor}{500} \leq t \leq 0.26 + \frac{\lfloor 20R \rfloor}{500} \\ p_o(t) + \sum_{k=1}^{k=4} \sin(2\pi(95 + \lfloor 15R \rfloor)t) & 0.40 + \frac{\lfloor 20R \rfloor}{500} \leq t \leq 0.60 + \frac{\lfloor 20R \rfloor}{500} \\ p_o(t) + \sum_{k=1}^{k=6} \sin(\lfloor 2\pi 250R \rfloor\, t) & 0.84 + \frac{\lfloor 20R \rfloor}{500} \leq t \leq 0.90 + \frac{\lfloor 25R \rfloor}{500} \\ p_o(t) & \text{otherwise} \end{cases} \tag{17}$$

$$s_{2_i}(t) = \begin{cases} p_o(t) + \sum_{k=1}^{k=6} \sin(\lfloor 2\pi 250R \rfloor\, t) & 0.04 + \frac{\lfloor 30R \rfloor}{500} \leq t \leq 0.26 + \frac{\lfloor 20R \rfloor}{500} \\ p_o(t) + \sum_{k=1}^{k=4} \sin(2\pi(60 + \lfloor 15R \rfloor)t) & 0.58 + \frac{\lfloor 20R \rfloor}{500} \leq t \leq 0.74 + \frac{\lfloor 20R \rfloor}{500} \\ p_o(t) + \sum_{k=1}^{k=6} \sin(\lfloor 2\pi 250R \rfloor\, t) & 0.84 + \frac{\lfloor 20R \rfloor}{500} \leq t \leq 0.90 + \frac{\lfloor 25R \rfloor}{500} \\ p_o(t) & \text{otherwise} \end{cases} \tag{18}$$

where

$$p_o(t) = 0.8[\sin(2\pi 10t) + \sin(2\pi 15t) + \sin(2\pi 18t)] \tag{19}$$

and $R \sim |\mathcal{N}(0, 1)|$ simulates the uncertainties in the signals with $t \in [0, 1]$. $\lfloor x \rfloor$ represents the greatest integer function, which gives the largest integer less than or equal to x.

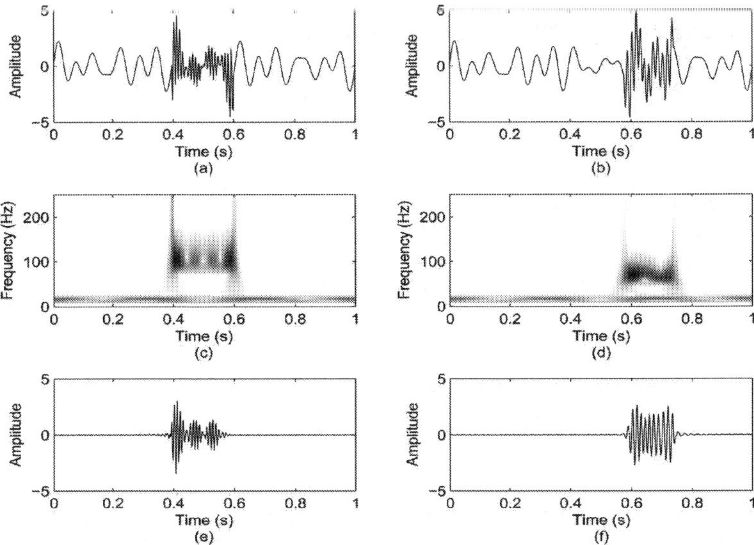

Fig. 2. Time-domain and time-frequency domain representations of dual templates: (a) time domain representation of template of the first template; (b) time domain representation of template of the second template; (c) time-frequency domain representation of the first template; (d) time-frequency domain representation of the second template; (e) time domain representation of the first template after pre-processing; (f) time domain representation of the second template after pre-processing.

The templates are depicted by the top two graphs in Fig. 2. They have the same low frequency content, but the transients that occur in the templates represent two different phenomena as described by (15) and (16). The time-frequency representations of the templates are obtained according to (1) using the S-transform. Their main characteristics can be summarized by the following equations:

$$Tp_1(t,\omega) = \begin{cases} \Omega_{p_{11}} = \{(t,\omega) : t \in [0.38, 0.62], \quad \omega \in [50, 160] \text{ Hz}\} \\ \Omega_{p_{12}} = \{(t,\omega) : t \in [0,1], \quad \omega \in [8, 26] \text{ Hz}\} \end{cases} \tag{20}$$

$$Tp_2(t,\omega) = \begin{cases} \Omega_{p_{21}} = \{(t,\omega) : t \in [0.55, 0.77], \quad \omega \in [40, 120] \text{ Hz}\} \\ \Omega_{p_{22}} = \{(t,\omega) : t \in [0,1] \quad \omega \in [8, 26] \text{ Hz}\} \end{cases} \tag{21}$$

with the regions of support including the bands in which the amplitude of time-frequency representations is greater than or equal to one percent of its maximum amplitude. The overlapped time-frequency areas are excluded by windowing in order to form the mutually exclusive templates $p_1^{(1)}(t)$ and $p_2^{(1)}(t)$. The time domain representations of these mutually exclusive templates are shown in the bottom two graphs of Fig. 2.

Furthermore, ten thousand test signals, $s_i(t)$ where $i = 1...10000$, were constructed according to (17) and (18); with half of the signals containing the patterns similar to $p_1(t)$ and the other half similar to $p_2(t)$. Since each of these signals can contain either of the templates, a window function is needed to capture all the variations. In this case, a window, $W_{gd}(t,\omega)$ was designed to support the region $\Omega_{gd} = \{(t, \omega) : t \in [0.38, 0.77], \omega \in [40, 160] \text{ Hz}\}$.

The correlations were performed by using general correlation and the SRC, and the results are presented in Table 2. These results represent an average of 10000 trials. In Table 2, ρ_M represents the situation where the signal matches the template as specified, while ρ_{NM} represents the situation where the signal does not match the template. Also, $\varphi = \rho_M - \rho_{NM}$ denotes the resolution, and the error percentage (EP) is calculated according to $EP = MC/(MC + CC) * 100\%$, where CC and MC represent the number of correct classifications and misclassifications, respectively.

Method		ρ_M	ρ_{NM}	φ	EP
SRC	STFT	0.5827	0.0823	0.5004	0.0001%
	CWT	0.4856	0.3207	0.1649	1.9600%
	S-transform	0.5835	0.0789	0.5046	0.0000%
General Correlation		0.6127	0.5625	0.0502	19.4900%

Table 2. Comparison of the peak correlation coefficients for SRC and general correlation.

The SRC performed significantly better than general correlation as shown in Table 2, especially when the S-transform and STFT are used. Furthermore, the error percentage for the SRC-based classifier is only 0-2%, while for the conventional correlation-based classifier is almost 20%.

To be useful in practice, any pattern recognition scheme should possess a high degree of sensitivity to the template, and be robust to slight variations in the signals being analyzed. Therefore, the robustness of the SRC has been examined by stretching and shrinking the signals at three different levels. The results of such an analysis are presented in Table 3 and these represent an average of 10000 trials with the S-transform used as a time-frequency representation. Also, each trial represents the mean value of the two operations: expansion and compression.

Amount of expansion and compression			
	0%	10%	15%	20%
ρ_M	0.5835	0.5064	0.4057	0.2834
ρ_{NM}	0.0789	0.0848	0.1197	0.1611
φ	0.5046	0.4215	0.2860	0.1223
EP	0.0000%	0.0000%	0.0002%	7.7400%

Table 3. Robustness of the proposed scheme to expansion and compression.

As demonstrated, slight variations in the range of 0 - 15% have no major effect on the performance of the SRC based pattern classifier since the accuracy remains almost the same as shown in Table 3, even though the resolution has decreased by a factor of 2. However, deterioration in performance can be seen for variations larger than 20%. Therefore, the SRC can be considered very robust.

4. Heart sound classification by SRC based scheme

Despite numerous advances and decades of declining death rates, cardiovascular diseases (CVDs) remain the leading cause of death worldwide; contributing to more than 17 million deaths or one-third of all deaths each year. CVD is becoming increasingly prevalent in developing countries and, by 2010, CVDs are expected to kill more people in developing countries than infectious diseases according to World Health Organization (W. H. Organization, 2006). Fortunately, clinical experience has shown that heart sounds analysis can be an effective tool to noninvasively diagnose some of the diseases (Khan, 1996; Ravin, 1977), since they provide clinicians with valuable diagnostic and prognostic information concerning the heart valves and hemodynamics. Heart auscultation is an important technique for detecting abnormal heart behaviour before using more sophisticated techniques such as the ECG or ultrasound imaging (Durand & Pibarot, 1995; Erickson, 1997; Obadiat, 1993).

Heart sounds are the result of a sudden closure of the heart valves at different phases of the cardiac contraction. They are non-stationary, non-deterministic signals that carry information about the anatomical and physiological state of the heart. Heart sounds are result of the interplay of dynamic events associated with the contraction and relaxation of atria and ventricles, valve movements and blood flow (Ravin, 1977; Durand & Pibarot, 1995). Each heart beat consists of at least the first heart sound (S1) and second heart sound (S2). S1 occurs at the onset of the ventricular contraction during closure of the mitral and the tricuspid valves. It indicates the beginning of the ventricular systole. The intensity of S1 is closely related to that event. S1 consists of four components with frequency range 70-110 Hz. It starts with a low-frequency component (M1) synchronous with the first myocardial contraction after the onset of rise in the ventricular pressure. The second component (T1) has a higher frequency and is caused by tension of the left ventricular structures; contraction of myocardium and deceleration of blood. The third occurs at the time of opening of the aortic valve and is related to sudden acceleration of blood into the ventricular walls. The fourth component is due to turbulence in the blood flow in the ascending aorta. The intensity of S1 varies depending on the following factors: position of auscultation, the anatomy of chest, the vigor of ventricular contraction, valve position at the onset of ventricular contraction, and the pathological alternation of the valve structure (Erickson, 1997; Horovitz, 1988). S2 marks the end of ventricular systole and the beginning of ventricular relaxation following the closure of the aortic and the pulmonary valves. Therefore, two different components could be heard in S2, and those are A2 and P2. These are produced by vibrations initiated by the closure of the aortic and the pulmonary semilunar valves, and by sudden cessation of backflow of the blood (Khan, 1996; Ravin, 1977).

A heart problem known as mitral stenosis is caused by a rheumatic heart disease in the majority of cases. This leads to narrowing of the mitral valve. As a result, it slows down the free flow of blood from the left atrium to the left ventricle. Blood returning from the lungs backs up in the left atrium and in the lungs. As a consequence, there is a gradual increase in pressure in the left atrium and in the pulmonary (lung) circulation. This condition can eventually lead to enlargement of the left atrium, weakening of the atrium wall, and gradually result in more serious conditions due to the reduced ability to propel blood efficiently (Horovitz, 1988). Mitral stenosis is very often manifested through a heart sound known as the opening snap (OS); a short, sharp sound occurring in the early diastole. It is caused by the abrupt halting at its maximal opening of an abnormal atrioventricular valve and the OS usually occurs 0.08-0.10 s after S2 (Ravin, 1977; Erickson, 1997). However, the difficulty, as shown in the top two graphs of Fig. 3, lies in the fact that the OS sounds very similar to the third heart sound (S3), which is often heard in normal children or young adults. When S3 is heard in individuals over the age of 40, it usually reflects cardiac disease characterized by ventricular dilatation, decreased systolic function, and elevated ventricular diastolic filling pressure. It is generally difficult to distinguish these two sounds without going through proper training (Khan, 1996; Ravin, 1977; Erickson, 1997).

The objective of this study is to examine the suitability of the SRC for classification of aforementioned conditions. For full details of the study, please refer to (Sejdić & Jiang, 2007). For the purpose of clear illustration, one signal from each group is selected as the template for that group and both templates are depicted in the top two graphs of Fig. 3. As shown, most of the energy associated with an OS is concentrated between 50 and 300 Hz, while that of S3 lies between 30 and 150 Hz (boxed regions in Fig. 3). The templates have to be decoupled, since there is an overlap in some frequency ranges between the two signals. Based on the numerical analysis, it is concluded that the template for OS, $p_{OS}(t)$, should have frequency range between 120 and 300 Hz and its time duration should be around 50 ms, while the template for S3, $p_{S3}(t)$, should have frequency range between 30 and 70 Hz and its time duration should be near 100 ms. Since the signal being analyzed could contain either OS or S3, the frequency band for the window is chosen as $\omega \in [30\ 300]$ Hz.

Similar to the previous case, the performance of the SRC is again evaluated by comparing it with that of the general correlation, and the results are shown in Table 4. These results represent an average of thirty trials. σ_M, σ_{NM} and σ are the standard deviations of ρ_M, ρ_{NM} and φ, respectively. A comparison of the values of these two states shows that the SRC performs significantly better than the general correlation. Furthermore, T-test is used to inspect whether ρ_M and ρ_{NM} are statistically different for classifiers based both on SRC and general correlation. The analysis concludes that the null hypothesis (the means are equal) can be rejected at the 0.05 significance level for the SRC based classifier, but not for the classifier based on the general correlation.

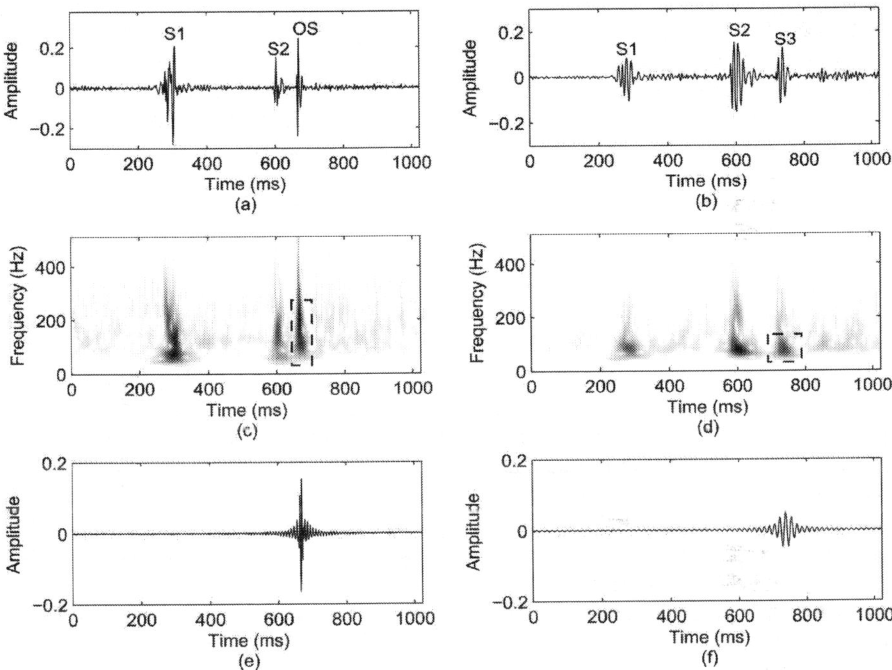

Fig. 3. Time domain, time-frequency domain representations and the templates: (a) time domain representation of heart sounds with a typical OS; (b) time domain representation of heart sounds with a typical S3; (c) time-frequency representation of (a); (d) time-frequency representation of (b); (e) the template based on the typical OS; (f) the template based on the typical S3.

Method		ρ_M	σ_M	ρ_{NM}	σ_{NM}	φ	σ_φ	EP
SRC	STFT	0.5533	0.1627	0.2413	0.0942	0.3120	0.2263	10.00%
	CWT	0.6731	0.1546	0.5248	0.1097	0.1483	0.1347	16.67%
	S-transform	0.4905	0.1043	0.1661	0.0708	0.3244	0.1582	6.670%
General Correlation		0.3477	0.1087	0.3352	0.0562	0.0126	0.1122	56.67%

Table 4. Heart sound classification with different techniques.

5. Fault diagnosis of servo drives in machine tools

There are many potential sources for mechanical failure in the main positioning system of a machine tool including DC servomotor brush seizing, drive belt wear or stretching, and wear in the bearings and lead screws. Each of these problems exhibits a specific characteristic signature. These signatures can be used for machine condition monitoring (MCM). The key is to identify a set of features that correspond unambiguously to either the healthy mode or possible faulty modes of the machine. Such features can be found in vibration signals of the axes during machining. By comparing the measured data to the failure signature, the health of the machine tool positioning drives can be determined.

This study focuses on brush seizing faults in a DC servo motor drive that controls the position of the spindle block on the machine tool. This fault originates from the design and construction of the brush holders, which are plastic and often warp with exposure to heat and lubricant. Whenever this happens, the spindle block experiences excessive vibration. When one of the servos is faulty, the axis jumps along the guideways rather than moving smoothly. Experience has shown that this type of fault always leads to failure.

It has been found that, for a healthy spindle, there are no fixed patterns in the vibration signals. However, periodic phenomena arise when a fault starts to develop in the system (Rehorn, 2003). These phenomena become much more apparent in the time-frequency domain because they often appear as transient spikes of short durations. It is difficult to detect them either in the time domain or in the frequency domain alone. This is because both the healthy and the faulty drives contain energy in the same frequency bands. However, there are increased periodic fluctuations with energy concentrated in the 20-200 Hz band when the system is faulty. Thus, a faulty system will exhibit a regular pattern of spikes in this frequency range, while a healthy one will not (Rehorn, 2003).

Templates are selected using three different 2D windows, with each of the windows isolating a feature in the time-frequency domain which exists for a range $R = \{(t, \omega) : t \in [540, 630], \omega \in [20, 200]\}$ (Rehorn et al., 2006). The selection of a specific template with the rectangular window in the X direction is shown in Fig. 4. The upper graph depicts the S-transform of the entire vibration signal, $Tv_F(t, \omega)$, and the boxed region on the graph represents the area covered by the 2D window. The middle graph displays the windowed and isolated feature of interest in the time-frequency domain, $Tv_{F1}(t, \omega)$. The bottom graph shows the corresponding time domain signal, $v_{F1}(t)$, that is used in SRC.

SRC improves the ability to distinguish between similar and dissimilar patterns beyond conventional correlation by improving the resolution for different states of the system. The results are presented in Tables 5-8. The values for ρ_M and ρ_{NM} are the average values over twelve tests. From these results, several interesting observations can be made. The highest values of φ for a specified time-frequency method are generally in Z direction, although this is not the case for the S-transform. Also, changing the time-frequency method used has a more pronounced effect on the SRC resolution than do the shape and type of the window employed for feature extraction. It should also be noted that the S-transform has achieved the best resolution among all three time-frequency methods used, with the STFT being the runner up. The CWT has the poorest resolution of the three methods tested in the X and Y directions, but its resolution is equal to, or even better than, the others in Z direction. Of the three windows considered, the Kaiser yields the highest resolution while the Gaussian window performs the worst.

By comparing the values in Tables 5 - 7, with those in Table 8, the values generated by general correlation for similar events are much smaller than those calculated using time-frequency methods and SRC in the given direction. General correlation of similar events generates only 10% similarity at the most; well below the value of ρ_{NM} produced by any of the time-frequency methods. This is mainly due to the non-stationary nature of the vibration signals in this case. The resolution of general correlation is extremely poor as well, and never exceeds 5%, while any combination of time-frequency method and 2D window with SRC results in very high resolution between the two states. Thus, an MCM system that relies on general correlation will not be able to perform as effectively as the one based on time-frequency methods and SRC.

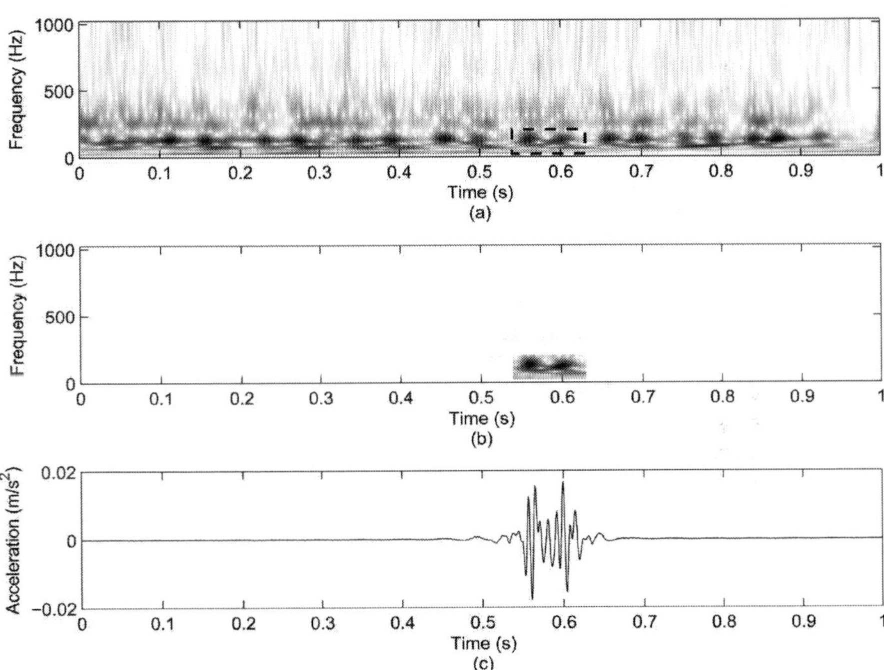

Fig. 4. Template signal selection from the S-transform of a faulty drive: (a) time-frequency representation of a faulty drive; (b) extracted template in time-frequency domain; and (c) the template in the time domain.

| | Selective Regional Correlation | | | | | | | | |
| | STFT | | | CWT | | | S-transform | | |
Directions	X	Y	Z	X	Y	Z	X	Y	Z
ρ_M	0.4531	0.5177	0.6701	0.2994	0.1688	0.7343	0.5522	0.6557	0.5981
ρ_{NM}	0.2413	0.2342	0.3298	0.1399	0.1075	0.2574	0.1810	0.1762	0.1433
φ	0.2118	0.2835	0.3403	0.1595	0.0613	0.4769	0.3712	0.4795	0.4548

Table 5. Performance of SRC using a 2D rectangular window.

Directions	Selective Regional Correlation								
	STFT			CWT			S-transform		
	X	Y	Z	X	Y	Z	X	Y	Z
ρ_M	0.4836	0.5521	0.6918	0.3467	0.1978	0.7960	0.5847	0.6951	0.6230
ρ_{NM}	0.3141	0.3064	0.3849	0.2206	0.1489	0.3965	0.2768	0.2524	0.2851
φ	0.1695	0.2457	0.3069	0.1261	0.0489	0.3995	0.3079	0.4427	0.3379

Table 6. Performance of SRC using a 2D Gaussian window.

Directions	Selective Regional Correlation								
	STFT			CWT			S-transform		
	X	Y	Z	X	Y	Z	X	Y	Z
ρ_M	0.6171	0.6643	0.7243	0.4823	0.1931	0.8210	0.6211	0.7184	0.6673
ρ_{NM}	0.3318	0.3397	0.3322	0.2631	0.1143	0.3829	0.2293	0.2219	0.3049
φ	0.2853	0.3246	0.3912	0.2192	0.0788	0.4381	0.3918	0.4965	0.3624

Table 7. Performance of SRC using a 2D Kaiser window.

Directions	X	Y	Z
ρ_M	0.0652	0.0560	0.1002
ρ_{NM}	0.0581	0.0285	0.0536
φ	0.0071	0.0275	0.0466

Table 8. Performance of classifier using general correlation.

6. Conclusion

In this chapter, a recently developed technique for pattern classification based on time-frequency decomposition is presented. The essence of the scheme is that the correlation between the observed signal and the template is conducted only in selected regions of interest in the time-frequency domain. The results of two applications have indicated conclusively that the proposed technique provides a consistent improvement over the traditional correlation-based pattern classification schemes.

7. References

W. Chou and B. H. Juang, Eds., *Pattern Recognition in Speech and Language Processing.* London: CRC Press, 2003.

J. Jiang, "Design of reconfigurable control systems using eigenstructure assignments," *International Journal of Control*, vol. 59, pp. 395-410, 1994.

J. L. Blue, G. T. Candela, P. J. Grother, R. Chellappa, C. L. Wilson, and J. D. Blue, "Evaluation of pattern classifiers for fingerprint and OCR applications," *Pattern Recognition*, vol. 27, no. 4, pp. 485-501, Apr. 1994.

A. Milosavljević, "Algorithmic significance, mutual information, and DNA sequence comparisons," in *Proceedings of the Data Compression Conference*, Mar. 29-31, 1994, p. 457.

P. Moreels and S. Smrekar, "Watershed identification of polygonal patterns in noisy SAR images," *IEEE Transactions on Signal Processing*, vol. 12, no. 7, pp. 740-750, Jul. 2003.

R. Shiavi, *Introduction to Applied Statistical Signal Analysis*, 2nd ed. San Diego: Academic Press, 1999.

L. L. Scharf, *Statistical Signal Processing: Detection, Estimation, and Time Series Analysis*. Addison Wesley, 1991.

D. H. Kil and F. B. *Shin, Pattern Recognition and Prediction with Applications to Signal Characterization*. Woodbury, NY: AIP Press, 1996.

E. Sejdić and J. Jiang, "Selective regional correlation for pattern recognition," *IEEE Transactions on Systems, Man and Cybernetics - Part A*, vol. 37, no. 1, pp. 82-93, Jan. 2007.

A. G. Rehorn, E. Sejdić, and J. Jiang, "Fault diagnosis in machine tools using selective regional correlation," *Mechanical Systems and Signal Processing*, vol. 20, no. 5, pp. 1221-1238, Jul. 2006.

S. G. Mallat, *A Wavelet Tour of Signal Processing*, 2nd ed. San Diego: Academic Press, 1999.

K. Gröchenig, *Foundations of Time-Frequency Analysis*. Boston: Birkhäuser, 2001.

I. Daubechies, *Ten Lectures on Wavelets*. Philadelphia: Society for Industrial and Applied Mathematics, 1992.

R. G. Stockwell, L. Mansinha, and R. P. Lowe, "Localization of the complex spectrum: The S-transform," *IEEE Transactions on Signal Processing*, vol. 44, no. 4, pp. 998-1001, Apr. 1996.

R. Pinnegar, "The generalized S-transform and TT-transform, in one and two dimensions," Ph.D. dissertation, The University of Western Ontario, London, Ontario, Canada, Sep. 2001.

W. H. Organization, "Cardiovascular disease: prevention and control,"Apr. 2006. [Online]. Available: http://www.who.int/dietphysicalactivity/publications/facts/cvd/en/

M. G. Khan, Heart Disease Diagnosis and Therapy: A Practical Approach. Baltimore: Williams and Wilkins, 1996.

A. Ravin, *Auscultation of the Heart*, 3rd ed. Chicago: Year Book Medical Publishers, 1977.

L. Durand and P. Pibarot, "Digital signal processing of the phonocardiogram: Review of the most recent advancements," *Critical Reviews in Biomedical Engineering*, vol. 23, no. 3-4, pp. 169-219, 1995.

B. Erickson, *Heart Sounds and Murmurs: A Practical Guide*, 3rd ed. St. Louis: Mosby-Year Book, 1997.

M. Obadiat, "Phonocardiogram signal analysis: Techniques and performance analysis," *Journal of Medical Engineering and Technology*, vol. 17, no. 6, pp. 221-227, Nov./Dec. 1993.

E. Horovitz, *Heart Beat: A Complete Guide to Understanding and Preventing Heart Disease*. Los Angeles, CA: Health Trend Publishing, 1988.

A. G. Rehorn, P. E. Orban, and J. Jiang, "Vibration-based machine condition monitoring with attention to the use of time-frequency methods," in *Proc. of SPIE Conference on Intelligent Manufacturing*, vol. 5263, Providence, RI, USA, Oct. 29, 2003, pp. 10-21.